ETHNOLOGUE INDEX

TWELFTH EDITION • BARBARA F. GRIMES, EDITOR

Summer Institute of Linguistics, Inc.
Dallas, Texas

Cover photo provided by Anton and Joanne Bucher

This is a computer produced index to the names that are associated with the 6,528 languages listed in *Ethnologue: Languages of the World,* Twelfth Edition, 1992. It identifies all the language names and their alternates, and all the dialect names and their alternates. For each language it gives it main name, its three-letter Language Identification Code, the country with which the language is most centrally identified, and other countries where it (including all of its dialects) is spoken. For alternate names and dialect names it gives the main language name and Language Identification Code.

The computer produced 37,370 index entries. Unfortunately some of them were duplicates, so we have no exact count of names.

We have followed our sources in using conventional symbols for 'click' sounds, such as /, //, !, "; used to write Khoisan languages and a few others in southern Africa.

Additional copies of this Index and of the *Ethnologue* itself may be obtained from

Summer Institute of Linguistics
International Academic Book Center
7500 West Camp Wisdom Road
Dallas, Texas 75236 USA

!GÃ!NE alt for !GA!NGE dial of SEROA [KQU]
!GÃ!NE alt for !GÃ!NGE dial of SEROA [KQU]
!GA!NGE dial of SEROA [KQU]
!GÃ!NGE dial of SEROA [KQU]
!GINGKWE dial of NHARON [NHR]
!HU alt for KUNG-EKOKA [KNW]
!HUKWE alt for XUN [XUU]
!KABBAKWE dial of NHARON [NHR]
!KÕ alt for /HUA-OWANI [HUC]
!KORA alt for KORANA [KQZ]
!KU alt for KUNG-EKOKA [KNW]
!KUNG alt for KUNG-EKOKA [KNW]
!O!KUNG alt for !O!UNG [OUN]
!ORA alt for KORANA [KQZ]
!XON alt for /HUA-OWANI [HUC]
!XONG alt for /HUA-OWANI [HUC]
!XU alt for KUNG-EKOKA [KNW]
'ABD-EL-KURI dial of SOQOTRI [SQT]
'ABOTEE alt for VUTE [VUT]
'ABWETEE alt for VUTE [VUT]
'AEKE alt for HAEKE [AEK]
'ALA'ALA alt for NARA [NRZ]
'AMAARA dial of ARABIC, MESOPOTAMIAN
    COLLOQUIAL [ACM]
'AMAARA-MI'DAAN dial of ARABIC,
    MESOPOTAMIAN COLLOQUIAL [ACM]
'ANAH dial of ARABIC, SYRO-MESOPOTAMIAN
    [AYP]
'ARAB alt for BAHRAINI ARABIC dial of AYIZO-GBE
    [AYB]
'ARAGURE alt for XARAGURE [ARG]
'ARE'ARE dial of 'ARE'ARE [ALU]
'AVEKE alt for HAVEKE [AVE]
'AZUMEINA alt for MARBA [MPG]
'BA alt for BUA [BUB]
'BALI'BA dial of MORU [MGD]
'BALO alt for KPASAM [PBN]
'BELI alt for BELI [BLM]
'BIDIO alt for BIDIO [BID]
'BIDIYO alt for BIDIO [BID]
'BURULO dial of MADI [MHI]
'DI'DINGA alt for DIDINGA [DID]
'MOAEKE alt for VAMALE [MKT]
'MOAVEKE alt for HMWAVEKE [MRK]
'OBOYGUNO dial of BIDIO [BID]
'UGONG alt for UGONG [UGO]
'UM FALIN alt for JIMI [JIM]
'UNAR alt for BESME [BES]
//'AIYE dial of SHUA [SHG]
//AI//EI alt for NHARON [NHR]
//AI//EN alt for NHARON [NHR]
//AIKWE alt for NHARON [NHR]
//AISAN alt for NHARON [NHR]
//AU//EI alt for 'AKHOE [AKE]
//AU//EĨ alt for 'AKHOE [AKE]
//AU//EI alt for KUNG-GOBABIS [AUE]
//AU//EN alt for 'AKHOE [AKE]
//AUKWE alt for 'AKHOE [AKE]
//KAU-//-EN alt for 'AKHOE [AKE]
//K"AU-//-EN alt for 'AKHOE [AKE]
//KU//E dial of SEROA [KQU]
//KXAU dial of NG'HUKI [NGH]
//NG alt for //NG!KE dial of NG'HUKI [NGH]
//NG!KE dial of NG'HUKI [NGH]
//U//EN alt for NG/U//EN dial of NG/AMANI [NMN]
//U//EN alt for NG/U//EN dial of NG/AMANI [NMN]

//XEGWE alt for //XEGWI [XEG]
//XEKWI alt for //XEGWI [XEG]
/AAYE alt for //'AIYE dial of SHUA [SHG]
/AIKWE alt for NHARON [NHR]
/AIS alt for /HAISE dial of SHUA [SHG]
/AMKWE dial of NHARON [NHR]
/ANEKWE dial of NHARON [NHR]
/AU-//EN alt for 'AKHOE [AKE]
/AUKWE alt for 'AKHOE [AKE]
/AUNI alt for AUNI dial of NG/AMANI [NMN]
/AUO alt for AUNI dial of NG/AMANI [NMN]
/EIKUSI alt for XATIA dial of NG/AMANI [NMN]
/HAIS alt for /HAISE dial of SHUA [SHG]
/HAISE dial of SHUA [SHG]
/HÛ alt for /HUA-OWANI [HUC]
/HUA alt for /HUA-OWANI [HUC]
/ING/KE alt for //NG!KE dial of NG'HUKI [NGH]
/KAMKA!E alt for /XAM [XAM]
/KHAM-KA-!K'E alt for /XAM [XAM]
/KHESSÁKHOE dial of GANA-KHWE [GNK]
/KHOMANI dial of NG'HUKI [NGH]
/KOREE-KHOE alt for /OREE-KHWE dial of SHUA
    [SHG]
/KUSI alt for XATIA dial of NG/AMANI [NMN]
/KUSI alt for XATIA dial of NG/AMANI [NMN]
/NU//EN alt for NG/U/EN dial of NG/AMANI [NMN]
/NU//EN alt for NG/U//EN dial of NG/AMANI [NMN]
/OREE alt for /OREE-KHWE dial of SHUA [SHG]
/OREE-KHWE dial of SHUA [SHG]
/U//EIN alt for NG/U//EN dial of NG/AMANI [NMN]
/XAISE alt for /HAISE dial of SHUA [SHG]
/XAM-KA-!K'E alt for /XAM [XAM]
A'A SAMA alt for SAMA dial of SAMA, SOUTHERN
    [SIT]
A'ARA alt for CHEKE HOLO [MRN]
A'E alt for REMPI [RMP]
A'I alt for COFÁN [CON]
A'WE alt for XAVÁNTE [XAV]
A-DHAM alt for ADHAM dial of RADE [RAD]
A-LA CONG alt for ALAKONG dial of BAHNAR [BDQ]
A-PUCIKWAR [APQ] lang, India
A-REM alt for AREM [AEM]
AAGE alt for ESIMBI [AGS]
AAIMASA alt for AIMARA dial of KUNAMA [KUM]
AALEIRA alt for LARO [LRO]
AARAI alt for AARI [AIZ]
AARI [AIZ] lang, Ethiopia
AARIYA [AAR] lang, India
AASÁX [AAS] lang, Tanzania
ABA alt for SHOR [CJS]
ABA alt for AMBA [UTP]
ABÁ alt for AVÁ-CANOEIRO [AVV]
ABAANGI alt for GWAMHI dial of GWAMHI-WURI
    [BGA]
ABACA alt for ABAKA dial of ILONGOT [ILK]
ABACAMA alt for BACAMA [BAM]
ABACHA alt for RUBASA [BZW]
ABADEKH alt for ABADZEX dial of ADYGHE [ADY]
ABADI alt for AWADHI [AWD]
ABADI alt for VADI dial of GADI-SHINGINI-VADI-
    BAANGI [KAM]
ABADZEX dial of ADYGHE [ADY]
ABAGA [ABG] lang, Papua New Guinea
ABAI dial of PUTOH [PUT]
ABAI SUNGAI [ABF] lang, Malaysia, Sabah
ABAKA dial of ILONGOT [ILK]

ABAKAN alt for KPAN [KPK]
ABAKAN TATAR alt for KHAKAS [KJH]
ABAKAY SPANISH alt for DAVAWENYO
    ZAMBOANGUENYO dial of CHAVACANO [CBK]
ABAKNON alt for SAMA, ABAKNON [ABX]
ABAKOUM alt for KWAKUM [KWU]
ABAKPA alt for SOUTHERN EJAGHAM dial of
    EJAGHAM [ETU]
ABAKPA alt for SOUTHERN EJAGHAM dial of
    EJAGHAM [ETU]
ABAKUM alt for KWAKUM [KWU]
ABAKWARIGA alt for HAUSA [HUA]
ABALETTI dial of YELE [YLE]
ABAM dial of GIDRA [GDR]
ABANE alt for BANIVA [BVV]
ABANGBA alt for BANGBA [BBE]
ABANLIKU alt for OBANLIKU [BZY]
ABANYAI alt for NYAI dial of KALANGA [KCK]
ABANYOM alt for BAKOR [ABM]
ABANYUM alt for BAKOR [ABM]
ABARAMBO alt for BARAMBU [BRM]
ABASAKUR [ABW] lang, Papua New Guinea
ABATHWA alt for //XEGWI [XEG]
ABATONGA alt for TONGA dial of NDAU [NDC]
ABATSA alt for RUBASA [BZW]
ABAU [AAU] lang, Papua New Guinea, Indonesia,
    Irian Jaya
ABAW alt for ABO [ABB]
ABAYONGO dial of AGWAGWUNE [YAY]
ABAZA [ABQ] lang, Russia, Europe, Turkey, Turkey
ABAZA alt for ABAZA [ABQ]
ABAZIN alt for ABAZA [ABQ]
ABAZINTSY alt for ABAZA [ABQ]
ABBÉ alt for ABÉ [ABA]
ABBEY alt for ABÉ [ABA]
ABBEY-VE dial of ABÉ [ABA]
ABBRUZZESI dial of ROMANI, SINTE [RMO]
ABDAL alt for AYNU [AIB]
ABDEDAL alt for GAGADU [GBU]
ABÉ [ABA] lang, Côte d'Ivoire
ABECHE dial of ARABIC, SHUWA [SHU]
ABEDJU-AZAKI dial of LUGBARA, HIGH [LUG]
ABEFANG alt for BEFANG dial of BEFANG [BBY]
ABELAM alt for AMBULAS [ABT]
ABENAGO alt for NIPSAN [YAC]
ABENAKI alt for WESTERN ABNAKI dial of ABNAKI-
    PENOBSCOT [ABE]
ABENAKI alt for WESTERN ABNAKI dial of ABNAKI-
    PENOBSCOT [ABE]
ABENAQUI alt for WESTERN ABNAKI dial of
    ABNAKI-PENOBSCOT [ABE]
ABENG dial of GARO [GRT]
ABENGYA dial of GARO [GRT]
ABENLEN alt for AYTA, ABENLEN [ABP]
ABI alt for ABÉ [ABA]
ABI alt for AMA [AMM]
ABIA alt for ANEME WAKE [ABY]
ABIDDUL alt for GAGADU [GBU]
ABIDJI [ABI] lang, Côte d'Ivoire
ABIE alt for ANEME WAKE [ABY]
ABIEM dial of DINKA, SOUTHWESTERN [DIK]
ABIGAR dial of NUER [NUS]
ABIGAR alt for EASTERN NUER dial of NUER [NUS]
ABIGIRA alt for ABISHIRA [ASH]
ABIJI alt for ABIDJI [ABI]
ABIJI ANYIN dial of ANYIN [ANY]

ABILIANG dial of DINKA, NORTHEASTERN [DIP]
ABINI dial of AGWAGWUNE [YAY]
ABINSI [JUB] lang, Nigeria
ABIQUIRA alt for ABISHIRA [ASH]
ABIRA alt for PANARE [PBH]
ABIRI alt for MARARIT [MGB]
ABIRI alt for ABINI dial of AGWAGWUNE [YAY]
ABISHIRA [ASH] lang, Peru
ABISI alt for PITI [PCN]
ABIYI alt for MARARIT [MGB]
ABKAR dial of MABA [MDE]
ABKHAZ [ABK] lang, Georgia, Turkey, Turkey
ABKHAZ alt for ABKHAZ [ABK]
ABLEG-SALEGSEG dial of KALINGA, LUBUAGAN
    [KNB]
ABNAKI-PENOBSCOT [ABE] lang, USA, Canada
ABO [ABB] lang, Cameroon
ABO alt for TOPOSA [TOQ]
ABO alt for MULAM [MLM]
ABO alt for ABONG [ABO]
ABOA dial of AMA [AMM]
ABOH dial of UKWUANI-ABOH [UKW]
ABOHI alt for AWADHI [AWD]
ABON alt for ABONG [ABO]
ABONG [ABO] lang, Nigeria
ABONWA alt for ABURE [ABU]
ABOR alt for ADI [ADI]
ABOR-MIRI alt for ADI [ADI]
ABORIGINAL ENGLISH dial of ENGLISH [ENG]
ABORLAN TAGBANWA alt for TAGBANWA [TBW]
ABORO alt for BEROM [BOM]
ABOU CHARIB dial of MARARIT [MGB]
ABOURÉ alt for ABURE [ABU]
ABRA-DE-ILOG dial of IRAYA [IRY]
ABRAKO alt for FROUKOU dial of AIZI [AHI]
ABRI alt for KOALIB [KIB]
ABRON [ABR] lang, Ghana, Côte d'Ivoire
ABRUZZESE dial of ITALIAN [ITN]
ABU [ADO] lang, Papua New Guinea
ABU dial of BOKYI [BKY]
ABU CHARIN dial of MABA [MDE]
ABU LEILA dial of MORO [MOR]
ABU SHARIB alt for ABOU CHARIB dial of MARARIT
    [MGB]
ABU SHARIN alt for ABU CHARIN dial of MABA
    [MDE]
ABU SINUN dial of KANGA [KCP]
ABUA [ABN] lang, Nigeria
ABUAN alt for ABUA [ABN]
ABUI [ABZ] lang, Indonesia, Nusa Tenggara
ABUJHMARIA alt for ABUJMARIA [ABJ]
ABUJMAR MARIA alt for ABUJMARIA [ABJ]
ABUJMARIA [ABJ] lang, India
ABUJMARIYA alt for ABUJMARIA [ABJ]
ABUKEIA alt for AVOKAYA [AVU]
ABULAS alt for AMBULAS [ABT]
ABULDUGU dial of BURUN [BDI]
ABULE alt for ABURE [ABU]
ABULOMA alt for OBULOM [OBU]
ABUN [KGR] lang, Indonesia, Irian Jaya
ABUN JE dial of ABUN [KGR]
ABUN JI dial of ABUN [KGR]
ABUN TAT dial of ABUN [KGR]
ABUNG [ABL] lang, Indonesia, Sumatra
ABURE [ABU] lang, Côte d'Ivoire
ABURLIN NEGRITO alt for AYTA, ABENLEN [ABP]

ABUYA alt for AGEER dial of DINKA, NORTHEASTERN [DIP]
ABXAZO alt for ABKHAZ [ABK]
ABYSSINIAN alt for AMHARIC [AMH]
ABZHUI dial of ABKHAZ [ABK]
AC'YE alt for LASHI [LSI]
ACADIAN alt for FRENCH, CAJUN [FRC]
ACAHUAYO alt for AKAWAIO [ARB]
ACANG alt for ACHANG [ACN]
ACATEC alt for KANJOBAL, WESTERN [KNJ]
ACATECO alt for KANJOBAL, WESTERN [KNJ]
ACATLÁN MIXTECO alt for MIXTECO, SOUTHERN PUEBLA [MIT]
ACAWAYO alt for AKAWAIO [ARB]
ACCHAMI dial of NEPALI [NEP]
ACCRA alt for GA-ADANGME-KROBO [GAC]
ACEH [ATJ] lang, Indonesia, Sumatra
ACEWAIO alt for AKAWAIO [ARB]
ACH'ANG alt for ACHANG [ACN]
ACHAGUA [ACA] lang, Colombia, Venezuela, Venezuela
ACHAGUA alt for ACHAGUA [ACA]
ACHANG [ACN] lang, China, Myanmar, Myanmar
ACHANG alt for ACHANG [ACN]
ACHANG dial of ACHANG [ACN]
ACHANTI alt for ASANTE dial of AKAN [TWS]
ACHAWA alt for YAO [YAO]
ACHÉ [GUQ] lang, Paraguay
ACHEHNESE alt for ACEH [ATJ]
ACHERON dial of MORO HILLS [TAZ]
ACHERON dial of MORO [MOR]
ACHÍ, CUBULCO [ACC] lang, Guatemala
ACHÍ, RABINAL [ACR] lang, Guatemala
ACHICK dial of GARO [GRT]
ACHIK dial of GARO [GRT]
ACHIK alt for ACHICK dial of GARO [GRT]
ACHINESE alt for ACEH [ATJ]
ACHIPA alt for ACIPA [AWA]
ACHLO alt for IGO [AHL]
ACHODE alt for GIKYODE [ACD]
ACHOLI [ACO] lang, Uganda, Sudan
ACHOMAWI alt for ACHUMAWI [ACH]
ACHUAL alt for ACHUAR-SHIWIAR [ACU]
ACHUALE alt for ACHUAR-SHIWIAR [ACU]
ACHUAR alt for ACHUAR-SHIWIAR [ACU]
ACHUAR-SHIWIAR [ACU] lang, Peru, Ecuador
ACHUARA alt for ACHUAR-SHIWIAR [ACU]
ACHUMAWI [ACH] lang, USA
ACHUNG alt for ACHANG [ACN]
ACI alt for ATSI [ATB]
ACILOWE alt for LOMWE [NGL]
ACIPA [AWA] lang, Nigeria
ACIPANCI alt for ACIPA [AWA]
ACIRA alt for ADZERA [AZR]
ACOLI alt for ACHOLI [ACO]
ACOMA dial of KERES, WESTERN [KJQ]
ACOOLI alt for ACHOLI [ACO]
ACRA alt for GA-ADANGME-KROBO [GAC]
ACROÁ [ACS] lang, Brazil
ACULO alt for DEG [MZW]
AD'N'AMADANA alt for ADYNYAMATHANHA [ADT]
ADA alt for KUTURMI [KHJ]
ADABE [ADB] lang, Indonesia, Nusa Tenggara
ADAMAWA FULANI alt for FULFULDE, ADAMAWA [FUB]
ADAMOROBE SIGN LANGUAGE [ADS] lang, Ghana

ADANG dial of LUNDAYEH [LND]
ADANGBE alt for ADANGME dial of GA-ADANGME-KROBO [GAC]
ADANGME dial of GA-ADANGME-KROBO [GAC]
ADAP [ADP] lang, Bhutan
ADARA alt for KADARA [KAD]
ADARE [HAR] lang, Ethiopia
ADARU dial of CARÚTANA [CRU]
ADASEN [TIU] lang, Philippines
ADASEN ITNEG alt for ADASEN [TIU]
ADDASEN alt for ADASEN [TIU]
ADDASEN TINGUIAN alt for ADASEN [TIU]
ADDO alt for EDO [EDO]
ADE BHASHA alt for ARE [AAG]
ADEA alt for HADIYYA [HDY]
ADEEYAH alt for BUBE [BVB]
ADELE [ADE] lang, Ghana, Togo, Togo
ADELE alt for ADELE [ADE]
ADELI alt for ADELE [ADE]
ADENI dial of ARABIC, YEMENI [ACQ]
ADERE alt for DZODINKA [ADD]
ADERINYA alt for ADARE [HAR]
ADEWADA dial of MARIA [MRR]
ADGAWAN dial of MANOBO, AGUSAN [MSM]
ADHAM dial of RADE [RAD]
ADHIANG alt for TUIC dial of DINKA, SOUTHWESTERN [DIK]
ADHO-ADHOM alt for DJANGUN [DJF]
ADHOLA [ADH] lang, Uganda
ADI [ADI] lang, India, China
ADI dial of KOWIAI [KWH]
ADI dial of ADI [ADI]
ADI DRAVIDA dial of TAMIL [TCV]
ADI-GALO alt for GALONG [GBH]
ADIANGOK alt for BISOO dial of BAKOKO [BKH]
ADIE dial of BAKOKO [BKH]
ADIJA alt for BUBE [BVB]
ADIKIMMU SUKUR alt for SUKUR [SUK]
ADILABAD alt for NIRMAL dial of GONDI, SOUTHERN [GGO]
ADIM dial of AGWAGWUNE [YAY]
ADIOUKROU [ADJ] lang, Côte d'Ivoire
ADIVASI ORIYA alt for ORIYA, ADIWASI [ORT]
ADIWASI GIRASIA alt for GIRASIA, ADIWASI [GAS]
ADIWASI ORIYA alt for ORIYA, ADIWASI [ORT]
ADIYAN [ADN] lang, India
ADIYE alt for HADIYYA [HDY]
ADJA alt for AJA-GBE [AJG]
ADJABDURAH dial of NARUNGGA [NNR]
ADJAHDURAH alt for ADJABDURAH dial of NARUNGGA [NNR]
ADJER alt for AZER dial of SONINKE [SNN]
ADJER alt for AZER dial of SONINKE [SNN]
ADJIGA alt for AJIGU dial of AVOKAYA [AVU]
ADJIO alt for TAJIO [TDJ]
ADJORA alt for ABU [ADO]
ADJORIA alt for ABU [ADO]
ADJUKRU alt for ADIOUKROU [ADJ]
ADJUMBA alt for AJUMBA dial of MYENE [MYE]
ADKIBBA alt for MURLE [MUR]
ADKURI dial of HALBI [HLB]
ADLAI alt for ROGLAI, NORTHERN [ROG]
ADO dial of KAILI, LEDO [LEW]
ADOMA dial of LELA [DRI]
ADONA alt for RER BARE [RER]
ADONARA alt for SOUTH LAMAHOLOT dial of

LAMAHOLOT [SLP]
ADONG alt for IDUN [LDB]
ADONG alt for RUNGU dial of MAMBWE-LUNGU [MGR]
ADOR alt for CIEC dial of DINKA, SOUTH CENTRAL [DIB]
ADORA alt for AIRORAN [AIR]
ADOUMA alt for DUMA [DMA]
ADOWEN alt for DJAUAN [DJN]
ADOYO dial of ANUAK [ANU]
ADSAWA alt for YAO [YAO]
ADSOA alt for YAO [YAO]
ADU dial of TABARU [TBY]
ADUGE [ADU] lang, Nigeria
ADULU alt for ATURU [AUP]
ADUMA alt for DUMA [DMA]
ADUN dial of MBEMBE, CROSS RIVER [MFN]
ADYAKTYE alt for KAKANDA dial of NUPE [NUP]
ADYGEI alt for ADYGHE [ADY]
ADYGEY alt for ADYGHE [ADY]
ADYGHE [ADY] lang, Russia, Europe, Iraq, Israel, Jordan, Syria, Turkey, Yugoslavia
ADYGHE alt for ADYGHE [ADY]
ADYNYAMATHANHA [ADT] lang, Australia
ADYOUKROU alt for ADIOUKROU [ADJ]
ADYUKRU alt for ADIOUKROU [ADJ]
ADYUMBA alt for AJUMBA dial of MYENE [MYE]
ADZERA [AZR] lang, Papua New Guinea
ADZERMA alt for DYERMA [DJE]
ADZU BALAKA alt for ASSAKA dial of CAKA [CKX]
ADZU BATANGA alt for BATANGA dial of CAKA [CKX]
AEJAUROH alt for SAWI [SAW]
AEKA [AIG] lang, Papua New Guinea
AEKE alt for HAEKE [AEK]
AEKYOM alt for AWIN [AWI]
AERORAN alt for AIRORAN [AIR]
AETA NEGRITO alt for SAMBAL, BOTOLAN [SBL]
AF-ASHRAAF dial of SOMALI [SOM]
AF-BAJUUN alt for BAJUNI dial of SWAHILI [SWA]
AF-BOON alt for BOON [BNL]
AF-CHIMWIINI alt for MWINI dial of SWAHILI [SWA]
AF-DABARRE alt for DABARRE [DBR]
AF-GARRE alt for GARRE [GEX]
AF-HELLEDI dial of MAAY [QMA]
AF-IROOLE alt for IROOLE dial of DABARRE [DBR]
AF-JIIDDU alt for JIIDDU [JII]
AF-KARETI alt for KOMSO [KXC]
AF-MAAY alt for MAAY [QMA]
AF-MAAY TIRI alt for MAAY [QMA]
AF-MAXAAD TIRI alt for SOMALI [SOM]
AF-MAY alt for MAAY [QMA]
AF-MAYMAY alt for MAAY [QMA]
AF-SOOMAALI alt for SOMALI [SOM]
AF-TUNNI alt for TUNNI [TQQ]
AFA alt for PA'A [AFA]
AFA alt for AFFA dial of AKOKO, NORTH [AKK]
AFADA alt for AFADE [AAL]
AFADE [AAL] lang, Nigeria, Cameroon
AFADEH alt for AFADE [AAL]
AFAK alt for APAK dial of ATUOT [ATU]
AFAKANI alt for DEFAKA [AFN]
AFAN MAO alt for KOMA, NORTH [KMQ]
AFAN OROMO alt for OROMO, BORANA-ARUSI-GUJI [GAX]
AFANCI alt for PA'A [AFA]

AFANGO alt for BEROM [BOM]
AFAO alt for ELOYI [AFO]
AFAR [AFR] lang, Ethiopia, Djibouti
AFARAF alt for AFAR [AFR]
AFATIME alt for AVATIME [AVA]
AFAWA alt for PA'A [AFA]
AFENMAI alt for YEKHEE [ETS]
AFERIKE alt for AFRIKE dial of UTUGWANG [AFE]
AFFA dial of AKOKO, NORTH [AKK]
AFFADE alt for AFADE [AAL]
AFFIÑIAM dial of GUSILAY [GSL]
AFFITTI alt for AFITTI [AFT]
AFGHAN alt for PASHTO, WESTERN [PBT]
AFGHAN FARSI alt for DARI dial of FARSI, EASTERN [PRS]
AFGHANA-YI NASFURUSH alt for PARYA [PAQ]
AFGHANA-YI SIYARUI alt for PARYA [PAQ]
AFGHANTSY alt for PASHTO, WESTERN [PBT]
AFIKPO dial of IGBO [IGR]
AFITTI [AFT] lang, Sudan
AFIZARE alt for IZERE [FIZ]
AFIZAREK alt for IZERE [FIZ]
AFKABIYE alt for GUDUF [GDF]
AFO alt for ELOYI [AFO]
AFO alt for BAFAW dial of BAFAW-BALONG [BWT]
AFORE dial of MANAGALASI [MCQ]
AFORIT alt for HARSUSI [HSS]
AFORO alt for KALAM [KMH]
AFRIDI dial of PASHTO, EASTERN [PBU]
AFRIKAANS [AFK] lang, South Africa, Malawi, Namibia, Zambia, Zimbabwe
AFRIKAANS alt for AFRIKAANS [AFK]
AFRIKE dial of UTUGWANG [AFE]
AFRO-SEMINOLE alt for AFRO-SEMINOLE CREOLE [AFS]
AFRO-SEMINOLE CREOLE [AFS] lang, USA, Mexico
AFSAR alt for AFSHARI dial of AZERBAIJANI, SOUTH [AZB]
AFSHAR alt for AFSHARI dial of AZERBAIJANI, SOUTH [AZB]
AFSHARI dial of AZERBAIJANI, SOUTH [AZB]
AFU alt for ELOYI [AFO]
AFUGHE alt for BUFE dial of BAFUT [BFD]
AFUNATA alt for NTA dial of NDE-NSELE-NTA [NDD]
AFUSARE alt for IZERE [FIZ]
AFUTU alt for AWUTU [AFU]
AGA alt for KANURI, YERWA [KPH]
AGA dial of BURIAT, MONGOLIA [BXM]
AGA dial of BURIAT, CHINA [BXU]
AGA BEREHO alt for BARIJI [BJC]
AGADEZ alt for AIR dial of TAMAJEQ, AIR [THZ]
AGADI alt for GADI dial of GADI-SHINGINI-VADI-BAANGI [KAM]
AGALA [AGL] lang, Papua New Guinea
AGAM dial of MINANGKABAU [MPU]
AGAMORU alt for AJIGU dial of AVOKAYA [AVU]
AGAR alt for DINKA, SOUTH CENTRAL [DIB]
AGAR dial of DINKA, SOUTH CENTRAL [DIB]
AGARA'IWA dial of AGAUSHI-KIMBA-NGWANCI [KDL]
AGARABE alt for AGARABI [AGD]
AGARABI [AGD] lang, Papua New Guinea
AGARI alt for GBIRI dial of GBIRI-NIRAGU [GRH]
AGARI alt for GURA dial of LAME [BMA]
AGARIYA [AGI] lang, India
AGATU [AGC] lang, Nigeria

AGAU alt for AWNGI [AWN]
AGAU alt for NOGAU dial of KUNG-TSUMKWE [KTZ]
AGAUSHI dial of AGAUSHI-KIMBA-NGWANCI [KDL]
AGAUSHI-KIMBA-NGWANCI [KDL] lang, Nigeria
AGAVOTAGUERRA [AVO] lang, Brazil
AGAVOTOKUENG alt for AGAVOTAGUERRA [AVO]
AGAW alt for AWNGI [AWN]
AGBARAGBA alt for EFUTOP [OFU]
AGBARHO dial of URHOBO [URH]
AGBAWI alt for KWANGE dial of GBARI [GBY]
AGBI dial of NUPE [NUP]
AGBIRI alt for GBIRI dial of GBIRI-NIRAGU [GRH]
AGBIRI alt for GURA dial of LAME [BMA]
AGBO alt for LEGBO [AGB]
AGE alt for ESIMBI [AGS]
AGEER dial of DINKA, NORTHEASTERN [DIP]
AGEIR alt for AGEER dial of DINKA,
  NORTHEASTERN [DIP]
AGER alt for AGEER dial of DINKA, NORTHEASTERN
  [DIP]
AGERLEP alt for AIKLEP [MWG]
AGEW alt for AWNGI [AWN]
AGHARIA alt for AGARIYA [AGI]
AGHEM [AGQ] lang, Cameroon
AGHEM dial of AGHEM [AGQ]
AGHU [AHH] lang, Indonesia, Irian Jaya
AGHU THARNGGALU [GGR] lang, Australia
AGHUL [AGX] lang, Russia, Europe
AGHULSHUY alt for AGHUL [AGX]
AGI [AIF] lang, Papua New Guinea
AGI dial of MORU [MGD]
AGIBA alt for MURLE [MUR]
AGIRYAMA alt for GIRYAMA [NYF]
AGIYAN alt for AGTA, CAMARINES NORTE [ABD]
AGNAGAN alt for ANYANGA [AYG]
AGNANG alt for DENYA [ANV]
AGNI alt for ANYIN [ANY]
AGO alt for IGO [AHL]
AGŎB [KIT] lang, Papua New Guinea
AGOI [IBM] lang, Nigeria
AGOLOK alt for KAGORO dial of KATAB [KCG]
AGOMA alt for KAGOMA [KDM]
AGOMES alt for HERMIT [LLF]
AGONA dial of AKAN [TWS]
AGORIA alt for AGARIYA [AGI]
AGOUISIRI alt for ABISHIRA [ASH]
AGOW alt for AWNGI [AWN]
AGTA, ALABAT ISLAND [DUL] lang, Philippines
AGTA, CAMARINES NORTE [ABD] lang, Philippines
AGTA, CASIGURAN DUMAGAT [DGC] lang,
  Philippines
AGTA, CENTRAL CAGAYAN [AGT] lang, Philippines
AGTA, DICAMAY [DUY] lang, Philippines
AGTA, DUPANINAN [DUO] lang, Philippines
AGTA, ISAROG [AGK] lang, Philippines
AGTA, MT. IRAYA [ATL] lang, Philippines
AGTA, MT. IRIGA [AGZ] lang, Philippines
AGTA, REMONTADO [AGV] lang, Philippines
AGTA, UMIRAY DUMAGET [DUE] lang, Philippines
AGTA, VILLAVICIOSA [DYG] lang, Philippines
AGU dial of RAWANG [RAW]
AGUA alt for OMAGUA [OMG]
AGUACATEC alt for AGUACATECO [AGU]
AGUACATECO [AGU] lang, Guatemala
AGUAJUN alt for AGUARUNA [AGR]
AGUALINDA GUAHIBO alt for MACAGUÁN [MBN]

AGUANO [AGA] lang, Peru
AGUANU alt for AGUANO [AGA]
AGUARICO dial of COFÁN [CON]
AGUARUNA [AGR] lang, Peru
AGUAS BLANCAS alt for TUNEBO, WESTERN [TNB]
AGUFI dial of FAGANI [FAF]
AGUL alt for AGHUL [AGX]
AGUL dial of AGHUL [AGX]
AGULIS dial of ARMENIAN [ARM]
AGULY alt for AGHUL [AGX]
AGUNA [AUG] lang, Benin
AGUNACO alt for AGUNA [AUG]
AGUOK dial of DINKA, SOUTHWESTERN [DIK]
AGURO alt for KAGORO dial of KATAB [KCG]
AGUSAN alt for MANOBO, AGUSAN [MSM]
AGUTAYNEN [AGN] lang, Philippines
AGUTAYNO alt for AGUTAYNEN [AGN]
AGUTAYNON alt for AGUTAYNEN [AGN]
AGVALI-RICHAGANIK-TSUMADA-URUKH alt for
  GAKVARI dial of CHAMALAL [CJI]
AGWAGUNA alt for AGWAGWUNE [YAY]
AGWAGWUNE [YAY] lang, Nigeria
AGWAGWUNE dial of AGWAGWUNE [YAY]
AGWAMIN [AWG] lang, Australia
AGWARA alt for NGWANCI dial of AGAUSHI-
  KIMBA-NGWANCI [KDL]
AGWATASHI dial of ALAGO [ALA]
AGWOK alt for AGUOK dial of DINKA,
  SOUTHWESTERN [DIK]
AGWOLOK alt for KAGORO dial of KATAB [KCG]
AGWOT alt for KAGORO dial of KATAB [KCG]
AHAAN alt for AHAN dial of AKOKO, NORTH [AKK]
AHAFO dial of AKAN [TWS]
AHAGGAREN alt for HOGGAR dial of TAMAHAQ,
  HOGGAR [THV]
AHAHNELIN alt for GROS VENTRE [ATS]
AHAMB alt for AXAMB [AHB]
AHAN dial of AKOKO, NORTH [AKK]
AHANTA [AHA] lang, Ghana
AHASA alt for AKASSA dial of IJO, SOUTHEAST
  [IJO]
AHCHAN alt for ACHANG [ACN]
AHE [AHE] lang, Indonesia, Kalimantan
AHE alt for GROS VENTRE [ATS]
AHE DAYAK alt for AHE [AHE]
AHEAVE dial of KEURU [QQK]
AHEIMA dial of NGILE [MAS]
AHERI dial of GONDI, SOUTHERN [GGO]
AHIRANI dial of KHANDESI [KHN]
AHIRI alt for AHIRANI dial of KHANDESI [KHN]
AHIZI alt for AIZI [AHI]
AHKA alt for AKHA [AKA]
AHLŎ alt for IGO [AHL]
AHLON alt for IGO [AHL]
AHLON-BOGO alt for IGO [AHL]
AHMEDABAD GAMADIA alt for GAMADIA dial of
  GUJARATI [GJR]
AHO alt for ELOYI [AFO]
AHOLIO alt for SHOLIO dial of KATAB [KCG]
AHOM [AHO] lang, India
AHONLAN alt for IGO [AHL]
AHONLAN alt for ANLO [AOL]
AHTENA [AHT] lang, USA
AHTIAGO alt for BOBOT [BTY]
AHTNA alt for AHTENA [AHT]
AHUAJUN alt for AGUARUNA [AGR]

AHUATEMPAN POPOLOCA alt for POPOLOCA, SANTA INÉS AHUATEMPAN [PCA]
AHUS alt for ANDRA-HUS [ANX]
AI NAN alt for MAONAN [MMD]
AI SUI alt for SUI [SWI]
AI-CHAM [AIH] lang, China
AIBONDENI dial of WANDAMEN [WAD]
AICA alt for JAUARI dial of YANOMÁMI [WCA]
AIDUMA alt for KOWIAI [KWH]
AIEWOMBA dial of AMPEELI-WOJOKESO [APZ]
AIGA alt for AEKA [AIG]
AIGANG alt for KEIGA [KEC]
AIGANG alt for KEIGA dial of KEIGA [KEC]
AIGON dial of PSOHOH [BCL]
AIGUAVIVAN alt for NORTHWESTERN CATALAN dial of CATALAN [CLN]
AIKANÁ alt for TUBARÃO [TBA]
AIKE alt for AKE [AIK]
AIKEWARA alt for SURUÍ DO PARÁ [MDZ]
AIKI alt for RUNGA [ROU]
AIKLEP [MWG] lang, Papua New Guinea
AIKOA dial of MORI ATAS [MZQ]
AIKU [MZF] lang, Papua New Guinea
AIKWAKAI alt for SIKARITAI [TTY]
AILI GAILI alt for HINDI, CARIBBEAN [HNS]
AILUAKI dial of NAMIA [NNM]
AIMAQ [AIQ] lang, Afghanistan, Iran
AIMARA dial of KUNAMA [KUM]
AIMELE [AIL] lang, Papua New Guinea
AIMOL [AIM] lang, India
AIMOLI dial of KABOLA [KLZ]
AINBAI [AIC] lang, Papua New Guinea
AINE KURUBA dial of KANNADA [KJV]
AINI alt for AYNU [AIB]
AINI alt for AKHA [AKA]
AINU [AIN] lang, Japan, Russia, Asia, Russia, Asia
AINU alt for AINU [AIN]
AIOME [AKI] lang, Papua New Guinea
AION [AEW] lang, Papua New Guinea
AIPKI alt for SUKUBATONG [SBT]
AIR dial of TAMAJEQ, AIR [THZ]
AIR TABUN alt for KETUNGAU dial of IBAN [IBA]
AIRD HILLS dial of KIBIRI [PRM]
AIRIMAN alt for NGARINMAN [NBJ]
AIRMADIDI dial of TONSEA [TXS]
AIRMATI alt for KWERBA [KWE]
AIRORAN [AIR] lang, Indonesia, Irian Jaya
AIRYM dial of AZERBAIJANI, NORTH [AZE]
AISO alt for KAMPUNG BARU [KZM]
AISOR alt for ASSYRIAN [AII]
AISSOR alt for ASSYRIAN [AII]
AISSUARI alt for AIZUARE dial of OMAGUA [OMG]
AITA dial of ROTOKAS [ROO]
AITON [AIO] lang, India
AITONIA alt for AITON [AIO]
AITUTAKI dial of RAROTONGAN [RRT]
AIWANAT dial of YUPIK, CENTRAL SIBERIAN [ESS]
AIWIN alt for AWIN [AWI]
AĨWO alt for AYIWO [NFL]
AIYANGAR dial of TAMIL [TCV]
AIYAR dial of TAMIL [TCV]
AIZI [AHI] lang, Côte d'Ivoire
AIZI dial of AIZI [AHI]
AIZUARE dial of OMAGUA [OMG]
AJA alt for AJA-GBE [AJG]
AJA dial of KRESH [KRS]

AJA-GBE [AJG] lang, Benin, Togo, Togo
AJA-GBE alt for AJA-GBE [AJG]
AJAGUA alt for ACHAGUA [ACA]
AJAK alt for CIEC dial of DINKA, SOUTH CENTRAL [DIB]
AJAK alt for PALIET dial of DINKA, SOUTHWESTERN [DIK]
AJAM alt for AYAM dial of ASMAT, CENTRAL [AST]
AJAMARU alt for MAI BRAT [AYZ]
AJANJI alt for JANJI [JNI]
AJAU alt for AWYU [AWJ]
AJAWA alt for YAO [YAO]
AJE dial of AKOKO, NORTH [AKK]
AJER alt for AZER dial of SONINKE [SNN]
AJI dial of MALAY [MLI]
AJIBBA alt for MURLE [MUR]
AJIĒ [AJI] lang, New Caledonia
AJIGU dial of AVOKAYA [AVU]
AJIRI OF HAZARA dial of GUJARI [GJU]
AJJER alt for HOGGAR dial of TAMAHAQ, HOGGAR [THV]
AJMERI [AJM] lang, India
AJO alt for MAJANG [MPE]
AJOKOOT alt for MARGU [MHG]
AJOMANG alt for TALODI [TLO]
AJONG DIT alt for ABIEM dial of DINKA, SOUTHWESTERN [DIK]
AJONG THI alt for ABIEM dial of DINKA, SOUTHWESTERN [DIK]
AJUGU alt for AJIGU dial of AVOKAYA [AVU]
AJUH dial of LAWANGAN [LBX]
AJUJURE alt for ARÁRA, PARÁ [AAP]
AJUKRU alt for ADIOUKROU [ADJ]
AJUMBA dial of MYENE [MYE]
AJURAN dial of GARREH-AJURAN [GGH]
AJURE alt for KAJURU dial of KADARA [KAD]
AJURÚ alt for WAYORÓ [WYR]
AJUURAAN alt for AJURAN dial of GARREH-AJURAN [GGH]
AK [AKQ] lang, Papua New Guinea
AK alt for WHITE NOGAI dial of NOGAI [NOG]
AK'A alt for AKHA [AKA]
AKA [SOH] lang, Sudan
AKA [AXK] lang, Central African Republic, Congo
AKA alt for AKHA [AKA]
AKA alt for ASUA [ASV]
AKA alt for AKA [AXK]
AKA LEL dial of NISI [DAP]
AKA-BEA [ACE] lang, India
AKA-BEADA alt for AKA-BEA [ACE]
AKA-BO [AKM] lang, India
AKA-CARI [ACI] lang, India
AKA-JERU [AKJ] lang, India
AKA-KEDE [AKX] lang, India
AKA-KOL [AKY] lang, India
AKA-KORA [ACK] lang, India
AKAB alt for KAYAPA dial of KALLAHAN, KAYAPA [KAK]
AKABAFA dial of MANAGALASI [MCQ]
AKAJO alt for EKAJUK [EKA]
AKAJUK alt for EKAJUK [EKA]
AKALAK alt for KATLA [KCR]
AKAN [TWS] lang, Ghana
AKANDA alt for KAKANDA dial of NUPE [NUP]
AKANI dial of NANAI [GLD]
AKANY KOK alt for ABIEM dial of DINKA,

SOUTHWESTERN [DIK]
AKAPLASS alt for ABURE [ABU]
AKAR-BALE [ACL] lang, India
AKARA alt for TOPOSA [TOQ]
AKARA alt for AKERRE dial of ARANDA, WESTERN
    [ARE]
AKASELE alt for AKASELEM [AKS]
AKASELEM [AKS] lang, Togo
AKASSA dial of IJO, SOUTHEAST [IJO]
AKAWAI alt for AKAWAIO [ARB]
AKAWAIO [ARB] lang, Guyana, Brazil, Venezuela
AKAWAIO alt for AKAWAIO [ARB]
AKAYON alt for KIONG [KKM]
AKE [AIK] lang, Nigeria
AKEBOU [KEU] lang, Togo
AKEBU alt for AKEBOU [KEU]
AKEI [TSR] lang, Vanuatu
AKELE alt for KÉLÉ [KEB]
AKER alt for ALIAP dial of DINKA, SOUTH CENTRAL
    [DIB]
AKERN JOK alt for ABIEM dial of DINKA,
    SOUTHWESTERN [DIK]
AKEROA alt for TOPOSA [TOQ]
AKERRE dial of ARANDA, WESTERN [ARE]
AKEWERE alt for SURUÍ DO PARÁ [MDZ]
AKHA [AKA] lang, Myanmar, China, Myanmar, Laos,
    Thailand, Viet Nam
'AKHOE [AKE] lang, Namibia, Angola
AKHTY dial of LEZGI [LEZ]
AKHU alt for LATI [LBT]
AKHVAKH [AKV] lang, Russia, Europe
AKI alt for BANGGAI [BGZ]
AKI alt for NGORO dial of TUKI [BAG]
AKIAPMIN alt for SUARMIN [SEO]
"AKIDO" alt for TOLAKI [LBW]
AKIE alt for ATTIÉ [ATI]
AKIEK alt for OKIEK [OKI]
AKIMBA alt for KIMBA dial of AGAUSHI-KIMBA-
    NGWANCI [KDL]
AKIT dial of KERINCI [KVR]
AKIUM alt for AWIN [AWI]
AKIUM-PARE alt for PARE [PPT]
AKJUET alt for PALIOUPINY dial of DINKA,
    SOUTHWESTERN [DIK]
AKKA dial of CHECHEN [CJC]
AKKHUSHA alt for AKUSHA dial of DARGWA [DAR]
AKKIN alt for AKKA dial of CHECHEN [CJC]
AKLAN alt for AKLANON [AKL]
AKLANO alt for AKLANON [AKL]
AKLANON [AKL] lang, Philippines
AKLANON-BISAYAN alt for AKLANON [AKL]
AKN dial of ARMENIAN [ARM]
AKO dial of EKPEYE [EKP]
AKO dial of BADA [BHZ]
AKO dial of AKHA [AKA]
AKO alt for BORORRO dial of FULFULDE, KANO-
    KATSINA-BORORRO [FUV]
AKOERIO alt for AKURIO [AKO]
AKOINKAKE alt for ANGOYA [MIW]
AKOIYANG alt for KIONG [KKM]
AKOKO, NORTH [AKK] lang, Nigeria
AKOKOLEMU alt for KUMAM [KDI]
AKOLET [AKT] lang, Papua New Guinea
AKOLI alt for ACHOLI [ACO]
AKONO dial of YORUBA [YOR]
AKONTO alt for MBEMBE, TIGON [NZA]

AKOON alt for ABILIANG dial of DINKA,
    NORTHEASTERN [DIP]
AKOOSE [BSS] lang, Cameroon
AKOSI alt for AKOOSE [BSS]
AKOYE alt for ANGOYA [MIW]
AKPA dial of AKPA-YACHE [AKF]
AKPA-YACHE [AKF] lang, Nigeria
AKPAFU dial of AKPAFU-LOLOBI [AKP]
AKPAFU-LOLOBI [AKP] lang, Ghana
AKPANZHI alt for KPAN [KPK]
AKPANZHI alt for DONGA dial of JUKUN TAKUM
    [JBU]
AKPARABONG alt for EKPARAGONG dial of NDOE
    [NBB]
AKPE [AQP] lang, Togo
AKPES [IBE] lang, Nigeria
AKPES alt for AKUNNU dial of AKPES [IBE]
AKPESE alt for KPELLE, GUINEA [GKP]
AKPET alt for UKPET dial of UKPET-EHOM [AKD]
AKPET-EHOM alt for UKPET-EHOM [AKD]
AKPOSO [KPO] lang, Togo, Ghana
AKPOSSO alt for AKPOSO [KPO]
AKPOTO alt for IDOMA CENTRAL dial of IDOMA
    [IDO]
AKPWAKUM alt for KWAKUM [KWU]
AKRUKAY [AFI] lang, Papua New Guinea
AKSANA [KBG] lang, Chile
AKSANÁS alt for AKSANA [KBG]
AKSU dial of UYGHUR [UIG]
AKTO TÜRKMEN dial of UYGHUR [UIG]
AKU alt for LIO [LJL]
AKU dial of KRIO [KRI]
AKU alt for MODELE dial of BEFANG [BBY]
AKUAPEM dial of AKAN [TWS]
AKUAPIM alt for AKUAPEM dial of AKAN [TWS]
AKUÊN alt for XAVÁNTE [XAV]
AKUKU dial of OKPE-IDESA-OLOMA-AKUKU [OKP]
AKULIYO alt for AKURIO [AKO]
AKUM [AKU] lang, Cameroon, Nigeria
AKUM alt for KUMAM [KDI]
AKUM alt for BAGANGU dial of NGEMBA [NGE]
AKUNAKUNA alt for AGWAGWUNE [YAY]
AKUNNU dial of AKPES [IBE]
AKURAKURA alt for AGWAGWUNE [YAY]
AKURI alt for AKURIO [AKO]
AKURIJO alt for AKURIO [AKO]
AKURIO [AKO] lang, Surinam
AKURIYO alt for AKURIO [AKO]
AKURMI alt for KURAMA [KRH]
AKURUMI alt for KURAMA [KRH]
AKUSHA dial of DARGWA [DAR]
AKUWAGEL alt for BELI [BEY]
AKWA [AKW] lang, Congo
AKWA'ALA alt for PAIPAI [PPI]
AKWANG alt for PALIOUPINY dial of DINKA,
    SOUTHWESTERN [DIK]
AKWAPEM TWI alt for AKUAPEM dial of AKAN
    [TWS]
AKWAPI alt for AKUAPEM dial of AKAN [TWS]
AKWAYA alt for ASURINÍ [ASU]
AKWAYA MOTOM alt for MACI dial of ICEVE-MACI
    [BEC]
AKWETO alt for NSARI [ASJ]
AKWEYA alt for AKPA dial of AKPA-YACHE [AKF]
AKYE alt for AKE [AIK]
AKYE alt for ATTIÉ [ATI]

AKYEM BOSOME dial of AKAN [TWS]
AKYODE alt for GIKYODE [ACD]
AL-HASAA dial of ARABIC, GULF [AFB]
AL-QASIIM alt for CENTRAL NAJDI dial of ARABIC,
  NAJDI [ARS]
AL-SHIHUH alt for SHIHU [SSH]
ALA alt for WALI [WLX]
ALA alt for ASHE dial of KORO [KOR]
ALABA alt for ALLAABA [ALB]
ALABAMA [AKZ] lang, USA
ALABAT ISLAND DUMAGAT alt for AGTA, ALABAT
  ISLAND [DUL]
ALACALUF alt for KAWESQAR [ALC]
ALADA alt for GUN-GBE [GUW]
ALADA-GBE alt for GUN-GBE [GUW]
ALADIAN [ALD] lang, Côte d'Ivoire
ALADYAN alt for ALADIAN [ALD]
ALAG-BAKO dial of IRAYA [IRY]
ALAGIA alt for ALADIAN [ALD]
ALAGIAN alt for ALADIAN [ALD]
ALAGO [ALA] lang, Nigeria
ALAGWA alt for WASI [WBJ]
ALAI [AMB] lang, Papua New Guinea
ALAK 1 [ALK] lang, Laos
ALAK 2 [ALQ] lang, Laos
ALAKAMAN dial of ABUI [ABZ]
ALAKAMAT alt for HUAULU [HUD]
ALAKI alt for LEKI dial of LURI [LRI]
ALAKONG dial of BAHNAR [BDQ]
ALALAO alt for PADOE [PDO]
ALAM alt for MALA [PED]
ALAMA alt for QUICHUA, PASTAZA, NORTHERN
  [QLB]
ALAMA alt for QUICHUA, LOWLAND, NAPO [QLN]
ALAMATU alt for MBUTU dial of NGEMBA [NGE]
ALAMBLAK [AMP] lang, Papua New Guinea
ALAMBUK alt for ALAMBLAK [AMP]
ALANGAN [ALJ] lang, Philippines
ALANTE alt for BALANTA [BLE]
ALAR dial of BURIAT, RUSSIA [MNB]
ALAS dial of BATAK ALAS-KLUET [BTZ]
ALAS-KLUET BATAK alt for BATAK ALAS-KLUET
  [BTZ]
ALASAI dial of PASHAYI, NORTHWEST [GLH]
ALATENING dial of NGEMBA [NGE]
ALATESU dial of NAMBIKUÁRA, SOUTHERN [NAB]
ALATIL [ALX] lang, Papua New Guinea
ALATINING alt for ALATENING dial of NGEMBA
  [NGE]
ALAUAGAT alt for BRAGAT [AOF]
ALAWA [ALH] lang, Australia
ALAWA alt for WASI [WBJ]
ALBANIAN, ARVANITIKA [AAT] lang, Greece
ALBANIAN, GHEG [ALS] lang, Yugoslavia, Albania,
  Bulgaria
ALBANIAN, TOSK [ALN] lang, Albania, Italy, Italy,
  Turkey, Ukraine
ALBARRADAS ZAPOTEC alt for ZAPOTECO,
  ALBARRADAS [ZAS]
ALCANTARANON dial of INONHAN [LOC]
ALDAN TIMPTON dial of EVENKI [EVN]
ALE alt for NAKE [NBK]
ALEALUM alt for MALAYALAM [MJS]
ALEGE [ALF] lang, Nigeria
ALEGI alt for ALEGE [ALF]
ALEKANO [GAH] lang, Papua New Guinea

ALEMANNIC alt for SCHWYZERDÜTSCH [GSW]
ALEMANNISCH alt for SCHWYZERDÜTSCH [GSW]
ALENG alt for MON [MNW]
ALEPA dial of SINAGORO [SNC]
ALEUT [ALW] lang, USA, Russia, Asia, Russia, Asia
ALEUT alt for YUPIK, PACIFIC GULF [EMS]
ALEUT alt for ALEUT [ALW]
ALEVICA alt for KIRMANJKI [QKV]
ALFENDIO alt for ARAFUNDI [ARF]
ALFOLD dial of HUNGARIAN [HNG]
ALGERIAN alt for ARABIC, ALGERIAN [ARQ]
ALGERIAN SIGN LANGUAGE [ASP] lang, Algeria
ALGHERESE dial of CATALAN [CLN]
ALGIERS dial of ARABIC, ALGERIAN [ARQ]
ALGONKIN alt for ALGONQUIN [ALG]
ALGONQUIN [ALG] lang, Canada
ALI alt for YAKAMUL [YKM]
ALI dial of GBAYA [GYA]
ALI dial of YAKAMUL [YKM]
ALI dial of MANJA [MZV]
ALIAB alt for ALIAP dial of DINKA, SOUTH
  CENTRAL [DIB]
ALIAP dial of DINKA, SOUTH CENTRAL [DIB]
ALILE dial of PARAUJANO [PBG]
ALINGA alt for ELING dial of TUNEN [BAZ]
ALINGAR dial of PASHAYI, SOUTHEAST [DRA]
ALIS alt for TOMÁS-ALIS dial of QUECHUA,
  YAUYOS [QUX]
ALITTA alt for SIDRAP dial of BUGIS [BPR]
ALIUTOR alt for ALUTOR [ALR]
ALLAABA [ALB] lang, Ethiopia
ALLADIAN alt for ALADIAN [ALD]
ALLADYAN alt for ALADIAN [ALD]
ALLAGIR dial of OSETIN [OSE]
ALLANG dial of LARIKE-WAKASIHU [ALO]
ALLAR [ALL] lang, India
ALLAR alt for OLLARI [OLL]
ALLEMANNIC alt for SCHWYZERDÜTSCH [GSW]
ALLEMANNISCH alt for SCHWYZERDÜTSCH [GSW]
ALMATSON alt for SHOMBA dial of NGEMBA [NGE]
ALMOLONGA dial of POPOLOCA, WESTERN [POW]
ALNGITH [AID] lang, Australia
ALO dial of BANGBA [BBE]
ALO alt for ALU dial of MONO [MTE]
ALOA alt for NGAM dial of KWANG [KVI]
ALOAPAM ZAPOTECO alt for ZAPOTECO,
  WESTERN IXTLÁN [ZAE]
ALOEKOE alt for ALUKU dial of AUKAANS [DJK]
ALOMA alt for AROMA dial of KEOPARA [KHZ]
ALOMWE alt for LOMWE [NGL]
ALONG alt for ELONG dial of AKOOSE [BSS]
ALOR dial of DINKA, NORTHWESTERN [DIW]
ALOR alt for EAST LAMAHOLOT dial of
  LAMAHOLOT [SLP]
ALORESE alt for EAST LAMAHOLOT dial of
  LAMAHOLOT [SLP]
ALORO alt for ALUR [ALZ]
ALPIN alt for GAVOT dial of PROVENÇAL [PRV]
ALPINE LOMBARD dial of LOMBARD [LMO]
ALSATIAN alt for SCHWYZERDÜTSCH [GSW]
ALTA, NORTHERN [AQN] lang, Philippines
ALTA, SOUTHERN [AGY] lang, Philippines
ALTAI alt for ALTAI, SOUTHERN [ALT]
ALTAI PROPER dial of ALTAI, SOUTHERN [ALT]
ALTAI, NORTHERN [ATV] lang, Russia, Asia
ALTAI, SOUTHERN [ALT] lang, Russia, Asia

ALTAI-KIZHI alt for ALTAI PROPER dial of ALTAI, SOUTHERN [ALT]
ALTAJ KIZI alt for ALTAI PROPER dial of ALTAI, SOUTHERN [ALT]
ALTMARK alt for EAST LOW GERMAN dial of GERMAN, LOW [GEP]
ALTO BAYANO alt for BAYANO dial of KUNA, SAN BLAS [CUK]
ALTOARAGONES alt for ARAGONESE [AXX]
ALU [AUX] lang, India
ALU alt for DIA [DIA]
ALU alt for MONO [MTE]
ALU dial of MONO [MTE]
ALU KURUMBA alt for ALU [AUX]
ALU KURUMBA NONSTANDARD KANNADA alt for KURUMBA, ALU [QKA]
ALUA alt for ALUR [ALZ]
ALUKU dial of AUKAANS [DJK]
ALUKU alt for BONI dial of AUKAANS [DJK]
ALUKUYANA alt for WAYANA [WAY]
ALULU alt for ALUR [ALZ]
ALUMBIS dial of TAGAL MURUT [MVV]
ALUMBIS alt for LUMBIS dial of TAGAL MURUT [MVV]
ALUNE [ALP] lang, Indonesia, Maluku
ALUR [ALZ] lang, Zaïre, Uganda
ALURU dial of LUGBARA, HIGH [LUG]
ALUTIIQ alt for YUPIK, PACIFIC GULF [EMS]
ALUTOR [ALR] lang, Russia, Asia
ALUTORSKIJ dial of ALUTOR [ALR]
ALUU dial of IKWERE [IKW]
ALYAWARRA [ALY] lang, Australia
ALYK dial of KRYTS [KRY]
ALYUTOR alt for ALUTOR [ALR]
AMA [AMM] lang, Papua New Guinea
AMA alt for NYIMANG [NYI]
AMAARRO alt for KOORETE [KQY]
AMABI alt for AMFOAN-FATULEU-AMABI dial of ATONI [TMR]
AMABUSMANA alt for //XEGWI [XEG]
AMACACORE alt for IQUITO [IQU]
AMADI alt for MA [MSJ]
AMAGE alt for AMUESHA [AME]
AMAGUACO alt for AMAHUACA [AMC]
AMAGUES alt for AMUESHA [AME]
AMAHAI [AMQ] lang, Indonesia, Maluku
AMAHEI alt for AMAHAI [AMQ]
AMAHUACA [AMC] lang, Peru, Brazil
AMAIMON [ALI] lang, Papua New Guinea
AMAIZUHO dial of DANO [ASO]
AMAJE alt for AMUESHA [AME]
AMAJO alt for AMUESHA [AME]
AMAKERE alt for MAKERE dial of MANGBETU [MDJ]
AMAL [AAD] lang, Papua New Guinea
AMALA alt for MALA [RUY]
AMALE alt for AMELE [AMI]
AMAM alt for KOMA, NORTH [KMQ]
AMAM alt for BAMBESHI [MYF]
AMAMI-OSHIMA, NORTHERN [RYN] lang, Japan
AMAMI-OSHIMA, SOUTHERN [AMS] lang, Japan
AMAMPA alt for SHERBRO [BUN]
AMAN alt for AMANAVIL dial of EMAN [EMN]
AMANA alt for EMANE [AMD]
AMANAB [AMN] lang, Papua New Guinea, Indonesia, Irian Jaya
AMANAGE alt for AMANAYÉ [AMA]

AMANAJÉ alt for AMANAYÉ [AMA]
AMANATUN alt for AMANUBAN-AMANATUN dial of ATONI [TMR]
AMANAVIL dial of EMAN [EMN]
AMANAYÉ [AMA] lang, Brazil
AMANGBETU alt for MANGBETU [MDJ]
AMANI dial of NAMIA [NNM]
AMANI alt for AMANAVIL dial of EMAN [EMN]
AMANKGQWIGQWI alt for //XEGWI [XEG]
AMANUBAN alt for AMANUBAN-AMANATUN dial of ATONI [TMR]
AMANUBAN-AMANATUN dial of ATONI [TMR]
AMANUBANG alt for AMANUBAN-AMANATUN dial of ATONI [TMR]
AMANYÉ alt for AMANAYÉ [AMA]
AMAR alt for HAMER-BANNA [AMF]
AMARA [AIE] lang, Papua New Guinea
AMARACAIRE alt for AMARAKAERI [AMR]
AMARAG [AMG] lang, Australia
AMARAKAERI [AMR] lang, Peru
AMARAKAIRE alt for AMARAKAERI [AMR]
AMARASI dial of ATONI [TMR]
AMARCOCCHE alt for HAMER-BANNA [AMF]
AMARI dial of ADZERA [AZR]
AMARIBA dial of WAPISHANA [WAP]
AMARINYA alt for AMHARIC [AMH]
AMARRO alt for KOORETE [KQY]
AMASI alt for MANTA [MYG]
AMASSI alt for MANTA [MYG]
AMATAN dial of TZOTZIL, CHAMULA [TZC]
AMATENANGO DEL VALLE dial of TZELTAL, BACHAJÓN [TZB]
AMATLÁN ZAPOTECO alt for ZAPOTECO, NORTHEASTERN MIAHUATLÁN [ZPO]
AMAWACA alt for AMAHUACA [AMC]
AMAWAKA alt for AMAHUACA [AMC]
AMAWÁKA alt for AMAHUACA [AMC]
AMAYO dial of EMAN [EMN]
AMAZIGH alt for TAMAJEQ, AIR [THZ]
AMAZIGH alt for TAMAJEQ, TAHOUA [TTQ]
AMAZONAS alt for QUECHUA, CHACHAPOYAS [QUK]
"AMAZONAS MACUSA" alt for CARABAYO [CBY]
AMBA [UTP] lang, Solomon Islands
AMBA alt for KWAMBA [RWM]
AMBABIKO alt for MODELE dial of BEFANG [BBY]
AMBAE, EAST [OMB] lang, Vanuatu
AMBAE, WEST [NND] lang, Vanuatu
AMBAI [AMK] lang, Indonesia, Irian Jaya
AMBAI dial of AMBAI [AMK]
AMBAI-MENAWI alt for AMBAI [AMK]
AMBALA AGTA alt for AYTA, AMBALA [ABC]
AMBALA SAMBAL alt for AYTA, AMBALA [ABC]
AMBALI alt for BALI dial of TEKE, EASTERN [TEK]
AMBAQUISTA alt for MBAKA dial of MBUNDU, LOANDA [MLO]
AMBARI alt for AMPEELI-WOJOKESO [APZ]
AMBASI [AIT] lang, Papua New Guinea
AMBAWANG dial of KENDAYAN [KNX]
AMBEDE alt for MBERE [MDT]
AMBELAU [AMV] lang, Indonesia, Maluku
AMBELE [AEL] lang, Cameroon
AMBENG dial of GARO [GRT]
AMBENU (VAIKENU alt for BIBOKI-INSANA dial of ATONI [TMR]
AMBENU alt for ATONI [TMR]

AMBER alt for WAIGEO [WGO]
AMBER dial of WAIGEO [WGO]
AMBERBAKEN alt for MPUR [AKC]
AMBERI alt for WAIGEO [WGO]
AMBLAU alt for AMBELAU [AMV]
AMBLONG [ALM] lang, Vanuatu
AMBO alt for NDONGA [NDG]
AMBO dial of LALA-BISA [LEB]
AMBO dial of LALA-BISA [LEB]
AMBO-PASCO QUECHUA alt for QUECHUA, SAN
  RAFAEL-HUARIACA [QEG]
AMBODHI alt for AWADHI [AWD]
AMBONESE alt for MALAY, AMBONESE [ABS]
AMBRYM, NORTH [MMG] lang, Vanuatu
AMBRYM, SOUTHEAST [TVK] lang, Vanuatu
AMBUAL dial of KENINGAU MURUT [KXI]
AMBUELLA alt for MBWELA [MFU]
AMBUL alt for APALIK [PLI]
AMBULAS [ABT] lang, Papua New Guinea
AMBUMI dial of WANDAMEN [WAD]
AMBWELA dial of LUIMBI [LUM]
AMDANG [AMJ] lang, Chad, Sudan
AMDO [ADX] lang, China
AME alt for AMI [AMY]
AMEGI alt for BISENI [IJE]
AMELE [AMI] lang, Papua New Guinea
AMENFI dial of WASA [WSS]
AMENGI dial of MAMVU [MDI]
AMENGUACA alt for AMAHUACA [AMC]
AMER alt for HAMER-BANNA [AMF]
AMERAX [AEX] lang, USA
AMERICAN SIGN LANGUAGE [ASE] lang, USA,
  Canada
AMERICAN SPANISH dial of SPANISH [SPN]
AMESLAN alt for AMERICAN SIGN LANGUAGE
  [ASE]
AMEUHAQUE alt for AMAHUACA [AMC]
AMFOAN alt for AMFOAN-FATULEU-AMABI dial of
  ATONI [TMR]
AMFOAN-FATULEU-AMABI dial of ATONI [TMR]
AMFUANG alt for AMFOAN-FATULEU-AMABI dial of
  ATONI [TMR]
AMHARIC [AMH] lang, Ethiopia, Egypt, Israel
AMHARINYA alt for AMHARIC [AMH]
AMI [AMY] lang, Australia
AMI alt for AMIS [ALV]
AMIA alt for AMIS [ALV]
AMIANGBA alt for BARAMBU [BRM]
AMIANGBWA alt for BARAMBU [BRM]
AMIJANGAL alt for AMI [AMY]
AMIKOANA [AKN] lang, Brazil
AMINA alt for GA-ADANGME-KROBO [GAC]
AMINI alt for NAI [BIO]
AMIOL alt for TUIC dial of DINKA, SOUTHWESTERN
  [DIK]
AMIS [ALV] lang, Taiwan
AMIS, NATAORAN [AIS] lang, Taiwan
AMISH PENNSYLVANIA GERMAN dial of GERMAN,
  PENNSYLVANIA [PDC]
AMMAR alt for HAMER-BANNA [AMF]
AMNIAPÉ alt for KANOÉ [KXO]
AMO [AMO] lang, Nigeria
AMOAMO alt for NORTH MEKEO dial of MEKEO
  [MEK]
AMOISHE alt for AMUESHA [AME]
AMOK alt for MOK [MQT]

AMON alt for UMON [UMM]
AMON alt for AMO [AMO]
AMONDAWA [ADW] lang, Brazil
AMONG alt for AMO [AMO]
AMONO alt for MONO [MNH]
AMORUA alt for CHIRICOA dial of CUIBA [CUI]
AMOTA dial of MARIA [MDS]
AMOU OBLOU dial of AKPOSO [KPO]
AMOY alt for FUJIAN dial of CHINESE, MIN NAN
  [CFR]
AMOY alt for FUKIENESE dial of CHINESE, MIN NAN
  [CFR]
AMOY alt for HOKKIEN dial of CHINESE, MIN NAN
  [CFR]
AMPALE alt for AMPEELI-WOJOKESO [APZ]
AMPANANG [APG] lang, Indonesia, Kalimantan
AMPAS alt for MOLOF [MSL]
AMPEELI-WOJOKESO [APZ] lang, Papua New
  Guinea
AMPELE alt for AMPEELI-WOJOKESO [APZ]
AMPEYI alt for NUPE CENTRAL dial of NUPE [NUP]
AMPIBABO alt for LAUJE [LAW]
AMPIKA alt for BOLE [BOL]
AMRAVATI dial of GONDI, NORTHERN [GON]
AMRI dial of MIKIR [MJW]
AMSURA SADRI dial of SADRI, ORAON [SDR]
AMTO [AMT] lang, Papua New Guinea
AMTUL alt for TAL [TAL]
AMU dial of SWAHILI [SWA]
AMUBRE-KATSI dial of BRIBRI [BZD]
AMUEIXA alt for AMUESHA [AME]
AMUESE alt for AMUESHA [AME]
AMUESHA [AME] lang, Peru
AMUETAMO alt for AMUESHA [AME]
AMUGEN dial of ONO [ONS]
AMUN dial of PIVA [TGI]
AMUNG alt for DAMAL [UHN]
AMUNG dial of DAMAL [UHN]
AMUNG KAL alt for DAMAL [UHN]
AMUNGME alt for DAMAL [UHN]
AMUR dial of GILYAK [NIV]
AMURAG alt for AMARAG [AMG]
AMURU [AUZ] lang, Ethiopia
AMUTOURA alt for SAISIYAT [SAI]
AMUY alt for DAMAL [UHN]
AMUZGO DE SAN PEDRO AMUZGOS alt for
  AMUZGO, OAXACA [AZG]
AMUZGO, GUERRERO [AMU] lang, Mexico
AMUZGO, OAXACA [AZG] lang, Mexico
AMUZGO, SANTA MARÍA IPALAPA [AZM] lang,
  Mexico
AMWI [AML] lang, India
ANA alt for IFÈ [IFE]
ANA-IFÉ alt for IFÈ [IFE]
ANA-IFE alt for IFÈ [IFE]
ANAANG [ANW] lang, Nigeria
ANABEZE alt for BUJI dial of JERA [JER]
ANAFEJANZI alt for JANJI [JNI]
ANAGO alt for IFÈ [IFE]
ANAGUTA alt for IGUTA [NAR]
ANAKALANG alt for ANAKALANGU [AKG]
ANAKALANGU [AKG] lang, Indonesia, Nusa
  Tenggara
ANAKOLA alt for BATAK ANGKOLA [AKB]
ANAL [ANM] lang, India, Myanmar, Myanmar
ANAL alt for ANAL [ANM]

ANAMAGI alt for TORRICELLI [TEI]
ANAMBÉ [AAN] lang, Brazil
ANANA alt for GUANANO [GVC]
ANANDJOOBI alt for ANANJUBI dial of AKPE [AQP]
ANANG alt for ANAANG [ANW]
ANANJUBI dial of AKPE [AQP]
ANAPIA alt for OMAGUA [OMG]
ANAR alt for SAAMI, INARI [LPI]
ANARYA dial of BHILI [BHB]
ANATOLIAN alt for TURKISH [TRK]
ANATRI dial of CHUVASH [CJU]
ANAULI dial of TURKMEN [TCK]
ANAWLA alt for GAMADIA dial of GUJARATI [GJR]
ANCALONG KUTAI dial of MALAY, TENGGARONG
    KUTAI [VKT]
ANCHIX dial of KARATA [KPT]
ANCIENT ETHIOPIC alt for GEEZ [GEE]
ANCIENT HEBREW alt for HEBREW, OLD [HBO]
ANCUX dial of AVAR [AVR]
ANDAGARINYA alt for ANTAKARINYA [ANT]
ANDAHUAYLAS dial of QUECHUA, AYACUCHO
    [QUY]
ANDAKI alt for ANDAQUI [ANA]
ANDALAL-GXDATL dial of AVAR [AVR]
ANDALI alt for ANGWE dial of MANGBUTU [MDK]
ANDALUSIAN dial of SPANISH [SPN]
ANDANG alt for AMDANG [AMJ]
ANDANGTI alt for AMDANG [AMJ]
ANDAQUI [ANA] lang, Colombia
ANDARUM [AOD] lang, Papua New Guinea
ANDASA alt for NDASA [NDA]
ANDEGEREBINHA [ADG] lang, Australia
ANDELALE dial of UMBU-UNGU [UMB]
ANDH [ANR] lang, India
ANDHA alt for ANDH [ANR]
ANDHI alt for ANDH [ANR]
ANDHRA alt for TELUGU [TCW]
ANDHRA PRADESH LAMANI dial of LAMANI [LMN]
ANDI [ANI] lang, Russia, Europe
ANDIAN alt for MANDAR [MHN]
ANDII alt for ANDI [ANI]
ANDILJANGWA alt for ANINDILYAKWA [AOI]
ANDILYAUGWA alt for ANINDILYAKWA [AOI]
ANDINAI dial of MANGBUTU [MDK]
ANDIO [BZB] lang, Indonesia, Sulawesi
ANDIO'O alt for ANDIO [BZB]
ANDIRA alt for SATERÉ-MAWÉ [MAV]
ANDIY alt for ANDI [ANI]
ANDO alt for ANO dial of ANYIN [ANY]
ANDOA [ANB] lang, Peru
ANDOKE alt for ANDOQUE [ANO]
ANDONE alt for OBOLO [ANN]
ANDONI alt for OBOLO [ANN]
ANDONNI alt for OBOLO [ANN]
ANDOQUE [ANO] lang, Colombia
ANDRA-HUS [ANX] lang, Papua New Guinea
ANDRE dial of LUGBARA, LOW [LUC]
ANDRE-LEBATI alt for LUGBARA, LOW [LUC]
ANDRI dial of MORU [MGD]
ANDRO dial of KADO [KDV]
ANEGOROM alt for RIBINA dial of JERA [JER]
ANEI alt for ABIEM dial of DINKA, SOUTHWESTERN
    [DIK]
ANEITEUM alt for ANEITYUM [ATY]
ANEITEUMESE alt for ANEITYUM [ATY]
ANEITYUM [ATY] lang, Vanuatu

ANEJ alt for GULE [GLE]
ANEJOM alt for ANEITYUM [ATY]
ANEM [ANZ] lang, Papua New Guinea
ANEME WAKE [ABY] lang, Papua New Guinea
ANEMORO alt for LEMORO [LDJ]
ANEP alt for NDOE [NBB]
ANESU alt for XARACUU [ANE]
ANEWA alt for ANIWA dial of FUTUNA-ANIWA
    [FUT]
ANFILLO [MYO] lang, Ethiopia
ANGA [ANP] lang, India
ANGA alt for HANGA [HAG]
ANGAATIHA [AGM] lang, Papua New Guinea
ANGAATIYA alt for ANGAATIHA [AGM]
ANGADI dial of ASMAT, CENTRAL [AST]
ANGAITE [AIV] lang, Paraguay
ANGAL ENEN alt for ANGAL HENENG, SOUTH [AOE]
ANGAL HENENG, SOUTH [AOE] lang, Papua New
    Guinea
ANGAL HENENG, WEST [AKH] lang, Papua New
    Guinea
ANGAL, EAST [AGE] lang, Papua New Guinea
ANGAMIS alt for NAGA, ANGAMI [NJM]
ANGAN alt for KAMANTAN [KCI]
ANGANIWAI alt for KAHUA [AGW]
ANGANIWEI alt for KAHUA [AGW]
ANGAS [ANC] lang, Nigeria
ANGATAHA alt for ANGAATIHA [AGM]
ANGATE alt for ANGAITE [AIV]
ANGAUA alt for NENT [ANH]
ANGAVE alt for ANKAVE [AAK]
ANGBA alt for NGELIMA [AGH]
ANGEL ALBINO CORZO dial of TZOTZIL, HUIXTÁN
    [TZU]
ANGEVIN dial of FRENCH [FRN]
ANGGOR alt for ANGOR [AGG]
ANGGURUK alt for YALI, ANGGURUK [YLI]
ANGIE alt for NGIE [NGJ]
ANGIKA alt for ANGA [ANP]
ANGIKAR alt for ANGA [ANP]
ANGKOLA alt for BATAK ANGKOLA [AKB]
ANGLAT AGTA dial of AGTA, UMIRAY DUMAGET
    [DUE]
ANGLO dial of ÉWÉ [EWE]
ANGLOROMANI [RME] lang, United Kingdom, USA,
    Australia
ANGOCHE alt for KOTI [EKO]
ANGOLAR NGOLA dial of CRIOULO, GULF OF
    GUINEA [CRI]
ANGOLE dial of KUSAAL, EASTERN [KUS]
ANGOM alt for NGOM [NRA]
ANGOMERRY alt for NGENKIWUMERRI dial of
    NANGIKURRUNGGURR [NAM]
ANGONI alt for NGONI [NGU]
ANGOR [AGG] lang, Papua New Guinea
ANGORAM [AOG] lang, Papua New Guinea
ANGOTERO alt for SECOYA [SEY]
ANGOTERO dial of SECOYA [SEY]
ANGOXE alt for KOTI [EKO]
ANGOYA [MIW] lang, Papua New Guinea
ANGPHANG dial of NAGA, KONYAK [NBE]
ANGWE dial of MANGBUTU [MDK]
ANHAQUI dial of BIDYOGO [BJG]
ANIBAU alt for GUSU dial of JERA [JER]
ANIGIBI alt for ARIGIBI dial of KIWAI, NORTHEAST
    [KIW]

ANII [BLO] lang, Benin, Togo, Togo
ANII alt for ANII [BLO]
ANIMERE [ANF] lang, Ghana
ANINDILYAKWA [AOI] lang, Australia
ANINI-Y dial of KINARAY-A [KRJ]
ANIOCHA dial of IGBO [IGR]
ANIR dial of TANGGA [TGG]
ANIRAGO alt for NIRAGU dial of GBIRI-NIRAGU
   [GRH]
ANIULA alt for YANYUWA [JAO]
ANIWA dial of FUTUNA-ANIWA [FUT]
ANJAM [BOJ] lang, Papua New Guinea
ANJIE alt for AJIË [AJI]
ANJIMATANA alt for ADYNYAMATHANHA [ADT]
ANJIWATANA alt for ADYNYAMATHANHA [ADT]
ANJOUAN alt for SHINZWANI dial of COMORIAN
   [SWB]
ANJUSKI dial of UDIHE [UDE]
ANKAI dial of ANKAVE [AAK]
ANKAVE [AAK] lang, Papua New Guinea
ANKOBER dial of ARGOBBA [AGJ]
ANKPA dial of IGALA [IGL]
ANKULU alt for IKULU [IKU]
ANKWAI alt for GOEMAI [ANK]
ANKWE alt for GOEMAI [ANK]
ANKWEI alt for GOEMAI [ANK]
ANLO [AOL] lang, Togo
ANLO alt for IGO [AHL]
ANLOUR dial of KUY [KDT]
ANMATJIRRA [AMX] lang, Australia
ANNA alt for BIDEYAT [BIH]
ANNABERG alt for RAO [RAO]
ANNAMESE alt for VIETNAMESE [VIE]
ANNAMITE FRENCH alt for TAY BOI [TAS]
ANNANG alt for ANAANG [ANW]
ANNOBONESE dial of CRIOULO, GULF OF GUINEA
   [CRI]
ANO dial of ANYIN [ANY]
ANODÕUB alt for NADËB [MBJ]
ANOONG alt for NUNG [NUN]
ANOR [ANJ] lang, Papua New Guinea
ANORUBUNA alt for RIBINA dial of JERA [JER]
ANOSANGOBARI alt for GUSU dial of JERA [JER]
ANOWURU alt for LEMORO [LDJ]
ANPIKA alt for FIKA dial of BOLE [BOL]
ANSAKARA alt for NZAKARA [NZK]
ANSERMA [ANS] lang, Colombia
ANSERNA alt for ANSERMA [ANS]
ANSHUENKUAN NYARONG alt for ATUENCE [ATF]
ANSITA alt for SHITA [LGN]
ANSUS [AND] lang, Indonesia, Irian Jaya
ANTA alt for MANTA [MYG]
ANTAIMORO alt for TAIMORO dial of MALAGASY
   [MEX]
ANTAISAKA alt for TAISAKA dial of MALAGASY
   [MEX]
ANTAIVA alt for BEZANOZANO dial of MALAGASY
   [MEX]
ANTAKARINYA [ANT] lang, Australia
ANTAMBAHOAKA alt for TAMBAHOAKA dial of
   MALAGASY [MEX]
ANTANALA alt for TANALA dial of MALAGASY
   [MEX]
ANTANKA alt for BEZANOZANO dial of MALAGASY
   [MEX]
ANTARBEDI alt for BRAJ BHASHA [BFS]

ANTARBEDI dial of BRAJ BHASHA [BFS]
ANTARDROY 1 dial of MALAGASY [MEX]
ANTARDROY 2 dial of MALAGASY [MEX]
ANTARVEDI alt for BRAJ BHASHA [BFS]
ANTIPOLO IFUGAO alt for KALLAHAN, KELEY-I [IFY]
ANTIQUEÑO alt for KINARAY-A [KRJ]
ANTRA dial of KUY [KDT]
ANTSUKH alt for ANCUX dial of AVAR [AVR]
ANU [ANL] lang, Myanmar
ANU alt for NUNG [NUN]
ANU dial of GUA [LAR]
ANUAK [ANU] lang, Ethiopia, Sudan, Sudan
ANUAK alt for ANUAK [ANU]
ANUFO [CKO] lang, Togo, Benin, Ghana
ANUKI [AUI] lang, Papua New Guinea
ANULA alt for YANYUWA [JAO]
ANUM alt for ANU dial of GUA [LAR]
ANUNG alt for NUNG [NUN]
ANUPE alt for NUPE CENTRAL dial of NUPE [NUP]
ANUPECWAYI alt for NUPE CENTRAL dial of NUPE
   [NUP]
ANUPERI alt for NUPE CENTRAL dial of NUPE [NUP]
ANUS alt for SOBEI [SOB]
ANUS dial of SOBEI [SOB]
ANUTA [AUD] lang, Solomons
ANWAIN alt for ESAN [ISH]
ANYAH alt for DENYA [ANV]
ANYAMA dial of OGBIA [OGB]
ANYAN alt for DENYA [ANV]
ANYANG alt for DENYA [ANV]
ANYANG dial of NGEMBA [NGE]
ANYANGA [AYG] lang, Togo
ANYAR alt for AKUM [AKU]
ANYARAN alt for UKAAN [KCF]
ANYEP alt for NDOE [NBB]
ANYI alt for ANYIN [ANY]
ANYIMA alt for LENYIMA [LDG]
ANYIMERE alt for ANIMERE [ANF]
ANYIN [ANY] lang, Côte d'Ivoire, Ghana, Ghana
ANYIN alt for ANYIN [ANY]
ANYO alt for NAGA, MELURI [NLM]
ANYUAK alt for ANUAK [ANU]
ANYULA alt for YANYUWA [JAO]
ANYWA alt for ANUAK [ANU]
ANYWAK alt for ANUAK [ANU]
ANYX dial of LEZGI [LEZ]
AO alt for NAGA, AO [NJO]
AO TÁ dial of MUONG [MTQ]
AO YAO alt for MIEN [YOC]
AOAQUI alt for ARUTANI [ATX]
AOBA alt for AMBAE, EAST [OMB]
AOHENG [PNI] lang, Indonesia, Kalimantan
AOLA dial of LENGO [LGR]
AOMIE alt for ÖMIE [AOM]
AONA alt for ONA [ONA]
AONIKEN alt for TEHUELCHE [TEH]
AORE [AOR] lang, Vanuatu
AORR alt for NAGA, AO [NJO]
AOSHEDD alt for NAGA, KHIAMNGAN [NKY]
AOUDJILA alt for AWJILAH [AUJ]
AOWIN dial of ANYIN [ANY]
AP-NE-AP dial of TORRES STRAIT CREOLE [TCS]
APA alt for APATANI [APT]
APACHE, JICARILLA [APJ] lang, USA
APACHE, KIOWA [APK] lang, USA
APACHE, LIPAN [APL] lang, USA

APACHE, MESCALERO-CHIRICAHUA [APM] lang, USA
APACHE, WESTERN [APW] lang, USA
APAE'AA alt for SA'A [APB]
APAGIBETE alt for PAGABETE [PAG]
APAGIBETI alt for PAGABETE [PAG]
APAHAPSILI dial of NIPSAN [YAC]
APAK dial of ATUOT [ATU]
APAKA alt for AMA [AMM]
APAKABETI alt for PAGABETE [PAG]
APAKIBETI alt for PAGABETE [PAG]
APAL [ENA] lang, Papua New Guinea
APALAÍ [APA] lang, Brazil
APALAKIRI alt for KALAPÁLO [KPB]
APALAQUIRI alt for KALAPÁLO [KPB]
APALAY alt for APALAÍ [APA]
APALI alt for APAL [ENA]
APALIK [PLI] lang, Papua New Guinea
APAMBIA alt for PAMBIA [PAM]
APANHECRA alt for APANJEKRA dial of CANELA [RAM]
APANIEKRA alt for APANJEKRA dial of CANELA [RAM]
APANJEKRA dial of CANELA [RAM]
APAPOCUVA dial of CHIRIPA [NHD]
APARAI alt for APALAÍ [APA]
APATANI [APT] lang, India
API alt for LAMPUNG [LJP]
APIACÁ [API] lang, Brazil
APIAKÁ alt for APIACÁ [API]
APIAKE alt for APIACÁ [API]
APIAPUM dial of MBEMBE, CROSS RIVER [MFN]
APINAGÉ alt for APINAYÉ [APN]
APINAJÉ alt for APINAYÉ [APN]
APINAYÉ [APN] lang, Brazil
APINDJE alt for PINJI [PIC]
APINDJI alt for PINJI [PIC]
APINJI alt for PINJI [PIC]
APMA [APP] lang, Vanuatu
APMISIBIL dial of NGALUM [SZB]
APOI dial of IJO, CENTRAL-WESTERN [IJC]
APOKINSKIJ dial of KORYAK [KPY]
APOLO dial of QUECHUA, NORTH BOLIVIAN [QUL]
APONTE INGA dial of INGA [INB]
APOS dial of KWANGA [KWJ]
APOWASI dial of BITARA [BIT]
APPA alt for TAROK [YER]
APPOLO alt for NZEMA [NZE]
APRWE dial of AIZI [AHI]
APUI dial of WOISIKA [WOI]
APUK dial of DINKA, SOUTHWESTERN [DIK]
APUKIN alt for APOKINSKIJ dial of KORYAK [KPY]
APUOTH alt for ABIEM dial of DINKA, SOUTHWESTERN [DIK]
APURAHUANO alt for TAGBANWA [TBW]
APURÍ dial of QUECHUA, YAUYOS [QUX]
APURI dial of BLAGAR [BEU]
APURINÃ [APU] lang, Brazil
APURUCAYALI dial of CAMPA, ASHÉNINCA [CPU]
APUT alt for PUNAN APUT [PUD]
APUTAI [APX] lang, Indonesia, Maluku
APWOTH alt for ABIEM dial of DINKA, SOUTHWESTERN [DIK]
APYTARE alt for CHIRIPA [NHD]
AQSU alt for AKSU dial of UYGHUR [UIG]
AQUA alt for SOUTHERN EJAGHAM dial of

EJAGHAM [ETU]
AQUA alt for SOUTHERN EJAGHAM dial of EJAGHAM [ETU]
ARA alt for ARHÂ [ARN]
ARA alt for AARI [AIZ]
ARA alt for KONJO PESISIR dial of KONJO, COASTAL [KJC]
ARAB-SWAHILI alt for SWAHILI [SWA]
ARABANA [ARD] lang, Australia
ARABE CHOA alt for ARABIC, SHUWA [SHU]
ARABELA [ARL] lang, Peru
ARABIC, ALGERIAN [ARQ] lang, Algeria, Niger, Niger
ARABIC, ALGERIAN alt for ARABIC, ALGERIAN [ARQ]
ARABIC, BABALIA [BBZ] lang, Chad
ARABIC, CENTRAL ASIAN COLLOQUIAL [ABH] lang, Uzbekistan, Afghanistan
ARABIC, CLASSICAL [ARA] lang, Saudi Arabia
ARABIC, CYPRIOT [ACY] lang, Cyprus
ARABIC, EGYPTIAN COLLOQUIAL [ARZ] lang, Egypt, United Arab Emirates, Libya, Iraq, Jordan, Saudi Arabic, United Arab Emirates, Yemen
ARABIC, GULF [AFB] lang, Iraq, Iran, Oman, Qatar, Saudi Arabic, United Arab Emirates
ARABIC, GULF alt for ARABIC, NAJDI [ARS]
ARABIC, GULF alt for AYIZO-GBE [AYB]
ARABIC, HASSANIYA [MEY] lang, Mauritania, Mali, Morocco, Niger, Senegal
ARABIC, HIJAZI [ACW] lang, Saudi Arabia
ARABIC, JUDEO-MOROCCAN [AJU] lang, Israel, Morocco
ARABIC, JUDEO-TUNISIAN [AJT] lang, Tunisia, France, Israel
ARABIC, LEVANTINE [APC] lang, Syria, Israel, Jordan, Kuwait, Lebanon
ARABIC, LIBYAN [AYL] lang, Libya
ARABIC, MESOPOTAMIAN COLLOQUIAL [ACM] lang, Iraq, Iran
ARABIC, MODERN STANDARD [ABV] lang, Saudi Arabia, Algeria, Chad, Egypt, Ethiopia, Libya, Morocco, Somalia, Sudan, Tanzania, Tunisia, Bahrain, Iraq, Jordan, Kuwait, Lebanon, Oman, Qatar, Syria, United Arab Emirates, Yemen
ARABIC, MOROCCAN [ARY] lang, Morocco, Egypt
ARABIC, NAJDI [ARS] lang, Saudi Arabia, Iraq, Jordan, Kuwait, Syria
ARABIC, OMANI [ACX] lang, Oman, United Arab Emirates
ARABIC, SÁIDI [AEC] lang, Egypt
ARABIC, SHUWA [SHU] lang, Chad, Cameroon, Niger, Nigeria
ARABIC, SUDANESE [APD] lang, Sudan, Egypt, Ethiopia
ARABIC, SUDANESE CREOLE [PGA] lang, Sudan
ARABIC, SYRO-MESOPOTAMIAN [AYP] lang, Iraq, Syria, Syria, Turkey
ARABIC, TUNISIAN [AEB] lang, Tunisia, France
ARABIC, YEMENI [ACQ] lang, Yemen, Djibouti, Ethiopia, Tanzania
ARABINYA alt for ARABIC, YEMENI [ACQ]
ARABIZED HEBREW alt for ORIENTAL HEBREW dial of HEBREW [HBR]
ARABKIR dial of ARMENIAN [ARM]
ARADIGI alt for RATAGNON [BTN]
ARAFUNDI [ARF] lang, Papua New Guinea
ARAGO alt for ALAGO [ALA]

ARAGONES alt for ARAGONESE [AXX]
ARAGONESE [AXX] lang, Spain
ARAGONESE dial of SPANISH [SPN]
ARAGU alt for ALAGO [ALA]
ARAGURE alt for XARAGURE [ARG]
ARAGWA dial of TU [MJG]
ARAKANESE [MHV] lang, Myanmar, Bangladesh,
    India
ARAKH [AAH] lang, India
ARAKI [AKR] lang, Vanuatu
ARAKI dial of FARSI, WESTERN [PES]
ARALLE alt for ARALLE-TABULAHAN [ATQ]
ARALLE-TABULAHAN [ATQ] lang, Indonesia,
    Sulawesi
ARAMA alt for SOUTH WAIBUK dial of HARUAI
    [TMD]
ARAMANIK [AAM] lang, Tanzania
ARAMAUE alt for ARAMO dial of HAGAHAI [HAX]
ARAMBA [STK] lang, Papua New Guinea
ARAMIC alt for JUDEO-ARAMAIC [TRG]
ARAMO alt for HAGAHAI [HAX]
ARAMO dial of HAGAHAI [HAX]
ARANADAN [AAF] lang, India
ARANAIS alt for GASCON [GSC]
ARANDA alt for ARANDA, WESTERN [ARE]
ARANDA, WESTERN [ARE] lang, Australia
ARANDAI [JBJ] lang, Indonesia, Irian Jaya
ARANDAI dial of ARANDAI [JBJ]
ARANDUI alt for GAWAR-BATI [GWT]
ARANÉS alt for GASCON [GSC]
ARANESE alt for GASCON [GSC]
ARANESE OCCITAN alt for GASCON [GSC]
ARANGKA'A dial of TALAUD [TLD]
ARAONA [ARO] lang, Bolivia
ARAOUAN alt for WEST SONGAI dial of SONGAI
    [SON]
ARÁP dial of JARAI [JRA]
ARAPAÇO alt for ARAPASO [ARJ]
ARAPAHO [ARP] lang, USA
ARAPASO [ARJ] lang, Brazil
ARAPESH, BUMBITA [AON] lang, Papua New Guinea
ARAPESH, SOUTHERN [AOJ] lang, Papua New
    Guinea
ARAPIUM alt for SATERÉ-MAWÉ [MAV]
ARARA alt for JÚMA [JUA]
ARARA dial of CARÚTANA [CRU]
ARÁRA DO JIPARANÁ alt for ARÁRA, RONDÔNIA
    [ARR]
ARÁRA, ACRE [AXA] lang, Brazil
ARÁRA, MATO GROSSO [AXG] lang, Brazil
ARÁRA, PARÁ [AAP] lang, Brazil
ARÁRA, RONDÔNIA [ARR] lang, Brazil
ARARA-SHAWANAWA dial of KATUKÍNA, PANOAN
    [KNT]
ARARAPINA dial of KATUKÍNA, PANOAN [KNT]
ARARAWA dial of KATUKÍNA, PANOAN [KNT]
ARASAIRI dial of HUACHIPAERI [HUG]
ARASPASO alt for ARAPASO [ARJ]
ARAUCANO alt for MAPUDUNGUN [ARU]
ARAUINE alt for AWETÍ [AWE]
ARAUITE alt for AWETÍ [AWE]
ARAVA dial of TAMIL [TCV]
ARAVIA dial of HAHON [HAH]
ARAWAK [ARW] lang, Surinam, French Guiana,
    Guyana, Venezuela
ARAWAK alt for ARAWAK [ARW]

ARAWE alt for AROVE [AAW]
ARAWETÉ [AWT] lang, Brazil
ARAWUM [AWM] lang, Papua New Guinea
ARAY alt for ARE [AAG]
ARAYANS alt for MALARYAN [MJQ]
ARBANASI dial of ALBANIAN, TOSK [ALN]
ARBËRESHË alt for ALBANIAN, TOSK [ALN]
ARBËRESHË dial of ALBANIAN, TOSK [ALN]
ARBOR alt for ADI [ADI]
ARBORA alt for ARBORE [ARV]
ARBORE [ARV] lang, Ethiopia
ARBORENSE dial of SARDINIAN, CAMPIDANESE
    [SRO]
ARCHI [ARC] lang, Russia, Europe
ARCHIN alt for ARCHI [ARC]
ARCHINTSY alt for ARCHI [ARC]
ARCHUALDA alt for ADYNYAMATHANHA [ADT]
ARCTIC RED RIVER dial of GWICH'IN [KUC]
ARCTIC VILLAGE GWICH'IN dial of GWICH'IN [KUC]
ARDERI alt for DZODINKA [ADD]
ARE [AAG] lang, India
ARE [MWC] lang, Papua New Guinea
ARÉ alt for XETÁ [XET]
ARE alt for TOEMOETOE dial of KATI, NORTHERN
    [KTI]
'ARE'ARE [ALU] lang, Solomon Islands
AREBA [AEA] lang, Australia
ARECUNA dial of PEMON [AOC]
ARECUNA dial of PEMON [AOC]
AREGEREK alt for MUSAR [MMI]
AREGWE alt for IRIGWE [IRI]
AREKUNA alt for ARECUNA dial of PEMON [AOC]
AREKUNA alt for ARECUNA dial of PEMON [AOC]
AREM [AEM] lang, Viet Nam, Laos
ARENG alt for CHIN, KHUMI [CKM]
AREQUENA alt for GUAREQUENA [GAE]
AREQUIPA QUECHUA alt for QUECHUA,
    COTAHUASI [QAR]
ARET dial of PASHAYI, NORTHEAST [AEE]
ARFAK alt for MEAH [MEJ]
ARGO alt for ALAGO [ALA]
ARGOBBA [AGJ] lang, Ethiopia
ARGOBBINYA alt for ARGOBBA [AGJ]
ARGOENI alt for ARGUNI [AGF]
ARGUNI [AGF] lang, Indonesia, Irian Jaya
ARGUNI BAY alt for IRARUTU [IRH]
ARHÂ [ARN] lang, New Caledonia
ARHE dial of IVBIE NORTH-OKPELA-ARHE [ATG]
ARHÖ [AOK] lang, New Caledonia
ARHUACO alt for ICA [ARH]
ARI [AAC] lang, Papua New Guinea
ARI alt for AARI [AIZ]
ARI alt for ERRE [ERR]
ARI alt for ABIDJI [ABI]
ARIA alt for RAPANGKAKA dial of PAMONA [BCX]
ARIA alt for BANAHU dial of UMA [PPK]
ARIA-MOUK alt for MOUK-ARIA [MWH]
ARIANA alt for OMAGUA [OMG]
ARIANGULU alt for SANYE [SSN]
ARIAWIAI alt for MIKAREW [MSY]
ARIBWATSA alt for LAE [LAZ]
ARIBWAUNGG alt for YALU [YLU]
ARICAPÚ alt for ARIKAPÚ [ARK]
ARICUNA alt for ARECUNA dial of PEMON [AOC]
ARICUNA alt for ARECUNA dial of PEMON [AOC]
ARIÉGEOIS dial of GASCON [GSC]

ARIFAMA dial of ARIFAMA-MINIAFIA [AAI]
ARIFAMA-MINIAFIA [AAI] lang, Papua New Guinea
ARIGIBI dial of KIWAI, NORTHEAST [KIW]
ARIGIDI dial of AKOKO, NORTH [AKK]
ARIHINI alt for MANDAHUACA [MHT]
ARIHINI alt for BARÉ [BAE]
ARIKAPÚ [ARK] lang, Brazil
ARIKARA [ARI] lang, USA
ARIKUN dial of HOANYA [HON]
ARIL dial of ATUOT [ATU]
ARIMA alt for ARINUA [AUK]
ARINGA LUGBARA alt for LUGBARA, LOW [LUC]
ARINUA [AUK] lang, Papua New Guinea
ARINWA alt for ARINUA [AUK]
ARIOM dial of BIAK [BHW]
ARIPAKTSA alt for RIKBAKTSA [ART]
ARISEACHI TARAHUMARA alt for TARAHUMARA,
   NORTHERN [THH]
ARKANSAS alt for QUAPAW [QUA]
ARLENG dial of MIKIR [MJW]
ARLIJA dial of ROMANI, BALKAN [RMN]
ARLIJA dial of ROMANI, BALKAN [RMN]
ARMA [AOH] lang, Colombia
ARMAN dial of EVEN [EVE]
ARMANSKI alt for ARMENIAN [ARM]
ARMENIAN [ARM] lang, Armenia, Egypt, Bulgaria,
   Cyprus, France, Greece, India, Iran, Iraq, Israel,
   Jordan, Lebanon, Syria, Turkey
ARMENIAN alt for ARMENIAN [ARM]
ARMENIAN BOSA alt for LOMAVREN [RMI]
ARMENIAN BOSHA alt for LOMAVREN [RMI]
ARMENIAN SIGN LANGUAGE [AEN] lang, Armenia
ARMINA alt for RUMANIAN, MACEDO [RUP]
ARMJANSKI (YAZYK) alt for ARMENIAN [ARM]
ARMJANSKI alt for ARMENIAN [ARM]
ARMOPA alt for BONGGO [BPG]
ARNAUT alt for ALBANIAN, TOSK [ALN]
ARNIYA alt for KHOWAR [KHW]
ARO alt for AARI [AIZ]
ARO alt for ARHÖ [AOK]
AROBA dial of IRARUTU [IRH]
AROGBO dial of IJO, CENTRAL-WESTERN [IJC]
AROI alt for HAROI [HRO]
AROKWA alt for ERUWA [ERH]
AROMA dial of KEOPARA [KHZ]
AROMUNIAN alt for RUMANIAN, MACEDO [RUP]
ARONA alt for AROMA dial of KEOPARA [KHZ]
AROP alt for AROP-LOKEP [APR]
AROP alt for AROP-SISSANO [APS]
AROP-LOKEP [APR] lang, Papua New Guinea
AROP-SISSANO [APS] lang, Papua New Guinea
AROSARIO alt for MALAYO [MBP]
AROSI [AIA] lang, Solomon Islands
AROSI dial of AROSI [AIA]
AROVE [AAW] lang, Papua New Guinea
AROWAK alt for ARAWAK [ARW]
ARRAKH alt for ARAKH [AAH]
ARRAPAHOE alt for ARAPAHO [ARP]
ARRERNTE, EASTERN [AER] lang, Australia
ARREY alt for ARE [AAG]
ARRINGEU alt for PONGU [PON]
ARSARIO alt for MALAYO [MBP]
ARSI alt for ARUSI dial of OROMO, BORANA-ARUSI-
   GUJI [GAX]
ARSO alt for TAIKAT [AOS]
ARTA [ATZ] lang, Philippines

ARTHARE [RAA] lang, Nepal
ARTHARE-KHESANG alt for ARTHARE [RAA]
ARTVIN dial of ARMENIAN [ARM]
ARTVIN dial of ARMENIAN [ARM]
ARTWIN alt for ARTVIN dial of ARMENIAN [ARM]
ARU alt for JAQARU [JQR]
ARU alt for ALATIL [ALX]
ARUÁ [ARX] lang, Brazil
ARUA dial of TAIRORA [TBG]
ARUA LUGBARA dial of LUGBARA, HIGH [LUG]
ARUACHI alt for ARUÁSHI dial of ARUÁ [ARX]
ARUACO alt for ICA [ARH]
ARUAMU alt for MIKAREW [MSY]
ARUÁSHI dial of ARUÁ [ARX]
ARUEK [AUR] lang, Papua New Guinea
ARUFE alt for NAMBU [NCM]
ARUI alt for SERUI-LAUT [SEU]
ARUM-CESU [AAB] lang, Nigeria
ARUM-CHESSU alt for ARUM-CESU [AAB]
ARUMANIAN alt for RUMANIAN, MACEDO [RUP]
ARUMBI dial of LESE [LES]
ARUNDUM alt for RUNDUM dial of TAGAL MURUT
   [MVV]
ARUNDUM alt for RUNDUM MURUT dial of TAGAL
   MURUT [MVV]
ARUNG alt for NAGA, ZEME [NZM]
ARUOP [LSR] lang, Papua New Guinea
ARUPAI dial of MANITSAUÁ [MSP]
ARURO alt for KACHAMA [KCX]
ARUSA dial of MAASAI [MET]
ARUSA dial of MAASAI [MET]
ĀRUSHA alt for RUSHA [RUH]
ARUSHA alt for ARUSA dial of MAASAI [MET]
ARUSHA alt for ARUSA dial of MAASAI [MET]
ARUSI dial of OROMO, BORANA-ARUSI-GUJI [GAX]
ARUSSI alt for ARUSI dial of OROMO, BORANA-
   ARUSI-GUJI [GAX]
ARUTANI [ATX] lang, Brazil, Venezuela, Venezuela
ARUTANI alt for ARUTANI [ATX]
ARVANITIC alt for ALBANIAN, ARVANITIKA [AAT]
ARVANITIKA alt for ALBANIAN, ARVANITIKA [AAT]
ARWALA dial of TUGUN [TZN]
ARWUR alt for WARAY [WRZ]
ARYA alt for ARE [AAG]
ARZEU dial of TARIFIT [RIF]
AS [ASZ] lang, Indonesia, Irian Jaya
ASA dial of IRAQW [IRK]
ASAHYUE alt for SEHWI [SFW]
ASAK alt for KADO [KDV]
ASAKE alt for SAKE [SAG]
ASAMBE alt for ASSAMESE [ASM]
ASAMI alt for ASSAMESE [ASM]
ASANDE alt for ZANDE [ZAN]
ASANGA alt for GUSU dial of JERA [JER]
ASANTE dial of AKAN [TWS]
ASANTI alt for ASANTE dial of AKAN [TWS]
ASAPA dial of ÖMIE [AOM]
ASARO alt for DANO [ASO]
ASAS [ASD] lang, Papua New Guinea
ASAT [ASX] lang, Papua New Guinea
ASBALMIN alt for ATBALMIN dial of TIFAL [TIF]
ASCHINGINI alt for CHISHINGYINI [ASG]
ASEN dial of AKAN [TWS]
ASENGSENG alt for SENGSENG [SSZ]
ASER alt for AZER dial of SONINKE [SNN]
ASER alt for AZER dial of SONINKE [SNN]

ASERA dial of TOLAKI [LBW]
ASHAGANNA alt for CHISHINGYINI [ASG]
ASHANTE TWI alt for ASANTE dial of AKAN [TWS]
ASHE dial of KORO [KOR]
ASHINGINI alt for CHISHINGYINI [ASG]
ASHINGINI alt for SHINGINI dial of GADI-SHINGINI-
    VADI-BAANGI [KAM]
ASHIRAT dial of ASSYRIAN [AII]
ASHKARAUA dial of ABAZA [ABQ]
ASHKHARIK dial of ARMENIAN [ARM]
ASHKUN [ASK] lang, Afghanistan
ASHKUND alt for ASHKUN [ASK]
ASHKUNI alt for ASHKUN [ASK]
ASHLUSHLAY alt for CHULUPÍ [CAG]
ASHO alt for CHIN, ASHO [CSH]
ASHOLIO alt for SHOLIO dial of KATAB [KCG]
ASHRAAF alt for AF-ASHRAAF dial of SOMALI
    [SOM]
ASHREE alt for ASURI [ASR]
ASHRETI dial of PHALURA [PHL]
ASHTIANI [ATN] lang, Iran
ASHTIKULIN dial of LAK [LBE]
ASHU alt for CHIN, ASHO [CSH]
ASHUKU dial of MBEMBE, TIGON [NZA]
ASHURUVERI dial of ASHKUN [ASK]
ASHUWA alt for ABAZA [ABQ]
ASI alt for WASI [WBJ]
ASIAN SWAHILI alt for CUTCHI-SWAHILI [CCL]
ASIANARA alt for ASIENARA [ASI]
ASIAORO dial of MAILU [MGU]
ASIATIC ESKIMO alt for YUPIK, CENTRAL SIBERIAN
    [ESS]
ASIENARA [ASI] lang, Indonesia, Irian Jaya
ASIFABAD dial of KOLAMI, SOUTHEASTERN [NIT]
ASIGA alt for LEYIGHA [AYI]
ASILULU [ASL] lang, Indonesia, Maluku
ASILULU dial of ASILULU [ASL]
ASIQ alt for BANTOANON [BNO]
ASKOTI dial of KUMAUNI [KFY]
ASL alt for AMERICAN SIGN LANGUAGE [ASE]
ASMAT, CASUARINA COAST [ASC] lang, Indonesia,
    Irian Jaya
ASMAT, CENTRAL [AST] lang, Indonesia, Irian Jaya
ASMAT, YAOSAKOR [ASY] lang, Indonesia, Irian
    Jaya
ASOBSE alt for BASSOSSI [BSI]
ASOLIO alt for SHOLIO dial of KATAB [KCG]
ASOM alt for AZOM dial of POL [PMM]
ASONG alt for SUNGOR [SUN]
ASONG dial of AKHA [AKA]
ASONGORI alt for SUNGOR [SUN]
ASOWI alt for ITERI [ITR]
ASSAGORI alt for SUNGOR [SUN]
ASSAIKIO dial of ALAGO [ALA]
ASSAKA dial of CAKA [CKX]
ASSAM KHAMTI dial of KHAMTI [KHT]
ASSAMESE [ASM] lang, India, Bangladesh
ASSANGORI alt for SUNGOR [SUN]
ASSEM dial of JAGOI [SNE]
ASSIGA alt for LEYIGHA [AYI]
ASSINIBOIN alt for ASSINIBOINE [ASB]
ASSINIBOINE [ASB] lang, Canada, USA, USA
ASSINIBOINE alt for ASSINIBOINE [ASB]
ASSOUNGOR alt for SUNGOR [SUN]
ASSUMBO alt for IPULO [ASS]
ASSUR alt for ASURI [ASR]

ASSURINÍ alt for ASURINÍ [ASU]
ASSURINÍ DO TOCANTINS alt for ASURINÍ [ASU]
ASSYRIAN [AII] lang, Iraq, Cyprus, Iran, Russia,
    Europe, Syria, Turkey
ASSYRIAN alt for ASSYRIAN [AII]
ASTARIN dial of TALYSH [TLY]
ASTIANI alt for ASHTIANI [ATN]
ASTOR alt for ASTORI dial of SHINA [SCL]
ASTORI dial of SHINA [SCL]
ASTRACHAN alt for ASTRAKHAN dial of ARMENIAN
    [ARM]
ASTRAKHAN dial of ARMENIAN [ARM]
ASTRAKHAN dial of ARMENIAN [ARM]
ASTRAKHAN TATAR dial of TATAR [TTR]
ASTURIAN [AUB] lang, Spain
ASU [ASA] lang, Tanzania
ASU dial of NUPE [NUP]
ASUA [ASV] lang, Zaïre
ASUAE alt for ASUA [ASV]
ASUATI alt for ASUA [ASV]
ASUMBO alt for IPULO [ASS]
ASUMBOA [AUA] lang, Solomon Islands
ASUMBUA alt for ASUMBOA [AUA]
ASUMUO alt for ASUMBOA [AUA]
ASUNCIÓN MIXTEPEC ZAPOTECO alt for
    ZAPOTECO, NORTH CENTRAL ZIMATLÁN [ZOO]
ASUNCIÓN TLACOCULITA ZAPOTECO alt for
    ZAPOTECO, SOUTHEASTERN YAUTEPEC [ZPK]
ASUNGORE alt for SUNGOR [SUN]
ASURA alt for ASURI [ASR]
ASURI [ASR] lang, India
ASURINÍ [ASU] lang, Brazil
ASURINÍ, XINGÚ [ASN] lang, Brazil
ASWANIK alt for SONINKE [SNN]
ATA [ATM] lang, Philippines
ATA dial of PELE-ATA [ATA]
ATA OF DAVAO alt for MANOBO, ATA [ATD]
ATA-MAN alt for MAGAHAT [MTW]
ATABA dial of OBOLO [ANN]
ATACAMEÑO alt for KUNZA [KUZ]
ATAIYAL alt for ATAYAL [TAY]
ATAK alt for JIRU [JRR]
ATAKAPA [ALE] lang, USA
ATAKAR alt for ATAKAT dial of KATAB [KCG]
ATAKAT dial of KATAB [KCG]
ATALA alt for DEGEMA [DEG]
ATALA dial of DEGEMA [DEG]
ATAM alt for HATAM [HAD]
ATAM alt for NTA dial of NDE-NSELE-NTA [NDD]
ATAMANU alt for YALAHATAN [JAL]
ATAMPAYA [AMZ] lang, Australia
ATAO MANOBO alt for MANOBO, ATA [ATD]
ATAOUAT alt for KATU [KTV]
ATARIPOE dial of MALO [MLA]
ATAURA alt for ADABE [ADB]
ATAURU alt for ADABE [ADB]
ATAYAL [TAY] lang, Taiwan
ATBALMIN dial of TIFAL [TIF]
ATCHE alt for ATTIÉ [ATI]
ATCHIN dial of URIPIV-WALA-RANO-ATCHIN [UPV]
ATE alt for GARUS [GYB]
ATE alt for ARHE dial of IVBIE NORTH-OKPELA-
    ARHE [ATG]
ATEITA dial of WOISIKA [WOI]
ATEMBLE [ATE] lang, Papua New Guinea
ATEMPLE alt for ATEMBLE [ATE]

ATEMPLE-APRIS alt for ATEMBLE [ATE]
ATEN [GAN] lang, Nigeria
ATEPEC ZAPOTEC alt for ZAPOTECO, SIERRA DE
    JUÁREZ [ZAA]
ATESINO dial of LADIN [LLD]
ATESO alt for TESO [TEO]
ATHOC dial of DINKA, SOUTHEASTERN [DIN]
ATHOIC alt for ATHOC dial of DINKA,
    SOUTHEASTERN [DIN]
ATHPARE alt for ARTHARE [RAA]
ATHPARE RAI alt for ARTHARE [RAA]
ATHU alt for ASU [ASA]
ATI [ATK] lang, Philippines
ATI alt for OBOGWITAI [AFZ]
ATI alt for BUTMAS-TUR [BNR]
ATI alt for KUTEP [KUB]
ATI alt for KINARAY-A [KRJ]
ATIAHU alt for BOBOT [BTY]
ATICHERAK alt for KACHICHERE dial of KATAB
    [KCG]
ATICUM alt for UAMUÉ [UAM]
ATIE alt for ATTIÉ [ATI]
ATIHKAMEKW alt for ATIKAMEKW [TET]
ATIKAMEK alt for ATIKAMEKW [TET]
ATIKAMEKW [TET] lang, Canada
ATIKUM alt for UAMUÉ [UAM]
ATIMELANG dial of ABUI [ABZ]
ATINA dial of LAZ [LZZ]
ATINGGOLA dial of BOLANGO [BLD]
ATIRI alt for NOMATSIGUENGA [NOT]
ATISA dial of EPIE [EPI]
ATISSA alt for ATISA dial of EPIE [EPI]
ATITLÁN MIXE alt for MIXE, NORTHEASTERN [MVE]
ATIU dial of RAROTONGAN [RRT]
ATJEH alt for ACEH [ATJ]
ATJEHNESE alt for ACEH [ATJ]
ATKAN alt for WESTERN ALEUT dial of ALEUT
    [ALW]
ATKAN alt for BERINGOV dial of ALEUT [ALW]
ATLACOMULCO-TEMASCALCINGO dial of
    MAZAHUA [MAZ]
ATNA alt for AHTENA [AHT]
ATNEBAR alt for TANIMBAR KEI dial of KEI [KEI]
ATO alt for OGEA [ERI]
ATO MAJANG alt for MAJANG [MPE]
ATO MAJANGER-ONK alt for MAJANG [MPE]
ATOC alt for ATHOC dial of DINKA,
    SOUTHEASTERN [DIN]
ATOHWAIM [AQM] lang, Indonesia, Irian Jaya
ATOKTOU alt for MALUAL dial of DINKA,
    SOUTHWESTERN [DIK]
ATONG [ATO] lang, Cameroon
ATONG dial of GARO [GRT]
ATONGA alt for TONGA dial of NDAU [NDC]
ATONI [TMR] lang, Indonesia, Nusa Tenggara
ATOR'TI alt for ATORAI dial of WAPISHANA [WAP]
ATORAI dial of WAPISHANA [WAP]
ATORI alt for KAMPUNG BARU [KZM]
ATRATO alt for EMBERA, NORTHERN [EMP]
ATROAHY alt for ATRUAHÍ [ATR]
ATROAÍ alt for ATRUAHÍ [ATR]
ATROARÍ alt for ATRUAHÍ [ATR]
ATROWARI alt for ATRUAHÍ [ATR]
ATRUAHÍ [ATR] lang, Brazil
ATRUAHI dial of ATRUAHÍ [ATR]
ATSAHUACA [ATC] lang, Peru

ATSAM [CCH] lang, Nigeria
ATSANG alt for ACHANG [ACN]
ATSANG-BANGWA alt for YEMBA [BAN]
ATSCHOLI alt for ACHOLI [ACO]
ATSE alt for XIAO HUA dial of HMONG, WESTERN
    [HUJ]
ATSHE alt for ATTIÉ [ATI]
ATSHI alt for ATSI [ATB]
ATSI [ATB] lang, China, Myanmar, Myanmar
ATSI alt for ATSI [ATB]
ATSI-MARU alt for ATSI [ATB]
ATSILIMA dial of ROTOKAS [ROO]
ATSINA alt for GROS VENTRE [ATS]
ATSIRI alt for CAMPA, PAJONAL ASHÉNINCA [CJO]
ATSUGEWI [ATW] lang, USA
ATTA, FAIRE [ATH] lang, Philippines
ATTA, PAMPLONA [ATT] lang, Philippines
ATTA, PUDTOL [ATP] lang, Philippines
ATTAKA alt for ATAKAT dial of KATAB [KCG]
ATTAKAR alt for ATAKAT dial of KATAB [KCG]
ATTAYAL alt for ATAYAL [TAY]
ATTE alt for ARHE dial of IVBIE NORTH-OKPELA-
    ARHE [ATG]
ATTIÉ [ATI] lang, Côte d'Ivoire
ATTIMEWK alt for ATIKAMEKW [TET]
ATTO alt for GIANGAN [BGI]
ATTOCK HINDKO dial of HINDKO, SOUTHERN [HIN]
ATTOCK-HARIPUR HINDKO alt for ATTOCK HINDKO
    dial of HINDKO, SOUTHERN [HIN]
ATTOUAT alt for KATU [KTV]
ATTUAN alt for WESTERN ALEUT dial of ALEUT
    [ALW]
ATTUAN alt for MEDNOV dial of ALEUT [ALW]
ATUENCE [ATF] lang, China
ATUENTSE alt for ATUENCE [ATF]
ATUI dial of LESING-ATUI [LET]
ATUMFUOR dial of LIGBI [LIG]
ATUMFUOR-KASA alt for ATUMFUOR dial of LIGBI
    [LIG]
ATUOT [ATU] lang, Sudan
ATUOT dial of ATUOT [ATU]
ATURA alt for ATURU [AUP]
ATURU [AUP] lang, Papua New Guinea
ATWOT alt for ATUOT [ATU]
ATYAP alt for KATAB dial of KATAB [KCG]
ATYOTI alt for GIKYODE [ACD]
ATZERA alt for ADZERA [AZR]
ATZI alt for ATSI [ATB]
ATZINTECO alt for MATLATZINCA, ATZINGO [OCU]
AU [AVT] lang, Papua New Guinea
AU TÁ alt for AO TÁ dial of MUONG [MTQ]
AUA alt for IMBO UNGU [IMO]
AUA dial of PILENI [PIV]
AUA dial of WUVULU-AUA [WUV]
AUA-VIWULU alt for WUVULU-AUA [WUV]
AUAKE alt for ARUTANI [ATX]
AUAQUÉ alt for ARUTANI [ATX]
AUARIS dial of SANUMÁ [SAM]
"AUCA" alt for WAORANI [AUC]
AUCHI dial of YEKHEE [ETS]
AUEN alt for 'AKHOE [AKE]
AUEN alt for KUNG-GOBABIS [AUE]
AUETO alt for AWETÍ [AWE]
AUGA alt for UKAAN [KCF]
AUGA RIVER dial of FUYUGE [FUY]
AUGILA alt for AWJILAH [AUJ]

AUGU alt for ANGAL HENENG, WEST [AKH]
AUGU dial of ANGAL HENENG, WEST [AKH]
'AUHELAWA [KUD] lang, Papua New Guinea
AUIA-TARAUWI dial of KARKAR-YURI [YUJ]
AUISHIRI alt for ABISHIRA [ASH]
AUITI alt for AWETÍ [AWE]
AUJILA alt for AWJILAH [AUJ]
AUKA alt for LOSA dial of NAKANAI [NAK]
AUKAANS [DJK] lang, Surinam, French Guiana
AUKAN alt for AUKAANS [DJK]
AUKOV alt for AKKA dial of CHECHEN [CJC]
AUKSHTAICHIAI alt for AUKSHTAITISH dial of
     LITHUANIAN [LIT]
AUKSHTAITISH dial of LITHUANIAN [LIT]
AUKWE alt for 'AKHOE [AKE]
AULUA [AUL] lang, Vanuatu
AULUA BAY alt for AULUA [AUL]
AUNA alt for AGAUSHI dial of AGAUSHI-KIMBA-
     NGWANCI [KDL]
AUNA alt for KIMBA dial of AGAUSHI-KIMBA-
     NGWANCI [KDL]
AUNA-AGARAIWA KAMBARI alt for AGAUSHI-
     KIMBA-NGWANCI [KDL]
AUNALEI [AUN] lang, Papua New Guinea
AUNGE alt for NASIOI [NAS]
AUNI dial of NG/AMANI [NMN]
AUNUS alt for OLONETSIAN [OLO]
AURÃ alt for PURUBORÁ [PUR]
AURA alt for WAURÁ [WAU]
AURAMA alt for PAWAIA [PWA]
AURAMA dial of PAWAIA [PWA]
AURAMOT alt for URAMAT [URO]
AUREI dial of FOLOPA [PPO]
AUSHI [AUH] lang, Zambia
AUSHIRI [AUS] lang, Peru
AUSSA dial of AFAR [AFR]
AUSTRAL [AUT] lang, French Polynesia
AUSTRALIAN ABORIGINES SIGN LANGUAGE [ASW]
     lang, Australia
AUSTRALIAN SIGN LANGUAGE [ASF] lang, Australia
AUSTRALIAN STANDARD ENGLISH dial of ENGLISH
     [ENG]
AUSTRIAN SIGN LANGUAGE [ASQ] lang, Austria
AUSTRO-HUNGARIAN SIGN LANGUAGE alt for
     AUSTRIAN SIGN LANGUAGE [ASQ]
AUSTRONESIAN HIRI MOTU dial of MOTU, HIRI
     [POM]
AUTU alt for KAMNUM [KMN]
AUVERGNAT [AUV] lang, France
AUVERNHAS alt for AUVERGNAT [AUV]
AUWAKA dial of ANEME WAKE [ABY]
AUWJE alt for AUYE [AUU]
AUX alt for AKKA dial of CHECHEN [CJC]
AUXIRA alt for AUSHIRI [AUS]
AUYAKAWA alt for AUYOKAWA [AUO]
AUYANA alt for AWIYAANA [AUY]
AUYE [AUU] lang, Indonesia, Irian Jaya
AUYOKAWA [AUO] lang, Nigeria
AUYU alt for AWYU [AWJ]
AVA alt for CHIRIPA [NHD]
AVÁ alt for AVÁ-CANOEIRO [AVV]
AVA alt for PAI TAVYTERA [PTA]
AVA GUARANÍ alt for CHIRIPA [NHD]
AVÁ-CANOEIRO [AVV] lang, Brazil
AVADHI alt for AWADHI [AWD]
AVADI alt for VADI dial of GADI-SHINGINI-VADI-

BAANGI [KAM]
AVAM dial of NGANASAN [NIO]
AVAND alt for EVAND [BZZ]
AVANDE alt for EVAND [BZZ]
AVAÑE'E alt for GUARANÍ, PARAGUAYAN [GUG]
AVANI alt for BANIVA [BVV]
AVANKI alt for EVENKI [EVN]
AVANKIL alt for EVENKI [EVN]
AVAR [AVR] lang, Russia, Europe, Azerbaijan
AVARE alt for AVARI dial of NDO [NDP]
AVARI dial of NDO [NDP]
AVARI dial of NDO [NDP]
AVARO alt for AVAR [AVR]
AVASÕ dial of BABATANA [BAQ]
AVATIME [AVA] lang, Ghana
AVAU [AVB] lang, Papua New Guinea
AVAUSHI alt for AUSHI [AUH]
AVEKE alt for HAVEKE [AVE]
AVEKOM alt for AVIKAM [AVI]
AVERE alt for AVARI dial of NDO [NDP]
AVERE alt for AVARI dial of NDO [NDP]
AVERI dial of MANAGALASI [MCQ]
AVIANWU dial of YEKHEE [ETS]
AVIELE dial of YEKHEE [ETS]
AVIKAM [AVI] lang, Côte d'Ivoire
AVIO alt for AWYU [AWJ]
AVIRITU alt for AVARI dial of NDO [NDP]
AVIRITU alt for AVARI dial of NDO [NDP]
AVIRXIRI alt for ABISHIRA [ASH]
AVOKAYA [AVU] lang, Zaïre, Sudan
AVOKAYA PURE dial of AVOKAYA [AVU]
AVREAS alt for VURAS dial of MOSINA [MSN]
AVUKAYA alt for AVOKAYA [AVU]
AVUNATARI dial of MALO [MLA]
AWA [AWB] lang, Papua New Guinea
AWA alt for CHIN, KHUMI [CKM]
AWA alt for IMBO UNGU [IMO]
AWA alt for BUSUU [BJU]
AWA alt for CUAIQUER [KWI]
AWA-CUAIQUER alt for CUAIQUER [KWI]
AWABAGAL alt for AWABAKAL [AWK]
AWABAKAL [AWK] lang, Australia
AWADHI [AWD] lang, India, Nepal, Nepal
AWADHI alt for AWADHI [AWD]
AWAIAMA alt for AWAYAMA dial of TAWALA
     [TBO]
AWAIYA alt for YALAHATAN [JAL]
AWAK [AWO] lang, Nigeria
AWAKE alt for ARUTANI [ATX]
AWALAMA alt for AWAYAMA dial of TAWALA
     [TBO]
AWALE dial of DIODIO [DDI]
AWAN dial of DINKA, SOUTHWESTERN [DIK]
AWANA alt for AVÁ-CANOEIRO [AVV]
AWANO alt for AGUANO [AGA]
AWAR [AYA] lang, Papua New Guinea
AWAR dial of AWAR [AYA]
AWARA dial of WANTOAT [WNC]
AWARAI alt for WARAY [WRZ]
AWARRA alt for WARAY [WRZ]
AWATÉ alt for ASURINÍ, XINGÚ [ASN]
AWAU alt for AVAU [AVB]
AWAWAR alt for AWNGI [AWN]
AWAYAMA dial of TAWALA [TBO]
AWE alt for BIDEYAT [BIH]
AWE dial of GARO [GRT]

AWEER alt for BONI [BOB]
AWEERA alt for BONI [BOB]
AWEIKOMA alt for XOKLENG [XOK]
AWEMBAK dial of MONI [MNZ]
AWEMBIAK alt for AWEMBAK dial of MONI [MNZ]
AWERA [AWR] lang, Indonesia, Irian Jaya
AWETÍ [AWE] lang, Brazil
AWETÕ alt for AWETÍ [AWE]
AWI alt for AWNGI [AWN]
AWI alt for MBWE'WI dial of AWING [AZO]
AWIAKA alt for AUYOKAWA [AUO]
AWIN [AWI] lang, Papua New Guinea
AWING [AZO] lang, Cameroon
AWING alt for MBWE'WI dial of AWING [AZO]
AWIT dial of TALAUD [TLD]
AWIYA alt for AWNGI [AWN]
AWIYAANA [AUY] lang, Papua New Guinea
AWJE alt for AWYI [AUW]
AWJI alt for AWYI [AUW]
AWJILAH [AUJ] lang, Libya
AWJU alt for AWYU [AWJ]
AWNGI [AWN] lang, Ethiopia
AWO-SUMAKUYU alt for ULUMANDA' [ULM]
AWOK alt for AWAK [AWO]
AWON alt for AWUN [AWW]
AWORI dial of YORUBA [YOR]
AWORO dial of YORUBA [YOR]
AWUN [AWW] lang, Papua New Guinea
AWUNA alt for AGUNA [AUG]
AWUNA dial of ÉWÉ [EWE]
AWUTU [AFU] lang, Ghana
AWUTU dial of AWUTU [AFU]
AWYA alt for AWYU [AWJ]
AWYE alt for AWYI [AUW]
AWYI [AUW] lang, Indonesia, Irian Jaya
AWYU [AWJ] lang, Indonesia, Irian Jaya
AWYU alt for YAIR [YIR]
AXAMB [AHB] lang, Vanuatu
AXE alt for ACHÉ [GUQ]
AXLUSLAY alt for CHULUPÍ [CAG]
AXVAX alt for AKHVAKH [AKV]
AYA alt for AYU [AYU]
AYABADHU [AYD] lang, Australia
AYAM dial of ASMAT, CENTRAL [AST]
AYAMARU alt for MAI BRAT [AYZ]
AYAN alt for BASARI [BSC]
AYAN-MAYA dial of EVENKI [EVN]
AYANE alt for BANIVA [BVV]
AYANGAN IFUGAO dial of IFUGAO, BATAD [IFB]
AYAO alt for YAO [YAO]
AYAT alt for PALIOUPINY dial of DINKA,
    SOUTHWESTERN [DIK]
AYAWA alt for YAO [YAO]
AYAYA alt for GUAJÁ [GUJ]
AYERE dial of AKOKO, NORTH [AKK]
AYIGA alt for LEYIGHA [AYI]
AYIGHA alt for LEYIGHA [AYI]
AYIKIBEN alt for YUKUBEN [YBL]
AYIWO [NFL] lang, Solomon Islands
AYIZO alt for AYIZO-GBE [AYB]
AYIZO-GBE [AYB] lang, Benin, Bahrain
AYKI alt for RUNGA [ROU]
AYKINDANG alt for RUNGA [ROU]
AYMALLAL alt for SODDO dial of GURAGE, NORTH
    [GRU]
AYMARA, CENTRAL [AYM] lang, Bolivia, Argentina,

Chile, Peru
AYMARA, SOUTHERN [AYC] lang, Peru
AYMASA alt for AIMARA dial of KUNAMA [KUM]
AYMELLEL alt for SODDO dial of GURAGE, NORTH
    [GRU]
AYNALLU dial of AZERBAIJANI, SOUTH [AZB]
AYNU [AIB] lang, China
AYO alt for YAO [YAO]
AYOM alt for AIOME [AKI]
AYORÉ alt for AYOREO [AYO]
AYOREO [AYO] lang, Paraguay, Bolivia
AYOTZINTEPEC alt for CHINANTECO, OZUMACÍN
    [CHZ]
AYT WAZITEN dial of GHADAMÈS [GHA]
AYTA ABENLEN SAMBAL alt for AYTA, ABENLEN
    [ABP]
AYTA, ABENLEN [ABP] lang, Philippines
AYTA, AMBALA [ABC] lang, Philippines
AYTA, BATAAN [AYT] lang, Philippines
AYTA, MAG-ANCHI [SGB] lang, Philippines
AYTA, MAG-INDI [BLX] lang, Philippines
AYTA, SORSOGON [AYS] lang, Philippines
AYTA, TAYABAS [AYY] lang, Philippines
AYU [AYU] lang, Nigeria
AYUN dial of JOLA-KASA [CSK]
AYURÚ alt for WAYORÓ [WYR]
AYUTLA MIXTECO alt for MIXTECO, COASTAL
    GUERRERO [MIY]
AYZO alt for AYIZO-GBE [AYB]
AZA dial of TEDA [TUQ]
AZAGHVANA alt for DGHWEDE [DGH]
AZANDE alt for ZANDE [ZAN]
AZÁNGARO-HUANGÁSCAR-CHOCOS
    HUANGÁSCAR alt for MADEAN-VIÑAC dial of
    QUECHUA, YAUYOS [QUX]
AZANGORI alt for SUNGOR [SUN]
AZANGURI alt for SUNGOR [SUN]
AZAO alt for ABU [ADO]
AZELLE alt for JERE dial of JERA [JER]
AZER dial of SONINKE [SNN]
AZER dial of SONINKE [SNN]
AZERA alt for ADZERA [AZR]
AZERA dial of ADZERA [AZR]
AZERBAIJAN alt for AZERBAIJANI, NORTH [AZE]
AZERBAIJANI, NORTH [AZE] lang, Azerbaijan,
    Russia, Europe
AZERBAIJANI, SOUTH [AZB] lang, Iran,
    Afghanistan, Iraq, Syria, Turkey
AZERBAYDZHANI alt for AZERBAIJANI, NORTH
    [AZE]
AZERI alt for AZERBAIJANI, SOUTH [AZB]
AZERI TURK alt for AZERBAIJANI, NORTH [AZE]
AZI alt for ATSI [ATB]
AZIANA alt for KENATI [GAT]
AZOM dial of POL [PMM]
AZONYU dial of NAGA, RENGMA [NRE]
AZORA alt for IZORA [CBO]
AZUMEINA alt for MARBA [MPG]
AZUMU alt for KURAMA [KRH]
B'RU alt for BRU, WESTERN [BRV]
BA [KWB] lang, Nigeria
BA alt for AKA-BO [AKM]
BA alt for AMO [AMO]
BA MALI alt for BAH MALEI dial of KENYAH, SEBOB
    [SIB]
BA PAI [BPN] lang, China

BA'A alt for BAÄ-LOLEH dial of ROTI [ROT]
BA'ADU dial of AFAR [AFR]
BA'AMANG dial of NGAJU [NIJ]
BA'E alt for MANG [MGA]
BA-BUCHE alt for GAMO dial of GAMO-NINGI [BTE]
BA-HI alt for PAHI dial of PACOH [PAC]
BA-MBUTU alt for GAMO dial of GAMO-NINGI [BTE]
BAÄ alt for BAÄ-LOLEH dial of ROTI [ROT]
BAÄ-LOLEH dial of ROTI [ROT]
BAADA alt for KUNAMA [KUM]
BAADEN alt for KUNAMA [KUM]
BAADI [BCJ] lang, Australia
BAAGANDJI alt for DARLING [DRL]
BAAGANDJI alt for BAGUNDJI dial of DARLING
   [DRL]
BAAGATO dial of BANGANDU [BGF]
BAALI alt for BALI [BCP]
BAANGI dial of GADI-SHINGINI-VADI-BAANGI [KAM]
BAANGINGI' alt for SAMA, BALANGINGI [SSE]
BAARAAWAA alt for BARAWA [BWR]
BAARAVI alt for NUCLEAR WESTERN FIJIAN dial of
   FIJIAN, WESTERN [WYY]
BAARAVI alt for CENTRAL VANUA LEVU dial of
   FIJIAN [FJI]
BAATE alt for IFÈ [IFE]
BAATI alt for BWA [BWW]
BAATI alt for BATI dial of NGOMBE [NGC]
BAATO BALOI alt for BALOI [BIZ]
BAATONUM alt for BARIBA [BBA]
BAATONUN alt for BARIBA [BBA]
BAATONUN-KWARA alt for BARIBA [BBA]
BAAZA alt for KUNAMA [KUM]
BAAZAYN alt for KUNAMA [KUM]
BAAZEN alt for KUNAMA [KUM]
BABA [BBW] lang, Cameroon
BABA alt for MALAY, BABA [BAB]
BABA dial of TOGBO [TOR]
BABA dial of GALOLI [GAL]
BABA INDONESIAN alt for INDONESIAN,
   PERANAKAN [PEA]
BABA'ZHI alt for BEBA' dial of BAFUT [BFD]
BABADJI alt for BEBA' dial of BAFUT [BFD]
BABADJOU dial of NGOMBALE [NLA]
BABAGA dial of KEOPARA [KHZ]
BABAGARUPU dial of SINAGORO [SNC]
BABALIA alt for BERAKOU [BXV]
BABALIA alt for ARABIC, BABALIA [BBZ]
BABANGO [BBM] lang, Zaïre
BABANKI [BBK] lang, Cameroon
BABAR, NORTH [BCD] lang, Indonesia, Maluku
BABAR, SOUTHEAST [VBB] lang, Indonesia, Maluku
BABASI alt for BATOMO dial of MESAKA [IYO]
BABATA alt for UBAE dial of NAKANAI [NAK]
BABATANA [BAQ] lang, Solomon Islands
BABATANA dial of BABATANA [BAQ]
BABESSI alt for WUSHI [BSE]
BABETE alt for BAMETE dial of NGOMBA [NNO]
BABINE [BCR] lang, Canada
BABINE CARRIER alt for BABINE [BCR]
BABINGA alt for GIELI [BCB]
BABINGA alt for BAKA [BKC]
BABINGA alt for AKA [AXK]
"BABINGA" alt for AKA [AXK]
BABIR alt for BURA-PABIR [BUR]
BABIRUWA alt for BARUA [BAD]
BABLE alt for ASTURIAN [AUB]

BABLE alt for CENTRAL ASTURIAN dial of
   ASTURIAN [AUB]
BABOK alt for BOK dial of MANDYAK [MFV]
BABOK alt for BOK dial of MANDYAK [MFV]
BABOLE [BVX] lang, Congo
BABONG dial of MBO [MBO]
BABOUTE alt for VUTE [VUT]
BABRI alt for BAURIA [BGE]
BABRUA alt for BARUA [BAD]
BABRUWA alt for BARUA [BAD]
BABUE alt for BALUE dial of BAKUNDU-BALUE
   [BDU]
BABUL alt for LASSA dial of MARGHI CENTRAL
   [MAR]
BABUNGO alt for VENGO [BAV]
BABUR alt for BURA-PABIR [BUR]
BABURIWA alt for BARUA [BAD]
BABUSA alt for BABUZA [BZG]
BABUTE alt for VUTE [VUT]
BABUYAN alt for IBATAN [IVB]
BABUYAN alt for BATAK [BTK]
BABUZA [BZG] lang, Taiwan
BABWA alt for KWA' dial of KWA' [BKO]
BAC alt for BATS [BBL]
BACA alt for NUBACA [BAF]
BACA dial of SWATI [SWZ]
BACADIN dial of AVAR [AVR]
BACAIRÍ alt for BAKAIRÍ [BKQ]
BACAMA [BAM] lang, Nigeria
BACAN alt for MALAY, BACANESE [BTJ]
BACAVÈS alt for CATALAN [CLN]
BACENGA alt for TUKI [BAG]
BACENGA alt for TOCENGA dial of TUKI [BAG]
BACEVE alt for BACHEVE dial of ICEVE-MACI [BEC]
BACHA alt for KWEGU [YID]
BACHADI dial of MALVI [MUP]
BACHAMA alt for BACAMA [BAM]
BACHE alt for CHE [RUK]
BACHEVE alt for ICEVE-MACI [BEC]
BACHEVE dial of ICEVE-MACI [BEC]
BACHEVE dial of ICEVE-MACI [BEC]
BACHIT-GASHISH dial of BEROM [BOM]
BACO alt for BAKO dial of AARI [AIZ]
BACUISSO alt for KWISE dial of KWADI [KWZ]
BADA [BAU] lang, Nigeria
BADA [BHZ] lang, Indonesia, Sulawesi
BADA alt for KUNAMA [KUM]
BADA alt for CACUA [CBV]
BADA dial of TOGBO [TOR]
BADA dial of BADA [BHZ]
BADA' alt for BADA [BHZ]
BADAG alt for BADAGA [BFQ]
BADAGA [BFQ] lang, India
BADAGU alt for BADAGA [BFQ]
BADAK alt for BAURIA [BGE]
BADAKHSHI alt for FARSI, EASTERN [PRS]
BADANCHI alt for BADA [BAU]
BADANG alt for MADANG [MQD]
BADARA DUGURI dial of DUGURI [DBM]
BADAWA alt for BADA [BAU]
BADE [BDE] lang, Nigeria
BADE-KADO dial of BADE [BDE]
BADEN alt for KUNAMA [KUM]
BADERWALI alt for BHADRAWAHI [BHD]
BADESHI [BDZ] lang, Pakistan
BADHANI dial of GARHWALI [GBM]

BADIAN alt for BADYARA [PBP]
BADIE alt for BÉTÉ, GBADI [GBP]
BADITTU alt for KOORETE [KQY]
BADJANDE alt for ZANDE [ZAN]
BADJAVA alt for NGADA [NXG]
BADJAW alt for BAJAU, INDONESIAN [BDL]
BADJIA dial of EWONDO [EWO]
BADJIRI dial of NGURA [NBX]
BADJO alt for BAJAU, INDONESIAN [BDL]
BADJOUE dial of KOOZIME [NJE]
BADJOUE dial of KOOZIME [NJE]
BADONJUNGA alt for NGADJUNMAYA [NJU]
BADOU alt for LITIME dial of AKPOSO [KPO]
BADOUMA alt for DUMA [DMA]
BADROHI alt for BHADRAWAHI [BHD]
BADUGA alt for BADAGA [BFQ]
BADUGU alt for BADAGA [BFQ]
BADUI [BAC] lang, Indonesia, Java, Bali
BADUNG alt for LOWLAND BALI dial of BALI [BZC]
BADYARA [PBP] lang, Guinea Bissau, Guinea,
    Senegal
BADYARANKE alt for BADYARA [PBP]
BADZUMBO alt for IPULO [ASS]
BAEBUNTA alt for LEMOLANG [LEY]
BAEGGU dial of TO'ABAITA [MLU]
BAEGU alt for BAEGGU dial of TO'ABAITA [MLU]
BAEGWA alt for ZIMAKANI [ZIK]
BAELE alt for BIDEYAT [BIH]
BAELELEA dial of TO'ABAITA [MLU]
BAETORA [BTR] lang, Vanuatu
BAFANG alt for FE'FE' [FMP]
BAFANG alt for FA' dial of FE'FE' [FMP]
BAFANGI alt for BAFANJI [BFJ]
BAFANIO alt for WEST BAFWANGADA dial of BUDU
    [BUU]
BAFANJI [BFJ] lang, Cameroon
BAFANYI alt for BAFANJI [BFJ]
BAFATÁ CREOLE dial of CRIOULO, UPPER GUINEA
    [POV]
BAFAW dial of BAFAW-BALONG [BWT]
BAFAW-BALONG [BWT] lang, Cameroon
BAFEUK dial of EWONDO [EWO]
BAFFINLAND ESKIMO dial of INUIT, EASTERN
    CANADIAN [ESB]
BAFIA [KSF] lang, Cameroon
BAFMEN alt for MMEN [BFM]
BAFMENG alt for MMEN [BFM]
BAFO alt for BAFAW dial of BAFAW-BALONG [BWT]
BAFOU alt for YEMBA [BAN]
BAFOUMENG alt for MMEN [BFM]
BAFOWU alt for BAFAW dial of BAFAW-BALONG
    [BWT]
BAFRENG alt for NKWEN dial of MENDANKWE
    [MFD]
BAFUCHU alt for NGAMAMBO dial of META' [MGO]
BAFUMEN alt for MMEN [BFM]
BAFUN alt for MBWASE NGHUY dial of MBO [MBO]
BAFUT [BFD] lang, Cameroon
BAFUT alt for BUFE dial of BAFUT [BFD]
BAFWAKOYI dial of BUDU [BUU]
BAFWANDAKA dial of BALI [BCP]
BAG LACHI alt for LIPUTE dial of LATI [LBT]
BAGA BINARI [BCG] lang, Guinea
BAGA FORÉ alt for MBULUNGISH [MBV]
BAGA KOGA [BGO] lang, Guinea
BAGA MADURI [BMD] lang, Guinea

BAGA MBOTENI [BGM] lang, Guinea
BAGA MONSON alt for MBULUNGISH [MBV]
BAGA SITEMU [BSP] lang, Guinea
BAGA SOBANÉ [BSV] lang, Guinea
BAGADJI alt for KUUKU-YA'U [QKL]
BAGAHAK alt for BEGAHAK dial of IDA'AN [DBJ]
BAGAM alt for BAMENYAM [BCE]
BAGAM alt for MEGAKA [XMG]
BAGAM dial of BAMENYAM [BCE]
BAGANDJI alt for BAGUNDJI dial of DARLING [DRL]
BAGANDO alt for BANGANDU [BGF]
BAGANDO-NGOMBE alt for NGOMBE [NMJ]
BAGANDOU alt for NGANDO [NGD]
BAGANGTE alt for MEDUMBA [BYV]
BAGANGU dial of NGEMBA [NGE]
BAGANTOU alt for BANGANTU dial of
    MPONGMPONG [MGG]
BAGARI alt for BAGRI [BGQ]
BAGARMI alt for BAGIRMI [BMI]
BAGASIN alt for GIRAWA [BBR]
BAGAT alt for BAGATA [BFX]
BAGATA [BFX] lang, India
BAGBA dial of GBAYA [GYA]
BAGBOT alt for BAGATA [BFX]
BAGELKHANDI alt for BAGHELI [BFY]
BAGETO alt for BANGANTU dial of MPONGMPONG
    [MGG]
BAGHATI dial of MAHASUI [BFZ]
BAGHELI [BFY] lang, India, Nepal, Nepal
BAGHELI alt for BAGHELI [BFY]
BAGHELI dial of AWADHI [AWD]
BAGHI alt for KAREN, BWE [BWE]
BAGHIRMI alt for BAGIRMI [BMI]
BAGHIRMI PEUL alt for FULFULDE, BAGIRMI [FUI]
BAGHLIANI dial of MAHASUI [BFZ]
BAGI dial of MAHASUI [BFZ]
BAGIRMI [BMI] lang, Chad, Nigeria, Nigeria
BAGIRMI alt for BAGIRMI [BMI]
BAGIRMI FULA alt for FULFULDE, BAGIRMI [FUI]
BAGNOUN alt for BAINOUK [BCZ]
BAGO [BQG] lang, Togo
BAGO S'AAMAKK-ULO alt for TSAMAI [TSB]
BAGOBO alt for GIANGAN [BGI]
BAGOBO alt for MANOBO, OBO [OBO]
BAGRI [BGQ] lang, Pakistan, India
BAGRI LOHAR alt for GADE LOHAR [GDA]
BAGRIA alt for BAGRI [BGQ]
BAGRIMMA alt for BAGIRMI [BMI]
BAGRIS alt for BAGRI [BGQ]
BAGU alt for MIWA [VMI]
BAGUIRME alt for BAGIRMI [BMI]
BAGUIRMI alt for BAGIRMI [BMI]
BAGULAL alt for BAGVALAL [KVA]
BAGUNDJI dial of DARLING [DRL]
BAGUPI [BPI] lang, Papua New Guinea
BAGUSA [BQB] lang, Indonesia, Irian Jaya
BAGVALAL [KVA] lang, Russia, Europe
BAGVALIN alt for BAGVALAL [KVA]
BAGWA dial of ZIMAKANI [ZIK]
BAGWA ZIMAKANI alt for ZIMAKANI [ZIK]
BAGWAMA alt for KURAMA [KRH]
BAGWAMA alt for RUMA [RUZ]
BAGYELE dial of NGUMBA [NMG]
BAH MALEI dial of KENYAH, SEBOB [SIB]
BAHAM [BDW] lang, Indonesia, Irian Jaya
BAHAMAS CREOLE ENGLISH [BAH] lang, Bahamas,

USA
BAHANGA-LA alt for BANGGARLA [BJB]
BAHARLU dial of AZERBAIJANI, SOUTH [AZB]
BAHARNAH alt for BAHRAINI ARABIC dial of AYIZO-
GBE [AYB]
BAHASA ASLI alt for HUAULU [HUD]
BAHASA GERAGAU alt for MALACCAN CREOLE
PORTUGUESE [MCM]
BAHASA INDONESIA alt for INDONESIAN [INZ]
BAHASA MALAY alt for MALAY [MLI]
BAHASA MALAYSIA alt for MALAY [MLI]
BAHASA MALAYSIA KOD TANGAN alt for
MALAYSIAN SIGN LANGUAGE [XML]
BAHASA MALAYU alt for MALAY [MLI]
BAHASA MELAYU alt for MALAY [MLI]
BAHASA SERANI alt for MALACCAN CREOLE
PORTUGUESE [MCM]
BAHAU [BHV] lang, Indonesia, Kalimantan
BAHAU RIVER KENYA alt for KENYAH, BAHAU
RIVER [BWV]
BAHAWALPURI [BGB] lang, India
BAHAWALPURI alt for SIRAIKI [SKR]
BAHAWALPURI dial of SIRAIKI [SKR]
BAHE dial of RAJBANGSI [RJB]
BAHELIA alt for PARDHI [PCL]
BAHENG alt for PAHENG dial of PUNU [PNU]
BAHENGMAI alt for PAHENG dial of PUNU [PNU]
BAHGRI alt for BAGRI [BGQ]
BAHI alt for BHADRAWAHI [BHD]
BAHINEMO [BJH] lang, Papua New Guinea
BAHING [RAR] lang, Nepal
BAHNAR [BDQ] lang, Viet Nam, USA
BAHNAR BONOM dial of BAHNAR [BDQ]
BAHNAR CHAM alt for HAROI [HRO]
BAHNAR-RENGAO dial of RENGAO [REN]
BAHONSUAI [BSU] lang, Indonesia, Sulawesi
BAHR-EL-GHAZAL ARABIC alt for ARABIC,
SUDANESE CREOLE [PGA]
BAHRAIN dial of TORWALI [TRW]
BAHRAINI ARABIC dial of AYIZO-GBE [AYB]
BAHRI GIRINTI dial of BELI [BLM]
BAHUMONO alt for KOHUMONO [BCS]
BAI [PIQ] lang, China
BAI [BDJ] lang, Sudan
BAI alt for DUMUN [DUI]
BAI dial of SAKATA [SAT]
BAI alt for BALONG dial of BAFAW-BALONG [BWT]
BAIAP alt for DAKAKA [BPA]
BAIAWA dial of MAIWA [MTI]
BAIBAI [BBF] lang, Papua New Guinea
BAIBARA dial of MAILU [MGU]
BAICIT alt for KENDAYAN [KNX]
BAIGA [BFV] lang, India
BAIGANI alt for BAIGA [BFV]
BAIGANI dial of CHATTISGARHI [HNE]
BAIGO alt for BAYGO [BYG]
BAIKENU alt for ATONI [TMR]
BAILADILA dial of DANDAMI MARIA [DAQ]
BAILALA alt for OROKOLO [ORO]
BAILKO alt for NIJADALI [NAD]
BAIMAK [BMX] lang, Papua New Guinea
BAIMAK alt for GAL [GAP]
BAINAPI [PIK] lang, Papua New Guinea
BAING alt for BAHING [RAR]
BAINGE RAI alt for BAHING [RAR]
BAINING alt for QAQET [BYX]

BAINOUK [BCZ] lang, Senegal, Guinea Bissau
BAINUK alt for BAINOUK [BCZ]
BAIONG alt for BAYUNGU [BXJ]
BAIOT alt for BAYOT [BDA]
BAIOTE alt for BAYOT [BDA]
BAIRIN alt for JO-UDA dial of MONGOLIAN,
PERIPHERAL [MVF]
BAIRISCH alt for BAVARIAN [BAR]
BÁISHA dial of HLAI [LIC]
BAISO [BSW] lang, Ethiopia
BAISWARI alt for AWADHI [AWD]
BAITADI dial of NEPALI [NEP]
BAITE dial of CHIN, THADO [TCZ]
BAITSI dial of SIWAI [SIW]
BAIUNG alt for BAYUNGU [BXJ]
BAIYER alt for KYAKA [KYC]
BAJALANI alt for BAJELAN [BJM]
BAJAMA alt for GONGLA [GMM]
BAJAMA alt for GOLA dial of MUMUYE [MUL]
BAJAN dial of ENGLISH [ENG]
BAJANIA dial of KOLI, KACHI [GJK]
BAJAO alt for BAJAU, INDONESIAN [BDL]
BAJAT dial of KUBU [KVB]
BAJAU ASLI alt for BAJAU SEMPORNA dial of
SAMA, SOUTHERN [SIT]
BAJAU BANARAN dial of SAMA, SOUTHERN [SIT]
BAJAU BUKIT alt for PAPAR [DPP]
BAJAU DARAT dial of SAMA, SOUTHERN [SIT]
BAJAU KAGAYAN alt for MAPUN [SJM]
BAJAU LAUT dial of SAMA, SOUTHERN [SIT]
BAJAU SEMPORNA dial of SAMA, SOUTHERN [SIT]
BAJAU, INDONESIAN [BDL] lang, Indonesia,
Sulawesi
BAJAU, WEST COAST [BDR] lang, Malaysia, Sabah,
Brunei
BAJAVA alt for NGADA [NXG]
BAJAVA dial of NGADA [NXG]
BAJELAN [BJM] lang, Iraq
BAJELE alt for BAGYELE dial of NGUMBA [NMG]
BAJELI alt for BAGYELE dial of NGUMBA [NMG]
BAJHANGI dial of NEPALI [NEP]
BÀJII dial of SENOUFO, MAMARA [MYK]
BAJO alt for BAJAU, INDONESIAN [BDL]
BAJPURI alt for BHOJPURI [BHJ]
BAJUN alt for BAJUNI dial of SWAHILI [SWA]
BAJUN alt for BAJUNI dial of SWAHILI [SWA]
BAJUNGU alt for BAYUNGU [BXJ]
BAJUNI dial of SWAHILI [SWA]
BAJUNI dial of SWAHILI [SWA]
BAJURA alt for BAJURALI dial of NEPALI [NEP]
BAJURALI dial of NEPALI [NEP]
BAJWE'E alt for BADJOUE dial of KOOZIME [NJE]
BAJWO dial of DENYA [ANV]
BAKA [BDH] lang, Sudan, Zaïre, Zaïre
BAKA [BKC] lang, Cameroon, Gabon
BAKA alt for GIELI [BCB]
BAKA alt for BAKA [BDH]
BAKAA alt for KALANGA [KCK]
BAKAIRÍ [BKQ] lang, Brazil
BAKAKA dial of MBO [MBO]
BAKALANG dial of BLAGAR [BEU]
BAKANIKE alt for KANINGI [KZO]
BAKATAN alt for BUKITAN [BKN]
BAKATIQ alt for BEKATI' [BAT]
BAKAWALI dial of KASHMIRI [KSH]
BAKE dial of BERTA [WTI]

BAKEDI alt for TESO [TEO]
BAKELE alt for KUKELE [KEZ]
BAKEM dial of BASAA [BAA]
BAKHA dial of MABA [MDE]
BAKHA alt for BAXA dial of KARANGA [KTH]
BAKHTIARI dial of LURI [LRI]
BAKI [BKI] lang, Vanuatu
BAKI alt for TUKI [BAG]
BAKI dial of KWAKUM [KWU]
BAKIDI alt for TESO [TEO]
BAKISE alt for KWISE dial of KWADI [KWZ]
BAKITAN alt for BUKITAN [BKN]
BAKJO alt for BADJIA dial of EWONDO [EWO]
BAKKA alt for FAALA dial of KARANGA [KTH]
BAKO dial of NGWO [NGN]
BAKO dial of AARI [AIZ]
BAKO alt for BAGYELE dial of NGUMBA [NMG]
BAKOA alt for KWA' [BKO]
BAKOI dial of LAWANGAN [LBX]
BAKOKO [BKH] lang, Cameroon
BAKOLA alt for BAGYELE dial of NGUMBA [NMG]
BAKOLE [KME] lang, Cameroon
BAKOLLE alt for BAKOLE [KME]
BAKOMBE alt for KOMBE dial of TUKI [BAG]
BAKONG alt for KENYAH, BAKUNG [BOC]
BAKONG alt for WONGO [WON]
BAKONI dial of KENYANG [KEN]
BAKOR [ABM] lang, Nigeria
BAKOROKA alt for KWADI [KWZ]
BAKOSSI alt for AKOOSE [BSS]
BAKOTA alt for MBAMA [MBM]
BAKOTI alt for SANGAMESVARI dial of KONKANI [KNK]
BAKOUA alt for KWA' dial of KWA' [BKO]
BAKOVI alt for BOLA [BNP]
BAKPINKA [BBS] lang, Nigeria
BAKPWE alt for MOKPWE [BRI]
BAKSA alt for SIRAIYA [FOS]
BAKSAN dial of KABARDIAN [KAB]
BAKTA alt for BAGATA [BFX]
BAKTAPUR dial of NEWARI [NEW]
BAKU dial of AZERBAIJANI, NORTH [AZE]
BAKUISE alt for KWISE dial of KWADI [KWZ]
BAKULI alt for KULUNG [BBU]
BAKULU alt for KULUNG [BBU]
BAKULUNG alt for KULUNG [BBU]
BAKUM alt for KWAKUM [KWU]
BAKUMPAI [BKR] lang, Indonesia, Kalimantan
BAKUMPAI dial of MALAY [MLI]
BAKUMPAI dial of BAKUMPAI [BKR]
BAKUN dial of LOLODA [LOL]
BAKUN-KIBUNGAN dial of KANKANAEY [KNE]
BAKUNDU dial of BAKUNDU-BALUE [BDU]
BAKUNDU-BALUE [BDU] lang, Cameroon
BAKUNDUMU dial of BALI [BCP]
BAKUNG alt for KENYAH, BAKUNG [BOC]
BAKUNG KENYA alt for KENYAH, BAKUNG [BOC]
BAKURUT alt for AMIS [ALV]
BAKUTU alt for KUTU dial of MONGO-NKUNDU [MOM]
BAKWA alt for KWA' [BKO]
BAKWÉ [BAK] lang, Côte d'Ivoire
BAKWEDI alt for MOKPWE [BRI]
BAKWELE alt for MOKPWE [BRI]
BAKWELE alt for BEKWEL [BKW]
BAKWERI alt for MOKPWE [BRI]

BAKWIL alt for BEKWEL [BKW]
BAKWISSO alt for KWISE dial of KWADI [KWZ]
BALA'U alt for BALAU [BUG]
BALAABE alt for YUKUBEN [YBL]
BALAABEN alt for YUKUBEN [YBL]
BALABAN alt for TADYAWAN [TDY]
BALAESAN [BLS] lang, Indonesia, Sulawesi
BALAESANG alt for BALAESAN [BLS]
BALAFI alt for LA'FI dial of FE'FE' [FMP]
BALAGNINI alt for SAMA, BALANGINGI [SSE]
BALAHAIM alt for ISEBE [IGO]
BALAISANG alt for BALAESAN [BLS]
BALAIT dial of LUNDAYEH [LND]
BALAIT JATI dial of KIPUT [KYI]
BALAKEO dial of BENGGOI [BGY]
BALALI alt for LOHORONG [LBR]
BALAMATA alt for PALUMATA [PMC]
BALAMBU alt for BARAMBU [BRM]
BALAMULA dial of LEWADA-DEWARA [LWD]
BALANDA alt for BALANTA [BLE]
BALANGAO [BLW] lang, Philippines
BALANGAO BONTOC alt for BALANGAO [BLW]
BALANGAW alt for BALANGAO [BLW]
BALANGINGI dial of SAMA, BALANGINGI [SSE]
BALANGINGI BAJAU alt for SAMA, BALANGINGI [SSE]
BALANIAN alt for SAMA, BALANGINGI [SSE]
BALANINI alt for SAMA, BALANGINGI [SSE]
BALANIPA dial of MANDAR [MHN]
BALANT alt for BALANTA [BLE]
BALANTA [BLE] lang, Guinea Bissau, Cape Verde Islands, Senegal
BALANTA alt for BALANTA [BLE]
BALANTAK [BLZ] lang, Indonesia, Sulawesi
BALANTE alt for BALANTA [BLE]
BALANTIAN alt for NYADU [NXJ]
BALANTIANG alt for NYADU [NXJ]
BALATCHI dial of NGYEMBOON [NNH]
BALAU [BUG] lang, Malaysia, Sarawak
BALAWAIA dial of SINAGORO [SNC]
BALBALASANG dial of KALINGA, LUBUAGAN [KNB]
BALDA alt for MATAL [MFH]
BALDAM alt for BAYMUNA dial of MÍSKITO [MIQ]
BALDAMU [BDN] lang, Cameroon
BALE [BLL] lang, Ethiopia
BALE alt for LENDU [LED]
BALE alt for AKAR-BALE [ACL]
BALE alt for ZILMAMU [ZIL]
BALEARIC dial of CATALAN [CLN]
BALEGETE alt for EVAND [BZZ]
BALEN alt for BILEN [BYN]
BALENDRU alt for LENDU [LED]
BALEP dial of NDOE [NBB]
BALER NEGRITO alt for ALTA, NORTHERN [AQN]
BALESE alt for LESE [LES]
BALETHA alt for LENDU [LED]
BALETHA alt for ZILMAMU [ZIL]
BALETHI alt for ZILMAMU [ZIL]
BALGU alt for NIJADALI [NAD]
BALI [BBN] lang, Papua New Guinea
BALI [BZC] lang, Indonesia, Java, Bali
BALI [BCN] lang, Nigeria
BALI [BCP] lang, Zaïre
BALI alt for MUNGAKA [MHK]
BALI dial of TEKE, EASTERN [TEK]
BALI alt for BALI NYONGA dial of MUNGAKA [MHK]

"BALI AGA" alt for HIGHLAND BALI dial of BALI
  [BZC]
BALI NYONGA dial of MUNGAKA [MHK]
BALIET alt for PALIET dial of DINKA,
  SOUTHWESTERN [DIK]
BALIF dial of ARAPESH, SOUTHERN [AOJ]
BALIGNINI alt for SAMA, BALANGINGI [SSE]
BALIKPAPAN dial of MALAY [MLI]
BALINESE alt for BALI [BZC]
BALINGIAN dial of MELANAU [MEL]
BALIWON alt for GA'DANG [GDG]
BALKAN GAGAUZ TURKISH [BGX] lang, Turkey
BALKAN TURKIC alt for BALKAN GAGAUZ TURKISH
  [BGX]
BALKAR dial of KARACHAY-BALKAR [KRC]
BALKAR-TSALAKAN alt for BALXAR-CALAKAN dial
  of LAK [LBE]
BALKE dial of NDAU [NDC]
BALKH ARABIC dial of ARABIC, CENTRAL ASIAN
  COLLOQUIAL [ABH]
BALLANTE alt for BALANTA [BLE]
BALO [BQO] lang, Cameroon
BALOBO alt for LIKILA [LIE]
BALOBO alt for LOBO dial of MABAALE [MMZ]
BALOCHI alt for BALUCHI, WESTERN [BGN]
BALOCHI alt for BALUCHI, EASTERN [BGP]
BALOCHI alt for BALUCHI, SOUTHERN [BCC]
BALOCI alt for BALUCHI, WESTERN [BGN]
BALOCI alt for BALUCHI, EASTERN [BGP]
BALOCI alt for BALUCHI, SOUTHERN [BCC]
BALOGA alt for AYTA, MAG-INDI [BLX]
BALOI [BIZ] lang, Zaïre
BALOKI alt for BOLOKI [BKT]
BALOM dial of BAFIA [KSF]
BALON alt for BALONG dial of BAFAW-BALONG
  [BWT]
BALONDO dial of MBO [MBO]
BALONG dial of BAFAW-BALONG [BWT]
BALOUM alt for GHOMALA' [BBJ]
BALOUMBOU alt for LUMBU [LUP]
BALSAPUERTINO alt for CHAYAHUITA [CBT]
BALTAP alt for MONTOL [MTL]
BALTAP-LALIN dial of MONTOL [MTL]
BALTI [BFT] lang, Pakistan
BALTISTANI alt for BALTI [BFT]
BALUAN dial of BALUAN-PAM [BLQ]
BALUAN-PAM [BLQ] lang, Papua New Guinea
BALUCHI, EASTERN [BGP] lang, Pakistan, India
BALUCHI, SOUTHERN [BCC] lang, Pakistan, Iran,
  Oman, United Arab Emirates
BALUCHI, WESTERN [BGN] lang, Pakistan,
  Afghanistan, Iran, Turkmenistan
BALUCI alt for BALUCHI, WESTERN [BGN]
BALUCI alt for BALUCHI, EASTERN [BGP]
BALUCI alt for BALUCHI, SOUTHERN [BCC]
BALUD alt for BLAAN, SARANGANI [BIS]
BALUE dial of BAKUNDU-BALUE [BDU]
BALUGA alt for ALTA, SOUTHERN [AGY]
BALUNDU dial of BALUNDU-BIMA [NGO]
BALUNDU-BIMA [NGO] lang, Cameroon
BALUNG alt for BALONG dial of BAFAW-BALONG
  [BWT]
BALUOMBILA dial of POKE [POF]
BALURBI dial of DJINANG [DJI]
BALWA alt for AKAR-BALE [ACL]
BALXAR-CALAKAN dial of LAK [LBE]

BALYGU alt for NIJADALI [NAD]
BAM [BBH] lang, Papua New Guinea
BAM alt for BIEM [BMC]
BAMA alt for NAGUMI [NGV]
BAMA alt for BURMESE [BMS]
BAMACHAKA alt for BURMESE [BMS]
BAMALI [BBQ] lang, Cameroon
BAMANA alt for BAMBARA [BRA]
BAMANAKAN alt for BAMBARA [BRA]
BAMANYEKA alt for MANYIKA [MXC]
BAMASSA alt for BOMASSA [BME]
BAMBA alt for EAST SONGAI dial of SONGAI [SON]
BAMBAA alt for HUKUMINA [HUW]
BAMBAAMA alt for MBAMA [MBM]
BAMBADION-DOGOSO alt for DOGOSO [DGS]
BAMBADION-DOKHOSIÉ alt for DOGOSO [DGS]
BAMBADION-KHESO alt for KHE [KQG]
BAMBALA alt for BURJI [BJI]
BAMBALANG [BMO] lang, Cameroon
BAMBAM dial of PITU ULUNNA SALU [PTU]
BAMBAN alt for BAMBAM dial of PITU ULUNNA
  SALU [PTU]
BAMBANG alt for BAMBAM dial of PITU ULUNNA
  SALU [PTU]
BAMBANG HULU alt for BAMBAM dial of PITU
  ULUNNA SALU [PTU]
BAMBARA [BRA] lang, Mali, Burkina Faso, Côte
  d'Ivoire, Gambia, Senegal
BAMBARA alt for BAMBARA [BRA]
BAMBARA alt for BAMBARO dial of LAME [BMA]
BAMBARO dial of LAME [BMA]
BAMBEIRO alt for MBAMBA dial of MBUNDU,
  LOANDA [MLO]
BAMBELE alt for MBERE dial of TUKI [BAG]
"BAMBENGA" alt for AKA [AXK]
BAMBENZELE dial of AKA [AXK]
BAMBESHI [MYF] lang, Ethiopia
BAMBESHI MAO dial of BAMBESHI [MYF]
BAMBILI [BAW] lang, Cameroon
BAMBILI dial of BAMBILI [BAW]
BAMBO alt for AMBO dial of LALA-BISA [LEB]
BAMBOKO alt for WUMBOKO [BQM]
BAMBOLANG alt for BAMBALANG [BMO]
BAMBOMA alt for BOO dial of TEKE, CENTRAL
  [TEC]
BAMBOMA alt for BOMA dial of TEKE, CENTRAL
  [TEC]
BAMBOUTE alt for VUTE [VUT]
BAMBUBA alt for MVUBA [MXH]
BAMBUI alt for BAMBILI [BAW]
BAMBUI dial of BAMBILI [BAW]
BAMBUKA alt for KYAK [BKA]
BAMBUKU alt for WUMBOKO [BQM]
BAMBULUWE alt for MBWE'WI dial of AWING [AZO]
BAMBUR alt for KULUNG [BBU]
BAMBURO alt for BAMBARO dial of LAME [BMA]
BAMBUTU alt for MBUTU dial of NGEMBA [NGE]
BAMBUTUKU alt for VANUMA [VAU]
BAMECHOM alt for SHOMBA dial of NGEMBA [NGE]
BAMEKON alt for KOM [BKM]
BAMENDA alt for MENDANKWE dial of
  MENDANKWE [MFD]
BAMENDJIN alt for BAMENDJING dial of
  BAMENYAM [BCE]
BAMENDJINA alt for NGOMBALE [NLA]
BAMENDJINDA dial of NGOMBA [NNO]

BAMENDJING dial of BAMENYAM [BCE]
BAMENJOU alt for NGEMBA dial of GHOMALA'
    [BBJ]
BAMENKOUMBIT alt for BAMUKUMBIT dial of
    AWING [AZO]
BAMENYAM [BCE] lang, Cameroon
BAMENYAM dial of BAMENYAM [BCE]
BAMENYAN alt for BAMENYAM [BCE]
BAMESSING alt for KENSWEI NSEI [NDB]
BAMESSINGUE dial of NGOMBALE [NLA]
BAMESSO dial of NGOMBA [NNO]
BAMETA alt for META' [MGO]
BAMETA alt for MENEMO dial of META' [MGO]
BAMETE dial of NGOMBA [NNO]
BAMILEKE-BANDJOUN alt for GHOMALA' [BBJ]
BAMILEKE-MEDUMBA alt for MEDUMBA [BYV]
BAMINGE alt for NGIE [NGJ]
BAMITABA alt for BOMITABA [ZMX]
BAMONGO alt for BUSHOONG [BUF]
BAMOTA alt for MAGOBINENG dial of KÂTE [KMG]
BAMOUKOUMBIT alt for BAMUKUMBIT dial of
    AWING [AZO]
BAMOUM alt for BAMUN [BAX]
BAMOUN alt for BAMUN [BAX]
BAMOUNGONG dial of NGYEMBOON [NNH]
BAMU [BCF] lang, Papua New Guinea
BAMU KIWAI alt for BAMU [BCF]
BAMUKUMBIT dial of AWING [AZO]
BAMUM alt for BAMUN [BAX]
BAMUMBO dial of MUNDANI [MUN]
BAMUMBU alt for BAMUMBO dial of MUNDANI
    [MUN]
BAMUN [BAX] lang, Cameroon
BAMUNDUM 1 alt for MBREREWI dial of NGEMBA
    [NGE]
BAMUNDUM 2 alt for ANYANG dial of NGEMBA
    [NGE]
BAMUNKA [NDO] lang, Cameroon
BAMUNKUM alt for BAMUKUMBIT dial of AWING
    [AZO]
BAMUNKUN alt for BAMUNKA [NDO]
BAMUSSO alt for BAKOLE [KME]
BAMVELE alt for BEBELE [BEB]
BAMVELE dial of EWONDO [EWO]
BAMVELE alt for MBERE dial of TUKI [BAG]
BAMVUBA alt for MVUBA [MXH]
BAMWE [BMG] lang, Zaïre
BAMYILI CREOLE dial of KRIOL [ROP]
BANA [FLI] lang, Nigeria, Cameroon
BANA alt for BAHNAR [BDQ]
BANA dial of UMA [PPK]
BANA alt for IMBANA dial of MUNDANG [MUA]
BANA alt for NEE dial of FE'FE' [FMP]
BANA' alt for PHANA' [PHN]
BANABAN dial of KIRIBATI [GLB]
BANADAN alt for SAMA, BALANGINGI [SSE]
BANAG alt for PANANG [PCR]
BANAGERE alt for MESAKA [IYO]
BANAHU dial of UMA [PPK]
BANAI dial of KOCH [KDQ]
BANAKA alt for BANO'O dial of BATANGA [BNM]
BANAN BAY alt for BURMBAR [VRT]
"BANANA" alt for MASANA [MCN]
BANANA' dial of MALAYIC DAYAK [XDY]
BANANNA alt for MOSI [MSE]
BANANNA HO HO alt for MOSI [MSE]

BANAO ITNEG dial of KALINGA, LUBUAGAN [KNB]
BANAPARI dial of BAGHELI [BFY]
BANAPHARI dial of BUNDELI [BNS]
BANAR alt for BANARO [BYZ]
BANARA alt for BANARO [BYZ]
BANARA alt for MALA [PED]
BANARA alt for MAIANI [TNH]
BANARO [BYZ] lang, Papua New Guinea
BANAT dial of RUMANIAN [RUM]
BANAUÁ alt for BANAWÁ [BNH]
BANAUE IFUGAO dial of IFUGAO, AMGANAD [IFA]
BANAULE alt for BEBELI [BEK]
BANAVÁ alt for BANAWÁ [BNH]
BANAVA alt for UNDE dial of KAILI, DA'A [KZF]
BANAWÁ [BNH] lang, Brazil
BANAWA alt for UNDE dial of KAILI, DA'A [KZF]
BANCHAPAI dial of MURIA, WESTERN [MUT]
BANDA [BBP] lang, Central African Republic, Sudan,
    Sudan
BANDA [BND] lang, Indonesia, Maluku
BANDA alt for NAFAANRA [NFR]
BANDA alt for BANDA [BBP]
BANDA alt for LIGBI [LIG]
BANDA alt for SHOO dial of SHOO-MINDA-NYEM
    [BCV]
BANDA alt for NORTHERN CHUMBURUNG dial of
    CHUMBURUNG [NCU]
BANDA ACEH dial of ACEH [ATJ]
BANDA-BANDA [BPD] lang, Central African Republic
BANDA-KPAYA [BDT] lang, Sudan
BANDA-MINDA-KUNINI alt for SHOO-MINDA-NYEM
    [BCV]
BANDA-NDELE [BFL] lang, Central African Republic
BANDAL alt for GANJA [BLA]
BANDAS alt for DURR-BARAZA dial of DASS [DOT]
BANDAWA alt for SHOO dial of SHOO-MINDA-NYEM
    [BCV]
BANDE alt for BUDIK [TNR]
BANDE alt for BANDI [GBA]
BANDE alt for MANGKUNGE dial of NGEMBA [NGE]
BANDE' alt for MANGKUNGE dial of NGEMBA [NGE]
BANDEM alt for NDEMLI [NML]
BANDENG alt for MANGKUNGE dial of NGEMBA
    [NGE]
BANDENG alt for NDE dial of MUNGAKA [MHK]
BANDI [GBA] lang, Liberia
BANDIAL dial of GUSILAY [GSL]
BANDJA-BABOUNTOU alt for NJEE-POANTU dial of
    FE'FE' [FMP]
BANDJALANG [BDY] lang, Australia
BANDJARESE alt for BANJAR [BJN]
BANDJELANG alt for BANDJALANG [BDY]
BANDJIGALI [BJD] lang, Australia
BANDJIMA alt for PANYTYIMA [PNW]
BANDJOUN alt for GHOMALA' [BBJ]
BANDJOUN alt for GHOMALA CENTRAL dial of
    GHOMALA' [BBJ]
BANDOBO dial of TIKAR [TIK]
BANDOUGOU dial of SIAMOU [SIF]
BANDOUMOU alt for NDUMU [NMD]
BANDU dial of TAI, NORTHERN [NOD]
BANDZABI alt for NJEBI [NZB]
BANDZHOGI alt for CHIN, ZOTUNG [CZT]
BANDZHOGI alt for ZOTUNG dial of CHIN, HAKA
    [CNH]
BANE dial of EWONDO [EWO]

BANEKA dial of MBO [MBO]
BANEN alt for TUNEN [BAZ]
BANEND alt for TUNEN [BAZ]
BANFORA-SIENENA dial of CERMA [GOT]
BANG alt for MAMBILA, CAMEROON [MYA]
BANG alt for MAMBILA, NIGERIA [MZK]
BANG-GO dial of TUPURI [TUI]
BANG-LING dial of TUPURI [TUI]
BANG-WERE dial of TUPURI [TUI]
BANGA alt for RUKAI [DRU]
BANGA dial of KABA NA [KWV]
BANGA dial of MBOI [MOI]
BANGA alt for GWAMHI dial of GWAMHI-WURI
    [BGA]
BANGA-BHASA alt for BENGALI [BNG]
BANGAD dial of KALINGA, SOUTHERN [KSC]
BANGALA [BXG] lang, Zaïre
BANGALA alt for BANGGARLA [BJB]
BANGALA alt for LAMANI [LMN]
BANGALA alt for BENGALI [BNG]
BANGALAM alt for OLAM dial of MURLE [MUR]
BANGALEMA alt for NGELIMA [AGH]
BANGALORE-MADRAS SIGN LANGUAGE dial of
    INDIAN SIGN LANGUAGE [INS]
BANGAN alt for NGAM dial of FE'FE' [FMP]
BANGANCI alt for GWAMHI dial of GWAMHI-WURI
    [BGA]
BANGANDO alt for BANGANDU [BGF]
BANGANDO dial of GBAYA [GYA]
BANGANDO-NGOMBE alt for NGOMBE [NMJ]
BANGANDOU alt for NGANDO [NGD]
BANGANDU [BGF] lang, Cameroon, Congo, Congo
BANGANDU alt for BANGANDU [BGF]
BANGANG dial of MUNDANI [MUN]
BANGANGTE alt for MEDUMBA [BYV]
BANGANTO alt for BANGANTU dial of
    MPONGMPONG [MGG]
BANGANTOU alt for BANGANDU [BGF]
BANGANTU dial of MPONGMPONG [MGG]
BANGARU [BGC] lang, India
BANGARU PROPER dial of BANGARU [BGC]
BANGAWA alt for GWAMHI dial of GWAMHI-WURI
    [BGA]
BANGAY alt for BONGGI [DBG]
BANGBA [BBE] lang, Zaïre
BANGBINDA alt for NGBINDA [NBD]
BANGELA alt for LIKILA [LIE]
BANGELIMA alt for NGELIMA [AGH]
BANGER alt for BANGARU [BGC]
BANGGAI [BGZ] lang, Indonesia, Sulawesi
BANGGALA alt for BANGGARLA [BJB]
BANGGARLA [BJB] lang, Australia
BANGGI alt for BONGGI [DBG]
BANGGI DUSUN alt for BONGGI [DBG]
BANGI [BNI] lang, Zaïre, Central African Republic,
    Congo
BANGINDA BOKARI dial of GBAYA [GYA]
BANGINGI SAMA alt for SAMA, BALANGINGI [SSE]
BANGINGITA dial of BWA [BWW]
BANGKA dial of MALAY [MLI]
BANGKALAN dial of MADURA [MHJ]
BANGLA alt for BENGALI [BNG]
BANGLA dial of SAMBA LEKO [NDI]
BANGLA-BHASA alt for BENGALI [BNG]
BANGLORI alt for KANNADA [KJV]
BANGNI alt for NISI [DAP]

BANGO alt for NUBACA [BAF]
BANGO dial of BWA [BWW]
BANGOBANGO alt for BANGUBANGU [BNX]
BANGOLAN [BGJ] lang, Cameroon
BANGOM alt for NGOM [NRA]
BANGOMO alt for NGOM [NRA]
BANGON alt for TAWBUID, EASTERN [BNJ]
BANGON alt for BUHID [BKU]
BANGRI alt for BANGARU [BGC]
BANGRU alt for BANGARU [BGC]
BANGRU dial of KOMA [KMY]
BANGUBANGU [BNX] lang, Zaïre
BANGUI dial of BEFANG [BBY]
BANGUNJI alt for BANGWINJI [BSJ]
BANGWA alt for YEMBA [BAN]
BANGWA alt for SONGWA dial of NGEMBA [NGE]
BANGWE alt for BANGUI dial of BEFANG [BBY]
BANGWE alt for SENA BANGWE dial of SENA [SEH]
BANGWI alt for BANGUI dial of BEFANG [BBY]
BANGWINJI [BSJ] lang, Nigeria
BANHUM alt for BAINOUK [BCZ]
BANI KHAALID alt for NORTH NAJDI dial of
    ARABIC, NAJDI [ARS]
BANI KHAALID alt for KUWAITI ARABIC dial of
    ARABIC, NAJDI [ARS]
BANI KHAALID alt for NORTH NAJDI dial of
    ARABIC, NAJDI [ARS]
BANI KHALID alt for NORTH NAJDI dial of ARABIC,
    NAJDI [ARS]
BANI SAKHAR alt for NORTH NAJDI dial of ARABIC,
    NAJDI [ARS]
BANIATA [BNT] lang, Solomon Islands
BANIBA alt for BANIWA [BAI]
BANINGE alt for NGIE [NGJ]
BANIUA alt for BANIWA [BAI]
BANIUA DO IÇANA alt for BANIWA [BAI]
BANIVA [BVV] lang, Venezuela
BANIVA alt for BANIWA [BAI]
BANIVA dial of BANIVA [BVV]
BANIWA [BAI] lang, Brazil, Colombia, Colombia,
    Venezuela
BANIWA alt for BANIWA [BAI]
BANJA alt for NGAMAMBO dial of META' [MGO]
BANJANGI alt for KENYANG [KEN]
BANJAR [BJN] lang, Indonesia, Kalimantan,
    Malaysia, Sabah, Malaysia, Sabah
BANJAR alt for BANJAR [BJN]
BANJAR MALAY alt for BANJAR [BJN]
BANJARA alt for LAMANI [LMN]
BANJARESE alt for BANJAR [BJN]
BANJIMA alt for PANYTYIMA [PNW]
BANJOGI alt for CHIN, ZOTUNG [CZT]
BANJOGI alt for ZOTUNG dial of CHIN, HAKA [CNH]
BANJONG alt for NJONG dial of NGEMBA [NGE]
BANJORI alt for LAMANI [LMN]
BANJOUN-BAHAM alt for GHOMALA' [BBJ]
BANJUN alt for GHOMALA' [BBJ]
BANJUR alt for KETUNGAU dial of IBAN [IBA]
BANJURI alt for LAMANI [LMN]
BANKA alt for NKA' dial of FE'FE' [FMP]
BANKAL dial of JARAWA [JAR]
BANKALA alt for BANKAL dial of JARAWA [JAR]
BANKARA dial of KODA [KFN]
BANKON dial of BASAA [BAA]
BANKOTI alt for KONKANI [KNK]
BANKOTI alt for SANGAMESVARI dial of KONKANI

[KNK]
BANKUTU alt for NKUTU [NKW]
BANLOL dial of MA'YA [SLZ]
BANNA alt for HAMER-BANNA [AMF]
BANNOCHI alt for BANNUCHI dial of PASHTO,
    CENTRAL [PST]
BANNOCK dial of PAIUTE, NORTHERN [PAO]
BANNU alt for BANNUCHI dial of PASHTO,
    CENTRAL [PST]
BANNUCHI dial of PASHTO, CENTRAL [PST]
BANO'O alt for BATANGA [BNM]
BANO'O dial of BATANGA [BNM]
BANOHO alt for BATANGA [BNM]
BANOKO alt for BANO'O dial of BATANGA [BNM]
BANONI [BCM] lang, Papua New Guinea
BANOO alt for BATANGA [BNM]
BANOO alt for BANO'O dial of BATANGA [BNM]
BANPARA NAGA alt for NAGA, WANCHO [NNP]
BANSAW alt for LAMNSO' [NSO]
BANSBALI dial of CHAMEALI [CDH]
BANSO alt for LAMNSO' [NSO]
BANSO' alt for LAMNSO' [NSO]
BANSYARI dial of CHAMEALI [CDH]
BANTA alt for MANTA [MYG]
BANTA alt for THEMNE [TEJ]
BANTAENG dial of KONJO, COASTAL [KJC]
BANTAKPA alt for MANTA [MYG]
BANTALANG alt for RUKAI [DRU]
BANTAR dial of MAITHILI [MKP]
BANTAURANG alt for RUKAI [DRU]
BANTAWA [BAP] lang, Nepal
BANTAWA RAI alt for BANTAWA [BAP]
BANTAYAN dial of HILIGAYNON [HIL]
BANTEN dial of SUNDA [SUO]
BANTEN dial of JAVANESE [JAN]
BANTI dial of MUNDANI [MUN]
BANTIAN dial of LAWANGAN [LBX]
BANTIK [BNQ] lang, Indonesia, Sulawesi
BANTOANON [BNO] lang, Philippines
BANTON alt for BANTOANON [BNO]
BANTUANON alt for BANTOANON [BNO]
BANU alt for GBANU dial of GBAYA [GYA]
BANUWANG dial of LAWANGAN [LBX]
BANYA dial of NGWO [NGN]
BANYAI alt for NYAI dial of KALANGA [KCK]
BANYANG alt for KENYANG [KEN]
BANYANGI alt for KENYANG [KEN]
BANYOK dial of SIBU [SDX]
BANYUK alt for BAINOUK [BCZ]
BANYUM alt for BAINOUK [BCZ]
BANYUN alt for BAINOUK [BCZ]
BANYUNG alt for BAINOUK [BCZ]
BANYUQ alt for LONG BANYUQ dial of KAYAN,
    MURIK [MXR]
BANYUWANGI alt for OSING [OSI]
BANZ-NONDUGL dial of WAHGI [WAK]
BANZA dial of MABAALE [MMZ]
BANZIRI alt for GBANZIRI [GBG]
BAO dial of PSOHOH [BCL]
BAO'AN alt for BONAN [PEH]
BAOCHÉNG dial of HLAI [LIC]
BAODING dial of HLAI [LIC]
BAOKAN alt for BAUKAN dial of BAUKAN [BNB]
BAOL dial of WOLOF [WOL]
BAONAN alt for BONAN [PEH]
BAORI alt for BAURIA [BGE]

BAORIA dial of BHILI [BHB]
BAORIAS alt for BAGRI [BGQ]
BAOULE alt for BAULE [BCI]
BAPA alt for BABA [BBW]
BAPAI dial of YAQAY [JAQ]
BAPAKUM alt for BABA [BBW]
BAPE alt for KAALONG dial of BAFIA [KSF]
BAPINYI alt for PINYIN dial of PINYIN [PNY]
BAPO dial of KRUMEN, SOUTHERN [TED]
BAPU [BPO] lang, Indonesia, Irian Jaya
BAPUKU dial of BATANGA [BNM]
BAPUU alt for BAPUKU dial of BATANGA [BNM]
BAR alt for ANUAK [ANU]
BARA [BXC] lang, Brazil
"BARÁ" alt for WAIMAHA [BAO]
BARÁ alt for POKANGÁ [POK]
BARA alt for BODO [BRX]
BARA dial of BOLE [BOL]
BARA dial of MALAGASY [MEX]
BARA dial of FOLOPA [PPO]
BARA MAKÚ alt for BARA [BXC]
BARA SONA alt for POKANGÁ [POK]
BARA-BARE alt for BA'AMANG dial of NGAJU [NIJ]
BARA-DIA alt for KAPUAS dial of NGAJU [NIJ]
BARA-JIDA alt for BAKUMPAI [BKR]
BARAA alt for LIKES-UTSIA dial of MANDYAK [MFV]
BARAAMU [BRD] lang, Nepal
BARAAN alt for BLAAN, KORONADAL [BIK]
BARABA dial of TATAR [TTR]
BARABAIG dial of DATOGA [TCC]
BARABAIK alt for BARABAIG dial of DATOGA [TCC]
BARABARA dial of BUNAMA [BDD]
BARAGAON alt for BARAGAUNLE [BON]
BARAGAUN alt for BARAGAUNLE [BON]
BARAGAUNLE [BON] lang, Nepal
BARAGRA dial of TOGBO [TOR]
BARAGUYU dial of MAASAI [MET]
BARAI [BCA] lang, Papua New Guinea
BARAIN alt for FULFULDE, BARANI [FUP]
BARAIN alt for BAREIN [BVA]
BARAKA dial of BISSA [BIB]
BARAKAI [BAJ] lang, Indonesia, Maluku
BARAKAI dial of BARAKAI [BAJ]
BARAKE alt for DOMARI [RMT]
BARAKE dial of DOMARI [RMT]
BARAKS alt for ORMURI [ORU]
BARALA JULA dial of JULA [DYU]
BARALAKA dial of MAU [MXX]
BARAM dial of POLCI [POL]
BARAM DUTSE alt for DIR dial of POLCI [POL]
BARAM KAJAN alt for KAYAN, BARAM [KYS]
BARAMA [BBG] lang, Gabon
BARAMBO alt for BARAMBU [BRM]
BARAMBU [BRM] lang, Zaïre
BARAMU [BMZ] lang, Papua New Guinea
BARANCI alt for BANKAL dial of JARAWA [JAR]
BARANG alt for BARAM dial of POLCI [POL]
BARANG-BARANG dial of LAIYOLO [LJI]
BARANGAN alt for TAWBUID, EASTERN [BNJ]
BARAOG alt for PARAUK [PRK]
BARAPASI [BRP] lang, Indonesia, Irian Jaya
BARAS [BRS] lang, Indonesia, Sulawesi
BARAS dial of TAGBANWA, CALAMIAN [TBK]
BARASANA [BSN] lang, Colombia
BARASANO alt for WAIMAHA [BAO]
BARASANO alt for POKANGÁ [POK]

BARAT dial of ORYA [URY]
BARAU dial of KEMBERANO [BZP]
BARAUANA alt for BARÉ [BAE]
BARAUNA alt for BARÉ [BAE]
BARAWA [BWR] lang, Nigeria
BARAWAHING alt for ABUI [ABZ]
BARAWANA alt for BARÉ [BAE]
BARAWÂNA alt for BARÉ [BAE]
BARBA alt for BARIBA [BBA]
BARBACOAS [BPB] lang, Colombia
BARBADIAN ENGLISH alt for BAJAN dial of
ENGLISH [ENG]
BARBADOS alt for UMOTÍNA [UMO]
BARBAIG alt for BARABAIG dial of DATOGA [TCC]
BARBALIN alt for BAGVALAL [KVA]
BARBARI alt for AIMAQ [AIQ]
BARBARICINO dial of SARDINIAN, LOGUDORESE
[SRD]
BARBURR alt for BURA-PABIR [BUR]
BARD alt for BAADI [BCJ]
BARDESKARI dial of KONKANI, GOANESE [GOM]
BARDI alt for BAADI [BCJ]
BARDOJUNGA alt for NGADJUNMAYA [NJU]
BARÉ [BAE] lang, Venezuela, Brazil
BARE alt for BWAZZA dial of MBULA-BWAZZA
[MBU]
BARE'E alt for PAMONA [BCX]
BARE'E alt for PAMONA dial of PAMONA [BCX]
BARE'E alt for TOBAU dial of PAMONA [BCX]
"BAREA" alt for NARA [NRB]
BAREDJI alt for BAREJI dial of GAINA [GCN]
BAREE alt for PAMONA [BCX]
BAREI dial of MAITHILI [MKP]
BAREIN [BVA] lang, Chad
BAREJI dial of GAINA [GCN]
BAREKE dial of VANGUNU [MPR]
BAREKO dial of MBO [MBO]
BAREL alt for BARELI [BGD]
BARELI [BGD] lang, India
BARELI PAURI alt for BARELI [BGD]
BARERA alt for BURARRA [BVR]
BARESHE alt for RESHE [RES]
BARGA alt for MABAAN [MFZ]
BARGAM [MLP] lang, Papua New Guinea
BARGISTA alt for ORMURI [ORU]
BARGU alt for BARIBA [BBA]
BARGU dial of BURIAT, CHINA [BXU]
BARGU BURIAT alt for BURIAT, CHINA [BXU]
BARGUZIN dial of BURIAT, RUSSIA [MNB]
BARHAMU alt for BARAAMU [BRD]
BARI [BFA] lang, Sudan, Uganda, Uganda, Zaïre
BARI alt for BAI [BDJ]
BARI alt for BARI [BFA]
BARI alt for NIMBARI [NMR]
BARI alt for MOTILÓN [MOT]
BARI dial of LOGO [LOG]
BARI KAKWA alt for KAKWA [KEO]
BARI-LOGO alt for BARI dial of LOGO [LOG]
"BARIA" alt for NARA [NRB]
BARIA alt for SEDOA [TVW]
BARIA alt for MBELALA dial of PAMONA [BCX]
BARIAI [BCH] lang, Papua New Guinea
BARIBA [BBA] lang, Benin, Nigeria, Nigeria
BARIBA alt for BARIBA [BBA]
"BARIBARI" alt for KANURI, YERWA [KPH]
BARIJI [BJC] lang, Papua New Guinea

BARIK dial of BENGALI [BNG]
BARIKANCHI [BXO] lang, Nigeria
BARIM [BBV] lang, Papua New Guinea
BARIO dial of KELABIT [KZI]
BARITI alt for BARI dial of LOGO [LOG]
BARKA alt for BAGA KOGA [BGO]
BARKA alt for BAGA BINARI [BCG]
BARKA alt for BAGA SITEMU [BSP]
BARKA alt for BAGA SOBANÉ [BSV]
BARKA alt for BAGA MADURI [BMD]
BARKA dial of KUNAMA [KUM]
BARKA dial of BISSA [BIB]
BARKE alt for MBURKU [BBT]
BARKI alt for ORMURI [ORU]
BARKLY KRIOL dial of KRIOL [ROP]
BARKO alt for MBURKU [BBT]
BARKOUNDOUBA dial of FULFULDE, JELGOOJI
[FUM]
BARKUL alt for MABO-BARKUL [MAE]
BARLIG dial of BONTOC, EASTERN [BKB]
BARMA alt for BAGIRMI [BMI]
BARMA alt for ZUL dial of POLCI [POL]
BARMELI dial of MAITHILI [MKP]
BÄRNDÜTSCH alt for BERN dial of
SCHWYZERDÜTSCH [GSW]
BAROK [BJK] lang, Papua New Guinea
BAROK dial of BAROK [BJK]
BAROMBI [BBI] lang, Cameroon
BARON alt for BOKKOS [CLA]
BARONDO alt for BALUNDU dial of BALUNDU-BIMA
[NGO]
BARONGAGUNAY dial of AGTA, DUPANINAN [DUO]
BAROPASI alt for BARAPASI [BRP]
BAROTAC VIEJO NAGPANA dial of ATI [ATK]
BARRAWA dial of KURANKO [KHA]
BARROW POINT [BPT] lang, Australia
BARRU dial of BUGIS [BPR]
BARTA alt for BERTA [WTI]
BARTANG alt for BARTANGI dial of SHUGHNI [SGH]
BARTANGI dial of SHUGHNI [SGH]
BARU alt for BRU, WESTERN [BRV]
BARUA [BAD] lang, Indonesia, Irian Jaya
BARUA alt for BARUYA [BYR]
BARUE alt for ABUI [ABZ]
BARUE alt for BALUE dial of BAKUNDU-BALUE
[BDU]
BARUGA [BBB] lang, Papua New Guinea
BARUH dial of ACEH [ATJ]
BARUN alt for BURUN [BDI]
BARUYA [BYR] lang, Papua New Guinea
BARUYA dial of BARUYA [BYR]
BARWAANI alt for MWINI dial of SWAHILI [SWA]
"BARYA" alt for NARA [NRB]
BAS-AUVERGNAT dial of AUVERGNAT [AUV]
BAS-KENYANG alt for LOWER KENYANG dial of
KENYANG [KEN]
BAS-LANGUEDOCIEN dial of LANGUEDOCIEN [LNC]
BAS-LIMOUSIN dial of LIMOUSIN [LMS]
BASA [BQA] lang, Benin
BASA alt for BASAA [BAA]
BASA dial of NGWO [NGN]
BASA KUPANG dial of MALAY [MLI]
BASA KUTA alt for BASA-KADUNA [BSL]
BASA-BENUE alt for RUBASA [BZW]
BASA-KADUNA [BSL] lang, Nigeria
BASAA [BAA] lang, Cameroon

BASANG dial of OBANLIKU [BZY]
BASANGA alt for DOKO-UYANGA [UYA]
BASAP [BDB] lang, Indonesia, Kalimantan
BASAR alt for NTCHAM [BUD]
BASARE alt for NTCHAM [BUD]
BASARI [BSC] lang, Guinea, Gambia, Senegal
BASARI alt for BASARI [BSC]
BASARI alt for NTCHAM [BUD]
BASARI DU BANDEMBA alt for BUDIK [TNR]
BASAY [BYQ] lang, Taiwan
BASAYA alt for BISAYA, BRUNEI [BSB]
BASAYA alt for BISAYA, SABAH [BSY]
BASCO IVATAN dial of IVATAN [IVV]
BASECA alt for ANII [BLO]
BASEL dial of SCHWYZERDÜTSCH [GSW]
BASESE dial of AKA [AXK]
BASHALDO alt for ROMANI, CARPATHIAN [RMC]
BASHAMMA alt for BACAMA [BAM]
BASHAR [BSX] lang, Nigeria
BASHARAWA alt for BASHAR [BSX]
BASHGALI alt for KATI [BSH]
BASHGHARIK alt for KALAMI [GWC]
BASHILELE alt for LELE [LEL]
BASHIRI alt for BASHAR [BSX]
BASHKARDI [BSG] lang, Iran
BASHKARIK alt for KALAMI [GWC]
BASHKIR [BXK] lang, Russia, Asia
BASHO dial of DENYA [ANV]
BASIC ZULU alt for FANAGOLO [FAO]
BASILA alt for ANII [BLO]
BASILAKI alt for BOHILAI dial of TAWALA [TBO]
BASILI alt for SERE [SWF]
BASIMA dial of GALEYA [GAR]
BASING alt for MOKEN [MWT]
BASINYARI dial of NUNI [NNW]
BASIQ dial of ROMBLOMANON [ROL]
BASIRI alt for SERE [SWF]
BASKATTA alt for BASKETTO [BST]
BASKETO alt for BASKETTO [BST]
BASKETTO [BST] lang, Ethiopia
BASO [BSA] lang, Indonesia, Irian Jaya
BASOO alt for BAKOKO [BKH]
BASOO BA DIE alt for ADIE dial of BAKOKO [BKH]
BASOO BA LIKOL alt for BISOO dial of BAKOKO
  [BKH]
BASOO D'EDEA alt for ADIE dial of BAKOKO [BKH]
BASOSI alt for BASSOSSI [BSI]
BASOSSI alt for BASSOSSI [BSI]
BASQUE [BSQ] lang, Spain, France
BASQUE CALO dial of ROMANI, CALO [RMR]
BASQUORT alt for BASHKIR [BXK]
BASRIA alt for BAURIA [BGE]
BASSA [BAS] lang, Liberia, Sierra Leone, Sierra
  Leone
BASSA alt for BASSA [BAS]
BASSA alt for BASAA [BAA]
BASSA dial of DWANG [NNU]
BASSA alt for BASA dial of NGWO [NGN]
BASSA NGE dial of NUPE [NUP]
BASSA-KADUNA alt for BASA-KADUNA [BSL]
BASSA-KOMO alt for RUBASA [BZW]
BASSA-KONTAGORA [BSR] lang, Nigeria
BASSA-KWOMU alt for RUBASA [BZW]
BASSAR alt for NTCHAM [BUD]
BASSARI alt for BASARI [BSC]
BASSARI alt for NTCHAM [BUD]

BASSERI dial of FARSI, WESTERN [PES]
BASSILA alt for ANII [BLO]
BASSO dial of BASAA [BAA]
BASSO alt for BISOO dial of BAKOKO [BKH]
BASSOSSI [BSI] lang, Cameroon
BASTARI alt for HALBI [HLB]
BASTARI dial of HALBI [HLB]
BASTI alt for NORTHERN STANDARD BHOJPURI dial
  of BHOJPURI [BHJ]
BASTIA alt for NORTHERN CORSICAN dial of
  CORSICAN [COI]
BASUA dial of BOKYI [BKY]
BASUA alt for BOKYI [BKY]
BASURUDO alt for EPENA SAIJA [SJA]
BAT alt for BADA [BAU]
BATA [BTA] lang, Nigeria, Cameroon
BATA-NDEEWE alt for NDEEWE dial of BATA [BTA]
BATAAN dial of TAGALOG [TGL]
BATAAN AYTA alt for AYTA, BATAAN [AYT]
BATAAN SAMBAL alt for AYTA, BATAAN [AYT]
BATAD IFUGAO dial of IFUGAO, BATAD [IFB]
BATADJI alt for BEBA' dial of BAFUT [BFD]
BATAK [BTK] lang, Philippines
BATAK ALAS-KLUET [BTZ] lang, Indonesia, Sumatra
BATAK ANGKOLA [AKB] lang, Indonesia, Sumatra
BATAK DAIRI [BTD] lang, Indonesia, Sumatra
BATAK KARO [BTX] lang, Indonesia, Sumatra
BATAK MANDAILING [BTM] lang, Indonesia,
  Sumatra
BATAK SIMALUNGUN [BTS] lang, Indonesia,
  Sumatra
BATAK TOBA [BBC] lang, Indonesia, Sumatra
BATANG LUPAR dial of IBAN [IBA]
BATANGA [BNM] lang, Cameroon
BATANGA dial of BATANGA [BNM]
BATANGA dial of CAKA [CKX]
BATANGA-BAKOKO alt for DOTANGA dial of
  BALUNDU-BIMA [NGO]
BATANGAN alt for TAWBUID, EASTERN [BNJ]
BATANGAN alt for BUHID [BKU]
BATANGAS dial of TAGALOG [TGL]
BATANTA ISLAND dial of MA'YA [SLZ]
BATAVI alt for BETAWI [BEW]
BATAWI alt for BETAWI [BEW]
BATAXAN dial of DAUR [DTA]
BATCHAM dial of NGYEMBOON [NNH]
BATCHENGA alt for TUKI [BAG]
BATEG alt for BATEK [BTQ]
BATEK [BTQ] lang, Malaysia, Peninsular
BATEK DE' dial of BATEK [BTQ]
BATEK IGA dial of BATEK [BTQ]
BATEK NONG dial of BATEK [BTQ]
BATEK TEH dial of JEHAI [JHI]
BATEK TEQ dial of BATEK [BTQ]
BATEM-DA-KAI-EE alt for KATO [KTW]
BATEQ alt for BATEK [BTQ]
BATERAWAL alt for BATERI [BTV]
BATERAWAL KOHISTANI alt for BATERI [BTV]
BATERI [BTV] lang, Pakistan, India
BATERI KOHISTANI alt for BATERI [BTV]
BATHA alt for LENDU [LED]
BATHARI dial of MAHRI [MHR]
BATHUDI [BGH] lang, India
BATI [BTC] lang, Cameroon
BATI [BVT] lang, Indonesia, Maluku
BATI alt for BWA [BWW]

BATI dial of NGOMBE [NGC]
BATI dial of BAMENYAM [BCE]
BATI alt for TI dial of MUNGAKA [MHK]
BATI BA NGONG alt for BATI [BTC]
BATI DE BROUSSE alt for BATI [BTC]
BATIBO alt for META' [MGO]
BATIBO alt for MOGHAMO dial of META' [MGO]
BATICOLA dial of GUARANÍ, MBYÁ [GUN]
BATIE alt for GHOMALA' [BBJ]
BATIGI dial of WALI [WLX]
BATIWAI dial of NAMOSI-NAITASIRI-SERUA [BWB]
BATJAN alt for MALAY, BACANESE [BTJ]
BATLUX dial of AVAR [AVR]
BATOK alt for BATEK [BTQ]
BATOKA alt for TONGA dial of NDAU [NDC]
BATOMBU alt for BARIBA [BBA]
BATOMO dial of MESAKA [IYO]
BATONGA alt for TONGA dial of NDAU [NDC]
BATONGTOU dial of MEDUMBA [BYV]
BATONNUM alt for BARIBA [BBA]
BATONU alt for BARIBA [BBA]
BATS [BBL] lang, Georgia
BATSANGUI alt for TSAANGI [TSA]
BATSAW alt for BATS [BBL]
BATSBI alt for BATS [BBL]
BATSBIITSY alt for BATS [BBL]
BATSI alt for BATS [BBL]
BATSINGO alt for TSINGA dial of TUKI [BAG]
BATTA alt for BATAK TOBA [BBC]
BATTA alt for BATA [BTA]
BATTA alt for BATAK MANDAILING [BTM]
BATU [BTU] lang, Nigeria
BATU alt for NIAS [NIP]
BATU dial of NIAS [NIP]
BATU BELAH alt for BATU BLA dial of BERAWAN
   [LOD]
BATU BLA dial of BERAWAN [LOD]
BATU MERAH dial of LUHU [LCQ]
BATU SANGKAR-PARIANGAN dial of
   MINANGKABAU [MPU]
BATUA alt for BASQUE [BSQ]
BATUA dial of BASQUE [BSQ]
BATUAN alt for SIBUGUEY dial of SAMA,
   BALANGINGI [SSE]
BATUI dial of PAMONA [BCX]
BATULEY [BAY] lang, Indonesia, Maluku
BATURA dial of DAFFO-BATURA [DAM]
BATWA alt for //XEGWI [XEG]
BAU [BBD] lang, Papua New Guinea
BAU dial of FIJIAN [FJI]
BAU-JAGOI alt for JAGOI [SNE]
BAUAN alt for BAU dial of FIJIAN [FJI]
BAUBAU alt for WOLIO [WLO]
BAUCHI alt for BAUSHI [BSF]
BAUCI alt for BAUSHI [BSF]
BAUDI alt for BAUZI [PAU]
BAUDJI alt for BAUZI [PAU]
BAUDO [BDC] lang, Colombia
BAUDZI alt for BAUZI [PAU]
BAUKAN [BNB] lang, Malaysia, Sabah
BAUKAN dial of BAUKAN [BNB]
BAULE [BCI] lang, Côte d'Ivoire
BAUMAA alt for SOUTHEAST VANUA LEVU dial of
   FIJIAN [FJI]
BAUNGSHE alt for CHIN, HAKA [CNH]
BAURE [BRG] lang, Bolivia

BAURI alt for BAUZI [PAU]
BAURIA [BGE] lang, India
BAURO [BXA] lang, Solomon Islands
BAURO dial of BAURO [BXA]
BAUSHI [BSF] lang, Nigeria
BAUTAHARI alt for BATHARI dial of MAHRI [MHR]
BAUWAKI [BWK] lang, Papua New Guinea
BAUZI [PAU] lang, Indonesia, Irian Jaya
BAVARAMA alt for BARAMA [BBG]
BAVARIAN [BAR] lang, Austria, Germany,
   Czechoslovakia, Germany, Italy, Slovenia
BAVARIAN alt for BAVARIAN [BAR]
BAVARIAN AUSTRIAN alt for BAVARIAN [BAR]
BAVILLI alt for VILI [VIF]
BAWAKI alt for BAUWAKI [BWK]
BAWANDJI alt for WANDJI [WDD]
BAWARI alt for BAURIA [BGE]
BAWEAN dial of MADURA [MHJ]
BAWERA alt for BURARRA [BVR]
BAWM alt for CHIN, BAWM [BGR]
BAWN alt for CHIN, BAWM [BGR]
BAWNG alt for CHIN, BAWM [BGR]
BAWO alt for BAKUNDU dial of BAKUNDU-BALUE
   [BDU]
BAWOM alt for ABILIANG dial of DINKA,
   NORTHEASTERN [DIP]
BAWU dial of LAWANGAN [LBX]
BAWULE alt for BAULE [BCI]
BAWULI alt for BOWIRI [BOV]
BAXA dial of KARANGA [KTH]
BAY dial of ENETS [ENE]
BAY ISLANDS ENGLISH dial of ENGLISH [ENG]
BAY OF PLENTY dial of MAORI [MBF]
BAYA alt for GBAYA [GYA]
BAYAG dial of ISNAG [ISD]
BAYAKA alt for YAKPA [BYK]
BAYAKA alt for BEKA dial of AKA [AXK]
BAYALI [BJY] lang, Australia
BAYANGA [BYL] lang, Central African Republic
BAYANGI alt for KENYANG [KEN]
BAYANO dial of KUNA, SAN BLAS [CUK]
BAYASH dial of RUMANIAN [RUM]
BAYAT dial of AZERBAIJANI, SOUTH [AZB]
BAYGO [BYG] lang, Sudan
BAYI alt for BALONG dial of BAFAW-BALONG [BWT]
BAYINO alt for ABAYONGO dial of AGWAGWUNE
   [YAY]
BAYIT dial of KALMYK-OIRAT [KGZ]
BAYMUNA dial of MÍSKITO [MIQ]
BAYMUNANA alt for BAYMUNA dial of MÍSKITO
   [MIQ]
"BAYNAWA" alt for GIDAR [GID]
BAYNAWA alt for GIDAR [GID]
BAYNINAN dial of KALLAHAN, KELEY-I [IFY]
BAYO alt for BAJAU, INDONESIAN [BDL]
BAYOBIRI dial of UKPE-BAYOBIRI [UKP]
BAYOMBE alt for YOMBE [YOM]
BAYONG alt for NDEMLI [NML]
BAYONGHO alt for YANGHO [YNH]
BAYONO alt for ABAYONGO dial of AGWAGWUNE
   [YAY]
BAYOT [BDA] lang, Senegal, Gambia, Guinea Bissau
BAYOTTE alt for BAYOT [BDA]
BAYRISCH alt for BAVARIAN [BAR]
BAYSO alt for BAISO [BSW]
BAYUNGU [BXJ] lang, Australia

BAYYU dial of BONTOC, CENTRAL [BNC]
BAZA alt for NGBANDI [NGB]
BAZA alt for KUNAMA [KUM]
BAZA alt for BANA [FLI]
BAZAAR MALAY alt for MALAY, SABAH [MSI]
BAZAAR MALAY dial of MALAY [MLI]
BAZAAR MALAY alt for MELAYU PASAR dial of
    MALAY [MLI]
BAZEN alt for KUNAMA [KUM]
BAZENDA alt for ZANDE [ZAN]
BAZEZURU alt for ZEZURU dial of SHONA [SHD]
BAZHI alt for BEBA' dial of BAFUT [BFD]
BAZIGAR [BFR] lang, India
BAZUZURA alt for ZEZURU dial of SHONA [SHD]
BAZZA dial of KAMWE [HIG]
BBADHA alt for LENDU [LED]
BBALEDHA alt for LENDU [LED]
BÊ alt for LINGAO [ONB]
BE alt for DENO [DBB]
BEA alt for MAMBILA, CAMEROON [MYA]
BEA alt for AKA-BEA [ACE]
BEADA alt for AKA-BEA [ACE]
BEAFADA alt for BIAFADA [BIF]
BEAMI [BEO] lang, Papua New Guinea
BEARLAKE dial of SLAVEY [SLA]
BÉARNAIS dial of GASCON [GSC]
BEAUFORT dial of DUSUN, CENTRAL [DTP]
BEAUFORT MURUT dial of TIMUGON MURUT [TIH]
BEAVER [BEA] lang, Canada
BEBA' dial of BAFUT [BFD]
BEBA-BEFANG alt for BEFANG [BBY]
BEBA-BEFANG alt for BEFANG dial of BEFANG [BBY]
BEBADJI alt for BEBA' dial of BAFUT [BFD]
BEBAROE alt for YAMBA [YAM]
BEBAYAGA alt for BAKA [BKC]
BEBAYAKA alt for BAKA [BKC]
BEBE [BZV] lang, Cameroon
BEBELE [BEB] lang, Cameroon
BEBELI [BEK] lang, Papua New Guinea
BEBENDE alt for BEBENT dial of MAKAA [MCP]
BEBENT dial of MAKAA [MCP]
BEBI dial of OBANLIKU [BZY]
BEBIL [BXP] lang, Cameroon
BECHATI dial of MUNDANI [MUN]
BECHERE alt for ICEVE-MACI [BEC]
BECHERE alt for BACHEVE dial of ICEVE-MACI [BEC]
BECHEVE alt for ICEVE-MACI [BEC]
BECHEVE alt for BACHEVE dial of ICEVE-MACI [BEC]
BECHITIN alt for BEZHTA [KAP]
BEDA alt for VEDDAH [VED]
BEDAMINI alt for BEAMI [BEO]
BEDAMUNI alt for BEAMI [BEO]
BEDANGA dial of SOKORO [SOK]
BEDAUYE alt for BEJA [BEI]
BEDAWIYE alt for BEJA [BEI]
BEDAWYE alt for BEJA [BEI]
BEDDA alt for BADE [BDE]
BEDDA alt for VEDDAH [VED]
BEDDE alt for BADE [BDE]
BEDE alt for BADE [BDE]
BEDERE alt for ADELE [ADE]
BEDFOLA alt for BIAFADA [BIF]
BEDIA [BXD] lang, India
BEDIK alt for BUDIK [TNR]
BEDIYA alt for BEDIA [BXD]
BEDJA alt for BEJA [BEI]

BEDOANAS [BED] lang, Indonesia, Irian Jaya
BEDUANDA dial of TEMUAN [TMW]
BEDWI alt for BEJA [BEI]
BEDYA alt for BEJA [BEI]
BEEGE dial of MUSGU [MUG]
BEEKE [BKF] lang, Zaïre
BEEKURU alt for MODELE dial of BEFANG [BBY]
BEEMBE [BEJ] lang, Congo
BEEMBE alt for BEMBE [BMB]
BEER alt for AGEER dial of DINKA, NORTHEASTERN
    [DIP]
BEETJUANS alt for TSWANA [TSW]
BEEZEN [BNZ] lang, Cameroon
BEFANG [BBY] lang, Cameroon
BEFANG dial of BEFANG [BBY]
BEFANG alt for BEFANG dial of BEFANG [BBY]
BEFE alt for BAFUT [BFD]
BEFI alt for KENSWEI NSEI [NDB]
BEFON alt for NDE dial of NDE-NSELE-NTA [NDD]
BEFUN alt for BAKOR [ABM]
BEGA alt for GUMUZ [GUK]
BEGA alt for BAIGA [BFV]
BEGAHAK dial of IDA'AN [DBJ]
BEGAK alt for BEGAHAK dial of IDA'AN [DBJ]
BEGASIN alt for GIRAWA [BBR]
BEGBERE dial of KORO [KOR]
BEGE alt for NJALGULGULE [NJL]
BEGI alt for NJALGULGULE [NJL]
BEGI-MAO alt for HOZO-SEZO [HOZ]
BEGI-NIBUM alt for NIGII dial of YAMBETA [YAT]
BEGINCI dial of SEMANDANG [SDM]
BEGO alt for BAYGO [BYG]
BEGUA alt for BAGWA dial of ZIMAKANI [ZIK]
BEHE dial of DAYAK, LAND [DYK]
BEHEVE alt for BACHEVE dial of ICEVE-MACI [BEC]
BEHIE alt for NUGUNU [YAS]
BEHLI alt for BELI [BLM]
BEHOA alt for BESOA [BEP]
BEHRAN alt for THAYORE [THD]
BEIÇO DE PAU dial of SUYÁ [SUY]
BEIGO alt for BAYGO [BYG]
BEIJINGHUA alt for CHINESE, MANDARIN [CHN]
BEIK alt for MERGUESE dial of BURMESE [BMS]
BEILI alt for BELI [BLM]
BEILLA dial of KOMA, CENTRAL [KOM]
BEIR alt for MURLE [MUR]
BEIRA dial of PORTUGUESE [POR]
BEIRUT dial of DOMARI [RMT]
BEJA [BEI] lang, Sudan, Ethiopia
BEJAMSE alt for SOUTHERN CHUMBURUNG dial of
    CHUMBURUNG [NCU]
BEK alt for PAK dial of VATRATA [VLR]
BEKÁ alt for AKA [AXK]
BEKA dial of AKA [AXK]
BEKATI' [BAT] lang, Indonesia, Kalimantan
BEKE alt for NUGUNU [YAS]
BEKE alt for DAJU, DAR FUR [DAJ]
BEKETAN alt for BUKITAN [BKN]
BEKIAU alt for BISAYA, BRUNEI [BSB]
BEKIAU alt for BISAYA, SARAWAK [BSD]
BEKO alt for BAYGO [BYG]
BEKO alt for NJALGULGULE [NJL]
BEKOE alt for BAGYELE dial of NGUMBA [NMG]
BEKOL alt for KOL [BIW]
BEKOMBO alt for EKOMBE dial of BAKUNDU-BALUE
    [BDU]

BEKOOSE alt for AKOOSE [BSS]
BEKPAK alt for BAFIA [KSF]
BEKUNDE alt for BAKUNDU dial of BAKUNDU-BALUE [BDU]
BEKWA' alt for KWA' dial of KWA' [BKO]
BEKWARRA [BKV] lang, Nigeria
BEKWEL [BKW] lang, Congo, Cameroon, Gabon
BEKWEL alt for BEKWEL [BKW]
BEKWIE alt for BEKWEL [BKW]
BEKWIL alt for BEKWEL [BKW]
BEKWIRI alt for MOKPWE [BRI]
BEKWORRA alt for BEKWARRA [BKV]
BEL alt for GEDAGED [GDD]
BELA alt for MBELALA dial of PAMONA [BCX]
BELAGAR alt for BLAGAR [BEU]
BELALA alt for MBELALA dial of PAMONA [BCX]
BELANA alt for BELANDA dial of TEMUAN [TMW]
BELANA'U alt for MELANAU [MEL]
BELANAS alt for BELANDA dial of TEMUAN [TMW]
BELANDA alt for BELANDA VIRI [BVI]
BELANDA dial of TEMUAN [TMW]
BELANDA BOR [BXB] lang, Sudan
BELANDA VIRI [BVI] lang, Sudan
BELANDAS alt for BELANDA dial of TEMUAN [TMW]
BELANTE alt for BALANTA [BLE]
BELANYA dial of TUMMA [TBQ]
BELAYAN alt for KAYAN, BUSANG [BFG]
BELBALI alt for KORANJE dial of DAUSAHAQ [DSQ]
BELE [BXQ] lang, Nigeria
BELE dial of FALI, SOUTH [FLE]
BELEBELE dial of IDUNA [VIV]
BELEGETE alt for EVAND [BZZ]
BELEN alt for BILEN [BYN]
BELENI alt for BILEN [BYN]
BELEP dial of NYÂLAYU [YLY]
BELEPA alt for KEURU [QQK]
BELFAST dial of ENGLISH [ENG]
BELGIAN SIGN LANGUAGE [BVS] lang, Belgium
BELI [BLM] lang, Sudan
BELI [BEY] lang, Papua New Guinea
BELI alt for BEBELI [BEK]
BELIBI alt for ELIP [EKM]
BELIDE dial of MALAY [MLI]
BELIP alt for ELIP [EKM]
BELITUNG dial of MALAY [MLI]
BELIZE CREOLE ENGLISH [BZI] lang, Belize, USA
BELLA BELLA dial of HEILTSUK [HEI]
BELLA COOLA [BEL] lang, Canada
BELLARI [BRW] lang, India
BELLARI dial of TULU [TCY]
BELLE alt for KUWAA [BLH]
BELLEH alt for KUWAA [BLH]
BELLONA alt for MUNGIKI dial of RENNELL [MNV]
BELLONESE alt for MUNGIKI dial of RENNELL [MNV]
BELO alt for TETUN [TTM]
BELOH alt for KARAU dial of LAWANGAN [LBX]
BELOM alt for LOM [MFB]
BELORUSSIAN [RUW] lang, Belarus, Poland, Poland
BELTIR dial of KHAKAS [KJH]
BELU alt for TETUN [TTM]
BELUBN alt for KENSIU [KNS]
BELUDJI dial of DOMARI [RMT]
BELUDZHI alt for BALUCHI, WESTERN [BGN]
BELUDZNI alt for BALUCHI, WESTERN [BGN]
BELUJI alt for BALUCHI, WESTERN [BGN]
BEMAL [BMH] lang, Papua New Guinea

BEMBA [BEM] lang, Zambia, Tanzania, Zaïre
BEMBA [BMY] lang, Zaïre
BEMBALA alt for BURJI [BJI]
BEMBE [BMB] lang, Zaïre
BEMBE alt for BEEMBE [BEJ]
BEMBE dial of MABAALE [MMZ]
BEMBI [BEG] lang, Papua New Guinea
BEMBI alt for FAS [FAS]
BEMILI dial of BALI [BCP]
BEMINA alt for BEBENT dial of MAKAA [MCP]
BEN alt for BENG [NHB]
BEN alt for MOBA [MFQ]
BENA [BEZ] lang, Tanzania
BENA alt for BENABENA [BEF]
BENAADIR dial of SOMALI [SOM]
BENABENA [BEF] lang, Papua New Guinea
BENARSI alt for WESTERN STANDARD BHOJPURI dial of BHOJPURI [BHJ]
BENASQUESE alt for NORTHWESTERN CATALAN dial of CATALAN [CLN]
BENAULE alt for BEBELI [BEK]
BENBAKANJAMATA alt for ADYNYAMATHANHA [ADT]
BENCH dial of GIMIRA [BCQ]
BENCHO alt for BENCH dial of GIMIRA [BCQ]
BENCOOLEN alt for BENGKULU [BKE]
BENDE [BDP] lang, Tanzania
BENDE dial of WESTERN CARIBBEAN CREOLE ENGLISH [JAM]
BENDI [BCT] lang, Zaïre
BENDI alt for BETE-BENDE [BTT]
BENDI dial of HLAI [LIC]
BENE dial of BULU [BUM]
BENEHES dial of MODANG [MXD]
BENERAF alt for BONERIF [BNV]
BENESHO alt for BENCH dial of GIMIRA [BCQ]
BENG [NHB] lang, Côte d'Ivoire
BENGA [BEN] lang, Equatorial Guinea, Gabon, Gabon
BENGA alt for BENGA [BEN]
BENGALI [BNG] lang, Bangladesh, India, India, Singapore
BENGALI alt for BENGALI [BNG]
BENGE dial of BOBO FING [BBO]
BENGE alt for BATI dial of NGOMBE [NGC]
BENGE-BAATI alt for BWA [BWW]
BENGGAULU alt for KANTEWU dial of UMA [PPK]
BENGGOI [BGY] lang, Indonesia, Maluku
BENGGOI dial of BENGGOI [BGY]
BENGKULU [BKE] lang, Indonesia, Sumatra
BENGLONG alt for DE'ANG [BFP]
BENGOI alt for BENGGOI [BGY]
BENGUET-IGOROT alt for IBALOI [IBL]
BENI IZNASSEN dial of TARIFIT [RIF]
BENI IZNASSEN alt for IZNACEN dial of TARIFIT [RIF]
"BENI SHANGUL" alt for BERTA [WTI]
BENI-AAMIR alt for BEJA [BEI]
BENI-AMER alt for BEJA [BEI]
BENI-AMIR alt for BEJA [BEI]
BENIN alt for EDO [EDO]
BENKONJO alt for UKHWEJO [UKH]
BENKULAN alt for BENGKULU [BKE]
BENTENAN alt for RATAHAN [RTH]
BENTIAN alt for BANTIAN dial of LAWANGAN [LBX]
BENTOENI alt for WANDAMEN [WAD]
BENTONG [BNU] lang, Indonesia, Sulawesi

BENTUNI alt for WANDAMEN [WAD]
BENUA alt for TEMUAN [TMW]
BENUA dial of LAWANGAN [LBX]
BENYADU' [BYD] lang, Indonesia, Kalimantan
BENYI alt for MMAALA [MMU]
BENZA dial of LIGENZA [LGZ]
BEO dial of NGELIMA [AGH]
BEO dial of NGOMBE [NGC]
BEO dial of TALAUD [TLD]
BEPOUR [BIE] lang, Papua New Guinea
BERA [BRF] lang, Zaïre
BERA dial of KAKO [KKJ]
BERAD dial of TELUGU [TCW]
BERAKOU [BXV] lang, Chad
BERANG alt for GUGUBERA [KKP]
BERANG dial of DAYAK, LAND [DYK]
BERAR MARATHI alt for VARHADI-NAGPURI [VAH]
BERARI alt for VARHADI-NAGPURI [VAH]
BERAU alt for MALAY, BERAU [BVE]
BERAU dial of BASAP [BDB]
BERAUR alt for KALABRA [KZZ]
BERAWAN [LOD] lang, Malaysia, Sarawak
BERBA alt for BARIBA [BBA]
BERBA alt for BIALI [BEH]
BERBER alt for TAMAZIGHT [TZM]
BERBERI alt for AIMAQ [AIQ]
BERBICE CREOLE DUTCH [BRC] lang, Guyana
BERDAMA alt for NAMA [NAQ]
BERE alt for BWAZZA dial of MBULA-BWAZZA
    [MBU]
BEREGADOUGOU-TOUMOUSSENI dial of TURKA
    [TUZ]
BEREINA dial of RORO [RRO]
BEREMBUN dial of TEMUAN [TMW]
BEREPO alt for PERIHO dial of OROKAIVA [ORK]
BEREYA [BYH] lang, Central African Republic
BERGAMASCO [BEQ] lang, Italy
BERGDAMARA alt for NAMA [NAQ]
BERGISH alt for LOW FRANCONIAN dial of
    GERMAN, LOW [GEP]
BERGIT alt for BIRGIT [BTF]
BERGUID alt for BIRGIT [BTF]
BERI alt for CHEWONG [CWG]
BERI alt for ZAGHAWA [ZAG]
BERI alt for BARI [BFA]
BERI-AA alt for ZAGHAWA [ZAG]
"BERIBERI" alt for KANURI, YERWA [KPH]
BERICK alt for BERIK [BER]
BERIK [BER] lang, Indonesia, Irian Jaya
BERIN alt for JUMJUM [JUM]
BERING alt for BERINGOV dial of ALEUT [ALW]
BERING STRAIT ESKIMO dial of INUIT, NORTHWEST
    ALASKA INUPIAT [ESK]
BERINGOV dial of ALEUT [ALW]
BERIYA alt for BEDIA [BXD]
BERKA alt for BARKA dial of KUNAMA [KUM]
BERMEJO VEJOZ dial of WICHÍ LHAMTÉS VEJOZ
    [MAD]
BERN dial of SCHWYZERDÜTSCH [GSW]
BERO alt for OWINIGA [OWI]
BERO dial of MESME [ZIM]
BEROM [BOM] lang, Nigeria
BERONK alt for CENTRAL KANUM dial of KANUM
    [KCD]
BERREMBEEL alt for WIRADHURI [WRH]
BERRI alt for ZAGHAWA [ZAG]

BERRICHON dial of FRENCH [FRN]
BERRIK alt for BERIK [BER]
BERRINGEN alt for MARITHIEL [MFR]
BERTA [WTI] lang, Ethiopia, Sudan, Sudan
BERTA alt for BERTA [WTI]
BERTHA alt for BERTA [WTI]
BERTI [BYT] lang, Sudan
BERUM alt for BEROM [BOM]
BESALI dial of MUNDANI [MUN]
BESAYA alt for BISAYA, BRUNEI [BSB]
BESAYA alt for BISAYA, SABAH [BSY]
BESEKI alt for SEKI [SYI]
BESEMA alt for BACAMA [BAM]
BESEMAH alt for PASEMAH [PSE]
BESEMBO dial of KAKO [KKJ]
BESEME alt for BESME [BES]
BESEMME alt for BESME [BES]
BESEP dial of BYEP [MKK]
BESHA alt for BESEP dial of BYEP [MKK]
BESHADA alt for HAMER-BANNA [AMF]
BESI alt for PASI [PSI]
BESI alt for MOGHAMO dial of META' [MGO]
BESISI [MHE] lang, Malaysia, Peninsular
BESLENEI alt for KABARDIAN [KAB]
BESLENEI dial of KABARDIAN [KAB]
BESLENEJ alt for BESLENEI dial of KABARDIAN
    [KAB]
BESLERI [HNA] lang, Cameroon
BESLERI dial of BESLERI [HNA]
BESME [BES] lang, Chad
BESOA [BEP] lang, Indonesia, Sulawesi
BETA alt for KUAP dial of DAYAK, LAND [DYK]
BETA alt for KUAP dial of DAYAK, LAND [DYK]
BETAU dial of SEMAI [SEA]
BETAWI [BEW] lang, Indonesia, Java, Bali
BETAYA alt for TUCANO [TUO]
BETCHAMUP dial of ASMAT, CENTRAL [AST]
BETE [BYF] lang, Nigeria
BETE alt for BIETE [BIU]
BETE alt for BATA [BTA]
BETE alt for BETE-BENDE [BTT]
BÉTÉ, DALOA [BEV] lang, Côte d'Ivoire
BÉTÉ, GAGNOA [BTG] lang, Côte d'Ivoire
BÉTÉ, GBADI [GBP] lang, Côte d'Ivoire
BÉTÉ, GUIBEROUA [BET] lang, Côte d'Ivoire
BETE-BENDE [BTT] lang, Nigeria
BETEF alt for ITIK [ITX]
BETEN dial of KWAKUM [KWU]
BETHEN dial of POL [PMM]
BETI [BTB] lang, Cameroon
BETI dial of EWONDO [EWO]
BETIBE alt for EOTILE [EOT]
BETISE' dial of BESISI [MHE]
BETISEK alt for BETISE' dial of BESISI [MHE]
BETOYA alt for TUCANO [TUO]
BETSILEO dial of MALAGASY [MEX]
BETSIMARAKA alt for BETSIMISARAKA dial of
    MALAGASY [MEX]
BETSIMISARAKA dial of MALAGASY [MEX]
BETSINGA alt for TUKI [BAG]
BETTA KURUMBA NONSTANDARD TAMIL alt for
    KURUMBA, BETTA [QKB]
BETTE alt for BETE-BENDE [BTT]
BETTE-BENDI alt for BETE-BENDE [BTT]
BETUL dial of GONDI, NORTHERN [GON]
BETZINGA alt for TUKI [BAG]

BEU dial of GUÉRÉ [GXX]
BEWIL alt for BEBENT dial of MAKAA [MCP]
BEXITA alt for BEZHTA [KAP]
BEYGO alt for BAYGO [BYG]
BEYIDZOLO dial of ETON [ETO]
BEZANOZANO dial of MALAGASY [MEX]
BEZHEDUKH dial of ADYGHE [ADY]
BEZHEHUX-TEMIRGOI alt for BEZHEDUKH dial of
   ADYGHE [ADY]
BEZHETA alt for BEZHTA [KAP]
BEZHITA alt for BEZHTA [KAP]
BEZHTA [KAP] lang, Russia, Europe
BEZHTA dial of BEZHTA [KAP]
BEZSHAGH alt for ABAZA [ABQ]
BGHAI KAREN alt for KAREN, BWE [BWE]
BGHE alt for KAREN, BWE [BWE]
BGU alt for BONGGO [BPG]
BHABARI OF RAMPUR dial of KUMAUNI [KFY]
BHADAURI dial of BUNDELI [BNS]
BHADERBHAI JAMU alt for BHADRAWAHI [BHD]
BHADERWALI PAHARI alt for BHADRAWAHI [BHD]
BHADRAVA alt for BHADRAWAHI [BHD]
BHADRAWAHI [BHD] lang, India
BHADRI alt for BHADRAWAHI [BHD]
BHAGIRA dial of LOGO [LOG]
BHAIPEI alt for VAIPHEI [VAP]
BHAKHA alt for KANAUJI [BJJ]
BHAKTA alt for BAGATA [BFX]
BHALAY [BHX] lang, India
BHALESI dial of BHADRAWAHI [BHD]
BHAMANI alt for BHAMANI MARIA dial of MARIA
   [MRR]
BHAMANI MARIA dial of MARIA [MRR]
BHAMRAGARH dial of GONDI, SOUTHERN [GGO]
BHANDARA dial of GONDI, NORTHERN [GON]
BHANDARI dial of KONKANI [KNK]
BHAR alt for BHARIA [BHA]
BHARAT alt for BHARIA [BHA]
BHARIA [BHA] lang, India
BHARMAURI dial of GADDI [GBK]
BHARMAURI BHADI alt for GADDI [GBK]
BHATBALI dial of DOGRI-KANGRI [DOJ]
BHATEALI [BHT] lang, India
BHATEALI dial of GADDI [GBK]
BHATEALI GADI dial of GADDI [GBK]
BHATIA dial of SINDHI [SND]
BHATIALI alt for BHATEALI [BHT]
BHATIARI dial of BENGALI [BNG]
BHATIYALI alt for BHATEALI [BHT]
BHATNERI [BHN] lang, India, Pakistan, Pakistan
BHATNERI alt for BHATNERI [BHN]
BHATOLA [BTL] lang, India
BHATRA alt for BHATRI [BGW]
BHATRI [BGW] lang, India
BHATRI dial of ORIYA [ORY]
BHATTIANI dial of GARHWALI [GBM]
BHATTIYALI alt for BHATEALI [BHT]
BHATTRA alt for BHATRI [BGW]
BHATTRI alt for BHATRI [BGW]
BHAWALPURI alt for BAHAWALPURI [BGB]
BHAWNAGARI alt for KATHIYAWADI dial of
   GUJARATI [GJR]
BHELE [PER] lang, Zaïre
BHIÉT alt for BIAT dial of MNONG, CENTRAL [MNC]
BHIL alt for BHILI [BHB]
BHILALA [BHI] lang, India

BHILALI alt for BHILALA [BHI]
BHILBARI alt for BHILI [BHB]
BHILBOLI alt for BHILI [BHB]
BHILI [BHB] lang, India
BHILLA alt for BHILI [BHB]
BHILODI alt for BHILORI [BQI]
BHILODI dial of BHILORI [BQI]
BHILORI [BQI] lang, India
BHIM [BMM] lang, India
BHIMCHAURA dial of BHILI [BHB]
BHINA alt for BHIM [BMM]
BHOI-KHASI dial of KHASI [KHI]
BHOJAPURI alt for BHOJPURI [BHJ]
BHOJPURI [BHJ] lang, India, Nepal, Nepal
BHOJPURI alt for BHOJPURI [BHJ]
BHOJPURI THARU dial of BHOJPURI [BHJ]
BHOMIYARI alt for BHOYARI [BHY]
BHONDA alt for BONDO [BFW]
BHOO dial for YAOURÉ [YRE]
BHORIA alt for BAURIA [BGE]
BHOTIA alt for TIBETAN [TIC]
BHOTIA OF BALTISTAN alt for BALTI [BFT]
BHOTIA OF BHUTAN alt for DZONGKHA [DZO]
BHOTIA OF DUKPA alt for DZONGKHA [DZO]
BHOTIA OF LAHUL alt for LAHULI, TINAN [LBF]
BHOTIA OF UPPER KANAWAR alt for NESANG [NES]
BHOTIA OF UPPER KANAWAR alt for PUH [PUH]
BHOTTADA alt for BHOTTARA [BHR]
BHOTTARA [BHR] lang, India
BHOYARI [BHY] lang, India
BHOYARI dial of MALVI [MUP]
BHOYAROO alt for BHOYARI [BHY]
BHOZPURI alt for BHOJPURI [BHJ]
BHRAMU alt for BARAAMU [BRD]
BHUANI dial of NIMADI [NOE]
BHUBALIYA LOHAR alt for GADE LOHAR [GDA]
BHUBHI alt for BUBI [BUW]
BHUGELKHUD alt for BAGHELI [BFY]
BHUI dial of MIKIR [MJW]
BHUINHAR alt for BHUIYA [BHC]
BHUINYA alt for BHUIYA [BHC]
BHUIYA [BHC] lang, India
BHUIYALI alt for BHUIYA [BHC]
BHUIYAR alt for BHOYARI [BHY]
BHUJEL KHAM dial of KHAM, NISI [KIF]
BHUKSA dial of BRAJ BHASHA [BFS]
BHULIA dial of CHATTISGARHI [HNE]
BHUMIA alt for BHARIA [BHA]
BHUMIA alt for BHUIYA [BHC]
BHUMIA alt for BAIGA [BFV]
BHUMIJ [BHM] lang, India
BHUMIJ MUNDA alt for BHUMIJ [BHM]
BHUMIYA alt for BHARIA [BHA]
BHUMJIYA alt for BHUNJIA [BHU]
BHUMTAM alt for BUMTHANGKHA dial of
   KEBUMTAMP [KJZ]
BHUMTANG alt for BUMTHANGKHA dial of
   KEBUMTAMP [KJZ]
BHUNGIYAS alt for BHUIYA [BHC]
BHUNJIA [BHU] lang, India
BHUNJIYA alt for BHUNJIA [BHU]
BHURIA alt for BHOYARI [BHY]
BHUTANESE alt for DZONGKHA [DZO]
BHUYAN ORIYA alt for BHUIYA [BHC]
BIA alt for GUHU-SAMANE [GHS]
BIABO dial of GREBO, GBOLOO [GEC]

BIADA alt for AKA-BEA [ACE]
BIADJU alt for NGAJU [NIJ]
BIAFADA [BIF] lang, Guinea Bissau
BIAFAR alt for BIAFADA [BIF]
BIAI dial of KRAHN, WESTERN [KRW]
BIAK [BHW] lang, Indonesia, Irian Jaya
BIAK-NUMFOR alt for BIAK [BHW]
BIAKA alt for NAI [BIO]
BIAKPAN dial of UBAGHARA [BYC]
BIALI [BEH] lang, Benin, Burkina Faso, Burkina Faso
BIALI alt for BIALI [BEH]
BIAMI alt for PIAME [PIN]
BIAN alt for MARIND, BIAN [BPV]
BIANDA dial of GBAYA [GYA]
BIANGAI [BIG] lang, Papua New Guinea
BIANGWALA dial of LAMMA [LEV]
BIAO MIEN [BMT] lang, China
BIAO-JIAO alt for BIAO MIEN [BMT]
BIAOMAN dial of IU MIEN [IUM]
BIAOMIN dial of BIAO MIEN [BMT]
BIAPIM alt for WASEMBO [GSP]
BIARU-WARIA dial of WERI [WER]
BIAT dial of MNONG, CENTRAL [MNC]
BIAT dial of MNONG, CENTRAL [MNC]
BIATAH [BTH] lang, Malaysia, Sarawak, Indonesia,
    Kalimantan
BIATE for BIETE [BIU]
BIBA alt for BEBA' dial of BAFUT [BFD]
BIBA-BIFANG alt for BEFANG [BBY]
BIBASA [BHE] lang, Papua New Guinea
BIBAYA alt for BAKA [BKC]
BIBENG dial of BASAA [BAA]
BIBLING alt for AMARA [AIE]
BIBO dial of SAMO-KUBO [SMQ]
BIBOKI alt for BIBOKI-INSANA dial of ATONI [TMR]
BIBOKI-INSANA dial of ATONI [TMR]
BIBOT alt for BOTO dial of ZARI [ZAZ]
BIBRIARI alt for ANGOR [AGG]
BICEK alt for BASAA [BAA]
BICHELAMAR alt for BISLAMA [BCY]
BICOLANO, ALBAY [BHK] lang, Philippines
BICOLANO, CENTRAL [BKL] lang, Philippines
BICOLANO, IRIGA [BTO] lang, Philippines
BICOLANO, NORTHERN CATANDUANES [CTS] lang,
    Philippines
BICOLANO, SOUTHERN CATANDUANES [BLN] lang,
    Philippines
BICOLI alt for MABA [MQA]
BIDA alt for MANKON dial of NGEMBA [NGE]
BIDA-BIDA alt for PITTA PITTA [PIT]
BIDAYAH alt for BUKAR BIDAYUH dial of BUKAR
    SADONG [SDO]
BIDAYUH alt for BUKAR BIDAYUH dial of BUKAR
    SADONG [SDO]
BIDEYAT [BIH] lang, Chad
BIDEYU alt for BIATAH [BTH]
BIDHABIDHA alt for PITTA PITTA [PIT]
BIDIO [BID] lang, Chad
BIDIRE alt for ADELE [ADE]
BIDIYA alt for BIDIO [BID]
BIDIYO-WAANA alt for BIDIO [BID]
BIDJARA dial of NGURA [NBX]
BIDJOUKI alt for BIDJUKI dial of MPYEMO [MCX]
BIDJUKI dial of MPYEMO [MCX]
BIDOR dial of SEMAI [SEA]
BIDUANDA alt for BEDUANDA dial of TEMUAN

[TMW]
BIDYARA [BYM] lang, Australia
BIDYO alt for BIDIO [BID]
BIDYOGO [BJG] lang, Guinea Bissau
BIDYOLA alt for BIAFADA [BIF]
BIELORUSSIAN alt for BELORUSSIAN [RUW]
BIEM [BMC] lang, Papua New Guinea
BIEREBO [BNK] lang, Vanuatu
BIERI alt for BIERIA [BRJ]
BIERI alt for BIALI [BEH]
BIERIA [BRJ] lang, Vanuatu
BIERIA dial of BIERIA [BRJ]
BIETE [BIU] lang, India
BIFANG alt for BEFANG [BBY]
BIFANG alt for BEFANG dial of BEFANG [BBY]
BIG BAY alt for TOLOMAKO [TLM]
BIG FLOWERY alt for TA HUA dial of HMONG,
    WESTERN [HUJ]
BIG SEPIK alt for IATMUL [IAN]
BIGA alt for SOBEI [SOB]
BIGAWGUNO dial of BIDIO [BID]
BIGOLA alt for BADYARA [PBP]
BIH dial of RADE [RAD]
BIHAK dial of SEMANDANG [SDM]
BIHAR HO alt for HO [HOC]
BIHARI alt for MAGAHI [MQM]
BIHARI alt for BHOJPURI [BHJ]
BIHARI alt for MAITHILI [MKP]
BIHOR alt for BIRHOR [BIY]
BIIRA alt for FULFULDE, ADAMAWA [FUB]
BIISA alt for BISA dial of LALA-BISA [LEB]
BIISHAH alt for CENTRAL NAJDI dial of ARABIC,
    NAJDI [ARS]
BIJAGO alt for BIDYOGO [BJG]
BIJAPUR dial of KANNADA [KJV]
BIJAPURI dial of DECCAN [DCC]
BIJBHASHA alt for BRAJ BHASHA [BFS]
BIJIM dial of KWANKA [BIJ]
BIJOBE alt for SOLA [SOY]
BIJOGO alt for BIDYOGO [BJG]
BIJORI [BIX] lang, India
BIJOUGOT alt for BIDYOGO [BJG]
BIJUGA alt for BIDYOGO [BJG]
BIK alt for TAT, HEBREW [TAT]
BIKAKA dial of UKHWEJO [UKH]
BIKANERI alt for NORTHERN MARWARI dial of
    MARWARI [MKD]
BIKARU [BIC] lang, Papua New Guinea
BIKARU alt for PIKARU dial of BISORIO [BIR]
BIKELE dial of KOL [BIW]
BIKELE-BIKAY alt for KOL [BIW]
BIKELE-BIKENG alt for KOL [BIW]
BIKEN alt for BEBENT dial of MAKAA [MCP]
BIKENG dial of KOL [BIW]
BIKENU alt for ATONI [TMR]
BIKIN dial of UDIHE [UDE]
BIKOL alt for BICOLANO, CENTRAL [BKL]
BIKOL SORSOGON alt for SORSOGON, WARAY
    [SRV]
BIKOM alt for KOM [BKM]
BIKSI [BDX] lang, Indonesia, Irian Jaya, Papua New
    Guinea
BIKSI alt for BIKSI [BDX]
BIKUAB alt for KUAP dial of DAYAK, LAND [DYK]
BIKUAP alt for KUAP dial of DAYAK, LAND [DYK]
BIKYA [BYB] lang, Cameroon

BIKYEK alt for BASAA [BAA]
BIL dial of SEMAI [SEA]
BILA [BIP] lang, Zaïre
BILA dial of TSONGA [TSO]
BILAAN alt for BLAAN, SARANGANI [BIS]
BILADABA [BXI] lang, Australia
BILAKURA [BQL] lang, Papua New Guinea
BILALA [BKX] lang, Chad
BILANES alt for BLAAN, KORONADAL [BIK]
BILASPURI alt for KAHLURI [KFS]
BILASPURI PAHARI alt for KAHLURI [KFS]
BILAYN alt for BILEN [BYN]
BILBA alt for BILBA-DIU-LELENUK dial of ROTI [ROT]
BILBA-DIU-LELENUK dial of ROTI [ROT]
BILBIL [BRZ] lang, Papua New Guinea
BILE [BIL] lang, Nigeria
BILEIN alt for BILEN [BYN]
BILEKI dial of NAKANAI [NAK]
BILEN [BYN] lang, Ethiopia
BILENINYA alt for BILEN [BYN]
BILENO alt for BILEN [BYN]
BILI alt for BILE [BIL]
BILI alt for BHELE [PER]
BILI dial of MONO [MNH]
BILIAU [BCU] lang, Papua New Guinea
BILIAU dial of BILIAU [BCU]
BILIBIL alt for BILBIL [BRZ]
BILICHI dial of KAREN, PAKU [KPP]
BILIN alt for BILEN [BYN]
BILINARA dial of NGARINMAN [NBJ]
BILIRI [BIA] lang, Nigeria
BILKIRE FULANI dial of FULFULDE, ADAMAWA
  [FUB]
BILKIRI alt for BILKIRE FULANI dial of FULFULDE,
  ADAMAWA [FUB]
BILLANCHI alt for BILE [BIL]
BILLE alt for BILE [BIL]
BILTINE alt for AMDANG [AMJ]
BILTUM alt for BURUSHASKI [BSK]
BILUA [BLB] lang, Solomon Islands
BILUR [BXF] lang, Papua New Guinea
BIMA [BHP] lang, Indonesia, Nusa Tenggara
BIMA dial of BIMA [BHP]
BIMA dial of BALUNDU-BIMA [NGO]
BIMANESE alt for BIMA [BHP]
BIMBIA alt for ISU [SZV]
BIMIN [BHL] lang, Papua New Guinea
BIMOBA [BIM] lang, Ghana
BIMU alt for MPYEMO [MCX]
BINA [BYJ] lang, Nigeria
BINA [BMN] lang, Papua New Guinea
BINADAN alt for SAMA, BALANGINGI [SSE]
BINAHARI [BXZ] lang, Papua New Guinea
BINAMARIR alt for BINUMARIEN [BJR]
BINANA dial of KENGA [KYQ]
BINANDERE [BHG] lang, Papua New Guinea
BINARI alt for BAGA BINARI [BCG]
BINATANG dial of BASAP [BDB]
BINATANGAN alt for TAWBUID, EASTERN [BNJ]
BINAWA alt for BINA [BYJ]
BINBARNJA alt for ADYNYAMATHANHA [ADT]
BINBINGA dial of WAMBAYA [WMB]
BINDAFUM alt for BESEP dial of BYEP [MKK]
BINDDIBU alt for PINTUPI-LURITJA [PIU]
BINDI alt for NGITI [NIY]
BINDJI alt for BINJI [BIN]

BINE [ORM] lang, Papua New Guinea
BING alt for BILIAU [BCU]
BINGA alt for AKA [AXK]
BINGA dial of YULU [YUL]
BINGKOKAK alt for MEKONGGA [MWK]
BINI alt for PINI [PII]
BINI alt for EDO [EDO]
BINI dial of ANYIN [ANY]
BINI alt for BUNU dial of YORUBA [YOR]
BINIGUNI dial of MAIWA [MTI]
BINIGURA alt for PINIGURA [PNV]
BINISAYA alt for WARAY-WARAY [WRY]
BINISAYA alt for CEBUANO [CEB]
BINJA alt for SONGOORA [SOD]
BINJA dial of NGOMBE [NGC]
BINJARA alt for MULURIDYI [VMU]
BINJHAL alt for BINJHWARI [BGG]
BINJHAWAR alt for BINJHWARI [BGG]
BINJHAWARI alt for BINJHWARI [BGG]
BINJHIA alt for BIJORI [BIX]
BINJHWAR alt for BINJHWARI [BGG]
BINJHWARI [BGG] lang, India
BINJHWARI dial of CHATTISGARHI [HNE]
BINJI [BIN] lang, Zaïre
BINLI dial of HANUNOO [HNN]
BINNA alt for YUNGUR [YUN]
BINOKID alt for BINUKID [BKD]
BINONGKO dial of TUKANGBESI SOUTH [BHQ]
BINTA' alt for BEAUFORT MURUT dial of TIMUGON
  MURUT [TIH]
BINTAUNA [BNE] lang, Indonesia, Sulawesi
BINTUK alt for ICA [ARH]
BÍNTUKUA alt for ICA [ARH]
BINTULU [BNY] lang, Malaysia, Sarawak
BINTUNI alt for WANDAMEN [WAD]
BINTUNI dial of WANDAMEN [WAD]
BINUANG alt for PATTAE' dial of MAMASA [MQJ]
BINUANG-PAKI-BATETANGA-ANTEAPI alt for
  PATTAE' dial of MAMASA [MQJ]
BINUKID [BKD] lang, Philippines
BINUKID MANOBO alt for BINUKID [BKD]
BINUMARIA alt for BINUMARIEN [BJR]
BINUMARIEN [BJR] lang, Papua New Guinea
BINZA alt for BINJA dial of NGOMBE [NGC]
BINZABI alt for NJEBI [NZB]
BIO alt for BIYO [BYO]
BIO alt for BIYO dial of AARI [AIZ]
BIONAH alt for SERMAH dial of DAYAK, LAND
  [DYK]
BIOTU alt for URHOBO [URH]
BIOTU alt for ISOKO [ISO]
BIPI [BIQ] lang, Papua New Guinea
BIPIM alt for WARKAY-BIPIM [BGV]
BIPIM AS-SO alt for WARKAY-BIPIM [BGV]
BIQUENO alt for ATONI [TMR]
BIRA alt for IGU dial of EBIRA [IGB]
BIRA alt for KONJO PESISIR dial of KONJO,
  COASTAL [KJC]
BIRAAN alt for BLAAN, KORONADAL [BIK]
BIRAHUI alt for BRAHUI [BRH]
BIRALE alt for 'ONGOTA [BXE]
BIRAO [BRR] lang, Solomon Islands
BIRAR alt for BILUR [BXF]
BIRAR dial of NANAI [GLD]
BIRATAK alt for SAU dial of DAYAK, LAND [DYK]
BIRBHUM dial of KODA [KFN]

BIRELLE alt for 'ONGOTA [BXE]
BIRGID alt for BIRKED [BRK]
BIRGID alt for BIRGIT [BTF]
BIRGIT [BTF] lang, Chad
BIRGUID alt for BIRKED [BRK]
BIRHAR alt for BIRHOR [BIY]
BIRHOR [BIY] lang, India
BIRHORE alt for BIRHOR [BIY]
BIRI [BZR] lang, Australia
BIRI alt for BELANDA VIRI [BVI]
BIRI alt for IGU dial of EBIRA [IGB]
BIRI alt for LOKATHAN dial of TESO [TEO]
BIRIFO alt for BIRIFOR, GHANA [BIV]
BIRIFO alt for BIRIFOR, MALBA [BFO]
BIRIFOR dial of BIRIFOR, MALBA [BFO]
BIRIFOR, GHANA [BIV] lang, Ghana
BIRIFOR, MALBA [BFO] lang, Burkina Faso, Côte
    d'Ivoire
BIRIJIA alt for BIJORI [BIX]
BIRIR alt for NORTHERN KALASHA dial of KALASHA
    [KLS]
BIRITAI alt for OBOGWITAI [AFZ]
BIRIWA-SAROKO-KALANTUBA-SUNKO alt for
    SOUTHERN LIMBA dial of LIMBA, EAST [LMA]
BIRKED [BRK] lang, Sudan
BIRKIT alt for BIRKED [BRK]
BIRMINGHAM dial of ENGLISH [ENG]
BIRMUN alt for BEREMBUN dial of TEMUAN [TMW]
BIRNI alt for PINI [PII]
BIROM alt for BEROM [BOM]
BIRQED alt for BIRKED [BRK]
BIRSA alt for BATA [BTA]
BIRWA [BRL] lang, Botswana, South Africa
BIRWA alt for BIRWA [BRL]
BISA alt for BISSA [BIB]
BISA alt for BUSA-BOKO [BUS]
BISA dial of LALA-BISA [LEB]
BISA dial of LALA-BISA [LEB]
BISAA alt for BASAA [BAA]
BISAIA alt for BISAYA, BRUNEI [BSB]
BISAIA alt for BISAYA, SABAH [BSY]
BISARIAB alt for BISHARIN dial of BEJA [BEI]
BISARIAB alt for BISHARIN dial of BEJA [BEI]
BISARIN alt for BISHARIN dial of BEJA [BEI]
BISAYA BUKIT alt for BISAYA, BRUNEI [BSB]
BISAYA BUKIT alt for BISAYA, SARAWAK [BSD]
BISAYA, BRUNEI [BSB] lang, Brunei
BISAYA, SABAH [BSY] lang, Malaysia, Sabah
BISAYA, SARAWAK [BSD] lang, Malaysia, Sarawak
BISAYAH alt for BISAYA, BRUNEI [BSB]
BISAYAH alt for BISAYA, SARAWAK [BSD]
BISAYAH alt for BISAYA, SABAH [BSY]
BISAYAN alt for CEBUANO [CEB]
BISCAYAN dial of BASQUE [BSQ]
BISENI [IJE] lang, Nigeria
BISHARIN dial of BEJA [BEI]
BISHARIN dial of BEJA [BEI]
BISHIRI dial of OBANLIKU [BZY]
BISHNUPURIYA dial of MEITHEI [MNR]
BISHUO [BWH] lang, Cameroon
BISI alt for PITI [PCN]
BISINGAI alt for SINGGI [SGS]
BISIO alt for KWASIO dial of NGUMBA [NMG]
BISIS [BNW] lang, Papua New Guinea
BISIWO alt for NGUMBA [NMG]
BISLAMA [BCY] lang, Vanuatu, New Caledonia

BISMAM dial of ASMAT, CENTRAL [AST]
BISON HORN MARIA alt for DANDAMI MARIA
    [DAQ]
BISOO dial of BAKOKO [BKH]
BISORIO [BIR] lang, Papua New Guinea
BISSA [BIB] lang, Burkina Faso, Ghana, Côte
    d'Ivoire, Ghana, Togo
BISSA alt for BISSA [BIB]
BISSAU-BOLAMA CREOLE dial of CRIOULO, UPPER
    GUINEA [POV]
BISSAULA dial of KPAN [KPK]
BISU [BII] lang, Thailand
BISU dial of OBANLIKU [BZY]
BIT [BGK] lang, Laos, China
BITAAMA alt for BITAMA dial of KUNAMA [KUM]
BITAAPUL dial of NTCHAM [BUD]
BITAMA dial of KUNAMA [KUM]
BITARA [BIT] lang, Papua New Guinea
BITARE [BRE] lang, Nigeria, Cameroon
BITHARA alt for BIDYARA [BYM]
BITI dial of MOROKODO [MGC]
BITIEKU dial of DENYA [ANV]
BITJARA alt for BIDYARA [BYM]
BITJOLI alt for MABA [MQA]
BITONGA alt for TONGA [TOH]
BITWI alt for NDAKTUP [NCP]
BIWANGAN dial of MAGINDANAON [MDH]
BIWAT [BWM] lang, Papua New Guinea
BIYALI alt for BAYALI [BJY]
BIYAM alt for BISHUO [BWH]
BIYAN alt for BASARI [BSC]
BIYO [BYO] lang, China
BIYO dial of AARI [AIZ]
BIYOBE alt for SOLA [SOY]
BIYOM [BPM] lang, Papua New Guinea
BIYORI alt for PHALURA [PHL]
BIZA-LALA alt for LALA-BISA [LEB]
BJERB alt for BIALI [BEH]
BJERI alt for BIALI [BEH]
BLAAN, KORONADAL [BIK] lang, Philippines
BLAAN, SARANGANI [BIS] lang, Philippines
BLABLANGA [BLP] lang, Solomon Islands
BLACK AMERICAN SIGN LANGUAGE dial of
    AMERICAN SIGN LANGUAGE [ASE]
BLACK BAGA alt for MBULUNGISH [MBV]
BLACK BOBO alt for BOBO FING [BBO]
BLACK BOLON dial of BOLON [BOF]
BLACK BUSHMAN alt for XUN [XUU]
BLACK DOGOSE alt for DOGOSO [DGS]
BLACK ENGLISH dial of ENGLISH [ENG]
BLACK KAREN alt for RIANG [RIL]
BLACK KAREN alt for KAREN, PA'O [BLK]
BLACK KHOANY dial of PHUNOI [PHO]
BLACK KONJO alt for TANA TOA dial of KONJO,
    COASTAL [KJC]
BLACK LACHI alt for LIPUTIÕ dial of LATI [LBT]
BLACK LAHU alt for NA dial of LAHU [LAH]
BLACK LISU alt for LIPO [TKL]
BLACK MIAO alt for HE MIAO dial of HMONG,
    EASTERN [HEA]
BLACK NOGAI dial of NOGAI [NOG]
BLACK RIANG alt for YINCHIA [YIN]
BLACK SEMINOLE alt for AFRO-SEMINOLE CREOLE
    [AFS]
BLACK TAI alt for TAI DAM [BLT]
BLACK YANG alt for RIANG [RIL]

BLACKFOOT [BLC] lang, Canada, USA, USA
BLAGAR [BEU] lang, Indonesia, Nusa Tenggara
BLANCHE BAY alt for TOLAI [KSD]
BLANDA alt for BELANDA dial of TEMUAN [TMW]
BLANG [BLR] lang, China, Myanmar, Myanmar, Thailand
BLANG alt for BLANG [BLR]
BLÉ [BXL] lang, Burkina Faso
BLE alt for MAMBILA, CAMEROON [MYA]
BLI alt for HLAI [LIC]
BLISS dial of JOLA-KASA [CSK]
BLIT dial of MANOBO, COTABATO [MTA]
BLITI alt for LEMBAK BLITI dial of LEMBAK [LIW]
BLO dial of RADE [RAD]
BLOOD dial of BLACKFOOT [BLC]
BLUE MEO alt for HMONG NJUA [BLU]
BLUE MIAO alt for HMONG NJUA [BLU]
BLUE MIAO alt for TAK dial of HMONG, WESTERN [HUJ]
BMOBA alt for BIMOBA [BIM]
BO [BGL] lang, Laos
BO [BPW] lang, Papua New Guinea
BO alt for BOLON [BOF]
BO alt for AKA-BO [AKM]
BO alt for ABO [ABB]
BŎ dial of MANINKA [MNI]
BO dial of BASAA [BAA]
BO RIVER VAN KIEU alt for PACOH [PAC]
BO'O dial of BIAK [BHW]
BO-I alt for BOUYEI [PCC]
BO-UNG alt for MBO-UNG [MUX]
BO-Y alt for BOUYEI [PCC]
BOA alt for BWA [BWW]
BOA alt for BUA [BUB]
BOADJI alt for BOAZI [KVG]
BOAN alt for BONAN [PEH]
BOANA alt for NUMANGGANG [NOP]
BOANAI alt for BOIANAKI [BMK]
BOANAKI alt for BOIANAKI [BMK]
BOANO [BZN] lang, Indonesia, Maluku
BOANO alt for BOLANO [BZL]
BOAR alt for KARA dial of GBAYA [GYA]
BOAZI [KVG] lang, Papua New Guinea
BOBA alt for BOMBOMA [BWS]
BOBANGI alt for BANGI [BNI]
BOBAR dial of JARAWA [JAR]
BOBASAN dial of GAYO [GYO]
BOBE alt for BUBIA [BBX]
BOBE alt for BUBE [BVB]
BOBEA alt for BUBIA [BBX]
BOBILI dial of POL [PMM]
BOBILIS alt for BEBIL [BXP]
BOBO alt for BOBO FING [BBO]
BOBO DA alt for BOBO FING [BBO]
BOBO DIOULA [BOD] lang, Burkina Faso
BOBO DYOULA alt for BOBO DIOULA [BOD]
BOBO FI alt for BOBO FING [BBO]
BOBO FIGN alt for BOBO FING [BBO]
BOBO FING [BBO] lang, Burkina Faso, Mali, Mali
BOBO FING alt for BOBO FING [BBO]
BOBO JULA alt for BOBO DIOULA [BOD]
BOBO MADARE alt for BOBO FING [BBO]
BOBO OULE alt for BOMU [BMQ]
BOBO WULE alt for BOMU [BMQ]
BOBONAZA alt for QUICHUA, PASTAZA, NORTHERN [QLB]

BOBONAZA QUICHUA alt for QUICHUA, PASTAZA, NORTHERN [QLB]
"BOBONGKO" alt for ANDIO [BZB]
BOBOT [BTY] lang, Indonesia, Maluku
BOBOTA alt for BUGLERE [SAB]
BOBWA-BOKIPA dial of BWA [BWW]
BOCAS DEL TORO dial of WESTERN CARIBBEAN CREOLE ENGLISH [JAM]
BOCHA dial of MANYIKA [MXC]
BOCHIL dial of TZOTZIL, CHAMULA [TZC]
BOCOTA alt for BUGLERE [SAB]
BOD-SKAD alt for NESANG [NES]
BODHO dial of THURI [THU]
BODI alt for BODO [BRX]
BODI dial of ME'EN [MYM]
BODIMAN dial of DUALA [DOU]
BODIN dial of ATTIÉ [ATI]
BODO [BOY] lang, Central African Republic
BODO [BRX] lang, India, Nepal, Nepal
BODO alt for BODO [BRX]
BODO alt for NAGA PIDGIN [NAG]
BODO alt for BUDU [BUU]
BODO dial of MPADE [MPI]
BODO alt for GUDWA dial of GADABA [GBJ]
BODO-GADABA alt for GUDWA dial of GADABA [GBJ]
BODOR alt for BESME [BES]
BODORO alt for KPATOGO [GBW]
BODZANGA alt for NGANDO [NGD]
BOE alt for BORÔRO [BOR]
BOE dial of DEG [MZW]
BOEGINEESCHE alt for BUGIS [BPR]
BOEGINEZEN alt for BUGIS [BPR]
BOËNG dial of TOBELO [TLB]
BOENGA KO MUZOK alt for YAMBA [YAM]
BOEROE alt for BURU [MHS]
BOETONEEZEN alt for CIA-CIA [CIA]
BOETONEEZEN alt for WOLIO [WLO]
BOEWE alt for OROWE [BPK]
BOFI dial of MANJA [MZV]
BOFOTA alt for BUGLERE [SAB]
BOGA alt for BUKA-KHWE [BUZ]
BOGA dial of GA'ANDA [GAA]
BOGADJIM alt for ANJAM [BOJ]
BOGAIA alt for BOGAYA [BOQ]
BOGAJIM alt for ANJAM [BOJ]
BOGANA alt for BINA [BYJ]
BOGANDÉ dial of FULFULDE, GOURMANTCHE [FUH]
BOGATI alt for ANJAM [BOJ]
BOGAYA [BOQ] lang, Papua New Guinea
BOGGANGER alt for BANDJALANG [BDY]
BOGGHOM alt for BOGHOM [BUX]
BOGH alt for BASHAR [BSX]
BOGHOM [BUX] lang, Nigeria
BOGHOROM alt for BOGHOM [BUX]
BOGIJIAB alt for AKA-BEA [ACE]
BOGNAK-ASUNGORUNG alt for SUNGOR [SUN]
BOGO alt for BILEN [BYN]
BOGOMIL alt for PALITYAN dial of BULGARIAN [BLG]
BOGON alt for ABULDUGU dial of BURUN [BDI]
BOGONGO dial of PANDE [BKJ]
BOGOR dial of SUNDA [SUO]
BOGOS alt for BILEN [BYN]
BOGOTA alt for BUGLERE [SAB]
BOGU alt for BONGGO [BPG]

BOGUE alt for ESIMBI [AGS]
BOGUNG alt for BARIBA [BBA]
BOGURU [BQU] lang, Zaïre
BOGURU dial of BOGURU [BQU]
BOGYEL alt for BAGYELE dial of NGUMBA [NMG]
BOGYELI alt for BAGYELE dial of NGUMBA [NMG]
BOH dial of KENYAH, MAHAKAM [XKM]
BOH BAKUNG dial of KENYAH, BAKUNG [BOC]
BOHAAN dial of BURIAT, RUSSIA [MNB]
BOHEMIAN alt for CZECH [CZC]
BOHENA dial of DANO [ASO]
BOHILAI dial of TAWALA [TBO]
BOHIRA'I alt for BOHILAI dial of TAWALA [TBO]
BOHOLANO dial of CEBUANO [CEB]
BOHOM alt for BOGHOM [BUX]
BOHOYERI alt for BHOYARI [BHY]
BOHUAI [RAK] lang, Papua New Guinea
BOHUAI dial of BOHUAI [RAK]
BOHUAI-TULU alt for BOHUAI [RAK]
BOHUTU alt for BUHUTU [BXH]
BOI dial of KWANKA [BIJ]
BOI BI dial of MUONG [MTQ]
BOIANAKI [BMK] lang, Papua New Guinea
BOIGU dial of MERIAM [ULK]
BOIKEN alt for BOIKIN [BZF]
BOIKIN [BZF] lang, Papua New Guinea
BOINAKI alt for BOIANAKI [BMK]
BOINELANG dial of AULUA [AUL]
BOJE dial of BOKYI [BKY]
BOJE alt for BUJI dial of AGÖB [KIT]
BOJIE alt for BOJE dial of BOKYI [BKY]
BOJIGNIJI alt for AKA-BEA [ACE]
BOJIGYAB alt for AKA-BEA [ACE]
BOJIIN alt for LIMBUM [LIM]
BOK alt for DABRA [DBA]
BOK dial of MANDYAK [MFV]
BOK dial of MANDYAK [MFV]
BOK dial of MANDYAK [MFV]
BOK alt for BOK PUNAN dial of PUNAN-NIBONG
   [PNE]
BOK alt for POK dial of SABAOT [SPY]
BOK PUNAN dial of PUNAN-NIBONG [PNE]
BOKA alt for BOLON [BOF]
BOKA alt for BOCHA dial of MANYIKA [MXC]
BOKA alt for BOGA dial of GA'ANDA [GAA]
BOKABO dial of GAGU [GGU]
BOKAI dial of ROTI [ROT]
BOKAN alt for BAUKAN dial of BAUKAN [BNB]
BOKARE dial of GBAYA [GYA]
BOKARI alt for BOKARE dial of GBAYA [GYA]
BOKEN alt for BAUKAN dial of BAUKAN [BNB]
BOKHAN alt for BOHAAN dial of BURIAT, RUSSIA
   [MNB]
BOKHARAN alt for BUKHARIC [BHH]
BOKHARIC alt for BUKHARIC [BHH]
BOKI alt for BOKYI [BKY]
BOKI dial of BOKYI [BKY]
BOKIYIM alt for BOGHOM [BUX]
BOKIYO alt for KENGA [KYQ]
BOKKOS [CLA] lang, Nigeria
BOKKOS dial of BOKKOS [CLA]
BOKMAL alt for NORWEGIAN, BOKMAL [NRR]
BOKO [BKP] lang, Zaïre
BOKO alt for LONGTO [WOK]
BOKO alt for BUSA-BOKO [BUS]
BOKO dial of BUSA-BOKO [BUS]

BOKO dial of BUSA-BOKO [BUS]
BOKOBARU alt for BUSA-BOKO [BUS]
BOKOBARU dial of BUSA-BOKO [BUS]
BOKOD dial of IBALOI [IBL]
BOKODO dial of GBAYA [GYA]
BOKOKI alt for BOLIA [BLI]
BOKON alt for BAUKAN dial of BAUKAN [BNB]
BOKONYA alt for BUSA-BOKO [BUS]
BOKONZI dial of BOMBOMA [BWS]
BOKOR alt for DAJU, DAR SILA [DAU]
BOKORIKE alt for DAJU, DAR SILA [DAU]
BOKORUGE alt for DAJU, DAR SILA [DAU]
BOKOTA alt for BUGLERE [SAB]
BOKOTÁ alt for BUGLERE [SAB]
BOKOY dial of LIGENZA [LGZ]
BOKU dial of SINAGORO [SNC]
BOKUN alt for BAUKAN dial of BAUKAN [BNB]
BOKWA dial of GLAVDA [GLV]
BOKWA dial of GAGU [GGU]
BOKWA-KENDEM alt for KENDEM [KVM]
BOKYI [BKY] lang, Nigeria, Cameroon
BOL MURUT alt for MALIGAN dial of TAGAL MURUT
   [MVV]
BOLA [BNP] lang, Papua New Guinea
BOLA alt for MANKANYA [MAN]
BOLA-BAKOVI alt for BOLA [BNP]
BOLAANG ITANG dial of KAIDIPANG [KZP]
BOLAANG MONGONDOW alt for MONGONDOW
   [MOG]
BOLAGHAIN dial of PASHAYI, NORTHWEST [GLH]
BOLANCHI alt for BOLE [BOL]
BOLANG ITANG alt for BOLAANG ITANG dial of
   KAIDIPANG [KZP]
BOLANGO [BLD] lang, Indonesia, Sulawesi
BOLANGO dial of BOLANGO [BLD]
BOLANO [BZL] lang, Indonesia, Sulawesi
BOLAWA alt for BOLE [BOL]
BOLE [BOL] lang, Nigeria
BOLE dial of VAGLA [VAG]
BOLE MURUT alt for MALIGAN dial of TAGAL
   MURUT [MVV]
BOLEKA alt for DESANO [DES]
BOLEKI alt for BOLOKI [BKT]
BOLEMBA dial of MBATI [MDN]
BOLERI alt for DADIYA [DBD]
BOLEWA alt for BOLE [BOL]
BOLGO [BVO] lang, Chad
BOLGO DUGAG alt for BOLGO [BVO]
BOLI alt for BALI [BCN]
BOLI alt for DOOKA dial of GBAYA [GYA]
BOLIA [BLI] lang, Zaïre
BOLINAO [SMK] lang, Philippines
BOLINAO SAMBAL alt for BOLINAO [SMK]
BOLINAO ZAMBAL alt for BOLINAO [SMK]
BOLIVIAN SIGN LANGUAGE [BVL] lang, Bolivia
BOLO [BLV] lang, Angola
BOLOI alt for BALOI [BIZ]
BOLOKI [BKT] lang, Zaïre
BOLOM alt for BULLOM SO [BUY]
BOLON [BOF] lang, Burkina Faso
BOLONDO [BZM] lang, Zaïre
BOLONGAN [BLJ] lang, Indonesia, Kalimantan
BOLONGO dial of KENGA [KYQ]
BOLONGO alt for LONGO dial of MONGO-NKUNDU
   [MOM]
BOLOS POINT dial of AGTA, DUPANINAN [DUO]

BOLOVEN alt for LAVEN [LBO]
BOLTON LANCASHIRE dial of ENGLISH [ENG]
BOLU dial of GEJI [GEZ]
BOLUPI dial of LIGENZA [LGZ]
BOM [BMF] lang, Sierra Leone
BOM alt for CHIN, BAWM [BGR]
BOM alt for ANJAM [BOJ]
BOM alt for BUM [BMV]
BOM FUTURO dial of JAMAMADÍ [JAA]
BOMA [BOH] lang, Zaïre
BOMA dial of TEKE, CENTRAL [TEC]
BOMA dial of IJO, CENTRAL-WESTERN [IJC]
BOMA KASAI alt for BOMA [BOH]
BOMA MBALI alt for BOMA dial of TEKE, CENTRAL
   [TEC]
BOMALI alt for BOMWALI [BMW]
BOMAM alt for BAHNAR BONOM dial of BAHNAR
   [BDQ]
BOMAN alt for MPOMAM dial of MPONGMPONG
   [MGG]
BOMANG dial of BURMESE [BMS]
BOMASA alt for BOMASSA [BME]
BOMASSA [BME] lang, Zaïre
BOMBALI dial of THEMNE [TEJ]
BOMBARO alt for BAMBARO dial of LAME [BMA]
BOMBAY GUJARATI alt for STANDARD GUJARATI
   dial of GUJARATI [GJR]
BOMBAY SIGN LANGUAGE dial of INDIAN SIGN
   LANGUAGE [INS]
BOMBE alt for BEBA' dial of BAFUT [BFD]
BOMBERAWA alt for BAMBARO dial of LAME [BMA]
BOMBO alt for MPONGMPONG [MGG]
BOMBOKO alt for WUMBOKO [BQM]
BOMBOLI [BML] lang, Zaïre
BOMBOMA [BWS] lang, Zaïre
BOMBONGO alt for BOMBOLI [BML]
BOMBORI dial of KATLA [KCR]
BOME alt for BOM [BMF]
BOMITABA [ZMX] lang, Congo, Central African
   Republic
BOMLA alt for GONGLA [GMM]
BOMO alt for BOM [BMF]
BOMPAKA alt for BOMPOKA dial of TERESSA [TEF]
BOMPOKA dial of TERESSA [TEF]
BOMU [BMQ] lang, Mali, Burkina Faso
BOMVANA dial of XHOSA [XOS]
BOMWALI [BMW] lang, Congo, Cameroon
BON alt for BONI [BOB]
BON alt for BON GULA [GLC]
BON dial of BASAA [BAA]
BON GULA [GLC] lang, Chad
BON SHWAI alt for PALIET dial of DINKA,
   SOUTHWESTERN [DIK]
BONA dial of ANYIN [ANY]
BONA BONA dial of SUAU [SWP]
BONAHOI dial of ARAPESH, BUMBITA [AON]
BONAN [PEH] lang, China
BONAPUTA-MOPU alt for MIANI [PLA]
BONARUA dial of SUAU [SWP]
BONDA alt for BONDO [BFW]
BONDE alt for BONDEI [BOU]
BONDEI [BOU] lang, Tanzania
BONDEYA alt for KORKU [KFQ]
BONDO [BFW] lang, India
BONDO-PORAJA alt for BONDO [BFW]
BONDONGA alt for NDUNGA [NDT]

BONDOY dial of KORKU [KFQ]
BONDUKU alt for KULANGO, BONDOUKOU [KZC]
BONE dial of BUGIS [BPR]
BONE HAU dial of KALUMPANG [KLI]
BONEFA alt for NISA [NIC]
BONEK alt for TUOTOMB [TTF]
BONEK dial of TUNEN [BAZ]
BONERATE [BNA] lang, Indonesia, Sulawesi
BONERATE dial of BONERATE [BNA]
BONERIF [BNV] lang, Indonesia, Irian Jaya
BONFIA alt for MASIWANG [BNF]
BONG alt for KINTAQ [KNQ]
BÒNG MIEU alt for CUA [CUA]
BONG MIEW alt for CUA [CUA]
BONG'OMEK dial of SABAOT [SPY]
BONGA alt for MALALAMAI [MMT]
BONGAMAISE alt for BONGOMAISI dial of KWANGA
   [KWJ]
BONGGI [DBG] lang, Malaysia, Sabah
BONGGO [BPG] lang, Indonesia, Irian Jaya
BONGILI [BUI] lang, Congo
BONGIMAN alt for YUPNA [YUT]
BONGIRI alt for BONGILI [BUI]
BONGKENG dial of MBO [MBO]
BONGLONG alt for DE'ANG [BFP]
BONGLUNG alt for DE'ANG [BFP]
BONGO [BOT] lang, Sudan
BONGO [BJO] lang, Central African Republic
BONGO alt for BONGGO [BPG]
BONGO alt for NUBACA [BAF]
BONGO TALK alt for JAMAICAN CREOLE ENGLISH
   dial of WESTERN CARIBBEAN CREOLE ENGLISH
   [JAM]
BONGOMAISI dial of KWANGA [KWJ]
BONGOR dial of MASANA [MCN]
BONGOR-JODO-TAGAL-BEREM-GUNU dial of MOSI
   [MSE]
BONGOS dial of KWANGA [KWJ]
BONGU [BPU] lang, Papua New Guinea
BONGWE alt for YASA [YKO]
BONI [BOB] lang, Kenya, Somalia, Somalia
BONI alt for BONI [BOB]
BONI dial of AUKAANS [DJK]
BONI alt for ALUKU dial of AUKAANS [DJK]
BONIANGE dial of LIBINZA [LIZ]
BONJO [BOK] lang, Congo
BONKIMAN [BOP] lang, Papua New Guinea
BONKOVIA-YEVALI alt for BIEREBO [BNK]
BONNY alt for IBANI [IBY]
BONOM alt for MONOM [MOO]
BONOTSEK alt for ATAYAL [TAY]
BONTAWA alt for BANTAWA [BAP]
BONTHAIN alt for BANTAENG dial of KONJO,
   COASTAL [KJC]
BONTOC, CENTRAL [BNC] lang, Philippines
BONTOC, EASTERN [BKB] lang, Philippines
BONTOK alt for BONTOC, CENTRAL [BNC]
BONUM dial of FALI, SOUTH [FLE]
BONZIO dial of MBATI [MDN]
BOO dial of TOURA [NEB]
BOO dial of TEKE, CENTRAL [TEC]
BOÒ alt for BOO dial of TEKE, CENTRAL [TEC]
BOO alt for BOMA dial of TEKE, CENTRAL [TEC]
BOO alt for BOKO dial of BUSA-BOKO [BUS]
BOOBE alt for BUBE [BVB]
BOODLA alt for ZUMBUL dial of DASS [DOT]

BOOLBOORA alt for YIDINY [YII]
BOOMBE alt for BUBE [BVB]
BOOMU alt for BOMU [BMQ]
BOON [BNL] lang, Somalia
BOONI dial of GURENNE [GUR]
BOORAN alt for OROMO, BORANA-ARUSI-GUJI
  [GAX]
BOORAN alt for BORANA dial of OROMO, BORANA-
  ARUSI-GUJI [GAX]
BOORDOONA alt for BURDUNA [BXN]
BOORIM dial of BOKYI [BKY]
BOORKUTTI alt for DYANGADI [DYN]
BOOT alt for BOTO dial of ZARI [ZAZ]
BOOW dial of DII [DUR]
BOPCHI alt for KORKU [KFQ]
BOR alt for DINKA, SOUTHEASTERN [DIN]
BOR dial of DINKA, SOUTHEASTERN [DIN]
BOR ATHOIC alt for ATHOC dial of DINKA,
  SOUTHEASTERN [DIN]
BOR GOK alt for BOR dial of DINKA,
  SOUTHEASTERN [DIN]
BOR MUTHUN dial of NAGA, WANCHO [NNP]
BOR MUTONIA alt for BOR MUTHUN dial of NAGA,
  WANCHO [NNP]
BORA [BOA] lang, Peru, Brazil, Colombia
BORA dial of BORA [BOA]
BORA MABANG alt for MABA [MDE]
BORAAN alt for OROMO, BORANA-ARUSI-GUJI
  [GAX]
BORAE alt for SOUTHERN CHUMBURUNG dial of
  CHUMBURUNG [NCU]
BORAI [MFX] lang, Indonesia, Irian Jaya
BORAIL SADRI dial of SADRI, ORAON [SDR]
BORAKA alt for BURAKA [BKG]
BORAN alt for OROMO, BORANA-ARUSI-GUJI [GAX]
BORAN dial of OROMO, BORANA-ARUSI-GUJI [GAX]
BORAN alt for BORANA dial of OROMO, BORANA-
  ARUSI-GUJI [GAX]
BORAN alt for BORANA dial of OROMO, BORANA-
  ARUSI-GUJI [GAX]
BORANA alt for OROMO, BORANA-ARUSI-GUJI
  [GAX]
BORANA dial of OROMO, BORANA-ARUSI-GUJI
  [GAX]
BORANA dial of OROMO, BORANA-ARUSI-GUJI
  [GAX]
BORATHOI alt for ATHOC dial of DINKA,
  SOUTHEASTERN [DIN]
BORCALA dial of AZERBAIJANI, NORTH [AZE]
BORCH dial of RUTUL [RUT]
BORDER KOMBA dial of KOMBA [KPF]
BORDO dial of KIMRÉ [KQP]
BORDURIA alt for NAGA, NOCTE [NJB]
BORE alt for BOMU [BMQ]
BOREBO dial of MAILU [MGU]
BOREI [GAI] lang, Papua New Guinea
BORENA alt for BORANA dial of OROMO, BORANA-
  ARUSI-GUJI [GAX]
BOREWAR dial of BOREI [GAI]
BORGAWA alt for BARIBA [BBA]
BORGOTKE alt for MABA [MDE]
BORGU alt for MABA [MDE]
BORGU alt for BARIBA [BBA]
BORI alt for BVERI dial of FALI, NORTH [FLL]
BORITSU alt for YUKUBEN [YBL]
BORNA [BXX] lang, Zaïre

BORNEO dial of MALAY [MLI]
BORNOUAN alt for KANURI, YERWA [KPH]
BORNOUANS alt for KANURI, YERWA [KPH]
BORNU alt for KANURI, YERWA [KPH]
BORO [BWO] lang, Ethiopia
BORO alt for BORA [BOA]
BORO alt for BODO [BRX]
BORO dial of FOLOPA [PPO]
BORO alt for BURU dial of NGELIMA [AGH]
BORO alt for BURU dial of NGOMBE [NGC]
BORO-ABORO alt for BEROM [BOM]
BOROA alt for //XEGWI [XEG]
BOROBO dial of GREBO, GLOBO [GRV]
BORODDA alt for WOLAYTTA [WBC]
BOROI dial of BOREI [GAI]
BOROMA dial of ACIPA [AWA]
BOROMESO alt for BURMESO [BZU]
BORONI alt for BODO [BRX]
BOROPA alt for AMA [AMM]
BORÔRO [BOR] lang, Brazil
BORORO alt for BORORRO dial of FULFULDE, KANO-
  KATSINA-BORORRO [FUV]
BORORRO dial of FULFULDE, KANO-KATSINA-
  BORORRO [FUV]
BOROU alt for BURU [BUH]
BORPIKA alt for BOLE [BOL]
BORROM alt for BASHAR [BSX]
BORROM alt for BOGHOM [BUX]
BORUCA [BRN] lang, Costa Rica
BORUMESSO alt for BURMESO [BZU]
BORUN alt for BURUN [BDI]
BORUNCA alt for BORUCA [BRN]
BOSA alt for LOMAVREN [RMI]
BOSAMBI dial of BUDZA [BJA]
BOSAVI alt for KALULI [BCO]
BOSHA alt for LOMAVREN [RMI]
BOSHA dial of KAFA [KBR]
BOSIKEN alt for DIMIR [DMC]
BOSILEWA [BOS] lang, Papua New Guinea
BOSKIEN alt for DIMIR [DMC]
BOSMAN alt for BOSNGUN [BQS]
BOSNGUN [BQS] lang, Papua New Guinea
BOSNIAN alt for SERBO-CROATIAN [SRC]
BOSNIK dial of BIAK [BHW]
BOSO dial of GUA [LAR]
BOSSOUM dial of FALI, NORTH [FLL]
BOTA alt for BUBIA [BBX]
BOTAI dial of GBARI [GBY]
BOTAN alt for JEZIRE dial of KURMANJI [KUR]
BOTBOT dial of BOREI [GAI]
BOTE-MAJHI [BMJ] lang, Nepal
BOTEL TABAGO alt for YAMI [YMI]
BOTEL TOBAGO alt for YAMI [YMI]
BOTHAR [BOW] lang, Papua New Guinea, Indonesia,
  Irian Jaya
BOTIN [KBX] lang, Papua New Guinea
BOTLIKH [BPH] lang, Russia, Europe
BOTLIKH dial of BOTLIKH [BPH]
BOTLIX alt for BOTLIKH [BPH]
BOTO dial of ZARI [ZAZ]
BOTOCUDOS alt for XOKLENG [XOK]
BOTOLAN ZAMBAL alt for SAMBAL, BOTOLAN
  [SBL]
BOTTENG dial of ULUMANDA' [ULM]
BOTTENG-TAPPALANG alt for ULUMANDA' [ULM]
BOTUNGA dial of MBOLE [MDQ]

BOU dial of YELE [YLE]
BOU BAAN alt for ZHUANG, SOUTHERN [CCY]
BOU LAU alt for ZHUANG, SOUTHERN [CCY]
BOU RAU alt for ZHUANG, SOUTHERN [CCY]
BOU-SHUUNG alt for ZHUANG, NORTHERN [CCX]
BOU-TSUUNG alt for ZHUANG, NORTHERN [CCX]
BOUA alt for BWA [BWW]
BOUA alt for BUA [BUB]
BOUAKA alt for NGBAKA MA'BO [NBM]
BOUAMOU alt for BWAMU [BOX]
BOUANILA alt for SOUTHERN BABOLE dial of
    BABOLE [BVX]
BOUDJOU alt for TONJO dial of TUKI [BAG]
BOUDOUMA alt for BUDUMA [BDM]
BOUENDE-TOROSSO dial of SAMBLA [SOS]
BOUIN alt for NGALKBUN [NGK]
BOUIOK alt for SAISIYAT [SAI]
BOUKA alt for BUKA [BQK]
BOULAHAY alt for MEFELE [MFJ]
BOULALA alt for BILALA [BKX]
BOULBA [BLY] lang, Benin
BOULBE alt for FULFULDE, ADAMAWA [FUB]
BOULOU alt for BULU [BUM]
BOUMOALI alt for BOMWALI [BMW]
BOUMPE alt for MENDE [MFY]
BOUN alt for NGALKBUN [NGK]
BOURAKA alt for BURAKA [BKG]
BOURBONNAIS dial of FRENCH [FRN]
BOURGIGNON dial of FRENCH [FRN]
BOURGU alt for MABA [MDE]
BOURIYA dial of KORKU [KFQ]
BOUSSA alt for BUSA-BOKO [BUS]
BOUTE alt for VUTE [VUT]
BOUYE [BYE] lang, Papua New Guinea
BOUYEI [PCC] lang, China, Viet Nam, Viet Nam
BOUYEI alt for BOUYEI [PCC]
"BOUZE" alt for LOMA [LOM]
BOVEN-MBIAN alt for MARIND, BIAN [BPV]
BOWAI alt for BOHUAI [RAK]
BOWILI alt for BOWIRI [BOV]
BOWIRI [BOV] lang, Ghana
BOWOM alt for ABILIANG dial of DINKA,
    NORTHEASTERN [DIP]
BOYA alt for LONGARIM [LOH]
BOYANESE alt for BAWEAN dial of MADURA [MHJ]
BOYELA alt for YELA [YEL]
BOZABA [BZO] lang, Zaïre
BOZE-GIRINGAREDE dial of BINE [ORM]
BOZO, HAINYAXO [BZX] lang, Mali
BOZO, SOROGAMA [BZE] lang, Mali
BOZO, TIÈMA CIÈWÈ [BOO] lang, Mali
BOZO, TIÉYAXO [BOZ] lang, Mali, Burkina Faso
BOZO, TIÉYAZO alt for BOZO, TIÉYAXO [BOZ]
BRABORI alt for DIDA, LAKOTA [DIC]
BRAGAT [AOF] lang, Papua New Guinea
BRAHMANI dial of VARHADI-NAGPURI [VAH]
BRAHMU alt for BARAAMU [BRD]
BRAHUI [BRH] lang, Pakistan, Afghanistan, Iran
BRAHUIDI alt for BRAHUI [BRH]
BRAHUIKI alt for BRAHUI [BRH]
BRAJ alt for KANAUJI [BJJ]
BRAJ alt for BRAJ BHASHA [BFS]
BRAJ BHAKHA alt for BRAJ BHASHA [BFS]
BRAJ BHASHA [BFS] lang, India
BRAJ BHASHA dial of BRAJ BHASHA [BFS]
BRAJ KANAUJI alt for KANAUJI [BJJ]

BRAME alt for MANKANYA [MAN]
BRAME dial of BURAMA [MAN]
BRANDENBURG alt for EAST LOW GERMAN dial of
    GERMAN, LOW [GEP]
BRAO [BRB] lang, Laos, Cambodia, Viet Nam
BRAO alt for BRAO [BRB]
BRAOU alt for BRAO [BRB]
BRASS IJO alt for IJO, SOUTHEAST [IJO]
BRASSA alt for BALANTA [BLE]
BRAT alt for MAI BRAT [AYZ]
BRATHELA alt for GAMADIA dial of GUJARATI
    [GJR]
BRAU alt for BRAO [BRB]
BRAVA ISLAND CREOLE dial of CRIOULO, UPPER
    GUINEA [POV]
BRAVANESE alt for MWINI dial of SWAHILI [SWA]
BRAWBAW dial of THAO [SSF]
BRAZILIAN CALÃO dial of ROMANI, CALO [RMR]
BRAZILIAN CALO dial of ROMANI, CALO [RMR]
BRAZILIAN GUARANÍ   alt for GUARANÍ, MBYÁ
    [GUN]
BRAZILIAN PORTUGUESE dial of PORTUGUESE
    [POR]
BRAZILIAN SIGN LANGUAGE [BZS] lang, Brazil
BREC alt for KAREN, BREK [KVL]
BREK alt for KAREN, BREK [KVL]
BREN alt for KHANG [KJM]
BRERI [BRQ] lang, Papua New Guinea
BRETON [BRT] lang, France, USA
BREZHONEG alt for BRETON [BRT]
BRI alt for BRAJ BHASHA [BFS]
BRI-LA alt for JEH BRI LA dial of JEH [JEH]
BRIBRI [BZD] lang, Costa Rica
BRIGNAN alt for AVIKAM [AVI]
BRIJ BHASHA alt for BRAJ BHASHA [BFS]
BRIJIA alt for BIJORI [BIX]
BRIJIA dial of ASURI [ASR]
BRIJU alt for BRAJ BHASHA [BFS]
"BRINGEN" alt for MARITHIEL [MFR]
"BRINKEN" alt for MARITHIEL [MFR]
BRINYA alt for AVIKAM [AVI]
BRISSA alt for AOWIN dial of ANYIN [ANY]
BRITISH SIGN LANGUAGE [BHO] lang, United
    Kingdom
BROKPA alt for BROKSKAT [BKK]
BROKPA alt for SAGTENGPA [SGT]
BROKPA OF DAH-HANU alt for BROKSKAT [BKK]
BROKSKAT [BKK] lang, India
BRON alt for ABRON [ABR]
BRONG alt for ABRON [ABR]
BRONGA alt for CENTRAL KANUM dial of KANUM
    [KCD]
BROOKE'S POINT PALAWAN alt for PALAWANO,
    BROOKE'S POINT [PLW]
BROSA alt for AOWIN dial of ANYIN [ANY]
BROU alt for BRAO [BRB]
BROU alt for BRU, EASTERN [BRU]
BROU alt for BURU [BUH]
BRŪ alt for BRU, EASTERN [BRU]
BRU, EASTERN [BRU] lang, Viet Nam, Laos
BRU, WESTERN [BRV] lang, Thailand, USA
BRUIT dial of MELANAU [MEL]
BRUJ alt for BRAJ BHASHA [BFS]
BRUNCA alt for BORUCA [BRN]
BRUNEI [KXD] lang, Brunei, Malaysia, Sabah,
    Malaysia, Sabah

BRUNEI alt for BRUNEI [KXD]
BRUNEI dial of BRUNEI [KXD]
BRUNEI MALAY dial of BRUNEI [KXD]
BRUNEI-KADAIAN alt for BRUNEI [KXD]
BRUNG dial of KELABIT [KZI]
BRUNKA alt for BORUCA [BRN]
BRUSHASKI alt for BURUSHASKI [BSK]
BRUU alt for BRU, WESTERN [BRV]
BSL alt for BRITISH SIGN LANGUAGE [BHO]
BU [BOE] lang, Cameroon
BU DANG dial of MNONG, CENTRAL [MNC]
BU DEH dial of STIENG [STI]
BU LO dial of STIENG [STI]
BU MAAN alt for ZHUANG, SOUTHERN [CCY]
BU NAR dial of MNONG, CENTRAL [MNC]
BU RUNG dial of MNONG, CENTRAL [MNC]
BU'U dial of ANKAVE [AAK]
BU-HWAN alt for TAROKO [TRV]
BU-NAO dial of PUNU [PNU]
BU-NONG alt for NUNG [NUT]
BUA [BUB] lang, Chad
BUA alt for BWA [BWW]
BUA dial of TAE' [ROB]
BUA dial of GREBO, FOPO-BUA [GEF]
BUA PONRANG alt for LUWU dial of BUGIS [BPR]
BUAGA dial of SINAGORO [SNC]
BUAL alt for BUWAL [BHS]
BUAL alt for BUOL [BLF]
BUAN alt for NGALKBUN [NGK]
BUANG, MANGGA [MMO] lang, Papua New Guinea
BUANG, MAPOS [BZH] lang, Papua New Guinea
BUANO alt for BOANO [BZN]
BUASI alt for VEHES [VAL]
BUBALIA alt for ARABIC, BABALIA [BBZ]
BUBANDA dial of MONO [MNH]
BUBANGI alt for BANGI [BNI]
BUBE [BVB] lang, Equatorial Guinea
BUBI [BUW] lang, Gabon
BUBI alt for BUBE [BVB]
BUBI dial of KÉLÉ [KEB]
BUBIA [BBX] lang, Cameroon
BUBIS dial of CITAK [TXT]
BUBU alt for NGURU dial of KARA [KCM]
BUBU alt for NGURU dial of KARA [KCM]
BUBUBUN alt for BUNABUN [BUQ]
BUBUKUN alt for BUNUN [BNN]
BUBURE alt for VUTE [VUT]
BUCHO dial of LEVEI-NDREHET [TLX]
BUD-KAT alt for NESANG [NES]
BUDAI dial of RUKAI [DRU]
BUDANG alt for MNONG, CENTRAL [MNC]
BUDANOH dial of DAYAK, LAND [DYK]
BUDIBUD [BTP] lang, Papua New Guinea
BUDIDJARA alt for PUDITARA dial of MARTU
    WANGKA [MPJ]
BUDIGRI dial of GBAYA [GYA]
BUDIK [TNR] lang, Senegal
BUDINA alt for BURDUNA [BXN]
BUDÍP alt for STIENG [STI]
BUDIP dial of STIENG [STI]
BUDJA alt for BUDZA [BJA]
BUDJAGO alt for BIDYOGO [BJG]
BUDON alt for KAKANDA dial of NUPE [NUP]
BUDONG alt for MNONG, CENTRAL [MNC]
BUDONG-BUDONG alt for TANGKOU [TGK]
BUDOONA alt for BURDUNA [BXN]

BUDU [BUU] lang, Zaïre
BUDUG alt for BUDUKH [BDK]
BUDUGI alt for BUDUKH [BDK]
BUDUGUM dial of MASANA [MCN]
BUDUGUM dial of MASANA [MCN]
BUDUKH [BDK] lang, Azerbaijan
BUDUKH dial of BUDUKH [BDK]
BUDUMA [BDM] lang, Chad, Cameroon, Niger,
    Nigeria
BUDUMA alt for BUDUMA [BDM]
BUDUMA dial of BUDUMA [BDM]
BUDUNA alt for BURDUNA [BXN]
BUDUX alt for BUDUKH [BDK]
BUDZA [BJA] lang, Zaïre
BUDZABA alt for BOZABA [BZO]
BUE alt for HUITOTO, MURUI [HUU]
BUELA alt for BWELA [BWL]
BUEM alt for LELEMI [LEF]
BUENDE alt for BWENDE dial of KONGO [KON]
BUENG dial of ACEH [ATJ]
BUFE alt for BAFUT [BFD]
BUFE dial of BAFUT [BFD]
BUFUMBWA dial of RWANDA [RUA]
BUG alt for MANGAYAT [MYJ]
BUGAGO alt for BIDYOGO [BJG]
BUGALU alt for BIKARU [BIC]
BUGAU dial of IBAN [IBA]
BUGE dial of VAGLA [VAG]
BUGHOTU [BGT] lang, Solomon Islands
BUGI alt for BUGIS [BPR]
BUGI alt for BUJI dial of AGÖB [KIT]
BUGINESE alt for BUGIS [BPR]
BUGIS [BPR] lang, Indonesia, Sulawesi, Malaysia,
    Sabah, Malaysia, Sabah
BUGIS alt for BUGIS [BPR]
BUGKALUT alt for ILONGOT [ILK]
BUGLERE [SAB] lang, Panama
BUGLIAL dial of MERIAM [ULK]
BUGOMBE dial of BHELE [PER]
BUGONGO alt for BOGONGO dial of PANDE [BKJ]
BUGOTA alt for BUGHOTU [BGT]
BUGOTO alt for BUGHOTU [BGT]
BUGOTU alt for BUGHOTU [BGT]
BUGRE alt for KAINGÁNG [KGP]
BUGRE alt for XOKLENG [XOK]
BUGSUK PALAWANO alt for SOUTH PALAWANO
    dial of PALAWANO, BROOKE'S POINT [PLW]
BUGUDUM alt for BUDUGUM dial of MASANA
    [MCN]
BUGULI alt for PUGULI [PUG]
BUGUMBE dial of KURIA [KUJ]
BUGURI alt for PUGULI [PUG]
BUHAGANA alt for MACUNA [MYY]
BUHI dial of BICOLANO, ALBAY [BHK]
BUHI'NON alt for BUHI dial of BICOLANO, ALBAY
    [BHK]
BUHID [BKU] lang, Philippines
BUHULU alt for BUHUTU [BXH]
BUHUTU [BXH] lang, Papua New Guinea
BUI alt for BOUYEI [PCC]
BUIAMANAMBU alt for YELOGU [YLG]
BUILE alt for BULI [BWU]
BUILSA alt for BULI [BWU]
BUIN [BUO] lang, Papua New Guinea
BUIN alt for NGALKBUN [NGK]
BUINAK dial of KUMYK [KSK]

BUJA alt for BUDZA [BJA]
BUJAL alt for GHARTI [GOR]
BUJHEL alt for GHARTI [GOR]
BUJI dial of AGÖB [KIT]
BUJI dial of JERA [JER]
BUJIYEL dial of SANGA [SGA]
BUJWE alt for BUYU [BYI]
BUKA [BQK] lang, Central African Republic
BUKA alt for BUKAR SADONG [SDO]
BUKA alt for BUKA-KHWE [BUZ]
BUKA-KHWE [BUZ] lang, Botswana
BUKA-KHWE dial of BUKA-KHWE [BUZ]
BUKABUKAN alt for PUKAPUKA [PKP]
BUKALA dial of MONGO-NKUNDU [MOM]
BUKALOT alt for ILONGOT [ILK]
BUKAR alt for BUKAR SADONG [SDO]
BUKAR BIDAYUH dial of BUKAR SADONG [SDO]
BUKAR SADONG [SDO] lang, Malaysia, Sarawak,
    Indonesia, Kalimantan
BUKAR SADONG dial of BUKAR SADONG [SDO]
BUKAT [BVK] lang, Indonesia, Kalimantan
BUKAU dial of TIMUGON MURUT [TIH]
BUKAUA alt for BUKAWA [BUK]
BUKAWA [BUK] lang, Papua New Guinea
BUKAWAC alt for BUKAWA [BUK]
BUKHARA ARABIC dial of ARABIC, CENTRAL ASIAN
    COLLOQUIAL [ABH]
BUKHARAN alt for BUKHARIC [BHH]
BUKHARIAN alt for BUKHARIC [BHH]
BUKHARIC [BHH] lang, Israel, Uzbekistan,
    Uzbekistan
BUKHARIC alt for BUKHARIC [BHH]
BUKIDNON alt for BINUKID [BKD]
BUKIDNON alt for MAGAHAT [MTW]
BUKIDNON alt for SULOD [SRG]
BUKIL alt for BUHID [BKU]
BUKIRA dial of KURIA [KUJ]
BUKIT alt for MALAY, BUKIT [BVU]
BUKITAN [BKN] lang, Malaysia, Sarawak, Indonesia,
    Kalimantan
BUKIYIP [APE] lang, Papua New Guinea
BUKIYÚP alt for BUKIYIP [APE]
BUKONGO alt for BOGONGO dial of PANDE [BKJ]
BUKOWJ dial of TIMUGON MURUT [TIH]
BUKPI dial of CHIN, TEDIM [CTD]
BUKU dial of CAMPALAGIAN [CML]
BUKUETA alt for BUGLERE [SAB]
BUKUKHI alt for BUDUKH [BDK]
BUKUM alt for BUKUR dial of BOGURU [BQU]
BUKUMA alt for OGBRONUAGUM [OGU]
BUKUN alt for BAUKAN dial of BAUKAN [BNB]
BUKUR dial of BOGURU [BQU]
BUKURU alt for BUKUR dial of BOGURU [BQU]
BUKURUMI alt for KURAMA [KRH]
BUKUSU [BUL] lang, Kenya
BUKUSU dial of BUKUSU [BUL]
BUL alt for THIANG dial of NUER [NUS]
BULA alt for MEFELE [MFJ]
BULA alt for MAFA [MAF]
BULACAN dial of TAGALOG [TGL]
BULACH dial of STIENG [STI]
BULAGAT dial of BURIAT, RUSSIA [MNB]
BULAHAI alt for MEFELE [MFJ]
BULAHAI alt for MAFA [MAF]
BULALA alt for BILALA [BKX]
BULALAKAW dial of INONHAN [LOC]

BULALAKAWNON dial of HANUNOO [HNN]
BULAMA alt for BURAMA dial of MANKANYA [MAN]
BULANDA alt for BALANTA [BLE]
BULANG alt for BLANG [BLR]
BULANGA alt for BOLANGO [BLD]
BULANGA-UKI alt for BOLANGO [BLD]
BULBA alt for BOULBA [BLY]
BULE alt for VUTE [VUT]
BULELENG alt for LOWLAND BALI dial of BALI [BZC]
BULEM alt for BULLOM SO [BUY]
BULGAI dial of MERIAM [ULK]
BULGAR alt for CHUVASH [CJU]
BULGAR GAGAUZ dial of GAGAUZ [GAG]
BULGAR GAGAUZI dial of GAGAUZ [GAG]
BULGARIAN [BLG] lang, Bulgaria, Romania, Greece,
    Moldova, Romania, Turkey, Yugoslavia
BULGARIAN alt for BULGARIAN [BLG]
BULGEBI [BMP] lang, Papua New Guinea
BULI [BWU] lang, Ghana, Burkina Faso
BULI [BZQ] lang, Indonesia, Maluku
BULI dial of GBAYA [GYA]
BULI dial of BULI [BZQ]
BULI dial of AKHA [AKA]
BULI dial of POLCI [POL]
BULI alt for PANGA dial of MONGO-NKUNDU [MOM]
BULIA alt for BOLIA [BLI]
BULISA alt for BULI [BWU]
BULLA dial of SHEKO [SHE]
BULLIN alt for BULLOM SO [BUY]
BULLOM SO [BUY] lang, Sierra Leone
BULLUN alt for BULLOM SO [BUY]
BULO dial of STIENG [STI]
BULO dial of PANNEI [PNC]
BULU [BJL] lang, Papua New Guinea
BULU [BUM] lang, Cameroon
BULU alt for SEKI [SYI]
BULUD UPI alt for IDA'AN [DBJ]
BULUF dial of JOLA-FOGNY [DYO]
BULU KUNING alt for SAMIHIM dial of MA'ANYAN
    [MHY]
BULUKI alt for BOLOKI [BKT]
BULUKUMBA alt for SINJAI dial of BUGIS [BPR]
BULUM alt for BURUM-MINDIK [BMU]
BULUM-BULUM alt for DYAABUGAY [DYY]
BULUNGAN alt for BOLONGAN [BLJ]
BULUNGAN dial of BASAP [BDB]
BULUNGE alt for BURUNGI [BDS]
BULUYIEMA dial of LOMA [LOM]
BUM [BMV] lang, Cameroon
BUM alt for BOM [BMF]
BUM alt for MBOUM dial of MBUM [MDD]
BUMA alt for BOMA [BOH]
BUMA alt for TEANU [TKW]
BUMA alt for TURKANA [TUV]
BUMAJI [BYP] lang, Nigeria
BUMAL dial of PITU ULUNNA SALU [PTU]
BUMALI alt for BOMWALI [BMW]
BUMBIRA dial of HAYA [HAY]
BUMBOKO alt for WUMBOKO [BQM]
BUMBONG alt for DIMBONG [DII]
BUMBORET alt for NORTHERN KALASHA dial of
    KALASHA [KLS]
BUME alt for TURKANA [TUV]
BUMO dial of IJO, CENTRAL-WESTERN [IJC]
BUMTANGKHA alt for BUMTHANGKHA dial of
    KEBUMTAMP [KJZ]

BUMTHANG alt for BUMTHANGKHA dial of
  KEBUMTAMP [KJZ]
BUMTHANGKHA dial of KEBUMTAMP [KJZ]
BUMWANGI dial of LUSENGO [LUS]
BUN [BUV] lang, Papua New Guinea
BUN alt for BON GULA [GLC]
BUNA [BVN] lang, Papua New Guinea
BUNA alt for MBUM [MDD]
BUNA alt for YUNGUR [YUN]
BUNA alt for KULANGO, BOUNA [NKU]
BUNA' alt for BUNAK [BUA]
BUNABA [BCK] lang, Australia
BUNABUN [BUQ] lang, Papua New Guinea
BUNAK [BUA] lang, Indonesia, Nusa Tenggara
BUNAKE alt for BUNAK [BUA]
BUNAKI alt for NAKI [MFF]
BUNAMA [BDD] lang, Papua New Guinea
BUNAMA dial of BUNAMA [BDD]
BUNAN [BFU] lang, India, China
BUNAN alt for BUNUN [BNN]
BUNAN alt for PUNAN dial of DAYAK, LAND [DYK]
BUNBERAWA alt for BAMBARO dial of LAME [BMA]
BUNDA alt for SUWAWA [SWU]
BUNDA dial of SUWAWA [SWU]
BUNDALA alt for BANDJALANG [BDY]
BUNDE dial of LOMA [LOM]
BUNDEL KHANDI alt for BUNDELI [BNS]
BUNDELI [BNS] lang, India
BUNDELI dial of BUNDELI [BNS]
BUNDHAMARA alt for PUNTHAMARA dial of NGURA
  [NBX]
BUNDI alt for GENDE [GAF]
BUNDU dial of DUSUN, CENTRAL [DTP]
BUNDUM dial of TUKI [BAG]
BUNGAIN [BUT] lang, Papua New Guinea
BUNGASE dial of LIGBI [LIG]
BUNGBINDA alt for NGBINDA [NBD]
BUNGEHA alt for BANGGARLA [BJB]
BUNGELA alt for BANGGARLA [BJB]
BUNGGU alt for KAILI, DA'A [KZF]
BUNGILI alt for BONGILI [BUI]
BUNGIRI alt for BONGILI [BUI]
BUNGKU [BKZ] lang, Indonesia, Sulawesi
BUNGKU dial of BUNGKU [BKZ]
BUNGNU alt for KAMKAM [BGU]
BUNGO dial of BONGO [BOT]
BUNGU [WUN] lang, Tanzania
BUNGU alt for BONGO [BOT]
BUNIABURA dial of ANEME WAKE [ABY]
BUNINGA dial of NAMAKURA [NMK]
BUNINGA dial of EFATE, NORTH [LLP]
BUNJI dial of MANYIKA [MXC]
BUNJIA alt for BHUNJIA [BHU]
BUNJU alt for TONJO dial of TUKI [BAG]
BUNJWALI dial of KASHMIRI [KSH]
BUNONG dial of MNONG, SOUTHERN [MNN]
BUNTI alt for BUNUN [BNN]
BUNU alt for KAMKAM [BGU]
BUNU alt for PUNU [PNU]
BUNU alt for BARGAM [MLP]
BUNU dial of YORUBA [YOR]
BUNU alt for RIBINA dial of JERA [JER]
BUNUBA alt for BUNABA [BCK]
BUNUBUN alt for BUNABUN [BUQ]
BUNUM alt for BUNUN [BNN]
BUNUN [BNN] lang, Taiwan

BUNUO alt for PUNU [PNU]
BUOL [BLF] lang, Indonesia, Sulawesi
BUONCWAI alt for PALIET dial of DINKA,
  SOUTHWESTERN [DIK]
BUPUL alt for NORTH YEI dial of YEI [JEI]
BUPURAN alt for PAPORA [PPU]
BUR:AAD alt for BURIAT, MONGOLIA [BXM]
BURA alt for BURA-PABIR [BUR]
BURA dial of TAITA [DAV]
BURA MABANG alt for MABA [MDE]
BURA-PABIR [BUR] lang, Nigeria
BURADA alt for BURARRA [BVR]
BURAIMI ARABIC dial of ARABIC, GULF [AFB]
BURAK [BYS] lang, Nigeria
BURAKA [BKG] lang, Central African Republic, Zaïre,
  Zaïre
BURAKA alt for BURAKA [BKG]
BURAM alt for BURAMA dial of MANKANYA [MAN]
BURAMA dial of MANKANYA [MAN]
BURARRA [BVR] lang, Australia
BURATE [BTI] lang, Indonesia, Irian Jaya
BURBA alt for BIALI [BEH]
BURDUNA [BXN] lang, Australia
BUREDA alt for BURARRA [BVR]
BURERA alt for BURARRA [BVR]
BURGADI alt for DYANGADI [DYN]
BURGANDI dial of TAMIL [TCV]
BURGU alt for BARIBA [BBA]
BURIAH-WETH-LATURAKE alt for CENTRAL EAST
  ALUNE dial of ALUNE [ALP]
BURIAT, CHINA [BXU] lang, China
BURIAT, MONGOLIA [BXM] lang, Mongolian Peoples
  Republic
BURIAT, RUSSIA [MNB] lang, Russia, Asia
BURIAT-MONGOLIAN alt for BURIAT, MONGOLIA
  [BXM]
BURIAT-MONGOLIAN alt for BURIAT, CHINA [BXU]
BURIAT-MONGOLIAN alt for BURIAT, RUSSIA [MNB]
BURIG alt for PURIK [BXR]
BURIGSKAT alt for PURIK [BXR]
BURIRAM dial of KHMER, NORTHERN [KXM]
BURJA alt for BIJORI [BIX]
BURJI [BJI] lang, Ethiopia, Kenya, Kenya
BURJI alt for BURJI [BJI]
BURJIN alt for ANUAK [ANU]
BURJINYA alt for BURJI [BJI]
BURKANAWA alt for MBURKU [BBT]
BURKENEJI alt for SAMBURU [SAQ]
BURMA alt for BOGHOM [BUX]
BURMA TAMIL dial of TAMIL [TCV]
BURMBAR [VRT] lang, Vanuatu
BURMESE [BMS] lang, Myanmar, Bangladesh
BURMESE dial of BURMESE [BMS]
BURMESE KAREN alt for KAREN, S'GAW [KSW]
BURMESO [BZU] lang, Indonesia, Irian Jaya
BURNAY IFUGAO dial of IFUGAO, AMGANAD [IFA]
BURO alt for DEG [MZW]
BUROM alt for BOGHOM [BUX]
BURRA alt for BURA-PABIR [BUR]
BURRUM alt for BASHAR [BSX]
BURRUM alt for BOGHOM [BUX]
BURTA alt for BERTA [WTI]
BURU [BUH] lang, Sudan
BURU [MHS] lang, Indonesia, Maluku, Netherlands
BURU alt for LISELA [LCL]
BURU alt for DEG [MZW]

BURU alt for TAMAGARIO [TCG]
BURU dial of NGELIMA [AGH]
BURU dial of NGOMBE [NGC]
BURUBORA alt for PURUBORÁ [PUR]
BURUCAKI alt for BURUSHASKI [BSK]
BURUCASKI alt for BURUSHASKI [BSK]
BURUESE alt for BURU [MHS]
BURUI [BRY] lang, Papua New Guinea
BURUI dial of SAWOS [SIC]
BURUM alt for BOGHOM [BUX]
BURUM alt for BURUM-MINDIK [BMU]
BURUM-MINDIK [BMU] lang, Papua New Guinea
BURUMBA alt for BAKI [BKI]
BURUN [BDI] lang, Sudan
BURUN alt for UDUK [UDU]
BURUNCA alt for BORUCA [BRN]
BURUNGE alt for BURUNGI [BDS]
BURUNGI [BDS] lang, Tanzania
BURUSA alt for BOULBA [BLY]
BURUSHAKI alt for BURUSHASKI [BSK]
BURUSHASKI [BSK] lang, Pakistan, India
BURUSHKI alt for BURUSHASKI [BSK]
BURUSU [BQR] lang, Indonesia, Kalimantan
BURUWA alt for BORDO dial of KIMRÉ [KQP]
BURUWAI alt for ASIENARA [ASI]
BURYAT alt for BURIAT, MONGOLIA [BXM]
BURYAT alt for BURIAT, CHINA [BXU]
BURYAT alt for BURIAT, RUSSIA [MNB]
BURZHAN dial of BASHKIR [BXK]
BUSA [BHF] lang, Papua New Guinea
BUSA alt for BUSA-BOKO [BUS]
BUSA-BOKO [BUS] lang, Benin, Nigeria, Nigeria
BUSA-BOKO alt for BUSA-BOKO [BUS]
BUSAGWE alt for BUSA-BOKO [BUS]
BUSAM [BXS] lang, Cameroon
BUSAMI [BSM] lang, Indonesia, Irian Jaya
BUSANCHI alt for BUSA-BOKO [BUS]
BUSANG alt for KAYAN, BUSANG [BFG]
BUSANG alt for PUNAN dial of DAYAK, LAND [DYK]
BUSANG alt for MURANG PUNAN dial of DAYAK,
   LAND [DYK]
BUSANSE alt for BUSA-BOKO [BUS]
BUSAWA alt for BUSA-BOKO [BUS]
BUSENI alt for BISENI [IJE]
BUSERE BONGO dial of BONGO [BOT]
BUSH MEKEO alt for MEKEO [MEK]
BUSH MEKEO alt for WEST MEKEO dial of MEKEO
   [MEK]
BUSH UNUA dial of UNUA [ONU]
BUSH-C alt for //XEGWI [XEG]
BUSHI alt for BAUSHI [BSF]
BUSHMAN alt for GIMSBOK NAMA [GEM]
BUSHMAN'S BAY alt for LINGARAK [LGK]
BUSHONG alt for BUSHOONG [BUF]
BUSHONGO alt for BUSHOONG [BUF]
BUSHOONG [BUF] lang, Zaïre
BUSI dial of OBANLIKU [BZY]
BUSILLU SISALA alt for SISAALA, WESTERN [SSL]
BUSILMIN dial of TIFAL [TIF]
BUSO [BSO] lang, Chad
BUSOA [BUP] lang, Indonesia, Sulawesi
BUSOONG alt for BUSHOONG [BUF]
BUSSA alt for DOBASE [DOX]
BUSSAGWE alt for BUSA-BOKO [BUS]
BUSSO alt for BUSO [BSO]
BUSU DJANGA dial of LUSENGO [LUS]

BUSUU [BJU] lang, Cameroon
"BUSY" alt for LOMA [LOM]
BUTA alt for GAMO dial of GAMO-NINGI [BTE]
BUTAM dial of TAULIL-BUTAM [TUH]
BUTANGLU alt for PAIWAN [PWN]
BUTE alt for VUTE [VUT]
BUTE BAMNYO dial of VUTE [VUT]
BUTELKUD-GUNTABAK alt for NOBANOB [GAW]
BUTI alt for VUTE [VUT]
BUTJU alt for DJANGUN [DJF]
BUTMAS-TUR [BNR] lang, Vanuatu
BUTON alt for CIA-CIA [CIA]
BUTON alt for WOLIO [WLO]
BUTONESE alt for CIA-CIA [CIA]
BUTONESE alt for WOLIO [WLO]
BUTUANON [BTW] lang, Philippines
BUTUNG alt for CIA-CIA [CIA]
BUTUNG alt for WOLIO [WLO]
BUTURA dial of BOKKOS [CLA]
BUU alt for ZARANDA dial of GEJI [GEZ]
BUU I dial of POKOMO, LOWER [POJ]
BUU II dial of POKOMO, LOWER [POJ]
BUU III dial of POKOMO, LOWER [POJ]
BUURAK alt for BURAK [BYS]
BUWAL [BHS] lang, Cameroon
BUWAN alt for NGALKBUN [NGK]
BUWEYEU dial of BUANG, MAPOS [BZH]
BUXARA alt for BUKHARA ARABIC dial of ARABIC,
   CENTRAL ASIAN COLLOQUIAL [ABH]
BUY alt for KOBIANA [KCJ]
BUYA [BYY] lang, Zaïre
BUYA dial of LOKO [LOK]
BUYAKA alt for SENTANI [SET]
BUYANG [BYU] lang, China
BUYEI alt for BOUYEI [PCC]
BUYI alt for BUYU [BYI]
BUYI alt for BOUYEI [PCC]
BUYU [BYI] lang, Zaïre
BUYUI alt for BOUYEI [PCC]
BUZABA alt for BOZABA [BZO]
BUZAWA dial of KALMYK-OIRAT [KGZ]
"BUZI" alt for LOMA [LOM]
BVANUMA alt for VANUMA [VAU]
BVERI dial of FALI, NORTH [FLL]
BVIRI alt for BELANDA VIRI [BVI]
BVUKOO alt for KUO [OKU]
BVUMBA dial of MANYIKA [MXC]
BWA [BWW] lang, Zaïre
BWA alt for BWAMU [BOX]
BWA alt for BUA [BUB]
BWABA alt for BWAMU [BOX]
BWADJI alt for BOAZI [KVG]
BWAGIRA dial of BANA [FLI]
BWAIDOGA alt for BWAIDOKA [BWD]
BWAIDOGA dial of BWAIDOKA [BWD]
BWAIDOKA [BWD] lang, Papua New Guinea
BWAKA alt for NGBAKA MA'BO [NBM]
BWAKA dial of MBATI [MDN]
BWAKERA dial of SEWA BAY [SEW]
BWAL alt for BWOL dial of KOFYAR [KWL]
BWAMU [BOX] lang, Burkina Faso
BWANA dial of NUNI [NNW]
BWANABWANA alt for TUBETUBE [TTE]
BWAREBA alt for BACAMA [BAM]
BWATNAPNI dial of APMA [APP]
BWATOO [BWA] lang, New Caledonia

BWATVENUA alt for HANO [LML]
BWAZZA dial of MBULA-BWAZZA [MBU]
BWE alt for KAREN, BWE [BWE]
BWELA [BWL] lang, Zaïre
BWENDE dial of KONGO [KON]
BWILE [BWC] lang, Zambia
BWILIM alt for MWANA dial of DIJIM [CFA]
BWIREGE dial of KURIA [KUJ]
BWISHA dial of RWANDA [RUA]
BWISI [BWZ] lang, Congo, Gabon
BWISI alt for BWISI [BWZ]
BWISSI alt for TALINGA-BWISI [TLJ]
BWO'OL alt for BUOL [BLF]
BWOL dial of KOFYAR [KWL]
BWONCWAI alt for PALIET dial of DINKA,
    SOUTHWESTERN [DIK]
BWORO alt for BORO [BWO]
BYABE dial of NORRA [NOR]
BYANGSI [BEE] lang, Nepal
BYANSKAT alt for CHANGTHANG [CNA]
BYELORUSSIAN alt for BELORUSSIAN [RUW]
BYEP [MKK] lang, Cameroon
BYEP dial of BYEP [MKK]
BYETRI alt for EOTILE [EOT]
BYOKI alt for BOKYI [BKY]
BYRRE alt for GBETE dial of MBUM [MDD]
BYRRE alt for KEPERE dial of MBUM [MDD]
BZEDUX alt for BEZHEDUKH dial of ADYGHE [ADY]
BZYB dial of ABKHAZ [ABK]
CA GIONG alt for KAYONG [KXY]
CA TUA alt for KATUA [KTA]
CA' dial of FE'FE' [FMP]
CAABE alt for CABE [CBJ]
CAAC [MSQ] lang, New Caledonia
CABANATIT alt for TOBA-MASKOY [TMF]
CABARAN alt for KAVALAN [CKV]
CABE [CBJ] lang, Benin
CABEÇA SECA dial of GAVIÃO DO JIPARANÁ
    [GVO]
CABÉCAR [CJP] lang, Costa Rica
CABICHÍ alt for KABIXÍ [KBD]
CABINDA alt for KONGO [KON]
CABISHI alt for KABIXÍ [KBD]
CABIUARÍ alt for CABIYARÍ [CBB]
CABIYARÍ [CBB] lang, Colombia
CABO dial of MÍSKITO [MIQ]
CABRAI alt for KABIYÉ [KBP]
CABRAIS alt for KABIYÉ [KBP]
CAC'CHIQUEL MAM alt for CHICOMUCELTEC [COB]
CACA WERANOS alt for CHIMILA [CBG]
CACAHUE alt for KAKAUHUA [KBF]
CACALOXTEPEC MIXTECO alt for MIXTECO,
    HUAJUAPAN [MIU]
CACATAIBO dial of CASHIBO-CACATAIBO [CBR]
CACCHÉ alt for KEKCHÍ [KEK]
CACHARI alt for KACHARI [QKC]
CACHEU-ZIGUINCHOR CREOLE dial of CRIOULO,
    UPPER GUINEA [POV]
CACHIBO alt for CASHIBO-CACATAIBO [CBR]
"CACHOMASHIRI" alt for CAQUINTE [COT]
CACHUENA alt for KATAWIAN dial of WAIWAI
    [WAW]
CACHUY alt for CAUQUI dial of JAQARU [JQR]
CACI alt for TIRMA dial of MURSI [MUZ]
CACIBO alt for CASHIBO-CACATAIBO [CBR]
CACRA-HONGOS dial of QUECHUA, YAUYOS [QUX]

CACUA [CBV] lang, Colombia
CADAUAPURITANA alt for UNHUN dial of
    CURRIPACO [KPC]
CADDO [CAD] lang, USA
CADDOE alt for CADDO [CAD]
CADOE LOANG alt for CHRU [CJE]
CADONG alt for SEDANG [SED]
CADORINO dial of LADIN [LLD]
CADUVÉO alt for KADIWÉU [KBC]
CAELI alt for KAYELI [KZL]
CAFFINO alt for KAFA [KBR]
CAFFRE alt for XHOSA [XOS]
CAFRE alt for XHOSA [XOS]
CAFUNDO CREOLE [CCD] lang, Brazil
CAGA alt for ENGA [ENQ]
CAGABA alt for COGUI [KOG]
CAGAYAN alt for GADDANG [GAD]
CAGAYAN DE SULU alt for MAPUN [SJM]
CAGAYANCILLO alt for KAGAYANEN [CGC]
CAGAYANO alt for MAPUN [SJM]
CAGAYANO CILLO alt for KAGAYANEN [CGC]
CAGAYANON alt for MAPUN [SJM]
CAGLIARE dial of SARDINIAN, CAMPIDANESE [SRO]
CAGLIARITAN alt for CAGLIARE dial of SARDINIAN,
    CAMPIDANESE [SRO]
CAGUA [CBH] lang, Colombia
CAHIVO alt for CASHIBO-CACATAIBO [CBR]
CAHTO alt for KATO [KTW]
CAHUAPA alt for CHAYAHUITA [CBT]
CAHUAPANA dial of CHAYAHUITA [CBT]
CAHUARANO [CAH] lang, Peru
CAHUILLA [CHL] lang, USA
CAI alt for BURUN [BDI]
CAI alt for TIRMA dial of MURSI [MUZ]
CAIABI alt for KAYABÍ [KYZ]
CAIMAN NUEVO alt for KUNA, PAYA-PUCURO
    [KUA]
CAINGANG alt for KAINGÁNG [KGP]
CAINGUA alt for KAIWÁ [KGK]
CAIUA alt for KAIWÁ [KGK]
CAIWÁ alt for KAIWÁ [KGK]
CAJAN alt for FRENCH, CAJUN [FRC]
CAJELI alt for KAYELI [KZL]
CAJONOS ZAPOTEC alt for ZAPOTECO, SOUTHERN
    VILLA ALTA [ZAD]
CAJUN alt for FRENCH, CAJUN [FRC]
CAKA [CKX] lang, Cameroon
CAKCHIQUEL MAM alt for CHICOMUCELTEC [COB]
CAKCHIQUEL, CENTRAL [CAK] lang, Guatemala
CAKCHIQUEL, EASTERN [CKE] lang, Guatemala
CAKCHIQUEL, NORTHERN [CKC] lang, Guatemala
CAKCHIQUEL, SANTA MARÍA DE JESÚS [CKI] lang,
    Guatemala
CAKCHIQUEL, SANTO DOMINGO XENACOJ [CKJ]
    lang, Guatemala
CAKCHIQUEL, SOUTH CENTRAL [CKD] lang,
    Guatemala
CAKCHIQUEL, SOUTHERN [CKF] lang, Guatemala
CAKCHIQUEL, SOUTHWESTERN, ACATENANGO
    [CKK] lang, Guatemala
CAKCHIQUEL, SOUTHWESTERN, YEPOCAPA [CBM]
    lang, Guatemala
CAKCHIQUEL, WESTERN [CKW] lang, Guatemala
CAKFEM dial of MWAGHAVUL [SUR]
CAKKE dial of DURI [MVP]
CALA alt for CHALA [CHA]

CALA-CALA alt for LELA [DRI]
CALABAR alt for EFIK [EFK]
CALABASH BIGHT dial of ENGLISH [ENG]
CALABRESE dial of NEAPOLITAN-CALABRESE [NPL]
CALABRIAN alt for CALABRESE dial of
   NEAPOLITAN-CALABRESE [NPL]
CALABRIAN ALBANIAN dial of ALBANIAN, TOSK
   [ALN]
CALAMIANO alt for TAGBANWA, CALAMIAN [TBK]
CALANASAN dial of ISNAG [ISD]
CALÃO alt for ROMANI, CALO [RMR]
CALÃO alt for PORTUGUESE CALÃO dial of
   ROMANI, CALO [RMR]
CALATRAVANHON alt for BANTOANON [BNO]
CALCUTTA SIGN LANGUAGE dial of INDIAN SIGN
   LANGUAGE [INS]
CALDERÓN QUICHUA alt for QUICHUA, HIGHLAND,
   CALDERÓN [QUD]
CALDOCHE alt for KALDOSH [CKS]
CALEBASSES alt for KENSWEI NSEI [NDB]
CALIANA alt for SAPÉ [SPC]
CALIBUGAN SUBANON dial of SUBANON,
   WESTERN [SUC]
CALLAHUAYA alt for CALLAWALLA [CAW]
CALLAWALLA [CAW] lang, Bolivia
CALO alt for BRU, EASTERN [BRU]
CALO alt for ROMANI, CALO [RMR]
CALUYANEN alt for CALUYANUN [CAU]
CALUYANHON alt for CALUYANUN [CAU]
CALUYANUN [CAU] lang, Philippines
CAM dial of DIJIM [CFA]
CAM MU alt for KHMU [KJG]
CAMA alt for EBRIÉ [EBR]
CAMAIURA alt for KAMAYURÁ [KAY]
CAMALAL alt for CHAMALAL [CJI]
CAMAN alt for EBRIÉ [EBR]
CAMARACOTA dial of PEMON [AOC]
CAMARACOTO dial of PEMON [AOC]
CAMBA alt for KAMBA [QKZ]
CAMBA dial of BUGIS [BPR]
CAMBEBA alt for OMAGUA [OMG]
CAMBELA alt for OMAGUA [OMG]
CAMBODIAN alt for KHMER, CENTRAL [KMR]
CAMBODIAN CHAM alt for CHAM, WESTERN [CJA]
CAMERIJA dial of ALBANIAN, TOSK [ALN]
CAMERON dial of SEMAI [SEA]
CAMEROON CREOLE ENGLISH alt for PIDGIN,
   CAMEROON [WES]
CAMILEROI alt for KAMILAROI [KLD]
CAMO dial of KUDU-CAMO [KOV]
CAMONAYAN dial of AGTA, DUPANINAN [DUO]
CAMORTA dial of NICOBARESE, CENTRAL [NCB]
CAMOTES alt for POROHANON [PRH]
CAMPA, ASHÁNINCA [CNI] lang, Peru
CAMPA, ASHÉNINCA [CPU] lang, Peru, Brazil
CAMPA, PAJONAL ASHÉNINCA [CJO] lang, Peru
CAMPALAGIAN [CML] lang, Indonesia, Sulawesi
CAMPALAGIAN dial of CAMPALAGIAN [CML]
CAMPEBA alt for OMAGUA [OMG]
CAMPIDANESE alt for SARDINIAN, CAMPIDANESE
   [SRO]
CAMPO alt for TIPAI [TIP]
CAMPO MARINO ALBANIAN dial of ALBANIAN,
   TOSK [ALN]
CAMPUON alt for TAMPUAN [TPU]
CAMSÁ [KBH] lang, Colombia

CAMUCONES alt for TIDONG [TID]
CAMUHI alt for CEMUHÎ [CAM]
CAMUKI alt for CEMUHÎ [CAM]
CAMURU alt for KAMURÚ dial of KARIRI-XUCO
   [KZW]
CANADIAN SIGN LANGUAGE [CSD] lang, Canada
CANALA alt for XARACUU [ANE]
CANAMANTI alt for KANAMANTI [QKN]
CANAMARÍ alt for KANAMARÍ [KNM]
CANARESE alt for KANNADA [KJV]
CAÑARIS dial of QUECHUA, LAMBAYEQUE [QUF]
CANARY ISLANDS SPANISH dial of SPANISH [SPN]
CANDELARIA LOXICHA ZAPOTECO dial of
   ZAPOTECO, NORTHEASTERN POCHUTLA [ZTP]
CANDOSHI alt for CANDOSHI-SHAPRA [CBU]
CANDOSHI-SHAPRA [CBU] lang, Peru
CANDOXI alt for CANDOSHI-SHAPRA [CBU]
CANE alt for NCANE [NCR]
CANEJAN ARANÉS dial of GASCON [GSC]
CANELA [RAM] lang, Brazil
CANGA-PEBA alt for OMAGUA [OMG]
CANICHANA [CAZ] lang, Bolivia
CANOA alt for AVÁ-CANOEIRO [AVV]
CANOE alt for AVÁ-CANOEIRO [AVV]
CANOÉ alt for KANOÉ [KXO]
CANOEIRO alt for RIKBAKTSA [ART]
CANOEIROS alt for AVÁ-CANOEIRO [AVV]
CANT alt for SHELTA [STH]
CANTEL QUICHÉ alt for QUICHÉ, WEST CENTRAL
   [QUT]
CANTILAN dial of SURIGAONON [SUL]
CANTONESE alt for CHINESE, YUE [YUH]
CANTONESE dial of CHINESE, YUE [YUH]
CANTONESE alt for GUANGZHOU dial of CHINESE,
   YUE [YUH]
CAO alt for KATU [KTV]
CAO LAN alt for MAN CAO LAN [MLC]
CAOLAN alt for MAN CAO LAN [MLC]
CAPANAHUA [KAQ] lang, Peru
CAPE AFRIKAANS dial of AFRIKAANS [AFK]
CAPE CORS alt for NORTHERN CORSICAN dial of
   CORSICAN [COI]
CAPE HOTTENTOT alt for XIRI [XII]
CAPE YORK CREOLE alt for TORRES STRAIT
   CREOLE [TCS]
CAPISANO alt for CAPIZNON [CPS]
CAPISEÑO alt for CAPIZNON [CPS]
CAPIZNON [CPS] lang, Philippines
CAPOSHO alt for MAXAKALÍ [MBL]
CAPUL alt for SAMA, ABAKNON [ABX]
CAPULEÑO alt for SAMA, ABAKNON [ABX]
CAQUETÁ alt for KOREGUAJE [COE]
CAQUINTE [COT] lang, Peru
CAQUINTE CAMPA alt for CAQUINTE [COT]
CAR alt for NICOBARESE, CAR [CAQ]
CARA [CFD] lang, Nigeria
CARABAYO [CBY] lang, Colombia
CARAMANTA [CRF] lang, Colombia
CARAPANA [CBC] lang, Colombia, Brazil
CARAPANA-TAPUYA alt for CARAPANA [CBC]
CARAS-PRETAS alt for MUNDURUKÚ [MYU]
CARAVARE alt for KURUÁYA [KYR]
CARE alt for SENA-CARE dial of SENA [SEH]
CARGESE dial of GREEK [GRK]
CARI alt for AKA-CARI [ACI]
CARIB alt for KALIHNA [CRB]

CARIB MOTILÓN alt for YUKPA [YUP]
CARIB, BLACK [CAB] lang, Guatemala, Belize, Honduras, Nicaragua
CARIB, BLACK alt for CARIB, BLACK [CAB]
CARIB, ISLAND [CAI] lang, Dominica, St. Vincent and the Grenadines
CARIB, ISLAND alt for CARIB, ISLAND [CAI]
CARIBE alt for CARIB, BLACK [CAB]
CARIBE alt for KALIHNA [CRB]
CARIBOU ESKIMO dial of INUIT, WESTERN CANADIAN [ESC]
CARIHONA alt for CARIJONA [CBD]
CARIJONA [CBD] lang, Colombia
CARIÑA alt for KALIHNA [CRB]
CARIPUNA alt for KARIPUNÁ DO GUAPORÉ [KUQ]
CARITIANA alt for KARITIÂNA [KTN]
CARNICO dial of FRIULIAN [FRL]
CARNIJÓ alt for FULNIÔ [FUN]
CAROLINIAN [CAL] lang, Micronesia
CARPATHIAN alt for RUSYN [RUE]
CARPATHO-RUSYN alt for RUSYN [RUE]
CARRAGA MANDAYA alt for MANDAYA, KARAGA [MRY]
CARRIACOU CREOLE ENGLISH dial of LESSER ANTILLEAN CREOLE ENGLISH [VIB]
CARRIER [CAR] lang, Canada
CARRIER, SOUTHERN [CAF] lang, Canada
CARÚTANA [CRU] lang, Brazil
CASA alt for JOLA-KASA [CSK]
CASABLANCA dial of ARABIC, MOROCCAN [ARY]
CASHIBO dial of CASHIBO-CACATAIBO [CBR]
CASHIBO-CACATAIBO [CBR] lang, Peru
CASHINAHUA [CBS] lang, Peru, Brazil
CASHMEEREE alt for KASHMIRI [KSH]
CASHMIRI alt for KASHMIRI [KSH]
CASHQUIHA alt for GUANA [GVA]
CASHUBIAN alt for KASHUBIAN [CSB]
CASIGURAN DUMAGAT alt for AGTA, CASIGURAN DUMAGAT [DGC]
CASKA alt for KASKA [KKZ]
CASSANGA alt for KASANGA [CCJ]
CASSUBIAN alt for KASHUBIAN [CSB]
CASTELLANO alt for SPANISH [SPN]
CASTILIAN alt for SPANISH [SPN]
CASTILIAN dial of SPANISH [SPN]
CASU alt for ASU [ASA]
CATALÀ alt for CATALAN [CLN]
CATALAN [CLN] lang, Spain, Andorra, France, Italy
CATALÁN alt for CATALAN [CLN]
CATALAN-ROUSILLONESE dial of CATALAN [CLN]
CATALONIAN alt for CATALAN [CLN]
CATALONIAN CALO dial of ROMANI, CALO [RMR]
CATALONIAN SIGN LANGUAGE [CSC] lang, Spain
CATAUIAN alt for KATAWIAN dial of WAIWAI [WAW]
CATAUICHI alt for KATAWIXI [QKI]
CATAUIXI alt for KATAWIXI [QKI]
CATAWBA [CHC] lang, USA
CATAWIAN alt for KATAWIAN dial of WAIWAI [WAW]
CATAWISHI alt for KATAWIXI [QKI]
CATAWIXI alt for KATAWIXI [QKI]
CATEELENYO alt for MANDAYA, CATAELANO [MST]
CATÍO [CTO] lang, Colombia, Panama, Panama
CATÍO alt for CATÍO [CTO]

CATU alt for KATU [KTV]
CATUQUINA alt for KATUKÍNA, PANOAN [KNT]
CATUQUINA alt for KATUKÍNA [KAV]
CAUQUI dial of JAQARU [JQR]
CAURA dial of SANUMÁ [SAM]
CAUYARÍ alt for CABIYARÍ [CBB]
"CAUZUH" alt for XHOSA [XOS]
CAVCUVENSKIJ dial of KORYAK [KPY]
CAVDUR dial of TURKMEN [TCK]
CAVINA alt for ARAONA [ARO]
CAVINEÑA [CAV] lang, Bolivia
CAVITEÑO dial of CHAVACANO [CBK]
CAWAI alt for ATSAM [CCH]
CAWE alt for ATSAM [CCH]
CAWI alt for ATSAM [CCH]
CAXIBO alt for CASHIBO-CACATAIBO [CBR]
CAXINAWA alt for CASHINAHUA [CBS]
CAXINAWÁ alt for CASHINAHUA [CBS]
CAXUR alt for TSAKHUR [TKR]
CAYAMBE QUICHUA alt for QUICHUA, HIGHLAND, CALDERÓN [QUD]
CAYAPA alt for CHACHI [CBI]
CAYLLOMA QUECHUA dial of QUECHUA, CUZCO [QUZ]
CAYOR dial of WOLOF [WOL]
CAYUA alt for KAIWÁ [KGK]
CAYUBABA [CAT] lang, Bolivia
CAYUGA [CAY] lang, Canada, USA, USA
CAYUGA dial of CAYUGA [CAY]
CAYUVAVA alt for CAYUBABA [CAT]
CAYUWABA alt for CAYUBABA [CAT]
CEBU dial of CEBUANO [CEB]
CEBUANO [CEB] lang, Philippines, USA
CECEN alt for CHECHEN [CJC]
CEEMBA dial of NTCHAM [BUD]
CELLATE alt for BESISI [MHE]
CELLE S. VITO dial of FRANCO-PROVENÇAL [FRA]
CEMBA alt for AKASELEM [AKS]
CEMDALSK dial of EVENKI [EVN]
CEMUAL alt for NANDI dial of KALENJIN [KLN]
CEMUHÎ [CAM] lang, New Caledonia
CENGA dial of KENGA [KYQ]
CENGE alt for KENGA [KYQ]
CENKA [CEN] lang, Benin
CENRANA alt for SENDANA dial of MANDAR [MHN]
CENTRAL dial of LIMBA, WEST-CENTRAL [LIA]
CENTRAL ABUAN dial of ABUA [ABN]
CENTRAL AFAR dial of AFAR [AFR]
CENTRAL ALASKAN YUPIK alt for YUPIK, CENTRAL [ESU]
CENTRAL AMBON alt for LAHA [LAD]
CENTRAL AMERICAN CARIB alt for CARIB, BLACK [CAB]
CENTRAL AMIS dial of AMIS [ALV]
CENTRAL AND NORTH POHJANMAA dial of FINNISH [FIN]
CENTRAL ANGOR alt for NAI dial of ANGOR [AGG]
CENTRAL ARAGONESE dial of ARAGONESE [AXX]
CENTRAL ASTURIAN dial of ASTURIAN [AUB]
CENTRAL ATLAS dial of TAMAZIGHT [TZM]
CENTRAL AZTEC alt for NAHUATL, CENTRAL [NHN]
CENTRAL BABOLE dial of BABOLE [BVX]
CENTRAL BASSA dial of BASSA [BAS]
CENTRAL BAVARIAN dial of BAVARIAN [BAR]
CENTRAL BELORUSSIAN dial of BELORUSSIAN [RUW]

CENTRAL BÉTÉ alt for BÉTÉ, GUIBEROUA [BET]
CENTRAL BOHEMIAN dial of CZECH [CZC]
CENTRAL BOIKIN dial of BOIKIN [BZF]
CENTRAL BOLIVIAN QUECHUA alt for QUECHUA,
    SOUTH BOLIVIAN [QUH]
CENTRAL BOMITABA dial of BOMITABA [ZMX]
CENTRAL BUANG alt for BUANG, MAPOS [BZH]
CENTRAL BUNUN dial of BUNUN [BNN]
CENTRAL BURU dial of BURU [MHS]
CENTRAL CAMPIDANESE dial of SARDINIAN,
    CAMPIDANESE [SRO]
CENTRAL CARRIER alt for CARRIER [CAR]
CENTRAL CATALAN dial of CATALAN [CLN]
CENTRAL CHWABO dial of CHWABO [CHW]
CENTRAL COLLOQUIAL MAITHILI dial of MAITHILI
    [MKP]
CENTRAL CRIMEAN dial of CRIMEAN TURKISH
    [CRH]
CENTRAL CUMBERLAND dial of ENGLISH [ENG]
CENTRAL DANGALEAT dial of DANGALEAT [DAA]
CENTRAL DINKA alt for DINKA, SOUTH CENTRAL
    [DIB]
CENTRAL DIODIO dial of DIODIO [DDI]
CENTRAL DOBU dial of DOBU [DOB]
CENTRAL EAST ALUNE dial of ALUNE [ALP]
CENTRAL EAST SASAK alt for NGENO-NGENE dial
    of SASAK [SAS]
CENTRAL GOURMANCHEMA dial of
    GOURMANCHÉMA [GUX]
CENTRAL HUANCAYO alt for WAYCHA dial of
    QUECHUA, HUANCA, HUAYLLA [QHU]
CENTRAL HUASTECA NAHUATL dial of NAHUATL,
    HUASTECA, WESTERN [NHW]
CENTRAL IGEDE alt for OJU dial of IGEDE [IGE]
CENTRAL ISAN dial of TAI, NORTHEASTERN [TTS]
CENTRAL JIBBALI dial of JIBBALI [SHV]
CENTRAL KADAZAN alt for DUSUN, CENTRAL [DTP]
CENTRAL KAINGANG dial of KAINGÁNG [KGP]
CENTRAL KANKANAEY alt for KANKANAEY [KNE]
CENTRAL KANUM dial of KANUM [KCD]
CENTRAL KERALA dial of MALAYALAM [MJS]
CENTRAL KLAOH dial of KLAO [KLU]
CENTRAL KOMBA dial of KOMBA [KPF]
CENTRAL KOMBIO dial of KOMBIO [KOK]
CENTRAL KONGO dial of KONGO [KON]
CENTRAL KONKAN alt for KONKANI [KNK]
CENTRAL KONO dial of KONO [KNO]
CENTRAL LAAMANG dial of LAMANG [HIA]
CENTRAL LATVIAN alt for WEST LATVIAN dial of
    LATVIAN [LAT]
CENTRAL LISU alt for LISU [LIS]
CENTRAL LYELE dial of LYÉLÉ [LEE]
CENTRAL MAFA dial of MAFA [MAF]
CENTRAL MAGAHI dial of MAGAHI [MQM]
CENTRAL MAMASA dial of MAMASA [MQJ]
CENTRAL MANGGARAI dial of MANGGARAI [MQY]
CENTRAL MARCHIGIANO dial of ITALIAN [ITN]
CENTRAL MARING dial of MARING [MBW]
CENTRAL MARSELA alt for MASELA, CENTRAL
    [MKH]
CENTRAL MBULA alt for MBULA dial of MBULA
    [MNA]
CENTRAL METAFONETICA dial of SICILIAN [SCN]
CENTRAL MON alt for MATABAN-MOULMEIN dial of
    MON [MNW]
CENTRAL MONGOLIAN alt for MONGOLIAN, HALH

[KHK]
CENTRAL MOUNTAIN ALBANIAN dial of ALBANIAN,
    TOSK [ALN]
CENTRAL MUNJI dial of MUNJI [MNJ]
CENTRAL MURUT alt for KENINGAU MURUT [KXI]
CENTRAL NAJDI dial of ARABIC, NAJDI [ARS]
CENTRAL NAJDI dial of ARABIC, NAJDI [ARS]
CENTRAL NAJDI dial of ARABIC, NAJDI [ARS]
CENTRAL NGADA dial of NGADA [NXG]
CENTRAL NOCHISTLÁN MIXTECO alt for MIXTECO,
    DIUXI-TILANTONGO [MIS]
CENTRAL NOGAI dial of NOGAI [NOG]
CENTRAL OCOTL#AN ZAPOTECO alt for
    ZAPOTECO, WESTERN OCOTLÁN [ZAC]
CENTRAL OROMO alt for OROMO, WELLEGA-
    CENTRAL [GAZ]
CENTRAL POCOMAM alt for POKOMAM, CENTRAL
    [POC]
CENTRAL POMO dial of POMO [POO]
CENTRAL PRASUN dial of PRASUNI [PRN]
CENTRAL RAGA alt for APMA [APP]
CENTRAL RUSSIAN dial of RUSSIAN [RUS]
CENTRAL SAKAI alt for SEMAI [SEA]
CENTRAL SANGTAM alt for THUKUMI dial of NAGA,
    SANGTAM [NSA]
CENTRAL SARDINIAN alt for SARDINIAN,
    LOGUDORESE [SRD]
CENTRAL SASAK alt for MENO-MENE dial of SASAK
    [SAS]
CENTRAL SAWOS dial of SAWOS [SIC]
CENTRAL SEDANG dial of SEDANG [SED]
CENTRAL SENTANI dial of SENTANI [SET]
CENTRAL SEWA BAY dial of SEWA BAY [SEW]
CENTRAL SHILHA alt for TAMAZIGHT [TZM]
CENTRAL SIKKA alt for SARA KROW dial of SIKKA
    [SKI]
CENTRAL SINAMA alt for SAMA, CENTRAL [SML]
CENTRAL SOLA DE VEGA ZAPOTECO alt for
    ZAPOTECO, SAN LORENZO TEXMELUCAN [ZPZ]
CENTRAL SONGAI dial of SONGAI [SON]
CENTRAL SOUTH SASAK alt for MRIAK-MRIKU dial
    of SASAK [SAS]
CENTRAL TABUKANG dial of SANGIR [SAN]
CENTRAL TAI alt for THAI [THJ]
CENTRAL TAIRORA dial of TAIRORA [TBG]
CENTRAL THARAKA alt for NTUGI dial of THARAKA
    [THA]
CENTRAL TIGAK dial of TIGAK [TGC]
CENTRAL TIMBE dial of TIMBE [TIM]
CENTRAL TUVIN dial of TUVIN [TUN]
CENTRAL URAT dial of URAT [URT]
CENTRAL VANUA LEVU dial of FIJIAN [FJI]
CENTRAL VEPS dial of VEPS [VEP]
CENTRAL VIETNAMESE dial of VIETNAMESE [VIE]
CENTRAL VIVIGANI dial of IDUNA [VIV]
CENTRAL VLACH ROMANI dial of ROMANI, VLACH
    [RMY]
CENTRAL WAIBUK dial of HARUAI [TMD]
CENTRAL WAKHI dial of WAKHI [WBL]
CENTRAL WEST ALUNE dial of ALUNE [ALP]
CENTRAL WEST SASAK alt for NGENO-NGENE dial
    of SASAK [SAS]
CENTRAL YAMALELE dial of IAMALELE [YML]
CENTRAL YAWA dial of YAWA [YVA]
CENTRAL YI dial of YI, SICHUAN [III]
CEP dial of ACIPA [AWA]

CERMA [GOT] lang, Burkina Faso, Côte d'Ivoire,
Côte d'Ivoire
CERMA alt for CERMA [GOT]
CERUMBA dial of SHWAI [SHW]
CESAR dial of YUKPA [YUP]
CEVENDA alt for VENDA [VEN]
CEWA alt for CHEWA dial of NYANJA [NYJ]
CEWA alt for CHICHEWA dial of NYANJA [NYJ]
CEZ alt for DIDO [DDO]
CH'IANG alt for QIANG [CNG]
CH'IEN-CHIANG alt for QIANJIANG [CCV]
CH'OPA alt for RAWANG [RAW]
CH'UNGCH'ONGDO dial of KOREAN [KKN]
CHA' dial of AGHEM [AGQ]
CHA' PALAACHI alt for CHACHI [CBI]
CHAARI alt for DANSHE dial of ZEEM [ZUA]
CHABAKANO alt for CHAVACANO [CBK]
CHACHI [CBI] lang, Ecuador
CHACO PILAGÁ dial of PILAGÁ [PLG]
CHACO SUR alt for TOBA [TOB]
CHÁCOBO [CAO] lang, Bolivia
CHAD ARABIC alt for ARABIC, SHUWA [SHU]
CHADIAN ARABIC alt for ARABIC, SHUWA [SHU]
CHADIAN SIGN LANGUAGE [CDS] lang, Chad
CHADIC ARABIC alt for ARABIC, SHUWA [SHU]
CHAECUNG dial of AKHA [AKA]
CHAGA alt for CHAGGA [KAF]
CHAGATAI [CGT] lang, Turkmenistan
CHAGATAI alt for TEKE dial of TURKMEN [TCK]
CHAGGA [KAF] lang, Tanzania
CHAGHATAY alt for CHAGATAI [CGT]
CHAHA dial of GURAGE, CENTRAL WEST [GUY]
CHAHAR dial of MONGOLIAN, PERIPHERAL [MVF]
CHAHAR-AIMAQ alt for AIMAQ [AIQ]
CHAHI dial of NYATURU [RIM]
CHAI alt for TIRMA dial of MURSI [MUZ]
CHAIBASA-THAKURMUNDA dial of HO [HOC]
CHAIL dial of TORWALI [TRW]
CHAIMA alt for CHAYMA dial of KALIHNA [CRB]
CHAK [CKH] lang, Myanmar, Bangladesh
CHAKALI [CLI] lang, Ghana
CHAKAVIAN dial of SERBO-CROATIAN [SRC]
CHAKFEM alt for CAKFEM dial of MWAGHAVUL
[SUR]
CHAKHAR alt for CHAHAR dial of MONGOLIAN,
PERIPHERAL [MVF]
CHAKHESANG alt for NAGA, CHOKRI [NRI]
CHAKMA [CCP] lang, India, Bangladesh
CHAKOSI alt for ANUFO [CKO]
CHAKPA dial of KADO [KDV]
CHAKRIABA alt for XAKRIABÁ [XKR]
CHAKRIMA NAGA alt for NAGA, CHOKRI [NRI]
CHAKROMA dial of NAGA, ANGAMI [NJM]
CHAKRU alt for NAGA, CHOKRI [NRI]
CHAL alt for RUTUL [RUT]
CHALA [CHA] lang, Ghana
CHALAH dial of CHRAU [CHR]
CHALAS dial of PASHAYI, NORTHEAST [AEE]
CHALDEAN [CLD] lang, Iraq, USA
CHALDEAN alt for SURYOYO [SYR]
CHALGARI alt for WANECI [WNE]
CHALI dial of SÔ [SSS]
CHALI dial of KOMA, CENTRAL [KOM]
CHALLA alt for DAFFO-BATURA [DAM]
CHALUN dial of CHRAU [CHR]
CHAM alt for CHAM, WESTERN [CJA]

CHAM dial of MIEN [YOC]
CHAM alt for CHING dial of CHING [MKG]
CHAM alt for CAM dial of DIJIM [CFA]
CHAM CHANG alt for NAGA, TASE [NST]
CHAM, EASTERN [CJM] lang, Viet Nam, USA (West
Coast, San Diego)
CHAM, WESTERN [CJA] lang, Cambodia, Viet Nam,
Viet Nam
CHAM, WESTERN alt for CHAM, WESTERN [CJA]
CHAM-RE alt for HRE [HRE]
"CHAMA" alt for ESE EJJA [ESE]
CHAMACOCO [CEG] lang, Paraguay
CHAMACOCO BRAVO dial of CHAMACOCO [CEG]
CHAMALAL [CJI] lang, Russia, Europe
CHAMALIN alt for CHAMALAL [CJI]
CHAMAN alt for MANG [MGA]
CHAMAR alt for CHAMARI [CDG]
CHAMARI [CDG] lang, India
CHAMARWA alt for BANGARU [BGC]
CHAMAYA alt for CHAMEALI [CDH]
CHAMBA alt for LAHULI, CHAMBA [LAE]
CHAMBA alt for AKASELEM [AKS]
CHAMBA DAKA alt for SAMBA DAKA [CCG]
CHAMBA LEEKO alt for SAMBA LEKO [NDI]
CHAMBA LEKO alt for SAMBA LEKO [NDI]
CHAMBHAR BOLI alt for CHAMARI [CDG]
CHAMBHARI alt for CHAMARI [CDG]
CHAMBIALI alt for CHAMEALI [CDH]
CHAMBIYALI alt for CHAMEALI [CDH]
CHAMBOA alt for KARAJÁ [KPJ]
CHAMBRI [CAN] lang, Papua New Guinea
CHAMEALI [CDH] lang, India
CHAMÍ [CMI] lang, Colombia
CHAMICOLO alt for CHAMICURO [CCC]
CHAMICURA alt for CHAMICURO [CCC]
CHAMICURO [CCC] lang, Peru
CHAMIN alt for XAMIR [XAI]
CHAMIR alt for XAMIR [XAI]
CHAMIYALI PAHARI alt for CHAMEALI [CDH]
CHAMLING [RAB] lang, Nepal
CHAMLINGE RAI alt for CHAMLING [RAB]
CHAMO alt for CAMO dial of KUDU-CAMO [KOV]
CHAMORRO [CJD] lang, Guam, Northern Mariana
Islands, Northern Mariana Islands
CHAMORRO alt for CHAMORRO [CJD]
CHAMORRO dial of CHAMORRO [CJD]
CHAMPHUNG alt for NAGA, TANGKHUL [NMF]
CHAMULA alt for TZOTZIL, CHAMULA [TZC]
CHAMUS dial of SAMBURU [SAQ]
CHAMYA alt for CHAMEALI [CDH]
CHAN alt for LAZ [LZZ]
CHANA alt for GUANA [QKS]
CHAÑABAL alt for TOJOLABAL [TOJ]
CHANCO alt for WAUMEO [NOA]
CHANDARI dial of HALBI [HLB]
CHANDINAHUA dial of SHARANAHUA [MCD]
CHANÉ [CAJ] lang, Argentina
CHANÉ dial of CHIRIGUANO [GUI]
CHANG alt for NAGA, CHANG [NBC]
CHANG CHÁ alt for BOUYEI [PCC]
CHANGA dial of NDAU [NDC]
CHANGA dial of NDAU [NDC]
CHANGA alt for CHANGANA dial of TSONGA [TSO]
CHANGANA alt for TSONGA [TSO]
CHANGANA dial of TSONGA [TSO]
CHANGANA dial of TSONGA [TSO]

CHANGDE dial of CHINESE, XIANG [HSN]
CHANGKI dial of NAGA, AO [NJO]
CHANGNOI dial of NAGA, WANCHO [NNP]
CHANGNYU dial of NAGA, KONYAK [NBE]
CHANGO alt for SANGU [SNQ]
CHANGRIWA [CGA] lang, Papua New Guinea
CHANGSEN dial of CHIN, THADO [TCZ]
CHANGSHA dial of CHINESE, XIANG [HSN]
CHANGTHANG [CNA] lang, India
CHANGTING dial of CHINESE, HAKKA [HAK]
CHANGYANGUH alt for NAGA, CHANG [NBC]
CHANKA alt for QUECHUA, AYACUCHO [QUY]
CHANTEL [CHX] lang, Nepal
CHANZAN alt for LAZ [LZZ]
CHAO SHAN dial of CHINESE, MIN NAN [CFR]
"CHAOBON" alt for NYAHKUR [CBN]
CHAOCHA PAI alt for KOREGUAJE [COE]
CHAOCHOW dial of CHINESE, MIN NAN [CFR]
CHAOCHOW dial of CHINESE, MIN NAN [CFR]
CHAOCHOW dial of CHINESE, MIN NAN [CFR]
CHAOCHOW dial of CHINESE, MIN NAN [CFR]
CHAOCHOW alt for CHAO SHAN dial of CHINESE,
   MIN NAN [CFR]
CHAOCHOW alt for TEOCHEW dial of CHINESE, MIN
   NAN [CFR]
"CHAODON" alt for NYAHKUR [CBN]
CHAOUE alt for SHOE dial of MPADE [MPI]
CHAOUIA alt for SHAWIYA [SHY]
CHAOXIAN alt for KOREAN [KKN]
CHAOZHOU alt for CHAO SHAN dial of CHINESE,
   MIN NAN [CFR]
CHAOZHOU alt for TEOCHEW dial of CHINESE, MIN
   NAN [CFR]
CHAOZHOU alt for CHAOCHOW dial of CHINESE,
   MIN NAN [CFR]
CHAPACURA alt for URUPÁ [URP]
CHAPARA dial of CANDOSHI-SHAPRA [CBU]
CHAPLINO dial of YUPIK, CENTRAL SIBERIAN [ESS]
CHAPOGIR alt for EVENKI [EVN]
CHAR alt for ZAKATALY dial of AVAR [AVR]
CHARA [CRA] lang, Ethiopia
CHARA alt for CARA [CFD]
CHARANI dial of BHILI [BHB]
CHARARANA alt for ECHOALDI dial of GUANA
   [GVA]
CHARAZANI dial of QUECHUA, NORTH BOLIVIAN
   [QUL]
CHARBERD alt for KHARBERD dial of ARMENIAN
   [ARM]
CHARCHAN dial of UYGHUR [UIG]
CHARI alt for CHALI dial of SÔ [SSS]
CHARI CHONG dial of CHIN, FALAM [HBH]
CHARIAR alt for AKA-CARI [ACI]
CHAROTARI alt for GAMADIA dial of GUJARATI
   [GJR]
CHARUMBUL alt for BAYALI [BJY]
CHASAN YAO alt for MIEN [YOC]
CHASHAN alt for LASHI [LSI]
CHASU alt for ASU [ASA]
CHATANS alt for ALLAR [ALL]
CHATINO DE LA ZONA ALTA OCCIDENTAL alt for
   CHATINO, WEST HIGHLAND [CTP]
CHATINO, LACHAO-YOLOTEPEC [CLY] lang, Mexico
CHATINO, NOPALA [CYA] lang, Mexico
CHATINO, TATALTEPEC [CTA] lang, Mexico
CHATINO, WEST HIGHLAND [CTP] lang, Mexico

CHATINO, YAITEPEC [CUC] lang, Mexico
CHATINO, ZACATEPEC [CTZ] lang, Mexico
CHATINO, ZENZONTEPEC [CZE] lang, Mexico
CHATTISGARHI [HNE] lang, India
CHATTISGARHI PROPER dial of CHATTISGARHI
   [HNE]
CHAU KO' alt for MOKEN [MWT]
CHAU POK alt for MOKLEN [MKM]
CHAUDANGSI [CDN] lang, Nepal, India
CHAUDHARI alt for CHODRI [CDI]
CHAUDRI alt for CHODRI [CDI]
CHAUGARKHIYA dial of KUMAUNI [KFY]
CHAUMA alt for MAA [CMA]
CHAUN dial of CHUKOT [CKT]
CHAUNGTHA [CCQ] lang, Myanmar
CHAURA [CHO] lang, India
CHAURASIA alt for TSAURASYA [TSU]
CHAURASYA alt for TSAURASYA [TSU]
CHAURO alt for CHRAU [CHR]
CHAVACANO [CBK] lang, Philippines, Malaysia,
   Sabah
CHAVACANO alt for ZAMBOANGUEÑO dial of
   CHAVACANO [CBK]
CHAVANTE alt for OTI [OTI]
CHAVANTE alt for XAVÁNTE [XAV]
CHAVCHUVEN alt for CAVCUVENSKIJ dial of
   KORYAK [KPY]
CHAVDUR dial of TURKMEN [TCK]
CHAW TALAY alt for URAK LAWOI' [URK]
CHAWAI alt for ATSAM [CCH]
CHAWE alt for ATSAM [CCH]
CHAWI alt for CHAYAHUITA [CBT]
CHAWI alt for ATSAM [CCH]
CHAWIA dial of TAITA [DAV]
CHAWIYANA alt for HIXKARYÁNA [HIX]
CHAWNAM alt for URAK LAWOI' [URK]
CHAWNG alt for CHONG [COG]
"CHAWUNCU" alt for CHIRIGUANO [GUI]
CHAYABITA alt for CHAYAHUITA [CBT]
CHAYAHUITA [CBT] lang, Peru
CHAYAHUITA dial of CHAYAHUITA [CBT]
CHAYAWITA alt for CHAYAHUITA [CBT]
CHAYHUITA alt for CHAYAHUITA [CBT]
CHAYMA dial of KALIHNA [CRB]
CHAYUCU MIXTECO alt for MIXTECO, EASTERN
   JAMILTEPEC-CHAYUCO [MIH]
CHE [RUK] lang, Nigeria
CHE MA alt for MAA [CMA]
CHE'WONG alt for CHEWONG [CWG]
CHE-HWAN alt for TAROKO [TRV]
CHEBERLOEV alt for CHEBERLOT dial of CHECHEN
   [CJC]
CHEBERLOT dial of CHECHEN [CJC]
CHEBERO alt for JEBERO [JEB]
CHECHEK alt for NDREHET dial of LEVEI-NDREHET
   [TLX]
CHECHEN [CJC] lang, Russia, Europe, Jordan
CHECK-CULL alt for DYAABUGAY [DYY]
CHEDEPO dial of GREBO, E JE [GRB]
CHEDI alt for LISU [LIS]
CHEHA alt for CHAHA dial of GURAGE, CENTRAL
   WEST [GUY]
CHEHALIS alt for CHEHALIS, UPPER [CJH]
CHEHALIS, LOWER [CEA] lang, USA
CHEHALIS, UPPER [CJH] lang, USA
CHEJU ISLAND dial of KOREAN [KKN]

CHEKE alt for GUDE [GDE]
CHEKE HOLO [MRN] lang, Solomon Islands
CHEKIRI alt for ISEKIRI [ITS]
CHELI alt for LISU [LIS]
CHEMANT alt for QIMANT [QIM]
CHEMEHUEVI dial of UTE-SOUTHERN PAIUTE [UTE]
CHEMGUI alt for BEZHEDUKH dial of ADYGHE [ADY]
CHEN dial of NAGA, KONYAK [NBE]
CHENALÓ alt for TZOTZIL, CHENALHÓ [TZE]
CHENAP alt for CHENAPIAN [CJN]
CHENAPIAN [CJN] lang, Papua New Guinea
CHENBEROM alt for BEROM [BOM]
CHENCHU [CDE] lang, India
CHENCHUCOOLAM alt for CHENCHU [CDE]
CHENCHWAR alt for CHENCHU [CDE]
CHENG alt for JENG [JEG]
CHENGFENG dial of HMONG, EASTERN [HEA]
CHENGKUNG-KWANGSHAN dial of AMIS [ALV]
CHENSWAR alt for CHENCHU [CDE]
CHENTEL MAGAR alt for CHANTEL [CHX]
CHEPANG [CDM] lang, Nepal
CHEQ WONG alt for CHEWONG [CWG]
CHERANGANY dial of KALENJIN [KLN]
CHERE alt for SERE [SWF]
CHEREMIS alt for MARI, LOW [MAL]
CHEREMISS alt for MARI, HIGH [MRJ]
CHEREPON alt for OKERE dial of GUA [LAR]
CHERES alt for ULU CERES dial of JAH HUT [JAH]
CHERIBON alt for CIREBON dial of JAVANESE [JAN]
CHERKES alt for ADYGHE [ADY]
CHERKES dial of KABARDIAN [KAB]
CHERO [CRR] lang, India
CHERRAPUNJI alt for KHASI dial of KHASI [KHI]
CHERRE alt for KARO [KXH]
CHETA alt for XETÁ [XET]
CHETCO [CHE] lang, USA
CHEVA alt for CHEWA dial of NYANJA [NYJ]
CHEWA dial of NYANJA [NYJ]
CHEWA dial of NYANJA [NYJ]
CHEWA alt for CHICHEWA dial of NYANJA [NYJ]
CHEWLIE alt for DYAABUGAY [DYY]
CHEWONG [CWG] lang, Malaysia, Peninsular
CHEYENNE [CHY] lang, USA
CHHATHAR [CTH] lang, Nepal
CHHATHAR LIMBU alt for CHHATHAR [CTH]
CHHINDWARA BUNDELI dial of BUNDELI [BNS]
CHHINTANG dial of BANTAWA [BAP]
CHHORI alt for CHIRU [CDF]
CHI dial of CHING [MKG]
CHIANGLO dial of CHINESE, HAKKA [HAK]
CHIANGRAI dial of MIEN [YOC]
CHIANGRAI dial of KAREN, PWO OMKOI [PWW]
CHIAPANECO [CIP] lang, Mexico
CHIARONG alt for JIARONG [JYA]
CHIASU alt for ASU [ASA]
CHIBBAK alt for CIBAK [CKL]
CHIBBUK alt for CIBAK [CKL]
CHIBCHA [CBF] lang, Colombia
CHIBEMBA alt for BEMBA [BEM]
CHIBHALI alt for PAHARI-POTWARI [PHR]
CHIBHALI dial of PAHARI-POTWARI [PHR]
CHIBITO alt for HIBITO [HIB]
CHIBUK alt for CIBAK [CKL]
CHICANO alt for YUWANA [YAU]
CHICAO alt for TXIKÃO [TXI]

CHICHAMACHU alt for BAJELAN [BJM]
CHICHANGA alt for CHANGA dial of NDAU [NDC]
CHICHANGA alt for CHANGA dial of NDAU [NDC]
CHICHEWA dial of NYANJA [NYJ]
CHICHEWA alt for CHEWA dial of NYANJA [NYJ]
CHICHEWA alt for CHEWA dial of NYANJA [NYJ]
CHICHICAPAN ZAPOTECO alt for ZAPOTECO,
    CHICHICAPAN-TILQUIAPAN [ZPV]
CHICHIMECA alt for CHICHIMECA-JONAZ [PEI]
CHICHIMECA DE ALAQUINES PAME alt for
    CHICHIMECA PAME, NORTHERN [PMQ]
CHICHIMECA PAME, NORTHERN [PMQ] lang,
    Mexico
CHICHIMECA-JONAZ [PEI] lang, Mexico
CHICHIMECA-PAME CENTRAL alt for PAME,
    CENTRAL [PBS]
CHICHIMECO alt for CHICHIMECA-JONAZ [PEI]
CHICHONYI alt for CHONYI [COH]
CHICHWABO alt for CHWABO [CHW]
CHICOMUCELTEC [COB] lang, Mexico, Guatemala
CHICUNDA alt for KUNDA [KDN]
CHIDIGO alt for DIGO [DIG]
CHIECH alt for CIEC dial of DINKA, SOUTH
    CENTRAL [DIB]
CHIEHN alt for TCHIEN dial of KRAHN, EASTERN
    [KQO]
CHIEM alt for CHAM, WESTERN [CJA]
CHIEM alt for CHAM, EASTERN [CJM]
CHIEM THÀNH alt for CHAM, EASTERN [CJM]
CHIENGMAI SIGN LANGUAGE [CSG] lang, Thailand
CHIENTUNG MIAO alt for HMONG, EASTERN [HEA]
CHIGA [CHG] lang, Uganda
CHIGOGO alt for GOGO [GOG]
CHIHLI alt for ZHILI dial of CHINESE, MANDARIN
    [CHN]
CHIIKUHANE alt for SUBIA [SBS]
CHIILA alt for ILA [ILB]
CHIK-BARIK [CKB] lang, India
CHIKACHIKI dial of MAITHILI [MKP]
CHIKAGULU alt for KAGULU [KKI]
CHIKAHONDE alt for KAONDE [KQN]
CHIKALANGA alt for KALANGA [KCK]
CHIKAMANGA dial of TUMBUKA [TUW]
CHIKAMANGA dial of TUMBUKA [TUW]
CHIKANO alt for YUWANA [YAU]
CHIKAONDE alt for KAONDE [KQN]
CHIKARANGA alt for KARANGA dial of SHONA
    [SHD]
CHIKBARAIK alt for CHIK-BARIK [CKB]
CHIKENA alt for SIKIANA [SIK]
CHIKIDE alt for CIKIDE dial of GUDUF [GDF]
CHIKOBO alt for IZORA [CBO]
CHIKRIABA alt for XAKRIABÁ [XKR]
CHIKUNDA alt for KUNDA [KDN]
CHIKUNDA dial of NYANJA [NYJ]
CHIKUYA alt for TEKE, SOUTHERN [KKW]
CHIL dial of KOHO [KPM]
CHIL dial of MNONG, EASTERN [MNG]
CHILALA alt for LELA [DRI]
CHILAMBA alt for LAMBA [LAB]
CHILAO alt for GELO [KKF]
CHILAPALAPA dial of FANAGOLO [FAO]
CHILAS alt for CHILASI KOHISTANI dial of SHINA
    [SCL]
CHILAS alt for CHALAS dial of PASHAYI,
    NORTHEAST [AEE]

CHILASI KOHISTANI dial of SHINA [SCL]
CHILCOTIN [CHI] lang, Canada
CHILELA alt for LELA [DRI]
CHILENJE alt for LENJE [LEH]
CHILISS alt for CHILISSO [CLH]
CHILISSO [CLH] lang, Pakistan
CHILIWACK dial of HALKOMELEM [HUR]
CHILOWE alt for LOMWE [NGL]
CHILU WUNDA alt for RUUND [RND]
CHILUCHAZI alt for LUCHAZI [LCH]
CHILUIMBI alt for LUIMBI [LUM]
CHILUNDA alt for LUNDA [LVN]
CHILUVALE alt for LUVALE [LUE]
CHILUWUNDA alt for RUUND [RND]
CHIMA-NISHEY dial of WAIGALI [WBK]
CHIMABIHA alt for MAVIHA [MHP]
CHIMAKONDE alt for MAKONDE [KDE]
CHIMANÉ alt for TSIMANÉ [CAS]
CHIMANYIKA alt for MANYIKA [MXC]
CHIMATENGO alt for MATENGO [MGV]
CHIMAVIHA alt for MAVIHA [MHP]
CHIMBA alt for ZEMBA [DHM]
CHIMBALAZI alt for BAJUNI dial of SWAHILI [SWA]
CHIMBALAZI alt for BAJUNI dial of SWAHILI [SWA]
CHIMBARI alt for SIMBARI [SMB]
CHIMBIAN dial of SAWOS [SIC]
CHIMBU alt for KUMAN [KUE]
CHIMBULUK dial of BUANG, MAPOS [BZH]
CHIMBUNDA alt for MBUNDA [MCK]
CHIMILA [CBG] lang, Colombia
CHIMIRA alt for GIMIRA [BCQ]
CHIMMEZYAN alt for TSIMSHIAN [TSI]
CHIMONA dial of MANAGALASI [MCQ]
CHIMPOTO alt for MPOTO [MPA]
CHIMWERA alt for MWERA [MWE]
CHIMWIINI alt for MWINI dial of SWAHILI [SWA]
CHIN, ASHO [CSH] lang, Myanmar, Bangladesh, China
CHIN, BAWM [BGR] lang, India, Bangladesh, Myanmar
CHIN, BAWM alt for CHIN, BAWM [BGR]
CHIN, CHINBON [CNB] lang, Myanmar
CHIN, CHO [CCN] lang, Myanmar
CHIN, DAAI [DAO] lang, Myanmar
CHIN, FALAM [HBH] lang, Myanmar, Bangladesh, India
CHIN, HAKA [CNH] lang, Myanmar, Bangladesh, India
CHIN, KHUMI [CKM] lang, Myanmar, Bangladesh, India
CHIN, KHUMI AWA [CKA] lang, Myanmar
CHIN, MARA [MRH] lang, India, Myanmar, Myanmar
CHIN, MARA alt for CHIN, MARA [MRH]
CHIN, MÜN [MWQ] lang, Myanmar
CHIN, NGAWN [CNW] lang, Myanmar
CHIN, PAITE [PCK] lang, India, Myanmar, Myanmar
CHIN, PAITE alt for CHIN, PAITE [PCK]
CHIN, SENTHANG [SEZ] lang, Myanmar
CHIN, SIYIN [CSY] lang, Myanmar
CHIN, TAWR [TCP] lang, Myanmar
CHIN, TEDIM [CTD] lang, Myanmar, India
CHIN, THADO [TCZ] lang, India, Myanmar, Myanmar
CHIN, THADO alt for CHIN, THADO [TCZ]
CHIN, ZOTUNG [CZT] lang, Myanmar
CHINAMBYA alt for NAMBYA [NMQ]
CHINAMUKUNI alt for LENJE [LEH]

CHINANTECO, CHILTEPEC [CSA] lang, Mexico
CHINANTECO, COMALTEPEC [CCO] lang, Mexico
CHINANTECO, LALANA [CNL] lang, Mexico
CHINANTECO, LEALAO [CLE] lang, Mexico
CHINANTECO, OJITLÁN [CHJ] lang, Mexico
CHINANTECO, OZUMACÍN [CHZ] lang, Mexico
CHINANTECO, PALANTLA [CPA] lang, Mexico
CHINANTECO, QUIOTEPEC [CHQ] lang, Mexico
CHINANTECO, SOCHIAPAN [CSO] lang, Mexico
CHINANTECO, TEPETOTUTLA [CNT] lang, Mexico
CHINANTECO, TEPINAPA [CTE] lang, Mexico
CHINANTECO, TLACOATZINTEPEC [CTL] lang, Mexico
CHINANTECO, USILA [CUS] lang, Mexico
CHINANTECO, VALLE NACIONAL [CHV] lang, Mexico
CHINATU dial of TARAHUMARA, CENTRAL [TAR]
"CHINBOK" alt for CHIN, MÜN [MWQ]
CHINBON alt for CHIN, CHINBON [CNB]
CHINDAU alt for NDAU [NDC]
CHINDERI alt for SOUTHERN CHUMBURUNG dial of CHUMBURUNG [NCU]
CHINDWARA dial of GONDI, NORTHERN [GON]
CHINDWIN CHIN alt for CHIN, CHINBON [CNB]
CHINESE INDONESIAN alt for INDONESIAN, PERANAKAN [PEA]
CHINESE MALAY alt for MALAY, BABA [BAB]
CHINESE NUNG alt for CHINESE, YUE [YUH]
CHINESE PIDGIN ENGLISH [CPE] lang, Nauru
CHINESE SHAN alt for TAI NÜA [TDD]
CHINESE SHAN alt for TAI MAO dial of SHAN [SJN]
CHINESE SIGN LANGUAGE [CSL] lang, China, Hongkong, Hong Kong
CHINESE SIGN LANGUAGE alt for CHINESE SIGN LANGUAGE [CSL]
CHINESE TAI alt for DAI [TIZ]
CHINESE, GAN [KNN] lang, China
CHINESE, HAKKA [HAK] lang, China, French Guiana, Panama, Surinam, Brunei, Hong Kong, Indonesia, Java, Bali, Malaysia, Peninsular, Singapore, Taiwan, Thailand, French Polynesia
CHINESE, HAKKA alt for CHINESE, HAKKA [HAK]
CHINESE, MANDARIN [CHN] lang, China, South Africa, Brunei, Cambodia, Hong Kong, Indonesia, Java, Bali, Laos, Malaysia, Peninsular, Mongolian Peoples Republic, Philippines, Singapore, Taiwan, Thailand, Nauru
CHINESE, MANDARIN alt for CHINESE, MANDARIN [CHN]
CHINESE, MIN NAN [CFR] lang, China, Brunei, Hong Kong, Indonesia, Java, Bali, Malaysia, Peninsular, Philippines, Singapore, Taiwan, Thailand
CHINESE, MIN NAN alt for CHINESE, MIN NAN [CFR]
CHINESE, MIN PEI [MNP] lang, China, Brunei, Indonesia, Java, Bali, Malaysia, Peninsular, Singapore, Thailand
CHINESE, MIN PEI alt for CHINESE, MIN PEI [MNP]
CHINESE, WU [WUU] lang, China
CHINESE, XIANG [HSN] lang, China
CHINESE, YUE [YUH] lang, China, Costa Rica, Panama, Brunei, Hong Kong, Indonesia, Java, Bali, Macau, Malaysia, Peninsular, Philippines, Singapore, Thailand, Viet Nam, Nauru, New Zealand
CHINESE, YUE alt for CHINESE, YUE [YUH]
CHING [MKG] lang, China

CHING alt for VIETNAMESE [VIE]
CHING dial of CHING [MKG]
CHINGA alt for TSINGA dial of TUKI [BAG]
CHINGALEE alt for DJINGILI [JIG]
CHINGCHANG alt for TAIKUNG dial of HMONG,
    EASTERN [HEA]
CHINGHIZI dial of AIMAQ [AIQ]
CHINGKAO dial of NAGA, KONYAK [NBE]
CHINGLANG dial of NAGA, KONYAK [NBE]
CHINGMENGU alt for NAGA, PHOM [NPH]
CHINGONI alt for NGONI [NGU]
CHINGONI dial of NYANJA [NYJ]
CHINGP'O alt for JINGPHO [CGP]
CHINGPAW alt for JINGPHO [CGP]
CHINGPO alt for JINGPHO [CGP]
CHINIMAKONDE alt for MAKONDE [KDE]
CHINOOK [CHH] lang, USA
CHINOOK JARGON alt for CHINOOK WAWA [CRW]
CHINOOK PIDGIN alt for CHINOOK WAWA [CRW]
CHINOOK WAWA [CRW] lang, Canada, USA, USA
CHINOOK WAWA alt for CHINOOK WAWA [CRW]
CHINSENGA alt for NSENGA [NSE]
CHINTOOR KOYA dial of KOYA [KFF]
CHINYANJA alt for NYANJA [NYJ]
CHINYUNGWI alt for NYUNGWE [NYU]
CHIP alt for MISHIP [CHP]
CHIPAYA [CAP] lang, Bolivia
CHIPETA alt for PETA dial of NYANJA [NYJ]
CHIPEWYAN [CPW] lang, Canada
CHIPIAJES [CBE] lang, Colombia
CHIPODZO alt for PODZO [POZ]
CHIPOGOLO alt for POGOLO [POY]
CHIPOGORO alt for POGOLO [POY]
CHIPOKA dial of TUMBUKA [TUW]
CHIPOKA alt for POKA dial of TUMBUKA [TUW]
CHIPPEWA alt for OJIBWA, WESTERN [OJI]
CHIPPEWA dial of OJIBWA, EASTERN [OJG]
CHIQUENA alt for SIKIANA [SIK]
CHIQUIANA alt for SIKIANA [SIK]
CHIQUITANO [CAX] lang, Bolivia
CHIQUITO alt for CHIQUITANO [CAX]
CHIR alt for MANDARI [MQU]
CHIRICAHUA dial of APACHE, MESCALERO-
    CHIRICAHUA [APM]
CHIRICHANO alt for SANUMÁ [SAM]
CHIRICHANO alt for SAPÉ [SPC]
CHIRICOA dial of CUIBA [CUI]
CHIRICOA dial of CUIBA [CUI]
CHIRIGUANO [GUI] lang, Bolivia, Argentina,
    Paraguay
CHIRIGUANO alt for CHIRIGUANO [GUI]
CHIRIMA alt for MAKHUWA-NIASSA [VMK]
CHIRIMA RIVER dial of FUYUGE [FUY]
CHIRIPA [NHD] lang, Paraguay, Argentina, Brazil
CHIRIPÁ alt for CHIRIPA [NHD]
CHIRIPO dial of CUIBA [CUI]
CHIRIPON alt for OKERE dial of GUA [LAR]
CHIRIPONG alt for OKERE dial of GUA [LAR]
CHIRIPUNO alt for ARABELA [ARL]
CHIRIPUNU alt for ARABELA [ARL]
CHIRIQUI alt for GUAYMÍ [GYM]
CHIRIQUI alt for EASTERN GUAYMÍ dial of GUAYMÍ
    [GYM]
CHIRMAR dial of BENGALI [BNG]
CHIRORO-KURSI dial of KANGA [KCP]
CHIRR dial of NAGA, YIMCHUNGRU [YIM]

CHIRRIPÓ alt for CABÉCAR [CJP]
CHIRRIPÓ dial of CABÉCAR [CJP]
CHIRU [CDF] lang, India
CHIRUE alt for RUE dial of SENA [SEH]
CHISAK dial of GARO [GRT]
CHISALAMPASU alt for SALAMPASU [SLX]
CHISENA alt for SENA [SEH]
CHISENJI alt for CHANGA dial of NDAU [NDC]
CHISHINGA dial of BEMBA [BEM]
CHISHINGYINI [ASG] lang, Nigeria
CHISHONA alt for SHONA [SHD]
CHISINGINI alt for CHISHINGYINI [ASG]
CHISOLI alt for SOLI [SBY]
CHITA PARDHI alt for PARDHI [PCL]
CHITAPAVANI dial of KONKANI, GOANESE [GOM]
CHITAWAN THARU alt for THARU, CHITWAN [THE]
CHITEMBO alt for TEMBO [TBT]
CHITIMACHA [CHM] lang, USA
CHITKHULI alt for CHITKULI [CIK]
CHITKULI [CIK] lang, India
CHITONGA alt for TONGA [TOG]
CHITONGA alt for TONGA [TOI]
CHITONGA dial of TONGA [TOI]
CHITRALI alt for KHOWAR [KHW]
CHITRARI alt for KHOWAR [KHW]
CHITTAGONG dial of CHIN, ASHO [CSH]
CHITTIES CREOLE MALAY alt for MALACCAN
    CREOLE MALAY [CCM]
CHITUAN THARU alt for THARU, CHITWAN [THE]
CHITUMBUKA alt for TUMBUKA [TUW]
CHITUMBUKA dial of TUMBUKA [TUW]
CHIUPEI alt for QIUBEI dial of ZHUANG, NORTHERN
    [CCX]
CHIUTSE alt for RAWANG [RAW]
CHIUTZU alt for RAWANG [RAW]
CHIVENDA alt for VENDA [VEN]
CHIVIDUNDA alt for VIDUNDA [VID]
CHIWARO alt for SHUAR [JIV]
CHIWEI dial of HMONG, NORTHERN [MUQ]
CHIWEMBA alt for BEMBA [BEM]
CHIWERE alt for OTO [OTO]
CHIXANGA alt for CHANGA dial of NDAU [NDC]
CHIXANGA alt for CHANGA dial of NDAU [NDC]
CHIYAO alt for YAO [YAO]
CHIZEZURU alt for ZEZURU dial of SHONA [SHD]
CHIZIMA alt for NAGA, LOTHA [NJH]
CHO-RAI alt for JARAI [JRA]
CHOA alt for ARABIC, SHUWA [SHU]
CHOAPAM ZAPOTEC alt for ZAPOTECO, CHOAPAN
    [ZPC]
CHOBBA alt for HUBA [KIR]
CHOCAMA alt for WAUMEO [NOA]
CHOCHO [COZ] lang, Mexico
CHOCHOTECO alt for CHOCHO [COZ]
CHOCTAW-CHICKASAW [CCT] lang, USA
CHODHARI alt for CHODRI [CDI]
CHODRI [CDI] lang, India
CHOHA dial of NAGA, KONYAK [NBE]
CHOI-SALMST alt for KHVOY-SALMST dial of
    ARMENIAN [ARM]
CHOIMI alt for NAGA, LOTHA [NJH]
CHOKFEM alt for CAKFEM dial of MWAGHAVUL
    [SUR]
CHOKOBO alt for IZORA [CBO]
CHOKOSI alt for ANUFO [CKO]
CHOKOSSI alt for ANUFO [CKO]

CHOKRI alt for NAGA, CHOKRI [NRI]
CHOKWE [CJK] lang, Zaïre, Angola, Zambia
CHOKWE alt for CHOKWE [CJK]
CHOL, TILA [CTI] lang, Mexico
CHOL, TUMBALÁ [CTU] lang, Mexico
CHOLIMI alt for NAGA, AO [NJO]
CHOLLADO dial of KOREAN [KKN]
CHOLO alt for EPENA SAIJA [SJA]
CHOLO alt for EMBERA, NORTHERN [EMP]
CHOLO dial of NUNG [NUN]
CHOLON [CHT] lang, Peru
CHOLUTECA alt for CHOROTEGA [CJR]
CHOM alt for HRE [HRE]
CHOMO alt for COMO KARIM [CFG]
CHONA alt for CHONI [CDA]
CHONCHARU alt for CHENCHU [CDE]
CHONE alt for CHONI [CDA]
CHONG [COG] lang, Cambodia, Thailand, Thailand
CHONG alt for CHONG [COG]
CHONG'E alt for KUSHI [KUH]
CHONGLI dial of NAGA, AO [NJO]
CHONI [CDA] lang, China
CHONTAL OF OAXACA, HIGHLAND [CHD] lang,
    Mexico
CHONTAL OF OAXACA, LOWLAND [CLO] lang,
    Mexico
CHONTAL OF TABASCO [CHF] lang, Mexico
CHONYI [COH] lang, Kenya
CHOPI [CCE] lang, Mozambique
CHOPI alt for DHOPALUO dial of ACHOLI [ACO]
CHOR alt for JARAI [JRA]
CHOREI dial of CHIN, FALAM [HBH]
CHORI alt for CORI dial of HAM [JAB]
CHORO alt for CHRAU [CHR]
CHOROBA alt for CHORUBA dial of GONJA [DUM]
CHOROTE, IYO'WUJWA alt for CHOROTE,
    IYO'WUJWA [CRQ]
CHOROTE, IYOJWA'JA [CRT] lang, Argentina
CHOROTE, IYO'WUJWA [CRQ] lang, Argentina,
    Paraguay, Bolivia, Paraguay
CHOROTEGA [CJR] lang, Costa Rica
CHOROTEGA dial of CHOROTEGA [CJR]
CHOROTI alt for CHOROTE, IYO'WUJWA [CRQ]
CHOROTI alt for CHOROTE, IYOJWA'JA [CRT]
CHORTÍ [CAA] lang, Guatemala
CHORU alt for CHRU [CJE]
CHORUBA dial of GONJA [DUM]
CHOTA NAGPURI alt for SADANI [SCK]
CHOTE dial of BODO [BRX]
CHOTHE alt for NAGA, CHOTHE [NCT]
CHOUDHARA alt for CHODRI [CDI]
CHOUGOULE alt for SHUGULE dial of MEFELE [MFJ]
CHOUSHAN alt for CHAO SHAN dial of CHINESE,
    MIN NAN [CFR]
CHOWA alt for ARABIC, SHUWA [SHU]
CHOWRA alt for CHAURA [CHO]
CHRAU [CHR] lang, Viet Nam
CHRAU HMA alt for CHRU [CJE]
CHRU [CJE] lang, Viet Nam, USA
CHU alt for CHRU [CJE]
CHUABO alt for CHWABO [CHW]
CHUALA alt for GUANA [QKS]
CHUAMBO alt for CHWABO [CHW]
CHUAN alt for PEH dial of HMONG, WESTERN [HUJ]
CHUANA alt for TSWANA [TSW]
CHUANA dial of KUNA, SAN BLAS [CUK]

CHUANCHIENTIEN MIAO alt for HMONG, WESTERN
    [HUJ]
CHUANG alt for ZHUANG, NORTHERN [CCX]
CHUANGCHIA alt for ZHONGJIA dial of ZHUANG,
    NORTHERN [CCX]
CHUANQIANDIAN MIAO alt for HMONG, WESTERN
    [HUJ]
CHUAVE [CJV] lang, Papua New Guinea
CHUAVE dial of CHUAVE [CJV]
CHUBA alt for CHEWONG [CWG]
CHUBO alt for META' [MGO]
CHUCHEE alt for CHUKOT [CKT]
CHUCKCHANSI alt for YOKUTS [YOK]
"CHUDY" alt for VEPS [VEP]
CHUF alt for KHUFI dial of SHUGHNI [SGH]
CHUGACH ESKIMO alt for YUPIK, PACIFIC GULF
    [EMS]
CHUH alt for CHUJ, SAN MATEO IXTATÁN [CNM]
"CHUHARI" alt for VEPS [VEP]
CHUHE alt for CHUJ, SAN MATEO IXTATÁN [CNM]
CHUI-HUAN alt for THAO [SSF]
CHUIHWAN alt for THAO [SSF]
CHUIL QUICHÉ alt for QUICHE, CUNÉN [CUN]
CHUJ, SAN MATEO IXTATÁN [CNM] lang,
    Guatemala, Mexico, Mexico
CHUJ, SAN MATEO IXTATÁN alt for CHUJ, SAN
    MATEO IXTATÁN [CNM]
CHUJ, SAN SEBASTIÁN COATÁN [CAC] lang,
    Guatemala
CHUJE alt for CHUJ, SAN MATEO IXTATÁN [CNM]
CHUKA [CUH] lang, Kenya
CHUKCHA alt for CHUKOT [CKT]
CHUKCHEE alt for CHUKOT [CKT]
CHUKCHI alt for CHUKOT [CKT]
"CHUKHARI" alt for VEPS [VEP]
CHUKOT [CKT] lang, Russia, Asia
CHUKU alt for CHUKA [CUH]
CHULIKATA [CLK] lang, India
CHULIM alt for CHULYM [CHU]
CHULLA alt for SHILLUK [SHK]
CHULUPE alt for CHULUPÍ [CAG]
CHULUPÍ [CAG] lang, Paraguay, Argentina
CHULUPIE alt for CHULUPÍ [CAG]
CHULYM [CHU] lang, Russia, Asia
CHULYM TATAR alt for CHULYM [CHU]
CHULYM-TURKISH alt for CHULYM [CHU]
CHUMA dial of QUECHUA, NORTH BOLIVIAN [QUL]
CHUMASH [CHS] lang, USA
CHUMBURUNG [NCU] lang, Ghana
CHUNDAWAN dial of TINPUTZ [TPZ]
CHUNG alt for LISU [LIS]
CHUNG CHA alt for NHANG [NHA]
CHUNGCHIA alt for ZHONGJIA dial of ZHUANG,
    NORTHERN [CCX]
CHUNGKI alt for DJANGUN [DJF]
CHUNGLI alt for CHONGLI dial of NAGA, AO [NJO]
CHUNGSHAN alt for ZHONGSHAN dial of CHINESE,
    YUE [YUH]
CHUNGULOO alt for DJINGILI [JIG]
CHUNKUMBERRIES alt for DJANGUN [DJF]
CHUNKUNBURRA alt for DJANGUN [DJF]
CHUNUPI alt for CHULUPÍ [CAG]
CHUQUISACA dial of QUECHUA, SOUTH BOLIVIAN
    [QUH]
CHURAHI [CDJ] lang, India
CHURAHI GADI dial of GADDI [GBK]

CHURAHI PAHARI alt for CHURAHI [CDJ]
CHURARI dial of ROMANI, VLACH [RMY]
CHURARI dial of ROMANI, VLACH [RMY]
CHURARÍCKO alt for CHURARI dial of ROMANI,
    VLACH [RMY]
CHURI alt for SURMA [SUQ]
CHURI-WALI dial of DOMARI [RMT]
CHURIN dial of JAPANESE [JPN]
CHURO alt for CUR dial of MANDYAK [MFV]
CHURU alt for CHRU [CJE]
CHURUPI alt for CHULUPÍ [CAG]
CHUTIYA alt for DEORI [DER]
CHUTY dial of JARAI [JRA]
CHUUFI alt for BAFANJI [BFJ]
CHUUK alt for TRUK [TRU]
CHUVASH [CJU] lang, Russia, Europe
CHUWARE alt for GABAKE-NTSHORI [GZZ]
CHUWAU alt for HIOTSHUWAU [HIO]
CHUY alt for TALANGIT dial of ALTAI, SOUTHERN
    [ALT]
CHWABO [CHW] lang, Mozambique
CHWAGGA dial of SAN [HGM]
CHWAKA dial of GIRYAMA [NYF]
CHWAMPO alt for CHWABO [CHW]
CHWANA alt for TSWANA [TSW]
CHWANG alt for ZHUANG, NORTHERN [CCX]
CHWARE alt for HIECHWARE [HIE]
CHXALA dial of LAZ [LZZ]
CI alt for CI-GBE [CIB]
CI alt for PAICÎ [PRI]
CI'ULI alt for TS'OLE' dial of ATAYAL [TAY]
CI-GBE [CIB] lang, Benin
CIA-CIA [CIA] lang, Indonesia, Sulawesi
CIARA alt for CHARA [CRA]
CIBAANGI alt for BAANGI dial of GADI-SHINGINI-
    VADI-BAANGI [KAM]
CIBAK [CKL] lang, Nigeria
CIBALKE alt for BALKE dial of NDAU [NDC]
CIBECUE dial of APACHE, WESTERN [APW]
CIC alt for CIEC dial of DINKA, SOUTH CENTRAL
    [DIB]
CICAK alt for CITAK [TXT]
CICEWA alt for CHEWA dial of NYANJA [NYJ]
CICOLANO-REATINO-AQUILANO dial of ITALIAN
    [ITN]
CICOPI alt for CHOPI [CCE]
CICUABO alt for CHWABO [CHW]
CIEC dial of DINKA, SOUTH CENTRAL [DIB]
CIEN dial of NUER [NUS]
CIFIPA alt for FIPA [FIP]
CIGA alt for CHIGA [CHG]
CIGÁNY alt for ROMANI, CARPATHIAN [RMC]
CIINA alt for LENJE [LEH]
CIITA alt for SHITA [LGN]
CIKABANGA dial of FANAGOLO [FAO]
CIKIDE dial of GUDUF [GDF]
CIKOBU alt for IZORA [CBO]
CIKUNDA alt for KUNDA [KDN]
CILE dial of FIPA [FIP]
CILOWE alt for LOMWE [NGL]
CILUNGU alt for RUNGU dial of MAMBWE-LUNGU
    [MGR]
CIMABIHA alt for MAVIHA [MHP]
CIMAKALE alt for MAKALE dial of YAO [YAO]
CIMAKONDE alt for MAKONDE [KDE]
CIMANGANJA alt for MANGANJA dial of NYANJA

[NYJ]
CIMASHANGA alt for CHANGA dial of NDAU [NDC]
CIMASSANINGA alt for MASSANINGA dial of YAO
    [YAO]
CIMBA alt for ZEMBA [DHM]
CIMBANGALA alt for MBANGALA [MXG]
CIMBRIAN [CIM] lang, Italy
CIMEL alt for PALIOUPINY dial of DINKA,
    SOUTHWESTERN [DIK]
CIMWERA alt for MWERA [MWE]
CIN HAW alt for HO dial of CHINESE, MANDARIN
    [CHN]
CINAMIGUIN alt for MANOBO, CINAMIGUIN [MKX]
CINDA dial of KAMUKU [KAU]
CINDANDA alt for NDANDA dial of NDAU [NDC]
CINENI dial of GLAVDA [GLV]
CINGALESE alt for SINHALA [SNH]
CINGONI alt for NGONI dial of NYANJA [NYJ]
CINI alt for TCHINI dial of NIELLIM [NIE]
CINSENGA alt for NSENGA dial of NYANJA [NYJ]
CINTA LARGA dial of GAVIÃO DO JIPARANÁ [GVO]
CINYAMBE alt for NYAMBE dial of TONGA [TOH]
CINYANJA alt for NYANJA dial of NYANJA [NYJ]
CINYUNGWE alt for NYUNGWE [NYU]
CIOKWE alt for CHOKWE [CJK]
CIP alt for MISHIP [CHP]
CIPETA alt for PETA dial of NYANJA [NYJ]
CIPETA alt for PETA dial of NYANJA [NYJ]
CIPIMBWE alt for PIMBWE [PIW]
CIPODZO alt for PODZO [POZ]
CIRCASSIAN alt for ADYGHE [ADY]
CIREBON dial of SUNDA [SUO]
CIREBON dial of JAVANESE [JAN]
CIRI alt for TIRI [CIR]
CIRIMBA alt for NYA CERIYA dial of LONGUDA
    [LNU]
CIRMA alt for TIRMA dial of MURSI [MUZ]
CÎRO dial of ANUAK [ANU]
CIS-BAIKALIA dial of EVENKI [EVN]
CISAFWA alt for SAFWA [SBK]
CISENA alt for SENA [SEH]
CISHINGINI alt for SHINGINI dial of GADI-SHINGINI-
    VADI-BAANGI [KAM]
CISUUNDI alt for SUUNDI dial of KONGO [KON]
CITA alt for SHITA [LGN]
CITAK [TXT] lang, Indonesia, Irian Jaya
CITAK, TAMNIM [TML] lang, Indonesia, Irian Jaya
CITRALI alt for KHOWAR [KHW]
CIVILI alt for VILI [VIF]
CIYAO alt for YAO [YAO]
CIYEI alt for YEYE [YEY]
CIYOOMBE alt for YOOMBE dial of VILI [VIF]
CIYOOMBE alt for YOOMBE dial of VILI [VIF]
CKHALA alt for CHXALA dial of LAZ [LZZ]
CLACKAMA dial of CHINOOK [CHH]
CLALLAM [CLM] lang, USA
CLASSICAL AZTEC alt for NAHUATL, CLASSICAL
    [NCI]
CLASSICAL GREEK dial of GREEK, ANCIENT [GKO]
CLATA alt for GIANGAN [BGI]
CLELA alt for LELA [DRI]
CO alt for KOL dial of CUA [CUA]
CO-DON alt for KODU dial of KOHO [KPM]
COAIQUER alt for CUAIQUER [KWI]
COANA alt for TSWANA [TSW]
COAST KIWAI dial of KIWAI, SOUTHERN [KJD]

COAST MIWOK dial of MIWOK [SKD]
COAST TARANGAN dial of TARANGAN, WEST [TXN]
COASTAL ALORESE alt for EAST LAMAHOLOT dial of LAMAHOLOT [SLP]
COASTAL ARAPESH dial of BUKIYIP [APE]
COASTAL BALUCHI dial of BALUCHI, SOUTHERN [BCC]
COASTAL CHONTAL OF OAXACA alt for CHONTAL OF OAXACA, LOWLAND [CLO]
COASTAL CREE alt for CREE, COASTAL EASTERN [CRL]
COASTAL MAKHUWA alt for MACA [XMC]
COASTAL MIXTECO alt for MIXTECO, WESTERN JAMILTEPEC [MIO]
COASTAL QUICHÉ dial of QUICHÉ, WEST CENTRAL [QUT]
COASTAL TIHAAMAH dial of ARABIC, HIJAZI [ACW]
COASTAL TUPIAN alt for NHENGATU [YRL]
COATEPEC AZTEC alt for NAHUATL, COATEPEC [NAZ]
COATZOSPAN MIXTECO alt for MIXTECO, SAN JUAN COATZOSPAN [MIZ]
COBARI dial of YANOMAMÖ [GUU]
COBARÍA TUNEBO alt for TUNEBO, CENTRAL [TUF]
COBARIWA alt for COBARI dial of YANOMAMÖ [GUU]
COBIANA alt for KOBIANA [KCJ]
COC MUN alt for MUN [MJI]
COCAMA alt for COCAMA-COCAMILLA [COD]
COCAMA dial of COCAMA-COCAMILLA [COD]
COCAMA-COCAMILLA [COD] lang, Peru, Brazil, Colombia
COCAMILLA dial of COCAMA-COCAMILLA [COD]
COCAMILLA dial of COCAMA-COCAMILLA [COD]
COCCHE alt for HAMER-BANNA [AMF]
COCHABAMBA dial of QUECHUA, SOUTH BOLIVIAN [QUH]
COCHE alt for CAMSÁ [KBH]
COCHITI dial of KERES, EASTERN [KEE]
COCHOAPA dial of AMUZGO, GUERRERO [AMU]
COCKNEY dial of ENGLISH [ENG]
COCOLI alt for LANDOMA [LAO]
COCOPA [COC] lang, Mexico, USA, USA
COCOPA alt for COCOPA [COC]
COCOPAH alt for COCOPA [COC]
COCOS alt for MALAY, COCOS ISLANDS [COA]
CODOZZI dial of YUKPA [YUP]
COEUR D'ALENE [CRD] lang, USA
COFÁN [CON] lang, Ecuador, Colombia
COGAPACORI [COX] lang, Peru
COGHUI alt for COGUI [KOG]
COGNIAGUI alt for KONYAGI [COU]
COGUI [KOG] lang, Colombia
COHO alt for KOHO [KPM]
COICOYÁN dial of MIXTECO, METLATONOC [MXV]
COK alt for GOK dial of DINKA, SOUTH CENTRAL [DIB]
COKOBANCI alt for IZORA [CBO]
COKOBO alt for IZORA [CBO]
COKOSI alt for ANUFO [CKO]
COKWE alt for CHOKWE [CJK]
COL alt for KOL dial of CUA [CUA]
COLH alt for MUNDARI [MUW]
COLLA alt for QUECHUA, NORTHWEST JUJUY [QUO]

COLO alt for SHILLUK [SHK]
COLO dial of THURI [THU]
COLOMBIA CUNA alt for KUNA, PAYA-PUCURO [KUA]
COLOMBIAN SIGN LANGUAGE [CSN] lang, Colombia
COLÓN dial of WESTERN CARIBBEAN CREOLE ENGLISH [JAM]
COLORADO [COF] lang, Ecuador
COLUMBIA RIVER SAHAPTIN alt for UMATILLA [UMA]
COLUMBIA-WENATCHI [COL] lang, USA
COLUMBIAN alt for COLUMBIA-WENATCHI [COL]
COLVILLE dial of OKANAGAN [OKA]
COMA alt for KOMA, CENTRAL [KOM]
COMALTEPEC dial of ZAPOTECO, CHOAPAN [ZPC]
COMANCHE [COM] lang, USA
COMBE alt for NGUMBI [NUI]
COMEMATSA dial of BARASANA [BSN]
COMITANCILLO MAM alt for MAM, CENTRAL [MVC]
COMITECO alt for TOJOLABAL [TOJ]
COMMON SOMALI alt for SOMALI [SOM]
COMO alt for KOMA, CENTRAL [KOM]
COMO KARIM [CFG] lang, Nigeria
COMORES SWAHILI alt for COMORIAN [SWB]
COMORIAN [SWB] lang, Comoros Islands, Mayotte, Madagascar, Mayotte
COMORIAN alt for COMORIAN [SWB]
COMORIAN, SHINGAZIDJA [SWS] lang, Comoros Islands
COMORO alt for COMORIAN [SWB]
COMOX [COO] lang, Canada
COMOX-SLIAMMON alt for COMOX [COO]
COMPEVA alt for OMAGUA [OMG]
CON [CNO] lang, Laos
CONCEPCIÓN dial of CHIQUITANO [CAX]
CONCEPCIÓN PÁPALO dial of CUICATECO, TEPEUXILA [CUX]
CONCORINUM alt for KONKANI [KNK]
CONDUL dial of NICOBARESE, SOUTHERN [NIK]
CONE alt for JONE dial of KHAM [KHG]
CONGO alt for KONGO [KON]
CONGO alt for KONGO, SAN SALVADOR [KWY]
CONGO POL alt for POL [PMM]
CONGO SWAHILI alt for SWAHILI, ZAÏRE [SWC]
CONHAGUE alt for KONYAGI [COU]
CONIAGUI alt for KONYAGI [COU]
CONIBA alt for CONIBO dial of SHIPIBO-CONIBO [SHP]
CONIBO dial of SHIPIBO-CONIBO [SHP]
CONNACHT dial of GAELIC, IRISH [GLI]
CONOB alt for KANJOBAL, WESTERN [KNJ]
CONOB alt for KANJOBAL, EASTERN [KJB]
CONSO alt for KOMSO [KXC]
CONSTANTINE dial of ARABIC, ALGERIAN [ARQ]
CONSTANTINOPLE dial of ARMENIAN [ARM]
CONTA alt for KONTA dial of KULLO [KLO]
CONTA-REDDI alt for MUKHA-DORA [MMK]
CONTAQUIRO alt for PIRO [PIB]
COOK ISLAND alt for RAROTONGAN [RRT]
COOK ISLANDS MAORI alt for RAROTONGAN [RRT]
CÔÔNG alt for PHUNOI [PHO]
COONGURRI alt for KUNGGARI [KGL]
COORGE alt for KODAGU [KFA]
COOS [COS] lang, USA

COPALA TRIQUE alt for TRIQUE, SAN JUAN COPALA [TRC]
COPI alt for CHOPI [CCE]
COPI dial of CHOPI [CCE]
COPPER alt for MEDNOV dial of ALEUT [ALW]
COPPER ESKIMO alt for COPPER INUIT dial of INUIT, WESTERN CANADIAN [ESC]
COPPER INUIT dial of INUIT, WESTERN CANADIAN [ESC]
COPPER INUKTITUT alt for COPPER INUIT dial of INUIT, WESTERN CANADIAN [ESC]
COPPER RIVER alt for AHTENA [AHT]
COPPERSMITH alt for KALDERASH dial of ROMANI, VLACH [RMY]
COPTIC [COP] lang, Egypt
COQUILLE [COQ] lang, USA
COR alt for KOL dial of CUA [CUA]
CORA [COR] lang, Mexico
CORAPAN dial of CORA [COR]
COREGUAJE alt for KOREGUAJE [COE]
CORI dial of HAM [JAB]
CORINA alt for CULINA [CUL]
CORNISH [CRN] lang, United Kingdom
CORNOUAILLAIS dial of BRETON [BRT]
CORNWALL dial of ENGLISH [ENG]
COROÁ alt for ACROÁ [ACS]
COROADO alt for KAINGÁNG [KGP]
COROADO alt for PURI [PRR]
COROADOS alt for KAINGÁNG [KGP]
COROGAMA alt for BOZO, SOROGAMA [BZE]
COROMA dial of BRIBRI [BZD]
CORREGUAJE alt for KOREGUAJE [COE]
CORSE alt for CORSICAN [COI]
CORSI alt for CORSICAN [COI]
CORSICAN [COI] lang, France, Canada, Italy
CORSICAN alt for CORSICAN [COI]
CORSO alt for CORSICAN [COI]
CORSU alt for CORSICAN [COI]
CORUMBIARA alt for TUBARÃO [TBA]
COSSYAH alt for KHASI [KHI]
COSTA RICAN SIGN LANGUAGE [CSR] lang, Costa Rica
COTI alt for KOTI [EKO]
COTO alt for OREJÓN [ORE]
COTOBATO CHAVACANO dial of CHAVACANO [CBK]
COTOCOLI alt for TEM [KDH]
COTU alt for KATU [KTV]
COULAILAI alt for KULERE [KXE]
COUNTRY SIGN alt for JAMAICAN COUNTRY SIGN LANGUAGE [JCS]
COUSHATTA alt for KOASATI [CKU]
COWICHAN dial of HALKOMELEM [HUR]
COWLITZ [COW] lang, USA
COXIMA [KOX] lang, Colombia
COYAIMA [COY] lang, Colombia
COYAVITIS alt for ANGAITE [AIV]
COYOTERO alt for APACHE, WESTERN [APW]
COYULTITA dial of HUICHOL [HCH]
CRAIG COVE alt for LONWOLWOL [CRC]
CRANGE alt for KREYE [XRE]
CRAVEN YORKSHIRE dial of ENGLISH [ENG]
CREE alt for OJIBWA, NORTHERN [OJB]
CREE, CENTRAL [CRM] lang, Canada
CREE, COASTAL EASTERN [CRL] lang, Canada

CREE, INLAND EASTERN [CRE] lang, Canada
CREE, WESTERN [CRP] lang, Canada, USA, USA
CREE, WESTERN alt for CREE, WESTERN [CRP]
CREE-SAULTEAUX alt for OJIBWA, NORTHERN [OJB]
CREEK alt for MUSKOGEE [CRK]
CREEK dial of MUSKOGEE [CRK]
CRENGE alt for KREYE [XRE]
CRENYE alt for KREYE [XRE]
CREOLA alt for BELIZE CREOLE ENGLISH [BZI]
CREOLE alt for KRIO [KRI]
CREOLE ENGLISH OF HAWAII alt for HAWAI'I CREOLE ENGLISH [HAW]
CREOLESE alt for GUYANESE [GYN]
CREOLIZED ATTUAN alt for MEDNOV dial of ALEUT [ALW]
CREQ dial of HRE [HRE]
CREYE alt for KREYE [XRE]
CRICHANA alt for NINAM [SHB]
CRIMEA dial of ARMENIAN [ARM]
CRIMEAN GOTHIC dial of GOTHIC [GOF]
CRIMEAN NOGAI alt for NORTHERN CRIMEAN dial of CRIMEAN TURKISH [CRH]
CRIMEAN TARTAR alt for CRIMEAN TURKISH [CRH]
CRIMEAN TATAR alt for CRIMEAN TURKISH [CRH]
CRIMEAN TURKISH [CRH] lang, Uzbekistan, Bulgaria, Romania, Turkey
CRIOULO alt for KARIPÚNA CREOLE [KMV]
CRIOULO, GULF OF GUINEA [CRI] lang, Sao Tome e Principe, Equatorial Guinea
CRIOULO, UPPER GUINEA [POV] lang, Guinea Bissau, Cape Verde Islands, Gambia, Senegal
CRIOULO, UPPER GUINEA alt for CRIOULO, UPPER GUINEA [POV]
CRISCA alt for XAVÁNTE [XAV]
CROAT alt for CROATIAN dial of SERBO-CROATIAN [SRC]
CROATAN alt for LUMBEE [LUA]
CROATIAN alt for SERBO-CROATIAN [SRC]
CROATIAN dial of SERBO-CROATIAN [SRC]
CROATIAN dial of SERBO-CROATIAN [SRC]
CROW [CRO] lang, USA
CRU alt for CHRU [CJE]
CSL alt for CANADIAN SIGN LANGUAGE [CSD]
CÙ TE alt for LATI [LBT]
CU THO alt for KHMER, CENTRAL [KMR]
CUA [CUA] lang, Viet Nam
CUABO alt for CHWABO [CHW]
CUAIQUER [KWI] lang, Colombia, Ecuador, Ecuador
CUAIQUER alt for CUAIQUER [KWI]
CUAMBO alt for CHWABO [CHW]
CUANA alt for TSWANA [TSW]
CUANHOCA alt for KWADI [KWZ]
CUBEO [CUB] lang, Colombia, Brazil
CUBEU alt for CUBEO [CUB]
CUCAPA alt for COCOPA [COC]
CUCHI alt for KACHCHI [KFR]
CUCHUDUA dial of JAMAMADÍ [JAA]
CUCUPA alt for COCOPA [COC]
CUDAXAR dial of DARGWA [DAR]
CUEPE alt for KWADI [KWZ]
CUEVA dial of KUNA, SAN BLAS [CUK]
CUGANI alt for KONKANI [KNK]
CUGURDE alt for NOUMOU [NOW]
CÙI CHU alt for NHANG [NHA]
CUIBA [CUI] lang, Colombia, Venezuela, Venezuela

CUIBA alt for CUIBA [CUI]
CUIBA-WÁMONAE alt for CUIBA [CUI]
CUICATECO, TEPEUXILA [CUX] lang, Mexico
CUICATECO, TEUTILA [CUT] lang, Mexico
CUICUTL alt for KUIKÚRO [KUI]
CUINI alt for KWINI [GWW]
CUIVA alt for CUIBA [CUI]
CUJARENO alt for MASHCO PIRO [CUJ]
CUJAREÑO alt for MASHCO PIRO [CUJ]
CUJUBI alt for PURUBORÁ [PUR]
CULE alt for TSAMAI [TSB]
CULINA [CUL] lang, Brazil, Peru, Peru
CULINA alt for CULINA [CUL]
CULLO alt for KULLO [KLO]
CULTIVATED CAIRENE ARABIC dial of ARABIC,
  EGYPTIAN COLLOQUIAL [ARZ]
CUMANASHO alt for MAXAKALÍ [MBL]
CUMATA alt for IPEKA-TAPUIA [PAJ]
CUMBERLAND dial of ENGLISH [ENG]
CUMERAL [CUM] lang, Colombia
CUN [CUQ] lang, China
CUNA alt for KUNA, PAYA-PUCURO [KUA]
CUNAMA alt for KUNAMA [KUM]
CUNG [CUG] lang, Cameroon
CUNG [CUU] lang, China
CUNHUA alt for NGAO FON [NFO]
CUNI alt for TCHINI dial of NIELLIM [NIE]
CUNIPUSANA alt for MANDAHUACA [MHT]
CUNIPUSANA alt for BARÉ [BAE]
CUNUANA alt for MAQUIRITARI [MCH]
CUNUANA dial of MAQUIRITARI [MCH]
CUÓI alt for HUNG [HNU]
CUOI alt for KUY [KDT]
CUPEÑO [CUP] lang, USA
CUR dial of MANDYAK [MFV]
CUR CUL alt for KHMER, CENTRAL [KMR]
CURACIRARI dial of OMAGUA [OMG]
CURAÇOLEÑO alt for PAPIAMENTU [PAE]
CURAMA alt for TURKA [TUZ]
CURASICANA dial of YABARANA [YAR]
CURASSESE alt for PAPIAMENTU [PAE]
CURAUA alt for YOHORAA dial of TUCANO [TUO]
CURAZICARI alt for CURACIRARI dial of OMAGUA
  [OMG]
CURIPACO alt for CURRIPACO [KPC]
CUROCA alt for KWADI [KWZ]
CURRIPACO [KPC] lang, Colombia, Brazil, Venezuela
CURRIPACO alt for CURRIPACO [KPC]
CURUAIA alt for KURUÁYA [KYR]
CURUCICURI dial of OMAGUA [OMG]
CURUCURU alt for KURUKURU dial of PAUMARÍ
  [PAD]
CURUZICARI alt for CURUCICURI dial of OMAGUA
  [OMG]
CUSCO QUECHUA alt for QUECHUA, CUZCO [QUZ]
CUTCH alt for KACHCHI [KFR]
CUTCHI alt for KACHCHI [KFR]
CUTCHI-SWAHILI [CCL] lang, Kenya
CUTIADAPA dial of KATUKÍNA [KAV]
CUVEO alt for CUBEO [CUB]
CUVOK [CUV] lang, Cameroon
CUYANAWA dial of NUKUINI [NUC]
CUYARE alt for CABIYARÍ [CBB]
CUYO alt for CUYONON [CYO]
CUYONO alt for CUYONON [CYO]
CUYONON [CYO] lang, Philippines

CUYUNON alt for CUYONON [CYO]
CYMRAEG alt for WELSH [WLS]
CYPRIOT MARONITE ARABIC alt for ARABIC,
  CYPRIOT [ACY]
CZECH [CZC] lang, Czechoslovakia, Austria, Ukraine
CZECH alt for CZECH [CZC]
CZECH SIGN LANGUAGE [CSE] lang, Czechoslovakia
CZECHO-MORAVIAN dial of CZECH [CZC]
D'OOPACE alt for DOBASE [DOX]
D'OPAASUNTE alt for DOBASE [DOX]
DA alt for DAN [DAF]
DA KINE alt for HAWAI'I CREOLE ENGLISH [HAW]
DA'A alt for MAJERA [XMJ]
DA'A alt for KAILI, DA'A [KZF]
DA'A alt for KAILI, DA'A [KZF]
DA'AN alt for ULU AI' dial of DOHOI [OTD]
DA'ANG alt for LAIYOLO [LJI]
DA'ANG dial of DE'ANG [BFP]
DA-ANG alt for DA'ANG dial of DE'ANG [BFP]
DAADIYA alt for DADIYA [DBD]
DAAN alt for BULLA dial of SHEKO [SHE]
DAANYIR alt for BULLA dial of SHEKO [SHE]
DAASANECH [DSH] lang, Ethiopia, Kenya, Kenya
DAASANECH alt for DAASANECH [DSH]
DAASENECH alt for DAASANECH [DSH]
DAASH alt for BURJI [BJI]
DABA [DAB] lang, Cameroon
DABA alt for SAMO-KUBO [SMQ]
DABA DE GORE dial of NGAMBAI [SBA]
DABA KOLA alt for KOLA dial of DABA [DAB]
DABA MOUSGOY alt for MUSGOI dial of DABA
  [DAB]
DABAI dial of LELA [DRI]
DABAI alt for NABAY dial of KENINGAU MURUT
  [KXI]
DABAN YAO alt for YERONG [YRN]
DABARRE [DBR] lang, Somalia
DABARRE dial of DABARRE [DBR]
DABAY alt for NABAY dial of KENINGAU MURUT
  [KXI]
DABBA alt for DABA [DAB]
DABE [DBE] lang, Indonesia, Irian Jaya
DABI dial of DJINBA [DJB]
DABIDA alt for TAITA [DAV]
DABOSA alt for TOPOSA [TOQ]
DABRA [DBA] lang, Indonesia, Irian Jaya
DABU alt for AGÖB [KIT]
DABUGUS dial of TIMUGON MURUT [TIH]
DABURA alt for MORIGI [MDB]
DABUSO dial of BERTA [WTI]
DACCA dial of GARO [GRT]
DACE alt for DACHE [DCH]
DACHE [DCH] lang, Ethiopia
DACHSEA alt for TUCANO [TUO]
DACO-RUMANIAN alt for RUMANIAN [RUM]
DADIA alt for DADIYA [DBD]
DADIANCI alt for DADIYA [DBD]
DADIBI [MPS] lang, Papua New Guinea
DADIYA [DBD] lang, Nigeria
DADJA dial of IFÈ [IFE]
DADJO alt for DAJU, DAR DADJU [DJC]
DADJO alt for DAJU, DAR SILA [DAU]
DADUA dial of GALOLI [GAL]
DADUWA alt for GURUNG, EASTERN [GGN]
DAENG alt for TAI DAENG [TYR]
DAFFO dial of DAFFO-BATURA [DAM]

DAFFO-BATURA [DAM] lang, Nigeria
DAFI alt for MARKA [MWR]
DAFIIR alt for NORTH NAJDI dial of ARABIC, NAJDI [ARS]
DAFIIR alt for NORTH NAJDI dial of ARABIC, NAJDI [ARS]
DAFING alt for MARKA [MWR]
DAFLA alt for NISI [DAP]
DAFUHU dial of BELIZE CREOLE ENGLISH [BZI]
DAFWEGILONG dial of BELIZE CREOLE ENGLISH [BZI]
DAGA [DGZ] lang, Papua New Guinea
DAGAARI DIOULA [DGD] lang, Burkina Faso
DAGAARI JULA alt for DAGAARI DIOULA [DGD]
DAGAARI, NORTHERN [DGI] lang, Burkina Faso
DAGAARI, SOUTHERN [DGA] lang, Ghana
DAGAGA alt for FATALUKU [DDG]
DAGANONGA alt for SAMBA BALI dial of SAMBA LEKO [NDI]
DAGANYONGA dial of SAMBA LEKO [NDI]
DAGARA alt for DAGAARI, SOUTHERN [DGA]
DAGARA alt for DAGAARI, NORTHERN [DGI]
DAGARA dial of KANURI, YERWA [KPH]
DAGARI alt for DAGAARI, SOUTHERN [DGA]
DAGARI DYOULA alt for DAGAARI DIOULA [DGD]
DAGARRO dial of OTORO [OTR]
DAGATI alt for DAGAARI, SOUTHERN [DGA]
DAGATI alt for DAGAARI, NORTHERN [DGI]
DAGBA dial of VALE [VAE]
DAGBAMBA alt for DAGBANI [DAG]
DAGBANE alt for DAGBANI [DAG]
DAGBANI [DAG] lang, Ghana, Togo
DAGEL dial of KIBET [KIE]
DAGENAVA dial of YAGARIA [YGR]
DAGESTANI alt for AVAR [AVR]
DAGGAL alt for DAGEL dial of KIBET [KIE]
DAGI dial of KORUPUN [KPQ]
DAGLI dial of GODIÉ [GOD]
DAGO' LAWNG BIT dial of MARU [MHX]
DAGODA' alt for FATALUKU [DDG]
DAGOI alt for MALA [PED]
DAGOMBA alt for DAGBANI [DAG]
DAGPAKHA dial of DZONGKHA [DZO]
DAGU alt for DAJU, DAR FUR [DAJ]
DAGUI alt for MALA [PED]
DAGUOR alt for DAUR [DTA]
DAGUR alt for DAUR [DTA]
DAHALO [DAL] lang, Kenya
DAHANMU dial of BOMU [BMQ]
DAHATI alt for MAITHILI, DEHATI [MTR]
DAHATING [DAH] lang, Papua New Guinea
DAHIT alt for KOL [KFO]
DAHO-DOO [DAS] lang, Côte d'Ivoire
DAHOMEEN alt for FON-GBE [FOA]
DAHUNI dial of SUAU [SWP]
DAI [DIJ] lang, Indonesia, Maluku
DAI [TIZ] lang, China
DAI alt for HLAI [LIC]
DAI alt for DAY [DAI]
DAI alt for CHIN, DAAI [DAO]
DAI dial of LAU [LLU]
DAI KONG alt for TAI NÜA [TDD]
DAI NUEA alt for TAI NÜA [TDD]
DAIAMUNI alt for DAIO dial of WAGAWAGA [WGW]
DAIDO alt for SINOHOAN dial of PAMONA [BCX]
DAIER alt for DAIR [DRB]

DAIGOK alt for ARECUNA dial of PEMON [AOC]
DAIM alt for ME'EN [MYM]
DAINGGATI alt for DYANGADI [DYN]
DAIO dial of WAGAWAGA [WGW]
DAIOMUNI alt for DAIO dial of WAGAWAGA [WGW]
DAIR [DRB] lang, Sudan
DAIRI alt for BATAK DAIRI [BTD]
DAISO alt for DHAISO [SEG]
DAIYA-ATAIYAL alt for TAROKO [TRV]
DAJA dial of ACEH [ATJ]
DAJA dial of AKPES [IBE]
DAJO alt for DAJU, DAR DADJU [DJC]
DAJOU alt for DAJU, DAR DADJU [DJC]
DAJOU alt for DAJU, DAR SILA [DAU]
DAJU alt for DAJU, DAR DADJU [DJC]
DAJU alt for DAJU, DAR SILA [DAU]
DAJU FERNE alt for DAJU, DAR FUR [DAJ]
DAJU MONGO alt for DAJU, DAR DADJU [DJC]
DAJU OUM HADJER alt for DAJU, DAR DADJU [DJC]
DAJU, DAR DADJU [DJC] lang, Chad
DAJU, DAR FUR [DAJ] lang, Sudan
DAJU, DAR SILA [DAU] lang, Chad, Sudan, Sudan
DAJU, DAR SILA alt for DAJU, DAR SILA [DAU]
DAK SUT SEDANG dial of SEDANG [SED]
DAKA alt for DIRIM [DIR]
DAKA alt for SAMBA DAKA [CCG]
DAKAKA [BPA] lang, Vanuatu
DAKAKARI alt for LELA [DRI]
DAKALLA alt for KADUGLI dial of KATCHA-KADUGLI-MIRI [KAT]
DAKANI alt for DAKHINI dial of URDU [URD]
DAKARKARI alt for LELA [DRI]
DAKDUNG dial of CHIN, TEDIM [CTD]
DAKHECZJHA alt for DEHEJIA dial of BONAN [PEH]
DAKHINI dial of URDU [URD]
DAKKA [DKK] lang, Indonesia, Sulawesi
DAKKA alt for DIRIM [DIR]
DAKKARKARI alt for LELA [DRI]
DAKLAN dial of IBALOI [IBL]
DAKOTA [DHG] lang, USA, Canada
DAKOTA dial of DAKOTA [DHG]
DAKPA [DKP] lang, Central African Republic
DAKPA alt for SAGTENGPA [SGT]
DAKTJERAT alt for TYARAITY [WOA]
DAKUNZA dial of GUMUZ [GUK]
DAKUNZA dial of GUMUZ [GUK]
DAKWA alt for BAZZA dial of KAMWE [HIG]
DAL [DLL] lang, India
DAL'GARI alt for DHARGARI [DHR]
DALA alt for FUR [FUR]
DALABON alt for NGALKBUN [NGK]
DALAD alt for DALAT dial of MELANAU [MEL]
DALAI alt for TIBETAN [TIC]
DALANDJI alt for DHALANDJI [DHL]
DALAT dial of MELANAU [MEL]
DALDI dial of KONKANI, GOANESE [GOM]
DALENDI alt for DHALANDJI [DHL]
DALI dial of LELAK [LLK]
DALIT MURUT dial of PALUAN [PLZ]
DALMATIAN [DLM] lang, Croatia
DALOKA alt for NGILE [MAS]
DALOKA alt for NGILE [MAS]
DALONG alt for PAI [PAI]
DALOUA BÉTÉ alt for BÉTÉ, DALOA [BEV]
DALY RIVER KRIOL dial of KRIOL [ROP]

DAM alt for BUSO [BSO]
DAM alt for NDAM [NDM]
DAMA [DMM] lang, Cameroon
DAMA alt for NAMA [NAQ]
DAMA alt for BETE-BENDE [BTT]
DAMA alt for MURSI [MUZ]
DAMA alt for DAASANECH [DSH]
DAMA alt for NAMA dial of MBEMBE, TIGON [NZA]
DAMA alt for NAMA dial of MBEMBE, TIGON [NZA]
DAMAL [UHN] lang, Indonesia, Irian Jaya
DAMAL dial of DAMAL [UHN]
DAMALO alt for TAMALU dial of RAWANG [RAW]
DAMANGO dial of HANGA [HAG]
DAMANI alt for PARABHI dial of KONKANI [KNK]
DAMAQUA alt for NAMA [NAQ]
DAMAR, EAST [DMR] lang, Indonesia, Maluku
DAMAR, WEST [DRN] lang, Indonesia, Maluku
DAMARA alt for HERERO [HER]
DAMARA alt for NAMA [NAQ]
DAMAT dial of MAASAI [MET]
DAMATA dial of MAMBAI [MGM]
DAMBI dial of SAGALLA [TGA]
DAMBI dial of MUMENG [MZI]
DAMBRO alt for TAI, SOUTHERN [SOU]
DAMEDI alt for DAMELI [DML]
DAMEL alt for DAMELI [DML]
DAMELI [DML] lang, Pakistan
DAMI [DAD] lang, Papua New Guinea
DAMIA alt for DAMELI [DML]
DAMINYU dial of YELE [YLE]
DAMLALE alt for PELASLA dial of PELASLA [MLR]
DAMOT alt for AWNGI [AWN]
DAMPAL [DMP] lang, Indonesia, Sulawesi
DAMPELAS alt for DAMPELASA [DMS]
DAMPELASA [DMS] lang, Indonesia, Sulawesi
DAMREY dial of KUY [KDT]
DAMULIAN alt for TAMIL [TCV]
DAN [DAF] lang, Côte d'Ivoire, Liberia, Guinea,
    Liberia
DAN alt for DYAN [DYA]
DAN alt for DAN [DAF]
DAN alt for BULLA dial of SHEKO [SHE]
DAN MUURE dial of PEERE [KUT]
"DANAKIL" alt for AFAR [AFR]
DANAL alt for DANGALEAT [DAA]
DANARU [DNR] lang, Papua New Guinea
DANAU [DNU] lang, Myanmar
DANAW alt for DANAU [DNU]
DANDA dial of NDAU [NDC]
DANDAMI MARIA [DAQ] lang, India
DANDAWA alt for DENDI [DEN]
DANG alt for KEDANG [KSX]
DANG alt for NHANG [NHA]
DANG alt for TUNGAG [LCM]
DANGADI alt for DYANGADI [DYN]
DANGAL [DAC] lang, Papua New Guinea
DANGAL alt for DANGALEAT [DAA]
DANGALEAT [DAA] lang, Chad
DANGALI alt for THARU, DANG [THL]
DANGALI alt for HUMLA BHOTIA [HUT]
DANGARIK alt for PHALURA [PHL]
DANGATI alt for DYANGADI [DYN]
DANGBE alt for ADANGME dial of GA-ADANGME-
    KROBO [GAC]
DANGBON alt for NGALKBUN [NGK]
DANGEDL dial of YIR YORONT [YIY]

DANGGADI alt for DYANGADI [DYN]
DANGGAL alt for DANGAL [DAC]
DANGGETTI alt for DYANGADI [DYN]
DANGHA alt for THARU, DANG [THL]
DANGI [DAT] lang, India
DANGI dial of BRAJ BHASHA [BFS]
DANGI alt for DANGRI dial of KHANDESI [KHN]
DANGLA alt for DANGALEAT [DAA]
DANGME alt for ADANGME dial of GA-ADANGME-
    KROBO [GAC]
DANGRI alt for DANGI [DAT]
DANGRI dial of KHANDESI [KHN]
DANGS BHIL alt for DANGI [DAT]
DANGU alt for DHANGU [GLA]
DANGURA alt for THARU, DANG [THL]
DANI alt for DENÍ [DAN]
DANI BARAT alt for DANI, WESTERN [DNW]
DANI, LOWER GRAND VALLEY [DNI] lang,
    Indonesia, Irian Jaya
DANI, MID GRAND VALLEY [DNT] lang, Indonesia,
    Irian Jaya
DANI, WESTERN [DNW] lang, Indonesia, Irian Jaya
DANI-KURIMA alt for LOWER GRAND VALLEY
    HITIGIMA dial of DANI, LOWER GRAND VALLEY
    [DNI]
DANIEL CARRION alt for QUECHUA, PASCO-
    YANAHUANCA [QUR]
DANISA alt for DANISIN [DNA]
DANISH [DNS] lang, Denmark, Greenland, Germany
DANISH alt for DANISH [DNS]
DANISH SIGN LANGUAGE [DSL] lang, Denmark
DANISIN [DNA] lang, Botswana
DANJONGKA alt for SIKKIMESE [SIP]
DANKYIRA dial of AKAN [TWS]
DANO [ASO] lang, Papua New Guinea
DANO-NORWEGIAN alt for NORWEGIAN, BOKMAL
    [NRR]
DANPURIYA dial of KUMAUNI [KFY]
DANSHE dial of ZEEM [ZUA]
DANU dial of MADAK [MMX]
DANU dial of BURMESE [BMS]
DANUBE-TISZA dial of HUNGARIAN [HNG]
DANUBIAN alt for ROMANI, VLACH [RMY]
DANUBIAN dial of TURKISH [TRK]
DANUWAR alt for DHANWAR [DHA]
DANUWAR RAI alt for DHANWAR [DHW]
DAO alt for MIEN [YOC]
DAONDA [DND] lang, Papua New Guinea
DAONGDUNG dial of SAMA, BALANGINGI [SSE]
DAOUSSAHAQ alt for DAUSAHAQ [DSQ]
DAOUSSAK alt for DAUSAHAQ [DSQ]
DAP alt for SAGTENGPA [SGT]
DAPALAN dial of TALAUD [TLD]
DAPERA alt for OUNE [OUE]
DAPHLA alt for NISI [DAP]
DAPITAN dial of SUBANON, TUBOY [STB]
DAPO dial of KRUMEN, SOUTHERN [TED]
DAPZAL dial of CHIN, TEDIM [CTD]
DAR EL KABIRA dial of TULISHI [TEY]
DARAGA dial of BICOLANO, ALBAY [BHK]
DARAGAWAN alt for KARAGAWAN dial of ISNAG
    [ISD]
DARAI [DRY] lang, Nepal
DARAMANDOUGOU-NYARAFO dial of TIÉFO [TIQ]
DARAMBAL alt for BAYALI [BJY]
DARANG dial of DE'ANG [BFP]

DEBBARMA dial of KOK BOROK [TRP]
DÉBO dial of BOZO, SOROGAMA [BZE]
DEBRI [DEB] lang, Sudan
DECCAN [DCC] lang, India
DECCAN alt for DAKHINI dial of URDU [URD]
DEDIEBO dial of GREBO, GBOLOO [GEC]
DEDUA [DED] lang, Papua New Guinea
DEDUAE alt for DEDUA [DED]
DEENU dial of SAMBA LEKO [NDI]
DEFA dial of BAKWÉ [BAK]
DEFAKA [AFN] lang, Nigeria
DEFALE dial of LAMA [LAS]
DEFORO alt for KURUMFÉ [KFZ]
DEG [MZW] lang, Ghana, Côte d'Ivoire
DEGARU [DGR] lang, India
DEGATI alt for DAGAARI, SOUTHERN [DGA]
DEGATI alt for DAGAARI, NORTHERN [DGI]
DEGEMA [DEG] lang, Nigeria
DEGENAN [DGE] lang, Papua New Guinea
DEGEXIT'AN [ING] lang, USA
DEGHA alt for DEG [MZW]
DEGHWARI alt for DEHWARI [DEH]
DEGOJA alt for DAKUNZA dial of GUMUZ [GUK]
DEGOJA alt for DAKUNZA dial of GUMUZ [GUK]
DEGUBA alt for GUMUZ [GUK]
DEHATI alt for MAITHILI, DEHATI [MTR]
DEHEJIA dial of BONAN [PEH]
DEHENDA alt for GUMUZ [GUK]
DEHES alt for EL MOLO [ELO]
DEHONG alt for TAI NÜA [TDD]
DEHONG dial of TAI NÜA [TDD]
DEHONG DAI alt for TAI NÜA [TDD]
DEHOXDE alt for DGHWEDE [DGH]
DEHU [DEU] lang, New Caledonia
DEHWARI [DEH] lang, Pakistan
DEI alt for DEWOIN [DEE]
DEIBULA dial of KORUPUN [KPQ]
DEING dial of TEWA [TWE]
DEJAH alt for DUSUN DEYAH [DUN]
DEJBUK dial of DARGWA [DAR]
DÉJING dial of ZHUANG, SOUTHERN [CCY]
DEK [DEK] lang, Cameroon
DEKINI alt for DECCAN [DCC]
DEKKA alt for SAMBA DAKA [CCG]
DEKOKA dial of GUMUZ [GUK]
DEKWAMBRE alt for MPUR [AKC]
DELA alt for OENALE-DELHA dial of ROTI [ROT]
DELANG dial of MALAYIC DAYAK [XDY]
DELAWARE alt for UNAMI [DEL]
DELAWARE alt for MUNSEE [UMU]
DELEN alt for DILLING [DIL]
DELHA alt for OENALE-DELHA dial of ROTI [ROT]
DELHI SIGN LANGUAGE dial of INDIAN SIGN
  LANGUAGE [INS]
DELI dial of MALAY [MLI]
DELO [NTR] lang, Ghana, Togo, Togo
DELO alt for DELO [NTR]
DELTA ARABIC dial of ARABIC, EGYPTIAN
  COLLOQUIAL [ARZ]
DEM [DEM] lang, Indonesia, Irian Jaya
DEMA alt for TUPURI [TUI]
DEMAM alt for KETUNGAU dial of IBAN [IBA]
DEMBIYA [DEY] lang, Ethiopia
DEMBO alt for BODHO dial of THURI [THU]
DEMBYA alt for DEMBIYA [DEY]
DEMEN alt for BODHO dial of THURI [THU]

DEMENGGONG-WAIBRON-BANO alt for MEKWEI
  [MSF]
DEMIK alt for KEIGA [KEC]
DEMIK dial of KEIGA [KEC]
DEMISA [DEI] lang, Indonesia, Irian Jaya
DEMISA alt for DANISIN [DNA]
DEMSA dial of BATA [BTA]
DEMSA BATA alt for BATA [BTA]
DEMSHIN dial of MIYA [MKF]
DEMTA [DMY] lang, Indonesia, Irian Jaya
DEMWA dial of PELASLA [MLR]
DENAWA alt for DENO [DBB]
DENDI [DEN] lang, Niger, Benin, Nigeria
DENDI alt for DENDI [DEN]
DENDJE (DINDJE alt for DUNJE dial of KABA NA
  [KWV]
DENG alt for SAMBA DAKA [CCG]
DENG alt for DE dial of GOLA [GOL]
DENGALU [DEA] lang, Papua New Guinea
DENGEBU [DEC] lang, Sudan
DENGESE [DEZ] lang, Zaïre
DENGKA alt for DENGKA-LELAIN dial of ROTI [ROT]
DENGKA-LELAIN dial of ROTI [ROT]
DENGKWOP alt for GHOMALA SOUTH dial of
  GHOMALA' [BBJ]
DENGURUME alt for NGURIMI [NGQ]
DENÍ [DAN] lang, Brazil
DENI alt for NDENI dial of SANTA CRUZ [STC]
DENJE alt for DUNJE dial of KABA NA [KWV]
DENJONKA alt for SIKKIMESE [SIP]
DENJONKE alt for SIKKIMESE [SIP]
"DENKEL" alt for AFAR [AFR]
DENO [DBB] lang, Nigeria
DENTONG alt for BENTONG [BNU]
DENWA alt for DENO [DBB]
DENYA [ANV] lang, Cameroon
DEO TIEN dial of MIEN [YOC]
DEOKHAR alt for THARU, DEOKRI [THG]
DEORI [DER] lang, India
DEPLE dial of BAKWÉ [BAK]
DEQ alt for BATEK DE' dial of BATEK [BTQ]
DERA alt for KANAKURU [KNA]
DERA alt for KAMBERATARO [KBV]
DERA dial of KANAKURU [KNA]
DERASA alt for GEDEO [DRS]
DERASANYA alt for GEDEO [DRS]
DERAWALI dial of SIRAIKI [SKR]
DERBENT dial of AZERBAIJANI, NORTH [AZE]
DERBET alt for DÖRBÖT dial of KALMYK-OIRAT
  [KGZ]
DEREBAI dial of MAILU [MGU]
DERESA alt for GEDEO [DRS]
DERMUHA dial of KAREN, PAKU [KPP]
DERSIMKI alt for KIRMANJKI [QKV]
DERU alt for KANAKURU [KNA]
DESA dial of IBAN [IBA]
DESÂNA alt for DESANO [DES]
DESANO [DES] lang, Brazil, Colombia, Colombia
DESANO alt for DESANO [DES]
DESARI alt for BANGARU [BGC]
DESHIYA alt for MAITHILI, DEHATI [MTR]
DESI alt for DECCAN [DCC]
DESIA alt for ORIYA, ADIWASI [ORT]
DESIA alt for DAKHINI dial of URDU [URD]
DESIA ORIYA alt for KORAPUT ORIYA dial of ORIYA
  [ORY]

DESIN DOLA' alt for DUANO' [DUP]
DESSANA alt for DESANO [DES]
DESSAULYA dial of GARHWALI [GBM]
DESUA alt for DISOHA dial of GUMUZ [GUK]
DESWALI dial of BANGARU [BGC]
DETI alt for DETI-KHWE [DET]
DETI-KHWE [DET] lang, Botswana
DEURI alt for DEORI [DER]
DEUTSCHE GEBÄRDENSPRACHE alt for GERMAN
SIGN LANGUAGE [GSG]
DEVONSHIRE dial of ENGLISH [ENG]
DEWALA dial of LEWADA-DEWARA [LWD]
DEWALA-LEWADA alt for LEWADA-DEWARA [LWD]
DEWALA-LEWADA alt for LEWADA-DEWARA dial of
TIRIO [TCR]
DEWIYA dial of GUMUZ [GUK]
DEWOI alt for DEWOIN [DEE]
DEWOIN [DEE] lang, Liberia
DEY alt for DEWOIN [DEE]
DFOLA alt for BIAFADA [BIF]
DGERNESIAIS dial of FRENCH [FRN]
DGHWEDE [DGH] lang, Nigeria
DGIÉH alt for TRIENG [STG]
DGS alt for GERMAN SIGN LANGUAGE [GSG]
DHA'I alt for DAYI [DAX]
DHAISO [SEG] lang, Tanzania
DHALANDJI [DHL] lang, Australia
DHALLA alt for KADUGLI dial of KATCHA-KADUGLI-
MIRI [KAT]
DHALWANGU dial of DAYI [DAX]
DHANAGARI alt for VARHADI-NAGPURI [VAH]
DHANAGARI dial of KONKANI [KNK]
DHANGAR alt for KURUX, NEPALI [KXL]
DHANGON dial of KODA [KFN]
DHANGU [GLA] lang, Australia
DHANGU'MI alt for DHANGU [GLA]
DHANGU-DJANGU dial of DHANGU [GLA]
DHANKA [DHN] lang, India
DHANKI alt for DHANKA [DHN]
DHANORA dial of MURIA, WESTERN [MUT]
DHANU'UN alt for DANGEDL dial of YIR YORONT
[YIY]
DHANVAR alt for DHANWAR [DHA]
DHANVAR alt for DHANWAR [DHW]
DHANWAR [DHA] lang, India
DHANWAR [DHW] lang, Nepal
DHARAWAAL alt for THURAWAL [TBH]
DHARAWAL alt for THURAWAL [TBH]
DHARBA dial of DURUWA [PCI]
DHARGARI [DHR] lang, Australia
DHARWAR alt for KALVADI dial of DECCAN [DCC]
DHATAKI alt for DHATKI [MKI]
DHATI alt for DHATKI [MKI]
DHATKI [MKI] lang, Pakistan
DHATKI BHIL dial of DHATKI [MKI]
DHAY'YI alt for DAYI [DAX]
DHE BOODHO alt for BODHO dial of THURI [THU]
DHE COLO alt for COLO dial of THURI [THU]
DHE LUWO alt for LUWO [LWO]
DHE LWO alt for LUWO [LWO]
DHE THURI alt for THURI [THU]
DHEBANG alt for HEIBAN [HEB]
DHED alt for MAHARI dial of KONKANI [KNK]
DHED GUJARI alt for KHANDESI [KHN]
DHEDI alt for MAHARI dial of VARHADI-NAGPURI
[VAH]

DHEKARU alt for DEGARU [DGR]
DHELKI KHARIA dial of KHARIA [KHR]
DHIBALI alt for BALI [BCP]
DHIMAL [DHI] lang, Nepal
DHIMBA alt for ZEMBA [DHM]
DHIMORONG alt for MORO [MOR]
DHIRAILA dial of NGURA [NBX]
DHITORO alt for OTORO [OTR]
DHO ALUR alt for ALUR [ALZ]
DHO ANYWAA alt for ANUAK [ANU]
DHOBI alt for DHODIA [DHO]
DHOCOLO alt for SHILLUK [SHK]
DHODHRI dial of BHILI [BHB]
DHODIA [DHO] lang, India
DHOFAR dial of ARABIC, OMANI [ACX]
DHOGARYALI alt for DOGRI-KANGRI [DOJ]
DHOLEWARI dial of MALVI [MUP]
DHOLUBI alt for KATCHA dial of KATCHA-KADUGLI-
MIRI [KAT]
DHOLUO alt for LUO [LUO]
DHOPADHOLA alt for ADHOLA [ADH]
DHOPALUO dial of ACHOLI [ACO]
DHORE alt for DHODIA [DHO]
DHOWARI alt for DHODIA [DHO]
DHRUVA alt for DURUWA [PCI]
DHU'RGA alt for DHURGA [DHU]
DHUNDI-KAIRALI alt for PAHARI-POTWARI [PHR]
DHUNDI-KAIRALI alt for PAHARI dial of PAHARI-
POTWARI [PHR]
DHUNGRI BHILI alt for GIRASIA, RAJPUT [GRA]
DHUNGRI GIRASIA alt for GIRASIA, RAJPUT [GRA]
DHURGA [DHU] lang, Australia
DHURI alt for SURMA [SUQ]
DHURU alt for DANDAMI MARIA [DAQ]
DHURWA alt for DURUWA [PCI]
DHUWAL [DUJ] lang, Australia
DHUWAL dial of DHUWAL [DUJ]
DHUWAYA dial of DHUWAL [DUJ]
DI alt for DING [DIZ]
DI-ANG alt for PALAUNG, PALE [PCE]
DI-PRI alt for DIH BRI dial of MNONG, CENTRAL
[MNC]
DIA [DIA] lang, Papua New Guinea
DIA alt for BUOL [BLF]
DIA alt for DJIA dial of SAKATA [SAT]
DIABE alt for DJOABLIN dial of ANYIN [ANY]
DIAHÔI dial of TENHARIM [PAH]
DIAHOUE alt for JAWE [JAZ]
DIAKHANKE alt for JAHANKA [JAD]
DIAKKANKE alt for JAHANKA [JAD]
DIALONKE alt for YALUNKA [YAL]
DIAN alt for DYAN [DYA]
DIAN alt for DAMPELASA [DMS]
DIANBAO [TST] lang, China
DIANG dial of KURANKO [KHA]
DIARBEKIR alt for TIGRANAKERT dial of ARMENIAN
[ARM]
DIAWARA alt for SONINKE [SNN]
DIBA alt for TUVIN [TUN]
DIBABAON alt for MANOBO, DIBABAWON [MBD]
DIBAGAT-KABUGAO dial of ISNAG [ISD]
DIBAGAT-KABUGAO-ISNEG alt for ISNAG [ISD]
DIBIASU alt for BAINAPI [PIK]
DIBO alt for GANAGANA dial of NUPE [NUP]
DIBOUM dial of BASAA [BAA]
DICAMAY DUMAGAT alt for AGTA, DICAMAY

[DUY]
DIDA, LAKOTA [DIC] lang, Côte d'Ivoire
DIDA, YOCOBOUÉ [GUD] lang, Côte d'Ivoire
DIDAYI alt for GATA' [GAQ]
DIDEI alt for GATA' [GAQ]
DIDESSA [DIQ] lang, Ethiopia
DIDI dial of KALIKO-MA'DI [XKZ]
DIDIGARU dial of MARIA [MDS]
DIDIGAVU dial of IAMALELE [YML]
DIDINGA [DID] lang, Sudan
DIDO [DDO] lang, Russia, Europe
DIDOI alt for DIDO [DDO]
DIDRA alt for TODRAH [TDR]
DIDRAH alt for TODRAH [TDR]
DIE alt for JEH [JEH]
DIEGUENO [DIH] lang, Mexico, USA, USA
DIEGUEÑO alt for DIEGUENO [DIH]
DIEGUEÑO dial of DIEGUENO [DIH]
DIEKO alt for DIDA, LAKOTA [DIC]
DIERI [DIF] lang, Australia
DIÉS alt for EGA [DIE]
DIGAM dial of MPADE [MPI]
DIGARO [MHU] lang, India
DIGARU alt for DIGARO [MHU]
DIGENJA alt for LIGENZA [LGZ]
DIGO [DIG] lang, Kenya, Tanzania, Tanzania
DIGO alt for DIGO [DIG]
DIGOEL alt for KATI, SOUTHERN [KTS]
DIGOR dial of OSETIN [OSE]
DIGUEÑO alt for DIEGUENO [DIH]
DIGUL alt for KATI, SOUTHERN [KTS]
DIGUT alt for GAVIÃO DO JIPARANÁ [GVO]
DIH BRI dial of MNONG, CENTRAL [MNC]
DIH BRI dial of MNONG, CENTRAL [MNC]
DIHINA [DIY] lang, Ethiopia
DII [DUR] lang, Cameroon
DII alt for BATA [BTA]
DIILA alt for KUNAMA [KUM]
DIIR alt for DIR dial of POLCI [POL]
DIJAMA dial of OTORO [OTR]
DIJE alt for TUMAK [TMC]
DIJIM [CFA] lang, Nigeria
DIK-NDAM alt for NDAM-DIK dial of NDAM [NDM]
DIKAYU dial of SUBANON, TUBOY [STB]
DIKELE alt for KÉLÉ [KEB]
DIKKU KAJI alt for SADANI [SCK]
DIKO dial of GBAGYI [GBR]
DIKOTA dial of NGANDO [NGD]
DIKUTA dial of NGANDO [NGD]
DILAUT-BADJAO dial of SAMA, CENTRAL [SML]
DILAVA RIVER dial of FUYUGE [FUY]
DILI TETUN dial of TETUN [TTM]
DILLING [DIL] lang, Sudan
DIM dial of CHIN, TEDIM [CTD]
DIM alt for ADIM dial of AGWAGWUNE [YAY]
DIMA alt for DIME [DIM]
DIMA alt for KANASI [SOQ]
DIMA alt for JIMAJIMA [JMA]
DIMADOKO dial of MAYOGO [MDM]
DIMASA [DIS] lang, India
DIMASA dial of DIMASA [DIS]
DIMASA KACHARI alt for KACHARI [QKC]
DIMBAMBANG alt for MBANG dial of BAKOKO [BKH]
DIMBONG [DII] lang, Cameroon
DIME [DIM] lang, Ethiopia
DIME alt for GINUMAN [GNM]
DIMEO dial of MOFU, SOUTH [MIF]
DIMILI alt for DIMLI [ZZZ]
DIMILKI alt for KIRMANJKI [QKV]
DIMIR [DMC] lang, Papua New Guinea
DIMISI alt for IDI [IDI]
DIMLI [ZZZ] lang, Turkey, Germany
DIMMUK dial of KOFYAR [KWL]
DIMODONGO alt for KRONGO [KGO]
DIMOTIKI dial of GREEK [GRK]
DIMSISI alt for IDI [IDI]
DIMU alt for TIMU dial of SAWU [HVN]
DIMUGA alt for DAGA [DGZ]
DIMUK alt for DIMMUK dial of KOFYAR [KWL]
DIN alt for DING [DIZ]
DING [DIZ] lang, Zaïre
DINGANDO alt for NGANDO [NGD]
DINGI alt for DUNGU [DBV]
DINIK alt for AFITTI [AFT]
DINJE alt for DUNJE dial of KABA NA [KWV]
DINKA IBRAHIM alt for ABILIANG dial of DINKA, NORTHEASTERN [DIP]
DINKA, NORTHEASTERN [DIP] lang, Sudan
DINKA, NORTHWESTERN [DIW] lang, Sudan
DINKA, SOUTH CENTRAL [DIB] lang, Sudan
DINKA, SOUTHEASTERN [DIN] lang, Sudan
DINKA, SOUTHWESTERN [DIK] lang, Sudan
DINLER dial of TURKISH [TRK]
DIO alt for KAIDIPANG [KZP]
DIO dial of ZANDE [ZAN]
DIODIO [DDI] lang, Papua New Guinea
DIOI alt for NHANG [NHA]
DIOI alt for BOUYEI [PCC]
DIOLA-FOGNY alt for JOLA-FOGNY [DYO]
DIOLA-KASA alt for JOLA-KASA [CSK]
DIONGOR BOURMA TAGIL alt for JEGU [JEU]
DIONGOR GUERA alt for MOKULU [MOZ]
DIONKOR alt for MIGAAMA [MMY]
DIORE alt for XIKRIN dial of KAYAPÓ [TXU]
DIOS dial of TINPUTZ [TPZ]
DIOULA alt for JULA [DYU]
DIOULA VÉHICULAIRE dial of BAMBARA [BRA]
DIR dial of POLCI [POL]
DIRAASHA alt for DIRASHA [GDL]
DIRARI [DIT] lang, Australia
DIRASHA [GDL] lang, Ethiopia
DIRAYTA alt for DIRASHA [GDL]
DIRE alt for GATA' [GAQ]
DIRI [DWA] lang, Nigeria
DIRI alt for KALAMI [GWC]
DIRIA alt for CHOROTEGA [CJR]
DIRIA dial of CHOROTEGA [CJR]
DIRIKO alt for DIRIKU [DIU]
DIRIKU [DIU] lang, Namibia, Angola
DIRIM [DIR] lang, Nigeria
DIRIN alt for DIRIM [DIR]
DIRIYA alt for DIRI [DWA]
DIRMA alt for TIRMA dial of MURSI [MUZ]
DIRONG-GURUF dial of ZAGHAWA [ZAG]
DIRRIM alt for DIRIM [DIR]
DIRWALI alt for KALAMI [GWC]
DIRYA alt for DIRI [DWA]
DIRYAWA alt for DIRI [DWA]
DISA [DIV] lang, Chad
DISO alt for MARU [MHX]
DISOHA dial of GUMUZ [GUK]

DISPOHOLNON dial of INONHAN [LOC]
DITAMARI alt for DITAMMARI [TBZ]
DITAMMARI [TBZ] lang, Benin
DITAYLIN ALTA alt for ALTA, NORTHERN [AQN]
DITAYLIN DUMAGAT alt for ALTA, NORTHERN
[AQN]
DITTI alt for AFITTI [AFT]
DİU alt for MIEN [YOC]
DIU alt for BOLANGO [BLD]
DIU alt for BILBA-DIU-LELENUK dial of ROTI [ROT]
DIULA alt for JULA [DYU]
DIVEHI alt for MALDIVIAN [SNM]
DIVEHI BAS alt for MALDIVIAN [SNM]
DIVEHLI alt for MALDIVIAN [SNM]
DIVINAI alt for TAWALA dial of TAWALA [TBO]
DIVO dial of DIDA, YOCOBOUÉ [GUD]
DIWALA alt for DUALA [DOU]
DIWINAI alt for TAWALA dial of TAWALA [TBO]
DIXON REEF [DIX] lang, Vanuatu
DIYARBAKIR alt for TIGRANAKERT dial of
ARMENIAN [ARM]
DIYARBEKIR dial of ARABIC, SYRO-
MESOPOTAMIAN [AYP]
DIYARI alt for DIERI [DIF]
DIYI alt for JUKUN TAKUM [JBU]
DIZI [MDX] lang, Ethiopia
DIZI-MAJI alt for DIZI [MDX]
DIZU alt for GIMIRA [BCQ]
DJA alt for DJIA dial of SAKATA [SAT]
DJABUGAI alt for DYAABUGAY [DYY]
DJADHA dial of LENDU [LED]
DJADIWITJIBI dial of DJINANG [DJI]
DJAFOLO dial of SENOUFO, DJIMINI [DYI]
DJAGA alt for CHAGGA [KAF]
DJAIR alt for AGHU [AHH]
DJAKUN alt for JAKUN [JAK]
DJALENDI alt for DHALANDJI [DHL]
DJALLONKE alt for YALUNKA [YAL]
DJAMA dial of IFÈ [IFE]
DJAMALA alt for SENOUFO, DIAMALA [SEB]
DJAMBARBWINGU alt for DJAMBARRPUYNGU
[DJR]
DJAMBARRPUYNGU [DJR] lang, Australia
DJAMBI dial of KUBU [KVB]
DJAMCHIDI alt for JAMSHIDI dial of AIMAQ [AIQ]
DJAMINDJUNG [DJD] lang, Australia
DJANET alt for GHAT dial of TAMAHAQ, HOGGAR
[THV]
DJANG alt for REJANG [REJ]
DJANG alt for ARUEK [AUR]
DJANG BELE TEBO alt for REJANG [REJ]
DJANG LEBONG alt for LEBONG dial of REJANG
[REJ]
DJANGGU alt for JANGGU [DJA]
DJANGGUN alt for DJANGUN [DJF]
DJANGU alt for DHANGU [GLA]
DJANGUN [DJF] lang, Australia
DJANTI alt for TIBEA [NGY]
DJAO alt for YAO [YAO]
DJAPU dial of DHUWAL [DUJ]
DJARAI alt for JARAI [JRA]
DJARRWARK dial of DAYI [DAX]
DJARU alt for JARU [DDJ]
DJARU dial of JARU [DDJ]
DJASING alt for YASING dial of MUNDANG [MUA]
DJAU alt for ENDE dial of ENDE [END]

DJAUAN [DJN] lang, Australia
DJAUL alt for TIANG [TBJ]
DJAWA alt for JAVANESE [JAN]
DJAWALI alt for MANGALA [MEM]
DJAWI [DJW] lang, Australia
DJEDJI alt for FON-GBE [FOA]
DJEEBBANA [DJJ] lang, Australia
DJEM alt for NDJEM dial of KOOZIME [NJE]
DJEMBE dial of BUSHOONG [BUF]
DJERADJ alt for TYARAITY [WOA]
DJERBA alt for JERBA [JEA]
DJERMA alt for DYERMA [DJE]
DJIA dial of SAKATA [SAT]
DJIBO alt for FULFULDE, JELGOOJI [FUM]
DJIDANAN dial of SENOUFO, TAGWANA [TGW]
DJIDJA alt for BOLANO [BZL]
DJIKINI alt for NJININGI dial of TEKE, NORTHERN
[TEG]
DJIME alt for MESME [ZIM]
DJIMI alt for JIMI [JIM]
DJIMI dial of JIMI [JIM]
DJIMINI alt for SENOUFO, DJIMINI [DYI]
DJIMU alt for KOOZIME [NJE]
DJINANG [DJI] lang, Australia
DJINBA [DJB] lang, Australia
DJINGBURU alt for JUNGURU [JGR]
DJINGILA alt for DJINGILI [JIG]
DJINGILI [JIG] lang, Australia
DJIRI alt for LOPA [LOP]
DJIRUBAL alt for DYIRBAL [DBL]
DJIWARLI [DJL] lang, Australia
DJIWE alt for MESME [ZIM]
DJOABLIN dial of ANYIN [ANY]
"DJOEKA" alt for AUKAANS [DJK]
DJOK alt for CHOKWE [CJK]
DJOLOF alt for DYOLOF dial of WOLOF [WOL]
DJONBI alt for ZONGBI dial of PEERE [KUT]
DJONGA alt for JONGA dial of TSONGA [TSO]
DJONGGUNU alt for MONI [MNZ]
DJONGKANG [DJO] lang, Indonesia, Kalimantan
DJONKOR alt for MIGAAMA [MMY]
DJONKOR ABOU TELFANE alt for MIGAAMA [MMY]
DJONKOR BOURMA TAGIL alt for JEGU [JEU]
DJONKOR GUERA alt for MOKULU [MOZ]
DJUDJAN alt for DANGEDL dial of YIR YORONT
[YIY]
"DJUKA" alt for AUKAANS [DJK]
DJULA alt for JULA [DYU]
DJULOI alt for PUNAN dial of DAYAK, LAND [DYK]
DJULOI alt for MURANG PUNAN dial of DAYAK,
LAND [DYK]
DJUWALI alt for MANGALA [MEM]
DJUWARLINY dial of WALMAJARRI [WMT]
DJWARLI alt for DJIWARLI [DJL]
DLI alt for HLAI [LIC]
DLOGO dial of GODIÉ [GOD]
DOA alt for TAUSE [TAD]
DOAN alt for HALANG DOAN [HLD]
DOAYO alt for DOYAYO [DOW]
DOBASE [DOX] lang, Ethiopia
DOBEL [KVO] lang, Indonesia, Maluku
DOBI alt for GOGOT dial of GURAGE, NORTH [GRU]
DOBODURU dial of OROKAIVA [ORK]
DOBU [DOB] lang, Papua New Guinea
DOCHKAFUARA alt for TUYUCA [TUE]
DODA' alt for SARUDU [SDU]

DODINGA dial of TOBELO [TLB]
DODOS dial of KARAMOJONG [KDJ]
DODOTH alt for DODOS dial of KARAMOJONG
  [KDJ]
DOE [DOE] lang, Tanzania
DOFANA dial of SENOUFO, DJIMINI [DYI]
DOGA [DGG] lang, Papua New Guinea
DOGA dial of MIGAAMA [MMY]
DOGAARI alt for DAGAARI, SOUTHERN [DGA]
DOGAARI alt for DAGAARI, NORTHERN [DGI]
DOGARI alt for DOGRI-KANGRI [DOJ]
DOGBA alt for GIZIGA, NORTH [GIS]
DÒGBÓ-GBÈ dial of AJA-GBE [AJG]
DOGHOSE alt for DOGHOSIÉ [DOS]
DOGHOSIÉ [DOS] lang, Burkina Faso
DOGO dial of KALIKO-MA'DI [XKZ]
DOGON [DOG] lang, Mali, Burkina Faso
DOGORINDI dial of OTORO [OTR]
DOGORO [DGO] lang, Papua New Guinea
DOGOSÉ alt for DOGHOSIÉ [DOS]
DOGOSO [DGS] lang, Burkina Faso
DOGOTUKI SAQANI alt for NORTHEAST VANUA
  LEVU dial of FIJIAN [FJI]
DOGRI alt for DOGRI-KANGRI [DOJ]
DOGRI dial of DOGRI-KANGRI [DOJ]
DOGRI JAMMU alt for DOGRI-KANGRI [DOJ]
DOGRI PAHARI alt for DOGRI-KANGRI [DOJ]
DOGRI-KANGRA alt for DOGRI-KANGRI [DOJ]
DOGRI-KANGRI [DOJ] lang, India
DOGRI-KANGRI dial of PANJABI, EASTERN [PNJ]
DOGRIB [DGB] lang, Canada
DOGWA alt for TLOKWA dial of SOTHO, NORTHERN
  [SRT]
DOHE alt for DOE [DOE]
DOHOI [OTD] lang, Indonesia, Kalimantan
DOHOI dial of DOHOI [OTD]
DOI dial of KAILI, LEDO [LEW]
DOI dial of TAI LOI [TLQ]
DOIBEL alt for DOBEL [KVO]
DOK ACOLI alt for ACHOLI [ACO]
DOKA [DBI] lang, Nigeria
DOKA dial of LOGO [LOG]
DOKA dial of MISHIP [CHP]
DOKÁ-POARA alt for TUYUCA [TUE]
DOKHOBE alt for DOGHOSIÉ [DOS]
DOKHOSIÉ alt for DOGHOSIÉ [DOS]
DOKO dial of NGOMBE [NGC]
DOKO-UYANGA [UYA] lang, Nigeria
DOKSHI alt for LUSHI dial of ZEEM [ZUA]
DOKSKAT alt for BROKSKAT [BKK]
DOKWARA dial of OTORO [OTR]
DOLAKHA alt for DOLKHALI dial of NEWARI [NEW]
DOLAN dial of UYGHUR [UIG]
DOLGAN [DLG] lang, Russia, Asia
DOLIKI dial of MOKULU [MOZ]
DOLKHALI dial of NEWARI [NEW]
DOLNA LUZICA alt for WEND, LOWER [WEE]
DOLNA LUZICA alt for LOWER LUSATIAN dial of
  WEND, UPPER [WEN]
DOLOMITE alt for LADIN [LLD]
DOLPA TIBETAN alt for DOLPO [DRE]
DOLPO [DRE] lang, Nepal
DOM [DOA] lang, Papua New Guinea
DOM alt for DOMU [DOF]
DOMA alt for DOMAAKI [DMK]
DOMA alt for ABRON [ABR]

DOMA dial of ALAGO [ALA]
DOMA dial of ANEME WAKE [ABY]
DOMAAKI [DMK] lang, Pakistan
DOMAKI dial of DOMARI [RMT]
DOMARA dial of MAILU [MGU]
DOMARI [RMT] lang, Iran, Egypt, Libya,
  Afghanistan, India, Iraq, Russia, Europe, Syria,
  Turkey
DOMBA dial of MANYIKA [MXC]
DOMBANO alt for ARANDAI [JBJ]
DOMBE alt for NDOMBE [NDQ]
DOMBO alt for BODHO dial of THURI [THU]
DOMDOM alt for GUMAWANA [GVS]
DOMINICA CREOLE dial of LESSER ANTILLEAN
  CREOLE FRENCH [DOM]
DOMINICAN ENGLISH dial of ENGLISH [ENG]
DOMKHOE dial of GANA-KHWE [GNK]
DOMMARA dial of TELUGU [TCW]
DOMO dial of MASANA [MCN]
DOMONA alt for FULFULDE, ADAMAWA [FUB]
DOMPA alt for TOBAKU dial of UMA [PPK]
DOMPAGO alt for LUKPA [DOP]
DOMRA dial of BHOJPURI [BHJ]
DOMU [DOF] lang, Papua New Guinea
DOMUNG [DEV] lang, Papua New Guinea
DONDE alt for VADONDE dial of MAKONDE [KDE]
DONDI dial of POL [PMM]
DONDO [DOK] lang, Indonesia, Sulawesi
DONDO alt for DOONDO [DOD]
DONDONGO dial of MABA [MDE]
DONEGAL dial of GAELIC, IRISH [GLI]
DONG [DOH] lang, Nigeria
DONG [KMC] lang, China
DONG alt for MIEN [YOC]
DONG dial of MUMUYE [MUL]
DONG alt for TRAW dial of CUA [CUA]
DONGA alt for KAMBAATA [KTB]
DONGA alt for DONG [DOH]
DONGA alt for DONGO [DOO]
DONGA dial of JUKUN TAKUM [JBU]
DONGARI alt for DOGRI-KANGRI [DOJ]
DONGAY dial of JAGOI [SNE]
DONGIRO alt for DONYIRO dial of TOPOSA [TOQ]
DONGJOL dial of DINKA, NORTHEASTERN [DIP]
DONGO [DOO] lang, Zaïre
DONGO alt for MBUNDU, LOANDA [MLO]
DONGO dial of KRESH [KRS]
DONGOLA dial of KENUZI-DONGOLA [KNC]
DONGOLA-KENUZ alt for KENUZI-DONGOLA [KNC]
DONGOLAWI alt for KENUZI-DONGOLA [KNC]
DONGOTONO [DDD] lang, Sudan
DONGXIANG [SCE] lang, China
DONYANYO alt for DOYAYO [DOW]
DONYAYO alt for DOYAYO [DOW]
DONYIRO dial of TOPOSA [TOQ]
DONYIRO alt for TOPOSA [TOQ]
DONYORO alt for DONYIRO dial of TOPOSA [TOQ]
DOOHYAAYO alt for DOYAYO [DOW]
DOOKA dial of GBAYA [GYA]
DOOMPAS alt for DUMPAS [DMV]
DOONDO [DOD] lang, Congo
DOOR alt for EASTERN NUER dial of NUER [NUS]
DOOR alt for DOR dial of NUER [NUS]
DOORA alt for NUGUNU [NNV]
DOOWAAYO alt for DOYAYO [DOW]
DOOYAAYO alt for DOYAYO [DOW]

DOOYAYO alt for DOYAYO [DOW]
DOR alt for BONGO [BOT]
DOR dial of NUER [NUS]
DOR dial of CHRAU [CHR]
DOR KOI alt for DORLI [DOL]
DORA alt for DORLI [DOL]
DORA KOI alt for DORLI [DOL]
DORAM alt for DOROMU [KQC]
DÖRBÖD alt for DÖRBÖT dial of KALMYK-OIRAT [KGZ]
DORBOR dial of GBII [GGB]
DÖRBÖT dial of KALMYK-OIRAT [KGZ]
DORDAR dial of NAGA, AO [NJO]
DORHOSIÉ-FINNG alt for DOGOSO [DGS]
DORHOSIÉ-NOIRS alt for DOGOSO [DGS]
DORHOSSIÉ alt for DOGHOSIÉ [DOS]
DORHOSYE alt for DOGHOSIÉ [DOS]
DORI alt for FULFULDE, LIPTAAKO [FUO]
DORIA alt for DHODIA [DHO]
DORI'O [DOR] lang, Solomon Islands
DORIRI alt for MOIKODI [DOI]
DORIRI alt for DORORO [DRR]
DORLA alt for DORLI [DOL]
DORLA KOITUR alt for DORLI [DOL]
DORLA KOITUR alt for CHINTOOR KOYA dial of KOYA [KFF]
DORLA KOYA alt for DORLI [DOL]
DORLI [DOL] lang, India
DORO alt for DOR dial of CHRAU [CHR]
DOROBÉ alt for DOGHOSIÉ [DOS]
DOROBO alt for MEDIAK [MWX]
DOROBO alt for MOSIRO [MWY]
"DOROBO" alt for ARAMANIK [AAM]
"DOROBO" alt for KISANKASA [KQH]
DOROBO dial of GREBO, GLOBO [GRV]
DOROGORI dial of GIDRA [GDR]
DOROMBE dial of OTORO [OTR]
DOROMU [KQC] lang, Papua New Guinea
DOROMU dial of DOROMU [KQC]
DORONG alt for LEBU dial of MORO [MOR]
DORORO [DRR] lang, Solomon Islands
DOROSIE alt for DOGHOSIÉ [DOS]
DOROSSÉ alt for DOGHOSIÉ [DOS]
DOROSSIÉ-FING alt for DOGOSO [DGS]
DOROT dial of GAYO [GYO]
DORPAT alt for TARTU dial of ESTONIAN [EST]
DORRO [DOQ] lang, Papua New Guinea
DORSET dial of ENGLISH [ENG]
DORSHA dial of SHEKO [SHE]
DORZE [DOZ] lang, Ethiopia
DORZINYA alt for DORZE [DOZ]
DOSANGA alt for DOKO-UYANGA [UYA]
DOT dial of DASS [DOT]
DOT alt for KOL dial of CUA [CUA]
DOTANGA dial of BALUNDU-BIMA [NGO]
DOTELI dial of NEPALI [NEP]
DOTT alt for DOT dial of DASS [DOT]
DOU alt for EDOPI [DBF]
DOUALA alt for DUALA [DOU]
DOUDOUMA alt for BUDUMA [BDM]
DOUFOU alt for EDOPI [DBF]
DOUGOUR alt for DUGWOR [DME]
DOUGUIA dial of MALGBE [MXF]
DOUMA alt for DUMA [DMA]
DOUMBOU alt for NDUMU [NMD]
DOUME alt for DEMWA dial of PELASLA [MLR]

DOUMORI dial of KIWAI, SOUTHERN [KJD]
DOUNA dial of TURKA [TUZ]
DOUPA alt for DUUPA [DAE]
DOURA [DON] lang, Papua New Guinea
DOURBEYE dial of FALI, NORTH [FLL]
DOUROU alt for DII [DUR]
DOUROUN dial of MOFU, NORTH [MFK]
DOUTAI alt for TOLITAI [TDS]
DOUVANGAR alt for MOFU, NORTH [MFK]
DOWAYAYO alt for DOYAYO [DOW]
DOWAYO alt for DOYAYO [DOW]
DOYAAYO alt for DOYAYO [DOW]
DOYAU alt for DOYAYO [DOW]
DOYAYO [DOW] lang, Cameroon
DRA alt for KAMBERATARO [KBV]
DRA alt for DIR dial of POLCI [POL]
DRAS alt for ASTORI dial of SHINA [SCL]
DRASI dial of SHINA [SCL]
DREHU alt for DEHU [DEU]
DRIAFLEISUMA alt for MEHEK [NUX]
DRO dial of MALGBE [MXF]
DROMOIS alt for DAUPHINOIS dial of PROVENÇAL [PRV]
DRORI alt for DEORI [DER]
DRUBEA alt for DUMBEA [DUF]
DRUKAI alt for RUKAI [DRU]
DRUKAY alt for RUKAI [DRU]
DRUKHA alt for DZONGKHA [DZO]
DRUKKE alt for DZONGKHA [DZO]
DRUNA alt for NGITI [NIY]
DRUNG [DUU] lang, China
DSCHAGGA alt for CHAGGA [KAF]
DSCHANG alt for YEMBA [BAN]
DSCHANG alt for FOREKE DSCHANG dial of YEMBA [BAN]
DSCHUGHA alt for DZHULFA dial of ARMENIAN [ARM]
DSCHULFA alt for DZHULFA dial of ARMENIAN [ARM]
DU-ROPP-RIM dial of BEROM [BOM]
DUA BOCCOE alt for BONE dial of BUGIS [BPR]
DUAL alt for DHUWAL [DUJ]
DUALA [DOU] lang, Cameroon
DUALA alt for DHUWAL [DUJ]
DUALLA alt for DUALA [DOU]
DUAN alt for HALANG DOAN [HLD]
DUANO' [DUP] lang, Malaysia, Peninsular
DUAU [DUA] lang, Papua New Guinea
DUAU dial of DUAU [DUA]
DUAU PWATA alt for SEWA BAY [SEW]
DUAURU alt for NUMEE [KDK]
DUBALA alt for DUBLA [DUB]
DUBEA alt for DUMBEA [DUF]
DUBER-KANDIA dial of KOHISTANI, INDUS [MVY]
DUBLA [DUB] lang, India
DUBLI alt for DUBLA [DUB]
DUBU [DMU] lang, Indonesia, Irian Jaya
DUBUDURU alt for DOBODURU dial of OROKAIVA [ORK]
DUCLIGAN IFUGAO dial of IFUGAO, BATAD [IFB]
DUDH KHARIA dial of KHARIA [KHR]
DUDI alt for TIRIO [TCR]
DUDI alt for MUTUM [MCC]
DUDJYM alt for DANGEDL dial of YIR YORONT [YIY]
DUDUELA [DUK] lang, Papua New Guinea
DUFF alt for TAUMAKO dial of PILENI [PIV]

DUGARWA alt for DUGURI [DBM]
DUGBO dial of KRUMEN, NORTHEASTERN [PYE]
DUGUN alt for PAPE [NDU]
DUGUNZ alt for DAKUNZA dial of GUMUZ [GUK]
DUGUNZA alt for DAKUNZA dial of GUMUZ [GUK]
DUGUNZA alt for DAKUNZA dial of GUMUZ [GUK]
DUGUR dial of MEREY [MEQ]
DUGURANCHI alt for DUGURI [DBM]
DUGURAWA alt for DUGURI [DBM]
DUGURI [DBM] lang, Nigeria
DUGURILA dial of OTORO [OTR]
DUGUSA alt for DUGUZA [DZA]
DUGUZA [DZA] lang, Nigeria
DUGWOR [DME] lang, Cameroon
DUGWUJUR dial of OTORO [OTR]
DUHTU dial of TSOU [TSY]
DUI alt for DULI [DUZ]
DUI alt for DII [DUR]
DUINDUI alt for NDUINDUI dial of AMBAE, WEST
     [NND]
DUKA [DUD] lang, Nigeria
DUKA alt for KONYAGI [COU]
DUKA-EKOR dial of KAMBERATARO [KBV]
DUKAI alt for RUKAI [DRU]
DUKAIYA dial of OCAINA [OCA]
DUKANCHI alt for DUKA [DUD]
DUKANCI alt for DUKA [DUD]
DUKAWA alt for DUKA [DUD]
DUKE [NKE] lang, Solomon Islands
DUKE OF YORK alt for RAMOAAINA [RAI]
DUKPA alt for DZONGKHA [DZO]
DUKPU [DKU] lang, Central African Republic, Sudan
DUKSHI alt for LUKSHI dial of DASS [DOT]
DUKSLINU dial of SINDHI [SND]
DUKUNA alt for DAKUNZA dial of GUMUZ [GUK]
DUKUNA alt for DAKUNZA dial of GUMUZ [GUK]
DUKUNZA alt for DAKUNZA dial of GUMUZ [GUK]
DUKUNZA alt for DAKUNZA dial of GUMUZ [GUK]
DUKURI alt for DUGURI [DBM]
DUKWA alt for DUKA [DUD]
DULBU [DBO] lang, Nigeria
DULI [DUZ] lang, Cameroon
DULIEN alt for LUSHAI [LSH]
DULIEN dial of LUSHAI [LSH]
DULIIT alt for MALUAL dial of DINKA,
     SOUTHWESTERN [DIK]
DULONG alt for DRUNG [DUU]
DUMA [DMA] lang, Gabon
DUMAKI alt for DOMAAKI [DMK]
DUMARING dial of BASAP [BDB]
DUMBEA [DUF] lang, New Caledonia
DUMBO alt for KEMEZUNG [DMO]
DUMBU alt for NDUMU [NMD]
DUMBULE [MLB] lang, Cameroon
DUMOGA dial of MONGONDOW [MOG]
DUMPAS [DMV] lang, Malaysia, Sabah
DUMPO dial of GONJA [DUM]
DUMPU [WTF] lang, Papua New Guinea
DUMU alt for KAIRI [KLQ]
DUMUN [DUI] lang, Papua New Guinea
DUMUT alt for KAETI [KZH]
DUNA [DUC] lang, Papua New Guinea
DUNG dial of MOKEN [MWT]
DUNGAN [DNG] lang, Kyrghyzstan, Kazakhstan
DUNGARI GIRASIA alt for GIRASIA, RAJPUT [GRA]
DUNGI alt for DUNGU [DBV]

DUNGMALI dial of BANTAWA [BAP]
DUNGRI GRASIA alt for GIRASIA, RAJPUT [GRA]
DUNGU [DBV] lang, Nigeria
DUNJAWA alt for DUNGU [DBV]
DUNJE dial of KABA NA [KWV]
DUNMALI alt for DUNGMALI dial of BANTAWA
     [BAP]
DUNU alt for BATA [BTA]
DUON alt for LÜ [KHB]
DUPA alt for DUUPA [DAE]
DUPANINAN AGTA alt for AGTA, DUPANINAN
     [DUO]
DURAM alt for KORUPUN dial of KORUPUN [KPQ]
DURANGO AZTEC alt for NAHUATL, DURANGO
     [NLN]
DURANI dial of PASHTO, WESTERN [PBT]
DURANMIN alt for SUARMIN [SEO]
DURGA alt for DHURGA [DHU]
DURHAM dial of ENGLISH [ENG]
DURI [MVP] lang, Indonesia, Sulawesi
DURIANKARI alt for DURIANKERE [DBN]
DURIANKERE [DBN] lang, Indonesia, Irian Jaya
DUROP alt for KOROP [KRP]
DURP-BARAZA dial of DASS [DOT]
DURRU alt for DII [DUR]
DURU alt for DII [DUR]
DURUM alt for DOUROUN dial of MOFU, NORTH
     [MFK]
DURUMA [DUG] lang, Kenya
DURUWA [PCI] lang, India
DURVA alt for DURUWA [PCI]
DUSAN alt for DUSUN, CENTRAL [DTP]
DUSNER [DSN] lang, Indonesia, Irian Jaya
DUSNIR alt for DUSNER [DSN]
DUSUM alt for DUSUN, CENTRAL [DTP]
DUSUN alt for DUSUN, CENTRAL [DTP]
DUSUN alt for DUSUN, SUGUT [KZS]
DUSUN BALANGAN dial of MA'ANYAN [MHY]
DUSUN DAYAK alt for RUNGUS [DRG]
DUSUN DEYAH [DUN] lang, Indonesia, Kalimantan
DUSUN MALANG [DUQ] lang, Indonesia, Kalimantan
DUSUN MURUT dial of KENINGAU MURUT [KXI]
DUSUN SEGAMA dial of KINABATANGAN, UPPER
     [DMG]
DUSUN SINULIHAN dial of DUSUN, CENTRAL [DTP]
DUSUN WITU [DUW] lang, Indonesia, Kalimantan
DUSUN, CENTRAL [DTP] lang, Malaysia, Sabah
DUSUN, SUGUT [KZS] lang, Malaysia, Sabah
DUSUN, TAMBUNAN [KZT] lang, Malaysia, Sabah
DUSUN, TEMPASUK [TDU] lang, Malaysia, Sabah
DUSUR alt for DUSUN, CENTRAL [DTP]
DUTCH [DUT] lang, Netherlands, Netherlands
     Antilles, Surinam, Belgium, France
DUTCH CREOLE [DCR] lang, U.S. Virgin Islands,
     Puerto Rico
DUTCH SIGN LANGUAGE [DSE] lang, Netherlands
DUU alt for DUUN [DUX]
DUUN [DUX] lang, Mali, Burkina Faso
DUUNGIDJAWU dial of WAKAWAKA [WKW]
DUUPA [DAE] lang, Cameroon
DUVDE alt for DUVLE [DUV]
DUVELE alt for DUVLE [DUV]
DUVLE [DUV] lang, Indonesia, Irian Jaya
DUVRE alt for DUVLE [DUV]
DUWAI [DBP] lang, Nigeria
DUWAMISH dial of SALISH, SOUTHERN PUGET

SOUND [SLH]
DUWE alt for MURA dial of WANDALA [MFI]
DUWET alt for GUWOT [GVE]
DWALA alt for DUALA [DOU]
DWAN alt for DWANG [NNU]
DWANG [NNU] lang, Ghana
DWAR dial of BIAK [BHW]
DWAT alt for DOT dial of DASS [DOT]
DWELA alt for DUALA [DOU]
DWEMU dial of BOMU [BMQ]
DWERA dial of LIGBI [LIG]
DWINGI alt for DUNGU [DBV]
DYA alt for DYAN [DYA]
DYAABUGAY [DYY] lang, Australia
DYAABUGAY dial of DYAABUGAY [DYY]
DYABARMA alt for DYERMA [DJE]
DYABERDYABER [DYB] lang, Australia
DYABUGAY alt for DYAABUGAY [DYY]
DYAIR alt for AGHU [AHH]
DYAKANKE alt for JAHANKA [JAD]
DYALA alt for BLÉ [BXL]
DYALANU alt for BLÉ [BXL]
DYALONKE alt for YALUNKA [YAL]
DYAMALA alt for SENOUFO, DIAMALA [SEB]
DYAN [DYA] lang, Burkina Faso
DYANE alt for DYAN [DYA]
DYANGADI [DYN] lang, Australia
DYANGIRTE dial of BAMBARA [BRA]
DYANU alt for DYAN [DYA]
DYARMA alt for DYERMA [DJE]
DYE alt for NGANGAM [GNG]
DYEGUEME dial of SERERE-SINE [SES]
DYERAIDY alt for TYARAITY [WOA]
DYERMA [DJE] lang, Niger, Benin, Burkina Faso,
   Nigeria
DYERMA alt for DYERMA [DJE]
DYIMINI alt for SENOUFO, DJIMINI [DYI]
DYIRBAL [DBL] lang, Australia
DYOBA alt for NON [SNF]
DYOKAY alt for RUKAI [DRU]
DYOLA alt for JOLA-FOGNY [DYO]
DYOLOF dial of WOLOF [WOL]
DYONGOR alt for MIGAAMA [MMY]
DYONGOR GUERA alt for MOKULU [MOZ]
DYOULA alt for JULA [DYU]
DYUGUN [DYD] lang, Australia
DYULA alt for JULA [DYU]
DYUMBA alt for AJUMBA dial of MYENE [MYE]
DYUROP alt for KOROP [KRP]
DZA [JEN] lang, Nigeria
DZALAMO alt for ZALAMO [ZAJ]
DZAMA alt for NAFAANRA [NFR]
DZAMBA alt for BANGI [BNI]
DZAMBA dial of BALOI [BIZ]
DZAMBA alt for NZAMBA dial of KONGO [KON]
DZAMBAZI dial of ROMANI, BALKAN [RMN]
DZANDO [DZN] lang, Zaïre
DZANGGALI alt for JANGGALI [JNL]
DZAUI dial of CARÚTANA [CRU]
DZAWI alt for DZAUI dial of CARÚTANA [CRU]
DZAZE alt for PIAPOCO [PIO]
DZEK alt for KRYTS [KRY]
DZEKE alt for NORTHERN BABOLE dial of BABOLE
   [BVX]
DZEM alt for NDJEM dial of KOOZIME [NJE]
DZEMAY alt for FULFULDE, ADAMAWA [FUB]

DZER alt for GULAK dial of MARGHI CENTRAL
   [MAR]
DZHEK alt for KRYTS [KRY]
DZHEK dial of KRYTS [KRY]
DZHEKI alt for KRYTS [KRY]
DZHIDI [DZH] lang, Iran
DZHUDEZMO alt for LADINO [SPJ]
DZHUHURIC alt for TAT, HEBREW [TAT]
DZHULFA dial of ARMENIAN [ARM]
DZHULFA alt for JOLFA dial of ARMENIAN [ARM]
DZHUNYAN alt for DUNGAN [DNG]
DZIBI-DZONGA alt for TSWA dial of TSWA [TSC]
DZIBI-DZONGA alt for TSWA dial of TSWA [TSC]
DZIHANA alt for JIBANA dial of GIRYAMA [NYF]
DZILI dial of JINGPHO [CGP]
DZIMOU alt for KOOZIME [NJE]
DZINDA alt for ZINZA [JIN]
DZING alt for DING [DIZ]
DZIVI alt for TSWA dial of TSWA [TSC]
DZODINKA [ADD] lang, Cameroon
DZONGA alt for JONGA dial of TSONGA [TSO]
DZONGA alt for JONGA dial of TSONGA [TSO]
DZONGA-DZIBI alt for TSWA dial of TSWA [TSC]
DZONGKHA [DZO] lang, Bhutan, Nepal, Nepal
DZONGKHA alt for DZONGKHA [DZO]
DZORGAI dial of QIANG [CNG]
DZOWO alt for LIGBI [LIG]
DZU'OASI alt for KUNG-TSUMKWE [KTZ]
DZU'OASI dial of KUNG-TSUMKWE [KTZ]
DZU/'OÄSI dial of KUNG-TSUMKWE [KTZ]
DZUBUCUA alt for DZUBUKUÁ dial of KARIRI-XUCO
   [KZW]
DZUBUKUÁ dial of KARIRI-XUCO [KZW]
DZUKISH dial of LITHUANIAN [LIT]
DZUMBO alt for KEMEZUNG [DMO]
DZUMDZUM alt for JINGJING dial of BESLERI [HNA]
DZUNA dial of NAGA, ANGAMI [NJM]
DZUNGO [SBE] lang, Burkina Faso
DZUNGO dial of DZUNGO [SBE]
DZUNZA dial of POKOMO, LOWER [POJ]
DZWABO dial of SOTHO, NORTHERN [SRT]
E [EEE] lang, China
E alt for ERE [TWP]
E JE dial of GREBO, E JE [GRB]
E LOKOP alt for SAMBURU [SAQ]
E'DA alt for MANGKI dial of KALUMPANG [KLI]
E-DE alt for RADE [RAD]
EALEBA alt for YALEBA dial of TAWALA [TBO]
EAST ANGLIA dial of ENGLISH [ENG]
EAST AWIN dial of AWIN [AWI]
EAST BAFWANGADA dial of BUDU [BUU]
EAST BANGGAI dial of BANGGAI [BGZ]
EAST BOIKIN dial of BOIKIN [BZF]
EAST BULGARIAN ROMANI dial of ROMANI,
   BALKAN [RMN]
EAST CAPE alt for KEHELALA dial of TAWALA
   [TBO]
EAST CAPE AFRIKAANS dial of AFRIKAANS [AFK]
EAST CENTRAL FRIULIAN dial of FRIULIAN [FRL]
EAST CHACHAPOYAS alt for GRENADA-MENDOZA
   dial of QUECHUA, CHACHAPOYAS [QUK]
EAST CHOISEUL alt for BABATANA [BAQ]
EAST CIRCASSIAN alt for KABARDIAN [KAB]
EAST DANGALEAT dial of DANGALEAT [DAA]
EAST DEVONSHIRE dial of ENGLISH [ENG]
EAST DOGRI dial of DOGRI-KANGRI [DOJ]

EAST ELEMA alt for TOARIPI [TPI]
EAST GIMI dial of GIMI [GIM]
EAST GODAVERI,RAYALSEEMA dial of TELUGU
[TCW]
EAST GORONTALO dial of GORONTALO [GRL]
EAST GREENLANDIC dial of INUIT, GREENLANDIC
[ESG]
EAST GUIZHOU HMONG alt for HMONG, EASTERN
[HEA]
EAST HIGHLAND CHATINO alt for CHATINO,
NOPALA [CYA]
EAST INLAND dial of JIMAJIMA [JMA]
EAST INLAND KAULONG dial of KAULONG [PSS]
EAST KALAMSE alt for KASOMA dial of KALAMSE
[KNZ]
EAST KARA dial of KARA [LEU]
EAST KAREKARE alt for NGWAJUM dial of
KAREKARE [KAI]
EAST KASEM dial of KASEM [KAS]
EAST KHOWAR dial of KHOWAR [KHW]
EAST KOITA dial of KOITA [KQI]
EAST KOMBA dial of KOMBA [KPF]
EAST KONGO dial of KONGO [KON]
EAST LAGOON dial of TRUK [TRU]
EAST LAMAHOLOT dial of LAMAHOLOT [SLP]
EAST LATVIAN dial of LATVIAN [LAT]
EAST LOW GERMAN dial of GERMAN, LOW [GEP]
EAST MAFA dial of MAFA [MAF]
EAST MAKIAN dial of MAKIAN, EAST [MKY]
EAST MAPE dial of MAPE [MLH]
EAST MARSELA alt for MASELA, EAST [VME]
EAST MEKEO dial of MEKEO [MEK]
EAST MORI alt for MORI BAWAH [XMZ]
EAST NDA'NDA alt for UNDIMEHA dial of NDA'NDA
[NNZ]
EAST NEK dial of NEK [NIF]
EAST NUMANGGANG dial of NUMANGGANG [NOP]
EAST NYALA dial of LUYIA [LUY]
EAST OKI-NO-ERABU dial of OKI-NO-ERABU [OKN]
EAST PARANÁ alt for GUANA [QKS]
EAST PUA PRAY alt for LUA' [PRB]
EAST RORO alt for RORO dial of RORO [RRO]
EAST SAKHALIN dial of GILYAK [NIV]
EAST SENTANI dial of SENTANI [SET]
EAST SLOVAKIAN ROMANI dial of ROMANI,
CARPATHIAN [RMC]
EAST SONGAI dial of SONGAI [SON]
EAST SUMBANESE alt for SUMBA [SMI]
EAST SUTHERLANDSHIRE dial of GAELIC, SCOTS
[GLS]
EAST TANNA dial of TANNA, NORTH [TNN]
EAST TORAJA alt for TAE' [ROB]
EAST TORAJA alt for TOALA' [TLZ]
EAST TORRICELLI dial of TORRICELLI [TEI]
EAST TRANGAN alt for TARANGAN, EAST [TRE]
EAST UKRAINIAN dial of UKRAINIAN [UKR]
EAST UMANAKAINA dial of UMANAKAINA [GDN]
EAST URAT dial of URAT [URT]
EAST UREPARAPARA alt for LEHALURUP [URR]
EAST URII dial of URI [UVH]
EAST UVEAN alt for WALLISIAN [WAL]
EAST VALLEY ZAPOTECO alt for ZAPOTECO, EAST
CENTRAL TLACOLULA [ZAW]
EAST VOD dial of VOD [VOD]
EAST WAYLLA dial of QUECHUA, HUANCA,
HUAYLLA [QHU]

EAST YAMBES dial of YAMBES [YMB]
EAST YAWA dial of YAWA [YVA]
EASTER ISLAND alt for RAPANUI [PBA]
EASTERN dial of ROMANI, VLACH [RMY]
EASTERN ABNAKI alt for PENOBSCOT dial of
ABNAKI-PENOBSCOT [ABE]
EASTERN ACIPANCI alt for BOROMA dial of ACIPA
[AWA]
EASTERN ADDASEN dial of ADASEN [TIU]
EASTERN AKA alt for BASESE dial of AKA [AXK]
EASTERN ALEUT dial of ALEUT [ALW]
EASTERN ANGAMI alt for NAGA, CHOKRI [NRI]
EASTERN ARAGONESE dial of ARAGONESE [AXX]
EASTERN ARANDA alt for ARRERNTE, EASTERN
[AER]
EASTERN ARCTIC ESKIMO alt for INUIT, EASTERN
CANADIAN [ESB]
EASTERN ARGENTINA GUARANI alt for GUARANÍ,
MBYÁ [GUN]
EASTERN ARMENIAN dial of ARMENIAN [ARM]
EASTERN ASTURIAN dial of ASTURIAN [AUB]
EASTERN BÉTÉ alt for BÉTÉ, GAGNOA [BTG]
EASTERN BISA alt for BARAKA dial of BISSA [BIB]
EASTERN BOBO OULE alt for BWAMU [BOX]
EASTERN BOBO WULE alt for BWAMU [BOX]
EASTERN BOKYI dial of BOKYI [BKY]
EASTERN BOLIVIAN GUARANÍ alt for CHIRIGUANO
[GUI]
EASTERN BROACH GUJARATI alt for GAMADIA dial
of GUJARATI [GJR]
EASTERN CAGAYAN AGTA alt for AGTA,
DUPANINAN [DUO]
EASTERN CANADIAN ESKIMO alt for INUIT,
EASTERN CANADIAN [ESB]
EASTERN CARIB alt for TYREWUJU dial of KALIHNA
[CRB]
EASTERN CHEPANG dial of CHEPANG [CDM]
EASTERN CHIPPEWA dial of OJIBWA, EASTERN
[OJG]
EASTERN COASTAL CREE alt for CREE, COASTAL
EASTERN [CRL]
EASTERN DINKA alt for DINKA, SOUTHEASTERN
[DIN]
EASTERN DUKA dial of DUKA [DUD]
EASTERN DUVLE dial of DUVLE [DUV]
EASTERN EFATE alt for ETON dial of EFATE, SOUTH
[ERK]
EASTERN EJAGHAM dial of EJAGHAM [ETU]
EASTERN EMILIANO dial of EMILIANO [EML]
EASTERN FIJIAN alt for FIJIAN [FJI]
EASTERN FULANI alt for FULFULDE, ADAMAWA
[FUB]
EASTERN GOE alt for ZOUMOU dial of SAMO [SBD]
EASTERN GUAYMÍ dial of GUAYMÍ [GYM]
EASTERN GUJARI dial of GUJARI [GJU]
EASTERN HAUSA dial of HAUSA [HUA]
EASTERN HUASTECA AZTEC alt for NAHUATL,
HUASTECA, EASTERN [NAI]
EASTERN HUICHOL alt for SAN SEBASTIÁN-SANTA
CATARINA dial of HUICHOL [HCH]
EASTERN INLAND CREE alt for CREE, INLAND
EASTERN [CRE]
EASTERN ISIRAWA dial of ISIRAWA [SRL]
EASTERN JIBBALI dial of JIBBALI [SHV]
EASTERN JIKANY dial of NUER [NUS]
EASTERN KADAZAN alt for KADAZAN, LABUK-

EDO dial of KAILI, LEDO [LEW]
EDOLO alt for ETORO [ETR]
EDOLO ADO alt for ETORO [ETR]
EDOPI [DBF] lang, Indonesia, Irian Jaya
EDULIA alt for BARASANA [BSN]
EDURIA alt for BARASANA [BSN]
EDZU dial of NUPE [NUP]
EENTHLIT alt for NORTHERN LENGUA dial of
    LENGUA [LEG]
EERWEE alt for IRRUAN dial of BOKYI [BKY]
EFATE, NORTH [LLP] lang, Vanuatu
EFATE, SOUTH [ERK] lang, Vanuatu
EFE [EFE] lang, Zaïre
EFE alt for ÉWÉ [EWE]
EFFIUM alt for UFIOM dial of ORING [ORI]
EFFURUN alt for UVBIE [EVH]
EFIFA dial of AKPES [IBE]
EFIK [EFK] lang, Nigeria, Cameroon
EFIRA alt for FILA dial of MELE-FILA [MXE]
EFTAWAGARIA dial of ROMANI, SINTE [RMO]
EFUTOP [OFU] lang, Nigeria
EFUTU alt for AWUTU [AFU]
EFUTU dial of AWUTU [AFU]
EGA [DIE] lang, Côte d'Ivoire
EGBA dial of YORUBA [YOR]
EGBEDA dial of IKWERE [IKW]
EGBEMA dial of IGBO [IGR]
EGBEMA dial of IJO, CENTRAL-WESTERN [IJC]
EGBIRA alt for EBIRA [IGB]
EGBURA alt for EBIRA [IGB]
EGEDE alt for IGEDE [IGE]
EGEJO alt for GEZON dial of PAGABETE [PAG]
EGENE alt for ENGENNI [ENN]
EGEZO alt for GEZON dial of PAGABETE [PAG]
EGEZON alt for GEZON dial of PAGABETE [PAG]
EGGAN dial of NUPE [NUP]
EGGON [EGO] lang, Nigeria
EGHOM alt for OKOM dial of MBEMBE, CROSS
    RIVER [MFN]
EGI dial of OGBAH [OGC]
EGON alt for EGGON [EGO]
EGONGOT dial of ILONGOT [ILK]
EGU alt for IGU dial of EBIRA [IGB]
EGUN alt for GUN-GBE [GUW]
EGWA alt for EGA [DIE]
EH JE alt for GREBO, E JE [GRB]
EHOB MKAA alt for BAKAKA dial of MBO [MBO]
EHODE BELON alt for BALONDO dial of MBO [MBO]
EHOM dial of UKPET-EHOM [AKD]
ÉHOUÉ alt for HWÉ [HWE]
EHOW MBA alt for BAREKO dial of MBO [MBO]
EHWE alt for ÉWÉ [EWE]
EIBE alt for ÉWÉ [EWE]
EIPO alt for EIPOMEK [EIP]
EIPOMEK [EIP] lang, Indonesia, Irian Jaya
EITIEP [EIT] lang, Papua New Guinea
EIVO [EIV] lang, Papua New Guinea
EIWAJA alt for IWAIDJA [IBD]
EJAGAM alt for EJAGHAM [ETU]
EJAGHAM [ETU] lang, Nigeria, Cameroon
EJAHAM alt for EJAGHAM [ETU]
EJAMAT [EJA] lang, Guinea Bissau, Senegal,
    Senegal
EJAMAT alt for EJAMAT [EJA]
EJAR dial of KORO [KOR]
EJINE dial of MONGOLIAN, PERIPHERAL [MVF]

EK NII alt for NII [NII]
EKAGI alt for EKARI [EKG]
EKAJUK [EKA] lang, Nigeria
EKAMA dial of MBEMBE, CROSS RIVER [MFN]
EKAMTULUFU alt for NDE dial of NDE-NSELE-NTA
    [NDD]
EKAMU alt for EKAMA dial of MBEMBE, CROSS
    RIVER [MFN]
EKARI [EKG] lang, Indonesia, Irian Jaya
EKAW alt for AKHA [AKA]
EKBEBE alt for AKEBOU [KEU]
EKEGUSII alt for GUSII [GUZ]
EKELE alt for KELE [KHY]
EKET alt for EKIT [EKE]
EKHINGA alt for MACA [XMC]
EKHIRIT dial of BURIAT, RUSSIA [MNB]
EKI dial of BEBELE [BEB]
EKIBENA alt for BENA [BEZ]
EKIGURIA alt for KURIA [KUJ]
EKIHAYA alt for HAYA [HAY]
EKIKEREBE alt for KEREBE [KED]
EKIKINGA alt for KINGA [KIX]
EKIKIRA alt for SWAGA dial of NANDI [NNB]
EKIKUMBULE alt for KUMBULE dial of NANDI [NNB]
EKIMATE alt for MATE dial of NANDI [NNB]
EKIN alt for SOUTHERN EJAGHAM dial of EJAGHAM
    [ETU]
EKIN alt for SOUTHERN EJAGHAM dial of EJAGHAM
    [ETU]
EKINYAMBO alt for NYAMBO [NYM]
EKIPANGWA alt for PANGWA [PBR]
EKISANZA alt for SANZA dial of KONJO [KOO]
EKISANZA alt for SANZA dial of NANDI [NNB]
EKISHU alt for SHU dial of NANDI [NNB]
EKISONGOORA dial of NANDI [NNB]
EKISWAGA alt for SWAGA dial of NANDI [NNB]
EKIT [EKE] lang, Nigeria
EKITANGI alt for TANGI dial of NANDI [NNB]
EKITI dial of YORUBA [YOR]
EKIYIRA alt for YIRA dial of NANDI [NNB]
EKIZIBA dial of HAYA [HAY]
EKLENJUY alt for CHOROTE, IYOJWA'JA [CRT]
EKLEP alt for AIKLEP [MWG]
EKOI alt for EJAGHAM [ETU]
EKOKA-!XÛ alt for KUNG-EKOKA [KNW]
EKOKOMA alt for MBEMBE, CROSS RIVER [MFN]
EKOMBE dial of BAKUNDU-BALUE [BDU]
EKONDA MONGO dial of MONGO-NKUNDU [MOM]
EKOS-YENABI-MARAGIN dial of KWOMTARI [KWO]
EKOTI alt for KOTI [EKO]
EKPARAGONG dial of NDOE [NBB]
EKPARI [EKR] lang, Nigeria
EKPENMEN alt for UKUE-EHUEN [UKU]
EKPENMI alt for UKUE-EHUEN [UKU]
EKPERI alt for IKWERI dial of NGWO [NGN]
EKPESHE alt for IKPESHI [IKP]
EKPETIAMA dial of IJO, CENTRAL-WESTERN [IJC]
EKPEYE [EKP] lang, Nigeria
EKPON dial of ESAN [ISH]
EKPWO alt for KUO [OKU]
EKUMBE alt for EKOMBE dial of BAKUNDU-BALUE
    [BDU]
EKUMTAK alt for MBE [MFO]
EKUMURU alt for KOHUMONO [BCS]
EKURI alt for NKUKOLI [NBO]
EKWA alt for AKHA [AKA]

EKWARE alt for MPUR [AKC]
EKWE alt for EJAGHAM [ETU]
EL AKHEIMAR alt for AHEIMA dial of NGILE [MAS]
EL AMIRA alt for JEBEL EL AMIRA dial of LAFOFA [LAF]
EL HUGEIRAT [ELH] lang, Sudan
EL MOLO [ELO] lang, Kenya
EL ODEIN dial of ARABIC, YEMENI [ACQ]
EL SALVADORAN SIGN LANGUAGE [ESN] lang, El Salvador
ELAKA alt for AMANAVIL dial of EMAN [EMN]
ELAT dial of BANDA [BND]
ELBASAN-TIRANA dial of ALBANIAN, GHEG [ALS]
ELEKO alt for ILIKU dial of LUSENGO [LUS]
ELEKU alt for ILIKU dial of LUSENGO [LUS]
ELELE dial of IKWERE [IKW]
ELEMBE dial of NKUTU [NKW]
ELEME [ELM] lang, Nigeria
ELEPI [ELE] lang, Papua New Guinea
ELEUTH alt for OLOT dial of KALMYK-OIRAT [KGZ]
ELGEYO alt for KEIYO dial of KALENJIN [KLN]
ELGUMI alt for TESO [TEO]
ELI dial of BANDA [BND]
ELIMBARI dial of CHUAVE [CJV]
ELING dial of TUNEN [BAZ]
ELIP [EKM] lang, Cameroon
ELIRI alt for NDING [ELI]
ELKEI [ELK] lang, Papua New Guinea
ELLICE alt for TUVALUAN [ELL]
ELLICEAN alt for TUVALUAN [ELL]
ELLYRIA alt for LOKOYA [LKY]
ELMOLO alt for EL MOLO [ELO]
ELOG MPOO alt for ADIE dial of BAKOKO [BKH]
ELOMAY alt for BAINOUK [BCZ]
ELOMWE alt for LOMWE [NGL]
ELONG dial of AKOOSE [BSS]
ELOWA dial of LIGENZA [LGZ]
ELOYI [AFO] lang, Nigeria
ELPAPUTI alt for ELPAPUTIH [ELP]
ELPAPUTIH [ELP] lang, Indonesia, Maluku
ELPIRA alt for WARLPIRI [WBP]
ELT ULID dial of GHADAMÈS [GHA]
ELU [ELU] lang, Papua New Guinea
ELU dial of DADIBI [MPS]
ELU-KARA alt for LELE [UGA]
ELUN [ELN] lang, Senegal
ELUNAY alt for BAINOUK [BCZ]
ELUNCHUN alt for OROQEN [ORH]
ELUNG alt for ELONG dial of AKOOSE [BSS]
ELUOSI alt for RUSSIAN [RUS]
ELYUT alt for OLOT dial of KALMYK-OIRAT [KGZ]
EM alt for GARUS [GYB]
EMA alt for KEMAK [KEM]
EMAE [MMW] lang, Vanuatu
EMAI alt for EMAE [MMW]
EMAI dial of EMAI-IULEHA-ORA [EMA]
EMAI-IULEHA-ORA [EMA] lang, Nigeria
EMAKA alt for MACA [XMC]
EMAKHUWANA alt for MAKHUWA-MAKHUWANA [VMW]
EMAN [EMN] lang, Cameroon
EMANE [AMD] lang, Nigeria
EMARENDJE alt for MARENDJE [VMR]
EMAREVONI alt for MAREVONI dial of MAKHUWA [MAK]
EMARLE alt for EMHALHE dial of OKPAMHERI [OPA]

EMAU dial of EFATE, NORTH [LLP]
EMBA alt for HEMBA [HEM]
EMBALOH [EMB] lang, Indonesia, Kalimantan
EMBENA alt for CATÍO [CTO]
EMBENÁ TADÓ alt for TADÓ [TDC]
EMBERA, NORTHERN [EMP] lang, Panama, Colombia
EMBU [EBU] lang, Kenya
EMBU dial of EMBU [EBU]
EMBUDJA alt for BUDZA [BJA]
EME-EME alt for MINANIBAI [MCV]
EMEEJE alt for MEJE dial of MANGBETU [MDJ]
EMEETTO alt for MEDO dial of MAKHUWA [MAK]
EMEREÑON alt for EMERILLON [EME]
EMERILLON [EME] lang, French Guiana
EMERILON alt for EMERILLON [EME]
EMERUM alt for APAL [ENA]
EMETO alt for MEDO dial of MAKHUWA [MAK]
EMETO alt for MEDO dial of MAKHUWA [MAK]
EMFINU alt for MFINU [ZMF]
EMHALHE dial of OKPAMHERI [OPA]
EMILIAN alt for EMILIANO [EML]
EMILIANO [EML] lang, Italy
EMIRA [EMI] lang, Papua New Guinea
EMIRA dial of EMIRA [EMI]
EMIRA-MUSSAU alt for EMIRA [EMI]
EMO RIVER dial of BARAI [BCA]
EMOA alt for MACUNA [MYY]
EMOK [EMO] lang, Paraguay
EMORO alt for LEMORO [LDJ]
EMOWHUA dial of IKWERE [IKW]
EMPAWA dial of JAGOI [SNE]
EMPERA alt for EMBERA, NORTHERN [EMP]
EMPESA POKO dial of LUSENGO [LUS]
EMPLAWAS [EMW] lang, Indonesia, Maluku
EMPUI alt for NAGA, ZEME [NZM]
EMUGHAN dial of ABUA [ABN]
EMUMU [ENR] lang, Indonesia, Irian Jaya
EMVANE SO dial of SO [SOX]
EMWAE alt for EMAE [MMW]
EMWAE ISLAND alt for MAKURA dial of NAMAKURA [NMK]
EMWUIKARI alt for MACA [XMC]
EN dial of VO [WBM]
ENA alt for ENYA [GEY]
ENAHARA alt for NAHARA dial of MAKHUWA [MAK]
ENAWENÉ-NAWÉ alt for SALUMÃ [UNK]
ENCABELLADO alt for SECOYA [SEY]
ENDAGANY alt for GURAGE, INDEGEGN [GIE]
ENDANGEN alt for KOMBIO [KOK]
ENDE [END] lang, Indonesia, Nusa Tenggara
ENDE alt for BARAS [BRS]
ENDE dial of ENDE [END]
ENDE MALAY alt for LARANTUKA dial of MALAY [MLI]
ENDEGEN alt for GURAGE, INDEGEGN [GIE]
ENDEH alt for ENDE [END]
ENDEH alt for ENDE dial of ENDE [END]
ENDEKAN alt for ENREKANG [PTT]
ENDEKAN TIMUR alt for ENREKANG [PTT]
ENDO alt for ENDO-MARAKWET [ENB]
ENDO-MARAKWET [ENB] lang, Kenya
ENDU dial of AMBRYM, SOUTHEAST [TVK]
ENEBY alt for YIDINY [YII]
ENEDEGENY alt for GURAGE, INDEGEGN [GIE]
ENEEME dial of MBEMBE, TIGON [NZA]
ENEEME alt for NAMA dial of MBEMBE, TIGON

[NZA]
ENENGA dial of MYENE [MYE]
ENENLHIT alt for TOBA-MASKOY [TMF]
ENER alt for ENOR dial of GURAGE, PERIPHERAL WEST [GPW]
ENETS [ENE] lang, Russia, Asia
ENEUENE-MARE alt for SALUMÃ [UNK]
ENGA [ENQ] lang, Papua New Guinea
ENGA-KYAKA alt for KYAKA [KYC]
ENGENNI [ENN] lang, Nigeria
ENGGANESE alt for ENGGANO [ENO]
ENGGANO [ENO] lang, Indonesia, Sumatra
ENGGIPILOE alt for DAMAL [UHN]
ENGGIPILU dial of DAMAL [UHN]
ENGLISH [ENG] lang, United Kingdom, Anguilla, Antigua, Bahamas, Barbados, Belize, Bermuda, British Virgin Islands, British West Indies, Canada, Dominica, Falkland Islands, Grenada, Guyana, Honduras, Jamaica, Netherlands Antilles, Puerto Rico, St. Pierre and Miquelon, St. Kitts-Nevis, St. Lucia, St. Vincent and the Grenadines, Surinam, Trinidad and Tobago, USA, U.S. Virgin Islands, Botswana, British Indian Ocean Territory, Cameroon, Ethiopia, Gambia, Ghana, Kenya, Lesotho, Liberia, Malawi, Mauritius, Mozambique, Namibia, Nigeria, Seychelles, Sierra Leone, Somalia, South Africa, St. Helena, Swaziland, Tanzania, Uganda, Zambia, Zimbabwe, India, Gibraltar, Hong Kong, India, Ireland, Israel, Malaysia, Peninsular, Malta, Pakistan, Philippines, Singapore, Sri Lanka, American Samoa, Australia, Belau, Cook Islands, Fiji, Guam, Kiribati, Micronesia, Midway Islands, Nauru, New Zealand, Niue, Norfolk Island, Papua New Guinea, Pitcairn, Samoa, Solomon Islands, Tokelau, Tonga, Vanuatu, Wake Island
ENGLISH alt for ENGLISH [ENG]
ENGLISH ROMANI alt for ANGLOROMANI [RME]
ENGLISH, AMERICAN [EGA] lang, USA
ENGRIAN alt for LOW SAXON dial of GERMAN, LOW [GEP]
ENGUTUK-ELOIKOB dial of MAASAI [MET]
ENHEN alt for UNHUN dial of CURRIPACO [KPC]
ENI dial of OKO-ENI-OSAYEN [OKS]
ENIBURA alt for WAKAWAKA [WKW]
ENIM [ENI] lang, Indonesia, Sumatra
ENIMACA alt for MACA [MCA]
ENIMAGA alt for MACA [MCA]
ENINDHILYAGWA alt for ANINDILYAKWA [AOI]
ENINDILJAUGWA alt for ANINDILYAKWA [AOI]
ENKELEMBU alt for KANUM [KCD]
ENLIT alt for ANGAITE [AIV]
ENMYLINSKIJ dial of CHUKOT [CKT]
ENNA alt for EREI dial of AGWAGWUNE [YAY]
ENNA alt for SINJAI dial of BUGIS [BPR]
ENNAMOR alt for GURAGE, INNEMOR [GII]
ENNEMOR alt for GURAGE, INNEMOR [GII]
ENNEQOR dial of GURAGE, EAST [GRE]
ENOAH dial of EWONDO [EWO]
ENOR dial of GURAGE, PERIPHERAL WEST [GPW]
ENREKANG [PTT] lang, Indonesia, Sulawesi
ENREKANG dial of ENREKANG [PTT]
ENURMIN dial of CHUKOT [CKT]
ENYA [GEY] lang, Zaïre
ENYAU alt for YOKU dial of SIE [ERG]
ENYEMBE dial of ABIDJI [ABI]

ENYONG dial of IBIBIO [IBB]
ENZEB alt for HUNZIB [HUZ]
EOTILE [EOT] lang, Côte d'Ivoire
EPAI alt for IPIKO [IPK]
EPE alt for ELOYI [AFO]
EPENA alt for CENTRAL BOMITABA dial of BOMITABA [ZMX]
EPENA SAIJA [SJA] lang, Colombia
EPERA alt for CATÍO [CTO]
EPERA PEDEE alt for EPENA SAIJA [SJA]
EPIE [EPI] lang, Nigeria
EPIE-ATISSA alt for EPIE [EPI]
EPIGI dial of NDUMU [NMD]
EPINMI alt for UKUE-EHUEN [UKU]
EPWAU alt for ETON dial of EFATE, SOUTH [ERK]
EQUINAO alt for GUANA [QKS]
ER-GWAR alt for ROR dial of PUKU-GEERI-KERI-WIPSI [GEL]
ERA dial of KUMAN [KUE]
ERA RIVER alt for KOPE dial of KIWAI, NORTHEAST [KIW]
ERAANS alt for IDA'AN [DBJ]
ERAI alt for ILIUN [ILU]
ERAKOR alt for EFATE, SOUTH [ERK]
ERAKOR dial of EFATE, SOUTH [ERK]
ERAKWA alt for ERUWA [ERH]
ERANADANS alt for ARANADAN [AAF]
ERAP alt for URI [UVH]
ERAVALLAN alt for IRULA [IRU]
ERAVAS alt for ADIYAN [ADN]
ERAVE dial of DADIBI [MPS]
ERAWA alt for RAWA [RWO]
ERBORE alt for ARBORE [ARV]
ERE [TWP] lang, Papua New Guinea
ERE alt for ERRE [ERR]
ERE dial of KIM [KIA]
EREI dial of AGWAGWUNE [YAY]
EREMAGOK alt for PATAMONA [PBC]
EREMPI alt for REMPI [RMP]
ERENGA alt for SUNGOR [SUN]
ERENGA dial of SUNGOR [SUN]
ERENGA dial of TAMA [TMA]
EREVAN dial of ARMENIAN [ARM]
EREVAN dial of ARMENIAN [ARM]
EREVAN dial of AZERBAIJANI, NORTH [AZE]
EREWA alt for RAWA [RWO]
ERIKBATSA alt for RIKBAKTSA [ART]
ERIKPATSA alt for RIKBAKTSA [ART]
ERIMA alt for OGEA [ERI]
ERITAI alt for BARUA [BAD]
ERIWAN alt for EREVAN dial of ARMENIAN [ARM]
ERLI alt for ARLIJA dial of ROMANI, BALKAN [RMN]
ERMENICE (ERMENI DILI) alt for ARMENIAN [ARM]
ERMENICE alt for ARMENIAN [ARM]
ERMITAÑO dial of CHAVACANO [CBK]
ERMITEÑO alt for ERMITAÑO dial of CHAVACANO [CBK]
ERNGA alt for KORWA [KFP]
EROHWA alt for ERUWA [ERH]
EROKH alt for IRAQW [IRK]
EROKWANAS [ERW] lang, Indonesia, Irian Jaya
EROMANGA alt for SIE [ERG]
ERORUP alt for KOROP [KRP]
ERRAMANGA alt for SIE [ERG]
ERRE [ERR] lang, Australia
ERRONAN alt for FUTUNA-ANIWA [FUT]

ERSARI dial of TURKMEN [TCK]
ERŞE alt for GAELIC, IRISH [GLI]
ERU alt for ALATIL [ALX]
ERU-EU-WAU-WAU alt for URU-EU-UAU-UAU [URZ]
ERUKALA alt for YERUKALA [YEU]
ERUKALA alt for IRULA [IRU]
ERUSU dial of AKOKO, NORTH [AKK]
ERUWA [ERH] lang, Nigeria
ERVATO-VENTUARI dial of SANUMÁ [SAM]
ERWAN alt for IRRUAN dial of BOKYI [BKY]
ERYUAN dial of BAI [PIQ]
ERZENKA alt for KHARBERD dial of ARMENIAN
    [ARM]
ERZERUM alt for KARIN dial of ARMENIAN [ARM]
ERZGEBIRGISCH dial of GERMAN, STANDARD [GER]
ERZINCAN alt for KHARBERD dial of ARMENIAN
    [ARM]
ERZURUM alt for KARIN dial of ARMENIAN [ARM]
ERZYA [MYV] lang, Russia, Europe
ES-SAARE alt for WESTERN DUKA dial of DUKA
    [DUD]
ESA alt for ESAN [ISH]
ESAKA alt for SAKA dial of MAKHUWA [MAK]
ESAKAJI alt for SAKAJI [SKN]
ESAMBI KIPYA alt for WESTERN KALEBWE dial of
    SONGE [SOP]
ESAN [ISH] lang, Nigeria
ESARI dial of TURKMEN [TCK]
ESARI dial of TURKMEN [TCK]
ESARO alt for DURIANKERE [DBN]
ESARY alt for ESARI dial of TURKMEN [TCK]
ESAUN dial of CITAK [TXT]
ESE EJA alt for ESE EJJA [ESE]
ESE EJJA [ESE] lang, Bolivia, Peru, Peru
ESE EJJA alt for ESE EJJA [ESE]
ESE EXA alt for ESE EJJA [ESE]
ESEL dial of BEKWEL [BKW]
ESHIRA alt for SIRA [SWJ]
ESHIRIMA alt for MAKHUWA-NIASSA [VMK]
ESHISANGO alt for SANGU [SBP]
ESHKASHIMI alt for ISHKASHIMI dial of
    SANGLECHI-ISHKASHIMI [SGL]
ESHKASHMI alt for ISHKASHIMI dial of SANGLECHI-
    ISHKASHIMI [SGL]
ESILUYANA alt for LUYANA [LAV]
ESIMBI [AGS] lang, Cameroon
ESIMBOWE alt for MBOWE [MXO]
ESIMBOWE alt for MBOWE dial of LUYANA [LAV]
ESINGEE alt for NGEE dial of TEKE, EASTERN [TEK]
ESIRIUN alt for WATUBELA [WAH]
ESKIMO SIGN LANGUAGE [ESL] lang, Canada
ESKISEHIR dial of TURKISH [TRK]
ESKUARA alt for BASQUE [BSQ]
ESO alt for SO [SOC]
ESPAÑOL alt for SPANISH [SPN]
ESPERANTO [ESP] lang, France
ESPIEGLE BAY alt for MALUA BAY [MLL]
ESSANG dial of TALAUD [TLD]
ESSEL alt for ESEL dial of BEKWEL [BKW]
ESSELE dial of ETON [ETO]
ESSEQUIBO dial of SKEPI CREOLE DUTCH [SKW]
ESSIMBI alt for ESIMBI [AGS]
ESSOUMA alt for ESUMA [ESM]
ESTONIAN [EST] lang, Estonia, Canada, Finland,
    Sweden
ESTONIAN alt for ESTONIAN [EST]

ESTONIAN ROMANI dial of ROMANI, BALTIC [ROM]
ESTRACHARIA dial of ROMANI, SINTE [RMO]
ESTRELLA dial of CABÉCAR [CJP]
ESTREMENHO dial of PORTUGUESE [POR]
ESULALU dial of JOLA-KASA [CSK]
ESUMA [ESM] lang, Côte d'Ivoire
ESUMBU dial of LUSENGO [LUS]
ET-HUN alt for EASTERN DUKA dial of DUKA [DUD]
ET-JIIR alt for JIIR dial of PUKU-GEERI-KERI-WIPSI
    [GEL]
ET-KAG alt for KAG dial of PUKU-GEERI-KERI-WIPSI
    [GEL]
ET-MAROR alt for ROR dial of PUKU-GEERI-KERI-
    WIPSI [GEL]
ET-US alt for US dial of PUKU-GEERI-KERI-WIPSI
    [GEL]
ET-ZUKSUN alt for ZUKSUN dial of PUKU-GEERI-
    KERI-WIPSI [GEL]
ETAPALLY GONDI dial of GONDI, SOUTHERN [GGO]
ETAPALLY MARIA dial of MARIA [MRR]
ETELENA alt for TERÊNA [TEA]
ETHIOPIAN alt for AMHARIC [AMH]
ETHIOPIC alt for GEEZ [GEE]
ETIEN alt for ATEN [GAN]
ETKYE alt for BISSAULA dial of KPAN [KPK]
ETKYWA alt for ICEN [ICH]
ETLA ZAPOTECO alt for ZAPOTECO, SANTO
    TOMÁS MAZALTEPEC [ZPY]
ETLA ZAPOTECO alt for ZAPOTECO, WESTERN
    IXTLÁN [ZAE]
ETNA BAY alt for SEMIMI [ETZ]
ETO alt for GIANGAN [BGI]
ETON [ETO] lang, Cameroon
ETON dial of EFATE, SOUTH [ERK]
ETONO dial of AGWAGWUNE [YAY]
ETONO dial of UBAGHARA [BYC]
ETORO [ETR] lang, Papua New Guinea
ETOSSIO alt for TESO [TEO]
ETSAKO alt for YEKHEE [ETS]
ETSAKOR alt for YEKHEE [ETS]
ETTHWARI alt for MACA [XMC]
ETULO [UTR] lang, Nigeria
ETUNG alt for EJAGHAM [ETU]
ETUNO alt for IGARA dial of EBIRA [IGB]
ETUNO alt for ETONO dial of AGWAGWUNE [YAY]
ETURO alt for ETULO [UTR]
ETYEE alt for TYEE dial of TEKE, WESTERN [TEZ]
EUCHAVANTE alt for OTI [OTI]
EUE alt for ÉWÉ [EWE]
EUPHRATES dial of ARABIC, MESOPOTAMIAN
    COLLOQUIAL [ACM]
EUROPEAN OIRAT alt for KALMYK-OIRAT [KGZ]
EUROPEANIZED HEBREW alt for STANDARD
    HEBREW dial of HEBREW [HBR]
EUSKARA alt for BASQUE [BSQ]
EUSKERA alt for BASQUE [BSQ]
EUSKUARA alt for BASQUE [BSQ]
EUZKADI alt for BASQUE [BSQ]
EVADI alt for VADI dial of GADI-SHINGINI-VADI-
    BAANGI [KAM]
EVAND [BZZ] lang, Cameroon, Nigeria, Nigeria
EVAND alt for EVAND [BZZ]
EVANT alt for EVAND [BZZ]
EVAV alt for KEI [KEI]
EVE alt for ÉWÉ [EWE]
EVEN [EVE] lang, Russia, Asia

EVENKI [EVN] lang, China, Mongolian Peoples
Republic, Russia, Asia
EVENKI alt for EVENKI [EVN]
"EVHRO" alt for UVBIE [EVH]
EVIIA alt for BUBI [BUW]
EVORRA alt for PURARI [IAR]
EVOUZOK dial of EWONDO [EWO]
EVRIE alt for UVBIE [EVH]
EWAGE alt for EWAGE-NOTU [NOU]
EWAGE-NOTU [NOU] lang, Papua New Guinea
EWDOKIA dial of ARMENIAN [ARM]
ÉWÉ [EWE] lang, Ghana, Togo, Togo
ÉWÉ alt for ÉWÉ [EWE]
EWEN alt for EVEN [EVE]
EWENKI alt for EVENKI [EVN]
EWOASE dial of DWANG [NNU]
EWODI alt for OLI dial of DUALA [DOU]
EWONDO [EWO] lang, Cameroon
EWOTA alt for BUBIA [BBX]
EWUMBONGA alt for OFOMBONGA dial of
MBEMBE, CROSS RIVER [MFN]
EWUNDU alt for EWONDO [EWO]
EXTREMADURAN dial of SPANISH [SPN]
EYABIDA alt for CATÍO [CTO]
EYAK [EYA] lang, USA
EYAN alt for DENYA [ANV]
EYE alt for PANARE [PBH]
EZA alt for EZAA dial of IZI-EZAA-IKWO-MGBO [IZI]
EZA alt for EZHA dial of GURAGE, CENTRAL WEST
[GUY]
EZAA dial of IZI-EZAA-IKWO-MGBO [IZI]
EZEI alt for EREI dial of AGWAGWUNE [YAY]
EZEKWE alt for UZEKWE [EZE]
EZELLE alt for JERE dial of JERA [JER]
EZESHIO alt for KAMAKAN [VKM]
EZHA dial of GURAGE, CENTRAL WEST [GUY]
EZO alt for HOKKAIDO dial of AINU [AIN]
EZOPONG alt for OSOPONG dial of MBEMBE,
CROSS RIVER [MFN]
FA D'AMBU alt for ANNOBONESE dial of CRIOULO,
GULF OF GUINEA [CRI]
FA SAPOSA alt for SAPOSA dial of SAPOSA [SPS]
FA' dial of FE'FE' [FMP]
FA'AWA alt for PA'A [AFA]
FA-C-AKA alt for AKA [SOH]
FAAKE alt for PHAKE [PHK]
FAALA dial of KARANGA [KTH]
FAALE-PIYEW dial of TUPURI [TUI]
FABLA ARAGONESA alt for ARAGONESE [AXX]
FABLAS dial of HAITIAN CREOLE FRENCH [HAT]
FACÉ alt for FACEI dial of SULA [SZN]
FACEI dial of SULA [SZN]
FACHARA alt for CARA [CFD]
FADA alt for BIAFADA [BIF]
FADA NGURMA dial of FULFULDE, JELGOOJI [FUM]
FADASHI dial of BERTA [WTI]
FADAWA dial of KANURI, YERWA [KPH]
FADICCA alt for MAHAS-FIADIDJA [FIA]
FADICCA alt for FIYADIKKA dial of MAHAS-
FIADIDJA [FIA]
FADICHA alt for MAHAS-FIADIDJA [FIA]
FADICHA alt for FIYADIKKA dial of MAHAS-
FIADIDJA [FIA]
FADIJA alt for MAHAS-FIADIDJA [FIA]
FADIJA alt for FIYADIKKA dial of MAHAS-FIADIDJA
[FIA]

FADIRO alt for BAMBESHI [MYF]
FADJULU alt for PÖJULU dial of BARI [BFA]
FADJULU alt for PÖJULU dial of BARI [BFA]
FADL dial of ARABIC, SYRO-MESOPOTAMIAN [AYP]
FADYUT-PALMERIN alt for SERERE-SINE [SES]
FAETO dial of FRANCO-PROVENÇAL [FRA]
FAGA-UVEA alt for UVEAN, WEST [UVE]
FAGALULU alt for FAGULULU dial of MOLIMA
[MOX]
FAGANI [FAF] lang, Solomon Islands
FAGANI dial of FAGANI [FAF]
FAGHANI alt for FAGANI [FAF]
FAGNIA alt for FANIA [FAN]
FAGUDU dial of SULA [SZN]
FAGULULU dial of MOLIMA [MOX]
FAIAMA alt for CENTRAL KONO dial of KONO [KNO]
FAIRI dial of BIAK [BHW]
FAISHANG dial of MIYA [MKF]
FAITA [FAT] lang, Papua New Guinea
FAIWOL [FAI] lang, Papua New Guinea
FAIWOLMIN alt for FAIWOL [FAI]
FAJELU alt for PÖJULU dial of BARI [BFA]
FAJELU alt for PÖJULU dial of BARI [BFA]
FAJULU alt for PÖJULU dial of BARI [BFA]
FAK alt for BALOM dial of BAFIA [KSF]
FAKANCHI alt for KAG dial of PUKU-GEERI-KERI-
WIPSI [GEL]
FAKANCHI alt for ROR dial of PUKU-GEERI-KERI-
WIPSI [GEL]
FAKARA alt for CARA [CFD]
FALA alt for FAALA dial of KARANGA [KTH]
FALAHU dial of SULA [SZN]
FALAM alt for CHIN, FALAM [HBH]
FALI alt for LONWOLWOL [CRC]
FALI alt for BANA [FLI]
FALI DU BELE-FERE alt for BELE dial of FALI, SOUTH
[FLE]
FALI DU PESKE-BORI alt for BVERI dial of FALI,
NORTH [FLL]
FALI KANGOU alt for KANGOU dial of FALI, SOUTH
[FLE]
FALI OF MUBI alt for VIN [VIM]
FALI OF MUCHELLA alt for VIN [VIM]
FALI, NORTH [FLL] lang, Cameroon
FALI, SOUTH [FLE] lang, Cameroon
FALI-BELE alt for BELE dial of FALI, SOUTH [FLE]
FALI-BOSSOUM alt for BOSSOUM dial of FALI,
NORTH [FLL]
FALI-DOURBEYE alt for DOURBEYE dial of FALI,
NORTH [FLL]
FALI-TINGUELIN dial of FALI, SOUTH [FLE]
FALL INDIANS alt for GROS VENTRE [ATS]
FALLAM alt for CHIN, FALAM [HBH]
FALOR alt for PALOR [FAP]
FAM [FAM] lang, Nigeria
FAMA-TEIS-KUA dial of KRONGO [KGO]
FAN-FORON-HEIKPANG dial of BEROM [BOM]
FANA alt for FANIA [FAN]
FANAGOLO [FAO] lang, South Africa, Zambia,
Zambia, Zimbabwe
FANAGOLO alt for FANAGOLO [FAO]
FANAKALO alt for FANAGOLO [FAO]
FANEKOLO alt for FANAGOLO [FAO]
FANG [FNG] lang, Equatorial Guinea, Cameroon,
Congo, Gabon
FANG alt for FANG [FNG]

FIOME alt for GOROWA [GOW]
FIOT alt for VILI [VIF]
FIOTE alt for VILI [VIF]
FIOTE alt for WEST KONGO dial of KONGO [KON]
FIOTE alt for WEST KONGO dial of KONGO [KON]
FIOTI alt for WEST KONGO dial of KONGO [KON]
FIPA [FIP] lang, Tanzania
FIRA alt for FILA dial of MELE-FILA [MXE]
FIRAN [FIR] lang, Nigeria
FIRIA dial of YALUNKA [YAL]
FIROZKOHI dial of AIMAQ [AIQ]
FITI alt for SURUBU [SDE]
FITZROY VALLEY KRIOL dial of KRIOL [ROP]
FIU alt for KWARA'AE [KWF]
FIWAGA [FIW] lang, Papua New Guinea
FIYADIKKA dial of MAHAS-FIADIDJA [FIA]
FIYADIKKYA alt for MAHAS-FIADIDJA [FIA]
FIZERE alt for IZERE [FIZ]
FLAAI TAAL alt for FLY TAAL [FLY]
FLAMAND alt for DUTCH [DUT]
FLATHEAD-KALISPEL [FLA] lang, USA
FLEMISH alt for DUTCH [DUT]
FLEO dial of GUÉRÉ [GXX]
FLINDERS ISLAND [FLN] lang, Australia
FLORIDA ISLANDS alt for GELA [NLG]
FLOUP alt for EJAMAT [EJA]
FLOWERED MEO alt for HMONG, WESTERN [HUJ]
FLOWERY alt for HUA dial of HMONG, WESTERN
   [HUJ]
FLOWERY LACHI alt for LIPULIONGTCO dial of LATI
   [LBT]
FLOWERY LISU alt for HUA LISU dial of LISU [LIS]
FLOWERY LISU alt for HWA LISU dial of LISU [LIS]
FLUP alt for EJAMAT [EJA]
FLUVIAL dial of JOLA-KASA [CSK]
FLY TAAL [FLY] lang, South Africa
FO alt for FON-GBE [FOA]
FO alt for SO [SOX]
FO dial of FON-GBE [FOA]
FOAU [FLH] lang, Indonesia, Irian Jaya
FODARA dial of SENOUFO, CEBAARA [SEF]
FOE alt for FOI [FOI]
FOGBE alt for FON-GBE [FOA]
FOGI dial of BURU [MHS]
FOGNY dial of JOLA-FOGNY [DYO]
FOHR-AMRUM alt for FERRING dial of FRISIAN,
   NORTHERN [FRR]
FOI [FOI] lang, Papua New Guinea
FOI alt for IAU [TMU]
FOJA alt for FOYA [FJA]
FOLEPI dial of MUNDANI [MUN]
FOLOPA [PPO] lang, Papua New Guinea
FOMA [FOM] lang, Zaïre
FOMOPEA alt for NGWE [NWE]
FON alt for FON-GBE [FOA]
FON-GBE [FOA] lang, Benin, Togo, Togo
FON-GBE alt for FON-GBE [FOA]
FONDANTI alt for NTII dial of FE'FE' [FMP]
FONDEBOUGOU dial of SENOUFO, TAGWANA
   [TGW]
FONDJOMEKWET alt for MKWET dial of FE'FE'
   [FMP]
FONG dial of EWONDO [EWO]
FONGONDENG alt for NGWE [NWE]
FONGORO [FGR] lang, Sudan
FONI alt for PA'A [AFA]

FONNU alt for FON-GBE [FOA]
FONTEM alt for NGWE [NWE]
FONY alt for FOGNY dial of JOLA-FOGNY [DYO]
FOOCHOW dial of CHINESE, MIN PEI [MNP]
FOOCHOW dial of CHINESE, MIN PEI [MNP]
FOOCHOW dial of CHINESE, MIN PEI [MNP]
FOOCHOW alt for FUZHOU dial of CHINESE, MIN PEI
   [MNP]
FOOCHOW alt for FUCHOW dial of CHINESE, MIN
   PEI [MNP]
FOODO [FOD] lang, Benin, Ghana
FOOLO dial of SENOUFO, DJIMINI [DYI]
FOPO dial of GREBO, FOPO-BUA [GEF]
FORA alt for FUR [FUR]
FORA dial of BALANTA [BLE]
FORABA alt for FOLOPA [PPO]
FORAK [FRO] lang, Papua New Guinea
FORAN alt for WAGI [FAD]
FORCALQUIEREN alt for GAVOT dial of PROVENÇAL
   [PRV]
FORDAT alt for FORDATA [FRD]
FORDATA [FRD] lang, Indonesia, Maluku
FORDATA dial of FORDATA [FRD]
FORDATE alt for FORDATA [FRD]
FORDUNGA alt for FUR [FUR]
FORE [FOR] lang, Papua New Guinea
FOREDAFA alt for MORUNAHUA [MNY]
FOREKE DSCHANG dial of YEMBA [BAN]
FOREST BIRA alt for BILA [BIP]
FOREST CHULUPI dial of CHULUPÍ [CAG]
FOREST ENETS alt for BAY dial of ENETS [ENE]
FOREST YURAK dial of NENETS [YRK]
FORMOSAN alt for SIRAIYA [FOS]
FORMOSAN alt for CHINESE, MIN NAN [CFR]
FORMOSAN alt for TAIWANESE dial of CHINESE,
   MIN NAN [CFR]
FORNIÓ alt for FULNIÔ [FUN]
FOROK alt for FUR [FUR]
FORT YUKON GWICH'IN dial of GWICH'IN [KUC]
FORTA alt for FUR [FUR]
FORTSENAL [FRT] lang, Vanuatu
FOTO alt for NGWE [NWE]
FOTOUNI alt for FE'FE' [FMP]
FOTOUNI alt for TUNGI' dial of FE'FE' [FMP]
FOTUNA alt for WEST FUTUNA dial of FUTUNA-
   ANIWA [FUT]
FOULA alt for LATI [LBT]
FOULA FOUTA alt for FUUTA JALON [FUF]
FOULFOULDE alt for FULFULDE, ADAMAWA [FUB]
FOULSÉ alt for KURUMFÉ [KFZ]
FOUR alt for FUR [FUR]
FOURGOULA dial of SENOUFO, TAGWANA [TGW]
FOUTA DYALON alt for FUUTA JALON [FUF]
FOUTE alt for VUTE [VUT]
FOX dial of MESQUAKIE [SAC]
FOYA [FJA] lang, Indonesia, Irian Jaya
FRAFRA alt for GURENNE [GUR]
FRAFRA dial of GURENNE [GUR]
FRANC-COMTOIS dial of FRENCH [FRN]
FRANÇAIS alt for FRENCH [FRN]
FRANÇAIS ACADIEN alt for FRENCH, CAJUN [FRC]
FRANCO-PROVENÇAL [FRA] lang, France, Italy, Italy
FRANCO-PROVENÇAL alt for FRANCO-PROVENÇAL
   [FRA]
FRANCONIAN alt for MAINFRÄNKISCH [VMF]
FRANKISH [FRK] lang, Germany

FRASE alt for BALANTA [BLE]
FRENCH [FRN] lang, France, Canada, French Guiana,
  Guadeloupe, Haiti, Martinique, Puerto Rico, St.
  Pierre and Miquelon, Algeria, Benin, Burkina Faso,
  Burundi, Cameroon, Central African Republic,
  Chad, Comoros Islands, Congo, Côte d'Ivoire,
  Djibouti, Gabon, Guinea, Madagascar, Mali,
  Mauritania, Mayotte, Mozambique, Niger,
  Reunion, Rwanda, Senegal, Seychelles, Togo,
  Tunisia, Zaïre, Andorra, Belgium, Italy,
  Luxembourg, Monaco, Switzerland, United
  Kingdom, French Polynesia, New Caledonia,
  Vanuatu, Wallis and Futuna
FRENCH alt for FRENCH [FRN]
FRENCH CANADIAN SIGN LANGUAGE [FCS] lang,
  Canada
FRENCH CREE alt for MITCHIF [CRG]
FRENCH GUIANESE [FRE] lang, French Guiana
FRENCH SIGN LANGUAGE [FSL] lang, France, Togo
FRENCH, CAJUN [FRC] lang, USA
FRIES alt for FRISIAN, WESTERN [FRI]
FRIOULAN alt for FRIULIAN [FRL]
FRIOULIAN alt for FRIULIAN [FRL]
FRISIAN, EASTERN [FRS] lang, Germany
FRISIAN, NORTHERN [FRR] lang, Germany
FRISIAN, WESTERN [FRI] lang, Netherlands, USA
FRIULANO alt for FRIULIAN [FRL]
FRIULIAN [FRL] lang, Italy, Slovenia, Slovenia
FRIULIAN alt for FRIULIAN [FRL]
FROUKOU dial of AIZI [AHI]
FRYSK alt for FRISIAN, WESTERN [FRI]
FSL alt for FRENCH SIGN LANGUAGE [FSL]
FTOUR alt for TUR dial of HEDI [TUR]
FU alt for BAFUT [BFD]
FU'DA alt for NGEMBA dial of GHOMALA' [BBJ]
FUCH'YE alt for NUNG [NUN]
FUCHOW dial of CHINESE, MIN PEI [MNP]
FUCHYE alt for NUNG [NUN]
FUGA OF JIMMA dial of YEMSA [JNJ]
FUGAR alt for AVIANWU dial of YEKHEE [ETS]
FUJIAN dial of CHINESE, MIN NAN [CFR]
FUJIAN dial of CHINESE, MIN NAN [CFR]
FUJIAN alt for HOKKIEN dial of CHINESE, MIN NAN
  [CFR]
FUJIANESE alt for FUKIENESE dial of CHINESE, MIN
  NAN [CFR]
FUJUGE alt for FUYUGE [FUY]
FUKAC dial of MAPE [MLH]
FUKIEN alt for FUJIAN dial of CHINESE, MIN NAN
  [CFR]
FUKIEN alt for FUJIAN dial of CHINESE, MIN NAN
  [CFR]
FUKIENESE dial of CHINESE, MIN NAN [CFR]
FUKIENESE alt for HOKKIEN dial of CHINESE, MIN
  NAN [CFR]
FUL alt for FULFULDE, ADAMAWA [FUB]
FUL alt for FULFULDE, JELGOOJI [FUM]
FULA alt for FULFULDE, ADAMAWA [FUB]
FULA alt for LATI [LBT]
FULA FORRO dial of FULACUNDA [FUC]
FULA FULBE alt for FULFULDE, ADAMAWA [FUB]
FULA PETA dial of FUUTA JALON [FUF]
FULA PRETO alt for FULACUNDA [FUC]
FULACUNDA [FUC] lang, Senegal, Gambia, Guinea,
  Guinea Bissau
FULAKUNDA alt for FULACUNDA [FUC]

FULANI alt for FULFULDE, ADAMAWA [FUB]
FULANNARA dial of TU [MJG]
FULATANCHI alt for FULFULDE, ADAMAWA [FUB]
FULBE alt for FULFULDE, ADAMAWA [FUB]
FULBE alt for FUUTA JALON [FUF]
FULBE alt for FULFULDE, MAASINA [FUL]
FULBE alt for FULFULDE, KANO-KATSINA-BORORRO
  [FUV]
FULBE ATAKORA dial of FULFULDE, BENIN-TOGO
  [FUE]
FULBE JEERI [FUA] lang, Senegal, Mali
FULBE-BORGU dial of FULFULDE, BENIN-TOGO [FUE]
FULERO alt for FULIIRU [FLR]
FULFULDE alt for FULFULDE, ADAMAWA [FUB]
FULFULDE JALON alt for FUUTA JALON [FUF]
FULFULDE, ADAMAWA [FUB] lang, Cameroon,
  Nigeria, Chad, Nigeria, Sudan
FULFULDE, ADAMAWA alt for FULFULDE,
  ADAMAWA [FUB]
FULFULDE, BAGIRMI [FUI] lang, Central African
  Republic, Chad, Chad
FULFULDE, BAGIRMI alt for FULFULDE, BAGIRMI
  [FUI]
FULFULDE, BARANI [FUP] lang, Burkina Faso
FULFULDE, BENIN-TOGO [FUE] lang, Benin, Togo,
  Togo
FULFULDE, BENIN-TOGO alt for FULFULDE, BENIN-
  TOGO [FUE]
FULFULDE, GOURMANTCHE [FUH] lang, Burkina
  Faso
FULFULDE, JELGOOJI [FUM] lang, Burkina Faso
FULFULDE, KANO-KATSINA-BORORRO [FUV] lang,
  Nigeria, Cameroon, Chad, Niger
FULFULDE, LIPTAAKO [FUO] lang, Burkina Faso
FULFULDE, MAASINA [FUL] lang, Mali, Côte d'Ivoire,
  Ghana
FULFULDE, SOKOTO [FUQ] lang, Nigeria, Niger
FULIIRU [FLR] lang, Zaïre
FULILWA dial of TUMBUKA [TUW]
FULIRU alt for FULIIRU [FLR]
FULIRWA alt for FULILWA dial of TUMBUKA [TUW]
FULKUNDA alt for FULACUNDA [FUC]
FULLO FUUTA alt for FUUTA JALON [FUF]
FULNIÔ [FUN] lang, Brazil
FULSE alt for KURUMFÉ [KFZ]
FULUKA alt for KUSU [KSV]
FULUNKE dial of MALINKE [MLQ]
FULUP alt for EJAMAT [EJA]
FUMA alt for FOMA [FOM]
FUNAFUTI alt for SOUTH TUVALUAN dial of
  TUVALUAN [ELL]
FUNDI dial of SWAHILI [SWA]
FUNG alt for NI NYO'O dial of TUNEN [BAZ]
FUNGI alt for GULE [GLE]
FUNGOM [FUG] lang, Cameroon
FUNGOR alt for KO [FUJ]
FUNGUR alt for KO [FUJ]
FUNGWA [ULA] lang, Nigeria
FUNGWE dial of TUMBUKA [TUW]
FUNIARA dial of IRARUTU [IRH]
FUNIKA alt for MFINU [ZMF]
FUNJ alt for GULE [GLE]
FUR [FUR] lang, Sudan, Chad
FURA-PAWA alt for EL MOLO [ELO]
FURAKANG alt for FUR [FUR]
FURAN alt for KAMBA [XAB]

FURAWI alt for FUR [FUR]
FURNIÔ alt for FULNIÔ [FUN]
FURSUM dial of MIYA [MKF]
FURU [FUU] lang, Zaïre
FURU alt for BISHUO [BWH]
FURU alt for BIKYA [BYB]
FURU alt for BUSUU [BJU]
FURUPAGHA dial of IJO, CENTRAL-WESTERN [IJC]
FUSAP alt for GHOMALA NORTH dial of GHOMALA'
    [BBJ]
FUT alt for BAFUT [BFD]
FUTA FULA alt for FUUTA JALON [FUF]
FUTA JALLON alt for FUUTA JALON [FUF]
FUTE alt for VUTE [VUT]
FUTU dial of KAMWE [HIG]
FUTUNA, EAST [FUD] lang, Wallis and Futuna, New
    Caledonia
FUTUNA-ANIWA [FUT] lang, Vanuatu
FUTUNIAN alt for FUTUNA, EAST [FUD]
FUUMU dial of TEKE, SOUTH CENTRAL [IFM]
FUUTA JALON [FUF] lang, Guinea, Sierra Leone,
    Guinea Bissau, Mali, Senegal, Sierra Leone
FUUTA JALON alt for FUUTA JALON [FUF]
FUYUGE [FUY] lang, Papua New Guinea
FUYUGHE alt for FUYUGE [FUY]
FUZHOU dial of CHINESE, MIN PEI [MNP]
FUZHOU alt for FOOCHOW dial of CHINESE, MIN PEI
    [MNP]
FUZHOU alt for FUCHOW dial of CHINESE, MIN PEI
    [MNP]
FWA-GOUMAK alt for KUMAK [NEE]
FWÂI [FWA] lang, New Caledonia
FWE alt for WE dial of TONGA [TOI]
FYAM [PYM] lang, Nigeria
FYER [FIE] lang, Nigeria
G!INKWE dial of NHARON [NHR]
G!OKWE dial of NHARON [NHR]
GIWIKWE alt for GWI-KHWE [GWJ]
G'KELENDEG alt for MBARA [MPK]
G'KELENDENG alt for MBARA [MPK]
G//AA alt for G//AAKHWE dial of GANA-KHWE
    [GNK]
G//AAKHWE dial of GANA-KHWE [GNK]
G//ABAKE alt for GABAKE-NTSHORI [GZZ]
G//ABAKE-NTSHORI alt for GABAKE-NTSHORI [GZZ]
G//ABAKETSHORI alt for GABAKE-NTSHORI [GZZ]
G//ANA alt for GANA-KHWE [GNK]
G//ANA-KHWE alt for GANA-KHWE [GNK]
G//ANAKHWE dial of GANA-KHWE [GNK]
G//ANIKHWE dial of GANI-KHWE [GNX]
G//WI alt for GWI-KHWE [GWJ]
G//WIHWE alt for GWI-KHWE [GWJ]
G//WIKHWE alt for GWI-KHWE [GWJ]
GÃ alt for KAANSE [GNA]
GA dial of GA-ADANGME-KROBO [GAC]
GA-ADANGME-KROBO [GAC] lang, Ghana, Togo,
    Togo
GA-ADANGME-KROBO alt for GA-ADANGME-
    KROBO [GAC]
GAALPU dial of DHANGU [GLA]
GAAM [TBI] lang, Sudan, Ethiopia
GA'ANDA [GAA] lang, Nigeria
GAANDA dial of GA'ANDA [GAA]
GAANDU alt for GA'ANDA [GAA]
GAAWRO alt for KALAMI [GWC]
GABA [GAY] lang, Ethiopia

GABADI alt for KABADI [KBT]
GABAKE-NTSHORI [GZZ] lang, Botswana
GABAR KHEL alt for GOWRO [GWF]
GABARO alt for GOWRO [GWF]
GABBRA alt for GABRA dial of OROMO, BORANA-
    ARUSI-GUJI [GAX]
GABERE alt for GABRI [GAB]
GABERI alt for GABRI [GAB]
GABERO alt for EAST SONGAI dial of SONGAI [SON]
GABIANO alt for NIKSEK [GBE]
GABIANO dial of NIKSEK [GBE]
GABIN dial of GA'ANDA [GAA]
GABLAI alt for KABALAI [KVF]
GABLET alt for JIBBALI [SHV]
GABO alt for DIDA, LAKOTA [DIC]
GABOBORA alt for ANUKI [AUI]
GABOU alt for GUBU [GOX]
GABRA dial of OROMO, BORANA-ARUSI-GUJI [GAX]
GABRI [GAB] lang, Chad
GABRI [GBZ] lang, Iran
GABRI-KIMRE alt for KIMRÉ [KQP]
GABRI-NORD alt for TOBANGA [TNG]
GABU alt for GUBU [GOX]
GABU dial of IGEDE [IGE]
GABUTAMON [GAV] lang, Papua New Guinea
GACHIKOLO dial of HALBI [HLB]
GACHITL-KVANKHI alt for GADYRI dial of
    CHAMALAL [CJI]
GADABA [GBJ] lang, India
GADABA [GDB] lang, India
GADAISU alt for SINAKI dial of SUAU [SWP]
GADALA alt for BUWAL [BHS]
GADALA dial of GAVAR [GOU]
GA'DANG [GDG] lang, Philippines
GADANG [GDK] lang, Chad
GADANG alt for WORIMI [KDA]
GADBA alt for GADABA [GBJ]
GADBA alt for GADABA [GDB]
GADBA dial of GADABA [GBJ]
GADDANG [GAD] lang, Philippines
GADDI [GBK] lang, India
GADDYALI alt for GADDI [GBK]
GADE [GED] lang, Nigeria
GADE LOHAR [GDA] lang, India
GADHANG alt for WORIMI [KDA]
GADHAVALI alt for GARHWALI [GBM]
GADHAWALA alt for GARHWALI [GBM]
GADI alt for GADDI [GBK]
GADI dial of GADI-SHINGINI-VADI-BAANGI [KAM]
GADI CHAMEALI dial of CHAMEALI [CDH]
GADI-SHINGINI-VADI-BAANGI [KAM] lang, Nigeria
GADJERAWANG [GDH] lang, Australia
GADJERONG alt for GADJERAWANG [GDH]
GADJNJAMADA alt for ADYNYAMATHANHA [ADT]
GADO alt for KADO [KDV]
GADRE alt for ADELE [ADE]
GADSCHKENE dial of ROMANI, SINTE [RMO]
GADSUP [GAJ] lang, Papua New Guinea
GADSUP dial of GADSUP [GAJ]
GADU alt for KADO [KDV]
GADULIYA LOHAR alt for GADE LOHAR [GDA]
GADUWA [GDW] lang, Cameroon
GADWAHI alt for GARHWALI [GBM]
GADYAGA alt for SONINKE [SNN]
GADYRI dial of CHAMALAL [CJI]
GAE alt for ANDOA [ANB]

GAE dial of GHARI [GRI]
GAEJAWA alt for GEJI dial of GEJI [GEZ]
GAELI alt for KAYELI [KZL]
GAELIC alt for GAELIC, SCOTS [GLS]
GAELIC, IRISH [GLI] lang, Ireland, United Kingdom, United Kingdom
GAELIC, IRISH alt for GAELIC, IRISH [GLI]
GAELIC, SCOTS [GLS] lang, United Kingdom, Canada
GAFAT [GFT] lang, Ethiopia
GAFATINYA alt for GAFAT [GFT]
GAFUKU alt for ALEKANO [GAH]
GAGADU [GBU] lang, Australia
GAGATL dial of ANDI [ANI]
GAGAUZ [GAG] lang, Moldova, Bulgaria, Romania
GAGAUZ alt for GAGAUZ [GAG]
GAGAUZI alt for GAGAUZ [GAG]
GAGE alt for TOLITOLI [TXE]
GAGNOUA-BÉTÉ alt for BÉTÉ, GAGNOA [BTG]
GAGOU alt for GAGU [GGU]
GAGU [GGU] lang, Côte d'Ivoire
GAGUDJARA alt for KARTUJARRA dial of MARTU WANGKA [MPJ]
GAGUDJU alt for GAGADU [GBU]
GAH alt for BATI [BVT]
GAHOM alt for BAHINEMO [BJH]
GAHORE dial of BAGHELI [BFY]
GAHRI alt for BUNAN [BFU]
GAHUKU alt for ALEKANO [GAH]
GAIDASU alt for SINAKI dial of SUAU [SWP]
GAIDIDJ [GBB] lang, Australia
GAIKA dial of XHOSA [XOS]
GAIKUNDI [GBF] lang, Papua New Guinea
GAIKUNTI alt for GAIKUNDI [GBF]
GAIN alt for GA-ADANGME-KROBO [GAC]
GAINA [GCN] lang, Papua New Guinea
GAINA dial of OROKAIVA [ORK]
GAINA dial of GAINA [GCN]
GAIRIN dial of JAPANESE [JPN]
GAJ alt for GANTS [GAO]
GAJ alt for BAJAU, INDONESIAN [BDL]
GAJADILT alt for GAYARDILT [GYD]
GAJARDILD alt for GAYARDILT [GYD]
GAJILA dial of KUNIMAIPA [KUP]
GAJILI alt for GAJILA dial of KUNIMAIPA [KUP]
GAJO alt for GAYO [GYO]
GAJOL dial of BALKAN GAGAUZ TURKISH [BGX]
GAJOMANG alt for TALODI [TLO]
GAKPA alt for LOZOUA dial of DIDA, YOCOBOUÉ [GUD]
GAKTAI alt for MALI [GCC]
GAKVARI dial of CHAMALAL [CJI]
GAL [GAP] lang, Papua New Guinea
GALA dial of MIYA [MKF]
GALAAGU alt for KALARKO [KBA]
GALABA dial of MONO [MNH]
GALAMBE alt for GALAMBU [GLO]
GALAMBI alt for GALAMBU [GLO]
GALAMBU [GLO] lang, Nigeria
GALANCHOG dial of CHECHEN [CJC]
GALAVDA alt for GLAVDA [GLV]
GALAVI alt for BOIANAKI [BMK]
GALCHA alt for TAJIKI [PET]
GALEBAGLA alt for GIL BAGALE dial of SISAALA, TUMULUNG [SIL]
GALEG dial of BILIAU [BCU]

GALEGO alt for GALICIAN [GLN]
GALELA [GBI] lang, Indonesia, Maluku
GALEMBI alt for GALAMBU [GLO]
GALERA dial of NAMBIKUÁRA, SOUTHERN [NAB]
GALESHI dial of GILAKI [GLK]
GALEYA [GAR] lang, Papua New Guinea
GALGADUNGU alt for KALKUTUNG [KTG]
GALGADUUN alt for KALKUTUNG [KTG]
GALI alt for ROINJI [ROE]
GALIBI alt for KALIHNA [CRB]
GALIBÍ alt for KALIHNA [CRB]
GALICE [GCE] lang, USA
GALICIAN [GLN] lang, Spain, Portugal
GALICIAN dial of PORTUGUESE [POR]
GALICIAN dial of ROMANI, CARPATHIAN [RMC]
GALILA dial of AARI [AIZ]
GALIM alt for SUGA [SGI]
GALITS dial of KARAIM [KDR]
GALKE alt for NDAI [GKE]
"GALLA" alt for OROMO, BORANA-ARUSI-GUJI [GAX]
GALLA alt for OROMO, WELLEGA-CENTRAL [GAZ]
GALLAB alt for DAASANECH [DSH]
GALLE GURUNG alt for GHALE [GHE]
GALLEGO alt for GALICIAN [GLN]
GALLER alt for BRU, EASTERN [BRU]
GALLINAS alt for VAI [VAI]
GALLINES alt for VAI [VAI]
"GALLINYA" alt for OROMO, BORANA-ARUSI-GUJI [GAX]
GALLO alt for GALONG [GBH]
GALLOA alt for GALWA dial of MYENE [MYE]
GALLONG alt for GALONG [GBH]
GALLOT dial of FRENCH [FRN]
GALLURESE alt for SARDINIAN, GALLURESE [SDN]
GALO alt for GALONG [GBH]
GALOA alt for GALWA dial of MYENE [MYE]
GALOLE alt for GALOLI [GAL]
GALOLENG alt for TALUR [ILW]
GALOLI [GAL] lang, Indonesia, Nusa Tenggara
GALOLI alt for GALOLI [GAL]
GALOMA alt for AROMA dial of KEOPARA [KHZ]
GALONG [GBH] lang, India
GALOS alt for CHILISSO [CLH]
GALU alt for SINAGEN [SIU]
GALU alt for DIA [DIA]
GALUA alt for GALWA dial of MYENE [MYE]
GALUBA alt for DAASANECH [DSH]
GALUEWA dial of DOBU [DOB]
GALUMPANG alt for KALUMPANG [KLI]
GALUNG alt for PATTAE dial of PITU ULUNNA SALU [PTU]
GALVAXDAXA alt for GLAVDA [GLV]
GALWA dial of MYENE [MYE]
GAM alt for DONG [KMC]
GAM alt for NGAM dial of KWANG [KVI]
GAMA alt for PIRUPIRU dial of BAMU [BCF]
GAMADIA dial of GUJARATI [GJR]
GAMAEWE dial of GIDRA [GDR]
GAMAI alt for BOREI [GAI]
GAMARGU dial of WANDALA [MFI]
GAMARGU alt for WANDALA [MFI]
GAMARI alt for GAWARI [GBO]
GAMATI alt for GAMIT [GBL]
GAMAWA alt for NGAMO [NBH]
GAMBA alt for NGAMBAI [SBA]

GAMBA alt for BELANDA VIRI [BVI]
GAMBADI dial of PEREMKA [PEP]
GAMBAI alt for NGAMBAI [SBA]
GAMBAI dial of TIKAR [TIK]
GAMBAR LEERE alt for ZAAR dial of SAYA [SAY]
GAMBAYE alt for NGAMBAI [SBA]
GAMBERA [GMA] lang, Australia
GAMBERA dial of WUNAMBAL [WUB]
GAMBLAI alt for NGAMBAI [SBA]
GAMBO alt for NAFAANRA [NFR]
GAMBOURA dial of BANA [FLI]
GAMBRE alt for GAMBERA [GMA]
GAMDUGUN dial of BESLERI [HNA]
GAMEI alt for BOREI [GAI]
GAMERGOU alt for GAMARGU dial of WANDALA
 [MFI]
GAMERGU alt for GAMARGU dial of WANDALA
 [MFI]
GAMERGU alt for GAMARGU dial of WANDALA
 [MFI]
GAMETA dial of GALEYA [GAR]
GAMGRE alt for GAMBERA [GMA]
GAMILA [GML] lang, Ethiopia
GAMILARAAY alt for KAMILAROI [KLD]
GAMILAROI alt for KAMILAROI [KLD]
GAMIT [GBL] lang, India
GAMITH alt for GAMIT [GBL]
GAMIYA dial of MIGAAMA [MMY]
GAMKONORA [GAK] lang, Indonesia, Maluku
GAMO [GMO] lang, Ethiopia
GAMO alt for NGAMO [NBH]
GAMO dial of GAMO-NINGI [BTE]
GAMO-NINGI [BTE] lang, Nigeria
GAMOR alt for KAMU [QKY]
GAMTA alt for GAMIT [GBL]
GAMTI alt for GAMIT [GBL]
GAMTI dial of MAWCHI [MKE]
GAMUSO alt for TOKANO [ZUH]
GAN alt for CHINESE, GAN [KNN]
GAN alt for KAANSE [GNA]
GAN alt for BENG [NHB]
GAN dial of BAMBARA [BRA]
GANA [GNQ] lang, Malaysia, Sabah
GANA alt for GAN dial of BAMBARA [BRA]
GANA' alt for GANA [GNQ]
GANA-KHWE [GNK] lang, Botswana
GANAAN dial of KADO [KDV]
GANÁDE [GNE] lang, Botswana
GANAGANA dial of NUPE [NUP]
GANAGAWA alt for GANAGANA dial of NUPE [NUP]
GANALBINGU dial of DJINBA [DJB]
GANAN alt for GANAAN dial of KADO [KDV]
GANANG-FAISHANG dial of IZERE [FIZ]
GANANWA dial of SOTHO, NORTHERN [SRT]
GANAQ alt for GANA [GNQ]
GANATI alt for KENATI [GAT]
GANAWURI alt for ATEN [GAN]
GANCHING dial of GARO [GRT]
GANDA [LAP] lang, Uganda, Tanzania
GANDA alt for GA'ANDA [GAA]
GANDANJU alt for KANJU [KBE]
GANDJU alt for KANJU [KBE]
GANDUA dial of WAWA [WWW]
GANE [GZN] lang, Indonesia, Maluku
GANE alt for KAANSE [GNA]
GANET alt for GHAT dial of TAMAHAQ, HOGGAR

[THV]
GANG alt for ACHOLI [ACO]
GANG alt for PUNAN GANG dial of PUNAN-NIBONG
 [PNE]
GANGA alt for BUSHOONG [BUF]
GANGAM alt for NGANGAM [GNG]
GANGAPARI dial of AWADHI [AWD]
GANGAPARIYA alt for TEHRI [THB]
GANGGAI alt for BAGHELI [BFY]
GANGGALIDA [GCD] lang, Australia
GANGGALITA alt for GANGGALIDA [GCD]
GANGLAU [GGL] lang, Papua New Guinea
GANGOLA dial of KUMAUNI [KFY]
GANGTE [GNB] lang, India, Myanmar, Myanmar
GANGTE alt for GANGTE [GNB]
GANGUELLA alt for NYEMBA [NBA]
GANGULU [GNL] lang, Australia
GANGUM alt for NGANGAM [GNG]
GANI alt for GANE [GZN]
GANI-KHWE [GNX] lang, Botswana
GANJA [BLA] lang, Senegal
GANJA alt for KANDAWO [GAM]
GANJA BLIP alt for GANJA [BLA]
GANJAWLE alt for GANJULE [GJE]
GANJULE [GJE] lang, Ethiopia
GANONGGA alt for GHANONGGA [GHN]
GANSU dial of DUNGAN [DNG]
GANTE alt for GANGTE [GNB]
GANTS [GAO] lang, Papua New Guinea
GANUNG-RAWANG alt for RAWANG [RAW]
GANZA [GZA] lang, Ethiopia
GANZA alt for DAKUNZA dial of GUMUZ [GUK]
GANZA alt for DAKUNZA dial of GUMUZ [GUK]
GANZI [GNZ] lang, Central African Republic
GANZI dial of GANZI [GNZ]
GANZO alt for GANZA [GZA]
GAO [GGA] lang, Solomon Islands
GAO alt for EAST SONGAI dial of SONGAI [SON]
GAPA alt for GAPAPAIWA [PWG]
GAPAPAIWA [PWG] lang, Papua New Guinea
GAPELTA alt for FULFULDE, ADAMAWA [FUB]
GAPIAN alt for GAVOT dial of PROVENÇAL [PRV]
GAPINJI alt for PINJI [PIC]
GAPUN [GPN] lang, Papua New Guinea
GAR dial of BADA [BAU]
GAR alt for MNONG GAR dial of MNONG, EASTERN
 [MNG]
GAR DUGURI dial of DUGURI [DBM]
GARADJIRI alt for KARADJERI [GBD]
GARADYARI alt for KARADJERI [GBD]
GARAGANZA alt for TAKAMA dial of NYAMWEZI
 [NYZ]
GARAKA alt for BADA [BAU]
GARAMA alt for MURRINH-PATHA [MWF]
GARANDALA dial of NGURA [NBX]
GARAP alt for JUMAM dial of KIM [KIA]
GARASIA alt for GIRASIA, ADIWASI [GAS]
GARASIA alt for GIRASIA, RAJPUT [GRA]
GARAWA [GBC] lang, Australia
GARAWA dial of KAPIN [TBX]
GARAWGINO dial of BIDIO [BID]
GARBABI dial of JIBU [JIB]
GARD'ARE alt for KARADJERI [GBD]
GARDENA dial of LADIN [LLD]
GARDUDJARA alt for KARTUJARRA dial of MARTU
 WANGKA [MPJ]

GARDULLA alt for DIRASHA [GDL]
GAREA alt for GALEYA [GAR]
GAREA dial of GALEYA [GAR]
GARHWALI [GBM] lang, India
GARI alt for GHARI [GRI]
GARI alt for GARREH dial of GARREH-AJURAN [GGH]
GARIA alt for SUMAU [SIX]
GARIA dial of KWALE [KSJ]
GARIERA alt for KARIYARRA [VKA]
GARÍFUNA alt for CARIB, BLACK [CAB]
GARKIN dial of LEZGI [LEZ]
GARKO alt for KARKO [KKO]
GARLALI alt for KALALI dial of NGURA [NBX]
GARMALANGGA dial of JARNANGO [JAY]
GARO [GRT] lang, India, Bangladesh
GARO alt for KOTA MARUDU TALANTANG [GRM]
GARO alt for BOSHA dial of KAFA [KBR]
GARO alt for TANDEK dial of KIMARAGANG [KQR]
GAROUA dial of FULFULDE, ADAMAWA [FUB]
GAROUA dial of BATA [BTA]
GARRE [GEX] lang, Somalia
GARRE alt for GARREH dial of GARREH-AJURAN [GGH]
GARREH dial of GARREH-AJURAN [GGH]
GARREH-AJURAN [GGH] lang, Kenya
GARROW alt for GARO [GRT]
GARUA alt for HARUA dial of BOLA [BNP]
GARUH alt for NOBANOB [GAW]
GARUS [GYB] lang, Papua New Guinea
GARUWAHI [GRW] lang, Papua New Guinea
GARWA alt for KALAMI [GWC]
GARWE dial of NDAU [NDC]
GARWI alt for KALAMI [GWC]
GASCON [GSC] lang, France, Spain, Spain
GASCON alt for GASCON [GSC]
GASCON, ARANESE alt for GASCON [GSC]
GASHAN dial of NAGA, TASE [NST]
GASHUA dial of BADE [BDE]
GASHWALI alt for GARHWALI [GBM]
GASMATA [GSA] lang, Papua New Guinea
GATA' [GAQ] lang, India
GATAQ alt for GATA' [GAQ]
GATO alt for KOMSO [KXC]
GATSAME alt for KACHAMA [KCX]
GATUE dial of THARAKA [THA]
GAUA alt for NUME [TGS]
GAUA alt for LAKONA [LKN]
GAUAR alt for GAVAR [GOU]
GAUDI alt for GONDI, NORTHERN [GON]
GAUK alt for GOK dial of DINKA, SOUTH CENTRAL [DIB]
GAUNGTO alt for KAREN, ZAYEIN [KXK]
GAUR KRISTEN dial of TEOR [TEV]
GAURI alt for KAURI dial of JINGPHO [CGP]
GAURI alt for KAURI dial of JINGPHO [CGP]
GAURU dial of MBULA [MNA]
GAUUARI alt for GAWARI [GBO]
GAUWADA alt for GAWWADA [GWD]
GAVA dial of GUDUF [GDF]
GAVAR [GOU] lang, Cameroon
GAVIÃO DO JIPARANÁ [GVO] lang, Brazil
GAVIÃO DO MARANHÃO dial of CANELA [RAM]
GAVIÃO DO PARÁ dial of CANELA [RAM]
GAVIÃO DO RONDÔNIA alt for GAVIÃO DO JIPARANÁ [GVO]

GAVIT alt for GAMIT [GBL]
GAVOKO alt for GEVOKO [NGS]
GAVOT dial of PROVENÇAL [PRV]
GAWA alt for LOUGAW dial of MUYUW [MYW]
GAWAAR alt for THIANG dial of NUER [NUS]
GAWAN NAW' dial of MARU [MHX]
GAWANGA alt for KWANGA [KWJ]
GAWAR alt for GAVAR [GOU]
GAWAR-BATI [GWT] lang, Afghanistan, Pakistan, Pakistan
GAWAR-BATI alt for GAWAR-BATI [GWT]
GAWARI [GBO] lang, India
GAWATA alt for GAWWADA [GWD]
GAWAWA alt for GARAWA dial of KAPIN [TBX]
GAWI dial of MSER [KQX]
GAWIGL alt for UMBU-UNGU [UMB]
GAWIL alt for UMBU-UNGU [UMB]
GAWIR alt for MARIND [MRZ]
GAWRI alt for KALAMI [GWC]
GAWWADA [GWD] lang, Ethiopia
GAYADILT alt for GAYARDILT [GYD]
GAYAM dial of JIBU [JIB]
GAYARDILT [GYD] lang, Australia
GAYE alt for ANDOA [ANB]
GAYEGI dial of GBARI [GBY]
GAYI dial of KPAN [KPK]
GAYI alt for BISU dial of OBANLIKU [BZY]
GAYMONA dial of GBAYA [GYA]
GAYO [GYO] lang, Indonesia, Sumatra
GAZI [GZI] lang, Iran
GAZIANTEP dial of TURKISH [TRK]
GAZILI alt for GAJILA dial of KUNIMAIPA [KUP]
GBA SOR dial of BASSA [BAS]
GBADIE alt for BÉTÉ, GBADI [GBP]
GBADO dial of MBANZA [ZMZ]
GBADOGO alt for KPATOGO [GBW]
GBADOK dial of GBAYA [GYA]
GBAESON dial of KRAHN, WESTERN [KRW]
GBAGA-1 [GGG] lang, Central African Republic
GBAGA-2 [GBX] lang, Central African Republic
GBAGIRI dial of GBAYA [GYA]
GBAGYI [GBR] lang, Nigeria
GBAISON alt for GBAESON dial of KRAHN, WESTERN [KRW]
GBAKA alt for NGBAKA MA'BO [NBM]
GBAKPATILI dial of TOGBO [TOR]
GBAKPWA alt for KPALA [KPL]
GBAMBIYA [GMY] lang, Central African Republic
GBAN alt for GAGU [GGU]
GBANDA alt for AVIKAM [AVI]
GBANDE alt for BANDI [GBA]
GBANDERE alt for GBANZIRI [GBG]
GBANDI alt for BANDI [GBA]
GBANE alt for PERIPHERAL KONO dial of KONO [KNO]
GBANE MAFINDO alt for PERIPHERAL KONO dial of KONO [KNO]
GBANG alt for BEROM [BOM]
GBANMI-SOKUN dial of NUPE [NUP]
GBANRAIN dial of IJO, CENTRAL-WESTERN [IJC]
GBANU dial of GBAYA [GYA]
GBANZILI alt for GBANZIRI [GBG]
GBANZIRI [GBG] lang, Central African Republic, Zaïre, Zaïre
GBANZIRI alt for GBANZIRI [GBG]
GBARA alt for MO'DA [GBN]

GBARANMATU alt for OPOROZA dial of IJO,
    CENTRAL-WESTERN [IJC]
GBARBO dial of KRAHN, WESTERN [KRW]
GBARI [GBY] lang, Nigeria
GBARI MATTAI alt for GBAGYI [GBR]
GBARI YAMMA alt for GBARI [GBY]
GBARZON alt for GBAESON dial of KRAHN,
    WESTERN [KRW]
GBATI-RI [GTI] lang, Zaïre
GBAYA [GYA] lang, Central African Republic,
    Cameroon, Congo, Nigeria
GBAYA dial of GBAYA [GYA]
GBAYA OF BODA dial of GBAYA [GYA]
GBAYA OF BORRO dial of GBAYA [GYA]
GBAYA-DARA dial of KRESH [KRS]
GBAYA-GBOKO dial of KRESH [KRS]
GBAYA-NDOGO dial of KRESH [KRS]
GBAYA-NGBONGBO dial of KRESH [KRS]
GBAYAKA alt for BEKA dial of AKA [AXK]
GBE alt for ÉWÉ [EWE]
GBEA alt for GBAYA [GYA]
GBÉAN alt for SÉMIEN dial of WOBE [WOB]
GBEAPO alt for GBEPO dial of GREBO, E JE [GRB]
GBEDDE dial of YORUBA [YOR]
GBEE alt for GBII [GGB]
GBEE dial of GBAYA [GYA]
GBENDEMBU dial of LOKO [LOK]
GBENDERE alt for YANGO [YNG]
GBENSE alt for CENTRAL KONO dial of KONO [KNO]
GBENYÅSE dial of DOGHOSIÉ [DOS]
GBEPO dial of GREBO, E JE [GRB]
GBERI alt for MO'DA [GBN]
GBESE alt for KPELLE, GUINEA [GKP]
GBESE alt for KPELLE, LIBERIA [KPE]
GBETE dial of MBUM [MDD]
GBEYA alt for GBAYA [GYA]
GBHU alt for NINZAM [NIN]
GBI [GBS] lang, Central African Republic, Zaïre, Zaïre
GBI alt for GBI [GBS]
GBI-DOWLU alt for GBII [GGB]
GBIGBIL alt for BEBIL [BXP]
GBII [GGB] lang, Liberia
GBIRI dial of GBIRI-NIRAGU [GRH]
GBIRI-NIRAGU [GRH] lang, Nigeria
GBLOU GREBO alt for GREBO, GBOLOO [GEC]
GBO alt for LEGBO [AGB]
GBO dial of SENOUFO, TAGWANA [TGW]
GBO dial of KRAHN, WESTERN [KRW]
GBOAO dial of GREBO, FOPO-BUA [GEF]
GBOARE alt for BACAMA [BAM]
GBOATI alt for BATA [BTA]
GBOBO alt for GBOO dial of GUÉRÉ [GXX]
GBOBO alt for GBORBO dial of KRAHN, WESTERN
    [KRW]
GBOFI dial of GBAYA [GYA]
GBOGOROSE dial of DOGHOSIÉ [DOS]
GBOLOO alt for GREBO, GBOLOO [GEC]
GBONGOGBO alt for CENTRAL dial of LIMBA,
    WEST-CENTRAL [LIA]
GBOO dial of GUÉRÉ [GXX]
GBOR dial of BASSA [BAS]
GBORBO dial of KRAHN, WESTERN [KRW]
GBOTE alt for GBATI-RI [GTI]
GBOWE-HRAN dial of KRUMEN, NORTHEASTERN
    [PYE]
GBUHWE alt for LAMANG [HIA]

GBUNDE alt for BANDI [GBA]
GBWATA alt for BATA [BTA]
GBWATE alt for BATA [BTA]
GCIRIKU alt for DIRIKU [DIU]
GE alt for GEN-GBE [GEJ]
GE alt for BEFANG dial of BEFANG [BBY]
GE'EZ alt for GEEZ [GEE]
GEAGEA dial of MAILU [MGU]
GEALEKA dial of XHOSA [XOS]
GEBA alt for KAREN, GEBA [KVQ]
GEBE [GEI] lang, Indonesia, Maluku
GEBETO alt for GOBATO [GTO]
GEBI alt for GEBE [GEI]
GEBI dial of MARIA [MDS]
GEBRA alt for GABRA dial of OROMO, BORANA-
    ARUSI-GUJI [GAX]
GEDAGED [GDD] lang, Papua New Guinea
GEDDEO alt for GEDEO [DRS]
GEDE alt for GADE [GED]
GEDEGEDE dial of AKPES [IBE]
GEDEO [DRS] lang, Ethiopia
GEDEROBO dial of GREBO, GBOLOO [GEC]
"GEECHEE" alt for SEA ISLANDS CREOLE ENGLISH
    [GUL]
GEEDAM dial of DANDAMI MARIA [DAQ]
GEEZ [GEE] lang, Ethiopia
GEG alt for ALBANIAN, GHEG [ALS]
GEGBE alt for GEN-GBE [GEJ]
GEI alt for QI dial of HLAI [LIC]
GEJA alt for NGULU [NGP]
GEJAWA alt for GEJI [GEZ]
GEJI [GEZ] lang, Nigeria
GEJI dial of GEJI [GEZ]
GEK'O alt for KAREN, GEKO [GHK]
GEKHO alt for KAREN, GEKO [GHK]
GEKOYO alt for GIKUYU [KIU]
GEKXUN dial of AGHUL [AGX]
GELA [NLG] lang, Solomon Islands
GELA alt for KELA [KCL]
GELAB alt for DAASANECH [DSH]
GELAKI alt for GILAKI [GLK]
GELAMA dial of MUNDANG [MUA]
GELANCHI alt for JIIR dial of PUKU-GEERI-KERI-
    WIPSI [GEL]
GELANGALI alt for GRANGALI [NLI]
GELAO alt for GELO [KKF]
GELDERSCH alt for LOW FRANCONIAN dial of
    GERMAN, LOW [GEP]
GELE alt for FONGORO [FGR]
GELE' alt for KELE [SBC]
GELEB alt for DAASANECH [DSH]
GELEBA alt for DAASANECH [DSH]
GELEBDA alt for GLAVDA [GLV]
GELEBINYA alt for DAASANECH [DSH]
GELEKIDORIA dial of NAGA, KONYAK [NBE]
GELIK alt for PATPATAR [GFK]
GELILLA alt for ZWAY [ZWA]
GELO [KKF] lang, Viet Nam, China
GELUBBA alt for DAASANECH [DSH]
GELVAXDAXA alt for GLAVDA [GLV]
GEM MUN alt for MUN [MJI]
GEMA alt for GYEM [GYE]
GEMA alt for BLABLANGA [BLP]
GEMASAKUN alt for SUKUR [SUK]
GEMAWA alt for GYEM [GYE]
GEMBANAWA alt for GIBANAWA [GIB]

GEMJEK alt for GEMZEK [GND]
GEMU alt for GAMO [GMO]
GEMU dial of WOLAYTTA [WBC]
GEMZEK [GND] lang, Cameroon
GEN-GBE [GEJ] lang, Togo, Benin
GENAGANE alt for NAGANE [GEN]
GENDE [GAF] lang, Papua New Guinea
GENDEKA alt for GENDE [GAF]
GENDJA alt for LIGENZA [LGZ]
GENDOK dial of KELON [KYO]
GENDZA-BALI alt for LIGENZA [LGZ]
GENE alt for GENDE [GAF]
GENERAL ISRAELI alt for STANDARD HEBREW dial
    of HEBREW [HBR]
GENGE alt for GBAGYI [GBR]
GENGE alt for NGENGE dial of GBAGYI [GBR]
GENGELE dial of SONGOORA [SOD]
GENGLE [GEG] lang, Nigeria
GENNAKEN alt for PUELCHE [PUE]
GENOAN alt for GENOESE dial of LIGURIAN [LIJ]
GENOESE dial of LIGURIAN [LIJ]
GENOGANI alt for NAGANE [GEN]
GENOVESE alt for GENOESE dial of LIGURIAN [LIJ]
GENTOO alt for TELUGU [TCW]
GENYA alt for ENYA [GEY]
GEORDIE dial of ENGLISH [ENG]
GEORGIA dial of SEA ISLANDS CREOLE ENGLISH
    [GUL]
GEORGIAN [GEO] lang, Georgia, Turkey, Iran, Turkey
GEORGIAN alt for GEORGIAN [GEO]
GEPMA KWUDI alt for IATMUL [IAN]
GEPMA KWUNDI alt for IATMUL [IAN]
GERA [GEW] lang, Nigeria
GERAI dial of SEMANDANG [SDM]
GERAL alt for NHENGATU [YRL]
GERAWA alt for GERA [GEW]
GERE alt for GUÉRÉ [GXX]
GEREMA alt for GERUMA [GEA]
GEREP alt for JUMAM dial of KIM [KIA]
GEREZE alt for DACHE [DCH]
GERGERE [GEQ] lang, Ethiopia
GERI dial of GHARI [GRI]
GERKA alt for YIWOM [GEK]
GERKANCHI alt for YIWOM [GEK]
GERKAWA alt for YIWOM [GEK]
GERLOVO TURKS dial of BALKAN GAGAUZ
    TURKISH [BGX]
GERMA alt for GERUMA [GEA]
GERMAN SIGN LANGUAGE [GSG] lang, Germany
GERMAN, HUTTERITE [GEH] lang, Canada, USA
GERMAN, HUTTERITE alt for GERMAN, HUTTERITE
    [GEH]
GERMAN, LOW [GEP] lang, Germany
GERMAN, PENNSYLVANIA [PDC] lang, USA, Canada
GERMAN, STANDARD [GER] lang, Germany, Bolivia,
    Paraguay, Puerto Rico, Austria, Belgium,
    Czechoslovakia, Denmark, Hungary, Italy,
    Liechtenstein, Luxembourg, Poland, Romania,
    Russia, Europe, Slovenia, Switzerland
GERMAN, STANDARD alt for GERMAN, STANDARD
    [GER]
GERRAH alt for YIDINY [YII]
GERSE alt for KPELLE, GUINEA [GKP]
GERUMA [GEA] lang, Nigeria
GERZE alt for KPELLE, GUINEA [GKP]
GESA alt for GESER-GOROM [GES]

GESAWA alt for GUSU dial of JERA [JER]
GESDA DAE dial of BAUZI [PAU]
GESER alt for GESER-GOROM [GES]
GESER-GOROM [GES] lang, Indonesia, Maluku
GESINAN alt for ADARE [HAR]
GETA' alt for GATA' [GAQ]
GETAQ alt for GATA' [GAQ]
GETMATA [GET] lang, Papua New Guinea
GETO dial of GURAGE, PERIPHERAL WEST [GPW]
GETSAAYI alt for TSAAYI dial of TEKE, WESTERN
    [TEZ]
GETSAAYI alt for TSAAYI dial of TEKE, WESTERN
    [TEZ]
GETSOGO alt for TSOGO [TSV]
GEVOKO [NGS] lang, Nigeria, Cameroon
GEWE alt for GEY [GUV]
GEY [GUV] lang, Cameroon
GEZAWA alt for GEJI [GEZ]
GEZAWA alt for GEJI dial of GEJI [GEZ]
GEZON dial of PAGABETE [PAG]
GHAANGALA dial of KONGO [KON]
GHADAMÈS [GHA] lang, Libya, Tunisia
GHAGAR dial of ROMANI, VLACH [RMY]
GHAIMUTA dial of LENGO [LGR]
GHALE [GHE] lang, Nepal
GHAM alt for MEGAKA [XMG]
GHANAIAN SIGN LANGUAGE [GSE] lang, Ghana
GHANGATTY alt for DYANGADI [DYN]
GHANONGGA [GHN] lang, Solomon Islands
GHARA alt for BUNAN [BFU]
GHARDAIA alt for MZAB [MZB]
GHARI [GRI] lang, Solomon Islands
GHARI dial of GHARI [GRI]
GHARTI [GOR] lang, Nepal
GHAT dial of TAMAHAQ, HOGGAR [THV]
GHATI dial of KONKANI [KNK]
GHBOKO alt for GEVOKO [NGS]
GHEG alt for ALBANIAN, GHEG [ALS]
GHEKHOL alt for KAREN, GEKO [GHK]
GHEKHU alt for KAREN, GEKO [GHK]
GHEKO alt for KAREN, GEKO [GHK]
GHELEBA alt for DAASANECH [DSH]
GHETSOGO alt for TSOGO [TSV]
GHIBARAMA alt for BARAMA [BBG]
GHIDOLE alt for DIRASHA [GDL]
GHILZAI dial of PASHTO, WESTERN [PBT]
GHIMARRA alt for GIMIRA [BCQ]
GHISADI alt for TARIMUKI dial of GUJARATI [GJR]
GHODOBERI [GDO] lang, Russia, Europe
GHOL dial of DINKA, SOUTHEASTERN [DIN]
GHOMALA' [BBJ] lang, Cameroon
GHOMALA CENTRAL dial of GHOMALA' [BBJ]
GHOMALA NORTH dial of GHOMALA' [BBJ]
GHOMALA SOUTH dial of GHOMALA' [BBJ]
GHOMARA [GHO] lang, Morocco
GHOND alt for GONDI, NORTHERN [GON]
GHONE dial of VARISI [VRS]
GHORANI alt for SHUGHNI dial of SHUGHNI [SGH]
GHOTUO [AAA] lang, Nigeria
GHUA alt for GHAIMUTA dial of LENGO [LGR]
GHUJULAN dial of PARACHI [PRC]
GHULFAN [GHL] lang, Sudan
GHUMGHUM alt for TABASSARAN [TAB]
GHUNA alt for PIDLIMDI dial of TERA [TER]
GHYE alt for HYA [HYA]
GI/KXIGWI alt for //XEGWI [XEG]

GIA-RAI alt for JARAI [JRA]
GIAHOI alt for DIAHÓI dial of TENHARIM [PAH]
GIAI alt for NHANG [NHA]
GIAMBA alt for NGIYAMBAA dial of
    WANGAAYBUWAN-NGIYAMBAA [WYB]
GIANG alt for NHANG [NHA]
GIANG dial of NUNG [NUT]
GIANG RAY alt for TRIENG [STG]
GIANGAN [BGI] lang, Philippines
GIANYAR alt for LOWLAND BALI dial of BALI [BZC]
GIÁY alt for NHANG [NHA]
GIBAIO alt for KIWAI, NORTHEAST [KIW]
GIBAIO dial of KIWAI, NORTHEAST [KIW]
GIBANAWA [GIB] lang, Nigeria
GIBARAMA alt for BARAMA [BBG]
GIBARIO dial of KEREWO [KXZ]
GICHODE alt for GIKYODE [ACD]
GICHUGU dial of GIKUYU [KIU]
GIDABAL alt for BANDJALANG [BDY]
GIDABAL dial of BANDJALANG [BDY]
GIDAR [GID] lang, Cameroon, Chad, Chad
GIDAR alt for GIDAR [GID]
GIDDER alt for GIDAR [GID]
GIDERE alt for ADELE [ADE]
GIDGID alt for BADE [BDE]
GIDICCHO alt for GIDICHO dial of KOORETE [KQY]
GIDICHO dial of KOORETE [KQY]
GIDJA alt for KITJA [GIA]
GIDOLE alt for DIRASHA [GDL]
GIDOLINYA alt for DIRASHA [GDL]
GIDRA [GDR] lang, Papua New Guinea
GIDRE alt for ADELE [ADE]
GIE alt for JEH [JEH]
GIE-TRIENG alt for TRIENG [STG]
GIELI [BCB] lang, Cameroon, Gabon
GIETA alt for GETO dial of GURAGE, PERIPHERAL
    WEST [GPW]
GIGATL dial of CHAMALAL [CJI]
GIGIKUYU alt for GIKUYU [KIU]
GIHA alt for HA [HAQ]
GIIWO [KKS] lang, Nigeria
GIJOW alt for YIDINY [YII]
GIKLSAN alt for GITKSIAN dial of NASS-GITKSIAN
    [NCG]
GIKOLODJYA dial of ANII [BLO]
GIKUYU [KIU] lang, Kenya
GIKYODE [ACD] lang, Ghana
GIL BAGALE dial of SISAALA, TUMULUNG [SIL]
GILAKI [GLK] lang, Iran
GILANI alt for GILAKI [GLK]
GILBAGALA dial of PASAALA [SIG]
GILBERTESE alt for KIRIBATI [GLB]
GILEMPLA dial of ANII [BLO]
GILGIT alt for GILGITI dial of SHINA [SCL]
GILGITI dial of SHINA [SCL]
GILI dial of BANA [FLI]
GILI alt for GUILI dial of BANA [FLI]
GILIKA [GIK] lang, Indonesia, Irian Jaya
GILIMA [GIX] lang, Zaïre
GILIPANES alt for IFUGAO, TUWALI [IFK]
GILLAH alt for YIDINY [YII]
GILYAK [NIV] lang, Russia, Asia
GIMAN alt for GANE [GZN]
GIMARAS alt for GUIMARAS ISLAND dial of
    KINARAY-A [KRJ]
GIMARRA alt for GIMIRA [BCQ]

GIMBA dial of SAGALLA [TGA]
GIMBAAMA alt for MBAMA [MBM]
GIMBALA alt for MBALA [MDP]
GIMBANAWA alt for GIBANAWA [GIB]
GIMBE alt for GIMNIME [KMB]
GIMBUNDA alt for MBUNDA [MCK]
GIMBUNDA alt for MPUUN dial of MPUONO [ZMP]
GIMI [GIM] lang, Papua New Guinea
GIMI [GIP] lang, Papua New Guinea
GIMIRA [BCQ] lang, Ethiopia
GIMMA alt for GIMME [KMP]
GIMME [KMP] lang, Cameroon
GIMMIRA alt for GIMIRA [BCQ]
GIMNIME [KMB] lang, Cameroon
GIMR dial of TAMA [TMA]
GIMR dial of TAMA [TMA]
GIMSBOK NAMA [GEM] lang, South Africa
GIN alt for VIETNAMESE [VIE]
GIN dial of KORYAK [KPY]
GINABWAL alt for GA'DANG [GDG]
GINAOUROU dial of NATIORO [NTI]
GINGA alt for NJINGA dial of MBUNDU, LOANDA
    [MLO]
GINGWAK dial of JARAWA [JAR]
GINUKH alt for HINUKH [GIN]
GINUKHTSY alt for HINUKH [GIN]
GINUMAN [GNM] lang, Papua New Guinea
GINUX alt for HINUKH [GIN]
GINYAMUNYINGANYI dial of NYATURU [RIM]
GIO alt for DAN [DAF]
GIO-DAN alt for DAN [DAF]
GIO-LANG alt for JOLONG dial of BAHNAR [BDQ]
GIONG alt for BAYUNGU [BXJ]
GIPENDE alt for PHENDE [PEM]
GIPHENDE alt for PHENDE [PEM]
GIRA [GRG] lang, Papua New Guinea
GIRANGO dial of ZANAKI [ZAK]
GIRASIA, ADIWASI [GAS] lang, India
GIRASIA, RAJPUT [GRA] lang, India
GIRAWA [BBR] lang, Papua New Guinea
GIRE alt for KIRE [GEB]
GIRGA dial of SUNGOR [SUN]
GIRI alt for KIRE [GEB]
GIRIAMA alt for GIRYAMA [NYF]
GIRIWE alt for YREWE dial of KRUMEN,
    NORTHEASTERN [PYE]
GIRONGA alt for RONGA [RON]
GIRWALI alt for GARHWALI [GBM]
GIRWANA dial of NYATURU [RIM]
GIRYAMA [NYF] lang, Kenya
GIRYAMA alt for GIRYAMA [NYF]
GISAMJANG alt for KISAMAJENG dial of DATOGA
    [TCC]
GISAMJANGA alt for KISAMAJENG dial of DATOGA
    [TCC]
GISEDA dial of ANII [BLO]
GISÈME dial of AKPE [AQP]
GISEWI alt for SEWI dial of TONGA [TOH]
GISEY alt for GIZAY dial of MASANA [MCN]
GISHU alt for LUGISU dial of MASABA [MYX]
GISI alt for KISSI, SOUTHERN [KSS]
GISIDA alt for ANII [BLO]
GISIGA alt for GIZIGA, NORTH [GIS]
GISIGA alt for GIZIGA, SOUTH [GIZ]
GISIKA alt for GIZIGA, NORTH [GIS]
GISIKA alt for GIZIGA, SOUTH [GIZ]

GISIRA alt for SIRA [SWJ]
GISSI alt for KISSI, SOUTHERN [KSS]
GISU alt for MASABA [MYX]
GITANO alt for ROMANI, CALO [RMR]
GITKSAN alt for GITKSIAN dial of NASS-GITKSIAN [NCG]
GITKSIAN dial of NASS-GITKSIAN [NCG]
GITOA alt for GITUA [GIL]
GITONGA alt for TONGA [TOH]
GITONGA GY KHOGANI dial of TONGA [TOH]
GITUA [GIL] lang, Papua New Guinea
GITYSKYAN alt for GITKSIAN dial of NASS-GITKSIAN [NCG]
GIUR alt for LUWO [LWO]
GIVEROM alt for GWORAM dial of KOFYAR [KWL]
GIYUG [GIY] lang, Australia
GIZAY dial of MASANA [MCN]
GIZAY dial of MASANA [MCN]
GIZI alt for KISSI, SOUTHERN [KSS]
GIZI alt for KISSI, NORTHERN [KQS]
GIZIGA DE MAROUA alt for GIZIGA, NORTH [GIS]
GIZIGA DE MIDJIVIN alt for MI MIJIVIN dial of GIZIGA, SOUTH [GIZ]
GIZIGA DE MOUTOUROUA alt for MUTURAMI dial of GIZIGA, SOUTH [GIZ]
GIZIGA, NORTH [GIS] lang, Cameroon
GIZIGA, SOUTH [GIZ] lang, Cameroon
GIZIMA dial of LOMA [LOM]
GIZRA [TOF] lang, Papua New Guinea
GJUNEJ dial of LEZGI [LEZ]
GLANDA alt for GLAVDA [GLV]
GLANDA-KHWE alt for XUN [XUU]
GLARO dial of GLARO-TWABO [GLR]
GLARO-TWABO [GLR] lang, Liberia
GLAVDA [GLV] lang, Nigeria, Cameroon
GLAVDA dial of GLAVDA [GLV]
GLAWLO dial of KRUMEN, SOUTHERN [TED]
GLIBEWA dial of GODIÉ [GOD]
GLIO alt for GLIO-OUBI [OUB]
GLIO-OUBI [OUB] lang, Liberia, Côte d'Ivoire
GLOBO dial of GREBO, GLOBO [GRV]
GNALLUMA alt for NGARLUMA [NRL]
GNALOUMA alt for NGARLUMA [NRL]
GNAMEI alt for NAGA, ANGAMI [NJM]
GNAMO alt for NYAMAL [NLY]
GNAU [GNU] lang, Papua New Guinea
GNI alt for YI, SICHUAN [III]
GNI alt for YI, YUNNAN [NOS]
GNIVO alt for AYIWO [NFL]
GNOORE dial of MUMUYE [MUL]
GNORMBUR alt for NGURMBUR [NRX]
GNUMBU alt for NGURMBUR [NRX]
GOA alt for MAKASSAR [MSR]
GOA alt for GOWA dial of MAKASSAR [MSR]
GOAHIBO alt for GUAHIBO [GUH]
GOAHIVA alt for GUAHIBO [GUH]
GOAJIRO alt for GUAJIRO [GUC]
GOAN alt for KONKANI, GOANESE [GOM]
GOANESE alt for KONKANI, GOANESE [GOM]
GOANESE alt for STANDARD KONKANI dial of KONKANI, GOANESE [GOM]
GOARI alt for GAWARI [GBO]
GOARIBARI alt for GIBARIO dial of KEREWO [KXZ]
GOBA alt for NGWABA [NGW]
GOBA alt for KOREKORE dial of SHONA [SHD]
GOBA alt for KOREKORE dial of SHONA [SHD]

GOBABINGO alt for GUPAPUYNGU [GUF]
GOBASI [GOI] lang, Papua New Guinea
GOBATO [GTO] lang, Ethiopia
GOBEYO alt for LONGTO [WOK]
GOBEZE alt for DOBASE [DOX]
GOBLA alt for MANAGOBLA dial of GOLA [GOL]
GOBU alt for GUBU [GOX]
GOBUGDUA alt for SISIBNA dial of KORUPUN [KPQ]
GODAULI alt for GARHWALI [GBM]
GODAVARI KOYA alt for JAGANATHAPURAM KOYA dial of KOYA [KFF]
GODE alt for GADE [GED]
GODI alt for GONDI, NORTHERN [GON]
GODIÉ [GOD] lang, Côte d'Ivoire
GODOBERI alt for GHODOBERI [GDO]
GODOBERIN alt for GHODOBERI [GDO]
GODWANI dial of BAGHELI [BFY]
GODYE alt for GODIÉ [GOD]
GOEMAI [ANK] lang, Nigeria
GOFA dial of WOLAYTTA [WBC]
GOG alt for LAKONA [LKN]
GOGGOT alt for GOGOT dial of GURAGE, NORTH [GRU]
GOGO [GOG] lang, Tanzania
GOGODALA [GOH] lang, Papua New Guinea
GOGODARA alt for GOGODALA [GOH]
GOGOT dial of GURAGE, NORTH [GRU]
GOGRI alt for GUJARI [GJU]
GOGULICH alt for MANSI [MNS]
GOGWAMA alt for KOMA, NORTH [KMQ]
GOHAR-HERKERI alt for LAMANI [LMN]
GOHILWADI alt for KATHIYAWADI dial of GUJARATI [GJR]
GOI alt for BLABLANGA [BLP]
GOIALA dial of IDUNA [VIV]
GOJAL dial of WAKHI [WBL]
GOJARI alt for GUJARI [GJU]
GOJRI alt for GUJARI [GJU]
GOK dial of DINKA, SOUTH CENTRAL [DIB]
GOKANA [GKN] lang, Nigeria
GOKLAN alt for GOKLEN dial of TURKMEN [TCK]
GOKLEN dial of TURKMEN [TCK]
GOKLEN dial of TURKMEN [TCK]
GOKWOM alt for KOMA, CENTRAL [KOM]
GOLA [GOL] lang, Liberia, Sierra Leone, Sierra Leone
GOLA alt for GOLA [GOL]
GOLA alt for BADYARA [PBP]
GOLA dial of MUMUYE [MUL]
GOLAR dial of JARAI [JRA]
GOLAR dial of BAHNAR [BDQ]
GOLARI dial of TELUGU [TCW]
GOLARI-KANNADA alt for HOLIYA [HOY]
GOLD alt for NANAI [GLD]
GOLDEN PALAUNG alt for PALAUNG, SHWE [SWE]
GOLDI alt for NANAI [GLD]
GOLIATH alt for UNA [MTG]
GOLIN [GVF] lang, Papua New Guinea
GOLIN dial of GOLIN [GVF]
GOLLANGO [GOV] lang, Ethiopia
GOLLUM alt for GOLIN [GVF]
GOLO [GYC] lang, Sudan
GOLOG [GOC] lang, China
GOLUMALA dial of DHANGU [GLA]
GOMA alt for KOMA, NORTH [KMQ]
GOMADJ alt for GUMATJ [GNN]
GOMANTAKI alt for BARDESKARI dial of KONKANI,

GOANESE [GOM]
GOMATAKI alt for KONKANI, GOANESE [GOM]
GOMBARA dial of BARUGA [BBB]
GOMBE dial of FULFULDE, ADAMAWA [FUB]
GOMBE dial of SENA [SEH]
GOMBI alt for NGWABA [NGW]
GOMBO alt for GUMUZ [GUK]
GOMBO dial of GUMUZ [GUK]
GOMIA dial of CHUAVE [CJV]
GOMJUER alt for PALIOUPINY dial of DINKA,
  SOUTHWESTERN [DIK]
GOMMU KOYA alt for JAGANATHAPURAM KOYA
  dial of KOYA [KFF]
GON SHAN alt for KHÜN [KKH]
GONA alt for YEGA [YGG]
GONDI alt for GONDI, NORTHERN [GON]
GONDI, NORTHERN [GON] lang, India
GONDI, SOUTHERN [GGO] lang, India
GONDIVA alt for GONDI, NORTHERN [GON]
GONDLA alt for LAHULI, TINAN [LBF]
GONDU alt for GONDI, NORTHERN [GON]
GONDWADI alt for GONDI, NORTHERN [GON]
GONE DAU [GOO] lang, Fiji
GONEDAU alt for GONE DAU [GOO]
GONG alt for NGONG [NNX]
GONG alt for UGONG [UGO]
GONGE dial of PANA [PNZ]
GONGE dial of NZAKMBAY [NZY]
GONGLA [GMM] lang, Nigeria
GONGO alt for WONGO [WON]
GONGON LOBI dial of LOBI [LOB]
GONI alt for YERETUAR [GOP]
GONJA [DUM] lang, Ghana
GONJA dial of GONJA [DUM]
GONSOMON dial of RUNGUS [DRG]
GOOLA alt for LAMANI [LMN]
GOOM dial of DII [DUR]
GOOM-GHARRA alt for KUNGGARA [KVS]
GOONAN alt for KWINI [GWW]
GOONDILE alt for GONDI, NORTHERN [GON]
GOONIYANDI [GNI] lang, Australia
GOPE alt for KOPE dial of KIWAI, NORTHEAST [KIW]
GOR dial of NGAMBAI [SBA]
GORA-BOMAHOUJI dial of ÖMIE [AOM]
GORACHOUQUA alt for KORANA [KQZ]
GORAKHPURI alt for NORTHERN STANDARD
  BHOJPURI dial of BHOJPURI [BHJ]
GORAKOR dial of YANTA [YNT]
GORAM alt for GESER-GOROM [GES]
GORAM alt for GWORAM dial of KOFYAR [KWL]
GORAM LAUT dial of GESER-GOROM [GES]
GORAN alt for GESER-GOROM [GES]
GORANI alt for HAWRAMI [HAC]
GORAP [GOQ] lang, Indonesia, Maluku
GORAU dial of IKOBI-MENA [MEB]
GORAZE alt for DOBASE [DOX]
GORBO dial of KRAHN, EASTERN [KQO]
GORI alt for LAAL [GDM]
GORI dial of NUNI [NNW]
GORKHALI alt for NEPALI [NEP]
GORKHALI dial of NEPALI [NEP]
GORLOS alt for JIRIM dial of MONGOLIAN,
  PERIPHERAL [MVF]
GORMA KONO alt for PERIPHERAL KONO dial of
  KONO [KNO]
GORMATI alt for LAMANI [LMN]

GORMINANG dial of YIR YORONT [YIY]
GORNO-MARIY alt for MARI, HIGH [MRJ]
GOROA alt for GOROWA [GOW]
GOROGONE alt for GURAGONE [GGE]
GOROM alt for GESER-GOROM [GES]
GORONG alt for GESER-GOROM [GES]
GORONTALO [GRL] lang, Indonesia, Sulawesi
GORONTALO dial of GORONTALO [GRL]
GOROSE [GOS] lang, Ethiopia
GOROVA alt for GOROVU [GRQ]
GOROVU [GRQ] lang, Papua New Guinea
GOROWA [GOW] lang, Tanzania
GORROSE alt for GOROSE [GOS]
GORUM alt for PARENGI [PCJ]
GORWALI alt for GARHWALI [GBM]
GOSHUTE alt for GOSIUTE dial of SHOSHONI [SHH]
GOSIUTE dial of SHOSHONI [SHH]
GÖTA dial of SWEDISH [SWD]
GOTHIC [GOF] lang, Ukraine, Bulgaria
GOTOMI dial of YAGARIA [YGR]
GOTTE KOYA alt for PODIA KOYA dial of KOYA
  [KFF]
GOUDE alt for GUDE [GDE]
GOUDI alt for GONDI, NORTHERN [GON]
GOUDOU alt for LOZOUA dial of DIDA, YOCOBOUÉ
  [GUD]
GOUDWAL alt for GONDI, NORTHERN [GON]
GOUIN alt for CERMA [GOT]
GOUINDOUGOUBA dial of CERMA [GOT]
GOULA alt for GULA [GLU]
GOULA alt for GULA dial of KARA [KCM]
GOULA D'IRO alt for GULA IRO [GLJ]
GOULA IRO alt for GULA IRO [GLJ]
GOULAI [GVL] lang, Chad
GOULAY alt for GOULAI [GVL]
GOULAYE alt for GOULAI [GVL]
GOULEI alt for GOULAI [GVL]
GOULFEI alt for MALGBE [MXF]
GOULFEI alt for MALGBE dial of MALGBE [MXF]
GOULFEY alt for MALGBE [MXF]
GOULIMANCEMA alt for GOURMANCHÉMA [GUX]
GOULMACEMA alt for GOURMANCHÉMA [GUX]
GOULMANCEMA alt for GOURMANCHÉMA [GUX]
GOUMAYE alt for GUMAY dial of MASANA [MCN]
GOUN alt for GUN-GBE [GUW]
GOUNO alt for WEST GIMI dial of GIMI [GIM]
GOUNOU alt for NUGUNU [YAS]
GOURAGHIE alt for GURAGE, CENTRAL WEST
  [GUY]
GOURARA [GRR] lang, Algeria
GOURMA alt for GOURMANCHÉMA [GUX]
GOURMANCHÉMA [GUX] lang, Burkina Faso, Benin,
  Niger, Togo
GOURMANCHÉMA alt for GOURMANCHÉMA [GUX]
GOURMANTCHE alt for GOURMANCHÉMA [GUX]
GOURO alt for GURO [GOA]
GOUWAR alt for GAVAR [GOU]
GOVA alt for MBUKUSHU [MHW]
GOVA alt for KOREKORE dial of SHONA [SHD]
GOVA alt for KOREKORE dial of SHONA [SHD]
GOVARI dial of VARHADI-NAGPURI [VAH]
GOVBORO alt for GOVORO [GOY]
GOVERNOR GENEROSO MANOBO dial of MANOBO,
  SARANGANI [MBS]
GOVORO [GOY] lang, Sudan
GOWA dial of MAKASSAR [MSR]

GOWA alt for KOREKORE dial of SHONA [SHD]
GOWAR-BATI alt for GAWAR-BATI [GWT]
GOWARI alt for GAWAR-BATI [GWT]
GOWASE alt for DOBASE [DOX]
GOWLAN [GOJ] lang, India
GOWLI [GOK] lang, India
GOWRI alt for KALAMI [GWC]
GOWRO [GWF] lang, Pakistan
GOWRO dial of BAIGA [BFV]
GOZZA dial of AARI [AIZ]
GRAECAE alt for GREEK [GRK]
GRAGED alt for GEDAGED [GDD]
GRAMSUKRAVIRI dial of ASHKUN [ASK]
GRAMYA alt for GAMADIA dial of GUJARATI [GJR]
GRANGALI [NLI] lang, Afghanistan
GRANGALI dial of GRANGALI [NLI]
GRASIA alt for GIRASIA, RAJPUT [GRA]
GRASSLAND MARI dial of MARI, LOW [MAL]
GREAT NICOBAR dial of NICOBARESE, SOUTHERN
  [NIK]
GREAT THAI alt for SHAN [SJN]
GREATER CHECHEN dial of CHECHEN [CJC]
GREATER KABARDIAN dial of KABARDIAN [KAB]
GREATER KABYLE dial of KABYLE [KYL]
GREATER SEDANG dial of SEDANG [SED]
GREBO, BARCLAYVILLE [GRY] lang, Liberia
GREBO, E JE [GRB] lang, Liberia
GREBO, FOPO-BUA [GEF] lang, Liberia
GREBO, GBOLOO [GEC] lang, Liberia
GREBO, GLEBO [GEU] lang, Liberia
GREBO, GLOBO [GRV] lang, Liberia
GREBO, JABO [GRJ] lang, Liberia
GREBO, NORTHEASTERN [GRP] lang, Liberia
GREBO, SEASIDE [GRF] lang, Liberia
GREC alt for GREEK [GRK]
GRECO alt for GREKURJA dial of ROMANI, VLACH
  [RMY]
GREEK [GRK] lang, Greece, Egypt, Albania, Bulgaria,
  Cyprus, France, Italy, Romania, Russia, Europe,
  Turkey
GREEK alt for GREEK [GRK]
GREEK ROMANI dial of ROMANI, BALKAN [RMN]
GREEK SIGN LANGUAGE [GSS] lang, Greece
GREEK, ANCIENT [GKO] lang, Greece
GREEN MIAO alt for HMONG NJUA [BLU]
GREEN MIAO alt for TAK dial of HMONG, WESTERN
  [HUJ]
GREEN RIVER alt for ABAU [AAU]
GREENLANDIC alt for INUIT, GREENLANDIC [ESG]
GREENLANDIC ESKIMO alt for INUIT, GREENLANDIC
  [ESG]
GREKURJA dial of ROMANI, VLACH [RMY]
GREKURJA dial of ROMANI, VLACH [RMY]
GRENADA-MENDOZA dial of QUECHUA,
  CHACHAPOYAS [QUK]
GRENADIAN ENGLISH dial of ENGLISH [ENG]
GRESI [GRS] lang, Indonesia, Irian Jaya
GRESIK alt for GRESI [GRS]
GRIFFIN POINT dial of SUDEST [TGO]
GRIK dial of TEMIAR [TMH]
GRIKWA alt for XIRI [XII]
GRIQUA alt for XIRI [XII]
GRISONS alt for LOWER ENGADINE dial of RHETO-
  ROMANCE [RHE]
GRODNEN-BARANOVICH alt for SOUTHWEST
  BELORUSSIAN dial of BELORUSSIAN [RUW]

GROGO dial of JAGOI [SNE]
GROMA [GRO] lang, India, China
GROOTE EYLANDT alt for ANINDILYAKWA [AOI]
GROS VENTRE [ATS] lang, USA
GROS VENTRE alt for HIDATSA [HID]
GROS VENTRES alt for GROS VENTRE [ATS]
GRÜDNO alt for GARDENA dial of LADIN [LLD]
GRUZIN alt for GEORGIAN [GEO]
GRY alt for XIRI [XII]
GTA' alt for GATA' [GAQ]
GTSANG dial of TIBETAN [TIC]
GU alt for GUN-GBE [GUW]
GU dial of GELO [KKF]
GUA [LAR] lang, Ghana
GUADELOUPE CREOLE dial of LESSER ANTILLEAN
  CREOLE FRENCH [DOM]
GUADEMA alt for YANOMAM dial of YANOMÁMI
  [WCA]
GUAGA-TAGARE alt for CHAYMA dial of KALIHNA
  [CRB]
GUAGUA alt for PIAROA [PID]
GUAHARIBO alt for YANOMAMÖ [GUU]
GUAHIBO [GUH] lang, Colombia, Venezuela,
  Venezuela
GUAHIBO alt for GUAHIBO [GUH]
"GUAIAQUI" alt for ACHÉ [GUQ]
GUAICA alt for YANOMAMÖ [GUU]
GUAIGUA alt for GUAHIBO [GUH]
GUAIKA alt for SANUMÁ [SAM]
GUAJÁ [GUJ] lang, Brazil
GUAJAJÁRA [GUB] lang, Brazil
GUAJARIBO alt for YANOMAMÖ [GUU]
GUAJIBO alt for GUAHIBO [GUH]
GUAJIRA alt for GUAJIRO [GUC]
GUAJIRO [GUC] lang, Colombia, Venezuela,
  Venezuela
GUAJIRO alt for GUAJIRO [GUC]
GUAMAKA alt for MALAYO [MBP]
GUAMBIA alt for GUAMBIANO [GUM]
GUAMBIANO [GUM] lang, Colombia
GUANA [QKS] lang, Brazil
GUANA [GVA] lang, Paraguay
GUANANO [GVC] lang, Brazil, Colombia, Colombia
GUANANO alt for GUANANO [GVC]
GUANCHE [GNC] lang, Spain
GUANGA alt for GIANGAN [BGI]
GUANGDONG alt for CHAO SHAN dial of CHINESE,
  MIN NAN [CFR]
GUANGFU alt for CHINESE, YUE [YUH]
GUANGZHOU alt for CHINESE, YUE [YUH]
GUARANÍ, BOLIVIAN, WESTERN [GNW] lang, Bolivia
GUARANÍ, MBYÁ [GUN] lang, Paraguay, Argentina,
  Brazil
GUARANÍ, PARAGUAYAN [GUG] lang, Paraguay,
  Brazil
GUARAO alt for WARAO [WBA]
GUARATEGAJA alt for KANOÉ [KXO]
GUARATÉGAYA alt for KANOÉ [KXO]
GUARATIRA alt for KANOÉ [KXO]
GUARAUNO alt for WARAO [WBA]
"GUARAYO" alt for GUARAYU [GYR]
GUARAYO alt for TAPIETÉ [TAI]
GUARAYO alt for CHIRIGUANO [GUI]
GUARAYU [GYR] lang, Bolivia
GUARAYU-TA alt for PAUSERNA [PSM]
GUAREKENA alt for GUAREQUENA [GAE]

GUAREQUENA [GAE] lang, Venezuela, Brazil
GUARIBA MAKU [GBQ] lang, Brazil
GUARIJÍO alt for HUARIJÍO [VAR]
GUASURANGO alt for TAPIETÉ [TAI]
GUASURANGO alt for CHIRIGUANO [GUI]
GUASURANGUE alt for TAPIETÉ [TAI]
GUATÓ [GTA] lang, Brazil
GUATUSO alt for MALÉKU JAÍKA [GUT]
GUAVA alt for ORAMI dial of NASIOI [NAS]
GUAXARE alt for GUAJÁ [GUJ]
GUAYABERO [GUO] lang, Colombia
"GUAYAKÍ" alt for ACHÉ [GUQ]
GUAYAKI-ACHE alt for ACHÉ [GUQ]
GUAYANA alt for WAYANA [WAY]
GUAYBA alt for GUAHIBO [GUH]
GUAYMÍ [GYM] lang, Panama, Costa Rica
GUAYQUERI alt for WOKIARE dial of YABARANA
    [YAR]
GUAYUYACO dial of INGA, JUNGLE [INJ]
GUAZAZARA alt for GUAJAJÁRA [GUB]
GUBA [GBV] lang, Ethiopia
GUBA alt for SHIKI [GUA]
GUBABWINGU alt for GUPAPUYNGU [GUF]
GUBAT alt for SORSOGON, WARAY [SRV]
GUBAT alt for GUBATNON dial of HANUNOO [HNN]
GUBATNON dial of HANUNOO [HNN]
GUBAWA alt for SHIKI [GUA]
GUBI alt for SHIKI [GUA]
GUBI dial of SHIKI [GUA]
GUBU [GOX] lang, Zaïre, Central African Republic
GUDAL dial of MOFU, SOUTH [MIF]
GUDANDJI dial of WAMBAYA [WMB]
GUDE [GDE] lang, Nigeria, Cameroon
"GUDEILLA" alt for HADIYYA [HDY]
"GUDELLA" alt for HADIYYA [HDY]
GUDENI dial of GURENNE [GUR]
GUDENI dial of GURENNE [GUR]
GUDENNE alt for GUDENI dial of GURENNE [GUR]
GUDI dial of NUNGU [RIN]
GUDO alt for GUDU [GDU]
GUDOJI alt for DAMELI [DML]
GUDU [GDU] lang, Nigeria
GUDUF [GDF] lang, Nigeria, Cameroon
GUDUF dial of GUDUF [GDF]
GUDUPE alt for GUDUF [GDF]
GUDWA alt for GADABA [GBJ]
GUDWA dial of GADABA [GBJ]
GUÉBIE alt for DIDA, LAKOTA [DIC]
GUEBIE dial of BÉTÉ, GAGNOA [BTG]
GUEGUE alt for ALBANIAN, GHEG [ALS]
GUELAVÍA ZAPOTEC alt for ZAPOTECO, WESTERN
    TLACOLULA [ZAB]
GUELEBDA alt for GLAVDA [GLV]
GUELENGDENG alt for MBARA [MPK]
GUEMSHEK alt for GEMZEK [GND]
GUERA dial of ARABIC, SHUWA [SHU]
GUÉRÉ [GXX] lang, Côte d'Ivoire
GUERRERO AZTEC alt for NAHUATL, GUERRERO
    [NAH]
GUERZE alt for KPELLE, GUINEA [GKP]
GUEVE alt for GEY [GUV]
GUEVEA DE HUMBOLT ZAPOTECO alt for
    ZAPOTECO, NORTHERN ISTHMUS [ZPG]
GUGADA alt for KOKATA [KTD]
GUGADJ [GGD] lang, Australia
GUGADJA alt for KUKATJA [KUX]

GUGBE alt for GUN-GBE [GUW]
GUGIKO dial of MOKULU [MOZ]
GUGU dial of DAYAK, LAND [DYK]
GUGU BADHUN [GDC] lang, Australia
GUGU WARRA [WRW] lang, Australia
GUGU YIMIJIR alt for GUGUYIMIDJIR [KKY]
GUGUBERA [KKP] lang, Australia
GUGUDAYOR alt for THAYORE [THD]
GUGUMINJEN alt for KUNJEN [KJN]
GUGUWARRA alt for GUGU WARRA [WRW]
GUGUYALANJI alt for KUKU-YALANJI [GVN]
GUGUYIMIDJIR [KKY] lang, Australia
GUHA alt for HOLOHOLO [HOO]
GUHJALI alt for WAKHI [WBL]
GUHU-SAMANE [GHS] lang, Papua New Guinea
GUI alt for JUI dial of ZHUANG, NORTHERN [CCX]
GUIAM dial of GIDRA [GDR]
GUIARAK [GKA] lang, Papua New Guinea
GUÌBEI dial of ZHUANG, NORTHERN [CCX]
GUIBEROUA dial of BÉTÉ, GUIBEROUA [BET]
GÙIBIAN dial of ZHUANG, NORTHERN [CCX]
GUICURÚ alt for KUIKÚRO [KUI]
GUIDAR alt for GIDAR [GID]
GUIDER alt for GIDAR [GID]
GUILI dial of BANA [FLI]
GUILI alt for GILI dial of BANA [FLI]
GUIMARAS ISLAND dial of KINARAY-A [KRJ]
GUIN alt for CERMA [GOT]
GUIN alt for GEN-GBE [GEJ]
GUINAANG dial of KALINGA, LUBUAGAN [KNB]
GUINAANG BONTOC dial of BONTOC, CENTRAL
    [BNC]
GUINZADAN dial of KANKANAEY [KNE]
GUIPUZCOAN dial of BASQUE [BSQ]
GUIRVIDIG alt for MUZUK dial of MUSGU [MUG]
GÙISNAY alt for WICHÍ LHAMTÉS GÜISNAY [MZH]
GUISSEY alt for GIZAY dial of MASANA [MCN]
GUISSEY alt for GIZAY dial of MASANA [MCN]
GUITRY alt for LOZOUA dial of DIDA, YOCOBOUÉ
    [GUD]
GUIZIGA alt for GIZIGA, NORTH [GIS]
GUIZIGA alt for GIZIGA, SOUTH [GIZ]
GUJAAXET dial of BAINOUK [BCZ]
GUJALABIYA alt for BURARRA [BVR]
GUJAR alt for GUJARI [GJU]
GUJARATI [GJR] lang, India, South Africa, Tanzania,
    Uganda, Zambia, Zimbabwe, Pakistan, Singapore
GUJARATI alt for GUJARATI [GJR]
GUJARI [GJU] lang, India, Afghanistan, Pakistan
GUJARI alt for GUJARI [GJU]
GUJER alt for GUJARI [GJU]
GUJERATHI alt for GUJARATI [GJR]
GUJERATI alt for GUJARATI [GJR]
GUJI dial of OROMO, BORANA-ARUSI-GUJI [GAX]
GUJINGALIA alt for BURARRA [BVR]
GUJJARI alt for GUJARI [GJU]
GUJJI alt for GUJI dial of OROMO, BORANA-ARUSI-
    GUJI [GAX]
GUJRATHI alt for GUJARATI [GJR]
GUJURI alt for GUJARI [GJU]
GUJURI RAJASTHANI alt for GUJARI [GJU]
GULA [GLU] lang, Chad
GULA alt for GOLA [GOL]
GULA dial of KARA [KCM]
GULA GUERA alt for ZAN GULA [ZNA]
GULA GUERA alt for BON GULA [GLC]

GULA IRO [GLJ] lang, Chad
GULA'ALAA [GMB] lang, Solomon Islands
GULAI alt for GOULAI [GVL]
GULAI dial of SAR [MWM]
GULAK dial of MARGHI CENTRAL [MAR]
GULANGA alt for GIANGAN [BGI]
GULAY dial of DYAABUGAY [DYY]
GULBAHAR dial of PASHAYI, NORTHWEST [GLH]
GULE [GLE] lang, Sudan
GULEGULEU dial of DUAU [DUA]
GULEI alt for GOULAI [GVL]
GULFAN alt for GHULFAN [GHL]
GULFE alt for MALGBE [MXF]
GULFEI alt for MALGBE [MXF]
GULI alt for NDAM [NDM]
GULICHA dial of BARUYA [BYR]
GULIGULI [GLG] lang, Solomon Islands
GULILI alt for GULIGULI [GLG]
GULIMANCEMA alt for GOURMANCHÉMA [GUX]
"GULLAH" alt for SEA ISLANDS CREOLE ENGLISH
     [GUL]
GULUD alt for JULUD dial of KATLA [KCR]
GUMADIR dial of GUNWINGGU [GUP]
GUMAHI dial of BUKA-KHWE [BUZ]
GUMAIT alt for GUMATJ [GNN]
GUMAJ alt for GUMATJ [GNN]
GUMALU [GMU] lang, Papua New Guinea
GUMAS dial of MUNA [MYN]
GUMASI alt for GUMAWANA [GVS]
GUMATJ [GNN] lang, Australia
GUMAWANA [GVS] lang, Papua New Guinea
GUMAY dial of MASANA [MCN]
GUMBA alt for BELANDA VIRI [BVI]
GUMBAINGARI alt for KUMBAINGGAR [KGS]
GUMBANG dial of JAGOI [SNE]
GUMBAYNGGIR alt for KUMBAINGGAR [KGS]
GUMER dial of GURAGE, CENTRAL WEST [GUY]
GUMIA alt for IRUMU [IOU]
GUMINE alt for GOLIN [GVF]
GUMIS alt for GUMUZ [GUK]
GUMSAI dial of KUI [KXU]
GUMUZ [GUK] lang, Ethiopia, Sudan
GUMUZ alt for GUMUZ [GUK]
GUN alt for GUN-GBE [GUW]
GUN-ALADA alt for GUN-GBE [GUW]
GUN-GBE [GUW] lang, Benin, Nigeria, Nigeria
GUN-GBE alt for GUN-GBE [GUW]
GUN-GURAGONE alt for GURAGONE [GGE]
GUN-GURAGONE alt for BURARRA [BVR]
GUNA dial of SINASINA [SST]
GUNA alt for NGUNA dial of EFATE, NORTH [LLP]
GUNAGORAGONE alt for GURAGONE [GGE]
GUNANTUNA alt for TOLAI [KSD]
GUNAVIDJI alt for DJEEBBANA [DJJ]
GUNAWITJI alt for GUNWINGGU [GUP]
GUNBALANG alt for KUNBARLANG [WLG]
GUNDANGBON alt for NGALKBUN [NGK]
GUNDI [GDI] lang, Central African Republic
GUNDJEIPME dial of GUNWINGGU [GUP]
GUNEI dial of GUNWINGGU [GUP]
GUNERAKAN alt for KUNGARAKANY [GGK]
GUNGA alt for RESHE [RES]
GUNGABULA [GNF] lang, Australia
GUNGALANG alt for KUNBARLANG [WLG]
GUNGANCHI alt for RESHE [RES]
GUNGARAGAN alt for KUNGARAKANY [GGK]

GUNGARI alt for KUNGGARI [KGL]
GUNGAWA alt for RESHE [RES]
GUNGAWA dial of RESHE [RES]
GUNGDEKHA dial of KEBUMTAMP [KJZ]
GUNGGARA alt for KUNGGARA [KVS]
GUNGGARI alt for KUNGGARI [KGL]
GUNGGAY dial of YIDINY [YII]
GUNGOROGONE alt for GURAGONF [GGE]
GUNGU [RUB] lang, Uganda
GUNGU alt for NYORO [NYR]
GUNIAN alt for GOONIYANDI [GNI]
GUNIANDI alt for GOONIYANDI [GNI]
GUNIN alt for KWINI [GWW]
GUNIYAN alt for GOONIYANDI [GNI]
GUNIYN alt for GOONIYANDI [GNI]
GUNMARUNG alt for MAUNG [MPH]
GUNTUR dial of TELUGU [TCW]
GUNU alt for NUGUNU [YAS]
GUNUA-KENA alt for TEHUELCHE [TEH]
GUNUNA-KENA alt for TEHUELCHE [TEH]
GUNWINGGU [GUP] lang, Australia
GUNYA [GYY] lang, Australia
GUNYA alt for BAJUNI dial of SWAHILI [SWA]
GUNYAMOLO dial of BAINOUK [BCZ]
GUNZA alt for DAKUNZA dial of GUMUZ [GUK]
GUNZA alt for DAKUNZA dial of GUMUZ [GUK]
GUNZIB alt for HUNZIB [HUZ]
GUO GARIMANI alt for DAHALO [DAL]
"GUOYAGUI" alt for ACHÉ [GUQ]
GUOYU alt for CHINESE, MANDARIN [CHN]
GUPA dial of NUPE [NUP]
GUPAPUYNGU [GUF] lang, Australia
GUPAPUYNGU dial of GUPAPUYNGU [GUF]
GURA alt for MABAAN [MFZ]
GURA dial of LAME [BMA]
GURA dial of GURAGE, CENTRAL WEST [GUY]
GURA alt for GBIRI dial of GBIRI-NIRAGU [GRH]
GURADJARA alt for KARADJERI [GBD]
GURAGE, CENTRAL WEST [GUY] lang, Ethiopia
GURAGE, EAST [GRE] lang, Ethiopia
GURAGE, INDEGEGN [GIE] lang, Ethiopia
GURAGE, INNEMOR [GII] lang, Ethiopia
GURAGE, NORTH [GRU] lang, Ethiopia
GURAGE, PERIPHERAL WEST [GPW] lang, Ethiopia
GURAGIE alt for GURAGE, CENTRAL WEST [GUY]
GURAGONE [GGE] lang, Australia
GURAGUE alt for GURAGE, CENTRAL WEST [GUY]
GURAGUREU alt for GULEGULEU dial of DUAU
     [DUA]
GURAMA alt for KURRAMA [VKU]
GURAMALUM [GRZ] lang, Papua New Guinea
GURANI alt for HAWRAMI [HAC]
GURANI alt for BAJELAN [BJM]
GURARA alt for GOURARA [GRR]
GURDJAR [GDJ] lang, Australia
GURE alt for GBIRI dial of GBIRI-NIRAGU [GRH]
GURE-KAHUGU alt for GBIRI-NIRAGU [GRH]
GURENG GURENG [GNR] lang, Australia
GURENNE [GUR] lang, Ghana, Burkina Faso
GURENNE alt for GUDENI dial of GURENNE [GUR]
GURESHA alt for BULI [BWU]
GUREZI dial of SHINA [SCL]
GUREZI alt for ASTORI dial of SHINA [SCL]
GURGO dial of DAYAK, LAND [DYK]
GURIAN-ADZHAR dial of GEORGIAN [GEO]
GURIASO [GRX] lang, Papua New Guinea

GURINDJI alt for GURINJI [GUE]
GURINJI [GUE] lang, Australia
GURJAR alt for GUJARI [GJU]
GURJINDI dial of JARNANGO [JAY]
GURKA alt for YIWOM [GEK]
GURKHALI alt for NEPALI [NEP]
GURMA alt for GOURMANCHÉMA [GUX]
GURMANA [GRC] lang, Nigeria
GURMARTI alt for LAMANI [LMN]
GURMUKHI alt for PANJABI, EASTERN [PNJ]
GURO [GOA] lang, Côte d'Ivoire
GURREH alt for GARREH dial of GARREH-AJURAN
    [GGH]
GURROGONE alt for GURAGONE [GGE]
GURRUM alt for RIBINA dial of JERA [JER]
GURU alt for RUGURU [RUF]
GURU alt for SHIKI [GUA]
GURUBI alt for SOUTHERN CHUMBURUNG dial of
    CHUMBURUNG [NCU]
GURUF alt for NGARIAWAN [NGG]
GURUF/NGARIAWANG dial of ADZERA [AZR]
GURUKU alt for SAFWA [SBK]
GURUMUKHI alt for PANJABI, EASTERN [PNJ]
GURUNE alt for GUDENI dial of GURENNE [GUR]
GURUNG [GVR] lang, Nepal, India
GURUNG KURA alt for GURUNG [GVR]
GURUNG, EASTERN [GGN] lang, Nepal
GURUNTUM alt for GURUNTUM-MBAARU [GRD]
GURUNTUM-MBAARU [GRD] lang, Nigeria
GURVALI alt for GARHWALI [GBM]
GUSAN [GSN] lang, Papua New Guinea
GUSAP alt for WASEMBO [GSP]
GUSAWA alt for GUSU dial of JERA [JER]
GUSII [GUZ] lang, Kenya
GUSILAAY alt for GUSILAY [GSL]
GUSILAY [GSL] lang, Senegal
GUSSUM alt for GUSU dial of JERA [JER]
GUSU alt for SANGA [SGA]
GUSU dial of JERA [JER]
GUTA dial of MANYIKA [MXC]
GUTJERTABIA alt for GURAGONE [GGE]
GUTOB alt for GADABA [GBJ]
GUTOBI alt for BONDO [BFW]
GUTU alt for GUDU [GDU]
GUUGU YIMITHIRR alt for GUGUYIMIDJIR [KKY]
GUVJA dial of KANURI, YERWA [KPH]
GUWAMAL alt for YIDINY [YII]
GUWAMU [GWU] lang, Australia
GUWAN alt for GAMBERA [GMA]
GUWET alt for GUWOT [GVE]
GUWIDJ dial of NGARINYIN [UNG]
GUWII dial of KURMANJI [KUR]
GUWOT [GVE] lang, Papua New Guinea
GUXHOU alt for FOOCHOW dial of CHINESE, MIN
    PEI [MNP]
GUYANAIS alt for FRENCH GUIANESE [FRE]
GUYANE alt for FRENCH GUIANESE [FRE]
GUYANE CREOLE alt for FRENCH GUIANESE [FRE]
GUYANESE [GYN] lang, Guyana, Surinam, Surinam
GUYANESE alt for GUYANESE [GYN]
GUYANESE CREOLE alt for GUYANESE [GYN]
GUYANESE CREOLE ENGLISH alt for GUYANESE
    [GYN]
GUYANESE ENGLISH dial of ENGLISH [ENG]
GUYENNAIS dial of LANGUEDOCIEN [LNC]
GUYUK alt for NYA GUYUWA dial of LONGUDA

    [LNU]
GUZAWA alt for GUSU dial of JERA [JER]
GUZII alt for GUSII [GUZ]
GVEDE alt for UMANAKAINA [GDN]
GVOKO alt for GEVOKO [NGS]
GWA [GWB] lang, Nigeria
GWA alt for MBATO [GWA]
GWABEGWABE dial of IAMALELE [YML]
GWADARA BASA alt for BASA-KADUNA [BSL]
GWADI PAREKWA alt for PARKWA [PBI]
GWAK alt for GINGWAK dial of JARAWA [JAR]
GWAKA alt for NGBAKA MA'BO [NBM]
GWAMA alt for KOMA, NORTH [KMQ]
GWAMBA alt for TSONGA [TSO]
GWAMBA dial of TSONGA [TSO]
GWAMFANCI alt for GWAMHI dial of GWAMHI-
    WURI [BGA]
GWAMFI alt for GWAMHI dial of GWAMHI-WURI
    [BGA]
GWAMHI dial of GWAMHI-WURI [BGA]
GWAMHI-WURI [BGA] lang, Nigeria
GWANDARA [GWN] lang, Nigeria
GWANDARA CENTRAL dial of GWANDARA [GWN]
GWANDARA EASTERN dial of GWANDARA [GWN]
GWANDARA GITATA dial of GWANDARA [GWN]
GWANDARA SOUTHERN dial of GWANDARA [GWN]
GWANDARA WESTERN dial of GWANDARA [GWN]
GWANDERA alt for YIR YORONT [YIY]
GWANJE dial of WANDALA [MFI]
GWANO dial of POKOMO, UPPER [PKB]
GWANTO alt for GWANTU dial of NUMANA-NUNKU-
    GWANTU-NUMBU [NBR]
GWANTU dial of NUMANA-NUNKU-GWANTU-
    NUMBU [NBR]
GWAPA alt for GWAMBA dial of TSONGA [TSO]
GWARI MATAI alt for GBAGYI [GBR]
GWARI MATAYI alt for GBAGYI [GBR]
GWARI YAMMA alt for GBARI [GBY]
GWATALEY alt for BATULEY [BAY]
GWATE alt for BATA [BTA]
GWATIKE alt for DAHATING [DAH]
GWAVILI alt for YALEBA dial of TAWALA [TBO]
GWAWILI alt for YALEBA dial of TAWALA [TBO]
GWAZA dial of NUNG [NUN]
GWE alt for CERMA [GOT]
GWE alt for SUKUMA [SUA]
GWEDA alt for UMANAKAINA [GDN]
GWEDE alt for UMANAKAINA [GDN]
GWEDENA alt for UMANAKAINA [GDN]
GWEMARA alt for GUMER dial of GURAGE,
    CENTRAL WEST [GUY]
GWEN alt for CERMA [GOT]
GWENDELE alt for PELASLA dial of PELASLA [MLR]
GWENO [GWE] lang, Tanzania
GWÉÒ dial of TOURA [NEB]
GWERE [GWR] lang, Uganda
GWERI alt for MO'DA [GBN]
GWI-KHWE [GWJ] lang, Botswana
GWIBWEN alt for NEYO [NEY]
GWICH'IN [KUC] lang, USA, Canada
GWIINI alt for KWINI [GWW]
GWINI alt for KWINI [GWW]
GWOMO alt for GWOMU [GWG]
GWOMO alt for DZA [JEN]
GWOMU [GWG] lang, Nigeria
GWONG alt for KAGOMA [KDM]

GWORAM alt for LALA-ROBA [LLA]
GWORAM dial of KOFYAR [KWL]
GWUNE alt for AGWAGWUNE [YAY]
GXON alt for /HUA-OWANI [HUC]
GYAAZI alt for GEJI dial of GEJI [GEZ]
GYANGE alt for NGENGE dial of GBAGYI [GBR]
GYANGIYA alt for NYANG'I [NYP]
GYARONG alt for JIARONG [JYA]
GYARUNG alt for JIARONG [JYA]
GYEGEM alt for DYEGUEME dial of SERERE-SINE
   [SES]
GYELL-KURU-VWANG dial of BEROM [BOM]
GYEM [GYE] lang, Nigeria
GYEM alt for FYAM [PYM]
GYEMAWA alt for GYEM [GYE]
GYENGYEN alt for NGENGE dial of GBAGYI [GBR]
GYETA alt for GETO dial of GURAGE, PERIPHERAL
   WEST [GPW]
GYETO alt for GETO dial of GURAGE, PERIPHERAL
   WEST [GPW]
GYIRONG alt for KYERUNG [KGY]
GYO alt for DAN [DAF]
GYOGO dial of LIGBI [LIG]
GYONG alt for KAGOMA [KDM]
GYPSY alt for ROMANI, KALO FINNISH [RMF]
GYPSY alt for ROMANI, BALKAN [RMN]
GYPSY alt for DOMARI [RMT]
GYPSY alt for ROMANI, VLACH [RMY]
HA [HAQ] lang, Tanzania
HA alt for KATU [KTV]
HA dial of HLAI [LIC]
HA MEA alt for MEA [MEG]
HÀ NHÌ alt for HANI [HNI]
HA XA PHANG alt for CHINESE, YUE [YUH]
HA'AANG dial of TA'OIH, UPPER [TTH]
HA'US alt for ANDRA-HUS [ANX]
HA'UWA alt for RAMPI [LJE]
HA-TIRI alt for TIRI [CIR]
HAAL alt for KASANGA [CCJ]
HAALPULAAR alt for TOUCOULEUR [TOU]
HAAVU alt for HAVU [HAV]
HAAYIL alt for CENTRAL NAJDI dial of ARABIC,
   NAJDI [ARS]
HABAU dial of JARAI [JRA]
HABE alt for HAUSA [HUA]
HABU [HBU] lang, Indonesia, Nusa Tenggara
HABURI dial of BHILI [BHB]
HADAAREB alt for HADAREB dial of BEJA [BEI]
HADANG alt for SEDANG [SED]
HADAREB dial of BEJA [BEI]
HADAUTI alt for HARAUTI [HOJ]
HADEM dial of HRANGKHOL [HRA]
HADENDOA dial of BEJA [BEI]
HADENDOWA alt for HADENDOA dial of BEJA [BEI]
HADIA alt for HADIYYA [HDY]
HADIIDIIN dial of ARABIC, SYRO-MESOPOTAMIAN
   [AYP]
HADIMU alt for PEMBA dial of SWAHILI [SWA]
HADIYA alt for HADIYYA [HDY]
HADIYYA [HDY] lang, Ethiopia
HADOTI alt for HARAUTI [HOJ]
HADYA alt for HADIYYA [HDY]
HADZA alt for HATSA [HTS]
HADZABI alt for HATSA [HTS]
HADZAPI alt for HATSA [HTS]
HAEKE [AEK] lang, New Caledonia

HAGAHAI [HAX] lang, Papua New Guinea
HAGEN alt for MEDLPA [MED]
HAGEULU dial of BUGHOTU [BGT]
HAGUETI alt for CASHIBO-CACATAIBO [CBR]
HAHAINTESU dial of NAMBIKUÁRA, SOUTHERN
   [NAB]
HAHAK dial of GALOLI [GAL]
HAHON [HAH] lang, Papua New Guinea
HAHUTAN alt for ILIUN [ILU]
HAHUTAU alt for ILIUN [ILU]
HAI [HAF] lang, Central African Republic
HAI alt for LELE [UGA]
HAI NAM alt for CHINESE, YUE [YUH]
HAIAN AMI alt for CENTRAL AMIS dial of AMIS
   [ALV]
HAIAO alt for YAO [YAO]
HAIDA [HAI] lang, Canada, USA, USA
HAIDA alt for HAIDA [HAI]
HAIEREN alt for ARMENIAN [ARM]
HAIHTE alt for CHIN, PAITE [PCK]
HAIJONG alt for HAJONG [HAJ]
HAILAR dial of DAUR [DTA]
HAIN alt for BOZO, HAINYAXO [BZX]
HAIN//UM dial of SAN [HGM]
HAINAN dial of CHINESE, MIN NAN [CFR]
HAINAN dial of CHINESE, MIN NAN [CFR]
HAINAN CHAM alt for UTSAT [HUQ]
HAINANESE dial of CHINESE, MIN NAN [CFR]
HAINANESE dial of CHINESE, MIN NAN [CFR]
HAINANESE alt for HAINAN dial of CHINESE, MIN
   NAN [CFR]
HAININH dial of MIEN [YOC]
HAINMAN alt for NGARINMAN [NBJ]
HAINYAXO alt for BOZO, HAINYAXO [BZX]
HAIRA alt for OROKOLO [ORO]
HAISLA [HAS] lang, Canada
HAITHE alt for CHIN, PAITE [PCK]
HAITIAN CREOLE FRENCH [HAT] lang, Haiti,
   Dominican Republic, Puerto Rico
HAITIAN CREOLE FRENCH alt for HAITIAN CREOLE
   FRENCH [HAT]
HAITSHUARI alt for HIECHWARE [HIE]
HAITSHUWAU alt for HIECHWARE [HIE]
HAJONG [HAJ] lang, India, Bangladesh
HAKA alt for BOLO [BLV]
HAKARI dial of KURMANJI [KUR]
HAKEI dial of GELO [KKF]
HAKETIA alt for LADINO [SPJ]
HAKETIYA alt for LADINO [SPJ]
HAKITIA alt for LADINO [SPJ]
HAKKA alt for CHINESE, HAKKA [HAK]
HAKKARI dial of KURMANJI [KUR]
HAKÖ [HAO] lang, Papua New Guinea
HAKOA [HKO] lang, Papua New Guinea
HAKU alt for HAKÖ [HAO]
HALABA alt for ALLAABA [ALB]
HALABI alt for HALBI [HLB]
HALAKWALIP alt for KAWESQAR [ALC]
HALAM alt for CHIN, FALAM [HBH]
HALAM dial of CHIN, FALAM [HBH]
HALAM dial of KOK BOROK [TRP]
HALAM CHIN alt for CHIN, FALAM [HBH]
HALANG [HAL] lang, Viet Nam, Laos
HALANG DOAN [HLD] lang, Viet Nam, Laos
HALANG DUAN alt for HALANG DOAN [HLD]
HALBA alt for HALBI [HLB]

HALBI [HLB] lang, India
HALBI dial of ORIYA [ORY]
HALERMAN dial of KELON [KYO]
HALH alt for MONGOLIAN, HALH [KHK]
HALH dial of MONGOLIAN, HALH [KHK]
HALH alt for KHALKHA dial of MONGOLIAN, HALH [KHK]
HALIA [HLA] lang, Papua New Guinea
HALIFOERSCH alt for MARIND [MRZ]
HALITI alt for PARECÍS [PAB]
HALKOMELEM [HUR] lang, Canada
HALLAM alt for CHIN, FALAM [HBH]
HALLAM CHIN alt for CHIN, FALAM [HBH]
HALLARI alt for OLLARI [OLL]
HALÓ TÉ SÚ [HLO] lang, Brazil
HALVAS alt for HALBI [HLB]
HALVI alt for HALBI [HLB]
HAM [JAB] lang, Nigeria
HAM alt for DAMI [DAD]
HAM dial of HAM [JAB]
HAM dial of MASANA [MCN]
HAMACORE alt for IQUITO [IQU]
HAMADANI dial of FARSI, WESTERN [PES]
HAMAP dial of KABOLA [KLZ]
HAMAR alt for HMAR [HMR]
HAMAR alt for HAMER-BANNA [AMF]
HAMAR-KOKE alt for HAMER-BANNA [AMF]
HAMBA [HBA] lang, Zaïre
HAMBA alt for KWAMBA [RWM]
HAMBA dial of HAYA [HAY]
HAMBA dial of NKUTU [NKW]
HAMBA alt for KIGUMU dial of KWAMBA [RWM]
HAMBO alt for KWAMBA [RWM]
HAMDAY alt for HAMTAI [HMT]
HAMDE alt for HAMTAI [HMT]
HÄME dial of FINNISH [FIN]
HAMEHA alt for MEA [MEG]
HAMEJ alt for GULE [GLE]
HAMER alt for HAMER-BANNA [AMF]
HAMER-BANNA [AMF] lang, Ethiopia
HAMGYONGDO dial of KOREAN [KKN]
HAMI alt for KUMUL dial of UYGHUR [UIG]
HAMIL alt for NORTH WAIBUK dial of HARUAI [TMD]
HAMMER alt for HAMER-BANNA [AMF]
HAMMERCOCHE alt for HAMER-BANNA [AMF]
HAMSCHEN alt for HAMSHEN dial of ARMENIAN [ARM]
HAMSHEN dial of ARMENIAN [ARM]
HAMTAI [HMT] lang, Papua New Guinea
HAMTAI dial of HAMTAI [HMT]
HAMTIK dial of KINARAY-A [KRJ]
HAMTIKNON alt for KINARAY-A [KRJ]
HAMUNG alt for DAMAL [UHN]
HAN [HAA] lang, USA, Canada
HAN alt for CHINESE, YUE [YUH]
HAN LACHI alt for LIPUTCIO dial of LATI [LBT]
HAN-KUTCHIN alt for HAN [HAA]
HANAHAN alt for HALIA [HLA]
HANAK dial of CZECH [CZC]
HANANWA alt for GANANWA dial of SOTHO, NORTHERN [SRT]
HANDÁ [HNH] lang, Botswana
HANDA dial of MBOI [MOI]
HANDA-KHWE alt for HANDÁ [HNH]
HANDÁDAM alt for HANDÁ [HNH]

HANDÁKWE-DAM alt for HANDÁ [HNH]
HANDURI dial of MAHASUI [BFZ]
HANG alt for KHANG [KJM]
HÀNG TONG alt for TAI HANG TONG [THC]
HANGA [HAG] lang, Ghana
HANGA dial of NGELIMA [AGH]
HANGA alt for WANGA dial of LUYIA [LUY]
HANGA HUNDI alt for KWASENGEN [WOS]
HANGALA alt for GHAANGALA dial of KONGO [KON]
HANGAN dial of HALIA [HLA]
HANGANU alt for CHANGANA dial of TSONGA [TSO]
HANGAZA [HAN] lang, Tanzania
HANGCHOW alt for HANGZHOU dial of CHINESE, WU [WUU]
HANGIRO dial of HAYA [HAY]
HANGZHOU dial of CHINESE, WU [WUU]
HANHI alt for HANI [HNI]
HANI [HNI] lang, China, Myanmar, Laos, Myanmar, Viet Nam
HANI alt for HANI [HNI]
HANIS alt for COOS [COS]
HANO [LML] lang, Vanuatu
HANO dial of TEWA [TEW]
HANOI alt for NORTHERN VIETNAMESE dial of VIETNAMESE [VIE]
HANON alt for HAHON [HAH]
HANONOO alt for HANUNOO [HNN]
HANTONG' dial of TA'OIH, LOWER [TTO]
HANTY alt for KHANTY [KCA]
HANUNOO [HNN] lang, Philippines
HANYAXO alt for BOZO, HAINYAXO [BZX]
HAOULO alt for WLUWE-HAWLO dial of KRUMEN, NORTHEASTERN [PYE]
HAOUSSA alt for HAUSA [HUA]
HAPA alt for LABU [LBU]
HAPAO IFUGAO dial of IFUGAO, TUWALI [IFK]
HAPOOL alt for SAPOIN [SPH]
HAQ'ARU alt for JAQARU [JQR]
HAQARU alt for JAQARU [JQR]
HAQEARU alt for JAQARU [JQR]
HAR alt for SANTALI [SNT]
HARAGURE alt for XARAGURE [ARG]
HARAHU alt for BARA dial of FOLOPA [PPO]
HARAHUI alt for BARA dial of FOLOPA [PPO]
HARAMOSH alt for GILGITI dial of SHINA [SCL]
HARANEU alt for XARACUU [ANE]
HARAR alt for OROMO, EASTERN [HAE]
HARAR dial of ARGOBBA [AGJ]
HARARI alt for ADARE [HAR]
HARARRI alt for ADARE [HAR]
HARAUTI [HOJ] lang, India
HARAUTI dial of HARAUTI [HOJ]
HARBAN alt for CHILASI KOHISTANI dial of SHINA [SCL]
HARE dial of SLAVEY [SLA]
HARENGAN dial of SORI-HARENGAN [SBH]
HARER alt for OROMO, EASTERN [HAE]
HARER alt for HARAR dial of ARGOBBA [AGJ]
HARIA alt for KHARIA [KHR]
HARIAMBA dial of DIMASA [DIS]
HARIANI alt for BANGARU [BGC]
HARIGAYA dial of KOCH [KDQ]
HARIJAN dial of TAMIL [TCV]
HARIJAN KINNAURI dial of KANAURI [KFK]

HARIPMOR dial of BOIKIN [BZF]
HAROI [HAB] lang, Papua New Guinea
HAROI [HRO] lang, Viet Nam
HARRO alt for GIDICHO dial of KOORETE [KQY]
HARSO [HRS] lang, Ethiopia
HARSUSI [HSS] lang, Saudi Arabia
HARUA dial of BOLA [BNP]
HARUAI [TMD] lang, Papua New Guinea
HARUKU [HRK] lang, Indonesia, Maluku
HARURO alt for KACHAMA [KCX]
HARWAY alt for HARUAI [TMD]
HARZANI [HRZ] lang, Iran
HASADA dial of MUNDARI [MUW]
HASADA' dial of MUNDARI [MUW]
HASANA alt for CENTRAL NAJDI dial of ARABIC,
    NAJDI [ARS]
HASANYA alt for ARABIC, HASSANIYA [MEY]
HASSANI alt for ARABIC, HASSANIYA [MEY]
HASSANIYYA alt for ARABIC, HASSANIYA [MEY]
HAT alt for O DU [TYH]
HAT dial of KHMU [KJG]
HATAM [HAD] lang, Indonesia, Irian Jaya
HATANG-KAYEY alt for AGTA, REMONTADO [AGV]
HATE alt for KATE dial of KUNIMAIPA [KUP]
HATERUMA dial of YAEYAMA [RYS]
HATIGORIA alt for NAGA, AO [NJO]
HATOMA dial of YAEYAMA [RYS]
HATSA [HTS] lang, Tanzania
HATTAM alt for HATAM [HAD]
HATUE alt for SALEMAN [SAU]
HATUMETEN alt for BOBOT [BTY]
HATUOLU dial of MANUSELA [WHA]
HATUSUA dial of KAIBOBO [KZB]
HATUTU dial of MARQUESAN, NORTH [MRQ]
HATZFELDHAFEN alt for MALA [PED]
HAUHUNU alt for HAUNUNU dial of BAURO [BXA]
HAUNUNU dial of BAURO [BXA]
HAURA alt for KEURU [QQK]
HAURA alt for GIMR dial of TAMA [TMA]
HAURA HAELA alt for KEURU [QQK]
HAURUHA dial of PAWAIA [PWA]
HAUSA [HUA] lang, Nigeria, Benin, Burkina Faso,
    Cameroon, Chad, Ghana, Niger, Sudan, Togo
HAUSA alt for HAUSA [HUA]
HAUSAWA alt for HAUSA [HUA]
HAUSSA alt for HAUSA [HUA]
HAUT-AUVERGNAT dial of AUVERGNAT [AUV]
HAUT-KENYANG alt for UPPER KENYANG dial of
    KENYANG [KEN]
HAUT-LANGUEDOCIEN dial of LANGUEDOCIEN
    [LNC]
HAUT-LIMOUSIN dial of LIMOUSIN [LMS]
HAVANNAH HARBOUR alt for LELEPA dial of EFATE,
    NORTH [LLP]
HAVASUPAI dial of HAVASUPAI-WALAPAI-
    YAVAPAI [YUF]
HAVASUPAI-WALAPAI-YAVAPAI [YUF] lang, USA
HAVE dial of NAGA, TASE [NST]
HAVEKE [AVE] lang, New Caledonia
HAVU [HAV] lang, Zaïre
HAVUNESE alt for SAWU [HVN]
HAW alt for HANI [HNI]
HAW alt for HO dial of CHINESE, MANDARIN [CHN]
HAWAI'I alt for HAWAIIAN [HWI]
HAWAI'I CREOLE ENGLISH [HAW] lang, USA
HAWAII PIDGIN ENGLISH alt for HAWAI'I CREOLE

ENGLISH [HAW]
HAWAI'I PIDGIN SIGN LANGUAGE [HPS] lang, USA
HAWAIIAN [HWI] lang, USA
HAWKIP dial of CHIN, THADO [TCZ]
HAWRAMANI alt for HAWRAMI [HAC]
HAWRAMI [HAC] lang, Iraq, Iran
HAWSA alt for HAUSA [HUA]
HAWU alt for SAWU [HVN]
HAYA [HAY] lang, Tanzania
HAYA alt for WEST TELUTI dial of TELUTI [TLT]
HAYAHAYA alt for KOMA, CENTRAL [KOM]
HAYU alt for VAYU [VAY]
HAZAKE alt for KAZAKH [KAZ]
HAZARA alt for HAZARAGI [HAZ]
HAZARA HINDKO alt for HINDKO, NORTHERN [HNO]
HAZARAGI [HAZ] lang, Afghanistan, Pakistan, Iran,
    Pakistan
HAZARAGI alt for HAZARAGI [HAZ]
HAZILI alt for GAJILA dial of KUNIMAIPA [KUP]
HBROGPA dial of AMDO [ADX]
HBRUGCHU dial of KHAM [KHG]
HDANG alt for SEDANG [SED]
HDRUNG alt for HODRUNG dial of JARAI [JRA]
HE LISU alt for LIPO [TKL]
HE MIAO dial of HMONG, EASTERN [HEA]
HE'DÉ alt for HERDÉ [HED]
HEBA alt for SEBA dial of SAWU [HVN]
HEBBAR dial of TAMIL [TCV]
HEBREW [HBR] lang, Israel, USA
HEBREW TATI alt for TAT, HEBREW [TAT]
HEBREW, OLD [HBO] lang, Israel
HECHE alt for NANAI [GLD]
HEDI [TUR] lang, Cameroon, Nigeria, Nigeria
HEDI alt for HEDI [TUR]
HEH alt for HE MIAO dial of HMONG, EASTERN
    [HEA]
HEHE [HEH] lang, Tanzania
HEHENAWA alt for CUBEO [CUB]
HEI alt for MINANIBAI [MCV]
HEI alt for HE MIAO dial of HMONG, EASTERN [HEA]
HEI//OM alt for HAIN//UM dial of SAN [HGM]
HEIBAN [HEB] lang, Sudan
HEIKOM alt for HAIN//UM dial of SAN [HGM]
HEIKOM BUSHMAN alt for HAIN//UM dial of SAN
    [HGM]
HEIKUM alt for HAIN//UM dial of SAN [HGM]
HEILTSUK [HEI] lang, Canada
HEITU dial of HLAI [LIC]
HELAMBU SHERPA [SCP] lang, Nepal
HELEBI dial of DOMARI [RMT]
HELEWORURU alt for TOBELO dial of TOBELO [TLB]
HELGOLAND dial of FRISIAN, NORTHERN [FRR]
HELLENOROMANI alt for ROMANO-GREEK [RGE]
HELON alt for HELONG [HEG]
HELONG [HEG] lang, Indonesia, Nusa Tenggara
HEMA alt for HEMA-SUD [NIX]
HEMA alt for ORUHEMA dial of HIMA [HIM]
HEMA-NORD alt for LENDU [LED]
HEMA-SUD [NIX] lang, Zaïre
HEMBA [HEM] lang, Zaïre
HENALIMA alt for NEGERI LIMA dial of ASILULU
    [ASL]
HENGA alt for CHIKAMANGA dial of TUMBUKA
    [TUW]
HENGA alt for CHIKAMANGA dial of TUMBUKA
    [TUW]

HENGCH'UN AMIS alt for SOUTHERN AMIS dial of AMIS [ALV]
HENGHUA dial of CHINESE, MIN PEI [MNP]
HENGYANG alt for CHANGSHA dial of CHINESE, XIANG [HSN]
HER [HHR] lang, Senegal
HERA alt for HUTU dial of RWANDA [RUA]
HERATI alt for DARI dial of FARSI, EASTERN [PRS]
HERDÉ [HED] lang, Chad, Cameroon
HERE dial of MANYIKA [MXC]
HERERO [HER] lang, Namibia
HERKI [HEK] lang, Iraq, Iran, Turkey
HERKI alt for HERKI [HEK]
HERMIT [LLF] lang, Papua New Guinea
HERRERO alt for HERERO [HER]
HESO alt for SO [SOC]
HEUSKARA alt for BASQUE [BSQ]
HEWA [HAM] lang, Papua New Guinea
HEWA alt for HEWE dial of TUMBUKA [TUW]
HEWE dial of TUMBUKA [TUW]
HEYO alt for ARINUA [AUK]
HEZARE'I alt for HAZARAGI [HAZ]
HEZAREH alt for HAZARAGI [HAZ]
HEZHE alt for NANAI [GLD]
HEZHEN alt for NANAI [GLD]
HIANACOTO-UMAUA alt for CARIJONA [CBD]
HIAO alt for YAO [YAO]
HIBARADAI alt for WAIA [KNV]
HIBITO [HIB] lang, Peru
HICAQUE alt for TOL [JIC]
HICHKARYANA alt for HIXKARYÁNA [HIX]
HID dial of AVAR [AVR]
HIDALGO AZTEC alt for NAHUATL, HUASTECA, EASTERN [NAI]
HIDALGO TEPEHUA alt for TEPEHUA, HUEHUETLA [TEE]
HIDATSA [HID] lang, USA
HIDE alt for HEDI [TUR]
HIECHWARE [HIE] lang, Botswana, Zimbabwe, Zimbabwe
HIECHWARE alt for GABAKE-NTSHORI [GZZ]
HIECHWARE alt for HIECHWARE [HIE]
HIGA alt for IPIKO [IPK]
HIGAONON alt for MANOBO, HIGAONON [MBA]
HIGH ARABIC alt for ARABIC, CLASSICAL [ARA]
HIGH ARABIC alt for ARABIC, MODERN STANDARD [ABV]
HIGH ARAGONESE alt for ARAGONESE [AXX]
HIGH GERMAN alt for GERMAN, STANDARD [GER]
HIGH KATU alt for KANTU [KTT]
HIGH LATVIAN alt for EAST LATVIAN dial of LATVIAN [LAT]
HIGH LITHUANIAN alt for AUKSHTAITISH dial of LITHUANIAN [LIT]
HIGH PIEMONTESE dial of PIEMONTESE [PMS]
HIGHLAND AREQUIPA dial of QUECHUA, COTAHUASI [QAR]
HIGHLAND BALI dial of BALI [BZC]
HIGHLAND CHINANTECO alt for CHINANTECO, QUIOTEPEC [CHQ]
HIGHLAND GUERRERO MIXTECO alt for MIXTECO, ALACATLATZALA [MIM]
HIGHLAND HUARIJIO dial of HUARIJÍO [VAR]
HIGHLAND INGA alt for INGA [INB]
HIGHLAND MAZATECO alt for MAZATECO, HUAUTLA DE JIMENEZ [MAU]

HIGHLAND NUNG alt for NUNG [NUT]
HIGHLAND POPOLUCA alt for POPOLUCA, SIERRA [POI]
HIGHLAND PUEBLA NAHUATL alt for NAHUATL, SIERRA DE PUEBLA [AZZ]
HIGHLAND TOTONACO alt for TOTONACO, SIERRA [TOS]
HIGHLAND YAO alt for MIEN [YOC]
HIGI alt for KAMWE [HIG]
HIGIR alt for NARA [NRB]
HIIT dial of ARABIC, SYRO-MESOPOTAMIAN [AYP]
HIJAZI alt for ARABIC, HIJAZI [ACW]
HIJI alt for KAMWE [HIG]
HIJUK [HIJ] lang, Cameroon
HILA dial of HITU [HIT]
HILA-KAITETU alt for SEIT-KAITETU [HIK]
HILDI dial of MARGHI SOUTH [MFM]
HILEMAN alt for DYAABUGAY [DYY]
HILIGAINON alt for HILIGAYNON [HIL]
HILIGAYNON [HIL] lang, Philippines, USA
HILIGAYNON dial of HILIGAYNON [HIL]
HILL ANGAS dial of ANGAS [ANC]
HILL BURA alt for PELA dial of BURA-PABIR [BUR]
HILL COUNTRY SIGN LANGUAGE [HST] lang, Thailand
HILL DUSUN alt for KUIJAU [DKR]
HILL GETA' dial of GATA' [GAQ]
HILL JARAWA alt for IZERE [FIZ]
HILL MADA dial of EGGON [EGO]
HILL MARIA alt for ABUJMARIA [ABJ]
HILL PANTARAM alt for MALAPANDARAM [MJP]
HILL TAROK dial of TAROK [YER]
HIMA [HIM] lang, Rwanda, Burundi, Zaïre
HIMA alt for HIMA [HIM]
HIMA dial of EBIRA [IGB]
HIMA dial of NYANKOLE [NYN]
HIMA alt for ORUHIMA dial of HIMA [HIM]
HIMARIMÃ [HIR] lang, Brazil
HIMBA alt for ZEMBA [DHM]
HIN alt for NYAHEUN [NEV]
HINA alt for BESLERI [HNA]
HINA alt for PIDLIMDI dial of TERA [TER]
HINAPAVOSA alt for PAPORA [PPU]
HINARAY-A alt for KINARAY-A [KRJ]
HINDI [HND] lang, India, Mauritius, South Africa, Uganda, Nepal, Singapore, New Zealand
HINDI alt for URDU [URD]
HINDI alt for HINDI [HND]
HINDI DOGRI alt for DOGRI-KANGRI [DOJ]
HINDI, CARIBBEAN [HNS] lang, Surinam, Guyana, Trinidad and Tobago
HINDI, CARIBBEAN alt for HINDI, CARIBBEAN [HNS]
HINDI, FIJIAN [HIF] lang, Fiji
HINDKI alt for HINDKO, NORTHERN [HNO]
HINDKO, NORTHERN [HNO] lang, Pakistan
HINDKO, SOUTHERN [HIN] lang, Pakistan
HINDU SINDHI alt for DUKSLINU dial of SINDHI [SND]
HINDUSTANI alt for HINDI, CARIBBEAN [HNS]
HINGHUA alt for HSINGHUA dial of CHINESE, MIN PEI [MNP]
HINGHUA MIN alt for CHINESE, MIN PEI [MNP]
HINIHON [HIH] lang, Papua New Guinea
HINNA alt for PIDLIMDI dial of TERA [TER]
HINUKH [GIN] lang, Russia, Europe
HINUX alt for HINUKH [GIN]

HIOCHUWAU alt for HIOTSHUWAU [HIO]
HIOTSHUWAU [HIO] lang, Botswana
HIOWE alt for SANIYO-HIYOWE [SNY]
HIRA dial of YAGARIA [YGR]
HIRARA alt for MIYAKO-JIMA dial of MIYAKO [MVI]
HIRI alt for MOTU, HIRI [POM]
HIROI-LAMGANG alt for LAMKANG [LMK]
HISHKARYANA alt for HIXKARYÁNA [HIX]
HISPANOROMANI alt for ROMANI, CALO [RMR]
HISSALA alt for SISAALA, TUMULUNG [SIL]
HISSALA alt for SISAALA, WESTERN [SSL]
HITADIPA NDUGA dial of NDUGA [NDX]
HITAU-PORORAN dial of PETATS [PEX]
HITCHITI alt for MIKASUKI [MIK]
HITU [HIT] lang, Indonesia, Maluku
HITU dial of HITU [HIT]
HIVA OA dial of MARQUESAN, SOUTH [QMS]
HIW [HIW] lang, Vanuatu
HIWI alt for WAIA [KNV]
HIXKARIANA alt for HIXKARYÁNA [HIX]
HIXKARYÁNA [HIX] lang, Brazil
HIYOWE alt for SANIYO-HIYOWE [SNY]
HKA-HKU alt for HKAKU dial of JINGPHO [CGP]
HKAKU dial of JINGPHO [CGP]
HKAKU dial of JINGPHO [CGP]
HKAKU HKA-HKU dial of JINGPHO [CGP]
HKALUK dial of NAGA, TASE [NST]
HKAMTI alt for KHAMTI [KHT]
HKANUNG alt for RAWANG [RAW]
HKAURI alt for KAURI dial of JINGPHO [CGP]
HKAWA alt for BLANG [BLR]
HKUN alt for KHÜN [KKH]
HLAI [LIC] lang, China
HLANGANU alt for CHANGANA dial of TSONGA
     [TSO]
HLAVE dial of TSONGA [TSO]
HLAWTHAI dial of CHIN, MARA [MRH]
HLENGWE dial of TSWA [TSC]
HLENGWE dial of TSWA [TSC]
HLENGWE dial of TSWA [TSC]
HLO'LAN dial of MARU [MHX]
HLOKA alt for DZONGKHA [DZO]
HLOTA alt for NAGA, LOTHA [NJH]
HLUBI dial of SWATI [SWZ]
HM NAI alt for NGNAI dial of PUNU [PNU]
HMANGGONA [TVL] lang, Indonesia, Irian Jaya
HMAR [HMR] lang, India
HMARI alt for HMAR [HMR]
HMONG DAW [MWW] lang, Thailand, Laos, Viet
     Nam
HMONG DAW alt for HMONG DAW [MWW]
HMONG GU MBA dial of HMONG DAW [MWW]
HMONG GU MBA dial of HMONG DAW [MWW]
HMONG LENG alt for HMONG NJUA [BLU]
HMONG NJUA [BLU] lang, Laos, Viet Nam,
     Myanmar, Thailand, Viet Nam
HMONG NJUA alt for HMONG NJUA [BLU]
HMONG NJWA alt for HMONG NJUA [BLU]
HMONG QUA MBA alt for HMONG GU MBA dial of
     HMONG DAW [MWW]
HMONG QUA MBA alt for HMONG GU MBA dial of
     HMONG DAW [MWW]
HMONG, DANANSHAN [HMO] lang, China
HMONG, EASTERN [HEA] lang, China, Thailand
HMONG, NORTHERN [MUQ] lang, China
HMONG, RED [MMR] lang, Viet Nam, China, Thailand

HMONG, WESTERN [HUJ] lang, China, Viet Nam,
     Viet Nam
HMONG, WESTERN alt for HMONG, WESTERN
     [HUJ]
HMONONO alt for HMANGGONA [TVL]
HMU alt for HMONG, EASTERN [HEA]
HMWAEKE alt for VAMALE [MKT]
HMWAEKE dial of VAMALE [MKT]
HMWAVEKE [MRK] lang, New Caledonia
HO [HOC] lang, India, Bangladesh
HO alt for HONI [HOW]
HO dial of CHINESE, MANDARIN [CHN]
HO'TEI alt for HOTE [HOT]
HO-BAU alt for HABAU dial of JARAI [JRA]
HO-NHI alt for HANI [HNI]
HOA alt for CHINESE, YUE [YUH]
HOAI PETEL alt for TITA [TDQ]
HOANNYA alt for HOANYA [HON]
HOANYA [HON] lang, Taiwan
HOANYA dial of HOANYA [HON]
HOAVA [HOA] lang, Solomon Islands
HOCHE alt for ULCH [ULC]
HOCKCHEW alt for FOOCHOW dial of CHINESE, MIN
     PEI [MNP]
HOD dial of KAREN, PWO OMKOI [PWW]
HODRUNG dial of JARAI [JRA]
HOEN alt for NYAHEUN [NEV]
HOFUF alt for CENTRAL NAJDI dial of ARABIC,
     NAJDI [ARS]
HOG HARBOUR alt for SAKAO [SKU]
HOGGAR alt for TAMAHAQ, HOGGAR [THV]
HOGGAR dial of TAMAHAQ, HOGGAR [THV]
HOGIRANO alt for CHEKE HOLO [MRN]
HOGO alt for TAROKO [TRV]
HOGRANO alt for CHEKE HOLO [MRN]
HOH dial of QUILEUTE [QUI]
HOHODENA alt for HOHODENÉ dial of BANIWA
     [BAI]
HOHODENÉ dial of BANIWA [BAI]
HOHUMONO alt for KOHUMONO [BCS]
HOI alt for HAROI [HRO]
HOISAN alt for TAISHAN dial of CHINESE, YUE
     [YUH]
HOJERIA dial of ARABIC, YEMENI [ACQ]
HOKCHIA dial of CHINESE, MIN PEI [MNP]
HOKING dial of BAI [PIQ]
HOKKA alt for CHINESE, HAKKA [HAK]
HOKKAIDO dial of AINU [AIN]
HOKKIEN dial of CHINESE, MIN NAN [CFR]
HOKKIEN dial of CHINESE, MIN NAN [CFR]
HOKKIEN alt for FUKIENESE dial of CHINESE, MIN
     NAN [CFR]
HOL-CHIH alt for ULCH [ULC]
HOLADI alt for KATHIYAWADI dial of GUJARATI
     [GJR]
HOLAR alt for HOLIYA [HOY]
HOLARI alt for HOLIYA [HOY]
HOLE alt for HOLIYA [HOY]
HOLI alt for IJE [IJJ]
HOLIA alt for MAHARI dial of KONKANI [KNK]
HOLIAN alt for HOLIYA [HOY]
HOLIKACHUK [HOI] lang, USA
HOLIYA [HOY] lang, India
HOLLANDS alt for DUTCH [DUT]
HOLLAR GADBAS alt for OLLARI [OLL]
HOLMA alt for NZANYI [NJA]

HOLMA dial of NZANYI [NJA]
HOLMESTRAND dial of NORWEGIAN SIGN
    LANGUAGE [NSL]
HOLO alt for CHEKE HOLO [MRN]
HOLO alt for HOLU [HOL]
HOLOHOLO [HOO] lang, Tanzania, Zaïre, Zaïre
HOLOHOLO alt for HOLOHOLO [HOO]
HOLOM alt for HWALEM dial of MAJERA [XMJ]
HOLOWON alt for YALI, NINIA [NLK]
HOLU [HOL] lang, Angola, Zaïre, Zaïre
HOLU alt for HOLU [HOL]
HOLU alt for HOLIYA [HOY]
HOM alt for GHOMALA CENTRAL dial of GHOMALA'
    [BBJ]
HOMA [HOM] lang, Sudan
HOMBO alt for OMBO [OML]
HOMBORI alt for CENTRAL SONGAI dial of SONGAI
    [SON]
HOME dial of DII [DUR]
HONA alt for HWANA [HWO]
HONDURAN MÍSKITO dial of MÍSKITO [MIQ]
HONDURAN SUMO dial of SUMO [SUM]
HONGALLA alt for NGALAKAN [NIG]
HÓNGSHUIHÉ dial of ZHUANG, NORTHERN [CCX]
HONI [HOW] lang, China
HONIBO dial of SAMO-KUBO [SMQ]
HONITETU alt for WEMALE, SOUTH [TLW]
HONO' dial of SEKO PADANG [SKX]
HONPO dial of KRUMEN, SOUTHERN [TED]
HONYA alt for TUPURI [TUI]
HOOPA alt for HUPA [HUP]
HOP alt for MARI [HOB]
HOPA alt for XOPA dial of LAZ [LZZ]
HOPAO dial of NAGA, KONYAK [NBE]
HOPI [HOP] lang, USA
HOR alt for SANTALI [SNT]
HORA alt for JORÁ [JOR]
HORALE dial of WEMALE, NORTH [WEO]
HORO [HOR] lang, Central African Republic
HORO alt for MUNDARI [MUW]
HOROHORO alt for HOLOHOLO [HOO]
HOROM [HOE] lang, Nigeria
HORORO dial of NYANKOLE [NYN]
HORPA dial of HSIFAN [HSI]
HORU MUTHUN dial of NAGA, WANCHO [NNP]
HORUDAHUA alt for MORUNAHUA [MNY]
HORUNAHUA alt for MORUNAHUA [MNY]
HORURU [HRR] lang, Indonesia, Maluku
HOSHANGABAD dial of MALVI [MUP]
HOSS dial of BEROM [BOM]
HOTAN-YUTIAN alt for KHOTAN-KERYA dial of
    UYGHUR [UIG]
HOTE [HOT] lang, Papua New Guinea
HOTEA alt for SEDANG [SED]
HOTEANG alt for SEDANG [SED]
HOTEC alt for HOTE [HOT]
HOTI [HTI] lang, Indonesia, Maluku
HOTI alt for YUWANA [YAU]
HOTON alt for CHINESE, MANDARIN [CHN]
HOTON alt for KHOTON dial of KALMYK-OIRAT
    [KGZ]
HOTTENTOT alt for NAMA [NAQ]
HOUAILOU alt for AJIË [AJI]
HOULOUF dial of MSER [KQX]
HOUNAR alt for BESME [BES]
HOVA alt for MERINA dial of MALAGASY [MEX]

HOVONGAN [HOV] lang, Indonesia, Kalimantan
HOVONGAN dial of HOVONGAN [HOV]
HOWI dial of HAMTAI [HMT]
HOZO dial of HOZO-SEZO [HOZ]
HOZO-SEZO [HOZ] lang, Ethiopia
HPALONE alt for KAREN, PWO [PWO]
HPALONE alt for KAREN, PWO OMKOI [PWW]
HPON [HPO] lang, Myanmar
HPŎN alt for HPON [HPO]
HPUNGSI dial of RAWANG [RAW]
HRANGKHOL [HRA] lang, Myanmar, India
HRE [HRE] lang, Viet Nam
HRE dial of HRE [HRE]
HRLAK 1 alt for ALAK 1 [ALK]
HRLAK 2 alt for ALAK 2 [ALQ]
HROI alt for HAROI [HRO]
HROY alt for HAROI [HRO]
HRWAY alt for HAROI [HRO]
HSEMTANG alt for CHIN, SENTHANG [SEZ]
HSEN-HSUM alt for MOK [MQT]
HSIANG alt for CHINESE, XIANG [HSN]
HSIANGHSI MEO alt for HMONG, NORTHERN [MUQ]
HSIENYU alt for XIANYOU dial of CHINESE, MIN PEI
    [MNP]
HSIFAN [HSI] lang, Myanmar
HSING-AN dial of MIEN [YOC]
HSINGHUA alt for CHINESE, MIN PEI [MNP]
HSINGHUA dial of CHINESE, MIN PEI [MNP]
HSINGNING alt for XINGNING dial of CHINESE,
    HAKKA [HAK]
HSIUKULAN AMI alt for CENTRAL AMIS dial of
    AMIS [ALV]
HTIN alt for MAL [MLF]
HTISELWANG dial of RAWANG [RAW]
HU [HUO] lang, China
HUA dial of HMONG, WESTERN [HUJ]
HUA HIN KAREN alt for KAREN, PWO RATCHABURI
    [KJF]
HUA HIN PWO KAREN alt for KAREN, PWO
    RATCHABURI [KJF]
HUA LISU dial of LISU [LIS]
HUA MIAO alt for HMONG, WESTERN [HUJ]
/HUA-OWANI [HUC] lang, Botswana
HUACHIEH dial of HMONG, WESTERN [HUJ]
HUACHIPAERI [HUG] lang, Peru
HUACHIPAIRE alt for HUACHIPAERI [HUG]
HUACHIPAIRE dial of HUACHIPAERI [HUG]
HUAILAS dial of QUECHUA, ANCASH, HUAYLAS
    [QAN]
HUALAN YAO alt for MIEN [YOC]
HUALLAGA alt for COCAMA-COCAMILLA [COD]
HUALNGO alt for LUSHAI [LSH]
HUALPAI alt for WALAPAI dial of HAVASUPAI-
    WALAPAI-YAVAPAI [YUF]
HUAMALIES dial of QUECHUA, HUÁNUCO,
    HUAMALÍES [QEJ]
HUAMBISA [HUB] lang, Peru
HUAMBIZA alt for HUAMBISA [HUB]
HUAMELULA CHONTAL alt for CHONTAL OF
    OAXACA, LOWLAND [CLO]
HUAMELULTECO alt for CHONTAL OF OAXACA,
    LOWLAND [CLO]
HUAMUÊ alt for UAMUÉ [UAM]
HUANA alt for HUNGANA [HUM]
HUANCAVELICA dial of QUECHUA, AYACUCHO
    [QUY]

HUANCAYA-VITIS dial of QUECHUA, YAUYOS [QUX]
HUAORANI alt for WAORANI [AUC]
HUARAYO alt for ESE EJJA [ESE]
HUARAZ dial of QUECHUA, ANCASH, HUAYLAS [QAN]
HUARIAPANO alt for PANOBO [PNO]
HUARIJÍO [VAR] lang, Mexico
HUASTECA NAHUATL alt for NAHUATL, HUASTECA, WESTERN [NHW]
HUASTECA NAHUATL alt for NAHUATL, HUASTECA, EASTERN [NAI]
HUASTECO, SAN LUIS POTOSÍ [HVA] lang, Mexico
HUASTECO, VERACRUZ [HUS] lang, Mexico
HUAULU [HUD] lang, Indonesia, Maluku
HUAVE, SAN FRANCISCO DEL MAR [HUE] lang, Mexico
HUAVE, SAN MATEO DEL MAR [HUV] lang, Mexico
HUAYANG dial of CHINESE, HAKKA [HAK]
HUAYCHA alt for WAYCHA dial of QUECHUA, HUANCA, HUAYLLA [QHU]
HUAYLAS alt for HUAILAS dial of QUECHUA, ANCASH, HUAYLAS [QAN]
HUAYU alt for CHINESE, MANDARIN [CHN]
HUAYUAN MIAO alt for HMONG, NORTHERN [MUQ]
HUBA [KIR] lang, Nigeria
HUBE alt for MONGI [KGF]
HUDE alt for DGHWEDE [DGH]
HUDU dial of ÉWÉ [EWE]
HUE alt for CENTRAL VIETNAMESE dial of VIETNAMESE [VIE]
HUEHUETENANGO MAM alt for MAM, NORTHERN [MAM]
HUEHUETLA OTOMÍ alt for OTOMÍ, EASTERN [OTM]
HUEHUETONOC dial of AMUZGO, GUERRERO [AMU]
HUEI alt for OY [OYB]
HUHUNA dial of TAWALA [TBO]
HUI alt for CHINESE, MANDARIN [CHN]
HUI alt for HO dial of CHINESE, MANDARIN [CHN]
HUI-TZE alt for HO dial of CHINESE, MANDARIN [CHN]
HUI-ZU alt for DUNGAN [DNG]
HUI-ZU alt for CHINESE, MANDARIN [CHN]
HUICHOL [HCH] lang, Mexico
HUIHUI alt for UTSAT [HUQ]
HUILA alt for MWILA dial of NYANEKA [NYK]
HUILICHE alt for HUILLICHE [HUH]
HUILLICHE [HUH] lang, Chile
HUITIUPAN dial of TZOTZIL, CHAMULA [TZC]
HUITOTO, MENECA [HTO] lang, Colombia, Peru, Peru
HUITOTO, MENECA alt for HUITOTO, MENECA [HTO]
HUITOTO, MUINANE [HUX] lang, Peru
HUITOTO, MURUI [HUU] lang, Peru, Brazil, Colombia
HUIXTÁN dial of TZOTZIL, HUIXTÁN [TZU]
HUIXTECO alt for TZOTZIL, HUIXTÁN [TZU]
HUIZAPULA alt for MALINALTEPEC dial of TLAPANECO [TLL]
HUKUMINA [HUW] lang, Indonesia, Maluku
HUKWE alt for XUN [XUU]
HULA [HUL] lang, Papua New Guinea
HULALIU dial of HARUKU [HRK]
HULI [HUI] lang, Papua New Guinea
HULI-HULIDANA alt for HULI [HUI]

HULO alt for MENDE [MFY]
HULON alt for ELUN [ELN]
HULONTALO alt for GORONTALO [GRL]
HULU dial of BANJAR [BJN]
HULUF dial of JOLA-KASA [CSK]
HULUNG [HUK] lang, Indonesia, Maluku
HUM alt for HAM [JAB]
HUMA alt for TOPOSA [TOQ]
HUMA alt for ORUHUMA dial of HIMA [HIM]
HUMAI alt for PALAUNG, RUMAI [RBB]
HUMBA alt for KWANYAMA [KUY]
HUMBE dial of NYANEKA [NYK]
HUMBE alt for LILIMA dial of KALANGA [KCK]
HUMBE alt for LILIMA dial of KALANGA [KCK]
HUMBOLDT JOTAFA alt for TOBATI [TTI]
HUMBU dial of LUNDA [LVN]
HUMENE [HUF] lang, Papua New Guinea
HUMENE dial of HUMENE [HUF]
HUMLA BHOTIA [HUT] lang, Nepal
HUMONO alt for KOHUMONO [BCS]
HUMU alt for KWAMBA [RWM]
HUMURANA alt for OMURANO [OMU]
HUN alt for NYAHEUN [NEV]
HUN alt for EASTERN DUKA dial of DUKA [DUD]
HUNA alt for HWANA [HWO]
HUNAN alt for CHINESE, XIANG [HSN]
HUNANESE alt for CHINESE, XIANG [HSN]
HUNDE [HKE] lang, Zaïre
HUNE alt for EASTERN DUKA dial of DUKA [DUD]
HUNER alt for BESME [BES]
HUNG [HNU] lang, Viet Nam
HUNGAAN alt for HUNGANA [HUM]
HUNGANA [HUM] lang, Zaïre
HUNGANNA alt for HUNGANA [HUM]
HUNGARIAN [HNG] lang, Hungary, Austria, Czechoslovakia, Israel, Romania, Ukraine, Yugoslavia
HUNGARIAN alt for HUNGARIAN [HNG]
HUNGARIAN-SLOVAK ROMANI alt for ROMANI, CARPATHIAN [RMC]
HUNGDUAN IFUGAO dial of IFUGAO, TUWALI [IFK]
HUNGHO dial of ZHUANG, NORTHERN [CCX]
HUNGWE dial of MANYIKA [MXC]
HUNGWORO [NAT] lang, Nigeria
HUNJARA [HUN] lang, Papua New Guinea
HUNTJARA alt for HUNJARA [HUN]
HUNZA dial of BURUSHASKI [BSK]
HUNZA-NAGAR alt for GILGITI dial of SHINA [SCL]
HUNZIB [HUZ] lang, Russia, Europe
HUO NTE alt for SHE [SHX]
HUPA [HUP] lang, USA
"HUPDÁ MAKÚ" alt for HUPDË [JUP]
HUPDË [JUP] lang, Brazil, Colombia
HUPDË alt for HUPDË [JUP]
HUPDË dial of HUPDË [JUP]
HUPLA [HAP] lang, Indonesia, Irian Jaya
HURI alt for HULI [HUI]
HURON alt for WYANDOT [WYA]
HURUTSHE dial of TSWANA [TSW]
HURZA dial of PELASLA [MLR]
HURZO alt for HURZA dial of PELASLA [MLR]
HUTTERIAN GERMAN alt for GERMAN, HUTTERITE [GEH]
HUTU dial of RWANDA [RUA]
HUVA dial of YAGARIA [YGR]
HUVE alt for BURA-PABIR [BUR]

HUVIYA alt for BURA-PABIR [BUR]
HUZHU dial of TU [MJG]
HWA dial of CHING [MKG]
HWA alt for HUA dial of HMONG, WESTERN [HUJ]
HWA LISU dial of LISU [LIS]
HWA MIAO alt for HMONG, WESTERN [HUJ]
HWALEM dial of MAJERA [XMJ]
HWANA [HWO] lang, Nigeria
HWANE alt for WANE [HWA]
HWANGHAEDO dial of KOREAN [KKN]
HWASO alt for KPAN [KPK]
HWAYE alt for KPAN [KPK]
HWÉ [HWE] lang, Togo
HWÈ alt for AJA-GBE [AJG]
HWEDA alt for HWÉ [HWE]
HWÈGBÈ dial of AJA-GBE [AJG]
HWEI alt for HO dial of CHINESE, MANDARIN [CHN]
HWELA dial of LIGBI [LIG]
HWEN GBA KON dial of BASSA [BAS]
HWETHOM dial of PHUNOI [PHO]
HWINDJA dial of SHI [SHR]
HWLA [HWL] lang, Togo
HWONA alt for HWANA [HWO]
HYA [HYA] lang, Cameroon
HYABE alt for KAKANDA dial of NUPE [NUP]
HYAM alt for HAM [JAB]
HYAM alt for HAM dial of HAM [JAB]
HYAO alt for YAO [YAO]
HYATAD alt for CHINESE, MANDARIN [CHN]
HYILHAWUL dial of BURA-PABIR [BUR]
I alt for YI, SICHUAN [III]
I alt for YI, YUNNAN [NOS]
I-HADJA alt for KASANGA [CCJ]
I-WAK [IWK] lang, Philippines
IAAI [IAI] lang, New Caledonia
IAI alt for IAAI [IAI]
IAI alt for PURARI [IAR]
IAI dial of PURARI [IAR]
IAIBU dial of MULAHA [MFW]
IAKA alt for YAKA [YAF]
IAMALELE [YML] lang, Papua New Guinea
IAMBI dial of NILAMBA [NIM]
IAMEGA dial of GIDRA [GDR]
IAPAMA [IAP] lang, Brazil
IATÊ alt for FULNIÔ [FUN]
IATMUL [IAN] lang, Papua New Guinea
IAU [TMU] lang, Indonesia, Irian Jaya
IAU alt for YAWA [YVA]
IAU dial of IAU [TMU]
IAUANAUÁ alt for YAWANAWA [YWN]
IAUGA dial of NAMBU [NCM]
IAUIAULA dial of DIODIO [DDI]
IAW alt for IAU [TMU]
IAZGULEM alt for YAZGULYAM [YAH]
IBA alt for LAIWONU dial of PAMONA [BCX]
IBAA dial of IKWERE [IKW]
IBADJO alt for IWAIDJA [IBD]
IBADOY alt for IBALOI [IBL]
IBAJI dial of IGALA [IGL]
IBALAO dial of ILONGOT [ILK]
IBALI alt for TEKE, EASTERN [TEK]
IBALOI [IBL] lang, Philippines
IBALOY alt for IBALOI [IBL]
IBAMI alt for AGOI [IBM]
IBAN [IBA] lang, Indonesia, Kalimantan, Brunei,
    Malaysia, Sarawak

IBAN alt for IBAN [IBA]
IBANAG [IBG] lang, Philippines
IBANGA [IGA] lang, Papua New Guinea
IBANI [IBY] lang, Nigeria
IBARA alt for EBIRA [IGB]
IBARA alt for BASSA NGE dial of NUPE [NUP]
IBARAM dial of AKPES [IBE]
IBARAM-EFIFA alt for AKPES [IBE]
IBATAAN alt for IBATAN [IVB]
IBATAN [IVB] lang, Philippines
IBEEKE alt for BEEKE [BKF]
IBEMBE alt for BEMBE [BMB]
IBENO alt for IBINO [IBN]
IBERIAN ROMANI alt for ROMANI, CALO [RMR]
IBETU alt for VADI dial of GADI-SHINGINI-VADI-
    BAANGI [KAM]
IBHUBHI alt for BUBI [BUW]
IBIBIO [IBB] lang, Nigeria
IBIE NORTH alt for IVBIE NORTH dial of IVBIE
    NORTH-OKPELA-ARHE [ATG]
IBILAO alt for IBALAO dial of ILONGOT [ILK]
IBINO [IBN] lang, Nigeria
IBITO alt for HIBITO [HIB]
IBO alt for IGBO [IGR]
IBO alt for MWANI [WMW]
IBO dial of MWANI [WMW]
IBO UGU alt for IMBO UNGU [IMO]
IBO'TSA dial of OCAINA [OCA]
IBOHO alt for TAROKO [TRV]
IBOKO alt for BOKO [BKP]
IBOT OBOLO dial of OBOLO [ANN]
IBU [IBU] lang, Indonesia, Maluku
IBUBI alt for BUBI [BUW]
IBUKAIRU alt for SESA dial of FOLOPA [PPO]
IBUKWO alt for KPAN [KPK]
IBUNO alt for IBINO [IBN]
IBUT alt for JIDA-ABU [JID]
IBUYA alt for BUYA [BYY]
IBWISI alt for BWISI [BWZ]
ICA [ICA] lang, Benin, Togo
ICA [ARH] lang, Colombia
ICAANGI alt for TSAANGI [TSA]
ICAANGUI alt for TSAANGI [TSA]
ICAICHE MAYA alt for ITZÁ [ITZ]
ICELANDIC [ICE] lang, Iceland, USA
ICEN [ICH] lang, Nigeria
ICEVE-MACI [BEC] lang, Cameroon, Nigeria, Nigeria
ICEVE-MACI alt for ICEVE-MACI [BEC]
ICHEN alt for ICEN [ICH]
ICHEVE alt for ICEVE-MACI [BEC]
ICHIA alt for YI, SICHUAN [III]
ICHIA alt for ZHONGJIA dial of ZHUANG,
    NORTHERN [CCX]
ICHIBEMBA alt for BEMBA [BEM]
ICHIBISA alt for BISA dial of LALA-BISA [LEB]
ICHIBISA alt for BISA dial of LALA-BISA [LEB]
ICHIFIPA alt for FIPA [FIP]
ICHIINAMWANGA alt for MWANGA [MWN]
ICHILALA alt for LALA dial of LALA-BISA [LEB]
ICHILAMBA alt for LAMBA [LAB]
ICHILAMBYA alt for LAMBYA [LAI]
ICHIMAMBWE alt for MAMBWE dial of MAMBWE-
    LUNGU [MGR]
ICHIMAMBWE alt for MAMBWE dial of MAMBWE-
    LUNGU [MGR]
ICHINAMWANGA alt for MWANGA [MWN]

ICHIPIMBWE alt for PIMBWE [PIW]
ICHIRA alt for SIRA [SWJ]
ICHIRUNGU alt for RUNGU dial of MAMBWE-LUNGU [MGR]
ICHIRUNGWA alt for RUNGWA [RNW]
ICHITAABWA alt for TAABWA [TAP]
ICHIWANDA alt for WANDA [WBH]
ICHUN dial of CHINESE, GAN [KNN]
IDA alt for CHULIKATA [CLK]
IDA'AN dial of IDA'AN [DBJ]
IDAACA alt for IDACA [IDD]
IDA'AN [DBJ] lang, Malaysia, Sabah
IDACA [IDD] lang, Benin
IDAFAN alt for IRIGWE [IRI]
IDAH dial of IGALA [IGL]
IDAHAN alt for IDA'AN [DBJ]
IDAKAMENAI dial of IDUNA [VIV]
IDAKHO dial of IDAKHO-ISUKHA-TIRIKI [IDA]
IDAKHO-ISUKHA-TIRIKI [IDA] lang, Kenya
IDAN alt for IDA'AN [DBJ]
IDATE [IDT] lang, Indonesia, Nusa Tenggara
IDAXO alt for IDAKHO dial of IDAKHO-ISUKHA-TIRIKI [IDA]
IDAYAN alt for IDA'AN [DBJ]
IDE alt for MACUNA [MYY]
IDELE alt for MODELE dial of BEFANG [BBY]
IDESA dial of OKPE-IDESA-OLOMA-AKUKU [OKP]
IDI [IDI] lang, Papua New Guinea
IDIN IDINDJI alt for YIDINY [YII]
IDIN-WUDJAR alt for YIDINY [YII]
IDINJI alt for YIDINY [YII]
IDNE alt for MALEU-KILENGE [MGL]
IDO alt for SINOHOAN dial of PAMONA [BCX]
IDOMA [IDO] lang, Nigeria
IDOMA CENTRAL dial of IDOMA [IDO]
IDOMA NOKWU alt for ALAGO [ALA]
IDOMA SOUTH dial of IDOMA [IDO]
IDOMA WEST dial of IDOMA [IDO]
IDON [IDC] lang, Nigeria
IDONG alt for IDON [IDC]
IDONGIRO alt for DONYIRO dial of TOPOSA [TOQ]
IDORE'E alt for SINOHOAN dial of PAMONA [BCX]
IDU alt for CHULIKATA [CLK]
IDUN [LDB] lang, Nigeria
IDUNA [VIV] lang, Papua New Guinea
IDUWINI dial of IJO, CENTRAL-WESTERN [IJC]
IFA'ONGOTA alt for 'ONGOTA [BXE]
IFÈ [IFE] lang, Benin, Togo
IFÈ alt for IFÈ [IFE]
IFIGI dial of FOI [FOI]
IFIRA alt for FILA dial of MELE-FILA [MXE]
IFO [IFF] lang, Vanuatu
IFO dial of SIE [ERG]
IFUGAO, AMGANAD [IFA] lang, Philippines
IFUGAO, BATAD [IFB] lang, Philippines
IFUGAO, MAYOYAO [IFU] lang, Philippines
IFUGAO, TUWALI [IFK] lang, Philippines
IFUNUBWA alt for MBEMBE, CROSS RIVER [MFN]
IFUUMU alt for FUUMU dial of TEKE, SOUTH CENTRAL [IFM]
"IGABO" alt for ISOKO [ISO]
IGABO alt for ISOKO dial of URHOBO [URH]
IGALA [IGL] lang, Nigeria
IGAN dial of MELANAU [MEL]
IGANA [IGG] lang, Papua New Guinea
IGARA alt for IGALA [IGL]

IGARA dial of EBIRA [IGB]
IGBARRA alt for EBIRA [IGB]
IGBENA dial of YORUBA [YOR]
IGBIRA alt for EBIRA [IGB]
IGBIRI alt for GBIRI dial of GBIRI-NIRAGU [GRH]
IGBIRRA alt for EBIRA [IGB]
IGBO [IGR] lang, Nigeria
IGBO alt for LEGBO [AGB]
IGBUDUYA dial of EKPEYE [EKP]
IGEDDE alt for IGEDE [IGE]
IGEDE [IGE] lang, Nigeria
IGEMBE dial of MERU [MER]
IGIKIGA dial of RWANDA [RUA]
IGIKURIA alt for KURIA [KUJ]
IGNACIANO [IGN] lang, Bolivia
IGO [AHL] lang, Togo
IGODOR alt for IBALOI [IBL]
IGOJI dial of MERU [MER]
IGOM [IGM] lang, Papua New Guinea
IGORA [KQF] lang, Papua New Guinea
IGORA dial of IGORA [KQF]
IGOROT alt for BONTOC, CENTRAL [BNC]
IGU dial of EBIRA [IGB]
IGUAMBO dial of MUNDANI [MUN]
IGUEBEN dial of ESAN [ISH]
IGUMALE alt for IDOMA SOUTH dial of IDOMA [IDO]
IGUMBO alt for IGUAMBO dial of MUNDANI [MUN]
IGUTA [NAR] lang, Nigeria
IGWAALE alt for IDOMA SOUTH dial of IDOMA [IDO]
IGWORMANY dial of LARO [LRO]
IGWURUTA dial of IKWERE [IKW]
IGZENNAIAN dial of TARIFIT [RIF]
IHA [IHP] lang, Indonesia, Irian Jaya
IHA-SAPARUA dial of SAPARUA [SPR]
IHA-SERAM dial of SAPARUA [SPR]
IHATUM alt for OSATU [OST]
IHEKWOT alt for MACI dial of ICEVE-MACI [BEC]
IHIMA alt for HIMA dial of EBIRA [IGB]
IHINI alt for MANDAHUACA [MHT]
IHINI alt for BARÉ [BAE]
IHOBE MBOG alt for BABONG dial of MBO [MBO]
IHURUANA dial of MAQUIRITARI [MCH]
IIKÓ dial of LIKA [LIK]
IILIIT alt for ILIT dial of KUNAMA [KUM]
IILIT alt for ILIT dial of KUNAMA [KUM]
IIMUTSU dial of TSOU [TSY]
IJA dial of KAILI, LEDO [LEW]
IJAW alt for IJO, SOUTHEAST [IJO]
IJCA alt for ICA [ARH]
IJE [IJJ] lang, Benin
IJEBU dial of YORUBA [YOR]
IJEN KUI alt for ZHONGJIA dial of ZHUANG, NORTHERN [CCX]
IJESHA dial of YORUBA [YOR]
IJIGBAM alt for IDOMA SOUTH dial of IDOMA [IDO]
IJKA alt for ICA [ARH]
IJO, CENTRAL-WESTERN [IJC] lang, Nigeria
IJO, SOUTHEAST [IJO] lang, Nigeria
IJOH dial of KENSIU [KNS]
IJOK alt for IJOH dial of KENSIU [KNS]
IK [IKX] lang, Uganda
IKA [IKK] lang, Nigeria
IKA alt for ICA [ARH]
IKA alt for IGU dial of EBIRA [IGB]
IKAIKU alt for KAIKU [KKQ]

IKALAHAN alt for KALLAHAN, KAYAPA [KAK]
IKALE dial of YORUBA [YOR]
IKALEBWE alt for EASTERN KALEBWE dial of
   SONGE [SOP]
IKAN alt for UKAAN [KCF]
IKAW alt for AKHA [AKA]
IKE alt for ICA [ARH]
IKEGA dial of SINAGORO [SNC]
IKELA alt for KELA [KEL]
IKELEVE dial of KITUBA [KTU]
IKERAM dial of AKPES [IBE]
IKHO alt for AKHA [AKA]
IKIBIRI dial of IJO, CENTRAL-WESTERN [IJC]
IKIBUNGU alt for KIMBU [KIV]
IKIHA alt for HA [HAQ]
IKIKURIA alt for KURIA [KUJ]
IKINATA alt for IKOMA [NTK]
IKINGONDE alt for NYAKYUSA-NGONDE [NYY]
IKINGURIMI alt for NGURIMI [NGQ]
IKINILAMBA alt for NILAMBA [NIM]
IKINIRAMBA alt for NILAMBA [NIM]
IKINYAKYUSA alt for NYAKYUSA-NGONDE [NYY]
IKINYARWANDA alt for RWANDA [RUA]
IKINYIKYUSA alt for NYAKYUSA-NGONDE [NYY]
IKIRIBATI alt for KIRIBATI [GLB]
IKIRUGURU alt for RUGURU [RUF]
IKISENYI alt for ISSENYI dial of IKOMA [NTK]
IKITO alt for IQUITO [IQU]
IKIZANAKI alt for ZANAKI [ZAK]
IKIZU [IKZ] lang, Tanzania
IKO alt for DOKO-UYANGA [UYA]
IKO dial of OBOLO [ANN]
IKO dial of AGOI [IBM]
IKÓ alt for IIKÓ dial of LIKA [LIK]
IKOBI KAIRI alt for IKOBI-MENA [MEB]
IKOBI-MENA [MEB] lang, Papua New Guinea
IKOKOLEMU alt for KUMAM [KDI]
IKOKU alt for NEMADI [NED]
IKOLU alt for IKULU [IKU]
IKOLU dial of SINAGORO [SNC]
IKOM dial of OLULUMO-IKOM [IKO]
IKOMA [NTK] lang, Tanzania
IKOR alt for AKHA [AKA]
IKOTA alt for KOTA [KOQ]
IKPAN alt for KPAN [KPK]
IKPESHE alt for IKPESHI [IKP]
IKPESHI [IKP] lang, Nigeria
IKPONU dial of AKPOSO [KPO]
IKPOSO alt for AKPOSO [KPO]
IKRANI [IKR] lang, India
IKU alt for IKU-GORA-ANKWA [IKV]
IKU alt for MODELE dial of BEFANG [BBY]
IKU-GORA-ANKWA [IKV] lang, Nigeria
IKULU [IKU] lang, Nigeria
IKUMAMA alt for TESO [TEO]
IKUMAMA alt for KUMAM [KDI]
IKUN dial of UBAGHARA [BYC]
IKUNDUN [IMI] lang, Papua New Guinea
IKUTA alt for KOTA [KOQ]
IKWERE [IKW] lang, Nigeria
IKWERI dial of NGWO [NGN]
IKWERRE alt for IKWERE [IKW]
IKWERRI alt for IKWERE [IKW]
IKWO dial of IZI-EZAA-IKWO-MGBO [IZI]
IKYOO dial of LENAKEL [TNL]
IL-ARUSA alt for ARUSA dial of MAASAI [MET]

ILA [ILB] lang, Zambia
ILA dial of ILA [ILB]
ILA dial of YORUBA [YOR]
ILAALI alt for LAALI dial of TEKE, WESTERN [TEZ]
ILAGA WESTERN DANI alt for DANI, WESTERN
   [DNW]
ILAHITA alt for FILIFITA dial of ARAPESH,
   SOUTHERN [AOJ]
ILAI dial of MAILU [MGU]
ILAJE dial of YORUBA [YOR]
ILAKIA dial of AWA [AWB]
ILAMBA alt for NILAMBA [NIM]
ILAMMU dial of LEPCHA [LEP]
ILANON alt for IRANUN dial of MAGINDANAON
   [MDH]
ILANUM alt for IRANUN dial of MAGINDANAON
   [MDH]
ILANUN [ILL] lang, Malaysia, Sabah
ILAO alt for GELO [KKF]
ILCAMUS alt for CHAMUS dial of SAMBURU [SAQ]
ILE MANDIRI alt for SOUTH LAMAHOLOT dial of
   LAMAHOLOT [SLP]
ILEME alt for UNEME [UNE]
ILENTUNGEN dial of MANOBO, WESTERN
   BUKIDNON [MBB]
ILEO alt for DENGESE [DEZ]
ILI dial of UYGHUR [UIG]
ILI TURKI [ILI] lang, China, Kazakhstan
ILI TURKI alt for ILI TURKI [ILI]
ILIAURA alt for ALYAWARRA [ALY]
ILIIT alt for ILIT dial of KUNAMA [KUM]
ILIKU dial of LUSENGO [LUS]
ILIMPEYA dial of EVENKI [EVN]
ILIT dial of KUNAMA [KUM]
ILIUN [ILU] lang, Indonesia, Maluku
ILIWAKI alt for TALUR [ILW]
ILLANOAN alt for ILANUN [ILL]
ILLANON alt for IRANUN dial of MAGINDANAON
   [MDH]
ILLANOON alt for ILANUN [ILL]
ILLANOS alt for ILANUN [ILL]
ILLANUN alt for ILANUN [ILL]
ILMAUMAU alt for ILIUN [ILU]
ILMEDU alt for TALUR [ILW]
ILOCANO [ILO] lang, Philippines, USA
ILOKANO alt for ILOCANO [ILO]
ILOKO alt for ILOCANO [ILO]
ILOM dial of IXIL, CHAJUL [IXJ]
ILOMWE alt for LOMWE [NGL]
ILONGGO alt for HILIGAYNON [HIL]
ILONGOT [ILK] lang, Philippines
ILOODOKILANI dial of MAASAI [MET]
ILPARA alt for WARLPIRI [WBP]
ILPUTIH alt for APUTAI [APX]
ILOAN alt for EVEN [EVE]
ILUD dial of MAGINDANAON [MDH]
ILUMBU alt for LUMBU [LUP]
ILWAKI alt for TALUR [ILW]
ILWANA alt for MALAKOTE [MLK]
IMABAN alt for LEGBO [AGB]
IMAFIN dial of TANNA, NORTH [TNN]
IMAKUA alt for MAKHUWA [MAK]
IMAN dial of UDIHE [UDE]
IMASI alt for SOBEI [SOB]
IMBANA dial of MUNDANG [MUA]
IMBAO'O alt for ANDIO [BZB]

IMBARA alt for IMBANA dial of MUNDANG [MUA]
IMBINIS [IMB] lang, Papua New Guinea
IMBO alt for MBO [ZMW]
IMBO UNGU [IMO] lang, Papua New Guinea
IMBONGGO alt for IMBO UNGU [IMO]
IMBONGU alt for IMBO UNGU [IMO]
IMENTI dial of MERU [MER]
IMERAGUEN [IME] lang, Mauritania
IMERETIAN dial of GEORGIAN [GEO]
IMERXEV dial of GEORGIAN [GEO]
IMERXEV KARTLIAN dial of GEORGIAN [GEO]
IMILA dial of MARIA [MDS]
IMILANGU dial of SIMAA [SIE]
IMILANGU alt for MDUNDULU dial of LUYANA [LAV]
IMONA dial of NTOMBA [NTO]
IMONDA dial of WARIS [WRS]
IMRAGUEN alt for IMERAGUEN [IME]
IMROIN alt for IMROING [IMR]
IMROING [IMR] lang, Indonesia, Maluku
IMURUD alt for IMURUT dial of YAMI [YMI]
IMURUT dial of YAMI [YMI]
IN alt for IR [IRR]
INABAKNON alt for SAMA, ABAKNON [ABX]
INAFOSA alt for TAUYA [TYA]
INAGTA OF MT. IRAYA alt for AGTA, MT. IRAYA
[ATL]
INAKONA alt for KOO dial of TALISE [TLR]
INALLU alt for AYNALLU dial of AZERBAIJANI,
SOUTH [AZB]
INAMARI alt for MASHCO PIRO [CUJ]
INAMWANGA alt for MWANGA [MWN]
INANLU alt for AYNALLU dial of AZERBAIJANI,
SOUTH [AZB]
INANWATAN [SZP] lang, Indonesia, Irian Jaya
IÑAPARI alt for MASHCO PIRO [CUJ]
INAQUEN alt for TEHUELCHE [TEH]
INARI "LAPPISH" alt for SAAMI, INARI [LPI]
INATI alt for ATI [ATK]
INAUINI dial of DENÍ [DAN]
INBAKNON alt for SAMA, ABAKNON [ABX]
INCAHUASI dial of QUECHUA, LAMBAYEQUE [QUF]
INCHAZI alt for CHE [RUK]
INDAAKA alt for NDAAKA [NDK]
INDAGEN alt for GURAGE, INDEGEGN [GIE]
INDE dial of KAILI, DA'A [KZF]
INDEGEGNE alt for GURAGE, INDEGEGN [GIE]
INDENIE dial of ANYIN [ANY]
INDI AYTA alt for AYTA, MAG-INDI [BLX]
INDIAN SIGN LANGUAGE [INS] lang, India,
Bangladesh, Pakistan
INDIAN SIGN LANGUAGE alt for INDIAN SIGN
LANGUAGE [INS]
INDIGIRKA dial of EVEN [EVE]
INDINDJI alt for YIDINY [YII]
INDINOGOSIMA alt for MEHEK [NUX]
ÍNDIOS DO COXODOÁ alt for ZURUAHÁ [ZUR]
INDO-PORTUGUESE [IDB] lang, Sri Lanka, India
INDONESIAN [INZ] lang, Indonesia, Java, Bali, USA
INDONESIAN SIGN LANGUAGE [INL] lang, Indonesia,
Java, Bali
INDONESIAN, PERANAKAN [PEA] lang, Indonesia,
Java, Bali
INDORODORO alt for TONDA [IND]
INDRAMAYU dial of JAVANESE [JAN]
INDRI [IDR] lang, Sudan
INDUS dial of KOHISTANI, INDUS [MVY]

INEDUA dial of ENGENNI [ENN]
INEME alt for UNEME [UNE]
INETA dial of BUDU [BUU]
INGA [INB] lang, Colombia
INGA alt for QUECHUA, PASTAZA, SOUTHERN
[QUP]
INGA, JUNGLE [INJ] lang, Colombia
"INGALIK" alt for DEGEXIT'AN [ING]
"INGALIT" alt for DEGEXIT'AN [ING]
INGANO alt for QUICHUA, LOWLAND, NAPO [QLN]
INGANO alt for INGA, JUNGLE [INJ]
INGARA alt for YINGGARDA [YIA]
INGARDA alt for YINGGARDA [YIA]
INGARICÓ alt for PEMON [AOC]
INGARIKO alt for AKAWAIO [ARB]
INGARIKO alt for PATAMONA [PBC]
INGARIKÓ alt for PEMON [AOC]
INGARRA alt for YINGGARDA [YIA]
INGARRAH alt for YINGGARDA [YIA]
INGASSANA alt for GAAM [TBI]
INGELSI dial of DAUSAHAQ [DSQ]
INGESSANA alt for GAAM [TBI]
INGGARDA alt for YINGGARDA [YIA]
INGILO dial of GEORGIAN [GEO]
INGLI alt for MABA [MQA]
INGRIAN [IZH] lang, Estonia, Sweden, Sweden
INGRIAN alt for INGRIAN [IZH]
INGUL alt for NGUL [NLO]
INGULU alt for LOMWE [NGL]
INGUNDI alt for NGUNDI [NDN]
INGUNDJI alt for LIPOTO dial of LUSENGO [LUS]
INGURA alt for ANINDILYAKWA [AOI]
INGUS alt for INGUSH [INH]
INGUSH [INH] lang, Russia, Europe
INGWE alt for HUNGWORO [NAT]
INGWO alt for HUNGWORO [NAT]
INHAMBANE alt for TONGA [TOH]
INIAI alt for NETE [NET]
INIAI alt for BISORIO [BIR]
INIBALOI alt for IBALOI [IBL]
INIDEM alt for NINDEM dial of KANUFI-KANINGDON-
NINDEM [KDP]
INJA dial of MBOLE [MDQ]
INJANG alt for NAGA, RENGMA [NRE]
INJEBI alt for NJEBI [NZB]
INKONGO alt for LUNA [LUJ]
INLAND CREE alt for CREE, INLAND EASTERN [CRE]
INLAND DOBEL dial of DOBEL [KVO]
INMEAS alt for ISINAI [INN]
INN TEA dial of OY [OYB]
INNEQOR alt for ENNEQOR dial of GURAGE, EAST
[GRE]
INNER SIRAGI dial of KULUI [KFX]
INNTHA alt for INTHA [INT]
INOKE alt for INOKE-YATE [INO]
INOKE-YATE [INO] lang, Papua New Guinea
INONHAN [LOC] lang, Philippines
INOR alt for GURAGE, INNEMOR [GII]
INPARRA alt for YINGGARDA [YIA]
INSANAO alt for BIBOKI-INSANA dial of ATONI
[TMR]
INSINAI alt for ISINAI [INN]
INSULAR CATALAN alt for BALEARIC dial of
CATALAN [CLN]
INTERIOR SALUAN alt for SALUAN,
KAHUMAMAHON [SLB]

INTHA [INT] lang, Myanmar
INUIT, EASTERN CANADIAN [ESB] lang, Canada
INUIT, GREENLANDIC [ESG] lang, Greenland, Denmark
INUIT, GREENLANDIC alt for INUIT, GREENLANDIC [ESG]
INUIT, NORTH ALASKAN [ESI] lang, USA, Canada
INUIT, NORTHWEST ALASKA INUPIAT [ESK] lang, USA
INUIT, WESTERN CANADIAN [ESC] lang, Canada
INUKTITUT alt for INUIT, EASTERN CANADIAN [ESB]
INUPIAQ alt for INUIT, NORTH ALASKAN [ESI]
INUPIAT ESKIMO alt for INUIT, NORTH ALASKAN [ESI]
INUPIAT ESKIMO dial of INUIT, NORTH ALASKAN [ESI]
INUPIK alt for INUIT, NORTH ALASKAN [ESI]
INUVAKEN dial of AMAHUACA [AMC]
INXOKVARI dial of KHVARSHI [KHV]
INYAI-GADIO-BISORIO alt for BISORIO [BIR]
INYANGATOM alt for NYANGATOM dial of TOPOSA [TOQ]
INYIMA alt for LENYIMA [LDG]
INYIMANG alt for NYIMANG [NYI]
INYVEN alt for SOUTH PERMYAK dial of KOMI-PERMYAK [KOI]
IOMA BINANDERE alt for BINANDERE [BHG]
IOULLEMMEDEN dial of TAMAJEQ, TAHOUA [TTQ]
IOULLEMMEDEN alt for TAWALLAMMET TAN DANNAG dial of TAMAJEQ, TAHOUA [TTQ]
IOULLEMMEDEN alt for TAWALLAMMAT TAN DANNAG dial of TAMAJEQ, TAHOUA [TTQ]
IOWA [IOW] lang, USA
IOWAY alt for IOWA [IOW]
IPANDE alt for PANDE [BKJ]
IPANGA alt for PANGA dial of MONGO-NKUNDU [MOM]
IPECA alt for IPEKA-TAPUIA [PAJ]
IPEKA-TAPUIA [PAJ] lang, Brazil
IPERE alt for BHELE [PER]
IPIKO [IPK] lang, Papua New Guinea
IPIKOI alt for IPIKO [IPK]
IPILI [IPI] lang, Papua New Guinea
IPILI-PAIELA alt for IPILI [IPI]
IPILI-PAYALA alt for IPILI [IPI]
IPITINERI alt for AMAHUACA [AMC]
IPOH dial of DAYAK, LAND [DYK]
IPULO [ASS] lang, Cameroon
IPUNU alt for PUNU [PUU]
IPURICOTO alt for CAMARACOTA dial of PEMON [AOC]
IPURINÃN alt for APURINÃ [APU]
IQUITA alt for IQUITO [IQU]
IQUITO [IQU] lang, Peru
IR [IRR] lang, Laos
IRABU-JIMA dial of MIYAKO [MVI]
IRAHUTU alt for IRARUTU [IRH]
IRAKU alt for IRAQW [IRK]
IRAMBA alt for LAMBYA [LAI]
IRAMBA alt for NILAMBA [NIM]
IRANCHE alt for IRÁNTXE [IRA]
IRANGI alt for LANGI [LAG]
IRANON alt for IRANUN dial of MAGINDANAON [MDH]
IRANON MARANAO alt for ILANUN [ILL]

IRÁNTXE [IRA] lang, Brazil
IRÁNTXE dial of IRÁNTXE [IRA]
IRANUM alt for ILANUN [ILL]
IRANUN alt for ILANUN [ILL]
IRANUN dial of MAGINDANAON [MDH]
IRANXE alt for IRÁNTXE [IRA]
IRAQW [IRK] lang, Tanzania
IRARUTU [IRH] lang, Indonesia, Irian Jaya
IRAVA alt for IRULA [IRU]
IRAYA [IRY] lang, Philippines
IRBORE alt for ARBORE [ARV]
IREGWE alt for IRIGWE [IRI]
IRESIM [IRE] lang, Indonesia, Irian Jaya
IRHOBO alt for ISEKIRI [ITS]
IRI dial of KADARA [KAD]
IRIA [IRX] lang, Indonesia, Irian Jaya
IRIANESE dial of MALAY [MLI]
IRIEMKENA alt for AIRORAN [AIR]
IRIGWE [IRI] lang, Nigeria
IRISH alt for GAELIC, IRISH [GLI]
IRISH SIGN LANGUAGE [ISG] lang, Ireland
IRISH TRAVELER CANT alt for SHELTA [STH]
IROKA dial of YUKPA [YUP]
IRON dial of OSETIN [OSE]
IRONWORKER ROMANI dial of ROMANI, BALKAN [RMN]
IROOLE dial of DABARRE [DBR]
IRRUAN dial of BOKYI [BKY]
IRTYSH dial of TATAR [TTR]
IRUAN dial of BOKYI [BKY]
IRULA [IRU] lang, India
IRULAR alt for IRULA [IRU]
IRULAR MOZHI alt for IRULA [IRU]
IRULIGA alt for IRULA [IRU]
IRULIGAR alt for IRULA [IRU]
IRUMU [IOU] lang, Papua New Guinea
IRUNGI alt for RUNGI [RUR]
IRUPI-DRAGELI dial of BINE [ORM]
IRUTU alt for IRARUTU [IRH]
ISA alt for ESAN [ISH]
ISAALUNG alt for SISAALA, TUMULUNG [SIL]
ISAAN alt for TAI, NORTHEASTERN [TTS]
ISABI [ISA] lang, Papua New Guinea
ISACHANURE alt for NAGA, SANGTAM [NSA]
ISAL alt for BENGGOI [BGY]
ISALA dial of SISAALA, TUMULUNG [SIL]
ISAM dial of PAGU [PGU]
ISAMAL dial of KALAGAN [KQE]
ISAN alt for TAI, NORTHEASTERN [TTS]
ISAN alt for YUPNA [YUT]
ISANGA alt for SANGA [SGA]
ISANGA alt for GUSU dial of JERA [JER]
ISANGELE alt for EFIK [EFK]
ISANGU alt for SANGU [SNQ]
ISANZU [ISN] lang, Tanzania
ISCOBAQUEBU alt for ISCONAHUA [ISC]
ISCONAHUA [ISC] lang, Peru
ISEBE [IGO] lang, Papua New Guinea
ISEKIRI [ITS] lang, Nigeria
ISELEMA-OTU alt for ISEKIRI [ITS]
ISENYI alt for ISSENYI dial of IKOMA [NTK]
ISFAHANI dial of FARSI, WESTERN [PES]
ISHAN alt for ESAN [ISH]
ISHARON KI ZABAN [ISR] lang, Pakistan
ISHBUKUN alt for SOUTH BUNUN dial of BUNUN [BNN]

ISHE dial of UKAAN [KCF]
ISHEKIRI alt for ISEKIRI [ITS]
ISHIBORI alt for NKEM dial of NKEM-NKUM [ISI]
ISHIGAKI dial of YAEYAMA [RYS]
ISHIM dial of TATAR [TTR]
ISHIMALILIA alt for MALILA [MGQ]
ISHINYIHA alt for NYIHA [NIH]
ISHIRA alt for SIRA [SWJ]
ISHIRO alt for CHAMACOCO [CEG]
ISHIRO alt for EBITOSO dial of CHAMACOCO [CEG]
ISHISAFWA alt for SAFWA [SBK]
ISHKASHIM alt for ISHKASHIMI dial of SANGLECHI-
  ISHKASHIMI [SGL]
ISHKASHIMI dial of SANGLECHI-ISHKASHIMI [SGL]
ISHKASHMI alt for ISHKASHIMI dial of SANGLECHI-
  ISHKASHIMI [SGL]
ISHKOMAN dial of WAKHI [WBL]
ISHPI dial of PASHAYI, SOUTHWEST [PSH]
ISHUA alt for UHAMI-IYAYU [UHA]
ISHUATAN dial of TZOTZIL, CHAMULA [TZC]
ISI [ISS] lang, Papua New Guinea
ISIBIRI alt for NKEM dial of NKEM-NKUM [ISI]
"ISIKULA" alt for FANAGOLO [FAO]
ISILOLOLO alt for FANAGOLO [FAO]
ISIMBI alt for ESIMBI [AGS]
ISINAI [INN] lang, Philippines
ISINAY alt for ISINAI [INN]
ISINDE'BELE alt for NDEBELE [NDF]
ISIOKPO dial of IKWERE [IKW]
ISIPIKI alt for FANAGOLO [FAO]
ISIRA alt for SIRA [SWJ]
ISIRAWA [SRL] lang, Indonesia, Irian Jaya
ISISWAZI alt for SWATI [SWZ]
ISIXHOSA alt for XHOSA [XOS]
ISIZULU alt for ZULU [ZUU]
ISKEN dial of PASHAYI, SOUTHWEST [PSH]
ISLAMI alt for URDU [URD]
ISLAND dial of MAILU [MGU]
ISLAND BOIKIN dial of BOIKIN [BZF]
ISLAND COMOX dial of COMOX [COO]
ISLAND KIWAI dial of KIWAI, SOUTHERN [KJD]
ISLAND TIGAK dial of TIGAK [TGC]
ISLETA dial of TIWA, SOUTHERN [TIX]
ISLETA PUEBLO alt for ISLETA dial of TIWA,
  SOUTHERN [TIX]
ISNAG [ISD] lang, Philippines
ISNAY alt for ISINAI [INN]
ISNEG alt for ISNAG [ISD]
ISOCENIO alt for IZOCENYO dial of CHIRIGUANO
  [GUI]
ISOKO [ISO] lang, Nigeria
ISOKO dial of URHOBO [URH]
ISOLE EOLIE dial of SICILIAN [SCN]
ISOMBI alt for WADIMBISA dial of BUDU [BUU]
ISONGO alt for MBATI [MDN]
ISRAELI SIGN LANGUAGE [ISL] lang, Israel
ISSA alt for SOMALI [SOM]
ISSALA alt for SISAALA, TUMULUNG [SIL]
ISSALA alt for SISAALA, WESTERN [SSL]
ISSAN alt for TAI, NORTHEASTERN [TTS]
ISSANA alt for BANIWA [BAI]
ISSENYI dial of IKOMA [NTK]
ISSILITA' dial of PITU ULUNNA SALU [PTU]
ISSONGO alt for MBATI [MDN]
ISTANBUL alt for CONSTANTINOPLE dial of
  ARMENIAN [ARM]

ISTHMUS AZTEC alt for NAHUATL, ISTHMUS [NAU]
ISTHMUS MIXE alt for MIXE, GUICHICOVI [MIR]
ISTHMUS NAHUAT alt for NAHUATL, ISTHMUS
  [NAU]
ISTRIAN dial of VENETIAN [VEC]
ISTRO-ROMANIAN alt for RUMANIAN, ISTRO [RUO]
ISU [ISU] lang, Cameroon
ISU [SZV] lang, Cameroon
ISUAMA alt for OWERRI dial of IGBO [IGR]
ISUBU alt for ISU [SZV]
ISUKHA dial of IDAKHO-ISUKHA-TIRIKI [IDA]
ISUWU alt for ISU [SZV]
ISUXA alt for ISUKHA dial of IDAKHO-ISUKHA-
  TIRIKI [IDA]
ITA alt for ALTA, SOUTHERN [AGY]
ITAEM [ITM] lang, Papua New Guinea
ITAKHO alt for IDAKHO dial of IDAKHO-ISUKHA-
  TIRIKI [IDA]
ITALIAN [ITN] lang, Italy, Puerto Rico, Ethiopia,
  Somalia, France, San Marino, Switzerland,
  Yugoslavia
ITALIAN SIGN LANGUAGE [ISE] lang, Italy
ITALIOT dial of GREEK [GRK]
ITALKIAN alt for JUDEO-ITALIAN [ITK]
ITALON dial of ILONGOT [ILK]
ITANGA alt for ITOGAPÚK [ITG]
ITANGIKOM alt for KOM [BKM]
ITAWES alt for ITAWIT [ITV]
ITAWIS alt for ITAWIT [ITV]
ITAWIS dial of ITAWIT [ITV]
ITAWIT [ITV] lang, Philippines
ITBAYAT dial of IVATAN [IVV]
ITBAYATEN alt for ITBAYAT dial of IVATAN [IVV]
ITBEG RUGNOT alt for AGTA, MT. IRAYA [ATL]
ITCHEN alt for ICEN [ICH]
ITEEJI dial of KUKELE [KEZ]
ITEGHE alt for TEKE, NORTHERN [TEG]
ITELMEN [ITL] lang, Russia, Asia
ITELMEN dial of ITELMEN [ITL]
ITELYMEM alt for ITELMEN [ITL]
ITENE [ITE] lang, Bolivia
ITENEO alt for ITENE [ITE]
ITENEZ alt for ITENE [ITE]
ITERI [ITR] lang, Papua New Guinea
ITESO alt for TESO [TEO]
ITESYO alt for TESO [TEO]
ITIGIDI alt for LEGBO [AGB]
ITIK [ITX] lang, Indonesia, Irian Jaya
ITKAN dial of KORYAK [KPY]
ITNEG, BINONGAN [ITB] lang, Philippines
ITNEG, INLAOD [ITI] lang, Philippines
ITNEG, MASADIIT [TIS] lang, Philippines
ITNEG, SOUTHERN [ITT] lang, Philippines
ITO dial of IGEDE [IGE]
ITOGAPUC alt for ITOGAPÚK [ITG]
ITOGAPÚK [ITG] lang, Brazil
ITONAMA [ITO] lang, Bolivia
ITONGA dial of LENAKEL [TNL]
ITOREAUHIP dial of ITENE [ITE]
ITOTO alt for MACO dial of PIAROA [PID]
ITSAANGI alt for TSAANGI [TSA]
ITSANGI alt for TSAANGI [TSA]
ITSEKIRI alt for ISEKIRI [ITS]
ITSONG alt for SONGO [SOO]
ITTIK alt for ITIK [ITX]
ITTIK dial of ITIK [ITX]

ITTIK-TOR alt for ITIK [ITX]
ITTIK-TOR dial of ITIK [ITX]
ITTU alt for OROMO, EASTERN [HAE]
ITUCALI alt for URARINA [URA]
ITUMBA dial of SAGALA [SBM]
ITUMKALA dial of CHECHEN [CJC]
ITUNDU dial of TUNEN [BAZ]
ITURI dial of SWAHILI, ZAÏRE [SWC]
ITUTANG [ITU] lang, Papua New Guinea
ITYOO alt for TYOO dial of TEKE, CENTRAL [TEC]
ITZÁ [ITZ] lang, Guatemala, Belize
IU MIEN [IUM] lang, China
IU MIEN alt for MIEN [YOC]
IUI alt for SALT-YUI [SLL]
IULEHA dial of EMAI-IULEHA-ORA [EMA]
IURUNA alt for JURÚNA [JUR]
IVANGA alt for IBANGA [IGA]
IVATAN [IVV] lang, Philippines
IVATAN alt for IBATAN [IVB]
IVBIE NORTH dial of IVBIE NORTH-OKPELA-ARHE
   [ATG]
IVBIE NORTH-OKPELA-ARHE [ATG] lang, Nigeria
IVBIOSAKON alt for EMAI-IULEHA-ORA [EMA]
IVHIADAOBI dial of YEKHEE [ETS]
IVHIMION dial of EMAI-IULEHA-ORA [EMA]
IVORI alt for TAINAE [AGO]
IVRIT alt for HEBREW [HBR]
IWA dial of MWANGA [MWN]
IWAAK alt for I-WAK [IWK]
IWAIDJA [IBD] lang, Australia
IWAIDJI alt for IWAIDJA [IBD]
IWAL [KBM] lang, Papua New Guinea
IWAM [IWM] lang, Papua New Guinea
IWAM, SEPIK [IWS] lang, Papua New Guinea
IWAM-NAGALEMB dial of ARAPESH, SOUTHERN
   [AOJ]
IWATENU alt for NENGONE [NEN]
IWERE alt for ISEKIRI [ITS]
IWI dial of AKPOSO [KPO]
IWOER alt for IWUR [IWO]
IWORRO dial of YORUBA [YOR]
IWUR [IWO] lang, Indonesia, Irian Jaya
IWUUMU alt for WUUMU dial of TEKE, SOUTH
   CENTRAL [IFM]
IXCATECO [IXC] lang, Mexico
IXIGNOR alt for ABISHIRA [ASH]
IXIL, CHAJUL [IXJ] lang, Guatemala
IXIL, NEBAJ [IXI] lang, Guatemala
IXIL, SAN JUAN COTZAL [IXL] lang, Guatemala
IXREKO-MUXREK dial of RUTUL [RUT]
IXTAPA dial of TZOTZIL, CHAMULA [TZC]
IXTENCO OTOMÍ alt for OTOMÍ, SOUTHEASTERN
   [OTA]
IXTLÁN ZAPOTECO alt for ZAPOTECO, SIERRA DE
   JUÁREZ [ZAA]
IYAA alt for YAA dial of TEKE, WESTERN [TEZ]
IYAA alt for YAKA dial of TEKE, WESTERN [TEZ]
IYACE alt for YACHE dial of AKPA-YACHE [AKF]
IYAKA alt for YAKA [YAF]
IYAKA alt for YAA dial of TEKE, WESTERN [TEZ]
IYAKA alt for YAKA dial of TEKE, WESTERN [TEZ]
IYALA alt for YALA [YBA]
IYANI dial of AKPES [IBE]
IYANZI alt for YANS [YNS]
IYEKHEE alt for YEKHEE [ETS]
IYIRIKUM alt for MOGHAMO dial of META' [MGO]

IYIVE alt for YIIVE dial of TIV [TIV]
IYO alt for ROCKY PEAK [ROK]
IYON alt for MESAKA [IYO]
IYONGIYONG alt for BAKPINKA [BBS]
IYONGUT dial of ILONGOT [ILK]
IYONIYONG alt for KIONG [KKM]
IZALE alt for NZARE dial of MBEMBE, TIGON [NZA]
IZARE alt for NZARE dial of MBEMBE, TIGON [NZA]
IZAREK alt for IZERE [FIZ]
IZEM dial of GBARI [GBY]
IZERE [FIZ] lang, Nigeria
IZHA alt for EZHA dial of GURAGE, CENTRAL WEST
   [GUY]
IZHOR alt for INGRIAN [IZH]
IZI dial of IZI-EZAA-IKWO-MGBO [IZI]
IZI-EZAA-IKWO-MGBO [IZI] lang, Nigeria
IZMIR alt for SMYRNA dial of ARMENIAN [ARM]
IZNACEN dial of TARIFIT [RIF]
IZO alt for IJO, CENTRAL-WESTERN [IJC]
IZOCENIO alt for IZOCEÑO dial of CHIRIGUANO
   [GUI]
IZOCEÑO dial of CHIRIGUANO [GUI]
IZOCEÑO alt for IZOCENYO dial of CHIRIGUANO
   [GUI]
IZOCENYO dial of CHIRIGUANO [GUI]
IZON alt for IJO, CENTRAL-WESTERN [IJC]
IZORA [CBO] lang, Nigeria
IZZI alt for IZI dial of IZI-EZAA-IKWO-MGBO [IZI]
JA alt for DZA [JEN]
JA'ALI dial of ARABIC, SUDANESE [APD]
JA'O alt for ENDE dial of ENDE [END]
JA-IT dial of MOKEN [MWT]
JAAKO alt for MARGU [MHG]
JAAN alt for YANA [YAN]
JAAN alt for YANGA dial of MOORE [MHM]
JAANG alt for DINKA, NORTHEASTERN [DIP]
JAB alt for YELMEK [JEL]
JABA alt for HAM [JAB]
JABA alt for HAM dial of HAM [JAB]
JABAAL dial of TAMA [TMA]
JABAAL dial of TAMA [TMA]
JABAANA alt for YABAÂNA [YBN]
JABAL NAFUSAH [JBN] lang, Libya
JABAN alt for ARANDAI [JBJ]
JABANA alt for ZABANA [KJI]
JABBA alt for HAM [JAB]
JABEM alt for YABEM [JAE]
JABI alt for YABI dial of EKARI [EKG]
JABIM alt for YABEM [JAE]
JABO dial of GREBO, JABO [GRJ]
JABORLANG alt for BABUZA [BZG]
JABSCH alt for YELMEK [JEL]
JABUDA alt for KANJU [KBE]
JABUNG dial of ABUNG [ABL]
JABUTÍ [JBT] lang, Brazil
JACALTECO, EASTERN [JAC] lang, Guatemala
JACALTECO, WESTERN [JAI] lang, Guatemala,
   Mexico, Mexico
JACALTECO, WESTERN alt for JACALTECO,
   WESTERN [JAI]
JACARIA dial of KARIPUNÁ DO GUAPORÉ [KUQ]
JADEJI dial of KACHCHI [KFR]
JADEJI dial of SINDHI [SND]
JADGALI [JAV] lang, Pakistan
JADOBAFI dial of BRAJ BHASHA [BFS]
JAFGA alt for BEEGE dial of MUSGU [MUG]

JAFI alt for BANAWÁ [BNH]
JAFI alt for YAFI [WFG]
JAFI dial of KURDI [KDB]
JAFRI dial of SIRAIKI [SKR]
JAGA AAD alt for JAGANNATHI [JAG]
JAGAI alt for THIANG dial of NUER [NUS]
JAGANATHAPURAM KOYA dial of KOYA [KFF]
JAGANATHI alt for JAGANNATHI [JAG]
JAGANNATHA BHASHA alt for JAGANNATHI [JAG]
JAGANNATHI [JAG] lang, India
JAGATAI alt for CHAGATAI [CGT]
JAGATAI alt for TEKE dial of TURKMEN [TCK]
JAGGOI alt for JAGOI [SNE]
JAGOI [SNE] lang, Malaysia, Sarawak
JAH HET alt for JAH HUT [JAH]
JAH HUT [JAH] lang, Malaysia, Peninsular
JAHADIAN alt for YAHADIAN [NER]
JAHAI alt for JEHAI [JHI]
JAHALATAN alt for YALAHATAN [JAL]
JAHALATANE alt for YALAHATAN [JAL]
JAHANKA [JAD] lang, Senegal, Gambia, Guinea,
  Guinea Bissau
JAHANQUE alt for JAHANKA [JAD]
JAHONQUE alt for JAHANKA [JAD]
JAHROMI dial of FARSI, WESTERN [PES]
JAHUI alt for DIAHÓI dial of TENHARIM [PAH]
JAINTIA dial of KHASI [KHI]
JAINTIA dial of PNAR [PBV]
JAIPURI dial of MARWARI [MKD]
JAIPURIA alt for NAGA, NOCTE [NJB]
JAISELMER alt for MARWARI, SOUTHERN [MQH]
JAISELMER alt for MARWARI, NORTHERN [MRI]
JAJAO alt for ZAZAO [JAJ]
JAJURU alt for KAJURU dial of KADARA [KAD]
JAKAI alt for YAQAY [JAQ]
JAKANCI alt for LABIR [JKU]
JAKARTA dial of MALAY [MLI]
JAKARTA MALAY alt for BETAWI [BEW]
JAKATI [JAT] lang, Moldova, Afghanistan
JAKHACHIN dial of KALMYK-OIRAT [KGZ]
JAKOON alt for JAKUN [JAK]
JAKPHANG dial of NAGA, KONYAK [NBE]
JAKU alt for LABIR [JKU]
JAKU'D alt for JAKUN [JAK]
JAKUD'N alt for JAKUN [JAK]
JAKULA alt for GANGGALIDA [GCD]
JAKUN [JAK] lang, Malaysia, Peninsular
JAKUN alt for LABIR [JKU]
JAL alt for ATEN [GAN]
JALAIT alt for JIRIM dial of MONGOLIAN,
  PERIPHERAL [MVF]
JALALUM dial of KAREKARE [KAI]
JALINGO dial of MUMUYE [MUL]
JALKOTI dial of SHINA, KOHISTANI [PLK]
JALOC alt for YALU [YLU]
JALON alt for FUUTA JALON [FUF]
JALONKÉ alt for YALUNKA [YAL]
JALONKE alt for YALUNKA [YAL]
JALTEPEC MIXTECO alt for MIXTECO, SOUTHERN
  NOCHIXTLÁN [MAB]
JAMA alt for SAMBA DAKA [CCG]
JAMA MAPUN alt for MAPUN [SJM]
JAMAICAN COUNTRY SIGN LANGUAGE [JCS] lang,
  Jamaica
JAMAICAN CREOLE ENGLISH dial of WESTERN
  CARIBBEAN CREOLE ENGLISH [JAM]

JAMAICAN PATWA alt for JAMAICAN CREOLE
  ENGLISH dial of WESTERN CARIBBEAN CREOLE
  ENGLISH [JAM]
JAMAMADÍ [JAA] lang, Brazil
JAMATIA dial of KOK BOROK [TRP]
JAMBA alt for DZAMBA dial of BALOI [BIZ]
JAMBAPUING alt for DJAMBARRPUYNGU [DJR]
JAMBAPUINGO alt for DJAMBARRPUYNGU [DJR]
JAMBO alt for ANUAK [ANU]
JAMDEN alt for YAMDENA [JMD]
JAMDENA alt for YAMDENA [JMD]
JAMINAWÁ alt for YAMINAHUA [YAA]
JAMINAWA alt for YAMINAHUA [YAA]
JAMINJUNG alt for DJAMINDJUNG [DJD]
JAMPALAM dial of WANDALA [MFI]
JAMPEA dial of BAJAU, INDONESIAN [BDL]
JAMRAL dial of MALVI [MUP]
JAMSHEDI alt for JAMSHIDI dial of AIMAQ [AIQ]
JAMSHIDI dial of AIMAQ [AIQ]
JANAMA alt for NORTHERN PONDORI dial of BOZO,
  SOROGAMA [BZE]
JANAMA alt for SOUTHERN PONDORI dial of BOZO,
  SOROGAMA [BZE]
JANDALI alt for ADYNYAMATHANHA [ADT]
JANDIJINUNG alt for DJINANG [DJI]
JANELA alt for DEG [MZW]
JANERA dial of BARASANA [BSN]
JANG alt for REJANG [REJ]
JANG-KALA alt for NYANGGA [NNY]
JANGA alt for NYANGGA [NNY]
JANGAA alt for NYANGGA [NNY]
JANGAD alt for KURUX, NEPALI [KXL]
JANGALI alt for JANGGALI [JNL]
JANGAN alt for GIANGAN [BGI]
JANGGA alt for NYANGGA [NNY]
JANGGALI [JNL] lang, Nepal, India
JANGGU [DJA] lang, Indonesia, Irian Jaya
JANGHARD alt for KURUX, NEPALI [KXL]
JANGKUNDJARA alt for YANKUNTATJARA [KDD]
JANGLI dial of SIRAIKI [SKR]
JANGRAMI alt for JANGSHUNG [JNA]
JANGSHEN dial of CHIN, THADO [TCZ]
JANGSHUNG [JNA] lang, India
"JANJERINYA" alt for YEMSA [JNJ]
"JANJERO" alt for YEMSA [JNJ]
JANJI [JNI] lang, Nigeria
JANJO alt for DZA [JEN]
"JANJOR" alt for YEMSA [JNJ]
JANJULA alt for YANYUWA [JAO]
JANSAURI alt for JAUNSARI [JNS]
JAO alt for YAO [YAO]
JAOPING HAKKA dial of CHINESE, HAKKA [HAK]
JAPANESE [JPN] lang, Japan, USA, Singapore,
  Taiwan, Thailand
JAPANESE alt for JAPANESE [JPN]
JAPANESE SIGN LANGUAGE [JSL] lang, Japan
JAPRERÍA [JRU] lang, Venezuela
JAQAI alt for YAQAY [JAQ]
JAQARU [JQR] lang, Peru
JAR alt for BADA [BAU]
JAR alt for JARAWA [JAR]
JARA [JAF] lang, Nigeria
JARA alt for JARAWA [JAR]
JARACIN KASA alt for GINGWAK dial of JARAWA
  [JAR]
JARAI [JRA] lang, Viet Nam, USA

JARANCHI alt for JARAWA [JAR]
JARAW-DOMO dial of MOSI [MSE]
JARAWA [JAR] lang, Nigeria
JARAWA [ANQ] lang, India
JARAWA alt for IZERE [FIZ]
JARAWAN BUNUNU alt for GINGWAK dial of
    JARAWA [JAR]
JARAWAN DUTSE alt for IZERE [FIZ]
JARAWAN KOGI alt for BADA [BAU]
JARAWAN KOGI alt for JARAWA [JAR]
JARAWARA [JAP] lang, Brazil
JARENG alt for GONGLA [GMM]
JARI alt for DAGAARI DIOULA [DGD]
JARI alt for IZERE [FIZ]
JARI dial of ANEME WAKE [ABY]
JARICUNA alt for ARECUNA dial of PEMON [AOC]
JARICUNA alt for ARECUNA dial of PEMON [AOC]
JARNANGO [JAY] lang, Australia
JARONG alt for JIARONG [JYA]
JAROO alt for JARU [DDJ]
JARU [DDJ] lang, Australia
JARU alt for LAVEN [LBO]
JARU alt for PAKAÁSNOVOS [PAV]
JARU dial of YELE [YLE]
JARUÁRA alt for JARAWARA [JAP]
JARUM dial of KENSIU [KNS]
JARUMÁ alt for YARUMÁ [YRM]
JARUNA alt for JURÚNA [JUR]
JAS alt for ASMAT, CENTRAL [AST]
JASING alt for YASING dial of MUNDANG [MUA]
JASOA dial of MPYEMO [MCX]
JASOA alt for JASUA dial of MPYEMO [MCX]
JASUA dial of MPYEMO [MCX]
JASUA alt for JASOA dial of MPYEMO [MCX]
JAT alt for JAKATI [JAT]
JAT alt for JADGALI [JAV]
JATAPU [JTP] lang, India
JATGALI alt for JADGALI [JAV]
JATI alt for JAKATI [JAT]
JATKI alt for JADGALI [JAV]
JATKI dial of SIRAIKI [SKR]
JATU alt for JAKATI [JAT]
JAU-NAVO alt for KARIPUNÁ DO GUAPORÉ [KUQ]
JAUARETE dial of CARÚTANA [CRU]
JAUARI dial of YANOMÁMI [WCA]
JAULAPITI alt for YAWALAPITÍ [YAW]
JAUN-JAUN dial of SURIGAONON [SUL]
JAUNA alt for NIJADALI [NAD]
JAUNDE alt for EWONDO [EWO]
JAUNSARI [JNS] lang, India
JAUNSAURI alt for JAUNSARI [JNS]
JAUR alt for YAUR [JAU]
JAVAÉ dial of KARAJÁ [KPJ]
JAVAHE alt for JAVAÉ dial of KARAJÁ [KPJ]
JAVANESE [JAN] lang, Indonesia, Java, Bali,
    Malaysia, Sabah, Malaysia, Sabah, Singapore
JAVANESE alt for JAVANESE [JAN]
JAVANESE, CARIBBEAN [JVN] lang, Surinam,
    French Guiana
JAVANESE, NEW CALEDONIAN [JAS] lang, New
    Caledonia
JAVIERANO dial of TRINITARIO [TRN]
JAVIERANO alt for SAN JAVIER dial of
    CHIQUITANO [CAX]
JAWA alt for JAVANESE [JAN]
JAWA HALUS dial of JAVANESE [JAN]

JAWAN alt for DJAUAN [DJN]
JAWANAUA alt for YAWANAWA [YWN]
JAWANLI alt for WAYAMLI dial of BULI [BZQ]
JAWAPERI alt for NINAM [SHB]
JAWAPERI dial of ATRUAHÍ [ATR]
JAWARI alt for NINAM [SHB]
JAWE [JAZ] lang, New Caledonia
JAWONY alt for DJAUAN [DJN]
JAYA BAKTI dial of BAJAU, INDONESIAN [BDL]
JAYAPURA alt for TOBATI [TTI]
JAYE dial of KENGA [KYQ]
JE alt for YEI [JEI]
JEBA alt for HAM [JAB]
JEBEL alt for JEBEL TEKEIM dial of LAFOFA [LAF]
JEBEL EL AMIRA dial of LAFOFA [LAF]
JEBEL NEFUSA alt for JABAL NAFUSAH [JBN]
JEBEL SILAK alt for AKA [SOH]
JEBEL TEKEIM dial of LAFOFA [LAF]
JEBELAWI alt for BERTA [WTI]
JEBELS SILLOK alt for AKA [SOH]
JEBERO [JEB] lang, Peru
JEDEPO dial of GREBO, E JE [GRB]
JEERE alt for JERA [JER]
JEGA alt for GIBANAWA [GIB]
JEGARATA-KAKENDETTA dial of OROKAIVA [ORK]
JEGASI SARUHU dial of OROKAIVA [ORK]
JEGU [JEU] lang, Chad
JEH [JEH] lang, Viet Nam, Laos
JEH BRI LA dial of JEH [JEH]
JEH BRI LA dial of JEH [JEH]
JEH MANG RAM dial of JEH [JEH]
JEHAI [JHI] lang, Malaysia, Peninsular
JEHAI dial of JEHAI [JHI]
JEHER dial of KENSIU [KNS]
JEI alt for YEI [JEI]
JEIDJI alt for WUNAMBAL [WUB]
JEINU KURUBA dial of KANNADA [KJV]
JEITHI alt for WUNAMBAL [WUB]
JEKANG alt for EASTERN JIKANY dial of NUER
    [NUS]
JEKKINO dial of BIDIO [BID]
JEKRI alt for ISEKIRI [ITS]
JELAI dial of SEMAI [SEA]
JELALONG PUNAN dial of PUNAN-NIBONG [PNE]
JELGOOJI alt for FULFULDE, JELGOOJI [FUM]
JELMEK alt for YELMEK [JEL]
JELTULAK dial of EVENKI [EVN]
JEMBAYAN dial of BASAP [BDB]
JEMBRANA alt for LOWLAND BALI dial of BALI
    [BZC]
JEME alt for NAGA, ZEME [NZM]
JEMEZ [TOW] lang, USA
JEMHWA dial of GUMUZ [GUK]
JEMJEM alt for SUGA [SGI]
JEMMARI dial of JABAL NAFUSAH [JBN]
JEN alt for DZA [JEN]
JEN KURUMBA alt for KURUMBA, JENNU [QKJ]
JENAMA alt for BOZO, SOROGAMA [BZE]
JENEPONTO alt for TURATEA dial of MAKASSAR
    [MSR]
JENG [JEG] lang, Laos
JENG alt for NZANYI [NJA]
JENG dial of MUMUYE [MUL]
JENGE alt for NZANYI [NJA]
JENGJENG alt for LANOH [LNH]
JENGRE alt for JERE dial of JERA [JER]

JENIMU alt for SIAGHA-YENIMU [OSR]
JENISCH alt for YENICHE [YEC]
JENJI alt for JANJI [JNI]
JENJO alt for DZA [JEN]
JENNE alt for WEST SONGAI dial of SONGAI [SON]
JENNU KURUMBA NONSTANDARD KANNADA alt
   for KURUMBA, JENNU [QKJ]
JENURES dial of BIAK [BHW]
JENUWA dial of KUTEP [KUB]
JEPA-MATSI [JEP] lang, Brazil
JEPAL alt for JIPAL dial of KOFYAR [KWL]
JEPEL alt for JIPAL dial of KOFYAR [KWL]
JERA [JER] lang, Nigeria
JERA alt for JARA [JAF]
JERBA [JEA] lang, Tunisia
JERE dial of JERA [JER]
JERIYAWA alt for JERE dial of JERA [JER]
JERRIAIS dial of FRENCH [FRN]
JERU alt for AKA-JERU [AKJ]
JESÚS MARÍA dial of CORA [COR]
JETI alt for MANEM [JET]
JETO alt for JOTO [JOT]
JEWISH TAT alt for TAT, HEBREW [TAT]
JEYWO alt for CHAMACOCO [CEG]
JEZHU dial of GBARI [GBY]
JEZIRE dial of KURMANJI [KUR]
JHADPI dial of VARHADI-NAGPURI [VAH]
JHALAWADI alt for KATHIYAWADI dial of
   GUJARATI [GJR]
JHALIYA alt for JHARIA [JHA]
JHANGAL alt for JANGGALI [JNL]
JHANGAR alt for JANGGALI [JNL]
JHANGER alt for KURUX, NEPALI [KXL]
JHARAWAN dial of BRAHUI [BRH]
JHARIA [JHA] lang, India
JHARKOT dial of BARAGAUNLE [BON]
JHARWA dial of ASSAMESE [ASM]
JHORIA alt for MURIA, WESTERN [MUT]
JHUE dial of JARAI [JRA]
JI alt for EASTERN NUER dial of NUER [NUS]
JIAMÀO [JIO] lang, China
JIAOGONGMIAN dial of BIAO MIEN [BMT]
JIARONG [JYA] lang, China
JIBA alt for KONA [JUO]
JIBANA dial of GIRYAMA [NYF]
JIBANCHI alt for JIBU [JIB]
JIBANCI alt for JIBU [JIB]
JIBARO alt for SHUAR [JIV]
JIBAWA alt for JIBU [JIB]
JIBBALI [SHV] lang, Oman
JIBI alt for KONA [JUO]
JIBITO alt for HIBITO [HIB]
JIBLA dial of ARABIC, YEMENI [ACQ]
JIBU [JIB] lang, Nigeria
JIBU alt for GIDRA [GDR]
JIBU KOINE dial of JIBU [JIB]
JIBYAL alt for JIPAL dial of KOFYAR [KWL]
JICAQUE alt for TOL [JIC]
JIDA alt for JIDA-ABU [JID]
JIDA-ABU [JID] lang, Nigeria
JIDDA alt for JIDA-ABU [JID]
JIDDA-ABU alt for JIDA-ABU [JID]
JIDDU alt for JIIDDU [JII]
JIDINDJI alt for YIDINY [YII]
JIE dial of KARAMOJONG [KDJ]
JIIDDU [JII] lang, Somalia

JIIR dial of PUKU-GEERI-KERI-WIPSI [GEL]
JIJAL alt for INDUS dial of KOHISTANI, INDUS
   [MVY]
JIJI [JIJ] lang, Tanzania
JIKAI alt for BURARRA [BVR]
JIKAIN alt for EASTERN JIKANY dial of NUER [NUS]
JIKANY alt for EASTERN NUER dial of NUER [NUS]
JILAMA BAWANG alt for BISAYA, BRUNEI [BSB]
JILAMA BAWANG alt for BISAYA, SABAH [BSY]
JILAMA SUNGAI alt for BISAYA, BRUNEI [BSB]
JILAMA SUNGAI alt for BISAYA, SABAH [BSY]
JILBE [JIE] lang, Nigeria
JILI alt for DZILI dial of JINGPHO [CGP]
JILIM [JIL] lang, Papua New Guinea
JIM MUN alt for MUN [MJI]
JIMAJIMA [JMA] lang, Papua New Guinea
JIMBIN [JMB] lang, Nigeria
JIMBINAWA alt for JIMBIN [JMB]
JIMI [JIM] lang, Cameroon
JIMI [JMI] lang, Nigeria
JIMJIMEN alt for JIMI [JIM]
JIMO dial of JIMI [JIM]
JIMO alt for ZUMU dial of BATA [BTA]
JIMO alt for ZUMU dial of BATA [BTA]
JIMUNI dial of MANAGALASI [MCQ]
JINA [JIA] lang, Cameroon
JINA dial of JINA [JIA]
JINAK dial of CITAK [TXT]
JINDA alt for CINDA dial of KAMUKU [KAU]
JINDJIBANDI alt for YINDJIBARNDI [YIJ]
JINDWI dial of MANYIKA [MXC]
JING alt for VIETNAMESE [VIE]
JINGA alt for NJINGA dial of MBUNDU, LOANDA
   [MLO]
JINGALI alt for DJINGILI [JIG]
JINGGARDA alt for YINGGARDA [YIA]
JINGHPAW alt for JINGPHO [CGP]
JINGJING dial of BESLERI [HNA]
JINGPHO [CGP] lang, Myanmar, China, India
JINGULU alt for DJINGILI [JIG]
JINHUA dial of CHINESE, WU [WUU]
JINJA alt for ZINZA [JIN]
JINJO dial of YELE [YLE]
JINKUM alt for WAPAN [JUK]
JINLERI alt for SHOO-MINDA-NYEM [BCV]
JINMEN dial of IU MIEN [IUM]
JINMINI alt for SENOUFO, DJIMINI [DYI]
JINO [JIU] lang, China
JINPING DAI alt for TAI DAM [BLT]
JINUO alt for JINO [JIU]
JIONGNAI alt for QIUNGNAI dial of PUNU [PNU]
JIPAL dial of KOFYAR [KWL]
JIR JORONT alt for YIR YORONT [YIY]
JIR'JOROND dial of YIR YORONT [YIY]
JIRAI dial of BATA [BTA]
JIREL [JUL] lang, Nepal
JIRI alt for JIREL [JUL]
JIRIM dial of MONGOLIAN, PERIPHERAL [MVF]
JIRIM dial of MONGOLIAN, PERIPHERAL [MVF]
JIRMEL MEL-JIR alt for JIR'JOROND dial of YIR
   YORONT [YIY]
JIRU [JRR] lang, Nigeria
JITA [JIT] lang, Tanzania
JITOTOL dial of TZOTZIL, CHAMULA [TZC]
JIVARO alt for ACHUAR-SHIWIAR [ACU]
JIVARO alt for SHUAR [JIV]

JIW alt for GUAYABERO [GUO]
JIWADJA alt for IWAIDJA [IBD]
JIWALI alt for MANGALA [MEM]
JIYE dial of TOPOSA [TOQ]
JIYE alt for JIE dial of KARAMOJONG [KDJ]
JJU [KAJ] lang, Nigeria
JLUKO dial of GODIÉ [GOD]
JO [JOW] lang, Mali
JO alt for GHOMALA CENTRAL dial of GHOMALA'
    [BBJ]
JO ALUR alt for ALUR [ALZ]
JO COLO alt for COLO dial of THURI [THU]
JO LWO alt for LUWO [LWO]
JO THURI alt for THURI [THU]
JO-UDA dial of MONGOLIAN, PERIPHERAL [MVF]
JOARI alt for JAUARI dial of YANOMÁMI [WCA]
JOBA [JOB] lang, Zaïre
JOBI dial of POM [PMO]
JOBOKA alt for NAGA, WANCHO [NNP]
JOHAHI dial of MAITHILI [MKP]
JOHARI dial of KUMAUNI [KFY]
JOHODE alt for DGHWEDE [DGH]
JOHOR alt for RIAU dial of MALAY [MLI]
JOI alt for JUI dial of ZHUANG, NORTHERN [CCX]
JOK alt for NGOK-SOBAT dial of DINKA,
    NORTHEASTERN [DIP]
JOKOT dial of ALUR [ALZ]
JOLA alt for JOLA-FOGNY [DYO]
JOLA-FOGNY [DYO] lang, Senegal, Gambia
JOLA-KASA [CSK] lang, Senegal, Gambia
JOLFA dial of ARMENIAN [ARM]
JOLOANO SULU alt for TAUSUG [TSG]
JOLOF alt for DYOLOF dial of WOLOF [WOL]
JOLONG dial of BAHNAR [BDQ]
JOMANG alt for TALODI [TLO]
"JOMPRE" alt for KUTEP [KUB]
JONAM dial of ALUR [ALZ]
JONAZ alt for CHICHIMECA-JONAZ [PEI]
JONE dial of KHAM [KHG]
JONGA dial of TSONGA [TSO]
JONGA dial of TSONGA [TSO]
JONGGUNU alt for MONI [MNZ]
JONGOR alt for MIGAAMA [MMY]
JONKHA alt for DZONGKHA [DZO]
JONKOR-BOURMA TAGUIL alt for JEGU [JEU]
JONKOR-GERA alt for MOKULU [MOZ]
JÓOLA alt for JOLA-FOGNY [DYO]
JÓOLA-KASA alt for JOLA-KASA [CSK]
JOORE alt for ZAORÉ [ZRE]
JOPARA alt for GUARANÍ, PARAGUAYAN [GUG]
JORÁ [JOR] lang, Bolivia
JORAI alt for JARAI [JRA]
JORTO [JRT] lang, Nigeria
JOS-ZARAZON alt for IZERE [FIZ]
JOSTU dial of MONGOLIAN, PERIPHERAL [MVF]
JOSTU dial of MONGOLIAN, PERIPHERAL [MVF]
JOTAFA alt for TOBATI [TTI]
JOTI alt for YUWANA [YAU]
JOTO [JOT] lang, Central African Republic
JOWULU alt for JO [JOW]
JRO dial of CHRAU [CHR]
JU [JUU] lang, Nigeria
JU BA dial of MAMBILA, CAMEROON [MYA]
JU NAARE dial of MAMBILA, CAMEROON [MYA]
JU'OASI alt for KUNG-TSUMKWE [KTZ]
JUANAUO alt for KARIPUNÁ DO GUAPORÉ [KUQ]

JUANEÑO dial of LUISEÑO [LUI]
JUANG [JUN] lang, India
JUANGA alt for YUAGA [NUA]
JUANGA dial of YUAGA [NUA]
JUARZON dial of SAPO [KRN]
JUBA ARABIC alt for ARABIC, SUDANESE CREOLE
    [PGA]
JUCHEN alt for NANAI [GLD]
JUDEO SPANISH alt for LADINO [SPJ]
JUDEO-ARABIC alt for YAHUDIC [YHD]
JUDEO-ARABIC alt for YUDI [YUD]
JUDEO-ARAMAIC [TRG] lang, Israel
JUDEO-BERBER [JBE] lang, Israel, Morocco
JUDEO-COMTADINE alt for SHUADIT [SDT]
JUDEO-CRIMEAN TATAR [JCT] lang, Uzbekistan,
    Georgia
JUDEO-CRIMEAN TURKISH alt for JUDEO-CRIMEAN
    TATAR [JCT]
JUDEO-FRENCH alt for ZARPHATIC [ZRP]
JUDEO-GEORGIAN [JGE] lang, Georgia, Israel, Israel
JUDEO-GEORGIAN alt for JUDEO-GEORGIAN [JGE]
JUDEO-GERMAN alt for YIDDISH [YDD]
JUDEO-GREEK alt for YEVANIC [YEJ]
JUDEO-ITALIAN [ITK] lang, Italy
JUDEO-KURDISH [JKR] lang, Azerbaijan
JUDEO-PERSIAN alt for DZHIDI [DZH]
JUDEO-PROVENÇAL alt for SHUADIT [SDT]
JUDEO-TAJIK alt for BUKHARIC [BHH]
JUDEO-TAT alt for TAT, HEBREW [TAT]
JUDEO-TATIC alt for TAT, HEBREW [TAT]
JUDEZMO alt for LADINO [SPJ]
JUGARI alt for ARABIC, CENTRAL ASIAN
    COLLOQUIAL [ABH]
JUGULA alt for GANGGALIDA [GCD]
JUGUMBIR alt for YUGAMBAL [YUB]
JUI dial of ZHUANG, NORTHERN [CCX]
JUKAGIR alt for YUKAGHIR, NORTHERN [YKG]
JUKAGIR alt for YUKAGHIR, SOUTHERN [YUX]
JUKAMBA alt for YUGAMBAL [YUB]
JUKON alt for WAPAN [JUK]
JUKU alt for WAPAN [JUK]
JUKU JUNKUN alt for WAPAN [JUK]
JUKUM alt for WAPAN [JUK]
JUKUN alt for DYUGUN [DYD]
JUKUN alt for JUKUN TAKUM [JBU]
JUKUN ABINSI alt for ABINSI [JUB]
JUKUN KONA alt for KONA [JUW]
JUKUN TAKUM [JBU] lang, Nigeria, Cameroon
JUKUN WAPAN alt for WAPAN [JUK]
JUKUN WASE alt for WASE [JUW]
JUKUN WUKARI alt for WAPAN [JUK]
JUKUN WURKUM [JUI] lang, Nigeria
JULA [DYU] lang, Burkina Faso, Côte d'Ivoire, Côte
    d'Ivoire, Mali
JULA alt for JULA [DYU]
JULI alt for MAMBILA, CAMEROON [MYA]
JULUD dial of KATLA [KCR]
JÚMA [JUA] lang, Brazil
JUMAM dial of KIM [KIA]
JUMIAKI alt for GRANGALI [NLI]
JUMJUM [JUM] lang, Sudan
JUMLA alt for JUMLELI dial of NEPALI [NEP]
JUMLELI dial of NEPALI [NEP]
JUMU dial of YORUBA [YOR]
JUNA alt for TATUYO [TAV]
JUNGCHIANG dial of HMONG, EASTERN [HEA]

JUNGMAN alt for YANGMAN [JNG]
JUNGURU [JGR] lang, Central African Republic, Sudan
JUNÍN QUECHUA alt for QUECHUA, NORTH JUNÍN [QJU]
JUNOI alt for OKO-JUWOI [OKJ]
"JUPDÁ MACÚ" alt for HUPDË [JUP]
JUR BELI alt for BELI [BLM]
JUR LUO alt for LUWO [LWO]
JUR LWO alt for LUWO [LWO]
JUR MANANGEER alt for MANANGEER dial of THURI [THU]
JUR MODO [BEX] lang, Sudan
JUR MODO alt for MODO dial of JUR MODO [BEX]
JUR SHOL alt for COLO dial of THURI [THU]
JURAY [JUY] lang, India
JURCHEN [JUC] lang, China
JURITI alt for YURUTI [YUI]
JURITI-TAPUIA alt for YURUTI [YUI]
JURUA dial of JAMAMADÍ [JAA]
JURÚNA [JUR] lang, Brazil
JURUPARI dial of CARÚTANA [CRU]
JURUTI alt for YURUTI [YUI]
JURUTI-TAPUIA alt for YURUTI [YUI]
JUWOI alt for OKO-JUWOI [OKJ]
JUXTLAHUACA dial of MIXTECO, SILACAYOAPAN [MKS]
JWIRA dial of JWIRA-PEPESA [JWI]
JWIRA-PEPESA [JWI] lang, Ghana
JWISINCE alt for MASALIT [MSA]
JYARUNG alt for JIARONG [JYA]
K'ABENA alt for QEBENA dial of KAMBAATA [KTB]
K'ALA alt for BLANG [BLR]
K'ARK'ARTE alt for GERGERE [GEQ]
K'AWA alt for VO [WBM]
K'ERE-KHWE dial of DETI-KHWE [DET]
K'WA alt for BLANG [BLR]
KA [XKK] lang, Central African Republic
KA alt for TAI PONG dial of TAI NÜA [TDD]
KA BAO alt for LAQUA [LAQ]
KA BEO alt for LAQUA [LAQ]
KA BIAO alt for LAQUA [LAQ]
KA'DO HERDÉ alt for HERDÉ [HED]
KA'DO NGUETÉ alt for NGUETÉ [NNN]
KA'DO PEVÉ alt for PEVÉ [LME]
KA'KAS alt for KAKAS dial of TONDANO [TDN]
KA'U alt for KAO [KAX]
KA'UR alt for KAUR [VKK]
KA-ANG dial of DE'ANG [BFP]
KAADENÕ alt for MARANSÉ [MSC]
KAADKIINE alt for MARANSÉ [MSC]
KAADO alt for CENTRAL SONGAI dial of SONGAI [SON]
KAADO alt for CENTRAL SONGAI dial of SONGAI [SON]
KAADO alt for CENTRAL SONGAI dial of SONGAI [SON]
KAAGAN alt for KALAGAN, KAGAN [KLL]
KAAKYI alt for KRACHE [KYE]
KAALONG dial of BAFIA [KSF]
KAAMBA dial of DOONDO [DOD]
KAAN alt for KAANSE [GNA]
KAANA MASALA alt for MASALIT [MSA]
KAANG alt for KANGOU dial of FALI, SOUTH [FLE]
KAANSE [GNA] lang, Burkina Faso
KAANTYU alt for KANJU [KBE]

KAANU alt for KANU [KHX]
KAAPA alt for GABA [GAY]
KAAPO alt for GABA [GAY]
KÄASE alt for KAANSE [GNA]
KAAWLU dial of KRAHN, WESTERN [KRW]
KABA 'DEM alt for KABA DEME [KWG]
KABA [KSP] lang, Central African Republic, Chad, Chad
KABA alt for KABA [KSP]
KABA alt for KAREN, GEBA [KVQ]
KABA alt for SHE dial of GIMIRA [BCQ]
KABA DE BAIBOKOUM alt for KABA [KSP]
KABA DE PAOUA alt for KABA [KSP]
KABA DEME [KWG] lang, Chad
KABA DEMI alt for KABA DEME [KWG]
KABA DUNJO [KOJ] lang, Central African Republic
KABA KURUMI alt for KABA SO [KXJ]
KABA NA [KWV] lang, Chad
KABA NAA alt for KABA NA [KWV]
KABA NAR alt for KABA NA [KWV]
KABA SO [KXJ] lang, Chad
KABA-LAI alt for KABALAI [KVF]
KABADE dial of SAPO [KRN]
KABADI [KBT] lang, Papua New Guinea
KABAENA alt for TOKOTU'A dial of MORONENE [MQN]
KABAKADA dial of TOLAI [KSD]
KABALAI [KVF] lang, Chad
KABALAN alt for KAVALAN [CKV]
KABANA alt for BARIAI [BCH]
KABARAN alt for KAVALAN [CKV]
KABARDIAN [KAB] lang, Russia, Europe, Turkey, Turkey
KABARDIAN alt for KABARDIAN [KAB]
KABARDINO-CHERKES alt for KABARDIAN [KAB]
KABARDO-CHERKES alt for KABARDIAN [KAB]
KABARI alt for NADËB [MBJ]
KABARI dial of KANURI, YERWA [KPH]
KABAYAN dial of IBALOI [IBL]
KABBA alt for KABA [KSP]
KABBA alt for KAMKAM [BGU]
KABBA LAKA alt for LAKA [LAM]
KABE dial of MSER [KQX]
KABEN alt for KIBET [KIE]
KABENDE dial of BEMBA [BEM]
KABENTANG alt for KIBET [KIE]
KABEO alt for LAQUA [LAQ]
KABIANO alt for NIKSEK [GBE]
KABILA alt for LUBILA [KCC]
KABINGA'AN dial of SAMA, BALANGINGI [SSE]
KABIRA dial of YAEYAMA [RYS]
KABIRE alt for LUBILA [KCC]
KABIXÍ [KBD] lang, Brazil
KABIXI alt for SARARÉ [SRR]
KABIYÉ [KBP] lang, Togo, Benin, Ghana
KABO dial of IJO, CENTRAL-WESTERN [IJC]
KABO alt for CABO dial of MÍSKITO [MIQ]
KABOK alt for BOK dial of MANDYAK [MFV]
KABOLA [KLZ] lang, Indonesia, Nusa Tenggara
KABOLI alt for DARI dial of FARSI, EASTERN [PRS]
KABOLOAN alt for ALTA, SOUTHERN [AGY]
KABORI alt for NADËB [MBJ]
KABOTIRAI dial of RAMOAAINA [RAI]
KABRAS dial of LUYIA [LUY]
KABRE alt for KABIYÉ [KBP]
KABU alt for AKEBOU [KEU]

KABUI alt for NAGA, KABUI [NKF]
KABULI alt for DARI dial of FARSI, EASTERN [PRS]
KABULOWAN alt for ALTA, SOUTHERN [AGY]
KABULUEN alt for ALTA, SOUTHERN [AGY]
KABULUWAN alt for ALTA, SOUTHERN [AGY]
KABULUWEN alt for ALTA, SOUTHERN [AGY]
KABUNAYE dial of JOLA-FOGNY [DYO]
KABURE alt for KABIYÉ [KBP]
KABURUANG dial of TALAUD [TLD]
KABWA [CWA] lang, Tanzania
KABWARI [KCW] lang, Zaïre
KABYE alt for KABIYÉ [KBP]
KABYLE [KYL] lang, Algeria, France
KACA alt for KATCHA dial of KATCHA-KADUGLI-
   MIRI [KAT]
KACA alt for KACHA dial of KHAKAS [KJH]
KACCHI alt for KACHCHI [KFR]
KACHA alt for NAGA, ZEME [NZM]
KACHA dial of KHAKAS [KJH]
KACHA dial of KHAKAS [KJH]
KACHAMA [KCX] lang, Ethiopia
KACHARI [QKC] lang, India
KACHARI BENGALI alt for NAGA PIDGIN [NAG]
KACHARI-BENGALI dial of BENGALI [BNG]
KACHCHA alt for NAGA, ZEME [NZM]
KACHCHHI dial of SINDHI [SND]
KACHCHI [KFR] lang, India, Kenya, Tanzania
KACHCHI alt for KOLI, KACHI [GJK]
KACHCHI dial of KOLI, KACHI [GJK]
KACHCHI dial of SINDHI [SND]
KACHE alt for JJU [KAJ]
KACHEL alt for KATCHAL dial of NICOBARESE,
   CENTRAL [NCB]
KACHI alt for KACHCHI [KFR]
KACHI alt for KOLI, KACHI [GJK]
KACHI alt for KACHCHI dial of KOLI, KACHI [GJK]
KACHIA dial of KADARA [KAD]
KACHICHERE dial of KATAB [KCG]
KACHIN alt for JINGPHO [CGP]
KACHUANA alt for KAXUIÂNA [KBB]
KACIPO [KOE] lang, Sudan
KACMIRI alt for KASHMIRI [KSH]
KAD CHENSU alt for IRULA [IRU]
KADA alt for GIDAR [GID]
KADA alt for KADAR [KEJ]
KADA-GBE alt for KADAGBE dial of AYIZO-GBE
   [AYB]
KADADDJARA alt for KARTUJARRA dial of MARTU
   WANGKA [MPJ]
KADAGBE dial of AYIZO-GBE [AYB]
KADAGI alt for KODAGU [KFA]
KADAI [KZD] lang, Indonesia, Maluku
KADAI dial of GALELA [GBI]
KADAIAN dial of BRUNEI [KXD]
KADAIAN alt for KEDAYAN dial of BRUNEI [KXD]
KADAKLAN dial of BONTOC, EASTERN [BKB]
KADAKLAN-BARLIG BONTOC alt for BONTOC,
   EASTERN [BKB]
KADAM alt for GIMNIME [KMB]
KADAR [KEJ] lang, India
KADARA [KAD] lang, Nigeria
KADARO alt for KADARU [KDU]
KADARU [KDU] lang, Sudan
KADAS alt for RUKAI [DRU]
KADAS alt for PAIWAN [PWN]
KADAS alt for PYUMA [PYU]

KADASAN alt for DUSUN, CENTRAL [DTP]
KADAUPURITANA alt for HOHODENÉ dial of
   BANIWA [BAI]
KADAVU dial of FIJIAN [FJI]
KADAYAN alt for DUSUN, CENTRAL [DTP]
KADAYAN alt for DUSUN, SUGUT [KZS]
KADAYAN alt for KEDAYAN dial of BRUNEI [KXD]
KADAYAN alt for KADAIAN dial of BRUNEI [KXD]
KADAZAN, COASTAL [KZJ] lang, Malaysia, Sabah
KADAZAN, KLIAS RIVER [KQT] lang, Malaysia,
   Sabah
KADAZAN, LABUK-KINABATANGAN [DTB] lang,
   Malaysia, Sabah
KADAZAN-TAGARO dial of DUSUN, CENTRAL [DTP]
KADERO alt for KADARU [KDU]
KADERU alt for KADARU [KDU]
KADIAN alt for KEDAYAN dial of BRUNEI [KXD]
KADIAN alt for KADAIAN dial of BRUNEI [KXD]
KADIEN alt for KEDAYAN dial of BRUNEI [KXD]
KADIEN alt for KADAIAN dial of BRUNEI [KXD]
KADIM-KABAN alt for CAKFEM dial of
   MWAGHAVUL [SUR]
KADINA dial of GALELA [GBI]
KADIRGI alt for FUR [FUR]
KADIRO dial of MORU [MGD]
KADIWÉU [KBC] lang, Brazil
KADJAKSE alt for KAJAKSE [CKQ]
KADJALLA dial of LAMA [LAS]
KADJANG alt for TANA TOA dial of KONJO,
   COASTAL [KJC]
KADO [KDV] lang, Myanmar, China, Laos
KADO alt for KATU [KTV]
KADO alt for ULUMANDA' [ULM]
KADO alt for HERDÉ [HED]
KADO alt for CADDO [CAD]
KADO alt for HAUSA [HUA]
KADO alt for PEVÉ [LME]
KADO alt for CENTRAL SONGAI dial of SONGAI
   [SON]
KADOHADACHO alt for CADDO [CAD]
KADU alt for KADO [KDV]
KADU dial of KADO [KDV]
KADUGLI dial of KATCHA-KADUGLI-MIRI [KAT]
KADUKALI alt for KURUX [KVN]
KADUMODI alt for KRONGO [KGO]
KADUN alt for KWANKA dial of KWANKA [BIJ]
KADUNA dial of GBAGYI [GBR]
KADUO [KTP] lang, Laos
KADYAN alt for KEDAYAN dial of BRUNEI [KXD]
KADYAN alt for KADAIAN dial of BRUNEI [KXD]
KAELE alt for MUNDANG [MUA]
KAELE dial of TUPURI [TUI]
KAESABU dial of CIA-CIA [CIA]
KAETI [KZH] lang, Indonesia, Irian Jaya, Papua New
   Guinea, Papua New Guinea
KAETI alt for KAETI [KZH]
KAFA [KBR] lang, Ethiopia
KAFA dial of FOI [FOI]
KAFA dial of KAFA [KBR]
KAFANCHAN dial of KATAB [KCG]
KAFFA alt for KAFA [KBR]
KAFFER alt for XHOSA [XOS]
KAFFICHO alt for KAFA [KBR]
KAFFIR alt for XHOSA [XOS]
KAFIRE dial of SENOUFO, CEBAARA [SEF]
KAFOA [KPU] lang, Indonesia, Nusa Tenggara

KAFU dial of BULLOM SO [BUY]
KAFUGU alt for NIRAGU dial of GBIRI-NIRAGU [GRH]
KAG dial of PUKU-GEERI-KERI-WIPSI [GEL]
KAGA dial of KANURI, YERWA [KPH]
KAGA dial of MONO [MNH]
KAGABA alt for COGUI [KOG]
KAGAMA alt for KAGA dial of KANURI, YERWA
  [KPH]
KAGAN KALAGAN alt for KALAGAN, KAGAN [KLL]
KAGANI alt for HINDKO, NORTHERN [HNO]
KAGANKAN dial of HANUNOO [HNN]
KAGARI alt for KANJARI [KFT]
KAGATE [SYW] lang, Nepal
KAGATE BHOTE alt for KAGATE [SYW]
KAGAYAN alt for MAPUN [SJM]
KAGAYANEN [CGC] lang, Philippines
KAGBENI dial of BARAGAUNLE [BON]
KAGBO dial of GODIÉ [GOD]
KAGGABA alt for COGUI [KOG]
KAGHANI alt for HINDKO, NORTHERN [HNO]
KAGIUONG alt for KAYONG [KXY]
KAGOMA [KDM] lang, Nigeria
KAGORO [XKG] lang, Mali
KAGORO alt for KATAB [KCG]
KAGOSHIMA dial of JAPANESE [JPN]
KAGOUÉ alt for LOZOUA dial of DIDA, YOCOBOUÉ
  [GUD]
KAGU alt for NIRAGU dial of GBIRI-NIRAGU [GRH]
KAGULU [KKI] lang, Tanzania
KAGURU alt for KAGULU [KKI]
KAGWAHIV dial of TENHARIM [PAH]
KAH SO alt for SÔ [SSS]
KAHABU dial of PAZEH [PZH]
KAHAIAN alt for KAHAYAN [XAH]
KAHAJAN alt for KAHAYAN [XAH]
KAHASI alt for KHASI [KHI]
KAHAYAN [XAH] lang, Indonesia, Kalimantan
KAHE [HKA] lang, Tanzania
KAHEDUPA alt for KALEDUPA dial of TUKANGBESI
  NORTH [KHC]
KAHLURI [KFS] lang, India
KAHUA [AGW] lang, Solomon Islands
KAHUA dial of KAHUA [AGW]
KAHUGU alt for NIRAGU dial of GBIRI-NIRAGU [GRH]
KAI alt for NUMANGGANG [NOP]
KAI alt for KEI [KEI]
KAI alt for KÂTE [KMG]
KAI PO-MO alt for KATO [KTW]
KAI-IRI alt for KAIRI [KLQ]
KAIADILT alt for GAYARDILT [GYD]
KAIAMA dial of BUSA-BOKO [BUS]
KAIAMA alt for BOKOBARU dial of BUSA-BOKO
  [BUS]
KAIAN [KCT] lang, Papua New Guinea
KAIBI alt for KAIVI [KCE]
KAIBOBO [KZB] lang, Indonesia, Maluku
KAIBOBO dial of KAIBOBO [KZB]
KAIBU dial of FASU [FAA]
KAIBUBU alt for KAIBOBO [KZB]
KAIBUS alt for TEHIT [KPS]
KAIDEMUI alt for BUANG, MANGGA [MMO]
KAIDIPAN alt for KAIDIPANG [KZP]
KAIDIPAN dial of KAIDIPANG [KZP]
KAIDIPANG [KZP] lang, Indonesia, Sulawesi
KAIDITJ alt for GAIDIDJ [GBB]
KAIEP [KBW] lang, Papua New Guinea

KAIKADI [KEP] lang, India
KAIKADIA alt for KAIKADI [KEP]
KAIKAI alt for KAIKADI [KEP]
KAIKE [KZQ] lang, Nepal
KAIKU [KKQ] lang, Zaïre
KAILI dial of HMONG, EASTERN [HEA]
KAILI, DA'A [KZF] lang, Indonesia, Sulawesi
KAILI, LEDO [LEW] lang, Indonesia, Sulawesi
KAILIKAILI alt for KORAFE [KPR]
KAILOLO dial of HARUKU [HRK]
KAIMANGA dial of MBULA [MNA]
KAIMBÉ [QKQ] lang, Brazil
KAIMBULAWA [ZKA] lang, Indonesia, Sulawesi
KAINA dial of ENGA [ENQ]
KAINGÁNG [KGP] lang, Brazil
KAINGANG, SÃO PAULO [ZKS] lang, Brazil
KAINTIBA dial of HAMTAI [HMT]
KAIOVA alt for KAIWÁ [KGK]
KAIPANG dial of CHIN, FALAM [HBH]
KAIPI alt for OROKOLO [ORO]
KAIPI dial of TOARIPI [TPI]
KAIPU alt for KAIBU dial of FASU [FAA]
KAIRAK [CKR] lang, Papua New Guinea
KAIRATU dial of ALUNE [ALP]
KAIRI [KLQ] lang, Papua New Guinea
KAIRIRU [KXA] lang, Papua New Guinea
KAIRU-KAURA alt for OROKOLO [ORO]
KAIRUI dial of KAIRUI-MIDIKI [KRD]
KAIRUI-MIDIKI [KRD] lang, Indonesia, Nusa Tenggara
KAIS alt for KAMPUNG BARU [KZM]
KAISAK alt for KAZAKH [KAZ]
KAITAK alt for KAJTAK dial of DARGWA [DAR]
KAITAROLEA alt for KILENGE dial of MALEU-
  KILENGE [MGL]
KAITERO alt for IRARUTU [IRH]
KAITETU dial of SEIT-KAITETU [HIK]
KAITITJ alt for GAIDIDJ [GBB]
KAIVI [KCE] lang, Nigeria
KAIWÁ [KGK] lang, Brazil, Argentina
KAIWA alt for IWAL [KBM]
KAIWÁ dial of KAIWÁ [KGK]
KAIWAI alt for KOWIAI [KWH]
KAIXIEN alt for LAHU [LAH]
KAIY [TCQ] lang, Indonesia, Irian Jaya
KAJABÍ alt for KAYABÍ [KYZ]
KAJAGAR alt for KAYGIR [KYT]
KAJAJA alt for TINGAL [TIG]
KAJAKAJA dial of ASMAT, CENTRAL [AST]
KAJAKJA alt for TINGAL [TIG]
KAJAKSE [CKQ] lang, Chad
KAJAMAN [KAG] lang, Malaysia, Sarawak
KAJAN alt for KAYAN, BUSANG [BFG]
KAJANG alt for KAYAN, KAYAN RIVER [XKN]
KAJANG alt for KAYAN, BUSANG [BFG]
KAJANG alt for TANA TOA dial of KONJO,
  COASTAL [KJC]
KAJANGA dial of MABA [MDE]
KAJANGAN alt for KAJANGA dial of MABA [MDE]
KAJAWO alt for KANDAWO [GAM]
KAJE alt for JJU [KAJ]
KAJELI alt for KAYELI [KZL]
KAJESKE alt for KAJAKSE [CKQ]
KAJIRE-'DULO dial of MAJERA [XMJ]
KAJIRRAWUNG alt for GADJERAWANG [GDH]
KAJJARA alt for BIRKED [BRK]
KAJJI alt for JJU [KAJ]

KAJKAVIAN dial of SERBO-CROATIAN [SRC]
KAJOA dial of BAJAU, INDONESIAN [BDL]
KAJOA alt for KAYOA dial of MAKIAN, EAST [MKY]
KAJTAK dial of DARGWA [DAR]
KAJUMERAH alt for KOWIAI [KWH]
KAJUPULAU alt for KAYUPULAU [KZU]
KAJURU dial of KADARA [KAD]
KAKA alt for YAMBA [YAM]
KAKA alt for KAKO [KKJ]
KAKA dial of GBAYA [GYA]
KAKAA alt for KURI dial of BUDUMA [BDM]
KAKABA alt for KAMKAM [BGU]
KAKABAI alt for IGORA [KQF]
KAKABAI dial of IGORA [KQF]
KAKACHHU-KI BOLI alt for DANGI [DAT]
KAKADU alt for GAGADU [GBU]
KAKAKTA alt for GAGADU [GBU]
KAKAMEGA alt for IDAKHO dial of IDAKHO-
    ISUKHA-TIRIKI [IDA]
KAKANDA dial of NUPE [NUP]
KAKARAKALA alt for YINGGARDA [YIA]
KAKARI dial of GUJARATI [GJR]
KAKAS dial of TONDANO [TDN]
KAKASA dial of BARUGA [BBB]
KAKAT alt for QAQET [BYX]
KAKAUHUA [KBF] lang, Chile
KAKAYAMBA alt for YAMBA [YAM]
KAKDJU alt for GAGADU [GBU]
KAKDJUAN alt for GAGADU [GBU]
KAKHETIAN alt for KAXETIAN dial of GEORGIAN
    [GEO]
KAKIA dial of NG/AMANI [NMN]
KAKIHUM alt for GADI dial of GADI-SHINGINI-VADI-
    BAANGI [KAM]
KAKIRU alt for APOWASI dial of BITARA [BIT]
KAKO [KKJ] lang, Cameroon, Central African
    Republic, Central African Republic, Congo
KAKO alt for KAKO [KKJ]
KAKOLI alt for UMBU-UNGU [UMB]
KAKOLO alt for KAGORO [XKG]
KAKUA alt for KAKWA [KEO]
KAKUMEGA alt for IDAKHO dial of IDAKHO-
    ISUKHA-TIRIKI [IDA]
KAKUMO alt for UKAAN [KCF]
KAKUMO dial of UKAAN [KCF]
KAKUNA alt for MAMUSI [KDF]
KAKUNA alt for MELKOI dial of MAMUSI [KDF]
KAKUS PENAN dial of KENYAH, WESTERN [XKY]
KAKUYA BUSHMAN NASIE alt for NAMA [NAQ]
KAKWA [KEO] lang, Uganda, Sudan, Zaïre
KAKWA alt for CACUA [CBV]
KAKWA alt for KAKWA [KEO]
KAKWAK alt for KAKWA [KEO]
KAKWERE alt for KWERE [CWE]
KAL alt for ZAAR dial of SAYA [SAY]
KAL-UWAN alt for KALINGA, MABAKA VALLEY
    [KKG]
KALA dial of MBANZA [ZMZ]
KALA dial of UMBU-UNGU [UMB]
KALA alt for BUKALA dial of MONGO-NKUNDU
    [MOM]
KALA DEGEMA alt for USOKUN dial of DEGEMA
    [DEG]
KALA LAGAU LANGGUS alt for KALA LAGAW YA
    [MWP]
KALA LAGAW alt for KALA LAGAW YA [MWP]

KALA LAGAW YA [MWP] lang, Australia
KALA MORU alt for MORU [MGD]
KALA YAGAW YA alt for KALA LAGAW YA [MWP]
KALAALLISUT alt for INUIT, GREENLANDIC [ESG]
KALABAKAN [KVE] lang, Malaysia, Sabah
KALABAKAN MURUT alt for KALABAKAN [KVE]
KALABARI [IJN] lang, Nigeria
KALABAT ATAS dial of TONSEA [TXS]
KALABIT alt for KELABIT [KZI]
KALABRA [KZZ] lang, Indonesia, Irian Jaya
KALABUAN dial of KINABATANGAN, UPPER [DMG]
KALADDARSCH alt for KIMAGHAMA [KIG]
KALAGAN [KQE] lang, Philippines
KALAGAN, KAGAN [KLL] lang, Philippines
KALAGAN, TAGAKAULU [KLG] lang, Philippines
KALAI dial of CHIN, FALAM [HBH]
KALAK alt for KATLA [KCR]
KALAKAFRA alt for KALO dial of MSER [KQX]
KALAKO alt for KALARKO [KBA]
KALAKU alt for KALARKO [KBA]
KALAKUL alt for KALARKO [KBA]
KALALI dial of NGURA [NBX]
KALAM [KMH] lang, Papua New Guinea
KALAM dial of KALAMI [GWC]
KALAMI [GWC] lang, Pakistan
KALAMI KOHISTANI alt for KALAMI [GWC]
KALAMIAN alt for TAGBANWA, CALAMIAN [TBK]
KALAMIANON alt for TAGBANWA, CALAMIAN
    [TBK]
KALAMO [KKC] lang, Papua New Guinea
KALAMSE [KNZ] lang, Burkina Faso
KALANA alt for KALANGA [KCK]
KALANGA [KCK] lang, Botswana, Zimbabwe,
    Zimbabwe
KALANGA alt for KALANGA [KCK]
KALANGA alt for HOLOHOLO [HOO]
KALANGA dial of CHATTISGARHI [HNE]
KALANGA dial of RONGA [RON]
KALANGOYA alt for KALLAHAN, KAYAPA [KAK]
KALANGOYA-IKALAHAN alt for KALLAHAN,
    KAYAPA [KAK]
KALANGUYYA alt for KALLAHAN, KAYAPA [KAK]
KALANKE [CKN] lang, Gambia
KALAO [KLY] lang, Indonesia, Sulawesi
KALAOTOA alt for KALAO [KLY]
KALAPÁLO [KPB] lang, Brazil
KALAPUYA [KAL] lang, USA
KALAR dial of EVENKI [EVN]
KALARKO [KBA] lang, Australia
KALASH alt for KALASHA [KLS]
KALASHA [KLS] lang, Pakistan
KALASHA-ALA alt for WAIGALI [WBK]
KALASHAMON alt for KALASHA [KLS]
KALAT dial of BRAHUI [BRH]
KALAUNA dial of IDUNA [VIV]
KALAW KAWAW dial of KALA LAGAW YA [MWP]
KALBU alt for GAALPU dial of DHANGU [GLA]
KALDANI alt for CHALDEAN [CLD]
KALDARÁRI alt for KALDERASH dial of ROMANI,
    VLACH [RMY]
KALDERASH dial of ROMANI, VLACH [RMY]
KALDERASH dial of ROMANI, VLACH [RMY]
KALDERASH dial of ROMANI, VLACH [RMY]
KALDOSH [CKS] lang, New Caledonia
KALDOYO alt for CHALDEAN [CLD]
KALE-WHAN alt for PAIWAN [PWN]

KALEBWE alt for SONGE [SOP]
KALEDUPA dial of TUKANGBESI NORTH [KHC]
KALEMSE alt for KALAMSE [KNZ]
KALENDE dial of PANCANA [PNP]
KALENGA alt for KALAMSE [KNZ]
KALENJIN [KLN] lang, Kenya
"KALERI" alt for MABO-BARKUL [MAE]
"KALERI" alt for HOROM [HOE]
KALERNG alt for CENTRAL ISAN dial of TAI,
   NORTHEASTERN [TTS]
KALEU dial of SÔ [SSS]
KALEUNG alt for CENTRAL ISAN dial of TAI,
   NORTHEASTERN [TTS]
KALI alt for KARI [KBN]
KALI alt for HOANYA [HON]
KALI dial of LAWANGAN [LBX]
KALIAI alt for LUSI [KHL]
KALIAI dial of LUSI [KHL]
KALIÁNA alt for SAPÉ [SPC]
KALIANDA dial of PESISIR, SOUTHERN [PEC]
KALIBUGAN alt for CALIBUGAN SUBANON dial of
   SUBANON, WESTERN [SUC]
KALIGE alt for FEROGE [FER]
KALIGI alt for FEROGE [FER]
KALIHNA [CRB] lang, Venezuela, Brazil, French
   Guiana, Guyana, Surinam
KALIKA ARYA BHASHA alt for ARE [AAG]
KALIKE alt for FEROGE [FER]
KALIKI alt for FEROGE [FER]
KALIKO [KBO] lang, Sudan
KALIKO alt for KALIKO-MA'DI [XKZ]
KALIKO-MA'DI [XKZ] lang, Zaïre
KALIKO-OMI alt for OMI [OMI]
KALINDI dial of POKOMO, LOWER [POJ]
KALINGA alt for GA'DANG [GDG]
KALINGA, BUTBUT [KYB] lang, Philippines
KALINGA, LIMOS [KMK] lang, Philippines
KALINGA, LOWER TANUDAN [KML] lang, Philippines
KALINGA, LUBUAGAN [KNB] lang, Philippines
KALINGA, MABAKA VALLEY [KKG] lang, Philippines
KALINGA, MADUKAYANG [KMD] lang, Philippines
KALINGA, SOUTHERN [KSC] lang, Philippines
KALINGA, UPPER TANUDAN [KGH] lang, Philippines
KALINGE RAI alt for KHALING [KLR]
KALININ alt for TVER dial of KARELIAN [KRL]
KALINYA alt for KALIHNA [CRB]
KALIS dial of EMBALOH [EMB]
KALIS DAYAK alt for KALIS dial of EMBALOH [EMB]
KALIS MALOH alt for KALIS dial of EMBALOH [EMB]
KALISPEL dial of FLATHEAD-KALISPEL [FLA]
KALISPEL-FLATHEAD alt for FLATHEAD-KALISPEL
   [FLA]
KALISUSU alt for KULISUSU [VKL]
KALITAMI alt for KEMBERANO [BZP]
KALKADOON alt for KALKUTUNG [KTG]
KALKALI alt for KALLAHAN, KAYAPA [KAK]
KALKATUNGU alt for KALKUTUNG [KTG]
KALKOTI [XKA] lang, Pakistan
KALKUS alt for LIKES-UTSIA dial of MANDYAK
   [MFV]
KALKUTUNG [KTG] lang, Australia
KALLA alt for YAÁYUWEE dial of GBAYA [GYA]
KALLA alt for YAAYUWEE dial of GBAYA [GYA]
KALLAHAN, KAYAPA [KAK] lang, Philippines
KALLAHAN, KELEY-I [IFY] lang, Philippines
KALLAHAN, TINOC [TNE] lang, Philippines

KALLANA alt for ALAWA [ALH]
KALMACK alt for KALMYK-OIRAT [KGZ]
KALMUCK alt for KALMYK-OIRAT [KGZ]
KALMUK alt for KALMYK-OIRAT [KGZ]
KALMYK-OIRAT [KGZ] lang, Russia, Europe, China,
   Mongolian Peoples Republic
KALMYTSKII JAZYK alt for KALMYK-OIRAT [KGZ]
KALO alt for BRU, EASTERN [BRU]
KALO dial of KEOPARA [KHZ]
KALO dial of MSER [KQX]
KALO alt for LOKALO dial of NKUTU [NKW]
KALOKALO [KLX] lang, Papua New Guinea
KALONDAMA dial of LAMMA [LEV]
KALONG alt for DIMBONG [DII]
KALONGO dial of BAMBARA [BRA]
KALOP dial of KOHO [KPM]
KALOSI dial of DURI [MVP]
KALOU [KLF] lang, Papua New Guinea
KALOUNAY dial of JOLA-FOGNY [DYO]
KALP alt for URIM [URI]
KALTO alt for NIHALI [NHL]
KALULI [BCO] lang, Papua New Guinea
KALUM alt for BAGA BINARI [BCG]
KALUMPANG [KLI] lang, Indonesia, Sulawesi
KALVADI dial of DECCAN [DCC]
KALYOKENGNYU alt for NAGA, KHIAMNGAN [NKY]
KALYOKENGNYU, alt for NAGA, KHIAMNGAN [NKY]
KAM [KDX] lang, Nigeria
KAM alt for KHAM [KHG]
KAM alt for DONG [KMC]
KAM MU'ANG alt for TAI, NORTHERN [NOD]
KAM TI alt for KHAMTI [KHT]
KAMÃ [KWA] lang, Brazil
KAMA dial of KISSI, SOUTHERN [KSS]
KAMA dial of KISSI, NORTHERN [KQS]
KAMÃ MAKÚ alt for KAMÃ [KWA]
KAMA PERMYAK alt for KOMI-PERMYAK [KOI]
KAMAIURÁ alt for KAMAYURÁ [KAY]
KAMAKAN [VKM] lang, Brazil
KAMALAN alt for KAVALAN [CKV]
KAMAN alt for MIJU [MXJ]
KAMANA dial of WOISIKA [WOI]
KAMANAWA alt for KATUKÍNA, PANOAN [KNT]
KAMANG alt for KAMANA dial of WOISIKA [WOI]
KAMANGA alt for CHIKAMANGA dial of TUMBUKA
   [TUW]
KAMANIDI alt for GAAM [TBI]
KAMANNAUA alt for KATUKÍNA, PANOAN [KNT]
KAMANO [KBQ] lang, Papua New Guinea
KAMANO-KAFE alt for KAMANO [KBQ]
KAMANT alt for QIMANT [QIM]
KAMANTAN [KCI] lang, Nigeria
KAMANTON alt for KAMANTAN [KCI]
KAMAONI alt for KUMAUNI [KFY]
KAMAR [KEQ] lang, India
KAMARA alt for CENTRAL KONO dial of KONO
   [KNO]
KAMARA alt for MARA dial of HANGA [HAG]
KAMARAGAKOK alt for ARECUNA dial of PEMON
   [AOC]
KAMARI alt for KAWARI [KFV]
KAMARI-SANTALI dial of SANTALI [SNT]
KAMARIAN [KZX] lang, Indonesia, Maluku
KAMARIANG alt for KAMARIAN [KZX]
KAMARU [KGX] lang, Indonesia, Sulawesi
KAMAS [XAS] lang, Russia, Asia

KAMAS alt for KARAGAS [KIM]
KAMASA [KLP] lang, Papua New Guinea
KAMASAU [KMS] lang, Papua New Guinea
KAMASAU-TRING-WAU dial of KAMASAU [KMS]
KAMASSIAN alt for KAMAS [XAS]
KAMASSIAN dial of KHAKAS [KJH]
KAMASSIAN dial of KAMAS [XAS]
KAMATE dial of YAGARIA [YGR]
KAMATHI dial of TELUGU [TCW]
KAMAU alt for JIAMÀO [JIO]
KAMAYIRÁ alt for KAMAYURÁ [KAY]
KAMAYO [KYK] lang, Philippines
KAMAYURÁ [KAY] lang, Brazil
KAMBA [QKZ] lang, Brazil
KAMBA [KIK] lang, Kenya
KAMBA [XAB] lang, Papua New Guinea
KAMBA alt for AKASELEM [AKS]
KAMBA alt for WAGI [FAD]
KAMBAATA [KTB] lang, Ethiopia
KAMBAIRA [KYY] lang, Papua New Guinea
KAMBARA alt for KAMBAATA [KTB]
KAMBARAMBA dial of BOTIN [KBX]
KAMBARI alt for GADI-SHINGINI-VADI-BAANGI [KAM]
KAMBARIIRE dial of FULFULDE, ADAMAWA [FUB]
KAMBATA alt for KAMBAATA [KTB]
KAMBATTA alt for KAMBAATA [KTB]
KAMBE dial of GIRYAMA [NYF]
KAMBE-KAMBERO dial of KAIMBULAWA [ZKA]
KAMBEBA alt for OMAGUA [OMG]
KAMBEGL dial of MARING [MBW]
KAMBERA alt for GAMBERA [GMA]
KAMBERA alt for SUMBA [SMI]
KAMBERA dial of SUMBA [SMI]
KAMBERATARO [KBV] lang, Indonesia, Irian Jaya, Papua New Guinea
KAMBERATARO alt for KAMBERATARO [KBV]
KAMBERATORO alt for KAMBERATARO [KBV]
KAMBERAU alt for IRIA [IRX]
KAMBERCHI alt for GADI-SHINGINI-VADI-BAANGI [KAM]
KAMBERRI alt for GADI-SHINGINI-VADI-BAANGI [KAM]
KAMBIA dial of WAHGI [WAK]
KAMBIWÁ [QKH] lang, Brazil
KAMBOI-RAMBOI alt for KWERBA [KWE]
KAMBOLÉ [XKB] lang, Togo
KAMBONSENGA alt for AMBO dial of LALA-BISA [LEB]
KAMBOT alt for BOTIN [KBX]
KAMBOWA dial of KIOKO [UES]
KAMBURWAMA dial of WANDALA [MFI]
KAMCHADAL alt for ITELMEN [ITL]
KAMCHATKA alt for ITELMEN [ITL]
KAMCHATKA dial of EVEN [EVE]
KAMDANG dial of TULISHI [TEY]
KAMDESHI alt for KAMVIRI [QMV]
KAMDHUE alt for KANJU [KBE]
KAMEA alt for HAMTAI [HMT]
KAMEMTXA alt for CAMSÁ [KBH]
KAMEN alt for KAMENSKIJ dial of KORYAK [KPY]
KAMENGMI dial of WOISIKA [WOI]
KAMENSKIJ dial of KORYAK [KPY]
KAMER dial of BIAK [BHW]
KAMESH alt for BAHARLU dial of AZERBAIJANI, SOUTH [AZB]

KAMET alt for LAMET [LBN]
KAMETSU dial of TOKU-NO-SHIMA [TKN]
KAMHAO alt for KAMHAU dial of CHIN, TEDIM [CTD]
KAMHAU dial of CHIN, TEDIM [CTD]
KAMHMU alt for KHMU [KJG]
KAMHOW alt for KAMHAU dial of CHIN, TEDIM [CTD]
KAMI [KCU] lang, Tanzania
KAMI alt for CHIN, KHUMI [CKM]
KAMI alt for YAGARIA [YGR]
KAMI dial of NUPE [NUP]
KAMI-KULAKA dial of YAGARIA [YGR]
KAMIA dial of DIEGUENO [DIH]
KAMIGIN alt for MANOBO, CINAMIGUIN [MKX]
KAMIK alt for KAMVIRI [QMV]
KAMILAROI [KLD] lang, Australia
KAMINDJO alt for ROUKU [TCI]
KAMIR alt for XAMIR [XAI]
KAMKAM [BGU] lang, Nigeria, Cameroon
KAMMU alt for KHMU [KJG]
KAMMYANG alt for TAI, NORTHERN [NOD]
KAMNUM [KMN] lang, Papua New Guinea
KAMO [KCQ] lang, Nigeria
KAMORA alt for KAMORO [KGQ]
KAMORO [KGQ] lang, Indonesia, Irian Jaya
KAMORTA alt for CAMORTA dial of NICOBARESE, CENTRAL [NCB]
KAMOT dial of WOISIKA [WOI]
KAMPA alt for CAMPA, ASHÉNINCA [CPU]
KAMPAR alt for ULU KAMPAR dial of SEMAI [SEA]
KAMPONG BARU alt for KAMPUNG BARU [KZM]
KAMPUNG BARU [KZM] lang, Indonesia, Irian Jaya
KAMRAU alt for IRIA [IRX]
KAMRUP dial of GARO [GRT]
KAMSA alt for CAMSÁ [KBH]
KAMSE alt for CAMSÁ [KBH]
KAMSIKI alt for PSIKYE [KVJ]
KAMSILI dial of UKHWEJO [UKH]
KAMTUK alt for KEMTUIK [KMT]
KAMU [QKY] lang, Australia
KAMU alt for KAMO [KCQ]
KAMU alt for KHMU [KJG]
KAMU alt for PSIKYE dial of PSIKYE [KVJ]
KAMUAN' dial of TA'OIH, UPPER [TTH]
KAMUKU [KAU] lang, Nigeria
KAMULA [KHM] lang, Papua New Guinea
KAMURA alt for KAMULA [KHM]
KAMURÚ dial of KARIRI-XUCO [KZW]
KAMVIRI [QMV] lang, Afghanistan, Pakistan, Pakistan
KAMVIRI alt for KAMVIRI [QMV]
KAMVIRI dial of KAMVIRI [QMV]
KAMWE [HIG] lang, Nigeria
KAN alt for CHINESE, GAN [KNN]
KAN alt for KAANSE [GNA]
KAN dial of MBAI [MYB]
KANA alt for KOANA [KEH]
KANA dial of TOGBO [TOR]
KANA MABANG alt for MABA [MDE]
KANABU alt for KANAKANABU [QNB]
KANAD alt for TAICHIANG dial of HMONG, EASTERN [HEA]
KANAKANABU [QNB] lang, Taiwan
KANAKANAVU alt for KANAKANABU [QNB]
KANAKHOE alt for GANA-KHWE [GNK]

KANAKHOE alt for G//ANAKHWE dial of GANA-
  KHWE [GNK]
KANAKURU [KNA] lang, Nigeria
KANALA alt for XARACUU [ANE]
KANALU alt for BAROK [BJK]
KANAM alt for KOENOEM [KCS]
KANAM dial of JARAWA [JAR]
KANAMANTI [QKN] lang, Brazil
KANAMARÉ alt for KANAMARÍ [KNM]
KANAMARÍ [KNM] lang, Brazil
KANAMBU alt for KANEMBU [KBL]
KANANA alt for KALANGA [KCK]
KANANDJOHO dial of NDUMU [NMD]
KANAPIT alt for BAROK [BJK]
KANARA alt for KUKNA [KEX]
KANARESE alt for KANNADA [KJV]
KANASHI [QAS] lang, India
KANASI [SOQ] lang, Papua New Guinea
KANASI alt for KANASHI [QAS]
KANATANG dial of SUMBA [SMI]
KANAUJI [BJJ] lang, India
KANAUJI PROPER dial of KANAUJI [BJJ]
KANAURI [KFK] lang, India
KANAWA dial of KYAK [BKA]
KANAWARI alt for KANAURI [KFK]
KANAWI alt for KANAURI [KFK]
KANCHANABURI alt for KAREN, PWO KANCHANA
  BURI [KJP]
KANDA alt for KANDE [KBS]
KANDA alt for KUI [KXU]
KANDAK dial of PASHAYI, NORTHEAST [AEE]
KANDAR dial of SANGIR [SAN]
KANDAR dial of SELARU [SLU]
KANDAS [KQW] lang, Papua New Guinea
KANDASI dial of FIPA [FIP]
KANDAWIRE dial of TUMBUKA [TUW]
KANDAWO [GAM] lang, Papua New Guinea
KANDE [KBS] lang, Gabon
KANDE dial of TSONGA [TSO]
KANDEPE dial of ENGA [ENQ]
KANDERE dial of SENOUFO, CEBAARA [SEF]
KANDERMA alt for KINDERMA dial of TIRA [TIR]
KANDH alt for KUI [KXU]
KANDIALI dial of DOGRI-KANGRI [DOJ]
KANDJU alt for KANJU [KBE]
KANDOASHI dial of CANDOSHI-SHAPRA [CBU]
KANDOMIN alt for YAGAWAK [YGK]
KANDOSHI alt for CANDOSHI-SHAPRA [CBU]
KANDYU alt for KANJU [KBE]
KANELA alt for CANELA [RAM]
KANEMBOU alt for KANEMBU [KBL]
KANEMBU [KBL] lang, Chad, Niger, Niger
KANEMBU alt for KANEMBU [KBL]
KANG [KYP] lang, Laos, China
KANG-LO dial of BONAN [PEH]
KANGA [KCP] lang, Sudan
KANGANA dial of LUSENGO [LUS]
KANGAR BHAT alt for KANJARI [KFT]
KANGARRAGA alt for KUNGARAKANY [GGK]
KANGEAN [KKV] lang, Indonesia, Java, Bali
KANGEJU alt for HATSA [HTS]
KANGGEWOT dial of KATI, NORTHERN [KTI]
KANGITE alt for APURINÃ [APU]
KANGO [KTY] lang, Zaïre
KANGOU dial of FALI, SOUTH [FLE]
KANGRA alt for KANGRI dial of DOGRI-KANGRI

[DOJ]
KANGRI alt for KANJARI [KFT]
KANGRI dial of DOGRI-KANGRI [DOJ]
KANGU alt for KANGOU dial of FALI, SOUTH [FLE]
KANGWONDO alt for SEOUL dial of KOREAN [KKN]
KANGYE alt for KWANGE dial of GBARI [GBY]
KANHOBAL alt for KANJOBAL, EASTERN [KJB]
KANI-KHOE alt for GANI-KHWE [GNX]
KANICHANA alt for CANICHANA [CAZ]
KANIET [KTK] lang, Papua New Guinea
KANIGURAMI dial of ORMURI [ORU]
KANIKEH dial of MANUSELA [WHA]
KANIKKAR alt for KANIKKARAN [KEV]
KANIKKARAN [KEV] lang, India
KANINGARA alt for KANINGRA [KNR]
KANINGDOM dial of KANUFI-KANINGDON-NINDEM
  [KDP]
KANINGI [KZO] lang, Gabon
KANINGKON alt for KANINGDOM dial of KANUFI-
  KANINGDON-NINDEM [KDP]
KANINGKWOM alt for KANINGDOM dial of KANUFI-
  KANINGDON-NINDEM [KDP]
KANINGRA [KNR] lang, Papua New Guinea
KANINJAL alt for KENINJAL [KNL]
KANINJAL DAYAK alt for KENINJAL [KNL]
KANINKON alt for KANINGDOM dial of KANUFI-
  KANINGDON-NINDEM [KDP]
KANIOKA alt for KANYOK [KNY]
KANIRAN alt for MAIRASI [FRY]
KANITE [KMU] lang, Papua New Guinea
KANJAGA alt for BULI [BWU]
KANJARI [KFT] lang, India
KANJIMATA alt for ADYNYAMATHANHA [ADT]
KANJININGI alt for NJININGI dial of TEKE,
  NORTHERN [TEG]
KANJOBAL, EASTERN [KJB] lang, Guatemala, USA
KANJOBAL, WESTERN [KNJ] lang, Guatemala, USA
KANJRI alt for KANJARI [KFT]
KANJU [KBE] lang, Australia
KANKANAEY [KNE] lang, Philippines
KANKANAI alt for KANKANAEY [KNE]
KANKANAY alt for KANKANAEY [KNE]
KANKANAY, NORTHERN [KAN] lang, Philippines
KANNA alt for BADA [BAU]
KANNADA [KJV] lang, India
KANNADA, SOUTHERN [SKJ] lang, India
KANNEH dial of KRAHN, EASTERN [KQO]
KANNIKAN alt for KANIKKARAN [KEV]
KANNIKARAN alt for KANIKKARAN [KEV]
KANNIKHARAN alt for KANIKKARAN [KEV]
KANO alt for KANU [KHX]
KANO-KATSINA dial of FULFULDE, KANO-KATSINA-
  BORORRO [FUV]
KANOÉ [KXO] lang, Brazil
KANOREUNU SKADD alt for KANAURI [KFK]
KANORUG SKADD alt for KANAURI [KFK]
KANOURI alt for KANURI, MANGA [KBY]
KANOURI alt for KANURI, YERWA [KPH]
KANOURY alt for KANURI, MANGA [KBY]
KANOURY alt for KANURI, YERWA [KPH]
KANOWIT [KXN] lang, Malaysia, Sarawak
KANSA [KAA] lang, USA
KANTANA [MMA] lang, Nigeria
KANTANA dial of BADA [BAU]
KANTE dial of LAMA [LAS]
KANTEWU dial of UMA [PPK]

KANTILAN alt for CANTILAN dial of SURIGAONON [SUL]
KANTOHE dial of BALANTA [BLE]
KANTONSI alt for KANTOSI [XKT]
KANTOSI [XKT] lang, Ghana
KANTU [KTT] lang, Laos
KANTU PILU' dial of KANTU [KTT]
KANTU TANGPRIL-TALUY dial of KANTU [KTT]
KANTU' dial of IBAN [IBA]
KANTUA alt for TA'OIH, UPPER [TTH]
KANU [KHX] lang, Zaïre
KANUFI dial of KANUFI-KANINGDON-NINDEM [KDP]
KANUFI-KANINGDON-NINDEM [KDP] lang, Nigeria
KANUM [KCD] lang, Papua New Guinea, Indonesia, Irian Jaya
KANURI, MANGA [KBY] lang, Niger, Nigeria
KANURI, MANGA alt for KANURI, MANGA [KBY]
KANURI, YERWA [KPH] lang, Nigeria, Cameroon, Chad, Niger, Sudan
KANURI, YERWA alt for KANURI, YERWA [KPH]
KANY alt for EASTERN NUER dial of NUER [NUS]
KANYAK alt for NAGA, KONYAK [NBE]
KANYAW alt for KAREN, S'GAW [KSW]
KANYAY alt for KENYAH, UPPER BARAM [UBM]
KANYAY alt for KENYAH, WESTERN [XKY]
KANYOK [KNY] lang, Zaïre
KANYOKA alt for KANYOK [KNY]
KANYOP alt for MANDYAK [MFV]
KANYU alt for KANJU [KBE]
KAO [KAX] lang, Indonesia, Maluku
KAO alt for KATU [KTV]
KAOKEEP dial of CHIN, THADO [TCZ]
KAOKONAU alt for KAMORO [KGQ]
KAONDE [KQN] lang, Zambia, Zaïre
KAORA alt for KODA [KFN]
KAOUARA-TIMBA-SINDOU-KORONI dial of NATIORO [NTI]
KAOWLU alt for KAAWLU dial of KRAHN, WESTERN [KRW]
KAPAGALAN dial of TIMUGON MURUT [TIH]
KAPAL dial of GIDRA [GDR]
KAPAMPANGAN alt for PAMPANGAN [PMP]
KAPANAWA alt for CAPANAHUA [KAQ]
KAPANGAN dial of KANKANAEY [KNE]
KAPARI dial of KEOPARA [KHZ]
KAPAU alt for HAMTAI [HMT]
KAPAUKU alt for EKARI [EKG]
KAPAUR alt for IHA [IHP]
KAPAURI alt for KAPORI [KHP]
KAPIANGAN alt for PAIWAN [PWN]
KAPIN [TBX] lang, Papua New Guinea
KAPINAWÁ [QKP] lang, Brazil
KAPINGAMARANGI [KPG] lang, Micronesia
KAPO alt for YREPO dial of KRUMEN, SOUTHERN [TED]
KAPONA dial of ENGA [ENQ]
KAPONE alt for NUMEE [KDK]
KAPONTORI dial of PANCANA [PNP]
KAPORE alt for BEBELI [BEK]
KAPORI [KHP] lang, Indonesia, Irian Jaya
KAPRIMAN [DJU] lang, Papua New Guinea
KAPRIMAN dial of KAPRIMAN [DJU]
KAPSIKI alt for PSIKYE [KVJ]
KAPSIKI alt for PSIKYE dial of PSIKYE [KVJ]
KAPUAS dial of NGAJU [NIJ]
KAPUCHA alt for BEZHTA [KAP]

KAPUCHIN alt for BEZHTA [KAP]
KAPUGU alt for NIRAGU dial of GBIRI-NIRAGU [GRH]
KAPUL alt for SAMA, ABAKNON [ABX]
KAPUTIEI dial of MAASAI [MET]
KAPWI alt for NAGA, KABUI [NKF]
KAR alt for KARABORO, EASTERN [KAR]
KAR alt for KUR dial of PUKU-GEERI-KERI-WIPSI [GEL]
KAR BHOTE alt for LHOMI [LHM]
KARA [REG] lang, Tanzania
KARA [LEU] lang, Papua New Guinea
KARA [KCM] lang, Central African Republic, Sudan, Sudan
KARA [CFL] lang, Ethiopia
KARA alt for NGALA [NUD]
KARA alt for KARA [KCM]
KARA alt for KIRGHIZ [KDO]
KARA dial of GBAYA [GYA]
KARA dial of HAMER-BANNA [AMF]
KARA dial of KARA [CFL]
KARA alt for BLACK NOGAI dial of NOGAI [NOG]
KARA-KIRGIZ alt for KIRGHIZ [KDO]
KARABAGH dial of ARMENIAN [ARM]
KARABAGH SHAMAKHI dial of ARMENIAN [ARM]
KARABAKH alt for SUSA dial of AZERBAIJANI, NORTH [AZE]
KARABORO, EASTERN [KAR] lang, Burkina Faso, Côte d'Ivoire
KARABORO, WESTERN [KZA] lang, Burkina Faso
KARACAYLAR alt for KARACHAY-BALKAR [KRC]
KARACHAI alt for KARACHAY-BALKAR [KRC]
KARACHAITSY alt for KARACHAY-BALKAR [KRC]
KARACHAY alt for KARACHAY-BALKAR [KRC]
KARACHAY dial of KARACHAY-BALKAR [KRC]
KARACHAY-BALKAR [KRC] lang, Russia, Europe, USA
KARACHAYLA alt for KARACHAY-BALKAR [KRC]
KARACHI dial of DOMARI [RMT]
KARADJEE alt for IWAIDJA [IBD]
KARADJERI [GBD] lang, Australia
KARAGAN dial of DAYAK, LAND [DYK]
KARAGAS [KIM] lang, Russia, Asia
KARAGAS dial of MATOR [MTM]
KARAGASS alt for KARAGAS [KIM]
KARAGAWAN dial of ISNAG [ISD]
KARAGINSKIJ dial of ALUTOR [ALR]
KARAGWE alt for NYAMBO [NYM]
KARAHAWYANA [XKH] lang, Brazil
KARAI KARAI alt for KAREKARE [KAI]
KARAIAI alt for ANEM [ANZ]
KARAIKARAI alt for KAREKARE [KAI]
KARAIM [KDR] lang, Lithuania, Ukraine
KARAITE alt for KARAIM [KDR]
KARAJÁ [KPJ] lang, Brazil
KARAJARRI alt for KARADJERI [GBD]
KARAKALPAK [KAC] lang, Uzbekistan, Afghanistan
KARAKATI alt for KRIKATI [XRI]
KARAKELANG alt for SOUTH KARAKELONG dial of TALAUD [TLD]
KARAKELONG alt for SOUTH KARAKELONG dial of TALAUD [TLD]
KARAKH alt for KARAX dial of AVAR [AVR]
KARAKLOBUK alt for KARAKALPAK [KAC]
KARAM alt for KALAM [KMH]
KARAMA alt for KURRAMA [VKU]
KARAMANLI dial of BALKAN GAGAUZ TURKISH

[BGX]
KARAMANLI dial of TURKISH [TRK]
KARAMBA dial of MARING [MBW]
KARAMBIT dial of KAPRIMAN [DJU]
KARAMI [XAR] lang, Papua New Guinea
KARAMIANANEN alt for TAGBANWA, CALAMIAN
[TBK]
KARAMOJONG [KDJ] lang, Uganda
KARANG [KZR] lang, Cameroon, Chad, Chad
KARANG alt for ANGAS [ANC]
KARANG alt for KARANG [KZR]
KARANG dial of KARANG [KZR]
KARANGA [KTH] lang, Chad
KARANGA dial of KARANGA [KTH]
KARANGA dial of SHONA [SHD]
KARANGAN dial of BASAP [BDB]
KARANGAN alt for KARAGAN dial of DAYAK, LAND
[DYK]
KARANGASEM alt for LOWLAND BALI dial of BALI
[BZC]
KARANGI alt for WELIKI [KLH]
KARANKASSO dial of SAMBLA [SOS]
KARAO [KYJ] lang, Philippines
KARAPANÃ alt for CARAPANA [CBC]
KARAPANO alt for CARAPANA [CBC]
KARAPAPAK dial of AZERBAIJANI, NORTH [AZE]
KARAPAPAKH dial of AZERBAIJANI, SOUTH [AZB]
KARARAÓ dial of KAYAPÓ [TXU]
KARAS [KGV] lang, Indonesia, Irian Jaya
KARASHI dial of GWANDARA [GWN]
KARATA [KPT] lang, Russia, Europe
KARATAI alt for KARATA [KPT]
KARATAUN dial of KALUMPANG [KLI]
KARATE alt for KOMSO [KXC]
KARATIN alt for KARATA [KPT]
KARAU dial of LAWANGAN [LBX]
KARAW alt for KARAO [KYJ]
KARAWA [QKR] lang, Papua New Guinea
KARAWA alt for GARAWA [GBC]
KARAWARI alt for TABRIAK [TZX]
KARAWARI dial of ALAMBLAK [AMP]
KARAX dial of AVAR [AVR]
KARAXAHAR alt for QARASHAHR dial of UYGHUR
[UIG]
KARAY-A alt for KINARAY-A [KRJ]
KARAYAN alt for KEDAYAN dial of BRUNEI [KXD]
KARAYAN alt for KADAIAN dial of BRUNEI [KXD]
KARBARDAE alt for KABADE dial of SAPO [KRN]
KARBI alt for MIKIR [MJW]
KARDUTJARA alt for KARTUJARRA dial of MARTU
WANGKA [MPJ]
KARDUTJARRA alt for KARTUJARRA dial of MARTU
WANGKA [MPJ]
KARE [KMF] lang, Papua New Guinea
KARE alt for TOPOSA [TOQ]
KARE alt for KARI [KBJ]
KARE alt for KARI [KBN]
KARE alt for CREQ dial of HRE [HRE]
KAREKARE [KAI] lang, Nigeria
KARELIAN [KRL] lang, Russia, Europe, Finland
KARELY alt for KARELIAN [KRL]
KAREN, BREK [KVL] lang, Myanmar
KAREN, BWE [BWE] lang, Myanmar, Thailand,
Thailand
KAREN, BWE alt for KAREN, BWE [BWE]
KAREN, GEBA [KVQ] lang, Myanmar

KAREN, GEKO [GHK] lang, Myanmar
KAREN, LAHTA [KVT] lang, Myanmar
KAREN, MANUMANAW [KXF] lang, Myanmar
KAREN, NORTHERN PWO [KJT] lang, Thailand
KAREN, PA'O alt for KAREN, PA'O [BLK]
KAREN, PADAUNG [PDU] lang, Myanmar, Thailand,
Thailand
KAREN, PADAUNG alt for KAREN, PADAUNG [PDU]
KAREN, PAKU [KPP] lang, Myanmar
KAREN, PA'O [BLK] lang, Myanmar, Thailand,
Thailand
KAREN, PWO [PWO] lang, Myanmar
KAREN, PWO KANCHANA BURI [KJP] lang, Thailand
KAREN, PWO OMKOI [PWW] lang, Thailand
KAREN, PWO RATCHABURI [KJF] lang, Thailand
KAREN, S'GAW alt for KAREN, S'GAW [KSW]
KAREN, S'GAW [KSW] lang, Myanmar, Thailand,
Thailand
KAREN, YINBAW [KVU] lang, Myanmar
KAREN, YINTALE [KVY] lang, Myanmar
KAREN, ZAYEIN [KXK] lang, Myanmar
KARENBYU alt for KAREN, GEBA [KVQ]
KARENG alt for KARANG [KZR]
KARENJO alt for DZA [JEN]
KARENNYI alt for KAYAH, EASTERN [EKY]
KARENNYI alt for KAYAH, WESTERN [KYU]
KAREOVAN dial of KAVALAN [CKV]
KAREOWAN alt for KAREOVAN dial of KAVALAN
[CKV]
KARETI alt for KOMSO [KXC]
KAREY [KYD] lang, Indonesia, Maluku
KAREZ-I-MULLA dial of MOGHOLI [MLG]
KARFA [KBZ] lang, Nigeria
KARFASIA alt for SAMAROKENA [TMJ]
KARHADI dial of KONKANI [KNK]
KARI [KBJ] lang, Central African Republic, Zaïre,
Zaïre
KARI [KBN] lang, Central African Republic,
Cameroon
KARI alt for SUMAU [SIX]
KARI alt for KARI [KBJ]
KARI alt for USINO [URW]
KARI dial of KARI [KBN]
KARIA dial of KOLI, KACHI [GJK]
KARIANA alt for SAPÉ [SPC]
KARIERA alt for KARIYARRA [VKA]
KARIJONA alt for CARIJONA [CBD]
KARIKITANG dial of SANGIR [SAN]
KARIM alt for COMO KARIM [CFG]
KARIME alt for NANOMAM dial of YANOMÁMI
[WCA]
KARIMOJONG alt for KARAMOJONG [KDJ]
KARIMUI alt for DADIBI [MPS]
KARIN dial of ARMENIAN [ARM]
KARINGAL alt for MALARYAN [MJQ]
KARINGANI [KGN] lang, Iran
KARIPÚNA [KGM] lang, Brazil
KARIPÚNA CREOLE [KMV] lang, Brazil
KARIPUNÁ DE RONDÔNIA alt for KARIPUNÁ DO
GUAPORÉ [KUQ]
KARIPÚNA DO AMAPÁ alt for KARIPÚNA [KGM]
KARIPUNÁ DO GUAPORÉ [KUQ] lang, Brazil
KARIPÚNA DO UAÇÁ alt for KARIPÚNA [KGM]
KARIPUNA JACI PARANÁ dial of TENHARIM [PAH]
KARIRA dial of MANAGALASI [MCQ]
KARIRÍ alt for KARIRI-XUCO [KZW]

KARIRI XOCÓ alt for KARIRI-XUCO [KZW]
KARIRI-XUCO [KZW] lang, Brazil
KARITIÃNA [KTN] lang, Brazil
KARIYA [KIL] lang, Nigeria
KARIYARRA [VKA] lang, Australia
KARIYU alt for KARIYA [KIL]
KARKAR alt for KARKAR-YURI [YUJ]
KARKAR-YURI [YUJ] lang, Papua New Guinea
KARKAWU dial of KANEMBU [KBL]
KARKO [KKO] lang, Sudan
KARLUKO-CHIGILE-UIGHUR dial of UZBEK,
    NORTHERN [UZB]
KARLUKO-CHIGILE-UIGHUR dial of UZBEK,
    NORTHERN [UZB]
KARMALI [KFL] lang, India
KARMALI dial of SANTALI [SNT]
KARNATAK LAMANI dial of LAMANI [LMN]
KARNU alt for KANJU [KBE]
KARO [KXH] lang, Ethiopia
KARO alt for RAWA [RWO]
KARO BATAK alt for BATAK KARO [BTX]
KAROK [KYH] lang, USA
KAROKA dial of KATLA [KCR]
KAROLANOS [KYN] lang, Philippines
KAROMBE dial of MANYIKA [MXC]
KAROMPA dial of BONERATE [BNA]
KARON [KRX] lang, Senegal, Gambia
KARON DORI [KGW] lang, Indonesia, Irian Jaya
KARON PANTAI alt for ABUN TAT dial of ABUN
    [KGR]
KARONDI dial of TUMTUM [TBR]
KARONSIE dial of MORI BAWAH [XMZ]
KARORE [XKX] lang, Papua New Guinea
KARRAJARRA alt for KARADJERI [GBD]
KARRÉ alt for KARI [KBN]
KARRIARA alt for KARIYARRA [VKA]
KARS dial of AZERBAIJANI, SOUTH [AZB]
KARSHI alt for KANUFI dial of KANUFI-KANINGDON-
    NINDEM [KDP]
KARTUJARRA dial of MARTU WANGKA [MPJ]
KARTUTJARA alt for KARTUJARRA dial of MARTU
    WANGKA [MPJ]
KARU dial of GBAGYI [GBR]
KARUA alt for HARUA dial of BOLA [BNP]
KARUAMA dial of KUNIMAIPA [KUP]
KARUFA alt for ASIENARA [ASI]
KARUK alt for KAROK [KYH]
KARUPAKA alt for KORRIPAKO dial of CURRIPACO
    [KPC]
KARUTANA alt for CARÚTANA [CRU]
KASAA dial of MUMUYE [MUL]
KASANGA [CCJ] lang, Guinea Bissau, Senegal,
    Senegal
KASANGA alt for KASANGA [CCJ]
KASARA dial of SENOUFO, CEBAARA [SEF]
KASCHEMIRI alt for KASHMIRI [KSH]
KASELE alt for AKASELEM [AKS]
KASEM [KAS] lang, Burkina Faso, Ghana, Ghana
KASEM alt for KASEM [KAS]
KASEM dial of KASEM [KAS]
KASENA alt for KASEM [KAS]
KASENE alt for KASEM [KAS]
KASENG alt for KASSENG [KGC]
KASERE alt for IKOBI-MENA [MEB]
KASHANI dial of FARSI, WESTERN [PES]
KASHAYA dial of POMO [POO]

KASHGAR-YARKAND dial of UYGHUR [UIG]
KASHGAR-YARKAND dial of UYGHUR [UIG]
KASHGAR-YARKAND dial of UYGHUR [UIG]
KASHI-SHACHE alt for KASHGAR-YARKAND dial of
    UYGHUR [UIG]
KASHKADARYA ARABIC dial of ARABIC, CENTRAL
    ASIAN COLLOQUIAL [ABH]
KASHKAI alt for QASHQAI [QSQ]
KASHKARI alt for KHOWAR [KHW]
KASHMERE alt for KECHMERRE dial of MABA [MDE]
KASHMIR GUJURI alt for GUJARI [GJU]
KASHMIRI [KSH] lang, India, Pakistan, Pakistan
KASHMIRI alt for KASHMIRI [KSH]
KASHTAWARI alt for STANDARD KASHMIRI dial of
    KASHMIRI [KSH]
KASHTWARI alt for KISHTWARI [KGA]
KASHUBIAN [CSB] lang, Poland
KASHUBIAN PROPER dial of KASHUBIAN [CSB]
KASHUJANA alt for KAXUIÂNA [KBB]
KASHUYANA alt for KAXUIANA [KBB]
KASIEH dial of WEMALE, NORTH [WEO]
KASIGAU dial of SAGALLA [TGA]
KASIGURANIN [KSN] lang, Philippines
KASIM alt for KASEM [KAS]
KASIMBAR alt for TAJIO [TDJ]
KASIMOV-TATAR dial of TATAR [TTR]
KASIRA alt for IRARUTU [IRH]
KASIUI alt for WATUBELA [WAH]
KASIWA alt for NINGGERUM [NXR]
KASKA [KKZ] lang, Canada
KASKI GURUNG alt for WESTERN GURUNG dial of
    GURUNG [GVR]
KASKIHÁ alt for GUANA [GVA]
KASOMA dial of KALAMSE [KNZ]
KASON BURA alt for KASEM [KAS]
KASON FRA alt for KASEM [KAS]
KASONKE alt for KASSONKE [KAO]
KASRAPAI alt for NINAM [SHB]
KASSANGA alt for KASANGA [CCJ]
KASSEM alt for KASEM [KAS]
KASSENA alt for KASEM [KAS]
KASSENG [KGC] lang, Laos
KASSI alt for KHASI [KHI]
KASSO alt for KASSONKE [KAO]
KASSON alt for KASSONKE [KAO]
KASSONKE [KAO] lang, Mali, Gambia, Senegal
KASSONKE alt for KASSONKE [KAO]
KASTANITAS-SITENA dial of TSAKONIAN [TSD]
KASUA [KHS] lang, Papua New Guinea
KASUI alt for WATUBELA [WAH]
KASUVA dial of TAMIL [TCV]
KASUWA dial of NINGGERUM [NXR]
KASUWERI [QKW] lang, Indonesia, Irian Jaya
KASUWERI dial of KASUWERI [QKW]
KATAANG [KGD] lang, Laos
KATAB [KCG] lang, Nigeria
KATAB dial of KATAB [KCG]
KATABAGA [KTQ] lang, Philippines
KATAKARI alt for KATKARI [KFU]
KATAN alt for ULLATAN [ULL]
KATANG alt for KATAANG [KGD]
KATANG alt for KAYONG [KXY]
KATARI alt for KATKARI [KFU]
KATAUIXI alt for JÚMA [JUA]
KATAUSAN alt for PAIWAN [PWN]
KATAWA alt for EBIRA [IGB]

KATAWIAN dlal ot WAIWAI [WAW]
KATAWIAN dial of WAIWAI [WAW]
KATAWINA alt for KATAWIAN dial of WAIWAI [WAW]
KATAWINA alt for KATAWIAN dial of WAIWAI [WAW]
KATAWIXI [QKI] lang, Brazil
KATAZI dial of BABATANA [BAQ]
KATBOL [TMB] lang, Vanuatu
KATCH alt for KACHCHI [KFR]
KATCHA dial of KATCHA-KADUGLI-MIRI [KAT]
KATCHA-KADUGLI-MIRI [KAT] lang, Sudan
KATCHAL dial of NICOBARESE, CENTRAL [NCB]
KATCHI alt for KOLI, KACHI [GJK]
KATCHI alt for KACHCHI dial of KOLI, KACHI [GJK]
KÂTE [KMG] lang, Papua New Guinea
KATE dial of KUNIMAIPA [KUP]
KÂTE DONG alt for KÂTE [KMG]
KATEGE alt for TEKE, NORTHERN [TEG]
KATEGE alt for TEGEKALI dial of TEKE, NORTHERN [TEG]
KATEGHE dial of TEKE, NORTHERN [TEG]
KATEIK dial of KATLA [KCR]
KATH BHOTE alt for LHOMI [LHM]
KATHAREVOUSA dial of GREEK [GRK]
KATHARIYA dial of THARU, DANG [THL]
KATHE alt for MEITHEI [MNR]
KATHI alt for MEITHEI [MNR]
KATHIAWARI alt for KISHTWARI [KGA]
KATHIYAWADI dial of GUJARATI [GJR]
KATHMANDU dial of NEWARI [NEW]
KATHODI alt for KATKARI [KFU]
KATI [BSH] lang, Afghanistan, Pakistan, Pakistan
KATI alt for KATI [BSH]
KATI dial of DAYAK, LAND [DYK]
KATI, NORTHERN [KTI] lang, Indonesia, Irian Jaya
KATI, SOUTHERN [KTS] lang, Indonesia, Irian Jaya
KATI-METOMKA alt for KATI, SOUTHERN [KTS]
KATI-NINANTI alt for KATI, NORTHERN [KTI]
KATIA alt for XATIA dial of NG/AMANI [NMN]
KATIA alt for XATIA dial of NG/AMANI [NMN]
KATIARA dial of SENOUFO, TAGWANA [TGW]
KATIATI [KQA] lang, Papua New Guinea
KATINGAN [KXG] lang, Indonesia, Kalimantan
KATINGAN dial of MADAK [MMX]
KATINJA [KTJ] lang, Papua New Guinea
KATIO alt for CATÍO [CTO]
KATIOLA dial of SENOUFO, TAGWANA [TGW]
KATIVA alt for NINGGERUM [NXR]
KATIVIRI alt for KATI [BSH]
KATIYAI dial of MALVI [MUP]
KATKARI [KFU] lang, India
KATLA [KCR] lang, Sudan
KATO [KTW] lang, USA
KATO alt for KADO [KDV]
KATOVA alt for LAGHU [LGB]
KATSY alt for KRYTS [KRY]
KATTALAN alt for ULLATAN [ULL]
KATTANG alt for WORIMI [KDA]
KATTEA alt for XATIA dial of NG/AMANI [NMN]
KATTEA alt for XATIA dial of NG/AMANI [NMN]
KATU [KTV] lang, Viet Nam, Laos
KATU alt for KADO [KDV]
KATUA [KTA] lang, Viet Nam
KATUENA alt for KATAWIAN dial of WAIWAI [WAW]

KATUKÍNA [KAV] lang, Brazil
KATUKINA DO JURUÁ alt for KATUKÍNA, PANOAN [KNT]
KATUKINA DO JUTAÍ alt for KATUKÍNA [KAV]
KATUKÍNA, PANOAN [KNT] lang, Brazil
KATUMENE alt for KAPIN [TBX]
KATVADI alt for KATKARI [KFU]
KATWENA alt for KATAWIAN dial of WAIWAI [WAW]
KATWENA alt for KATAWIAN dial of WAIWAI [WAW]
KAU alt for KO [FUJ]
KAU alt for KAO [KAX]
KAU dial of KO [FUJ]
KAU BRU alt for RIANG [RIA]
KAU-//-EN alt for 'AKHOE [AKE]
KAUDITAN dial of TONSEA [TXS]
KAUESCAR alt for AKSANA [KBG]
KAUGAT alt for ATOHWAIM [AQM]
KAUGEL alt for UMBU-UNGU [UMB]
KAUIL alt for UMBU-UNGU [UMB]
KAUKAU alt for 'AKHOE [AKE]
KAUKAU alt for KUNG-GOBABIS [AUE]
KAUKAUE alt for KAKAUHUA [KBF]
KAULI alt for KULUI [KFX]
KAULONG [PSS] lang, Papua New Guinea
KAULONG dial of KAULONG [PSS]
KAUMA dial of GIRYAMA [NYF]
KAUNAK alt for CITAK [TXT]
KAUNGA alt for YELOGU [YLG]
KAUR [VKK] lang, Indonesia, Sumatra
KAURE [BPP] lang, Indonesia, Irian Jaya
KAUREH alt for KAURE [BPP]
KAURI dial of JINGPHO [CGP]
KAURI dial of JINGPHO [CGP]
KAURU alt for KUZAMANI [KSA]
KAUTCHY alt for KACHCHI [KFR]
KAUVIA alt for AMA [AMM]
KAUWERAWEC [QKX] lang, Indonesia, Irian Jaya
KAUWERAWETJ alt for KAUWERAWEC [QKX]
KAUWOL [KYW] lang, Papua New Guinea, Indonesia, Irian Jaya
KAUYARÍ alt for CABIYARÍ [CBB]
KAUYAWA alt for KARIYA [KIL]
KAVAH dial of KOLI, KACHI [GJK]
KAVALAN [CKV] lang, Taiwan
KAVANAN alt for KAVALAN [CKV]
KAVAR alt for KAWARI [KFV]
KAVARAUAN alt for KAVALAN [CKV]
KAVIRONDO alt for LUO [LUO]
KAVIRONDO LUO alt for LUO [LUO]
KAVIXI alt for SARARÉ [SRR]
KAVOR alt for KOYA [KFF]
KAVU alt for BUKIYIP [APE]
KAVWOL alt for KAUWOL [KYW]
KAW alt for KANSA [KAA]
KAW alt for AKHA [AKA]
KAW alt for KOSKIN [KID]
KAWA alt for VO [WBM]
KAWA alt for BLANG [BLR]
KAWA alt for BUKAWA [BUK]
KAWA dial of LISABATA-NUNIALI [LCS]
KAWA TADIMINI alt for KAJAKSE [CKQ]
KAWAAWILA GYPSIES dial of ARABIC, MESOPOTAMIAN COLLOQUIAL [ACM]
KAWAC alt for BUKAWA [BUK]

KAWACHA [KCB] lang, Papua New Guinea
KAWAIB alt for KAGWAHIV dial of TENHARIM [PAH]
KAWAIISU [KAW] lang, USA
KAWAKARUBI alt for WAIA [KNV]
KAWALIB alt for KOALIB [KIB]
KAWAMA alt for OTORO [OTR]
KAWANG dial of BAJAU, WEST COAST [BDR]
KAWANGA alt for WANGA dial of LUYIA [LUY]
KAWANUWAN alt for BASAY [BYQ]
KAWAR alt for KAWARI [KFV]
KAWAR dial of MAITHILI [MKP]
KAWARI [KFV] lang, India
KAWARMA alt for OTORO [OTR]
KAWASKAR alt for KAWESQAR [ALC]
KAWATHI alt for BAGHELI [BFY]
KAWATSA alt for KAWACHA [KCB]
KAWAYAN dial of HILIGAYNON [HIL]
KAWE [KGB] lang, Indonesia, Irian Jaya
KAWEL alt for LEMBUR dial of WOISIKA [WOI]
KAWESQAR [ALC] lang, Chile
KAWIKU dial of LUNDA [LVN]
KAWILLARY alt for CABIYARÍ [CBB]
KAWIT dial of MA'YA [SLZ]
KAWKI alt for CAUQUI dial of JAQARU [JQR]
KAWOL alt for KAUWOL [KYW]
KAWONDE alt for KAONDE [KQN]
KAWWAD'A alt for GAWWADA [GWD]
KAWWADA alt for GAWWADA [GWD]
KAXARARÍ [KTX] lang, Brazil
KAXARIRI alt for KAXARARÍ [KTX]
KAXETIAN dial of GEORGIAN [GEO]
KAXIB dial of AKHVAKH [AKV]
KAXIB dial of AVAR [AVR]
KAXINAUÁ alt for CASHINAHUA [CBS]
KAXINAWÁ alt for CASHINAHUA [CBS]
KAXUIÃNA [KBB] lang, Brazil
KAXÚYANA alt for KAXUIÃNA [KBB]
KAXYNAWA alt for CASHINAHUA [CBS]
KAYA alt for KOYA [KFF]
KAYABÍ [KYZ] lang, Brazil
KAYAGAR alt for KAYGIR [KYT]
KAYAH alt for KAYAH, EASTERN [EKY]
KAYAH, EASTERN [EKY] lang, Thailand
KAYAH, WESTERN [KYU] lang, Myanmar
KAYAM alt for KAREN, PADAUNG [PDU]
KAYAMAN alt for KAJAMAN [KAG]
KAYAN alt for KAIAN [KCT]
KAYAN MAHAKAM [XAY] lang, Indonesia,
  Kalimantan
KAYAN RIVER BAKUNG dial of KENYAH, BAKUNG
  [BOC]
KAYAN RIVER KAJAN alt for KAYAN, KAYAN RIVER
  [XKN]
KAYAN RIVER KENYA alt for KENYAH, KAYAN
  RIVER [KNH]
KAYAN, BARAM [KYS] lang, Malaysia, Sarawak,
  Brunei
KAYAN, BUSANG [BFG] lang, Indonesia, Kalimantan
KAYAN, KAYAN RIVER [XKN] lang, Indonesia,
  Kalimantan
KAYAN, MENDALAM [XKD] lang, Indonesia,
  Kalimantan
KAYAN, MURIK [MXR] lang, Malaysia, Sarawak
KAYAN, REJANG [REE] lang, Malaysia, Sarawak
KAYAN, WAHAU [WHU] lang, Indonesia, Kalimantan
KAYANI alt for JAKATI [JAT]

KAYANIYUT KAYAN dial of KAYAN, KAYAN RIVER
  [XKN]
KAYANIYUT KENYAH dial of KENYAH, KAYAN
  RIVER [KNH]
KAYAPA dial of KALLAHAN, KAYAPA [KAK]
KAYAPÓ [TXU] lang, Brazil
KAYAPO-KRADAÚ [KAH] lang, Brazil
KAYAPWE alt for ZÁPARO [ZRO]
KAYASTHI dial of SINDHI [SND]
KAYASTHI alt for PARABHI dial of KONKANI [KNK]
KAYAVAR dial of MALAYALAM [MJS]
KAYAY alt for KAYAH, EASTERN [EKY]
KAYAY alt for KAYAH, WESTERN [KYU]
KAYELI [KZL] lang, Indonesia, Maluku
KAYELI dial of KAYELI [KZL]
KAYGIR [KYT] lang, Indonesia, Irian Jaya
KAYIK alt for WANAP [WNP]
KAYIN alt for KAREN, BWE [BWE]
KAYINBYU alt for KAREN, GEBA [KVQ]
KAYLA alt for QWARA dial of KARA [CFL]
KAYOA dial of MAKIAN, EAST [MKY]
KAYOBE alt for SOLA [SOY]
KAYONG [KXY] lang, Viet Nam
KAYONG alt for KAYUNG dial of MALAYIC DAYAK
  [XDY]
KAYORT [KYV] lang, Nepal
KAYOVA alt for KAIWÁ [KGK]
KAYTAK alt for KAJTAK dial of DARGWA [DAR]
KAYU AGUNG [VKY] lang, Indonesia, Sumatra
KAYUMERAH alt for KOWIAI [KWH]
KAYUNG dial of MALAYIC DAYAK [XDY]
KAYUPULAU [KZU] lang, Indonesia, Irian Jaya
KAZAK alt for KAZAKH [KAZ]
KAZAKH [KAZ] lang, Kazakhstan, Afghanistan,
  China, Iran, Mongolian Peoples Republic, Turkey
KAZAKH alt for KAZAKH [KAZ]
KAZAKH dial of AZERBAIJANI, NORTH [AZE]
KAZAKHI alt for KAZAKH [KAZ]
KAZAN TATAR dial of TATAR [TTR]
KAZAX alt for KAZAKH [KAZ]
KAZERUNI dial of FARSI, WESTERN [PES]
KAZIKUMUKHTSY alt for LAK [LBE]
KAZUKURU [KZK] lang, Solomon Islands
KBALAN alt for KAVALAN [CKV]
KDANG alt for KEDANG [KSX]
KDRAO alt for KODRAO dial of RADE [RAD]
KE alt for CHINESE, HAKKA [HAK]
KE'BU alt for NDO [NDP]
KE'ERKEZI alt for KIRGHIZ [KDO]
KE'YAGANA alt for KEYAGANA [KYG]
KE-WOYA-YAKA alt for NORTHERN LIMBA dial of
  LIMBA, EAST [LMA]
KEAI alt for RO dial of FOLOPA [PPO]
KEAKA alt for EJAGHAM [ETU]
KEANA dial of ALAGO [ALA]
KEAPARA alt for KEOPARA [KHZ]
KEB-KAYE alt for KABALAI [KVF]
KEBA-WOPASALI dial of FOLOPA [PPO]
KEBADI alt for ZAGHAWA [ZAG]
KEBAI dial of CHUAVE [CJV]
KEBAR alt for MPUR [AKC]
KEBEIRKA alt for UDUK [UDU]
KEBENA alt for QEBENA dial of KAMBAATA [KTB]
KEBU alt for AKEBOU [KEU]
KEBU alt for NDO [NDP]
KEBU alt for OKE'BU dial of NDO [NDP]

KEBU FULA dial of FUUTA JALON [FUF]
KEBUMTAMP [KJZ] lang, Bhutan
KEBUTU alt for NDO [NDP]
KEBUTU alt for OKE'BU dial of NDO [NDP]
KECHAN alt for QUECHAN [YUM]
KECHI dial of BALUCHI, SOUTHERN [BCC]
KECHIA alt for CHINESE, HAKKA [HAK]
KECHMERRE dial of MABA [MDE]
KEDAH dial of KENSIU [KNS]
KEDAH dial of MALAY [MLI]
KEDAMAIAN DUSUN alt for DUSUN, TEMPASUK [TDU]
KEDANG [KSX] lang, Indonesia, Nusa Tenggara
KEDANGESE alt for KEDANG [KSX]
KEDAYAN alt for DUSUN, CENTRAL [DTP]
KEDAYAN dial of BRUNEI [KXD]
KEDAYAN alt for KEDAYAN dial of BRUNEI [KXD]
KEDAYAN alt for KADAIAN dial of BRUNEI [KXD]
KEDDE alt for KEDI dial of SAN [HGM]
KEDDI alt for KEDI dial of SAN [HGM]
KEDE alt for AKA-KEDE [AKX]
KEDER [KDY] lang, Indonesia, Irian Jaya
KEDI alt for LABA [LAU]
KEDI dial of SAN [HGM]
KEDIEN alt for KADAIAN dial of BRUNEI [KXD]
KEDIEN. KERAYAN alt for KEDAYAN dial of BRUNEI [KXD]
KEDYAN alt for KEDAYAN dial of BRUNEI [KXD]
KEDYAN alt for KADAIAN dial of BRUNEI [KXD]
KEEKONYOKIE dial of MAASAI [MET]
KEEMBO dial of MBOLE [MDQ]
KEENGE dial of BEEMBE [BEJ]
KEENOK dial of ASMAT, CENTRAL [AST]
KEER [KKE] lang, India
KEEWATIN alt for CARIBOU ESKIMO dial of INUIT, WESTERN CANADIAN [ESC]
KEFA alt for KAFA [KBR]
KEFFA alt for KAFA [KBR]
KEFFI alt for ELOYI [AFO]
KEFINYA alt for KAFA [KBR]
KEGBERIKE alt for AKEBOU [KEU]
KEGENGELE alt for GENGELE dial of SONGOORA [SOD]
KEH-DEO dial of HMONG, EASTERN [HEA]
KEH-LAO alt for GELO [KKF]
KEHA dial of TUKUDEDE [TKD]
KEHELALA dial of TAWALA [TBO]
KEHENA dial of NAGA, ANGAMI [NJM]
KEHERARA alt for KEHELALA dial of TAWALA [TBO]
KEHIA alt for CHINESE, HAKKA [HAK]
KEHJA alt for KENYAH, KAYAN RIVER [KNH]
KEHJA alt for KENYAH, KELINYAU [XKL]
KEHJA alt for KENYAH, MAHAKAM [XKM]
KEHLOORI PAHARI alt for KAHLURI [KFS]
KEI [KEI] lang, Indonesia, Maluku
KEI BESAR dial of KEI [KEI]
KEI KECIL dial of KEI [KEI]
KEIA alt for KEHA dial of TUKUDEDE [TKD]
KEIAGANA alt for KEYAGANA [KYG]
KEIGA [KEC] lang, Sudan
KEIGA dial of KEIGA [KEC]
KEIGA GIRRU alt for KEIGA JIRRU [KEG]
KEIGA JIRRU [KEG] lang, Sudan
KEIGA-AL-KHEIL alt for KEIGA [KEC]
KEIGA-TIMERO alt for KEIGA [KEC]
KEIGANA alt for KEYAGANA [KYG]

KEIN alt for BEMAL [BMH]
KEIYO dial of KALENJIN [KLN]
KEJAMAN alt for KAJAMAN [KAG]
KEJENG alt for BABANKI [BBK]
KEK alt for CHINESE, HAKKA [HAK]
KEKA alt for TERMANU-TALAE-KEKA dial of ROTI [ROT]
KEKAMBA alt for KAMBA [KIK]
KEKAR alt for KJAKELA dial of OROCH [OAC]
KEKAUNGDU alt for KAREN, GEKO [GHK]
KEKCHÍ [KEK] lang, Guatemala, Belize, El Salvador
KEKHONG alt for KAREN, GEKO [GHK]
KEKU alt for KAREN, GEKO [GHK]
KEL ALKASEYBATEN alt for EAST SONGAI dial of SONGAI [SON]
KELA [KCL] lang, Papua New Guinea
KELA [KEL] lang, Zaïre
KELABIT [KZI] lang, Malaysia, Sarawak, Indonesia, Kalimantan
KELAI dial of SEGAI [SGE]
KELANA alt for GITUA [GIL]
KELANA alt for KELA [KCL]
KELANCHI alt for KUR dial of PUKU-GEERI-KERI-WIPSI [GEL]
KELANG dial of LUHU [LCQ]
KELANGI alt for LANGI [LAG]
KELANTAN dial of MALAY [MLI]
KELAO alt for GELO [KKF]
KELDERASHÍCKO alt for KALDERASH dial of ROMANI, VLACH [RMY]
KÉLÉ alt for KÉLÉ [KEB]
KELE [SBC] lang, Papua New Guinea
KELE [KHY] lang, Zaïre
KÉLÉ [KEB] lang, Gabon, Congo
KELE alt for LIPOTO dial of LUSENGO [LUS]
KELEB dial of AVAR [AVR]
KELENGA alt for BOZO, HAINYAXO [BZX]
KELEO alt for GELO [KKF]
KELEYQIQ IFUGAO alt for KALLAHAN, KELEY-I [IFY]
KELHURI dial of LURI [LRI]
KELI dial of BOHUAI [RAK]
KELIKO alt for KALIKO [KBO]
KELIKO alt for KALIKO-MA'DI [XKZ]
KELIMURI dial of GESER-GOROM [GES]
KELINCI alt for KUR dial of PUKU-GEERI-KERI-WIPSI [GEL]
KÉLINGA alt for BOZO, HAINYAXO [BZX]
KELINGAN dial of MABA [MDE]
KELINGAN dial of MODANG [MXD]
KELINGI alt for SINDANG KELINGI [SDI]
KELINJAU alt for KENYAH, KELINYAU [XKL]
KELINYAU alt for KENYAH, KELINYAU [XKL]
KELLI-NI alt for KUR dial of PUKU-GEERI-KERI-WIPSI [GEL]
KÉLLINGUA alt for BOZO, HAINYAXO [BZX]
KELO [TSN] lang, Sudan
KELO-BENI SHEKO alt for KELO [TSN]
KELON [KYO] lang, Indonesia, Nusa Tenggara
KELONG alt for KELON [KYO]
KEM DEGNE dial of BLANG [BLR]
KEMAI alt for GOEMAI [ANK]
KEMAK [KEM] lang, Indonesia, Nusa Tenggara
KEMAK dial of KEMAK [KEM]
KEMANAT alt for QIMANT [QIM]
KEMANT alt for QIMANT [QIM]
KEMATA alt for KAMBAATA [KTB]

KEMBATA alt for KAMBAATA [KTB]
KEMBATINYA alt for KAMBAATA [KTB]
KEMBAYAN [XEM] lang, Indonesia, Kalimantan
KEMBERANO [BZP] lang, Indonesia, Irian Jaya
KEMELOM alt for MOMBUM [MSO]
KEMENA PENAN dial of KENYAH, WESTERN [XKY]
KEMEZUNG [DMO] lang, Cameroon
KEMMUNGAM alt for NAGA, KHIAMNGAN [NKY]
KEMTUIK [KMT] lang, Indonesia, Irian Jaya
KEMTUK alt for KEMTUIK [KMT]
KEMU alt for KHMU [KJG]
KEMU dial of WAN [WAN]
KENAT alt for BAGHELI [BFY]
KENATHI alt for KENATI [GAT]
KENATI [GAT] lang, Papua New Guinea
KENDARI alt for KONAWE dial of TOLAKI [LBW]
KENDATA dial of OROKAIVA [ORK]
KENDAYAN [KNX] lang, Indonesia, Kalimantan
KENDAYAN dial of KENDAYAN [KNX]
KENDAYAN DAYAK alt for KENDAYAN [KNX]
KENDAYAN-AMBAWANG alt for KENDAYAN [KNX]
KENDEM [KVM] lang, Cameroon
KENDERONG dial of TEMIAR [TMH]
KENEDIBI alt for WAIA [KNV]
KEÑELE alt for KYENELE [KQL]
KENEN BIRANG alt for KYENELE [KQL]
KENERING dial of TEMIAR [TMH]
KENG alt for KHENKHA dial of KEBUMTAMP [KJZ]
KENGA [KYQ] lang, Chad
KENGA alt for TYENGA dial of SHANGA [SHO]
KENGE alt for KENGA [KYQ]
KENI dial of CHAGGA [KAF]
KENINGAU DUSUN alt for GANA [GNQ]
KENINGAU MURUT [KXI] lang, Malaysia, Sabah
KENINJAL [KNL] lang, Indonesia, Kalimantan
KENJA alt for KENYAH, UPPER BARAM [UBM]
KENJA alt for KENYAH, KAYAN RIVER [KNH]
KENJA alt for KENYAH, KELINYAU [XKL]
KENJA alt for KENYAH, MAHAKAM [XKM]
KENJA alt for KENYAH, WESTERN [XKY]
KENKÜ alt for MÜNKÜ dial of IRÁNTXE [IRA]
KENSE alt for KENSIU [KNS]
KENSENSE alt for KENSWEI NSEI [NDB]
KENSEU alt for KENSIU [KNS]
KENSIEU alt for KENSIU [KNS]
KENSIU [KNS] lang, Malaysia, Peninsular, Thailand,
   Thailand
KENSIU alt for KENSIU [KNS]
KENSIU BATU dial of KENSIU [KNS]
KENSIU SIONG dial of KENSIU [KNS]
KENSIW alt for KENSIU [KNS]
KENSWEI NSEI [NDB] lang, Cameroon
KENTA alt for KINTAQ [KNQ]
KENTA alt for KENSIU [KNS]
KENTA-BOGN alt for KENSIU [KNS]
KENTAQ NAKIL dial of KENSIU [KNS]
KENTIN dial of KUTEP [KUB]
KENTU alt for ICEN [ICH]
KENTU alt for BISSAULA dial of KPAN [KPK]
KENTUNG WA dial of VO [WBM]
KENUZ dial of KENUZI-DONGOLA [KNC]
KENUZ alt for KENUZI dial of KENUZI-DONGOLA
   [KNC]
KENUZI dial of KENUZI-DONGOLA [KNC]
KENUZI alt for KENUZ dial of KENUZI-DONGOLA
   [KNC]

KENUZI-DONGOLA [KNC] lang, Egypt, Sudan
KENUZI-DONGOLA alt for KENUZI-DONGOLA [KNC]
KENYA alt for KENYAH, KAYAN RIVER [KNH]
KENYA alt for KENYAH, KELINYAU [XKL]
KENYA alt for KENYAH, MAHAKAM [XKM]
KENYA alt for KENGA [KYQ]
KENYAH alt for KENYAH, UPPER BARAM [UBM]
KENYAH alt for KENYAH, KAYAN RIVER [KNH]
KENYAH alt for KENYAH, KELINYAU [XKL]
KENYAH alt for KENYAH, MAHAKAM [XKM]
KENYAH, BAHAU RIVER [BWV] lang, Indonesia,
   Kalimantan
KENYAH, BAKUNG [BOC] lang, Indonesia,
   Kalimantan, Malaysia, Sarawak, Malaysia,
   Sarawak
KENYAH, BAKUNG alt for KENYAH, BAKUNG [BOC]
KENYAH, KAYAN RIVER [KNH] lang, Indonesia,
   Kalimantan
KENYAH, KELINYAU [XKL] lang, Indonesia,
   Kalimantan
KENYAH, MAHAKAM [XKM] lang, Indonesia,
   Kalimantan
KENYAH, SEBOB [SIB] lang, Malaysia, Sarawak
KENYAH, TUTOH [TTW] lang, Malaysia, Sarawak
KENYAH, UPPER BARAM [UBM] lang, Malaysia,
   Sarawak, Brunei, Indonesia, Kalimantan
KENYAH, WAHAU [WHK] lang, Indonesia,
   Kalimantan
KENYAH, WESTERN [XKY] lang, Malaysia, Sarawak
KENYAN SIGN LANGUAGE [XKI] lang, Kenya
KENYANG [KEN] lang, Cameroon
KENYI alt for SOGA [SOG]
KENYI dial of SOGA [SOG]
KENYI alt for ZHIRE dial of HAM [JAB]
KENYING BULANG alt for KYENELE [KQL]
KENZI alt for KENUZ dial of KENUZI-DONGOLA
   [KNC]
KEO [XXK] lang, Indonesia, Nusa Tenggara
KEOPARA [KHZ] lang, Papua New Guinea
KEOPARA dial of KEOPARA [KHZ]
KEPERE dial of MBUM [MDD]
KEPERE alt for GBETE dial of MBUM [MDD]
KEPO' [KUK] lang, Indonesia, Nusa Tenggara
KEPOQ alt for KEPO' [KUK]
KER alt for KARABORO, EASTERN [KAR]
KERA [KER] lang, Chad, Cameroon
KERA dial of MUNDARI [MUW]
KERA' dial of MUNDARI [MUW]
KERABIT alt for KELABIT [KZI]
KERANG alt for SOGA [SOG]
KERAWARA dial of RAMOAAINA [RAI]
KERAYAN alt for KADAIAN dial of BRUNEI [KXD]
KERDAU dial of JAH HUT [JAH]
KERE alt for KARO [KXH]
KERE dial of BAMBESHI [MYF]
KERE alt for KUR dial of PUKU-GEERI-KERI-WIPSI
   [GEL]
KEREBE [KED] lang, Tanzania
KEREHO-UHENG [XKE] lang, Indonesia, Kalimantan
KEREI alt for KAREY [KYD]
KEREK [KRK] lang, Russia, Asia
KEREKERE alt for KAREKARE [KAI]
KEREMA alt for NISA [NIC]
KEREMI alt for NYATURU [RIM]
KEREN dial of AGHUL [AGX]
KEREPUNU alt for KEOPARA [KHZ]

KERES, EASTERN [KEE] lang, USA
KERES, WESTERN [KJQ] lang, USA
KEREWA alt for KEREWO [KXZ]
KEREWA-GOARI alt for KEREWO [KXZ]
KEREWE alt for KEREBE [KED]
KEREWO [KXZ] lang, Papua New Guinea
KEREYU dial of OROMO, BORANA-ARUSI-GUJI
    [GAX]
KERI alt for KERA [KER]
KERI dial of GOLIN [GVF]
KERI-NI alt for KUR dial of PUKU-GEERI-KERI-WIPSI
    [GEL]
KERIAKA [KJX] lang, Papua New Guinea
KERIFA alt for KARFA [KBZ]
KERINCHI alt for KERINCI [KVR]
KERINCI [KVR] lang, Indonesia, Sumatra
KERINCI-MINANGKABAU dial of MINANGKABAU
    [MPU]
KERINTJI alt for KERINCI [KVR]
KERMANI dial of FARSI, WESTERN [PES]
KERMANJI alt for KURMANJI [KUR]
KERMANSHAHI dial of KURDI [KDB]
KEROROGEA dial of DUAU [DUA]
KERRE alt for HAMER-BANNA [AMF]
KERRE alt for KARO [KXH]
KERRIKERRI alt for KAREKARE [KAI]
KESAWAI [QKE] lang, Papua New Guinea
KESENGELE alt for SENGELE [SZG]
KESHIKTEN alt for JO-UDA dial of MONGOLIAN,
    PERIPHERAL [MVF]
KESHUR alt for KASHMIRI [KSH]
KESONGOLA alt for SONGOORA [SOD]
KESSI alt for SOPPENG dial of BUGIS [BPR]
KESTANE alt for SODDO dial of GURAGE, NORTH
    [GRU]
KESU' alt for RANTEPAO dial of TORAJA-SA'DAN
    [SDA]
KESUI alt for WATUBELA [WAH]
KET [KET] lang, Russia, Asia
KETAGALAN alt for KETANGALAN [KAE]
KETANGALAN [KAE] lang, Taiwan
KETE [KCV] lang, Zaïre
KETEBO alt for LOKATHAN dial of TESO [TEO]
KETEGHE dial of TEKE, NORTHERN [TEG]
KETEGO alt for TEKE, NORTHERN [TEG]
KETENENEYU dial of NAGA, RENGMA [NRE]
KETENGBAN [KIN] lang, Indonesia, Irian Jaya
KETIAR KRAU dial of JAH HUT [JAH]
KETIEPO dial of GREBO, NORTHEASTERN [GRP]
KETIN dial of ATTIÉ [ATI]
KETUEN alt for MBE [MFO]
KETUNGAU dial of IBAN [IBA]
KETY alt for TYM dial of SELKUP [SAK]
KEURO alt for KEURU [QQK]
KEURU [QQK] lang, Papua New Guinea
KEVAT BOLI alt for BAGHELI [BFY]
KEVATI alt for BAGHELI [BFY]
KEWA, EAST [KJS] lang, Papua New Guinea
KEWA, SOUTH [KJY] lang, Papua New Guinea
KEWA, WEST [KEW] lang, Papua New Guinea
KEWAH dial of FOLOPA [PPO]
KEWANI alt for BAGHELI [BFY]
KEWAT alt for BAGHELI [BFY]
KEWATI alt for BAGHELI [BFY]
KEWIENG [XEW] lang, Papua New Guinea
KEWOT alt for BAGHELI [BFY]

KEYAGANA [KYG] lang, Papua New Guinea
KEYDNJMARDA alt for ADYNYAMATHANHA [ADT]
KEYO alt for KEIYO dial of KALENJIN [KLN]
KEZAMI alt for NAGA, KHEZHA [NKH]
KGAGA dial of SOTHO, NORTHERN [SRT]
KGATLA dial of TSWANA [TSW]
KHA CAU alt for KHMU [KJG]
KHA KHMU alt for KHMU [KJG]
KHA KO alt for AKHA [AKA]
KHA LAMET alt for LAMET [LBN]
KHA NIANG alt for PUOC [PUO]
KHA PHAY alt for PHAI [PRT]
KHA PHONG alt for PONG 1 [KPN]
KHA PONG alt for PONG 1 [KPN]
KHA PUHOC alt for PUOC [PUO]
KHA TAMPUON alt for TAMPUAN [TPU]
KHA TONG LUANG [KHQ] lang, Laos
KHABIT alt for BIT [BGK]
KHADIA alt for KHARIA [KHR]
KHAE alt for LISU [LIS]
KHAGA alt for KGAGA dial of SOTHO, NORTHERN
    [SRT]
KHAIDAK dial of KUMYK [KSK]
KHAIRA dial of KODA [KFN]
KHAJUNA alt for BURUSHASKI [BSK]
KHAKAS [KJH] lang, USSR, Asia, China, Russia,
    Asia
KHAKHAS alt for KHAKAS [KJH]
KHAKHASS alt for KHAKAS [KJH]
KHAKO alt for AKHA [AKA]
KHAL:MAG alt for KALMYK-OIRAT [KGZ]
KHALAJ [KLJ] lang, Iran
KHALCHIGUOR dial of TU [MJG]
KHALENGE RAI alt for KHALING [KLR]
KHALING [KLR] lang, Nepal
KHALKHA alt for MONGOLIAN, HALH [KHK]
KHALKHA dial of MONGOLIAN, HALH [KHK]
KHALKHA alt for HALH dial of MONGOLIAN, HALH
    [KHK]
KHALKHA MONGOLIAN alt for MONGOLIAN, HALH
    [KHK]
KHALKHAL dial of TAKESTANI [TKS]
KHAM [KHG] lang, China
KHAM, GAMALE [KGJ] lang, Nepal
KHAM, MAIKOTI [ZKM] lang, Nepal
KHAM, NISI [KIF] lang, Nepal
KHAM, SHESHI [KIP] lang, Nepal
KHAM, TAKALE [KJL] lang, Nepal
KHAM-MAGAR alt for KHAM, TAKALE [KJL]
KHAM-TAI alt for KHAMTI [KHT]
KHAMA alt for ASSYRIAN [AII]
KHAMBA alt for KHAM [KHG]
KHAMBANA-MAKWAKWE alt for HLENGWE dial of
    TSWA [TSC]
KHAMBANI dial of CHOPI [CCE]
KHAMBANI alt for HLENGWE dial of TSWA [TSC]
KHAMED alt for LAMET [LBN]
KHAMEN-BORAN alt for KUY [KDT]
KHAMET alt for LAMET [LBN]
KHAMI alt for CHIN, KHUMI [CKM]
KHAMI dial of CHIN, KHUMI [CKM]
KHAMIR alt for XAMIR [XAI]
KHAMIT alt for XAMIR [XAI]
KHAMLA dial of GOWLI [GOK]
KHAMNIGAN alt for EVENKI [EVN]
KHAMPTI alt for KHAMTI [KHT]

KHAMPTI SHAN alt for KHAMTI [KHT]
KHAMS alt for KHAM [KHG]
KHAMS BHOTIA alt for KHAM [KHG]
KHAMS-YAL alt for KHAM [KHG]
KHAMTA alt for XAMTA [XAT]
KHAMTANGA alt for XAMTANGA [XAN]
KHAMTI [KHT] lang, Myanmar, India
KHAMTI SHAN alt for KHAMTI [KHT]
KHAMU alt for KHMU [KJG]
KHAMUK alt for KHMU [KJG]
KHAMYANG [KSU] lang, India
KHANA alt for KOANA [KEH]
KHANAG alt for NORTH TABASARAN dial of
    TABASSARAN [TAB]
KHANDESHI alt for KHANDESI [KHN]
KHANDESI [KHN] lang, India
KHANDESI dial of KHANDESI [KHN]
KHANDI SHAN alt for KHAMTI [KHT]
KHANDISH alt for KHANDESI [KHN]
KHANG [KJM] lang, Viet Nam
KHANG AI dial of KHANG [KJM]
KHANG CLAU dial of KHANG [KJM]
KHANGOI dial of NAGA, TANGKHUL [NMF]
KHANTI alt for KHANTY [KCA]
KHANTIS alt for KHAMTI [KHT]
KHANTY [KCA] lang, Russia, Asia
KHANUNG alt for RAWANG [RAW]
KHANUNG alt for NUNG [NUN]
KHAO [XAO] lang, Viet Nam
KHAO KHA KO alt for AKHA [AKA]
KHAPUT alt for XAPUT dial of KRYTS [KRY]
KHARACHIN alt for JOSTU dial of MONGOLIAN,
    PERIPHERAL [MVF]
KHARACHIN alt for JOSTU dial of MONGOLIAN,
    PERIPHERAL [MVF]
KHARAQAN dial of TAKESTANI [TKS]
KHARBERD dial of ARMENIAN [ARM]
KHARCHIN alt for JOSTU dial of MONGOLIAN,
    PERIPHERAL [MVF]
KHARCHIN-TUMUT alt for JOSTU dial of
    MONGOLIAN, PERIPHERAL [MVF]
KHARI BOLI alt for HINDI [HND]
KHARIA [KHR] lang, India, Nepal
KHARIA THAR [KSY] lang, India
KHARIYA alt for KHARIA [KHR]
KHARMANGI alt for ASTORI dial of SHINA [SCL]
KHARTOUM dial of ARABIC, SUDANESE [APD]
KHARTOUM ARABIC alt for ARABIC, SUDANESE
    [APD]
KHARVI alt for KHARIA [KHR]
KHARWA dial of GUJARATI [GJR]
KHARWARI alt for SOUTHERN STANDARD
    BHOJPURI dial of BHOJPURI [BHJ]
KHARYUZ dial of ITELMEN [ITL]
KHASA alt for KHASI [KHI]
KHASA alt for TIGRÉ [TIE]
KHASARLI dial of TURKMEN [TCK]
KHASAV-YURT dial of KUMYK [KSK]
KHASHI alt for KHASI [KHI]
KHASI [KHI] lang, India, Bangladesh
KHASI dial of KHASI [KHI]
KHASIE alt for KHASI [KHI]
KHASIYAS alt for KHASI [KHI]
KHASKHONG dial of PHUNOI [PHO]
KHASKURA alt for NEPALI [NEP]
KHASONKE alt for KASSONKE [KAO]

KHASPARJIYA dial of KUMAUNI [KFY]
KHASSEE alt for KHASI [KHI]
KHASSONKE alt for KASSONKE [KAO]
KHAT alt for KATU [KTV]
KHATAHI alt for CHATTISGARHI [HNE]
KHATAK alt for KOHAT dial of PASHTO, EASTERN
    [PBU]
KHATANG dial of NGANASAN [NIO]
KHATIA alt for XATIA dial of NG/AMANI [NMN]
KHATIN alt for MAL [MLF]
KHATKI alt for MULTANI dial of SIRAIKI [SKR]
KHATOLA dial of BUNDELI [BNS]
KHATRIA alt for KHARIA [KHR]
KHATYRKA dial of KEREK [KRK]
KHAUNGTOU alt for KAREN, ZAYEIN [KXK]
KHAVA dial of INGRIAN [IZH]
KHAWAR alt for KHOWAR [KHW]
KHAYO dial of SAAMIA [SBU]
KHE [KQG] lang, Burkina Faso, Côte d'Ivoire
KHEHEK alt for NDREHET dial of LEVEI-NDREHET
    [TLX]
KHEK alt for CHINESE, HAKKA [HAK]
KHELMA dial of CHIN, FALAM [HBH]
KHELOBEDU alt for LOBEDU dial of SOTHO,
    NORTHERN [SRT]
KHEMSING dial of NAGA, TASE [NST]
KHEMUNGAN alt for NAGA, KHIAMNGAN [NKY]
KHEN alt for KHENKHA dial of KEBUMTAMP [KJZ]
KHEN LÂI dial of NUNG [NUT]
KHENKHA dial of KEBUMTAMP [KJZ]
KHERIA alt for KHARIA [KHR]
KHESO alt for KHE [KQG]
KHETRANI [QKT] lang, Pakistan
KHEYSUR alt for XEVSUR dial of GEORGIAN [GEO]
KHEZHA alt for NAGA, KHEZHA [NKH]
KHEZHAMA alt for NAGA, KHEZHA [NKH]
KHI alt for KHISA [KQM]
KHI alt for GELO [KKF]
KHI KHIPA alt for KHISA [KQM]
KHIA PHLAO alt for LAHA [LHA]
KHIAMNGAN alt for NAGA, KHIAMNGAN [NKY]
KHIAMNIUNGAN alt for NAGA, KHIAMNGAN [NKY]
KHIENG alt for SHENDU [SHL]
KHIENMUNGAN alt for NAGA, KHIAMNGAN [NKY]
KHIK alt for WAKHI [WBL]
KHILI alt for KOHISTANI, INDUS [MVY]
KHILI alt for DUBER-KANDIA dial of KOHISTANI,
    INDUS [MVY]
KHIMI alt for CHIN, KHUMI [CKM]
KHIMI dial of CHIN, KHUMI [CKM]
KHINALUG alt for KHINALUGH [KJJ]
KHINALUGH [KJJ] lang, Azerbaijan
KHINALUGI alt for KHINALUGH [KJJ]
KHINGA alt for MACA [XMC]
KHIRWAR [KWX] lang, India
KHIRWARA alt for KHIRWAR [KWX]
KHISA [KQM] lang, Côte d'Ivoire, Burkina Faso
KHITHAULHU dial of NAMBIKUÁRA, SOUTHERN
    [NAB]
KHIURKILINSKII alt for DARGWA [DAR]
KHLOR [LLO] lang, Laos
KHMER, CENTRAL [KMR] lang, Cambodia, Viet Nam,
    Laos, Thailand, Viet Nam
KHMER, NORTHERN [KXM] lang, Thailand
KHMU [KJG] lang, Laos, China, Myanmar, Thailand,
    Viet Nam

KHMU' alt for KHMU [KJG]
KHO ME alt for KHMER, CENTRAL [KMR]
KHOCHARKHOTIN dial of BEZHTA [KAP]
KHOI alt for NAMA [NAQ]
KHOI-SALMST dial of ARMENIAN [ARM]
KHOIBU alt for NAGA, KHOIBU MARING [NKB]
KHOIBU MARING alt for NAGA, KHOIBU MARING
   [NKB]
KHOIRAO alt for NAGA, KHOIRAO [NKI]
KHOKE alt for KOKE [KOU]
KHOLE alt for KARMALI dial of SANTALI [SNT]
KHOLI alt for KOLI, KACHI [GJK]
KHOLIFA dial of THEMNE [TEJ]
KHOME KROM alt for KHMER, CENTRAL [KMR]
KHOMU alt for KHMU [KJG]
KHON DOI alt for BLANG [BLR]
KHON MUNG alt for TAI, NORTHERN [NOD]
KHON MYANG alt for TAI, NORTHERN [NOD]
KHOND alt for KUI [KXU]
KHONDI alt for KUI [KXU]
KHONDI alt for KUVI [KXV]
KHONDI dial of KUI [KXU]
KHONDO alt for KUI [KXU]
KHONGZAI dial of CHIN, THADO [TCZ]
KHONOMA dial of NAGA, ANGAMI [NJM]
KHOR dial of UDIHE [UDE]
KHORASANI alt for DARI dial of FARSI, EASTERN
   [PRS]
KHORASANI TURKISH [KMZ] lang, Iran
KHORAT THAI dial of THAI [THJ]
KHORCHIN alt for JIRIM dial of MONGOLIAN,
   PERIPHERAL [MVF]
KHORCHIN alt for JIRIM dial of MONGOLIAN,
   PERIPHERAL [MVF]
KHORI dial of BURIAT, MONGOLIA [BXM]
KHORI dial of BURIAT, CHINA [BXU]
KHOSHUT dial of KALMYK-OIRAT [KGZ]
KHOSHUUD alt for KHOSHUT dial of KALMYK-
   OIRAT [KGZ]
KHOTAN-KERYA dial of UYGHUR [UIG]
KHOTOGOIT dial of MONGOLIAN, HALH [KHK]
KHOTON dial of KALMYK-OIRAT [KGZ]
KHOTTA alt for EASTERN MAITHILI dial of MAITHILI
   [MKP]
KHOUEN [KHF] lang, Laos, USA
KHOWAR [KHW] lang, Pakistan
KHOWARI alt for KHOWAR [KHW]
KHÖWSÖGÖL UIGUR dial of TUVIN [TUN]
KHROONG dial of KHMU [KJG]
KHUA [XHU] lang, Viet Nam, Laos
KHUALSHIM dial of CHIN, FALAM [HBH]
KHUANO dial of CHIN, TEDIM [CTD]
KHUCHIA alt for KHASI [KHI]
KHUEN alt for KHOUEN [KHF]
KHUEN alt for KHÜN [KKH]
KHUF alt for KHUFI dial of SHUGHNI [SGH]
KHUFI dial of SHUGHNI [SGH]
KHUGNI alt for SHUGHNI dial of SHUGHNI [SGH]
KHUGNI alt for SHUGHNI dial of SHUGHNI [SGH]
KHULUNGE RAI alt for KULUNG [KLE]
KHUMBI alt for NKHUMBI [KHU]
KHUMI alt for TOPOSA [TOQ]
KHUMI alt for CHIN, KHUMI [CKM]
KHÜN [KKH] lang, Myanmar, Thailand, Thailand
KHÜN alt for KHÜN [KKH]
KHUN SHAN alt for KHÜN [KKH]

KHUNGARI dial of UDIHE [UDF]
KHUNGGOI dial of NAGA, TANGKHUL [NMF]
KHUNI alt for CHIN, KHUMI [CKM]
KHUNSARI [KFM] lang, Iran
KHUNZAL alt for HUNZIB [HUZ]
KHUNZALY alt for HUNZIB [HUZ]
KHUPANG alt for NUNG [NUN]
KHURGI alt for KODAGU [KFA]
KHUTSWE dial of SOTHO, NORTHERN [SRT]
KHUTSWI alt for KHUTSWE dial of SOTHO,
   NORTHERN [SRT]
KHUTU alt for KUTU [KDC]
KHVARSHI [KHV] lang, Russia, Europe
KHVARSHIN alt for KHVARSHI [KHV]
KHVEK alt for KRAVET [KRV]
KHVOY alt for KHOI-SALMST dial of ARMENIAN
   [ARM]
KHVOY-SALMST dial of ARMENIAN [ARM]
KHWE alt for XUN [XUU]
KHWEEN alt for KHOUEN [KHF]
KHWEYMI alt for CHIN, KHUMI [CKM]
KHYANG alt for CHIN, ASHO [CSH]
KHYANG dial of CHIN, ASHO [CSH]
KHYEN alt for SHENDU [SHL]
KHYENG alt for CHIN, ASHO [CSH]
KHYENG alt for SHENDU [SHL]
KHYN alt for KHÜN [KKH]
KI alt for TUKI [BAG]
KI alt for AMTO [AMT]
KI'NYA alt for ATRUAHÍ [ATR]
KI-NUBI alt for NUBI [KCN]
KI//KXIGWI alt for //XEGWI [XEG]
KI/HAZI dial of NG/AMANI [NMN]
KIA alt for ZABANA [KJI]
KIA dial of GOLIN [GVF]
KIADJARA alt for KARTUJARRA dial of MARTU
   WANGKA [MPJ]
KIAKH alt for ADYGHE [ADY]
KIAMBA dial of TBOLI [TBL]
KIAMBU alt for NDIA dial of GIKUYU [KIU]
KIAMEROP alt for EMUMU [ENR]
KIANGAN IFUGAO alt for IFUGAO, TUWALI [IFK]
KIAOTUNG alt for LIAODONG dial of CHINESE,
   MANDARIN [CHN]
KIARI dial of NOMANE [NOF]
KIARI alt for KIA dial of GOLIN [GVF]
KIBAALI alt for BALI [BCP]
KIBAI alt for BAI dial of SAKATA [SAT]
KIBAJUNI alt for BAJUNI dial of SWAHILI [SWA]
KIBALA alt for BALI [BCP]
KIBALAN alt for KAVALAN [CKV]
KIBALI alt for BALI [BCP]
KIBALLO [KCH] lang, Nigeria
KIBANGOBANGO alt for BANGUBANGU [BNX]
KIBANGUBANGU alt for BANGUBANGU [BNX]
KIBBAKU alt for CIBAK [CKL]
KIBBO alt for BEROM [BOM]
KIBBUN alt for BEROM [BOM]
KIBEEMBE alt for BEEMBE [BEJ]
KIBEET alt for KIBET [KIE]
KIBEIT alt for KIBET [KIE]
KIBET [KIE] lang, Chad
KIBET dial of KIBET [KIE]
KIBILA alt for BILA [BIP]
KIBIN alt for LOWER KIMBIN dial of DANI, LOWER
   GRAND VALLEY [DNI]

KIBIRA alt for BERA [BRF]
KIBIRI [PRM] lang, Papua New Guinea
KIBIRI alt for KAIRI [KLQ]
KIBIRI alt for AIRD HILLS dial of KIBIRI [PRM]
KIBO alt for BEROM [BOM]
KIBOMA alt for BOMA [BOH]
KIBOMBO dial of CHAGGA [KAF]
KIBONDEI alt for BONDEI [BOU]
KIBOSHO dial of CHAGGA [KAF]
KIBUA alt for BWA [BWW]
KIBUDU alt for BUDU [BUU]
KIBUM alt for NIGII dial of YAMBETA [YAT]
KIBUYU alt for BUYU [BYI]
KIBWA alt for BWA [BWW]
KIBYEN alt for BEROM [BOM]
KICHAGA alt for CHAGGA [KAF]
KICHAI alt for KITSAI [KII]
KICHÉ alt for QUICHÉ, CENTRAL [QUC]
KICHEPO alt for KACIPO [KOE]
KICHI [KCY] lang, Tanzania
KICHO alt for QUICHUA, LOWLAND, NAPO [QLN]
KICKAPOO alt for KIKAPOO [KIC]
KICWE alt for BAKONI dial of KENYANG [KEN]
KIDABIDA alt for TAITA [DAV]
KIDAL alt for TADGHAQ dial of TAMASHEQ,
   TIMBUKTU [TAQ]
KIDAPAWAN MANOBO alt for MANOBO, OBO
   [OBO]
KIDDU dial of KATLA [KCR]
KIDHAISO alt for DHAISO [SEG]
KIDIE alt for LAFOFA [LAF]
KIDIGO alt for DIGO [DIG]
KIDJA alt for KITJA [GIA]
KIDJIA alt for DJIA dial of SAKATA [SAT]
KIDOONDO alt for DOONDO [DOD]
KIDZEM alt for BABANKI [BBK]
KIDZOM alt for BABANKI [BBK]
KIEFO alt for TIÉFO [TIQ]
KIEMBA alt for HEMBA [HEM]
KIEMBARA dial of SAMO [SBD]
KIEMBU alt for EMBU [EBU]
KIETA alt for NASIOI [NAS]
KIETA TALK alt for NASIOI [NAS]
KIFULERO alt for FULIIRU [FLR]
KIFULIRU alt for FULIIRU [FLR]
KIGA alt for CHIGA [CHG]
KIGA alt for IGIKIGA dial of RWANDA [RUA]
KIGALA dial of LEGA-SHABUNDA [LEA]
KIGHAANGALA alt for GHAANGALA dial of KONGO
   [KON]
KIGIRIAMA alt for GIRYAMA [NYF]
KIGUMU dial of KWAMBA [RWM]
KIGWE alt for GWE dial of SUKUMA [SUA]
KIGWENO alt for GWENO [GWE]
KIGYOMA dial of LEGA-SHABUNDA [LEA]
KIHA alt for HA [HAQ]
KIHAI dial of CHAGGA [KAF]
KIHANGAZA alt for HANGAZA [HAN]
KIHAVU alt for HAVU [HAV]
KIHEHE alt for HEHE [HEH]
KIHEMA dial of HIMA [HIM]
KIHEMA-NORD alt for LENDU [LED]
KIHEMBA alt for HEMBA [HEM]
KIHOLO alt for HOLU [HOL]
KIHOLOHOLO alt for HOLOHOLO [HOO]
KIHOLU alt for HOLU [HOL]

KIHUMU alt for KWAMBA [RWM]
KIHUNDE alt for HUNDE [HKE]
KIHUNGANA alt for HUNGANA [HUM]
KIHYANZI dial of KWAMBA [RWM]
KIHYANZI alt for KYANZI dial of KWAMBA [RWM]
KIJA alt for KITJA [GIA]
KIJAU alt for KUIJAU [DKR]
KIJOBA alt for JOBA [JOB]
KIKAAMBA alt for KAAMBA dial of DOONDO [DOD]
KIKAI [KZG] lang, Japan
KIKALANGA alt for HOLOHOLO [HOO]
KIKAMBA alt for KAMBA [KIK]
KIKAMI alt for KAMI [KCU]
KIKAPOO [KIC] lang, USA, Mexico
KIKAPU alt for KIKAPOO [KIC]
KIKEENGE alt for KEENGE dial of BEEMBE [BEJ]
KIKETE alt for KETE [KCV]
KIKIMA alt for COCOPA [COC]
KIKIMBU alt for KIMBU [KIV]
KIKINGA alt for KINGA [KIX]
KIKOMO alt for KOMO [KMW]
KIKONGO alt for KONGO [KON]
KIKONGO alt for KONGO, SAN SALVADOR [KWY]
KIKONGO SIMPLIFIÉ alt for KITUBA [KTU]
KIKONGO YA LETA alt for KITUBA [KTU]
KIKONGO-KUTUBA alt for KITUBA [KTU]
KIKONJUNKULU alt for DYAABUGAY [DYY]
KIKOONGO alt for KONGO [KON]
KIKOONGO alt for KONGO, SAN SALVADOR [KWY]
KIKUK alt for CIBAK [CKL]
KIKUMO alt for KOMO [KMW]
KIKUMU alt for KOMO [KMW]
KIKUNYI alt for KUNYI [KNF]
KIKUSU alt for KUSU [KSV]
KIKUTU alt for KUTU [KDC]
KIKUUMU alt for KOMO [KMW]
KIKUWA alt for TEKE, SOUTHERN [KKW]
KIKUYU alt for GIKUYU [KIU]
KIKWAME alt for KWAMI [KTF]
KIKWAMI alt for KWAMI [KTF]
KIKWESE alt for KWESE [KWS]
KIL alt for CHIL dial of KOHO [KPM]
KILA alt for SOMYEWE [KGT]
KILA dial of NANAI [GLD]
KILAKILANA alt for DAIO dial of WAGAWAGA
   [WGW]
KILANGI alt for LANGI [LAG]
KILBA alt for HUBA [KIR]
KILDANEAN alt for CHALDEAN [CLD]
"KILDIN LAPPISH" alt for SAAMI, KILDIN [LPD]
KILEGA alt for LEGA-SHABUNDA [LEA]
KILEGA alt for LEGA-MWENGA [LGM]
KILEMA dial of CHAGGA [KAF]
KILENDU alt for LENDU [LED]
KILENGE dial of MALEU-KILENGE [MGL]
KILENGE alt for LENGUE dial of CHOPI [CCE]
KILENGOLA alt for LENGOLA [LEJ]
KILETA alt for KITUBA [KTU]
KILI alt for KELE [KHY]
KILIA dial of BWAIDOKA [BWD]
KILIKA alt for LIKA [LIK]
KILIKIEN dial of ARMENIAN [ARM]
KILIVILA alt for KIRIWINA [KIJ]
KILIWA alt for KILIWI [KLB]
KILIWI [KLB] lang, Mexico
KILMERA alt for KILMERI [KIH]

KILMERI [KIH] lang, Papua New Guinea
KILOKAKA alt for ZAZAO [JAJ]
KILOMBENO KIBYA alt for EASTERN KALEBWE dial of SONGE [SOP]
KILUBA alt for LUBA-SHABA [LUH]
KIM [KIA] lang, Chad
KIM alt for KRIM [KRM]
KIM-RUWA alt for KIMRUWA dial of KIMRÉ [KQP]
KIMAGHAMA [KIG] lang, Indonesia, Irian Jaya
KIMAKUA alt for MAKHUWA [MAK]
KIMAMBWE alt for MAMBWE dial of MAMBWE-LUNGU [MGR]
KIMANDA alt for MANDA [MGS]
KIMANGA alt for MBA [MFC]
KIMANT alt for QIMANT [QIM]
KIMANTINYA alt for QIMANT [QIM]
KIMARA alt for MARA dial of HANGA [HAG]
KIMARAGAN alt for KIMARAGANG [KQR]
KIMARAGANG [KQR] lang, Malaysia, Sabah
KIMARAGANGAN alt for KIMARAGANG [KQR]
KIMASHAMI dial of CHAGGA [KAF]
KIMATENGO alt for MATENGO [MGV]
KIMATUMBI alt for MATUMBI [MGW]
KIMAWANDA alt for NDONDE [NDS]
KIMAWIHA alt for MAVIHA [MHP]
KIMBA dial of AGAUSHI-KIMBA-NGWANCI [KDL]
KIMBAMBA alt for MBAMBA dial of MBUNDU, LOANDA [MLO]
KIMBANGA alt for MBA [MFC]
KIMBEERE alt for MBEERE dial of EMBU [EBU]
KIMBO alt for MBO [ZMW]
KIMBU [KIV] lang, Tanzania
KIMBUNDA alt for MBUNDA [MCK]
KIMBUNDU alt for MBUNDU, LOANDA [MLO]
KIMBUUN alt for MPUUN dial of MPUONO [ZMP]
KIMERU alt for MERU [MER]
KIMGI alt for SUKUBATONG [SBT]
KIMI alt for KRIM [KRM]
KIMJAL alt for HMANGGONA [TVL]
KIMMUN alt for JINMEN dial of IU MIEN [IUM]
KIMOSHI alt for MOSI [OLD]
KIMRÉ [KQP] lang, Chad
KIMRE alt for KIMRUWA dial of KIMRÉ [KQP]
KIMRUWA dial of KIMRÉ [KQP]
KIMUSHUNGULU alt for MUSHUNGULU [XMA]
KIMVITA alt for MVITA dial of SWAHILI [SWA]
KIMWANI alt for MWANI [WMW]
KIMWIMBI alt for MWIMBI dial of MWIMBI-MUTHAMBI [MWS]
KIMYAL alt for HMANGGONA [TVL]
KIMYAL OF KORUPUN alt for KORUPUN [KPQ]
KINA alt for SHITA [LGN]
KINABATANGAN MURUT alt for TENGARA dial of BAUKAN [BNB]
KINABATANGAN SUNGEI alt for SUNGAI, KINABATANGAN [DSB]
KINABATANGAN, UPPER [DMG] lang, Malaysia, Sabah
KINAKOMBA dial of POKOMO, UPPER [PKB]
KINALAKNA [KCO] lang, Papua New Guinea
KINAMI alt for CENTRAL BABOLE dial of BABOLE [BVX]
KINAMIGIN alt for MANOBO, CINAMIGUIN [MKX]
KINAMWANGA alt for MWANGA [MWN]
KINANDI alt for NANDI [NNB]
KINARAY-A [KRJ] lang, Philippines

KINBAKKA dial of SONINKE [SNN]
KINCHAI alt for KERINCI [KVR]
KINDA alt for PORI KINDA dial of POL [PMM]
KINDERMA dial of TIRA [TIR]
KINDIGA alt for HATSA [HTS]
KINDJIN alt for KENYAH, UPPER BARAM [UBM]
KINDJIN alt for KENYAH, KAYAN RIVER [KNH]
KINDJIN alt for KENYAH, KELINYAU [XKL]
KINDJIN alt for KENYAH, MAHAKAM [XKM]
KINDJIN alt for KENYAH, WESTERN [XKY]
KINDONGO alt for MBUNDU, LOANDA [MLO]
KING alt for KANDAS [KQW]
KING'S PASS HUNGARIAN dial of HUNGARIAN [HNG]
KINGA [KIX] lang, Tanzania
KINGBETU alt for MANGBETU [MDJ]
KINGENGEREKO alt for NDENGEREKO [NDE]
KINGETI alt for NGITI [NIY]
KINGHWELE alt for NGHWELE [NHE]
KINGINDO alt for NGINDO [NNQ]
KINGITI alt for NGITI [NIY]
KINGONI alt for ZULU [ZUU]
KINGONI alt for NGONI [NGU]
KINGULU alt for NGULU [NGP]
KINGWANA alt for SWAHILI, ZAÏRE [SWC]
KINH alt for VIETNAMESE [VIE]
KINHWA alt for JINHUA dial of CHINESE, WU [WUU]
KINIHINAO alt for GUANA [QKS]
KINIKINAO alt for GUANA [QKS]
KININANGGUNAN dial of TOLAI [KSD]
KININGO alt for KAGULU [KKI]
KINIRAMBA alt for NILAMBA [NIM]
KINIRAY-A alt for KINARAY-A [KRJ]
KINJAKI dial of BARUGA [BBB]
KINJIN alt for KENYAH, UPPER BARAM [UBM]
KINJIN alt for KENYAH, KAYAN RIVER [KNH]
KINJIN alt for KENYAH, KELINYAU [XKL]
KINJIN alt for KENYAH, MAHAKAM [XKM]
KINJIN alt for KENYAH, WESTERN [XKY]
KINKI dial of JAPANESE [JPN]
KINKWA alt for NKONGHO dial of MBO [MBO]
KINNAURAYANUSKAD alt for LOWER KANAURI dial of KANAURI [KFK]
KINNAURI alt for KANAURI [KFK]
KINNER alt for KANAURI [KFK]
KINOME dial of KETENGBAN [KIN]
KINORI alt for KANAURI [KFK]
KINTA SAKAI alt for ULU KINTA dial of TEMIAR [TMH]
KINTAK alt for KINTAQ [KNQ]
KINTAK alt for KENSIU [KNS]
KINTAQ [KNQ] lang, Malaysia, Peninsular, Thailand, Thailand
KINTAQ alt for KINTAQ [KNQ]
KINTAQ alt for KENSIU [KNS]
KINTAQ BONG alt for KINTAQ [KNQ]
KINTAQ BONG alt for KENSIU [KNS]
KINUBI alt for NUBI [KCN]
KINUGU alt for KINUKU [KKD]
KINUKA alt for KINUKU [KKD]
KINUKU [KKD] lang, Nigeria
KINYA-MITUKU alt for MITUKU [ZMQ]
KINYAANGA alt for NYAANGA dial of KUNYI [KNF]
KINYABANGA dial of LEGA-SHABUNDA [LEA]
KINYABEMBA alt for BEMBA [BMY]
KINYABWISHA alt for BWISHA dial of RWANDA

[RUA]
KINYAMBO alt for NYAMBO [NYM]
KINYAMULENGE alt for MULENGE dial of RWANDA
  [RUA]
KINYAMUNSANGE dial of LEGA-SHABUNDA [LEA]
KINYAMWESI alt for NYAMWEZI [NYZ]
KINYAMWEZI alt for NYAMWEZI [NYZ]
KINYANGA alt for NYANGA [NYA]
KINYARWANDA alt for RWANDA [RUA]
KINYASA alt for MPOTO [MPA]
KINYASA alt for MANDA [MGS]
KINYATURU alt for NYATURU [RIM]
KINYIKA alt for GIRYAMA [NYF]
KIOKI alt for LAIWUI dial of MEKONGGA [MWK]
KIOKO [UES] lang, Indonesia, Sulawesi
KIOKO dial of KIOKO [UES]
KIOMBI alt for YOMBE [YOM]
KIONG [KKM] lang, Nigeria
KIONG NAI alt for QIUNGNAI dial of PUNU [PNU]
KIORR [XKO] lang, Myanmar
KIOWA [KIO] lang, USA
KIPEÁ dial of KARIRI-XUCO [KZW]
KIPEÁ KIRIRÍ alt for KARIRI-XUCO [KZW]
KIPENDE alt for PHENDE [PEM]
KIPERE alt for BHELE [PER]
KIPGEN dial of CHIN, THADO [TCZ]
KIPILI alt for BHELE [PER]
KIPOKOMO alt for POKOMO, LOWER [POJ]
KIPSIGIS dial of KALENJIN [KLN]
KIPSIIKIS alt for KIPSIGIS dial of KALENJIN [KLN]
KIPSIKIIS alt for KIPSIGIS dial of KALENJIN [KLN]
KIPSIKIS alt for KIPSIGIS dial of KALENJIN [KLN]
KIPUT [KYI] lang, Brunei, Malaysia, Sarawak,
  Malaysia, Sarawak
KIPUT alt for KIPUT [KYI]
KIPUT dial of KIPUT [KYI]
KIR alt for JIRU [JRR]
KIR alt for MANDARI [MQU]
KIR alt for KEER [KKE]
KIR alt for KIR-BALAR [KKR]
KIR-BALAR [KKR] lang, Nigeria
KIRA alt for VAGLA [VAG]
KIRAMANG dial of KUI [KVD]
KIRAWA dial of WANDALA [MFI]
KIRDASI alt for KURMANJI [KUR]
KIRDI alt for KARATA [KPT]
KIRDI-MORA alt for MURA dial of WANDALA [MFI]
KIRE [GEB] lang, Papua New Guinea
KIRE-PUIRE alt for KIRE [GEB]
KIREGA alt for LEGA-SHABUNDA [LEA]
KIREGA alt for LEGA-MWENGA [LGM]
KIREMI alt for NYATURU [RIM]
KIRFI alt for GIIWO [KKS]
KIRGHIZ [KDO] lang, Kyrghyzstan, Afghanistan,
  China, Turkey
KIRGHIZ alt for KIRGHIZ [KDO]
KIRGHIZI alt for KIRGHIZ [KDO]
KIRGIZ alt for KIRGHIZ [KDO]
KIRI dial of KANAKURU [KNA]
KIRIBATI [GLB] lang, Kiribati, Fiji, Nauru, Solomon
  Islands, Tuvalu, Vanuatu
KIRIBATI alt for KIRIBATI [GLB]
KIRIFAWA alt for GIIWO [KKS]
KIRIFI alt for GIIWO [KKS]
KIRIKE alt for OKRIKA [OKR]
KIRIKIRI [KIY] lang, Indonesia, Irian Jaya

KIRIKJIR alt for LOPA [LOP]
KIRIM alt for KRIM [KRM]
KIRIM alt for KARIM dial of COMO KARIM [CFG]
KIRIMI alt for NYATURU [RIM]
KIRIRA alt for KIRIKIRI [KIY]
KIRIRÍ alt for KIRIRÍ-XOKÓ [XOO]
KIRIRÍ-XOKÓ [XOO] lang, Brazil
KIRISTAV dial of KONKANI [KNK]
KIRIWINA [KIJ] lang, Papua New Guinea
KIRIYENTEKEN dial of MANOBO, WESTERN
  BUKIDNON [MBB]
KIRKPONG dial of KATLA [KCR]
KIRKUK dial of AZERBAIJANI, SOUTH [AZB]
KIRMA alt for CERMA [GOT]
KIRMANJI alt for KURMANJI [KUR]
KIRMANJKI [QKV] lang, Turkey, Germany
KIRMICO-LEK dial of TSAKHUR [TKR]
KIROBA dial of KURIA [KUJ]
KIROVABAD dial of AZERBAIJANI, NORTH [AZE]
KIRR alt for KIR-BALAR [KKR]
KIRTIPUR dial of NEWARI [NEW]
KIRUIHI alt for RUFIJI [RUI]
KIRUNDI alt for RUNDI [RUD]
KIRWO alt for RWO [RWK]
KIS [KIS] lang, Papua New Guinea
KISA dial of LUYIA [LUY]
KISAGALA alt for SAGALLA [TGA]
KISAGALA alt for SAGALA [SBM]
KISAGALLA alt for SAGALLA [TGA]
KISAGARA alt for SAGALA [SBM]
KISAKATA alt for SAKATA [SAT]
KISAMAJENG dial of DATOGA [TCC]
KISAMBAA alt for SHAMBALA [KSB]
KISAMBAERI dial of AMARAKAERI [AMR]
KISAN dial of MAITHILI [MKP]
KISAN-BHUMIJ dial of BHUMIJ [BHM]
KISANGA alt for SANGA [SNG]
KISANKASA [KQH] lang, Tanzania
KISANZI alt for SANZI of BANGUBANGU [BNX]
KISAR [KJE] lang, Indonesia, Maluku
KISEDE dial of LEGA-SHABUNDA [LEA]
KISETLA alt for SETTLA [STA]
KISETTLA alt for SETTLA [STA]
KISHAKA alt for CHAGGA [KAF]
KISHAMBA dial of SAGALLA [TGA]
KISHAMBA alt for SHAMBA dial of SWAHILI [SWA]
KISHAMBAA alt for SHAMBALA [KSB]
KISHAMBALA alt for SHAMBALA [KSB]
KISHANGANGIA alt for KISHANGANJIA [KFW]
KISHANGANJIA [KFW] lang, India
KISHTWARI [KGA] lang, India
KISHTWARI dial of KASHMIRI [KSH]
KISI [KIZ] lang, Tanzania
KISI alt for KISSI, SOUTHERN [KSS]
KISI alt for KISSI, NORTHERN [KQS]
KISIE alt for KISSI, NORTHERN [KQS]
KISII alt for GUSII [GUZ]
KISIKONGO alt for KONGO, SAN SALVADOR [KWY]
KISONDE alt for SONDE [SHC]
KISONGA alt for SONGA [SGO]
KISONGE alt for SONGE [SOP]
KISONGO alt for SONGO [SOO]
KISONGYE alt for SONGE [SOP]
KISONKO dial of MAASAI [MET]
KISOONDE alt for SONDE [SHC]
KISSAMA alt for SAMA [SMD]

KO'REUAJU alt for KOREGUAJE [COE]
KO-GBE [KQK] lang, Benin
KOA alt for KOYA [KFF]
KOALGURDI alt for MANGALA [MEM]
KOALIB [KIB] lang, Sudan
KOANA [KEH] lang, Nigeria
KOARATIRA alt for KANOÉ [KXO]
KOARNBUT alt for NGURMBUR [NRX]
KOASATI [CKU] lang, USA
KOASSA alt for KWERBA [KWE]
KOBA [KPD] lang, Indonesia, Maluku
KOBA alt for YEYE [YEY]
KOBAI alt for KOVAI [KQB]
KOBALI alt for COBARI dial of YANOMAMÖ [GUU]
KOBE alt for FANIA [FAN]
KOBE dial of SAWAI [SZW]
KOBE-KAPKA dial of ZAGHAWA [ZAG]
KOBEUA alt for CUBEO [CUB]
KOBEWA alt for CUBEO [CUB]
KOBÉWA alt for CUBEO [CUB]
KOBI alt for HUNDE [HKE]
KOBI dial of LIANA-SETI [STE]
KOBI-BENGGOI alt for BENGGOI [BGY]
KOBIANA [KCJ] lang, Guinea Bissau, Senegal,
  Senegal
KOBIANA alt for KOBIANA [KCJ]
KOBO alt for MOM JANGO [VER]
KOBOCHI alt for NZANYI [NJA]
KOBOI alt for NAGA, KABUI [NKF]
KOBOLA dial of ABUI [ABZ]
KOBON [KPW] lang, Papua New Guinea
KOBOTACHI dial of BATA [BTA]
KOBOTSHI alt for NZANYI [NJA]
KOBRO'OR alt for DOBEL [KVO]
KOBROOR alt for DOBEL [KVO]
KOBUK RIVER ESKIMO dial of INUIT, NORTHWEST
  ALASKA INUPIAT [ESK]
KOBUK SOUND INUPIAT alt for KOTZEBUE SOUND
  INUPIAT dial of INUIT, NORTH ALASKAN [ESI]
KOC alt for KOCH [KDQ]
KOCCH alt for KOCH [KDQ]
KOCE alt for KOCH [KDQ]
KOCH [KDQ] lang, India, Bangladesh
KOCH [KXS] lang, India
KOCHBOLI alt for KOCH [KDQ]
KOCHI alt for RAMPURI dial of MAHASUI [BFZ]
KOCHIN-KAM alt for NORTH PERMYAK dial of
  KOMI-PERMYAK [KOI]
KOCHUVELAN alt for ULLATAN [ULL]
KODA [KFN] lang, India
KODAGU [KFA] lang, India
KODAVA THAK alt for KODAGU [KFA]
KODE dial of BAULE [BCI]
KODEOHA [VKO] lang, Indonesia, Sulawesi
KODGOTTO alt for DYAABUGAY [DYY]
KODHIN alt for KADARU [KDU]
KODHINNIAI alt for KADARU [KDU]
KODI [KOD] lang, Indonesia, Nusa Tenggara
KODI BANGEDO dial of KODI [KOD]
KODI BOKOL dial of KODI [KOD]
KODIAK ALEUT alt for EASTERN ALEUT dial of
  ALEUT [ALW]
KODIÉ alt for GODIÉ [GOD]
KODOÏ dial of MABA [MDE]
KODORO alt for KADARU [KDU]
KODRA alt for TODRAH [TDR]

KODRAO dial of RADE [RAD]
KODU alt for KUI [KXU]
KODU dial of KOHO [KPM]
KODULU alt for KUI [KXU]
KOEGU alt for KWEGU [YID]
KOENOEM [KCS] lang, Nigeria
KOFA [KFJ] lang, Cameroon
KOFA alt for KOFFA dial of MOGUM [MOU]
KOFÁN alt for COFÁN [CON]
KOFAN alt for COFÁN [CON]
KOFANE alt for COFÁN [CON]
KOFEI [KPI] lang, Indonesia, Irian Jaya
KOFFA dial of MOGUM [MOU]
KOFYAR [KWL] lang, Nigeria
KOFYAR dial of KOFYAR [KWL]
KOGA alt for BAGA KOGA [BGO]
KOGI alt for COGUI [KOG]
KOGORO alt for BOGURU [BQU]
KOGUMAN [QKG] lang, Papua New Guinea
KOGURU alt for BOGURU [BQU]
KOGURU dial of BOGURU [BQU]
KOH alt for KUO [KHO]
KOHAMA dial of YAEYAMA [RYS]
KOHAT dial of PASHTO, EASTERN [PBU]
KOHAT HINDKO dial of HINDKO, SOUTHERN [HIN]
KOHATI alt for KOHAT HINDKO dial of HINDKO,
  SOUTHERN [HIN]
KOHIMA dial of NAGA, ANGAMI [NJM]
KOHISTANI alt for SHINA, KOHISTANI [PLK]
KOHISTANI alt for KOHISTANI, INDUS [MVY]
KOHISTANI alt for KALAMI [GWC]
KOHISTANI, INDUS [MVY] lang, Pakistan
KOHISTYO alt for SHINA, KOHISTANI [PLK]
KOHLE alt for KARMALI [KFL]
KOHLI alt for KOLI, KACHI [GJK]
KOHLI alt for KOLI, PARKARI [KVX]
KOHLI alt for KUNBAN dial of VARHADI-NAGPURI
  [VAH]
KOHNADEH dial of PASHAYI, NORTHWEST [GLH]
KOHO [KPM] lang, Viet Nam, USA
KOHOROXITARI [KOB] lang, Brazil
KOHUMONO [BCS] lang, Nigeria
KOI [KKT] lang, Nepal
KOI alt for KOYA [KFF]
KOI GONDI alt for KOYA [KFF]
KOIALI, MOUNTAIN [KPX] lang, Papua New Guinea
KOIANU dial of KOROMIRA [KQJ]
KOIARI alt for KOIARI, GRASS [KBK]
KOIARI, GRASS [KBK] lang, Papua New Guinea
KOIBAL dial of KAMAS [XAS]
KOIJOE alt for KUIJAU [DKR]
KOINE GREEK dial of GREEK, ANCIENT [GKO]
KOIO alt for KWAIO [KWD]
KOIRENG [NKD] lang, India
KOIRNG alt for KOIRENG [NKD]
KOITA [KQI] lang, Papua New Guinea
KOITABU alt for KOITA [KQI]
KOITAR alt for KOYA [KFF]
KOIWAI alt for KOWIAI [KWH]
KOIWAT [KXT] lang, Papua New Guinea
KOIWAT dial of SAWOS [SIC]
KOJALI alt for AWADHI [AWD]
KOK BOROK [TRP] lang, India, Bangladesh
KOK CHIANG dial of UGONG [UGO]
KÖK MUNGAK alt for TUVIN [TUN]
KOKADI alt for KAIKADI [KEP]

KOKAMA alt for COCAMA-COCAMILLA [COD]
KOKAMILLA alt for COCAMILLA dial of COCAMA-
  COCAMILLA [COD]
KOKANT SHAN dial of SHAN [SJN]
KOKATA [KTD] lang, Australia
KOKATHA alt for KOKATA [KTD]
KOKCHULUTAN dial of TUVIN [TUN]
KOKE [KOU] lang, Chad
KOKILA dial of DOROMU [KQC]
KOKITTA alt for KOKATA [KTD]
KOKNA alt for KUKNA [KEX]
KOKNA dial of BHILI [BHB]
KOKNI alt for KUKNA [KEX]
KOKO alt for 'AKHOE [AKE]
KOKO alt for KUNG-GOBABIS [AUE]
KOKO alt for HUNJARA [HUN]
KOKO alt for BASAA [BAA]
KOKO dial of BANGBA [BBE]
KOKO BERA alt for GUGUBERA [KKP]
KOKO IMUDJI alt for GUGUYIMIDJIR [KKY]
KOKO PERA alt for GUGUBERA [KKP]
KOKO-JA'O alt for KUUKU-YA'U [QKL]
KOKO-MUDJU alt for DJANGUN [DJF]
KOKO-TJUMBUNDJI alt for DYAABUGAY [DYY]
KOKO-TYANKUN alt for DJANGUN [DJF]
KOKO-YALANJI alt for KUKU-YALANJI [GVN]
KOKO// //AU-KWE alt for 'AKHOE [AKE]
KOKOLA [KZN] lang, Malawi
KOKOMINDJEN alt for YIR YORONT [YIY]
KOKOMOLOROIJ alt for MULURIDYI [VMU]
KOKOMOLOROITJI alt for MULURIDYI [VMU]
KOKONYUNGALO alt for DYAABUGAY [DYY]
KOKOPO dial of TOLAI [KSD]
KOKORA dial of BARAI [BCA]
KOKORI alt for NAKARA [NCK]
KOKOROTON MURUT dial of BAUKAN [BNB]
KOKOS alt for MALAY, COCOS ISLANDS [COA]
KOKOTA [KKK] lang, Solomon Islands
KOKOYAO alt for KUUKU-YA'U [QKL]
KOKRAIMORO alt for KAYAPÓ [TXU]
KOKWAIYAKWA alt for YAGWOIA [YGW]
KOL [KFO] lang, India
KOL [KOL] lang, Papua New Guinea
KOL [BIW] lang, Cameroon
KOL alt for AKA-KOL [AKY]
KOL dial of KOL [KOL]
KOL dial of CUA [CUA]
KOL NORTH dial of KOL [BIW]
KOL SOUTH dial of KOL [BIW]
KOLA [KVV] lang, Indonesia, Maluku
KOLA alt for KOL [KOL]
KOLA dial of DABA [DAB]
KOLABOLI alt for KOL [KFO]
KOLAI [KKX] lang, India
KOLAI dial of SHINA, KOHISTANI [PLK]
KOLAKA alt for TOLAKI [LBW]
KOLAM alt for KOLAMI, NORTHWESTERN [KFB]
KOLAMBOLI alt for KOLAMI, NORTHWESTERN
  [KFB]
KOLAMI, NORTHWESTERN [KFB] lang, India
KOLAMI, SOUTHEASTERN [NIT] lang, India
KOLANA [KVW] lang, Indonesia, Nusa Tenggara
KOLANA-WERSIN alt for KOLANA [KVW]
KOLANGO alt for KULANGO, BONDOUKOU [KZC]
KOLAR alt for KOL [KFO]
KOLARI alt for KOL [KFO]

KOLATA alt for ASHURUVERI dial of ASHKUN [ASK]
KOLBAFFO alt for KORBAFFO dial of ROTI [ROT]
KOLBILA [KLC] lang, Cameroon
KOLBILARI alt for KOLBILA [KLC]
KOLBILI alt for KOLBILA [KLC]
KOLBILLA alt for KOLBILA [KLC]
KOLDRONG dial of KATLA [KCR]
KOLE alt for KOL [KFO]
KOLE alt for KOL [KOL]
KOLE alt for KANURI, YERWA [KPH]
KOLE alt for FONGORO [FGR]
KOLE alt for BAKOLE [KME]
KOLELA alt for LELA [DRI]
KOLENA alt for KOLBILA [KLC]
KOLENSUSU alt for KULISUSU [VKL]
KOLERE alt for KANURI, YERWA [KPH]
KOLHI alt for KOLI, KACHI [GJK]
KOLHRENG dial of KOM [KMM]
KOLI dial of KONKANI [KNK]
KOLI dial of DOMARI [RMT]
KOLI alt for OLI dial of DUALA [DOU]
KOLI, KACHI [GJK] lang, Pakistan
KOLI, PARKARI [KVX] lang, Pakistan
KOLI, THARADARI [KXQ] lang, Pakistan
KOLI, WADIYARA [KXP] lang, Pakistan
KOLIAN alt for KOL [KFO]
KOLIKU [KSL] lang, Papua New Guinea
KOLINSUSU alt for KULISUSU [VKL]
KOLLANKO alt for GOLLANGO [GOV]
KOLLINA alt for CULINA [CUL]
KOLMI alt for KOLAMI, NORTHWESTERN [KFB]
KOLO dial of BIMA [BHP]
KOLO dial of OGBIA [OGB]
KOLOBO dial of KIM [KIA]
KOLOBUAN alt for KALABUAN dial of
  KINABATANGAN, UPPER [DMG]
KOLOD alt for OKOLOD [KQV]
KOLOKUMA alt for KOLUKUMA dial of IJO,
  CENTRAL-WESTERN [IJC]
KOLOLO alt for LOZI [LOZ]
KOLOM [KLM] lang, Papua New Guinea
KOLOMBANGARA alt for DUKE [NKE]
KOLONG alt for MARBA [MPG]
KOLOO dial of SENOUFO, MAMARA [MYK]
KOLOUR alt for OKOLOD [KQV]
KOLS alt for KO [KST]
KOLSI alt for KO [KST]
KOLTA alt for SAAMI, SKOLT [LPK]
KOLTTA alt for SAAMI, SKOLT [LPK]
KOLUBE alt for BAROK [BJK]
KOLUKUMA dial of IJO, CENTRAL-WESTERN [IJC]
KOLUMBIARA alt for TUBARÃO [TBA]
KOLUR alt for OKOLOD [KQV]
KOLUR dial of LUNDAYEH [LND]
KOLYA alt for NAGA, KHOIRAO [NKI]
KOLYM alt for YUKAGHIR, SOUTHERN [YUX]
KOLYMA alt for YUKAGHIR, SOUTHERN [YUX]
KOLYMA-OMOLON dial of EVEN [EVE]
KOM [KMM] lang, India
KOM [BKM] lang, Cameroon
KOM alt for RASHAD dial of TEGALI [RAS]
KOM KOMBA alt for KONKOMBA [KOS]
KOM REM alt for KOM [KMM]
KOMA [KMY] lang, Nigeria, Cameroon
KOMA alt for GANZA [GZA]
KOMA alt for KONNI [KMA]

KOMA DAMTI dial of KOMA [KMY]
KOMA KA-BANA alt for BANA [FLI]
KOMA KADAM alt for GIMNIME [KMB]
KOMA KOMPANA alt for GIMME [KMP]
KOMA NDERA dial of KOMA [KMY]
KOMA OF ASOSA alt for KOMA, NORTH [KMQ]
KOMA OF BEGI alt for KOMA, SOUTH [KMJ]
KOMA OF DAGA alt for KOMA, CENTRAL [KOM]
KOMA, CENTRAL [KOM] lang, Sudan, Ethiopia
KOMA, NORTH [KMQ] lang, Ethiopia
KOMA, SOUTH [KMJ] lang, Ethiopia
KOMALU alt for BAROK [BJK]
KOMASMA dial of CITAK [TXT]
KOMBA [KPF] lang, Papua New Guinea
KOMBAI [KGU] lang, Indonesia, Irian Jaya
KOMBE alt for NGUMBI [NUI]
KOMBE dial of TUKI [BAG]
KOMBE dial of LUSI [KHL]
KOMBERATORO alt for KAMBERATARO [KBV]
KOMBIO [KOK] lang, Papua New Guinea
KOMBO dial of JOLA-FOGNY [DYO]
KOMBOY alt for KOMBAI [KGU]
KOMBU SANGARA dial of OROKAIVA [ORK]
KOME alt for RASHAD dial of TEGALI [RAS]
KOMERIN alt for KOMERING [KGE]
KOMERING [KGE] lang, Indonesia, Sumatra
KOMFANA alt for KOMPANE [KVP]
KOMI alt for KOMI-ZYRIAN [KPV]
KOMI-PERM alt for KOMI-PERMYAK [KOI]
KOMI-PERMYAK [KOI] lang, Russia, Europe
KOMI-PERMYAT alt for KOMI-PERMYAK [KOI]
KOMI-ZYRIAN [KPV] lang, Russia, Europe
KOMINIMUNG [QKM] lang, Papua New Guinea
KOMLAMA alt for GIMNIME [KMB]
KOMO [KMW] lang, Zaïre
KOMO alt for KOMA, CENTRAL [KOM]
KOMODO [KVH] lang, Indonesia, Nusa Tenggara
KOMOFIO dial of BEAMI [BEO]
KOMOGU alt for KOMONGGU dial of SIANE [SNP]
KOMONGGU dial of SIANE [SNP]
KOMONO alt for KHISA [KQM]
KOMORO alt for COMORIAN [SWB]
KOMPANA alt for GIMME [KMP]
KOMPANE [KVP] lang, Indonesia, Maluku
KOMPARA alt for GIMME [KMP]
KOMPONG THOM alt for PEAR [PCB]
KOMSO [KXC] lang, Ethiopia
KOMTAO dial of TELUGU [TCW]
KOMUDAGO alt for KASUWERI [QKW]
KOMUNG alt for KONNI [KMA]
KOMUTU [KLT] lang, Papua New Guinea
KON HRING SEDANG dial of SEDANG [SED]
KON KEU [ANG] lang, China
KONA [JUO] lang, Nigeria
KONABEM alt for KUNABEMBE dial of
    MPONGMPONG [MGG]
KONABEMBE alt for KUNABEMBE dial of
    MPONGMPONG [MGG]
KONAI [KXW] lang, Papua New Guinea
KONAWE dial of TOLAKI [LBW]
KONCH alt for KOCH [KDQ]
KOND alt for KUVI [KXV]
KONDA [KND] lang, Indonesia, Irian Jaya
KONDA dial of NGWO [NGN]
KONDA dial of KONDA-DORA [KFC]
KONDA dial of MONGO-NKUNDU [MOM]

KONDA-DORA [KFC] lang, India
KONDA-REDDI dial of TELUGU [TCW]
KONDAIR alt for PALIET dial of DINKA,
    SOUTHWESTERN [DIK]
KONDE alt for MAKONDE [KDE]
KONDE alt for NYAKYUSA-NGONDE [NYY]
KONDE dial of RONGA [RON]
KONDEHA alt for KODEOHA [VKO]
KONDIN alt for EASTERN VOGUL dial of MANSI
    [MNS]
KONDJA alt for KWANJA [KNP]
KONDJARA alt for FUR [FUR]
KONDJO alt for KONJO, COASTAL [KJC]
KONDKOR alt for OLLARI [OLL]
KONDOA dial of SAGALA [SBM]
KONDOMA dial of SHOR [CJS]
KONDOMA TATAR alt for SHOR [CJS]
KONE alt for KONI dial of SOTHO, NORTHERN [SRT]
KONEÁ alt for ARAPASO [ARJ]
KONEJANDI alt for GOONIYANDI [GNI]
KONERAW [KDW] lang, Indonesia, Irian Jaya
KONEYANDI alt for GOONIYANDI [GNI]
KONG alt for KOM [BKM]
KONG alt for TAI NÜA [TDD]
KONG dial of TIKAR [TIK]
KONG dial of GBARI [GBY]
KONG JULA dial of JULA [DYU]
KONGAMPANI alt for KOMPANE [KVP]
KONGAR dial of TAMIL [TCV]
KONGARA dial of NASIOI [NAS]
KONGBAA dial of GOLA [GOL]
KONGBO dial of TIBETAN [TIC]
KONGDER alt for PALIET dial of DINKA,
    SOUTHWESTERN [DIK]
KONGI dial of DANO [ASO]
KONGO [KON] lang, Zaïre, Angola, Congo
KONGO, SAN SALVADOR [KWY] lang, Zaïre, Angola
KONGOLA alt for KUSU [KSV]
KONGOLA-MENO dial of NKUTU [NKW]
KONGON dial of NAGA, KONYAK [NBE]
KONI alt for KONNI [KMA]
KONI dial of SOTHO, NORTHERN [SRT]
KONIAGI alt for KONYAGI [COU]
KONIKE dial of THEMNE [TEJ]
KONIO dial of MEKONGGA [MWK]
KONJA alt for KWANJA [KNP]
KONJARA alt for FUR [FUR]
KONJO [KOO] lang, Uganda
KONJO PEGUNUNGAN alt for KONJO, HIGHLAND
    [KJK]
KONJO PESISIR dial of KONJO, COASTAL [KJC]
KONJO, COASTAL [KJC] lang, Indonesia, Sulawesi
KONJO, HIGHLAND [KJK] lang, Indonesia, Sulawesi
KONKAN STANDARD alt for KONKANI [KNK]
KONKANASTHS alt for CHITAPAVANI dial of
    KONKANI, GOANESE [GOM]
KONKANESE alt for KONKANI [KNK]
KONKANI [KNK] lang, India
KONKANI, GOANESE [GOM] lang, India, Kenya
KONKOMBA [KOS] lang, Ghana, Togo, Togo
KONKOMBA alt for KONKOMBA [KOS]
KONNI [KMA] lang, Ghana
KONNOH alt for KONO [KNO]
KONO [KNO] lang, Sierra Leone
KONO [KLK] lang, Nigeria
KONO dial of KPELLE, GUINEA [GKP]

KONOBO dial of KRAHN, EASTERN [KQO]
KONOMALA [KOA] lang, Papua New Guinea
KONOMALA dial of KONOMALA [KOA]
KONONGO [KCZ] lang, Tanzania
KONONGO alt for MWERI dial of NYAMWEZI [NYZ]
KONOSAROLA alt for VAGLA [VAG]
KONSINYA alt for KOMSO [KXC]
KONSO alt for KOMSO [KXC]
KONSTANTINOPEL alt for CONSTANTINOPLE dial of
   ARMENIAN [ARM]
KONTA dial of KULLO [KLO]
KONTOI alt for BLANG [BLR]
KONTU dial of LAVATBURA-LAMUSONG [LBV]
KONTUM dial of BAHNAR [BDQ]
KONU alt for KONO [KLK]
KONUA alt for KUNUA [KYX]
KONY dial of SABAOT [SPY]
KONYA alt for KONYANKA dial of MANINKA [MNI]
KONYAGI [COU] lang, Guinea, Senegal, Senegal
KONYAK alt for NAGA, KONYAK [NBE]
KONYANKA dial of MANINKA [MNI]
KONYAR alt for YURUK dial of BALKAN GAGAUZ
   TURKISH [BGX]
KONYARE dial of KARANGA [KTH]
KONYO alt for KONJO, HIGHLAND [KJK]
KONZIME alt for KOOZIME [NJE]
KONZO alt for KONJO [KOO]
KOO dial of TALISE [TLR]
KOO'RA alt for NATIORO [NTI]
KOOCATHO alt for KOKATA [KTD]
KOOGURDA alt for KOKATA [KTD]
KOOINMARBURRA alt for BAYALI [BJY]
KOOKANOONA alt for MULURIDYI [VMU]
KOOKI dial of GANDA [LAP]
KOOLA alt for DEENU dial of SAMBA LEKO [NDI]
KOON alt for /HUA-OWANI [HUC]
KOONCIMO alt for KOOZIME [NJE]
KOOPEI dial of SIMEKU [SMZ]
KOOR dial of PUKU-GEERI-KERI-WIPSI [GEL]
KOORETE [KQY] lang, Ethiopia
KOOSA alt for XHOSA [XOS]
KOOSA alt for KOSA dial of LUNDA [LVN]
KOOSE alt for AKOOSE [BSS]
KOOTENAI alt for KUTENAI [KUN]
KOOZHIME alt for KOOZIME [NJE]
KOOZIME [NJE] lang, Cameroon, Congo, Congo
KOPA dial of SOTHO, NORTHERN [SRT]
KOPAR [QKO] lang, Papua New Guinea
KOPE dial of KIWAI, NORTHEAST [KIW]
KOPEI alt for KOOPEI dial of SIMEKU [SMZ]
KOPO-MONIA alt for IKOBI-MENA [MEB]
KOPTI alt for ZARI dial of ZARI [ZAZ]
KOR alt for KOL dial of CUA [CUA]
KORA alt for KODA [KFN]
KORA alt for AKA-KORA [ACK]
KORA alt for LAMANI [LMN]
KORAFE [KPR] lang, Papua New Guinea
KORAFE dial of KORAFE [KPR]
KORAFI alt for KORAFE [KPR]
KORAGA, KORRA [KFD] lang, India
KORAGA, MUDU [VMD] lang, India
KORAGAR alt for KORAGA, KORRA [KFD]
KORAGARA alt for KORAGA, KORRA [KFD]
KORAK [KOZ] lang, Papua New Guinea
KORAKU [KSZ] lang, India
KORALI alt for KODA [KFN]

KORAMA alt for KURRAMA [VKU]
KORAMBAR alt for KURUMBA [KFI]
KORANA [KQZ] lang, South Africa
KORANGI alt for KORAGA, KORRA [KFD]
KORANIC ARABIC alt for ARABIC, CLASSICAL
   [ARA]
KORANJE dial of DAUSAHAQ [DSQ]
KORANKO alt for KURANKO [KHA]
KORANNA alt for KORANA [KQZ]
KORANTI alt for BRIJIA dial of ASURI [ASR]
KORAPE alt for KORAFE [KPR]
KORAPUN alt for KORUPUN [KPQ]
KORAPUT ORIYA dial of ORIYA [ORY]
KORAQUA alt for KORANA [KQZ]
KORARA alt for UDUK [UDU]
KORATI alt for KODA [KFN]
KORAVA alt for YERUKALA [YEU]
KORAVA alt for IRULA [IRU]
KORAVA dial of TAMIL [TCV]
KORBAFFO dial of ROTI [ROT]
KORBO alt for WEST DANGALEAT dial of
   DANGALEAT [DAA]
KORCA dial of ALBANIAN, TOSK [ALN]
KORCHI dial of TAMIL [TCV]
KORE alt for KODA [KFN]
KORE dial of MAASAI [MET]
KOREAN [KKN] lang, Korea, South, China, Japan,
   Korea, North, Russia, Asia, Singapore, Thailand
KOREAN SIGN LANGUAGE [KVK] lang, Korea, South
KOREGUAJE [COE] lang, Colombia
KOREIPA dial of SIANE [SNP]
KOREKORE dial of SHONA [SHD]
KORI alt for KOLI, KACHI [GJK]
KORI alt for RAIO dial of KAILI, LEDO [LEW]
KORIDO dial of BIAK [BHW]
KORIKI alt for PURARI [IAR]
KORIKO dial of DOROMU [KQC]
KORIKORI alt for KOREKORE dial of SHONA [SHD]
KORIM dial of BIAK [BHW]
KORINDI alt for KARONDI dial of TUMTUM [TBR]
KORING alt for ORING [ORI]
KORINTAL dial of GULA IRO [GLJ]
KORIOK dial of OTUHO [LOT]
KORIPAKO alt for CURRIPACO [KPC]
KORISPASO alt for CURRIPACO [KPC]
KORKI alt for KORKU [KFQ]
KORKU [KFQ] lang, India
KORLAI CREOLE PORTUGUESE [VKP] lang, India
KORO [KOR] lang, Nigeria
KORO [KXR] lang, Papua New Guinea
KORO [KRF] lang, Vanuatu
KORO alt for GWANDARA WESTERN dial of
   GWANDARA [GWN]
KORO LAFIA alt for LIJILI [MGI]
KOROBORÉ [KBI] lang, Burkina Faso
KOROBORO alt for SONGAI [SON]
KOROK alt for MALUAL dial of DINKA,
   SOUTHWESTERN [DIK]
KOROKA alt for KWADI [KWZ]
KOROKA dial of MAU [MXX]
KOROKO alt for VALMAN [VAN]
KOROKORO alt for MUNYO dial of ORMA [ORC]
KOROLAU alt for NORTHEAST VANUA LEVU dial of
   FIJIAN [FJI]
KOROM BOYE alt for KULERE [KUL]
KOROMIRA [KQJ] lang, Papua New Guinea

KORONADAL BILAAN alt for BLAAN, KORONADAL [BIK]
KORONGO alt for KRONGO [KGO]
KORONI [XKQ] lang, Indonesia, Sulawesi
KOROP [KRP] lang, Nigeria, Cameroon
KOROWAI [KHE] lang, Indonesia, Irian Jaya
KORRA alt for FUR [FUR]
KORRA alt for KORAGA, KORRA [KFD]
KORRIPAKO dial of CURRIPACO [KPC]
KORROSE alt for GOROSE [GOS]
KORTABINA alt for BANGGARLA [BJB]
KORTCHI alt for GAVAR [GOU]
KORTSE dial of QIANG [CNG]
KORUBO [QKF] lang, Brazil
KORUPUN [KPQ] lang, Indonesia, Irian Jaya
KORUPUN dial of KORUPUN [KPQ]
KORWA [KFP] lang, India
KORYAK [KPY] lang, Russia, Asia
KOS dial of ABÉ [ABA]
KOSA dial of LUNDA [LVN]
KOSACH alt for KAZAKH [KAZ]
KOSADLE [KIQ] lang, Indonesia, Irian Jaya
KOSALI alt for AWADHI [AWD]
KOSAP alt for KOSOP dial of KIM [KIA]
KOSARE alt for KOSADLE [KIQ]
KOSAREK alt for YALE, KOSAREK [KKL]
KOSENA [KZE] lang, Papua New Guinea
KOSENG alt for KASSENG [KGC]
KOSHAN dial of AGHUL [AGX]
KOSHIN alt for KOSKIN [KID]
KOSHTI dial of BUNDELI [BNS]
KOSI alt for AKOOSE [BSS]
KOSIAN alt for BALANTAK [BLZ]
KOSIN alt for KOSKIN [KID]
KOSIRAVA dial of MAISIN [MBQ]
KOSKIN [KID] lang, Cameroon
KOSO alt for PANAMINT dial of SHOSHONI [SHH]
KOSOP dial of KIM [KIA]
KOSORONG [KSR] lang, Papua New Guinea
KOSOVA alt for GUSII [GUZ]
KOSOVE alt for SHIP dial of ALBANIAN, GHEG [ALS]
KOSRAE alt for KUSAIE [KSI]
KOSRAEAN alt for KUSAIE [KSI]
KOSSA alt for MENDE [MFY]
KOSSEE [KSO] lang, Botswana
KOSSEE-NTSHORI alt for KOSSEE [KSO]
KOSSEE-TSHORI alt for KOSSEE [KSO]
KOSSO alt for MENDE [MFY]
KOSTI dial of VARHADI-NAGPURI [VAH]
KOTA [KOQ] lang, Gabon, Congo
KOTA [KFE] lang, India
KOTA alt for DIKOTA dial of NGANDO [NGD]
KOTA AGUNG dial of PESISIR, SOUTHERN [PEC]
KOTA BELUD dial of BAJAU, WEST COAST [BDR]
KOTA BUMI dial of ABUNG [ABL]
KOTA MARUDU SONSOGON dial of SONSOGON [SGN]
KOTA MARUDU TALANTANG [GRM] lang, Malaysia, Sabah
KOTA MARUDU TINAGAS [KTR] lang, Malaysia, Sabah
KOTA-WARINGIN dial of MALAY [MLI]
KOTAFOA dial of ÉWÉ [EWE]
KOTAFON dial of ÉWÉ [EWE]
KOTAFOU dial of FON-GBE [FOA]
KOTAGU alt for KODAGU [KFA]

KOTALI dial of BHILI [BHB]
KOTALI BHIL dial of KHANDESI [KHN]
KÓTEDIA alt for GUANANO [GVC]
KOTET dial of YAU [YUW]
KOTI [EKO] lang, Mozambique
KOTIA ORIYA alt for ORIYA, ADIWASI [ORT]
KOTIRIA alt for GUANANO [GVC]
KÓTIRYA alt for GUANANO [GVC]
KOTIYA alt for ORIYA, ADIWASI [ORT]
KOTO alt for OREJÓN [ORE]
KOTOFO alt for PEERE [KUT]
KOTOFO alt for DAN MUURE dial of PEERE [KUT]
KOTOGÛT [KVZ] lang, Indonesia, Irian Jaya
KOTOKO-GANA alt for LOGONE-GANA dial of LAGWAN [KOT]
KOTOKO-KUSERI alt for MSER [KQX]
KOTOKO-LOGONE alt for LAGWAN [KOT]
KOTOKOLI alt for TEM [KDH]
KOTOKORI alt for EBIRA [IGB]
KOTOPO alt for PEERE [KUT]
KOTOPO alt for DAN MUURE dial of PEERE [KUT]
KOTPOJO alt for PEERE [KUT]
KOTTA alt for KOTA [KFE]
KOTU alt for KOTA [KOQ]
KOTUA SEDANG dial of SEDANG [SED]
KOTULE alt for TULA [TUL]
KOTVALI dial of BHILI [BHB]
KOTYA dial of BOZO, SOROGAMA [BZE]
KOTYAXO alt for KOTYA dial of BOZO, SOROGAMA [BZE]
KOTZEBUE SOUND INUPIAT dial of INUIT, NORTH ALASKAN [ESI]
KOUANG alt for KWANG [KVI]
KOUKA alt for KUKA [KUF]
KOUKOUYA alt for TEKE, SOUTHERN [KKW]
KOULANGO alt for KULANGO, BOUNA [NKU]
KOULANGO alt for KULANGO, BONDOUKOU [KZC]
KOUMAC alt for KUMAK [NEE]
KOUMONGOU dial of NGANGAM [GNG]
KOURA alt for KARA [CFL]
KOURI alt for KURI dial of BUDUMA [BDM]
KOUSERI alt for MSER [KQX]
KOUSERI alt for MSER dial of MSER [KQX]
KOUSSASSÉ alt for KUSAAL, WESTERN [KNU]
KOUSSERI alt for MSER [KQX]
KOUSSERI alt for MSER dial of MSER [KQX]
KOUSSERI alt for MSER dial of MSER [KQX]
KOUSSOUNTOU alt for BAGO [BQG]
KOUTIN alt for PEERE [KUT]
KOUTINE alt for PEERE [KUT]
KOUYA [KYF] lang, Côte d'Ivoire
KOVAI [KQB] lang, Papua New Guinea
KOVE [KVC] lang, Papua New Guinea
KOVIO alt for MEKEO [MEK]
KOVIO alt for NORTHWEST MEKEO dial of MEKEO [MEK]
KOW alt for ASAS [ASD]
KOW alt for SINSAURU [SNZ]
KOWAAO alt for KUWAA [BLH]
KOWAI alt for KOVAI [KQB]
KOWAKI [QKK] lang, Papua New Guinea
KOWALIB alt for KOALIB [KIB]
KOWAN dial of BAI [PIQ]
KOWET alt for KRAVET [KRV]
KOWIAI [KWH] lang, Indonesia, Irian Jaya
KOWLONG alt for KAULONG [PSS]

KOWYA alt for KOUYA [KYF]
KOXIMA alt for COXIMA [KOX]
KOYA [KFF] lang, India
KOYA dial of THEMNE [TEJ]
KOYA dial of LOKO [LOK]
KOYAGA JULA alt for WORODOUGOU JULA dial of
    JULA [DYU]
KOYATO alt for KOYA [KFF]
KOYI alt for KOYA [KFF]
KOYO [KOH] lang, Congo
KOYO alt for LOKOYA [LKY]
KOYO dial of GODIÉ [GOD]
KOYO alt for NGURU dial of KARA [KCM]
KOYO alt for NGURU dial of KARA [KCM]
KOYONG alt for HALANG [HAL]
KOYRA alt for KOORETE [KQY]
KOYSHA alt for KUCHA dial of KULLO [KLO]
KOYTA alt for NARA [NRB]
KOYUKON [KOY] lang, USA
KOZYMODEMYAN dial of MARI, HIGH [MRJ]
KPA alt for BAFIA [KSF]
KPA dial of MENDE [MFY]
KPA dial of BAFIA [KSF]
KPA alt for RDE KPA dial of RADE [RAD]
KPAGUA [KUW] lang, Zaïre
KPAKOLO dial of BÉTÉ, GAGNOA [BTG]
KPAKUM alt for KWAKUM [KWU]
KPALA [KPL] lang, Zaïre
KPALA alt for KRESH [KRS]
KPALA alt for KOLA dial of DABA [DAB]
KPALAGHA alt for SENOUFO, PALAKA [PLR]
KPAN [KPK] lang, Nigeria
KPANGO alt for DZUNGO [SBE]
KPANGO dial of DZUNGO [SBE]
KPANKPAM alt for KONKOMBA [KOS]
KPANTEN alt for KPAN [KPK]
KPANZON alt for KPAN [KPK]
KPANZON alt for KUMBO dial of KPAN [KPK]
KPARA alt for KRESH [KRS]
KPARLA alt for KRESH [KRS]
KPASAM [PBN] lang, Nigeria
KPASHAM alt for KPASAM [PBN]
KPASHAN alt for KAFANCHAN dial of KATAB [KCG]
KPATI [KOC] lang, Nigeria
KPATILI [KYM] lang, Central African Republic
KPATILI alt for GBAKPATILI dial of TOGBO [TOR]
KPATIRI alt for KPATILI [KYM]
KPATOGO [GBW] lang, Burkina Faso
KPATOGOSO alt for KPATOGO [GBW]
KPEAPLY dial of KRAHN, WESTERN [KRW]
KPELE alt for KPELLE, GUINEA [GKP]
KPELE alt for KPELLE, LIBERIA [KPE]
KPELESE alt for KPELLE, GUINEA [GKP]
KPELESETINA alt for KPELLE, GUINEA [GKP]
KPELLE, GUINEA [GKP] lang, Guinea
KPELLE, LIBERIA [KPE] lang, Liberia
KPERE alt for GBETE dial of MBUM [MDD]
KPERE alt for KEPERE dial of MBUM [MDD]
KPERESE alt for KPELLE, GUINEA [GKP]
KPESE alt for KPELLE, GUINEA [GKP]
KPESI alt for KPESSI [KEF]
KPESSI [KEF] lang, Togo
KPÉTSI alt for KPESSI [KEF]
KPILAKPILA alt for PILA [PIL]
KPLANG [PRA] lang, Ghana
KPLEBO dial of GREBO, BARCLAYVILLE [GRY]

KPLOR dial of GBII [GGB]
KPO dial of GOLA [GOL]
KPONGO alt for LIKA [LIK]
KPORO dial of MBEMBE, TIGON [NZA]
KPORO alt for NAMA dial of MBEMBE, TIGON [NZA]
KPOSO alt for AKPOSO [KPO]
KPOTOPO alt for DAN MUURE dial of PEERE [KUT]
KPWAALA alt for KPALA [KPL]
KPWATE alt for KPAN [KPK]
KPWESSI alt for KPELLE, GUINEA [GKP]
KPWESSI alt for KPELLE, LIBERIA [KPE]
KRACHE [KYE] lang, Ghana
KRACHI alt for KRACHE [KYE]
KRAHN alt for KRAHN, WESTERN [KRW]
KRAHN, EASTERN [KQO] lang, Liberia
KRAHN, WESTERN [KRW] lang, Liberia, Côte d'Ivoire
KRAHÔ [XRA] lang, Brazil
KRAKYE alt for KRACHE [KYE]
KRAMANG alt for KIRAMANG dial of KUI [KVD]
KRANARIA dial of ROMANI, SINTE [RMO]
KRANGKU alt for RAWANG [RAW]
KRANTIKI dial of ROMANI, SINTE [RMO]
KRANYEU dial of OY [OYB]
KRAOL dial of KUY [KDT]
KRASENG alt for KASSENG [KGC]
KRAU dial of JAH HUT [JAH]
KRAVET [KRV] lang, Cambodia
KRAWANG alt for BOGOR dial of SUNDA [SUO]
KRE alt for CREQ dial of HRE [HRE]
KREDJ alt for KRESH [KRS]
KREEN-AKARORE [KRE] lang, Brazil
KREI alt for KAREY [KYD]
KREICH alt for KRESH [KRS]
KREISH alt for KRESH [KRS]
KREM dial of BAHNAR [BDQ]
KREM-YE alt for KREYE [XRE]
KREN AKARORE alt for KREEN-AKARORE [KRE]
KRENAK [KQQ] lang, Brazil
KREOLE alt for MORISYEN [MFE]
KREPE alt for ÉWÉ [EWE]
KREPI alt for ÉWÉ [EWE]
KRESH [KRS] lang, Sudan, Central African Republic
KRESH-BORO alt for NAKA dial of KRESH [KRS]
KRESH-HOFRA alt for GBAYA-NGBONGBO dial of
    KRESH [KRS]
KRESH-NDOGO alt for GBAYA-NDOGO dial of
    KRESH [KRS]
KREYE [XRE] lang, Brazil
KRIANG alt for NGEQ [NGT]
KRIKATI [XRI] lang, Brazil
KRIM [KRM] lang, Sierra Leone
KRIM alt for CRIMEA dial of ARMENIAN [ARM]
KRINKATI alt for KRIKATI [XRI]
KRIO [KRI] lang, Sierra Leone, Equatorial Guinea,
    Gambia
KRIO FULA dial of FUUTA JALON [FUF]
KRIOL [ROP] lang, Australia
KRIOL alt for BELIZE CREOLE ENGLISH [BZI]
KRISA [KRO] lang, Papua New Guinea
KRISTANG alt for MALACCAN CREOLE
    PORTUGUESE [MCM]
KRIULO alt for CRIOULO, UPPER GUINEA [POV]
KROBO dial of GA-ADANGME-KROBO [GAC]
KROBOU alt for KROBU [KXB]
KROBU [KXB] lang, Côte d'Ivoire
KROE alt for KRUI [KRQ]

KROKONG dial of DAYAK, LAND [DYK]
KRONG alt for KHROONG dial of KHMU [KJG]
KRONGO [KGO] lang, Sudan
KRONGO ABDALLAH dial of TUMMA [TBQ]
KROO alt for KLAO [KLU]
KROUMEN alt for KRUMEN, SOUTHERN [TED]
KROUMEN alt for KRUMEN, NORTHEASTERN [PYE]
KRU alt for KRUMEN, SOUTHERN [TED]
KRU alt for CHRU [CJE]
KRU alt for KLAO [KLU]
KRU PIDGIN ENGLISH dial of LIBERIAN ENGLISH
  [LIR]
KRU'I alt for KRUI [KRQ]
KRUI [KRQ] lang, Indonesia, Sumatra
KRUMEN alt for KRUMEN, SOUTHERN [TED]
KRUMEN, NORTHEASTERN [PYE] lang, Côte d'Ivoire
KRUMEN, SOUTHERN [TED] lang, Côte d'Ivoire,
  Liberia, Liberia
KRUMEN, SOUTHERN alt for KRUMEN, SOUTHERN
  [TED]
KRUNG 1 dial of RADE [RAD]
KRU'NG 2 [KRR] lang, Cambodia
KRYC alt for KRYTS [KRY]
KRYTS [KRY] lang, Azerbaijan
KRYTS dial of KRYTS [KRY]
KRYZ alt for KRYTS [KRY]
KRYZY alt for KRYTS [KRY]
KSAKAUTENH alt for KHANG [KJM]
KTUNAXA alt for KUTENAI [KUN]
KU-AMBA alt for KWAMBA [RWM]
KUAKUA alt for PIAROA [PID]
KUAL alt for KOL [KFO]
KUALA dial of BANJAR [BJN]
KUALA LANGOT BESISI dial of BESISI [MHE]
KUALA LUMPUR SIGN LANGUAGE [KGI] lang,
  Malaysia, Peninsular
KUALA MONSOK DUSUN dial of DUSUN, CENTRAL
  [DTP]
KUALA TEMBELING dial of JAH HUT [JAH]
KUAMBA alt for KWAMBA [RWM]
KUAMBA alt for KIGUMU dial of KWAMBA [RWM]
KUAN [UAN] lang, Laos
KUANG alt for KWANG [KVI]
KUANGA alt for BRERI [BRQ]
KUANGFU alt for TAVALONG-VATAAN dial of AMIS
  [ALV]
KUANGSU-BONGGRANG alt for KWANSU [KJA]
KUANUA alt for TOLAI [KSD]
KUANYAMA alt for KWANYAMA [KUY]
KUAP dial of DAYAK, LAND [DYK]
KUAP dial of DAYAK, LAND [DYK]
KUAT alt for KUOT [KTO]
KUBA alt for YEYE [YEY]
KUBA alt for KUBI [KOF]
KUBA alt for LUNA [LUJ]
KUBA alt for LIKUBA [KXX]
KUBA alt for BUSHOONG [BUF]
KUBA dial of LEZGI [LEZ]
KUBA dial of AZERBAIJANI, NORTH [AZE]
KUBACHI dial of DARGWA [DAR]
KUBACHIN alt for KUBACHI dial of DARGWA [DAR]
KUBACHINTSY alt for KUBACHI dial of DARGWA
  [DAR]
KUBAI alt for NAGA, KABUI [NKF]
KUBAN dial of KABARDIAN [KAB]
KUBANG alt for BAJAU SEMPORNA dial of SAMA,

SOUTHERN [SIT]
KUBAWA alt for KUBI [KOF]
KUBE alt for MONGI [KGF]
KUBI [KOF] lang, Nigeria
KUBI dial of KONDA-DORA [KFC]
KUBIRI alt for UBIR [UBR]
KUBO dial of SAMO-KUBO [SMQ]
KUBOKOTA alt for GHANONGGA [GHN]
KUBONITU alt for CHEKE HOLO [MRN]
KUBORO dial of BABATANA [BAQ]
KUBU [KVB] lang, Indonesia, Sumatra
KUBULI dial of SINAGORO [SNC]
KUBUNG alt for SIKUBUNG dial of SAMA,
  SOUTHERN [SIT]
KUBWA alt for CUBEO [CUB]
KUCHA dial of UYGHUR [UIG]
KUCHA dial of KULLO [KLO]
KUCHBANDHI dial of KANJARI [KFT]
KUCHE alt for CHE [RUK]
KUCHI dial of MATUMBI [MGW]
KUCHIKOLI alt for KOLI, KACHI [GJK]
KUCHIKOLI alt for KACHCHI dial of KOLI, KACHI
  [GJK]
KUCONG alt for LAHU SHI [KDS]
KUDA alt for KUDU dial of KUDU-CAMO [KOV]
KUDA-CHAMO alt for KUDU-CAMO [KOV]
KUDAKA dial of OKINAWAN, CENTRAL [RYU]
KUDALA alt for PARKWA [PBI]
KUDALI dial of KONKANI, GOANESE [GOM]
KUDAWA alt for KUDU-CAMO [KOV]
KUDI alt for KODI [KOD]
KUDIYA [KFG] lang, India
KUDO alt for KADO [KDV]
KUDU dial of KUDU-CAMO [KOV]
KUDU-CAMO [KOV] lang, Nigeria
KUDUGLI alt for KADUGLI dial of KATCHA-
  KADUGLI-MIRI [KAT]
KUEI alt for ZHONGJIA dial of ZHUANG, NORTHERN
  [CCX]
KUEIPIEN alt for GÙIBIAN dial of ZHUANG,
  NORTHERN [CCX]
KUFA alt for KANGA [KCP]
KUFA-LIMA dial of KANGA [KCP]
KUFO alt for KANGA [KCP]
KUFURU dial of SENOUFO, CEBAARA [SEF]
KUGAMA [KOW] lang, Nigeria
KUGAMMA alt for KUGAMA [KOW]
KUGBO [KES] lang, Nigeria
KUGNI alt for KUNYI [KNF]
KUGONG dial of MUMUYE [MUL]
KUGU-MANGK alt for KUKU-MANGK [XMQ]
KUGU-MU'INH alt for KUKU-MU'INH [XMP]
KUGU-MUMINH alt for KUKU-MUMINH [XMH]
KUGU-UGBANH alt for KUKU-UGBANH [UGB]
KUGU-UWANH alt for KUKU-UWANH [UWA]
KUGURDA alt for KOKATA [KTD]
KUGWE alt for MOGHAMO dial of META' [MGO]
KUHPANG alt for NUNG [NUN]
KUI [KVD] lang, Indonesia, Nusa Tenggara
KUI [KXU] lang, India
KUI alt for LAHU SHI [KDS]
KUI alt for KUY [KDT]
KUI dial of KUI [KVD]
KUI SOUEI alt for KUY [KDT]
KUIJAU [DKR] lang, Malaysia, Sabah
KUIKÚRO [KUI] lang, Brazil

KUIKURU alt for KUIKÚRO [KUI]
KUILE alt for TSAMAI [TSB]
KUINGA alt for KUI [KXU]
KUINMURBARA alt for BAYALI [BJY]
KUIWAI alt for KOWIAI [KWH]
KUIYOW alt for KUIJAU [DKR]
KUJAA dial of SENOUFO, MAMARA [MYK]
KUJARGE [VKJ] lang, Chad
KUJARKE alt for KAJAKSE [CKQ]
KUJAU alt for KUIJAU [DKR]
KUJINGA dial of MABA [MDE]
KUK dial of AGHEM [AGQ]
KUKA [KUF] lang, Chad
KUKAJA alt for KUKATJA [KUX]
KUKANAR dial of DURUWA [PCI]
KUKATA alt for KOKATA [KTD]
KUKATJA [KUX] lang, Australia
KUKELE [KEZ] lang, Nigeria
KUKI alt for CHIN, THADO [TCZ]
KUKI AIRANI alt for RAROTONGAN [RRT]
KUKI CHIN alt for ZOME [ZOM]
KUKI-THADO alt for CHIN, THADO [TCZ]
KUKNA [KEX] lang, India
KUKTAYOR alt for THAYORE [THD]
KUKU dial of BARI [BFA]
KUKU-LUMUN alt for LUMUN dial of MORO HILLS
    [TAZ]
KUKU-MANGK [XMQ] lang, Australia
KUKU-MU'INH [XMP] lang, Australia
KUKU-MUMINH [XMH] lang, Australia
KUKU-UGBANH [UGB] lang, Australia
KUKU-UWANH [UWA] lang, Australia
KUKU-YALANGI alt for KUKU-YALANJI [GVN]
KUKU-YALANJI [GVN] lang, Australia
KUKUBERA alt for GUGUBERA [KKP]
KUKUDAYORE alt for THAYORE [THD]
KUKUI dial of KULUI [KFX]
"KUKUKUKU" alt for HAMTAI [HMT]
KUKULA dial of MANGSING [MBH]
KUKULIM alt for JUKUN WURKUM [JUI]
KUKULUNG alt for KULUNG [BBU]
KUKUM alt for FER dial of PUKU-GEERI-KERI-WIPSI
    [GEL]
KUKUMINDJEN alt for KUNJEN [KJN]
"KUKURUKU" alt for YEKHEE [ETS]
KUKUS alt for MALAY, COCOS ISLANDS [COA]
KUKUYA alt for TEKE, SOUTHERN [KKW]
KUKUYA alt for MINAVEHA [MVN]
KUKUYIMIDIR alt for GUGUYIMIDJIR [KKY]
KUKWA alt for TEKE, SOUTHERN [KKW]
KUKWAYA dial of GUMUZ [GUK]
KUKWE alt for NYAKYUSA-NGONDE [NYY]
KUKWE dial of NYAKYUSA-NGONDE [NYY]
KULA alt for DARLING [DRL]
KULA dial of DARLING [DRL]
KULAAL alt for GULA IRO [GLJ]
KULAHA alt for KOLA [KVV]
KULAMANEN dial of MANOBO, MATIGSALUG [MBT]
KULANGE alt for KULANGO, BOUNA [NKU]
KULANGE alt for KULANGO, BONDOUKOU [KZC]
KULANGO, BONDOUKOU [KZC] lang, Côte d'Ivoire,
    Ghana, Ghana
KULANGO, BONDOUKOU alt for KULANGO,
    BONDOUKOU [KZC]
KULANGO, BOUNA [NKU] lang, Côte d'Ivoire,
    Ghana, Ghana

KULANGO, BOUNA alt for KULANGO, BOUNA [NKU]
KULAWI alt for MOMA [MYL]
KULE alt for TSAMAI [TSB]
KULELE alt for KULERE [KXE]
KULERE [KUL] lang, Nigeria
KULERE [KXE] lang, Côte d'Ivoire
KULESA dial of POKOMO, LOWER [POJ]
KULI alt for KOL [KFO]
KULINA alt for CULINA [CUL]
KULÍNA alt for CULINA [CUL]
KULINO alt for CULINA [CUL]
KULIOW alt for KUIJAU [DKR]
KULISUSU [VKL] lang, Indonesia, Sulawesi
KULIVIU alt for MASKELYNES [KLV]
KULJA alt for ILI dial of UYGHUR [UIG]
KULJA alt for TARANCHI dial of UYGHUR [UIG]
KULLO [KLO] lang, Ethiopia
KULLU PAHARI alt for KULUI [KFX]
KULLUI alt for KULUI [KFX]
KULLUI PAHARI alt for KULUI [KFX]
KULME alt for KOLAMI, NORTHWESTERN [KFB]
KULON alt for KULUN [KNG]
KULPANTJA alt for YANKUNTATJARA [KDD]
KULU alt for KULUNG [BBU]
KULU dial of SARUDU [SDU]
KULU alt for KOOR dial of PUKU-GEERI-KERI-WIPSI
    [GEL]
KULU BOLI alt for KULUI [KFX]
KULU PAHARI alt for KULUI [KFX]
KULUBA dial of LUGBARA, LOW [LUC]
KULUBI alt for BAROK [BJK]
KULUI [KFX] lang, India
KULUN [KNG] lang, Taiwan
KULUNG [BBU] lang, Nigeria
KULUNG [KLE] lang, Nepal
KULUNG alt for MARBA [MPG]
KULUNG MUTHUN dial of NAGA, WANCHO [NNP]
KULUNO alt for KULUNG [BBU]
KULUR dial of SAPARUA [SPR]
KULVI alt for KULUI [KFX]
KULWALI alt for KULUI [KFX]
KULYNA alt for CULINA [CUL]
KUMA alt for KOMA [KMY]
KUMA alt for RUSHA [RUH]
KUMAI [KMI] lang, Papua New Guinea
KUMAI alt for KUP-MINJ dial of WAHGI [WAK]
KUMAIYA PACHHAI dial of KUMAUNI [KFY]
KUMAJU alt for KEMEZUNG [DMO]
KUMAK [NEE] lang, New Caledonia
KUMAK dial of KUMAK [NEE]
KUMALU alt for KUMARA dial of MUMENG [MZI]
KUMAM [KDI] lang, Uganda
KUMAN [KUE] lang, Papua New Guinea
KUMAN alt for KUMAM [KDI]
KUMAN dial of KUMAN [KUE]
KUMAON alt for KUMAUNI [KFY]
KUMAONI dial of KUMAUNI [KFY]
KUMARA dial of MUMENG [MZI]
KUMARAHU dial of DUAU [DUA]
KUMARBHAG MALTO dial of MALTO [MJT]
KUMAU alt for KUMAUNI [KFY]
KUMAUNI [KFY] lang, India, Nepal, Nepal
KUMAUNI alt for KUMAUNI [KFY]
KUMAWANI alt for KUMAUNI [KFY]
KUMBA [KSM] lang, Nigeria
KUMBA dial of LUSENGO [LUS]

KUMBAINGERI alt for KUMBAINGGAR [KGS]
KUMBAINGGAR [KGS] lang, Australia
KUMBERE dial of VUTE [VUT]
KUMBHARI alt for VARHADI-NAGPURI [VAH]
KUMBHARI dial of BUNDELI [BNS]
KUMBHARI dial of BHOYARI [BHY]
KUMBI dial of GUDU [GDU]
KUMBO dial of IJO, CENTRAL-WESTERN [IJC]
KUMBO dial of KPAN [KPK]
KUMBOKOTA alt for GHANONGGA [GHN]
KUMBORO alt for KUBORO dial of BABATANA
  [BAQ]
KUMBULE dial of NANDI [NNB]
KUMERTUO alt for DJAUAN [DJN]
KUMFEL alt for KUNFAL [XUF]
KUMFUTU dial of AGHEM [AGQ]
KUMGONI alt for KUMAUNI [KFY]
KUMHALI [KRA] lang, Nepal
KUMI alt for TOPOSA [TOQ]
KUMI alt for CHIN, KHUMI [CKM]
KUMIYANA alt for HIXKARYÁNA [HIX]
KUMKH alt for KUMUX dial of LAK [LBE]
KUMMAN alt for KUMAUNI [KFY]
KUMO alt for KOMO [KMW]
KUMOKIO alt for KUMUKIO [KUO]
KUMU alt for KOMO [KMW]
KUMUK alt for KUMYK [KSK]
KUMUKIO [KUO] lang, Papua New Guinea
KUMUKLAR alt for KUMYK [KSK]
KUMUL dial of UYGHUR [UIG]
KUMUM alt for KUMAM [KDI]
KUMUS alt for UDUK [UDU]
KUMUX dial of LAK [LBE]
KUMWENU alt for KHISA [KQM]
KUMYK [KSK] lang, Russia, Europe, USA, Turkey
KUMYK alt for KUMYK [KSK]
KUMYKI alt for KUMYK [KSK]
KUMZAI alt for KUMZARI [ZUM]
KUMZARI [ZUM] lang, Oman
KUN TO alt for ZHUANG, SOUTHERN [CCY]
KUNA, PAYA-PUCURO [KUA] lang, Colombia,
  Panama, Panama
KUNA, PAYA-PUCURO alt for KUNA, PAYA-PUCURO
  [KUA]
KUNA, SAN BLAS [CUK] lang, Panama
KUNABE dial of KUTEP [KUB]
KUNABEEB alt for KUNABEMBE dial of
  MPONGMPONG [MGG]
KUNABEMBE dial of MPONGMPONG [MGG]
KUNABI alt for KONKANI [KNK]
KUNAI dial of BOIKIN [BZF]
KUNAMA [KUM] lang, Ethiopia
KUNAN alt for KWINI [GWW]
KUNAN alt for GOONIYANDI [GNI]
KUNANA alt for LARDIL [LBZ]
KUNANT alt for MANSOANKA [MSW]
KUNANTE alt for MANSOANKA [MSW]
KUNAR dial of PASHAYI, SOUTHEAST [DRA]
KUNAWARI alt for KANAURI [KFK]
KUNAWUR alt for KANAURI [KFK]
KUNAYAONI alt for KUMAUNI [KFY]
KUNBAN dial of VARHADI-NAGPURI [VAH]
KUNBARLANG [WLG] lang, Australia
KUNBAU alt for KUNBI dial of KHANDESI [KHN]
KUNBI dial of KHANDESI [KHN]
KUNBI dial of VARHADI-NAGPURI [VAH]

KUNBILLE alt for BILE [BIL]
KUNDA [KDN] lang, Zimbabwe, Mozambique, Zambia
KUNDA alt for SEBA [KDG]
KUNDA alt for ANIMERE [ANF]
KUNDA dial of LUSENGO [LUS]
KUNDRI dial of BUNDELI [BNS]
KUNDU alt for BAKUNDU dial of BAKUNDU-BALUE
  [BDU]
KUNDUR dial of MOGHOLI [MLG]
KUNFAL [XUF] lang, Ethiopia
KUNFEL alt for KUNFAL [XUF]
KUNG alt for KUNG-TSUMKWE [KTZ]
KUNG alt for KUNG-EKOKA [KNW]
KUNG dial of AGHEM [AGQ]
KUNG-EKOKA [KNW] lang, Namibia, Angola
KUNG-GOBABIS [AUE] lang, Namibia
KUNG-TSUMKWE [KTZ] lang, Namibia, Angola
KUNGARA alt for FUR [FUR]
KUNGARAKAN alt for KUNGARAKANY [GGK]
KUNGARAKANY [GGK] lang, Australia
KUNGGARA [KVS] lang, Australia
KUNGGARI [KGL] lang, Australia
KUNGGERA alt for KUNGGARA [KVS]
KUNI [KSE] lang, Papua New Guinea
KUNI dial of BOAZI [KVG]
KUNIAN alt for GOONIYANDI [GNI]
KUNIBUM alt for EMAI-IULEHA-ORA [EMA]
KUNIE alt for NUMEE [KDK]
KUNIE alt for KWENYII dial of NUMEE [KDK]
KUNIGAMI [XUG] lang, Japan
KUNIMAIPA [KUP] lang, Papua New Guinea
KUNINI dial of BINE [ORM]
KUNINI alt for NYEM dial of SHOO-MINDA-NYEM
  [BCV]
KUNIYAN alt for GOONIYANDI [GNI]
KUNJEN [KJN] lang, Australia
KUNJIP dial of WAHGI [WAK]
KUNJUT alt for BURUSHASKI [BSK]
KUNLANG dial of RAWANG [RAW]
KUNMING alt for YUNNANESE dial of CHINESE,
  MANDARIN [CHN]
KUNRUKH alt for KURUX [KVN]
KUNTEMBA alt for KUNTENI dial of NATENI [NTM]
KUNTENI dial of NATENI [NTM]
KUNUA [KYX] lang, Papua New Guinea
KUNUZI alt for KENUZ dial of KENUZI-DONGOLA
  [KNC]
KUNUZI alt for KENUZI dial of KENUZI-DONGOLA
  [KNC]
KUNWINJKU alt for GUNWINGGU [GUP]
KUNYI [KNF] lang, Congo
KUNZA [KUZ] lang, Chile
KUNZAKH dial of AVAR [AVR]
KUO [OKU] lang, Cameroon
KUO [KHO] lang, Chad, Cameroon
KUOP alt for KUAP dial of DAYAK, LAND [DYK]
KUOT [KTO] lang, Papua New Guinea
KUOY alt for KUY [KDT]
KUOYU alt for CHINESE, MANDARIN [CHN]
KUP-MINJ dial of WAHGI [WAK]
KUPA dial of DAYAK, LAND [DYK]
KUPA dial of NUPE [NUP]
KUPANG alt for HELONG [HEG]
KUPANG alt for BASA KUPANG dial of MALAY [MLI]
KUPEL alt for KETENGBAN [KIN]
KUPERE dial of GIZRA [TOF]

KUPIA [KEY] lang, India
KUPOME dial of NAGA, TANGKHUL [NMF]
KUPSABINY [KPZ] lang, Uganda
KUPSABINY alt for SABINY dial of KUPSABINY [KPZ]
KUPSAPINY alt for SABINY dial of KUPSABINY [KPZ]
KUPTO [KPA] lang, Nigeria
KUPUCA alt for BEZHTA [KAP]
KUQA alt for KUCHA dial of UYGHUR [UIG]
KUR [KUV] lang, Indonesia, Maluku
KUR dial of PUKU-GEERI-KERI-WIPSI [GEL]
KUR GALLI alt for BRAHUI [BRH]
KUR-URMI dial of EVENKI [EVN]
KURA alt for BAKAIRÍ [BKQ]
KURADA ('URADA) alt for 'AUHELAWA [KUD]
KURAMA [KRH] lang, Nigeria
KURAMA alt for KURRAMA [VKU]
KURAMWARI alt for KURUMBA [KFI]
KURANGAL dial of PASHAYI, NORTHEAST [AEE]
KURANKO [KHA] lang, Sierra Leone, Guinea
KURATEG alt for MAKURÁPI [MAG]
KURBAT alt for DOMARI [RMT]
KURBATI dial of DOMARI [RMT]
KURDAR dial of PASHAYI, NORTHEAST [AEE]
KURDI [KDB] lang, Iraq, Iran
KURDIT alt for JUDEO-ARAMAIC [TRG]
KURDY alt for KURDI [KDB]
KURI alt for KORKU [KFQ]
KURI alt for NABI [NBN]
KURI dial of BUDUMA [BDM]
KURIA [KUJ] lang, Tanzania, Kenya
KURICHIYA [KFH] lang, India
KURIL dial of AINU [AIN]
KURIMA [VKR] lang, Indonesia, Irian Jaya
KURINA alt for CULINA [CUL]
KURIPACO alt for CURRIPACO [KPC]
KURIPAKO alt for CURRIPACO [KPC]
KURIYO alt for KUIJAU [DKR]
KURJA alt for KODAGU [KFA]
KURKA alt for FUR [FUR]
KURKA alt for KURUX [KVN]
KURKU alt for KORKU [KFQ]
KURKURO alt for KUIKÚRO [KUI]
KURLYAD alt for WESTERN LIVONIAN dial of LIV
    [LIV]
KURMANJI [KUR] lang, Turkey, Iran, Iraq, Lebanon,
    Russia, Europe, Syria
KURMANJIKI alt for KIRMANJKI [QKV]
KURMI dial of BHUMIJ [BHM]
KURO alt for NGURU dial of KARA [KCM]
KURO-URMI dial of NANAI [GLD]
KURONDI alt for KARONDI dial of TUMTUM [TBR]
KUROSHIMA dial of YAEYAMA [RYS]
KURRAMA [VKU] lang, Australia
KURRIPACO alt for CURRIPACO [KPC]
KURRIPAKO alt for CURRIPACO [KPC]
KURTAT dial of OSETIN [OSE]
KURTHA dial of RAJBANGSI [RJB]
KURTI [KTM] lang, Papua New Guinea
KURTJJAR alt for GURDJAR [GDJ]
KURTOPAKHA dial of KEBUMTAMP [KJZ]
KURU dial of GIDRA [GDR]
KURUÁYA [KYR] lang, Brazil
KURUBA alt for KURUMBA [KFI]
KURUDU [KJR] lang, Indonesia, Irian Jaya
KURUG alt for KODAGU [KFA]
KURUKH alt for KURUX [KVN]

KURUKO alt for PIU [PIX]
KURUKURU dial of PAUMARÍ [PAD]
KURUMAR alt for KURUMBA [KFI]
KURUMBA [KFI] lang, India
KURUMBA alt for KURUMFÉ [KFZ]
KURUMBA, ALU [QKA] lang, India
KURUMBA, BETTA [QKB] lang, India
KURUMBA, JENNU [QKJ] lang, India
KURUMBAN alt for KURUMBA [KFI]
KURUMBAR alt for KURUMBA [KFI]
KURUMFÉ [KFZ] lang, Burkina Faso, Mali
KURUMVARI alt for KURUMBA [KFI]
KURUNGA alt for KARANGA [KTH]
KURUNGA alt for KARANGA dial of KARANGA [KTH]
KURUNGTUFU dial of MONGI [KGF]
KURUNGU alt for KRONGO [KGO]
KURUPI alt for GARUS [GYB]
KURUR dial of HAHON [HAH]
KURUTI alt for KURTI [KTM]
KURUTI-PARE alt for KURTI [KTM]
KURUWER dial of KABA DEME [KWG]
KURUX [KVN] lang, India, Bangladesh
KURUX, NEPALI [KXL] lang, Nepal
KURYA alt for KURIA [KUJ]
KURYE alt for KURIA [KUJ]
KURZEME alt for WESTERN LIVONIAN dial of LIV
    [LIV]
KUSA alt for KUSA-MANLEA dial of ATONI [TMR]
KUSA-MANLEA dial of ATONI [TMR]
KUSAAL, EASTERN [KUS] lang, Ghana
KUSAAL, WESTERN [KNU] lang, Burkina Faso
KUSAGE alt for KUSAGHE [KSG]
KUSAGHE [KSG] lang, Solomon Islands
KUSAIE [KSI] lang, Micronesia, Nauru, Nauru
KUSAIE alt for KUSAIE [KSI]
KUSAIEAN alt for KUSAIE [KSI]
KUSALE alt for KUSAAL, WESTERN [KNU]
KUSALE alt for KUSAAL, EASTERN [KUS]
KUSANDA [KGG] lang, Nepal
KUSASI alt for KUSAAL, WESTERN [KNU]
KUSASI alt for KUSAAL, EASTERN [KUS]
KUSEKI dial of YENDANG [YEN]
KUSERI alt for MSER [KQX]
KUSERI alt for MSER dial of MSER [KQX]
KUSHA alt for KUCHA dial of KULLO [KLO]
KUSHANI alt for SHUGHNI dial of SHUGHNI [SGH]
KUSHAR alt for BOTE-MAJHI [BMJ]
KUSHE alt for KUSHI [KUH]
KUSHI [KUH] lang, Nigeria
KUSHI alt for BAUSHI [BSF]
KUSIBI alt for DESANO [DES]
KUSILAAY alt for GUSILAY [GSL]
KUSKOKWIM ESKIMO dial of YUPIK, CENTRAL
    [ESU]
KUSKOKWIM, UPPER [KUU] lang, USA
KUSSO alt for MBUKUSHU [MHW]
KUSU [KSV] lang, Zaïre
KUSUNDA alt for KUSANDA [KGG]
KUSURI dial of TUGUTIL [TUJ]
KUSUWA dial of KWAMBA [RWM]
KUSUWA alt for SUWA dial of KWAMBA [RWM]
KUTA dial of GBAGYI [GBR]
KUTAI alt for MALAY, TENGGARONG KUTAI [VKT]
KUTANG BHOTIA [KTE] lang, Nepal
KUTCHA alt for NAGA, ZEME [NZM]
KUTCHIN alt for GWICH'IN [KUC]

KUTEB alt for KUTEP [KUB]
KUTELE alt for TULA [TUL]
KUTENAI [KUN] lang, Canada, USA, USA
KUTENAI alt for KUTENAI [KUN]
KUTEP [KUB] lang, Nigeria, Cameroon
KUTEV alt for KUTEP [KUB]
KUTHANT [QKD] lang, Australia
KUTIA-DYAPA alt for CUTIADAPA dial of KATUKÍNA
    [KAV]
KUTIN alt for PEERE [KUT]
KUTINE alt for PEERE [KUT]
KUTINN alt for PEERE [KUT]
KUTKASEN dial of AZERBAIJANI, NORTH [AZE]
KUTO-KUTE dial of SASAK [SAS]
KUTSU alt for KUSU [KSV]
KUTSUNG alt for LAHU SHI [KDS]
KUTSWE alt for KHUTSWE dial of SOTHO,
    NORTHERN [SRT]
KUTU [KDC] lang, Tanzania
KUTU alt for YELA [YEL]
KUTU dial of LIBINZA [LIZ]
KUTU dial of MONGO-NKUNDU [MOM]
KUTUBU dial of FOI [FOI]
KUTURMI [KHJ] lang, Nigeria
KUUK THAAYOORE alt for THAYORE [THD]
KUUKU-YA'U [QKL] lang, Australia
KUUMU alt for KOMO [KMW]
KUVAKAN dial of BASHKIR [BXK]
KUVALAN alt for KAVALAN [CKV]
KUVARAWAN alt for KAVALAN [CKV]
KUVENMAS dial of ALAMBLAK [AMP]
KUVI [KXV] lang, India
KUVI KOND alt for KUVI [KXV]
KUVINGA alt for KUVI [KXV]
KUVOKO alt for GEVOKO [NGS]
KUVURI alt for KABARI dial of KANURI, YERWA
    [KPH]
KUWAA [BLH] lang, Liberia
KUWAITI ARABIC dial of ARABIC, NAJDI [ARS]
KUWAMA [QKU] lang, Australia
KUWAMA alt for PUNGUPUNGU dial of WADJIGINY
    [WDJ]
KUWANI [XKU] lang, Indonesia, Irian Jaya
KUWARAWAN alt for KAVALAN [CKV]
KUWATAAY alt for KWATAY [CWT]
KUWI alt for KUVI [KXV]
KUY [KDT] lang, Cambodia, Thailand, Laos, Thailand
KUY alt for KUY [KDT]
KUY alt for KUI [KXU]
KUYA alt for KOUYA [KYF]
KUYA dial of NDUMU [NMD]
KUYOBE alt for SOLA [SOY]
KUYONON alt for CUYONON [CYO]
KUYUBI alt for PURUBORÁ [PUR]
KUYUK alt for ZAGHAWA [ZAG]
KUYUNON alt for CUYONON [CYO]
KUZAMANI [KSA] lang, Nigeria
KUZNETS TATAR alt for SHOR [CJS]
KVALAN alt for KAVALAN [CKV]
KVANADA alt for BAGVALAL [KVA]
KVANADIN alt for BAGVALAL [KVA]
KVANXIDATL dial of ANDI [ANI]
KWA' [BKO] lang, Cameroon
KWA alt for BA [KWB]
KWA alt for EJAGHAM [ETU]
KWA dial of FIPA [FIP]

KWA alt for SOUTHERN EJAGHAM dial of
    EJAGHAM [ETU]
KWA alt for SOUTHERN EJAGHAM dial of
    EJAGHAM [ETU]
KWA' dial of KWA' [BKO]
KWA'ALANG alt for KWAGALLAK dial of KOFYAR
    [KWL]
KWAA alt for KUWAA [BLH]
KWAAMI [KSQ] lang, Nigeria
KWABZAK alt for TAL [TAL]
KWAC alt for CIEC dial of DINKA, SOUTH CENTRAL
    [DIB]
KWADI [KWZ] lang, Angola
KWADIA [KWP] lang, Côte d'Ivoire
KWADYA alt for KWADIA [KWP]
KW'ADZA [WKA] lang, Tanzania
KWAFI dial of FIPA [FIP]
KWAGALLAK dial of KOFYAR [KWL]
KWAGIUTL alt for KWAKIUTL [KWK]
KWAI alt for GULA'ALAA [GMB]
KWAIBIDA dial of SINAGORO [SNC]
KWAIBO dial of SINAGORO [SNC]
KWAIKER alt for CUAIQUER [KWI]
KWAIO [KWD] lang, Solomon Islands
KWAJA [KDZ] lang, Cameroon
KWAJI dial of MUMUYE [MUL]
KWAK dial of YAMBA [YAM]
KWAKIUTL [KWK] lang, Canada
KWAKUM [KWU] lang, Cameroon
KWAKUM dial of KWAKUM [KWU]
KWAKWA alt for AVIKAM [AVI]
KWAKWAGOM dial of BOKYI [BKY]
KWAKWAK alt for KAKWA [KEO]
KWAKWALA alt for KWAKIUTL [KWK]
KWAKWI dial of ATEN [GAN]
KWAL alt for IRIGWE [IRI]
KWALA alt for LIKWALA [KWC]
KWALA alt for KPALA [KPL]
KWALE [KSJ] lang, Papua New Guinea
KWALE dial of KWALE [KSJ]
KWALE alt for UKWUANI dial of UKWUANI-ABOH
    [UKW]
KWALI dial of GBARI [GBY]
KWALLA alt for KWAGALLAK dial of KOFYAR [KWL]
KWAM alt for KWAAMI [KSQ]
KWAMA alt for KOMA, NORTH [KMQ]
KWAMANCHI alt for KWAAMI [KSQ]
KWAMBA [RWM] lang, Uganda, Zaïre, Zaïre
KWAMBA alt for KWAMBA [RWM]
KWAMBI [KWM] lang, Namibia
KWAME alt for KWAMI [KTF]
KWAME-DANSO dial of DWANG [NNU]
KWAMERA [TNK] lang, Vanuatu
KWAMI [KTF] lang, Zaïre
KWAMI alt for KWAAMI [KSQ]
KWAN alt for IRIGWE [IRI]
KWANCAMA alt for KWANYAMA [KUY]
KWANDANG [KJW] lang, Indonesia, Sulawesi
KWANDARA alt for GWANDARA [GWN]
KWANDI dial of LUYANA [LAV]
KWANG [KVI] lang, Chad
KWANG dial of KWANG [KVI]
KWANGA [KWJ] lang, Papua New Guinea
KWANGA dial of LUYANA [LAV]
KWANGALI [KWN] lang, Namibia, Angola
KWANGARE alt for KWANGALI [KWN]

KWANGARI alt for KWANGALI [KWN]
KWANGE dial of GBARI [GBY]
KWANGFU alt for TAVALONG-VATAAN dial of AMIS [ALV]
KWANGSHUN dial of HMONG, WESTERN [HUJ]
KWANGSU-BONGGRANG alt for KWANSU [KJA]
KWANGTUNG alt for CHAO SHAN dial of CHINESE, MIN NAN [CFR]
KWANIM PA alt for UDUK [UDU]
KWANJA [KNP] lang, Cameroon
KWANJAMA alt for KWANYAMA [KUY]
KWANKA [BIJ] lang, Nigeria
KWANKA dial of KWANKA [BIJ]
KWANSU [KJA] lang, Indonesia, Irian Jaya
KWANSU-BONGGRANG alt for KWANSU [KJA]
KWANYAMA [KUY] lang, Angola, Namibia, Namibia
KWANYAMA alt for KWANYAMA [KUY]
KWAPM alt for ZARI dial of ZARI [ZAZ]
KWARA alt for QWARA dial of KARA [CFL]
KWARA'AE [KWF] lang, Solomon Islands
KWARAFE alt for KORAFE [KPR]
KWARASA alt for KARA [CFL]
KWARE [KWR] lang, Papua New Guinea
KWARE alt for KWALE [KSJ]
KWAREKWAREO alt for DORI'O [DOR]
KWARRA alt for KANTANA [MMA]
KWARSENGEN alt for KWASENGEN [WOS]
KWARUWIKWUNDI alt for SAWOS [SIC]
KWASANG dial of BUANG, MANGGA [MMO]
KWASENGA alt for KWASENGEN [WOS]
KWASENGAN alt for KWASENGEN [WOS]
KWASENGEN [WOS] lang, Papua New Guinea
KWASIO dial of NGUMBA [NMG]
KWASSIO alt for NGUMBA [NMG]
KWATAY [CWT] lang, Senegal
KWATO [KOP] lang, Papua New Guinea
KWAVI [CKG] lang, Tanzania
KWAWU dial of AKAN [TWS]
KWAYA [KYA] lang, Tanzania
KWAYA alt for MACI dial of ICEVE-MACI [BEC]
KWAYA alt for MACI dial of ICEVE-MACI [BEC]
KWAYAM dial of KANURI, YERWA [KPH]
KWE alt for KWE-ETSHORI [KWQ]
KWE dial of TEKE, CENTRAL [TEC]
KWE-ETSHORI [KWQ] lang, Botswana
KWE-TSHORI alt for KWE-ETSHORI [KWQ]
KWEDI alt for MOKPWE [BRI]
KWEE alt for KWE-ETSHORI [KWQ]
KWEEN alt for KHOUEN [KHF]
KWEGI alt for KWEGU [YID]
KWEGU [YID] lang, Ethiopia
KWEICHU dial of HMONG, WESTERN [HUJ]
KWELE alt for KWERE [CWE]
KWELI alt for MOKPWE [BRI]
KWELSHIN alt for KHUALSHIM dial of CHIN, FALAM [HBH]
KWEM alt for KAETI [KZH]
KWENA dial of TSWANA [TSW]
KWÉNDRÉ alt for GURO [GOA]
KWENGO alt for XUN [XUU]
KWENI alt for GURO [GOA]
KWENY dial of SAGALA [SBM]
KWENYII alt for NUMEE [KDK]
KWENYII dial of NUMEE [KDK]
KWERBA [KWE] lang, Indonesia, Irian Jaya
KWERE [CWE] lang, Tanzania

KWERISA [KKB] lang, Indonesia, Irian Jaya
KWESE [KWS] lang, Zaïre
KWESTEN [KWT] lang, Indonesia, Irian Jaya
KWÉYÒL alt for LESSER ANTILLEAN CREOLE FRENCH [DOM]
KWI alt for LAHU SHI [KDS]
KWIFA alt for NKWIFIYA dial of SAGALA [SBM]
KWIJAU alt for KUIJAU [DKR]
KWIKAPA alt for COCOPA [COC]
KWILI alt for MOKPWE [BRI]
KWINA alt for SHITA [LGN]
KWINGSANG alt for NUNG [NUN]
KWINI [GWW] lang, Australia
KWINP'ANG alt for NUNG [NUN]
KWINPANG alt for NUNG [NUN]
KWINTI [KWW] lang, Surinam
KWIRI alt for MOKPWE [BRI]
KWISE dial of KWADI [KWZ]
KWISSO alt for KWISE dial of KWADI [KWZ]
KWIVA alt for NKWIFIYA dial of SAGALA [SBM]
KWOIRENG alt for KOIRENG [NKD]
KWOJEFFA alt for BURA-PABIR [BUR]
KWOLL alt for IRIGWE [IRI]
KWOLLANYOCH alt for AWNGI [AWN]
KWOM alt for KWAAMI [KSQ]
KWOMA [KMO] lang, Papua New Guinea
KWOMA dial of KWOMA [KMO]
KWOMTARI [KWO] lang, Papua New Guinea
KWONG alt for KAGOMA [KDM]
KWONG alt for KOFYAR dial of KOFYAR [KWL]
KWONO alt for KONO [KLK]
KWOTTO alt for EBIRA [IGB]
KWOTTU alt for OROMO, EASTERN [HAE]
KWUSAUN dial of BOIKIN [BZF]
KXAXA alt for KGAGA dial of SOTHO, NORTHERN [SRT]
KXHALAXADI dial of TSWANA [TSW]
KXOE alt for XUN [XUU]
KYABRAT dial of MAITHILI [MKP]
KYAK [BKA] lang, Nigeria
KYAKA [KYC] lang, Papua New Guinea
KYAMA alt for EBRIÉ [EBR]
KYAN KYAR alt for GWANDARA SOUTHERN dial of GWANDARA [GWN]
KYANG alt for CHIN, ASHO [CSH]
KYANGO alt for BROKSKAT [BKK]
KYANZI dial of KWAMBA [RWM]
KYATO alt for ICEN [ICH]
KYENELE [KQL] lang, Papua New Guinea
KYENGA alt for TYENGA dial of SHANGA [SHO]
KYENTU alt for BISSAULA dial of KPAN [KPK]
KYENYING-BARANG alt for KYENELE [KQL]
KYERUNG [KGY] lang, Nepal, China
KYI alt for KHASI [KHI]
KYIBAKU alt for CIBAK [CKL]
KYIRONG alt for KYERUNG [KGY]
KYO dial of NAGA, LOTHA [NJH]
KYOKOSI alt for ANUFO [CKO]
KYON dial of NAGA, LOTHA [NJH]
KYONG dial of NAGA, LOTHA [NJH]
KYONGBORONG alt for CHUMBURUNG [NCU]
KYONGGIDO alt for SEOUL dial of KOREAN [KKN]
KYONGSANGDO dial of KOREAN [KKN]
KYOPI alt for NYORO [NYR]
KYOU dial of NAGA, LOTHA [NJH]
KYPCHAK dial of UZBEK, NORTHERN [UZB]

KYZYL dial of KHAKAS [KJH]
KYZYLBASH dial of BALKAN GAGAUZ TURKISH
 [BGX]
KYZYLBASH dial of AZERBAIJANI, NORTH [AZE]
L'ARABE DU TCHAD alt for ARABIC, SHUWA [SHU]
L'BE dial of MOKEN [MWT]
L'ELE alt for LYÉLÉ [LEE]
L'WA alt for LAWA, WESTERN [LCP]
L-ARUSA alt for ARUSA dial of MAASAI [MET]
LA alt for HLAI [LIC]
LA dial of VO [WBM]
LA alt for TAI PONG dial of TAI NÜA [TDD]
LA CONCEPTION dial of CAAC [MSQ]
LA CONCORDIA dial of TZOTZIL, HUIXTÁN [TZU]
LA HA UNG alt for LAHA [LHA]
LA JALCA dial of QUECHUA, CHACHAPOYAS [QUK]
LA NYA alt for TAI, NORTHERN [NOD]
LA PALMA PAME dial of CHICHIMECA PAME,
 NORTHERN [PMQ]
LA QUA alt for LATI [LBT]
LA'ALUA alt for SAAROA [SXR]
LA'FI dial of FE'FE' [FMP]
LA-DANG alt for NOANG dial of CHRU [CJE]
LA-OANG alt for ROGLAI, NORTHERN [ROG]
LA-OOR dial of LAWA, WESTERN [LCP]
LAADI dial of KONGO [KON]
LAADI dial of KONGO [KON]
LAAK alt for THIANG dial of NUER [NUS]
LAAL [GDM] lang, Chad
LAALI dial of TEKE, WESTERN [TEZ]
LAAMANG alt for LAMANG [HIA]
LAAME alt for GIMNIME [KMB]
LAAMOOT alt for OMOTIK [OMT]
LAANY alt for DANI, WESTERN [DNW]
LABA [LAU] lang, Indonesia, Maluku
LABASA alt for NORTHEAST VANUA LEVU dial of
 FIJIAN [FJI]
LABE dial of TAWALA [TBO]
LABEL [LBB] lang, Papua New Guinea
LABHANI MUKA alt for LAMANI [LMN]
LA'BI [LBI] lang, Cameroon
LABIR [JKU] lang, Nigeria
LABO [MWI] lang, Vanuatu
LABO alt for LABU [LBU]
LABOURDIN dial of BASQUE [BSQ]
LABRADOR ESKIMO dial of INUIT, EASTERN
 CANADIAN [ESB]
LABU [LBU] lang, Papua New Guinea
LABU alt for LAUA [LUF]
LABU dial of MALAY [MLI]
LABU BASAP alt for LABU dial of MALAY [MLI]
LABU' alt for LABU [LBU]
LABUAN dial of RUKAI [DRU]
LABUANDIRI dial of PANCANA [PNP]
LABUK dial of KADAZAN, LABUK-KINABATANGAN
 [DTB]
LABUK KADAZAN alt for KADAZAN, LABUK-
 KINABATANGAN [DTB]
LABWOR dial of ACHOLI [ACO]
LAC dial of KOHO [KPM]
LACANDÓN [LAC] lang, Mexico
LACH dial of CZECH [CZC]
LACH alt for LAC dial of KOHO [KPM]
LACHAO dial of CHATINO, LACHAO-YOLOTEPEC
 [CLY]
LACHÍ alt for LATI [LBT]

LACHI alt for LATI [LBT]
LACHIKWAW alt for LASHI [LSI]
LACHIROAG alt for ZAPOTECO, SAN CRISTOBAL
 LACHIRUAJ [ZTC]
LACHIXIO ZAPOTECO alt for ZAPOTECO, EASTERN
 ZIMATLÁN [ZPL]
LACONDE alt for YALAPMUNXTE dial of
 NAMBIKUÁRA, NORTHERN [MBG]
LACTAN alt for RATAGNON [BTN]
LACTAN dial of KALAGAN [KQE]
LADAK alt for LADAKHI [LBJ]
LADAKHI [LBJ] lang, India
LADAPHI alt for LADAKHI [LBJ]
LADHAKHI alt for LADAKHI [LBJ]
LADIL alt for LARDIL [LBZ]
LADIN [LLD] lang, Italy, USA
LADINO [SPJ] lang, Israel, USA, Turkey
LADINO alt for LADINO [SPJ]
LADINO alt for LADIN [LLD]
LADWAGS alt for LADAKHI [LBJ]
LAE [LAZ] lang, Papua New Guinea
LAEKO alt for LAEKO-LIBUAT [LKL]
LAEKO alt for SAMBA LEKO dial of SAMBA LEKO
 [NDI]
LAEKO-LIBUAT [LKL] lang, Papua New Guinea
LAEKO-LIMBUAT alt for LAEKO-LIBUAT [LKL]
LAEWAMBA alt for WAMPAR [LBQ]
LAEWOMBA alt for WAMPAR [LBQ]
LAFANA alt for LELEMI [LEF]
LAFIIT alt for LOPIT [LPX]
LAFIT alt for LOPIT [LPX]
LAFITE alt for LOPIT [LPX]
LAFOFA [LAF] lang, Sudan
LAFOFA dial of LAFOFA [LAF]
LAGANYAN alt for LEGENYEM [LCC]
LAGAWE IFUGAO dial of IFUGAO, TUWALI [IFK]
LAGBA alt for LANGBA [LNL]
LAGHMAN dial of PASHAYI, SOUTHEAST [DRA]
LAGHMANI alt for PARYA [PAQ]
LAGHU [LGB] lang, Solomon Islands
LAGIS dial of BUANG, MANGGA [MMO]
LAGO alt for POK dial of SABAOT [SPY]
LAGOUANE alt for LAGWAN [KOT]
LAGOWA dial of DAJU, DAR FUR [DAJ]
LAGU alt for LAGHU [LGB]
LAGUBI alt for MAMBILA, CAMEROON [MYA]
LAGUBI alt for MAMBILA, NIGERIA [MZK]
LAGUME dial of HUMENE [HUF]
LAGUNA dial of TRIQUE, SAN ANDRÉS
 CHICAHUAXTLA [TRS]
LAGUNA alt for ACOMA dial of KERES, WESTERN
 [KJQ]
LAGUNAN MURUT alt for PENSIANGAN MURUT dial
 of TAGAL MURUT [MVV]
LAGUNAN MURUT alt for PENSIANGAN MURUT dial
 of TAGAL MURUT [MVV]
LAGWAN [KOT] lang, Cameroon, Chad, Chad,
 Nigeria
LAGWAN alt for LAGWAN [KOT]
LAGWANE alt for LAGWAN [KOT]
LAHA [LAD] lang, Indonesia, Maluku
LAHA [LHA] lang, Viet Nam
LAHA SERANI dial of TELUTI [TLT]
LAHANAN [LHN] lang, Malaysia, Sarawak
LAHANDA alt for PANJABI, WESTERN [PNB]
LAHAULI alt for LAHULI, TINAN [LBF]

LAHE alt for LAE [LAZ]
LAHNDA alt for PANJABI, WESTERN [PNB]
LAHNDI alt for PANJABI, WESTERN [PNB]
LAHOULI alt for LAHULI, TINAN [LBF]
LAHTA alt for KAREN, LAHTA [KVT]
LAHU [LAH] lang, China, Myanmar, Laos, Myanmar,
    Thailand, Viet Nam
LAHU alt for LAHU [LAH]
LAHU alt for AVIKAM [AVI]
LAHU SHI [KDS] lang, Myanmar, China, Thailand
LAHU SHI alt for LAHU SHI [KDS]
LAHULI alt for LAHULI, TINAN [LBF]
LAHULI OF BUNAN alt for BUNAN [BFU]
LAHULI, CHAMBA [LAE] lang, India
LAHULI, TINAN [LBF] lang, India, China
LAHUNA alt for LAHU [LAH]
LAI alt for PALYU [PLY]
LAI alt for KABALAI [KVF]
LAI alt for HLAI [LIC]
LAI dial of GBAYA [GYA]
LAI dial of CHIN, HAKA [CNH]
LAIA dial of LOKO [LOK]
LAIAGAM dial of ENGA [ENQ]
LAIERDILA alt for LARDIL [LBZ]
LAISO alt for LAIZO dial of CHIN, FALAM [HBH]
LAITOKITOK dial of MAASAI [MET]
LAIWOMBA alt for WAMPAR [LBQ]
LAIWONU dial of PAMONA [BCX]
LAIWUI dial of MEKONGGA [MWK]
LAIYOLO [LJI] lang, Indonesia, Sulawesi
LAIYOLO dial of LAIYOLO [LJI]
LAIZAO alt for LAIZO dial of CHIN, FALAM [HBH]
LAIZO dial of CHIN, FALAM [HBH]
LAIZO dial of ANAL [ANM]
LAIZO-SHIMHRIN alt for LAIZO dial of CHIN, FALAM
    [HBH]
LAJIA alt for LAKA [LBC]
LAJOLO alt for LAIYOLO [LJI]
LAK [LBE] lang, Russia, Europe
LAKA [LAK] lang, Nigeria
LAKA [LAM] lang, Chad, Central African Republic
LAKA [LBC] lang, China
LAKA alt for KARANG [KZR]
LAKAALONG alt for KAALONG dial of BAFIA [KSF]
LAKAHIA alt for KAMORO [KGQ]
LAKALAI alt for BILEKI dial of NAKANAI [NAK]
LAKALEI [LKA] lang, Indonesia, Nusa Tenggara
LAKAMA'DI dial of MORU [MGD]
LAKATAKURA-TIKA alt for TIKA dial of KUNAMA
    [KUM]
LAKE alt for MOSES LAKE dial of OKANAGAN [OKA]
LAKE BUHI EAST alt for AGTA, MT. IRAYA [ATL]
LAKE BUHI WEST alt for AGTA, MT. IRIGA [AGZ]
LAKE MIWOK dial of MIWOK [SKD]
LAKE OF THE WOODS OJIBWA dial of OJIBWA,
    WESTERN [OJI]
LAKET dial of KONOMALA [KOA]
LAKHER alt for CHIN, MARA [MRH]
LAKI alt for LAK [LBE]
LAKI alt for TOLAKI [LBW]
LAKI alt for LEKI dial of LURI [LRI]
LAKIA alt for LAKA [LBC]
LAKING dial of MARU [MHX]
LAKIUNG alt for GOWA dial of MAKASSAR [MSR]
LAKJA alt for LAKA [LBC]
LAKKA alt for LAKA [LAK]

LAKKA alt for KARANG [KZR]
LAKKIA alt for LAKA [LBC]
LAKKJA alt for LAKA [LBC]
LAKON alt for LAKONA [LKN]
LAKONA [LKN] lang, Vanuatu
LAKOTA [LKT] lang, USA, Canada
LAKU alt for LAHU [LAH]
LAKUME alt for LAGUME dial of HUMENE [HUF]
LAKUNDU alt for BAKUNDU dial of BAKUNDU-
    BALUE [BDU]
LALA alt for NARA [NRZ]
LALA alt for LEHAR [CAE]
"LALA" alt for YUNGUR [YUN]
LALA dial of ZULU [ZUU]
LALA dial of LALA-BISA [LEB]
LALA dial of LALA-ROBA [LLA]
LALA-BISA [LEB] lang, Zambia, Zaïre
LALA-ROBA [LLA] lang, Nigeria
LALAKI alt for TOLAKI [LBW]
LALANG dial of KUBU [KVB]
LALAURA dial of KEOPARA [KHZ]
LALAWA alt for LELA [DRI]
LALI alt for FUR [FUR]
LALIA [LAL] lang, Zaïre
LALLA alt for LALA dial of LALA-ROBA [LLA]
LALLERE dial of ROMANI, SINTE [RMO]
LALOK alt for ANJAM [BOJ]
LALOMERUI dial of WARU [WRU]
LALUNG [LAX] lang, India
LAM dial of GIDAR [GID]
LAM-SI-HOAN alt for AMIS [ALV]
LAMA [LAS] lang, Togo, Benin
LAMA [LAY] lang, Myanmar, China
LAMA alt for QUECHUA, SAN MARTÍN [QSA]
LAMA dial of KABIYÉ [KBP]
LAMAG SUNGAI alt for SUNGAI, KINABATANGAN
    [DSB]
LAMAG SUNGAI dial of KADAZAN, LABUK-
    KINABATANGAN [DTB]
LAMAHOLOT [SLP] lang, Indonesia, Nusa Tenggara
LAMAI dial of SIRAIYA [FOS]
LAMALAMA alt for LAMU-LAMU [LBY]
LAMALANGA alt for HANO [LML]
LAMAM [LMM] lang, Cambodia
LAMANG [HIA] lang, Nigeria
LAMANI [LMN] lang, India
LAMANO alt for QUECHUA, SAN MARTÍN [QSA]
LAMASONG alt for LAVATBURA-LAMUSONG [LBV]
LAMASONG dial of LAMUSONG dial of
    LAVATBURA-LAMUSONG [LBV]
LAMBA [LAB] lang, Zambia, Zaïre
LAMBA alt for LAMA [LAS]
LAMBA dial of LAMBA [LAB]
LAMBADI alt for LAMANI [LMN]
LAMBARA alt for LAMANI [LMN]
LAMBAU dial of SIANE [SNP]
LAMBI alt for BAROMBI [BBI]
LAMBIA alt for LAMBYA [LAI]
LAMBON alt for SIAR [SJR]
LAMBONG alt for KAALONG dial of BAFIA [KSF]
LAMBOYA [LMY] lang, Indonesia, Nusa Tenggara
LAMBOYA dial of LAMBOYA [LMY]
LAMBU alt for RAMPI dial of RAMPI [LJE]
LAMBUMBU alt for VINMAVIS [VNM]
LAMBUNAO dial of KINARAY-A [KRJ]
LAMBWA alt for LAMBYA [LAI]

LAMBWE dial of CHOPI [CCE]
LAMBYA [LAI] lang, Tanzania, Malawi
LAME [BMA] lang, Nigeria
LAMÉ alt for PEVÉ [LME]
LAMENU [LMU] lang, Vanuatu
LAMERTIVIRI alt for KAMVIRI [QMV]
LAMET [LBN] lang, Laos, Thailand, Thailand
LAMET alt for LAMET [LBN]
LAMETIN [LMB] lang, Vanuatu
LAMGANG alt for LAMKANG [LMK]
LAMINUSA dial of SAMA, SOUTHERN [SIT]
LAMINUSA SINAMA alt for LAMINUSA dial of
SAMA, SOUTHERN [SIT]
LAMISTA alt for QUECHUA, SAN MARTÍN [QSA]
LAMISTO alt for QUECHUA, SAN MARTÍN [QSA]
LAMJA [LDH] lang, Nigeria
LAMJUNG alt for GURUNG, EASTERN [GGN]
LAMKANG [LMK] lang, India
LAMMA [LEV] lang, Indonesia, Nusa Tenggara
LAMNSO' [NSO] lang, Cameroon
LAMNSOK alt for LAMNSO' [NSO]
LAMOGAI [LMG] lang, Papua New Guinea
LAMPONG alt for LAMPUNG [LJP]
LAMPUNG [LJP] lang, Indonesia, Sumatra
LAMPUNG alt for BAKOI dial of LAWANGAN [LBX]
LAMSO alt for LAMNSO' [NSO]
LAMSSA alt for SIAR [SJR]
LAMTI alt for LAMUTI dial of KALAMI [GWC]
LAMU-LAMU [LBY] lang, Australia
LAMUD dial of QUECHUA, CHACHAPOYAS [QUK]
LAMULAMUL alt for LAMU-LAMU [LBY]
LAMUNKHIN dial of EVEN [EVE]
LAMUSONG dial of LAVATBURA-LAMUSONG [LBV]
LAMUT alt for EVEN [EVE]
LAMUTI dial of KALAMI [GWC]
LAMZANG dial of CHIN, TEDIM [CTD]
LAN NA alt for TAI, NORTHERN [NOD]
LAN TEN alt for MUN [MJI]
LAN TIN alt for MUN [MJI]
LANAN alt for LAHANAN [LHN]
LANAPSUA alt for SANAPANÁ [SAP]
LANATAI alt for TAI, NORTHERN [NOD]
LAND BAJAW alt for BAJAU, WEST COAST [BDR]
LANDA alt for BELANDA dial of TEMUAN [TMW]
LANDAIS dial of GASCON [GSC]
LANDAWE dial of TULAMBATU [MFG]
LANDIKMA dial of NIPSAN [YAC]
LANDOGO alt for LOKO [LOK]
LANDOMA [LAO] lang, Guinea
LANDOUMAN alt for LANDOMA [LAO]
LANDSMAL alt for NORWEGIAN, NYNORSK [NRN]
LANDU alt for BIATAH [BTH]
LANDU alt for LANDU-RINGGOU-OEPAO dial of ROTI
[ROT]
LANDU-RINGGOU-OEPAO dial of ROTI [ROT]
LANDUMA alt for LANDOMA [LAO]
LANG alt for MARU [MHX]
LANG alt for GHOMALA NORTH dial of GHOMALA'
[BBJ]
LANGA alt for SHITA [LGN]
LANGAGE GESTUELLE alt for SWISS SIGN
LANGUAGE [SSR]
LANGALANGA [LGL] lang, Solomon Islands
LANGAM [LNM] lang, Papua New Guinea
LANGANU alt for CHANGANA dial of TSONGA
[TSO]

LANGAS dial of POLCI [POL]
LANGBA [LNL] lang, Central African Republic
LANGBASE alt for LANGBASHE [LNA]
LANGBASHE [LNA] lang, Central African Republic,
Zaïre, Zaïre
LANGBASHE alt for LANGBASHE [LNA]
LANGBASI alt for LANGBASHE [LNA]
LANGBWASSE alt for LANGBASHE [LNA]
LANGDA alt for UNA [MTG]
LANGE alt for BURUN [BDI]
LANGGO alt for LANGO [LNO]
LANGI [LAG] lang, Tanzania
LANGILAN dial of MANOBO, MATIGSALUG [MBT]
LANGILANG alt for MANOBO, ATA [ATD]
LANGIMAR alt for ANGAATIHA [AGM]
LANGIUNG dial of CHIN, THADO [TCZ]
LANGKURU-KOLOMANO dial of WOISIKA [WOI]
LANGO [LNO] lang, Sudan
LANGO [LAJ] lang, Uganda
LANGO alt for DIDINGA [DID]
LANGO PARDHI alt for PARDHI [PCL]
LANGOAN dial of TONTEMBOAN [TNT]
LANGRONG dial of AIMOL [AIM]
LANGSHIN dial of NAGA, TASE [NST]
LANGUDA alt for LONGUDA [LNU]
LANGUE DES SIGNES FRANÇAISE alt for FRENCH
SIGN LANGUAGE [FSL]
LANGUE DES SIGNES QUÉBÉCOISE alt for FRENCH
CANADIAN SIGN LANGUAGE [FCS]
LANGUEDOC alt for LANGUEDOCIEN [LNC]
LANGUEDOCIEN [LNC] lang, France
LANGUEDOCIEN MOYEN dial of LANGUEDOCIEN
[LNC]
LANGULO alt for SANYE [SSN]
LANGUS alt for KALA LAGAW YA [MWP]
LANGWA dial of ATSI [ATB]
LANGWASI alt for LANGBASHE [LNA]
LANGYA alt for TAKUA [TKZ]
LANI alt for DANI, WESTERN [DNW]
LANJODA dial of MURIA, EASTERN [EMU]
LANJUNG alt for GURUNG, EASTERN [GGN]
LANKA KOL alt for HO [HOC]
LANKATERE dial of HANGA [HAG]
LANKAVIRI dial of MUMUYE [MUL]
LANNA alt for TAI, NORTHERN [NOD]
LANNATAI alt for TAI, NORTHERN [NOD]
LANOH [LNH] lang, Malaysia, Peninsular
LANOH KOBAK dial of TEMIAR [TMH]
LANOON alt for ILANUN [ILL]
LANSU alt for MARU [MHX]
LANTANAI [LNI] lang, Papua New Guinea
LANTEN alt for MUN [MJI]
LANTIN alt for MUN [MJI]
LANTOI dial of KAIMBULAWA [ZKA]
LANUN alt for ILANUN [ILL]
LANUN alt for LAHANAN [LHN]
LANZOG alt for PIU [PIX]
LAO [NOL] lang, Laos, Cambodia
LÀO alt for LAO [NOL]
LAO alt for GELO [KKF]
LAO HABE alt for LAKA [LAK]
LAO KAO alt for LAO [NOL]
LAO MUH alt for PUOC [PUO]
LAO PHUAN alt for PHUAN [PHU]
LAO SONG alt for SONG [SOA]
LAO SONG DAM alt for SONG [SOA]

LAO TERNG alt for KHMU [KJG]
LAO WIANG alt for LAO [NOL]
LAO-KAO dial of LAO [NOL]
LAO-KHRANG dial of LAO [NOL]
LAO-LUM alt for LAO [NOL]
LAO-NOI alt for LAO [NOL]
LAOPA alt for LAOPANG [LBG]
LAOPANG [LBG] lang, Myanmar, China
LAOTIAN alt for LAO [NOL]
LAOTIAN TAI alt for LAO [NOL]
LAPALAMA 1 dial of ENGA [ENQ]
LAPALAMA 2 dial of ENGA [ENQ]
LAPCHE alt for LEPCHA [LEP]
"LAPP" alt for SAAMI, PITE [LPB]
"LAPP" alt for SAAMI, SOUTHERN [LPC]
"LAPP" alt for SAAMI, KILDIN [LPD]
"LAPP" alt for SAAMI, INARI [LPI]
"LAPP" alt for SAAMI, SKOLT [LPK]
"LAPP" alt for SAAMI, LULE [LPL]
"LAPP" alt for SAAMI, NORTHERN [LPR]
"LAPP" alt for SAAMI, TER [LPT]
"LAPP" alt for SAAMI, UME [LPU]
LAPUYEN alt for SUBANUN, LAPUYAN [LAA]
LAQI alt for ZWAY [ZWA]
LAQUA [LAQ] lang, Viet Nam, China
LARA' [LRA] lang, Indonesia, Kalimantan, Malaysia,
    Sarawak, Malaysia, Sarawak
LARA' alt for LARA' [LRA]
LARAGIA [LRG] lang, Australia
LARAGIYA alt for LARAGIA [LRG]
LARAKIA alt for LARAGIA [LRG]
LARAKIYA alt for LARAGIA [LRG]
LARAMANIK alt for ARAMANIK [AAM]
LARANCHI alt for LARU [LAN]
LARANTUKA dial of MALAY [MLI]
LARAOS dial of QUECHUA, YAUYOS [QUX]
LARAT alt for FORDATA [FRD]
LARAT dial of FORDATA [FRD]
LARAT-FORDATA alt for LARAT dial of FORDATA
    [FRD]
LARAT-FORDATA II alt for FORDATA dial of
    FORDATA [FRD]
LARAVAT alt for LAREVAT [LRV]
LARAWA alt for LARU [LAN]
LARDIL [LBZ] lang, Australia
LARDILL alt for LARDIL [LBZ]
LARE dial of KANURI, YERWA [KPH]
LARE dial of KANURI, YERWA [KPH]
LARESTANI alt for LARI [LRL]
LAREVAT [LRV] lang, Vanuatu
LARI [LRL] lang, Iran
LARI dial of SINDHI [SND]
LARI alt for LAADI dial of KONGO [KON]
LARIA alt for CHATTISGARHI [HNE]
LARIANG alt for KULU dial of SARUDU [SDU]
LARIKE dial of LARIKE-WAKASIHU [ALO]
LARIKE-WAKASIHU [ALO] lang, Indonesia, Maluku
LARIM alt for LONGARIM [LOH]
LARIMINIT alt for LONGARIM [LOH]
LARKYE alt for KUTANG BHOTIA [KTE]
LARO [LRO] lang, Sudan
LARO alt for LARU [LAN]
LARO alt for ROCKY PEAK [ROK]
LARTEH alt for LATE dial of GUA [LAR]
LARTEH-CHEREPON-ANUM-BOSO alt for GUA [LAR]
LARU [LAN] lang, Nigeria

LARU alt for LARO [LRO]
LASALIMU [LLM] lang, Indonesia, Sulawesi
LASHI [LSI] lang, Myanmar, China
LASHI-MARU alt for LASHI [LSI]
LASHX dial of SVAN [SVA]
LASI [LSS] lang, Pakistan
LASI alt for LASHI [LSI]
LASI dial of SINDHI [SND]
LASSA dial of MARGHI CENTRAL [MAR]
LASSI alt for LASI [LSS]
LAT alt for LAC dial of KOHO [KPM]
LATAGNUN alt for RATAGNON [BTN]
LATAN alt for RATAGNON [BTN]
LATANI CHINANTECO alt for CHINANTECO,
    LEALAO [CLE]
LATAR dial of MUNDARI [MUW]
LATE dial of GUA [LAR]
LATEP [LTP] lang, Papua New Guinea
LATGALIAN alt for EAST LATVIAN dial of LATVIAN
    [LAT]
LATI [LBT] lang, Viet Nam, China
LATI, WHITE [LWH] lang, Viet Nam
LATIN [LTN] lang, Vatican State
LATIN ANAUNICO dial of LOMBARD [LMO]
LATIN FIAMAZZO dial of LOMBARD [LMO]
LATOD alt for LOTUD [DTR]
LATOMA [LTM] lang, Papua New Guinea
LATOOKA alt for OTUHO [LOT]
LATTUKA alt for OTUHO [LOT]
LATU [LTU] lang, Indonesia, Maluku
LATUD alt for LOTUD [DTR]
LATUKA alt for OTUHO [LOT]
LATUKO alt for OTUHO [LOT]
LATUNDÊ alt for YALAPMUNXTE dial of
    NAMBIKUÁRA, NORTHERN [MBG]
LATUVI ZAPOTECO alt for ZAPOTECO,
    SOUTHEASTERN IXTLÁN [ZPD]
LATVIAN [LAT] lang, Latvia, Germany, Sweden
LATVIAN alt for LATVIAN [LAT]
LATVIAN ROMANI dial of ROMANI, BALTIC [ROM]
LATVIAN SIGN LANGUAGE [LSL] lang, Latvia
LAU [LLU] lang, Solomon Islands
LAU alt for LAKA [LAK]
LAU alt for LAUAN [LLX]
LAU dial of DINKA, SOUTHWESTERN [DIK]
LAU dial of LAU [LLU]
LAU dial of LAUAN [LLX]
LAU alt for LOU dial of NUER [NUS]
LAU'U alt for ARUOP [LSR]
LAUA [LUF] lang, Papua New Guinea
LAUAN [LLX] lang, Fiji
LAUBE alt for LAVUKALEVE [LVK]
LAUDA alt for LOWUDO dial of OTUHO [LOT]
LAUDJE alt for LAUJE [LAW]
LAUISARANGA alt for ARUOP [LSR]
LAUJE [LAW] lang, Indonesia, Sulawesi
LAUKANU alt for KELA [KCL]
LAULABU alt for YABEM [JAE]
LAULI dial of WEYEWA [WEW]
LAUMBE alt for LAVUKALEVE [LVK]
LAUNA alt for LAHU [LAH]
LAUNGAW alt for MARU [MHX]
LAUNGWAW alt for MARU [MHX]
LAURA dial of WEYEWA [WEW]
LAURENTIAN [LRE] lang, Canada
LAUROWAN dial of PASHAYI, NORTHWEST [GLH]

LAUWELA dial of BWAIDOKA [BWD]
LAVA alt for LAWA, WESTERN [LCP]
LAVANGAI alt for TUNGAG [LCM]
LAVANI alt for LAMANI [LMN]
LAVATBURA dial of LAVATBURA-LAMUSONG [LBV]
LAVATBURA-LAMUSONG [LBV] lang, Papua New
   Guinea
LAVE alt for BRAO [BRB]
LAVEH alt for BRAO [BRB]
LAVEN [LBO] lang, Laos, USA
LAVIAM dial of TAUPOTA [TPA]
LAVONGAI alt for TUNGAG [LCM]
LAVUA alt for LAWA, WESTERN [LCP]
LAVŪA alt for LAWA, WESTERN [LCP]
LAVUKALEVE [LVK] lang, Solomon Islands
LAWA alt for UGONG [UGO]
LAWA alt for NYAHKUR [CBN]
LAWA dial of LAWANGAN [LBX]
LAWA, EASTERN [LWL] lang, Thailand
LAWA, WESTERN [LCP] lang, China, Thailand,
   Thailand
LAWA, WESTERN alt for LAWA, WESTERN [LCP]
LAWANGAN [LBX] lang, Indonesia, Kalimantan
LAWAS alt for TRUSAN dial of LUNDAYEH [LND]
LAWEENJRU alt for LAVEN [LBO]
LAWELE alt for KALENDE dial of PANCANA [PNP]
LAWNG alt for MARU [MHX]
LAWNG HSU dial of MARU [MHX]
LAWO dial of NAMIA [NNM]
LAWOI alt for URAK LAWOI' [URK]
LAWRA LOBI alt for NURA dial of DAGAARI,
   NORTHERN [DGI]
LAWTA alt for URAK LAWOI' [URK]
LAY alt for KABALAI [KVF]
LAY alt for LAI dial of GBAYA [GYA]
LAYA dial of MAGINDANAON [MDH]
LAYA dial of KOHO [KPM]
LAYA LINGZHI dial of DZONGKHA [DZO]
LAYANA dial of GUANA [GVA]
LAYAPO dial of ENGA [ENQ]
LAYDO dial of AARI [AIZ]
LAYIPING dial of HMONG, NORTHERN [MUQ]
LAYOLO alt for LAIYOLO [LJI]
LAZ [LZZ] lang, Turkey, Georgia
LAZE alt for LAZ [LZZ]
LAZEMI dial of NAGA, SEMA [NSM]
LAZIALE dial of ITALIAN [ITN]
LDES alt for EL MOLO [ELO]
LE alt for LUSHAI [LSH]
LE alt for HLAI [LIC]
LEANGBA alt for NGELIMA [AGH]
LEB-LANO alt for LANGO [LAJ]
LEBANESE-CENTRAL SYRIAN dial of ARABIC,
   LEVANTINE [APC]
LEBANG dial of TEWA [TWE]
LEBATI dial of LUGBARA, LOW [LUC]
LEBEI alt for LEVEI dial of LEVEI-NDREHET [TLX]
LEBEJ alt for LEVEI dial of LEVEI-NDREHET [TLX]
LEBIR dial of BISSA [BIB]
LEBIR dial of BISSA [BIB]
LEBONG dial of REJANG [REJ]
LEBONI alt for RAMPI [LJE]
LEBORO alt for BURU dial of NGELIMA [AGH]
LEBORO alt for BURU dial of NGOMBE [NGC]
LEBOU dial of WOLOF [WOL]
LEBOU dial of WOLOF [WOL]

LEBU dial of MORO [MOR]
LEBU alt for LABU dial of MALAY [MLI]
LEBU alt for LEBOU dial of WOLOF [WOL]
LECHI alt for LASHI [LSI]
LECHKHUM alt for LEXCHXUM dial of GEORGIAN
   [GEO]
LECO [LEC] lang, Bolivia
LEDO alt for KAILI, LEDO [LEW]
LEDO dial of KAILI, LEDO [LEW]
LEE alt for DJINGILI [JIG]
LEEALOWA alt for ALAWA [ALH]
LEEANUWA alt for YANYUWA [JAO]
LEEARRAWA alt for GARAWA [GBC]
LEELALWARRA alt for MARA [MEC]
LEELAU [LDK] lang, Nigeria
LEELAWARRA alt for MARA [MEC]
LEELU dial of KOMA [KMY]
LEEM dial of TA'OIH, UPPER [TTH]
LEEMAK alt for MAK [PBL]
LEEMO alt for HADIYYA [HDY]
LEEWAKYA alt for WAGAYA [WGA]
LEFA' alt for BAFIA [KSF]
LEFANA alt for LELEMI [LEF]
LEGA-MWENGA [LGM] lang, Zaïre
LEGA-SHABUNDA [LEA] lang, Zaïre
LEGASPI dial of BICOLANO, CENTRAL [BKL]
LEGBA alt for LUKPA [DOP]
LEGBO [AGB] lang, Nigeria
LEGENYEM [LCC] lang, Indonesia, Irian Jaya
LEGERI dial of KWANKA [BIJ]
LEGO alt for SAMBA LEKO [NDI]
LEGO alt for SAMBA LEKO dial of SAMBA LEKO
   [NDI]
LEH dial of LADAKHI [LBJ]
LEHALI [TQL] lang, Vanuatu
LEHALURUP [URR] lang, Vanuatu
LEHAR [CAE] lang, Senegal
LEI alt for NORTHERN KONO dial of KONO [KNO]
LEIK alt for THIANG dial of NUER [NUS]
LEILEIAFA dial of SUAU [SWP]
LEINSTER dial of GAELIC, IRISH [GLI]
LEIPON [LEK] lang, Papua New Guinea
LEISU alt for LISU [LIS]
LEKANINGI alt for KANINGI [KZO]
LEKE dial of KAREN, PWO [PWO]
LEKE dial of KAREN, PWO OMKOI [PWW]
LEKI dial of LURI [LRI]
LEKI dial of LURI [LRI]
LEKO alt for SAMBA LEKO [NDI]
LEKO alt for ILIKU dial of LUSENGO [LUS]
LEKO alt for SAMBA LEKO dial of SAMBA LEKO
   [NDI]
LEKON alt for SAMBA LEKO [NDI]
LEKON dial of SIKULE [SKH]
LEKON alt for SAMBA LEKO dial of SAMBA LEKO
   [NDI]
LEKONGO alt for NKONGHO dial of MBO [MBO]
LEKU alt for ILIKU dial of LUSENGO [LUS]
LEKWHAN alt for PAZEH [PZH]
LEL alt for NISI [DAP]
LELA [DRI] lang, Nigeria
LELA alt for KASEM [KAS]
LELAIN alt for DENGKA-LELAIN dial of ROTI [ROT]
LELAK [LLK] lang, Malaysia, Sarawak
LELAK dial of LELAK [LLK]
LELAU alt for LEELAU [LDK]

LELE [UGA] lang, Papua New Guinea
LELE [LEL] lang, Zaïre
LELE [LLN] lang, Chad
LELE alt for LYÉLÉ [LEE]
LELE dial of MANINKA [MNI]
LELE HAI alt for LELE [UGA]
LELEHUDI dial of TAWALA [TBO]
LELEMI [LEF] lang, Ghana
LELENUK alt for BILBA-DIU-LELENUK dial of ROTI
   [ROT]
LELEPA dial of EFATE, NORTH [LLP]
LELET alt for MADAK [MMX]
LELET dial of MADAK [MMX]
LELIALI dial of KAYELI [KZL]
LELU-TAFUNSAK dial of KUSAIE [KSI]
LEM alt for DEM [DEM]
LEM alt for SASAR dial of VATRATA [VLR]
LEMADI alt for LAMANI [LMN]
LEMAKOT alt for KARA [LEU]
LEMANAK dial of IBAN [IBA]
LEMANDE alt for NOMAANDE [LEM]
LEMANTANG alt for LEMATANG [LMT]
LEMATANG [LMT] lang, Indonesia, Sumatra
LEMBA alt for MALIMBA [MZD]
LEMBA alt for KELA [KEL]
LEMBAAMBA alt for MBAMA [MBM]
LEMBAK [LIW] lang, Indonesia, Sumatra
LEMBAK BLITI dial of LEMBAK [LIW]
LEMBAK SINDANG dial of LEMBAK [LIW]
LEMBENA [LEQ] lang, Papua New Guinea
LEMBUE dial of BEMBA [BEM]
LEMBUR dial of WOISIKA [WOI]
LEMENA dial of KAYAN, REJANG [REE]
LEMET alt for LAMET [LBN]
LEMIO [LEI] lang, Papua New Guinea
LEMITING dial of KIPUT [KYI]
LEMMA alt for LAMMA [LEV]
LEMOI alt for MOI [MOW]
LEMOLANG [LEY] lang, Indonesia, Sulawesi
LEMORO [LDJ] lang, Nigeria
LEMOSIN alt for LIMOUSIN [LMS]
LEMUSMUS alt for KARA [LEU]
LEMYO dial of CHIN, ASHO [CSH]
LENAKEL [TNL] lang, Vanuatu
LENAPE alt for UNAMI [DEL]
LENCA [LEN] lang, Honduras, El Salvador
LENDU [LED] lang, Zaïre
LENDU-SUD alt for NGITI [NIY]
LENDUMU alt for NDUMU [NMD]
LENGADOUCIAN alt for LANGUEDOCIEN [LNC]
LENGE alt for LENGUE dial of CHOPI [CCE]
LENGI alt for LENJE [LEH]
LENGILU [LGI] lang, Indonesia, Kalimantan
LENGKAYAP dial of MALAY [MLI]
LENGO [LGR] lang, Solomon Islands
LENGO dial of LENGO [LGR]
LENGOLA [LEJ] lang, Zaïre
LENGORA alt for LENGOLA [LEJ]
LENGUA [LEG] lang, Paraguay
LENGUA alt for PALENQUERO [PLN]
LENGUA NORTE alt for NORTHERN LENGUA dial of
   LENGUA [LEG]
LENGUA SUR alt for SOUTHERN LENGUA dial of
   LENGUA [LEG]
LENGUAJE DE SEÑAS MEXICANAS alt for MEXICAN
   SIGN LANGUAGE [MFS]

LENGUE dial of CHOPI [CCE]
LENGWE alt for HLENGWE dial of TSWA [TSC]
LENIDI-PRASTOS dial of TSAKONIAN [TSD]
LENINGITIJ [LNJ] lang, Australia
LENJE [LEH] lang, Zambia
LENJE dial of LENJE [LEH]
LENKAITAHE alt for SALAS [SGU]
LENKAU [LER] lang, Papua New Guinea
LENKORAN dial of TALYSH [TLY]
LENKORAN dial of AZERBAIJANI, NORTH [AZE]
LENNI-LENAPE alt for UNAMI [DEL]
LENTE dial of CHIN, FALAM [HBH]
LENTEX dial of SVAN [SVA]
LENYIMA [LDG] lang, Nigeria
LEON dial of VATRATA [VLR]
LEONAIS dial of BRETON [BRT]
LEONESE dial of SPANISH [SPN]
LEPCHA [LEP] lang, India, Bhutan, Nepal
LEPCHA alt for LEPCHA [LEP]
LEPO TAU KENYA alt for MADANG [MQD]
LEPO TAU KENYAH alt for MADANG [MQD]
LEPO' KULIT dial of KENYAH, KELINYAU [XKL]
LEPOHA alt for LEPCHA [LEP]
LEPU POTONG dial of LUNDAYEH [LND]
LEPU POTONG dial of KELABIT [KZI]
LEQI alt for LASHI [LSI]
LERA alt for HUTU dial of RWANDA [RUA]
LERE alt for LARE dial of KANURI, YERWA [KPH]
LERIK dial of TALYSH [TLY]
LERON dial of WANTOAT [WNC]
LESA alt for SAKATA [SAT]
LESA alt for LESE [LES]
LESA dial of BENGGOI [BGY]
LESE [LES] lang, Zaïre
LESE DESE alt for NDESE dial of LESE [LES]
LESE KARO dial of LESE [LES]
LESHUOOPA alt for LISU [LIS]
LESIGHU alt for SIGHU [SXE]
LESING dial of LESING-ATUI [LET]
LESING-ATUI [LET] lang, Papua New Guinea
LESSE alt for LESE [LES]
LESSER ANTILLEAN CREOLE ENGLISH [VIB] lang,
   Trinidad and Tobago, Anguilla, Antigua, British
   Virgin Islands, British West Indies, Grenada, St.
   Kitts-Nevis, St. Vincent and the Grenadines, U.S.
   Virgin Islands
LESSER ANTILLEAN CREOLE ENGLISH alt for
   LESSER ANTILLEAN CREOLE ENGLISH [VIB]
LESSER ANTILLEAN CREOLE FRENCH [DOM] lang,
   St. Lucia, Dominica, Grenada, Guadeloupe,
   Martinique
LESSER KABARDIAN dial of KABARDIAN [KAB]
LESSER KABYLE dial of KABYLE [KYL]
LESUO alt for LISU [LIS]
LETE alt for LATE dial of GUA [LAR]
LETEMBOI [NMS] lang, Vanuatu
LETI [LTI] lang, Indonesia, Maluku
LETI [LEO] lang, Cameroon
LETRI LGONA alt for LUANG [LEX]
LETSI alt for LASHI [LSI]
LETTA-BATULAPPA-KASSA alt for PATTINJO dial of
   ENREKANG [PTT]
"LETTISH" alt for LATVIAN [LAT]
LETTISH ROMANI alt for LATVIAN ROMANI dial of
   ROMANI, BALTIC [ROM]
LETUAMA alt for TANIMUCA-RETUARÃ [TNC]

LETUHAMA alt for TANIMUCA-RETUARĂ [TNC]
LÊTZBURGESCH alt for LUXEMBOURGEOIS [LUX]
LETZBURGISCH alt for LUXEMBOURGEOIS [LUX]
LÊTZEBURGESCH alt for LUXEMBOURGEOIS [LUX]
LEU alt for LEUN [LLE]
LEUANGIUA alt for ONTONG JAVA [LUN]
LEUN [LLE] lang, Laos
LEUNG alt for LEUN [LLE]
LEVANT alt for ARABIC, LEVANTINE [APC]
LEVEI alt for LEVEI-NDREHET [TLX]
LEVEI dial of LEVEI-NDREHET [TLX]
LEVEI-NDREHET [TLX] lang, Papua New Guinea
LEW dial of MOSI [MSE]
LEWA dial of SUMBA [SMI]
LEWADA alt for LEWADA-DEWARA [LWD]
LEWADA dial of LEWADA-DEWARA [LWD]
LEWADA-DEWARA [LWD] lang, Papua New Guinea
LEWADA-DEWARA dial of TIRIO [TCR]
LEWO [LWW] lang, Vanuatu
LEWO alt for LAMENU [LMU]
LEWOLAGA alt for SOUTH LAMAHOLOT dial of
    LAMAHOLOT [SLP]
LEWOTOBI alt for SOUTH LAMAHOLOT dial of
    LAMAHOLOT [SLP]
LEXCHXUM dial of GEORGIAN [GEO]
LEYA dial of TONGA [TOI]
LEYIGHA [AYI] lang, Nigeria
LEYTE dial of CEBUANO [CEB]
LEZGHI alt for LEZGI [LEZ]
LEZGI [LEZ] lang, Russia, Europe, Azerbaijan
LEZGIAN alt for LEZGI [LEZ]
LEZGIN alt for LEZGI [LEZ]
LGALIGE alt for KOALIB [KIB]
LGONA alt for LUANG [LEX]
LHASA alt for TIBETAN [TIC]
LHENGWE alt for HLENGWE dial of TSWA [TSC]
LHO-PA alt for LHOBA [LON]
LHOBA [LON] lang, India, China
LHOKA alt for DZONGKHA [DZO]
LHOKE alt for DZONGKHA [DZO]
LHOKET alt for LHOMI [LHM]
LHOMI [LHM] lang, Nepal, China, India
LHOSKAD alt for DZONGKHA [DZO]
LHOTA alt for NAGA, LOTHA [NJH]
LI alt for HLAI [LIC]
LI alt for LISU [LIS]
LI alt for MUNGAKA [MHK]
LI EMTEBAN alt for FOGI dial of BURU [MHS]
LI ENYOROT alt for LISELA [LCL]
LI-HSAW alt for LISU [LIS]
LI-KARI-LI alt for KARI [KBJ]
LI-LI-SHA alt for PAIWAN [PWN]
LI-SHAW alt for LISU [LIS]
LIABUKU [LIX] lang, Indonesia, Sulawesi
LIAE dial of SAWU [HVN]
LIAH BING dial of MODANG [MXD]
LIAMBATA alt for SALAS [SGU]
LIAMBATA-KOBI alt for LIANA-SETI [STE]
LIANA alt for LIANA-SETI [STE]
LIANA-SETI [STE] lang, Indonesia, Maluku
LIANAN alt for LIANA-SETI [STE]
LIANG dial of TULEHU [TLU]
LIANGMAI alt for NAGA, LIANGMAI [NJN]
LIANGMEI alt for NAGA, LIANGMAI [NJN]
LIANHUA dial of SHE [SHX]
LIANSHAN dial of ZHUANG, NORTHERN [CCX]

LIAODONG dial of CHINESE, MANDARIN [CHN]
LIARA alt for LIVARA dial of SAKAO [SKU]
LIARO dial of KISSI, SOUTHERN [KSS]
LIARO dial of KISSI, NORTHERN [KQS]
LIAS dial of BONTOC, EASTERN [BKB]
LIBAALI alt for BALI [BCP]
LIBBO alt for LIBO [LDL]
LIBBUNG dial of KELABIT [KZI]
LIBENGE alt for BWA [BWW]
LIBERIAN ENGLISH [LIR] lang, Liberia
LIBERIAN PIDGIN ENGLISH alt for LIBERIAN
    ENGLISH [LIR]
LIBERIAN STANDARD ENGLISH dial of ENGLISH
    [ENG]
LIBIDO [LIQ] lang, Ethiopia
LIBIE alt for ELIP [EKM]
LIBINDJA alt for BINJA dial of NGOMBE [NGC]
LIBINJA alt for LIBINZA [LIZ]
LIBINJA alt for BINJA dial of NGOMBE [NGC]
LIBINZA [LIZ] lang, Zaïre
LIBISEGAHUN dial of LOKO [LOK]
LIBO [LDL] lang, Nigeria
LIBOLO alt for BOLO [BLV]
LIBOMBI dial of BILA [BIP]
LIBON dial of BICOLANO, ALBAY [BHK]
LIBUA alt for BWA [BWW]
LIBWALI alt for BWA [BWW]
LIBYAN COLLOQUIAL ARABIC alt for ARABIC,
    LIBYAN [AYL]
LICELA alt for LISELA dial of LISELA [LCL]
LICELLA alt for LISELA dial of LISELA [LCL]
LICHABOOL-NALONG dial of KONKOMBA [KOS]
LIDUMA alt for DUMA [DMA]
LIEM CHAU alt for CHINESE, YUE [YUH]
LIET ENJOROT alt for LISELA [LCL]
LIFOMA alt for FOMA [FOM]
LIFOU alt for DEHU [DEU]
LIFU alt for DEHU [DEU]
LIGBELN dial of KONKOMBA [KOS]
LIGBI [LIG] lang, Ghana, Burkina Faso, Côte d'Ivoire
LIGENZA [LGZ] lang, Zaïre
LIGGO alt for LIGO dial of BARI [BFA]
LIGILI alt for LIJILI [MGI]
LIGO dial of BARI [BFA]
LIGRI dial of JARAWA [JAR]
LIGURE alt for LIGURIAN [LIJ]
LIGURI [LIU] lang, Sudan
LIGURI dial of LIGURI [LIU]
LIGURIAN [LIJ] lang, Italy, France, Monaco
LIGURIAN alt for LIGURIAN [LIJ]
LIGWI alt for LIGBI [LIG]
LIHEN dial of KAMBERATARO [KBV]
LIHIR [LIH] lang, Papua New Guinea
LIJILI [MGI] lang, Nigeria
LIKA [LIK] lang, Zaïre
LIKÁ alt for LILIKÁ dial of LIKA [LIK]
LIKANANTAÍ alt for KUNZA [KUZ]
LIKANGO alt for KANGO [KTY]
LIKANU alt for KANU [KHX]
LIKAW dial of BOMBOMA [BWS]
LIKELO alt for KELE [KHY]
LIKES-UTSIA dial of MANDYAK [MFV]
LIKI alt for SOBEI [SOB]
LIKILA [LIE] lang, Zaïre
LIKÓ alt for LILIKÓ dial of LIKA [LIK]
LIKOKA dial of LOBALA [LOQ]

LIKOLO dial of POKE [POF]
LIKOONLI dial of KONKOMBA [KOS]
LIKOUALA alt for LIKWALA [KWC]
LIKPAKPALN alt for KONKOMBA [KOS]
LIKPE alt for SEKPELE [LIP]
LIKUBA [KXX] lang, Congo
LIKUM [LIB] lang, Papua New Guinea
LIKUPANG dial of TONSEA [TXS]
LIKWALA [KWC] lang, Congo
LILA dial of LELA [DRI]
LILAU [LLL] lang, Papua New Guinea
LILIALI alt for LELIALI dial of KAYELI [KZL]
LILIGA dial of LEGA-SHABUNDA [LEA]
LILIKÁ dial of LIKA [LIK]
LILIKÓ dial of LIKA [LIK]
LILIMA dial of KALANGA [KCK]
LILIMA dial of KALANGA [KCK]
LILLOOET [LIL] lang, Canada
LILSE alt for KURUMFÉ [KFZ]
LIMA dial of LAMBA [LAB]
LIMA alt for NEGERI LIMA dial of ASILULU [ASL]
LIMARAHING dial of BLAGAR [BEU]
LIMBA alt for MALIMBA [MZD]
LIMBA alt for IWAIDJA [IBD]
LIMBA, EAST [LMA] lang, Guinea, Sierra Leone
LIMBA, EAST alt for LIMBA, EAST [LMA]
LIMBA, WEST-CENTRAL [LIA] lang, Sierra Leone
LIMBANG alt for TRUSAN dial of LUNDAYEH [LND]
LIMBEDE alt for MBERE [MDT]
LIMBO alt for LIMBU [LIF]
LIMBOM alt for LIMBUM [LIM]
LIMBOTO [LJO] lang, Indonesia, Sulawesi
LIMBOTTO alt for LIMBOTO [LJO]
LIMBU [LIF] lang, Nepal, India
LIMBUDZA alt for BUDZA [BJA]
LIMBUM [LIM] lang, Cameroon
LIMBUR alt for LEMBUR dial of WOISIKA [WOI]
LIMBURGISCH alt for LOW FRANCONIAN dial of
    GERMAN, LOW [GEP]
LIMERA alt for ILIUN [ILU]
LIMI alt for NYATURU [RIM]
LIMILNGAN [LMC] lang, Australia
LIMIMA alt for LILIMA dial of KALANGA [KCK]
LIMKOW alt for LINGAO [ONB]
LIMÓN CREOLE dial of WESTERN CARIBBEAN
    CREOLE ENGLISH [JAM]
LIMONKPEL dial of KONKOMBA [KOS]
LIMORO alt for LEMORO [LDJ]
LIMORRO alt for LEMORO [LDJ]
LIMOS-LIWAN KALINGA alt for KALINGA, LIMOS
    [KMK]
LIMOUSIN [LMS] lang, France
LIMPESA dial of LUSENGO [LUS]
LINAFIEL dial of KONKOMBA [KOS]
LINANGMANLI dial of NTCHAM [BUD]
LINAW-QAUQAUL dial of BASAY [BYQ]
LINCHA alt for TANA-LINCHA dial of QUECHUA,
    YAUYOS [QUX]
LINDA [LIY] lang, Central African Republic
LINDAU alt for NYINDROU [LID]
LINDIRI alt for NUNGU [RIN]
LINDJA dial of SHI [SHR]
LINDROU alt for NYINDROU [LID]
LINDU [KLW] lang, Indonesia, Sulawesi
LINDUAN alt for LINDU [KLW]
LING-CHUN alt for LINGYUN dial of MIEN [YOC]

LINGAAYAT dial of GOWLI [GOK]
LINGALA [LIN] lang, Zaïre, Congo
LINGAO [ONB] lang, China
LINGARAK [LGK] lang, Vanuatu
LINGBE alt for NGBEE [NBL]
LINGBEE alt for NGBEE [NBL]
LINGGAU alt for LEMBAK [LIW]
LINGI alt for BWELA [BWL]
LINGKABAU SUGUT dial of TOMBONUWO [TXA]
LINGOMBE alt for NGOMBE [NGC]
LINGONDA dial of BOMBOMA [BWS]
LINGOTES alt for ILONGOT [ILK]
LÍNGUA GERAL alt for NHENGATU [YRL]
LINGUA GESTUAL PORTUGUESA alt for
    PORTUGUESE SIGN LANGUAGE [PSR]
LINGUA ITALIANA DEI SEGNI alt for ITALIAN SIGN
    LANGUAGE [ISE]
LINGYUN dial of MIEN [YOC]
LINKABAU alt for LINGKABAU SUGUT dial of
    TOMBONUWO [TXA]
LINNGITHIG alt for LENINGITIJ [LNJ]
LINNGITHIGH alt for LENINGITIJ [LNJ]
LINO alt for BOMWALI [BMW]
LINTANG [LNT] lang, Indonesia, Sumatra
LINXIA dial of TU [MJG]
LINXIANG dial of CHINESE, XIANG [HSN]
LINYALI alt for NYALI [NLJ]
LINYANGA-LE alt for NYANGA-LI [NYC]
LINYELI alt for PANDE dial of PANDE [BKJ]
LINZELI alt for PANDE dial of PANDE [BKJ]
LIO [LJL] lang, Indonesia, Nusa Tenggara
LIONESE alt for LIO [LJL]
LIP'A alt for LISU [LIS]
LIPANJA dial of MABAALE [MMZ]
LIPE alt for KUNZA [KUZ]
LIPIS dial of SEMAI [SEA]
LIPKAWA alt for MBURKU [BBT]
LIPKAWA alt for KARIYA [KIL]
LIPO [TKL] lang, China
LIPTAAKO alt for FULFULDE, LIPTAAKO [FUO]
LIPUKE dial of LATI [LBT]
LIPULIO alt for LATI [LBT]
LIPULIONGTCO dial of LATI [LBT]
LIPUPI dial of LATI [LBT]
LIPUPŎ alt for LATI, WHITE [LWH]
LIPUTCIO dial of LATI [LBT]
LIPUTE dial of LATI [LBT]
LIPUTIŎ dial of LATI [LBT]
LIR alt for LIHIR [LIH]
LIR TALO alt for TALUR [ILW]
LIRANG dial of TALAUD [TLD]
LIRONG dial of KENYAH, SEBOB [SIB]
LIS alt for ITALIAN SIGN LANGUAGE [ISE]
LIS alt for BAGIRMI [BMI]
LISABATA alt for LISABATA-NUNIALI [LCS]
LISABATA-NUNIALI [LCS] lang, Indonesia, Maluku
LISABATA-TIMUR dial of LISABATA-NUNIALI [LCS]
LISAW alt for LISU [LIS]
LISBON dial of PORTUGUESE SIGN LANGUAGE
    [PSR]
LISELA [LCL] lang, Indonesia, Maluku
LISELA dial of LISELA [LCL]
LISHANA alt for ASSYRIAN [AII]
LISHANIT TARGUM alt for JUDEO-ARAMAIC [TRG]
LISHU alt for LISU [LIS]

LISI alt for KUKA [KUF]
LISI alt for BAGIRMI [BMI]
LISO alt for LISU [LIS]
LISONGO alt for MBATI [MDN]
LISSAM dial of KUTEP [KUB]
LISSI alt for LESE [LES]
LISSONGO alt for MBATI [MDN]
LISSU alt for LISU [LIS]
LISU [LIS] lang, China, Myanmar, Myanmar, Thailand
LISU alt for LISU [LIS]
LISUM dial of KAYAN, REJANG [REE]
LITEMBO alt for TEMBO [TMV]
LITERI LAGONA alt for LUANG [LEX]
LITHIRO alt for TIRA [TIR]
LITHUANIAN [LIT] lang, Lithuania, USA
LITIME dial of AKPOSO [KPO]
LITORO alt for OTORO [OTR]
LITTLE NICOBAR dial of NICOBARESE, SOUTHERN [NIK]
LITZLITZ [LTZ] lang, Vanuatu
LITZLITZ-VISELE alt for LITZLITZ [LTZ]
LIU dial of KOMA [KMY]
LIUCHIANG alt for LIUJIANG dial of ZHUANG, NORTHERN [CCX]
LIUJIANG dial of ZHUANG, NORTHERN [CCX]
LIUTWA dial of POKE [POF]
LIV [LIV] lang, Latvia
LIVANUMA alt for VANUMA [VAU]
LIVARA dial of SAKAO [SKU]
LIVARA dial of EFATE, NORTH [LLP]
LIVE dial of NAGA, LOTHA [NJH]
LIVONIAN alt for LIV [LIV]
LIVUAN dial of TOLAI [KSD]
LIVUNGANEN dial of MANOBO, ILIANEN [MBI]
LIVVIKOVIAN alt for OLONETSIAN [OLO]
LIWULI alt for BOWIRI [BOV]
LIYA GALAWUMIRR dial of DHUWAL [DUJ]
LIYAGAWUMIRR dial of DHUWAL [DUJ]
LIYANG alt for NAGA, LIANGMAI [NJN]
LIYUWA dial of SIMAA [SIE]
LLAGUA alt for YAGUA [YAD]
LLARURO alt for YARURO [YAE]
LLEIDATÀ alt for NORTHWESTERN CATALAN dial of CATALAN [CLN]
LLIMBUMI alt for LIMBUM [LIM]
LLOA dial of HOANYA [HON]
LLOGOLE alt for LOGOOLI [RAG]
LLUGULE alt for LOGOOLI [RAG]
LMAM alt for LAMAM [LMM]
LNGNGAM alt for LYNGNGAM dial of KHASI [KHI]
LO [LDO] lang, Nigeria
LO alt for GURO [GOA]
LO alt for TOGA [LHT]
LO dial of LOPA [LOY]
LO MONTANG alt for LOPA [LOY]
LOA alt for LLOA dial of HOANYA [HON]
LOANATIT dial of LENAKEL [TNL]
LOANDE alt for MBUNDU, LOANDA [MLO]
LOBA alt for LOPA [LOY]
LOBAHA alt for LOMBAHA dial of AMBAE, EAST [OMB]
LOBALA [LOQ] lang, Zaïre, Congo
LOBAT alt for BEJA [BEI]
LOBEDU dial of SOTHO, NORTHERN [SRT]
LOBER dial of DAGAARI, NORTHERN [DGI]
LOBI [LOB] lang, Burkina Faso, Côte d'Ivoire, Côte

d'Ivoire
LOBI alt for LOBI [LOB]
LOBIRI alt for LOBI [LOB]
LOBO dial of MABAALE [MMZ]
LOBOBANGI alt for BANGI [BNI]
LOBODA dial of DOBU [DOB]
LOBR alt for LOBER dial of DAGAARI, NORTHERN [DGI]
LOBU alt for TOMBONUWO [TXA]
LOBU dial of LOBU, LANAS [RUU]
LOBU, LANAS [RUU] lang, Malaysia, Sabah
LOBU, TAMPIAS [LOW] lang, Malaysia, Sabah
LOCAL SIGN LANGUAGE alt for PHILIPPINE SIGN LANGUAGE [PSP]
LOCKHART CREOLE alt for TORRES STRAIT CREOLE [TCS]
LOCO alt for MUTÚS [MUF]
LODA alt for LOLODA [LOL]
LODANG dial of SEKO PADANG [SKX]
LODHA alt for LODHI [LBM]
LODHANTI dial of BUNDELI [BNS]
LODHI [LBM] lang, India
LODHI dial of BUNDELI [BNS]
LODI alt for LODHI [LBM]
LOEMBIS alt for ALUMBIS dial of TAGAL MURUT [MVV]
LOEMBIS alt for LUMBIS dial of TAGAL MURUT [MVV]
LOFIT alt for LOPIT [LPX]
LOFUCHAI dial of QIANG [CNG]
LOG dial of BASAA [BAA]
LOG ACOLI alt for ACHOLI [ACO]
LOGANANGA dial of TUNEN [BAZ]
LOGAR dial of ORMURI [ORU]
LOGBA [LGQ] lang, Ghana
LOGBA alt for LUKPA [DOP]
LOGBO dial of AKPOSO [KPO]
LOGEA dial of SUAU [SWP]
LOGHOMA alt for LOMA [LOM]
LOGHON alt for TÉÉN [LOR]
LOGIR alt for LOGIRI dial of OTUHO [LOT]
LOGIRI dial of OTUHO [LOT]
LOGMA alt for LOGREMMA dial of KALAMSE [KNZ]
LOGO [LOG] lang, Zaïre
LOGOKE alt for DAR EL KABIRA dial of TULISHI [TEY]
LOGOL [LOF] lang, Sudan
LOGONE alt for LAGWAN [KOT]
LOGONE-BIRNI dial of LAGWAN [KOT]
LOGONE-GANA dial of LAGWAN [KOT]
LOGONE-GANA dial of LAGWAN [KOT]
LOGOOLI [RAG] lang, Kenya
LOGORBAN alt for UMM DOREIN dial of MORO [MOR]
LOGOTI alt for LOGO [LOG]
LOGOTOK dial of OTUHO [LOT]
LOGREMMA dial of KALAMSE [KNZ]
LOGU alt for LONGGU [LGU]
LOGUDORESE alt for SARDINIAN, LOGUDORESE [SRD]
LOH-TOGA alt for TOGA [LHT]
LOHAR alt for KARIA dial of KOLI, KACHI [GJK]
LOHARA dial of HO [HOC]
LOHARI alt for GADE LOHAR [GDA]
LOHARI-MALPAHARIA dial of BENGALI [BNG]
LOHARI-SANTALI dial of SANTALI [SNT]

LOHBYA dial of GARHWALI [GBM]
LOHEI alt for LAHU [LAH]
LOHEIRN alt for NA dial of LAHU [LAH]
LOHI alt for LODHI [LBM]
LOHIKI alt for ANGOYA [MIW]
LOHORONG [LBR] lang, Nepal
LOHPITTA RAJPUT LOHAR alt for GADE LOHAR
    [GDA]
LOHU alt for DOBASE [DOX]
LOI alt for LUI [LBA]
LOI alt for BALOI [BIZ]
LOI alt for HLAI [LIC]
LOI alt for TAI LOI [TLQ]
LOI dial of BALOI [BIZ]
LOI-NGIRI alt for NGIRI [NGR]
LOIKERA alt for KISAR [KJE]
LOINANG alt for SALUAN, COASTAL [LOE]
LOINDANG alt for SALUAN, COASTAL [LOE]
LOIRYA alt for LOKOYA [LKY]
LOISU alt for LISU [LIS]
LOITAI dial of MAASAI [MET]
LOJA QUICHUA alt for QUICHUA, HIGHLAND, LOJA
    [QQU]
LOKAI dial of MADI [MHI]
LOKALO dial of NKUTU [NKW]
LOKATHAN dial of TESO [TEO]
LOKAY dial of DZANDO [DZN]
LOKE alt for LOKO [YAZ]
LOKELE alt for KELE [KHY]
LOKEP alt for AROP-LOKEP [APR]
LOKEP alt for LUKEP [LOA]
LOKHAY dial of UZBEK, NORTHERN [UZB]
LOKO [LOK] lang, Sierra Leone
LOKO [YAZ] lang, Nigeria
LOKO alt for GIMI [GIP]
LOKO alt for AIKLEP [MWG]
LOKOIYA alt for LOKOYA [LKY]
LOKOJA alt for LOKOYA [LKY]
LOKOLI alt for NKUKOLI [NBO]
LOKONO alt for ARAWAK [ARW]
LOKOP alt for SAMBURU [SAQ]
LOKORO [LKR] lang, Sudan
LOKOYA [LKY] lang, Sudan
LOKPA alt for LUKPA [DOP]
LOKUKOLI alt for NKUKOLI [NBO]
LOKURU dial for BANIATA [BNT]
LOKUTSU alt for KUSU [KSV]
LOLA [LCD] lang, Indonesia, Maluku
LOLA dial of LOLA [LCD]
LOLAK [LLQ] lang, Indonesia, Sulawesi
LOLAKI alt for TOLAKI [LBW]
LOLANG dial of LAWANGAN [LBX]
LOLATAVOLA dial of SA [SSA]
LOLAYAN dial of MONGONDOW [MOG]
LOLE alt for BAÄ-LOLEH dial of ROTI [ROT]
LOLEH alt for BAÄ-LOLEH dial of ROTI [ROT]
LOLEI dial of MAMBAI [MGM]
LOLEKO alt for ILIKU dial of LUSENGO [LUS]
LOLI alt for LAULI dial of WEYEWA [WEW]
"LOLO" alt for YI, SICHUAN [III]
LOLO alt for LOMWE [NGL]
LOLO alt for CHWABO [CHW]
LOLO alt for NKUNDO dial of MONGO-NKUNDU
    [MOM]
LOLOBI dial of AKPAFU-LOLOBI [AKP]
LOLOBI-AKPAFU alt for AKPAFU-LOLOBI [AKP]

LOLODA [LOL] lang, Indonesia, Maluku
LOLOKARA alt for LOLOKARO dial of AMBAE, EAST
    [OMB]
LOLOKARO dial of AMBAE, EAST [OMB]
LOLOLO alt for FANAGOLO [FAO]
LOLOPANI alt for ARINUA [AUK]
LOLSIWOI alt for LOLOKARO dial of AMBAE, EAST
    [OMB]
LOLTONG dial of APMA [APP]
LOLUBO alt for LULUBA [LUL]
LOLUE alt for BALUE dial of BAKUNDU-BALUE [BDU]
LOLYA dial of LOGO [LOG]
LOM [MFB] lang, Indonesia, Sumatra
LOMA [LOI] lang, Côte d'Ivoire
LOMA [LOM] lang, Liberia
LOMABAALE alt for MABAALE [MMZ]
LOMAIVITI [LMV] lang, Fiji
LOMAKKA alt for LOMA [LOI]
LOMAPO alt for LOMA [LOI]
LOMASSE alt for LOMA [LOI]
LÕMAUMBI dial of BABATANA [BAQ]
LOMAVREN [RMI] lang, Armenia, Syria, Syria
LOMAVREN alt for LOMAVREN [RMI]
LOMBAHA dial of AMBAE, EAST [OMB]
LOMBARD [LMO] lang, Italy
LOMBARDO alt for LOMBARD [LMO]
LOMBE alt for BAROMBI [BBI]
LOMBI [LMI] lang, Zaïre
LOMBI alt for BAROMBI [BBI]
LOMBI dial of BASAA [BAA]
LOMBO [LOO] lang, Zaïre
LOMBOK alt for SASAK [SAS]
LOMBOLE alt for MBOLE [MDQ]
LOMBOOKI dial of POKE [POF]
LOMBU dial of GBAYA [GYA]
LOMETIMETI dial of WHITESANDS [TNP]
LOMI alt for NAXI [NBF]
LOMIA alt for LOMYA dial of OTUHO [LOT]
LOMITAWA dial of DUAU [DUA]
LOMLOM alt for AYIWO [NFL]
LOMONGO alt for MONGO-NKUNDU [MOM]
LOMONGO alt for EKONDA MONGO dial of MONGO-
    NKUNDU [MOM]
LOMORIK alt for TIMA [TMS]
LOMOTUA dial of BEMBA [BEM]
LOMOTWA alt for LOMOTUA dial of BEMBA [BEM]
LOMUE alt for LOMWE [NGL]
LOMURIKI alt for TIMA [TMS]
LOMWE [NGL] lang, Mozambique, Malawi
LOMYA dial of OTUHO [LOT]
LON BANGAG dial of KELABIT [KZI]
LONCHONG alt for LONCONG [LCE]
LONCONG [LCE] lang, Indonesia, Sumatra
LONDAI dial of SANTA CRUZ [STC]
LONDO alt for BALUNDU dial of BALUNDU-BIMA
    [NGO]
LONG AKAHSEMUKA dial of KAYAN, BARAM [KYS]
LONG ATAU dial of KENYAH, BAHAU RIVER [BWV]
LONG ATIP dial of KAYAN, BARAM [KYS]
LONG ATUN dial of KENYAH, SEBOB [SIB]
LONG BADAN dial of KAYAN, REJANG [REE]
LONG BANGAN dial of KENYAH, WESTERN [XKY]
LONG BANO alt for SIMEULUE [SMR]
LONG BANYUQ dial of KAYAN, MURIK [MXR]
LONG BAWAN alt for LUN BAWANG dial of
    LUNDAYEH [LND]

LONG BENA dial of KENYAH, BAHAU RIVER [BWV]
LONG BENTO' dial of MODANG [MXD]
LONG BLEH dial of KAYAN, BUSANG [BFG]
LONG BULAN alt for UMA BAKAH dial of KENYAH, WESTERN [XKY]
LONG EKANG dial of KENYAH, SEBOB [SIB]
LONG GENG dial of KAYAN, REJANG [REE]
LONG GLAT dial of MODANG [MXD]
LONG HAIR CUNA alt for KUNA, PAYA-PUCURO [KUA]
LONG IKANG alt for LONG EKANG dial of KENYAH, SEBOB [SIB]
LONG JEGAN dial of BERAWAN [LOD]
LONG KEHOBO dial of KAYAN, REJANG [REE]
LONG KELAWIT dial of KENYAH, KAYAN RIVER [KNH]
LONG KIPUT alt for KIPUT [KYI]
LONG LABID dial of KENYAH, TUTOH [TTW]
LONG LUYANG dial of KENYAH, SEBOB [SIB]
LONG MURUN dial of KAYAN, REJANG [REE]
LONG NAWAN dial of KENYAH, KAYAN RIVER [KNH]
LONG PATA dial of BERAWAN [LOD]
LONG POKUN dial of KENYAH, SEBOB [SIB]
LONG PUYUNGAN dial of KENYAH, BAHAU RIVER [BWV]
LONG SEMIANG dial of KAYAN, MURIK [MXR]
LONG TERAWAN dial of BERAWAN [LOD]
LONG WAI alt for KELINGAN dial of MODANG [MXD]
LONG WAT dial of KENYAH, TUTOH [TTW]
LONG WE alt for KELINGAN dial of MODANG [MXD]
LONG-HAIRED LACHI alt for LIPUPI dial of LATI [LBT]
LONGA alt for AMARA [AIE]
LONGA alt for LONGTO [WOK]
LONGANA dial of AMBAE, EAST [OMB]
LONGANDU alt for NGANDO [NXD]
LONGARIM [LOH] lang, Sudan
LONGBIA dial of KENYAH, KAYAN RIVER [KNH]
LONGBO alt for LONGTO [WOK]
LONGCHING dial of NAGA, KONYAK [NBE]
LONGE-LONGE dial of SHI [SHR]
LONGGU [LGU] lang, Solomon Islands
LONGKHAI dial of NAGA, KONYAK [NBE]
LONGLA dial of NAGA, AO [NJO]
LONGMEIN dial of NAGA, KONYAK [NBE]
LONGMI dial of RAWANG [RAW]
LONGMI dial of RAWANG [RAW]
LONGO dial of MONGO-NKUNDU [MOM]
LONGORO dial of DEG [MZW]
LONGPHI dial of NAGA, TASE [NST]
LONGRI dial of NAGA, TASE [NST]
LONGTO [WOK] lang, Cameroon
LONGUDA [LNU] lang, Nigeria
LONGWA dial of NAGA, KONYAK [NBE]
LONIO alt for LONIU [LOS]
LONIU [LOS] lang, Papua New Guinea
LONKUNDO alt for NKUNDO dial of MONGO-NKUNDU [MOM]
LONKUNDU alt for NKUNDO dial of MONGO-NKUNDU [MOM]
LONTES dial of HALIA [HLA]
LONTJONG alt for LONCONG [LCE]
LONTO alt for LONGTO [WOK]
LONTO alt for SOUTHERN CHUMBURUNG dial of

CHUMBURUNG [NCU]
LONTOMBA alt for NTOMBA [NTO]
LONWOLWOL [CRC] lang, Vanuatu
LONZO [LNZ] lang, Zaïre
LOOCNON alt for INONHAN [LOC]
LOODIYA alt for DADIYA [DBD]
LOOKNON alt for INONHAN [LOC]
LOOKNON dial of INONHAN [LOC]
LOOMBO alt for OMBO [OML]
LOPA [LOP] lang, Nigeria
LOPA [LOY] lang, Nepal
LOPAR alt for SAAMI, SKOLT [LPK]
LOPAWA alt for LOPA [LOP]
LOPHOMI alt for NAGA, SANGTAM [NSA]
LOPI [LOV] lang, Myanmar
LOPID alt for LOPIT [LPX]
LOPIT [LPX] lang, Sudan
LOPNOR dial of UYGHUR [UIG]
LOPNUR alt for LOPNOR dial of UYGHUR [UIG]
LOQUIA alt for LOKOYA [LKY]
LOR alt for LURI [LRI]
LOR alt for KHLOR [LLO]
LORABADA alt for TATE [TBD]
LORANG [LRN] lang, Indonesia, Maluku
LORANG BUKIT alt for BISAYA, BRUNEI [BSB]
LORANG BUKIT alt for BISAYA, SARAWAK [BSD]
LORD HOWE alt for ONTONG JAVA [LUN]
LOREDIAKARKAR [LNN] lang, Vanuatu
LORENZO alt for AMUESHA [AME]
LORETANO alt for LORETO dial of TRINITARIO [TRN]
LORETO dial of TRINITARIO [TRN]
LORHON alt for TÉÉN [LOR]
LORI alt for LURI [LRI]
LORI dial of JUR MODO [BEX]
LORIDJA alt for PINTUPI-LURITJA [PIU]
LORMA alt for LOMA [LOM]
LORON alt for TÉÉN [LOR]
LORRAINE dial of FRENCH [FRN]
LORUNG alt for LOHORONG [LBR]
LORWAMA dial of OTUHO [LOT]
LOSA dial of NAKANAI [NAK]
LOSAKA alt for SAKA dial of NKUTU [NKW]
LOSAU dial of CHIN, TEDIM [CTD]
LOSENGO alt for LUSENGO [LUS]
LOSI dial of DEHU [DEU]
LOSIARA dial of TEOP [TIO]
LOSO alt for DOOKA dial of GBAYA [GYA]
LOSO alt for LOSA dial of NAKANAI [NAK]
LOSSO alt for LAMA [LAS]
LOSSO alt for NAWDM [NMZ]
LOSU alt for NAWDM [NMZ]
LOTE [UVL] lang, Papua New Guinea
LOTHA alt for NAGA, LOTHA [NJH]
LOTORA dial of MAEWO, CENTRAL [MWO]
LOTSU-PIRI [LDP] lang, Nigeria
LOTUD [DTR] lang, Malaysia, Sabah
LOTUHO alt for OTUHO [LOT]
LOTUKA alt for OTUHO [LOT]
LOTUKO alt for OTUHO [LOT]
LOTUNI dial of BALUCHI, SOUTHERN [BCC]
LOTUNI alt for MAKRANI dial of BALUCHI, SOUTHERN [BCC]
LOTUXO alt for OTUHO [LOT]
LOU [LOJ] lang, Papua New Guinea
LOU alt for TORRICELLI [TEI]

LOU alt for TATE [TBD]
LOU dial of NUER [NUS]
LOUCHEUX alt for WESTERN CANADA GWICH'IN dial of GWICH'IN [KUC]
LOUDO alt for LOWUDO dial of OTUHO [LOT]
LOUGAW dial of MUYUW [MYW]
LOUISIANA CREOLE FRENCH [LOU] lang, USA
LOULOU alt for MUTURAMI dial of GIZIGA, SOUTH [GIZ]
LOUN [LOX] lang, Indonesia, Maluku
LOUOME dial of GBAGYI [GBR]
LOUTA dial of SAMO [SBD]
LOUTO alt for RUTO dial of RUTO [NDY]
LOUTO alt for RUTO dial of RUTO [NDY]
LOUXIRU alt for OTUKE [OTU]
LOUYI alt for LUYANA [LAV]
LOVAEA alt for MAKU'A [LVA]
LOVAIA alt for MAKU'A [LVA]
LOVALE alt for LUVALE [LUE]
LOVARI dial of ROMANI, VLACH [RMY]
LOVARI alt for ROMANI, VLACH [RMY]
LOVARÍCKO alt for LOVARI dial of ROMANI, VLACH [RMY]
LOVE alt for BRAO [BRB]
LOVEDU alt for LOBEDU dial of SOTHO, NORTHERN [SRT]
LOVEN alt for LAVEN [LBO]
LOVONI alt for NORTHEAST VITI LEVU dial of FIJIAN [FJI]
LOW FRANCONIAN dial of GERMAN, LOW [GEP]
LOW GERMAN alt for PLAUTDIETSCH [GRN]
LOW LITHUANIAN alt for SHAMAITISH dial of LITHUANIAN [LIT]
LOW MALAY alt for BAZAAR MALAY dial of MALAY [MLI]
LOW PIEMONTESE dial of PIEMONTESE [PMS]
LOW SAXON dial of GERMAN, LOW [GEP]
LOWA alt for BARANG-BARANG dial of LAIYOLO [LJI]
LOWER ASARO dial of TOKANO [ZUH]
LOWER BAL dial of SVAN [SVA]
LOWER BELE dial of DANI, LOWER GRAND VALLEY [DNI]
LOWER BISAYA dial of BISAYA, SARAWAK [BSD]
LOWER CARNIOLA dial of SLOVENIAN [SLV]
LOWER CHEHALIS dial of QUINAULT [QUN]
LOWER CHINOOK alt for CHINOOK [CHH]
LOWER CHULYM dial of CHULYM [CHU]
LOWER CIRCASSIAN alt for ADYGHE [ADY]
LOWER COWLITZ alt for COWLITZ [COW]
LOWER EGYPT COLLOQUIAL ARABIC alt for ARABIC, EGYPTIAN COLLOQUIAL [ARZ]
LOWER ENGADINE dial of RHETO-ROMANCE [RHE]
LOWER GIO dial of DAN [DAF]
LOWER GRAND VALLEY HITIGIMA dial of DANI, LOWER GRAND VALLEY [DNI]
LOWER GROMA dial of GROMA [GRO]
LOWER KANAURI dial of KANAURI [KFK]
LOWER KAYAN KENYAH dial of KENYAH, KAYAN RIVER [KNH]
LOWER KENYANG dial of KENYANG [KEN]
LOWER KIMBIN dial of DANI, LOWER GRAND VALLEY [DNI]
LOWER LADAKHI alt for SHAMMA dial of LADAKHI [LBJ]
LOWER LAMET dial of LAMET [LBN]

LOWER LOZYVIN alt for WESTERN VOGUL dial of MANSI [MNS]
LOWER LUSATIAN alt for WEND, LOWER [WEE]
LOWER LUSATIAN dial of WEND, UPPER [WEN]
LOWER LUZH dial of INGRIAN [IZH]
LOWER MOREHEAD alt for PEREMKA [PEP]
LOWER MORI alt for MORI BAWAH [XMZ]
LOWER MORTLOCK dial of MORTLOCK [MRL]
LOWER MURUT dial of TIMUGON MURUT [TIH]
LOWER NEPA TUNGIR dial of EVENKI [EVN]
LOWER PIMAN alt for PIMA BAJO, SONORA [PIA]
LOWER PRASUN dial of PRASUNI [PRN]
LOWER PYRAMID alt for WALAK [WLW]
LOWER SAMENAGE dial of SILIMO [WUL]
LOWER WARIA alt for ZIA [ZIA]
LOWER YAZGULYAM dial of YAZGULYAM [YAH]
LOWLAND BALI dial of BALI [BZC]
LOWLAND HUARIJIO alt for HUARIJÍO [VAR]
LOWLAND INGA alt for INGA, JUNGLE [INJ]
LOWLAND JICALTEPEC MIXTECO alt for MIXTECO, WESTERN JAMILTEPEC [MIO]
LOWLAND MAZATECO alt for MAZATECO, SAN FELIPE JALAPA DE DIAZ [MAJ]
LOWLAND NAPO QUECHUA alt for QUICHUA, LOWLAND, NAPO [QLN]
LOWLAND NAPO QUICHUA alt for QUICHUA, LOWLAND, NAPO [QLN]
LOWLAND NUNG alt for CHINESE, YUE [YUH]
LOWLAND SCOTTISH dial of ENGLISH [ENG]
LOWLAND TOTONACO alt for TOTONACO, PAPANTLA [TOP]
LOWLAND TZELTAL alt for TZELTAL, BACHAJÓN [TZB]
LOWLAND YAO alt for MUN [MJI]
LOWOI alt for LOKOYA [LKY]
LOWUDO dial of OTUHO [LOT]
LOYU alt for LOPA [LOY]
LOZI [LOZ] lang, Zambia, Zimbabwe, Zimbabwe
LOZI alt for LODHI [LBM]
LOZI alt for LOZI [LOZ]
LOZOUA dial of DIDA, YOCOBOUÉ [GUD]
LSB alt for BRAZILIAN SIGN LANGUAGE [BZS]
LSF alt for FRENCH SIGN LANGUAGE [FSL]
LSM alt for MEXICAN SIGN LANGUAGE [MFS]
LSQ alt for FRENCH CANADIAN SIGN LANGUAGE [FCS]
LÜ [KHB] lang, China, Myanmar, Laos, Myanmar, Thailand, Viet Nam
LÜ alt for LÜ [KHB]
LU alt for LÜ [KHB]
LU alt for NUNG [NUN]
LU dial of LUGBARA, HIGH [LUG]
LU SHI LISU dial of LISU [LIS]
LU-TZU alt for LISU [LIS]
LUA' [PRB] lang, Thailand
LUA alt for LAWA, WESTERN [LCP]
LUA alt for NIELLIM [NIE]
LUA' alt for MAL [MLF]
LUAAN alt for BAJAU, INDONESIAN [BDL]
LUAC dial of DINKA, SOUTHWESTERN [DIK]
LUAC dial of DINKA, NORTHEASTERN [DIP]
LUAIC alt for LUAC dial of DINKA, NORTHEASTERN [DIP]
LUALABA dial of SWAHILI, ZAÏRE [SWC]
LUANA alt for LUYANA [LAV]
LUANDA alt for MBUNDU, LOANDA [MLO]

LUANG [LEX] lang, Indonesia, Maluku
LUANG dial of LUANG [LEX]
LUANG PRABANG dial of LAO [NOL]
LUANG PRABANG dial of KHMU [KJG]
LUANGIUA alt for ONTONG JAVA [LUN]
LUANGIUA dial of ONTONG JAVA [LUN]
LUANO alt for LUYANA [LAV]
LUANO dial of LALA-BISA [LEB]
LUAPULA alt for LUUNDA dial of BEMBA [BEM]
LUBA dial of DUSUN, CENTRAL [DTP]
LUBA KAONDE alt for KAONDE [KQN]
LUBA-GARENGANZE alt for SANGA [SNG]
LUBA-HEMBA alt for HEMBA [HEM]
LUBA-KASAI [LUB] lang, Zaïre
LUBA-KATANGA alt for LUBA-SHABA [LUH]
LUBA-LULUA alt for LUBA-KASAI [LUB]
LUBA-SANGA alt for SANGA [SNG]
LUBA-SHABA [LUH] lang, Zaïre
LUBA-SONGI alt for SONGE [SOP]
LUBA-TIEMPO ITNEG alt for ITNEG, SOUTHERN
   [ITT]
LUBALE alt for LUVALE [LUE]
LUBANG dial of TAGALOG [TGL]
LUBEDU alt for LOBEDU dial of SOTHO, NORTHERN
   [SRT]
LUBILA [KCC] lang, Nigeria
LUBILO alt for LUBILA [KCC]
LUBOLO alt for BOLO [BLV]
LUBU [LCF] lang, Indonesia, Sumatra
LUBUAGAN dial of KALINGA, LUBUAGAN [KNB]
LUBUKUSU alt for BUKUSU [BUL]
LUBULEBULE alt for KWAMBA [RWM]
LUBULEBULE alt for KIGUMU dial of KWAMBA
   [RWM]
LUBWISI alt for TALINGA-BWISI [TLJ]
LUBWISSI alt for TALINGA-BWISI [TLJ]
LUCAZI alt for LUCHAZI [LCH]
LUCERNE dial of SCHWYZERDÜTSCH [GSW]
LUCHAZI [LCH] lang, Angola, Zambia, Zambia
LUCHAZI alt for LUCHAZI [LCH]
LUCHU alt for OKINAWAN, CENTRAL [RYU]
LUDAMA alt for ADHOLA [ADH]
LUDIAN [LUD] lang, Russia, Europe
LUDIC alt for LUDIAN [LUD]
LUDIOPA dial of GANDA [LAP]
LUDUMOR alt for SHWAI [SHW]
LUE alt for LÜ [KHB]
LUE alt for BALUE dial of BAKUNDU-BALUE [BDU]
LUENA alt for LUVALE [LUE]
LUF alt for HERMIT [LLF]
LUFU [LDQ] lang, Nigeria
LUGAGON alt for NALIK [NAL]
LUGANDA alt for GANDA [LAP]
LUGAT dial of KENYAH, TUTOH [TTW]
LUGBA alt for LUKPA [DOP]
LUGBARA, HIGH [LUG] lang, Uganda, Zaïre, Zaïre
LUGBARA, HIGH alt for LUGBARA, HIGH [LUG]
LUGBARA, LOW [LUC] lang, Uganda
LUGGOY dial of MUSGU [MUG]
LUGISU alt for SAAMIA [SBU]
LUGISU dial of MASABA [MYX]
LUGITAMA alt for PAHI [LGT]
LUGOOLI alt for LOGOOLI [RAG]
LUGOVO MARI alt for MARI, LOW [MAL]
LUGULU alt for RUGURU [RUF]
LUGURU alt for RUGURU [RUF]

LUGWE alt for SAAMIA [SBU]
LUGWE dial of SAAMIA [SBU]
LUGWERE alt for GWERE [GWR]
LUHANGA alt for WANGA dial of LUYIA [LUY]
LUHISHI alt for NYI dial of LAHU [LAH]
LUHTU dial of TSOU [TSY]
LUHU [LCQ] lang, Indonesia, Maluku
LUHU dial of LUHU [LCQ]
LUHUPPA alt for NAGA, TANGKHUL [NMF]
LUHUSHI alt for NYI dial of LAHU [LAH]
LUHYA alt for LUYIA [LUY]
LUI [LBA] lang, Myanmar
LUI alt for LUYANA [LAV]
LUIMBI [LUM] lang, Angola
LUIMBI dial of LUIMBI [LUM]
LUISEÑO [LUI] lang, USA
LUISEÑO dial of LUISEÑO [LUI]
LUJASH alt for LUCHAZI [LCH]
LUJAZI alt for LUCHAZI [LCH]
LUKAMIUTE alt for KALAPUYA [KAL]
LUKANGA alt for TWA dial of LENJE [LEH]
LUKEISEL dial of MORTLOCK [MRL]
LUKENYI alt for SOGA [SOG]
LUKEP [LOA] lang, Papua New Guinea
LUKEP alt for AROP-LOKEP [APR]
LUKETE alt for KETE [KCV]
LUKHA alt for LOGOL [LOF]
LUKHAI alt for LUSHAI [LSH]
LUKO alt for LOKO [YAZ]
LUKOLWE dial of NKOYA [NKA]
LUKPA [DOP] lang, Benin, Togo, Togo
LUKPA alt for LUKPA [DOP]
LUKSHI dial of DASS [DOT]
LUKSHI alt for LUSHI dial of ZEEM [ZUA]
LUL dial of ANUAK [ANU]
LULE alt for SAAMI, LULE [LPL]
LULEKE dial of TSONGA [TSO]
LULI dial of DOMARI [RMT]
LULUBA [LUL] lang, Sudan, Uganda, Uganda
LULUBA alt for LULUBA [LUL]
LULUMO alt for OLULUMO-IKOM [IKO]
LULUYIA alt for LUYIA [LUY]
LUM LAO alt for LAO [NOL]
LUMA dial of AKHA [AKA]
LUMADALE alt for LAMANI [LMN]
LUMAETE dial of KAYELI [KZL]
LUMAITI alt for LUMAETE dial of KAYELI [KZL]
LUMAN alt for TIRA LUMUM dial of TIRA [TIR]
LUMARA alt for LUMAETE dial of KAYELI [KZL]
LUMASABA alt for MASABA [MYX]
LUMBEE [LUA] lang, USA
LUMBI alt for LOMBI [LMI]
LUMBIS alt for TAGAL MURUT [MVV]
LUMBIS alt for ALUMBIS dial of TAGAL MURUT
   [MVV]
LUMBU [LUP] lang, Gabon, Congo
LUMBU alt for LIMBU [LIF]
LUMBU dial of ILA [ILB]
LUMBWA alt for MAASAI [MET]
LUMMI dial of SALISH, STRAITS [STR]
LUMUN dial of MORO HILLS [TAZ]
LUN BAWANG alt for LUNDAYEH [LND]
LUN BAWANG dial of LUNDAYEH [LND]
LUN BAWANG dial of LUNDAYEH [LND]
LUN DAYA alt for LUNDAYEH [LND]
LUN DAYAH alt for LUNDAYEH [LND]

LUN DAYAH dial of LUNDAYEH [LND]
LUN DAYE alt for LUNDAYEH [LND]
LUN DAYE dial of LUNDAYEH [LND]
LUN DAYEH alt for LUNDAYEH [LND]
LUN DAYOH alt for LUNDAYEH [LND]
LUN LOD alt for LUNDAYEH [LND]
LUN'GWIYE alt for PRINCIPENSE dial of CRIOULO,
    GULF OF GUINEA [CRI]
LUNA [LUJ] lang, Zaïre
LUNAN dial of KENYAH, WESTERN [XKY]
LUND dial of MANDYAK [MFV]
LUNDA [LVN] lang, Zambia, Angola, Zaïre
LUNDA alt for MBUNDU, LOANDA [MLO]
LUNDA KALUNDA dial of LUNDA [LVN]
LUNDA KAMBOVE alt for RUUND [RND]
LUNDA KAMBOVE dial of LUNDA [LVN]
LUNDA NDEMBU dial of LUNDA [LVN]
LUNDA-KAMBORO alt for RUUND [RND]
LUNDAYA alt for LUNDAYEH [LND]
LUNDAYEH [LND] lang, Indonesia, Kalimantan,
    Brunei, Malaysia, Sabah
LUNDAYEH alt for LUNDAYEH [LND]
LUNDU alt for BIATAH [BTH]
LUNDU alt for BALUNDU dial of BALUNDU-BIMA
    [NGO]
LUNDUR alt for LANGAS dial of POLCI [POL]
LUNDWE dial of ILA [ILB]
LUNGALUNGA alt for MINIGIR [VMG]
LUNGCHANG dial of NAGA, TASE [NST]
LUNGCHOW dial of NUNG [NUT]
LUNGGA [LGA] lang, Solomon Islands
LUNGLI dial of HMONG, WESTERN [HUJ]
LUNGMI alt for LONGMI dial of RAWANG [RAW]
LUNGNAN dial of CHINESE, HAKKA [HAK]
LUNGRI dial of NAGA, TASE [NST]
LUNGU alt for IDUN [LDB]
LUNGU alt for RUNGU dial of MAMBWE-LUNGU
    [MGR]
LUNGU alt for RUNGU dial of MAMBWE-LUNGU
    [MGR]
LUNGULU alt for MWAMBA dial of NYAKYUSA-
    NGONDE [NYY]
LUNGWA alt for RUNGWA [RNW]
LUNIGIANO dial of EMILIANO [EML]
LUNTU dial of SALAMPASU [SLX]
LUNTUMBA alt for NTOMBA [NTO]
LUNUBE MADO dial of DANO [ASO]
LUNYANEKA alt for NYANEKA [NYK]
LUNYOLE alt for NYORE [NYD]
LUNYORE alt for NYORE [NYD]
LUO [LUO] lang, Kenya, Tanzania, Tanzania
LUO alt for LUO [LUO]
LUOBA alt for LHOBA [LON]
LUOFU dial of SHE [SHX]
LUORAVETLAN alt for CHUKOT [CKT]
LUPA alt for LOPA [LOP]
LUPPA alt for NAGA, TANGKHUL [NMF]
LUR alt for LURI [LRI]
LUR alt for ALUR [ALZ]
LURAGOLI alt for LOGOOLI [RAG]
LURI [LRI] lang, Iran, Iraq, Iraq
LURI [LDD] lang, Nigeria
LURI alt for LURI [LRI]
LURI alt for ALUR [ALZ]
LURI dial of LURI [LRI]
LURU alt for LARA' [LRA]

LURUTY-TAPUYA alt for YURUTI [YUI]
LUSA alt for ZAAR dial of SAYA [SAY]
LUSAAMIA alt for SAAMIA [SBU]
LUSAAMIA dial of SAAMIA [SBU]
LUSAGO alt for LUSHAI [LSH]
LUSAI alt for LUSHAI [LSH]
LUSAMIA alt for SAAMIA [SBU]
LUSATIAN alt for WEND, LOWER [WEE]
LUSATIAN alt for WEND, UPPER [WEN]
LUSENGO [LUS] lang, Zaïre
LUSENGO POTO dial of LUSENGO [LUS]
LUSHAI [LSH] lang, India, Bangladesh, China,
    Myanmar
LUSHAI alt for LUSHAI [LSH]
LUSHAN dial of HMONG, EASTERN [HEA]
LUSHANGI dial of NKOYA [NKA]
LUSHEI alt for LUSHAI [LSH]
LUSHI dial of ZEEM [ZUA]
LUSHISA alt for KISA dial of LUYIA [LUY]
LUSHOOTSEED [LUT] lang, USA
LUSI [KHL] lang, Papua New Guinea
LUSINGA alt for SINGA [SGM]
LUSITANO-ROMANI alt for PORTUGUESE CALÃO
    dial of ROMANI, CALO [RMR]
LUSOGA alt for SOGA [SOG]
LUSONG alt for PUNAN LUSONG dial of PUNAN-
    NIBONG [PNE]
LUSONGE alt for SONGE [SOP]
LUSU alt for LISU [LIS]
LUTANGAN dial of SAMA, BALANGINGI [SSE]
LUTANGO alt for LUTANGAN dial of SAMA,
    BALANGINGI [SSE]
LUTAOS alt for BAJAU, INDONESIAN [BDL]
LUTAYAOS alt for BAJAU, INDONESIAN [BDL]
LUTHA alt for NAGA, LOTHA [NJH]
LUTISE dial of DOGHOSIÉ [DOS]
LUTKUHWAR alt for YIDGHA [YDG]
LUTO alt for RUTO dial of RUTO [NDY]
LUTO alt for RUTO dial of RUTO [NDY]
LUTSHASE alt for LUCHAZI [LCH]
LUTU alt for SOUTHEAST VITI LEVU dial of FIJIAN
    [FJI]
LUTZE alt for NUNG [NUN]
LUTZU alt for NUNG [NUN]
LUU alt for KHMU [KJG]
LUUN alt for LEUN [LLE]
LUUNDA alt for RUUND [RND]
LUUNDA dial of BEMBA [BEM]
LUVA alt for LUBA-KASAI [LUB]
LUVALE [LUE] lang, Angola, Zambia, Zambia
LUVALE alt for LUVALE [LUE]
LUVUMA dial of GANDA [LAP]
LUVURE alt for VUTE [VUT]
LUWA alt for LAWA, WESTERN [LCP]
LUWA dial of HUBA [KIR]
LUWANGAN alt for LAWANGAN [LBX]
LUWO [LWO] lang, Sudan
LUWU alt for TAE' [ROB]
LUWU dial of BUGIS [BPR]
LUWU' alt for TOALA' [TLZ]
LUWU' alt for LUWU dial of BUGIS [BPR]
LUWUNDA alt for RUUND [RND]
LUXAGE alt for LUCHAZI [LCH]
LUXEMBOURGEOIS [LUX] lang, Luxembourg,
    Belgium, Germany
LUXEMBOURGISH alt for LUXEMBOURGEOIS [LUX]

LUXEMBURGIAN alt for LUXEMBOURGEOIS [LUX]
LUYANA [LAV] lang, Zambia, Angola
LUYI alt for LUYANA [LAV]
LUYIA [LUY] lang, Kenya, Uganda, Uganda
LUYIA alt for LUYIA [LUY]
LVOVA dial of SANTA CRUZ [STC]
LWALU [LWA] lang, Zaïre
LWENA alt for LUVALE [LUE]
LWIMBE alt for LUIMBI [LUM]
LWIMBI alt for LUIMBI [LUM]
LWINDJA alt for HWINDJA dial of SHI [SHR]
LWISUKHA alt for ISUKHA dial of IDAKHO-ISUKHA-
    TIRIKI [IDA]
LWO alt for LANGO [LAJ]
LWO alt for LUWO [LWO]
LWO alt for ACHOLI [ACO]
LWOWA alt for LVOVA dial of SANTA CRUZ [STC]
LXLOUKXLE alt for //XEGWI [XEG]
LY alt for LÜ [KHB]
LYAASA alt for YASA [YKO]
LYANGMAY alt for NAGA, LIANGMAI [NJN]
LYASE alt for GWAMHI-WURI [BGA]
LYASE-NE alt for GWAMHI-WURI [BGA]
LYÉLÉ [LEE] lang, Burkina Faso
LYEN-LYEM alt for ZAHAO dial of CHIN, FALAM
    [HBH]
LYENGMAI alt for NAGA, LIANGMAI [NJN]
LYENTE alt for LENTE dial of CHIN, FALAM [HBH]
LYNG-NGAM dial of KHASI [KHI]
LYNGNGAM dial of KHASI [KHI]
LYO dial of CHING [MKG]
LYONNAIS dial of FRANCO-PROVENÇAL [FRA]
LYONS SIGN LANGUAGE [LSG] lang, France
LYUDIC alt for LUDIAN [LUD]
LYUDIKOVIAN alt for LUDIAN [LUD]
LYY dial of KHMU [KJG]
M'BAHOUIN alt for MBANGWE [ZMN]
M'BATO alt for MBATO [GWA]
M'BUNAI alt for TITAN [TTV]
M'BUNDO alt for UMBUNDU [MNF]
M'KAANG alt for CHIN, DAAI [DAO]
MA [MSJ] lang, Zaïre
MA alt for MAA [CMA]
MA alt for BILALA [BKX]
MA dial of BINAHARI [BXZ]
MA BUWAL alt for BUWAL [BHS]
MA DALA alt for MANDALA dial of MABA [MDE]
MA KRUNG alt for MAA [CMA]
MA KU alt for MLABRI [MRA]
MA NDABA alt for MANDABA dial of MABA [MDE]
MA NGAN alt for MAA [CMA]
MA TO alt for MAA [CMA]
MA XOP alt for MAA [CMA]
MA'A alt for MBUGU [MHD]
MA'ADI alt for MADI [MHI]
MA'AGING dial of KAYAN, REJANG [REE]
MA'ANJAN alt for MA'ANYAN [MHY]
MA'BO alt for NGBAKA MA'BO [NBM]
MA'DI alt for MOROKODO [MGC]
MA'DI alt for KALIKO-MA'DI [XKZ]
MA'DI alt for MADI [MHI]
MA'DITI alt for MADI [MHI]
MA'DU dial of MOROKODO [MGC]
MA'KI alt for KALUMPANG [KLI]
MA'YA dial of MA'YA [SLZ]
MAA [CMA] lang, Viet Nam

MAA alt for MAASAI [MET]
MAA alt for MANO [MEV]
MAA' alt for MAA [CMA]
MAABAN alt for MABAAN [MFZ]
MAAKA [MEW] lang, Nigeria
MAALOULA alt for MA'LULA [AMW]
MAANGELLA alt for MADNGELE [ZML]
MAANYAK DAYAK alt for MA'ANYAN [MHY]
MA'ANYAN [MHY] lang, Indonesia, Kalimantan
MAAQ alt for MAA [CMA]
MAARO alt for OIRATA [OIA]
MAASA alt for YASA [YKO]
MAASAI [MET] lang, Kenya, Tanzania, Tanzania
MAASAI alt for MAASAI [MET]
MAAY [QMA] lang, Somalia
MABA [MDE] lang, Chad
MABA [MQA] lang, Indonesia, Maluku
MABAA alt for MABA [MDE]
MABAALE [MMZ] lang, Zaïre
MABAAN [MFZ] lang, Sudan, Ethiopia
MABAHN dial of BASSA [BAS]
MABAK alt for MABA [MDE]
MABAKA ITNEG alt for KALINGA, MABAKA VALLEY
    [KKG]
MABALE alt for MABAALE [MMZ]
MABAN alt for MABA [MDE]
MABANG alt for MABA [MDE]
MABANGI alt for MABA [MDE]
MABAS [VEM] lang, Cameroon, Nigeria, Nigeria
MABAS alt for MABAS [VEM]
MABAS dial of MABAS [VEM]
MABE alt for MAHEI [MJA]
MABEA alt for NGUMBA [NMG]
MABEA alt for MABI dial of NGUMBA [NMG]
MABENDI alt for BENDI [BCT]
MABENI alt for BENDI [BCT]
MABI alt for NGUMBA [NMG]
MABI dial of NGUMBA [NMG]
MABIHA alt for MAVIHA [MHP]
MABILA alt for MAMBILA, NIGERIA [MZK]
MABITI alt for LIKA [LIK]
MABLEI dial of KALUMPANG [KLI]
MABO-BARKUL [MAE] lang, Nigeria
MABOKO dial of DZANDO [DZN]
MABOZO dial of MAYOGO [MDM]
MABRI alt for MLABRI [MRA]
MABUE alt for SATERÉ-MAWÉ [MAV]
MABUIAG alt for KALA LAGAW YA [MWP]
MACA [XMC] lang, Mozambique
MACA [MCA] lang, Paraguay
MACAGUAJE [MCL] lang, Colombia
MACAGUÁN [MBN] lang, Colombia
MACAGUANE alt for MACAGUÁN [MBN]
MACAÍSTA dial of PIDGIN, TIMOR [TVY]
MACANESE [MZS] lang, Hong Kong, Macau
MACANESE alt for MACANESE [MZS]
MACANIPA alt for OMAGUA [OMG]
MACAO CREOLE PORTUGUESE alt for MACANESE
    [MZS]
MACASSAI alt for MAKASAI [MKZ]
MACASSAR alt for MAKASSAR [MSR]
MACASSARESE alt for MAKASSAR [MSR]
MACCHA alt for MECHA dial of OROMO, WELLEGA-
    CENTRAL [GAZ]
MACEDO-ROMANIAN alt for RUMANIAN, MACEDO
    [RUP]

MACEDONIAN [MKJ] lang, Yugoslavia, Albania, Bulgaria, Greece
MACEDONIAN dial of TURKISH [TRK]
MACEDONIAN GAGAUZ dial of BALKAN GAGAUZ TURKISH [BGX]
MACEDONIAN TURKISH dial of TURKISH [TRK]
MACHAME alt for KIMASHAMI dial of CHAGGA [KAF]
MACHARIA dial of SINDHI [SND]
MACHE alt for BODO [BRX]
MACHICUI alt for TOBA-MASKOY [TMF]
MACHIGUENGA [MCB] lang, Peru
MACHINERE alt for PIRO [PIB]
MACHINERE alt for MANITENERI dial of PIRO [PIB]
MACHINGA [MVW] lang, Tanzania
MACHONGRR alt for NAGA, CHANG [NBC]
MACHOTO alt for ITONAMA [ITO]
MACHVANÍCKO alt for MACHVANO dial of ROMANI, VLACH [RMY]
MACHVANICZKO alt for MACHVANO KALDERASH dial of ROMANI, VLACH [RMY]
MACHVANO dial of ROMANI, VLACH [RMY]
MACHVANO alt for SERBO-BOSNIAN dial of ROMANI, VLACH [RMY]
MACHVANO KALDERASH dial of ROMANI, VLACH [RMY]
MACHVAYA alt for MACHVANO KALDERASH dial of ROMANI, VLACH [RMY]
MACHWAYA alt for MACHVANO KALDERASH dial of ROMANI, VLACH [RMY]
MACHWAYA alt for SERBO-BOSNIAN dial of ROMANI, VLACH [RMY]
MACI dial of ICEVE-MACI [BEC]
MACINA alt for FULFULDE, MAASINA [FUL]
MACKENZIE ESKIMO dial of INUIT, NORTH ALASKAN [ESI]
MACKENZIE ESKIMO alt for WEST ARCTIC ESKIMO dial of INUIT, NORTH ALASKAN [ESI]
MACO dial of PIAROA [PID]
MACONDE alt for MAKONDE [KDE]
"MACU" alt for HUPDË [JUP]
MACÚ alt for MACUSA, GUAVIARE [MBR]
MACU DE CUBEO alt for CACUA [CBV]
MACU DE DESANO alt for CACUA [CBV]
MACU DE GUANANO alt for CACUA [CBV]
"MACÚ DE TUCANO" alt for HUPDË [JUP]
MACÚ-PARANÁ CACUA dial of CACUA [CBV]
MACUA alt for MAKHUWA [MAK]
MACUNA [MYY] lang, Colombia, Brazil
MACUNI alt for MAXAKALÍ [MBL]
MACURAP alt for MAKURÁPI [MAG]
MACURAPI alt for MAKURÁPI [MAG]
MACUSA, GUAVIARE [MBR] lang, Colombia
MACUSHI [MBC] lang, Brazil, Guyana, Guyana, Venezuela
MACUSHI alt for MACUSHI [MBC]
MACUSI alt for MACUSHI [MBC]
MACUSSI alt for MACUSHI [MBC]
MADA [MDA] lang, Nigeria
MADA [MXU] lang, Cameroon
MADA EGGON alt for EGGON [EGO]
MADAGLASHTI alt for FARSI, EASTERN [PRS]
MADAK [MMX] lang, Papua New Guinea
MADANG [MQD] lang, Malaysia, Sarawak
MADAR dial of TEWA [TWE]
MADARA alt for MANDARA [TBF]

MADARRPA dial of GUPAPUYNGU [GUF]
MADDA alt for MADA [MDA]
MADEÁN alt for MADEAN-VIÑAC dial of QUECHUA, YAUYOS [QUX]
MADEAN-VIÑAC dial of QUECHUA, YAUYOS [QUX]
MADEGGUSU alt for SIMBO [SBB]
MADEIRA-AZORES dial of PORTUGUESE [POR]
MADEN [XMX] lang, Indonesia, Irian Jaya
MADENASSA alt for DANISIN [DNA]
MADENASSE alt for DANISIN [DNA]
MADHESI dial of BHOJPURI [BHJ]
MADHURA alt for MADURA [MHJ]
MADHYA PRADESH MARATHI alt for VARHADI-NAGPURI [VAH]
MADI [MHI] lang, Uganda, Sudan
MADI alt for SALUAN, COASTAL [LOE]
MADI alt for MARIA [MRR]
MADI alt for MA [MSJ]
MADI alt for PÖJULU dial of BARI [BFA]
MADIA alt for MARIA [MRR]
MADIDWANA alt for ASIENARA [ASI]
MADIHÁ alt for CULINA [CUL]
MADIIN alt for KOMA, SOUTH [KMJ]
MADIIN alt for KOMA, CENTRAL [KOM]
MADIJA alt for CULINA [CUL]
MADIK alt for ABUN JI dial of ABUN [KGR]
MADINGO alt for MANINKA [MNI]
MADINNISANE alt for DANISIN [DNA]
MADITI alt for KALIKO-MA'DI [XKZ]
MADIYA alt for MARIA [MRR]
MADIYA alt for DANDAMI MARIA [DAQ]
MADJA NGAI alt for SAR [MWM]
MADJA NGAI alt for MAJINGAI dial of SAR [MWM]
MADJINGAY alt for MAJINGAI dial of SAR [MWM]
MADJINGAYE alt for SAR [MWM]
MADJINGAYE alt for MAJINGAI dial of SAR [MWM]
MADKA-KINWAT dial of KOLAMI, NORTHWESTERN [KFB]
MADL alt for MAL [MLF]
MADNGELA alt for MADNGELE [ZML]
MADNGELE [ZML] lang, Australia
MADOLE alt for MODOLE [MQO]
MADRASI dial of TAMIL [TCV]
MADRASSI alt for KANNADA [KJV]
MADU dial of ENETS [ENE]
MADUNGORE alt for SUNGOR [SUN]
MADURA [MHJ] lang, Indonesia, Java, Bali, Singapore, Singapore
MADURESE alt for MADURA [MHJ]
MADURI alt for BAGA MADURI [BMD]
MADUTARA alt for KOKATA [KTD]
MADUWONGA alt for KOKATA [KTD]
MADYAY dial of YIDINY [YII]
MADYO alt for MA [MSJ]
MAE [MME] lang, Vanuatu
MAE alt for ENGA [ENQ]
MAE alt for EMAE [MMW]
MAE dial of ENGA [ENQ]
MAE dial of JINA [JIA]
MAE SARIENG dial of KAREN, PWO OMKOI [PWW]
MAE-MORAE alt for MAII [MMM]
MAEVO alt for MAEWO, CENTRAL [MWO]
MAEWO, CENTRAL [MWO] lang, Vanuatu
MAFA [MAF] lang, Cameroon, Nigeria, Nigeria
MAFEA [MKV] lang, Vanuatu
MAFILAU alt for MAII [MMM]

MAFOOR alt for BIAK [BHW]
MAFOORSCH alt for BIAK [BHW]
MAFUFU alt for FUYUGE [FUY]
MAG-ANCHI SAMBAL alt for AYTA, MAG-ANCHI [SGB]
MAG-INDI SAMBAL alt for AYTA, MAG-INDI [BLX]
MAGA alt for MAAKA [MEW]
MAGA dial of RUKAI [DRU]
MAGABARA alt for DOGA [DGG]
MAGADHI alt for MAGAHI [MQM]
MAGADIGE [ZMG] lang, Australia
MAGAHAT [MTW] lang, Philippines
MAGAHI [MQM] lang, India
MAGAM dial of AMBRYM, NORTH [MMG]
MAGANG alt for BOLU dial of GEJI [GEZ]
MAGAR, EASTERN [MGP] lang, Nepal, Bhutan, India
MAGAR, WESTERN [MRD] lang, Nepal
MAGARI alt for MAGAR, EASTERN [MGP]
MAGARKURA alt for MAGAR, EASTERN [MGP]
MAGAYA alt for MAGAHI [MQM]
MAGBA dial of BAKWÉ [BAK]
MAGBAI dial of MAYOGO [MDM]
MAGBIAMBO dial of LOKO [LOK]
MAGE alt for BILALA [BKX]
MAGH alt for ARAKANESE [MHV]
MAGHAYA alt for MAGAHI [MQM]
MAGHI alt for ARAKANESE [MHV]
MAGHORI alt for MAGAHI [MQM]
MAGHREBI ARABIC alt for ARABIC, MOROCCAN [ARY]
MAGHRIBI COLLOQUIAL ARABIC alt for ARABIC, MOROCCAN [ARY]
MAGI alt for MAGAHI [MQM]
MAGI alt for MAILU [MGU]
MAGINDANAON [MDH] lang, Philippines
MAGINDANAW alt for MAGINDANAON [MDH]
MAGIRONA alt for MATSÉS [MCF]
MAGOBINENG dial of KÂTE [KMG]
MAGODHI alt for MAGAHI [MQM]
MAGODI alt for NGONI dial of TUMBUKA [TUW]
MAGODRO alt for WAYA dial of FIJIAN, WESTERN [WYY]
MAGON alt for /HUA-OWANI [HUC]
MAGONG alt for /HUA-OWANI [HUC]
MAGONGO alt for OSAYEN dial of OKO-ENI-OSAYEN [OKS]
MAGORI [MDR] lang, Papua New Guinea
MAGRI dial of BHILI [BHB]
MAGU alt for MVANON [MCJ]
MAGUINDANAO alt for MAGINDANAON [MDH]
MAGWARAM dial of BADE [BDE]
MAGYAR alt for HUNGARIAN [HNG]
MAH alt for MANO [MEV]
MAH MERI alt for BESISI [MHE]
MAHA alt for MAAKA [MEW]
MAHAA dial of BUDU [BUU]
MAHAGA alt for BUGHOTU [BGT]
MAHAKAM BUSANG dial of KAYAN, BUSANG [BFG]
MAHAKAM KENYA alt for KENYAH, MAHAKAM [XKM]
MAHAKAM KENYAH dial of KENYAH, MAHAKAM [XKM]
MAHALI [MJX] lang, India
MAHALI dial of SANTALI [SNT]
MAHALLATI dial of FARSI, WESTERN [PES]
MAHARALY dial of MALAGASY [MEX]

MAHARASHTRA alt for MARATHI [MRT]
MAHARASHTRA LAMANI dial of LAMANI [LMN]
MAHARATHI alt for MARATHI [MRT]
MAHARI alt for HALBI [HLB]
MAHARI dial of KONKANI [KNK]
MAHARI dial of VARHADI-NAGPURI [VAH]
MAHARRA dial of MACA [XMC]
MAHAS alt for MAHAS-FIADIDJA [FIA]
MAHAS dial of MAHAS-FIADIDJA [FIA]
MAHAS-FIADIDJA [FIA] lang, Sudan, Egypt
MAHAS-FIYADIKKYA alt for MAHAS-FIADIDJA [FIA]
MAHASI alt for MAHAS dial of MAHAS-FIADIDJA [FIA]
MAHASS alt for MAHAS dial of MAHAS-FIADIDJA [FIA]
MAHASU PAHARI alt for MAHASUI [BFZ]
MAHASUI [BFZ] lang, India
MAHE alt for MAHEI [MJA]
MAHEI [MJA] lang, Myanmar, China
MAHI alt for MAXI-GBE [MXL]
MAHIGI alt for TAO-SUAMATO [TSX]
MAHILI alt for MAHALI [MJX]
MAHINAKU alt for MEHINÁKU [MMH]
MAHL alt for MALDIVIAN [SNM]
MAHLE alt for MAHALI [MJX]
MAHLE alt for MAHALI dial of SANTALI [SNT]
MAHLI alt for MAHALI [MJX]
MAHONGWE [MHB] lang, Gabon
MAHOTTARI alt for THARU, MAHOTARI [THN]
MAHOU alt for MAU [MXX]
MAHRI [MHR] lang, Oman, Kuwait, Saudi Arabia, Yemen
MAHRI alt for MAHRI [MHR]
MAHSUDI alt for PASHTO, CENTRAL [PST]
MAHU alt for MAU [MXX]
MAHUAN alt for TUGUN [TZN]
MAHUAYANA alt for MAPIDIAN dial of WAPISHANA [WAP]
MAHUM alt for GHOMALA' [BBJ]
MAHWA [MCW] lang, Chad
MAI alt for SILIPUT [MKC]
MAI alt for EMAE [MMW]
MAI alt for HARUA dial of BOLA [BNP]
MAI alt for MAE dial of ENGA [ENQ]
MAI BRAT [AYZ] lang, Indonesia, Irian Jaya
MAI JA alt for OREJÓN [ORE]
MAI-HEA-RI alt for ANGOYA [MIW]
MAIA [SKS] lang, Papua New Guinea
MAIABARE dial of SEWA BAY [SEW]
MAIAK dial of BURUN [BDI]
MAIANI [TNH] lang, Papua New Guinea
MAIBI dial of LEMBENA [LEQ]
MAIBRAT alt for MAI BRAT [AYZ]
MAIDU [MAI] lang, USA
MAIDUGURI dial of KANURI, YERWA [KPH]
MAIGO alt for MAYOGO [MDM]
MAIHIRI alt for ANGOYA [MIW]
MAII [MMM] lang, Vanuatu
MAIKEL alt for NAGA, MAO [NBI]
MAIKO alt for MAYOGO [MDM]
MAILANG alt for NGAING [NNF]
MAILU [MGU] lang, Papua New Guinea
MAIMA alt for CUCHUDUA dial of JAMAMADÍ [JAA]
MAIMAI alt for SILIPUT [MKC]
MAIMAKA dial of MAI BRAT [AYZ]
MAIMBIE alt for YIDINY [YII]

MAINA alt for ACHUAR SHIWIAR [ACU]
MAINA-KIZHI alt for ALTAI PROPER dial of ALTAI, SOUTHERN [ALT]
MAINFRÄNKISCH [VMF] lang, Germany
MAINGTHA dial of ACHANG [ACN]
MAINLAND FRISIAN alt for MOORINGER dial of FRISIAN, NORTHERN [FRR]
MAINOKE alt for MAINOKI dial of SIMEKU [SMZ]
MAINOKI dial of SIMEKU [SMZ]
MAINYPILGINO dial of KEREK [KRK]
MAIO-YESAN dial of YESSAN-MAYO [YSS]
MAIODOM dial of IAMALELE [YML]
MAIONGONG alt for MAQUIRITARI [MCH]
MAIOPITIAN alt for MAPIDIAN dial of WAPISHANA [WAP]
MAIPUA alt for PURARI [IAR]
MAIR alt for KOHISTANI, INDUS [MVY]
MAIRASI [FRY] lang, Indonesia, Irian Jaya
MAIRIRI alt for MARIRI [MQI]
MAISAN alt for MAISIN [MBQ]
MAISAWIET dial of MAI BRAT [AYZ]
MAISEFA dial of MAI BRAT [AYZ]
MAISIN [MBQ] lang, Papua New Guinea
MAITARIA dial of RABHA [RAH]
MAITE dial of MAI BRAT [AYZ]
MAITHILI [MKP] lang, India, Nepal, Nepal
MAITHILI alt for MAITHILI [MKP]
MAITHILI, DEHATI [MTR] lang, India, Nepal, Nepal
MAITHILI, DEHATI alt for MAITHILI, DEHATI [MTR]
MAITILI alt for MAITHILI [MKP]
MAITLI alt for MAITHILI [MKP]
MAITSI dial of MAQUIRITARI [MCH]
MAIVARA dial of TAUPOTA [TPA]
MAIWA [WMM] lang, Indonesia, Sulawesi
MAIWA [MTI] lang, Papua New Guinea
MAIYA alt for KOHISTANI, INDUS [MVY]
MAIYACH alt for KARON DORI [KGW]
MAIYAH dial of MAI BRAT [AYZ]
MAIYON alt for KOHISTANI, INDUS [MVY]
MAJAK alt for MANDYAK [MFV]
MAJANG [MPE] lang, Ethiopia
MAJANJIRO alt for MAJANG [MPE]
MAJE alt for BAYANO dial of KUNA, SAN BLAS [CUK]
MAJENE dial of MANDAR [MHN]
MAJERA [XMJ] lang, Cameroon, Chad, Chad
MAJERA alt for MAJERA [XMJ]
MAJERA alt for MAJERA [XMJ]
MAJH-KUMAIYA dial of GARHWALI [GBM]
MAJHI [MJH] lang, India, Pakistan, Pakistan
MAJHI [MJZ] lang, Nepal, India
MAJHI alt for MAJHI [MJH]
MAJHI-KORWA dial of KORWA [KFP]
MAJHVAR alt for MAJHWAR [MMJ]
MAJHWAR [MMJ] lang, India
MAJI alt for DIZI [MDX]
MAJINDA alt for CINDA dial of KAMUKU [KAU]
MAJINGAI dial of SAR [MWM]
MAJINGAI dial of SAR [MWM]
MAJINGAI-NGAMA alt for SAR [MWM]
MAJINNGAI alt for MAJINGAI dial of SAR [MWM]
MAJINNGAY alt for MAJINGAI dial of SAR [MWM]
MAJINYA alt for DIZI [MDX]
MAJNA-PIL'GINSKIJ alt for MAINYPILGINO dial of KEREK [KRK]
MAJUBIM alt for PARANAWÁT [PAF]

MAJUGU alt for MAYOGO [MDM]
MAJURUNA alt for MATSÉS [MCF]
MAJUU alt for MANGBELE [MKQ]
MAK [PBL] lang, Nigeria
MAK alt for CHING [MKG]
MAK dial of CHING [MKG]
MAK'Á alt for MACA [MCA]
MAKA alt for BYEP [MKK]
MAKA alt for MAAKA [MEW]
MAKA alt for MACA [XMC]
MAKA alt for MACA [MCA]
MAKAA [MCP] lang, Cameroon
MAKAA alt for TOMA dial of SAMO [SBD]
MAKABUKY dial of SANIYO-HIYOWE [SNY]
MAKADA alt for MAKADAM dial of RAMOAAINA [RAI]
MAKADAM dial of RAMOAAINA [RAI]
MAKAEYAM alt for ATURU [AUP]
MAKAH [MYH] lang, USA
MAKAHEELIGA dial of PALUAN [PLZ]
MAKAKAT alt for QAQET [BYX]
MAKAKAU dial of MALAY [MLI]
MAKAKWE-KHAMBANA alt for HLENGWE dial of TSWA [TSC]
MAKALAKA alt for KALANGA [KCK]
MAKALE alt for YAO [YAO]
MAKALE dial of TORAJA-SA'DAN [SDA]
MAKANGARA alt for CINDA dial of KAMUKU [KAU]
MAKARAKA dial of ZANDE [ZAN]
MAKARI alt for MPADE [MPI]
MAKARI alt for MPADE dial of MPADE [MPI]
MAKARIKI dial of AMAHAI [AMQ]
MAKARIM [MDV] lang, Papua New Guinea
MAKARUB alt for MIKAREW [MSY]
MAKARUP alt for MIKAREW [MSY]
MAKASAI [MKZ] lang, Indonesia, Nusa Tenggara
MAKASAI dial of MAKASAI [MKZ]
MAKASAR alt for MAKASSAR [MSR]
MAKASSA alt for MAKASSAR [MSR]
MAKASSAARSCHE alt for MAKASSAR [MSR]
MAKASSAI alt for MAKASAI [MKZ]
MAKASSAR [MSR] lang, Indonesia, Sulawesi
MAKASSARESE alt for MAKASSAR [MSR]
MAKASSARESE dial of MALAY [MLI]
MAKATAO dial of SIRAIYA [FOS]
MAKATIAN dial of SELUWASAN [SWH]
MAKATTAO alt for MAKATAO dial of SIRAIYA [FOS]
MAKAWE-KHAMBANA alt for HLENGWE dial of TSWA [TSC]
MAKE dial of FANG [FNG]
MAKELA'I-MAOTOW alt for TOMPASO dial of TONTEMBOAN [TNT]
MAKELAI alt for TOMPASO dial of TONTEMBOAN [TNT]
MAKEM alt for MALUAL dial of DINKA, SOUTHWESTERN [DIK]
MAKERE dial of MANGBETU [MDJ]
MAKERE dial of MANGBETU [MDJ]
MAKET dial of TANGGA [TGG]
MAKHUA alt for MAKHUWA [MAK]
MAKHUWA [MAK] lang, Mozambique, Tanzania, Tanzania
MAKHUWA alt for MAKHUWA [MAK]
MAKHUWA dial of MAKHUWA [MAK]
MAKHUWA-MAKHUWANA [VMW] lang,

Mozambique
MAKHUWA-NIASSA [VMK] lang, Mozambique
MAKHUWANA alt for MAKHUWA-MAKHUWANA
   [VMW]
MAKI alt for KALUMPANG [KLI]
MAKIALIGA alt for MAKAHEELIGA dial of PALUAN
   [PLZ]
MAKIAN BARAT alt for MAKIAN, WEST [MQS]
MAKIAN DALAM alt for MAKIAN, EAST [MKY]
MAKIAN LUAR alt for MAKIAN, WEST [MQS]
MAKIAN TIMUR alt for MAKIAN, EAST [MKY]
MAKIAN, EAST [MKY] lang, Indonesia, Maluku
MAKIAN, WEST [MQS] lang, Indonesia, Maluku
MAKIANG dial of KINABATANGAN, UPPER [DMG]
MAKIRITARE alt for MAQUIRITARI [MCH]
MAKKI alt for KALUMPANG [KLI]
MAKLERE dial of MAKASAI [MKZ]
MAKLEU alt for MAKLEW [MGF]
MAKLEW [MGF] lang, Indonesia, Irian Jaya
MAKO alt for MACO dial of PIAROA [PID]
MAKOA alt for MAKHUWA [MAK]
MAKOANE alt for MAKHUWA [MAK]
MAKODA dial of BUDU [BUU]
MAKOLKOL [ZMH] lang, Papua New Guinea
MAKOMA dial of SIMAA [SIE]
MAKONDA alt for MAKONDE [KDE]
MAKONDE [KDE] lang, Tanzania, Mozambique
MAKONDE alt for VAMAKONDE dial of MAKONDE
   [KDE]
MAKONG alt for MANGKONG [XMK]
MAKOREKORE alt for KOREKORE dial of SHONA
   [SHD]
MAKOROKO alt for KWADI [KWZ]
MAKRANA dial of MAITHILI [MKP]
MAKRANI alt for BALUCHI, SOUTHERN [BCC]
MAKRANI dial of BALUCHI, SOUTHERN [BCC]
MAKRANI alt for LOTUNI dial of BALUCHI,
   SOUTHERN [BCC]
MAKSELA alt for MOKSELA [VMS]
"MAKU" alt for YAHUP [YAB]
MAKÚ BARA alt for BARA [BXC]
MAKÚ NADÊB alt for NADÊB [MBJ]
MAKU-GUARIBA alt for GUARIBA MAKU [GBQ]
"MAKÚ-HUPDÁ" alt for HUPDË [JUP]
MAKÚ-YAHUP alt for YAHUP [YAB]
MAKU'A [LVA] lang, Indonesia, Nusa Tenggara
MAKUA alt for MAKHUWA [MAK]
MAKUANA alt for MAKHUWA-MAKHUWANA
   [VMW]
MAKUDUKUDU dial of BANGBA [BBE]
MAKUNA alt for MACUNA [MYY]
MAKUNADÔBÔ alt for NADÊB [MBJ]
MAKURA alt for NAMAKURA [NMK]
MAKURA dial of NAMAKURA [NMK]
MAKURÁP alt for MAKURÁPI [MAG]
MAKURÁPI [MAG] lang, Brazil
MAKUSHI alt for MACUSHI [MBC]
MAKUTANA dial of MANGBUTU [MDK]
MAKUTU dial of BALOI [BIZ]
MAKUXI alt for MACUSHI [MBC]
MAKUXÍ alt for MACUSHI [MBC]
MAKWAKWE-KHAMBANA alt for HLENGWE dial of
   TSWA [TSC]
MAKWARE alt for NAGA, KHIAMNGAN [NKY]
MAKWE dial of MWANI [WMW]
MAKYA alt for BYEP [MKK]

MAL [MLF] lang, Laos, Thailand, Thailand
MAL alt for MAL [MLF]
MALA [PED] lang, Papua New Guinea
MALA [RUY] lang, Nigeria
MALA alt for MARA [MEC]
MALA dial of TONGA [TOI]
MALABAR dial of MALAYALAM [MJS]
MALABU dial of BATA [BTA]
MALABU dial of JIMI [JIM]
MALACCAN alt for MALACCAN CREOLE
   PORTUGUESE [MCM]
MALACCAN CREOLE MALAY [CCM] lang, Malaysia,
   Peninsular
MALACCAN CREOLE PORTUGUESE [MCM] lang,
   Malaysia, Peninsular, Singapore, Singapore
MALACCAN CREOLE PORTUGUESE alt for
   MALACCAN CREOLE PORTUGUESE [MCM]
MALACHINI alt for POKOMO, LOWER [POJ]
MALAGASY [MEX] lang, Madagascar, Comoros
   Islands
MALAGHETI dial of TALISE [TLR]
MALAGMALAG alt for MULLUKMULLUK [MPB]
MALAI dial of TUAM-MUTU [TUC]
MALAK-MALAK alt for MULLUKMULLUK [MPB]
MALAKANAGIRI KOYA dial of KOYA [KFF]
MALAKHEL [MLD] lang, Afghanistan
MALAKKA BESISI dial of BESISI [MHE]
MALAKOTE [MLK] lang, Kenya
MALAL dial of THEMNE [TEJ]
MALALA alt for MALA [PED]
MALALAMAI [MMT] lang, Papua New Guinea
MALALULU dial of POKOMO, UPPER [PKB]
MALAMBA dial of BUDU [BUU]
MALAMUNI alt for MARAMUNI dial of ENGA [ENQ]
MALANG alt for MADANG [MQD]
MALANG-PASURUAN dial of JAVANESE [JAN]
MALANGA dial of MABA [MDE]
MALANGKE-USSU alt for LUWU dial of BUGIS [BPR]
MALANGO [MLN] lang, Solomon Islands
MALANKURAVAN [MJO] lang, India
MALAPANDARAM [MJP] lang, India
MALAPANTARAM alt for MALAPANDARAM [MJP]
MALAQUEIRO alt for MALACCAN CREOLE
   PORTUGUESE [MCM]
MALAQUENHO alt for MALACCAN CREOLE
   PORTUGUESE [MCM]
MALAQUENSE alt for MALACCAN CREOLE
   PORTUGUESE [MCM]
MALAQUÊS alt for MALACCAN CREOLE
   PORTUGUESE [MCM]
MALARKUTI alt for VISHAVAN [VIS]
MALARYAN [MJQ] lang, India
MALAS [MKR] lang, Papua New Guinea
MALASANGA [MQZ] lang, Papua New Guinea
MALASANGA dial of MALASANGA [MQZ]
MALATIA alt for MALATYA dial of ARMENIAN
   [ARM]
MALATYA dial of ARMENIAN [ARM]
MALAUEG alt for MALAWEG dial of ITAWIT [ITV]
MALAVEDAN [MJR] lang, India
MALAVETAN alt for MALAVEDAN [MJR]
MALAVI alt for MALVI [MUP]
MALAWEG dial of ITAWIT [ITV]
MALAWI alt for PETA dial of NYANJA [NYJ]
MALAWI alt for PETA dial of NYANJA [NYJ]
MALAY [MLI] lang, Malaysia, Peninsular, Brunei,

Indonesia, Sumatra, Singapore, Thailand
MALAY alt for MALAY [MLI]
MALAY dial of ATI [ATK]
MALAY, AMBONESE [ABS] lang, Indonesia, Maluku,
  Netherlands
MALAY, BABA [BAB] lang, Singapore, Malaysia,
  Peninsular
MALAY, BACANESE [BTJ] lang, Indonesia, Maluku
MALAY, BERAU [BVE] lang, Indonesia, Kalimantan
MALAY, BUKIT [BVU] lang, Indonesia, Kalimantan
MALAY, COCOS ISLANDS [COA] lang, Malaysia,
  Sabah, Australia, Australia
MALAY, COCOS ISLANDS alt for MALAY, COCOS
  ISLANDS [COA]
MALAY, JAMBI [JAX] lang, Indonesia, Sumatra
MALAY, KEDAH [MEO] lang, Thailand
MALAY, KOTA BANGUN KUTAI [MQG] lang,
  Indonesia, Kalimantan
MALAY, MENADONESE [XMM] lang, Indonesia,
  Sulawesi
MALAY, NORTH MOLUCCAN [MAX] lang, Indonesia,
  Maluku
MALAY, PATTANI [MFA] lang, Thailand
MALAY, SABAH [MSI] lang, Malaysia, Sabah
MALAY, TENGGARONG KUTAI [VKT] lang,
  Indonesia, Kalimantan
MALAYA TAMIL dial of TAMIL [TCV]
MALAYADIARS dial of MALANKURAVAN [MJO]
MALAYALAM [MJS] lang, India, Fiji, Singapore, Fiji
MALAYALAM alt for MALAYALAM [MJS]
MALAYALAM dial of MALAYALAM [MJS]
MALAYALANI alt for MALAYALAM [MJS]
MALAYALI alt for MALAYALAM [MJS]
MALAYARAYAN alt for MALARYAN [MJQ]
MALAYIC DAYAK [XDY] lang, Indonesia, Kalimantan
MALAYNON [MLZ] lang, Philippines
MALAYO [MBP] lang, Colombia
MALAYO-PORTUGUESE alt for MALACCAN CREOLE
  PORTUGUESE [MCM]
MALAYSIAN CREOLE PORTUGUESE alt for
  MALACCAN CREOLE PORTUGUESE [MCM]
MALAYSIAN MINANGKABAU alt for NEGERI
  SEMBILAN MALAY [ZMI]
MALAYSIAN SIGN LANGUAGE [XML] lang,
  Malaysia, Peninsular
MALAYU alt for MALAY [MLI]
MALBA alt for KALARKO [KBA]
MALBA-BIRIFOR alt for BIRIFOR, MALBA [BFO]
MALBE alt for MALGBE [MXF]
MALDAVACA alt for MANDAHUACA [MHT]
MALDAVACA alt for BARÉ [BAE]
MALDIVIAN [SNM] lang, Maldives, India
MALDJANA alt for MALGANA [VML]
MALE [MDC] lang, Papua New Guinea
MALE [MDY] lang, Ethiopia
MALE ARAYANS alt for MALARYAN [MJQ]
MALE KURAVAN alt for MALANKURAVAN [MJO]
MALEAN alt for MALAYALAM [MJS]
MALECITE dial of MALECITE-PASSAMAQUODDY
  [MAC]
MALECITE-PASSAMAQUODDY [MAC] lang, Canada,
  USA, USA
MALECITE-PASSAMAQUODDY alt for MALECITE-
  PASSAMAQUODDY [MAC]
MALEK alt for AIKU [MZF]
MALÉKU JAÍKA [GUT] lang, Costa Rica

MALELE dial of MANGBETU [MDJ]
MALEN-UTWE dial of KUSAIE [KSI]
MALENI alt for SHAGAWU [ROA]
MALEPANTARAM alt for MALAPANDARAM [MJP]
MALEU dial of MALEU-KILENGE [MGL]
MALEU-KILENGE [MGL] lang, Papua New Guinea
MALEYARAYAN alt for MALARYAN [MJQ]
MALFAXAL [MLX] lang, Vanuatu
MALGACHE alt for MALAGASY [MEX]
MALGANA [VML] lang, Australia
MALGBE [MXF] lang, Cameroon, Chad, Chad
MALGBE alt for MALGBE [MXF]
MALGBE dial of MALGBE [MXF]
MALGO alt for GAMARGU dial of WANDALA [MFI]
MALGO alt for GAMARGU dial of WANDALA [MFI]
MALGWA alt for GAMARGU dial of WANDALA [MFI]
MALGWA alt for GAMARGU dial of WANDALA [MFI]
MALGWE alt for MALGBE [MXF]
MALHATEE alt for MARATHI [MRT]
MALHESTI dial of KANAURI [KFK]
MALI [MKA] lang, India
MALI [GCC] lang, Papua New Guinea
MALIGAN dial of TAGAL MURUT [MVV]
MALIGO [MWJ] lang, Angola
MALIKH alt for MALDIVIAN [SNM]
MALIKI dial of AIMAQ [AIQ]
MALILA [MGQ] lang, Tanzania
MALILIA alt for MALILA [MGQ]
MALIMBA [MZD] lang, Cameroon
MALIMIUT alt for KOTZEBUE SOUND INUPIAT dial
  of INUIT, NORTH ALASKAN [ESI]
MALIMIUT ESKIMO alt for KOBUK RIVER ESKIMO
  dial of INUIT, NORTHWEST ALASKA INUPIAT
  [ESK]
MALIMPUNG [MLT] lang, Indonesia, Sulawesi
MALINALTEPEC dial of TLAPANECO [TLL]
MALINKA alt for MALINKE [MLQ]
MALINKE [MLQ] lang, Mali, Guinea, Senegal
MALINKÉ alt for JULA [DYU]
MALINKE alt for MALINKE [MLQ]
MALINKE dial of JULA [DYU]
MALISEET alt for MALECITE dial of MALECITE-
  PASSAMAQUODDY [MAC]
MALIYAD alt for MALAYALAM [MJS]
MALJANNA alt for MALGANA [VML]
MALKA dial of KABARDIAN [KAB]
MALKAN alt for MOLO [ZMO]
MALKANA alt for MALGANA [VML]
MALKI alt for MALDIVIAN [SNM]
MALLANGO dial of KALINGA, SOUTHERN [KSC]
MALLEALLE alt for MALAYALAM [MJS]
MALLORCA-MINORCA alt for BALEARIC dial of
  CATALAN [CLN]
MALLORQUIN dial of CATALAN [CLN]
MALLORQUIN-MENORQUIN alt for BALEARIC dial of
  CATALAN [CLN]
MALLOW alt for MALVI [MUP]
MALMARIV [MNL] lang, Vanuatu
MALNGIN dial of GURINJI [GUE]
MALO [MLA] lang, Vanuatu
MALO alt for EMBALOH [EMB]
MALO alt for ZAYSE [ZAY]
MALOH alt for EMBALOH [EMB]
MALOL [MBK] lang, Papua New Guinea
MALOLO alt for MALOL [MBK]
MALOM dial of MADAK [MMX]

MALON alt for MALOL [MBK]
MALOPOLSKA dial of POLISH [PQL]
MALPA alt for KALARKO [KBA]
MALPAHARIA alt for MALTO [MJT]
MALPAHARIA dial of BENGALI [BNG]
MALPAHARIA MALTO dial of MALTO [MJT]
MALTAM alt for MASLAM dial of MASLAM [MSV]
MALTESE [MLS] lang, Malta
MALTI alt for MALTO [MJT]
MALTO [MJT] lang, India
MALTU alt for MALTO [MJT]
MALU alt for RAMOAAINA [RAI]
MALU alt for TO'ABAITA [MLU]
MALU alt for MARU [MHX]
MALU'U alt for TO'ABAITA [MLU]
MALUA BAY [MLL] lang, Vanuatu
MALUAL dial of DINKA, SOUTHWESTERN [DIK]
MA'LULA [AMW] lang, Syria
MALUNDA dial of MANDAR [MHN]
MALUNUNDA alt for GAYARDILT [GYD]
MALVANI alt for KUDALI dial of KONKANI,
    GOANESE [GOM]
MALVAXAL-TOMAN ISLAND alt for MALFAXAL
    [MLX]
MALVI [MUP] lang, India
MALVI PROPER dial of MALVI [MUP]
MALWADA alt for MALVI [MUP]
MALWAL alt for MALUAL dial of DINKA,
    SOUTHWESTERN [DIK]
MALWI alt for MALVI [MUP]
MAM alt for HONDURAN MÍSKITO dial of MÍSKITO
    [MIQ]
MAM MARQUENSE alt for MAM, CENTRAL [MVC]
MAM OCCIDENTAL alt for MAM, CENTRAL [MVC]
MAM QUETZALTECO alt for MAM, SOUTHERN
    [MMS]
MAM, CENTRAL [MVC] lang, Guatemala
MAM, NORTHERN [MAM] lang, Guatemala, Mexico,
    Mexico
MAM, NORTHERN alt for MAM, NORTHERN [MAM]
MAM, SOUTHERN [MMS] lang, Guatemala
MAM, TAJUMULCO [MPF] lang, Guatemala
MAM, TODOS SANTOS CUCHUMATÁN [MVJ] lang,
    Guatemala, Mexico, Mexico
MAM, TODOS SANTOS CUCHUMATÁN alt for
    MAM, TODOS SANTOS CUCHUMATÁN [MVJ]
MAMA alt for KANTANA [MMA]
MAMA alt for MAMAA [MHF]
MAMAA [MHF] lang, Papua New Guinea
MAMAINDÉ alt for NAMBIKUÁRA, NORTHERN
    [MBG]
MAMAINDÉ dial of NAMBIKUÁRA, NORTHERN
    [MBG]
MAMALA dial of HITU [HIT]
MAMALGHA MUNJI dial of MUNJI [MNJ]
MAMANWA [MMN] lang, Philippines
MAMANWA NEGRITO alt for MAMANWA [MMN]
MAMAQ dial of KERINCI [KVR]
MAMARA alt for SENOUFO, MAMARA [MYK]
MAMASA [MQJ] lang, Indonesia, Sulawesi
MAMBA dial of CHAGGA [KAF]
MAMBAE alt for MAMBAI [MGM]
MAMBAI [MCS] lang, Cameroon, Chad, Chad
MAMBAI [MGM] lang, Indonesia, Nusa Tenggara
MAMBAI alt for MAMBAI [MCS]
MAMBAI dial of MAMBAI [MGM]

MAMBANGURA dial of NGURA [NBX]
MAMBAR alt for CENTRAL WAIBUK dial of HARUAI
    [TMD]
MAMBAY alt for MAMBAI [MCS]
MAMBAYA dial of POL [PMM]
MAMBE alt for MUNIWARA [MWB]
MAMBE' dial of DII [DUR]
MAMBERE alt for MAMBILA, CAMEROON [MYA]
MAMBERE alt for MAMBILA, NIGERIA [MZK]
MAMBETTO alt for MANGBETU [MDJ]
MAMBI alt for ARALLE-TABULAHAN [ATQ]
MAMBILA DE GEMBU alt for JU NAARE dial of
    MAMBILA, CAMEROON [MYA]
MAMBILA, CAMEROON [MYA] lang, Cameroon
MAMBILA, NIGERIA [MZK] lang, Nigeria
MAMBILLA alt for MAMBILA, CAMEROON [MYA]
MAMBILLA alt for MAMBILA, NIGERIA [MZK]
MAMBISA dial of ALUR [ALZ]
MAMBORU [MVD] lang, Indonesia, Nusa Tenggara
MAMBUKUSH alt for MBUKUSHU [MHW]
MAMBULU-LAPORO alt for SAMPOLAWA dial of
    CIA-CIA [CIA]
MAMBUMP dial of BUANG, MAPOS [BZH]
MAMBWE dial of MAMBWE-LUNGU [MGR]
MAMBWE dial of MAMBWE-LUNGU [MGR]
MAMBWE-LUNGU [MGR] lang, Zambia, Tanzania
MAMÉ alt for TACANECO [MTZ]
MAMEDJA alt for GAAM [TBI]
MAMENYAN alt for BAMENYAM [BCE]
MAMGBAY alt for MAMBAI [MCS]
MAMGBEI alt for MAMBAI [MCS]
MAMIDZA alt for GAAM [TBI]
MAMISA alt for SESA dial of FOLOPA [PPO]
MAMNA'A dial of DII [DUR]
MAMOEDJOE alt for MAMUJU [MQX]
MAMOEDJOESCH alt for MAMUJU [MQX]
MAMORI alt for MAMORIA dial of JAMAMADÍ [JAA]
MAMORIA dial of JAMAMADÍ [JAA]
MAMPA alt for SHERBRO [BUN]
MAMPOKO dial of BALOI [BIZ]
MAMPRULE alt for MAMPRULI [MAW]
MAMPRULI [MAW] lang, Ghana, Togo
MAMPUKUSH alt for MBUKUSHU [MHW]
MAMPWA alt for SHERBRO [BUN]
MAMUDJU alt for MAMUJU [MQX]
MAMUGA alt for BILEKI dial of NAKANAI [NAK]
MAMUJU [MQX] lang, Indonesia, Sulawesi
MAMUJU dial of MAMUJU [MQX]
MAMUSI [KDF] lang, Papua New Guinea
MAMUSI dial of MAMUSI [KDF]
MAMVU [MDI] lang, Zaïre
MAMVU alt for MAMVU [MDI]
MAN alt for MANCHU [MJF]
MÁN alt for MAN CAO LAN [MLC]
MÁN alt for MIEN [YOC]
MAN alt for MIEN [YOC]
MAN dial of PANA [PNZ]
MAN CAO LAN [MLC] lang, Viet Nam, China
MAN CAO-LAN alt for MAN CAO LAN [MLC]
MAN DO dial of MIEN [YOC]
MAN LAN-TIEN alt for MUN [MJI]
MAN LANTIEN alt for MUN [MJI]
MAN MET [MML] lang, China
MÁN PA SENG alt for PA HNG [PHA]
MAN PA SENG alt for PA HNG [PHA]
MAN THANH alt for TAI MAN THANH [TMM]

MÁN TRÁNG alt for HMONG DAW [MWW]
MANA alt for FANIA [FAN]
MANABE-SHIMA dial of JAPANESE [JPN]
MANADJA alt for LIMILNGAN [LMC]
MANAGALASI [MCQ] lang, Papua New Guinea
MANAGARI alt for MAUNG [MPH]
MANAGOBLA dial of GOLA [GOL]
MANAGUA alt for CASHIBO-CACATAIBO [CBR]
MANAGULASI alt for MANAGALASI [MCQ]
MANAIRISU [MPD] lang, Brazil
MANAJO alt for AMANAYÉ [AMA]
MANALA alt for MANGALA [MEM]
MANALDJALI alt for YUGAMBAL [YUB]
MANAM [MVA] lang, Papua New Guinea
MANAMBU [MLE] lang, Papua New Guinea
MANANAHUA alt for SENSI [SNI]
MANANG alt for MANANGBA [NMM]
MANANGA dial of TALIABU [TLV]
MANANGBA [NMM] lang, Nepal
MANANGEER dial of THURI [THU]
MANANGI alt for MANANGBA [NMM]
MANAPE alt for GAPAPAIWA [PWG]
MAÑARIES alt for MACHIGUENGA [MCB]
MANAU alt for BURMESO [BZU]
MANAWI dial of AMBAI [AMK]
MANAXO alt for AMANAYÉ [AMA]
MANAY MANDAYAN alt for MANDAYA, KARAGA
     [MRY]
MANAZE alt for AMANAYÉ [AMA]
MANAZO alt for AMANAYÉ [AMA]
MANBAE alt for MAMBAI [MGM]
MANBAI alt for MAMBAI [MCS]
MANBU alt for MANG [MGA]
MANCAGNE alt for MANKANYA [MAN]
MANCANG alt for MANKANYA [MAN]
MANCANHA alt for MANKANYA [MAN]
MANCHAD alt for LAHULI, CHAMBA [LAE]
MANCHATI alt for LAHULI, CHAMBA [LAE]
MANCHATI alt for MIKIR [MJW]
MANCHIA alt for YI, SICHUAN [III]
MANCHINERE alt for PIRO [PIB]
MANCHINERE alt for MANITENERI dial of PIRO [PIB]
MANCHINERI alt for PIRO [PIB]
MANCHINERI alt for MANITENERI dial of PIRO [PIB]
MANCHU [MJF] lang, China
MANDA [MGS] lang, Tanzania
MANDA [MHA] lang, India
MANDA [ZMA] lang, Australia
MANDABA dial of MABA [MDE]
MANDAEAN alt for MANDAIC [MID]
MANDAGE alt for MSER [KQX]
MANDAHUACA [MHT] lang, Venezuela, Brazil
MANDAIC [MID] lang, Iran
MANDAILING BATAK alt for BATAK MANDAILING
     [BTM]
MANDAK alt for MADAK [MMX]
MANDAL alt for BAGHELI [BFY]
MANDALA dial of MABA [MDE]
MANDAN [MHQ] lang, USA
MANDAN dial of RAMOAAINA [RAI]
MANDANDANYI [ZMK] lang, Australia
MANDANKWE alt for MENDANKWE [MFD]
MANDAR [MHN] lang, Indonesia, Sulawesi
MANDARA [TBF] lang, Papua New Guinea
MANDARA alt for WANDALA [MFI]
MANDARA alt for WANDALA dial of WANDALA

[MFI]
MANDARA MONTAGNARD alt for WANDALA [MFI]
MANDARI [MQU] lang, Sudan
MANDARI alt for MUNDARI [MUW]
MANDARI alt for BAGA MADURI [BMD]
MANDARI alt for MONDARI dial of BARI [BFA]
MANDARIN alt for CHINESE, MANDARIN [CHN]
MANDAUACA alt for MANDAHUACA [MHT]
MANDAWAKA alt for MANDAHUACA [MHT]
MANDAWÁKA alt for MANDAHUACA [MHT]
MANDAYA alt for MANOBO, DIBABAWON [MBD]
MANDAYA MANSAKA alt for MANSAKA [MSK]
MANDAYA, CATAELANO [MST] lang, Philippines
MANDAYA, KARAGA [MRY] lang, Philippines
MANDAYA, SANGAB [MYT] lang, Philippines
MANDE alt for NOMAANDE [LEM]
MANDE alt for GARO [GRT]
MANDE alt for MANINKA [MNI]
MANDE alt for MANDINKA [MNK]
MANDEALI [MJL] lang, India
MANDEGHUGHUSU alt for SIMBO [SBB]
MANDELAUT alt for BAJAU LAUT dial of SAMA,
     SOUTHERN [SIT]
MANDELLA alt for MADNGELE [ZML]
MANDER [MQR] lang, Indonesia, Irian Jaya
MANDHARSCHE alt for MANDAR [MHN]
MANDI [TUA] lang, Papua New Guinea
MANDI alt for MANDEALI [MJL]
MANDI alt for NOMAANDE [LEM]
MANDIALI alt for MANDEALI [MJL]
MANDING alt for MANDINKA [MNK]
MANDINGI alt for BULLOM SO [BUY]
MANDINGO alt for MANYA [MZJ]
MANDINGO alt for MANINKA [MNI]
MANDINGO alt for MANDINKA [MNK]
MANDINGUE alt for MANDINKA [MNK]
MANDINKA [MNK] lang, Senegal, Gambia, Guinea
     Bissau
MANDINQUE alt for MANDINKA [MNK]
MANDJA alt for MANJA [MZV]
MANDJALPINGU dial of DJINBA [DJB]
MANDJAQUE alt for MANDYAK [MFV]
MANDJOEN alt for YIR YORONT [YIY]
MANDJU alt for GHOMALA' [BBJ]
MANDLA dial of TSWA [TSC]
MANDLA dial of GONDI, NORTHERN [GON]
MANDLAHA alt for GODWANI dial of BAGHELI [BFY]
MANDO dial of KANEMBU [KBL]
MANDOBBO alt for KAETI [KZH]
MANDOBO alt for KAETI [KZH]
MANDOK dial of TUAM-MUTU [TUC]
MANDOP alt for MANGDIKHA dial of KEBUMTAMP
     [KJZ]
MANDRICA dial of ALBANIAN, GHEG [ALS]
MANDUKA dial of NAMBIKUÁRA, SOUTHERN [NAB]
MANDUSIR dial of BIAK [BHW]
MANDYAK [MFV] lang, Guinea Bissau, Cape Verde
     Islands, Gambia, Senegal
MANDYAK alt for MANDYAK [MFV]
MANDYAM BRAHMIN dial of TAMIL [TCV]
MANE dial of BALANTA [BLE]
MANEHAS dial of MBO [MBO]
MANEM [JET] lang, Indonesia, Irian Jaya, Papua
     New Guinea, Papua New Guinea
MANEM alt for MANEM [JET]
MANENGOUBA dial of MBO [MBO]

MANENGUBA alt for MANENGOUBA dial of MBO [MBO]
MANEO dial of MANUSELA [WHA]
MANG [MGA] lang, Viet Nam, China, Thailand
MANG dial of MUMUYE [MUL]
MANG alt for MANGEI dial of TALIABU [TLV]
MANG CONG alt for MANGKONG [XMK]
MANG U alt for MANG [MGA]
MANG-KOONG alt for MANGKONG [XMK]
MANGA alt for KANURI, MANGA [KBY]
MANGA alt for MBA [MFC]
MANGA BUANG alt for BUANG, MANGGA [MMO]
MANGAABA alt for MBULA [MNA]
MANGAAVA alt for MBULA [MNA]
MANGAAWA alt for MBULA [MNA]
MANGAHERI alt for KAGULU [KKI]
MANGAIA dial of RAROTONGAN [RRT]
MANGALA [MEM] lang, Australia
MANGALA [MGH] lang, Congo
MANGALAA alt for MANGALA [MEM]
MANGALILI dial of GUMATJ [GNN]
MANGALORE dial of KONKANI, GOANESE [GOM]
MANGANITU dial of SANGIR [SAN]
MANGANJA dial of NYANJA [NYJ]
MANGANJA dial of NYANJA [NYJ]
MANGANJI dial of NGIRI [NGR]
MANGAP alt for MBULA [MNA]
MANGAP-MBULA alt for MBULA [MNA]
MANGAR dial of DAFFO-BATURA [DAM]
MANGARAGAN MANDAYA alt for MANDAYA, KARAGA [MRY]
MANGARAI alt for MANGARAYI [MPC]
MANGARAYI [MPC] lang, Australia
MANGAREVA [MRV] lang, French Polynesia
MANGAREVAN alt for MANGAREVA [MRV]
MANGARI alt for MAGAR, EASTERN [MGP]
MANGARLA alt for MANGALA [MEM]
MANGARONGARO alt for PENRHYN [PNH]
MANGAS [MAH] lang, Nigeria
MANGASARA alt for MAKASSAR [MSR]
MANGATI alt for DATOGA [TCC]
MANGAYA alt for MANGAYAT [MYJ]
MANGAYAT [MYJ] lang, Sudan
MANGBAI alt for MAMBAI [MCS]
MANGBEI alt for MAMBAI [MCS]
MANGBELE [MKQ] lang, Zaïre
MANGBELE-MAYOGO dial of MAYOGO [MDM]
MANGBETTU alt for MANGBETU [MDJ]
MANGBETU [MDJ] lang, Zaïre, Uganda
MANGBETU dial of MANGBETU [MDJ]
MANGBUTU [MDK] lang, Zaïre
MANGDIKHA dial of KEBUMTAMP [KJZ]
MANGE alt for MANGEI dial of TALIABU [TLV]
MANGE'E alt for MANGEI dial of TALIABU [TLV]
MANGEI dial of TALIABU [TLV]
MANGELAS [MVL] lang, India
MANGEREI alt for MANGERR [ZME]
MANGERI alt for MANGERR [ZME]
MANGERR [ZME] lang, Australia
MANGGALILI dial of GUPAPUYNGU [GUF]
MANGGANG alt for NUMANGGANG [NOP]
MANGGAR alt for MAGAR, EASTERN [MGP]
MANGGARAI [MQY] lang, Indonesia, Nusa Tenggara
MANGGARAU alt for MANGARAYI [MPC]
MANGGUAR alt for KAMBERATARO [KBV]
MANGILI-WAIJELO dial of SUMBA [SMI]

MANGISA alt for MENGISA [MCT]
MANGKAAK dial of KADAZAN, LABUK-KINABATANGAN [DTB]
MANGKAHAK alt for MANGKAAK dial of KADAZAN, LABUK-KINABATANGAN [DTB]
MANGKAK alt for MANGKAAK dial of KADAZAN, LABUK-KINABATANGAN [DTB]
MANGKATIP alt for MENGKATIP dial of BAKUMPAI [BKR]
MANGKETTAN alt for BUKITAN [BKN]
MANGKI alt for KALUMPANG [KLI]
MANGKI dial of KALUMPANG [KLI]
MANGKIR alt for KALUMPANG [KLI]
MANGKOK alt for MANGKAAK dial of KADAZAN, LABUK-KINABATANGAN [DTB]
MANGKONG [XMK] lang, Laos, Viet Nam, Viet Nam
MANGKONG alt for MANGKONG [XMK]
MANGKUNGE dial of NGEMBA [NGE]
MANGO alt for FALI-TINGUELIN dial of FALI, SOUTH [FLE]
MANGOLE [MQC] lang, Indonesia, Maluku
MANGOLI alt for MANGOLE [MQC]
MANGSENG alt for MANGSING [MBH]
MANGSING [MBH] lang, Papua New Guinea
MANGU-NGUTU alt for MANGBUTU [MDK]
MANGUAGAN MANOBO dial of MANOBO, DIBABAWON [MBD]
MANGUE alt for CHOROTEGA [CJR]
MANGUM dial of DEG [MZW]
MANGWATO alt for NGWATU dial of TSWANA [TSW]
MANI alt for SHOE dial of MPADE [MPI]
MANI alt for INDUS dial of KOHISTANI, INDUS [MVY]
MANI-ILING alt for MANILING dial of MUSGU [MUG]
MANIBA alt for BANIWA [BAI]
MANIDE alt for AGTA, CAMARINES NORTE [ABD]
MANIF alt for ABUN [KGR]
MANIHIKI-RAKAHANGA alt for RAKAHANGA-MANIHIKI [RKH]
MANIKA alt for MANYIKA [MXC]
MANIKION alt for MANTION [MNX]
MANILA dial of TAGALOG [TGL]
MANILING dial of MUSGU [MUG]
MANIMO alt for VANIMO [VAM]
MANINKA [MNI] lang, Guinea, Liberia, Liberia, Sierra Leone
MANINKA alt for MANINKA [MNI]
MANINKA-MORI alt for MANINKA [MNI]
MANIPA [MQP] lang, Indonesia, Maluku
MANIPURI alt for MEITHEI [MNR]
MANIQ alt for KENSIU [KNS]
MANITENERE alt for PIRO [PIB]
MANITENERE alt for MANITENERI dial of PIRO [PIB]
MANITENERÍ alt for PIRO [PIB]
MANITENERI dial of PIRO [PIB]
MANITSAUÁ [MSP] lang, Brazil
MANITSAWÁ alt for MANITSAUÁ [MSP]
MANJA [MZV] lang, Central African Republic
MANJA dial of MANJA [MZV]
MANJACA alt for MANDYAK [MFV]
MANJACK alt for MANDYAK [MFV]
MANJACO alt for MANDYAK [MFV]
MANJACU alt for MANDYAK [MFV]
MANJAKU alt for MANDYAK [MFV]
MANJAR alt for MANDAR [MHN]

MANJHI alt for MAJHI [MJZ]
MANJHI alt for MAJHWAR [MMJ]
MANJHI dial of ASURI [ASR]
MANJHI dial of SANTALI [SNT]
MANJHIA alt for MAJHWAR [MMJ]
MANJI-KASA alt for DWERA dial of LIGBI [LIG]
MANJIAK alt for MANDYAK [MFV]
MANJO alt for KAFA [KBR]
MANJUKE alt for MANUKAI dial of DAYAK, LAND [DYK]
MANJUY alt for CHOROTE, IYO'WUJWA [CRQ]
MANKAGNE alt for MANKANYA [MAN]
MANKALIYA dial of KURANKO [KHA]
MANKANHA alt for MANKANYA [MAN]
MANKANYA [MAN] lang, Guinea Bissau, Gambia, Senegal
MANKANYA alt for MANKANYA [MAN]
MANKAYAN-BUGUIAS dial of KANKANAEY [KNE]
MANKETA alt for BUKITAN [BKN]
MANKIM dial of TIKAR [TIK]
MANKON dial of NGEMBA [NGE]
MANKOONG alt for MANGKONG [XMK]
MANLEA alt for KUSA-MANLEA dial of ATONI [TMR]
MANMIT alt for MAN MET [MML]
MANNA-DORA [MJU] lang, India
MANNADI alt for BAGHELI [BFY]
MANNAN [MJV] lang, India
MANNE alt for MANNAN [MJV]
MANNYOD alt for MANNAN [MJV]
MANO [MEV] lang, Liberia, Guinea
MANOA alt for PANOBO [PNO]
MANOBAI [WOO] lang, Indonesia, Maluku
MANOBO, AGUSAN [MSM] lang, Philippines
MANOBO, ATA [ATD] lang, Philippines
MANOBO, CINAMIGUIN [MKX] lang, Philippines
MANOBO, COTABATO [MTA] lang, Philippines
MANOBO, DIBABAWON [MBD] lang, Philippines
MANOBO, HIGAONON [MBA] lang, Philippines
MANOBO, ILIANEN [MBI] lang, Philippines
MANOBO, MATIGSALUG [MBT] lang, Philippines
MANOBO, OBO [OBO] lang, Philippines
MANOBO, RAJAH KABUNSUWAN [MQK] lang, Philippines
MANOBO, SARANGANI [MBS] lang, Philippines
MANOBO, TAGABAWA [BGS] lang, Philippines
MANOBO, WESTERN BUKIDNON [MBB] lang, Philippines
MANOITA alt for SHETEBO dial of SHIPIBO-CONIBO [SHP]
MANOUCHE alt for ROMANI, SINTE [RMO]
MANOUCHE dial of ROMANI, SINTE [RMO]
MANOUCHE dial of ROMANI, SINTE [RMO]
MANOWEE alt for ASMAT, CENTRAL [AST]
MANPELLE alt for MAMPRULI [MAW]
MANSAKA [MSK] lang, Philippines
MANSI [MNS] lang, Russia, Asia
MANSIBABER alt for MEAH [MEJ]
MANSIM alt for BORAI [MFX]
MANSINYO dial of YURACARE [YUE]
MANSIY alt for MANSI [MNS]
MANSO alt for MUSU dial of KURANKO [KHA]
MANSOANCA alt for MANSOANKA [MSW]
MANSOANKA [MSW] lang, Guinea Bissau, Gambia
MANTA [MYG] lang, Cameroon
MANTANGAI dial of NGAJU [NIJ]
MANTARAREN dial of LAWANGAN [LBX]

MANTAURAN dial of RUKAI [DRU]
MANTEMBU alt for YAWA [YVA]
MANTION [MNX] lang, Indonesia, Irian Jaya
MANTIZULA alt for MANITSAUÁ [MSP]
MANTJILTJARA alt for MANYJILYJARA dial of MARTU WANGKA [MPJ]
MANTON dial of DE'ANG [BFP]
MANTOVANO dial of EMILIANO [EML]
MANTRA dial of TEMUAN [TMW]
MANTZU alt for YI, SICHUAN [III]
MANU PARK PANOAN alt for YORA [MTS]
MANUA dial of MAMBAI [MGM]
MANUBARA alt for MARIA [MDS]
MANUCHE alt for ROMANI, SINTE [RMO]
MANUCHE alt for MANOUCHE dial of ROMANI, SINTE [RMO]
MANUK dial of JAVANESE [JAN]
MANUKAI dial of DAYAK, LAND [DYK]
MANUKAI alt for MANYUKAI dial of DAYAK, LAND [DYK]
MANUKOLU alt for LAGUME dial of HUMENE [HUF]
MANUM alt for MANAM [MVA]
MANUMANAW alt for KAREN, MANUMANAW [KXF]
MANUS alt for LELE [UGA]
MANUS alt for TITAN [TTV]
MANUSELA [WHA] lang, Indonesia, Maluku
MANUSH alt for MANOUCHE dial of ROMANI, SINTE [RMO]
MANX [MJD] lang, United Kingdom
MANYA [MZJ] lang, Liberia
MANYA KAN alt for MANYA [MZJ]
MANYAK dial of HSIFAN [HSI]
MANYANG alt for KENYANG [KEN]
MANYARRING dial of DJINANG [DJI]
MANYEMAN alt for BAKONI dial of KENYANG [KEN]
MANYEMEN alt for BAKONI dial of KENYANG [KEN]
MANYIKA [MXC] lang, Zimbabwe, Mozambique
MANYJILYJARA dial of MARTU WANGKA [MPJ]
MANYOK dial of BEBELE [BEB]
MANYUKAI dial of DAYAK, LAND [DYK]
MANYUKE alt for MANYUKAI dial of DAYAK, LAND [DYK]
MANYUKE alt for MANUKAI dial of DAYAK, LAND [DYK]
MANZA alt for MANJA [MZV]
MANZANERO alt for MOLUCHE dial of MAPUDUNGUN [ARU]
MANZARI alt for DUBER-KANDIA dial of KOHISTANI, INDUS [MVY]
MAO alt for NAGA, MAO [NBI]
MAO dial of KANURI, YERWA [KPH]
MAO alt for TAI MAO dial of SHAN [SJN]
MAOLI alt for GHATI dial of KONKANI [KNK]
MAONAN [MMD] lang, China
MAOPA dial of KEOPARA [KHZ]
MAOPITYAN alt for MAPIDIAN dial of WAPISHANA [WAP]
MAOPITYAN alt for MAPIDIAN dial of WAPISHANA [WAP]
MAORI [MBF] lang, New Zealand
MAOU alt for MAU [MXX]
MAOUKA alt for MAU [MXX]
MAPACHE dial of CARÚTANA [CRU]
MAPAN alt for MAPUN dial of MWAGHAVUL [SUR]
MAPAYO alt for MAPOYO [MCG]
MAPE [MLH] lang, Papua New Guinea

MAPENA [MNM] lang, Papua New Guinea
MAPI alt for YAQAY [JAQ]
MAPIA [MPY] lang, Indonesia, Irian Jaya
MAPIA dial of BIAK [BHW]
MAPIAN alt for MAPIA [MPY]
MAPIDIAN dial of WAPISHANA [WAP]
MAPIDIAN dial of WAPISHANA [WAP]
MAPIYA-KEGATA dial of EKARI [EKG]
MAPODI alt for GUDE [GDE]
MAPOR alt for LOM [MFB]
MAPORESE alt for LOM [MFB]
MAPOS alt for BUANG, MAPOS [BZH]
MAPOS dial of BUANG, MAPOS [BZH]
MAPOYE alt for MAPOYO [MCG]
MAPOYO [MCG] lang, Venezuela
MAPPA-PANA alt for TORAJA BARAT dial of
    TORAJA-SA'DAN [SDA]
MAPRIK dial of AMBULAS [ABT]
MAPUCHE alt for MAPUDUNGUN [ARU]
MAPUDA alt for GUDE [GDE]
MAPUDUNGU alt for MAPUDUNGUN [ARU]
MAPUDUNGUN [ARU] lang, Chile, Argentina
MAPUN [SJM] lang, Philippines, Malaysia, Sabah
MAPUN dial of MWAGHAVUL [SUR]
MAPUTE alt for WARU [WRU]
MAPUTONGO alt for MAPUDUNGUN [ARU]
MAQAQET alt for QAQET [BYX]
MAQUIRI alt for KAYABÍ [KYZ]
MAQUIRITAI alt for MAQUIRITARI [MCH]
MAQUIRITARE alt for MAQUIRITARI [MCH]
MAQUIRITARI [MCH] lang, Venezuela, Brazil
MAQUOUA alt for MAKHUWA [MAK]
MARA [MEC] lang, Australia
MARA alt for CHIN, MARA [MRH]
MARA dial of MALGBE [MXF]
MARA dial of HANGA [HAG]
MARA dial of KABA DEME [KWG]
MARA MA-SIKI alt for OROHA [ORA]
MARA-GOMU dial of MBO-UNG [MUX]
MARABA [XMW] lang, Central African Republic
MARABA alt for MARBA [MPG]
MARACAS dial of YUKPA [YUP]
MARACASERO alt for MALAYO [MBP]
MARACHI dial of SAAMIA [SBU]
MARAGANG alt for KIMARAGANG [KQR]
MARAGAUS alt for MARAGUS [MRS]
MARAGOLI alt for LOGOOLI [RAG]
MARAGOOLI alt for LOGOOLI [RAG]
MARAGUA alt for SATERÉ-MAWÉ [MAV]
MARAGUS [MRS] lang, Vanuatu
MARAJONA [MPQ] lang, Brazil
MARAKA alt for SONINKE [SNN]
MARAKO alt for LIBIDO [LIQ]
MARAKUET alt for MARAKWET dial of ENDO-
    MARAKWET [ENB]
MARAKWET alt for TALAI [TLE]
MARAKWET dial of ENDO-MARAKWET [ENB]
MARALANGKO alt for MARALANGO [MCY]
MARALANGO [MCY] lang, Papua New Guinea
MARALIINAN alt for SILISILI [MPL]
MARALINAN alt for SILISILI [MPL]
MARAM alt for CHIN, MARA [MRH]
MARAM alt for NAGA, MARAM [NMA]
MARAMA dial of LUYIA [LUY]
MARAMANANDJI alt for MARIMANINDJI [ZMM]
MARAMANUNGGU alt for MARINGARR [ZMT]

MARAMARANDJI alt for MARIMANINDJI [ZMM]
MARAMBA [MYD] lang, Papua New Guinea
MARAMUNI dial of ENGA [ENQ]
MARAN alt for AMIS [ALV]
MARANAO [MRW] lang, Philippines
MARANAW alt for MARANAO [MRW]
MARANGAI dial of TUAMOTUAN [PMT]
MARANGIS alt for WATAM [WAX]
MARANGU alt for KIWUNJO dial of CHAGGA [KAF]
MARANSÉ [MSC] lang, Burkina Faso
MARANUNGGU [ZMR] lang, Australia
MARANUNGGU alt for MARINGARR [ZMT]
MARAQO alt for LIBIDO [LIQ]
MARARET alt for MARARIT [MGB]
MARARI dial of BHOYARI [BHY]
MARARI dial of BAGHELI [BFY]
MARARIT [MGB] lang, Chad
MARASHI dial of DOMARI [RMT]
MARATHI [MRT] lang, India
MARAU [MVR] lang, Indonesia, Irian Jaya
MARAU dial of 'ARE'ARE [ALU]
MARAU SOUND alt for MARAU dial of 'ARE'ARE
    [ALU]
MARAVE alt for PETA dial of NYANJA [NYJ]
MARAVE alt for PETA dial of NYANJA [NYJ]
MARAVI alt for PETA dial of NYANJA [NYJ]
MARAVI alt for PETA dial of NYANJA [NYJ]
MARAWAR alt for MARWARI, SOUTHERN [MQH]
MARAWAR alt for MARWARI, NORTHERN [MRI]
MARAWORNO alt for KALIHNA [CRB]
MARBA [MPG] lang, Chad
MARBA alt for MARFA [MVU]
MARCHIGIANO dial of EMILIANO [EML]
MARDA dial of KUNAMA [KUM]
MARDALA alt for ADYNYAMATHANHA [ADT]
MARDIN dial of ARABIC, SYRO-MESOPOTAMIAN
    [AYP]
MARÉ alt for NENGONE [NEN]
MARE alt for BONE dial of BUGIS [BPR]
MARE-AMMU dial of MARITHIEL [MFR]
MAREDYERBIN alt for MARIDJABIN [ZMJ]
MAREGAON dial of KOLAMI, NORTHWESTERN
    [KFB]
MAREMGI [MRX] lang, Indonesia, Irian Jaya
MARENDJE [VMR] lang, Mozambique
MARENG alt for MARING [MBW]
MARENGGAR alt for MARINGARR [ZMT]
MARENGGE alt for MAREMGI [MRX]
MARENJE alt for MARENDJE [VMR]
MARENSÉ alt for CENTRAL SONGAI dial of SONGAI
    [SON]
MARENSE alt for CENTRAL SONGAI dial of SONGAI
    [SON]
MAREOTI ARABIC dial of ARABIC, MOROCCAN
    [ARY]
MARETYABIN alt for MARIDJABIN [ZMJ]
MAREVONI dial of MAKHUWA [MAK]
MAREWUMIRI alt for NGENKIWUMERRI dial of
    NANGIKURRUNGGURR [NAM]
MARFA [MVU] lang, Chad
MARGANY [ZMC] lang, Australia
MARGHI CENTRAL [MAR] lang, Nigeria
MARGHI SOUTH [MFM] lang, Nigeria
MARGHI WEST alt for PUTAI [MFL]
MARGI alt for MARGHI CENTRAL [MAR]
MARGOS CHAULÁN dial of QUECHUA, HUÁNUCO,

SOUTHERN DOS DE MAYO-MARGOS CHAULÁN [QEI]
MARGOSATUBIG alt for SUBANUN, LAPUYAN [LAA]
MARGU [MHG] lang, Australia
MARHAY alt for MUNDANG [MUA]
MARI [HOB] lang, Papua New Guinea
MARI [MBX] lang, Papua New Guinea
MARI alt for MARI, LOW [MAL]
MARI, HIGH [MRJ] lang, Russia, Europe
MARI, LOW [MAL] lang, Russia, Europe
MARI-HILLS alt for MARI, HIGH [MRJ]
MARI-WOODS alt for MARI, LOW [MAL]
MARIA [MDS] lang, Papua New Guinea
MARIA [MRR] lang, India
MARIA dial of MARIA [MDS]
MARIA GOND alt for DANDAMI MARIA [DAQ]
MARIAPE-NAHUQUA alt for MATIPUHY [MZO]
MARICOPA [MRC] lang, USA
MARIDAN [ZMD] lang, Australia
MARIDHIEL alt for MARITHIEL [MFR]
MARIDHIYEL alt for MARITHIEL [MFR]
MARIDJABIN [ZMJ] lang, Australia
MARIDYERBIN alt for MARIDJABIN [ZMJ]
MARIGANG alt for KIMARAGANG [KQR]
MARIGL dial of GOLIN [GVF]
MARILLE alt for DAASANECH [DSH]
MARIMANINDJI [ZMM] lang, Australia
MARIMANINDU alt for MARIMANINDJI [ZMM]
MARINA alt for TOLOMAKO [TLM]
MARINAHUA dial of SHARANAHUA [MCD]
MARINAHUA dial of SHARANAHUA [MCD]
MARINÁWA alt for MARINAHUA dial of SHARANAHUA [MCD]
MARINAWA alt for MARINAHUA dial of SHARANAHUA [MCD]
MARIND [MRZ] lang, Indonesia, Irian Jaya
MARIND, BIAN [BPV] lang, Indonesia, Irian Jaya
MARINDUQUE dial of TAGALOG [TGL]
MARING [MBW] lang, Papua New Guinea
MARING alt for NAGA, MARING [NNG]
MARINGA alt for MARINGARR [ZMT]
MARINGARR [ZMT] lang, Australia
MARINGE alt for CHEKE HOLO [MRN]
MARINGHE alt for CHEKE HOLO [MRN]
MARINO [MRB] lang, Vanuatu
MARIP alt for JINGPHO [CGP]
MARIPOSAS alt for TAMPIWI dial of CUIBA [CUI]
MARIRI [MQI] lang, Indonesia, Maluku
MARITHIEL [MFR] lang, Australia
MARITHIEL dial of MARITHIEL [MFR]
MARITHIYEL alt for MARITHIEL [MFR]
MARITIME GAGAUZ dial of GAGAUZ [GAG]
MARITIME GAGAUZI dial of GAGAUZ [GAG]
MARITIME PROVENÇAL dial of PROVENÇAL [PRV]
MARITSAUA alt for MANITSAUÁ [MSP]
MARIVELES AYTA alt for AYTA, BATAAN [AYT]
MARIYEDI [ZMY] lang, Australia
MARKA [MWR] lang, Burkina Faso
MARKA alt for SONINKE [SNN]
MARKE dial of DOYAYO [DOW]
MARKWETA alt for MARAKWET dial of ENDO-MARAKWET [ENB]
MARLASI alt for KOLA [KVV]
MARMA alt for ARAKANESE [MHV]
MARMAREGHO alt for BAURO [BXA]
MAROA alt for SHOLIO dial of KATAB [KCG]

MAROCASERO alt for MALAYO [MBP]
MARON alt for HERMIT [LLF]
MARONENE alt for MORONENE [MQN]
MARONITE alt for ARABIC, CYPRIOT [ACY]
MAROS-PANGKEP dial of MAKASSAR [MSR]
MAROUA dial of FULFULDE, ADAMAWA [FUB]
MAROVA alt for MARÚBO [MZR]
MAROVO [MVO] lang, Solomon Islands
MARPAHARIA [MKB] lang, India
MARQUESAN, NORTH [MRQ] lang, French Polynesia
MARQUESAN, SOUTH [QMS] lang, French Polynesia
MARQUINA dial of BASQUE [BSQ]
MARQUITO alt for MÍSKITO [MIQ]
MÁRQUITO alt for MÍSKITO [MIQ]
MARRA alt for MARA [MEC]
MARRAKULU dial of DHUWAL [DUJ]
MARRANGU dial of DHUWAL [DUJ]
MARRANUNGA alt for MARINGARR [ZMT]
MARREVONE dial of MACA [XMC]
MARRITHIYEL alt for MARITHIEL [MFR]
MARSEILLAIS alt for MARITIME PROVENÇAL dial of PROVENÇAL [PRV]
MARSEILLE SIGN LANGUAGE dial of FRENCH SIGN LANGUAGE [FSL]
MARSELA-SOUTH BABAR alt for MASELA, CENTRAL [MKH]
MARSHALLESE [MZM] lang, Marshall Islands, Nauru, Nauru
MARSHALLESE alt for MARSHALLESE [MZM]
MARTHA'S VINEYARD SIGN LANGUAGE [MRE] lang, USA
MARTHI alt for MARATHI [MRT]
MARTINIQUE CREOLE dial of LESSER ANTILLEAN CREOLE FRENCH [DOM]
MARTU WANGKA [MPJ] lang, Australia
MARTUYHUNIRA [VMA] lang, Australia
MARU [MHX] lang, Myanmar, China
MARÚBO [MZR] lang, Brazil
MARUBA alt for MARÚBO [MZR]
MARUHIA alt for ISABI [ISA]
MARUONGMAI alt for NAGA, RONGMEI [NBU]
MARUWA alt for SHOLIO dial of KATAB [KCG]
MARVARI alt for MARWARI [MKD]
MARWA alt for SHOLIO dial of KATAB [KCG]
MARWARI [MKD] lang, India
MARWARI BHIL alt for MARWARI, SOUTHERN [MQH]
MARWARI BHIL alt for MARWARI, NORTHERN [MRI]
MARWARI, NORTHERN [MRI] lang, Pakistan
MARWARI, SOUTHERN [MQH] lang, Pakistan
MARWARI-GUJERATI alt for SOUTHERN MARWARI dial of MARWARI [MKD]
MARWORNO alt for KALIHNA [CRB]
MASA alt for MASANA [MCN]
MASA DE NUNG-TIERE alt for NANCERE [NNC]
MASAABA alt for MASABA [MYX]
MASABA [MYX] lang, Uganda
MASAGAL dial of MOFU, SOUTH [MIF]
MASAI alt for MAASAI [MET]
MASAKÁ dial of TUBARÃO [TBA]
MASAKIN alt for DENGEBU [DEC]
MASAKIN alt for NGILE [MAS]
MASAKIN BURAM alt for MASAKIN GUSAR dial of NGILE [MAS]
MASAKIN DAGIG alt for MASAKIN GUSAR dial of NGILE [MAS]

MASAKIN GUSAR dial of NGILE [MAS]
MASAKIN TUWAL dial of NGILE [MAS]
MASAKU dial of KAMBA [KIK]
MASALE alt for MASALIT [MSA]
MASALIT [MSA] lang, Sudan, Chad
MASAMA alt for ANDIO [BZB]
MASAN dial of BUNA [BVN]
MASANA [MCN] lang, Cameroon, Chad
MASANA alt for MASANA [MCN]
MASANGO alt for MAJANG [MPE]
MASANZE dial of ZYOBA [ZYO]
MASARA alt for MASALIT [MSA]
MASARETE dial of BURU [MHS]
MASARWA alt for GABAKE-NTSHORI [GZZ]
MASARWA alt for KAKIA dial of NG/AMANI [NMN]
MASASI dial of BAMBARA [BRA]
MASAWA dial of TOLAI [KSD]
MASBATEÑO alt for MASBATENYO [MSB]
MASBATENYO [MSB] lang, Philippines
MASBUAR-TELA alt for TELA-MASBUAR [TVM]
MASEGI alt for MANGSING [MBH]
MASEKI alt for MANGSING [MBH]
MASELA, CENTRAL [MKH] lang, Indonesia, Maluku
MASELA, EAST [VME] lang, Indonesia, Maluku
MASELA, WEST [MSS] lang, Indonesia, Maluku
MASEMOLA dial of SOTHO, NORTHERN [SRT]
MASEMULA alt for MASEMOLA dial of SOTHO,
    NORTHERN [SRT]
MASENREMPULU alt for MAIWA [WMM]
MASENREMPULU alt for DURI [MVP]
MASEP alt for MASSEP [MVS]
MASFEIMA dial of WANDALA [MFI]
MASH alt for ARAKANESE [MHV]
MASHADI dial of FARSI, WESTERN [PES]
MASHANGA alt for CHANGA dial of NDAU [NDC]
MASHASHA dial of NKOYA [NKA]
MASHATI dial of CHAGGA [KAF]
"MASHCO" alt for MASHCO PIRO [CUJ]
"MASHCO" alt for AMARAKAERI [AMR]
"MASHCO" alt for HUACHIPAERI [HUG]
MASHCO PIRO [CUJ] lang, Peru
MASHELLE alt for DOBASE [DOX]
MASHI [MHO] lang, Zambia
MASHI alt for SHI [SHR]
MASHI dial of MASHI [MHO]
MASHILE alt for DOBASE [DOX]
MASHOLLE alt for DOBASE [DOX]
MASHUAKWE alt for SHUA [SHG]
MASHUAKWE alt for SHUA-KHWE dial of SHUA
    [SHG]
MASI alt for MASHI [MHO]
MASIGUARE dial of CUIBA [CUI]
MASIGUARE alt for MASIWARE dial of CUIBA [CUI]
MASIIN alt for AZER dial of SONINKE [SNN]
MASIMASI dial of IAMALELE [YML]
MASINGBI dial of THEMNE [TEJ]
MASINGLE dial of BINE [ORM]
MASIRI dial of CIA-CIA [CIA]
MASIWANG [BNF] lang, Indonesia, Maluku
MASIWARE dial of CUIBA [CUI]
MASKAN alt for MESQAN dial of GURAGE,
    PERIPHERAL WEST [GPW]
MASKELYNE ISLANDS alt for MASKELYNES [KLV]
MASKELYNES [KLV] lang, Vanuatu
MASKOY PIDGIN [MHH] lang, Paraguay
MASLAM [MSV] lang, Cameroon, Chad, Chad

MASLAM alt for MASLAM [MSV]
MASLAM dial of MASLAM [MSV]
MASLAVA alt for MBEREM dial of PELASLA [MLR]
MASMADJE alt for MASMAJE [MES]
MASMAJE [MES] lang, Chad
MASONGO alt for MAJANG [MPE]
MASQAN alt for MESQAN dial of GURAGE,
    PERIPHERAL WEST [GPW]
MASSA alt for MASANA [MCN]
MASSA DE GUELENGDENG alt for MBARA [MPK]
MASSACÁ alt for MASAKÁ dial of TUBARÃO [TBA]
MASSACHUSETT alt for WAMPANOAG [WAM]
MASSACHUSETTS alt for WAMPANOAG [WAM]
MASSAKA alt for MAKURÁPI [MAG]
MASSAKAL alt for MASAGAL dial of MOFU, SOUTH
    [MIF]
MASSALAT [MDG] lang, Chad
MASSALIN dial of TALYSH [TLY]
MASSALIT alt for MASALIT [MSA]
MASSANINGA dial of YAO [YAO]
MASSENREMPULU alt for DURI [MVP]
MASSEP [MVS] lang, Indonesia, Irian Jaya
MASSET dial of HAIDA [HAI]
MASSOLIT alt for MASALIT [MSA]
MASTANAHUA dial of YAMINAHUA [YAA]
MASWANKA alt for MANSOANKA [MSW]
MATA alt for TUPURI [TUI]
MATA dial of TUPURI [TUI]
MATABAN-MOULMEIN dial of MON [MNW]
MATABELLO alt for WATUBELA [WAH]
"MATACO" alt for WICHÍ LHAMTÉS GÜISNAY
    [MZH]
MATACO GÜISNAY alt for WICHÍ LHAMTÉS
    GÜISNAY [MZH]
MATACO NOCTEN alt for WICHÍ LHAMTÉS
    NOCTEN [MTP]
MATACO PILCOMAYO alt for WICHÍ LHAMTÉS
    GÜISNAY [MZH]
MATACO VEJOZ alt for WICHÍ LHAMTÉS VEJOZ
    [MAD]
MATAGALPA [MTN] lang, Nicaragua
MATAITAI dial of BWAIDOKA [BWD]
MATAKAM alt for MAFA [MAF]
"MATAKAM" alt for MAFA [MAF]
MATAL [MFH] lang, Cameroon
MATALAANG dial of BAJAU, INDONESIAN [BDL]
MATAMBWE alt for MAKONDE [KDE]
MATAN dial of DAYAK, LAND [DYK]
MATANA'I-MAORE' alt for SONDER dial of
    TONTEMBOAN [TNT]
MATANAI alt for SONDER dial of TONTEMBOAN
    [TNT]
MATANGNGA dial of PITU ULUNNA SALU [PTU]
MATAPI alt for YUCUNA [YCN]
MATAPO alt for MAASAI [MET]
MATARU alt for BALAMULA dial of LEWADA-
    DEWARA [LWD]
MATASO dial of NAMAKURA [NMK]
MATATARWA dial of EGGON [EGO]
MATATLÁN ZAPOTECO alt for ZAPOTECO,
    SANTIAGO MATATLÁN [ZAQ]
MATAWAI alt for MATAWARI [MWL]
MATAWARI [MWL] lang, Surinam
MATBAT [XMT] lang, Indonesia, Irian Jaya
MATCHI dial of GARO [GRT]
MATCHI alt for MACI dial of ICEVE-MACI [BEC]

MATCHI alt for MACI dial of ICEVE-MACI [BEC]
MATE dial of NANDI [NNB]
MATE-NUL-FILAKARA dial of LEWO [LWW]
MATEMA dial of PILENI [PIV]
MATENGALA dial of EGGON [EGO]
MATENGO [MGV] lang, Tanzania, Mozambique
MATEPI [MQE] lang, Papua New Guinea
MATHIRA dial of GIKUYU [KIU]
MATIA [MMC] lang, India
MATIG-SALUD dial of MANOBO, MATIGSALUG
    [MBT]
MATIG-SALUG MANOBO alt for MANOBO,
    MATIGSALUG [MBT]
MATINO alt for DAVAWENYO [DAW]
MATIPU alt for MATIPUHY [MZO]
MATIPUHY [MZO] lang, Brazil
MATIPUHY dial of MATIPUHY [MZO]
MATLALA-MOLETSHI dial of SOTHO, NORTHERN
    [SRT]
MATLATZINCA, ATZINGO [OCU] lang, Mexico
MATLATZINCA, FRANCISCO DE LOS RANCHOS
    [MAT] lang, Mexico
MATLIWAG dial of MERLAV [MRM]
MATNGALA alt for MADNGELE [ZML]
MATO alt for MAKHUWA [MAK]
MATOEWARI alt for MATAWARI [MWL]
MATOH alt for EMBALOH [EMB]
MATOKI alt for NORTHERN BOMITABA dial of
    BOMITABA [ZMX]
MATONDON' dial of SWAHILI [SWA]
MATOR [MTM] lang, Russia, Asia
MATOR dial of MATOR [MTM]
MATSE alt for MATSÉS [MCF]
MATSÉS [MCF] lang, Peru, Brazil
MATSIGANGA alt for MACHIGUENGA [MCB]
MATSIGENKA alt for MACHIGUENGA [MCB]
MATSUNGAN dial of PETATS [PEX]
MATTOLE [MVB] lang, USA
MATU alt for MARU [MHX]
MATU dial of CHIN, KHUMI [CKM]
MATU dial of DARO-MATU [DRO]
MATUARI alt for MATAWARI [MWL]
MATUKAR [MJK] lang, Papua New Guinea
MATUMBI [MGW] lang, Tanzania
MATUPIT dial of TOLAI [KSD]
MATWANLY dial of RAWANG [RAW]
MATYA alt for TOUGAN dial of SAMO [SBD]
MAU [MXX] lang, Côte d'Ivoire
MAU alt for TAI MAO dial of SHAN [SJN]
MAUCHI alt for MAWCHI [MKE]
MAUE alt for SATERÉ-MAWÉ [MAV]
MAUKA alt for MAU [MXX]
MAUKE alt for MAU [MXX]
MAUKE dial of RAROTONGAN [RRT]
MAULA alt for WARLUWARA [WRB]
MAULIGAN alt for MALIGAN dial of TAGAL MURUT
    [MVV]
MAUMBI dial of TONSEA [TXS]
MAUNG [MPH] lang, Australia
MAUNG alt for KETUNGAU dial of IBAN [IBA]
MAURE alt for ARABIC, HASSANIYA [MEY]
MAURI alt for ARABIC, HASSANIYA [MEY]
MAURITIAN alt for MORISYEN [MFE]
MAURITIAN BHOJPURI dial of HINDI [HND]
MAURITIUS CREOLE FRENCH alt for MORISYEN
    [MFE]

MAUTUTU dial of NAKANAI [NAK]
MAUULA alt for WARLUWARA [WRB]
MAUWAKE [MHL] lang, Papua New Guinea
MAVAR alt for MOVAR dial of KANURI, YERWA
    [KPH]
MAVAR alt for MOVAR dial of KANURI, YERWA
    [KPH]
MAVCHI alt for MAWCHI [MKE]
MAVEA alt for MAFEA [MKV]
MAVIA alt for MAVIHA [MHP]
MAVIHA [MHP] lang, Tanzania, Mozambique
MAW alt for TAI MAO dial of SHAN [SJN]
MAWA [MJE] lang, Chad
MAWAALI dial of ARABIC, SYRO-MESOPOTAMIAN
    [AYP]
MAWACHI alt for MAWCHI [MKE]
MAWAE [MXW] lang, Papua New Guinea
MAWAK [MJJ] lang, Papua New Guinea
MAWAKE alt for MAUWAKE [MHL]
MAWAN [MCZ] lang, Papua New Guinea
MAWANDA alt for NDONDE [NDS]
MAWAS alt for KENSIU [KNS]
MAWASI dial of KORKU [KFQ]
MAWAYANA alt for MAPIDIAN dial of WAPISHANA
    [WAP]
MAWAYANA alt for MAPIDIAN dial of WAPISHANA
    [WAP]
MAWCHI [MKE] lang, India
MAWCHI dial of MAWCHI [MKE]
MAWE alt for MANO [MEV]
MAWER [MTB] lang, Chad
MAWES [MGK] lang, Indonesia, Irian Jaya
MAWIA alt for MAVIHA [MHP]
MAWISSI alt for TALINGA-BWISI [TLJ]
MAWKEN alt for MOKEN [MWT]
MAWRANG dial of NAGA, TASE [NST]
MAWSHANG alt for NAGA, MONSANG [NMH]
MAWTEIK alt for KADO [KDV]
MAWULA alt for WARLUWARA [WRB]
MAWUNCHI alt for CHISHINGYINI [ASG]
MAXAKALÍ [MBL] lang, Brazil
MAXI alt for MAXI-GBE [MXL]
MAXI-GBE [MXL] lang, Benin, Togo, Togo
MAXI-GBE alt for MAXI-GBE [MXL]
MAXINÉRI alt for PIRO [PIB]
MAXINÉRI alt for MANITENERI dial of PIRO [PIB]
MAXIRONA alt for MATSÉS [MCF]
MAXUBÍ alt for ARIKAPÚ [ARK]
MAXURUNA alt for MATSÉS [MCF]
MAY [MVZ] lang, Viet Nam, Laos
MAY RIVER alt for IWAM [IWM]
MA'YA [SLZ] lang, Indonesia, Irian Jaya
MAYÁ [MGN] lang, Brazil
MAYA alt for MAIA [SKS]
MAYA alt for ITZÁ [ITZ]
MAYA alt for YUCATECO [YUA]
MAYA alt for KIEMBARA dial of SAMO [SBD]
MAYA ICAICHE dial of ITZÁ [ITZ]
MAYA ITZÁ dial of ITZÁ [ITZ]
MAYA MOPÁN alt for MOPÁN MAYA [MOP]
MAYA OF CHAN SANTA CRUZ alt for YUCATECO,
    CHAN SANTA CRUZ [YUS]
MAYAGUDUNA [XMY] lang, Australia
MAYALI alt for GUNWINGGU [GUP]
MAYAN SIGN LANGUAGE [MSD] lang, Mexico
MAYANG dial of ASSAMESE [ASM]

MAYANGKHANG alt for NAGA, KHOIRAO [NKI]
MAYAOYAW alt for IFUGAO, MAYOYAO [IFU]
MAYAYERO dial of CUIBA [CUI]
MAYEKA [MYC] lang, Central African Republic, Zaïre
MAYEKA alt for MAYEKA [MYC]
MAYI-KULAN alt for MAYKULAN [MNT]
MAYI-KUTUNA alt for MAYAGUDUNA [XMY]
MAYIRUNA alt for MATSÉS [MCF]
MAYKO alt for MAYOGO [MDM]
MAYKULAN [MNT] lang, Australia
MAYNA alt for OMURANO [OMU]
MAYO [MAY] lang, Mexico
MAYO alt for YESSAN-MAYO [YSS]
MAYO alt for MAYÁ [MGN]
MAYO-PAS alt for PASI [PSI]
MAYO-YESAN alt for YESSAN-MAYO [YSS]
MAYOGO [MDM] lang, Zaïre
MAYOL alt for NAGA, MOYON [NMO]
MAYON NAGA alt for NAGA, MOYON [NMO]
MAYONGONG dial of MAQUIRITARI [MCH]
MAYORUNA alt for MATSÉS [MCF]
MAYOTTE alt for SHIMAORE dial of COMORIAN [SWB]
MAYOTTE alt for SHIMAORE dial of COMORIAN [SWB]
MAYOYAO alt for IFUGAO, MAYOYAO [IFU]
MAYU alt for MAYÁ [MGN]
MAYU dial of BERTA [WTI]
MAYUBO alt for MAYÁ [MGN]
MAYUGO alt for MAYOGO [MDM]
MAYUZUNA alt for MATSÉS [MCF]
MAYVASI alt for MEWASI dial of KOLI, WADIYARA [KXP]
MAZAGWA dial of WANDALA [MFI]
MAZAGWAY alt for MUSGOI dial of DABA [DAB]
MAZAHUA [MAZ] lang, Mexico
MAZANDERANI [MZN] lang, Iran
MAZARO [MZX] lang, Mozambique
MAZATECO, HUAUTLA DE JIMENEZ [MAU] lang, Mexico
MAZATECO, SAN FELIPE JALAPA DE DIAZ [MAJ] lang, Mexico
MAZATECO, SAN JERÓNIMO TECOATL [MAA] lang, Mexico
MAZATECO, SAN JUAN CHIQUIHUITLÁN [MAQ] lang, Mexico
MAZATECO, SAN PEDRO IXCATLÁN [MAO] lang, Mexico
MAZGARWA dial of BADE [BDE]
MAZIZURU alt for ZEZURU dial of SHONA [SHD]
MAZNOUG dial of DOMARI [RMT]
MAZOVIAN dial of POLISH [PQL]
MAZRA alt for MAJERA dial of MAJERA [XMJ]
MBA [MFC] lang, Zaïre
MBAAMA alt for MBAMA [MBM]
MBACCA alt for NGBAKA MA'BO [NBM]
MBADA alt for BADA [BAU]
MBADAWA alt for BADA [BAU]
MBAELELEA alt for BAELELEA dial of TO'ABAITA [MLU]
MBAENGGU alt for BAEGGU dial of TO'ABAITA [MLU]
MBAGANI dial of SONGE [SOP]
MBAGU alt for BOAZI [KVG]
MBAHOUIN alt for MBANGWE [ZMN]
MBAI [MYB] lang, Chad, Cameroon, Central African

Republic, Nigeria
MBAI alt for MBUM [MDD]
MBAI alt for MBAI [MYB]
MBAI alt for NZAKMBAY [NZY]
MBAI dial of KUPSABINY [KPZ]
MBAI DOBA alt for MBAY DOBA dial of NGAMBAI [SBA]
MBAI, BEDIONDO [MAP] lang, Chad
MBAKA alt for BAKA [BDH]
MBAKA alt for NGBAKA MA'BO [NBM]
MBAKA dial of MBUNDU, LOANDA [MLO]
MBAKARLA alt for UMBUGARLA [UMR]
MBAKI alt for BAKI dial of KWAKUM [KWU]
MBALA [MDP] lang, Zaïre
MBALA dial of YOMBE [YOM]
MBALAZI alt for BAJUNI dial of SWAHILI [SWA]
MBALAZI alt for BAJUNI dial of SWAHILI [SWA]
MBALE alt for BUSHOONG [BUF]
MBALE dial of TAITA [DAV]
MBALI alt for MABAALE [MMZ]
MBALI alt for UMBUNDU [MNF]
MBALOH alt for EMBALOH [EMB]
MBAMA [MBM] lang, Gabon, Congo
MBAMA alt for NAGUMI [NGV]
MBAMBA alt for MBAMA [MBM]
MBAMBA dial of MBUNDU, LOANDA [MLO]
MBAMBATANA alt for BABATANA [BAQ]
MBAMU dial of ELOYI [AFO]
MBANA alt for IMBANA dial of MUNDANG [MUA]
MBANDIERU dial of HERERO [HER]
MBANDJA alt for MBANJA [MDL]
MBANDZA alt for MBANZA [ZMZ]
MBANG dial of BAKOKO [BKH]
MBANG dial of BASAA [BAA]
MBANGA alt for BANGA dial of KABA NA [KWV]
MBANGALA [MXG] lang, Angola
MBANGALA dial of MBANGALA [MXG]
MBANGWE [ZMN] lang, Congo, Gabon
MBANGWE alt for MBANGWE [ZMN]
MBANIATA alt for BANIATA [BNT]
MBANJA [MDL] lang, Zaïre
MBANUA alt for SANTA CRUZ [STC]
MBANUA dial of SANTA CRUZ [STC]
MBANZA [ZMZ] lang, Zaïre, Congo
MBARA [MPK] lang, Chad
MBARA [VMB] lang, Australia
MBARA KWENGO alt for XUN [XUU]
MBARAKWENA alt for XUN [XUU]
MBARAM alt for BARAM of POLCI [POL]
MBAREKE alt for BAREKE dial of VANGUNU [MPR]
MBARI alt for UMBUNDU [MNF]
MBARIKE alt for KUTEP [KUB]
MBARIMAN-GUDHINMA [ZMV] lang, Australia
MBARMI alt for ZUL dial of POLCI [POL]
MBAT alt for BADA [BAU]
MBATI [MDN] lang, Central African Republic
MBATI OF MBAÏKI dial of MBATI [MDN]
MBATO [GWA] lang, Côte d'Ivoire
MBAU alt for BAU of FIJIAN [FJI]
MBAW alt for MBE' [MTK]
MBAY alt for NZAKMBAY [NZY]
MBAY BEDIONDO alt for MBAI, BEDIONDO [MAP]
MBAY BEJONDO alt for MBAI, BEDIONDO [MAP]
MBAY DOBA dial of NGAMBAI [SBA]
MBAY MOISSALA alt for MBAI [MYB]
MBAY-KAN alt for KAN dial of MBAI [MYB]

MBAYA-GUAIKURU alt for KADIWÉU [KBC]
MBAZIA alt for BALDAMU [BDN]
MBE' [MTK] lang, Cameroon
MBE [MFO] lang, Nigeria
MBE AFAL alt for UTUGWANG [AFE]
MBECI dial of ELOYI [AFO]
MBEDAM [XMD] lang, Cameroon
MBÉDÉ alt for MBERE [MDT]
MBEERE dial of EMBU [EBU]
MBEGUMBA alt for BELANDA VIRI [BVI]
MBELE alt for MBRE [XMR]
MBELE alt for BASAA [BAA]
MBELE alt for MBERE dial of TUKI [BAG]
MBELE alt for BAMBILI dial of BAMBILI [BAW]
MBELIME [MQL] lang, Benin
MBEM alt for YAMBA [YAM]
MBEMBE, CROSS RIVER [MFN] lang, Nigeria
MBEMBE, TIGON [NZA] lang, Cameroon, Nigeria, Nigeria
MBEMBE, TIGON alt for MBEMBE, TIGON [NZA]
MBENGUI-NIELLÉ alt for TAGBARI dial of SENOUFO, CEBAARA [SEF]
MBENKPE alt for NDE dial of NDE-NSELE-NTA [NDD]
MBERE [MDT] lang, Congo, Gabon, Gabon
MBERE alt for MBERE [MDT]
MBERE alt for MBRE [XMR]
MBERE dial of TUKI [BAG]
MBERE dial of GBAYA [GYA]
MBERE dial of MBUM [MDD]
MBERE dial of KARANG [KZR]
MBERE alt for MBEERE dial of EMBU [EBU]
MBEREM dial of PELASLA [MLR]
MBESA [ZMS] lang, Zaïre
MBÉTÉ alt for MBERE [MDT]
MBETE alt for BETE-BENDE [BTT]
MBI alt for MBIYI [XMV]
MBIÁ alt for GUARANÍ, MBYÁ [GUN]
MBIDA-BANI dial of EWONDO [EWO]
MBIKA alt for BAMUNKA [NDO]
MBILA alt for SAFWA [SBK]
MBILA dial of BUDZA [BJA]
MBILI alt for BAMBILI dial of BAMBILI [BAW]
MBILME alt for MBELIME [MQL]
MBILUA alt for BILUA [BLB]
MBIMOU alt for MPYEMO [MCX]
MBIMU alt for MPYEMO [MCX]
MBINGA dial of MABAALE [MMZ]
MBIRAO alt for BIRAO [BRR]
MBISU alt for BISU [BII]
MBIYI [XMV] lang, Central African Republic
MBIZENAKU dial of KOM [BKM]
MBO [MBO] lang, Cameroon
MBO [ZMW] lang, Zaïre
MBO alt for MBE' [MTK]
MBO-UNG [MUX] lang, Papua New Guinea
MBOA alt for MBONGA [XMB]
MBOBYENG dial of MPONGMPONG [MGG]
MBOCOBÍ alt for MOCOVÍ [MOC]
MBODOMO dial of GBAYA [GYA]
MBOFON alt for NDE dial of NDE-NSELE-NTA [NDD]
MBOGEDO alt for DIRIKU [DIU]
MBOGEDU alt for DIRIKU [DIU]
MBOGOE alt for BAMBILI dial of BAMBILI [BAW]
MBOI [MOI] lang, Nigeria
MBOI dial of MBOI [MOI]

MBOIRE alt for MBOI [MOI]
MBOIRE alt for MBOI dial of MBOI [MOI]
MBOKA dial of KONGO [KON]
MBOKO [MDU] lang, Congo
MBOKO alt for WUMBOKO [BQM]
MBOKOU alt for MBUKO [MQB]
MBOKU alt for MBUKO [MQB]
MBOL alt for BWOL dial of KOFYAR [KWL]
MBOLA alt for DUMBULE [MLB]
MBOLE [MDQ] lang, Zaïre
MBOLE alt for MBULI dial of OMBO [OML]
MBOLOLO dial of TAITA [DAV]
MBOMAN alt for MPOMAM dial of MPONGMPONG [MGG]
MBOMBO alt for MPONGMPONG [MGG]
MBOMITABA alt for BOMITABA [ZMX]
MBOMOTABA alt for BOMITABA [ZMX]
MBOMU alt for ZANDE [ZAN]
MBONG alt for KAALONG dial of BAFIA [KSF]
MBONGA [XMB] lang, Nigeria, Cameroon
MBONGE dial of BAKUNDU-BALUE [BDU]
MBONJOKU dial of KAKO [KKJ]
MBOO alt for MBO [MBO]
MBOPALO alt for DOOKA dial of GBAYA [GYA]
MBORORO alt for BORORRO dial of FULFULDE, KANO-KATSINA-BORORRO [FUV]
MBOSHE alt for MBOSI [MDW]
MBOSHI alt for MBOSI [MDW]
MBOSI [MDW] lang, Congo
MBOTU alt for MBUTU dial of NGEMBA [NGE]
MBOTU alt for GAMO dial of GAMO-NINGI [BTE]
MBOUGOU alt for MBUGU [MHD]
MBOUM alt for MBUM [MDD]
MBOUM dial of MBUM [MDD]
MBOUM dial of MBUM [MDD]
MBOUMTIBA alt for MBUM [MDD]
MBOUNDJA dial of GBAYA [GYA]
MBOWE [MXO] lang, Zambia
MBOWE dial of LUYANA [LAV]
MBOWELA dial of NKOYA [NKA]
MBOXO alt for MBOKO [MDU]
MBOYAKUM alt for BAMBALANG [BMO]
MBOYI alt for MBOI [MOI]
MBOYI alt for MBOI dial of MBOI [MOI]
MBRE [XMR] lang, Central African Republic
MBREME alt for PELASLA [MLR]
MBREME alt for MBEREM dial of PELASLA [MLR]
MBREREWI dial of NGEMBA [NGE]
MBROU alt for BURU [BUH]
MBRU alt for BURU [BUH]
MBU alt for NGAMAMBO dial of META' [MGO]
MBUA alt for GUARANÍ, MBYÁ [GUN]
MBUBA alt for MVUBA [MXH]
MBUBE EASTERN alt for UTUGWANG [AFE]
MBUBEM alt for YAMBA [YAM]
MBUDJA alt for BUDZA [BJA]
MBUELA alt for MBWELA [MFU]
MBUGHOTU alt for BUGHOTU [BGT]
MBUGU [MHD] lang, Tanzania
MBUGU alt for NGBUGU [NUB]
MBUGWE [MGZ] lang, Tanzania
MBUI alt for BAMBUI dial of BAMBILI [BAW]
MBUKAMBERO dial of KODI [KOD]
MBUKO [MQB] lang, Cameroon
MBUKU alt for MBUKO [MQB]
MBUKU alt for MBOKO [MDU]

MBUKUHU alt for MBUKUSHU [MHW]
MBUKUSHI alt for MBUKUSHU [MHW]
MBUKUSHU [MHW] lang, Namibia, Angola,
    Botswana, Zambia
MBUKUSHU alt for MBUKUSHU [MHW]
MBULA [MNA] lang, Papua New Guinea
MBULA alt for MBULA-BWAZZA [MBU]
MBULA dial of MBULA [MNA]
MBULA dial of MBULA-BWAZZA [MBU]
MBULA-BWAZZA [MBU] lang, Nigeria
MBULI dial of OMBO [OML]
MBULU alt for IRAQW [IRK]
MBULUGWE alt for BURUNGI [BDS]
MBULUNGISH [MBV] lang, Guinea
MBUM [MDD] lang, Cameroon, Chad, Chad
MBUM alt for MBUM [MDD]
MBUM alt for KARANG [KZR]
MBUM-EAST alt for KARANG [KZR]
MBUM-NZAKAMBAY alt for MBUM [MDD]
MBUMI dial of LUYANA [LAV]
MBUNDA [MCK] lang, Zambia, Angola
MBUNDA alt for MPUUN dial of MPUONO [ZMP]
MBUNDU BENGUELLA alt for UMBUNDU [MNF]
MBUNDU, LOANDA [MLO] lang, Angola
MBUNGA [MGY] lang, Tanzania
MBURKU [BBT] lang, Nigeria
MBURUGAM alt for ESIMBI [AGS]
MBUSUKU dial of GBAYA [GYA]
MBUTA alt for GAMO dial of GAMO-NINGI [BTE]
MBUTE alt for VUTE [VUT]
MBUTERE alt for VUTE [VUT]
MBUTI alt for LESE [LES]
MBUTU dial of NGEMBA [NGE]
MBUUN alt for MPUUN dial of MPUONO [ZMP]
MBUUNDA alt for MBUNDA [MCK]
MBWAANZ dial of MAKAA [MCP]
MBWAKA alt for NGBAKA MA'BO [NBM]
MBWASE NGHUY dial of MBO [MBO]
MBWE'WI dial of AWING [AZO]
MBWELA [MFU] lang, Angola
MBWELA alt for MBOWELA dial of NKOYA [NKA]
MBWERA alt for MBWELA [MFU]
MBWERA alt for MBOWELA dial of NKOYA [NKA]
MBWISI alt for BWISI [BWZ]
MBYÁ alt for GUARANÍ, MBYÁ [GUN]
MBYAM dial of KWA' [BKO]
MBYEMO alt for MPYEMO [MCX]
MCDERMITT alt for NORTH NORTHERN PAIUTE dial
    of PAIUTE, NORTHERN [PAO]
MCGRATH INGALIK alt for KUSKOKWIM, UPPER
    [KUU]
MDHUR alt for NDHUR dial of RADE [RAD]
MDUNDULU dial of LUYANA [LAV]
ME'EK alt for MEHEK [NUX]
ME-WUK alt for MIWOK [SKD]
MEA [MEG] lang, New Caledonia
MEAH [MEJ] lang, Indonesia, Irian Jaya
MEAKAMBUT dial of ARAFUNDI [ARF]
MEARIM dial of GUAJAJÁRA [GUB]
MEAUN alt for LABO [MWI]
MEAX alt for MEAH [MEJ]
MEBAN alt for MABAAN [MFZ]
MEBU [MJN] lang, Papua New Guinea
MECAYAPAN dial of NAHUATL, ISTHMUS [NAU]
MECH alt for BODO [BRX]
MECH dial of BODO [BRX]

MECHA dial of OROMO, WELLEGA-CENTRAL [GAZ]
MECHE alt for BODO [BRX]
MECHI alt for BODO [BRX]
MECI alt for BODO [BRX]
MECKLENBURG alt for EAST LOW GERMAN dial of
    GERMAN, LOW [GEP]
MECO alt for CHICHIMECA-JONAZ [PEI]
MEDANG alt for MADANG [MQD]
MEDEBUR [MJM] lang, Papua New Guinea
MEDIAK [MWX] lang, Tanzania
MEDJE alt for MEJE dial of MANGBETU [MDJ]
MEDJE alt for MEJE dial of MANGBETU [MDJ]
MEDLPA [MED] lang, Papua New Guinea
MEDNOV dial of ALEUT [ALW]
MEDO dial of MAKHUWA [MAK]
MEDO dial of MAKHUWA [MAK]
MEDOGO [MNE] lang, Chad
MEDUMBA [BYV] lang, Cameroon
MEDYE alt for MEJE dial of MANGBETU [MDJ]
MEDZIME alt for MENZIME dial of MPONGMPONG
    [MGG]
MEE alt for BASAA [BAA]
MEE MANA alt for EKARI [EKG]
MEEKA dial of MUMUYE [MUL]
MEEMBI alt for MEMBI dial of NDO [NDP]
ME'EN [MYM] lang, Ethiopia
MEFELE [MFJ] lang, Cameroon
MEFELE dial of MEFELE [MFJ]
MEFOOR alt for BIAK [BHW]
MEGAKA [XMG] lang, Cameroon
MEGAM [MEF] lang, Bangladesh
MEGAM dial of GARO [GRT]
MEGHWAR alt for MARWARI, SOUTHERN [MQH]
MEGHWAR alt for MARWARI, NORTHERN [MRI]
MEGI dial of KAGULU [KKI]
MEGI dial of ANGAL HENENG, SOUTH [AOE]
MEGIAR [MFP] lang, Papua New Guinea
MEGILI alt for LIJILI [MGI]
MEGIMBA alt for NGEMBA [NGE]
MEGLENITIC alt for RUMANIAN, MEGLENO [RUQ]
MEGONG alt for EGGON [EGO]
MEGREL alt for MINGRELIAN [XMF]
MEGYAW alt for HPON [HPO]
MEGYE alt for MEJE dial of MANGBETU [MDJ]
MEHALA'AN-EASTERN RANTEBULAHAN dial of
    PITU ULUNNA SALU [PTU]
MEHARA alt for MESARA dial of SAWU [HVN]
MEHARI alt for HALBI [HLB]
MEHARI dial of HALBI [HLB]
MEHEK [NUX] lang, Papua New Guinea
MEHER alt for KISAR [KJE]
MEHINACO alt for MEHINÁKU [MMH]
MEHINÁKU [MMH] lang, Brazil
MEHRI alt for MAHRI [MHR]
MEHUA alt for MENGHUA [MJB]
MEIDOB alt for MIDOB [MEI]
MEIFU dial of HLAI [LIC]
MEIN dial of IJO, CENTRAL-WESTERN [IJC]
MEISISE dial of DOGHOSIÉ [DOS]
MEITHE alt for MEITHEI [MNR]
MEITHEI [MNR] lang, India, Bangladesh, Myanmar
MEITHEI alt for MEITHEI [MNR]
MEIXIEN dial of CHINESE, HAKKA [HAK]
MEIYARI alt for NIKSEK [GBE]
MEIHSIEN alt for MEIXIEN dial of CHINESE, HAKKA
    [HAK]

MEJACH alt for MEAH [MEJ]
MEJAH alt for MEAH [MEJ]
MEJE dial of MANGBETU [MDJ]
MEJE dial of MANGBETU [MDJ]
MEKA alt for BYEP [MKK]
MEKA alt for NGEMBA dial of GHOMALA' [BBJ]
MEKAA alt for MAKAA [MCP]
MEKAE alt for BYEP [MKK]
MEKAF alt for NAKI [MFF]
MEKAN alt for ME'EN [MYM]
MEKAY alt for BYEP [MKK]
MEKEM [XME] lang, Brazil
MEKEO [MEK] lang, Papua New Guinea
MEKEO alt for EAST MEKEO dial of MEKEO [MEK]
MEKEO-KOVIO alt for MEKEO [MEK]
MEKEY alt for BYEP [MKK]
"MEKEYER" alt for SHABO [SBF]
MEKIBO alt for EOTILE [EOT]
MEKITELYU alt for LIMÓN CREOLE dial of WESTERN
   CARIBBEAN CREOLE ENGLISH [JAM]
MEKMEK [MVK] lang, Papua New Guinea
MEKONGGA [MWK] lang, Indonesia, Sulawesi
MEKONGKA alt for MEKONGGA [MWK]
MEKUK alt for MVUMBO dial of NGUMBA [NMG]
MEKWEI [MSF] lang, Indonesia, Irian Jaya
MEKYE alt for BYEP [MKK]
MEKYIBO alt for EOTILE [EOT]
MELAJU alt for MALAY [MLI]
MELAM dial of RAWANG [RAW]
MELAMBA alt for KENSWEI NSEI [NDB]
MELAMELA [MXM] lang, Papua New Guinea
MELAN SO dial of SO [SOX]
MELANAU [MEL] lang, Malaysia, Sarawak
MELANESIAN ENGLISH alt for TOK PISIN [PDG]
MELARIPI alt for KAIPI dial of TOARIPI [TPI]
MELAWI alt for SARAWAI dial of DOHOI [OTD]
MELAYU alt for MALAY [MLI]
MELAYU AMBON alt for MALAY, AMBONESE [ABS]
MELAYU BAHASA alt for SRI LANKAN CREOLE
   MALAY [SCI]
MELAYU JAKARTE alt for BETAWI [BEW]
MELAYU PASAR dial of MALAY [MLI]
MELE dial of MELE-FILA [MXE]
MELE-FILA [MXE] lang, Vanuatu
MELETE dial of TSWANA [TSW]
MELETS TATAR alt for CHULYM [CHU]
MELIGAN alt for MALIGAN dial of TAGAL MURUT
   [MVV]
MELILUP dial of TEOP [TIO]
MELKHIN dial of CHECHEN [CJC]
MELKOI dial of MAMUSI [KDF]
MELLA dial of CUIBA [CUI]
MELOBONG RUNGUS alt for RUNGUS [DRG]
MELOKWO [MLW] lang, Cameroon
MELOLO dial of SUMBA [SMI]
MELPA alt for MEDLPA [MED]
MELSISI dial of APMA [APP]
MELUORY alt for NAGA, MELURI [NLM]
MELURI alt for NAGA, MELURI [NLM]
MEMAGUN alt for RUNGUS [DRG]
MEMALOH alt for EMBALOH [EMB]
MEMBA alt for MOINBA [MOB]
MEMBAKUT KADAZAN alt for KADAZAN, COASTAL
   [KZJ]
MEMBI dial of NDO [NDP]
MEMBI dial of NDO [NDP]

MEMBITU alt for MEMBI dial of NDO [NDP]
MEMBORO alt for MAMBORU [MVD]
MEMI alt for NAGA, MAO [NBI]
MEMOGUN alt for RUNGUS [DRG]
MEN alt for ME'EN [MYM]
MENA dial of IKOBI-MENA [MEB]
MENABE-IKONGO alt for TANALA dial of
   MALAGASY [MEX]
MENADONESE dial of MALAY [MLI]
MENAM alt for MONOM [MOO]
MENANDON alt for AIKU [MZF]
MENBA alt for MOINBA [MOB]
MENCHUM alt for BEFANG [BBY]
MENDALAM KAJAN alt for KAYAN, MENDALAM
   [XKD]
MENDANKWE [MFD] lang, Cameroon
MENDANKWE dial of MENDANKWE [MFD]
MENDE [MFY] lang, Sierra Leone, Liberia
MENDE alt for WAMSAK [WBD]
MENDEYA alt for GUMUZ [GUK]
MENDI alt for ANGAL, EAST [AGE]
MENDI alt for KENSIU [KNS]
MENDO-KALA alt for KALA dial of UMBU-UNGU
   [UMB]
MENDRIQ alt for MINRIQ [MNQ]
MENDYAKO alt for MANDYAK [MFV]
MENDZIME alt for MENZIME dial of MPONGMPONG
   [MGG]
MENEMO dial of META' [MGO]
MENEMO-MOGAMO alt for META' [MGO]
MENGAKA alt for SUGA [SGI]
MENGAKA alt for MEGAKA [XMG]
MENGAMBO alt for BAMENYAM [BCE]
MENGAU dial of KAMBERATARO [KBV]
MENGEN [MEE] lang, Papua New Guinea
MENGERRDJI alt for MANGERR [ZME]
MENGGALA dial of ABUNG [ABL]
MENGGATAL dial of DUSUN, CENTRAL [DTP]
MENGGEI alt for MEKWEI [MSF]
MENGGU alt for MONGOLIAN, PERIPHERAL [MVF]
MENGGWEI alt for MEKWEI [MSF]
MENGHUA [MJB] lang, China
MENGHWA alt for MENGHUA [MJB]
MENGISA [MCT] lang, Cameroon
MENGISA-NJOWE alt for MENGISA [MCT]
MENGKASARA alt for MAKASSAR [MSR]
MENGKATIP dial of BAKUMPAI [BKR]
MENGO alt for KENSIU [KNS]
MENGWA alt for MENGHUA [MJB]
MENI alt for IKOBI-MENA [MEB]
MENI dial of IKOBI-MENA [MEB]
MENIA dial of HSIFAN [HSI]
MENIK alt for KENSIU [KNS]
MENINDAL alt for KUIJAU [DKR]
MENINDAQ alt for KUIJAU [DKR]
MENING [MYQ] lang, Uganda
MENINGGO alt for MOSKONA [MTJ]
MENINGO alt for MOSKONA [MTJ]
MENINKA alt for MANINKA [MNI]
MENJA alt for KWEGU [YID]
MENJUKE alt for MANYUKAI dial of DAYAK, LAND
   [DYK]
MENKA [MEA] lang, Cameroon
MENKU alt for MÜNKÜ dial of IRÁNTXE [IRA]
MENNAGI alt for MANGERR [ZME]
MENNONITE GERMAN alt for PLAUTDIETSCH [GRN]

MENNONITEN PLATT alt for PLAUTDIETSCH [GRN]
MENO-MENE dial of SASAK [SAS]
MENOMINEE alt for MENOMINI [MEZ]
MENOMINI [MEZ] lang, USA
MENPA alt for MOINBA [MOB]
MENRAQ alt for MINRIQ [MNQ]
MENRIK alt for MINRIQ [MNQ]
MENRIQ alt for MINRIQ [MNQ]
MENSA dial of TIGRÉ [TIE]
MENTA alt for MANTA [MYG]
MENTAWAI [MWV] lang, Indonesia, Sumatra
MENTAWEI alt for MENTAWAI [MWV]
MENTAWI alt for MENTAWAI [MWV]
MENTEBAH-SURUK dial of MALAYIC DAYAK [XDY]
MENTERA alt for MANTRA dial of TEMUAN [TMW]
MENTUH TAPUH dial of DAYAK, LAND [DYK]
MENUI dial of WAWONII [WOW]
MENYA [MCR] lang, Papua New Guinea
MENYAMA alt for MENYA [MCR]
MENYE alt for MENYA [MCR]
MENYUKAI alt for MANYUKAI dial of DAYAK, LAND
    [DYK]
MENYUKAI alt for MANUKAI dial of DAYAK, LAND
    [DYK]
MENZIME dial of MPONGMPONG [MGG]
MEO alt for HMONG, EASTERN [HEA]
MEO alt for HMONG, WESTERN [HUJ]
MEO alt for HMONG NJUA [BLU]
MEO DO alt for HMONG, RED [MMR]
MÈO HOA alt for HMONG, WESTERN [HUJ]
MEO KAO alt for HMONG DAW [MWW]
MÈO LÀI alt for PA HNG [PHA]
MEO LAI alt for PA HNG [PHA]
MEOHANG alt for NEWANG [RAF]
MEON alt for KARON DORI [KGW]
MEOSWAR [MVX] lang, Indonesia, Irian Jaya
MEQAN alt for ME'EN [MYM]
MEQUEM alt for MEKEM [XME]
MEQUEN alt for MEKEM [XME]
MEQUENS alt for KANOÉ [KXO]
MER [MNU] lang, Indonesia, Irian Jaya
MER alt for MERIAM [ULK]
MER dial of GIMIRA [BCQ]
MERADAN alt for MARIDAN [ZMD]
MERAMERA alt for MELAMELA [MXM]
MERARIT alt for MARARIT [MGB]
MERATEI dial of DAYAK, LAND [DYK]
MERATUS alt for MALAY, BUKIT [BVU]
MERAU MALAY alt for MALAY, BERAU [BVE]
MERDU alt for MURSI [MUZ]
MERE alt for MEREY [MEQ]
MEREI dial of BANGBA [BBE]
MERELAVA alt for MERLAV [MRM]
MEREO alt for EMERILLON [EME]
MERETEI alt for MERATEI dial of DAYAK, LAND
    [DYK]
MEREY [MEQ] lang, Cameroon
MEREYO alt for EMERILLON [EME]
MERGUESE dial of BURMESE [BMS]
MERGUI alt for MERGUESE dial of BURMESE [BMS]
MERI alt for MEREY [MEQ]
MERIAM [ULK] lang, Australia, Papua New Guinea,
    Papua New Guinea
MERIAM alt for MERIAM [ULK]
MERIDA alt for ZAGHAWA [ZAG]
MERIDIONALE dial of SARDINIAN, CAMPIDANESE

[SRO]
MERIG alt for MWERIG dial of MERLAV [MRM]
MERILE alt for DAASANECH [DSH]
MERILLE alt for DAASANECH [DSH]
MERINA dial of MALAGASY [MEX]
MERITU alt for MURSI [MUZ]
MERLAV [MRM] lang, Vanuatu
MERLAV-MERIG alt for MERLAV [MRM]
MERNYANG alt for MIRRIAM dial of KOFYAR [KWL]
MERONG alt for MIRIWUNG [MEP]
MERU [MER] lang, Kenya
MERU alt for RWO [RWK]
MERU dial of MERU [MER]
MERU alt for KIHAI dial of CHAGGA [KAF]
MERULE alt for MURLE [MUR]
MERWARI alt for MARWARI, SOUTHERN [MQH]
MERWARI alt for MARWARI [MKD]
MERWARI alt for MARWARI, NORTHERN [MRI]
MESA DEL NAYAR dial of CORA [COR]
MESAKA [IYO] lang, Cameroon
MESAKIN alt for NGILE [MAS]
MESAKIN QUSAR alt for MASAKIN GUSAR dial of
    NGILE [MAS]
MESARA dial of SAWU [HVN]
MESARI dial of MANAGALASI [MCQ]
MESCALERO dial of APACHE, MESCALERO-
    CHIRICAHUA [APM]
MESE dial of TUNEN [BAZ]
MESEM [MCI] lang, Papua New Guinea
MESENGO alt for MAJANG [MPE]
MESHED alt for MASHADI dial of FARSI, WESTERN
    [PES]
MESI dial of MADAK [MMX]
MESIANG dial of BARAKAI [BAJ]
MESING alt for KENSWEI NSEI [NDB]
MESKETO alt for BASKETTO [BST]
MESME [ZIM] lang, Chad
MESMEDJE alt for MASMAJE [MES]
MESMES [MYS] lang, Ethiopia
MESQAN dial of GURAGE, PERIPHERAL WEST
    [GPW]
MESQUAKIE [SAC] lang, USA
MESQUAKIE dial of MESQUAKIE [SAC]
MESSAGA alt for MESAKA [IYO]
MESSAGA-EKOL alt for MESAKA [IYO]
MESSAKA alt for MESAKA [IYO]
MESSENI alt for TAKPASYEERI dial of SENOUFO,
    CEBAARA [SEF]
MESSINESE dial of SICILIAN [SCN]
META' [MGO] lang, Cameroon
META' alt for MENEMO dial of META' [MGO]
METABI alt for GAAM [TBI]
METAN alt for MITANG [MTY]
METHLI alt for MAITHILI [MKP]
METIS alt for MITCHIF [CRG]
METLA-KINWAT dial of KOLAMI, SOUTHEASTERN
    [NIT]
METO alt for MEDO dial of MAKHUWA [MAK]
METO alt for MEDO dial of MAKHUWA [MAK]
METOKI alt for KENUZI-DONGOLA [KNC]
METOKO alt for MITUKU [ZMQ]
METOMKA alt for KATI, SOUTHERN [KTS]
METOMKA dial of KATI, SOUTHERN [KTS]
METRU alt for SINAGEN [SIU]
METRU alt for DIA [DIA]
METTA alt for META' [MGO]

METTA alt for MENEMO dial of METIA' [MGO]
METTO alt for MEDO dial of MAKHUWA [MAK]
METU dial of RAWANG [RAW]
METYIBO alt for EOTILE [EOT]
METZONTLA POPOLOCA alt for POPOLOCA, SOUTHERN [PBE]
MEUAY alt for TAI MUOI dial of TAI DAM [BLT]
MEUAY alt for TÁY MU'Ò'I dial of TAI DAM [BLT]
MEUDANA dial of DUAU [DUA]
MEWARI alt for MARWARI [MKD]
MEWARI alt for SOUTHERN MARWARI dial of MARWARI [MKD]
MEWASI dial of KOLI, WADIYARA [KXP]
MEWUN alt for LABO [MWI]
MEXICAN SIGN LANGUAGE [MFS] lang, Mexico
MEXICANERO alt for NAHUATL, DURANGO [NLN]
MEXICO dial of AFRO-SEMINOLE CREOLE [AFS]
MEXTÃ alt for CARAPANA [CBC]
MEYACH alt for MEAH [MEJ]
MEYAH alt for MEAH [MEJ]
MEYOBE alt for SOLA [SOY]
MEZAMA alt for NAGA, ZEME [NZM]
MEZIME alt for MENZIME dial of MPONGMPONG [MGG]
MEZIMKO dial of MOKULU [MOZ]
MFANTSE alt for FANTE dial of AKAN [TWS]
MFE dial of YAMBA [YAM]
MFINU [ZMF] lang, Zaïre
MFUMTE [NFU] lang, Cameroon
MFUMU alt for FUUMU dial of TEKE, SOUTH CENTRAL [IFM]
MFUNUNGA alt for MFINU [ZMF]
MFUTI alt for VUTE [VUT]
MGAO dial of SWAHILI [SWA]
MGBAKPA alt for HAUSA [HUA]
MGBATO alt for MBATO [GWA]
MGBO dial of IZI-EZAA-IKWO-MGBO [IZI]
MGOLOG alt for GOLOG [GOC]
MGOUMBA alt for NGUMBA [NMG]
MHAR alt for HMAR [HMR]
MI MARVA alt for GIZIGA, NORTH [GIS]
MI MIJIVIN dial of GIZIGA, SOUTH [GIZ]
MINICA WITOTO alt for HUITOTO, MENECA [HTO]
MIADEBA dial of SEWA BAY [SEW]
MIAG-AO dial of KINARAY-A [KRJ]
MIALÁT dial of TENHARIM [PAH]
MIAMI [MIA] lang, USA
MIAMI dial of MIAMI [MIA]
MIAMI-ILLINOIS alt for MIAMI [MIA]
MIAMIA alt for EJAR dial of KORO [KOR]
MIAMU dial of WAN [WAN]
MIAN alt for MIANMIN [MPT]
MIAN alt for MIEN [YOC]
MIAN-JIN alt for IU MIEN [IUM]
MIANGO alt for IRIGWE [IRI]
MIANI [PLA] lang, Papua New Guinea
MIANI NORTH alt for MIANI [PLA]
MIANI SOUTH alt for MAIANI [TNH]
MIANKA alt for SENOUFO, MAMARA [MYK]
MIANMIN [MPT] lang, Papua New Guinea
MIANMIN dial of MIANMIN [MPT]
MIAO alt for HMONG, EASTERN [HEA]
MIAO alt for HMONG, RED [MMR]
MIAO alt for HMONG, NORTHERN [MUQ]
MIAO alt for HMONG, WESTERN [HUJ]
MIAO alt for HMONG NJUA [BLU]

MIAO LAI alt for HMONG GU MBA dial of HMONG DAW [MWW]
MIARO dial of AWYU [AWJ]
MIARRÃ [XMI] lang, Brazil
MICARI dial of NUNI [NNW]
MICCOSUKEE alt for MIKASUKI [MIK]
MICHOACÁN AZTEC alt for NAHUATL, MICHOACÁN [NCL]
MICHOACÁN MAZAHUA dial of MAZAHUA [MAZ]
MICHOACÁN NAHUAL alt for NAHUATL, MICHOACÁN [NCL]
MICMAC [MIC] lang, Canada, USA, USA
MICMAC alt for MICMAC [MIC]
MID BISAYA dial of BISAYA, SARAWAK [BSD]
MID WAHGI alt for KUMAI [KMI]
MID-WAHGI dial of WAHGI [WAK]
MID-WARIA alt for GUHU-SAMANE [GHS]
MIDA'A alt for MAJERA [XMJ]
MIDAH alt for MAJERA [XMJ]
MIDDLE BAMU dial of BAMU [BCF]
MIDDLE CHEROKEE dial of CHEROKEE [CER]
MIDDLE CHULYM dial of CHULYM [CHU]
MIDDLE EASTERN ROMANI alt for DOMARI [RMT]
MIDDLE EGYPT ARABIC dial of ARABIC, EGYPTIAN COLLOQUIAL [ARZ]
MIDDLE LOZYVIN alt for WESTERN VOGUL dial of MANSI [MNS]
MIDDLE MUSA alt for YAREBA [YRB]
MIDDLE NAMBAS alt for MALUA BAY [MLL]
MIDDLE WATUT alt for SILISILI [MPL]
MIDHI alt for CHULIKATA [CLK]
MIDIK alt for MIDIKI dial of KAIRUI-MIDIKI [KRD]
MIDIKI dial of KAIRUI-MIDIKI [KRD]
MIDNAPORE ORIYA dial of ORIYA [ORY]
MIDOB [MEI] lang, Sudan
MIDOBI alt for MIDOB [MEI]
MIDSIVINDI [MZU] lang, Papua New Guinea
MIDU alt for CHULIKATA [CLK]
MIE'EN alt for ME'EN [MYM]
MIEKEN alt for ME'EN [MYM]
MIEN [YOC] lang, China, Thailand, Laos, Thailand, Viet Nam
MIEN alt for MIEN [YOC]
MIENGE dial of MBO [MBO]
MIERE alt for MER [MNU]
MIERU alt for MER dial of GIMIRA [BCQ]
MIGAAMA [MMY] lang, Chad
MIGAAMA dial of MIGAAMA [MMY]
MIGABA' alt for MIGABAC [MPP]
MIGABAC [MPP] lang, Papua New Guinea
MIGAM alt for MEGAM [MEF]
MIGAMA alt for MIGAAMA [MMY]
MIGANGAM alt for NGANGAM [GNG]
MIGANI alt for MONI [MNZ]
MIGILI alt for LIJILI [MGI]
MIGORI dial of TAROF [TCF]
MIGUELENHO alt for PURUBORÁ [PUR]
MIGUELENO alt for PURUBORÁ [PUR]
MIGUHNI alt for NGWO dial of NGWO [NGN]
MIGULIMANCEMA alt for GOURMANCHÉMA [GUX]
MIHAVANE alt for LOMWE [NGL]
MIHAVANI alt for LOMWE [NGL]
MIHAWANI alt for LOMWE [NGL]
MIHIROA dial of TUAMOTUAN [PMT]
MIJI alt for MIJU [MXJ]
MIJIEM alt for NGANGAM [GNG]

MIJILI alt for LIJILI [MGI]
MIJONG alt for MISSONG [MIJ]
MIJU [MXJ] lang, India
MÌJUU dial of SENOUFO, MAMARA [MYK]
MIKA alt for BYEP [MKK]
"MIKAIR" alt for SHABO [SBF]
MIKAREW [MSY] lang, Papua New Guinea
MIKAREW-ARIAW alt for MIKAREW [MSY]
MIKARU dial of DADIBI [MPS]
MIKARUP alt for MIKAREW [MSY]
MIKASUKI [MIK] lang, USA
MIKASUKI SEMINOLE alt for MIKASUKI [MIK]
MIKAURU alt for MIKARU dial of DADIBI [MPS]
MIKEA [QMK] lang, Madagascar
"MIKEYIR" alt for SHABO [SBF]
MIKIFORE dial of MANINKA [MNI]
MIKIK dial of TSAKHUR [TKR]
MIKIR [MJW] lang, India
MIKIRI alt for MIKIR [MJW]
MIKIRI alt for MELOKWO [MLW]
MIKLAI alt for NAGA, LOTHA [NJH]
MIKO dial of NUNG [NUN]
MILANAU alt for MELANAU [MEL]
MILANESE dial of LOMBARD [LMO]
MILANO alt for MELANAU [MEL]
MILCHANANG alt for MALHESTI dial of KANAURI
  [KFK]
MILCHANG alt for MALHESTI dial of KANAURI [KFK]
MILDJINGI dial of DJINANG [DJI]
MILEERE alt for JABAAL dial of TAMA [TMA]
MILEERE alt for JABAAL dial of TAMA [TMA]
MILIKIN [MIN] lang, Malaysia, Sarawak
MILLERA alt for YIR YORONT [YIY]
MILLIKIN alt for MILIKIN [MIN]
MILO dial of NICOBARESE, SOUTHERN [NIK]
MILRI alt for JABAAL dial of TAMA [TMA]
MILTOU alt for MILTU [MLJ]
MILTU [MLJ] lang, Chad
MIMA alt for AMDANG [AMJ]
MIMA dial of NAGA, ANGAMI [NJM]
MIME alt for MIMI [MIV]
MIMI [MIV] lang, Chad
MIMI alt for AMDANG [AMJ]
MIMIKA alt for KAMORO [KGQ]
MIN alt for DEHU [DEU]
MIN NAN alt for CHINESE, MIN NAN [CFR]
MIN NAN dial of CHINESE, MIN NAN [CFR]
MINA [MYI] lang, India
MINA alt for GEN-GBE [GEJ]
MINA BHIL alt for WAGDI [WBR]
MINA MINA GORONG dial of GESER-GOROM [GES]
MINA-GEN alt for GEN-GBE [GEJ]
MINACO alt for MEHINÁKU [MMH]
MINAHASA alt for TOMBULU [TOM]
MINAHASSA alt for MONGONDOW [MOG]
MINALA alt for MANGALA [MEM]
MINAMANWA alt for MAMANWA [MMN]
MINANG alt for MINANGKABAU [MPU]
MINANGKABAU [MPU] lang, Indonesia, Sumatra
MINANIBAI [MCV] lang, Papua New Guinea
MINANSUT alt for GANA [GNQ]
MINANSUT alt for KUIJAU [DKR]
MINASBATE alt for MASBATENYO [MSB]
MINAVEGA alt for MINAVEHA [MVN]
MINAVEHA [MVN] lang, Papua New Guinea
MINBU dial of CHIN, ASHO [CSH]

MINCHHANANG alt for MALHESTI dial of KANAURI
  [KFK]
MINCHHANG alt for MALHESTI dial of KANAURI
  [KFK]
MINCHIA alt for BAI [PIQ]
MIND'JANA alt for YIR YORONT [YIY]
MINDA dial of SHOO-MINDA-NYEM [BCV]
MINDANAO dial of SANGIL [SNL]
MINDANAO VISAYAN dial of CEBUANO [CEB]
MINDAT [VMT] lang, Myanmar
MINDIK alt for BURUM-MINDIK [BMU]
MINDIRI [MPN] lang, Papua New Guinea
MINDIVI alt for IKUNDUN [IMI]
MINDOUMOU alt for NDUMU [NMD]
MINDUMBU alt for NDUMU [NMD]
MINDUUMO alt for NDUMU [NMD]
MINE KAFFIR alt for FANAGOLO [FAO]
MINENDON alt for AIKU [MZF]
MINEO alt for ZULGWA [ZUL]
MINEO alt for MINEW dial of ZULGWA [ZUL]
MINEW alt for ZULGWA [ZUL]
MINEW dial of ZULGWA [ZUL]
MINEWE alt for MINEW dial of ZULGWA [ZUL]
MINGAN alt for ULANCHAB dial of MONGOLIAN,
  PERIPHERAL [MVF]
MINGAT dial of KALMYK-OIRAT [KGZ]
MINGBARI dial of NGURA [NBX]
MINGHO dial of TU [MJG]
MINGI alt for NGIE [NGJ]
MINGRELIAN [XMF] lang, Georgia
MINH HUONG alt for CHINESE, YUE [YUH]
MINHASA alt for TOMBULU [TOM]
MINHE dial of TU [MJG]
MINI [MGJ] lang, Nigeria
MINI alt for KAJAKSE [CKQ]
MINI alt for OMATI [MGX]
MINIAFIA dial of ARIFAMA-MINIAFIA [AAI]
MINIAFIA-ARIFAMA alt for ARIFAMA-MINIAFIA
  [AAI]
MINIANKA alt for SENOUFO, MAMARA [MYK]
MINIGIR [VMG] lang, Papua New Guinea
MINIR dial of NAGA, YIMCHUNGRU [YIM]
MINITARI alt for HIDATSA [HID]
MINITJI alt for LIMILNGAN [LMC]
MINJANBAL alt for YUGAMBAL [YUB]
MINJANTI alt for TIBEA [NGY]
MINJIMMINA alt for DAR EL KABIRA dial of TULISHI
  [TEY]
MINJORI dial of MANAGALASI [MCQ]
MINKIA alt for BAI [PIQ]
MINNA dial of KADARA [KAD]
MINNAN alt for CHINESE, MIN NAN [CFR]
MINOKOK [MQQ] lang, Malaysia, Sabah
MINRIQ [MNQ] lang, Malaysia, Peninsular
MINTAMANI alt for KAMPUNG BARU [KZM]
MINTIL [MZT] lang, Malaysia, Peninsular
MINTRA alt for MANTRA dial of TEMUAN [TMW]
MINUNGO dial of CHOKWE [CJK]
MINYA alt for SENOUFO, MAMARA [MYK]
MINYANKA alt for SENOUFO, MAMARA [MYK]
MIOKO dial of RAMOAAINA [RAI]
MIOMAFO alt for MOLLO-MIOMAFO dial of ATONI
  [TMR]
MIOS NUM dial of BIAK [BHW]
MIPA alt for KWA' dial of KWA' [BKO]
MIR alt for MERIAM [ULK]

MIRA alt for CHIN, MARA [MRH]
MIRA SAGTENGPA alt for SAGTENGPA [SGT]
MIRAÑA dial of BORA [BOA]
MIRAÑA dial of BORA [BOA]
MIRAÑA dial of BORA [BOA]
MIRANHA alt for MIRAÑA dial of BORA [BOA]
MIRANHA alt for MIRAÑA dial of BORA [BOA]
MIRÃNIA alt for MIRAÑA dial of BORA [BOA]
MIRAPMIN alt for KONAI [KXW]
MIRAPU dial of MANGSING [MBH]
MIRASKI dial of KASHMIRI [KSH]
MIRDHA [MJY] lang, India
MIRDHA-KHARIA dial of KHARIA [KHR]
MIRDHA-KORA dial of KODA [KFN]
MIRE [MVH] lang, Chad
MIRGAN alt for DAKHINI dial of URDU [URD]
MIRI dial of KATCHA-KADUGLI-MIRI [KAT]
MIRI dial of NAROM [NRM]
MIRI dial of ADI [ADI]
MIRIAM alt for MERIAM [ULK]
MIRIAM-MIR alt for MERIAM [ULK]
MIRITI [MMV] lang, Brazil
MIRITI TAPUYO alt for MIRITI [MMV]
MIRITI-TAPUIA alt for MIRITI [MMV]
MIRIWOONG alt for MIRIWUNG [MEP]
MIRIWUN alt for MIRIWUNG [MEP]
MIRIWUNG [MEP] lang, Australia
MIROY alt for ANUAK [ANU]
MIRRIAM dial of KOFYAR [KWL]
MIRUNG alt for MIRIWUNG [MEP]
MIRZAPURI dial of AWADHI [AWD]
MIS-KEMBA alt for WAGI [FAD]
MISAMIS HIGAONON MANOBO alt for MANOBO,
    HIGAONON [MBA]
MISATIK alt for MUSOM [MSU]
MISE dial of NGISHE [NSH]
MISHER dial of TATAR [TTR]
MISHIKHWUTMETUNEE alt for COQUILLE [COQ]
MISHING alt for MIRI dial of ADI [ADI]
MISHIP [CHP] lang, Nigeria
MISHMI alt for MIJU [MXJ]
MISHMI alt for DIGARO [MHU]
MISHULUNDU dial of LUYANA [LAV]
MISIM dial of HOTE [HOT]
MISIMA-PANEATI [MPX] lang, Papua New Guinea
MÍSKITO [MIQ] lang, Nicaragua, Honduras
MÍSKITO COAST CREOLE dial of WESTERN
    CARIBBEAN CREOLE ENGLISH [JAM]
MÍSKITU alt for MÍSKITO [MIQ]
MISLES dial of TSAKHUR [TKR]
MÍSQUITO alt for MÍSKITO [MIQ]
MISSIRII alt for JABAAL dial of TAMA [TMA]
MISSISSIOU alt for SIGHU [SXE]
MISSONG [MIJ] lang, Cameroon
MISSOURI dial of OTO [OTO]
MITAA alt for META' [MGO]
MITANG [MTY] lang, Papua New Guinea
MITCHIF [CRG] lang, USA, Canada
MITEBOG alt for GEDAGED [GDD]
MITEI alt for MEITHEI [MNR]
MITHAN alt for KULUNG MUTHUN dial of NAGA,
    WANCHO [NNP]
MITHIL alt for MAITHILI [MKP]
MITIARO dial of RAROTONGAN [RRT]
MITIL alt for MINTIL [MZT]
MITLA ZAPOTECO alt for ZAPOTECO, EAST

CENTRAL TLACOLULA [ZAW]
MITMIT dial of YAU [YUW]
MITSOGO alt for TSOGO [TSV]
MITTU [MWU] lang, Sudan
MITUA alt for MANDAHUACA [MHT]
MITUA alt for BARÉ [BAE]
MITUKU [ZMQ] lang, Zaïre
MIU [MPO] lang, Papua New Guinea
MIUTINI dial of MERU [MER]
MIWA [VMI] lang, Australia
MIWA alt for LOBI [LOB]
MIWA dial of WUNAMBAL [WUB]
MIWOK [SKD] lang, USA
MIXE, COATLÁN [MCO] lang, Mexico
MIXE, GUICHICOVI [MIR] lang, Mexico
MIXE, JUQUILA [MXQ] lang, Mexico
MIXE, MAZATLÁN [MZL] lang, Mexico
MIXE, NORTHEASTERN [MVE] lang, Mexico
MIXE, QUETZALTEPEC [MZC] lang, Mexico
MIXE, TLAHUITOLTEPEC [MXP] lang, Mexico
MIXE, TOTONTEPEC [MTO] lang, Mexico
MIXIZTLÁN MIXE alt for MIXE, NORTHEASTERN
    [MVE]
MIXTECO, ALACATLATZALA [MIM] lang, Mexico
MIXTECO, AMOLTEPEC [MBZ] lang, Mexico
MIXTECO, CENTRAL PUEBLA [MII] lang, Mexico
MIXTECO, COASTAL GUERRERO [MIY] lang, Mexico
MIXTECO, DIUXI-TILANTONGO [MIS] lang, Mexico
MIXTECO, EASTERN [MIL] lang, Mexico
MIXTECO, EASTERN JAMILTEPEC-CHAYUCO [MIH]
    lang, Mexico
MIXTECO, EASTERN JAMILTEPEC-SAN CRISTOBAL
    [MXT] lang, Mexico
MIXTECO, EASTERN JUXTLAHUACA [MIX] lang,
    Mexico
MIXTECO, EASTERN PUTLA [MCE] lang, Mexico
MIXTECO, HUAJUAPAN [MIU] lang, Mexico
MIXTECO, METLATONOC [MXV] lang, Mexico
MIXTECO, NORTH CENTRAL NOCHIXTLÁN [MTX]
    lang, Mexico
MIXTECO, NORTHERN TLAXIACO [MOS] lang,
    Mexico
MIXTECO, NORTHWEST OAXACA [MXA] lang,
    Mexico
MIXTECO, SAN ANTONIO HUITEPEC [MXS] lang,
    Mexico
MIXTECO, SAN BARTOLOMÉ YUCUAÑE [MVG]
    lang, Mexico
MIXTECO, SAN ESTEBAN ATATLAHUCA [MIB] lang,
    Mexico
MIXTECO, SAN JUAN COATZOSPAN [MIZ] lang,
    Mexico
MIXTECO, SAN JUAN COLORADO [MJC] lang,
    Mexico
MIXTECO, SAN MIGUEL EL GRANDE [MIG] lang,
    Mexico
MIXTECO, SAN PEDRO TUTUTEPEC [MTU] lang,
    Mexico
MIXTECO, SANTIAGO APOALA [MIP] lang, Mexico
MIXTECO, SANTIAGO YOSONDUA [MPM] lang,
    Mexico
MIXTECO, SANTO TOMÁS OCOTEPEC [MIE] lang,
    Mexico
MIXTECO, SILACAYOAPAN [MKS] lang, Mexico
MIXTECO, SOUTHEASTERN NOCHIXTLÁN [MXY]
    lang, Mexico

MIXTECO, SOUTHERN NOCHIXTLÁN [MAB] lang, Mexico
MIXTECO, SOUTHERN PUEBLA [MIT] lang, Mexico
MIXTECO, SOUTHERN PUTLA [MZA] lang, Mexico
MIXTECO, SOUTHWESTERN TLAXIACO [MEH] lang, Mexico
MIXTECO, TEZOATLÁN DE SEGURA Y LUNA [MXB] lang, Mexico
MIXTECO, WESTERN JAMILTEPEC [MIO] lang, Mexico
MIYA [MKF] lang, Nigeria
MIYAK [MVM] lang, Papua New Guinea
MIYAK alt for KYENELE [KQL]
MIYAKO [MVI] lang, Japan
MIYAKO-JIMA dial of MIYAKO [MVI]
MIYAMIYA alt for EJAR dial of KORO [KOR]
MIYANG-KHANG alt for NAGA, KHOIRAO [NKI]
MIYANGHO alt for YANGHO [YNH]
MIYATNU dial of ANKAVE [AAK]
MIYAWA alt for MIYA [MKF]
MIYEM alt for MIYEMU dial of MBO-UNG [MUX]
MIYEMU dial of MBO-UNG [MUX]
MIYOBE alt for SOLA [SOY]
MIZA dial of MORU [MGD]
MIZERAN alt for BANA [FLI]
MIZLIME alt for WUZLAM [UDL]
MIZMAST dial of AIMAQ [AIQ]
MIZO dial of LUSHAI [LSH]
MJILLEM alt for NIELLIM [NIE]
MKUU dial of CHAGGA [KAF]
MKWET dial of FE'FE' [FMP]
MLA alt for MLABRI [MRA]
MLA BRI alt for MLABRI [MRA]
MLABRI [MRA] lang, Thailand, Laos
MLOMP [QML] lang, Senegal
MLOMP NORTH alt for MLOMP [QML]
MMAALA [MMU] lang, Cameroon
MMALA alt for MMAALA [MMU]
MMANI alt for BULLOM SO [BUY]
MMANI dial of BULLOM SO [BUY]
MME alt for MMEN [BFM]
MMEN [BFM] lang, Cameroon
MMFO alt for DEG [MZW]
MNGAHRIS dial of TIBETAN [TIC]
MNONG GAR dial of MNONG, EASTERN [MNG]
MNONG KWANH dial of MNONG, EASTERN [MNG]
MNONG ROLOM dial of MNONG, EASTERN [MNG]
MNONG, CENTRAL [MNC] lang, Viet Nam, Cambodia
MNONG, EASTERN [MNG] lang, Viet Nam, USA
MNONG, SOUTHERN [MNN] lang, Viet Nam
MNYAMSKAD alt for NESANG [NES]
MO alt for CHING [MKG]
MO alt for DEG [MZW]
MO'OR dial of WAROPEN [WRP]
MOA alt for MOBA [MFQ]
MOAB alt for MOBA [MFQ]
MÒÁKA alt for AKA [AXK]
MOANUS alt for LELE [UGA]
MOANUS alt for TITAN [TTV]
MOAR alt for BIMOBA [BIM]
MOAR alt for SOBEI [SOB]
MOARAERI alt for MORAORI [MOK]
MOARE alt for MOBA [MFQ]
MOBA [MFQ] lang, Togo, Burkina Faso
MOBANGO dial of BUDZA [BJA]
MOBBER alt for MOVAR dial of KANURI, YERWA

[KPH]
MOBBER alt for MOVAR dial of KANURI, YERWA [KPH]
MOBER alt for MOVAR dial of KANURI, YERWA [KPH]
MOBER alt for MOVAR dial of KANURI, YERWA [KPH]
MOBESA alt for MBESA [ZMS]
MOBILIAN [MOD] lang, USA
MOBILIAN JARGON alt for MOBILIAN [MOD]
MOBOU dial of KWANG [KVI]
MOBU alt for MOBOU dial of KWANG [KVI]
MOBUTA alt for AWA [AWB]
MÔC-CHÂU alt for TAI DAENG [TYR]
MOCH'A alt for MOCHA [MOY]
MOCHA [MOY] lang, Ethiopia
MOCHDA alt for CARAPANA [CBC]
MOCHIA dial of CHING [MKG]
MOCHINYA alt for MOCHA [MOY]
MOCHO [MHC] lang, Mexico
MOCHUELO-CASANARE-CUIBA dial of CUIBA [CUI]
MOCHUMI alt for NAGA, CHANG [NBC]
MOCHUNGRR alt for NAGA, CHANG [NBC]
MOCI alt for MOSI [OLD]
MOCIGIN alt for GUDE [GDE]
MOCIMBOA DA PRAIA dial of MWANI [WMW]
MOCO dial of BANGBA [BBE]
MOCOA alt for INGA, JUNGLE [INJ]
MOCOBÍ alt for MOCOVÍ [MOC]
MOCOVÍ [MOC] lang, Argentina
MOD alt for MAWER [MTB]
MO'DA [GBN] lang, Sudan
MODAN alt for NABI [NBN]
MODANG [MXD] lang, Indonesia, Kalimantan
MODEA dial of GUMUZ [GUK]
MODELE dial of BEFANG [BBY]
MODELI alt for MODELE dial of BEFANG [BBY]
MODELLE alt for MODELE dial of BEFANG [BBY]
MODEN alt for MAWER [MTB]
MODERN LANGUS dial of TORRES STRAIT CREOLE [TCS]
MODERN LITERARY ARABIC alt for ARABIC, MODERN STANDARD [ABV]
MODERN MANDAIC alt for MANDAIC [MID]
MODERN TUPÍ alt for NHENGATU [YRL]
MODGEL alt for NGAM dial of KWANG [KVI]
MODH alt for MARIA [MRR]
MODI alt for MARIA [MRR]
MODIN alt for MAWER [MTB]
MODO dial of JUR MODO [BEX]
MODO LALI alt for MODO dial of JUR MODO [BEX]
MODOLE [MQO] lang, Indonesia, Maluku
MODRA alt for TODRAH [TDR]
MODUNGA alt for NDUNGA [NDT]
MOENEBENG alt for CAAC [MSQ]
MOERE [MVQ] lang, Papua New Guinea
MOEWEHAFEN alt for AIKLEP [MWG]
MOFA alt for MAFA [MAF]
MOFA dial of MAFA [MAF]
MOFOU alt for MOFU, SOUTH [MIF]
MOFOU DE GOUDOUR alt for MOFU, SOUTH [MIF]
MOFU dial of BIAK [BHW]
MOFU DE DOUROUM alt for DOUROUN dial of MOFU, NORTH [MFK]
MOFU DE MERI alt for MEREY [MEQ]
MOFU, NORTH [MFK] lang, Cameroon

MOFU, SOUTH [MIF] lang, Cameroon
MOFU-DOUVANGAR alt for MOFU, NORTH [MFK]
MOFU-GUDUR alt for MOFU, SOUTH [MIF]
MOFU-MOKONG alt for MOFU, SOUTH [MIF]
MOFU-SUD alt for MOFU, SOUTH [MIF]
MOG alt for ARAKANESE [MHV]
MOGAO alt for PURAGI [PRU]
MOGAREB alt for NARA [NRB]
MOGH alt for ARAKANESE [MHV]
MOGHAMO dial of META' [MGO]
MOGHAMO-MENEMO alt for META' [MGO]
MOGHOL alt for MOGHOLI [MLG]
MOGHOLI [MLG] lang, Afghanistan
MOGIMBA alt for NGEMBA [NGE]
MOGOGODO alt for YAAKU [MUU]
MOGOL alt for MOGHOLI [MLG]
MOGONI dial of BARAI [BCA]
MOGOU alt for MOTIEM dial of NGANGAM [GNG]
MOGOUM alt for MOGUM [MOU]
MOGUEZ alt for GUAMBIANO [GUM]
MOGUL alt for MOGHOLI [MLG]
MOGUM [MOU] lang, Chad
MOGUM ABU DEIA dial of MOGUM [MOU]
MOGUM MELFI dial of MOGUM [MOU]
MOHAVE [MOV] lang, USA
MOHAWK [MOH] lang, Canada, USA, USA
MOHEGAN-MONTAUK-NARRAGANSETT [MOF] lang,
     USA
MOHELI alt for SHIMWALI dial of COMORIAN [SWB]
MOHISA dial of BUKA-KHWE [BUZ]
MOHMAND dial of PASHTO, EASTERN [PBU]
MOHONGIA alt for NAGA, NOCTE [NJB]
MOHUNG dial of NAGA, KONYAK [NBE]
MOI [MXN] lang, Indonesia, Irian Jaya
MOI [MOW] lang, Congo
MOI 1 dial of MUONG [MTQ]
MOI alt for MEKWEI [MSF]
MOI alt for HRE [HRE]
MOI BI alt for BOI BI dial of MUONG [MTQ]
MOI DA VACH alt for HRE [HRE]
MOI LUY alt for HRE [HRE]
MOIFAU alt for MEIFU dial of HLAI [LIC]
MOIKODI [DOI] lang, Papua New Guinea
MOIL alt for TYEMERI dial of NANGIKURRUNGGURR
     [NAM]
MOINBA [MOB] lang, China, India, India
MOINGI [MWZ] lang, Zaïre
MOIRE alt for HATAM [HAD]
MOIRE dial of HATAM [HAD]
MOISSALA MBAI alt for MBAI [MYB]
MOITANIK dial of MAASAI [MET]
MOIUM alt for PAPEL [PBO]
MOIYUI alt for NAGA, RENGMA [NRE]
MOJAVE alt for MOHAVE [MOV]
MOJOS alt for IGNACIANO [IGN]
MOJOS alt for TRINITARIO [TRN]
MOJUNG alt for NAGA, CHANG [NBC]
MOK [MQT] lang, Thailand
MOK alt for MOUK dial of MOUK-ARIA [MWH]
MOKA alt for BYEP [MKK]
MOKAR alt for GA'ANDA [GAA]
MOKARENG alt for MOKERANG [MFT]
MOKEN [MWT] lang, Myanmar, Thailand, Thailand
MOKERANG [MFT] lang, Papua New Guinea
MOKHEV alt for MOXEV dial of GEORGIAN [GEO]
MOKIL [MNO] lang, Micronesia

MOKILESE alt for MOKIL [MNO]
MOKILKO alt for MOKULU [MOZ]
MOKILKO dial of MOKULU [MOZ]
MOKLEN [MKM] lang, Thailand
MOKLUM dial of NAGA, TASE [NST]
MOKMER alt for SAMPORI dial of BIAK [BHW]
MOKOLE [MKL] lang, Benin
MOKOLLÉ alt for MOKOLE [MKL]
MOKOMOKO alt for MUKO-MUKO [VMO]
MOKONG alt for MOFU, SOUTH [MIF]
MOKORENG alt for MOKERANG [MFT]
MOKORUA alt for YEGA dial of KORAFE [KPR]
MOKOULOU alt for MOKULU [MOZ]
MOKPE alt for MOKPWE [BRI]
MOKPWE [BRI] lang, Cameroon
MOKSELA [VMS] lang, Indonesia, Maluku
MOKSHA [MDF] lang, Russia, Europe
MOKSHAN alt for MOKSHA [MDF]
MOKULU [MOZ] lang, Chad
MOKURU alt for USHAKU dial of BEFANG [BBY]
MOKWALE alt for MOKOLE [MKL]
MOKYO alt for MELOKWO [MLW]
MOL dial of MUONG [MTQ]
MOLAO alt for MULAM [MLM]
MOLBOG [PWM] lang, Philippines, Malaysia, Sabah
MOLBOG PALAWAN alt for MOLBOG [PWM]
MOLDAVIAN alt for RUMANIAN [RUM]
MOLDAVIAN dial of RUMANIAN [RUM]
MOLE alt for MOORE [MHM]
MOLI dial of TALISE [TLR]
MOLIBA dial of DZANDO [DZN]
MOLIMA [MOX] lang, Papua New Guinea
MOLIMA dial of MOLIMA [MOX]
MOLISANO dial of ITALIAN [ITN]
MOLKO alt for MELOKWO [MLW]
MOLKOA alt for MELOKWO [MLW]
MOLKWO alt for MELOKWO [MLW]
MOLLO alt for MOLLO-MIOMAFO dial of ATONI
     [TMR]
MOLLO-MIOMAFO dial of ATONI [TMR]
MOLLOROIDYI alt for MULURIDYI [VMU]
MOLO [ZMO] lang, Sudan
MOLO dial of NYAMUSA-MOLO [NYO]
MOLOF [MSL] lang, Indonesia, Irian Jaya
MOLOKO alt for MELOKWO [MLW]
MOLOKWO alt for MELOKWO [MLW]
MOLOT dial of RAMOAAINA [RAI]
MOLU-MARU dial of FORDATA [FRD]
MOLUCHE dial of MAPUDUNGUN [ARU]
MOLUNGA dial of DZANDO [DZN]
MOM JANGO [VER] lang, Nigeria, Cameroon
MOM JANGO dial of MOM JANGO [VER]
MOMA [MYL] lang, Indonesia, Sulawesi
MOMALE alt for MOMARE [MSZ]
MOMALILI alt for MESEM [MCI]
MOMARE [MSZ] lang, Papua New Guinea
MOMBA alt for MOINBA [MOB]
MOMBASA alt for MVITA dial of SWAHILI [SWA]
MOMBE alt for NYAKYUSA-NGONDE [NYY]
MOMBE dial of GBAYA [GYA]
MOMBESA alt for MBESA [ZMS]
MOMBI alt for MEMBI dial of NDO [NDP]
MOMBO alt for MAMBAI [MCS]
MOMBU dial of NGEMBA [NGE]
MOMBUM [MSO] lang, Indonesia, Irian Jaya
MOMBUTTU alt for MANGBUTU [MDK]

MOME alt for MUMUYE [MUL]
MOMFU alt for MAMVU dial of MAMVU [MDI]
MOMI dial of MOM JANGO [VER]
MOMOGUN alt for RUNGUS [DRG]
MOMOLE alt for MOMARE [MSZ]
MOMOLILI alt for MESEM [MCI]
MOMPA alt for MOINBA [MOB]
MOMUNA [MQF] lang, Indonesia, Irian Jaya
MOMVEDA dial of PAGABETE [PAG]
MOMVU alt for MAMVU dial of MAMVU [MDI]
MON [MNW] lang, Myanmar, Thailand, Thailand
MON alt for NAGA, RENGMA [NRE]
MON alt for MON [MNW]
MON dial of NAGA, KONYAK [NBE]
MON NYA alt for YE dial of MON [MNW]
MON TANG alt for PEGU dial of MON [MNW]
MON TE alt for MATABAN-MOULMEIN dial of MON
  [MNW]
MON-NON alt for MONO [MRU]
MONA alt for MUAN [MOA]
MONA alt for MWANA dial of DIJIM [CFA]
MONAM alt for MONOM [MOO]
MONAO alt for BURMESO [BZU]
MONASTIC SIGN LANGUAGE [MZG] lang, Vatican
  State
MONAU alt for BURMESO [BZU]
MONAXO alt for MAXAKALÍ [MBL]
MONBA alt for MOINBA [MOB]
MONDARI alt for MANDARI [MQU]
MONDARI alt for MUNDARI [MUW]
MONDARI dial of BARI [BFA]
MONDÉ [MND] lang, Brazil
MONDJEMBO alt for MONZOMBO [MOJ]
MONDO alt for MUNDU [MUH]
MONDO alt for SULOD [SRG]
MONDROPOLON [MLY] lang, Papua New Guinea
MONDU alt for MUNDU [MUH]
MONDUGU alt for NDUNGA [NDT]
MONDUNGA alt for NDUNGA [NDT]
MONEBWA alt for KAREN, PAKU [KPP]
MONÉGASQUE dial of LIGURIAN [LIJ]
MONG LENG dial of HMONG DAW [MWW]
MONGA dial of ANGOR [AGG]
MONGAIYAT alt for MANGAYAT [MYJ]
MONGALA POTO dial of LUSENGO [LUS]
MONGBAI BIPARE alt for MAMBAI [MCS]
MONGBANDI alt for NGBANDI [NGB]
MONGBAPELE dial of PAGABETE [PAG]
MONGBAY alt for MAMBAI [MCS]
MONGGOL alt for MONGOLIAN, PERIPHERAL [MVF]
MŎNGHSA alt for ACHANG [ACN]
MONGI [KGF] lang, Papua New Guinea
MONGLWE alt for TAI LOI [TLQ]
MONGO alt for BUSHOONG [BUF]
MONGO alt for MONGO-NKUNDU [MOM]
MONGO dial of KURANKO [KHA]
MONGO dial of LUSENGO [LUS]
MONGO dial of DAJU, DAR SILA [DAU]
MONGO-NKUNDU [MOM] lang, Zaïre
MONGO-SILA alt for DAJU, DAR SILA [DAU]
MONGOL [MGT] lang, Papua New Guinea
MONGOL alt for MONGOLIAN, HALH [KHK]
MONGOL alt for MONGOLIAN, PERIPHERAL [MVF]
MONGOLIAN BURIAT alt for BURIAT, MONGOLIA
  [BXM]
MONGOLIAN, HALH [KHK] lang, Mongolian Peoples

Republic, Russia, Russia, Asia
MONGOLIAN, HALH alt for MONGOLIAN, HALH
  [KHK]
MONGOLIAN, PERIPHERAL [MVF] lang, China,
  Mongolian Peoples Republic
MONGOLIAN, PERIPHERAL alt for MONGOLIAN,
  PERIPHERAL [MVF]
MONGONDOU alt for MONGONDOW [MOG]
MONGONDOW [MOG] lang, Indonesia, Sulawesi
MONGOR alt for TU [MJG]
MONGOUR alt for TU [MJG]
MONGOUR dial of TU [MJG]
MONGSEN KHARI dial of NAGA, AO [NJO]
MONGUL alt for MOGHOLI [MLG]
MONGUNA dial of DAFFO-BATURA [DAM]
MONGWANDI alt for NGBANDI [NGB]
MONI [MNZ] lang, Indonesia, Irian Jaya
MONI alt for KENSIU [KNS]
MONIA dial of LIBINZA [LIZ]
MONIK alt for KENSIU [KNS]
MONIMBO [MOL] lang, Nicaragua
MONIQ alt for KENSIU [KNS]
MONJO alt for NGEMBA dial of GHOMALA' [BBJ]
MONJOMBO alt for MONZOMBO [MOJ]
MONJUL alt for MUBI [MUB]
MONKOLE alt for MOKOLE [MKL]
MONNEPWA alt for KAREN, PAKU [KPP]
MONO [MRU] lang, Cameroon
MONO [MTE] lang, Solomon Islands
MONO [MNH] lang, Zaïre
MONO [MON] lang, USA
MONO dial of MONO [MTE]
MONO-ALU alt for MONO [MTE]
MONOARFU dial of BIAK [BHW]
MONOCHO alt for MAXAKALÍ [MBL]
MONOGOY [MCU] lang, Chad
MONOM [MOO] lang, Viet Nam
MONPA alt for MOINBA [MOB]
MONPAKHA dial of SHARCHAGPAKHA [SCH]
MONR alt for NAGA, ANGAMI [NJM]
MONSHANG alt for NAGA, MONSANG [NMH]
MONTAGNAIS [MOE] lang, Canada
MONTAL alt for MONTOL [MTL]
MONTAUK dial of MOHEGAN-MONTAUK-
  NARRAGANSETT [MOF]
MONTE VERDE MIXTECO dial of MIXTECO,
  NORTHERN TLAXIACO [MOS]
MONTOL [MTL] lang, Nigeria
MONTOL dial of MONTOL [MTL]
MONU alt for KAREN, MANUMANAW [KXF]
MONUMBO [MXK] lang, Papua New Guinea
MONZAMBOLI dial of BUDZA [BJA]
MONZOMBO [MOJ] lang, Congo, Central African
  Republic, Zaïre
MONZOMBO alt for MONZOMBO [MOJ]
MONZÓN dial of QUECHUA, HUÁNUCO,
  HUAMALÍES [QEJ]
MONZUMBO alt for MONZOMBO [MOJ]
MOOI alt for MEKWEI [MSF]
MOOJANGA alt for ANUAK [ANU]
MOOLOROIJI alt for MULURIDYI [VMU]
MOOR alt for ARABIC, HASSANIYA [MEY]
MOORE [MHM] lang, Burkina Faso, Benin, Côte
  d'Ivoire, Ghana, Mali, Togo
MOORE alt for MOORE [MHM]
MOORINGA alt for MOORINGER dial of FRISIAN,

NORTHERN [FRR]
MOORINGER dial of FRISIAN, NORTHERN [FRR]
MOOSE alt for MOORE [MHM]
MOOSE CREE dial of CREE, CENTRAL [CRM]
MOOSEHIDE alt for HAN [HAA]
MOOYO dial of KARANGA [KTH]
MOPÁN MAYA [MOP] lang, Guatemala, Belize
MOPANE alt for MOPÁN MAYA [MOP]
MOPHA [MPW] lang, Myanmar, China
MOPLA alt for MALAYALAM [MJS]
MOPLAH dial of MALAYALAM [MJS]
MOPO alt for MUFWA dial of BURUN [BDI]
MOPOI alt for MAPOYO [MCG]
MOPUTE alt for WARU [WRU]
MOPWA alt for KAREN, PAKU [KPP]
MOQADDAM dial of AZERBAIJANI, SOUTH [AZB]
MOQUISE alt for KWISE dial of KWADI [KWZ]
MOQUISSE alt for KWISE dial of KWADI [KWZ]
MOR [MHZ] lang, Indonesia, Irian Jaya
MOR [MOQ] lang, Indonesia, Irian Jaya
MORA alt for YAWA [YVA]
MORA alt for CENTRAL YAWA dial of YAWA [YVA]
MORA BROUSSE alt for MURA dial of WANDALA
    [MFI]
MORA MASSIF alt for MURA dial of WANDALA
    [MFI]
MORAFA [MTV] lang, Papua New Guinea
MORAID [MSG] lang, Indonesia, Irian Jaya
MORANGIA dial of THARU, SAPTARI [THQ]
MORAORI [MOK] lang, Indonesia, Irian Jaya
MORARI alt for MORAORI [MOK]
MORAVIAN ROMANI dial of ROMANI, CARPATHIAN
    [RMC]
MORAWA [MZE] lang, Papua New Guinea
MORDOFF alt for MOKSHA [MDF]
MORDOV alt for MOKSHA [MDF]
MORDVIN alt for ERZYA [MYV]
MORDVIN-ERZYA alt for ERZYA [MYV]
MORDVIN-MOKSHA alt for MOKSHA [MDF]
MORE alt for ITENE [ITE]
MORE alt for MOORE [MHM]
MOREB dial of TAGOI [TAG]
MORELA dial of HITU [HIT]
MOREREBI [XMO] lang, Brazil
MORESADA [MSX] lang, Papua New Guinea
MORI [MRG] lang, Gambia
MORI dial of ANEME WAKE [ABY]
MORI ATAS [MZQ] lang, Indonesia, Sulawesi
MORI BAWAH [XMZ] lang, Indonesia, Sulawesi
MORIE dial of ABÉ [ABA]
MORIGI [MDB] lang, Papua New Guinea
MORIGI ISLAND alt for MORIGI [MDB]
MORIIL alt for ZAN GULA [ZNA]
MORIKO dial of MOKULU [MOZ]
MORILLE alt for DAASANECH [DSH]
MORIMA alt for MOLIMA [MOX]
MORIORI dial of MAORI [MBF]
MORIPI-IOKEA alt for TOARIPI dial of TOARIPI [TPI]
MORISYEN [MFE] lang, Mauritius
MORMA alt for ARAKANESE [MHV]
MORO [MOR] lang, Sudan
MORO alt for AYOREO [AYO]
MORO HILLS [TAZ] lang, Sudan
MORO JOLOANO alt for TAUSUG [TSG]
MOROA alt for SHOLIO dial of KATAB [KCG]
MOROCCAN SIGN LANGUAGE [XMS] lang, Morocco

MOROKODO [MGC] lang, Sudan
MOROKODO dial of MOROKODO [MGC]
MOROMIRANGA [MYZ] lang, Papua New Guinea
MORONENE [MQN] lang, Indonesia, Sulawesi
MORONENE alt for WITA EA dial of MORONENE
    [MQN]
MORONOU dial of ANYIN [ANY]
MOROTAI dial of GALELA [GBI]
MOROTOCO alt for AYOREO [AYO]
MOROUAS [MRP] lang, Vanuatu
MORTA alt for KADUGLI dial of KATCHA-KADUGLI-
    MIRI [KAT]
MORTLOCK [MRL] lang, Micronesia
MORTLOCK alt for TAKUU [NHO]
MORTLOCKESE alt for MORTLOCK [MRL]
MORU [MXZ] lang, Côte d'Ivoire
MORU [MGD] lang, Sudan
MORUAS alt for MOROUAS [MRP]
MORUBA alt for MARABA [XMW]
MORUBANMIN alt for YOLIAPI dial of HEWA [HAM]
MORUNAHUA [MNY] lang, Peru
MORUWA'DI dial of MORU [MGD]
MORWA alt for SHOLIO dial of KATAB [KCG]
MORWAP [MRF] lang, Indonesia, Irian Jaya
MOS alt for TONGA [TNZ]
MOS alt for KENSIU [KNS]
MOSANA alt for MOI [MXN]
MOSANGE alt for NDOLO [NDL]
MOSCA alt for CHIBCHA [CBF]
MOSELLE FRANCONIAN alt for LUXEMBOURGEOIS
    [LUX]
MOSES LAKE dial of OKANAGAN [OKA]
MOSETEN alt for TSIMANÉ [CAS]
MOSHANG alt for NAGA, MONSANG [NMH]
MOSHI alt for MOSI [OLD]
MOSHI alt for MOORE [MHM]
MOSI [OLD] lang, Tanzania
MOSI [MSE] lang, Chad, Cameroon
MOSIENO dial of TEKE, EASTERN [TEK]
MOSIMO [MQV] lang, Papua New Guinea
MOSIN alt for MOSINA [MSN]
MOSINA [MSN] lang, Vanuatu
MOSIRO [MWY] lang, Tanzania
MOSIYE alt for DOBASE [DOX]
MOSKONA [MTJ] lang, Indonesia, Irian Jaya
MOSO alt for LAHU [LAH]
"MOSO" alt for NAXI [NBF]
MOSQUITO alt for MÍSKITO [MIQ]
MOSSI alt for MOORE [MHM]
"MOSSO" alt for NAXI [NBF]
MOSUL dial of ARABIC, SYRO-MESOPOTAMIAN
    [AYP]
MOTA [MTT] lang, Vanuatu
MOTALAVA alt for MOTLAV [MLV]
MOTCHEKIN alt for GUDE [GDE]
MOTEMBO alt for TEMBO [TMV]
MOTIEM alt for NGANGAM [GNG]
MOTILÓN [MOT] lang, Colombia, Venezuela,
    Venezuela
MOTILÓN alt for QUECHUA, SAN MARTÍN [QSA]
MOTILÓN alt for MOTILÓN [MOT]
MOTILONE alt for MOTILÓN [MOT]
MOTIN alt for MAWER [MTB]
MOTLAV [MLV] lang, Vanuatu
MOTOM alt for MACI dial of ICEVE-MACI [BEC]
MOTOMO alt for MACI dial of ICEVE-MACI [BEC]

MOTOMO alt for MACI dial of ICEVE-MACI [BEC]
MOTOZINTLECO alt for MOCHO [MHC]
MOTOZINTLECO dial of MOCHO [MHC]
MOTU [MEU] lang, Papua New Guinea
MOTU, HIRI [POM] lang, Papua New Guinea
MOTUMOTU alt for TOARIPI [TPI]
MOTUNA alt for SIWAI [SIW]
MOU alt for KHMU [KJG]
MOUAMENAM dial of MBO [MBO]
MOUAN alt for MUAN [MOA]
MOUBI alt for MUBI [MUB]
MOUGULU alt for BEAMI [BEO]
MOUHOUR alt for MUHURA dial of MEFELE [MFJ]
MOUK dial of MOUK-ARIA [MWH]
MOUK-ARIA [MWH] lang, Papua New Guinea
MOUKTELE alt for MATAL [MFH]
MOUNAN alt for MUNA [MYN]
MOUNDAN alt for MUNDANG [MUA]
MOUNDANG alt for MUNDANG [MUA]
MOUNTAIN dial of SLAVEY [SLA]
MOUNTAIN ARAPESH alt for BUKIYIP [APE]
MOUNTAIN BASHKIR alt for KUVAKAN dial of
    BASHKIR [BXK]
MOUNTAIN KOIARI alt for KOIALI, MOUNTAIN
    [KPX]
MOUNTAIN LAWA alt for LAWA, WESTERN [LCP]
MOUNTAIN MAIDU alt for NORTHEAST MAIDU dial
    of MAIDU [MAI]
MOUNTAIN MINCHIA dial of BAI [PIQ]
MOUNTAIN PIMA alt for PIMA BAJO, SONORA [PIA]
MOUNTAIN TEQUISTLATECO alt for CHONTAL OF
    OAXACA, HIGHLAND [CHD]
MOUNTOU alt for MUNDU [MUH]
MOURLE alt for MURLE [MUR]
MOUROUM dial of NGAMBAI [SBA]
MOURRO alt for MURRU dial of KIBET [KIE]
MOUSGOU alt for MUSGU [MUG]
MOUSGOUM alt for MUSGU [MUG]
MOUSGOUM DE GUIRVIDIG alt for MUZUK dial of
    MUSGU [MUG]
MOUSGOUM DE GUIRVIDIK alt for MUZUK dial of
    MUSGU [MUG]
MOUSGOUM DE POUSS alt for MPUS dial of
    MUSGU [MUG]
MOUSGOUN alt for MUSGU [MUG]
MOUSSEI alt for MOSI [MSE]
MOUSSEY alt for MOSI [MSE]
MOUYENGE alt for MUYANG [MUY]
MOUYENGUE alt for MUYANG [MUY]
MOVAR dial of KANURI, YERWA [KPH]
MOVAR dial of KANURI, YERWA [KPH]
MOVE dial of YAGARIA [YGR]
MOVEAVE alt for TOARIPI dial of TOARIPI [TPI]
MOVIMA [MZP] lang, Bolivia
MOXDOA alt for CARAPANA [CBC]
MOXEV dial of GEORGIAN [GEO]
MOXO alt for IGNACIANO [IGN]
MOXOS alt for IGNACIANO [IGN]
MOXOS alt for TRINITARIO [TRN]
MOYAKA alt for BEKA dial of AKA [AXK]
MOYO dial of MADI [MHI]
MOYO alt for MOOYO dial of KARANGA [KTH]
MOYON alt for NAGA, MOYON [NMO]
MOYON-MONSHANG dial of ANAL [ANM]
MOZARABIC [MXI] lang, Spain
MOZDOK dial of KABARDIAN [KAB]

MOZHUMI alt for NAGA, RENGMA [NRE]
MOZOME dial of NAGA, ANGAMI [NJM]
MPADE [MPI] lang, Cameroon, Chad, Chad, Nigeria
MPADE alt for MPADE [MPI]
MPADE dial of MPADE [MPI]
MPAMA dial of MONGO-NKUNDU [MOM]
MPEZENI alt for NGONI dial of NSENGA [NSE]
MPI [MPZ] lang, Thailand
MPI-MI alt for MPI [MPZ]
MPIEMO alt for MPYEMO [MCX]
MPO alt for MPYEMO [MCX]
MPO dial of BASAA [BAA]
MPOMAM dial of MPONGMPONG [MGG]
MPOMPO alt for MPONGMPONG [MGG]
MPONDO dial of XHOSA [XOS]
MPONDOMISI alt for MPONDOMSE dial of XHOSA
    [XOS]
MPONDOMSE dial of XHOSA [XOS]
MPONGMPONG [MGG] lang, Cameroon
MPONGO alt for NTOMBA [NTO]
MPONGOUÉ alt for MPONGWE dial of MYENE [MYE]
MPONGWE dial of MYENE [MYE]
MPOPO alt for MPONGMPONG [MGG]
MPOTO [MPA] lang, Tanzania, Malawi
MPOTOVORO [MVT] lang, Vanuatu
MPU dial of TEKE, NORTHEASTERN [NGZ]
MPUMPUM alt for MPU dial of TEKE,
    NORTHEASTERN [NGZ]
MPUNGWE alt for MPONGWE dial of MYENE [MYE]
MPUONO [ZMP] lang, Zaïre
MPUONO dial of MPUONO [ZMP]
MPUR [AKC] lang, Indonesia, Irian Jaya
MPUS [MUG] lang, Musgu [MUG]
MPUS dial of MUSGU [MUG]
MPUUN dial of MPUONO [ZMP]
MPYEMO [MCX] lang, Central African Republic,
    Cameroon
MPYEMO dial of MPYEMO [MCX]
MRABRI alt for MLABRI [MRA]
MRAS TATAR alt for SHOR [CJS]
MRASSA dial of SHOR [CJS]
MRIAK-MRIKU dial of SASAK [SAS]
MRIMA dial of SWAHILI [SWA]
MRO alt for MRU [MRO]
MRO dial of CHRAU [CHR]
MRU [MRO] lang, Myanmar, Bangladesh, India
MRUNG alt for MRU [MRO]
MRUNG alt for KOK BOROK [TRP]
MSER [KQX] lang, Cameroon, Chad, Chad
MSER alt for MSER [KQX]
MSER dial of MSER [KQX]
MSER dial of MSER [KQX]
MSIR dial of MSER dial of MSER [KQX]
MT. ELGON MAASAI alt for SABAOT [SPY]
MT. GOLIATH alt for UNA [MTG]
MT. IRIGA NEGRITO alt for AGTA, MT. IRIGA [AGZ]
MTEZI dial of KUKELE [KEZ]
MTHUR alt for JARAI [JRA]
MTIUL dial of GEORGIAN [GEO]
MU alt for SEKPELE [LIP]
MU'ANG alt for TAI, NORTHERN [NOD]
MU'ANG YONG dial of LÜ [KHB]
MU:DU alt for KORAGA, MUDU [VMD]
MUAL dial of MUONG [MTQ]
MUALANG [MTD] lang, Indonesia, Kalimantan
MUAN [MOA] lang, Côte d'Ivoire

MUANA alt for MUAN [MOA]
MUANE alt for MWANI [WMW]
MUANG alt for TAI, NORTHERN [NOD]
MUASI alt for MAWASI dial of KORKU [KFQ]
MUATIAMVUA alt for RUUND [RND]
MUATURAINA dial of MANAGALASI [MCQ]
MUBADJI alt for BEBA' dial of BAFUT [BFD]
MUBAKO alt for NYONG [MUO]
MUBI [MUB] lang, Chad
MUBI alt for GUDE [GDE]
MUBI dial of FOI [FOI]
MUBI RIVER alt for FOI [FOI]
MUCKLESHOOT dial of SALISH, SOUTHERN PUGET
    SOUND [SLH]
MUCOROCA alt for KWADI [KWZ]
MUD alt for MEDOGO [MNE]
MUDA alt for MO'DA [GBN]
MUDAVAN alt for MUTHUVAN [MUV]
MUDAYE alt for GUDE [GDE]
MUDBURA [MWD] lang, Australia
MUDBURRA alt for MUDBURA [MWD]
MUDIA alt for MURIA, WESTERN [MUT]
MUDIKORA alt for KODA [KFN]
MUDIMA alt for MALIMBA [MZD]
"MUDJETÍRE" alt for SURUÍ DO PARÁ [MDZ]
"MUDJETÍRE-SURUÍ" alt for SURUÍ DO PARÁ [MDZ]
MUDUGAR alt for MUTHUVAN [MUV]
MUDUVAN alt for MUTHUVAN [MUV]
MUDUVAR alt for MUTHUVAN [MUV]
MUENAME alt for MUINANE [BMR]
MUFIAN alt for ARAPESH, SOUTHERN [AOJ]
MUFWA dial of BURUN [BDI]
MUGABA alt for MUNGGAVA dial of RENNELL
    [MNV]
MUGAJA alt for MUGHAJA dial of BURUN [BDI]
MUGALI [MUK] lang, Nepal
MUGALI KHAM dial of MUGALI [MUK]
MUGALY alt for ZAKATALY dial of AZERBAIJANI,
    NORTH [AZE]
MUGANGE dial of SAGALLA [TGA]
MUGHAJA dial of BURUN [BDI]
MUGHALBANDI dial of ORIYA [ORY]
MUGIKI alt for MUNGIKI dial of RENNELL [MNV]
MUGIL alt for BARGAM [MLP]
MUGO-MBORKOINA alt for ABULDUGU dial of
    BURUN [BDI]
MUGUJI dial of KWEGU [YID]
MUGUM alt for NGEMBA dial of GHOMALA' [BBJ]
MUGUMUTE alt for KAPRIMAN [DJU]
MUHANG alt for WEST LAMAHOLOT dial of
    LAMAHOLOT [SLP]
MUHER dial of GURAGE, CENTRAL WEST [GUY]
MUHIAN alt for ARAPESH, SOUTHERN [AOJ]
MUHIANG alt for ARAPESH, SOUTHERN [AOJ]
MUHSO alt for LAHU [LAH]
MUHSUR alt for LAHU [LAH]
MUHURA dial of MEFELE [MFJ]
MUILA alt for MWILA dial of NYANEKA [NYK]
MUINANA alt for MUINANE [BMR]
MUINANE [BMR] lang, Colombia, Peru, Peru
MUINANE alt for MUINANE [BMR]
MUINANI alt for MUINANE [BMR]
MUIRIN dial of DARGWA [DAR]
MUISCA alt for CHIBCHA [CBF]
MUKA alt for BAMUNKA [NDO]
MUKA alt for MUKAH-OYA dial of MELANAU [MEL]

MUKAH alt for MUKAH-OYA dial of MELANAU [MEL]
MUKAH-OYA dial of MELANAU [MEL]
MUKAJAI alt for SOUTHERN NINAM dial of NINAM
    [SHB]
MUKAMUGA alt for KAMORO [KGQ]
MUKAWA alt for ARE [MWC]
MUKHA-DORA [MMK] lang, India
MUKHAD alt for RUTUL [RUT]
MUKI alt for MEKEM [XME]
MUKILI alt for BELI [BEY]
MUKO-MUKO [VMO] lang, Indonesia, Sumatra
MUKOGODO alt for YAAKU [MUU]
MUKOHN alt for MANGKUNGE dial of NGEMBA
    [NGE]
MUKOQUODO alt for YAAKU [MUU]
MUKRI dial of KURDI [KDB]
MUKTELE alt for MATAL [MFH]
MUKTELE dial of MAFA [MAF]
MUKTILE alt for MATAL [MFH]
MUKU alt for BILEKI dial of NAKANAI [NAK]
MUKULU alt for MOKULU [MOZ]
MUKULU dial of BEMBA [BEM]
MUKUNI alt for LENJE [LEH]
MUKUNO alt for MINEW dial of ZULGWA [ZUL]
MUKURU alt for USHAKU dial of BEFANG [BBY]
MULAHA [MFW] lang, Papua New Guinea
MULAHA dial of MULAHA [MFW]
MULAI dial of MACA [XMC]
MULAK dial of MALAY [MLI]
MULAM [MLM] lang, China
MULAO alt for MULAM [MLM]
MULARITCHEE alt for MULURIDYI [VMU]
MULENGE dial of RWANDA [RUA]
MULGARNOO alt for BAYUNGU [BXJ]
MULGI alt for MULY dial of ESTONIAN [EST]
MULI dial of HSIFAN [HSI]
MULIA [MUC] lang, India
MULIMBA alt for MALIMBA [MZD]
MULLRIDGEY alt for MULURIDYI [VMU]
MULLUKMULLUK [MPB] lang, Australia
MULONGA dial of SIMAA [SIE]
MULSOM dial of ANAL [ANM]
MULTANI alt for SIRAIKI [SKR]
MULTANI dial of SIRAIKI [SKR]
MULU alt for MARU [MHX]
MULUNG dial of NAGA, KONYAK [NBE]
MULURIDYI [VMU] lang, Australia
MULURUTJI alt for MULURIDYI [VMU]
MULWI alt for MUSGU [MUG]
MULWI alt for VULUM dial of MUSGU [MUG]
MULWI alt for VULUM dial of MUSGU [MUG]
MULWI-MOGROUM alt for VULUM dial of MUSGU
    [MUG]
MULWYIN alt for MULYEN dial of BACAMA [BAM]
MULY dial of ESTONIAN [EST]
MULYEN dial of BACAMA [BAM]
MUMAITE alt for LUMAETE dial of KAYELI [KZL]
MUMBAKE alt for NYONG [MUO]
MUMBALA alt for MBALA dial of YOMBE [YOM]
MUMENG [MZI] lang, Papua New Guinea
MUMENG dial of MUMENG [MZI]
MUMONI dial of KAMBA [KIK]
MUMUGHADJA alt for MUGHAJA dial of BURUN
    [BDI]
MUMUYE [MUL] lang, Nigeria, Cameroon
MUMVIRI dial of KATI [BSH]

MUN [MJI] lang, Laos, China, Viet Nam
MŬN alt for CHIN, MŬN [MWQ]
MUN alt for MUN [MJI]
MUN alt for MON [MNW]
MUN XEN alt for KHMU [KJG]
MUNA [MYN] lang, Indonesia, Sulawesi
MUNARI alt for MUNDARI [MUW]
MUNDA alt for BHUMIJ [BHM]
MUNDA alt for MUNDARI [MUW]
MUNDA alt for MENDANKWE dial of MENDANKWE
   [MFD]
MUNDANG [MUA] lang, Cameroon, Chad, Chad
MUNDANG alt for MUNDANG [MUA]
MUNDANI [MUN] lang, Cameroon
MUNDARI [MUW] lang, India, Bangladesh, Nepal
MUNDARI alt for MANDARI [MQU]
MUNDARI alt for MUNDARI [MUW]
MUNDARI alt for MONDARI dial of BARI [BFA]
MUNDAT [MMF] lang, Nigeria
MUNDJUN alt for YIR YORONT [YIY]
MUNDO alt for MUNDU [MUH]
MUNDU [MUH] lang, Sudan, Zaïre, Zaïre
MUNDU alt for IRÁNTXE [IRA]
MUNDU alt for MUNDU [MUH]
MUNDUGUMA alt for BIWAT [BWM]
MUNDUGUMOR alt for BIWAT [BWM]
MUNDUM 1 alt for MBREREWI dial of NGEMBA
   [NGE]
MUNDUM 2 alt for ANYANG dial of NGEMBA [NGE]
MUNDURUCU alt for MUNDURUKÚ [MYU]
MUNDURUKÚ [MYU] lang, Brazil
MUNEGASC alt for MONÉGASQUE dial of LIGURIAN
   [LIJ]
MUNG dial of PHUNOI [PHO]
MUNGA [MKO] lang, Nigeria
MUNGA'KA alt for MUNGAKA [MHK]
MUNGAKA [MHK] lang, Cameroon
MUNGARAI alt for MANGARAYI [MPC]
MUNGERA OHALO alt for YIDINY [YII]
MUNGERRY alt for MANGARAYI [MPC]
MUNGGAI alt for MEKWEI [MSF]
MUNGGAVA dial of RENNELL [MNV]
MUNGGE alt for MEKWEI [MSF]
MUNGGUI [MTH] lang, Indonesia, Irian Jaya
MUNGIKI dial of RENNELL [MNV]
MUNGO dial of DUALA [DOU]
MUNGOM alt for MUNGONG [XMN]
MUNGONG [XMN] lang, Cameroon
MUNGU alt for MUNGO dial of DUALA [DOU]
MUNGYEN alt for NGAMAMBO dial of META' [MGO]
MUNICHE [MYR] lang, Peru
MUNICHI alt for MUNICHE [MYR]
MUNICHINO alt for MUNICHE [MYR]
MUNIN dial of ANDI [ANI]
MUNIT [MTC] lang, Papua New Guinea
MUNIWARA [MWB] lang, Papua New Guinea
MUNJANI alt for MUNJI [MNJ]
MUNJHAN alt for MUNJI [MNJ]
MUNJI [MNJ] lang, Afghanistan
MUNJI dial of BOIKIN [BZF]
MUNJIWAR alt for MUNJI [MNJ]
MUNJUK alt for MUSGU [MUG]
MUNKAF alt for NAKI [MFF]
MUNKAN alt for WIK-MUNGKAN [WIM]
MUNKEI alt for MEKWEI [MSF]
MUNKIP [MPV] lang, Papua New Guinea

MŬNKŬ dial of IRÁNTXE [IRA]
MUNSEE [UMU] lang, Canada
"MUNSHI" alt for TIV [TIV]
MUNSTER dial of GAELIC, IRISH [GLI]
MUNTABI alt for GAAM [TBI]
MUNTENIAN dial of RUMANIAN [RUM]
MUNUKUTUBA [MKW] lang, Congo
MUNYO dial of ORMA [ORC]
MUNYUKU dial of GUPAPUYNGU [GUF]
MUONG [MTQ] lang, Viet Nam
MUONG LEUNG alt for LEUN [LLE]
MUP dial of YAU [YUW]
MUPUN alt for MAPUN dial of MWAGHAVUL [SUR]
MURA dial of WANDALA [MFI]
MÚRA-PIRAHÃ [MYP] lang, Brazil
MURALIDBAN dial of GUNWINGGU [GUP]
MURANG PUNAN dial of DAYAK, LAND [DYK]
MURANG PUNAN alt for PUNAN dial of DAYAK,
   LAND [DYK]
MURANG'A alt for GICHUGU dial of GIKUYU [KIU]
MURATO alt for CANDOSHI-SHAPRA [CBU]
MURATO dial of KALIHNA [CRB]
MURAWARI alt for MURUWARI [ZMU]
MURBA dial of KENGA [KYQ]
MURCIAN dial of SPANISH [SPN]
MURELEI alt for MURLE [MUR]
MURGI alt for BIRKED [BRK]
MURI alt for MER [MNU]
MURI alt for GUHU-SAMANE [GHS]
MURI dial of HALBI [HLB]
MURIA alt for MURI dial of HALBI [HLB]
MURIA GONDI alt for MURIA, WESTERN [MUT]
MURIA, EASTERN [EMU] lang, India
MURIA, FAR WESTERN [FMU] lang, India
MURIA, WESTERN [MUT] lang, India
MURIK [MTF] lang, Papua New Guinea
MURINBADA alt for MURRINH-PATHA [MWF]
MURINBATA alt for MURRINH-PATHA [MWF]
MURINMANINDJI alt for MARIMANINDJI [ZMM]
MURIRE alt for BUGLERE [SAB]
MURIS alt for DEMTA [DMY]
MURISAPA alt for MORESADA [MSX]
MURLE [MUR] lang, Sudan, Ethiopia
MURMI alt for TAMANG, NORTHWESTERN [TDG]
MURO alt for OROKOLO [ORO]
MURO alt for MURRU dial of KIBET [KIE]
MURRINH-PATHA [MWF] lang, Australia
MURRINHDIMININ dial of MURRINH-PATHA [MWF]
MURRINHKURA dial of MURRINH-PATHA [MWF]
MURRINHPATHA dial of MURRINH-PATHA [MWF]
MURRU dial of KIBET [KIE]
MURRUNGUN dial of DJINANG [DJI]
MURSI [MUZ] lang, Ethiopia, Sudan
MURSI alt for MURSI [MUZ]
MURSUM dial of CHIN, FALAM [HBH]
MURU [XMU] lang, Brazil
MURU alt for OROKOLO [ORO]
MURUA alt for MUYUW [MYW]
MURUGU dial of HANGA [HAG]
MURULE alt for MURLE [MUR]
MURUNG 1 alt for OT MURUNG 1 dial of DOHOI
   [OTD]
MURUNG alt for MRU [MRO]
MURUNG 2 dial of SIANG [SYA]
MURUPI [MQW] lang, Papua New Guinea
MURUSAPA-SAREWA alt for MORESADA [MSX]

MURUT PADASS dial of TIMUGON MURUT [TIH]
MURUTHU alt for MARATHI [MRT]
MURUWA alt for MUYUW [MYW]
MURUWARI [ZMU] lang, Australia
MURZI alt for MURSI [MUZ]
MURZU alt for MURSI [MUZ]
MUS dial of ARMENIAN [ARM]
MUSA alt for MUSAN [MMP]
MUSAHAR alt for MUSASA [SMM]
MUSAHARI dial of BHOJPURI [BHJ]
MUSAIA dial of YALUNKA [YAL]
MUSAK [MMQ] lang, Papua New Guinea
MUSALI alt for JAKATI [JAT]
MUSAN [MMP] lang, Papua New Guinea
MUSAR [MMI] lang, Papua New Guinea
MUSAR dial of MAITHILI [MKP]
MUSASA [SMM] lang, Nepal
MUSAU alt for MUSSAU dial of EMIRA [EMI]
MUSAYNA alt for MOSI [MSE]
MUSCH alt for MUS dial of ARMENIAN [ARM]
MUSEI alt for MOSI [MSE]
MUSEMBAN alt for MUNDANG [MUA]
MUSEY alt for MOSI [MSE]
MUSEYNA alt for MOSI [MSE]
MUSGOI dial of DABA [DAB]
MUSGOY alt for MUSGOI dial of DABA [DAB]
MUSGU [MUG] lang, Cameroon, Chad, Chad
MUSGU alt for MUSGU [MUG]
MUSGUM alt for MUSGU [MUG]
MUSGUM-POUSS alt for MPUS dial of MUSGU
    [MUG]
MUSHANG alt for NAGA, MONSANG [NMH]
MUSHERE dial of MWAGHAVUL [SUR]
MUSHUNGULI alt for MUSHUNGULU [XMA]
MUSHUNGULU [XMA] lang, Somalia
MUSI [MUI] lang, Indonesia, Sumatra
MUSIAN alt for MUSAN [MMP]
MUSIINA alt for MOSI [MSE]
MUSIYE alt for DOBASE [DOX]
MUSKOGEE [CRK] lang, USA
MUSLIM SINDHI dial of SINDHI [SND]
MUSLIM SINDHI alt for SINDHI MUSALMANI dial of
    SINDHI [SND]
MUSLIM TAT alt for TAT, MUSSULMAN [TTT]
MUSOI alt for MOSI [MSE]
MUSOM [MSU] lang, Papua New Guinea
MUSQUEAM dial of HALKOMELEM [HUR]
MUSSAR alt for LAHU [LAH]
MUSSAU dial of EMIRA [EMI]
MUSSAU-EMIRA alt for EMIRA [EMI]
MUSSEH DAENG alt for NYI dial of LAHU [LAH]
MUSSEH DAENG alt for NYI dial of LAHU [LAH]
MUSSEH KWI alt for LAHU SHI [KDS]
MUSSEH LYANG alt for LAHU SHI [KDS]
MUSSELMANI dial of BENGALI [BNG]
MUSSER alt for LAHU [LAH]
MUSSER DAM alt for NA dial of LAHU [LAH]
MUSSER DAM alt for NA dial of LAHU [LAH]
MUSSO alt for LAHU [LAH]
MUSSOI alt for MOSI [MSE]
MUSSOY alt for MOSI [MSE]
MUSSUH alt for LAHU [LAH]
MUSSULMAN TATI alt for TAT, MUSSULMAN [TTT]
MUSTANG alt for LOPA [LOY]
MUSU dial of KURANKO [KHA]
MUSUK alt for MUSGU [MUG]

MUTA alt for META' [MGO]
MUTAIR alt for CENTRAL NAJDI dial of ARABIC,
    NAJDI [ARS]
MUTANI alt for SIRAIKI [SKR]
MUTHAMBI dial of MWIMBI-MUTHAMBI [MWS]
MUTHEIT alt for KAREN, PWO [PWO]
MUTHEIT alt for KAREN, PWO OMKOI [PWW]
MUTHUVAN [MUV] lang, India
MUTTANGULLA alt for MADNGELE [ZML]
MUTÚ alt for MUTÚS [MUF]
MUTU alt for TUAM-MUTU [TUC]
MUTU dial of TUAM-MUTU [TUC]
MUTUM [MCC] lang, Papua New Guinea
MUTURAMI dial of GIZIGA, SOUTH [GIZ]
MUTURUA alt for MUTURAMI dial of GIZIGA,
    SOUTH [GIZ]
MUTURWA alt for MUTURAMI dial of GIZIGA,
    SOUTH [GIZ]
MUTÚS [MUF] lang, Venezuela
MUTUTU alt for AMDANG [AMJ]
MUTUVAR alt for MUTHUVAN [MUV]
MUTWANG dial of RAWANG [RAW]
MUTYU alt for DJANGUN [DJF]
MUUNGO alt for MUNGO dial of DUALA [DOU]
MUWASI alt for MAWASI dial of KORKU [KFQ]
MUXER alt for MUHER dial of GURAGE, CENTRAL
    WEST [GUY]
MUXULE dial of JINA [JIA]
MUXULI alt for MUXULE dial of JINA [JIA]
MUYA alt for MIYA [MKF]
MUYANG [MUY] lang, Cameroon
MUYENGE alt for MUYANG [MUY]
MUYU alt for KATI, SOUTHERN [KTS]
MUYU alt for MUYUW [MYW]
MUYU alt for NINGGERUM [NXR]
MUYUA alt for MUYUW [MYW]
MUYUW [MYW] lang, Papua New Guinea
MUYWI alt for MOGHAMO dial of META' [MGO]
MUZUK alt for MUSGU [MUG]
MUZUK dial of MUSGU [MUG]
MUZUK dial of MUSGU [MUG]
MVAE dial of FANG [FNG]
MVAN alt for MVAE dial of FANG [FNG]
MVANIP alt for MVANON [MCJ]
MVANLIP alt for MVANON [MCJ]
MVANON [MCJ] lang, Nigeria
MVAY alt for MVAE dial of FANG [FNG]
MVEDERE alt for VIDIRI [VIR]
MVEDERE dial of BANDA [BBP]
MVEGUMBA alt for BELANDA VIRI [BVI]
MVELE alt for BASAA [BAA]
MVELE alt for MBERE dial of TUKI [BAG]
MVELE alt for BAMVELE dial of EWONDO [EWO]
MVETE dial of EWONDO [EWO]
MVITA dial of SWAHILI [SWA]
MVO-NANGKOK dial of ETON [ETO]
MVOG-NAMVE dial of ETON [ETO]
MVOG-NIENGUE dial of EWONDO [EWO]
MVUBA [MXH] lang, Zaïre, Uganda
MVUBA-A alt for MVUBA [MXH]
MVUMBO alt for NGUMBA [NMG]
MVUMBO dial of NGUMBA [NMG]
MWA alt for MUAN [MOA]
MWAE alt for EMAE [MMW]
MWAGHAVUL [SUR] lang, Nigeria
MWAHED alt for MANEHAS dial of MBO [MBO]

MWALU alt for VAMWALU dial of MAKONDE [KDE]
MWALUKWASIA dial of DUAU [DUA]
MWAMBA alt for NYAKYUSA-NGONDE [NYY]
MWAMBE alt for VAMWAMBE dial of MAKONDE
   [KDE]
MWAMBONG dial of AKOOSE [BSS]
MWAN alt for MUAN [MOA]
MWANA dial of DIJIM [CFA]
MWANDA dial of TAITA [DAV]
MWANE alt for MWANI [WMW]
MWANEKA alt for BANEKA dial of MBO [MBO]
MWANGA [MWN] lang, Zambia, Tanzania
MWANI [WMW] lang, Mozambique
MWANI dial of HAYA [HAY]
MWANO alt for MWANA dial of DIJIM [CFA]
MWATEBU [MWA] lang, Papua New Guinea
MWELA alt for MWERA [MWE]
MWENYI dial of SIMAA [SIE]
MWERA [MWE] lang, Tanzania
MWERI dial of NYAMWEZI [NYZ]
MWERIG dial of MERLAV [MRM]
MWIINI alt for MWINI dial of SWAHILI [SWA]
MWIKARI alt for MACA [XMC]
MWILA dial of NYANEKA [NYK]
MWIMBI dial of MWIMBI-MUTHAMBI [MWS]
MWIMBI-MUTHAMBI [MWS] lang, Kenya
MWINA dial of POKOMO, LOWER [POJ]
MWINI dial of SWAHILI [SWA]
MWOKILESE alt for MOKIL [MNO]
MWOMO alt for MWANA dial of DIJIM [CFA]
MWONA alt for MWANA dial of DIJIM [CFA]
MYAGATWA alt for ZALAMO [ZAJ]
MYAMKAT alt for NESANG [NES]
MYANG alt for TAI, NORTHERN [NOD]
MYAU alt for MUYANG [MUY]
MYEN alt for MIEN [YOC]
MYEN alt for BURMESE [BMS]
MYENE [MYE] lang, Gabon
MYENGE alt for MUYANG [MUY]
MYET alt for TAPSHIN [TDL]
MYFOORSCH alt for BIAK [BHW]
MYIMU dial of NAGA, TASE [NST]
MYKHANIDY alt for RUTUL [RUT]
MYKY alt for MÜNKÜ dial of IRÁNTXE [IRA]
MYNKY alt for MÜNKÜ dial of IRÁNTXE [IRA]
MYRATO alt for MURATO dial of KALIHNA [CRB]
MYSORE LAMANI alt for KARNATAK LAMANI dial
   of LAMANI [LMN]
MYUNDUNO alt for YIR YORONT [YIY]
MZAB [MZB] lang, Algeria
MZABI alt for MZAB [MZB]
MZIEME alt for NAGA, MZIEME [NME]
N'BUNDO alt for MBUNDU, LOANDA [MLO]
N'DA dial of GAGU [GGU]
N'DJAMENA dial of ARABIC, SHUWA [SHU]
N'KOMI alt for NKOMI dial of MYENE [MYE]
N'SAKARA alt for NZAKARA [NZK]
N'WALUNGU dial of TSONGA [TSO]
N-BATTO alt for MBATO [GWA]
N//HAI alt for N/HAI-NTSE'E [NKT]
N//OOKHWE alt for N/OO-KHWE dial of SHUA [SHG]
N/OO alt for N/OO-KHWE dial of SHUA [SHG]
N/OO-KHWE dial of SHUA [SHG]
NA dial of LAHU [LAH]
NA dial of LAHU [LAH]
NA dial of KABA NA [KWV]

NA NAHEK dial of GALOLI [GAL]
NA NHYANG dial of KUY [KDT]
NA'AHAI alt for ORIERH dial of MALFAXAL [MLX]
NA'O alt for NAO [NOZ]
NA-ANG dial of DE'ANG [BFP]
NAA DUBEA alt for DUMBEA [DUF]
NAA NUMEE alt for NUMEE [KDK]
NAA-WEE alt for NUMEE [KDK]
NAADH alt for NUER [NUS]
NAAHAI alt for SOUTH WEST BAY [SNS]
NAANDI alt for NANDI dial of KALENJIN [KLN]
NAANI alt for SÉNOUFO, NANERIGÉ [SEN]
NAANI dial of GURENNE [GUR]
NAAPA [NAO] lang, Nepal
NAAPAA alt for NAAPA [NAO]
NAASIOI alt for NASIOI [NAS]
NAATH alt for NUER [NUS]
NABA alt for NABAK [NAF]
NABA alt for NAAPA [NAO]
NABAI alt for NABAY dial of KENINGAU MURUT
   [KXI]
NABAK [NAF] lang, Papua New Guinea
NABALEBALE alt for CENTRAL VANUA LEVU dial of
   FIJIAN [FJI]
NABALOI alt for IBALOI [IBL]
NABANDI alt for NGBANDI [NGB]
NABANJ dial of KULANGO, BOUNA [NKU]
NABAY dial of KENINGAU MURUT [KXI]
NABDAM alt for NABT dial of MAMPRULI [MAW]
NABDE alt for NABT dial of MAMPRULI [MAW]
NABDUG alt for NABT dial of MAMPRULI [MAW]
NABE alt for TÉEN [LOR]
NABESNA alt for TANANA, UPPER [TAU]
NABI [NBN] lang, Indonesia, Irian Jaya
NABIT alt for NABT dial of MAMPRULI [MAW]
NABLOS dial of DOMARI [RMT]
NABNAM alt for NABT dial of MAMPRULI [MAW]
NABRUG alt for NABT dial of MAMPRULI [MAW]
NABT dial of MAMPRULI [MAW]
NABT dial of GURENNE [GUR]
NABTE alt for NABT dial of MAMPRULI [MAW]
NABU alt for NAHU [NCA]
NABUKELEVU alt for KADAVU dial of FIJIAN [FJI]
NAD'A alt for NGADA [NXG]
NADA alt for BUDIBUD [BTP]
NADÊB [MBJ] lang, Brazil
NADEB MACU alt for NADÊB [MBJ]
NADÕBÕ alt for NADÊB [MBJ]
NADROGA alt for FIJIAN, WESTERN [WYY]
NADROGAA alt for NUCLEAR WESTERN FIJIAN dial
   of FIJIAN, WESTERN [WYY]
NADRONGA alt for FIJIAN, WESTERN [WYY]
NAFÃÃ dial of SENOUFO, MAMARA [MYK]
NAFAANRA [NFR] lang, Ghana, Côte d'Ivoire
NAFAARA alt for NAFAANRA [NFR]
NAFANA alt for NAFAANRA [NFR]
NAFAR dial of AZERBAIJANI, SOUTH [AZB]
NAFARPI alt for KAMORO [KGQ]
NAFI [SRF] lang, Papua New Guinea
NAFRI [NXX] lang, Indonesia, Irian Jaya
NAFUKWÁ alt for NAHUKUÁ dial of MATIPUHY
   [MZO]
NAFUNFIA alt for SHAGAWU [ROA]
NAGA dial of MAPE [MLH]
NAGA dial of BICOLANO, CENTRAL [BKL]
NAGA dial of BALANTA [BLE]

NAGA CREOLE ASSAMESE alt for NAGA PIDGIN [NAG]
NAGA PIDGIN [NAG] lang, India
NAGA, ANGAMI [NJM] lang, India
NAGA, AO [NJO] lang, India
NAGA, CHANG [NBC] lang, India
NAGA, CHOKRI [NRI] lang, India
NAGA, CHOTHE [NCT] lang, India
NAGA, KABUI [NKF] lang, India
NAGA, KHEZHA [NKH] lang, India
NAGA, KHIAMNGAN [NKY] lang, India, Myanmar, Myanmar
NAGA, KHIAMNGAN alt for NAGA, KHIAMNGAN [NKY]
NAGA, KHOIBU MARING [NKB] lang, India
NAGA, KHOIRAO [NKI] lang, India
NAGA, KONYAK [NBE] lang, India
NAGA, LIANGMAI [NJN] lang, India
NAGA, LOTHA [NJH] lang, India
NAGA, MAO [NBI] lang, India
NAGA, MARAM [NMA] lang, India
NAGA, MARING [NNG] lang, India
NAGA, MELURI [NLM] lang, India
NAGA, MONSANG [NMH] lang, India
NAGA, MOYON [NMO] lang, India
NAGA, MZIEME [NME] lang, India
NAGA, NOCTE [NJB] lang, India
NAGA, NTENYI [NNL] lang, India
NAGA, PHOM [NPH] lang, India
NAGA, POCHURI [NPO] lang, India
NAGA, POUMEI [PMX] lang, India
NAGA, PUIMEI [NPU] lang, India
NAGA, RENGMA [NRE] lang, India
NAGA, RONGMEI [NBU] lang, India
NAGA, SANGTAM [NSA] lang, India
NAGA, SEMA [NSM] lang, India
NAGA, TANGKHUL [NMF] lang, India
NAGA, TARAO [TRO] lang, India
NAGA, TASE [NST] lang, India, Myanmar, Myanmar
NAGA, TASE alt for NAGA, TASE [NST]
NAGA, WANCHO [NNP] lang, India
NAGA, YIMCHUNGRU [YIM] lang, India
NAGA, ZEME [NZM] lang, India
NAGA-ASSAMESE alt for NAGA PIDGIN [NAG]
NAGAMESE alt for NAGA PIDGIN [NAG]
NAGANE [GEN] lang, Papua New Guinea
NAGAR alt for NAGARCHAL [NBG]
NAGAR dial of BURUSHASKI [BSK]
NAGARA alt for NAKARA [NCK]
NAGARCHAL [NBG] lang, India
NAGARCHI alt for NAGARCHAL [NBG]
NAGARI alt for STANDARD GUJARATI dial of GUJARATI [GJR]
NAGARI-MALAYALAM dial of MALAYALAM [MJS]
NAGARIGE alt for PIVA [TGI]
NAGAROTTE dial of NAMBIKUÁRA, NORTHERN [MBG]
NAGATIMAN alt for YADË [NCE]
NAGATMAN alt for YADË [NCE]
NAGBANMBA dial of LOKO [LOK]
NAGE [NXE] lang, Indonesia, Nusa Tenggara
NAGIR alt for NAGAR dial of BURUSHASKI [BSK]
NAGIRA alt for NINGERA [NBY]
NAGO [NQG] lang, Benin
NAGO dial of KUNIGAMI [XUG]
NAGOT alt for NAGO [NQG]

NAGOTS alt for NAGO [NQG]
NAGOVIS alt for NAGOVISI [NCO]
NAGOVISI [NCO] lang, Papua New Guinea
NAGPUR dial of GONDI, NORTHERN [GON]
NAGPURI alt for SADANI [SCK]
NAGPURI HINDI dial of BUNDELI [BNS]
NAGPURI MARATHI alt for BAGHELI [BFY]
NAGPURIA alt for SADANI [SCK]
NAGPURIYA dial of GARHWALI [GBM]
NAGRAMADU alt for KAMORO [KGQ]
NAGRANDAN dial of CHOROTEGA [CJR]
NAGUMI [NGV] lang, Cameroon
NAGURI dial of MUNDARI [MUW]
NAHA dial of OKINAWAN, CENTRAL [RYU]
NAHAL alt for NIHALI [NHL]
NAHALE alt for NIHALI [NHL]
NAHALI alt for NIHALI [NHL]
NAHANI alt for KASKA [KKZ]
NAHARA dial of MAKHUWA [MAK]
NAHARI [NHH] lang, India
NAHES dial of MODANG [MXD]
"NAHINA" alt for TOLAKI [LBW]
NAHINA alt for MORI BAWAH [XMZ]
NAHINA dial of MORI BAWAH [XMZ]
NAHINE alt for BUNGKU [BKZ]
NAHO alt for NAHU [NCA]
NAHOA alt for NUGURIA [NUR]
NAHSI alt for NAXI [NBF]
NAHU [NCA] lang, Papua New Guinea
NAHUA alt for YORA [MTS]
NÁHUATL DE LA SIERRA DE ZONGOLICA alt for NAHUATL, ORIZABA [NLV]
NAHUATL, CENTRAL [NHN] lang, Mexico
NAHUATL, CLASSICAL [NCI] lang, Mexico
NAHUATL, COATEPEC [NAZ] lang, Mexico
NAHUATL, DURANGO [NLN] lang, Mexico
NAHUATL, GUERRERO [NAH] lang, Mexico
NAHUATL, HUASTECA, EASTERN [NAI] lang, Mexico
NAHUATL, HUASTECA, WESTERN [NHW] lang, Mexico
NAHUATL, ISTHMUS [NAU] lang, Mexico
NAHUATL, MICHOACÁN [NCL] lang, Mexico
NAHUATL, MORELOS [NHM] lang, Mexico
NAHUATL, NORTH PUEBLA [NCJ] lang, Mexico
NAHUATL, OMETEPEC [NHT] lang, Mexico
NAHUATL, ORIZABA [NLV] lang, Mexico
NAHUATL, SIERRA DE PUEBLA [AZZ] lang, Mexico
NAHUATL, SOUTHEAST PUEBLA [NHS] lang, Mexico
NAHUATL, TABASCO [NHC] lang, Mexico
NAHUATL, TETELCINGO [NHG] lang, Mexico
NAHUKUÁ dial of MATIPUHY [MZO]
NAHUQUA alt for NAHUKUÁ dial of MATIPUHY [MZO]
NAI [BIO] lang, Papua New Guinea
NAI dial of ANGOR [AGG]
NAIALI dial of GUNWINGGU [GUP]
NAIBEDJ alt for KWERBA [KWE]
NAIK-KURUBA dial of KURUMBA [KFI]
NAIKI dial of BHILI [BHB]
NAIKI dial of KOLAMI, SOUTHEASTERN [NIT]
NAIM dial of ARABIC, SYRO-MESOPOTAMIAN [AYP]
NAIMAN alt for JO-UDA dial of MONGOLIAN, PERIPHERAL [MVF]
NAIMASIMASI alt for SOUTHEAST VITI LEVU dial of

FIJIAN [FJI]
NAINDIN dial of ATTIÉ [ATI]
NAIRIN dial of JAPANESE [JPN]
NAJIL dial of PASHAYI, NORTHWEST [GLH]
NAJRAAN alt for CENTRAL NAJDI dial of ARABIC, NAJDI [ARS]
NAKA dial of KRESH [KRS]
NAKA alt for BAPUKU dial of BATANGA [BNM]
NAKA'ELA [NAE] lang, Indonesia, Maluku
NAKAMA [NIB] lang, Papua New Guinea
NAKANAI [NAK] lang, Papua New Guinea
NAKANNA dial of EVENKI [EVN]
NAKANYARE alt for SAMBA DAKA [CCG]
NAKARA [NCK] lang, Australia
NAKARE alt for JIDA-ABU [JID]
NAKE [NBK] lang, Papua New Guinea
NAKGAKTAI alt for KOL dial of KOL [KOL]
NAKHI alt for NAXI [NBF]
NAKHICHEVAN dial of AZERBAIJANI, NORTH [AZE]
NAKI [MFF] lang, Cameroon
NAKIAI dial of SANIYO-HIYOWE [SNY]
NAKKARA alt for NAKARA [NCK]
NAKONAI alt for NAKANAI [NAK]
NAKOROBOYA alt for WAYA dial of FIJIAN, WESTERN [WYY]
NAKOTA dial of DAKOTA [DHG]
NAKUKWÁ alt for NAHUKUÁ dial of MATIPUHY [MZO]
NAKWI dial of NIMO [NIW]
NALA alt for NARA [NRZ]
NALABON alt for NGALKBUN [NGK]
NALCA alt for HMANGGONA [TVL]
NALE alt for ATCHIN dial of URIPIV-WALA-RANO-ATCHIN [UPV]
NALEA dial of NAMOSI-NAITASIRI-SERUA [BWB]
NALGUNO dial of BIDIO [BID]
NALI [NSS] lang, Papua New Guinea
NALI dial of NAGA, ANGAMI [NJM]
NALIK [NAL] lang, Papua New Guinea
NALOU alt for NALU [NAJ]
NALTJE alt for HMANGGONA [TVL]
NALTYA alt for HMANGGONA [TVL]
NALU [NAJ] lang, Guinea, Guinea Bissau, Guinea Bissau
NALU alt for NALU [NAJ]
NAM HSAN dial of DE'ANG [BFP]
NAMA [NAQ] lang, Namibia, South Africa, South Africa
NAMA alt for NAMA [NAQ]
NAMA dial of MBEMBE, TIGON [NZA]
NAMA dial of MBEMBE, TIGON [NZA]
NAMADI alt for NEMADI [NED]
NAMAKABAN alt for TSOU [TSY]
NAMAKERE alt for MAKERE dial of MANGBETU [MDJ]
NAMAKERETI alt for MAKERE dial of MANGBETU [MDJ]
NAMAKURA [NMK] lang, Vanuatu
NAMAKWA alt for NAMA [NAQ]
NAMAN alt for NAMA [NAQ]
NAMAQUA alt for NAMA [NAQ]
NAMASA alt for LIGBI [LIG]
NAMATALAKI alt for ABUI [ABZ]
NAMATOTA dial of KOWIAI [KWH]
NAMATOTE alt for NAMATOTA dial of KOWIAI [KWH]

NAMAU alt for PURARI [IAR]
NAMAU alt for IAI dial of PURARI [IAR]
NAMBAKAENGÖ alt for SANTA CRUZ [STC]
NAMBAS, BIG [NMB] lang, Vanuatu
NAMBE dial of TEWA [TEW]
NAMBI alt for MITANG [MTY]
NAMBIKUÁRA, NORTHERN [MBG] lang, Brazil
NAMBIKUÁRA, SOUTHERN [NAB] lang, Brazil
NAMBIKWARA alt for NAMBIKUÁRA, SOUTHERN [NAB]
NAMBIQUARA alt for NAMBIKUÁRA, SOUTHERN [NAB]
NAMBLOMON-MABUR dial of YAQAY [JAQ]
NAMBO alt for NAMBU [NCM]
NAMBOODIRI dial of MALAYALAM [MJS]
NAMBRONG alt for NIMBORAN [NIR]
NAMBU [NCM] lang, Papua New Guinea
NAMBYA [NMQ] lang, Zimbabwe
NAMBZYA alt for NAMBYA [NMQ]
"NAMCHI" alt for DOYAYO [DOW]
"NAMCI" alt for DOYAYO [DOW]
NAMEJETI alt for MEJE dial of MANGBETU [MDJ]
NAMEL alt for NYAMAL [NLY]
NAMEN alt for LAHU [LAH]
NAMENA alt for NORTHEAST VITI LEVU dial of FIJIAN [FJI]
NAMFAU alt for ANAL [ANM]
NAMI dial of MANAGALASI [MCQ]
NAMIA [NNM] lang, Papua New Guinea
NAMIE alt for NAMIA [NNM]
NAMLUNG dial of KULUNG [KLE]
NAMNAM alt for NABT dial of MAMPRULI [MAW]
NAMOME alt for FASU [FAA]
NAMOME dial of FASU [FAA]
NAMONUITO [NMT] lang, Micronesia
NAMOSI-NAITAASIRI-SEERUA alt for NAMOSI-NAITASIRI-SERUA [BWB]
NAMOSI-NAITASIRI-SERUA [BWB] lang, Fiji
NAMPAMELA dial of MACA [XMC]
NAMSANGIA alt for NAGA, NOCTE [NJB]
"NAMSHI" alt for DOYAYO [DOW]
NAMU dial of REMBONG [REB]
NAMU alt for NAMA dial of MBEMBE, TIGON [NZA]
NAMU alt for NAMA dial of MBEMBE, TIGON [NZA]
NAMUMI alt for NAMOME dial of FASU [FAA]
NAMUNI alt for NAMOME dial of FASU [FAA]
NAMUNKA dial of OROCH [OAC]
NAMUYA alt for KESAWAI [QKE]
NAMWANGA alt for MWANGA [MWN]
NAMWEZI alt for NYAMWEZI [NYZ]
NAN dial of TAI, NORTHERN [NOD]
NANA HUNDI alt for KWASENGEN [WOS]
ÑANAGUA alt for TAPIETÉ [TAI]
NANAI [GLD] lang, Russia, Asia, China
NANAIMO dial of HALKOMELEM [HUR]
NANAJ alt for NANAI [GLD]
NANCERE [NNC] lang, Chad
NANCHANG dial of CHINESE, GAN [KNN]
NANCHERE alt for NANCERE [NNC]
NANCOURY alt for NANCOWRY dial of NICOBARESE, CENTRAL [NCB]
NANCOWRY dial of NICOBARESE, CENTRAL [NCB]
NANCSHERA alt for NANCERE [NNC]
NAND alt for GOWLI [GOK]
NAND dial of GOWLI [GOK]
NANDE alt for NANDI [NNB]

NATAKAN alt for MAFA [MAF]
NATANZI [NTZ] lang, Iran
NATCHABA dial of MOBA [MFQ]
NATCHAMBA alt for NTCHAM [BUD]
NATCHEZ [NCZ] lang, USA
NATEMBA alt for NATENI dial of NATENI [NTM]
NATENI [NTM] lang, Benin
NATENI dial of NATENI [NTM]
NATICK alt for WAMPANOAG [WAM]
NATIMBA alt for NATENI dial of NATENI [NTM]
NATIORO [NTI] lang, Burkina Faso
NATJORO alt for NATIORO [NTI]
NÀTÓU dial of HLAI [LIC]
NATUAK alt for MACUSA, GUAVIARE [MBR]
NATŨGU alt for SANTA CRUZ [STC]
NATUKHAI alt for NATUZAJ dial of ADYGHE [ADY]
NATURALIS dial of SURIGAONON [SUL]
NATÜRLICHE GEBÄRDE alt for SWISS SIGN
    LANGUAGE [SSR]
NATUZAJ dial of ADYGHE [ADY]
NATYORO alt for NATIORO [NTI]
NAUDM alt for NAWDM [NMZ]
NAUETI [NXA] lang, Indonesia, Nusa Tenggara
NAUKAN alt for YUPIK, NAUKAN [YNK]
NAUKANSKI alt for YUPIK, NAUKAN [YNK]
NAUMIK dial of NAUETI [NXA]
NAUNA [NCN] lang, Papua New Guinea
NAUNE alt for NAUNA [NCN]
NAURUAN [NRU] lang, Nauru
NAVAHO [NAV] lang, USA
NAVAJO alt for NAVAHO [NAV]
NAVARRESE dial of BASQUE [BSQ]
NAVARRESE dial of SPANISH [SPN]
NAVATU-C alt for SOUTHEAST VANUA LEVU dial of
    FIJIAN [FJI]
NAVUT [NSW] lang, Vanuatu
NAWA SHERPA alt for NAAPA [NAO]
NAWAITS alt for DALDI dial of KONKANI, GOANESE
    [GOM]
NAWAR alt for DOMARI [RMT]
NAWAR dial of DOMARI [RMT]
NAWARU [NWR] lang, Papua New Guinea
NAWDAM alt for NAWDM [NMZ]
NAWDM [NMZ] lang, Togo, Ghana
NAWENI alt for SOUTHEAST VANUA LEVU dial of
    FIJIAN [FJI]
NAWP alt for DAGA [DGZ]
NAWURI [NAW] lang, Ghana
NAWYEM dial of MUYUW [MYW]
NAXI [NBF] lang, China
NAYAR dial of MALAYALAM [MJS]
NAYINI [NYQ] lang, Iran
NAZE dial of AMAMI-OSHIMA, NORTHERN [RYN]
NBANGAM alt for NGANGAM [GNG]
NBULE alt for VUTE [VUT]
NBUNDU alt for MBUNDU, LOANDA [MLO]
NBWAKA alt for NGBAKA MA'BO [NBM]
NCANE [NCR] lang, Cameroon
NCANM dial of NTCHAM [BUD]
NCHA [NCH] lang, Cameroon
NCHAM alt for NTCHAM [BUD]
NCHANTI alt for NCANE [NCR]
NCHIMBURU alt for CHUMBURUNG [NCU]
NCHINCHEGE [NCQ] lang, Congo
NCHOBELA alt for BABADJOU dial of NGOMBALE
    [NLA]

NCHUMBULU [NLU] lang, Ghana
NCHUMBURUNG alt for CHUMBURUNG [NCU]
NCHUMMURU alt for CHUMBURUNG [NCU]
NCHUMUNU alt for DWANG [NNU]
NCQIKA alt for GAIKA dial of XHOSA [XOS]
NDA alt for MUNDANG [MUA]
NDA DIA alt for DADIYA [DBD]
NDAAKA [NDK] lang, Zaïre
NDAGAM alt for BALI [BCN]
NDAGAM alt for SAMBA BALI dial of SAMBA LEKO
    [NDI]
NDAI [GKE] lang, Cameroon
NDAI alt for DAI dial of LAU [LLU]
NDAKA alt for NDAAKA [NDK]
NDAKTUP [NCP] lang, Cameroon
NDALI [NDH] lang, Tanzania
NDALI dial of ZANAKI [ZAK]
NDAM [NDM] lang, Chad
NDAM dial of NDAM [NDM]
NDAM KOUNO alt for NDAM dial of NDAM [NDM]
NDAM-DIK dial of NDAM [NDM]
NDAM-NDAM alt for NDAM dial of NDAM [NDM]
NDAMBA [NDJ] lang, Tanzania
NDAMM alt for NDAM [NDM]
NDAMM,GUILLI alt for NDAM [NDM]
NDA'NDA' [NNZ] lang, Cameroon
NDANDA dial of NDAU [NDC]
NDANDE alt for NANDI [NNB]
NDANO dial of SHWAI [SHW]
NDAO [NFA] lang, Indonesia, Nusa Tenggara
NDAOE alt for PENDAU [UMS]
NDAONESE alt for NDAO [NFA]
NDARA alt for WANDALA [MFI]
NDARA dial of TOGBO [TOR]
NDARA alt for HUTU dial of RWANDA [RUA]
NDASA [NDA] lang, Congo, Gabon, Gabon
NDASA alt for NDASA [NDA]
NDASH alt for NDASA [NDA]
NDASSA alt for NDASA [NDA]
NDAU [NDC] lang, Zimbabwe, Mozambique
NDAU alt for PENDAU [UMS]
NDAUNDAU alt for NDAO [NFA]
NDAUWA alt for NDUGA [NDX]
NDE dial of NDE-NSELE-NTA [NDD]
NDE dial of MUNGAKA [MHK]
NDE-NSELE-NTA [NDD] lang, Nigeria
NDEBELE [NEL] lang, South Africa
NDEBELE [NDF] lang, Zimbabwe
NDEEWE dial of BATA [BTA]
NDELE dial of IKWERE [IKW]
NDEM alt for DEM [DEM]
NDEM alt for NNAM [NBP]
NDEMA SHERBRO dial of SHERBRO [BUN]
NDEMBA alt for NDEMLI [NML]
NDEMBU dial of LUNDA [LVN]
NDEMLI [NML] lang, Cameroon
NDENDEULE [DNE] lang, Tanzania
NDENDEULI alt for NDENDEULE [DNE]
NDENGELEKO alt for NDENGEREKO [NDE]
NDENGEREKO [NDE] lang, Tanzania
NDENGESE alt for DENGESE [DEZ]
NDENI dial of SANTA CRUZ [STC]
NDERA dial of POKOMO, UPPER [PKB]
NDESE dial of LESE [LES]
NDHUR dial of RADE [RAD]
NDI [NHI] lang, Central African Republic

NDI dial of GHARI [GRI]
NDIA dial of GIKUYU [KIU]
NDII alt for SAMBA LEKO [NDI]
NDII alt for SAMBA LEKO dial of SAMBA LEKO [NDI]
NDING [ELI] lang, Sudan
NDINGI dial of KONGO [KON]
NDIRMA alt for HUBA [KIR]
NDITAM dial of TIKAR [TIK]
NDJABI alt for NJEBI [NZB]
NDJÉBBANA alt for DJEEBBANA [DJJ]
NDJELI alt for PANDE dial of PANDE [BKJ]
NDJEM dial of KOOZIME [NJE]
NDJEM dial of KOOZIME [NJE]
NDJEM alt for NDJEM dial of KOOZIME [NJE]
NDJEMBE alt for WONGO [WON]
NDJEME alt for NJEME dial of KOOZIME [NJE]
NDJEVI alt for NJEBI [NZB]
NDJININI alt for NJININGI dial of TEKE, NORTHERN
   [TEG]
NDJUKÁ alt for AUKAANS [DJK]
NDLAMBE dial of XHOSA [XOS]
NDMPO alt for DUMPO dial of GONJA [DUM]
NDO [NDP] lang, Zaïre, Uganda
NDO alt for MEMBI dial of NDO [NDP]
NDO OKE'BU alt for OKE'BU dial of NDO [NDP]
NDOB alt for TIKAR [TIK]
NDOBO [NDW] lang, Zaïre
NDOE [NBB] lang, Nigeria
NDOGBANG dial of TUNEN [BAZ]
NDOGO [NDZ] lang, Sudan, Central African Republic
NDOGO alt for HUTU dial of RWANDA [RUA]
NDOKAMA dial of BASAA [BAA]
NDOKBELE dial of BASAA [BAA]
NDOKBIAKAT dial of TUNEN [BAZ]
NDOKPA [NKC] lang, Central African Republic
NDOKPENDA dial of BASAA [BAA]
NDOKPWA alt for NDOKPA [NKC]
NDOKTUNA dial of TUNEN [BAZ]
NDOLO [NDL] lang, Zaïre
NDOM [NQM] lang, Indonesia, Irian Jaya
NDOMBE [NDQ] lang, Angola
NDOMDE alt for NDONDE [NDS]
NDOME alt for TIKAR [TIK]
NDONDE [NDS] lang, Tanzania
NDONDE alt for VADONDE dial of MAKONDE [KDE]
NDONGA [NDG] lang, Namibia, Angola
NDONGE dial of CHOPI [CCE]
NDONGO alt for MBUNDU, LOANDA [MLO]
NDOOBO alt for NDOBO [NDW]
NDOOLA [NDR] lang, Nigeria, Cameroon
NDOOLO alt for NDOLO [NDL]
NDOORE alt for TUPURI [TUI]
NDOP-BAMESSING alt for KENSWEI NSEI [NDB]
NDOP-BAMUNKA alt for BAMUNKA [NDO]
NDORE alt for TUPURI [TUI]
NDORE dial of TUPURI [TUI]
NDORO alt for NDOOLA [NDR]
"NDOROBO" alt for OKIEK [OKI]
NDOROBO alt for MEDIAK [MWX]
NDOROBO alt for MOSIRO [MWY]
"NDOROBO" alt for OMOTIK [OMT]
"NDOROBO" alt for EL MOLO [ELO]
"NDOROBO" alt for ARAMANIK [AAM]
"NDOROBO" alt for KISANKASA [KQH]
"NDOROBO" alt for YAAKU [MUU]
NDOUDJA alt for FALI-TINGUELIN dial of FALI,

SOUTH [FLE]
NDOUKA alt for NDUKA dial of RUTO [NDY]
NDOUTE alt for NDUT [NDV]
NDREHET dial of LEVEI-NDREHET [TLX]
NDREME alt for PELASLA [MLR]
NDREME dial of PELASLA [MLR]
NDRENG dial of NAGA, LOTHA [NJH]
NDRI alt for NDI [NHI]
NDROKU alt for LONIU [LOS]
NDRUNA alt for NGITI [NIY]
NDU-FAA-KEELO alt for KELO [TSN]
NDUGA [NDX] lang, Indonesia, Irian Jaya
NDUGHORE alt for DUKE [NKE]
NDUGWA alt for NDUGA [NDX]
NDUINDUI dial of AMBAE, WEST [NND]
NDUKA dial of RUTO [NDY]
NDUKE alt for DUKE [NKE]
NDUM alt for OSO [OSO]
NDUMBEA alt for DUMBEA [DUF]
NDUMBO alt for NDUMU [NMD]
NDUMBU alt for NDUMU [NMD]
NDUMU [NMD] lang, Gabon, Congo
NDUNDA alt for VIDUNDA [VID]
NDUNGA [NDT] lang, Zaïre
NDURA dial of POKOMO, UPPER [PKB]
NDUT [NDV] lang, Senegal
NDUUMO alt for NDUMU [NMD]
NDUUPA alt for DUUPA [DAE]
NDUVUM dial of VUTE [VUT]
NDXHONGE dial of TSWA [TSC]
NDYAK alt for MANDYAK [MFV]
NDYANGER dial of WOLOF [WOL]
NDYUKÁ alt for AUKAANS [DJK]
NDZALE alt for NZARE dial of MBEMBE, TIGON
   [NZA]
NDZAWU alt for NDAU [NDC]
NDZEM alt for NDJEM dial of KOOZIME [NJE]
NDZIKOU alt for NJINJU dial of TEKE, CENTRAL
   [TEC]
NDZINDZIJU alt for NJINJU dial of TEKE, CENTRAL
   [TEC]
NDZUNDZA alt for NDEBELE [NEL]
NDZUNGLE alt for LIMBUM [LIM]
NDZUNGLI alt for LIMBUM [LIM]
NEA dial of SANTA CRUZ [STC]
NEABO alt for NEAO dial of GUÉRÉ [GXX]
NEAO dial of GUÉRÉ [GXX]
NEAPOLITAN dial of NEAPOLITAN-CALABRESE
   [NPL]
NEAPOLITAN-CALABRESE [NPL] lang, Italy
NEBAJI dial of OREJÓN [ORE]
NEBEE alt for NABAY dial of KENINGAU MURUT
   [KXI]
NEBES alt for TAROF [TCF]
NEBOME alt for PAPAGO-PIMA [PAP]
NEBOME alt for PIMA BAJO, SONORA [PIA]
NEBRASKA dial of WINNEBAGO [WIN]
NEDEBANG [NEC] lang, Indonesia, Nusa Tenggara
NEDEK dial of YAMBETA [YAT]
NEDERLANDS alt for DUTCH [DUT]
NEE dial of FE'FE' [FMP]
ÑEEGATÚ alt for NHENGATU [YRL]
NEELISHIKARI dial of BHILI [BHB]
NEELISHIKARI dial of PARDHI [PCL]
NEENOÁ alt for MIRITI [MMV]
NEFARPI alt for KAMORO [KGQ]

NEFERIPI alt for KAMORO [KGQ]
NEFUSI alt for JABAL NAFUSAH [JBN]
NEGAROTE [NRT] lang, Brazil
NEGERHOLLANDS alt for DUTCH CREOLE [DCR]
NEGERI BESAR dial of KASUWERI [QKW]
NEGERI LIMA dial of ASILULU [ASL]
NEGERI SEMBILAN MALAY [ZMI] lang, Malaysia,
    Peninsular
NEGIDAL [NEG] lang, Russia, Asia
NEGIDALY alt for NEGIDAL [NEG]
NEGRITO alt for KENSIU [KNS]
NEGUENI-KLANI dial of WARA [WBF]
NEHAN [NSN] lang, Papua New Guinea
"NEHINA" alt for TOLAKI [LBW]
NĚHUP dial of HUPDĚ [JUP]
NEJUU dial of SENOUFO, MAMARA [MYK]
NEK [NIF] lang, Papua New Guinea
NEKEDI dial of BÉTÉ, GAGNOA [BTG]
NEKGINI [NKG] lang, Papua New Guinea
NEKO [NEJ] lang, Papua New Guinea
NEKU [NEK] lang, New Caledonia
NELEMA alt for NENEMA dial of KUMAK [NEE]
NELLORE dial of TELUGU [TCW]
NEMADI [NED] lang, Mauritania, Mali
NEMADI alt for NIMADI [NOE]
NEMANGBETU alt for MANGBETU [MDJ]
NEMBAO alt for AMBA [UTP]
NEMBE dial of IJO, SOUTHEAST [IJO]
NEMBI [NMX] lang, Papua New Guinea
NEME dial of BINAHARI [BXZ]
NEMEA alt for NEME dial of BINAHARI [BXZ]
NEMEEJE alt for MEJE dial of MANGBETU [MDJ]
NEMEYAM [NMY] lang, Papua New Guinea
NEMI [NEM] lang, New Caledonia
NEMIA alt for NAMIA [NNM]
NENAYA [NIU] lang, Papua New Guinea
NENDŎ alt for SANTA CRUZ [STC]
NENEC alt for NENETS [YRK]
NENEMA alt for KUMAK [NEE]
NENEMA dial of KUMAK [NEE]
NENETS [YRK] lang, Russia, Asia
NENETSY alt for NENETS [YRK]
NENGAYA alt for NENAYA [NIU]
NENGONE [NEN] lang, New Caledonia
NENNI NYO'O alt for TUNEN [BAZ]
NENT [ANH] lang, Papua New Guinea
NENTSE alt for NENETS [YRK]
NENUSA-MAINGAS dial of TALAUD [TLD]
NENYA dial of TUMBUKA [TUW]
NEO-EGYPTIAN alt for COPTIC [COP]
NEO-HELLENIC alt for GREEK [GRK]
NEO-NYUNGAR dial of ENGLISH [ENG]
NEO-SOLOMONIC alt for PIJIN [PIS]
NEOGULADA alt for KANJU [KBE]
NEOMELANESIAN alt for TOK PISIN [PDG]
NEPA dial of EVENKI [EVN]
NEPALESE alt for NEPALI [NEP]
NEPALESE SIGN LANGUAGE [NSP] lang, Nepal
NEPALI [NEP] lang, Nepal, Bhutan, India
NEPALI dial of NEPALI [NEP]
NEPO alt for BARRU dial of BUGIS [BPR]
NEPOYE alt for MAPOYO [MCG]
NERA alt for NARA [NRB]
NERAUYA dial of LENAKEL [TNL]
NERĚ alt for ZIRE [SIH]
NEREYAMA [NRY] lang, Brazil

NEREZIM dial of TURKMEN [TCK]
NERIGO alt for YAHADIAN [NER]
NESANG [NES] lang, India
NESTORIAN alt for ASSYRIAN [AII]
NETE [NET] lang, Papua New Guinea
NETHANAR dial of DURUWA [PCI]
NETSILIK dial of INUIT, WESTERN CANADIAN [ESC]
NEUCATELAIS dial of FRANCO-PROVENÇAL [FRA]
NEVOME alt for PAPAGO-PIMA [PAP]
NEW BARGU alt for BARGU dial of BURIAT, CHINA
    [BXU]
NEW BRITAIN LANGUAGE alt for TOLAI [KSD]
NEW CHAM alt for CHAM, WESTERN [CJA]
NEW GUINEA PIDGIN ENGLISH alt for TOK PISIN
    [PDG]
NEW NORSE alt for NORWEGIAN, NYNORSK [NRN]
NEW ZEALAND MAORI alt for MAORI [MBF]
NEW ZEALAND SIGN LANGUAGE [NZS] lang, New
    Zealand
NEWAHANG alt for NEWANG [RAF]
NEWANG [RAF] lang, Nepal
NEWANGE RAI alt for NEWANG [RAF]
NEWARI [NEW] lang, Nepal, India
NEWBOLD'S SEMANG alt for ORANG BENUA dial of
    SEMANG, LOWLAND [ORB]
NEWCASTLE NORTHUMBERLAND dial of ENGLISH
    [ENG]
NEYA dial of KURANKO [KHA]
NEYO [NEY] lang, Côte d'Ivoire
NEZ PERCE [NEZ] lang, USA
NFACHARA alt for CARA [CFD]
NFUA alt for BOKYI [BKY]
NFUMTE alt for MFUMTE [NFU]
NG'UMBO dial of BEMBA [BEM]
NG'WERE alt for KWERE [CWE]
NG//-/E alt for //NGIKE dial of NG'HUKI [NGH]
NG/AMANI alt for NG/AMANI [NMN]
NG/U//EN dial of NG/AMANI [NMN]
NG/U/EI alt for NG/U/EN dial of NG/AMANI [NMN]
NG/U/EI alt for NG/U//EN dial of NG/AMANI [NMN]
NG/U/EN dial of NG/AMANI [NMN]
NG/USAN alt for NUSAN dial of NG/AMANI [NMN]
NG/USAN alt for NUSAN dial of NG/AMANI [NMN]
NGA alt for NGAMAMBO dial of META' [MGO]
NGA'KA alt for MUNGAKA [MHK]
NGA'O dial of ENDE [END]
NGAAKA alt for MUNGAKA [MHK]
NGAANYATJARA alt for NGAANYATJARRA [NTJ]
NGAANYATJARRA [NTJ] lang, Australia
NGÄBERE alt for GUAYMÍ [GYM]
NGABRE alt for GABRI [GAB]
NGAC'ANG alt for ACHANG [ACN]
NGAC'ANG alt for NGACANG dial of ACHANG
    [ACN]
NGACANG dial of ACHANG [ACN]
NGACHANG alt for ACHANG [ACN]
NGACHANG alt for NGACANG dial of ACHANG
    [ACN]
NGAD'A alt for NGADA [NXG]
NGADA [NXG] lang, Indonesia, Nusa Tenggara
NGADANJA dial of WIKALKAN [WIK]
NGADHA alt for NGADA [NXG]
NGADJU alt for NGAJU [NIJ]
NGADJU alt for NGADJUNMAYA [NJU]
NGADJUMAJA alt for NGADJUNMAYA [NJU]
NGADJUNMAIA alt for NGADJUNMAYA [NJU]

NGADJUNMAYA [NJU] lang, Australia
NGADOTHO alt for DODOS dial of KARAMOJONG [KDJ]
NGAIGUNGO alt for DJANGUN [DJF]
NGAIMAN alt for NGARINMAN [NBJ]
NGAIMBOM alt for LILAU [LLL]
NGAIN alt for NUMANGGANG [NOP]
NGAIN alt for BENG [NHB]
NGAING [NNF] lang, Papua New Guinea
NGAJU [NIJ] lang, Indonesia, Kalimantan
NGAJU alt for KAPUAS dial of NGAJU [NIJ]
NGAJU DAYAK alt for NGAJU [NIJ]
NGAKARIMOJONE dial of KARAMOJONG [KDJ]
NGAKARIMONJONG alt for KARAMOJONG [KDJ]
NGAKOM alt for RASHAD dial of TEGALI [RAS]
NGALA [NUD] lang, Papua New Guinea
NGALA alt for BANGALA [BXG]
NGALA alt for MANGALA [MGH]
NGALA alt for LINGALA [LIN]
NGALA dial of CHIN, KHUMI [CKM]
NGALABO [NLB] lang, Central African Republic
NGALAKAN [NIG] lang, Australia
NGALAM alt for OLAM dial of MURLE [MUR]
NGALANGAN alt for NGALAKAN [NIG]
NGALIWERRA alt for NGALIWURU dial of DJAMINDJUNG [DJD]
NGALIWURU dial of DJAMINDJUNG [DJD]
NGALKBON alt for NGALKBUN [NGK]
NGALKBUN [NGK] lang, Australia
NGALLOOMA alt for NGARLUMA [NRL]
NGALUM [SZB] lang, Indonesia, Irian Jaya, Papua New Guinea, Papua New Guinea
NGALUM alt for NGALUM [SZB]
NGALUM dial of NGALUM [SZB]
NGALUMA alt for NGARLUMA [NRL]
NGAM [NMC] lang, Chad, Central African Republic
NGAM dial of FE'FE' [FMP]
NGAM dial of KWANG [KVI]
NGAMA alt for NGAM [NMC]
NGAMA dial of SAR [MWM]
NGAMAMBO alt for META' [MGO]
NGAMAMBO dial of META' [MGO]
NG/AMANI [NMN] lang, Namibia, Botswana, South Africa
NGAMAWA alt for NGAMO [NBH]
NGAMBA'WANDH alt for JIR'JOROND dial of YIR YORONT [YIY]
NGAMBAI [SBA] lang, Chad, Cameroon
NGAMBAY alt for NGAMBAI [SBA]
NGAMI alt for NAGA, ANGAMI [NJM]
NGAMINI [NMV] lang, Australia
NGAMO [NBH] lang, Nigeria
NGAN alt for BENG [NHB]
NGAN alt for THO [THO]
NGANASAN [NIO] lang, Russia, Asia
NGANDI [NID] lang, Australia
NGANDJARA alt for WIKNGENCHERA [WUA]
NGANDJARA alt for WIK-NGANDJARA dial of WIKALKAN [WIK]
NGANDO [NGD] lang, Central African Republic
NGANDO [NXD] lang, Zaïre
NGANDO-KOTA alt for NGANDO [NGD]
NGANDU alt for NGANDO [NXD]
NGANDYERA [NNE] lang, Angola
NGANDYERA dial of NDONGA [NDG]
NGANGALA dial of LUIMBI [LUM]

NGANGAM [GNG] lang, Togo, Benin
NGANGAN alt for NGANGAM [GNG]
NGANGCHING dial of NAGA, KONYAK [NBE]
NGANGEA alt for NYANG'I [NYP]
NGANGELA alt for NYEMBA [NBA]
NGANGIKARANGURR alt for NANGIKURRUNGGURR [NAM]
NGANGOMORI alt for NGENKIWUMERRI dial of NANGIKURRUNGGURR [NAM]
NGANGOULOU alt for TEKE, NORTHEASTERN [NGZ]
NGANKIKURRUNKURR alt for NANGIKURRUNGGURR [NAM]
NGANKIKURRUNKURR alt for TYEMERI dial of NANGIKURRUNGGURR [NAM]
NGANSHUENKUAN alt for ATUENCE [ATF]
NGANTJERI alt for WIKNGENCHERA [WUA]
NGANYAYWANA [NYX] lang, Australia
NGANYGIT dial of MARITHIEL [MFR]
NGAO [NAX] lang, Central African Republic
NGAO alt for NGA'O dial of ENDE [END]
NGAO FON [NFO] lang, China
NGAONDÉRÉ dial of FULFULDE, ADAMAWA [FUB]
NGAPO [NPG] lang, Central African Republic
NGAPORE alt for NYANG'I [NYP]
NGAPU alt for NGAPO [NPG]
NGARE dial of MBOKO [MDU]
NGARI alt for NAGA, KHOIRAO [NKI]
NGARI alt for MNGAHRIS dial of TIBETAN [TIC]
NGARIAWAN [NGG] lang, Papua New Guinea
NGARIAWANG alt for NGARIAWAN [NGG]
NGARINMAN [NBJ] lang, Australia
NGARINYERI alt for NARRINYERI [NAY]
NGARINYIN [UNG] lang, Australia
NGARIWAN alt for NGARIAWAN [NGG]
NGARLA [NLR] lang, Australia
NGARLKAJIE alt for DYAABUGAY [DYY]
NGARLUMA [NRL] lang, Australia
NGARNDJI [NJI] lang, Australia
NGAROWAPUM dial of ADZERA [AZR]
NGASA [NSG] lang, Tanzania
NGATANA dial of POKOMO, LOWER [POJ]
NGATIK [NGM] lang, Micronesia
NGATJUMAY alt for NGADJUNMAYA [NJU]
NGATSANG alt for NGACANG dial of ACHANG [ACN]
NGATURKANA alt for TURKANA [TUV]
NGATURKWANA alt for TURKANA [TUV]
NGAU alt for NGAO [NAX]
NGAWN alt for CHIN, NGAWN [CNW]
NGAWUN [NXN] lang, Australia
NGAYABA alt for TIBEA [NGY]
NGAYABA dial of BAFIA [KSF]
NGAYMIL dial of DHANGU [GLA]
NGAZAR dial of KANURI, YERWA [KPH]
NGBAKA [NGA] lang, Zaïre, Central African Republic, Congo
NGBAKA GBAYA alt for NGBAKA [NGA]
NGBAKA LIMBA alt for NGBAKA MA'BO [NBM]
NGBAKA MA'BO alt for NGBAKA MA'BO [NBM]
NGBAKA MA'BO [NBM] lang, Central African Republic, Zaïre, Congo, Zaïre
NGBAKA MINANGENDE alt for NGBAKA [NGA]
NGBAKO dial of KAKO [KKJ]
NGBANDI [NGB] lang, Zaïre, Central African Republic
NGBANG dial of DII [DUR]
NGBANYITO alt for GONJA [DUM]

NGBEE [NBL] lang, Zaïre
NGBINDA [NBD] lang, Zaïre
NGBO alt for MGBO dial of IZI-EZAA-IKWO-MGBO [IZI]
NGBUGU [NUB] lang, Zaïre, Central African Republic
NGBUNDU [NUU] lang, Zaïre
NGBWANDI alt for NGBANDI [NGB]
NGE alt for VENGO [BAV]
NGE' alt for NGEQ [NGT]
NGE'DÉ alt for NGUETÉ [NNN]
NGEE dial of TEKE, EASTERN [TEK]
NGEH alt for NGEQ [NGT]
NGELIMA [AGH] lang, Zaïre
NGELL-KURU-VWANG alt for GYELL-KURU-VWANG dial of BEROM [BOM]
NGEMBA [NGE] lang, Cameroon
NGEMBA dial of GHOMALA' [BBJ]
NGEMBA alt for MANGKUNGE dial of NGEMBA [NGE]
NGEMBO alt for NGAMAMBO dial of META' [MGO]
NGEN alt for BENG [NHB]
NGEN alt for BASSOSSI [BSI]
NGENDE dial of BUSHOONG [BUF]
NGENE alt for ENGENNI [ENN]
NGENGE dial of GBAGYI [GBR]
NGENKIKURRUNGGUR alt for NANGIKURRUNGGURR [NAM]
NGENKIWUMERRI dial of NANGIKURRUNGGURR [NAM]
NGENO-NGENE dial of SASAK [SAS]
NGENTE dial of LUSHAI [LSH]
"NGEO" alt for SHAN [SJN]
NGEPMA KWUNDI alt for IATMUL [IAN]
NGEQ [NGT] lang, Laos
NGETI alt for NGITI [NIY]
NGETO-NGETE dial of SASAK [SAS]
NGEUMBA alt for NGIYAMBAA dial of WANGAAYBUWAN-NGIYAMBAA [WYB]
NGEZZIM alt for NGIZIM [NGI]
NGGAE alt for GAE dial of GHARI [GRI]
NGGAO alt for GAO [GGA]
NGGAURA dial of LAMBOYA [LMY]
NGGELA alt for GELA [NLG]
NGGEM [NBQ] lang, Indonesia, Irian Jaya
NGGERI alt for GERI dial of GHARI [GRI]
NGGWAHYI [NGX] lang, Nigeria
NGGWESHE alt for GEVOKO [NGS]
NG'HUKI [NGH] lang, South Africa
NGHWELE [NHE] lang, Tanzania
NGI alt for NGIE [NGJ]
NGIAMBA alt for NGIYAMBAA dial of WANGAAYBUWAN-NGIYAMBAA [WYB]
NGIANGEYA alt for NYANG'I [NYP]
"NGIAO alt for SHAN [SJN]
NGIAW alt for SHAN [SJN]
"NGIAW" alt for SHAN [SJN]
NGIE [NGJ] lang, Cameroon
NGILE [MAS] lang, Sudan
NGILEMONG dial of MUSGU [MUG]
NGILI alt for PANDE dial of PANDE [BKJ]
NGIN alt for BENG [NHB]
NGINDO [NNQ] lang, Tanzania
NGINIA dial of GHARI [GRI]
NGINYUKWUR dial of KOALIB [KIB]
NGIO alt for SHAN [SJN]
"NGIO" alt for SHAN [SJN]

NGIOW alt for SHAN [SJN]
"NGIOW" alt for SHAN [SJN]
NGIRERE alt for KOALIB [KIB]
NGIRERE dial of KOALIB [KIB]
NGIRI [NGR] lang, Zaïre
NGIRI dial of NGIRI [NGR]
NGISHE [NSH] lang, Cameroon
NGITI [NIY] lang, Zaïre
NGITURKWANA alt for TURKANA [TUV]
NGIUMBA alt for NGIYAMBAA dial of WANGAAYBUWAN-NGIYAMBAA [WYB]
NGIYAMBAA alt of WANGAAYBUWAN-NGIYAMBAA [WYB]
NGIZIM [NGI] lang, Nigeria
NGIZMAWA alt for NGIZIM [NGI]
NGJAMBA alt for NGIYAMBAA dial of WANGAAYBUWAN-NGIYAMBAA [WYB]
NGMAMPERLI alt for MAMPRULI [MAW]
NGNAI dial of PUNU [PNU]
NGO alt for VENGO [BAV]
NGO dial of OBOLO [ANN]
NGO CHANG alt for ACHANG [ACN]
NGO CHANG alt for NGACANG dial of ACHANG [ACN]
NGOAHU dial of LOKO [LOK]
NGOBERE alt for GUAYMÍ [GYM]
NGOBO alt for GUBU [GOX]
NGOBU alt for GUBU [GOX]
NGODENI alt for MUXULE dial of JINA [JIA]
NGOE alt for BAFAW-BALONG [BWT]
NGOK PA alt for KENSIU [KNS]
NGOK-KORDOFAN dial of DINKA, NORTHWESTERN [DIW]
NGOK-SOBAT dial of DINKA, NORTHEASTERN [DIP]
NGOLA [NLL] lang, Central African Republic
NGOLA dial of MBUNDU, LOANDA [MLO]
NGOLAK-WONGA alt for MULLUKMULLUK [MPB]
NGOLI alt for NGUL [NLO]
NGOLO dial of BALUNDU-BIMA [NGO]
NGOLOK alt for GOLOG [GOC]
NGOLUCHE alt for MOLUCHE dial of MAPUDUNGUN [ARU]
NGOM [NRA] lang, Congo, Gabon
NGOM alt for NGOM [NRA]
NGOMA dial of BEMBA [BEM]
NGOMBA [NNO] lang, Cameroon
NGOMBA alt for NGEMBA [NGE]
NGOMBALE [NLA] lang, Cameroon
NGOMBE [NGC] lang, Zaïre
NGOMBE [NMJ] lang, Central African Republic
NGOMBE dial of BUSHOONG [BUF]
NGOMBE-KAKA alt for NGOMBE [NMJ]
NGOMBIA alt for NGOMBE dial of BUSHOONG [BUF]
NGOMI dial of KARANG [KZR]
NGOMO alt for NGOM [NRA]
NGONDE alt for NYAKYUSA-NGONDE [NYY]
NGONDE dial of NYAKYUSA-NGONDE [NYY]
NGONDI alt for GUNDI [GDI]
NGONDI alt for NGUNDI [NDN]
NGONG [NNX] lang, Cameroon
NGONGE alt for GONGE dial of NZAKMBAY [NZY]
NGONGO [NOQ] lang, Zaïre
NGONGO dial of NKUTU [NKW]
NGONGO dial of BUSHOONG [BUF]
NGONGOSILA alt for GULA'ALAA [GMB]
NGONI [NGU] lang, Tanzania, Malawi, Mozambique

NGONI alt for ZULU [ZUU]
NGONI dial of NSENGA [NSE]
NGONI dial of NYANJA [NYJ]
NGONI dial of NYANJA [NYJ]
NGONI dial of TUMBUKA [TUW]
NGONI alt for CHINGONI dial of NYANJA [NYJ]
NGOOBECHOP alt for BAMALI [BBQ]
NGOONGO dial of YAKA [YAF]
NGOREME alt for NGURIMI [NGQ]
NGORK alt for NGOK-SOBAT dial of DINKA,
     NORTHEASTERN [DIP]
NGORMBUR alt for NGURMBUR [NRX]
NGORN alt for CHIN, NGAWN [CNW]
NGORO dial of TUKI [BAG]
NGORO dial of VUTE [VUT]
NGORO alt for NGOLO dial of BALUNDU-BIMA
     [NGO]
NGOSHE SAMA alt for GEVOKO [NGS]
NGOSHE-NDHANG alt for GEVOKO [NGS]
NGOSHI alt for GEVOKO [NGS]
NGOSHIE dial of GLAVDA [GLV]
NGOSSI alt for GEVOKO [NGS]
NGOUMBA alt for NGUMBA [NMG]
NGOUMBA alt for MVUMBO dial of NGUMBA [NMG]
NGOUTCHOUMI alt for BELE dial of FALI, SOUTH
     [FLE]
NGOWIYE dial of BIANGAI [BIG]
NGRARMUN alt for NGARINMAN [NBJ]
NGRUIMI alt for NGURIMI [NGQ]
NGU NGWONI alt for NGUNGWONI [NGF]
NGUBU alt for NGBUGU [NUB]
NGUEMBA alt for NGYEMBOON [NNH]
NGUEMBA alt for NGEMBA [NGE]
NGUETÉ [NNN] lang, Chad
NGUETTÉ alt for NGUETÉ [NNN]
NGUILI alt for NGIRI [NGR]
NGUIN alt for BENG [NHB]
NGUL [NLO] lang, Zaïre
NGULAK alt for IK [IKX]
NGULGULE alt for NJALGULGULE [NJL]
NGULI alt for NGUL [NLO]
NGULU [NGP] lang, Tanzania
NGULU alt for LOMWE [NGL]
NGULU alt for NGUL [NLO]
NGULUWONGGA alt for MULLUKMULLUK [MPB]
NGUMBA [NMG] lang, Cameroon, Equatorial Guinea,
     Equatorial Guinea
NGUMBA alt for NGUMBA [NMG]
NGUMBA alt for MVUMBO dial of NGUMBA [NMG]
NGUMBARR alt for NGIYAMBAA dial of
     WANGAAYBUWAN-NGIYAMBAA [WYB]
NGUMBI [NUI] lang, Equatorial Guinea
NGUMBUR alt for NGURMBUR [NRX]
NGUNA dial of EFATE, NORTH [LLP]
NGUNDI [NDN] lang, Congo, Central African Republic
NGUNDI alt for GUNDI [GDI]
NGUNDI dial of LUSENGO [LUS]
NGUNDI-OUEST alt for NGUNDI [NDN]
NGUNDU [NUE] lang, Zaïre
NGUNDUNA dial of KOALIB [KIB]
NGUNESE alt for NGUNA dial of EFATE, NORTH
     [LLP]
NGUNGULU alt for TEKE, NORTHEASTERN [NGZ]
NGUNGWEL alt for TEKE, NORTHEASTERN [NGZ]
NGUNGWONI [NGF] lang, Congo
NGUNI alt for NGWO dial of NGWO [NGN]

NGUNU alt for NGWO dial of NGWO [NGN]
NGUÔN [NUO] lang, Viet Nam, Laos
NGUQWURANG dial of KOALIB [KIB]
NGURA [NBX] lang, Australia
NGURAWARLA dial of NGURA [NBX]
NGURI dial of KANEMBU [KBL]
NGURIMI [NGQ] lang, Tanzania
NGURMBUR [NRX] lang, Australia
NGURU alt for LOMWE [NGL]
NGURU alt for NGULU [NGP]
NGURU alt for JUNGURU [JGR]
NGURU dial of KARA [KCM]
NGURU dial of KARA [KCM]
NGURUIMI alt for NGURIMI [NGQ]
NGUU alt for VENGO [BAV]
NGUU alt for NGULU [NGP]
NGWA alt for VENGO [BAV]
NGWA dial of IGBO [IGR]
NGWA alt for SONGWA dial of NGEMBA [NGE]
NGWABA [NGW] lang, Nigeria
NGWACI alt for NGWANCI dial of AGAUSHI-KIMBA-
     NGWANCI [KDL]
NGWAJUM dial of KAREKARE [KAI]
NGWAKETSE dial of TSWANA [TSW]
NGWALKWE alt for MALGBE [MXF]
NGWALUNGU dial of TSONGA [TSO]
NGWANA alt for SWAHILI, ZAÏRE [SWC]
NGWANCI dial of AGAUSHI-KIMBA-NGWANCI [KDL]
NGWANDI alt for NGBANDI [NGB]
NGWANÉ alt for WANE [HWA]
NGWATO dial of TSWANA [TSW]
NGWATU dial of TSWANA [TSW]
NGWATU dial of TSWANA [TSW]
NGWAW alt for NGWO [NGN]
NGWAW alt for NGWO dial of NGWO [NGN]
NGWAXI alt for NGGWAHYI [NGX]
NGWE [NWE] lang, Cameroon
NGWE alt for HUNGWORO [NAT]
NGWE PALAUNG alt for PALAUNG, PALE [PCE]
NGWELE alt for NGHWELE [NHE]
NGWESHE alt for NGOSHIE dial of GLAVDA [GLV]
NGWESHE-NDAGHAN alt for GEVOKO [NGS]
NGWII dial of MBERE [MDT]
NGWILI alt for NGIRI [NGR]
NGWO [NGN] lang, Cameroon
NGWO dial of NGWO [NGN]
NGWOHI alt for NGGWAHYI [NGX]
NGWOI alt for HUNGWORO [NAT]
NGWULLARO alt for LARO [LRO]
NGYEMBOON [NNH] lang, Cameroon
NGYEME alt for NJEME dial of KOOZIME [NJE]
NGYEPU alt for NYEPU dial of BARI [BFA]
NGYEPU alt for NYEPU dial of BARI [BFA]
NHA HEUN alt for NYAHEUN [NEV]
NHAANG alt for NHANG [NHA]
N/HAI-NTSE'E [NKT] lang, Botswana
NHANDEVA alt for CHIRIPA [NHD]
NHANECA alt for NYANEKA [NYK]
NHANG [NHA] lang, Viet Nam, China
NHARON [NHR] lang, Botswana
NHAURU alt for NHARON [NHR]
NHAURUN alt for NHARON [NHR]
NHAYI dial of TSWA [TSC]
NHEENGATU alt for NHENGATU [YRL]
NHENGATU [YRL] lang, Brazil, Colombia, Colombia,
     Venezuela

199

NHENGATU alt for NHENGATU [YRL]
NHLANGANU dial of TSONGA [TSO]
NHO alt for BAFAW dial of BAFAW-BALONG [BWT]
NHUON alt for LÜ [KHB]
NHUWALA [NHF] lang, Australia
NI NYO'O dial of TUNEN [BAZ]
NIA HOEN alt for NYAHEUN [NEV]
NIABO alt for NEAO dial of GUÉRÉ [GXX]
NIABOUA alt for NYABWA [NIA]
NIABRE dial of BÉTÉ, GAGNOA [BTG]
NIAHON alt for NYAHEUN [NEV]
NIAKARAMADOUGOU dial of SENOUFO, TAGWANA
    [TGW]
NIAKUOL alt for NYAHKUR [CBN]
NIAKUOLL alt for NYAHKUR [CBN]
NIAMNIAM alt for NIMBARI [NMR]
NIANG alt for NHANG [NHA]
NIANGBO dial of SENOUFO, TAGWANA [TGW]
NIANGOLOKO-DIARABAKOKO dial of CERMA [GOT]
NIAP alt for TEMUAN [TMW]
NIARDIAY dial of KOLI, KACHI [GJK]
NIAS [NIP] lang, Indonesia, Sumatra
NIAS dial of NIAS [NIP]
NIBAK alt for IXTAPA dial of TZOTZIL, CHAMULA
    [TZC]
NIBHATTA dial of BUNDELI [BNS]
NIBON alt for PUNAN-NIBONG [PNE]
NIBONG alt for PUNAN-NIBONG [PNE]
NIBONG dial of PUNAN-NIBONG [PNE]
NIBULU alt for NUNI [NNW]
NICARAGUAN SIGN LANGUAGE [NCS] lang,
    Nicaragua
NICARAGUAN SUMO dial of SUMO [SUM]
NIÇARD dial of PROVENÇAL [PRV]
NICOBAR alt for NICOBARESE, CENTRAL [NCB]
NICOBARA alt for NICOBARESE, SOUTHERN [NIK]
NICOBARESE, CAR [CAQ] lang, India
NICOBARESE, CENTRAL [NCB] lang, India
NICOBARESE, SOUTHERN [NIK] lang, India
NIÇOIS alt for NIÇARD dial of PROVENÇAL [PRV]
NICOYA dial of CHOROTEGA [CJR]
NIDE alt for LABO [MWI]
NIDEM alt for NINDEM dial of KANUFI-KANINGDON-
    NINDEM [KDP]
NIDROU alt for KAAWLU dial of KRAHN, WESTERN
    [KRW]
NIDRU alt for KAAWLU dial of KRAHN, WESTERN
    [KRW]
NIDZH dial of UDI [UDI]
NIÉDÉBOUA alt for NYEDEBWA dial of NYABWA
    [NIA]
NIEDIEKAHA dial of SENOUFO, TAGWANA [TGW]
NIEL alt for AGEER dial of DINKA, NORTHEASTERN
    [DIP]
NIELIM alt for NIELLIM [NIE]
NIELLIM [NIE] lang, Chad
NIELLIM dial of NIELLIM [NIE]
NIEMENG alt for BAMUNKA [NDO]
"NIENDE" alt for MBELIME [MQL]
NIENDE dial of TAMBERMA [SOF]
"NIENDI" alt for MBELIME [MQL]
NIENG Ó alt for MANG [MGA]
NIENI alt for KURANKO [KHA]
NIFE alt for NUPE CENTRAL dial of NUPE [NUP]
NIFILOLE alt for AYIWO [NFL]
NIGAC dial of MAPE [MLH]

NIGBI alt for LIGBI [LIG]
NIGERIAN CREOLE ENGLISH alt for PIDGIN,
    NIGERIAN [PCM]
NIGERIAN PIDGIN ENGLISH alt for PIDGIN,
    NIGERIAN [PCM]
NIGERIAN SIGN LANGUAGE [NSI] lang, Nigeria
NIGI alt for NIGII dial of YAMBETA [YAT]
NIGII dial of YAMBETA [YAT]
NIGUECACTEMIGI alt for LAYANA dial of GUANA
    [GVA]
NIGWI alt for LIGBI [LIG]
NIHAL alt for NIHALI [NHL]
NIHALI [NHL] lang, India
NIHAMBER alt for WAMSAK [WBD]
NIHAN alt for NEHAN [NSN]
NII [NII] lang, Papua New Guinea
NIINATI alt for KATI, NORTHERN [KTI]
NIITAKA alt for TSOU [TSY]
NIJADALI [NAD] lang, Australia
NIJRAU dial of PARACHI [PRC]
NIKA alt for GIRYAMA [NYF]
NIKSEK [GBE] lang, Papua New Guinea
NIKUDA dial of ONIN [ONI]
NIKULKAN-MURNATEN-WAKOLO alt for NORTH
    COASTAL ALUNE dial of ALUNE [ALP]
NILA [NIL] lang, Indonesia, Maluku
NILAMBA [NIM] lang, Tanzania
NILE NUBIAN alt for KENUZI-DONGOLA [KNC]
NILE NUBIAN alt for MAHAS-FIADIDJA [FIA]
NILOTIC KAVIRONDO alt for LUO [LUO]
NILYAMBA alt for NILAMBA [NIM]
NIMADI [NOE] lang, India
NIMADI alt for NEMADI [NED]
NIMALDA alt for ADYNYAMATHANHA [ADT]
NIMALTO alt for NYIMATLI dial of TERA [TER]
NIMANA alt for NUMANA dial of NUMANA-NUNKU-
    GWANTU-NUMBU [NBR]
NIMANBUR [NMP] lang, Australia
NIMARI alt for NIMADI [NOE]
NIMBARI [NMR] lang, Cameroon
NIMBARI-KEBI alt for NIMBARI [NMR]
NIMBE alt for NEMBE dial of IJO, SOUTHEAST [IJO]
NIMBORAN [NIR] lang, Indonesia, Irian Jaya
NIMI [NIS] lang, Papua New Guinea
NIMI KORO alt for PERIPHERAL KONO dial of KONO
    [KNO]
NIMI YEMA alt for PERIPHERAL KONO dial of KONO
    [KNO]
NIMO [NIW] lang, Papua New Guinea
NIMO-WASNAI dial of NIMO [NIW]
NIMOA [NMW] lang, Papua New Guinea
NIMOIS alt for RHODANIEN dial of PROVENÇAL
    [PRV]
NIMOWA alt for NIMOA [NMW]
NIMPO alt for NOMOPO dial of SAPO [KRN]
NINAM [SHB] lang, Brazil, Venezuela, Venezuela
NINAM alt for NINAM [SHB]
NINATIE alt for KATI, NORTHERN [KTI]
NINDEM dial of KANUFI-KANINGDON-NINDEM [KDP]
NINE HILLS dial of SUDEST [TGO]
NINEBULO dial of SA [SSA]
NINEIA alt for NENAYA [NIU]
NINGALAMI alt for NANGALAMI dial of GRANGALI
    [NLI]
NINGBO dial of CHINESE, WU [WUU]
NINGEBAL alt for BAYALI [BJY]

NINGERA [NBY] lang, Papua New Guinea
NINGERUM alt for NINGGERUM [NXR]
NINGGERA alt for NINGERA [NBY]
NINGGEROEM alt for NINGGERUM [NXR]
NINGGERUM [NXR] lang, Papua New Guinea,
  Indonesia, Irian Jaya
NINGGIRUM alt for NINGGERUM [NXR]
NINGGRUM alt for NINGGERUM [NXR]
NINGI dial of GAMO-NINGI [BTE]
NINGIL [NIZ] lang, Papua New Guinea
NINGPO alt for NINGBO dial of CHINESE, WU [WUU]
NINGRAHARIAN PASHTO alt for PASHTO, EASTERN
  [PBU]
NINGTING dial of BONAN [PEH]
NINGUESSEN alt for MESE dial of TUNEN [BAZ]
NINIA alt for YALI, NINIA [NLK]
NINIARI-PIRU-RIRING-LUMOLI alt for CENTRAL
  WEST ALUNE dial of ALUNE [ALP]
NINIGO alt for SEIMAT [SSG]
NINONG dial of AKOOSE [BSS]
NINZAM [NIN] lang, Nigeria
NINZNE-UDINSK dial of BURIAT, RUSSIA [MNB]
NINZO alt for NINZAM [NIN]
NIO dial of LUGBARA, HIGH [LUG]
NIOMINKA dial of NON [SNF]
NIOMOUN alt for BLISS dial of JOLA-KASA [CSK]
NIOPRENG alt for MRU [MRO]
NIOU dial of NIELLIM [NIE]
NIPA dial of ANGAL HENENG, WEST [AKH]
NIPOREN alt for NYANG'I [NYP]
NIPORI alt for NYANG'I [NYP]
NIPSAN [YAC] lang, Indonesia, Irian Jaya
NIRAGU dial of GBIRI-NIRAGU [GRH]
NIRAMBA alt for NILAMBA [NIM]
NIRERE alt for KOALIB [KIB]
NIRMAL dial of GONDI, SOUTHERN [GGO]
NISA [NIC] lang, Indonesia, Irian Jaya
NISEL alt for KHAM, NISI [KIF]
NISENAN dial of MAIDU [MAI]
NISHANG alt for NISI [DAP]
NISHEL KHAM alt for KHAM, NISI [KIF]
NISHI alt for NISI [DAP]
NISHKA alt for NISKA dial of NASS-GITKSIAN [NCG]
NISI [DAP] lang, India
NISI alt for KHAM, NISI [KIF]
NISK'A alt for NISKA dial of NASS-GITKSIAN [NCG]
NISKA dial of NASS-GITKSIAN [NCG]
NISQUALLY dial of SALISH, SOUTHERN PUGET
  SOUND [SLH]
NISSAN alt for NEHAN [NSN]
NISSI alt for NISI [DAP]
NITEN alt for ATEN [GAN]
NITIABO dial of GREBO, NORTHEASTERN [GRP]
NITIABO GREBO alt for GREBO, NORTHEASTERN
  [GRP]
NITINAT dial of NOOTKA [NOO]
NIUAFO'OU [NUM] lang, Tonga
NIUATOPUTAPU [NKP] lang, Tonga
NIUE [NIQ] lang, Niue, Cook Islands, New Zealand,
  Tonga
NIUE alt for NIUE [NIQ]
NIUEAN alt for NIUE [NIQ]
"NIUEFEKAI" alt for NIUE [NIQ]
NIUTAO alt for NORTH TUVALUAN dial of
  TUVALUAN [ELL]
NIVACLÉ alt for CHULUPÍ [CAG]

NIVAKLÉ alt for CHULUPÍ [CAG]
NIVE dial of DABA [DAB]
NIVKH alt for GILYAK [NIV]
NIVKHI alt for GILYAK [NIV]
NIVO alt for AYIWO [NFL]
NIZH alt for NIDZH dial of UDI [UDI]
NIZOVSK dial of NEGIDAL [NEG]
NJABI alt for NJEBI [NZB]
NJADU alt for NYADU [NXJ]
NJAI alt for NZANYI [NJA]
NJAKALI dial of DYAABUGAY [DYY]
NJALGULGULE [NJL] lang, Sudan
NJAMAL alt for NYAMAL [NLY]
NJAMARL alt for NYAMAL [NLY]
NJAMBETA alt for YAMBETA [YAT]
NJANG alt for NYANJANG dial of KWANJA [KNP]
NJANGGA alt for NYANGGA [NNY]
NJANGGA alt for WIRANGU [WIW]
NJANGGALA alt for NYANGGA [NNY]
NJANGULGULE alt for NJALGULGULE [NJL]
NJANTI alt for TIBEA [NGY]
NJANYI alt for NZANYI [NJA]
NJAO alt for AWYI [AUW]
NJAO alt for NDAU [NDC]
NJARI alt for NZARE dial of MBEMBE, TIGON [NZA]
NJAUNA dial of NAGA, ZEME [NZM]
NJAWE alt for JAWE [JAZ]
NJAWLO dial of LENDU [LED]
NJEBI [NZB] lang, Gabon, Congo
NJEE-POANTU dial of FE'FE' [FMP]
NJEGN alt for NZANYI [NJA]
NJEI alt for NZANYI [NJA]
NJEING alt for NZANYI [NJA]
NJELENG alt for MOFU, SOUTH [MIF]
NJELI alt for PANDE dial of PANDE [BKJ]
NJEM alt for NDJEM dial of KOOZIME [NJE]
NJEM alt for NDJEM dial of KOOZIME [NJE]
NJEME dial of KOOZIME [NJE]
NJEME dial of KOOZIME [NJE]
NJEMNJEM alt for SUGA [SGI]
NJEMPS alt for CHAMUS dial of SAMBURU [SAQ]
NJEN [MEN] lang, Cameroon
NJENG alt for DZA [JEN]
NJENY alt for NZANYI [NJA]
NJERUP [NJR] lang, Nigeria
NJESKO dial of KANURI, YERWA [KPH]
NJEVI alt for NJEBI [NZB]
NJIJAPALI alt for NIJADALI [NAD]
NJIKINI alt for NJININGI dial of TEKE, NORTHERN
  [TEG]
NJIKUM alt for JUKUN TAKUM [JBU]
NJINDO alt for NGINDO [NNQ]
NJINGA dial of MBUNDU, LOANDA [MLO]
NJININGI dial of TEKE, NORTHERN [TEG]
NJINJU dial of TEKE, CENTRAL [TEC]
NJIUNJIU alt for NJYUNJYU dial of TEKE, CENTRAL
  [TEC]
NJO alt for KOMERING [KGE]
NJO alt for KRUI [KRQ]
NJONG dial of NGEMBA [NGE]
NJOYAME alt for NDOOLA [NDR]
NJUGUNA alt for NUGUNU [NNV]
NJUKÁ alt for AUKAANS [DJK]
NJUKA alt for AUKAANS [DJK]
NJUMIT dial of LAWANGAN [LBX]
NJUNGENE alt for LIMBUM [LIM]

NJWANDE alt for BITARE [BRE]
NJYUNJYU dial of TEKE, CENTRAL [TEC]
NJYUNJYU alt for NJINJU dial of TEKE, CENTRAL
    [TEC]
NKA' dial of FE'FE' [FMP]
NKAFA dial of KAMWE [HIG]
NKANGALA [NKN] lang, Angola
NKAP alt for NAKI [MFF]
NKARI dial of IBIBIO [IBB]
NKARIGWE alt for IRIGWE [IRI]
NKEM dial of NKEM-NKUM [ISI]
NKEM-NKUM [ISI] lang, Nigeria
NKEMBE alt for NKIMBE dial of MBOLE [MDQ]
NKHUMBI [KHU] lang, Angola
NKI alt for BOKYI [BKY]
NKIM alt for NKEM dial of NKEM-NKUM [ISI]
NKIMBE dial of MBOLE [MDQ]
NKO dial of MUNDANI [MUN]
NKOGNA alt for NKONYA [NKO]
NKOKOLLE alt for NKUKOLI [NBO]
NKOLE alt for NYANKOLE [NYN]
NKOLE dial of NTOMBA [NTO]
NKOM alt for KOM [BKM]
NKOMI dial of MYENE [MYE]
NKONDE alt for NYAKYUSA-NGONDE [NYY]
NKONDE dial of NYAKYUSA-NGONDE [NYY]
NKONG alt for NKO dial of MUNDANI [MUN]
NKONGHO dial of MBO [MBO]
NKONYA [NKO] lang, Ghana
NKOOSI alt for AKOOSE [BSS]
NKORO alt for NKOROO [NKX]
NKOROO [NKX] lang, Nigeria
NKOSI alt for AKOOSE [BSS]
NKOT dial of YAMBA [YAM]
NKOXO alt for KAKO [KKJ]
NKOYA [NKA] lang, Zambia
NKOYA dial of NKOYA [NKA]
NKPANI dial of LOKO [YAZ]
NKQESHE alt for //XEGWI [XEG]
NKRIANG alt for NGEQ [NGT]
NKUCHU alt for NKUTU [NKW]
NKUKOLI [NBO] lang, Nigeria
NKUM dial of YALA [YBA]
NKUM dial of NKEM-NKUM [ISI]
NKUM AKPAMBE dial of YALA [YBA]
NKUMA dial of TSONGA [TSO]
NKUMABEM alt for KUNABEMBE dial of
    MPONGMPONG [MGG]
NKUMBI alt for NKHUMBI [KHU]
NKUNDO dial of MONGO-NKUNDU [MOM]
NKUNDU alt for BAKUNDU dial of BAKUNDU-BALUE
    [BDU]
NKUNDU alt for NKUNDO dial of MONGO-NKUNDU
    [MOM]
NKUNE alt for MANGKUNGE dial of NGEMBA [NGE]
NKUNYA alt for NKONYA [NKO]
NKURAENG alt for KULANGO, BOUNA [NKU]
NKURAENG alt for KULANGO, BONDOUKOU [KZC]
NKURANGE alt for KULANGO, BOUNA [NKU]
NKURANGE alt for KULANGO, BONDOUKOU [KZC]
NKUTSHU alt for NKUTU [NKW]
NKUTU [NKW] lang, Zaïre
NKUTUK alt for SAMBURU [SAQ]
NKWA alt for GBARI [GBY]
NKWEN dial of MENDANKWE [MFD]
NKWIFIYA dial of SAGALA [SBM]

NKWOI alt for HUNGWORO [NAT]
NLONG alt for BALONG dial of BAFAW-BALONG
    [BWT]
NLONG alt for ELONG dial of AKOOSE [BSS]
NNAM [NBP] lang, Nigeria
NNERIGWE alt for IRIGWE [IRI]
NNGAS alt for ANGAS [ANC]
NO dial of SAR [MWM]
NO-PENGE alt for PENGE dial of UMBU-UNGU [UMB]
NOALE alt for MBEMBE, TIGON [NZA]
NOANAMA alt for WAUMEO [NOA]
NOANG alt for ROGLAI, NORTHERN [ROG]
NOANG dial of CHRU [CJE]
NOATAK RIVER ESKIMO dial of INUIT, NORTHWEST
    ALASKA INUPIAT [ESK]
NOATIA dial of KOK BOROK [TRP]
NOBANOB [GAW] lang, Papua New Guinea
NOBIIN alt for MAHAS-FIADIDJA [FIA]
NOBIIN dial of MAHAS-FIADIDJA [FIA]
NOBNOB alt for NOBANOB [GAW]
NOBONOB alt for NOBANOB [GAW]
NOBUK alt for NOPUK [NOB]
NOCAMAN [NOM] lang, Peru
NOCOMAN alt for NOCAMAN [NOM]
NOCTE alt for NAGA, NOCTE [NJB]
NOCTEN alt for WICHÍ LHAMTÉS NOCTEN [MTP]
NOCTENES alt for WICHÍ LHAMTÉS NOCTEN [MTP]
NODUP dial of TOLAI [KSD]
NOEFOOR alt for BIAK [BHW]
NOENAMA alt for WAUMEO [NOA]
NOGAI [NOG] lang, Russia, Europe
NOGAI dial of TATAR [TTR]
NOGAITSY alt for NOGAI [NOG]
NOGALAR alt for NOGAI [NOG]
NOGAU alt for KUNG-TSUMKWE [KTZ]
NOGAU dial of KUNG-GOBABIS [AUE]
NOGAY alt for NOGAI [NOG]
NOGHAI alt for NOGAI [NOG]
NOGHAY alt for NOGAI [NOG]
NOGHAYLAR alt for NOGAI [NOG]
NOGLIKI-VAL alt for VAL-NOGLIKI dial of OROK
    [OAÀ]
NOGN alt for BATEK [BTQ]
NOGO dial of KEMAK [KEM]
NOGUGU alt for NOKUKU [NKK]
NOGUKWABAI alt for KWERBA [KWE]
"NOHINA" alt for TOLAKI [LBW]
NOHO alt for BATANGA [BNM]
NOHON dial of AWYU [AWJ]
NOHU alt for BATANGA [BNM]
NOHUR alt for NOKHURLI dial of TURKMEN [TCK]
NOHYA SIGN LANGUAGE alt for MAYAN SIGN
    LANGUAGE [MSD]
"NOIE" alt for TOLAKI [LBW]
"NOIHE" alt for TOLAKI [LBW]
NOIKORO alt for WAYA dial of FIJIAN, WESTERN
    [WYY]
NOIRI dial of BHILORI [BQI]
NOKANOKA alt for KOMA, NORTH [KMQ]
NOKAW alt for NAGA, KHIAMNGAN [NKY]
NOKHURLI dial of TURKMEN [TCK]
NOKHURLI dial of TURKMEN [TCK]
NOKOPO [NON] lang, Papua New Guinea
NOKU alt for BATANGA [BNM]
NOKUKU [NKK] lang, Vanuatu
NOKUNNA alt for NUGUNU [NNV]

NOMAANDE [LEM] lang, Cameroon
NOMAD alt for SAMO-KUBO [SMQ]
NOMAD alt for KALAMO [KKC]
NOMADI alt for NEMADI [NED]
NOMADIC FULFULDE dial of FULFULDE, ADAMAWA [FUB]
NOMADIC FULFULDE alt for BORORRO dial of FULFULDE, KANO-KATSINA-BORORRO [FUV]
NOMADIC KUBU dial of KUBU [KVB]
NOMAI alt for DOYAYO [DOW]
NOMANE [NOF] lang, Papua New Guinea
NOMANE dial of NOMANE [NOF]
NOMATSIGUENGA [NOT] lang, Peru
NOMATSIGUENGA CAMPA alt for NOMATSIGUENGA [NOT]
NOME dial of WALI [WLX]
NOMLAKI dial of WINTU [WIT]
NOMOPO dial of SAPO [KRN]
NOMU [NOH] lang, Papua New Guinea
NON [SNF] lang, Senegal
NON dial of NON [SNF]
NON-AMISH PENNSYLVANIA GERMAN dial of GERMAN, PENNSYLVANIA [PDC]
NON-AMISH PENNSYLVANIA GERMAN dial of GERMAN, PENNSYLVANIA [PDC]
NON-PLAIN PENNSYLVANIA GERMAN alt for NON-AMISH PENNSYLVANIA GERMAN dial of GERMAN, PENNSYLVANIA [PDC]
NONAMA alt for WAUMEO [NOA]
NONE alt for NON [SNF]
NONE alt for NON dial of NON [SNF]
NONES dial of LADIN [LLD]
NONES BLOT alt for NONES dial of LADIN [LLD]
NONESH alt for NONES dial of LADIN [LLD]
NONG alt for NUNG [NUT]
NONG alt for BATEK NONG dial of BATEK [BTQ]
NONG alt for BUNONG dial of MNONG, SOUTHERN [MNN]
NONGTUNG dial of KHASI [KHI]
NONGTUNG dial of PNAR [PBV]
NONI alt for NOONE [NHU]
NONIALI alt for LISABATA-NUNIALI [LCS]
NONUKAN alt for TIDONG [TID]
NONUKAN dial of TIDONG [TID]
NOOCOONA alt for NUGUNU [NNV]
NOOHALIT dial of YUPIK, CENTRAL SIBERIAN [ESS]
NOOKOONA alt for NUGUNU [NNV]
NOOKSACK [NOK] lang, USA
NOOLI dial of SANTA CRUZ [STC]
NOOMAANTE alt for NOMAANDE [LEM]
NOON alt for NON [SNF]
NOONE [NHU] lang, Cameroon
NOONGABURRAH alt for NGIYAMBAA dial of WANGAAYBUWAN-NGIYAMBAA [WYB]
NOORI alt for NOONE [NHU]
NOOSAN alt for NUSAN dial of NG/AMANI [NMN]
NOOTKA [NOO] lang, Canada
NOOTKA dial of NOOTKA [NOO]
NOOTRE alt for BOULBA [BLY]
NOOTSACK alt for NOOKSACK [NOK]
NOP dial of KOHO [KPM]
NOPUK [NOB] lang, Indonesia, Irian Jaya
NOR alt for MAMBILA, CAMEROON [MYA]
NOR alt for MURIK [MTF]
NOR TAGBO alt for MAMBILA, NIGERIA [MZK]
NOR-MURIK LAKES alt for MURIK [MTF]

NORA alt for NORRA [NOR]
NORA dial of NORRA [NOR]
NORFOLK dial of ENGLISH [ENG]
NORFOLK ENGLISH dial of PITCAIRN-NORFOLK [PIH]
NORGOROD dial of KARELIAN [KRL]
NORIO dial of MEKONGGA [MWK]
NORMAN dial of FRENCH [FRN]
NORRA [NOR] lang, Myanmar, China
NORTENYO alt for BUGLERE [SAB]
NORTENYO alt for TERIBE [TFR]
NORTH AGAW alt for BILEN [BYN]
NORTH ALASKAN ESKIMO alt for INUIT, NORTH ALASKAN [ESI]
NORTH ALBANIAN dial of ROMANI, VLACH [RMY]
NORTH ARABIAN COLLOQUIAL ARABIC alt for ARABIC, GULF [AFB]
NORTH ARABIAN COLLOQUIAL ARABIC alt for ARABIC, NAJDI [ARS]
NORTH ARABIAN COLLOQUIAL ARABIC alt for AYIZO-GBE [AYB]
NORTH ARABIAN COLLOQUIAL ARABIC alt for ARABIC, SYRO-MESOPOTAMIAN [AYP]
NORTH ASMAT dial of ASMAT, CENTRAL [AST]
NORTH AUCKLAND dial of MAORI [MBF]
NORTH AWIN dial of AWIN [AWI]
NORTH BALASORE ORIYA dial of ORIYA [ORY]
NORTH BANGATO dial of BANGANDU [BGF]
NORTH BANTAWA dial of BANTAWA [BAP]
NORTH BAVARIAN dial of BAVARIAN [BAR]
NORTH BEAMI dial of BEAMI [BEO]
NORTH BELGIUM SIGN LANGUAGE dial of BELGIAN SIGN LANGUAGE [BVS]
NORTH BINJA dial of SONGOORA [SOD]
NORTH BOAZI dial of BOAZI [KVG]
NORTH BOBE dial of BUBE [BVB]
NORTH BORNEO MURUT alt for TAGAL dial of TAGAL MURUT [MVV]
NORTH BUNA dial of BUNA [BVN]
NORTH BUNUN dial of BUNUN [BNN]
NORTH BURMA KHAMTI dial of KHAMTI [KHT]
NORTH BURU alt for LISELA [LCL]
NORTH CENTRAL FORE dial of FORE [FOR]
NORTH CENTRAL YURI dial of KARKAR-YURI [YUJ]
NORTH CH'UNGCH'ONG alt for CH'UNGCH'ONGDO dial of KOREAN [KKN]
NORTH CHOLLADO alt for CHOLLADO dial of KOREAN [KKN]
NORTH COAST MENGEN dial of MENGEN [MEE]
NORTH COASTAL ALUNE dial of ALUNE [ALP]
NORTH DAMAR alt for DAMAR, WEST [DRN]
NORTH DEDUA dial of DEDUA [DED]
NORTH DOGRI dial of DOGRI-KANGRI [DOJ]
NORTH HAMGYONGDO alt for HAMGYONGDO dial of KOREAN [KKN]
NORTH HAUSA dial of HAUSA [HUA]
NORTH HIBERNO ENGLISH dial of ENGLISH [ENG]
NORTH HIJAZI dial of ARABIC, HIJAZI [ACW]
NORTH IBANAG dial of IBANAG [IBG]
NORTH IDOMA alt for AGATU [AGC]
NORTH ISAN dial of TAI, NORTHEASTERN [TTS]
NORTH IZON alt for KOLUKUMA dial of IJO, CENTRAL-WESTERN [IJC]
NORTH KAMAYO dial of KAMAYO [KYK]
NORTH KAMBERATARO dial of KAMBERATARO [KBV]
NORTH KANUM dial of KANUM [KCD]

NORTH KAREKARE alt for PAKARO dial of KAREKARE [KAI]
NORTH KERALA dial of MALAYALAM [MJS]
NORTH KHANA dial of KOANA [KEH]
NORTH KHOWAR dial of KHOWAR [KHW]
NORTH KITUI dial of KAMBA [KIK]
NORTH KOMBIO dial of KOMBIO [KOK]
NORTH KOMEDIA dial of ARMENIAN [ARM]
NORTH KONKAN alt for KONKANI [KNK]
NORTH KORDOFAN ARABIC dial of ARABIC, SUDANESE [APD]
NORTH KWANDU dial of MASHI [MHO]
NORTH KYONGSANGDO alt for KYONGSANGDO dial of KOREAN [KKN]
NORTH LA PAZ QUECHUA alt for QUECHUA, NORTH BOLIVIAN [QUL]
NORTH LAAMANG dial of LAMANG [HIA]
NORTH LANCASHIRE dial of ENGLISH [ENG]
NORTH LOLODA alt for LOLODA [LOL]
NORTH LOW SAXON alt for LOW SAXON dial of GERMAN, LOW [GEP]
NORTH MAEWO alt for MARINO [MRB]
NORTH MAKAA alt for BYEP [MKK]
NORTH MALO alt for AVUNATARI dial of MALO [MLA]
NORTH MBUNDU alt for MBUNDU, LOANDA [MLO]
NORTH MEKEO dial of MEKEO [MEK]
NORTH MIANMIN alt for SUGANGA [SUG]
NORTH MIGABAC dial of MIGABAC [MPP]
NORTH MODOLE dial of MODOLE [MQO]
NORTH MOEJOE alt for KATI, NORTHERN [KTI]
NORTH MUYU alt for KATI, NORTHERN [KTI]
NORTH NAJDI dial of ARABIC, NAJDI [ARS]
NORTH NAJDI dial of ARABIC, NAJDI [ARS]
NORTH NAJDI dial of ARABIC, NAJDI [ARS]
NORTH NAJDI dial of ARABIC, NAJDI [ARS]
NORTH NAKAMA dial of NAKAMA [NIB]
NORTH NGALIK alt for YALI, NINIA [NLK]
NORTH NORTHERN PAIUTE dial of PAIUTE, NORTHERN [PAO]
NORTH NUK dial of NUK [NOC]
NORTH NYALI alt for NYALI-KILO dial of NYALI [NLJ]
NORTH OLO alt for PAYI dial of OLO [ONG]
NORTH P'YONG'ANDO alt for P'YONG'ANDO dial of KOREAN [KKN]
NORTH PAAMA dial of PAAMA [PMA]
NORTH PERMYAK dial of KOMI-PERMYAK [KOI]
NORTH PUEBLA AZTEC alt for NAHUATL, NORTH PUEBLA [NCJ]
NORTH QATARI ARABIC dial of ARABIC, GULF [AFB]
NORTH QUCHANI dial of KHORASANI TURKISH [KMZ]
NORTH RAGA alt for HANO [LML]
NORTH RUSSIAN dial of RUSSIAN [RUS]
NORTH RUSSIAN ROMANI dial of ROMANI, BALTIC [ROM]
NORTH SAISET alt for TAAI dial of SAISIYAT [SAI]
NORTH SAKHALIN dial of GILYAK [NIV]
NORTH SASAK alt for KUTO-KUTE dial of SASAK [SAS]
NORTH SELEPET dial of SELEPET [SEL]
NORTH SENA alt for SENA-CARE dial of SENA [SEH]
NORTH SIBERUT dial of MENTAWAI [MWV]
NORTH SMALL NAMBAS dial of MAE [MME]

NORTH SYRIAN dial of ARABIC, LEVANTINE [APC]
NORTH TABASARAN dial of TABASSARAN [TAB]
NORTH TABUKANG dial of SANGIR [SAN]
NORTH THARAKA alt for GATUE dial of THARAKA [THA]
NORTH TIMBE dial of TIMBE [TIM]
NORTH TUKEN alt for TUGEN, NORTH [TUY]
NORTH TUVALUAN dial of TUVALUAN [ELL]
NORTH UDMURT dial of UDMURT [UDM]
NORTH VEPS alt for PRIONEZH dial of VEPS [VEP]
NORTH WAIBUK dial of HARUAI [TMD]
NORTH WATUT alt for UNANK [UNA]
NORTH WILTSHIRE dial of ENGLISH [ENG]
NORTH YAMDENA dial of YAMDENA [JMD]
NORTH YAWA dial of YAWA [YVA]
NORTH YEI dial of YEI [JEI]
NORTH YORKSHIRE dial of ENGLISH [ENG]
NORTHEAST AMBAE alt for AMBAE, EAST [OMB]
NORTHEAST AMBON alt for TULEHU [TLU]
NORTHEAST AOBA alt for AMBAE, EAST [OMB]
NORTHEAST AWA dial of AWA [AWB]
NORTHEAST BARITO alt for LAWANGAN [LBX]
NORTHEAST BELORUSSIAN dial of BELORUSSIAN [RUW]
NORTHEAST BOHEMIAN dial of CZECH [CZC]
NORTHEAST DOBEL dial of DOBEL [KVO]
NORTHEAST DUGURI dial of DUGURI [DBM]
NORTHEAST FLORIDA COAST dial of SEA ISLANDS CREOLE ENGLISH [GUL]
NORTHEAST HUNGARIAN dial of HUNGARIAN [HNG]
NORTHEAST IZERE dial of IZERE [FIZ]
NORTHEAST KARAKALPAK dial of KARAKALPAK [KAC]
NORTHEAST LAMPUNG alt for MENGGALA dial of ABUNG [ABL]
NORTHEAST LUBA alt for SONGE [SOP]
NORTHEAST LUWU dial of TAE' [ROB]
NORTHEAST MAIDU dial of MAIDU [MAI]
NORTHEAST QUCHANI alt for NORTH QUCHANI dial of KHORASANI TURKISH [KMZ]
NORTHEAST SAHAPTIN alt for WALLA WALLA [WAA]
NORTHEAST SASAK alt for NGETO-NGETE dial of SASAK [SAS]
NORTHEAST VANUA LEVU dial of FIJIAN [FJI]
NORTHEAST VITI LEVU dial of FIJIAN [FJI]
NORTHEAST ZACATEPEC MIXE dial of MIXE, QUETZALTEPEC [MZC]
NORTHEASTERN GOE alt for KIEMBARA dial of SAMO [SBD]
NORTHEASTERN KARAKALPAK dial of KARAKALPAK [KAC]
NORTHEASTERN KAZAKH dial of KAZAKH [KAZ]
NORTHEASTERN MAIRASI dial of MAIRASI [FRY]
NORTHEASTERN OTOMÍ alt for OTOMÍ, TEXCATEPEC [OTX]
NORTHEASTERN PASHTO alt for PASHTO, EASTERN [PBU]
NORTHEASTERN POMO dial of POMO [POO]
NORTHEASTERN SARDINIAN alt for SARDINIAN, GALLURESE [SDN]
NORTHEASTERN TUVIN dial of TUVIN [TUN]
NORTHERN AFAR dial of AFAR [AFR]
NORTHERN AKHVAKH dial of AKHVAKH [AKV]
NORTHERN AKOKO alt for AKOKO, NORTH [AKK]

NORTHERN AMAMI-OSIMA alt for AMAMI-OSHIMA, NORTHERN [RYN]

NORTHERN AMIS dial of AMIS [ALV]

NORTHERN ARAMIC dial of JUDEO-ARAMAIC [TRG]

NORTHERN AREQUIPA dial of QUECHUA, COTAHUASI [QAR]

NORTHERN ASSYRIAN dial of ASSYRIAN [AII]

NORTHERN BABOLE dial of BABOLE [BVX]

NORTHERN BAKOSSI dial of AKOOSE [BSS]

NORTHERN BALONG alt for BAKONI dial of KENYANG [KEN]

NORTHERN BARASANO alt for WAIMAHA [BAO]

NORTHERN BÉTÉ alt for BÉTÉ, DALOA [BEV]

NORTHERN BIRIFOR alt for BIRIFOR, MALBA [BFO]

NORTHERN BOLON alt for BLACK BOLON dial of BOLON [BOF]

NORTHERN BOMITABA dial of BOMITABA [ZMX]

NORTHERN BULLOM alt for BULLOM SO [BUY]

NORTHERN CAGAYAN NEGRITO alt for ATTA, PAMPLONA [ATT]

NORTHERN CAROLINIAN dial of CAROLINIAN [CAL]

NORTHERN CARRIER alt for BABINE [BCR]

NORTHERN CATALÁN alt for CATALAN-ROUSILLONESE dial of CATALAN [CLN]

NORTHERN CHATINO alt for CHATINO, ZENZONTEPEC [CZE]

NORTHERN CHINESE alt for CHINESE, MANDARIN [CHN]

NORTHERN CHUMBURUNG dial of CHUMBURUNG [NCU]

NORTHERN CORSICAN dial of CORSICAN [COI]

NORTHERN CRIMEAN dial of CRIMEAN TURKISH [CRH]

NORTHERN DAGARI alt for DAGAARI, NORTHERN [DGI]

NORTHERN DONG dial of DONG [KMC]

NORTHERN DOS DE MAYO dial of QUECHUA, HUÁNUCO, HUAMALÍES [QEJ]

NORTHERN ESTONIAN alt for TALLINN dial of ESTONIAN [EST]

NORTHERN FUNGOM alt for FUNGOM [FUG]

NORTHERN GABRI alt for TOBANGA [TNG]

NORTHERN GOE alt for LOUTA dial of SAMO [SBD]

NORTHERN GOURMANCHEMA dial of GOURMANCHÉMA [GUX]

NORTHERN GUNU dial of NUGUNU [YAS]

NORTHERN GURUNG alt for MANANGBA [NMM]

NORTHERN HAIDA alt for MASSET dial of HAIDA [HAI]

NORTHERN KALASHA dial of KALASHA [KLS]

NORTHERN KALINGA alt for KALINGA, LIMOS [KMK]

NORTHERN KARELIAN dial of KARELIAN [KRL]

NORTHERN KHAMS dial of KHAM [KHG]

NORTHERN KHANTI dial of KHANTY [KCA]

NORTHERN KIRGIZ dial of KIRGHIZ [KDO]

NORTHERN KONO dial of KONO [KNO]

NORTHERN KORONDOUGOU dial of BOZO, SOROGAMA [BZE]

NORTHERN KPELE alt for KPELLE, GUINEA [GKP]

NORTHERN KRAHN alt for KRAHN, WESTERN [KRW]

NORTHERN KURDISH alt for KURMANJI [KUR]

NORTHERN KUTAI dial of MALAY, TENGGARONG KUTAI [VKT]

NORTHERN LAHU alt for NA dial of LAHU [LAH]

NORTHERN LAPP alt for SAAMI, NORTHERN [LPR]

NORTHERN LAPPISH alt for SAAMI, NORTHERN [LPR]

"NORTHERN LAPPISH" alt for SAAMI, NORTHERN [LPR]

NORTHERN LAWA alt for LAWA, EASTERN [LWL]

NORTHERN LENGUA dial of LENGUA [LEG]

NORTHERN LIMBA dial of LIMBA, EAST [LMA]

NORTHERN LOGO alt for OGAMBI dial of LOGO [LOG]

NORTHERN LOGUDORESE dial of SARDINIAN, LOGUDORESE [SRD]

"NORTHERN LOLO" alt for YI, SICHUAN [III]

NORTHERN LUBA alt for LUNA [LUJ]

NORTHERN LUNDA alt for RUUND [RND]

NORTHERN LUSHOOTSEED dial of LUSHOOTSEED [LUT]

NORTHERN LYELE dial of LYÉLÉ [LEE]

NORTHERN MACEDONIAN dial of MACEDONIAN [MKJ]

NORTHERN MAGAHI dial of MAGAHI [MQM]

NORTHERN MAMASA dial of MAMASA [MQJ]

NORTHERN MARWARI dial of MARWARI [MKD]

NORTHERN MASALIT dial of MASALIT [MSA]

NORTHERN MBENE alt for BASAA [BAA]

NORTHERN MBULA alt for KAIMANGA dial of MBULA [MNA]

NORTHERN MIN alt for CHINESE, MIN PEI [MNP]

NORTHERN MIXE alt for MIXE, TOTONTEPEC [MTO]

NORTHERN MON alt for PEGU dial of MON [MNW]

NORTHERN MONGOLIAN alt for BURIAT, MONGOLIA [BXM]

NORTHERN MONGOLIAN alt for BURIAT, CHINA [BXU]

NORTHERN MONGOLIAN alt for BURIAT, RUSSIA [MNB]

NORTHERN MOTILÓN alt for YUKPA [YUP]

NORTHERN MUJU alt for KATI, NORTHERN [KTI]

NORTHERN MUNA alt for STANDARD MUNA dial of MUNA [MYN]

NORTHERN MUNJI dial of MUNJI [MNJ]

NORTHERN NANDE alt for NANDI [NNB]

NORTHERN NDEBELE alt for NDEBELE [NDF]

NORTHERN NINAM dial of NINAM [SHB]

NORTHERN NINAM dial of NINAM [SHB]

NORTHERN NOCHIXTLÁN MIXTECO alt for MIXTECO, SANTIAGO APOALA [MIP]

NORTHERN OGAMBI dial of AVOKAYA [AVU]

NORTHERN OJIBWE alt for OJIBWA, NORTHERN [OJB]

NORTHERN OROK alt for VAL-NOGLIKI dial of OROK [OAA]

NORTHERN PA'O dial of KAREN, PA'O [BLK]

NORTHERN PASTAZA QUICHUA alt for QUICHUA, PASTAZA, NORTHERN [QLB]

NORTHERN PHALURA dial of PHALURA [PHL]

NORTHERN POMO dial of POMO [POO]

NORTHERN PONDORI dial of BOZO, SOROGAMA [BZE]

NORTHERN PUGET SOUND SALISH alt for NORTHERN LUSHOOTSEED dial of LUSHOOTSEED [LUT]

NORTHERN QIANG dial of QIANG [CNG]

NORTHERN QUICHÉ alt for QUICHE, CUNÉN [CUN]

NORTHERN SAGARA alt for KAGULU [KKI]

NORTHERN SAKAI alt for TEMIAR [TMH]

NORTHERN SAMA alt for SAMA, BALANGINGI [SSE]

NORTHERN SAMAR dial of WARAY-WARAY [WRY]
NORTHERN SAMO alt for SAMO [SBD]
NORTHERN SANGTAM alt for PIRR dial of NAGA, SANGTAM [NSA]
NORTHERN SHAN alt for TAI MAO dial of SHAN [SJN]
NORTHERN SHILHA alt for TARIFIT [RIF]
NORTHERN SHONA alt for KOREKORE dial of SHONA [SHD]
NORTHERN SHONA alt for KOREKORE dial of SHONA [SHD]
NORTHERN SHONA alt for KOREKORE dial of SHONA [SHD]
NORTHERN SINAMA alt for SAMA, BALANGINGI [SSE]
NORTHERN SOMALI dial of SOMALI [SOM]
NORTHERN SONGAI dial of SONGAI [SON]
NORTHERN SORSOGON alt for SORSOGON, MASBATE [BKS]
NORTHERN STANDARD BHOJPURI dial of BHOJPURI [BHJ]
NORTHERN TAIRORA dial of TAIRORA [TBG]
NORTHERN TEHUELCHE alt for PUELCHE [PUE]
NORTHERN TETUN dial of TETUN [TTM]
NORTHERN THAI alt for TAI, NORTHERN [NOD]
NORTHERN TOBA dial of TOBA [TOB]
NORTHERN TURKANA dial of TURKANA [TUV]
NORTHERN TUTCHONE dial of TUTCHONE [TUT]
NORTHERN VIETNAMESE dial of VIETNAMESE [VIE]
NORTHERN VOGUL dial of MANSI [MNS]
NORTHERN YI alt for YI, SICHUAN [III]
NORTHERN YI dial of YI, SICHUAN [III]
NORTHERN YUKAGIR alt for YUKAGHIR, NORTHERN [YKG]
NORTHERN ZAZA alt for KIRMANJKI [QKV]
NORTHUMBERLAND dial of ENGLISH [ENG]
NORTHWEST ALASKA INUPIAT ESKIMO alt for INUIT, NORTHWEST ALASKA INUPIAT [ESK]
NORTHWEST ARABIAN COLLOQUIAL ARABIC alt for ARABIC, LEVANTINE [APC]
NORTHWEST COLLOQUIAL ARABIAN ARABIC alt for ARABIC, LEVANTINE [APC]
NORTHWEST HUNGARIAN dial of HUNGARIAN [HNG]
NORTHWEST IZERE dial of IZERE [FIZ]
NORTHWEST IZON alt for MEIN dial of IJO, CENTRAL-WESTERN [IJC]
NORTHWEST LAMPUNG alt for KOTA BUMI dial of ABUNG [ABL]
NORTHWEST MAIDU dial of MAIDU [MAI]
NORTHWEST MARIND alt for MARIND, BIAN [BPV]
NORTHWEST MEKEO dial of MEKEO [MEK]
NORTHWEST QUCHANI alt for WEST QUCHANI dial of KHORASANI TURKISH [KMZ]
NORTHWEST SELA dial of SELA [SLS]
NORTHWEST TARANGAN dial of TARANGAN, WEST [TXN]
NORTHWEST UKRAINIAN dial of UKRAINIAN [UKR]
NORTHWESTERN CATALAN dial of CATALAN [CLN]
NORTHWESTERN KARAIM dial of KARAIM [KDR]
NORTHWESTERN MANINKA alt for MALINKE [MLQ]
NORTHWESTERN ORIYA dial of ORIYA [ORY]
NORTHWESTERN SARDINIAN alt for SARDINIAN, SASSARESE [SDC]
NORTHWESTERN TLAXIACO MIXTECO alt for MIXTECO, NORTHERN TLAXIACO [MOS]

NORTHWESTERN YAUTEPEC ZAPOTECO alt for ZAPOTECO, SAN BARTOLO YAUTEPEC [ZPB]
NORWEGIAN alt for NORWEGIAN, BOKMAL [NRR]
NORWEGIAN LAPP alt for SAAMI, NORTHERN [LPR]
"NORWEGIAN LAPP" alt for SAAMI, NORTHERN [LPR]
NORWEGIAN SIGN LANGUAGE [NSL] lang, Norway
NORWEGIAN, BOKMAL [NRR] lang, Norway, USA
NORWEGIAN, NYNORSK [NRN] lang, Norway
NOSU alt for YI, YUNNAN [NOS]
NOTOZER dial of SAAMI, SKOLT [LPK]
NOTRE alt for BOULBA [BLY]
NOTSI [NCF] lang, Papua New Guinea
NOTU alt for EWAGE-NOTU [NOU]
NOUMOU [NOW] lang, Burkina Faso
NOUMOUNDARA-KOUMANDARA dial of TIÉFO [TIQ]
NOUNI alt for NUNI [NNW]
NOUNOUMA alt for NUNI [NNW]
NOUTZU alt for NUSU [NUF]
NOVA SCOTIAN SIGN LANGUAGE [NSR] lang, Canada
NOVARESE LOMBARD dial of LOMBARD [LMO]
NOVOUYGUR alt for UYGHUR [UIG]
NOWAI dial of TANNA, SOUTHWEST [NWI]
NOWGONG alt for NAGA, AO [NJO]
NOY [NOY] lang, Chad
NOZA alt for NORRA [NOR]
NPONGUÉ alt for MPONGWE dial of MYENE [MYE]
NPONGWE alt for MPONGWE dial of MYENE [MYE]
NREBELE alt for NDEBELE [NEL]
NRUANGHMEI alt for NAGA, RONGMEI [NBU]
NSA dial of IGBO [IGR]
NSADOP dial of BOKYI [BKY]
NSARE alt for NZARE dial of MBEMBE, TIGON [NZA]
NSARI [ASJ] lang, Cameroon
NSAW alt for LAMNSO' [NSO]
NSEI alt for KENSWEI NSEI [NDB]
NSELE dial of NDE-NSELE-NTA [NDD]
NSENGA [NSE] lang, Zambia, Mozambique, Zimbabwe
NSENGA alt for NSENGA [NSE]
NSENGA dial of NSENGA [NSE]
NSENGA dial of NYANJA [NYJ]
NSHO' alt for LAMNSO' [NSO]
NSIHAA dial of SISAALA, TUMULUNG [SIL]
NSINDAK alt for SIMBA [SBW]
NSO alt for LAMNSO' [NSO]
NSO' alt for LAMNSO' [NSO]
NSONGO [NSX] lang, Angola
NSONGWA alt for SONGWA dial of NGEMBA [NGE]
NSOSE alt for BASSOSSI [BSI]
NSUNGALI alt for LIMBUM [LIM]
NSUNGLI alt for LIMBUM [LIM]
NSUNGNI alt for LIMBUM [LIM]
NSWASE alt for BASSOSSI [BSI]
NSWOSE alt for BASSOSSI [BSI]
NTA dial of NDE-NSELE-NTA [NDD]
NTAAPUM dial of NTCHAM [BUD]
NTAU alt for BOBOT [BTY]
NTCHAM [BUD] lang, Togo, Ghana
NTEM dial of YAMBA [YAM]
NTENYI alt for NAGA, NTENYI [NNL]
NTHALI dial of TUMBUKA [TUW]
NTHENYI alt for NAGA, NTENYI [NNL]
NTII dial of FE'FE' [FMP]
NTLAKAPMUK alt for THOMPSON [THP]

NTOGAPID alt for ITOGAPÚK [ITG]
NTOGAPIG alt for ITOGAPÚK [ITG]
NTOLEH dial of LIGBI [LIG]
NTOMBA [NTO] lang, Zaïre
NTOMBA dial of NTOMBA [NTO]
NTOMBA-BIKORO dial of MONGO-NKUNDU [MOM]
NTOMBA-BOLIA alt for NTOMBA [NTO]
NTOMBA-INONGO dial of MONGO-NKUNDU [MOM]
NTONG dial of YAMBA [YAM]
NTOUMOU dial of FANG [FNG]
NTRIBOU alt for DELO [NTR]
NTRIBU alt for DELO [NTR]
NTRUBO alt for DELO [NTR]
NTSAAYI alt for TSAAYI dial of TEKE, WESTERN
    [TEZ]
NTSHANTI alt for NCANE [NCR]
NTSIAM dial of MFINU [ZMF]
NTSWAR dial of MFINU [ZMF]
NTUGI dial of THARAKA [THA]
NTUM dial of FANG [FNG]
NTUM dial of FANG [FNG]
NTUMBA alt for NTOMBA [NTO]
NTUMU alt for NTOUMOU dial of FANG [FNG]
NTUMU alt for NTUM dial of FANG [FNG]
NU alt for NUNG [NUN]
NU BACA alt for NUBACA [BAF]
NU GUNU alt for NUGUNU [YAS]
NU MHOU alt for PUNU [PNU]
NU-SAN alt for NUSAN dial of NG/AMANI [NMN]
NU//EN alt for NG/U/EN dial of NG/AMANI [NMN]
NU//EN alt for NG/U//EN dial of NG/AMANI [NMN]
NUA alt for YUAGA [NUA]
NUADHU alt for COMO KARIM [CFG]
NUAKATA alt for 'AUHELAWA [KUD]
NUANGEYA alt for NYANG'I [NYP]
NUAULU alt for NUAULU, NORTH [NNI]
NUAULU alt for NUAULU, SOUTH [NXL]
NUAULU, NORTH [NNI] lang, Indonesia, Maluku
NUAULU, SOUTH [NXL] lang, Indonesia, Maluku
NUB alt for KAETI [KZH]
NUBA alt for KOALIB [KIB]
NUBACA [BAF] lang, Cameroon
NUBI [KCN] lang, Kenya, Uganda, Uganda
NUBI alt for NUBI [KCN]
NUBIA dial of AWAR [AYA]
NUBRA dial of LADAKHI [LBJ]
NUBRI alt for KUTANG BHOTIA [KTE]
NUCHEN alt for JURCHEN [JUC]
NUCLEAR WESTERN FIJIAN dial of FIJIAN,
    WESTERN [WYY]
NUCUM alt for BOIKIN [BZF]
NUDOO dial of VUTE [VUT]
NUER [NUS] lang, Sudan, Ethiopia
NUFAWA alt for NUPE [NUP]
NUFOOR alt for BIAK [BHW]
NUGANE dial of VUTE [VUT]
NUGBO dial of GODIÉ [GOD]
NUGUEI dial of AKHA [AKA]
NUGUNA alt for NUGUNU [NNV]
NUGUNU [NNV] lang, Australia
NUGUNU [YAS] lang, Cameroon
NUGUOR alt for NUKUORO [NKR]
NUGURIA [NUR] lang, Papua New Guinea
NUJUM dial of VUTE [VUT]
NUK [NOC] lang, Papua New Guinea
NUKA-DORA [NUK] lang, India

NUKANA alt for NUGUNU [NNV]
NUKAPU dial of PILENI [PIV]
NUKHA dial of AZERBAIJANI, NORTH [AZE]
NUKORO alt for NUKUORO [NKR]
NUKU alt for MEHEK [NUX]
NUKU HIVA dial of MARQUESAN, NORTH [MRQ]
NUKUFETAU alt for SOUTH TUVALUAN dial of
    TUVALUAN [ELL]
NUKUINI [NUC] lang, Brazil
NUKULAILA alt for SOUTH TUVALUAN dial of
    TUVALUAN [ELL]
NUKUMA dial of KWOMA [KMO]
NUKUMANU [NUQ] lang, Papua New Guinea
NUKUNA alt for NUGUNU [NNV]
NUKUNNU alt for NUGUNU [NNV]
NUKUNU alt for NUGUNU [NNV]
NUKUNUKUBARA alt for WAKAWAKA [WKW]
NUKUORO [NKR] lang, Micronesia
NUKURIA alt for NUGURIA [NUR]
NULU dial of RUNGUS [DRG]
NUMANA dial of NUMANA-NUNKU-GWANTU-
    NUMBU [NBR]
NUMANA-NUNKU-GWANTU-NUMBU [NBR] lang,
    Nigeria
NUMAND alt for NOMAANDE [LEM]
NUMANGAN alt for NUMANGGANG [NOP]
NUMANGANG alt for NUMANGGANG [NOP]
NUMANGGANG [NOP] lang, Papua New Guinea
NUMAO alt for PUNU [PNU]
NUMBA dial of MANAGALASI [MCQ]
NUMBAMI [SIJ] lang, Papua New Guinea
NUMBIAÍ [NUH] lang, Brazil
NUMBU dial of NUMANA-NUNKU-GWANTU-NUMBU
    [NBR]
NUME [TGS] lang, Vanuatu
NUMEE [KDK] lang, New Caledonia
NUMEE dial of NUMEE [KDK]
ÑUMI MIXTECO alt for MIXTECO, NORTHERN
    TLAXIACO [MOS]
NUMUKAN alt for NOUMOU [NOW]
NUMURANA alt for OMURANO [OMU]
NUNA alt for NUNI [NNW]
NUNA alt for KOORETE [KQY]
NUNDORO alt for NDOOLA [NDR]
NUNE alt for NUNI [NNW]
NUNG [NUN] lang, China, Myanmar, Myanmar
NUNG [NUT] lang, Viet Nam, China, Laos
NUNG alt for RAWANG [RAW]
NUNG alt for NUNG [NUN]
NUNG alt for CHINESE, YUE [YUH]
NUNG dial of NUNG [NUN]
NÙNG AN dial of NUNG [NUT]
NÙNG CHÁO dial of NUNG [NUT]
NÙNG LÒI dial of NUNG [NUT]
NUNG RAWANG alt for RAWANG [RAW]
NUNGALI [NUG] lang, Australia
NUNGGUBUJU alt for NUNGGUBUYU [NUY]
NUNGGUBUYU [NUY] lang, Australia
NUNGU [RIN] lang, Nigeria
NUNGUDA alt for LONGUDA [LNU]
NUNGURA alt for LONGUDA [LNU]
NUNGURABA alt for LONGUDA [LNU]
NUNI [NNW] lang, Burkina Faso
NUNIALI alt for LISABATA-NUNIALI [LCS]
NUNIALI dial of LISABATA-NUNIALI [LCS]
NUNIYA dial of MAITHILI, DEHATI [MTR]

NUNKU dial of NUMANA-NUNKU-GWANTU-NUMBU [NBR]
NUNLIGRANSKIJ dial of CHUKOT [CKT]
NUNPA alt for LEPCHA [LEP]
NUNU alt for PUNU [PNU]
NUNU dial of NGIRI [NGR]
NUNU' dial of SARUDU [SDU]
NUNUKAN alt for NONUKAN dial of TIDONG [TID]
NUNUMA alt for NUNI [NNW]
NUNUMA dial of KASEM [KAS]
NUNZO alt for NINZAM [NIN]
NUORESE dial of SARDINIAN, LOGUDORESE [SRD]
NUPANI dial of PILENI [PIV]
NUPE [NUP] lang, Nigeria
NUPE CENTRAL dial of NUPE [NUP]
NUPE TAKO dial of NUPE [NUP]
NUPECI alt for NUPE [NUP]
NUPECIDJI alt for NUPE [NUP]
NUPECIZI alt for NUPE CENTRAL dial of NUPE [NUP]
NUPENCHI alt for NUPE [NUP]
NUPENCIZI alt for NUPE [NUP]
NUPENCIZI alt for NUPE CENTRAL dial of NUPE [NUP]
NUQUAY alt for NUGUEI dial of AKHA [AKA]
NUQUINI alt for NUKUINI [NUC]
NURA dial of DAGAARI, NORTHERN [DGI]
NURALDA alt for ADYNYAMATHANHA [ADT]
NURISTANI alt for KATI [BSH]
NURO alt for ANUAK [ANU]
NURRA alt for NORRA [NOR]
NURU alt for OGEA [ERI]
NURUMA alt for NUNI [NNW]
NUSA LAUT [NUL] lang, Indonesia, Maluku
NUSA PENIDA dial of BALI [BZC]
NUSALAUT alt for NUSA LAUT [NUL]
NUSAN dial of NG/AMANI [NMN]
NUSARI alt for WORIASI [WBB]
NUSU [NUF] lang, China
NUTKA alt for NOOTKA [NOO]
NUTZU alt for NUSU [NUF]
NUXAÁ MIXTEC alt for MIXTECO, SOUTHEASTERN NOCHIXTLÁN [MXY]
NUXALK alt for BELLA COOLA [BEL]
NUYOO MIXTECO alt for MIXTECO, SOUTHWESTERN TLAXIACO [MEH]
NUZHEN alt for JURCHEN [JUC]
NVHAL dial of TANNA, SOUTHWEST [NWI]
NWA alt for WAN [WAN]
NWE alt for NGWE [NWE]
NWESI dial of BEMBA [BEM]
NYA CERIYA dial of LONGUDA [LNU]
NYA DELE dial of LONGUDA [LNU]
NYA GUYUWA dial of LONGUDA [LNU]
NYA GWANDA dial of LONGUDA [LNU]
NYA KOPO alt for MUMUYE [MUL]
NYA TARIYA dial of LONGUDA [LNU]
NYAAJA dial of MUMUYE [MUL]
NYAANA alt for TOMA dial of SAMO [SBD]
NYAANGA dial of KUNYI [KNF]
NYABADAN dial of MABA [MDE]
NYABASI dial of KURIA [KUJ]
NYABEA alt for TIBEA [NGY]
NYABO dial of GREBO, JABO [GRJ]
NYABUNGU alt for TEMBO [TBT]
NYABWA [NIA] lang, Côte d'Ivoire
NYABWA dial of NYABWA [NIA]

NYABWA-NYÉDÉBWA alt for NYABWA [NIA]
NYADA alt for NYINDROU [LID]
NYADU [NXJ] lang, Indonesia, Kalimantan
NYAG DII alt for DII [DUR]
NYAGALI alt for NJAKALI dial of DYAABUGAY [DYY]
NYAGO dial of GODIÉ [GOD]
NYAH HEUNY alt for NYAHEUN [NEV]
NYAH KUR alt for NYAHKUR [CBN]
NYAHEUN [NEV] lang, Laos
NYAHKUR [CBN] lang, Thailand
NYAHÖN alt for NYAHEUN [NEV]
NYAI dial of KALANGA [KCK]
NYAKALI alt for NJAKALI dial of DYAABUGAY [DYY]
NYAKISISA dial of HAYA [HAY]
NYAKUR alt for NYAHKUR [CBN]
NYAKUSA alt for NYAKYUSA-NGONDE [NYY]
NYAKWAI dial of ACHOLI [ACO]
NYAKYUSA dial of NYAKYUSA-NGONDE [NYY]
NYAKYUSA-NGONDE [NYY] lang, Tanzania, Malawi
NYALA dial of DAJU, DAR FUR [DAJ]
NYALA-LAGOWA alt for DAJU, DAR FUR [DAJ]
NYÂLAYU [YLY] lang, New Caledonia
NYALI [NLJ] lang, Zaïre
NYALI-KILO dial of NYALI [NLJ]
NYALI-TCHABI dial of NYALI [NLJ]
NYAM-NYAM DU MAYO-KEBI alt for NIMBARI [NMR]
NYAMAL [NLY] lang, Australia
NYAMASA dial of BAMBARA [BRA]
NYAMATOM alt for NYANGATOM dial of TOPOSA [TOQ]
NYAMBARA alt for NYANGBARA dial of BARI [BFA]
NYAMBE dial of TONGA [TOH]
NYAMBO [NYM] lang, Tanzania
NYAMEL alt for NYAMAL [NLY]
NYAMKAT alt for NESANG [NES]
NYAMNYAM alt for SUGA [SGI]
NYAMNYAM alt for NIMBARI [NMR]
NYAMSKAD alt for NESANG [NES]
NYAMTAM dial of BASAA [BAA]
NYAMUKA dial of MANYIKA [MXC]
NYAMUSA dial of NYAMUSA-MOLO [NYO]
NYAMUSA-MOLO [NYO] lang, Sudan
NYAMWANGA alt for MWANGA [MWN]
NYAMWESI alt for NYAMWEZI [NYZ]
NYAMWEZI [NYZ] lang, Tanzania
NYAMZAX alt for LANGAS dial of POLCI [POL]
NYANDANG alt for YENDANG [YEN]
NYANDUNG dial of KWANJA [KNP]
NYANEKA [NYK] lang, Angola
NYANG alt for NHANG [NHA]
NYANG alt for KENYANG [KEN]
NYANG alt for DENYA [ANV]
NYANG alt for TUIC dial of DINKA, SOUTHWESTERN [DIK]
NYANG'ORI alt for TERIK dial of KALENJIN [KLN]
NYANGA [NYA] lang, Zaïre
NYANGA-LI [NYC] lang, Zaïre
NYANGALA alt for EKISONGOORA dial of NANDI [NNB]
NYANGANYATJARA alt for NGAANYATJARRA [NTJ]
NYANGATOM dial of TOPOSA [TOQ]
NYANGATOM dial of TOPOSA [TOQ]

NZAKARA [NZK] lang, Central African Republic,
Zaïre, Zaïre
NZAKARA alt for NZAKARA [NZK]
NZAKARA dial of ZANDE [ZAN]
NZAKMBAY [NZY] lang, Cameroon, Chad
NZAKMBAY alt for NZAKMBAY [NZY]
NZAMBA dial of KONGO [KON]
NZANGI alt for NZANYI [NJA]
NZANGYIM alt for NZANYI [NJA]
NZANYI [NJA] lang, Nigeria, Cameroon
NZARE dial of MBEMBE, TIGON [NZA]
NZARE alt for NAMA dial of MBEMBE, TIGON [NZA]
NZARI dial of AKA [AXK]
NZEBI alt for NJEBI [NZB]
NZEMA [NZE] lang, Ghana, Côte d'Ivoire
NZIKINI alt for KATEGHE dial of TEKE, NORTHERN
[TEG]
NZIKINI alt for NJININGI dial of TEKE, NORTHERN
[TEG]
NZIKU alt for NJINJU dial of TEKE, CENTRAL [TEC]
NZIMA alt for NZEMA [NZE]
NZIME alt for KOOZIME [NJE]
NZIME dial of KOOZIME [NJE]
NZINZIHU alt for NJINJU dial of TEKE, CENTRAL
[TEC]
NZONG alt for NAGA, RENGMA [NRE]
NZONYU alt for NAGA, RENGMA [NRE]
O dial of KUY [KDT]
O DU [TYH] lang, Viet Nam
O'ODHAM alt for PAPAGO-PIMA [PAP]
OA alt for TATUYO [TAV]
OAD alt for OD [ODK]
OAS dial of BICOLANO, ALBAY [BHK]
OASIS BERBER alt for SIWA [SIZ]
OAYANA alt for WAYANA [WAY]
OBA alt for AMBAE, EAST [OMB]
OBA-MIWAMON dial of YAQAY [JAQ]
OBAMBA alt for MBAMA [MBM]
OBANG alt for EJAGHAM [ETU]
OBANG dial of BEFANG [BBY]
OBANLIKU [BZY] lang, Nigeria
OBE alt for UTUGWANG [AFE]
OBELEBHA alt for OBILEBHA dial of LOGO [LOG]
OBERLAND dial of RHETO-ROMANCE [RHE]
OBERWART dial of HUNGARIAN [HNG]
OBGWO alt for NINGGERUM [NXR]
OBI alt for ANGOYA [MIW]
OBI alt for VUKUTU dial of LESE [LES]
OBIAN dial of SAMA, SOUTHERN [SIT]
OBIAN alt for UBIAN dial of SAMA, SOUTHERN [SIT]
OBILEBHA alt for OBILEBHA dial of LOGO [LOG]
OBILEBHA dial of LOGO [LOG]
OBINI alt for ABINI dial of AGWAGWUNE [YAY]
OBIOPO-MGBU-TOLU dial of IKWERE [IKW]
OBIYE alt for MVUBA [MXH]
OBLO [OBL] lang, Cameroon
OBO BAGOBO alt for MANOBO, OBO [OBO]
OBOGOLO alt for OGBOGOLO [OGG]
OBOGWITAI [AFZ] lang, Indonesia, Irian Jaya
OBOLO [ANN] lang, Nigeria
OBONYA alt for DENYA [ANV]
OBOSO dial of UTUGWANG [AFE]
OBULOM [OBU] lang, Nigeria
OBURA dial of TAIRORA [TBG]
OBWALD dial of SCHWYZERDÜTSCH [GSW]
OCAINA [OCA] lang, Peru, Colombia

OCCITAN alt for LANGUEDOCIEN [LNC]
OCCITANI alt for LANGUEDOCIEN [LNC]
OCEBE alt for ICEVE-MACI [BEC]
OCEVE alt for ICEVE-MACI [BEC]
OCHEBE alt for ICEVE-MACI [BEC]
OCHEKWU alt for AGATU [AGC]
OCHEVE alt for ICEVE-MACI [BEC]
OCHIHERERO alt for HERERO [HER]
OCHIKWANYAMA alt for KWANYAMA [KUY]
OCHINDONGA alt for NDONGA [NDG]
OCOTEPEC dial of ZOQUE, COPAINALÁ [ZOC]
OCOTLÁN ZAPOTEC alt for ZAPOTECO, WESTERN
OCOTLÁN [ZAC]
OCOZINGO dial of TZELTAL, BACHAJÓN [TZB]
OCOZOCOAUTLA dial of TZOTZIL, CHAMULA [TZC]
OCUILTECO alt for MATLATZINCA, ATZINGO [OCU]
OD [ODK] lang, Pakistan
ODASA alt for AIMARA dial of KUNAMA [KUM]
ODAWA alt for OTTAWA dial of OJIBWA, EASTERN
[OJG]
ODERAGO alt for KASUWERI [QKW]
ODERIGA alt for MBEMBE, CROSS RIVER [MFN]
ODIENNÉ JULA dial of JULA [DYU]
ODIM alt for ADIM dial of AGWAGWUNE [YAY]
ODIO alt for MAKARAKA dial of ZANDE [ZAN]
ODIONGANON dial of BANTOANON [BNO]
ODKI alt for OD [ODK]
ODODOP alt for KOROP [KRP]
ODRI alt for ORIYA [ORY]
ODRUM alt for ORIYA [ORY]
ODU alt for O DU [TYH]
ODUAL [ODU] lang, Nigeria
ODUAL alt for SAKATA [SAT]
ODUL alt for YUKAGHIR, NORTHERN [YKG]
ODUL alt for YUKAGHIR, SOUTHERN [YUX]
ODUT [ODA] lang, Nigeria
ODYALOMBITO alt for LOMBI [LMI]
ODZILA alt for OJILA dial of AVOKAYA [AVU]
ODZILIWA alt for OJILA dial of AVOKAYA [AVU]
OEHOENDOENI alt for DAMAL [UHN]
OELOEMANDA alt for ULUMANDA' [ULM]
OEMA alt for UMA [PPK]
OENALE alt for OENALE-DELHA dial of ROTI [ROT]
OENALE-DELHA dial of ROTI [ROT]
OEPAO alt for LANDU-RINGGOU-OEPAO dial of ROTI
[ROT]
OERINGOEP alt for DANI, WESTERN [DNW]
OEWAKU alt for ARUTANI [ATX]
OFAIÉ-XAVANTE alt for OPAYÉ [OPY]
OFAYÉ alt for OPAYÉ [OPY]
OFERIKPE dial of MBEMBE, CROSS RIVER [MFN]
OFOMBONGA dial of MBEMBE, CROSS RIVER [MFN]
OFONOKPAN dial of MBEMBE, CROSS RIVER [MFN]
OFOR alt for LUBILA [KCC]
OFUNOBWAM alt for MBEMBE, CROSS RIVER [MFN]
OFUTOP alt for EFUTOP [OFU]
OGA alt for MUKAH-OYA dial of MELANAU [MEL]
OGA BAKUNG dial of KENYAH, BAKUNG [BOC]
OGAMARU alt for OGAMBI dial of LOGO [LOG]
OGAMBI dial of LOGO [LOG]
OGAMI alt for MIYAKO-JIMA dial of MIYAKO [MVI]
OGAN [OGN] lang, Indonesia, Sumatra
OGANIBI [OGA] lang, Papua New Guinea
OGAR dial of ONIN [ONI]
OGBA alt for OGBAH [OGC]
OGBAH [OGC] lang, Nigeria

OGBAKIRI dial of IKWERE [IKW]
OGBE IJO dial of IJO, CENTRAL-WESTERN [IJC]
OGBIA [OGB] lang, Nigeria
OGBINYA alt for OGBIA [OGB]
OGBOGOLO [OGG] lang, Nigeria
OGBOIN dial of IJO, CENTRAL-WESTERN [IJC]
OGBOJA alt for NKEM dial of NKEM-NKUM [ISI]
OGBRONUAGUM [OGU] lang, Nigeria
OGBRU dial of ABIDJI [ABI]
OGE dial of AKOKO, NORTH [AKK]
OGEA [ERI] lang, Papua New Guinea
OGHUZ dial of UZBEK, NORTHERN [UZB]
OGIT alt for KONDA [KND]
OGLIASTRINO dial of SARDINIAN, CAMPIDANESE
    [SRO]
OGODA alt for BONI [BOB]
OGOJA alt for NKEM dial of NKEM-NKUM [ISI]
OGOKO dial of MADI [MHI]
OGONDYAN alt for OYKANGAND dial of KUNJEN
    [KJN]
OGONI alt for KOANA [KEH]
OGORI alt for OKO dial of OKO-ENI-OSAYEN [OKS]
OGORI-MAGONGO alt for OKO-ENI-OSAYEN [OKS]
OGOWE dial of FANG [FNG]
OGUA dial of ENGENNI [ENN]
OGULAGHA dial of IJO, CENTRAL-WESTERN [IJC]
OGUTA dial of IGBO [IGR]
OHANA-ONYEN alt for OKOM dial of MBEMBE,
    CROSS RIVER [MFN]
OHUHU alt for UMUAHIA dial of IGBO [IGR]
OI alt for OY [OYB]
OIAKIRI dial of IJO, CENTRAL-WESTERN [IJC]
OIAMPÍ alt for WAYAMPI, OIAPOQUE [OYA]
OIAMPIPUCU alt for WAYAMPI, AMAPARI [OYM]
OIANA alt for WAYANA [WAY]
OIBA dial of SAMO-KUBO [SMQ]
OIBU dial of MARIA [MDS]
OIRAT alt for KALMYK-OIRAT [KGZ]
OIRAT dial of KALMYK-OIRAT [KGZ]
OIRATA [OIA] lang, Indonesia, Maluku
OIROT alt for ALTAI, SOUTHERN [ALT]
OIRYA alt for LOKOYA [LKY]
OIUM alt for PAPEL [PBO]
OIUMPIAN alt for WAYAMPI, OIAPOQUE [OYA]
OJABOLI alt for OJHI [OJH]
OJANJUR alt for MAJANG [MPE]
OJHA alt for OJHI [OJH]
OJHE alt for OJHI [OJH]
OJHI [OJH] lang, India
OJHI dial of BHOYARI [BHY]
OJHI dial of BAGHELI [BFY]
OJIBWA, EASTERN [OJG] lang, Canada, USA, USA
OJIBWA, EASTERN alt for OJIBWA, EASTERN [OJG]
OJIBWA, NORTHERN [OJB] lang, Canada
OJIBWA, WESTERN [OJI] lang, Canada, USA, USA
OJIBWA, WESTERN alt for OJIBWA, WESTERN [OJI]
OJIGA alt for AJIGU dial of AVOKAYA [AVU]
OJILA dial of AVOKAYA [AVU]
OJILA dial of AVOKAYA [AVU]
OJOR alt for LUBILA [KCC]
OJU dial of IGEDE [IGE]
OKA dial of BURIAT, RUSSIA [MNB]
OKAINA alt for OCAINA [OCA]
OKAK alt for FANG dial of FANG [FNG]
OKAM alt for MBEMBE, CROSS RIVER [MFN]
OKANAGAN [OKA] lang, Canada, USA, USA

OKANAGAN alt for OKANAGAN [OKA]
OKANAGAN-COLVILLE alt for OKANAGAN [OKA]
OKANAGON alt for OKANAGAN [OKA]
OKANDE alt for KANDE [KBS]
OKANISI alt for AUKAANS [DJK]
OKE'BU alt for NDO [NDP]
OKE'BU dial of NDO [NDP]
OKE'BU dial of NDO [NDP]
OKE-AGBE dial of AKOKO, NORTH [AKK]
OKEINA alt for KORAFE [KPR]
OKEINA dial of YEGA [YGG]
OKELA alt for KELA [KEL]
OKENE alt for HIMA dial of EBIRA [IGB]
OKERE dial of GUA [LAR]
OKHOTSK dial of EVEN [EVE]
OKI alt for TUKI [BAG]
OKI dial of JAPANESE [JPN]
OKI-NO-ERABU [OKN] lang, Japan
OKIEK [OKI] lang, Kenya
OKII alt for BOKYI [BKY]
OKINAWAN alt for OKINAWAN, CENTRAL [RYU]
OKINAWAN, CENTRAL [RYU] lang, Japan
OKLAHOMA alt for AFRO-SEMINOLE CREOLE [AFS]
OKO alt for OKO-ENI-OSAYEN [OKS]
OKO dial of MANAGALASI [MCQ]
OKO dial of OKO-ENI-OSAYEN [OKS]
OKO-ENI-OSAYEN [OKS] lang, Nigeria
OKO-JUWOI [OKJ] lang, India
OKOBO [OKB] lang, Nigeria
OKODIA [OKD] lang, Nigeria
OKOLLO dial of MADI [MHI]
OKOLOD [KQV] lang, Malaysia, Sarawak, Indonesia,
    Kalimantan
OKOLOD MURUT alt for OKOLOD [KQV]
OKOM dial of MBEMBE, CROSS RIVER [MFN]
OKOMA alt for OKONI dial of NATENI [NTM]
OKOMANJANG dial of BEFANG [BBY]
OKONI dial of NATENI [NTM]
OKONYONG alt for KIONG [KKM]
OKORDIA alt for OKODIA [OKD]
OKOROBI dial of NGWO [NGN]
OKOROETE dial of OBOLO [ANN]
OKOROGUNG dial of UTUGWANG [AFE]
OKOROMANDJANG alt for OKOMANJANG dial of
    BEFANG [BBY]
OKOROTUNG dial of UTUGWANG [AFE]
OKOYONG alt for KIONG [KKM]
OKPAMHERI [OPA] lang, Nigeria
OKPE [OKE] lang, Nigeria
OKPE dial of OKPE-IDESA-OLOMA-AKUKU [OKP]
OKPE-IDESA-OLOMA-AKUKU [OKP] lang, Nigeria
OKPEDEN dial of ABUA [ABN]
OKPELA dial of IVBIE NORTH-OKPELA-ARHE [ATG]
OKPELE alt for BEKWEL [BKW]
OKPELLA alt for OKPELA dial of IVBIE NORTH-
    OKPELA-ARHE [ATG]
OKPOTO dial of ORING [ORI]
OKRIKA [OKR] lang, Nigeria
OKRO [OKO] lang, Papua New Guinea
OKSAPMIN [OPM] lang, Papua New Guinea
OKTENAI alt for WICHÍ LHAMTÉS NOCTEN [MTP]
OKTENGBAN alt for KETENGBAN [KIN]
OKU alt for KUO [OKU]
OKU dial of BOKYI [BKY]
OKULOSHO dial of OKPAMHERI [OPA]
OKUNI dial of OLULUMO-IKOM [IKO]

OKURIKAN alt for AGWAGWUNE [YAY]
OKUROSHO alt for OKULOSHO dial of OKPAMHERI
[OPA]
OKWASAR alt for ISIRAWA [SRL]
OLA dial of EVEN [EVE]
OLAL dial of AMBRYM, NORTH [MMG]
OLAM dial of MURLE [MUR]
OLANGCHUNG GOLA [OLA] lang, Nepal, India
OLCH alt for ULCH [ULC]
OLCHA alt for ULCH [ULC]
OLCHIS alt for ULCH [ULC]
OLD BARGU alt for BARGU dial of BURIAT, CHINA
[BXU]
OLD KENTISH SIGN LANGUAGE [OKL] lang, United
Kingdom
OLD KHMER alt for KUY [KDT]
OLD SIRENIK alt for YUPIK, SIRENIK [YSR]
OLD TUPÍ alt for TUPINAMBÁ [TPN]
OLEM alt for ANGORAM [AOG]
OLGA alt for JUMJUM [JUM]
OLGEL alt for OYKANGAND dial of KUNJEN [KJN]
OLGOL alt for OYKANGAND dial of KUNJEN [KJN]
OLI dial of DUALA [DOU]
OLIT alt for MACI dial of ICEVE-MACI [BEC]
OLIT alt for MACI dial of ICEVE-MACI [BEC]
OLITHI alt for MACI dial of ICEVE-MACI [BEC]
OLITHI alt for MACI dial of ICEVE-MACI [BEC]
OLITI alt for MACI dial of ICEVE-MACI [BEC]
OLITI-AKWAYA alt for MACI dial of ICEVE-MACI
[BEC]
OLITI-AKWAYA alt for MACI dial of ICEVE-MACI
[BEC]
OLIYA alt for ORIYA [ORY]
OLKOI alt for ELKEI [ELK]
OLLARI [OLL] lang, India
OLLARI dial of GADABA [GDB]
OLLARO alt for OLLARI [OLL]
OLO [ONG] lang, Papua New Guinea
OLODIAMA EAST dial of IJO, CENTRAL-WESTERN
[IJC]
OLODIAMA WEST dial of IJO, CENTRAL-WESTERN
[IJC]
OLOGUTI dial of YAGARIA [YGR]
OLOH MANGTANGAI alt for MANTANGAI dial of
NGAJU [NIJ]
OLOH MENGKATIP alt for MENGKATIP dial of
BAKUMPAI [BKR]
OLOIBIRI dial of OGBIA [OGB]
OLOMA dial of OKPE-IDESA-OLOMA-AKUKU [OKP]
OLOMBO alt for LOMBO [LOO]
OLONETS alt for OLONETSIAN [OLO]
OLONETSIAN [OLO] lang, Russia, Europe, Finland
OLOSSU alt for RUSSIAN [RUS]
OLOT dial of KALMYK-OIRAT [KGZ]
OLOTEPEC MIXE alt for MIXE, NORTHEASTERN
[MVE]
OLOTORIT alt for OTUHO [LOT]
OLU'BO alt for LULUBA [LUL]
OLUBOGO alt for LULUBA [LUL]
OLUBOTI alt for LULUBA [LUL]
OLUBWISI alt for TALINGA-BWISI [TLJ]
OLUCHIGA alt for CHIGA [CHG]
OLUGWERE alt for GWERE [GWR]
OLUHANGA alt for WANGA dial of LUYIA [LUY]
OLUKONJO alt for KONJO [KOO]
OLUKONZO alt for KONJO [KOO]

OLUKOOKI alt for KOOKI dial of GANDA [LAP]
OLULU dial of IPULO [ASS]
OLULUMO dial of OLULUMO-IKOM [IKO]
OLULUMO-IKOM [IKO] lang, Nigeria
OLUMUILA alt for MWILA dial of NYANEKA [NYK]
OLUNCHUN alt for OROQEN [ORH]
OLUNYOLE alt for NYORE [NYD]
OLUNYORE alt for NYORE [NYD]
OLUSAAMIA alt for SAAMIA [SBU]
OLUSESE alt for SESE dial of GANDA [LAP]
OLUSOGA alt for SOGA [SOG]
OLUWANGA alt for WANGA dial of LUYIA [LUY]
OLYUTOR alt for ALUTOR [ALR]
OMAGE alt for AMUESHA [AME]
OMAGUA [OMG] lang, Brazil, Peru, Peru
OMAGUA alt for OMAGUA [OMG]
OMAGUA alt for CARIJONA [CBD]
OMAGUA-YETE alt for OMAGUA [OMG]
OMAGWA dial of IKWERE [IKW]
OMAHA [OMA] lang, USA
OMANI dial of ARABIC, OMANI [ACX]
OMATI [MGX] lang, Papua New Guinea
OMAYAMNON dial of MANOBO, AGUSAN [MSM]
OMBA alt for AMBAE, EAST [OMB]
OMBESSA alt for NUGUNU [YAS]
OMBO [OML] lang, Zaïre
OMDURMAN dial of ARABIC, SUDANESE [APD]
OMEJES [OME] lang, Colombia
OMENE dial of SINAGORO [SNC]
OMERELU dial of IKWERE [IKW]
OMETAY alt for KULLO [KLO]
OMETEPEC AZTEC alt for NAHUATL, OMETEPEC
[NHT]
OMETO alt for WOLAYTTA [WBC]
OMG'OM alt for BONG'OMEK dial of SABAOT [SPY]
OMI [OMI] lang, Zaïre
ŌMIE [AOM] lang, Papua New Guinea
OMKOI dial of KAREN, PWO OMKOI [PWW]
OMO alt for TIGAK [TGC]
OMOTIK [OMT] lang, Kenya
OMPA alt for TOBAKU dial of UMA [PPK]
OMURANO [OMU] lang, Peru
OMVANG dial of EWONDO [EWO]
OMWUNRA-TOQURA dial of TAIRORA [TBG]
OMYENE alt for MYENE [MYE]
OMYENE alt for GALWA dial of MYENE [MYE]
ONA [ONA] lang, Argentina, Chile, Chile
ONA alt for ONA [ONA]
ONABASULU [ONN] lang, Papua New Guinea
ONAGE alt for FUR [FUR]
ONANDAGA alt for ONONDAGA [ONO]
ONANGE alt for ONONGE dial of FUYUGE [FUY]
ONANK alt for UNANK [UNA]
ONDO dial of YORUBA [YOR]
ONDOE alt for LULUBA [LUL]
ONDOUMBO alt for NDUMU [NMD]
ONDUMBO alt for NDUMU [NMD]
ONE alt for AUNALEI [AUN]
ONEIDA [ONE] lang, USA, Canada
ONELE alt for AUNALEI [AUN]
ONESSO dial of AULUA [AUL]
ONG [OOG] lang, Laos
ONG alt for ÖNGE [OON]
ONG-BE alt for LINGAO [ONB]
ONGAMO alt for NGASA [NSG]
ONGBE alt for LINGAO [ONB]

OROMO, WELLEGA-CENTRAL [GAZ] lang, Ethiopia, Egypt
ORON [ORX] lang, Nigeria
ORONCHON alt for OROQEN [ORH]
OROQEN [ORH] lang, China
OROSHANI alt for ROSHANI dial of SHUGHNI [SGH]
OROSHANI alt for RUSHANI dial of SHUGHNI [SGH]
OROSHOR dial of SHUGHNI [SGH]
OROSHOR dial of SHUGHNI [SGH]
OROSHORI alt for OROSHOR dial of SHUGHNI [SGH]
OROTINA alt for CHOROTEGA [CJR]
OROTINA alt for OROTINYA dial of CHOROTEGA [CJR]
OROTINYA dial of CHOROTEGA [CJR]
OROWE [BPK] lang, New Caledonia
ORRA alt for GIMR dial of TAMA [TMA]
ORRA alt for GIMR dial of TAMA [TMA]
ORRI alt for ORING [ORI]
ORRIN alt for ORING [ORI]
ORRINGORRIN alt for ORING [ORI]
ORUHEMA dial of HIMA [HIM]
ORUHIMA dial of HIMA [HIM]
ORUHUMA dial of HIMA [HIM]
ORUKIGA alt for CHIGA [CHG]
ORUM dial of AGWAGWUNE [YAY]
ORUMA [ORR] lang, Nigeria
ORUNDANDE alt for NANDI [NNB]
ORUNGU dial of MYENE [MYE]
ORUNYARWANDA alt for RWANDA [RUA]
ORUNYORO dial of NYORO [NYR]
ORUONE dial of SINAGORO [SNC]
ORURO dial of QUECHUA, SOUTH BOLIVIAN [QUH]
ORUTAGWENDA dial of NYANKOLE [NYN]
ORUTORO alt for TORO dial of HEMA-SUD [NIX]
ORUTORO alt for TORO dial of NYORO [NYR]
ORYA [URY] lang, Indonesia, Irian Jaya
OSA NANGA alt for TUKI [BAG]
OSAGE [OSA] lang, USA
OSANYIN alt for OSAYEN dial of OKO-ENI-OSAYEN [OKS]
OSATU [OST] lang, Cameroon
OSAYEN dial of OKO-ENI-OSAYEN [OKS]
OSER alt for SIAGHA-YENIMU [OSR]
OSETIN [OSE] lang, Georgia, Russia, Europe, Turkey
OSETIN alt for OSETIN [OSE]
OSHIE alt for NGISHE [NSH]
OSHIE dial of NGISHE [NSH]
OSHIMA alt for AMAMI-OSHIMA, NORTHERN [RYN]
OSHINDONGA alt for NDONGA [NDG]
OSHOLIO alt for SHOLIO dial of KATAB [KCG]
OSIDONGA alt for NDONGA [NDG]
OSIKOM alt for BOKYI [BKY]
OSIMA alt for OSSIMA [OSM]
OSIMA alt for AMAMI-OSHIMA, NORTHERN [RYN]
OSINDONGA alt for NDONGA [NDG]
OSING [OSI] lang, Indonesia, Java, Bali
OSLO dial of NORWEGIAN SIGN LANGUAGE [NSL]
OSMANLI alt for TURKISH [TRK]
OSO [OSO] lang, Cameroon
OSO MOKO dial of NAUETI [NXA]
OSOKOM dial of BOKYI [BKY]
OSOPHONG alt for OSOPONG dial of MBEMBE, CROSS RIVER [MFN]
OSOPONG dial of MBEMBE, CROSS RIVER [MFN]
OSOSO [OSS] lang, Nigeria
OSSATU alt for OSATU [OST]

OSSETE alt for OSETIN [OSE]
OSSIMA [OSM] lang, Papua New Guinea
OSSO alt for OSO [OSO]
OST-OBERDEUTSCH alt for BAVARIAN [BAR]
OSTROGOTH dial of GOTHIC [GOF]
OSTUACÁN dial of ZOQUE, COPAINALÁ [ZOC]
OSTUNCALCO MAM alt for MAM, SOUTHERN [MMS]
OSTYAK alt for KHANTY [KCA]
OSTYAK SAMOYED alt for SELKUP [SAK]
OSUKAM alt for BOKYI [BKY]
OSUM [OMO] lang, Papua New Guinea
OT BALAWAN dial of DOHOI [OTD]
OT BANU'U dial of DOHOI [OTD]
OT DANUM alt for DOHOI [OTD]
OT MURUNG 1 dial of DOHOI [OTD]
OT OLANG dial of DOHOI [OTD]
OT SIANG alt for SIANG [SYA]
OT TUHUP dial of DOHOI [OTD]
OTABHA dial of ABUA [ABN]
OTANABE alt for MUNICHE [MYR]
OTANAVE alt for MUNICHE [MYR]
OTANG alt for OTANK [UTA]
OTANGA alt for OTANK [UTA]
OTANK [UTA] lang, Nigeria
OTAPHA alt for OTABHA dial of ABUA [ABN]
OTAVALO QUICHUA alt for QUICHUA, HIGHLAND, IMBABURA [QHO]
OTETELA alt for TETELA [TEL]
OTHAN alt for UDUK [UDU]
OTI [OTI] lang, Brazil
OTJIDHIMBA alt for ZEMBA [DHM]
OTLALTEPEC dial of POPOLOCA, WESTERN [POW]
OTO [OTO] lang, USA
OTO dial of OTO [OTO]
OTOE alt for OTO [OTO]
OTOMÍ, EASTERN [OTM] lang, Mexico
OTOMÍ, MEZQUITAL [OTE] lang, Mexico, USA
OTOMÍ, NORTHWESTERN [OTQ] lang, Mexico
OTOMÍ, SOUTHEASTERN [OTA] lang, Mexico
OTOMÍ, STATE OF MEXICO [OTS] lang, Mexico
OTOMÍ, TEMOAYA [OTT] lang, Mexico
OTOMÍ, TENANGO [OTN] lang, Mexico
OTOMÍ, TEXCATEPEC [OTX] lang, Mexico
OTOMÍ, TILAPA [OTL] lang, Mexico
OTORO [OTR] lang, Sudan
OTSHO dial of LUGBARA, HIGH [LUG]
OTTAWA dial of OJIBWA, EASTERN [OJG]
OTUHO [LOT] lang, Sudan
OTUKE [OTU] lang, Brazil
OTUKWANG alt for UTUGWANG dial of UTUGWANG [AFE]
OTUO alt for GHOTUO [AAA]
OTUQUE alt for OTUKE [OTU]
OTUQUI alt for OTUKE [OTU]
OTURKPO alt for IDOMA CENTRAL dial of IDOMA [IDO]
OTUXO alt for OTUHO [LOT]
OTWA alt for GHOTUO [AAA]
OUADDA alt for WADA [WDA]
OUADDAÏ alt for MABA [MDE]
OUADDAIEN alt for MABA [MDE]
OUALA alt for WARA [WBF]
OUALA alt for WALI [WLX]
OUARA alt for WARA [WBF]
OUARGLA [OUA] lang, Algeria

OUARGLI alt for OUARGLA [OUA]
OUASSA alt for WASA [WSW]
OUATCHI alt for WACI-GBE [WCI]
OUATOUROU-NIASOGONI dial of WARA [WBF]
OUAYEONE alt for WAIWAI [WAW]
OUBATCH alt for JAWE [JAZ]
OUBI alt for GLIO-OUBI [OUB]
OUBYKH alt for UBYKH [UBY]
OUEDGHIR dial of OUARGLA [OUA]
OUEN alt for NUMEE [KDK]
OUEN dial of NUMEE [KDK]
OUHIGUYUA dial of FULFULDE, JELGOOJI [FUM]
OUINJI-OUINJI alt for ANII [BLO]
OULA alt for WULA dial of PSIKYE [KVJ]
OULDEME alt for WUZLAM [UDL]
OULED DJEMMA dial of MABA [MDE]
OUMA [OUM] lang, Papua New Guinea
OUNE [OUE] lang, Papua New Guinea
!O!UNG [OUN] lang, Angola
OUNGE alt for OUNE [OUE]
OUNI alt for HONI [HOW]
OUOBE alt for WOBE [WOB]
OUOLOF alt for WOLOF [WOL]
OUORODOUGOU JULA alt for WORODOUGOU JULA
    dial of JULA [DYU]
OURI alt for OLI dial of DUALA [DOU]
OURZA alt for HURZA dial of PELASLA [MLR]
OURZO alt for HURZA dial of PELASLA [MLR]
OUSSOUYE alt for ESULALU dial of JOLA-KASA
    [CSK]
OUZBEK alt for UZBEK, NORTHERN [UZB]
OUZZA alt for HURZA dial of PELASLA [MLR]
OVAMBO alt for KWANYAMA [KUY]
OVAND alt for EVAND [BZZ]
OVANDE alt for EVAND [BZZ]
OVANDO alt for EVAND [BZZ]
OVIEDO alt for EDO [EDO]
OVIMBUNDU alt for UMBUNDU [MNF]
OVIOBA alt for EDO [EDO]
OWA RAHA alt for SANTA ANA dial of KAHUA
    [AGW]
OWA RIKI alt for SANTA CATALINA dial of KAHUA
    [AGW]
OWE dial of YORUBA [YOR]
OWENA alt for OWENIA [WSR]
OWENDA alt for OWENIA [WSR]
OWENIA [WSR] lang, Papua New Guinea
OWENKE alt for EVENKI [EVN]
OWERRI dial of IGBO [IGR]
OWINIGA [OWI] lang, Papua New Guinea
OWOI alt for LOKOYA [LKY]
OXCHUC TZELTAL alt for TZELTAL, HIGHLAND
    [TZH]
OXORIOK alt for LOKOYA [LKY]
OY [OYB] lang, Laos
OYA alt for MUKAH-OYA dial of MELANAU [MEL]
OYA' alt for MUKAH-OYA dial of MELANAU [MEL]
OYAMPÍ alt for WAYAMPI, OIAPOQUE [OYA]
OYAMPIPUKU alt for WAYAMPI, AMAPARI [OYM]
OYANA alt for WAYANA [WAY]
OYANA dial of GADSUP [GAJ]
OYANPÍK alt for WAYAMPI, OIAPOQUE [OYA]
OYAPÍ alt for WAYAMPI, OIAPOQUE [OYA]
OYARICOULET alt for AKURIO [AKO]
OYDA [OYD] lang, Ethiopia
OYIN dial of AKOKO, NORTH [AKK]

OYKANGAND dial of KUNJEN [KJN]
OYO dial of YORUBA [YOR]
OYOKOM dial of BOKYI [BKY]
OYROT alt for ALTAI, SOUTHERN [ALT]
OYUWI dial of MADI [MHI]
OZA alt for OJHI [OJH]
ÖZBEK alt for UZBEK, NORTHERN [UZB]
OZBEK alt for UZBEK, NORTHERN [UZB]
OZHA alt for OJHI [OJH]
P'U LA alt for LATI [LBT]
P'UMAN alt for U [UUU]
P'UMI alt for PUMI [PMI]
P'YONG'ANDO dial of KOREAN [KKN]
PA alt for PARE [PPT]
PA alt for GHOMALA SOUTH dial of GHOMALA'
    [BBJ]
PA DI alt for THO [THO]
PA HNG [PHA] lang, China, Viet Nam, Viet Nam
PA HNG alt for PA HNG [PHA]
PÀ HUNG alt for PA HNG [PHA]
PA KEMBALOH alt for PUTOH [PUT]
PA OH alt for KAREN, PA'O [BLK]
PÀ THEN alt for PA HNG [PHA]
PA THEN alt for PA HNG [PHA]
PA'AWA alt for PA'A [AFA]
PA'DISUA dial of SAHU [SUX]
PA'NON alt for PAPE [NDU]
PA'O alt for KAREN, PA'O [BLK]
PA'UMOTU alt for TUAMOTUAN [PMT]
PA-U alt for KAREN, PA'O [BLK]
PA'A [AFA] lang, Nigeria
PAACI alt for PAICÎ [PRI]
PÁÁFANG [PFA] lang, Micronesia
PAAMA [PMA] lang, Vanuatu
PAAMA-LOPEVI alt for PAAMA [PMA]
PAAMESE alt for PAAMA [PMA]
PAANG alt for PANG dial of LUSHAI [LSH]
PAASALE alt for PASAALA [SIG]
PABIR alt for BURA-PABIR [BUR]
PABRA alt for PAO [PPA]
PACAAS-NOVOS alt for PAKAÁSNOVOS [PAV]
PACAHANOVO alt for PAKAÁSNOVOS [PAV]
PACAHUARA [PCP] lang, Bolivia
PACAWARA alt for PACAHUARA [PCP]
PACCHMI alt for KAHLURI [KFS]
PACHAGAN dial of PASHAYI, NORTHWEST [GLH]
PACHIEN alt for SAAROA [SXR]
PACHITEA QUECHUA alt for QUECHUA, HUÁNUCO,
    PANAO [QEM]
PACIFIC YUPIK alt for YUPIK, PACIFIC GULF [EMS]
PACO alt for PACOH [PAC]
PACOH [PAC] lang, Viet Nam, Laos
PACU alt for IPEKA-TAPUIA [PAJ]
PADA alt for TERMANU-TALAE-KEKA dial of ROTI
    [ROT]
PADAMO-ORINOCO alt for WESTERN YANOMAMI
    dial of YANOMAMÖ [GUU]
PADANG alt for MINANGKABAU [MPU]
PADANG alt for DINKA, NORTHEASTERN [DIP]
PADANG dial of MAMUJU [MQX]
PADANG dial of TALIABU [TLV]
PADARI dial of BHADRAWAHI [BHD]
PADAS dial of LUNDAYEH [LND]
PADAUNG alt for KAREN, PADAUNG [PDU]
PADOA dial of BIAK [BHW]
PADOE [PDO] lang, Indonesia, Sulawesi

PADOÉ alt for PADOE [PDO]
PADOGHO alt for KPATOGO [GBW]
PADOGO alt for PARKWA [PBI]
PADOKWA alt for PARKWA [PBI]
PADORHO alt for KPATOGO [GBW]
PADORO alt for KPATOGO [GBW]
PADUKO alt for PARKWA [PBI]
PADVI dial of BHILI [BHB]
PADVI dial of MAWCHI [MKE]
PÁEZ [PBB] lang, Colombia
PAGABETE [PAG] lang, Zaïre
PAGAI dial of MENTAWAI [MWV]
PAGALU alt for ANNOBONESE dial of CRIOULO,
   GULF OF GUINEA [CRI]
PAGANYAW alt for KAREN, S'GAW [KSW]
PAGBAHAN dial of IRAYA [IRY]
PAGCAH alt for AMIS [ALV]
PAGEI alt for PAGI [PGI]
PAGI [PGI] lang, Papua New Guinea
PAGO alt for PAGU [PGU]
PAGOE alt for PAGU [PGU]
PAGU [PGU] lang, Indonesia, Maluku
PAGU alt for KAREN, PAKU [KPP]
PAGU dial of PAGU [PGU]
PAGUANA dial of OMAGUA [OMG]
PAGUARA alt for PAGUANA dial of OMAGUA [OMG]
PAHARI alt for NEPALI [NEP]
PAHARI alt for BHATEALI [BHT]
PAHARI alt for JAUNSARI [JNS]
PAHARI dial of PAHARI-POTWARI [PHR]
PAHARI alt for SINDHUPALCHOK PAHRI dial of
   NEWARI [NEW]
PAHARI BHARMAURI alt for GADDI [GBK]
PAHARI GARHWALI alt for GARHWALI [GBM]
PAHARI KULLU alt for KULUI [KFX]
PAHARI MANDIYALI alt for MANDEALI [MJL]
PAHARI-PALPA alt for PALPA [PLP]
PAHARI-POTWARI [PHR] lang, Pakistan
PAHARIA dial of BENGALI [BNG]
PAHARIA dial of SANTALI [SNT]
PAHAVAI alt for BOHUAI [RAK]
PAHENBAQUEBO dial of CAPANAHUA [KAQ]
PAHENG dial of PUNU [PNU]
PAHI [LGT] lang, Papua New Guinea
PAHI dial of PACOH [PAC]
PAHI dial of PACOH [PAC]
PAHLAVANI [PHV] lang, Afghanistan
PAHOUIN alt for FANG [FNG]
PAHRI alt for SINDHUPALCHOK PAHRI dial of
   NEWARI [NEW]
PAHU dial of TUNJUNG [TJG]
PAHU' dial of DUSUN, CENTRAL [DTP]
PAI [PAI] lang, Nigeria
PAI alt for BAI [PIQ]
PAI alt for PEI [PPQ]
PAĬ alt for PAI TAVYTERA [PTA]
PAI alt for MALA [PED]
PAI dial of SOTHO, NORTHERN [SRT]
PAI LISU alt for WHITE LISU dial of LISU [LIS]
PAI TAVYTERA [PTA] lang, Paraguay
PAI'I' alt for LÜ [KHB]
PAI-I alt for LÜ [KHB]
PAI-YI alt for LÜ [KHB]
PAIAWA alt for GUHU-SAMANE [GHS]
PAICHIEN alt for SAAROA [SXR]
PAICĬ [PRI] lang, New Caledonia

PAIDIA alt for PARDHI [PCL]
PAIEM alt for FYAM [PYM]
PAIKO dial of GBARI [GBY]
PAIMI alt for NAGA, AO [NJO]
PAIPAI [PPI] lang, Mexico
PAIQUIZE alt for MUNDURUKÚ [MYU]
PAITAN alt for TOMBONUWO [TXA]
PAITE alt for CHIN, PAITE [PCK]
PAITHE alt for CHIN, PAITE [PCK]
PAIUAN alt for PAIWAN [PWN]
PAIUTE, NORTHERN [PAO] lang, USA
PAIWA alt for GAPAPAIWA [PWG]
PAIWAN [PWN] lang, Taiwan
PAIYAGE alt for SILIMO [WUL]
PAIYI dial of DAI [TIZ]
PAJADE alt for BADYARA [PBP]
PAJADINCA alt for BADYARA [PBP]
PAJADINKA alt for BADYARA [PBP]
PAJAPAN dial of NAHUATL, ISTHMUS [NAU]
PAJO alt for BALAESAN [BLS]
PAJOKUMBUH dial of MINANGKABAU [MPU]
PAJULU alt for PÖJULU dial of BARI [BFA]
PAJULU alt for PÖJULU dial of BARI [BFA]
PAJUNGU alt for BAYUNGU [BXJ]
PAK dial of PAK-TONG [PKG]
PAK dial of VATRATA [VLR]
PAK TAI alt for TAI, SOUTHERN [SOU]
PAK THAI alt for TAI, SOUTHERN [SOU]
PAK-TONG [PKG] lang, Papua New Guinea
PAKA alt for NZANYI [NJA]
PAKA dial of NIKSEK [GBE]
PAKAANOVA alt for PAKAÁSNOVOS [PAV]
PAKAANOVAS alt for PAKAÁSNOVOS [PAV]
PAKAÁSNOVOS [PAV] lang, Brazil
PAKADJI alt for KUUKU-YA'U [QKL]
PAKANG alt for POKANGÁ [POK]
PAKANHA [PKN] lang, Australia
PAKARA alt for CARA [CFD]
PAKARLA alt for BANGGARLA [BJB]
PAKARO dial of KAREKARE [KAI]
PAKATAN [PKT] lang, Laos
PAKATAN alt for BUKITAN [BKN]
PAKAWA alt for DA'A dial of KAILI, DA'A [KZF]
PAKEWA alt for TONTEMBOAN [TNT]
PAKHTO alt for PASHTO, EASTERN [PBU]
PAKHTOO alt for PASHTO, WESTERN [PBT]
PAKHTOO alt for PASHTO, EASTERN [PBU]
PAKHTU alt for PASHTO, WESTERN [PBT]
PAKI alt for BAKI [BKI]
PAKIA-SIDERONSI dial of NASIOI [NAS]
PAKKAU dial of PITU ULUNNA SALU [PTU]
PAKOT alt for PÖKOOT [PKO]
PAKPAK alt for BATAK DAIRI [BTD]
PAKPAK DAIRI alt for BATAK DAIRI [BTD]
PAKSE dial of LAO [NOL]
PAKTU alt for PASHTO, WESTERN [PBT]
PAKTYAN PASHTO alt for PASHTO, SOUTHERN
   [PBQ]
PAKU [PKU] lang, Indonesia, Kalimantan
PAKU alt for KAREN, PAKU [KPP]
PAKU-TAPUYA alt for IPEKA-TAPUIA [PAJ]
PAKUM alt for KWAKUM [KWU]
PAL KURUMBA dial of KURUMBA [KFI]
PALA alt for PA'A [AFA]
PALA dial of PATPATAR [GFK]
PALA'AU alt for BAJAU LAUT dial of SAMA,

SOUTHERN [SIT]
PALACHI alt for PALAKHI dial of KAREN, S'GAW [KSW]
PALAKA alt for SENOUFO, PALAKA [PLR]
PALAKHI dial of KAREN, S'GAW [KSW]
PALAKKA alt for BONE dial of BUGIS [BPR]
PALAMATA alt for PALUMATA [PMC]
PALAMUL [PLX] lang, Indonesia, Irian Jaya
PALAN dial of KORYAK [KPY]
PALANAN DUMAGAT dial of PARANAN [AGP]
PALANAN VALLEY AGTA alt for PALANAN
    DUMAGAT dial of PARANAN [AGP]
PALANAN VALLEY DUMAGAT alt for PALANAN
    DUMAGAT dial of PARANAN [AGP]
PALANENYO alt for PARANAN [AGP]
PALANSKIJ dial of ALUTOR [ALR]
PALARA alt for SENOUFO, PALAKA [PLR]
PALASI dial of SHINA, KOHISTANI [PLK]
PALASI-KOHISTANI alt for SHINA, KOHISTANI [PLK]
PALATA dial for FULFULDE, ADAMAWA [FUB]
PALATTAE alt for SINJAI dial of BUGIS [BPR]
PALAU alt for PALAUAN [PLU]
PALAUAN [PLU] lang, Belau, Guam, Guam
PALAUAN-CALAVITE dial of IRAYA [IRY]
PALAUI ISLAND dial of AGTA, DUPANINAN [DUO]
PALAUI ISLAND AGTA dial of AGTA, UMIRAY
    DUMAGET [DUE]
PALAUNG alt for DE'ANG [BFP]
PALAUNG, PALE [PCE] lang, Myanmar, China,
    Thailand
PALAUNG, PALE alt for PALAUNG, PALE [PCE]
PALAUNG, RUMAI [RBB] lang, Myanmar, China
PALAUNG, SHWE [SWE] lang, Myanmar, China
PALAW dial of BURMESE [BMS]
PALAWAN alt for PALAWANO, BROOKE'S POINT [PLW]
PALAWAN BATAK alt for BATAK [BTK]
PALAWANEN alt for PALAWANO, CENTRAL [PLC]
PALAWANO, BROOKE'S POINT [PLW] lang,
    Philippines
PALAWANO, CENTRAL [PLC] lang, Philippines
PALAWANO, SOUTHWEST [PLV] lang, Philippines
PALAWEÑO alt for PALAWANO, CENTRAL [PLC]
PALAY alt for PALAUNG, PALE [PCE]
PALAYA alt for PALIYAN [PCF]
PALAYAN alt for PALIYAN [PCF]
PALCHI alt for POLCI [POL]
PALCI alt for POLCI [POL]
PALCI alt for POLCI dial of POLCI [POL]
PALDENA alt for FULFULDE, ADAMAWA [FUB]
PALDIDA alt for FULFULDE, ADAMAWA [FUB]
PALE alt for PALAUNG, PALE [PCE]
PALEE'N dial of TA'OIH, UPPER [TTH]
PALEMBANG [PLM] lang, Indonesia, Sumatra
PALENQUE alt for PALENQUERO [PLN]
PALENQUERO [PLN] lang, Colombia
PALESTINIAN-JORDANIAN ARABIC dial of ARABIC,
    LEVANTINE [APC]
PALI [PLL] lang, India, Sri Lanka, Myanmar, Sri Lanka
PALICUR alt for PALIKÚR [PAL]
PALIET dial of DINKA, SOUTHWESTERN [DIK]
PALIHA alt for BHARIA [BHA]
PALIJUR alt for PALIKÚR [PAL]
PALIK alt for APALIK [PLI]
PALIKOUR alt for PALIKÚR [PAL]
PALIKÚR [PAL] lang, Brazil, French Guiana, French

Guiana
PALILI' dial of TOALA' [TLZ]
PALIMBEI dial of IATMUL [IAN]
PALIN alt for EMBALOH [EMB]
PALÍN POCOMAM alt for POKOMAM, SOUTHERN [POU]
PALIOARIENE alt for IPEKA-TAPUIA [PAJ]
PALIOPING alt for PALIOUPINY dial of DINKA,
    SOUTHWESTERN [DIK]
PALIOUPINY dial of DINKA, SOUTHWESTERN [DIK]
PALIPO dial of GREBO, E JE [GRB]
PALISUA alt for PA'DISUA dial of SAHU [SUX]
PALITIANI alt for PALITYAN dial of BULGARIAN [BLG]
PALITYAN dial of BULGARIAN [BLG]
PALIYAN [PCF] lang, India
PALJGU alt for NIJADALI [NAD]
PALLAKHA alt for SENOUFO, PALAKA [PLR]
PALLARESE alt for NORTHWESTERN CATALAN dial
    of CATALAN [CLN]
PALOC alt for AGEER dial of DINKA,
    NORTHEASTERN [DIP]
PALOESCH alt for KAILI, LEDO [LEW]
PALOIC alt for AGEER dial of DINKA,
    NORTHEASTERN [DIP]
PALOLA alt for PHALURA [PHL]
PALONG alt for DIMBONG [DII]
PALOR [FAP] lang, Senegal
PALPA [PLP] lang, Nepal
PALPA dial of NEPALI [NEP]
PALU [PBZ] lang, Myanmar
PALU alt for KAILI, LEDO [LEW]
PALU alt for LEDO dial of KAILI, LEDO [LEW]
PALUAN [PLZ] lang, Malaysia, Sabah
PALUAN dial of PALUAN [PLZ]
PALU'E [PLE] lang, Indonesia, Nusa Tenggara
PALULA alt for PHALURA [PHL]
PALUMATA [PMC] lang, Indonesia, Maluku
PALYU [PLY] lang, China
PAM [PMN] lang, Cameroon
PAM dial of BALUAN-PAM [BLQ]
PAMA alt for KULERE [KXE]
PAMA dial of KARIPUNÁ DO GUAPORÉ [KUQ]
PAMALE alt for VAMALE [MKT]
PAMANA alt for PAMA dial of KARIPUNÁ DO
    GUAPORÉ [KUQ]
PAMBADEQUE alt for COCAMILLA dial of COCAMA-
    COCAMILLA [COD]
PAMBIA [PAM] lang, Central African Republic
PAMBOANG dial of MANDAR [MHN]
PAMBUHAN dial of IRAYA [IRY]
PAME, CENTRAL [PBS] lang, Mexico
PAMEKESAN dial of MADURA [MHJ]
PAMELA dial of SUDEST [TGO]
PAMENYAN alt for BAMENYAM [BCE]
PAMIWA alt for CUBEO [CUB]
PAMMARI alt for PAUMARÍ dial of PAUMARÍ [PAD]
PAMOA alt for TATUYO [TAV]
PAMONA [BCX] lang, Indonesia, Sulawesi
PAMONA dial of PAMONA [BCX]
PAMPA alt for PUELCHE [PUE]
PAMPADEQUE alt for COCAMA-COCAMILLA [COD]
PAMPANGAN [PMP] lang, Philippines

PAMPANGO alt for PAMPANGAN [PMP]
PAMPANGUEÑO alt for PAMPANGAN [PMP]
PAMUE alt for FANG [FNG]
PAMUSA dial of FORE [FOR]
PAN ARU dial of DINKA, NORTHWESTERN [DIW]
PAN YAO alt for MIEN [YOC]
PANA [PNQ] lang, Burkina Faso, Mali, Mali
PANA [PNZ] lang, Central African Republic,
   Cameroon, Chad, Nigeria
PANA alt for PANOBO [PNO]
PANA alt for PANA [PNQ]
PANA alt for PANA [PNZ]
PANA dial of PANA [PNZ]
PANA NORTH dial of PANA [PNQ]
PANA SOUTH dial of PANA [PNQ]
PANA' alt for PHANA' [PHN]
PANAEATI alt for MISIMA-PANEATI [MPX]
PANAGS alt for PANANG [PCR]
PANAIETI alt for MISIMA-PANEATI [MPX]
PANAKHA alt for PANANG [PCR]
PANAMA EMBERA alt for EMBERA, NORTHERN
   [EMP]
PANAMINT dial of SHOSHONI [SHH]
PANANAG alt for PANANG [PCR]
PANANG [PCR] lang, China
PANAPANAYAN alt for PYUMA [PYU]
PANAPU dial of KAREN, S'GAW [KSW]
PANARAS alt for KUOT [KTO]
PANARE [PBH] lang, Venezuela
PANARI alt for PANARE [PBH]
PANASUAN [PSN] lang, Indonesia, Sulawesi
PANATINANI dial of NIMOA [NMW]
PANAWINA dial of NIMOA [NMW]
PANAY alt for AKLANON [AKL]
PANAYANO alt for KINARAY-A [KRJ]
PANAYETI alt for MISIMA-PANEATI [MPX]
PANRE alt for GIMME [KMP]
PANCANA [PNP] lang, Indonesia, Sulawesi
PANCARÉ alt for PANKARARÚ [PAZ]
PANCARU alt for PANKARARÚ [PAZ]
PANCHALI dial of BHILI [BHB]
PANCHGAUNLE [PNL] lang, Nepal
PANCHI BRAHMAURI RAJPUT alt for GADDI [GBK]
PANCHTHAR dial of LIMBU [LIF]
PANDA dial of EBIRA [IGB]
PANDAMA alt for SAKPU dial of KARANG [KZR]
PANDAN alt for BICOLANO, NORTHERN
   CATANDUANES [CTS]
PANDAN dial of KINARAY-A [KRJ]
PANDAU dial of PASHAYI, NORTHWEST [GLH]
PANDE [BKJ] lang, Central African Republic
PANDE dial of PANDE [BKJ]
PANDEQUEBO alt for COCAMA-COCAMILLA [COD]
PANDEWAN dial of PALUAN [PLZ]
PANDEWAN MURUT alt for PANDEWAN dial of
   PALUAN [PLZ]
PANDIKERI dial of MADI [MHI]
PANDJIMA alt for PANYTYIMA [PNW]
PANEATE alt for MISIMA-PANEATI [MPX]
PANEROA alt for BARASANA [BSN]
PANEROA alt for JEPA-MATSI [JEP]
PANEYATE alt for MISIMA-PANEATI [MPX]
PANG dial of LUSHAI [LSH]
PANG dial of LUSHAI [LSH]
PANGA dial of MONGO-NKUNDU [MOM]
PANGA alt for PIANGA dial of BUSHOONG [BUF]

PANGAN alt for JEHAI [JHI]
PANGASINAN [PNG] lang, Philippines
PANGGAR dial of KELON [KYO]
PANGHSE alt for HO dial of CHINESE, MANDARIN
   [CHN]
PANGI [PGG] lang, India
PANGI alt for KINYAMUNSANGE dial of LEGA-
   SHABUNDA [LEA]
PANGKAJENE alt for PANGKEP dial of BUGIS [BPR]
PANGKALA alt for BANGGARLA [BJB]
PANGKEP dial of BUGIS [BPR]
PANGKUMU alt for REREP [PGK]
PANGKUMU BAY alt for REREP [PGK]
PANGSENG dial of MUMUYE [MUL]
PANGSOIA-DOLATOK dial of SIRAIYA [FOS]
PANGTSAH alt for AMIS [ALV]
PANGWA [PBR] lang, Tanzania
PANGWE alt for FANG [FNG]
PANI alt for PANA [PNZ]
PANI DUI alt for PHAANI dial of DII [DUR]
PANIA alt for PANIYAN [PCG]
PANIDURIA alt for NAGA, NOCTE [NJB]
PANIKA [PNK] lang, India
PANIKITA alt for PANIQUITA dial of PÁEZ [PBB]
PANIM [PNR] lang, Papua New Guinea
PANINGESEN alt for MESE dial of TUNEN [BAZ]
PANIQUITA dial of PÁEZ [PBB]
PANIXTLAHUACA CHATINO dial of CHATINO,
   WEST HIGHLAND [CTP]
PANIYA alt for PANIYAN [PCG]
PANIYAN [PCG] lang, India
PANJABI PROPER dial of PANJABI, EASTERN [PNJ]
PANJABI, EASTERN [PNJ] lang, India, Bangladesh,
   Singapore
PANJABI, EASTERN alt for PANJABI, EASTERN
   [PNJ]
PANJABI, MIRPUR [PMU] lang, India, United
   Kingdom
PANJABI, WESTERN [PNB] lang, Pakistan, Great
   Britain
PANJIMA alt for PANYTYIMA [PNW]
PANKALLA alt for BANGGARLA [BJB]
PANKARARÁ alt for PANKARARÚ [PAZ]
PANKARARÉ [PAX] lang, Brazil
PANKARARÚ [PAZ] lang, Brazil
PANKARAVU alt for PANKARARÚ [PAZ]
PANKARORU alt for PANKARARÚ [PAZ]
PANKARÚ alt for PANKARARÚ [PAZ]
PANKHO alt for PANKHU [PKH]
PANKHU [PKH] lang, Bangladesh
PANKO alt for PANKHU [PKH]
PANNAI dial of LUSHAI [LSH]
PANNEI [PNC] lang, Indonesia, Sulawesi
PANO alt for PANOBO [PNO]
PANOBO [PNO] lang, Peru
PANON alt for PAPE [NDU]
PANTERA dial of NAFAANRA [NFR]
PANTERA-FANTERA alt for NAFAANRA [NFR]
PANTESCO dial of SICILIAN [SCN]
PANTHA alt for HO dial of CHINESE, MANDARIN
   [CHN]
PANTHE alt for HO dial of CHINESE, MANDARIN
   [CHN]
PANTJANA alt for PANCANA [PNP]
PANYAH alt for PANIYAN [PCG]
PANYAM alt for MAK [PBL]

PANYAM dial of MWAGHAVUL [SUR]
PANYJIMA alt for PANYTYIMA [PNW]
PANYTYIMA [PNW] lang, Australia
PAO [PPA] lang, India
PAOAN alt for BONAN [PEH]
PAOAN dial of BONAN [PEH]
PAOMATA dial of NAGA, MAO [NBI]
PAONGAN alt for BONAN [PEH]
PAOTING alt for BAODING dial of HLAI [LIC]
PAPABUCO alt for ZAPOTECO, SANTA MARÍA
ZANIZA [ZPW]
PAPABUCO alt for ZAPOTECO, SAN LORENZO
TEXMELUCAN [ZPZ]
PAPADI dial of LUNDAYEH [LND]
PAPAGO dial of PAPAGO-PIMA [PAP]
PAPAGO-PIMA [PAP] lang, USA, Mexico
PAPAKENE dial of BUANG, MAPOS [BZH]
PAPAPANA [PAA] lang, Papua New Guinea
PAPAR [DPP] lang, Malaysia, Sabah
PAPAR KADAZAN alt for KADAZAN, COASTAL
[KZJ]
PAPARA dial of SENOUFO, CEBAARA [SEF]
PAPASENA [PAS] lang, Indonesia, Irian Jaya
PAPAVÔ [PPV] lang, Brazil
PAPE [NDU] lang, Cameroon
PAPEI alt for PAPEL [PBO]
PAPEL [PBO] lang, Guinea Bissau, Guinea
PAPERYN alt for GUGUBERA [KKP]
PAPI [PPE] lang, Papua New Guinea
PAPIA alt for BABA [BBW]
PAPIA KRISTANG alt for MALACCAN CREOLE
PORTUGUESE [MCM]
PAPIAM alt for PAPIAMENTU [PAE]
PAPIAMENTO alt for PAPIAMENTU [PAE]
PAPIAMENTU [PAE] lang, Netherlands Antilles,
Netherlands, Puerto Rico, U.S. Virgin Islands
PAPIAMENTU alt for PAPIAMENTU [PAE]
PAPITALAI [PAT] lang, Papua New Guinea
PAPOLA alt for PAPORA [PPU]
PAPORA [PPU] lang, Taiwan
PAPUAN HIRI MOTU dial of MOTU, HIRI [POM]
PAPUMA [PPM] lang, Indonesia, Irian Jaya
PARA alt for PARAWEN [PRW]
PARA alt for NAGA, KHIAMNGAN [NKY]
PARABHI dial of KONKANI [KNK]
PARACHI [PRC] lang, Afghanistan
PARADI alt for PARDHI [PCL]
PARAENE alt for YAVITERO [YVT]
PARAHUJANO alt for PARAUJANO [PBG]
PARAHURI alt for YANOMÁMI [WCA]
PARAJA alt for DURUWA [PCI]
PARAJHI alt for DURUWA [PCI]
PARAKANÃ [PAK] lang, Brazil
PARAKANÃN alt for PARAKANÃ [PAK]
PARAKATÊJÊ alt for GAVIÃO DO PARÁ dial of
CANELA [RAM]
PARAMACCAN dial of AUKAANS [DJK]
PARAN alt for TAROKO [TRV]
PARANÁ KAINGANG dial of KAINGÁNG [KGP]
PARANAN [AGP] lang, Philippines
PARANAPURA alt for CHAYAHUITA [CBT]
PARANAUAT alt for PARANAWÁT [PAF]
PARANAWÁT [PAF] lang, Brazil
PARATA dial of TUAMOTUAN [PMT]
PARAUJANO [PBG] lang, Venezuela
PARAUK [PRK] lang, Myanmar, China

PARAWEN [PRW] lang, Papua New Guinea
PARAZHGHAN dial of PASHAYI, NORTHWEST [GLH]
PARB alt for IAUGA dial of NAMBU [NCM]
PARBATE alt for KHAM, TAKALE [KJL]
PARBATIYA alt for NEPALI [NEP]
PARDESI dial of AWADHI [AWD]
PARDHAN [PCH] lang, India
PARDHI [PCL] lang, India
PARE [PPT] lang, Papua New Guinea
PARE alt for ASU [ASA]
PARE-PARE alt for BARRU dial of BUGIS [BPR]
PAREC dial of KÂTE [KMG]
PARECÍS [PAB] lang, Brazil
PAREKWA alt for PARKWA [PBI]
PAREN dial of KORYAK [KPY]
PAREN dial of NAGA, ZEME [NZM]
PARENG alt for PARENGI [PCJ]
PARENGA alt for PARENGI [PCJ]
PARENGI [PCJ] lang, India
PARENJI alt for PARENGI [PCJ]
PARESÍ alt for PARECÍS [PAB]
PARESSÍ alt for PARECÍS [PAB]
PARI alt for EMBALOH [EMB]
PARI alt for MUNDURUKÚ [MYU]
PARI alt for LOKORO [LKR]
PARIA alt for PARDHI [PCL]
PARIANA alt for OMAGUA [OMG]
PARIGI alt for TARA dial of KAILI, LEDO [LEW]
PARIKALA dial of YERUKALA [YEU]
PARIKALA dial of TAMIL [TCV]
PARIMA alt for EASTERN YANOMAMI dial of
YANOMAMÖ [GUU]
PARINTINTÍN dial of TENHARIM [PAH]
PARIPAO dial of LENGO [LGR]
PARJA alt for DURUWA [PCI]
PARJHI alt for DURUWA [PCI]
PARJI alt for DURUWA [PCI]
PARKARI alt for KOLI, PARKARI [KVX]
PARKARI KACHCHHI alt for KOLI, PARKARI [KVX]
PARKWA [PBI] lang, Cameroon
PARLATA TRENTINA alt for NONES dial of LADIN
[LLD]
PARNKALA alt for BANGGARLA [BJB]
PARNKALLA alt for BANGGARLA [BJB]
PAROCANA alt for PARAKANÃ [PAK]
PAROLE DES BANA alt for BANA [FLI]
PARQUENAHUA alt for YORA [MTS]
PARSE-KHUMIJ dial of BHUMIJ [BHM]
PARSI alt for FARSI, EASTERN [PRS]
PARSI alt for FARSI, WESTERN [PES]
PARSI dial of GUJARATI [GJR]
PARSIWAN dial of FARSI, EASTERN [PRS]
PARTE alt for CHIN, PAITE [PCK]
PARUA alt for KAYABÍ [KYZ]
PARUCUTU alt for HIXKARYÁNA [HIX]
PARUCUTU alt for KATAWIAN dial of WAIWAI
[WAW]
PARUKOTO-CHARUMA alt for HIXKARYÁNA [HIX]
PARUKUTU alt for KATAWIAN dial of WAIWAI
[WAW]
PARUN alt for PRASUNI [PRN]
PARUWA-KENYARI dial of KAMASAU [KMS]
PARVARI alt for MAHARI dial of KONKANI [KNK]
PARYA [PAQ] lang, Tajikistan, Afghanistan
PASA alt for SIROI [SSD]
PASAALA [SIG] lang, Ghana

PASAALI dial of PASAALA [SIG]
PASALE alt for PASAALA [SIG]
PASALI alt for PASAALA [SIG]
PASAN alt for RATAHAN [RTH]
PASANGKAYU dial of BUGIS [BPR]
PASAR MALAY alt for MALAY, SABAH [MSI]
PASAR MALAY alt for BAZAAR MALAY dial of
  MALAY [MLI]
PASCUENSE alt for RAPANUI [PBA]
PASE dial of ACEH [ATJ]
PASEMAH [PSE] lang, Indonesia, Sumatra
PASHAGAR dial of PASHAYI, NORTHWEST [GLH]
PASHAI alt for PASHAYI, SOUTHEAST [DRA]
PASHAYI, NORTHEAST [AEE] lang, Afghanistan
PASHAYI, NORTHWEST [GLH] lang, Afghanistan
PASHAYI, SOUTHEAST [DRA] lang, Afghanistan
PASHAYI, SOUTHWEST [PSH] lang, Afghanistan
PASHCHIMI dial of KUMAUNI [KFY]
PASHTO, CENTRAL [PST] lang, Pakistan
PASHTO, EASTERN [PBU] lang, Pakistan, United
  Arab Emirates, United Arab Emirates
PASHTO, EASTERN alt for PASHTO, EASTERN [PBU]
PASHTO, SOUTHERN [PBQ] lang, Pakistan,
  Afghanistan
PASHTO, WESTERN [PBT] lang, Afghanistan, Iran,
  Iran, Tajikistan, United Arab Emirates
PASHTO, WESTERN alt for PASHTO, WESTERN
  [PBT]
PASHTU alt for PASHTO, WESTERN [PBT]
PASHTU alt for PASHTO, EASTERN [PBU]
PASI [PSI] lang, Papua New Guinea
PASI dial of MONGONDOW [MOG]
PASIR dial of LAWANGAN [LBX]
PASIR alt for MELAYU PASAR dial of MALAY [MLI]
PASIR MALAY alt for BAZAAR MALAY dial of
  MALAY [MLI]
PASISIR dial of JAVANESE [JAN]
PASISMANUA alt for KAULONG [PSS]
PASO REAL MIXE alt for MIXE, GUICHICOVI [MIR]
PASOOM dial of TA'OIH, UPPER [TTH]
PASPATIAN dial of ROMANI, BALKAN [RMN]
PASS VALLEY alt for NIPSAN [YAC]
PASS VALLEY dial of NIPSAN [YAC]
PASSAM alt for KPASAM [PBN]
PASSAMAQUODDY dial of MALECITE-
  PASSAMAQUODDY [MAC]
PASSTOO alt for PASHTO, WESTERN [PBT]
PASSTOO alt for PASHTO, EASTERN [PBU]
PASTAZA QUICHUA alt for QUICHUA, PASTAZA,
  NORTHERN [QLB]
PASUMA alt for KEWA, WEST [KEW]
PASWAM alt for MUTUM [MCC]
PATA dial of TOGBO [TOR]
PATAKAI alt for NUAULU, NORTH [NNI]
PATAKAI alt for NUAULU, SOUTH [NXL]
PATAMONA [PBC] lang, Guyana
PATANI [PTN] lang, Indonesia, Maluku
PATANI alt for GAMADIA dial of GUJARATI [GJR]
PATANI alt for KABO dial of IJO, CENTRAL-
  WESTERN [IJC]
PATAPORI alt for PEERE [KUT]
PATARA dial of SENOUFO, CEBAARA [SEF]
PATASHÓ alt for PATAXÓ-HÃHÃHÃI [PTH]
PATASIWA ALFOEREN alt for ALUNE [ALP]
PATAXI alt for PATAXÓ-HÃHÃHÃI [PTH]
PATAXÓ-HÃHÃHÃE alt for PATAXÓ-HÃHÃHÃI

[PTH]
PATAXÓ-HÃHÃHÃI [PTH] lang, Brazil
PATE dial of SWAHILI [SWA]
PATELIA [PTL] lang, India
PATELIYA alt for PATELIA [PTL]
PATELIYA BHIL alt for PATELIA [PTL]
PATEP alt for PTEP [PTP]
PATHEE alt for HO dial of CHINESE, MANDARIN
  [CHN]
PATI alt for PAICÎ [PRI]
PATI dial of JIARONG [JYA]
PATIDARI alt for GAMADIA dial of GUJARATI [GJR]
PATIMITHERI alt for YANAMAM dial of YANOMÁMI
  [WCA]
PATIMUNI alt for BAHAM [BDW]
PATIPI dial of ONIN [ONI]
PATLA-CHICONTLA TOTONACO alt for
  TOTONACO, PATLA [TOT]
PATNI alt for LAHULI, CHAMBA [LAE]
PATNULI alt for SAURASHTRA [SAZ]
PATNULI alt for STANDARD GUJARATI dial of
  GUJARATI [GJR]
PATO TAPUIA alt for IPEKA-TAPUIA [PAJ]
PATO-TAPUYA alt for IPEKA-TAPUIA [PAJ]
PATOIS alt for FRENCH GUIANESE [FRE]
PATOIS alt for TRINIDAD CREOLE FRENCH [TRF]
PATOIS alt for LESSER ANTILLEAN CREOLE
  FRENCH [DOM]
PATOIS alt for LESSER ANTILLEAN CREOLE
  ENGLISH [VIB]
PATOIS alt for KRIO [KRI]
PATOOL dial of GULA IRO [GLJ]
PATOXÓ alt for PATAXÓ-HÃHÃHÃI [PTH]
PATPARI alt for PATPATAR [GFK]
PATPATAR [GFK] lang, Papua New Guinea
PATPATAR dial of PATPATAR [GFK]
PATRA-SAARA alt for JUANG [JUN]
PATRI alt for KPATILI [KYM]
PATSOKA alt for YURUTI [YUI]
PATTA' BINUANG alt for PATTAE' dial of MAMASA
  [MQJ]
PATTAE dial of PITU ULUNNA SALU [PTU]
PATTAE' dial of MAMASA [MQJ]
PATTAN alt for INDUS dial of KOHISTANI, INDUS
  [MVY]
PATTANI alt for LAHULI, CHAMBA [LAE]
PATTAPU BHASHA dial of TAMIL [TCV]
PATTINJO dial of ENREKANG [PTT]
PATU alt for KHOWAR [KHW]
PATUA alt for JUANG [JUN]
PATUES alt for ARAGONESE [AXX]
PATVI dial of MALVI [MUP]
PATWA alt for FRENCH GUIANESE [FRE]
PATWA alt for LESSER ANTILLEAN CREOLE
  FRENCH [DOM]
PATWA alt for LESSER ANTILLEAN CREOLE
  ENGLISH [VIB]
PATWIN dial of WINTU [WIT]
PAU CERNE alt for PAUSERNA [PSM]
PAU THIN alt for NHANG [NHA]
PAUHUT alt for BOMPOKA dial of TERESSA [TEF]
PAUINI alt for JAMAMADÍ [JAA]
PAULOHI [PLH] lang, Indonesia, Maluku
PAUMA alt for PAAMA [PMA]
PAUMARÍ [PAD] lang, Brazil
PAUMARÍ dial of PAUMARÍ [PAD]

PAUMEI alt for NAGA, POUMEI [PMX]
PAUNANGIS dial of EFATE, NORTH [LLP]
PAUPE alt for PAPI [PPE]
PAURA alt for PAURI [PWR]
PAURI [PWR] lang, India
PAUSERNA [PSM] lang, Bolivia
PAUSERNA-GUARASUG'WE alt for PAUSERNA
    [PSM]
PAUWI [PKA] lang, Indonesia, Irian Jaya
PAVAIA alt for PAWAIA [PWA]
PAVIOTSO alt for PAIUTE, NORTHERN [PAO]
PAWAIA [PWA] lang, Papua New Guinea
PAWANA alt for MAQUIRITARI [MCH]
PAWARI alt for PAURI [PWR]
PAWARI dial of BUNDELI [BNS]
PAWATÉ alt for PARANAWÁT [PAF]
PAWDAWKWA alt for PARKWA [PBI]
PAWIXI alt for PAWIYANA dial of KAXUIÂNA [KBB]
PAWIYANA dial of KAXUIÂNA [KBB]
PAWNEE [PAW] lang, USA
PAWNEE dial of PAWNEE [PAW]
PAWRI alt for PAURI [PWR]
PAWU alt for PUNU [PNU]
PAWU dial of PUNU [PNU]
PAXALA alt for VAGLA [VAG]
PAY alt for MALA [PED]
PAY alt for PAYI dial of OLO [ONG]
PAYA alt for PECH [PAY]
PAYAGUA alt for OREJÓN [ORE]
PAYAP alt for TAI, NORTHERN [NOD]
PAYI dial of OLO [ONG]
PAYNAMAR [PMR] lang, Papua New Guinea
PAYOWAN alt for PAIWAN [PWN]
PAYUALIENE alt for IPEKA-TAPUIA [PAJ]
PAYULIENE alt for IPEKA-TAPUIA [PAJ]
PAZANDE alt for ZANDE [ZAN]
PAZEH [PZH] lang, Taiwan
PAZEH dial of PAZEH [PZH]
PAZEH-KAHABU alt for PAZEH [PZH]
PAZEHE alt for PAZEH [PZH]
PAZEX alt for PAZEH [PZH]
PAZZEHE alt for PAZEH [PZH]
PBHARYA alt for PARYA [PAQ]
PE dial of MOSI [MSE]
PE alt for PEH dial of HMONG, WESTERN [HUJ]
PE-BAE alt for BAY dial of ENETS [ENE]
PE-HOLOM-GAMÉ dial of MOSI [MSE]
PEANA dial of UMA [PPK]
PEAR [PCB] lang, Cambodia
PEAWA dial of GIDRA [GDR]
PECH [PAY] lang, Honduras
PECIXE alt for YU dial of MANDYAK [MFV]
PECIXE alt for YU dial of MANDYAK [MFV]
PEDI alt for SOTHO, NORTHERN [SRT]
PEDIR alt for PIDIE dial of ACEH [ATJ]
PEDRA BRANCA alt for SABUJÁ dial of KARIRI-
    XUCO [KZW]
PEEKIT alt for NOOHALIT dial of YUPIK, CENTRAL
    SIBERIAN [ESS]
PEER alt for PEERE [KUT]
PEER MUURE dial of PEERE [KUT]
PEERE [KUT] lang, Cameroon, Nigeria, Nigeria
PEERE alt for PEERE [KUT]
PEEWA alt for PEWA dial of KRAHN, WESTERN
    [KRW]
PEGU dial of MON [MNW]

PEGUAN alt for MON [MNW]
PEGULLO-BURA alt for YIDINY [YII]
PEH dial of HMONG, WESTERN [HUJ]
PEHUENCHE dial of MAPUDUNGUN [ARU]
PEI [PPQ] lang, Papua New Guinea
PEI alt for CHINESE, MANDARIN [CHN]
PEI alt for PEH dial of HMONG, WESTERN [HUJ]
PEINAN alt for SOUTHERN AMIS dial of AMIS [ALV]
PEKAL [PEL] lang, Indonesia, Sumatra
PEKAVA alt for DA'A dial of KAILI, DA'A [KZF]
PEKAWA alt for DA'A dial of KAILI, DA'A [KZF]
PEKHI alt for UBYKH [UBY]
PEKUREHUA alt for NAPU [NAP]
PELA dial of BURA-PABIR [BUR]
PELADO alt for PANOBO [PNO]
PELAM alt for PYUMA [PYU]
PELASLA [MLR] lang, Cameroon
PELASLA dial of PELASLA [MLR]
PELAU dial of ONTONG JAVA [LUN]
PELAUW dial of HARUKU [HRK]
PELE dial of PELE-ATA [ATA]
PELE-ATA [ATA] lang, Papua New Guinea
PELEATA alt for PELE-ATA [ATA]
PELENDE [PPP] lang, Zaïre
PELIMPO alt for PINYIN dial of PINYIN [PNY]
PELIPOWAI alt for BOHUAI [RAK]
PELLA alt for HUBA [KIR]
PELMUNG dial of KULUNG [KLE]
PELTA HAY alt for FULFULDE, ADAMAWA [FUB]
PELU alt for BOLU of GEJI [GEZ]
PELUAN alt for PALUAN dial of PALUAN [PLZ]
PELYM alt for WESTERN VOGUL dial of MANSI
    [MNS]
PEM alt for FYAM [PYM]
PEMBA dial of SWAHILI [SWA]
PEMBA dial of SWAHILI [SWA]
PEMBA dial of MWANI [WMW]
PEMBA dial of YANTILI dial of FIPA [FIP]
PEMON [AOC] lang, Venezuela, Brazil, Guyana
PEMON alt for ARECUNA dial of PEMON [AOC]
PEMONG alt for PEMON [AOC]
PEN dial of MBAI, BEDIONDO [MAP]
PEN TI LOLO alt for LAQUA [LAQ]
PEÑABLANCA dial of AGTA, DUPANINAN [DUO]
PENAMPANG KADAZAN alt for KADAZAN,
    COASTAL [KZJ]
PENAN alt for PUNAN-NIBONG [PNE]
PENAN APO dial of PUNAN-NIBONG [PNE]
PENANG SIGN LANGUAGE [PSG] lang, Malaysia,
    Peninsular
PENAPO dial of AMBRYM, SOUTHEAST [TVK]
PENASAK alt for PENESAK [PEN]
PENASIFU dial of BIAK [BHW]
PENCHAL [PEK] lang, Papua New Guinea
PENCHANGAN dial of TIDONG [TID]
PEND D'OREILLE dial of FLATHEAD-KALISPEL [FLA]
PENDAU [UMS] lang, Indonesia, Sulawesi
PENDE alt for PHENDE [PEM]
PENESAK [PEN] lang, Indonesia, Sumatra
PENGE dial of UMBU-UNGU [UMB]
PENGLUNG alt for DE'ANG [BFP]
PENGO [PEG] lang, India
PENGO alt for VENGO [BAV]
PENGU alt for PENGO [PEG]
PENI dial of SAR [MWM]
PENI alt for PEN dial of MBAI, BEDIONDO [MAP]

PENIHING alt for AOHENG [PNI]
PENIN alt for TUNEN [BAZ]
PENINSULA SHERBRO dial of SHERBRO [BUN]
PENNSYLVANIA DUTCH alt for GERMAN,
   PENNSYLVANIA [PDC]
PENNSYLVANISCH alt for GERMAN,
   PENNSYLVANIA [PDC]
PENNSYLVANISCH DEITSCH alt for NON-AMISH
   PENNSYLVANIA GERMAN dial of GERMAN,
   PENNSYLVANIA [PDC]
PENNSYLVANISH alt for GERMAN, PENNSYLVANIA
   [PDC]
PENOBSCOT dial of ABNAKI-PENOBSCOT [ABE]
PEÑOLES alt for SANTA MARÍA PEÑOLES dial of
   MIXTECO, EASTERN [MIL]
PEÑOLES MIXTECO alt for MIXTECO, EASTERN
   [MIL]
PENRHYN [PNH] lang, Cook Islands
PENSIANGAN MURUT dial of TAGAL MURUT [MVV]
PENSIANGAN MURUT dial of TAGAL MURUT [MVV]
PENSYLVANISCH DEITSCH alt for NON-AMISH
   PENNSYLVANIA GERMAN dial of GERMAN,
   PENNSYLVANIA [PDC]
PENTJANGAN alt for PENSIANGAN MURUT dial of
   TAGAL MURUT [MVV]
PÉNTJÁNGÁN alt for PENSIANGAN MURUT dial of
   TAGAL MURUT [MVV]
PENTLATCH [PTW] lang, Canada
PENYABUNG PUNAN alt for PUNAN dial of DAYAK,
   LAND [DYK]
PENYABUNG PUNAN alt for MURANG PUNAN dial of
   DAYAK, LAND [DYK]
PENYIN alt for TUNEN [BAZ]
PENYU dial of NGOMBALE [NLA]
PÉOMÉ dial of WOBE [WOB]
PEORIA dial of MIAMI [MIA]
PEPEHA alt for MINANIBAI [MCV]
PEPEL alt for PAPEL [PBO]
PEPESA dial of JWIRA-PEPESA [JWI]
PEPESA-JWIRA alt for JWIRA-PEPESA [JWI]
PEPO-HWAN alt for SIRAIYA [FOS]
PEPOHOAN alt for SIRAIYA [FOS]
PEQUOT-MOHEGAN dial of MOHEGAN-MONTAUK-
   NARRAGANSETT [MOF]
PERAI [WET] lang, Indonesia, Maluku
PERAK dial of MALAY [MLI]
PERAK I dial of SEMAI [SEA]
PERAK II dial of SEMAI [SEA]
PERANAKAN alt for INDONESIAN, PERANAKAN
   [PEA]
PERÄPOHJA dial of FINNISH [FIN]
PERAS dial of MIXTECO, METLATONOC [MXV]
PERE alt for PEERE [KUT]
PERE alt for WOM [WOM]
PERE alt for BHELE [PER]
PERE alt for GBETE dial of MBUM [MDD]
PERE alt for KEPERE dial of MBUM [MDD]
PEREBA alt for WOM [WOM]
PEREMA alt for WOM [WOM]
PEREMKA [PEP] lang, Papua New Guinea
PERENE dial of CAMPA, ASHÉNINCA [CPU]
PERI alt for BHELE [PER]
PERI dial of KALANGA [KCK]
PERIHO dial of OROKAIVA [ORK]
PERIM dial of TOUNIA [TUG]
PERIPHERAL KONO dial of KONO [KNO]

PERMYAK alt for KOMI-PERMYAK [KOI]
PERO [PIP] lang, Nigeria
PERSIAN alt for FARSI, EASTERN [PRS]
PERSIAN alt for FARSI, WESTERN [PES]
PERUVIAN SIGN LANGUAGE [PRL] lang, Peru
PESAA alt for NSARI [ASJ]
PESECHAM alt for NDUGA [NDX]
PESECHEM alt for NDUGA [NDX]
PESEGEM alt for NDUGA [NDX]
PESHAWAR alt for YUSUFZAI dial of PASHTO,
   EASTERN [PBU]
PESHAWAR HINDKO dial of HINDKO, SOUTHERN
   [HIN]
PESHAWARI alt for PESHAWAR HINDKO dial of
   HINDKO, SOUTHERN [HIN]
PESII alt for WUSHI [BSE]
PESISIR, SOUTHERN [PEC] lang, Indonesia, Sumatra
PESKE alt for BVERI dial of FALI, NORTH [FLL]
PESKI dial of BANA [FLI]
PESSA alt for KPELLE, GUINEA [GKP]
PESSA alt for KPELLE, LIBERIA [KPE]
PESSY alt for KPELLE, GUINEA [GKP]
PESSY alt for KPELLE, LIBERIA [KPE]
PETA dial of NYANJA [NYJ]
PETA dial of NYANJA [NYJ]
PETAPA alt for TAJE [PEE]
PETASIA dial of MORI BAWAH [XMZ]
PETATS [PEX] lang, Papua New Guinea
PETCHABUN dial of HMONG, WESTERN [HUJ]
PETCHABUN MIAO alt for HMONG DAW [MWW]
PETEM alt for BETEN dial of KWAKUM [KWU]
PETÉN ITZÁ MAYA alt for ITZÁ [ITZ]
PETERARA dial of MAEWO, CENTRAL [MWO]
PETH alt for MALUAL dial of DINKA,
   SOUTHWESTERN [DIK]
PETIMPUI dial of WOISIKA [WOI]
PETSPETS dial of TEOP [TIO]
PEUHL alt for FULFULDE, JELGOOJI [FUM]
PEUL alt for FULFULDE, ADAMAWA [FUB]
PEUL alt for FULACUNDA [FUC]
PEUL alt for FULFULDE, BENIN-TOGO [FUE]
PEUL alt for FULFULDE, BAGIRMI [FUI]
PEUL alt for FULFULDE, MAASINA [FUL]
PEUL alt for FULFULDE, JELGOOJI [FUM]
PEUL alt for FULFULDE, KANO-KATSINA-BORORRO
   [FUV]
PEULH alt for FULFULDE, ADAMAWA [FUB]
PEULH alt for FULFULDE, BENIN-TOGO [FUE]
PEVÉ [LME] lang, Chad, Cameroon
PEVEKSKIJ dial of CHUKOT [CKT]
PEWA dial of KRAHN, WESTERN [KRW]
PEWANEAN alt for SEKO TENGAH [SKO]
PEWANEANG alt for SEKO TENGAH [SKO]
PFOKOMO alt for POKOMO, LOWER [POJ]
PHAANI dial of DII [DUR]
PHADANG dial of NAGA, TANGKHUL [NMF]
PHAI [PRT] lang, Thailand, Laos
PHAILENG dial of CHIN, TEDIM [CTD]
PHAKE [PHK] lang, India
PHAKEY alt for PHAKE [PHK]
PHAKIAL alt for PHAKE [PHK]
PHALABORWA alt for SOTHO, NORTHERN [SRT]
PHALABURWA alt for PHALABORWA dial of
   SOTHO, NORTHERN [SRT]
PHALDAKOTIYA dial of KUMAUNI [KFY]
PHALO dial of LAWA, EASTERN [LWL]

PHALOK alt for PARAUK [PRK]
PHALURA [PHL] lang, Pakistan
PHẢN SINH dial of NUNG [NUT]
PHANA' [PHN] lang, Laos
PHANG dial of LAWA, EASTERN [LWL]
PHANG dial of BLANG [BLR]
PHANI dial of VENDA [VEN]
PHANS PARDHI alt for PARDHI [PCL]
PHARI KULU alt for KULUI [KFX]
PHAY alt for PHAI [PRT]
PHAYAP alt for TAI, NORTHERN [NOD]
PHAYENG dial of KADO [KDV]
PHELONGRE dial of NAGA, SANGTAM [NSA]
PHEMBA alt for PEMBA dial of SWAHILI [SWA]
PHEN alt for THO [THO]
PHENDE [PEM] lang, Zaïre
PHERA alt for XWELA-GBE [XWE]
PHERRONGRE dial of NAGA, YIMCHUNGRU [YIM]
PHI THONG LUANG alt for MLABRI [MRA]
PHI TONG LUANG alt for KHA TONG LUANG [KHQ]
PHILIPPINE SIGN LANGUAGE [PSP] lang, Philippines
PHLA alt for XWLA-GBE [XWL]
PHLON alt for KAREN, PWO OMKOI [PWW]
PHLON dial of KAREN, PWO [PWO]
PHLON alt for KAREN, PWO OMKOI [PWW]
PHLONG alt for KAREN, PWO OMKOI [PWW]
PHNONG alt for MNONG, CENTRAL [MNC]
PHO KAREN alt for KAREN, PWO [PWO]
PHO KAREN alt for KAREN, PWO OMKOI [PWW]
PHOKA alt for POKA dial of TUMBUKA [TUW]
PHOKE alt for TIBETAN [TIC]
PHOKE alt for HUMLA BHOTIA [HUT]
PHOKE DOLPA alt for DOLPO [DRE]
PHOLONG alt for KAREN, PWO [PWO]
PHOM alt for NAGA, PHOM [NPH]
PHON alt for NAGA, PHOM [NPH]
PHỔN alt for HPON [HPO]
PHON alt for HPON [HPO]
PHON SOUNG alt for PHON SUNG [PHS]
PHON SUNG [PHS] lang, Laos
PHONG alt for PONG 1 [KPN]
PHOTSIMI dial of NAGA, SANGTAM [NSA]
PHOU LAO alt for LAO [NOL]
PHRAE alt for KAREN, NORTHERN PWO [KJT]
PHSING alt for BIT [BGK]
PHU THAI [PHT] lang, Laos, Thailand, Thailand, Viet
 Nam
PHU THAI alt for PHU THAI [PHT]
PHU UN alt for PHUAN [PHU]
PHUAN [PHU] lang, Thailand, Laos
PHUANG alt for PHUONG [PHG]
PHÚC KIẾN alt for CHINESE, YUE [YUH]
PHUDAGI [PHD] lang, India
PHUDAGI alt for VADVAL [VAD]
PHULA alt for LATI [LBT]
PHUN alt for HPON [HPO]
PHUNOI [PHO] lang, Laos, Thailand, Thailand
PHUONG [PHG] lang, Viet Nam
PHUONG CATANG alt for PHUONG [PHG]
PHUTAI alt for PHU THAI [PHT]
PHUTHI dial of SWATI [SWZ]
PHUTHI dial of SOTHO, SOUTHERN [SSO]
PHUU THAI alt for PHU THAI [PHT]
PHYAP alt for TAI, NORTHERN [NOD]
PIA alt for PIYA [PIY]
PIAJAO [PIJ] lang, Colombia

PIAMATSINA [PTR] lang, Vanuatu
PIAME [PIN] lang, Papua New Guinea
PIANAKOTÓ alt for KATAWIAN dial of WAIWAI
 [WAW]
PIANGA dial of BUSHOONG [BUF]
PIANOCOTÓ dial of TRIÓ [TRI]
PIAPOCO [PIO] lang, Colombia, Venezuela,
 Venezuela
PIAROA [PID] lang, Venezuela
PIAROA dial of PIAROA [PID]
PICARD dial of FRENCH [FRN]
PICHINCHA QUICHUA alt for QUICHUA, HIGHLAND,
 CALDERÓN [QUD]
PICHIS dial of CAMPA, ASHÉNINCA [CPU]
PICUNCHE dial of MAPUDUNGUN [ARU]
PICURIS dial of TIWA, NORTHERN [TAO]
PIDÁ-DJAPÁ alt for KATUKÍNA [KAV]
PIDGIN alt for HAWAI'I CREOLE ENGLISH [HAW]
PIDGIN alt for TOK PISIN [PDG]
PIDGIN alt for JHARWA dial of ASSAMESE [ASM]
PIDGIN ARABIC alt for ARABIC, SUDANESE CREOLE
 [PGA]
PIDGIN BANTU alt for FANAGOLO [FAO]
PIDGIN MOTU alt for MOTU, HIRI [POM]
PIDGIN SIGN LANGUAGE alt for HAWAI'I PIDGIN
 SIGN LANGUAGE [HPS]
PIDGIN, CAMEROON [WES] lang, Cameroon
PIDGIN, NIGERIAN [PCM] lang, Nigeria
PIDGIN, TIMOR [TVY] lang, Indonesia, Nusa
 Tenggara
PIDHA dial of LENDU [LED]
PIDIE dial of ACEH [ATJ]
PIDISOI alt for LOHORONG [LBR]
PIDLIMDI dial of TERA [TER]
PIDO dial of WOISIKA [WOI]
PIE alt for TEMIAR [TMH]
PIE dial of KRUMEN, NORTHEASTERN [PYE]
PIE-PLI-MAHON-KUSE-GBLAPO-HENEKWE alt for PIE
 dial of KRUMEN, NORTHEASTERN [PYE]
PIEDMONT SINTÍ dial of ROMANI, SINTE [RMO]
PIEDMONTESE alt for PIEMONTESE [PMS]
PIEGAN dial of BLACKFOOT [BLC]
PIEMONTE dial of FRANCO-PROVENÇAL [FRA]
PIEMONTESE [PMS] lang, Italy
PIIGA dial of UKHWEJO [UKH]
PIJAO alt for PIAJAO [PIJ]
PIJE [PIZ] lang, New Caledonia
PIJIN [PIS] lang, Solomon Islands
PIKARU alt for BIKARU [BIC]
PIKARU dial of BISORIO [BIR]
PIKI alt for FANAGOLO [FAO]
PIKIWA alt for BAINAPI [PIK]
PIL alt for WESTERN TEMNE dial of THEMNE [TEJ]
PILA [PIL] lang, Benin
PILA alt for MIANI [PLA]
PILA alt for MAIA [SKS]
PILACA alt for PILAGÁ [PLG]
PILAGÁ [PLG] lang, Argentina
PILAM alt for PYUMA [PYU]
PILAPILA alt for PILA [PIL]
PILENI [PIV] lang, Solomon Islands
PILENI dial of PILENI [PIV]
PILHENI alt for PILENI [PIV]
PILI alt for BHELE [PER]
PILILO alt for AROVE [AAW]
PILIPINO alt for TAGALOG [TGL]

PIMA dial of PAPAGO-PIMA [PAP]
PIMA BAJO, CHIHUAHUA [PMB] lang, Mexico
PIMA BAJO, SONORA [PIA] lang, Mexico
PIMBI dial of NSENGA [NSE]
PIMBWE [PIW] lang, Tanzania
PIMENC alt for NOMAANDE [LEM]
PIMURU dial of IKOBI-MENA [MEB]
PIN alt for TRIENG [STG]
PINAI [PNN] lang, Papua New Guinea
PINAI 1 dial of PINAI [PNN]
PINAI 2 dial of PINAI [PNN]
PINAN dial of PYUMA [PYU]
PINATA dial of TAIRORA [TBG]
PINAYE alt for PINAI [PNN]
PINCHE alt for TAUSHIRO [TRR]
PINCHI alt for TAUSHIRO [TRR]
PINDARE dial of GUAJAJÁRA [GUB]
PINDI alt for KWESE [KWS]
PINDI alt for PHENDE [PEM]
PINDIINI alt for PINTIINI [PTI]
PINDJE alt for PIJE [PIZ]
PINE alt for BINE [ORM]
PINGAS alt for BAUKAN dial of BAUKAN [BNB]
PINGELAP [PIF] lang, Micronesia, USA
PINGELAPESE alt for PINGELAP [PIF]
PINGFANG dial of QIANG [CNG]
PINGILAPESE alt for PINGELAP [PIF]
PINGYANG dial of CHINESE, MIN NAN [CFR]
PINGYUAN dial of CHINESE, HAKKA [HAK]
PINI [PII] lang, Australia
PINIGURA [PNV] lang, Australia
PINIRITJARA alt for PINI [PII]
PINJARI dial of URDU [URD]
PINJE alt for PIJE [PIZ]
PINJI [PIC] lang, Gabon
PINJI alt for PHENDE [PEM]
PINNEEGOOROO alt for BURDUNA [BXN]
PINOTEPA NACIONAL MIXTECO alt for MIXTECO,
    WESTERN JAMILTEPEC [MIO]
PINRANG alt for SAWITTO dial of BUGIS [BPR]
PINRANG UTARA alt for SIDRAP dial of BUGIS [BPR]
PINTIINI [PTI] lang, Australia
PINTUBI alt for PINTUPI-LURITJA [PIU]
PINTUMBANG dial of KABOLA [KLZ]
PINTUPI-LURITJA [PIU] lang, Australia
PINYIN [PNY] lang, Cameroon
PINYIN dial of PINYIN [PNY]
PIOCHE-SIONI alt for SIONA [SIN]
PIOJE alt for SIONA [SIN]
PIOJÉ dial of SECOYA [SEY]
PIPERO alt for PERO [PIP]
PIPIKORO alt for UMA [PPK]
PIPIL [PPL] lang, El Salvador, Honduras, Honduras
PIPIL alt for PIPIL [PPL]
PIPIPAIA dial of ROTOKAS [ROO]
PIRA alt for PIRO [PIB]
PIRÁ-TAPUYA alt for PIRATAPUYO [PIR]
PIRABANAK dial of CITAK [TXT]
PIRAHÃ alt for MÚRA-PIRAHÃ [MYP]
PIRATAPUYO [PIR] lang, Brazil, Colombia, Colombia
PIRATAPUYO alt for PIRATAPUYO [PIR]
PIRI alt for BHELE [PER]
PIRIMI dial of BARAI [BCA]
PIRNIRITJARA alt for PINI [PII]
PIRO [PIB] lang, Peru, Brazil
PIRO dial of PIRO [PIB]

PIRR dial of NAGA, SANGTAM [NSA]
PIRRO alt for PIRO [PIB]
PIRU [PPR] lang, Indonesia, Maluku
PIRUPIRU dial of BAMU [BCF]
PISA [PSA] lang, Indonesia, Irian Jaya
PISABO [PIG] lang, Peru
PISAGUA alt for PISABO [PIG]
PISAHUA alt for PISABO [PIG]
PISHAGCHI dial of AZERBAIJANI, SOUTH [AZB]
PISHAUCO alt for ARECUNA dial of PEMON [AOC]
PISIN alt for TOK PISIN [PDG]
PISO dial of KALAGAN [KQE]
PISQUIBO dial of SHIPIBO-CONIBO [SHP]
PITA PITA alt for PITTA PITTA [PIT]
PITAS BAJAU dial of BAJAU, WEST COAST [BDR]
PITAS KIMARAGANG dial of KIMARAGANG [KQR]
PITAS SONSOGON dial of SONSOGON [SGN]
PITAYO dial of PÁEZ [PBB]
PITCAIRN ENGLISH alt for PITCAIRN-NORFOLK [PIH]
PITCAIRN ENGLISH dial of PITCAIRN-NORFOLK [PIH]
PITCAIRN-NORFOLK [PIH] lang, Norfolk Island,
    Australia, New Zealand, Pitcairn
PITCAIRN-NORFOLK alt for PITCAIRN-NORFOLK
    [PIH]
PITE alt for SAAMI, PITE [LPB]
PITI [PCN] lang, Nigeria
PITILU alt for LEIPON [LEK]
PITJANTJARA alt for PITJANTJATJARA [PJT]
PITJANTJATJARA [PJT] lang, Australia
PITONARA alt for POTIGUÁRA [POG]
PITT RIVER alt for ACHUMAWI [ACH]
PITTA PITTA [PIT] lang, Australia
PITTALA BHASHA dial of BHILI [BHB]
PITTALA BHASHA dial of PARDHI [PCL]
PITTI alt for PITI [PCN]
PITU ULUNA BINANGA alt for PITU ULUNNA SALU
    [PTU]
PITU ULUNNA SALU [PTU] lang, Indonesia, Sulawesi
PITU-ULUNA-SALO alt for PITU ULUNNA SALU
    [PTU]
PITYILU alt for LEIPON [LEK]
PIU [PIX] lang, Papua New Guinea
PIVA [TGI] lang, Papua New Guinea
PIYA [PIY] lang, Nigeria
PIYUMA alt for PYUMA [PYU]
PLADINA alt for FULFULDE, ADAMAWA [FUB]
PLAIN alt for NYA GUYUWA dial of LONGUDA [LNU]
PLAIN ANGAS dial of ANGAS [ANC]
PLAIN BURA alt for HYILHAWUL dial of BURA-PABIR
    [BUR]
PLAIN PENNSYLVANIA GERMAN alt for AMISH
    PENNSYLVANIA GERMAN dial of GERMAN,
    PENNSYLVANIA [PDC]
PLAIN TAROK dial of TAROK [YER]
PLAINS BIRA alt for BERA [BRF]
PLAINS CREE dial of CREE, WESTERN [CRP]
PLAINS GETA' dial of GATA' [GAQ]
PLAINS INDIAN SIGN LANGUAGE [PSD] lang, USA
PLAINS JARAWA alt for BADA [BAU]
PLAINS MIWOK dial of MIWOK [SKD]
PLAINS TARANGAN dial of TARANGAN, WEST
    [TXN]
PLANG alt for BLANG [BLR]
PLAPO dial of KRUMEN, SOUTHERN [TED]
PLASLA alt for PELASLA dial of PELASLA [MLR]
PLATA alt for PELASLA dial of PELASLA [MLR]

PLATEAU HAITIAN CREOLE dial of HAITIAN CREOLE FRENCH [HAT]
PLATEAU TONGA alt for TONGA [TOI]
PLATLA alt for PELASLA dial of PELASLA [MLR]
PLATTDEUTSCH alt for GERMAN, LOW [GEP]
PLAUTDIETSCH [GRN] lang, Canada, Belize, Bolivia, Brazil, Costa Rica, Mexico, Paraguay, USA, Germany, Russia, Europe
PLAUTDIETSCH alt for PLAUTDIETSCH [GRN]
PLAYERO [GOB] lang, Colombia
PLEIKLY dial of JARAI [JRA]
PLO dial of KRAHN, WESTERN [KRW]
PLOSKOST alt for AKKA dial of CHECHEN [CJC]
PLUS dial of KENSIU [KNS]
PMASA'A dial of HAMTAI [HMT]
PNAR [PBV] lang, India
PNONG alt for MNONG, CENTRAL [MNC]
PNONG alt for BUNONG dial of MNONG, SOUTHERN [MNN]
PO alt for BO [BPW]
PO RANG alt for PRANG dial of MNONG, SOUTHERN [MNN]
PO-KLO dial of TEMIAR [TMH]
POAI alt for FWÂI [FWA]
POAMEI alt for PWAAMEI [PME]
POAPOA alt for PWAPWA [POP]
POAVOSA alt for BABUZA [BZG]
POAVOSA dial of BABUZA [BZG]
POBYENG alt for MBOBYENG dial of MPONGMPONG [MGG]
POCHURI alt for NAGA, POCHURI [NPO]
POCHURY alt for NAGA, POCHURI [NPO]
POCOMAM ORIENTAL alt for POKOMAM, EASTERN [POA]
POCOMÁN alt for POKOMAM, CENTRAL [POC]
POCOMCHÍ alt for POKOMCHÍ, WESTERN [POB]
POCOMCHÍ alt for POKOMCHÍ, EASTERN [POH]
POCONCHÍ alt for POKOMCHÍ, EASTERN [POH]
PODARI dial of GIDRA [GDR]
PODENA alt for SOBEI [SOB]
PODI alt for BODI dial of ME'EN [MYM]
PODIA KOYA dial of KOYA [KFF]
PODKAMENNAYA TUNGUSKA dial of EVENKI [EVN]
PODOBA alt for FOLOPA [PPO]
PODOGO alt for PARKWA [PBI]
PODOKGE dial of TUPURI [TUI]
PODOKO alt for PARKWA [PBI]
PODOKWO alt for PARKWA [PBI]
PODOPA alt for FOLOPA [PPO]
PODRA alt for TODRAH [TDR]
PODZO [POZ] lang, Mozambique
POENG alt for MENGEN [MEE]
POGADI CHIB alt for ANGLOROMANI [RME]
POGARA dial of SENOUFO, CEBAARA [SEF]
POGAYA alt for BOGAYA [BOQ]
POGOLO [POY] lang, Tanzania
POGOLU alt for POGOLO [POY]
POGORA alt for POGOLO [POY]
POGORO alt for POGOLO [POY]
POGULI dial of KASHMIRI [KSH]
POHBETIAN alt for TIBETAN [TIC]
POHNPEIAN alt for PONAPEAN [PNF]
POHONEANG alt for SEKO TENGAH [SKO]
POHUAI alt for BOHUAI [RAK]
POI dial of IAU [TMU]
POIANÁUA alt for POYANÁWA [PYN]

POINT BARROW ESKIMO dial of INUIT, NORTH ALASKAN [ESI]
POITEVIN dial of FRENCH [FRN]
POJOAQUE dial of TEWA [TEW]
PŎJULU dial of BARI [BFA]
PÕJULU dial of BARI [BFA]
POK dial of SABAOT [SPY]
POKA dial of TUMBUKA [TUW]
POKANGÁ [POK] lang, Brazil
POKANGÁ-TAPUYA alt for POKANGÁ [POK]
POKAU alt for NARA [NRZ]
POKE [POF] lang, Zaïre
POKO dial of LOBALA [LOQ]
POKOH alt for PACOH [PAC]
POKOMAM, CENTRAL [POC] lang, Guatemala, El Salvador
POKOMAM, EASTERN [POA] lang, Guatemala
POKOMAM, SOUTHERN [POU] lang, Guatemala
POKOMCHÍ, EASTERN [POH] lang, Guatemala
POKOMCHÍ, WESTERN [POB] lang, Guatemala
POKOMO, LOWER [POJ] lang, Kenya
POKOMO, UPPER [PKB] lang, Kenya
POKONCHÍ alt for POKOMCHÍ, EASTERN [POH]
PŎKOOT [PKO] lang, Kenya, Uganda, Uganda
PÕKOOT alt for PÖKOOT [PKO]
POKOT alt for PÖKOOT [PKO]
POKPAPA dial of TINPUTZ [TPZ]
POL [PMM] lang, Congo, Cameroon, Central African Republic
POL dial of POL [PMM]
POL-BETHEN dial of POL [PMM]
POL-POMO alt for POL [PMM]
POLABIAN [POX] lang, Germany
POLAR ESKIMO dial of INUIT, GREENLANDIC [ESG]
POLARI [PLD] lang, United Kingdom
POLCHI alt for POLCI [POL]
POLCI [POL] lang, Nigeria
POLCI dial of POLCI [POL]
POLE alt for KEWA, SOUTH [KJY]
POLEANG alt for WITA EA dial of MORONENE [MQN]
POLEO dial of TALISE [TLR]
POLI alt for POL dial of POL [PMM]
POLI alt for TEERE dial of DOYAYO [DOW]
POLICE MOTU alt for MOTU, HIRI [POM]
POLIGUS dial of EVENKI [EVN]
POLISH [PQL] lang, Poland, Czechoslovakia, Germany, Israel, Romania, Ukraine
POLISH alt for POLISH [PQL]
POLISH ROMANI dial of ROMANI, BALTIC [ROM]
POLISH SIGN LANGUAGE [PSO] lang, Poland
POLO dial of ATSI [ATB]
POLOGOZOM dial of DABA [DAB]
POLOME alt for KIBIRI [PRM]
POLONOMBAUK [PLB] lang, Vanuatu
POLOPA alt for FOLOPA [PPO]
POLOTS alt for NORTHEAST BELORUSSIAN dial of BELORUSSIAN [RUW]
POLSHI alt for POLCI dial of POLCI [POL]
POM [PMO] lang, Indonesia, Irian Jaya
POMAK alt for BULGARIAN [BLG]
POMAK alt for BULGARIAN [BLG]
POMERANIA alt for EAST LOW GERMAN dial of GERMAN, LOW [GEP]
POMO [POO] lang, USA
POMO alt for POL [PMM]

POMO dial of POL [PMM]
PONAAL dial of GULA IRO [GLJ]
PONAM [NCC] lang, Papua New Guinea
PONAPE alt for PONAPEAN [PNF]
PONAPEAN [PNF] lang, Micronesia
PONAPEAN dial of PONAPEAN [PNF]
PONARES [POD] lang, Colombia
PONASAKAN alt for PONOSAKAN [PNS]
PONCA [PQN] lang, USA
PONDA alt for LUCHAZI [LCH]
PONDO alt for ANGORAM [AOG]
PONDO dial of PANA [PNZ]
PONDOMA [PDA] lang, Papua New Guinea
PONEK alt for TUOTOMB [TTF]
PONEK alt for BONEK dial of TUNEN [BAZ]
PONERIHOUEN alt for PAICÎ [PRI]
PONG 1 [KPN] lang, Laos, Viet Nam, Viet Nam
PONG 1 alt for PONG 1 [KPN]
PONG 2 [PGO] lang, Laos
PONG 3 [PNX] lang, Laos
PONG'OM alt for BONG'OMEK dial of SABAOT
    [SPY]
PONGO alt for PONGU [PON]
PONGO dial of DUALA [DOU]
PONGOUÉ alt for MPONGWE dial of MYENE [MYE]
PONGPONG alt for MPONGMPONG [MGG]
PONGU [PON] lang, Nigeria
PONNA alt for MEITHEI [MNR]
PONO alt for AROP-LOKEP [APR]
PONO alt for GBETE dial of MBUM [MDD]
PONORWAL dial of SA [SSA]
PONOSAKAN [PNS] lang, Indonesia, Sulawesi
PONTHAI dial of NAGA, TASE [NST]
PONTIANAK alt for RITOK dial of MALAY [MLI]
PONTIC [PNT] lang, Greece, USA
PONYO alt for NAGA, KHIAMNGAN [NKY]
POODENA alt for BURDUNA [BXN]
POONCHI alt for PUNCHHI dial of PAHARI-POTWARI
    [PHR]
POONG alt for PONG 1 [KPN]
POONG alt for PONG 2 [PGO]
POORDOONA alt for BURDUNA [BXN]
POPENGARE alt for APURINĂ [APU]
POPO alt for ÉWÉ [EWE]
POPO alt for GEN-GBE [GEJ]
POPOI dial of MANGBETU [MDJ]
POPOLOCA, COYOTEPEC [PBF] lang, Mexico
POPOLOCA, EASTERN [POE] lang, Mexico
POPOLOCA, NORTHERN [PLS] lang, Mexico
POPOLOCA, SANTA INÉS AHUATEMPAN [PCA]
    lang, Mexico
POPOLOCA, SOUTHERN [PBE] lang, Mexico
POPOLOCA, WESTERN [POW] lang, Mexico
POPOLUCA, OLUTA [PLO] lang, Mexico
POPOLUCA, SAYULA [POS] lang, Mexico
POPOLUCA, SIERRA [POI] lang, Mexico
POPOLUCA, TEXISTEPEC [POQ] lang, Mexico
POPONDETTA dial of OROKAIVA [ORK]
POR alt for PEAR [PCB]
POREN alt for NYANG'I [NYP]
PORI alt for POL [PMM]
PORI ASOM alt for AZOM dial of POL [PMM]
PORI KINDA dial of POL [PMM]
PORJA alt for KONDA-DORA [KFC]
PORMI alt for NDAI [GKE]
POROHANON [PRH] lang, Philippines

POROJA alt for PARENGI [PCJ]
POROME alt for KIBIRI [PRM]
POROME dial of KIBIRI [PRM]
PORONAISK dial of OROK [OAA]
POROS dial of TIMUGON MURUT [TIH]
PORT SANDWICH [PSW] lang, Vanuatu
PORT VATO [PTV] lang, Vanuatu
PORTUGUÊS DE BIDAU dial of PIDGIN, TIMOR [TVY]
PORTUGUÊS DE MALACA alt for MALACCAN
    CREOLE PORTUGUESE [MCM]
PORTUGUESE [POR] lang, Portugal, Brazil, Angola,
    Cape Verde Islands, Guinea Bissau, Mozambique,
    Sao Tome e Principe, France, Macau
PORTUGUESE CALÃO dial of ROMANI, CALO [RMR]
PORTUGUESE CALÃO dial of ROMANI, CALO [RMR]
PORTUGUESE CREOLE alt for CRIOULO, UPPER
    GUINEA [POV]
PORTUGUÊS DE MALACA alt for MALACCAN CREOLE
    PORTUGUESE [MCM]
PORTUGUESE SIGN LANGUAGE [PSR] lang, Portugal
POSA alt for POLCI dial of POLCI [POL]
POSH 'N' POSH alt for ANGLOROMANI [RME]
POSO alt for PAMONA [BCX]
POSO dial of BAJAU, INDONESIAN [BDL]
POTAWATOMI [POT] lang, USA, Canada
POTHOHARI alt for PAHARI-POTWARI [PHR]
POTHWARI dial of PAHARI-POTWARI [PHR]
POTIGUÁRA [POG] lang, Brazil
POTINHUA alt for CHINESE, MANDARIN [CHN]
POTNARIVEN dial of SIE [ERG]
POTOPO alt for PEERE [KUT]
POTOPO alt for DAN MUURE dial of PEERE [KUT]
POTOPORE alt for PEERE [KUT]
POTOSÍ dial of QUECHUA, SOUTH BOLIVIAN [QUH]
POTOTAN dial of KINARAY-A [KRJ]
POTSAWUGOK alt for ARECUNA dial of PEMON
    [AOC]
POTTANGI dial of GADABA [GDB]
POTTAWOTOMI alt for POTAWATOMI [POT]
POTU alt for MBATO [GWA]
POTULE dial of SISAALA, TUMULUNG [SIL]
POTWARI alt for PAHARI-POTWARI [PHR]
POTWARI alt for POTHWARI dial of PAHARI-
    POTWARI [PHR]
POUÉBO dial of CAAC [MSQ]
POUGOULI alt for PUGULI [PUG]
POUMEI alt for NAGA, POUMEI [PMX]
POUN alt for BON GULA [GLC]
POUNO alt for PUNU [PUU]
POUSS alt for MPUS dial of MUSGU [MUG]
POUSS alt for MPUS dial of MUSGU [MUG]
POUTENG alt for KHMU [KJG]
POUTENG alt for KHANG [KJM]
POVA dial of IGORA [KQF]
POVE alt for BUBI [BUW]
POWARI dial of BHOYARI [BHY]
POWARI dial of BAGHELI [BFY]
POWARI alt for PAWARI dial of BUNDELI [BNS]
POWHATAN [PIM] lang, USA
POYANÁWA [PYN] lang, Brazil
POYENISATI alt for CAQUINTE [COT]
PRADHAN alt for PARDHAN [PCH]
PRADHANI alt for PARDHAN [PCH]
PRAE alt for KAREN, NORTHERN PWO [KJT]
PRAI alt for PHAI [PRT]
PRAISTIKI dial of ROMANI, SINTE [RMO]

PRANG alt for KPLANG [PRA]
PRANG dial of MNONG, SOUTHERN [MNN]
PRANG dial of CHRAU [CHR]
PRAOK alt for PARAUK [PRK]
PRASUN alt for PRASUNI [PRN]
PRASUNI [PRN] lang, Afghanistan
PRAY 1 alt for PHAI [PRT]
PRAY 2 alt for LUA' [PRB]
PRAY 3 [PRY] lang, Thailand
PRE alt for PRÉH dial of MNONG, CENTRAL [MNC]
PREH dial of MNONG, CENTRAL [MNC]
PRÉH dial of MNONG, CENTRAL [MNC]
PREHAN dial of MELANAU [MEL]
PRIANGAN alt for SUNDA [SUO]
PRIBILOF ALEUT alt for EASTERN ALEUT dial of
   ALEUT [ALW]
PRIEGNITZ alt for EAST LOW GERMAN dial of
   GERMAN, LOW [GEP]
PRIMMI alt for PUMI [PMI]
PRINCIPENSE dial of CRIOULO, GULF OF GUINEA
   [CRI]
PRINGAN dial of SUNDA [SUO]
PRIONEZH dial of VEPS [VEP]
PRIULIAN alt for FRIULIAN [FRL]
PROBUR dial of KELON [KYO]
PROON alt for TAMPUAN [TPU]
PROONS alt for TAMPUAN [TPU]
PROUE alt for BRAO [BRB]
PROUVENÇAU alt for PROVENÇAL [PRV]
PROVENÇAL [PRV] lang, France, Italy, Italy, Monaco
PROVENÇAL alt for PROVENÇAL [PRV]
PROVENZALE alt for PROVENÇAL [PRV]
PROVIDENCIA SIGN LANGUAGE [PRO] lang,
   Colombia
PRSL alt for PUERTO RICAN SIGN LANGUAGE [PSL]
PRU dial of KOHO [KPM]
PRUUMI alt for PUMI [PMI]
PSHAV dial of GEORGIAN [GEO]
PSIKYE [KVJ] lang, Cameroon, Nigeria
PSIKYE dial of PSIKYE [KVJ]
PSOHOH [BCL] lang, Papua New Guinea
PSOHOH alt for SOKHOK dial of PSOHOH [BCL]
PSOKHOK alt for SOKHOK dial of PSOHOH [BCL]
PSOKOK alt for SOKHOK dial of PSOHOH [BCL]
PTAMO dial of CUIBA [CUI]
PTEP [PTP] lang, Papua New Guinea
PTSAKE alt for PSIKYE [KVJ]
PU alt for NICOBARESE, CAR [CAQ]
PU KO [PUK] lang, Laos
PÚ NÀ alt for NHANG [NHA]
PU NO alt for PUNU [PNU]
PU PEO alt for LAQUA [LAQ]
PU PÉO alt for LAQUA [LAQ]
PU THENH alt for KHMU [KJG]
PU TO alt for ZHUANG, SOUTHERN [CCY]
PU-I alt for BOUYEI [PCC]
PU-JUI alt for BOUYEI [PCC]
PU-NAM alt for NHANG [NHA]
PU-NONG alt for ZHUANG, SOUTHERN [CCY]
PUA alt for PUOC [PUO]
PUAN dial of JARAI [JRA]
PUARI [PUX] lang, Papua New Guinea
PUBIAN [PUN] lang, Indonesia, Sumatra
PUBIAO alt for LAQUA [LAQ]
PUCA-UMA alt for IQUITO [IQU]
PUCHIKWAR alt for A-PUCIKWAR [APQ]

PUCIKWAR alt for A-PUCIKWAR [APQ]
PUDITARA dial of MARTU WANGKA [MPJ]
PUEBLA TEPEHUA alt for TEPEHUA, PISA FLORES
   [TPP]
PUEBLO NUEVO SOLISTAHUACAN dial of TZOTZIL,
   CHAMULA [TZC]
PUELCHE [PUE] lang, Argentina
PUERTO RICAN SIGN LANGUAGE [PSL] lang, Puerto
   Rico
PUGLIESE dial of ITALIAN [ITN]
PUGOT alt for ALTA, SOUTHERN [AGY]
PUGULI [PUG] lang, Burkina Faso
PUH [PUH] lang, India
PUHOC alt for PUOC [PUO]
PUI alt for BOUYEI [PCC]
PUIMEI alt for NAGA, PUIMEI [NPU]
PUINABE alt for PUINAVE [PUI]
PUINAHUA alt for POYANÁWA [PYN]
PUINAVE [PUI] lang, Colombia, Venezuela, Venezuela
PUINAVE alt for PUINAVE [PUI]
PUJAI alt for BOUYEI [PCC]
PUJOLO ARANÉS dial of GASCON [GSC]
PUKAMIGL-ANDEGABU dial of WAHGI [WAK]
PUKAPUKA [PKP] lang, Cook Islands, New Zealand,
   New Zealand
PUKAPUKA alt for PUKAPUKA [PKP]
PUKAUNU alt for WEST LAMAHOLOT dial of
   LAMAHOLOT [SLP]
PUKI alt for POKE [POF]
PUKOBYÉ alt for GAVIÃO DO MARANHÃO dial of
   CANELA [RAM]
PUKU alt for BAPUKU dial of BATANGA [BNM]
PUKU alt for KAG dial of PUKU-GEERI-KERI-WIPSI
   [GEL]
PUKU-GEERI-KERI-WIPSI [GEL] lang, Nigeria
PUKUNNA alt for NUGUNU [NNV]
PUL alt for POL [PMM]
PUL alt for POL dial of POL [PMM]
PULA alt for TADYAWAN [TDY]
PULA alt for LATI [LBT]
PULA alt for BLANG [BLR]
PULAAR alt for TOUCOULEUR [TOU]
PULAAR alt for FUUTA JALON [FUF]
PULABU [PUP] lang, Papua New Guinea
PULANA dial of SOTHO, NORTHERN [SRT]
PULANG alt for BLANG [BLR]
PULANGIYEN dial of MANOBO, WESTERN
   BUKIDNON [MBB]
PULAP dial of PULUWAT [PUW]
PULAPESE alt for PULAP dial of PULUWAT [PUW]
PULAR alt for TOUCOULEUR [TOU]
PULAR alt for FUUTA JALON [FUF]
PULAR alt for FULFULDE, JELGOOJI [FUM]
PULAU GUAI dial of JAH HUT [JAH]
PULAYA dial of MALAYALAM [MJS]
PULE alt for FULFULDE, ADAMAWA [FUB]
PULENIYAN dial of MANOBO, ILIANEN [MBI]
PULGAON dial of KOLAMI, NORTHWESTERN [KFB]
PULHILH alt for YU dial of MANDYAK [MFV]
PULIE-RAUTO [PUL] lang, Papua New Guinea
PULLO alt for FULFULDE, ADAMAWA [FUB]
PULOPETAK dial of NGAJU [NIJ]
PULUSUK dial of PULUWAT [PUW]
PULUWAT [PUW] lang, Micronesia
PULUWAT dial of PULUWAT [PUW]
PULUWATESE alt for PULUWAT [PUW]

PUMA alt for TEANU [TKW]
PUMAN alt for U [UUU]
PUMANI dial of MAIWA [MTI]
PUMBORA alt for PURUBORÁ [PUR]
PUMÉ alt for YARURO [YAE]
PUMI [PMI] lang, China
PUNAN dial of DAYAK, LAND [DYK]
PUNAN APUT [PUD] lang, Indonesia, Kalimantan
PUNAN BA alt for PUNAN BAH dial of PUNAN BAH-BIAU [PNA]
PUNAN BAH dial of PUNAN BAH-BIAU [PNA]
PUNAN BAH-BIAU [PNA] lang, Malaysia, Sarawak
PUNAN BASAP dial of SAJAU BASAP [SAD]
PUNAN BATU 1 [PNM] lang, Malaysia, Sarawak
PUNAN BATU 2 dial of SAJAU BASAP [SAD]
PUNAN BIAU dial of PUNAN BAH-BIAU [PNA]
PUNAN BUNGAN alt for HOVONGAN [HOV]
PUNAN BUSANG dial of BUKITAN [BKN]
PUNAN GANG dial of PUNAN-NIBONG [PNE]
PUNAN KERIAU alt for KEREHO-UHENG [XKE]
PUNAN LANYING dial of PUNAN-NIBONG [PNE]
PUNAN LUSONG dial of PUNAN-NIBONG [PNE]
PUNAN MERAH [PUF] lang, Indonesia, Kalimantan
PUNAN MERAP [PUC] lang, Indonesia, Kalimantan
PUNAN RATAH alt for OT MURUNG 1 dial of DOHOI [OTD]
PUNAN SAJAU dial of SAJAU BASAP [SAD]
PUNAN SILAT dial of PUNAN-NIBONG [PNE]
PUNAN TUBU [PUJ] lang, Indonesia, Kalimantan
PUNAN UKIT dial of BUKITAN [BKN]
PUNAN-NIBONG [PNE] lang, Malaysia, Sarawak
PUNAPA alt for BUNABA [BCK]
PUNCHHI dial of PAHARI-POTWARI [PHR]
PUNDA-UMEDA dial of SOWANDA [SOW]
PUNGLUNG alt for DE'ANG [BFP]
PUNGUPUNGU alt for KUWAMA [QKU]
PUNGUPUNGU dial of WADJIGINY [WDJ]
PUNIAL alt for GILGITI dial of SHINA [SCL]
PUNJABI alt for PANJABI, EASTERN [PNJ]
PUNKALLA alt for BANGGARLA [BJB]
PUNO alt for PUNU [PUU]
PUNOI alt for PHUNOI [PHO]
PUNTHAMARA dial of NGURA [NBX]
PUNTLATCH alt for PENTLATCH [PTW]
PUNU [PNU] lang, China
PUNU [PUU] lang, Gabon, Congo
PUOC [PUO] lang, Viet Nam, Laos
PUOK alt for PUOC [PUO]
PUPEO alt for LAQUA [LAQ]
PUPITAU dial of FOLOPA [PPO]
PURAGI [PRU] lang, Indonesia, Irian Jaya
PURAI dial of LAWANGAN [LBX]
PURAM alt for PURUM [PUB]
PURARI [IAR] lang, Papua New Guinea
PURBI alt for WESTERN STANDARD BHOJPURI dial of BHOJPURI [BHJ]
PURDUMA alt for BURDUNA [BXN]
PURDUNA alt for BURDUNA [BXN]
PURE MOTU alt for MOTU [MEU]
PURI [PRR] lang, Brazil
PURIG alt for PURIK [BXR]
PURIGSKAD alt for PURIK [BXR]
PURIK [BXR] lang, India, China
PURIK BHOTIA alt for PURIK [BXR]
PURKI alt for PURIK [BXR]
PURKO dial of MAASAI [MET]

PUROBORÁ alt for PURUBORÁ [PUR]
PURR dial of NAGA, SANGTAM [NSA]
PURRA alt for YUNGUR [YUN]
PURUBA alt for PURUBORÁ [PUR]
PURUBORÁ [PUR] lang, Brazil
PURUCOTO alt for ARECUNA dial of PEMON [AOC]
PURUM [PUB] lang, Myanmar
PURUNG dial of LAWANGAN [LBX]
PURUPURÚ alt for PAUMARÍ [PAD]
PUS alt for PITU ULUNNA SALU [PTU]
PUS alt for MPUS dial of MUSGU [MUG]
PUS alt for MPUS dial of MUSGU [MUG]
PUSCITI alt for XAVÁNTE [XAV]
PUSHTO alt for PASHTO, WESTERN [PBT]
PUSHTO alt for PASHTO, EASTERN [PBU]
PUSHTU alt for PASHTO, WESTERN [PBT]
PUSTO alt for PASHTO, EASTERN [PBU]
PUTAHI alt for PARATA dial of TUAMOTUAN [PMT]
PUTAI [MFL] lang, Nigeria
PUTAI alt for PHU THAI [PHT]
PUTATAN dial of BAJAU, WEST COAST [BDR]
PUTE alt for VUTE [VUT]
PUTEIK alt for KADO [KDV]
PUTENH alt for KHANG [KJM]
PUTHAI alt for PHU THAI [PHT]
PUTHAY alt for PHU THAI [PHT]
PUTHSU alt for PODZO [POZ]
PUTIAN dial of CHINESE, MIN PEI [MNP]
PUTOH [PUT] lang, Indonesia, Kalimantan
PUTONGHUA alt for CHINESE, MANDARIN [CHN]
PUTRI dial of ZANDE [ZAN]
PUTRU dial of RONGA [RON]
PUTTOOAS alt for JUANG [JUN]
PUTU dial of SAPO [KRN]
PUTUJARA alt for PUDITARA dial of MARTU WANGKA [MPJ]
PUTUKWAM alt for UTUGWANG [AFE]
PUURI alt for NGONG [NNX]
PUXMETECÁN MIXE alt for MIXE, NORTHEASTERN [MVE]
PUYALLUP dial of SALISH, SOUTHERN PUGET SOUND [SLH]
PUYI alt for BOUYEI [PCC]
PUYOI alt for BOUYEI [PCC]
PUYUMA alt for PYUMA [PYU]
PWA alt for PUGULI [PUG]
PWAAMEI [PME] lang, New Caledonia
PWAKANYAW alt for KAREN, S'GAW [KSW]
PWAPWA [POP] lang, New Caledonia
PWEBO alt for POUÉBO dial of CAAC [MSQ]
PWO alt for PUGULI [PUG]
PWO alt for KAREN, PWO [PWO]
PWO alt for KAREN, PWO OMKOI [PWW]
PWO KANCHANABURI alt for KAREN, PWO KANCHANA BURI [KJP]
PWO KAYIN alt for KAREN, PWO [PWO]
PWO KAYIN alt for KAREN, PWO OMKOI [PWW]
PWO PHRAE alt for KAREN, NORTHERN PWO [KJT]
PWO UTHAI THANI alt for KAREN, PWO KANCHANA BURI [KJP]
PYAM alt for FYAM [PYM]
PYAPUN [PCW] lang, Nigeria
PYE alt for PIE dial of KRUMEN, NORTHEASTERN [PYE]
PYEM alt for FYAM [PYM]
PYEN [PYY] lang, Myanmar

PYETA YOVAI alt for AYOREO [AYO]
PYGMEE alt for BAKA [BKC]
PYGMÉE DE LA LOBAYE alt for AKA [AXK]
PYGMÉE DE MONGOUMBA alt for AKA [AXK]
PYGMEES DE L'EST alt for BAKA [BKC]
PYGMÉES DE LA SANGHAS alt for AKA [AXK]
PYGMY-E alt for BAKA [BKC]
PYU [PBY] lang, Indonesia, Irian Jaya, Papua New
  Guinea, Papua New Guinea
PYUMA [PYU] lang, Taiwan
QABÉKHOE dial of N/HAI-NTSE'E [NKT]
QABENA alt for QEBENA dial of KAMBAATA [KTB]
QAHAR alt for CHAHAR dial of MONGOLIAN,
  PERIPHERAL [MVF]
QAJAR dial of AZERBAIJANI, SOUTH [AZB]
QALMAQ alt for KALMYK-OIRAT [KGZ]
QANDAHAR PASHTO alt for SOUTHWEST PASHTO
  dial of PASHTO, SOUTHERN [PBQ]
QAQET [BYX] lang, Papua New Guinea
QARAGOZLU dial of AZERBAIJANI, SOUTH [AZB]
QARAQULPAQS alt for KARAKALPAK [KAC]
QARASHAHR dial of UYGHUR [UIG]
QARLUG alt for KARLUKO-CHIGILE-UIGHUR dial of
  UZBEK, NORTHERN [UZB]
QARQAN alt for CHARCHAN dial of UYGHUR [UIG]
QASHQA'I alt for QASHQAI [QSQ]
QASHQAI [QSQ] lang, Iran
QASHQARI alt for KHOWAR [KHW]
QASHQAY alt for QASHQAI [QSQ]
QATVENUA alt for HANO [LML]
QAU dial of GELO [KKF]
QAWASHQAR alt for KAWESQAR [ALC]
QAWASQAR alt for KAWESQAR [ALC]
QAWIARAQ dial of INUIT, NORTHWEST ALASKA
  INUPIAT [ESK]
QAZAQ alt for KAZAKH [KAZ]
QAZAQI alt for KAZAKH [KAZ]
QAZVINI dial of FARSI, WESTERN [PES]
QEBENA dial of KAMBAATA [KTB]
QEDAI NAO HAZARA AIMAQ dial of AIMAQ [AIQ]
QEMANT alt for QIMANT [QIM]
QI dial of HLAI [LIC]
QIANDONG MIAO alt for HMONG, EASTERN [HEA]
QIÀNDUÌ dial of HLAI [LIC]
QIANG [CNG] lang, China
QIANJIANG [CCV] lang, China
QIEMO alt for CHARCHAN dial of UYGHUR [UIG]
QIMANT [QIM] lang, Ethiopia
QIMR alt for GIMR dial of TAMA [TMA]
QIN alt for CHIN, ASHO [CSH]
QINATI dial of DOMARI [RMT]
QIQIHAR dial of DAUR [DTA]
QIUBEI dial of ZHUANG, NORTHERN [CCX]
QIUCE alt for RAWANG [RAW]
QIUNGNAI dial of PUNU [PNU]
QOM alt for TOBA [TOB]
QOTONG alt for CHINESE, MANDARIN [CHN]
QOTTU alt for OROMO, EASTERN [HAE]
QUA alt for SOUTHERN EJAGHAM dial of EJAGHAM
  [ETU]
QUAIQUER alt for CUAIQUER [KWI]
QUAN CHET dial of MIEN [YOC]
QUAN TRANG dial of MIEN [YOC]
QUANG DONG alt for CHINESE, YUE [YUH]
QUANG LAM alt for KHANG [KJM]
QUANG TIN KATU alt for TAKUA [TKZ]

QUANG TRI BRU alt for BRU, EASTERN [BRU]
QUAPAW [QUA] lang, USA
QUAQUA alt for PIAROA [PID]
QUARA alt for QWARA dial of KARA [CFL]
QUARASA alt for KARA [CFL]
QUARINA alt for KARA [CFL]
QUASHIE TALK alt for JAMAICAN CREOLE ENGLISH
  dial of WESTERN CARIBBEAN CREOLE ENGLISH
  [JAM]
QUCHANI alt for KHORASANI TURKISH [KMZ]
QUEBEC ESKIMO dial of INUIT, EASTERN
  CANADIAN [ESB]
QUECCHÍ alt for KEKCHÍ [KEK]
QUECHAN [YUM] lang, USA
QUECHUA BOLIVIANO alt for QUECHUA, SOUTH
  BOLIVIAN [QUH]
QUECHUA, ANCASH, CHIQUIAN [QEC] lang, Peru
QUECHUA, ANCASH, CONCHUCOS [QED] lang, Peru
QUECHUA, ANCASH, CORONGO [QEE] lang, Peru
QUECHUA, ANCASH, HUAYLAS [QAN] lang, Peru
QUECHUA, ANCASH, SIHUAS [QES] lang, Peru
QUECHUA, APURIMAC [QEA] lang, Peru
QUECHUA, AYACUCHO [QUY] lang, Peru
QUECHUA, CAJAMARCA [QNT] lang, Peru
QUECHUA, CHACHAPOYAS [QUK] lang, Peru
QUECHUA, CHILEAN [QUE] lang, Chile
QUECHUA, CLASSICAL [QCL] lang, Peru
QUECHUA, COTAHUASI [QAR] lang, Peru
QUECHUA, CUZCO [QUZ] lang, Peru
QUECHUA, HUANCA, HUAYLLA [QHU] lang, Peru
QUECHUA, HUANCA, JAUJA [QHJ] lang, Peru
QUECHUA, HUÁNUCO, HUALLAGA [QUB] lang, Peru
QUECHUA, HUÁNUCO, HUAMALÍES [QEJ] lang,
  Peru
QUECHUA, HUÁNUCO, MARAÑON [QEL] lang, Peru
QUECHUA, HUÁNUCO, PANAO [QEM] lang, Peru
QUECHUA, HUÁNUCO, SOUTHERN DOS DE MAYO-
  MARGOS CHAULÁN [QEI] lang, Peru
QUECHUA, LAMBAYEQUE [QUF] lang, Peru
QUECHUA, NORTH BOLIVIAN [QUL] lang, Bolivia,
  Peru
QUECHUA, NORTH JUNÍN [QJU] lang, Peru
QUECHUA, NORTH LIMA, CAJATAMBO [QNL] lang,
  Peru
QUECHUA, NORTHWEST JUJUY [QUO] lang,
  Argentina
QUECHUA, PACAROAS [QCP] lang, Peru
QUECHUA, PASCO, SANTA ANA DE TUSI [QEF]
  lang, Peru
QUECHUA, PASCO-YANAHUANCA [QUR] lang, Peru
QUECHUA, PASTAZA, SOUTHERN [QUP] lang, Peru
QUECHUA, PUNO [QEP] lang, Peru
QUECHUA, SAN MARTÍN [QSA] lang, Peru
QUECHUA, SAN RAFAEL-HUARIACA [QEG] lang,
  Peru
QUECHUA, SOUTH BOLIVIAN [QUH] lang, Bolivia,
  Argentina
QUECHUA, YAUYOS [QUX] lang, Peru
QUECL alt for QUECHAN [YUM]
QUEDAH alt for KEDAH dial of KENSIU [KNS]
QUEQUEXQUE alt for TERIBE [TFR]
QUERETARO OTOMÍ alt for OTOMÍ,
  NORTHWESTERN [OTQ]
QUETTA PASHTO alt for SOUTHEAST PASHTO dial
  of PASHTO, SOUTHERN [PBQ]
QUETZALTENANGO MAM alt for MAM, SOUTHERN

[MMS]
QUEUTHOE alt for KANTOHE dial of BALANTA [BLE]
QUEZON PALAWANO alt for PALAWANO, CENTRAL [PLC]
QUIANGAN alt for IFUGAO, TUWALI [IFK]
QUIATIVIS alt for SANAPANÁ [SAP]
QUICHÉ, CENTRAL [QUC] lang, Guatemala
QUICHE, CUNÉN [CUN] lang, Guatemala
QUICHÉ, EAST CENTRAL [QUU] lang, Guatemala
QUICHÉ, EASTERN [QIE] lang, Guatemala
QUICHÉ, JOYABAJ [QUJ] lang, Guatemala
QUICHÉ, WEST CENTRAL [QUT] lang, Guatemala
QUICHUA, HIGHLAND, CALDERÓN [QUD] lang, Ecuador
QUICHUA, HIGHLAND, CAÑAR [QQC] lang, Ecuador
QUICHUA, HIGHLAND, CHIMBORAZO [QUG] lang, Ecuador
QUICHUA, HIGHLAND, IMBABURA [QHO] lang, Ecuador
QUICHUA, HIGHLAND, LOJA [QQU] lang, Ecuador
QUICHUA, HIGHLAND, TUNGURAHUA [QQS] lang, Ecuador
QUICHUA, LOWLAND, NAPO [QLN] lang, Ecuador, Colombia, Peru
QUICHUA, LOWLAND, NAPO alt for QUICHUA, LOWLAND, NAPO [QLN]
QUICHUA, LOWLAND, TENA [QUW] lang, Ecuador
QUICHUA, PASTAZA, NORTHERN [QLB] lang, Ecuador, Peru
QUICHUA, PASTAZA, NORTHERN alt for QUICHUA, PASTAZA, NORTHERN [QLB]
QUICHUA, SANTIAGO DEL ESTERO [QUS] lang, Argentina
QUIEGOLANI ZAPOTEC alt for ZAPOTECO, WESTERN YAUTEPEC [ZPI]
QUIJO alt for QUICHUA, LOWLAND, NAPO [QLN]
QUILCENE dial of TWANA [TWA]
QUILEUTE [QUI] lang, USA
QUILEUTE dial of QUILEUTE [QUI]
QUILIGUA alt for KILIWI [KLB]
QUILYACMOC alt for SANAPANÁ [SAP]
QUILYILHRAYROM alt for TOBA-MASKOY [TMF]
QUIMBUNDO alt for UMBUNDU [MNF]
QUIMUANE alt for MWANI [WMW]
QUINAULT [QUN] lang, USA
QUINJIANG dial of BOUYEI [PCC]
QUINQUI [QUQ] lang, Spain
QUIOQUITANI ZAPOTECO alt for ZAPOTECO, SANTA CATARINA QUIERÍ [ZTQ]
QUIPEA alt for KIPEÁ dial of KARIRI-XUCO [KZW]
QUIRRUBA dial of BANIVA [BVV]
QUISSAMA alt for SAMA [SMD]
QUISSANGA dial of MWANI [WMW]
QUITURRAN alt for IQUITO [IQU]
QUIXO alt for QUICHUA, LOWLAND, NAPO [QLN]
QUOIRENG alt for KOIRENG [NKD]
QUOP alt for KUAP dial of DAYAK, LAND [DYK]
QUOP alt for KUAP dial of DAYAK, LAND [DYK]
QUOTTU alt for OROMO, EASTERN [HAE]
QURAMA dial of UZBEK, NORTHERN [UZB]
QURANIC ARABIC alt for ARABIC, CLASSICAL [ARA]
QÚY RIN dial of NUNG [NUT]
QWABE dial of ZULU [ZUU]
QWANNAB alt for ANDI [ANI]
QWARA dial of KARA [CFL]

QWERA alt for KARA [CFL]
QWOTTU alt for OROMO, EASTERN [HAE]
QXÛ alt for KUNG-EKOKA [KNW]
RA-ANG dial of DE'ANG [BFP]
RA-GLAI alt for ROGLAI, CACGIA [ROC]
RA-GLAI alt for ROGLAI, NORTHERN [ROG]
RAANDALIST alt for WESTERN LIVONIAN dial of LIV [LIV]
RABAH dial of HRE [HRE]
RABAI dial of DURUMA [DUG]
RABAI alt for NABAY dial of KENINGAU MURUT [KXI]
RABAUL CREOLE GERMAN alt for UNSERDEUTSCH [ULN]
RABAY alt for NABAY dial of KENINGAU MURUT [KXI]
RABE alt for LABE dial of TAWALA [TBO]
RABHA [RAH] lang, India
RABINAL QUICHÉ alt for ACHÍ, RABINAL [ACR]
RACHA dial of GEORGIAN [GEO]
RADAY alt for RADE [RAD]
RADCLIFFE LANCASHIRE dial of ENGLISH [ENG]
RADE [RAD] lang, Viet Nam, USA
RADLAI alt for ROGLAI, NORTHERN [ROG]
RAEPA TATI alt for TATE [TBD]
RAGA alt for HANO [LML]
RAGETTA alt for GEDAGED [GDD]
RAGOLI alt for LOGOOLI [RAG]
RAGREIG dial of BURUN [BDI]
RAGUSAN alt for DALMATIAN [DLM]
RAGWE alt for NYAMBO [NYM]
RAHABARI dial of KOLI, KACHI [GJK]
RAHAMBUU [RAZ] lang, Indonesia, Sulawesi
RAHANWEEN alt for MAAY [QMA]
RAHANWEYN alt for MAAY [QMA]
RAHIYA dial of BHUMIJ [BHM]
RAI alt for ROGLAI, SOUTHERN [RGS]
RAI dial of CHRU [CJE]
RAI dial of ROGLAI, SOUTHERN [RGS]
RAI dial of KAILI, LEDO [LEW]
RAIDJUA alt for RAIJUA dial of SAWU [HVN]
RAIGARH dial of MURIA, EASTERN [EMU]
RAIJUA dial of SAWU [HVN]
RAIK alt for REK dial of DINKA, SOUTHWESTERN [DIK]
RAINBARGO alt for REMBARUNGA [RMB]
RAIO dial of KAILI, LEDO [LEW]
RAIPUR dial of VARHADI-NAGPURI [VAH]
RAIVAVAE dial of AUSTRAL [AUT]
RAJ KOYA alt for KOYA [KFF]
RAJAH KABUNGSUAN MANOBO alt for MANOBO, RAJAH KABUNSUWAN [MQK]
RAJASTHANI alt for MARWARI, SOUTHERN [MQH]
RAJASTHANI alt for MARWARI [MKD]
RAJASTHANI alt for MARWARI, NORTHERN [MRI]
RAJASTHANI GUJURI alt for GUJARI [GJU]
RAJBANGSI [RJB] lang, Nepal, Bangladesh, India
RAJBANSI alt for RAJBANGSI [RJB]
RAJI [RJI] lang, Nepal
RAJKOTI dial of KALAMI [GWC]
RAJMAHALIA alt for MALTO [MJT]
RAJONG [RJG] lang, Indonesia, Nusa Tenggara
RAJPUT GARASIA alt for GIRASIA, RAJPUT [GRA]
RAJSHAHI dial of BENGALI [BNG]
RAJSHAHI SADRI dial of SADRI, ORAON [SDR]
RAJURA dial of GONDI, SOUTHERN [GGO]

[SKR]
REASITI alt for BAHAWALPURI [BGB]
REBAR dial of TOLAI [KSD]
REBINA alt for RIBINA dial of JERA [JER]
REBU alt for BANGI [BNI]
REBU alt for BALOI [BIZ]
RED alt for HMONG, RED [MMR]
RED BOBO alt for BWAMU [BOX]
RED KAREN alt for KAYAH, EASTERN [EKY]
RED KAREN alt for KAYAH, WESTERN [KYU]
RED LACHI alt for LIPUKE dial of LATI [LBT]
RED LAHU alt for NYI dial of LAHU [LAH]
RED LAHU alt for NYI dial of LAHU [LAH]
RED MEO alt for HMONG, RED [MMR]
RED MIAO alt for HMONG, RED [MMR]
RED TAI alt for TAI DAENG [TYR]
RED THAI alt for TAI DAENG [TYR]
REDDI alt for MUKHA-DORA [MMK]
REDDI-DORA alt for MUKHA-DORA [MMK]
REDJANG alt for REJANG [REJ]
REEF ISLANDS alt for AYIWO [NFL]
REEFS alt for AYIWO [NFL]
REGA alt for LEGA-SHABUNDA [LEA]
REGA alt for LEGA-MWENGA [LGM]
REGI alt for KARA [REG]
REGI dial of KAMUKU [KAU]
REI dial of LOU [LOJ]
REIKHA alt for DENGEBU [DEC]
REIWO alt for YAPUNDA [YEV]
REJANG [REJ] lang, Indonesia, Sumatra
REJANG KAJAN alt for KAYAN, REJANG [REE]
REJANG-LEBONG alt for REJANG [REJ]
REK alt for DINKA, SOUTHWESTERN [DIK]
REK dial of DINKA, SOUTHWESTERN [DIK]
REKHTA dial of URDU [URD]
REKHTI alt for REKHTA dial of URDU [URD]
RELI [REI] lang, India
REMBARRANGA alt for REMBARUNGA [RMB]
REMBARRNGA alt for REMBARUNGA [RMB]
REMBARUNGA [RMB] lang, Australia
REMBOKEN dial of TONDANO [TDN]
REMBONG [REB] lang, Indonesia, Nusa Tenggara
REMBONG dial of REMBONG [REB]
REMI alt for NYATURU [RIM]
REMO [REM] lang, Peru
REMO alt for BONDO [BFW]
REMPI [RMP] lang, Papua New Guinea
REMPIN alt for REMPI [RMP]
RENDILE alt for RENDILLE [REL]
RENDILLE [REL] lang, Kenya
RENDRE alt for NUNGU [RIN]
RENGAO [REN] lang, Viet Nam
RENGGOU alt for LANDU-RINGGOU-OEPAO dial of ROTI [ROT]
RENGJONGMU dial of LEPCHA [LEP]
RENGMA alt for NAGA, RENGMA [NRE]
RENNELL [MNV] lang, Solomon Islands
RENNELL alt for MUNGGAVA dial of RENNELL [MNV]
RENNELLESE alt for RENNELL [MNV]
RENNELLESE SIGN LANGUAGE [RSI] lang, Solomon Islands
RENNELLESE-BELLONESE alt for RENNELL [MNV]
REPANBITIP [RPN] lang, Vanuatu
RER BARE [RER] lang, Ethiopia
RERAU [REA] lang, Papua New Guinea
RERE alt for KOALIB [KIB]

REREBERE alt for RER BARE [RER]
REREP [PGK] lang, Vanuatu
RESHE [RES] lang, Nigeria
RESHIAT alt for DAASANECH [DSH]
RESÍGARO [RGR] lang, Peru
RESÍGERO alt for RESÍGARO [RGR]
RESTIGOUCHE alt for MICMAC [MIC]
RETTA 1 dial of BLAGAR [BEU]
RETTA 2 dial of BLAGAR [BEU]
RETUAMA alt for TANIMUCA-RETUARÃ [TNC]
RETUARÃ alt for TANIMUCA-RETUARÃ [TNC]
REUNION CREOLE FRENCH [RCF] lang, Reunion
REVAL alt for TALLINN dial of ESTONIAN [EST]
REWA dial of SUDEST [TGO]
REYESANO [REY] lang, Bolivia
RGYARONG alt for JIARONG [JYA]
RHADE alt for RADE [RAD]
RHAETIAN alt for RHETO-ROMANCE [RHE]
RHAETO-ROMANCE alt for RHETO-ROMANCE [RHE]
RHENGKITANG dial of MIKIR [MJW]
RHENO alt for REMO [REM]
RHETO-ROMANCE [RHE] lang, Switzerland
RHINYIHINYI dial of TEMBO [TBT]
RHODANIEN dial of PROVENÇAL [PRV]
RIAHOMA alt for PAHI [LGT]
RIANG [RIA] lang, India, Bangladesh
RIANG [RIL] lang, Myanmar, China
RIANG dial of KOK BOROK [TRP]
RIANG-LANG alt for RIANG [RIL]
RIANTANA [RAN] lang, Indonesia, Irian Jaya
RIASATI alt for BAHAWALPURI [BGB]
RIASATI alt for BAHAWALPURI dial of SIRAIKI [SKR]
RIASI dial of KASHMIRI [KSH]
RIASITI alt for SIRAIKI [SKR]
RIAU dial of MALAY [MLI]
RIBAGORÇAN alt for NORTHWESTERN CATALAN dial of CATALAN [CLN]
RIBAM alt for RIBAN dial of PITI [PCN]
RIBAN dial of PITI [PCN]
RIBAW dial of BATA [BTA]
RIBBI dial of LOKO [LOK]
RIBE dial of GIRYAMA [NYF]
RIBIA dial of THEMNE [TEJ]
RIBINA dial of JERA [JER]
RIBUN [RIR] lang, Indonesia, Kalimantan
RIDAN dial of KUBU [KVB]
RIDARNGO alt for RITARUNGO [RIT]
RIDDI alt for MUKHA-DORA [MMK]
RIEN [RIE] lang, Laos
RIF alt for TARIFIT [RIF]
RIFF alt for TARIFIT [RIF]
RIFI alt for TARIFIT [RIF]
RIFIA alt for TARIFIT [RIF]
RIGWE alt for IRIGWE [IRI]
RIHE alt for RIBE dial of GIRYAMA [NYF]
RIHU'A dial of FAGANI [FAF]
RIKBAKTSA [ART] lang, Brazil
RIKPA alt for BAFIA [KSF]
RIKPA' alt for BAFIA [KSF]
RIKSMAL alt for NORWEGIAN, BOKMAL [NRR]
RIKVANI dial of ANDI [ANI]
RIMATARA dial of AUSTRAL [AUT]
RIMI alt for NYATURU [RIM]
RIMI alt for GIRWANA dial of NYATURU [RIM]
RINCÓN ZAPOTECO alt for ZAPOTECO, NORTHERN VILLA ALTA [ZAR]

RINCON-SUR ZAPOTEC alt for ZAPOTECO, SOUTHERN RINCÓN [ZSR]
RINCONADA BICOLANO alt for BICOLANO, IRIGA [BTO]
RINDIRI alt for NUNGU [RIN]
RINDRE alt for NUNGU [RIN]
RINDRE dial of NUNGU [RIN]
RINGGOU alt for LANDU-RINGGOU-OEPAO dial of ROTI [ROT]
RIO alt for GEDAGED [GDD]
RIO ABAJO dial of WESTERN CARIBBEAN CREOLE ENGLISH [JAM]
RIO ARAUCA GUAHIBO alt for PLAYERO [GOB]
RIO TOMO GUAHIBO dial of GUAHIBO [GUH]
RION dial of KOHO [KPM]
RIOUW-LINGGA alt for RIAU dial of MALAY [MLI]
RIPERE alt for GBETE dial of MBUM [MDD]
RIPERE alt for KEPERE dial of MBUM [MDD]
RIPEY alt for BAFIA [KSF]
RIRIO [RRI] lang, Solomon Islands
RIRRATJINGU dial of DHANGU [GLA]
RISHUWA alt for KUZAMANI [KSA]
RITARNUGU alt for RITARUNGO [RIT]
RITARUNGO [RIT] lang, Australia
RITHARNGU alt for RITARUNGO [RIT]
RITIME dial of GIMNIME [KMB]
RITO alt for RUTO dial of RUTO [NDY]
RITO alt for RUTO dial of RUTO [NDY]
RITOK dial of MALAY [MLI]
RIUNG [RIU] lang, Indonesia, Nusa Tenggara
RIUNG alt for DAPALAN dial of TALAUD [TLD]
RIVER BUSHMAN alt for BUKA-KHWE [BUZ]
RIVER CESS GIO dial of DAN [DAF]
RIVER CHULUPI dial of CHULUPÍ [CAG]
RIVER JARAWA alt for BADA [BAU]
RIVER JUKUN alt for ABINSI [JUB]
RIVER RUKI alt for BOLOKI [BKT]
RIVER TARANGAN dial of TARANGAN, WEST [TXN]
RIVERCESS BASSA dial of BASSA [BAS]
RIWAI alt for BAGHELI [BFY]
RIYADH alt for CENTRAL NAJDI dial of ARABIC, NAJDI [ARS]
RIYAO dial of OY [OYB]
RLAM alt for MNONG ROLOM dial of MNONG, EASTERN [MNG]
RLIK dial of MARSHALLESE [MZM]
RO alt for CHRAU [CHR]
RO dial of FOLOPA [PPO]
RO BAMBAMI alt for AGOI [IBM]
RO-NGAO alt for RENGAO [REN]
ROAMAINA alt for OMURANO [OMU]
ROBA dial of LALA-ROBA [LLA]
ROBBA alt for ROBA dial of LALA-ROBA [LLA]
ROBIANA alt for ROVIANA [RUG]
ROBODA alt for LOBODA dial of DOBU [DOB]
ROCKY PEAK [ROK] lang, Papua New Guinea
ROCOROIBO TARAHUMARA alt for TARAHUMARA BAJA [TAC]
RODI alt for TRAVELLER DANISH [RMD]
RODI alt for TRAVELLER NORWEGIAN [RMG]
RODIYA dial of SINHALA [SNH]
RODONG alt for CHAMLING [RAB]
RODOSTO dial of ARMENIAN [ARM]
RODRIGUES CREOLE dial of MORISYEN [MFE]
ROEA alt for MACUNA [MYY]
ROFIK alt for DEMIK dial of KEIGA [KEC]

ROGLAI, CACGIA [ROC] lang, Viet Nam
ROGLAI, NORTHERN [ROG] lang, Viet Nam
ROGLAI, SOUTHERN [RGS] lang, Viet Nam
ROGO alt for ROKO dial of MANGSING [MBH]
ROHOMONI dial of HARUKU [HRK]
ROHRURI dial of MAHASUI [BFZ]
ROINJI [ROE] lang, Papua New Guinea
ROK dial of KHMU [KJG]
ROKO dial of MANGSING [MBH]
ROLAM alt for MNONG ROLOM dial of MNONG, EASTERN [MNG]
ROLOM alt for MNONG ROLOM dial of MNONG, EASTERN [MNG]
ROLONG dial of TSWANA [TSW]
ROM alt for ROMANI, VLACH [RMY]
ROM alt for OROM dial of TESO [TEO]
ROMA [RMM] lang, Indonesia, Maluku
ROMA-NA alt for ADOMA dial of LELA [DRI]
ROMAGNOLO dial of EMILIANO [EML]
ROMAIC alt for GREEK [GRK]
ROMAM [ROH] lang, Viet Nam
ROMANAU alt for RUMANAU dial of LOBU, LANAS [RUU]
ROMANCHE alt for RHETO-ROMANCE [RHE]
ROMANÉS alt for ROMANI, VLACH [RMY]
ROMANESE alt for ROMANI, VLACH [RMY]
ROMANG alt for ROMA [RMM]
ROMANI ENGLISH alt for ANGLOROMANI [RME]
ROMANI, BALKAN [RMN] lang, Yugoslavia, Bulgaria, France, Germany, Greece, Hungary, Iran, Italy, Moldova, Romania, Turkey
ROMANI, BALTIC [ROM] lang, Latvia, Estonia, Poland
ROMANI, BALTIC alt for ROMANI, BALTIC [ROM]
ROMANI, CALO [RMR] lang, Spain, Brazil, France, Portugal
ROMANI, CARPATHIAN [RMC] lang, Czechoslovakia, Hungary, Hungary, Poland, Romania, Ukraine
ROMANI, CARPATHIAN alt for ROMANI, CARPATHIAN [RMC]
ROMANI, KALO FINNISH [RMF] lang, Finland, Sweden, Sweden
ROMANI, KALO FINNISH alt for ROMANI, KALO FINNISH [RMF]
ROMANI, SINTE [RMO] lang, Yugoslavia, Austria, Czechoslovakia, France, Germany, Italy, Kazakhstan, Netherlands, Poland, Switzerland
ROMANI, VLACH [RMY] lang, Romania, Argentina, Brazil, Colombia, USA, Albania, Bosnia-Herzegovina, Bulgaria, Czechoslovakia, France, Germany, Greece, Hungary, Italy, Netherlands, Norway, Poland, Portugal, Spain, Sweden, Ukraine, United Kingdom
ROMANI, VLACH alt for ROMANI, VLACH [RMY]
ROMANI, WELSH [RMW] lang, United Kingdom
ROMANIAN alt for RUMANIAN [RUM]
ROMANICHAL alt for ANGLOROMANI [RME]
ROMANO-GREEK [RGE] lang, Greece
ROMANO-SERBIAN [RSB] lang, Yugoslavia
ROMANSCH alt for RHETO-ROMANCE [RHE]
ROMANSH alt for RHETO-ROMANCE [RHE]
ROMBI alt for BAROMBI [BBI]
ROMBI alt for LOMBI [LMI]
ROMBLOMANON [ROL] lang, Philippines
ROMBLON alt for ROMBLOMANON [ROL]
ROMBLON dial of ROMBLOMANON [ROL]

ROMBO alt for USSERI dial of CHAGGA [KAF]
ROMENES alt for ROMANI, VLACH [RMY]
ROMKUIN alt for ROMKUN [RMK]
ROMKUN [RMK] lang, Papua New Guinea
ROMMANES alt for ROMANI, SINTE [RMO]
ROMMANI alt for TRAVELLER SWEDISH [RMU]
ROMNIS alt for ANGLOROMANI [RME]
ROMUNGRE dial of ROMANI, VLACH [RMY]
ROMUNGRO alt for ROMANI, CARPATHIAN [RMC]
RON alt for BOKKOS [CLA]
RON alt for ROON [RNN]
RON-BOKKOS alt for BOKKOS [CLA]
RON-DAFFO alt for DAFFO-BATURA [DAM]
RONDAWAYA dial of AMBAI [AMK]
RONDU alt for GILGITI dial of SHINA [SCL]
RONE alt for TEMEIN [TEQ]
RONG alt for CHANGTHANG [CNA]
RONG alt for LEPCHA [LEP]
RONG KONG alt for LAO [NOL]
RONGA [RON] lang, Mozambique, South Africa,
    South Africa
RONGA alt for RONGA [RON]
RONGBA dial of AMDO [ADX]
RONGE alt for TEMEIN [TEQ]
RONGGA [ROR] lang, Indonesia, Nusa Tenggara
RONGKE alt for LEPCHA [LEP]
RONGKONG alt for TAE' [ROB]
RONGKONG dial of TAE' [ROB]
RONGKONG KANANDEDE alt for TAE' [ROB]
RONGMAHBROGPA dial of AMDO [ADX]
RONGMAI alt for NAGA, RONGMEI [NBU]
RONGMEI alt for NAGA, RONGMEI [NBU]
RONGO alt for ORUNGU dial of MYENE [MYE]
RONGPA alt for LEPCHA [LEP]
RONGRANG dial of NAGA, TASE [NST]
RONRANG dial of NAGA, TASE [NST]
ROOI NASIE alt for NAMA [NAQ]
ROOMARROWS alt for RUMANAU dial of LOBU,
    LANAS [RUU]
ROON [RNN] lang, Indonesia, Irian Jaya
ROONGAS alt for RUNGUS [DRG]
ROPER RIVER KRIOL dial of KRIOL [ROP]
ROPER RIVER PIDGIN alt for ROPER RIVER KRIOL
    dial of KRIOL [ROP]
ROPER-BAMYILI CREOLE alt for KRIOL [ROP]
ROPO alt for WLOPO dial of KRUMEN, SOUTHERN
    [TED]
ROR dial of PUKU-GEERI-KERI-WIPSI [GEL]
RORI alt for SANGU [SBP]
RORIA [RGA] lang, Vanuatu
RORO [RRO] lang, Papua New Guinea
RORO dial of RORO [RRO]
ROROVANA alt for TORAU [TTU]
ROSHANI dial of SHUGHNI [SGH]
ROSHANI alt for RUSHANI dial of SHUGHNI [SGH]
ROSO dial of AGTA, DUPANINAN [DUO]
ROSSEL alt for YELE [YLE]
ROTANESE CHAMORRO dial of CHAMORRO [CJD]
ROTE alt for ROTI [ROT]
ROTEA alt for SEDANG [SED]
ROTEANG alt for SEDANG [SED]
ROTI [ROT] lang, Indonesia, Nusa Tenggara
ROTI dial of BAJAU, INDONESIAN [BDL]
ROTINESE alt for ROTI [ROT]
ROTO alt for PULIE-RAUTO [PUL]
ROTOKAS [ROO] lang, Papua New Guinea

ROTORUA-TAUPO dial of MAORI [MBF]
ROTSE alt for LOZI [LOZ]
ROTTI alt for ROTI [ROT]
ROTUMAN [RTM] lang, Fiji
ROTUNA alt for ROTUMAN [RTM]
ROTWELSCH alt for TRAVELLER DANISH [RMD]
ROTWELSCH alt for TRAVELLER NORWEGIAN
    [RMG]
ROUCOUYENNE alt for WAYANA [WAY]
ROUCOUYENNE alt for RUCUYEN dial of WAYANA
    [WAY]
ROUKU [TCI] lang, Papua New Guinea
ROUMANIAN alt for RUMANIAN [RUM]
ROUNGA alt for RUNGA [ROU]
ROUNGO alt for RUNGA [ROU]
ROUTA dial of BUNGKU [BKZ]
ROUTO alt for RUTO dial of RUTO [NDY]
ROUTO alt for RUTO dial of RUTO [NDY]
ROUYI alt for LUYANA [LAV]
ROVIANA [RUG] lang, Solomon Islands
ROZI alt for LOZI [LOZ]
RTAHU dial of AMDO [ADX]
RTCHI alt for GAVAR [GOU]
RUA dial of WANUKAKA [WNK]
RUAFA alt for TARIFIT [RIF]
RUAL dial of GIDRA [GDR]
RUANDA alt for RWANDA [RUA]
RUAVATU alt for LENGO [LGR]
RUBASA [BZW] lang, Nigeria
RUBASSA alt for RUBASA [BZW]
RUBIANA alt for ROVIANA [RUG]
RUC [RUL] lang, Laos, Viet Nam
RUC alt for RUC [RUL]
RUCUYEN dial of WAYANA [WAY]
RUE dial of SENA [SEH]
RUFIJI [RUI] lang, Tanzania
RUFUMBIRA dial of RWANDA [RUA]
RUGA dial of GARO [GRT]
RUGARA alt for BUIN [BUO]
RUGCIRIKU alt for DIRIKU [DIU]
RUGNOT OF LAKE BUHI EAST alt for AGTA, MT.
    IRAYA [ATL]
RUGO alt for ROKO dial of MANGSING [MBH]
RUGUNGU alt for GUNGU [RUB]
RUGURU [RUF] lang, Tanzania
RUHAYA alt for HAYA [HAY]
RUIHI alt for RUFIJI [RUI]
RUIJA dial of SAAMI, NORTHERN [LPR]
RUK alt for TRUK [TRU]
RUKAI [DRU] lang, Taiwan
RUKARAGWE alt for NYAMBO [NYM]
RUKIGA alt for CHIGA [CHG]
RUKOBI alt for HUNDE [HKE]
RUKONJO alt for KONJO [KOO]
RUKONJO dial of KONJO [KOO]
RUKUBA alt for CHE [RUK]
RUKWANGALI alt for KWANGALI [KWN]
RULI [RUC] lang, Uganda
RUM dial of GIZIGA, SOUTH [GIZ]
RUMA [RUZ] lang, Nigeria
RUMA dial of KORKU [KFQ]
RUMAI alt for PALAUNG, RUMAI [RBB]
RUMAIYA alt for MALA [RUY]
RUMANAU dial of LOBU, LANAS [RUU]
RUMANAU ALAB alt for RUMANAU dial of LOBU,
    LANAS [RUU]

RUMANIAN [RUM] lang, Romania, Israel, Moldova
RUMANIAN SIGN LANGUAGE [RMS] lang, Romania
RUMANIAN, ISTRO [RUO] lang, Yugoslavia
RUMANIAN, MACEDO [RUP] lang, Greece, Albania,
  Bulgaria, Yugoslavia
RUMANIAN, MACEDO alt for RUMANIAN, MACEDO
  [RUP]
RUMANIAN, MEGLENO [RUQ] lang, Greece
RUMANTSCH alt for RHETO-ROMANCE [RHE]
RUMAYA alt for MALA [RUY]
RUMBALA alt for MBALA [MDP]
RUMBERPON dial of BIAK [BHW]
RUMBIA alt for WITA EA dial of MORONENE [MQN]
RUMBUR alt for NORTHERN KALASHA dial of
  KALASHA [KLS]
RUMDALI alt for BAHING [RAR]
RUMELIAN dial of TURKISH [TRK]
RUMLI alt for LOMBI [LMI]
RUMU alt for KAIRI [KLQ]
RUMUWA alt for KAIRI [KLQ]
RUNA [RUN] lang, Colombia
RUNDI [RUD] lang, Burundi, Uganda, Tanzania,
  Uganda
RUNDI alt for RUNDI [RUD]
RUNDUM dial of TAGAL MURUT [MVV]
RUNDUM MURUT dial of TAGAL MURUT [MVV]
RUNGA [ROU] lang, Chad, Central African Republic
RUNGA alt for RUNGWA [RNW]
RUNGA DE NDELE alt for RUNGA [ROU]
RUNGCHENBUNG dial of BANTAWA [BAP]
RUNGI [RUR] lang, Tanzania
RUNGU alt for TAABWA [TAP]
RUNGU dial of MAMBWE-LUNGU [MGR]
RUNGU dial of MAMBWE-LUNGU [MGR]
RUNGU alt for ORUNGU dial of MYENE [MYE]
RUNGUS [DRG] lang, Malaysia, Sabah
RUNGUS dial of RUNGUS [DRG]
RUNGUS DUSUN alt for RUNGUS [DRG]
RUNGWA [RNW] lang, Tanzania
RUNYAMBO alt for NYAMBO [NYM]
RUNYANKOLE alt for NYANKOLE [NYN]
RUNYARWANDA alt for RWANDA [RUA]
RUNYORO alt for HEMA-SUD [NIX]
RUNYORO alt for NYORO [NYR]
RUPINI dial of CHIN, FALAM [HBH]
RUPSHU alt for CHANGTHANG [CNA]
RUPUNUNI dial of GUYANESE [GYN]
RURAL PESHAWAR HINDKO dial of HINDKO,
  SOUTHERN [HIN]
RURAL SOUTHERN MOROCCO dial of ARABIC,
  MOROCCAN [ARY]
RURAMA alt for RUMA [RUZ]
RURI dial of KWAYA [KYA]
RURUHI'IP alt for YAHANG [RHP]
RURUHIP alt for YAHANG [RHP]
RURUHIP alt for ARINUA [AUK]
RURULI alt for RULI [RUC]
RURUMA alt for RUMA [RUZ]
RURUTU dial of AUSTRAL [AUT]
RUSA alt for RUSHA [RUH]
RUSHA [RUH] lang, Tanzania
RUSHAN alt for ROSHANI dial of SHUGHNI [SGH]
RUSHAN alt for RUSHANI dial of SHUGHNI [SGH]
RUSHANI dial of SHUGHNI [SGH]
RUSHANI alt for ROSHANI dial of SHUGHNI [SGH]
RUSS alt for RUSSIAN [RUS]

RUSSELL ISLAND alt for LAVUKALEVE [LVK]
RUSSIA alt for DAASANECH [DSH]
RUSSIAN [RUS] lang, Russia, Europe, USA, China,
  Israel, Mongolian Peoples Republic
"RUSSIAN LAPP" alt for SAAMI, SKOLT [LPK]
RUSSIAN LAPP alt for SAAMI, SKOLT [LPK]
RUSSIAN SIGN LANGUAGE [RSL] lang, Russia,
  Europe, Bulgaria
RUSURJA KALDERASH dial of ROMANI, VLACH
  [RMY]
RUSYN [RUE] lang, Ukraine, Czechoslovakia
RUT dial of DINKA, NORTHEASTERN [DIP]
RUTAGWENDA dial of NYORO [NYR]
RUTAH dial of AMAHAI [AMQ]
RUTAL alt for RUTUL [RUT]
RUTENG alt for CENTRAL MANGGARAI dial of
  MANGGARAI [MQY]
RUTHENIAN alt for RUSYN [RUE]
RUTKAI alt for RUKAI [DRU]
RUTO [NDY] lang, Central African Republic, Chad,
  Chad
RUTO alt for RUTO [NDY]
RUTO dial of RUTO [NDY]
RUTO dial of RUTO [NDY]
RUTORO alt for TORO dial of NYORO [NYR]
RUTSE alt for LOZI [LOZ]
RUTUL [RUT] lang, Russia, Europe
RUTULTSY alt for RUTUL [RUT]
RUTULY alt for RUTUL [RUT]
RUTUMAN alt for ROTUMAN [RTM]
RUTWA dial of RWANDA [RUA]
RUUL alt for LEUN [LLE]
RUUND [RND] lang, Zaïre, Angola
RUVIANA alt for ROVIANA [RUG]
RUWENG dial of DINKA, NORTHWESTERN [DIW]
RUWENZORI KIBIRA alt for KWAMBA [RWM]
RWALA alt for CENTRAL NAJDI dial of ARABIC,
  NAJDI [ARS]
RWALA alt for CENTRAL NAJDI dial of ARABIC,
  NAJDI [ARS]
RWAMBA alt for KWAMBA [RWM]
RWANDA [RUA] lang, Rwanda, Burundi, Tanzania,
  Uganda, Zaïre
RWANDA alt for RWANDA [RUA]
RWO [RWK] lang, Tanzania
S'AMAI alt for TSAMAI [TSB]
SA [SSA] lang, Vanuatu
SA alt for NHANG [NHA]
SA alt for NGEMBA dial of GHOMALA' [BBJ]
SA'ANG alt for HA'AANG dial of TA'OIH, UPPER
  [TTH]
SA'BAN alt for SA'BAN [SNV]
SA'DAN alt for TORAJA-SA'DAN [SDA]
SA'DANSCHE alt for TORAJA-SA'DAN [SDA]
SA'U alt for SAHU [SUX]
SAA [SZR] lang, Cameroon
SA'A [APB] lang, Solomon Islands
SAADJE alt for SAGZEE dial of DII [DUR]
SAAFI alt for SAFEN [SAV]
SAAFI-SAAFI alt for SAFEN [SAV]
SAAKYE alt for SAGZEE dial of DII [DUR]
SAAM [RAQ] lang, Nepal
SAAM alt for SAAMI, KILDIN [LPD]
SAAM alt for SAAMI, INARI [LPI]
SAAM alt for SAAMI, SKOLT [LPK]
SAAM alt for SAAMI, TER [LPT]

SAAM RAI alt for SAAM [RAQ]
SAAME alt for SAAMI, INARI [LPI]
SAAME alt for SAAMI, LULE [LPL]
SAAME alt for SAAMI, NORTHERN [LPR]
SAAMI alt for SAAMI, LULE [LPL]
SAAMI alt for SAAMI, NORTHERN [LPR]
SAAMI, INARI [LPI] lang, Finland
SAAMI, KILDIN [LPD] lang, Russia, Europe
SAAMI, LULE [LPL] lang, Sweden, Norway
SAAMI, NORTHERN [LPR] lang, Norway, Finland,
    Sweden
SAAMI, NORTHERN alt for SAAMI, NORTHERN
    [LPR]
SAAMI, PITE [LPB] lang, Sweden, Norway
SAAMI, SKOLT [LPK] lang, Russia, Europe, Finland
SAAMI, SOUTHERN [LPC] lang, Sweden, Norway
SAAMI, TER [LPT] lang, Russia, Europe
SAAMI, UME [LPU] lang, Sweden, Norway
SAAMIA [SBU] lang, Kenya, Uganda, Uganda
SAAMIA alt for SAAMIA [SBU]
SAAMIA dial of SAAMIA [SBU]
SAAN alt for SAN [HGM]
SAANICH dial of SALISH, STRAITS [STR]
SAAPA alt for SANAPANÁ [SAP]
SAAPA alt for SAA [SZR]
SAAROA [SXR] lang, Taiwan
SAARONGE alt for DAJU, DAR DADJU [DJC]
SAARUA alt for SAAROA [SXR]
SAAWA dial of MUMUYE [MUL]
SABA [SAA] lang, Chad
SABAH MURUT alt for TAGAL dial of TAGAL
    MURUT [MVV]
SA'BAN [SNV] lang, Indonesia, Kalimantan,
    Malaysia, Sarawak, Malaysia, Sarawak
SABANÊ alt for SABANÊS [SAE]
SABANERO dial of BUGLERE [SAB]
SABANÊS [SAE] lang, Brazil
SABANGA [SXA] lang, Central African Republic
SABANILLA dial of CHOL, TILA [CTI]
SABAOT [SPY] lang, Kenya
SABAR alt for SORA [SRB]
SABARA alt for SORA [SRB]
SABARI alt for AMIS [ALV]
SABARI dial of NIMOA [NMW]
SABENA alt for MOSKONA [MTJ]
SABERI alt for ISIRAWA [SRL]
SABEU dial of CHIN, MARA [MRH]
SABINY dial of KUPSABINY [KPZ]
SABO dial of GREBO, NORTHEASTERN [GRP]
SABON dial of LELE [UGA]
SABONES alt for SABANÊS [SAE]
SABU alt for SAWU [HVN]
SABUJÁ dial of KARIRI-XUCO [KZW]
SABŮM [SBO] lang, Malaysia, Peninsular
SABUNGO dial of DAYAK, LAND [DYK]
SABUP alt for KENYAH, SEBOB [SIB]
SABURI dial of LIGURI [LIU]
SABUTAN alt for BUKAR SADONG [SDO]
SABUYAN alt for SEBUYAU [SNB]
SABUYAU alt for SEBUYAU [SNB]
SAC dial of MESQUAKIE [SAC]
SAC AND FOX alt for MESQUAKIE [SAC]
SACAPULAS QUICHÉ alt for SACAPULTECO [QUV]
SACAPULTECO [QUV] lang, Guatemala
SACH [SCB] lang, Viet Nam
SADA alt for TAE' [ROB]

SADA alt for TOALA' [TLZ]
SADALIR alt for SEDALIR dial of TIDONG [TID]
SADALIR alt for SALALIR dial of TAGAL MURUT
    [MVV]
SADAN alt for TORAJA-SA'DAN [SDA]
SADANA alt for SADANI [SCK]
SADANG alt for TORAJA-SA'DAN [SDA]
SADANGA dial of BONTOC, CENTRAL [BNC]
SADANI [SCK] lang, India
SADAR alt for SHADAL dial of MANKANYA [MAN]
SADAR BHUMIJ alt for BHUMIJ [BHM]
SADARI alt for SADANI [SCK]
SADATI alt for SADANI [SCK]
SADHAN alt for SADANI [SCK]
SADNA alt for SADANI [SCK]
SADONG alt for BUKAR SADONG [SDO]
SADRI alt for SADANI [SCK]
SADRI dial of MAITHILI [MKP]
SADRI KORWA dial of CHATTISGARHI [HNE]
SADRI, ORAON [SDR] lang, Bangladesh
SADRIK alt for SADANI [SCK]
SAEDIQ alt for TAROKO [TRV]
SAEK [SKB] lang, Laos, Thailand, Thailand
SAEK alt for SAEK [SKB]
SAEP [SPD] lang, Papua New Guinea
SAFALABA alt for SAFALIBA [SAF]
SAFALBA alt for SAFALIBA [SAF]
SAFALIBA [SAF] lang, Ghana
SAFAZO alt for SAFALIBA [SAF]
SAFEN [SAV] lang, Senegal
SAFEYOKA alt for AMPEELI-WOJOKESO [APZ]
SAFI alt for SAFEN [SAV]
SAFI-SAFI alt for SAFEN [SAV]
SAFWA [SBK] lang, Tanzania
SAGA-I alt for DUSUN SEGAMA dial of
    KINABATANGAN, UPPER [DMG]
SAGADA IGOROT alt for KANKANAY, NORTHERN
    [KAN]
SAGADIN dial of DIDO [DDO]
SAGAI dial of KHAKAS [KJH]
SAGAI dial of KHAKAS [KJH]
SAGAJ alt for SAGAI dial of KHAKAS [KJH]
SAGALA [SBM] lang, Tanzania
SAGALA alt for SAGALLA [TGA]
SAGALLA [TGA] lang, Kenya
SAGARA alt for SAGALA [SBM]
SAGBEE dial of MUMUYE [MUL]
SAGEJU alt for DHAISO [SEG]
SAGHALA alt for SAGALLA [TGA]
SAGHILIN alt for SAKHALIN dial of AINU [AIN]
SAGI alt for KAMASAU [KMS]
SAGO alt for TSAGU [TGD]
SAGTENGPA [SGT] lang, Bhutan
SAGUYE alt for SAKUYE dial of OROMO, BORANA-
    ARUSI-GUJI [GAX]
SAGZEE dial of DII [DUR]
SAHAFTRA dial of MALAGASY [MEX]
SAHARIA [SRX] lang, India
SAHO [SSY] lang, Ethiopia
SAHU [SUX] lang, Indonesia, Maluku
SAHU alt for SAO dial of MASLAM [MSV]
SAHU'U alt for SAHU [SUX]
SAI dial of GUMUZ [GUK]
SAI alt for TAI PONG dial of TAI NÜA [TDD]
SAIGHANI alt for SHUGHNI dial of SHUGHNI [SGH]
SAIJA alt for EPENA SAIJA [SJA]

SAILAU alt for LUSHAI [LSH]
SAILEN alt for DURIANKERE [DBN]
SAILOLOF alt for MA'YA [SLZ]
SAINJI dial of KULUI [KFX]
SAIPA dial of SINSAURU [SNZ]
SAIPAN CAROLINIAN alt for CAROLINIAN [CAL]
SAIRANG dial of CHIN, THADO [TCZ]
SAIROPE dial of OROKAIVA [ORK]
SAISET alt for SAISIYAT [SAI]
SAISETT alt for SAISIYAT [SAI]
SAISIAT alt for SAISIYAT [SAI]
SAISIETT alt for SAISIYAT [SAI]
SAISIRAT alt for SAISIYAT [SAI]
SAISIYAT [SAI] lang, Taiwan
SAISYET alt for SAISIYAT [SAI]
SAISYETT alt for SAISIYAT [SAI]
SAIZANG dial of CHIN, TEDIM [CTD]
SAJAU alt for SAJAU BASAP [SAD]
SAJAU BASAP [SAD] lang, Indonesia, Kalimantan
SAK alt for KADO [KDV]
SAKA alt for SAKATA [SAT]
SAKA alt for ODUAL [ODU]
SAKA dial of MAKHUWA [MAK]
SAKA dial of NKUTU [NKW]
SAKAI alt for SEMANG, LOWLAND [ORB]
SAKAI alt for KENSIU [KNS]
SAKAI BUKIT OF TEMONGOH alt for PO-KLO dial of
   TEMIAR [TMH]
SAKAI OF PLUS KORBU dial of TEMIAR [TMH]
SAKAI TANJONG OF TEMONGOH alt for JEHER dial
   of KENSIU [KNS]
SAKAJI [SKN] lang, Mozambique
SAKALAGAN dial of MENTAWAI [MWV]
SAKALAVA dial of MALAGASY [MEX]
SAKAM [SKM] lang, Papua New Guinea
SAKANYI dial of NTOMBA [NTO]
SAKAO [SKU] lang, Vanuatu
SAKARA alt for NZAKARA [NZK]
SAKATA [SAT] lang, Zaïre
SAKATA dial of SAKATA [SAT]
SAKAU alt for SAKAO [SKU]
SAKE [SAG] lang, Gabon
SAKEI dial of KERINCI [KVR]
SAKER alt for BARGAM [MLP]
SAKHA alt for YAKUT [UKT]
SAKHALIN dial of AINU [AIN]
SAKHALIN dial of EVENKI [EVN]
SAKI alt for MAIA [SKS]
SAKIRAY alt for SAKIZAYA dial of AMIS,
   NATAORAN [AIS]
SAKIZAYA dial of AMIS, NATAORAN [AIS]
SAKKYRYR dial of EVEN [EVE]
SAKPU dial of KARANG [KZR]
SAKUYE dial of OROMO, BORANA-ARUSI-GUJI
   [GAX]
SALA [SHQ] lang, Zambia
SALA alt for SALAR [SLR]
SALABEKHA dial of KEBUMTAMP [KJZ]
SALAJAR alt for SELAYAR [SLY]
SALAKAHADI [SKF] lang, Papua New Guinea
SALALE dial of OROMO, BORANA-ARUSI-GUJI
   [GAX]
SALALIR dial of TAGAL MURUT [MVV]
SALALIR alt for SEDALIR dial of TIDONG [TID]
SALAMÃI alt for MONDÉ [MND]
SALAMAIKÃ alt for MONDÉ [MND]

SALAMPASU [SLX] lang, Zaïre
SALANI dial of GARHWALI [GBM]
SALAR [SLR] lang, China
SALARU alt for SELARU [SLU]
SALAS [SGU] lang, Indonesia, Maluku
SALAS GUNUNG alt for SALAS [SGU]
SALASACA QUICHUA alt for QUICHUA, HIGHLAND,
   TUNGURAHUA [QQS]
SALATAV dial of AVAR [AVR]
SALAWATI alt for MA'YA [SLZ]
SALAYAR alt for SELAYAR [SLY]
SALAYER alt for SELAYAR [SLY]
SALCHUQ [SLQ] lang, Iran
SALEBABU alt for LIRANG dial of TALAUD [TLD]
SALEIER alt for SELAYAR [SLY]
SALEMAN [SAU] lang, Indonesia, Maluku
SALEWARI dial of TELUGU [TCW]
SALI alt for NSARI [ASJ]
SALIANY dial of AZERBAIJANI, NORTH [AZE]
SÁLIBA [SLC] lang, Colombia, Venezuela, Venezuela
SÁLIBA alt for SÁLIBA [SLC]
SALIBABU alt for LIRANG dial of TALAUD [TLD]
SALIEN alt for NYINDROU [LID]
SALINAN [SAL] lang, USA
SALISH, SOUTHERN PUGET SOUND [SLH] lang,
   USA
SALISH, STRAITS [STR] lang, Canada, USA, USA
SALISH, STRAITS alt for SALISH, STRAITS [STR]
SALITRE-CABAGRA dial of BRIBRI [BZD]
SÁLIVA alt for SÁLIBA [SLC]
SALKA alt for SHINGINI dial of GADI-SHINGINI-
   VADI-BAANGI [KAM]
SALOG dial of SUBANON, TUBOY [STB]
SALON alt for MOKEN [MWT]
SALOR dial of TURKMEN [TCK]
SALRENG dial of FRISIAN, NORTHERN [FRR]
SALT alt for SALT-YUI [SLL]
SALT-IUI alt for SALT-YUI [SLL]
SALT-YUI [SLL] lang, Papua New Guinea
SALU MUKANAM dial of PITU ULUNNA SALU [PTU]
SALU MUKANG alt for SALU MUKANAM dial of
   PITU ULUNNA SALU [PTU]
SALUAN, COASTAL [LOE] lang, Indonesia, Sulawesi
SALUAN, KAHUMAMAHON [SLB] lang, Indonesia,
   Sulawesi
SALUG alt for SALOG dial of SUBANON, TUBOY
   [STB]
SALUMÁ [SLJ] lang, Brazil
SALUMÃ [UNK] lang, Brazil
SALUR dial of GADABA [GDB]
SALYA alt for SELYA dial of NYAKYUSA-NGONDE
   [NYY]
SALYR dial of TURKMEN [TCK]
SAM alt for SHAN [SJN]
SAMA [SMD] lang, Angola
SAMA alt for PANA [PNQ]
SAMA alt for BAJAU, INDONESIAN [BDL]
SAMA alt for SAMBA DAKA [CCG]
SAMA dial of SAMA, SOUTHERN [SIT]
SAMA KUBANG alt for BAJAU SEMPORNA dial of
   SAMA, SOUTHERN [SIT]
SAMA KUBUNG alt for SIKUBUNG dial of SAMA,
   SOUTHERN [SIT]
SAMA LAUT alt for BAJAU LAUT dial of SAMA,
   SOUTHERN [SIT]
SAMA MANDELAUT alt for BAJAU LAUT dial of

SAMA, SOUTHERN [SIT]
SAMA MAPUN alt for MAPUN [SJM]
SAMA PALA'AU alt for BAJAU LAUT dial of SAMA, SOUTHERN [SIT]
SAMA SIBUTU alt for SIBUTU dial of SAMA, SOUTHERN [SIT]
SAMA SIBUTU' alt for SAMA, SOUTHERN [SIT]
SAMA SIMUNUL alt for SIMUNUL dial of SAMA, SOUTHERN [SIT]
SAMA UBIAN alt for UBIAN dial of SAMA, SOUTHERN [SIT]
SAMA' alt for SAMA dial of SAMA, SOUTHERN [SIT]
SAMA, ABAKNON [ABX] lang, Philippines
SAMA, BALANGINGI [SSE] lang, Philippines, Malaysia, Sabah
SAMA, CENTRAL [SML] lang, Philippines, Malaysia, Sabah
SAMA, PANGUTARAN [SLM] lang, Philippines
SAMA, SOUTHERN [SIT] lang, Philippines, Malaysia, Sabah
SAMACHIQUE TARAHUMARA alt for TARAHUMARA, CENTRAL [TAR]
SAMADA alt for PADANG dial of TALIABU [TLV]
SAMAGIR dial of NANAI [GLD]
SAMAH alt for SAMA dial of SAMA, SOUTHERN [SIT]
SAMAH LUMBUH alt for SIBUTU dial of SAMA, SOUTHERN [SIT]
SAMAH-SAMAH alt for SIBUTU dial of SAMA, SOUTHERN [SIT]
SAMAL alt for SAMA, CENTRAL [SML]
SAMAL alt for SAMA dial of SAMA, SOUTHERN [SIT]
SAMALEK alt for KASUWERI [QKW]
SAMANÁ ENGLISH [SAX] lang, Dominican Republic
SAMANAI dial of ANGOR [AGG]
SAMAP alt for ELEPI [ELE]
SAMAP alt for KAIEP [KBW]
SAMAR alt for SAMA dial of SAMA, SOUTHERN [SIT]
SAMAR-LEYTE alt for WARAY-WARAY [WRY]
SAMAR-LEYTE dial of WARAY-WARAY [WRY]
SAMARAN alt for WARAY-WARAY [WRY]
SAMAREÑO alt for WARAY-WARAY [WRY]
SAMARGIN dial of UDIHE [UDE]
SAMARIA dial of BENGALI [BNG]
SAMARIA dial of MARPAHARIA [MKB]
SAMARITAN [SMP] lang, Israel
SAMARKENA alt for SAMAROKENA [TMJ]
SAMAROKENA [TMJ] lang, Indonesia, Irian Jaya
SAMATALI alt for SANUMÁ [SAM]
SAMATARI alt for SANUMÁ [SAM]
SAMATE alt for MA'YA [SLZ]
SAMAYA dial of KURANKO [KHA]
SAMBA [SMX] lang, Zaïre
SAMBA alt for SAMBA DAKA [CCG]
SAMBA alt for SAMBA LEKO [NDI]
SAMBA BALI dial of SAMBA LEKO [NDI]
SAMBA DAKA [CCG] lang, Nigeria
SAMBA DE WANGAI dial of SAMBA LEKO [NDI]
SAMBA LEEKO alt for SAMBA LEKO [NDI]
SAMBA LEKO [NDI] lang, Cameroon, Nigeria, Nigeria
SAMBA LEKO alt for SAMBA LEKO [NDI]
SAMBA LEKO dial of SAMBA LEKO [NDI]
SAMBAA alt for SHAMBALA [KSB]

SAMBAL, BOTOLAN [SBL] lang, Philippines
SAMBAL, TINA [SNA] lang, Philippines
SAMBALA alt for SHAMBALA [KSB]
SAMBALPURI alt for WESTERN ORIYA dial of ORIYA [ORY]
SAMBAN alt for SHAMANG dial of HAM [JAB]
SAMBARA alt for SHAMBALA [KSB]
SAMBAS dial of MALAY [MLI]
SAMBERI dial of BIAK [BHW]
SAMBERIGI [SSX] lang, Papua New Guinea
SAMBIO alt for KAPIN [TBX]
SAMBIO alt for SAMBYU dial of KWANGALI [KWN]
SAMBIRIR dial of ENDO-MARAKWET [ENB]
SAMBIU alt for SAMBYU dial of KWANGALI [KWN]
SAMBLA [SOS] lang, Burkina Faso
SAMBO dial of MBO [MBO]
SAMBU alt for WAMSAK [WBD]
SAMBUP alt for KENYAH, SEBOB [SIB]
SAMBUR alt for SAMBURU [SAQ]
SAMBURU [SAQ] lang, Kenya
SAMBYU dial of KWANGALI [KWN]
SAME alt for SAAMI, SKOLT [LPK]
SAME alt for SAAMI, NORTHERN [LPR]
SAME' dial of BAJAU, INDONESIAN [BDL]
SAMEI [SMH] lang, China
SAMIA dial of SAAMIA [SBU]
SAMIC alt for SAAMI, INARI [LPI]
SAMIC alt for SAAMI, NORTHERN [LPR]
SAMIHIM dial of MA'ANYAN [MHY]
SAMISH dial of SALISH, STRAITS [STR]
SAMO [SBD] lang, Burkina Faso, Mali
SÀMÓ alt for KALAMSE [KNZ]
SAMO alt for OWINIGA [OWI]
SAMO dial of SAMO-KUBO [SMQ]
SAMO-KUBO [SMQ] lang, Papua New Guinea
SAMOAN [SMY] lang, Samoa, American Samoa, Fiji, New Zealand, Tokelau
SAMOAN alt for SAMOAN [SMY]
SAMOBI alt for PAIWAN [PWN]
SAMOE alt for WARA [WBF]
SAMOGHO alt for JO [JOW]
SAMOGHO alt for DUUN [DUX]
SAMOGHO alt for DZUNGO [SBE]
SAMOGHO alt for SAMBLA [SOS]
SAMOGITIAN alt for SHAMAITISH dial of LITHUANIAN [LIT]
SAMOGO alt for DUUN [DUX]
SAMOGO alt for DZUNGO [SBE]
SAMOGOHIRI alt for DZUNGO dial of DZUNGO [SBE]
SAMOHAI alt for PAIWAN [PWN]
SAMOMA alt for KALAMSE [KNZ]
SAMONG alt for HPON [HPO]
SAMORO alt for DUUN [DUX]
SAMORO alt for DZUNGO [SBE]
SAMOROGOUAN alt for KPANGO dial of DZUNGO [SBE]
SAMOSA [SMO] lang, Papua New Guinea
SAMPANG [RAV] lang, Nepal
SAMPANG dial of MADURA [MHJ]
SAMPANGE RAI alt for SAMPANG [RAV]
SAMPANTABIL dial of MANGSING [MBH]
SAMPARA dial of SAMBA LEKO [NDI]
SAMPIT dial of MALAY [MLI]
SAMPIT alt for BA'AMANG dial of NGAJU [NIJ]
SAMPOLAWA dial of CIA-CIA [CIA]
SAMPORI dial of BIAK [BHW]

SAMPUR alt for SAMBURU [SAQ]
SAMRE [SCC] lang, Cambodia
SAMTALI alt for SANTALI [SNT]
SAMTAO [STU] lang, Myanmar
SAMTAU alt for SAMTAO [STU]
SAMTUAN alt for SAMTAO [STU]
SAMURZAKAN dial of ABKHAZ [ABK]
SAMURZAKAN-ZUGDIDI dial of LAZ [LZZ]
SAMVEDI [SMV] lang, India
SAMYA alt for SAAMIA [SBU]
SAN [HGM] lang, Namibia
SAN alt for SAMO [SBD]
SAN AGUST#IN LOXICHA ZAPOTECO dial of
    ZAPOTECO, NORTHEASTERN POCHUTLA [ZTP]
SAN ANDRÉS COHAMIATA dial of HUICHOL [HCH]
SAN ANDRÉS CREOLE dial of WESTERN
    CARIBBEAN CREOLE ENGLISH [JAM]
SAN ANDRÉS INGA dial of INGA [INB]
SAN ANDRÉS SAJCABAJÁ QUICHÉ alt for QUICHÉ,
    EASTERN [QIE]
SAN ANDRÉS SEMETABAJ alt for SANTA MARÍA
    DE JESÚS CAKCHIQUEL dial of CAKCHIQUEL,
    WESTERN [CKW]
SAN BALTAZAR CHICHICAPAN ZAPOTECO alt for
    ZAPOTECO, CHICHICAPAN-TILQUIAPAN [ZPV]
SAN BALTÁZAR LOXICHA ZAPOTECO alt for
    ZAPOTECO, NORTHWESTERN POCHUTLA [ZPX]
SAN BARTOLOMÉ VENUSTIANO CARRANZA dial of
    TZOTZIL, HUIXTÁN [TZU]
SAN BLAS CUNA alt for KUNA, SAN BLAS [CUK]
SAN BORJANO alt for REYESANO [REY]
SAN CARLOS dial of APACHE, WESTERN [APW]
SAN CHAY alt for MAN CAO LAN [MLC]
SAN CHI alt for MAN CAO LAN [MLC]
SAN CRISTOBAL AMATLÁN ZAPOTECO alt for
    ZAPOTECO, NORTHEASTERN MIAHUATLÁN
    [ZPO]
SAN CRISTOBAL LAS CASAS dial of TZOTZIL,
    CHAMULA [TZC]
SAN DIONISIO HUAVE dial of HUAVE, SAN
    FRANCISCO DEL MAR [HUE]
SAN FELIPE dial of KERES, EASTERN [KEE]
SAN FELIPE SANTIAGO OTOMÍ dial of OTOMÍ,
    STATE OF MEXICO [OTS]
SAN FRANCISCO LOGUECHE ZAPOTECO alt for
    ZAPOTECO, NORTHEASTERN MIAHUATLÁN
    [ZPO]
SAN GREGORIO OZOLOTEPEC ZAPOTECO dial of
    ZAPOTECO, OZOLOTEPEC [ZAO]
SAN IGNACIO DE VELAZCO dial of CHIQUITANO
    [CAX]
SAN ILDEFONSO dial of TEWA [TEW]
SAN JAVIER dial of CHIQUITANO [CAX]
SAN JORGE alt for CHIMILA [CBG]
SAN JOSÉ CHACAYA CAKCHIQUEL dial of
    CAKCHIQUEL, WESTERN [CKW]
SAN JOSÉ OZOLOTEPEC ZAPOTECO dial of
    ZAPOTECO, SANTA CATARINA XANAGUÍA
    [ZTG]
SAN JUAN dial of TEWA [TEW]
SAN JUAN ATZINGO POPOLOCA alt for
    POPOLOCA, EASTERN [POE]
SAN JUAN CHAMULA dial of TZOTZIL, CHAMULA
    [TZC]
SAN JUAN COTZOCÓN MIXE alt for MIXE,
    NORTHEASTERN [MVE]

SAN JUAN DEL BOSQUE dial of TZOTZIL,
    CHAMULA [TZC]
SAN JUAN EL PARAÍSO MIXE alt for MIXE,
    COATLÁN [MCO]
SAN JUAN ELOTEPEC ZAPOTECO dial of
    ZAPOTECO, SANTA MARÍA ZANIZA [ZPW]
SAN JUAN GUELAVÍA ZAPOTECO alt for
    ZAPOTECO, WESTERN TLACOLULA [ZAB]
SAN JUAN MIXTEPEC MIXTECO alt for MIXTECO,
    EASTERN JUXTLAHUACA [MIX]
SAN JUAN MIXTEPEC ZAPOTECO alt for
    ZAPOTECO, EASTERN MIAHUATLÁN [ZPM]
SAN JUAN ÑUMI MIXTECO alt for MIXTECO,
    NORTHERN TLAXIACO [MOS]
SAN JUAN OSTUNCALCO MAM alt for MAM,
    SOUTHERN [MMS]
SAN JUAN QUIAHIJE CHATINO dial of CHATINO,
    WEST HIGHLAND [CTP]
SAN JUAN TEITA MIXTECO alt for MIXTECO, SAN
    BARTOLOMÉ YUCUAÑE [MVG]
SAN LUCAS TOLIMÁN alt for SANTA MARÍA DE
    JESÚS CAKCHIQUEL dial of CAKCHIQUEL,
    WESTERN [CKW]
SAN MARCIAL OZOLOTEPEC ZAPOTECO dial of
    ZAPOTECO, OZOLOTEPEC [ZAO]
SAN MARCOS MAM alt for MAM, CENTRAL [MVC]
SAN MARCOS ZACATEPEC CHATINO alt for
    CHATINO, ZACATEPEC [CTZ]
SAN MARTÍN CHILE VERDE MAM alt for SAN
    MARTÍN SACATEPÉQUEZ MAM dial of MAM,
    SOUTHERN [MMS]
SAN MARTÍN SACATEPÉQUEZ MAM dial of MAM,
    SOUTHERN [MMS]
SAN MATEO dial of MAZATECO, HUAUTLA DE
    JIMENEZ [MAU]
SAN MATEO TEPANTEPEC dial of MIXTECO,
    EASTERN [MIL]
SAN MIGUEL dial of CHIQUITANO [CAX]
SAN MIGUEL dial of MAZATECO, HUAUTLA DE
    JIMENEZ [MAU]
SAN MIGUEL ACATÁN KANJOBAL alt for
    KANJOBAL, WESTERN [KNJ]
SAN MIGUEL ALBARRADAS dial of ZAPOTECO,
    ALBARRADAS [ZAS]
SAN MIGUEL CHIMALAPA dial of ZOQUE, SANTA
    MARÍA CHIMALAPA [ZOH]
SAN MIGUEL CREOLE FRENCH [SME] lang, Panama
SAN MIGUEL MITONTIC dial of TZOTZIL,
    CHENALHÓ [TZE]
SAN MIGUEL PIEDRAS MIXTECO alt for MIXTECO,
    SOUTHERN NOCHIXTLÁN [MAB]
SAN MIGUEL SOYALTEPEC dial of MAZATECO,
    SAN JERÓNIMO TECOATL [MAA]
SAN MIGUEL ZAPOTECO alt for ZAPOTECO,
    WESTERN MIAHUATLÁN [ZPS]
SAN PABLO CHALCHIHUITAN dial of TZOTZIL,
    CHENALHÓ [TZE]
SAN PEDRO CAJONOS ZAPOTECO alt for
    ZAPOTECO, SOUTHERN VILLA ALTA [ZAD]
SAN PEDRO CHENALHO dial of TZOTZIL,
    CHENALHÓ [TZE]
SAN PEDRO DE HUACARPANA dial of QUECHUA,
    YAUYOS [QUX]
SAN PEDRO EL ALTO ZAPOTECO alt for
    ZAPOTECO, SOUTH CENTRAL ZIMATLÁN [ZPP]
SAN PEDRO MOLINOS dial of MIXTECO, SAN

MIGUEL EL GRANDE [MIG]
SAN PEDRO QUIATONI ZAPOTECO alt for
  ZAPOTECO, EASTERN TLACOLULA [ZPF]
SAN PEDRO TOTOMACHAPAN ZAPOTECO alt for
  ZAPOTECO, WESTERN ZIMATLÁN [ZPH]
SAN RAMON INAGTA alt for AGTA, MT. IRIGA
  [AGZ]
SAN SEBASTIÁN-SANTA CATARINA dial of
  HUICHOL [HCH]
SAN SIMÓN ZAHUATLÁN dial of MIXTECO,
  SILACAYOAPAN [MKS]
SAN TUNG dial of SUI [SWI]
SAN VICENTE COATLÁN ZAPOTECO alt for
  ZAPOTECO, SOUTHERN EJUTLA [ZPT]
SÁN-CHI alt for MAN CAO LAN [MLC]
SANA'A dial of ARABIC, YEMENI [ACQ]
SANABERIGI alt for SAMBERIGI [SSX]
SANAGA alt for TUKI [BAG]
SANAINAWA dial of KATUKÍNA, PANOAN [KNT]
SANAM alt for SANAPANÁ [SAP]
SANAMAICA alt for MONDÉ [MND]
SANAMAIKÁ alt for MONDÉ [MND]
SANAMAYKÃ alt for MONDÉ [MND]
SANANA alt for SULA [SZN]
SANAPANÁ [SAP] lang, Paraguay
SANAROA dial of DOBU [DOB]
SANBALBE alt for MALGBE [MXF]
SANBIAU alt for PIU [PIX]
SANCHUAN dial of TU [MJG]
SANDA dial of THEMNE [TEJ]
SANDA dial of LOKO [LOK]
SANDAKAN BAJAU dial of BAJAU, WEST COAST
  [BDR]
SANDAL alt for SANTALI [SNT]
SANDAU! alt for SANDAWE [SBR]
SANDAWE [SBR] lang, Tanzania
SANDAWI alt for SANDAWE [SBR]
SANDAYO dial of KIMARAGANG [KQR]
SANDE alt for ZANDE [ZAN]
SANDEWAR dial of TIMUGON MURUT [TIH]
SANDIA dial of TIWA, SOUTHERN [TIX]
SANDIWAR dial of TIMUGON MURUT [TIH]
SANDO alt for NORTHERN KONO dial of KONO
  [KNO]
SANDOWAY dial of CHIN, ASHO [CSH]
SANDU alt for SHENDU [SHL]
SANDWE alt for SANDAWE [SBR]
SANE alt for SAMO [SBD]
SANEMA alt for SANUMÁ [SAM]
SANG dial of NAGA, KONYAK [NBE]
SANG PHANG alt for CHINESE, YUE [YUH]
SANGA [SNG] lang, Zaïre
SANGA [SGA] lang, Nigeria
SANGA alt for NUMANA-NUNKU-GWANTU-NUMBU
  [NBR]
SANGAGE alt for SAKAJI [SKN]
SANGAJI alt for SAKAJI [SKN]
SANGALI alt for TUMMA [TBQ]
SANGAMESVARI dial of KONKANI [KNK]
SANGANGALLA' alt for TAE' [ROB]
SANGANGALLA' alt for TOALA' [TLZ]
SANGAR dial of BIMA [BHP]
SANGASANGA alt for BOMWALI [BMW]
SANGAU alt for EMBALOH [EMB]
SANGBANGA alt for SABANGA [SXA]
SANGCHE dial of NAGA, TASE [NST]

SANGGAR alt for SANGAR dial of BIMA [BHP]
SANGGAU [SCG] lang, Indonesia, Kalimantan
SANGGAU alt for EMBALOH [EMB]
SANGGIL alt for SANGIL [SNL]
SANGHO alt for SANGO [SAJ]
SANGI alt for SANGIR [SAN]
SANGIHÉ alt for SANGIR [SAN]
SANGIL [SNL] lang, Philippines
SANGIR [SAN] lang, Indonesia, Sulawesi, Philippines,
  Philippines
SANGIR alt for SANGIR [SAN]
SANGIRÉ alt for SANGIL [SNL]
SANGIRESE alt for SANGIR [SAN]
SANGISARI [SGR] lang, Iran
SANGKE [SKG] lang, Indonesia, Irian Jaya
SANGLA alt for TSANGLA [TSJ]
SANGLECHI dial of SANGLECHI-ISHKASHIMI [SGL]
SANGLECHI-ISHKASHIMI [SGL] lang, Tajikistan,
  Afghanistan
SANGLICH dial of SANGLECHI-ISHKASHIMI [SGL]
SANGO [SAJ] lang, Central African Republic, Zaïre,
  Chad, Zaïre
SANGO alt for SANGO [SAJ]
SANGO alt for SANGU [SBP]
SANGO RIVERAIN dial of SANGO [SAJ]
SANGPANG alt for SAMPANG [RAV]
SANGRIMA alt for NAGA, ZEME [NZM]
SANGS-RGYAS alt for NESANG [NES]
SANGTAI dial of NAGA, TASE [NST]
SANGTAL alt for SANTALI [SNT]
SANGTAM alt for NAGA, SANGTAM [NSA]
SANGU [SBP] lang, Tanzania
SANGU [SNQ] lang, Gabon
SANGWE dial of SENA [SEH]
SANGYAS alt for NESANG [NES]
SANI dial of AMAMI-OSHIMA, NORTHERN [RYN]
SANINAWACANA alt for SANAINAWA dial of
  KATUKÍNA, PANOAN [KNT]
SANIO alt for SANIYO-HIYOWE [SNY]
SANIO-HIOWE alt for SANIYO-HIYOWE [SNY]
SANIYO alt for SANIYO-HIYOWE [SNY]
SANIYO-HIYOWE [SNY] lang, Papua New Guinea
SANJA alt for MALAYO [MBP]
SANJAN dial of PASHAYI, NORTHWEST [GLH]
SANJIANGE dial of DONG [KMC]
SANJO alt for SHANJO dial of TONGA [TOI]
SANKA alt for MALAYO [MBP]
SANKAJI alt for SAKAJI [SKN]
SANKARA-YERUKALA dial of YERUKALA [YEU]
SANKE dial of NAGA, TASE [NST]
SANKETI dial of TAMIL [TCV]
SANKURA dial of NUNI [NNW]
SANPAIL dial of OKANAGAN [OKA]
SANSI [SSI] lang, Pakistan
SANSKRIT [SKT] lang, India
SANSU [SCA] lang, Myanmar, China
SANTA alt for DONGXIANG [SCE]
SANTA ANA dial of KAHUA [AGW]
SANTA ANA dial of KERES, EASTERN [KEE]
SANTA ANA-GONZAGA dial of AGTA, DUPANINAN
  [DUO]
SANTA CATALINA dial of KAHUA [AGW]
SANTA CATARINA ALBARRADAS dial of
  ZAPOTECO, ALBARRADAS [ZAS]
SANTA CATARINA PANTELHO dial of TZOTZIL,
  CHENALHÓ [TZE]

SANTA CLARA dial of TEWA [TEW]
SANTA CRUCINO alt for AGUANO [AGA]
SANTA CRUZ [STC] lang, Solomon Islands
SANTA CRUZ dial of IRAYA [IRY]
SANTA CRUZ ITUNDUJIA MIXTECO alt for
  MIXTECO, EASTERN PUTLA [MCE]
SANTA CRUZ VERAPAZ POKOMCHÍ dial of
  POKOMCHÍ, WESTERN [POB]
SANTA EULALIA KANJOBAL alt for KANJOBAL,
  EASTERN [KJB]
SANTA INEZ YARENI alt for ZAPOTECO, WESTERN
  IXTLÁN [ZAE]
SANTA INEZ YATSECHE ZAPOTECO alt for
  ZAPOTECO, SOUTHEASTERN ZIMATLÁN [ZPN]
SANTA INEZ ZEGACHE ZAPOTECO alt for
  ZAPOTECO, SOUTHEASTERN ZIMATLÁN [ZPN]
SANTA MAGDALENA ZOQUE alt for ZOQUE,
  FRANCISCO LEÓN [ZOS]
SANTA MARGARITA dial of AGTA, DUPANINAN
  [DUO]
SANTA MARÍA ACAPULCO PAME alt for PAME,
  CENTRAL [PBS]
SANTA MARÍA ACATEPEC dial of MIXTECO, SAN
  PEDRO TUTUTEPEC [MTU]
SANTA MARÍA ALBARRADAS dial of ZAPOTECO,
  ALBARRADAS [ZAS]
SANTA MARÍA CHIGMECATITLÁN MIXTECO alt for
  MIXTECO, CENTRAL PUEBLA [MII]
SANTA MARÍA CHIMALAPA dial of ZOQUE, SANTA
  MARÍA CHIMALAPA [ZOH]
SANTA MARIA COATLÁN ZAPOTECO alt for
  ZAPOTECO, WESTERN MIAHUATLÁN [ZPS]
SANTA MARÍA DE JESÚS CAKCHIQUEL dial of
  CAKCHIQUEL, WESTERN [CKW]
SANTA MARÍA PEÑOLES dial of MIXTECO,
  EASTERN [MIL]
SANTA MARÍA QUIEGOLANI ZAPOTECO alt for
  ZAPOTECO, WESTERN YAUTEPEC [ZPI]
SANTA MARÍA ZACATEPEC MIXTECO alt for
  MIXTECO, SOUTHERN PUTLA [MZA]
SANTA ROSA dial of COFÁN [CON]
SANTA ROSA QUECHUA alt for QUICHUA,
  LOWLAND, NAPO [QLN]
SANTA ROSA QUECHUA dial of QUICHUA,
  LOWLAND, NAPO [QLN]
SANTA TERESA dial of CORA [COR]
SANTA TERESA dial of RATAGNON [BTN]
SANTAL alt for SANTALI [SNT]
SANTALI [SNT] lang, India, Bangladesh, Nepal
SANTALI alt for SANTALI [SNT]
SANTAN dial of DAYAK, LAND [DYK]
SANTARROSINO alt for QUICHUA, LOWLAND,
  NAPO [QLN]
SANTEE alt for DAKOTA dial of DAKOTA [DHG]
SANTHALI alt for SANTALI [SNT]
SANTHIALI alt for SANTALI [SNT]
SANTIAGO dial of CHIQUITANO [CAX]
SANTIAGO CHAZUMBA dial of MIXTECO,
  SOUTHERN PUEBLA [MIT]
SANTIAGO INGA dial of INGA [INB]
SANTIAGO LACHIGUIRI ZAPOTECO alt for
  ZAPOTECO, NORTHWESTERN TEHUANTEPEC
  [ZPA]
SANTIAGO NUYOO MIXTECO alt for MIXTECO,
  SOUTHWESTERN TLAXIACO [MEH]
SANTIAGO TLATEPUSCO dial of CHINANTECO,

PALANTLA [CPA]
SANTIAGO TLAZOYALTEPEC dial of MIXTECO,
  EASTERN [MIL]
SANTIAGUEÑO QUICHUA alt for QUICHUA,
  SANTIAGO DEL ESTERO [QUS]
SANTIAM alt for KALAPUYA [KAL]
SANTO alt for SAKAO [SKU]
SANTO alt for TANGOA [TGP]
SANTO DOMINGO dial of KERES, EASTERN [KEE]
SANTO DOMINGO ALBARRADAS dial of
  ZAPOTECO, ALBARRADAS [ZAS]
SANTO DOMINGO NUXAÁ MIXTECO alt for
  MIXTECO, SOUTHEASTERN NOCHIXTLÁN [MXY]
SANTO DOMINGO TOTONACO alt for TOTONACO,
  FILOMENO MATA-COAHUITLÁN [TLP]
SANTONGEAIS dial of FRENCH [FRN]
SANTORA alt for NARA [NRB]
SANTRI alt for SADANI [SCK]
SANTROKOFI alt for SELE [SNW]
SANUKI dial of JAPANESE [JPN]
SANUMÁ [SAM] lang, Brazil, Venezuela, Venezuela
SANUMÁ alt for SANUMÁ [SAM]
SANVI dial of ANYIN [ANY]
SANYA alt for SANYE [SSN]
SANYE [SSN] lang, Kenya
SANYE alt for BONI [BOB]
SANYE alt for DAHALO [DAL]
SANYE alt for WAATA dial of ORMA [ORC]
SANYO alt for FULFULDE, ADAMAWA [FUB]
SANZA dial of KONJO [KOO]
SANZA dial of NANDI [NNB]
SANZI dial of BANGUBANGU [BNX]
SAO alt for SAHO [SSY]
SAO alt for THAO [SSF]
SAO dial of MASLAM [MSV]
SÃO PAULO SIGN LANGUAGE alt for BRAZILIAN
  SIGN LANGUAGE [BZS]
SÃO TOMENSE dial of CRIOULO, GULF OF GUINEA
  [CRI]
SA'OCH [SCQ] lang, Cambodia
SAONEK dial of WAIGEO [WGO]
SAONRAS alt for SORA [SRB]
SAORA alt for SORA [SRB]
SAOTCH alt for SA'OCH [SCQ]
SAPALEWA alt for ALUNE [ALP]
SAPARUA [SPR] lang, Indonesia, Maluku
SAPÉ [SPC] lang, Venezuela
SAPEI alt for KUPSABINY [KPZ]
SAPINY alt for SABINY dial of KUPSABINY [KPZ]
SAPITERI dial of HUACHIPAERI [HUG]
SAPO [KRN] lang, Liberia
SAPOIN [SPH] lang, Laos
SAPONI [SPI] lang, Indonesia, Irian Jaya
SAPOSA [SPS] lang, Papua New Guinea
SAPOSA dial of SAPOSA [SPS]
SAPOUAN alt for SAPUAN [SPU]
SAPRAN alt for MADEN [XMX]
SAPREK alt for PAIWAN [PWN]
SAPSUG alt for SHAPSUG dial of ADYGHE [ADY]
SAPTARI alt for THARU, SAPTARI [THQ]
SAPUAN [SPU] lang, Laos
SAPUDI dial of MADURA [MHJ]
SAPULOT MURUT dial of TAGAL MURUT [MVV]
SAPULOT MURUT alt for PENSIANGAN MURUT dial
  of TAGAL MURUT [MVV]
SAPULUT MURUT alt for SAPULOT MURUT dial of

TAGAL MURUT [MVV]
SAPULUT MURUT alt for PENSIANGAN MURUT dial of TAGAL MURUT [MVV]
SAPUTAN alt for BUKAR SADONG [SDO]
SAR [MWM] lang, Chad, Central African Republic
SAR alt for WARJI [WJI]
SARA [SRE] lang, Indonesia, Kalimantan
SARA alt for SAR [MWM]
SARA alt for KABA [KSP]
SARA alt for NGAMBAI [SBA]
SARA alt for KABA DUNJO [KOJ]
SARA alt for BOK dial of MANDYAK [MFV]
SARA GOULA alt for GULA [GLU]
SARA GULA alt for GULA [GLU]
SARA KABA alt for KABA [KSP]
SARA KROW dial of SIKKA [SKI]
SARA MADJINGAY alt for SAR [MWM]
SARA MBAI alt for MBAI [MYB]
SARA NGAMBAI alt for NGAMBAI [SBA]
SARA SIKKA alt for SIKKA [SKI]
SARAGURO QUICHUA alt for QUICHUA, HIGHLAND, LOJA [QQU]
SARAIKI alt for SIRAIKI [SKR]
SARAKA alt for THARAKA [THA]
SARAKI dial of BENGALI [BNG]
SARAKOLE alt for SONINKE [SNN]
SARALIR alt for SEDALIR dial of TIDONG [TID]
SARALIR alt for SALALIR dial of TAGAL MURUT [MVV]
SARAMACCAN [SRM] lang, Surinam
SARAMO alt for ITONAMA [ITO]
SARAMO alt for ZALAMO [ZAJ]
SARANGANI dial of SANGIL [SNL]
SARAR dial of MANDYAK [MFV]
SARAR alt for BOK dial of MANDYAK [MFV]
SARARÉ [SRR] lang, Brazil
SARASIRA [SRA] lang, Papua New Guinea
SARASSARA dial of JINA [JIA]
SARASVAT BRAHMIN dial of KONKANI, GOANESE [GOM]
SARAVECA [SAR] lang, Bolivia
SARAWAI dial of DOHOI [OTD]
SARAWAK DAYAK alt for JAGOI [SNE]
SARAWAK MALAY dial of MALAY [MLI]
SARAWAK MURUT alt for LUN BAWANG dial of LUNDAYEH [LND]
SARAWAK MURUT alt for LUN BAWANG dial of LUNDAYEH [LND]
SARAWAN dial of BRAHUI [BRH]
SARAWANI dial of BALUCHI, WESTERN [BGN]
SARAWARIA alt for NORTHERN STANDARD BHOJPURI dial of BHOJPURI [BHJ]
SARAWULE alt for SONINKE [SNN]
SARCEE alt for SARSI [SRS]
SARCHAPKKHA alt for SHARCHAGPAKHA [SCH]
SARD alt for SARDINIAN, LOGUDORESE [SRD]
SARDARESE alt for SARDINIAN, LOGUDORESE [SRD]
SARDINIAN, CAMPIDANESE [SRO] lang, Italy
SARDINIAN, GALLURESE [SDN] lang, Italy
SARDINIAN, LOGUDORESE [SRD] lang, Italy
SARDINIAN, SASSARESE [SDC] lang, Italy
SARDIYYA alt for NORTH NAJDI dial of ARABIC, NAJDI [ARS]
SARE alt for SENA-CARE dial of SENA [SEH]
SAREMDE dial of MOORE [MHM]

SARI alt for SAA [SZR]
SARI dial of ENGA [ENQ]
SARI YOGUR alt for YUGUR, WEST [YBE]
SARIBA dial of SUAU [SWP]
SARIG alt for YUGUR, WEST [YBE]
SARIKEI dial of MELANAU [MEL]
SARIKOLI [SRH] lang, China
SARIQ dial of TURKMEN [TCK]
SARIRÁ alt for SIRIANO [SRI]
SARISEN alt for RUKAI [DRU]
SARNAMI HINDI alt for HINDI, CARIBBEAN [HNS]
SARNGAM alt for NGAM [NMC]
SAROA alt for SAAROA [SXR]
SAROA dial of SINAGORO [SNC]
SAROUA alt for SARUA [SWY]
SARPO alt for SAPO [KRN]
SARRABENSE dial of SARDINIAN, CAMPIDANESE [SRO]
SARSI [SRS] lang, Canada
SART dial of UZBEK, NORTHERN [UZB]
SART QALMAQ dial of KALMYK-OIRAT [KGZ]
SARTENAIS dial of CORSICAN [COI]
SARTUL dial of MONGOLIAN, HALH [KHK]
SARUA [SWY] lang, Chad, Cameroon
SARUDU [SDU] lang, Indonesia, Sulawesi
SARUGA [SRP] lang, Papua New Guinea
SARWA alt for SARUA [SWY]
SARWA alt for HIECHWARE [HIE]
SARY-UIGHUR alt for YUGUR, WEST [YBE]
SARYGH UYGUR alt for YUGUR, WEST [YBE]
SARYKOLY alt for SARIKOLI [SRH]
SARYQ dial of TURKMEN [TCK]
SASAK [SAS] lang, Indonesia, Nusa Tenggara
SASAR dial of VATRATA [VLR]
SASARU alt for SASARU-ENWAN IGWE [SSC]
SASARU-ENWAN IGWE [SSC] lang, Nigeria
SASAWA [SNK] lang, Indonesia, Irian Jaya
SASI alt for SIZAKI [SZK]
SASIME alt for BIYOM [BPM]
SASSARESE alt for SARDINIAN, SASSARESE [SDC]
SASTEAN alt for SHASTA [SHT]
SATAR alt for SANTALI [SNT]
SATARÉ alt for SATERÉ-MAWÉ [MAV]
SATAWAL [STW] lang, Micronesia
SATAWALESE alt for SATAWAL [STW]
SATE alt for KUMBA [KSM]
SATERÉ-MAWÉ [MAV] lang, Brazil
SATHEWKOK dial of CHINESE, HAKKA [HAK]
SATPARA alt for ASTORI dial of SHINA [SCL]
SATPARIYA dial of KOCH [KDQ]
SATPUDA NOIRI alt for NOIRI dial of BHILORI [BQI]
SATRE alt for GAWAR-BATI [GWT]
SATRO alt for DIDA, LAKOTA [DIC]
SATUN dial of TONGA [TNZ]
SAU alt for SAMBERIGI [SSX]
SAU alt for SAHU [SUX]
SAU alt for SAVI [SDG]
SAU alt for THAO [SSF]
SAU dial of DAYAK, LAND [DYK]
SAU dial of ENGA [ENQ]
SAU ENGA alt for SAU dial of ENGA [ENQ]
SAUCH alt for SA'OCH [SCQ]
SAUDI ARABIAN SIGN LANGUAGE [SDL] lang, Saudi Arabia
SAUH alt for SAU dial of DAYAK, LAND [DYK]
SAUJI alt for SAVI [SDG]

SAUK [SKC] lang, Papua New Guinea
SAUK-FOX alt for MESQUAKIE [SAC]
SAUKRANG dial of NAGA, TASE [NST]
SAULTEAUX alt for OJIBWA, WESTERN [OJI]
SAUMANGANJA dial of MENTAWAI [MWV]
SAURA alt for SORA [SRB]
SAURASHTRA [SAZ] lang, India
SAURASHTRA STANDARD alt for STANDARD
 GUJARATI dial of GUJARATI [GJR]
SAURASHTRI alt for SAURASHTRA [SAZ]
SAURI [SAH] lang, Indonesia, Irian Jaya
SAURIA MALTO alt for SAWRIYA MALTO dial of
 MALTO [MJT]
SAUSE [SAO] lang, Indonesia, Irian Jaya
SAUSI [SSJ] lang, Papua New Guinea
SAVANNAKHET dial of LAO [NOL]
SAVARA [SVR] lang, India
SAVARA alt for SORA [SRB]
SAVI [SDG] lang, Afghanistan
SAVO [SVS] lang, Solomon Islands
SAVO dial of FINNISH [FIN]
SAVO ISLAND alt for SAVO [SVS]
SAVOLAX alt for SAVO dial of FINNISH [FIN]
SAVOSAVO alt for SAVO [SVS]
SAVOYARD dial of FRANCO-PROVENÇAL [FRA]
SAVU alt for SAWU [HVN]
SAVUNESE alt for SAWU [HVN]
SAVUSAVU alt for CENTRAL VANUA LEVU dial of
 FIJIAN [FJI]
SAW dial of NTOMBA [NTO]
SAWA alt for JANGGU [DJA]
SAWABWALA dial of DUAU [DUA]
SAWAI [SZW] lang, Indonesia, Maluku
SAWAI alt for SALEMAN [SAU]
SAWAI dial of SAWAI [SZW]
SAWARIA alt for SORA [SRB]
SAWATUPWA dial of BUNAMA [BDD]
SAWERI alt for ISIRAWA [SRL]
SAWI [SAW] lang, Indonesia, Irian Jaya
SAWI alt for SAVI [SDG]
SAWITTO dial of BUGIS [BPR]
SAWIYANU alt for AMA [AMM]
SAWK alt for SOK [SKK]
SAWKNAH [SWN] lang, Libya
SAWOS [SIC] lang, Papua New Guinea
SAWRIYA MALTO dial of MALTO [MJT]
SAWU [HVN] lang, Indonesia, Nusa Tenggara
SAWUNESE alt for SAWU [HVN]
SAWUVE dial of ANKAVE [AAK]
SAWUY alt for SAWI [SAW]
SAXON LUSATIAN alt for WEND, LOWER [WEE]
SAXON LUSATIAN alt for LOWER LUSATIAN dial of
 WEND, UPPER [WEN]
SAXWE alt for SAXWE-GBE [SXW]
SAXWE-GBE [SXW] lang, Benin
SAYA [SAY] lang, Nigeria
SAYABURY dial of KHMU [KJG]
SAYACO alt for AMAHUACA [AMC]
SAYACU alt for AMAHUACA [AMC]
SAYAN SAMOYED alt for KARAGAS [KIM]
SAYANCI alt for SAYA [SAY]
SAYARA alt for SAYA [SAY]
SAYAWA alt for SAYA [SAY]
SAYMA alt for CHAYMA dial of KALIHNA [CRB]
SAYSAY alt for SESE dial of GUMUZ [GUK]
SAZEK alt for TAROKO [TRV]

SAZIN alt for CHILASI KOHISTANI dial of SHINA
 [SCL]
SBALTI alt for BALTI [BFT]
SBÀA alt for CENTRAL NAJDI dial of ARABIC,
 NAJDI [ARS]
SBÀÀ alt for CENTRAL NAJDI dial of ARABIC,
 NAJDI [ARS]
SBRANAG alt for PANANG [PCR]
SCANDINAVIAN PIDGIN SIGN LANGUAGE [SPF]
 lang, Sweden, Denmark, Finland, Norway
SCE alt for SHE dial of GIMIRA [BCQ]
SCHABIN-KARAHISSAR alt for SHABIN-
 KARAHISSAR dial of ARMENIAN [ARM]
SCHAMACHI alt for SHAMAKHI dial of ARMENIAN
 [ARM]
SCHAMBALA alt for SHAMBALA [KSB]
SCHEKERE alt for XUN [XUU]
SCHOE alt for SHOE dial of MPADE [MPI]
SCHWÄBISCH alt for SWABIAN [SWG]
SCHWYTZERTUETSCH alt for SCHWYZERDÜTSCH
 [GSW]
SCHWYZERDÜTSCH [GSW] lang, Switzerland,
 Austria, France, Germany
SCINACIA alt for BORO [BWO]
SCOTS [SCO] lang, United Kingdom
SCOTTISH CANT alt for TRAVELLER SCOTTISH
 [TRL]
SCOTTISH TRAVELLER CANT alt for TRAVELLER
 SCOTTISH [TRL]
SCOUSE dial of ENGLISH [ENG]
SCUTARI dial of ALBANIAN, GHEG [ALS]
SEA BAJAU alt for BAJAU LAUT dial of SAMA,
 SOUTHERN [SIT]
SEA DAYAK alt for IBAN [IBA]
SEA GYPSIES alt for BAJAU LAUT dial of SAMA,
 SOUTHERN [SIT]
SEA ISLANDS CREOLE ENGLISH [GUL] lang, USA
SEA LAPPISH dial of SAAMI, NORTHERN [LPR]
SEAQAAQAA alt for CENTRAL VANUA LEVU dial of
 FIJIAN [FJI]
SEBA [KDG] lang, Zaïre
SEBA dial of SAWU [HVN]
SEBARU' alt for KETUNGAU dial of IBAN [IBA]
SEBASTE dial of ARMENIAN [ARM]
SEBE dial of BINE [ORM]
SEBEI alt for KUPSABINY [KPZ]
SEBERUANG dial of IBAN [IBA]
SEBOB alt for KENYAH, SEBOB [SIB]
SEBOP alt for KENYAH, SEBOB [SIB]
SEBUANO alt for CEBUANO [CEB]
SEBUTUIA dial of GALEYA [GAR]
SEBUYAU [SNB] lang, Malaysia, Sarawak
SEBYAR alt for ARANDAI [JBJ]
SECHELT [SEC] lang, Canada
SECHUANA alt for TSWANA [TSW]
SECO alt for PECH [PAY]
SECOYA [SEY] lang, Ecuador, Peru, Peru
SECOYA alt for SECOYA [SEY]
SECUNDERABAD BRAHMIN dial of TAMIL [TCV]
SEDALIR dial of TIDONG [TID]
SEDÁLIR alt for SALALIR dial of TAGAL MURUT
 [MVV]
SEDANG [SED] lang, Viet Nam
SEDANG-RENGAO dial of RENGAO [REN]
SEDANKA dial of ITELMEN [ITL]
SEDE alt for TCHIDE dial of JINA [JIA]

SEDEHI dial of FARSI, WESTERN [PES]
SEDEK alt for TAROKO [TRV]
SEDENTARY BULGARIA dial of ROMANI, VLACH
[RMY]
SEDENTARY ROMANIA dial of ROMANI, VLACH
[RMY]
SEDEQ alt for TAROKO [TRV]
SEDIAKK alt for TAROKO [TRV]
SEDIK alt for TAROKO [TRV]
SEDIQ alt for TAROKO [TRV]
SEDOA [TVW] lang, Indonesia, Sulawesi
SEDUAN dial of SIBU [SDX]
SEDUAN-BANYOK alt for SIBU [SDX]
SEEBA-YAGA dial of FULFULDE, JELGOOJI [FUM]
SEEDEK alt for TAROKO [TRV]
SEEDEQ alt for TAROKO [TRV]
SEEDIK alt for TAROKO [TRV]
SEEPTSA alt for CHOLON [CHT]
SEEREER alt for SERERE-SINE [SES]
SEEX alt for SERERE-SINE [SES]
SEFARDI alt for LADINO [SPJ]
SEFWI alt for SEHWI [SFW]
SEGAH dial of SEGAI [SGE]
SEGAHAN dial of MELANAU [MEL]
SEGAI [SGE] lang, Indonesia, Kalimantan
SEGAI alt for DUSUN SEGAMA dial of
KINABATANGAN, UPPER [DMG]
SEGALANG dial of MELANAU [MEL]
SEGEJU alt for DHAISO [SEG]
SEGET [SBG] lang, Indonesia, Irian Jaya
SEGIDDI alt for SIGIDI dial of SAYA [SAY]
SEGINKI dial of MOKULU [MOZ]
SEGUHA alt for ZIGULA [ZIW]
SEGUM dial of SERERE-SINE [SES]
SEHRI alt for SAHARIA [SRX]
SEHWI [SFW] lang, Côte d'Ivoire, Ghana, Ghana
SEHWI alt for SEHWI [SFW]
SEIM [SIM] lang, Papua New Guinea
SEIM alt for WAMSAK [WBD]
SEIM dial of KWANGA [KWJ]
SEIMAT [SSG] lang, Papua New Guinea
SEIMBRI dial of IJO, CENTRAL-WESTERN [IJC]
SEIRA dial of FORDATA [FRD]
SEISIRAT alt for SAISIYAT [SAI]
SEIT dial of SEIT-KAITETU [HIK]
SEIT-KAITETU [HIK] lang, Indonesia, Maluku
SEITH alt for SEIT dial of SEIT-KAITETU [HIK]
SEIYAP dial of CHINESE, YUE [YUH]
SEIYARA alt for SAYA [SAY]
ŞEJIQ alt for TAROKO [TRV]
SEK alt for SAEK [SKB]
SEK alt for GEDAGED [GDD]
SEK-HWAN alt for PAZEH [PZH]
SEKA alt for SKO [SKV]
SEKA alt for SEKAR [SKZ]
SEKALAÑA alt for KALANGA [KCK]
SEKALANA alt for KALANGA [KCK]
SEKALAU alt for KETUNGAU dial of IBAN [IBA]
SEKANI [SEK] lang, Canada
SEKAPAN [SKP] lang, Malaysia, Sarawak
SEKAPAT alt for KETUNGAU dial of IBAN [IBA]
SEKAR [SKZ] lang, Indonesia, Irian Jaya
SEKARANG dial of IBAN [IBA]
SEKARE dial of GUHU-SAMANE [GHS]
SEKAYU [SYU] lang, Indonesia, Sumatra
SEKE [SKE] lang, Vanuatu

SEKE alt for SEKI [SYI]
SEKE dial of LOPA [LOY]
SEKEPAN alt for SEKAPAN [SKP]
SEKI [SYI] lang, Gabon
SEKIANA alt for SEKI [SYI]
SEKIANI alt for SEKI [SYI]
SEKIYANI alt for SEKI [SYI]
SEKO alt for SEKO TENGAH [SKO]
SEKO alt for SKO [SKV]
SEKO alt for SEKO PADANG [SKX]
SEKO PADANG [SKX] lang, Indonesia, Sulawesi
SEKO TENGAH [SKO] lang, Indonesia, Sulawesi
SEKOL alt for SKO [SKV]
SEKOU alt for SKO [SKV]
SEKPELE [LIP] lang, Ghana
SEKPELE dial of SEKPELE [LIP]
SEKUNDA dial of MAKAA [MCP]
SEKWA dial of KULANGO, BOUNA [NKU]
SEKWA dial of SEKPELE [LIP]
SEKYANI alt for SEKI [SYI]
SELA [SLS] lang, Indonesia, Irian Jaya
SELA alt for WESTERN LIMBA dial of LIMBA, WEST-
CENTRAL [LIA]
SELAKO [SKL] lang, Indonesia, Kalimantan
SELAKO DAYAK alt for SELAKO [SKL]
SELALE alt for SALALE dial of OROMO, BORANA-
ARUSI-GUJI [GAX]
SELALIR alt for SEDALIR dial of TIDONG [TID]
SELANGOR SAKAI dial of BESISI [MHE]
SELARU [SLU] lang, Indonesia, Maluku
SELAU [SLF] lang, Papua New Guinea
SELAYAR [SLY] lang, Indonesia, Sulawesi
SELE [SNW] lang, Ghana
SELEK dial of JOLA-KASA [CSK]
SELEKAU alt for SILAKAU [SLI]
SELEMAN alt for SALEMAN [SAU]
SELEMO alt for ISEKIRI [ITS]
SELEPE alt for SELEPET [SEL]
SELEPET [SEL] lang, Papua New Guinea
SELKIRK alt for TUTCHONE [TUT]
SELKNAM alt for ONA [ONA]
SELKUP [SAK] lang, Russia, Asia
SELONG alt for MOKEN [MWT]
SELTI alt for SILTI dial of GURAGE, EAST [GRE]
SELUNG alt for MOKEN [MWT]
SELUNGAI MURUT [SLG] lang, Malaysia, Sabah,
Indonesia, Kalimantan
SELUWASAN [SWH] lang, Indonesia, Maluku
SELUWASAN dial of SELUWASAN [SWH]
SELVASA alt for SELUWASAN [SWH]
SELWASA alt for SELUWASAN [SWH]
SELYA dial of NYAKYUSA-NGONDE [NYY]
SEMA alt for NAGA, SEMA [NSM]
SEMAI [SEA] lang, Malaysia, Peninsular
SEMAKHA dial of AZERBAIJANI, NORTH [AZE]
SEMAMBU alt for TAGAL MURUT [MVV]
SEMAMBU alt for SUMAMBU dial of TAGAL MURUT
[MVV]
SEMANDANG [SDM] lang, Indonesia, Kalimantan
SEMANDANG dial of SEMANDANG [SDM]
SEMANG alt for KENSIU [KNS]
SEMANG, LOWLAND [ORB] lang, Indonesia,
Sumatra
SEMAQ BERI [SZC] lang, Malaysia, Peninsular
SEMAQ BRI alt for SEMAQ BERI [SZC]
SEMARIJI dial of PEREMKA [PEP]

Greece, Hungary, Italy, Romania, Russia, Europe, Sweden, Turkey
SERBODJADI dial of GAYO [GYO]
SERE [SWF] lang, Zaïre, Central African Republic
SEREER alt for SERERE-SINE [SES]
SERER alt for NON [SNF]
SERER alt for SERERE-SINE [SES]
SERER-SAFEN alt for SAFEN [SAV]
SERER-SIN alt for SERERE-SINE [SES]
SERERE-NON alt for NON [SNF]
SERERE-SAFEN alt for SAFEN [SAV]
SERERE-SINE [SES] lang, Senegal, Gambia
SERHTA dial of RAWANG [RAW]
SERI [SEI] lang, Mexico
SERIA alt for SELYA dial of NYAKYUSA-NGONDE [NYY]
SERIAN alt for BUKAR SADONG [SDO]
SERIKENAM dial of KWERBA [KWE]
SERILI [SVE] lang, Indonesia, Maluku
SERING dial of DAYAK, LAND [DYK]
SERKI alt for ARAMBA [STK]
SERKISETAVI alt for ARAMBA [STK]
SERMAH dial of DAYAK, LAND [DYK]
SERNUR-MORKIN alt for GRASSLAND MARI dial of MARI, LOW [MAL]
SEROA [KQU] lang, South Africa, Lesotho
SEROQ alt for TEMIAR [TMH]
SERRA alt for SERA [SRY]
SERRA AZUL dial of NAMBIKUÁRA, SOUTHERN [NAB]
SERRANO [SER] lang, USA
SERRE alt for SERE [SWF]
SERRER alt for SERERE-SINE [SES]
SERU [SZD] lang, Malaysia, Sarawak
SERU dial of MELANAU [MEL]
SERUA [SRW] lang, Indonesia, Maluku
SERUAWAN alt for KAMARIAN [KZX]
SERUDONG alt for SERUDUNG MURUT [SRK]
SERUDUNG MURUT [SRK] lang, Malaysia, Sabah
SERUI-LAUT [SEU] lang, Indonesia, Irian Jaya
SERVHULI alt for SONINKE [SNN]
SERWA alt for SHERPA [SCR]
SERWANG dial of RAWANG [RAW]
SESA dial of FOLOPA [PPO]
SESAJAP alt for SESAYAP dial of TIDONG [TID]
SESAKE dial of EFATE, NORTH [LLP]
SESAN dial of JARAI [JRA]
SESARWA alt for HIECHWARE [HIE]
SESARWA SESARWA alt for HIECHWARE [HIE]
SESAYAP dial of TIDONG [TID]
SESE dial of GANDA [LAP]
SESE dial of GUMUZ [GUK]
SESE alt for MESE dial of TUNEN [BAZ]
SESELWA [CRS] lang, Seychelles, British Indian Ocean Territory
SESIVI dial of DAKAKA [BPA]
SESOTHO alt for SOTHO, SOUTHERN [SSO]
SETA [STF] lang, Papua New Guinea
SETA alt for XETÁ [XET]
SETAMAN [STM] lang, Papua New Guinea
SETEBO alt for SHETEBO dial of SHIPIBO-CONIBO [SHP]
SETI [SBI] lang, Papua New Guinea
"SETI" alt for LIANA-SETI [STE]
"SETI" dial of LIANA-SETI [STE]
SETIALI dial of NIKSEK [GBE]

SETIBO alt for SHETEBO dial of SHIPIBO-CONIBO [SHP]
SETIIT alt for TAKAZZE-SETIIT dial of KUNAMA [KUM]
SETIT alt for TAKAZZE-SETIIT dial of KUNAMA [KUM]
SETO alt for SETO-GBE [STS]
SETO-GBE [STS] lang, Benin, Nigeria, Nigeria
SETO-GBE alt for SETO-GBE [STS]
SETTENTRIONALE dial of EMILIANO [EML]
SETTLA [STA] lang, Zambia
SETU dial of ESTONIAN [EST]
SEUCE alt for SAUSE [SAO]
SEUCI alt for SIUSY-TAPUYA dial of BANIWA [BAI]
SEVERN OJIBWA dial of OJIBWA, NORTHERN [OJB]
SEWA alt for SEBA [KDG]
SEWA BAY [SEW] lang, Papua New Guinea
SEWARD PENINSULA ESKIMO dial of INUIT, NORTHWEST ALASKA INUPIAT [ESK]
SEWATAITAI dial of SEWA BAY [SEW]
SEWAWA dial of MENDE [MFY]
SEWE dial of DOYAYO [DOW]
SEWI dial of TONGA [TOH]
SEYA alt for SAYA [SAY]
SEYAWA alt for SAYA [SAY]
SEYCHELLES CREOLE FRENCH alt for SESELWA [CRS]
SEYCHELLOIS CREOLE alt for SESELWA [CRS]
SEYKI dial of AARI [AIZ]
SEYU alt for CHRU [CJE]
SEZO dial of HOZO-SEZO [HOZ]
SGAU alt for KAREN, S'GAW [KSW]
SGAW alt for KAREN, S'GAW [KSW]
SGAW KAYIN alt for KAREN, S'GAW [KSW]
SHA [SCW] lang, Nigeria
SHA alt for SHAN [SJN]
SHA'A alt for KUWAITI ARABIC dial of ARABIC, NAJDI [ARS]
SHAALE alt for SUNGOR [SUN]
SHAARI dial of MUMUYE [MUL]
SHABAK alt for BAJELAN [BJM]
SHABARI alt for SORA [SRB]
SHABIN-KARAHISSAR dial of ARMENIAN [ARM]
SHABO [SBF] lang, Ethiopia
SHABOGALA alt for ATAYAL [TAY]
SHABUN dial of SHWAI [SHW]
SHACRIABA alt for XAKRIABÁ [XKR]
SHADAL dial of MANKANYA [MAN]
SHAGAU alt for SHAGAWU [ROA]
SHAGAWU [ROA] lang, Nigeria
SHAH-MANSURI dial of KASHMIRI [KSH]
SHAHARI alt for JIBBALI [SHV]
SHAHO alt for SAHO [SSY]
SHAHRUDI dial of FARSI, WESTERN [PES]
SHAHSAVANI dial of AZERBAIJANI, SOUTH [AZB]
SHAHSEVEN alt for SHAHSAVANI dial of AZERBAIJANI, SOUTH [AZB]
SHAINI alt for SHENI [SCV]
SHAIRE alt for SERE [SWF]
SHAK alt for SHEKO [SHE]
SHAKA alt for NGASA [NSG]
SHAKE alt for SAKE [SAG]
SHAKO alt for SHABO [SBF]
SHAKO alt for SHEKO [SHE]
SHAL alt for SHALL dial of SHALL-ZWALL [SHA]
SHALKOTA alt for SHELKOTA dial of MIDOB [MEI]

SHALL dial of SHALL-ZWALL [SHA]
SHALL-ZWALL [SHA] lang, Nigeria
SHAM alt for SHAMMA dial of LADAKHI [LBJ]
SHAMAITISH dial of LITHUANIAN [LIT]
SHAMAKHI dial of ARMENIAN [ARM]
SHAMAKOT dial of PASHAYI, NORTHWEST [GLH]
SHAMANG dial of HAM [JAB]
SHAMATARI alt for YANOMAMÖ [GUU]
SHAMATHARI alt for YANOMAMÖ [GUU]
SHAMBA dial of SWAHILI [SWA]
SHAMBAA alt for SHAMBALA [KSB]
SHAMBALA [KSB] lang, Tanzania
SHAMMA dial of LADAKHI [LBJ]
SHAMMAR alt for NORTH NAJDI dial of ARABIC,
   NAJDI [ARS]
SHAMMARI alt for NORTH NAJDI dial of ARABIC,
   NAJDI [ARS]
SHAMNYUYANGA dial of NAGA, KONYAK [NBE]
SHAMSKAT alt for SHAMMA dial of LADAKHI [LBJ]
SHAMYA alt for SINYAR [SYS]
SHAN [SJN] lang, Myanmar, China, Thailand
SHAN alt for SHAN [SJN]
SHANDIA QUICHUA alt for QUICHUA, LOWLAND,
   TENA [QUW]
SHANDONG dial of CHINESE, MANDARIN [CHN]
SHANDU alt for SHENDU [SHL]
SHANGA [SHO] lang, Nigeria
SHANGA dial of SHANGA [SHO]
SHANGA alt for CHANGA dial of NDAU [NDC]
SHANGAAN alt for CHANGA dial of NDAU [NDC]
SHANGAAN alt for TSONGA [TSO]
SHANGAAN alt for CHANGANA dial of TSONGA
   [TSO]
SHANGAMA dial of AARI [AIZ]
SHANGANA alt for TSONGA [TSO]
SHANGANA alt for CHANGANA dial of TSONGA
   [TSO]
SHANGAWA alt for SHANGA [SHO]
SHANGGE alt for SANKE dial of NAGA, TASE [NST]
SHANGHAI dial of CHINESE, WU [WUU]
SHANGHAI SIGN LANGUAGE dial of CHINESE SIGN
   LANGUAGE [CSL]
"SHANGILLA" alt for DAASANECH [DSH]
SHANGO alt for SANGU [SNQ]
SHANI alt for SHENI [SCV]
SHANJO dial of TONGA [TOI]
SHANKADI alt for SAMBA [SMX]
"SHANKILLA" alt for AARI [AIZ]
"SHANKILLINYA" alt for AARI [AIZ]
SHANKILLINYA alt for GUMUZ [GUK]
"SHANKILLINYA" alt for GUMUZ [GUK]
SHANLANG dial of NAGA, KONYAK [NBE]
"SHANQILLA" alt for 'ONGOTA [BXE]
SHANQILLA alt for GUMUZ [GUK]
"SHANQILLA" alt for GUMUZ [GUK]
SHANTOU alt for CHAO SHAN dial of CHINESE, MIN
   NAN [CFR]
SHANTOU alt for CHAOCHOW dial of CHINESE, MIN
   NAN [CFR]
SHANTUNG alt for SHANDONG dial of CHINESE,
   MANDARIN [CHN]
SHANZI YAO alt for MIEN [YOC]
SHAO alt for THAO [SSF]
SHAOWU dial of CHINESE, HAKKA [HAK]
SHAOYANG dial of CHINESE, XIANG [HSN]
SHAPRA alt for CHAPARA dial of CANDOSHI-

SHAPRA [CBU]
SHAPSUG dial of ADYGHE [ADY]
SHARANAHUA [MCD] lang, Peru, Brazil
SHARCHAGPAKHA [SCH] lang, Bhutan
SHARCHAGPAKHA dial of SHARCHAGPAKHA [SCH]
SHARCHOP KHA alt for SHARCHAGPAKHA [SCH]
SHARCHUP alt for SHARCHAGPAKHA [SCH]
SHARI alt for CHALI dial of SÔ [SSS]
SHARK BAY [SSV] lang, Vanuatu
SHAROKA alt for THARAKA [THA]
SHARPA alt for SHERPA [SCR]
SHARPA BHOTIA alt for SHERPA [SCR]
SHARWA alt for SARUA [SWY]
SHASHA dial of NKOYA [NKA]
SHASHI alt for SIZAKI [SZK]
SHASTA [SHT] lang, USA
SHATT [SHJ] lang, Sudan
SHATT alt for THURI [THU]
SHATT dial of MUNDU [MUH]
SHATT AL-'ARAB AND LOWER KAARUUN RIVER
   dial of ARABIC, MESOPOTAMIAN COLLOQUIAL
   [ACM]
SHATT AL-ARAB AND LOWER KAARUUN dial of
   ARABIC, MESOPOTAMIAN COLLOQUIAL [ACM]
SHAUSHA WANKA QUECHUA alt for QUECHUA,
   HUANCA, JAUJA [QHJ]
SHAVANTE alt for XAVÁNTE [XAV]
SHAWANAWA-ARARA alt for ARARA-
   SHAWANAWA dial of KATUKÍNA, PANOAN
   [KNT]
SHAWE alt for SHOE dial of MPADE [MPI]
SHAWIA alt for SHAWIYA [SHY]
SHAWIYA [SHY] lang, Algeria
SHAWNEE [SJW] lang, USA
SHAYABIT alt for CHAYAHUITA [CBT]
SHE [SHX] lang, China
SHE dial of GIMIRA [BCQ]
SHEDE alt for GUDE [GDE]
SHEDEKKA alt for TAROKO [TRV]
SHEETSWA alt for TSWA [TSC]
SHEFFIELD YORKSHIRE dial of ENGLISH [ENG]
SHEHLEH dial of LAHU [LAH]
SHEKASIP dial of CHIN, FALAM [HBH]
SHEKE alt for SEKI [SYI]
SHEKHANI alt for KAMVIRI [QMV]
SHEKHANI dial of KAMVIRI [QMV]
SHEKHANI alt for EASTERN KATIVIRI dial of KATI
   [BSH]
SHEKHOAN alt for PAZEH [PZH]
SHEKICCO alt for MOCHA [MOY]
SHEKIRI alt for ISEKIRI [ITS]
SHEKIYANA alt for SEKI [SYI]
SHEKKA alt for SHEKO [SHE]
SHEKKA alt for MOCHA [MOY]
SHEKKO alt for SHEKO [SHE]
SHEKO [SHE] lang, Ethiopia
SHEKWAN alt for KAVALAN [CKV]
SHELKOTA dial of MIDOB [MEI]
SHELTA [STH] lang, Ireland, United Kingdom
SHEMINAHUA dial of CASHINAHUA [CBS]
SHEMYA alt for SINYAR [SYS]
SHENARA alt for SENOUFO, SHENARA [SHZ]
SHENDU [SHL] lang, Bangladesh, India, India
SHENDU alt for SHENDU [SHL]
SHENGE SHERBRO dial of SHERBRO [BUN]
SHENGHA dial of NAGA, KONYAK [NBE]

SHENGWE alt for TONGA [TOH]
SHENI [SCV] lang, Nigeria
SHENSI dial of DUNGAN [DNG]
SHERA YOGUR alt for YUGUR, EAST [YUY]
SHERBRO [BUN] lang, Sierra Leone
SHERDUKPEN [SDP] lang, India
SHERE alt for SERE [SWF]
SHERENTÉ alt for XERÉNTE [XER]
SHEREWYANA alt for HIXKARYÁNA [HIX]
SHERI alt for SERE [SWF]
SHERPA [SCR] lang, Nepal, China, India
SHERWIN alt for SARUA [SWY]
SHETA alt for XETÁ [XET]
SHETE TSERE alt for TSHIDI-KHWE dial of SHUA
    [SHG]
SHETEBO dial of SHIPIBO-CONIBO [SHP]
SHEVA alt for CHEWA dial of NYANJA [NYJ]
SHEWA alt for TULEMA dial of OROMO, WELLEGA-
    CENTRAL [GAZ]
SHI [SHR] lang, Zaïre
SHI alt for LAHU SHI [KDS]
SHIBA alt for SHERBRO [BUN]
SHIBUKUN dial of BUNUN [BNN]
SHICHOPI alt for CHOPI [CCE]
SHICOPI alt for CHOPI [CCE]
SHIGHNI alt for SHUGHNI dial of SHUGHNI [SGH]
SHIGHNI alt for SHUGHNI dial of SHUGHNI [SGH]
SHIHLANGANU alt for NHLANGANU dial of TSONGA
    [TSO]
SHIHO alt for SAHO [SSY]
SHIHU [SSH] lang, United Arab Emirates
SHIHUH alt for SHIHU [SSH]
SHIITA alt for SHITA [LGN]
SHIKAKI [SHF] lang, Iraq, Iran, Turkey
SHIKAKI alt for SHIKAKI [SHF]
SHIKI [GUA] lang, Nigeria
SHIKIANA alt for SIKIANA [SIK]
SHIKOTAN alt for KURIL dial of AINU [AIN]
SHILA dial of TAABWA [TAP]
SHILA dial of BEMBA [BEM]
SHILANGANU alt for CHANGANA dial of TSONGA
    [TSO]
SHILENGWE alt for HLENGWE dial of TSWA [TSC]
SHILHA alt for TARIFIT [RIF]
SHILHA alt for TACHELHIT [SHI]
SHILINGOL dial of MONGOLIAN, PERIPHERAL [MVF]
SHILLUK [SHK] lang, Sudan
SHILMANI dial of PASHTO, EASTERN [PBU]
SHIMACU alt for URARINA [URA]
SHIMAKONDE alt for MAKONDE [KDE]
SHIMAORE dial of COMORIAN [SWB]
SHIMAORE dial of COMORIAN [SWB]
SHIMAORI alt for SHIMAORE dial of COMORIAN
    [SWB]
SHIMBOGEDU alt for DIRIKU [DIU]
SHIMBWERA alt for MBWELA [MFU]
SHIMBWERA alt for MBOWELA dial of NKOYA
    [NKA]
SHIMIGAE alt for ANDOA [ANB]
SHIMIZYA alt for CHIMILA [CBG]
SHIMLA SIRAJI dial of MAHASUI [BFZ]
SHIMWALI dial of COMORIAN [SWB]
SHINA [SCL] lang, Pakistan, India
SHINA dial of RUTUL [RUT]
SHINA, KOHISTANI [PLK] lang, Pakistan
SHINABO [SHN] lang, Bolivia

SHINAKI alt for SHINA [SCL]
SHINASHA alt for BORO [BWO]
SHINASHA alt for AMURU [AUZ]
SHING SAAPA alt for LHOMI [LHM]
SHINGINI dial of GADI-SHINGINI-VADI-BAANGI
    [KAM]
SHINGSOL alt for SINGSON dial of CHIN, THADO
    [TCZ]
SHINGWALUNGU alt for NGWALUNGU dial of
    TSONGA [TSO]
SHINGWALUNGU alt for N'WALUNGU dial of
    TSONGA [TSO]
SHINKOYA alt for NKOYA [NKA]
SHINNECOCK-POOSEPATUCK alt for MONTAUK dial
    of MOHEGAN-MONTAUK-NARRAGANSETT
    [MOF]
SHINWARI dial of PASHTO, EASTERN [PBU]
SHINYIHA alt for NYIHA [NIH]
SHINZWANI dial of COMORIAN [SWB]
SHIOKO alt for CHOKWE [CJK]
SHIP alt for MISHIP [CHP]
SHIP dial of ALBANIAN, GHEG [ALS]
SHIPIBO dial of SHIPIBO-CONIBO [SHP]
SHIPIBO-CONIBO [SHP] lang, Peru
SHIPINAHUA alt for XIPINÁWA [XIP]
SHIPUTHSU alt for PODZO [POZ]
SHIR alt for MANDARI [MQU]
SHIRA alt for SIRA [SWJ]
SHIRA dial of CHAGGA [KAF]
SHIRA YUGUR alt for YUGUR, EAST [YUY]
SHIRAHO dial of YAEYAMA [RYS]
SHIRAWA [SCX] lang, Nigeria
SHIRAZI dial of FARSI, WESTERN [PES]
SHIRE alt for SIRA [SWJ]
SHIRIANA CASAPARE alt for NINAM [SHB]
SHIRINGOL dial of BONAN [PEH]
SHIRONGA alt for RONGA [RON]
SHIRUMBA alt for SHWAI [SHW]
SHIRUMBA alt for CERUMBA dial of SHWAI [SHW]
SHISA alt for KISA dial of LUYIA [LUY]
SHISAMBYU alt for SAMBYU dial of KWANGALI
    [KWN]
SHISHI alt for SEBA [KDG]
SHISHONG alt for BEBA' dial of BAFUT [BFD]
SHITA [LGN] lang, Ethiopia, Sudan, Sudan
SHITA alt for SHITA [LGN]
SHITAKO alt for GANAGANA dial of NUPE [NUP]
SHITHLOU dial of CHIN, THADO [TCZ]
SHITSONGA (XITSONGA alt for TSONGA [TSO]
SHITSONGA alt for TSONGA [TSO]
SHITSWA alt for TSWA [TSC]
SHKIP alt for ALBANIAN, TOSK [ALN]
SHO alt for CHIN, CHINBON [CNB]
SHO alt for CHIN, ASHO [CSH]
SHOA alt for CHIN, ASHO [CSH]
SHOA alt for TULEMA dial of OROMO, WELLEGA-
    CENTRAL [GAZ]
SHOBA alt for PIANGA dial of BUSHOONG [BUF]
SHOBANG [SSB] lang, India
SHOBWA alt for PIANGA dial of BUSHOONG [BUF]
SHOBYO alt for HUTU dial of RWANDA [RUA]
SHOCO alt for KIRIRÍ-XOKÓ [XOO]
SHOCU alt for KIRIRÍ-XOKÓ [XOO]
SHOE dial of MPADE [MPI]
SHOHO alt for SAHO [SSY]
SHOLAGA [SLE] lang, India

SIBUNDOY alt for CAMSÁ [KBH]
SIBURAN alt for BIATAH [BTH]
SIBUTU dial of SAMA, SOUTHERN [SIT]
SIBUTU alt for SIBUTU' dial of SAMA, SOUTHERN [SIT]
SIBUTU' dial of SAMA, SOUTHERN [SIT]
SIBUTUQ alt for SIBUTU dial of SAMA, SOUTHERN [SIT]
SIBUYAN alt for SEBUYAU [SNB]
SIBUYAN dial of ROMBLOMANON [ROL]
SIBUYAU alt for SEBUYAU [SNB]
SICHE alt for ZIRE [SIH]
SICHUAN-GUIZHOU-YUNNAN HMONG alt for HMONG, WESTERN [HUJ]
SICHULE alt for SIKULE [SKH]
SICILIAN [SCN] lang, Italy
SICILIAN ALBANIAN dial of ALBANIAN, TOSK [ALN]
SÌCÌRÉ alt for SÉNOUFO, SÌCÌTÉ [SEP]
SÌCÌTÉ alt for SÉNOUFO, SÌCÌTÉ [SEP]
SICUANE dial of CUIBA [CUI]
"SICUANI" alt for GUAHIBO [GUH]
SICUARI alt for SICUANE dial of CUIBA [CUI]
SIDAMINYA alt for SIDAMO [SID]
SIDÁMO 'AFÓ alt for SIDAMO [SID]
SIDAMO [SID] lang, Ethiopia
SIDDRI alt for SADANI [SCK]
SIDEIA alt for SIRAIYA [FOS]
SIDEIA alt for SIDEYA dial of TAWALA [TBO]
SIDEIS alt for SIRAIYA [FOS]
SIDEISCH alt for SIRAIYA [FOS]
SIDEME alt for AVATIME [AVA]
SIDENRANG alt for SIDRAP dial of BUGIS [BPR]
SIDEYA dial of TAWALA [TBO]
SIDIN dial of DAYAK, LAND [DYK]
SIDING alt for SIDIN dial of DAYAK, LAND [DYK]
SIDO dial of AARI [AIZ]
SIDRAP dial of BUGIS [BPR]
SIDUAN alt for SIBU [SDX]
SIDUANI alt for SIBU [SDX]
SIE [ERG] lang, Vanuatu
SIE dial of SIE [ERG]
SIEGU alt for YAAKU [MUU]
SIÉMOU alt for SIAMOU [SIF]
SIEMU alt for SIAMOU [SIF]
SIERRA AZTEC alt for NAHUATL, SIERRA DE PUEBLA [AZZ]
SIERRA CHONTAL alt for CHONTAL OF OAXACA, HIGHLAND [CHD]
SIERRA DE PUEBLA NAHUAT alt for NAHUATL, SIERRA DE PUEBLA [AZZ]
SIERRA MIWOK dial of MIWOK [SKD]
SIERRA OTOMÍ alt for OTOMÍ, EASTERN [OTM]
SIEVEMAKERS dial of ROMANI, VLACH [RMY]
SIGABAC alt for SIO [SIO]
SIGARAU alt for KETUNGAU dial of IBAN [IBA]
SIGDI alt for SIGIDI dial of SAYA [SAY]
SIGGOYO alt for BAMBESHI [MYF]
SIGHU [SXE] lang, Gabon
SIGI alt for IJA dial of KAILI, LEDO [LEW]
SIGIDI dial of SAYA [SAY]
SIGILA alt for PELASLA [MLR]
SIGISIGERO alt for BAITSI dial of SIWAI [SIW]
SIGLIT dial of INUIT, WESTERN CANADIAN [ESC]
SIGN LANGUAGE OF THE NETHERLANDS alt for DUTCH SIGN LANGUAGE [DSE]
SIHA dial of CHAGGA [KAF]

SIHAN [SNR] lang, Papua New Guinea
SIHAN alt for SIAN [SPG]
SIHANAKA dial of MALAGASY [MEX]
SIHONG dial of MA'ANYAN [MHY]
SIHZANG dial of CHIN, TEDIM [CTD]
SII alt for WUSHI [BSE]
SIIME dial of KABA DEME [KWG]
SIIRT dial of ARABIC, SYRO-MESOPOTAMIAN [AYP]
SIIS alt for YU dial of MANDYAK [MFV]
SIJAGHA alt for SIAGHA-YENIMU [OSR]
SIJALI alt for JUMLELI dial of NEPALI [NEP]
SIKA alt for SIKKA [SKI]
SIKAIANA [SKY] lang, Solomon Islands
SIKAMI alt for SIKKIMESE [SIP]
SIKARI alt for SIKARITAI [TTY]
SIKARITAI [TTY] lang, Indonesia, Irian Jaya
SIKARWARI dial of BRAJ BHASHA [BFS]
SIKAYANA alt for SIKAIANA [SKY]
SIKHOTA ALIN dial of UDIHE [UDE]
SIKHULE alt for SIKULE [SKH]
SIKIANA [SIK] lang, Brazil, Venezuela, Venezuela
SIKIANA alt for SIKIANA [SIK]
SIKIÂNA alt for SIKIANA [SIK]
SIKKA [SKI] lang, Indonesia, Nusa Tenggara
SIKKA NATAR dial of SIKKA [SKI]
SIKKANESE alt for SIKKA [SKI]
SIKKIM BHOTIA alt for SIKKIMESE [SIP]
SIKKIMESE [SIP] lang, India
SIKUBUNG dial of SAMA, SOUTHERN [SIT]
SIKULE [SKH] lang, Indonesia, Sumatra
SIKWANGALI alt for KWANGALI [KWN]
SILA [SLT] lang, Laos, Viet Nam, Viet Nam
SILA alt for SILA [SLT]
SILA alt for DAJU, DAR SILA [DAU]
SILA dial of DAJU, DAR SILA [DAU]
SILABE alt for SONINKE [SNN]
SILABU dial of MENTAWAI [MWV]
SILADJA alt for SELAYAR [SLY]
SILAIPUI dial of WOISIKA [WOI]
SILAJARA alt for SELAYAR [SLY]
SILAKAU [SLI] lang, Malaysia, Sarawak
SILANKE alt for SININKERE [SKQ]
SILEIBI [SBQ] lang, Papua New Guinea
SILEN alt for TELUTI [TLT]
SILESIAN dial of POLISH [PQL]
SILI alt for SERE [SWF]
SILI alt for PALOR [FAP]
SILI alt for TSHIDI-KHWE dial of SHUA [SHG]
SILI-SILI alt for PALOR [FAP]
SILIGI dial of FOLOPA [PPO]
SILIMIGA alt for FULFULDE, JELGOOJI [FUM]
SILIMO [WUL] lang, Indonesia, Irian Jaya
SILINKERE alt for SININKERE [SKQ]
SILIPUT [MKC] lang, Papua New Guinea
SILISILI [MPL] lang, Papua New Guinea
SILISILI dial of SILISILI [MPL]
SILLOK alt for AKA [SOH]
SILOPI [SOT] lang, Papua New Guinea
SILOZI alt for LOZI [LOZ]
SILTI alt for GURAGE, EAST [GRE]
SILTI dial of GURAGE, EAST [GRE]
SILVER PALAUNG alt for PALAUNG, PALE [PCE]
SIM dial of WERI [WER]
SIMA dial of NAGA, KONYAK [NBE]
SIMAA [SIE] lang, Zambia
SIMAA dial of SIMAA [SIE]

SIMALEGI dial of MENTAWAI [MWV]
SIMALUR alt for SIMEULUE [SMR]
SIMARANHON alt for BANTOANON [BNO]
SIMAY dial of ASMAT, CENTRAL [AST]
SIMBA [SBW] lang, Gabon
SIMBA alt for ZEMBA [DHM]
SIMBAKONG alt for SEMBAKUNG MURUT [SMA]
SIMBALI [SMG] lang, Papua New Guinea
SIMBARI [SMB] lang, Papua New Guinea
SIMBERI dial of MANDARA [TBF]
SIMBITI dial of KURIA [KUJ]
SIMBO [SBB] lang, Solomon Islands
SIMEKU [SMZ] lang, Papua New Guinea
SIMELUNGAN alt for BATAK SIMALUNGUN [BTS]
SIMEULOĚ alt for SIMEULUE [SMR]
SIMEULUE [SMR] lang, Indonesia, Sumatra
SIMI alt for NAGA, SEMA [NSM]
SIMIRANCH alt for PIRO [PIB]
SIMIRINCHE alt for PIRO [PIB]
SIMOG [SMF] lang, Papua New Guinea
SIMOJOVEL dial of TZOTZIL, CHAMULA [TZC]
SIMORI dial of EKARI [EKG]
SIMPI alt for ESIMBI [AGS]
SIMTE [SMT] lang, India
SIMULUL alt for SIMEULUE [SMR]
SIMUNUL dial of SAMA, SOUTHERN [SIT]
SIMUNUL dial of SAMA, SOUTHERN [SIT]
SINA alt for SHINA [SCL]
SINA dial of KAMWE [HIG]
SINABU alt for SINABU' dial of KINABATANGAN,
    UPPER [DMG]
SINABU' dial of KINABATANGAN, UPPER [DMG]
SINAGEN [SIU] lang, Papua New Guinea
SINAGORO [SNC] lang, Papua New Guinea
SINAK NDUGA dial of NDUGA [NDX]
SINAKETA dial of KIRIWINA [KIJ]
SINAKI dial of SUAU [SWP]
SINALE alt for AGALA [AGL]
SINALON dial of TBOLI [TBL]
SINAMA alt for SISSANO [SSW]
SINAMA alt for SAMA, CENTRAL [SML]
SINAN dial of DAYAK, LAND [DYK]
SINANO alt for SISSANO [SSW]
SINARUPA dial of KINABATANGAN, UPPER [DMG]
SINARUPO alt for SINARUPA dial of
    KINABATANGAN, UPPER [DMG]
SINASINA [SST] lang, Papua New Guinea
SINAUGORO alt for SINAGORO [SNC]
SINAUNA alt for AGTA, REMONTADO [AGV]
SINDAMON dial of YAU [YUW]
SINDANG KELINGI [SDI] lang, Indonesia, Sumatra
SINDANGAN SUBANUN alt for SUBANEN, CENTRAL
    [SUS]
SINDEBELE alt for NDEBELE [NDF]
SINDHI [SND] lang, Pakistan, Afghanistan, India,
    Singapore
SINDHI alt for SINDHI [SND]
SINDHI BHIL [SBN] lang, Pakistan
SINDHI MUSALMANI dial of SINDHI [SND]
SINDHUPALCHOK PAHRI dial of NEWARI [NEW]
SINDI alt for SINDHI [SND]
SINDING alt for SIDIN dial of DAYAK, LAND [DYK]
SINDUE-TAWAILI alt for RAI dial of KAILI, LEDO
    [LEW]
SINE dial of SERERE-SINE [SES]
SINE-SALOUM alt for SERERE-SINE [SES]

SINE-SINE alt for SERERE-SINE [SES]
SINESIP alt for SOUTH WEST BAY [SNS]
SING MUN alt for PUOC [PUO]
SINGA [SGM] lang, Uganda
SINGALA dial of SENOUFO, DJIMINI [DYI]
SINGALI alt for LAMANI [LMN]
SINGFO alt for JINGPHO [CGP]
SINGGI [SGS] lang, Malaysia, Sarawak
SINGGIE alt for SINGGI [SGS]
SINGHALA alt for SINHALA [SNH]
SINGHALESE alt for SINHALA [SNH]
SINGHI alt for SINGGI [SGS]
SINGKARAK dial of MINANGKABAU [MPU]
SINGKIL dial of BATAK KARO [BTX]
SINGLI alt for KORWA [KFP]
SINGORAKAI dial of MALASANGA [MQZ]
SINGPHO alt for JINGPHO [CGP]
SINGPO alt for JINGPHO [CGP]
SINGSON dial of CHIN, THADO [TCZ]
SINHALA [SNH] lang, Sri Lanka, Singapore, Thailand
SINHALA alt for SINHALA [SNH]
SINHALESE alt for SINHALA [SNH]
SININKERE [SKQ] lang, Burkina Faso
SINJA alt for SHUBI [SUJ]
SINJA alt for JUMLELI dial of NEPALI [NEP]
SINJAI dial of BUGIS [BPR]
SINKALING HKAMTI dial of KHAMTI [KHT]
SINKON dial of SAPO [KRN]
SINOHOAN dial of PAMONA [BCX]
SINSAURU [SNZ] lang, Papua New Guinea
SINTANG alt for BORNEO dial of MALAY [MLI]
SINTE alt for ROMANI, SINTE [RMO]
SINTI alt for ROMANI, SINTE [RMO]
SINTÍ alt for ROMANI, SINTE [RMO]
SINULIHAN alt for DUSUN SINULIHAN dial of
    DUSUN, CENTRAL [DTP]
SINYA alt for SINYAR [SYS]
SINYAR [SYS] lang, Sudan, Chad
SINYONYOI dial of MAMUJU [MQX]
SIO [SIO] lang, Papua New Guinea
SIOCON alt for SUBANON, WESTERN [SUC]
SIOMPU dial of MUNA [MYN]
SIONA [SIN] lang, Colombia, Ecuador, Ecuador
SIONA alt for SIONA [SIN]
SIONG alt for SIHONG dial of MA'ANYAN [MHY]
SIONI alt for SIONA [SIN]
SIORA dial of ZANAKI [ZAK]
SIOUA alt for SIWA [SIZ]
SIOUX alt for DAKOTA [DHG]
SIPACAPA QUICHÉ alt for SIPACAPENSE [QUM]
SIPACAPEÑO alt for SIPACAPENSE [QUM]
SIPACAPENSE [QUM] lang, Guatemala
SIPARI dial of HARAUTI [HOJ]
SIPENG dial of PUNAN-NIBONG [PNE]
SİPİİTÉ alt for SÉNOUFO, SİCİTÉ [SEP]
SIPOMA alt for NUMBAMI [SIJ]
SIPSONG PANNA DAI alt for LÜ [KHB]
SIPUPU dial of DUAU [DUA]
SIPURA dial of MENTAWAI [MWV]
SIRA [SWJ] lang, Gabon
SIRA alt for PAWAIA [PWA]
SIRAIA alt for SIRAIYA [FOS]
SIRAIKI [SKR] lang, Pakistan, India
SIRAIKI HINDKI dial of SIRAIKI [SKR]
SIRAIYA [FOS] lang, Taiwan
SIRAJI OF DODA dial of KASHMIRI [KSH]

SIRAJI-KASHMIRI dial of KASHMIRI [KSH]
SIRAK alt for NAFI [SRF]
SIRAK alt for SERAK dial of MEFELE [MFJ]
SIRALI dial of KUMAUNI [KFY]
SIRASIRA alt for SARASIRA [SRA]
SIRATA alt for KANURI, YERWA [KPH]
SIRAWA alt for SIRI [SIR]
SIRAYA alt for SIRAIYA [FOS]
SIRAYA dial of SIRAIYA [FOS]
SIRENIK alt for YUPIK, SIRENIK [YSR]
SIRENIKSKI alt for YUPIK, SIRENIK [YSR]
SIRHAAN alt for NORTH NAJDI dial of ARABIC,
   NAJDI [ARS]
SIRHE alt for ZIRE [SIH]
SIRI [SIR] lang, Nigeria
SIRI alt for SERE [SWF]
SIRI-SORI dial of SAPARUA [SPR]
SIRIA dial of MAASAI [MET]
SIRIANO [SRI] lang, Colombia, Brazil
SIRIO alt for NAWARU [NWR]
SIRIONÓ [SRQ] lang, Bolivia
SIRIPU dial of CUIBA [CUI]
SIRIPU alt for CHIRIPO dial of CUIBA [CUI]
SIRIPURIA alt for KISHANGANJIA [KFW]
SIRIPURIA dial of BENGALI [BNG]
SIRKAI dial of KETENGBAN [KIN]
SIRMAURI dial of MAHASUI [BFZ]
SIROI [SSD] lang, Papua New Guinea
SIROMI alt for BARAPASI [BRP]
SIRONCHA dial of GONDI, SOUTHERN [GGO]
SIROW dial of ASMAT, CENTRAL [AST]
SIRXIN dial of DARGWA [DAR]
SISAALA, TUMULUNG [SIL] lang, Ghana
SISAALA, WESTERN [SSL] lang, Ghana
SISAALI alt for SISSALA [SLD]
SISAI alt for SISAALA, TUMULUNG [SIL]
SISAI alt for SISAALA, WESTERN [SSL]
SISAKET dial of KHMER, NORTHERN [KXM]
SISALA TUMU alt for SISAALA, TUMULUNG [SIL]
SISANO alt for SISSANO [SSW]
SISI dial of BESISI [MHE]
SISI-BIPI alt for BIPI [BIQ]
SISIAME dial of BAMU [BCF]
SISIBNA dial of KORUPUN [KPQ]
SISIMIN alt for HEWA [HAM]
SISINGGA alt for SENGAN dial of BABATANA [BAQ]
SISKA alt for TONGA [TOG]
SISSALA [SLD] lang, Burkina Faso
SISSANO [SSW] lang, Papua New Guinea
SISUTHO alt for SOTHO, SOUTHERN [SSO]
SISWATI alt for SWATI [SWZ]
SISYA alt for TONGA [TOG]
SISYABAN alt for SAAROA [SXR]
SITEMU alt for BAGA SITEMU [BSP]
SITENG dial of MELANAU [MEL]
SITI alt for VAGLA [VAG]
SITIA SHERBRO dial of SHERBRO [BUN]
SITIGO alt for VAGLA [VAG]
SIU dial of SWAHILI [SWA]
SIUCI alt for SIUSY-TAPUYA dial of BANIWA [BAI]
SIUSI alt for SIUSY-TAPUYA dial of BANIWA [BAI]
SIUSLAW [SIS] lang, USA
SIUSY-TAPUYA dial of BANIWA [BAI]
SIVANDI [SIY] lang, Iran
SIVUKUN alt for SHIBUKUN dial of BUNUN [BNN]
SIWA [SIZ] lang, Egypt

SIWA dial of FIPA [FIP]
SIWAI [SIW] lang, Papua New Guinea
SIWANG alt for CHEWONG [CWG]
SIWU alt for AKPAFU-LOLOBI [AKP]
SIWURI alt for BOWIRI [BOV]
SIWUSI alt for AKPAFU-LOLOBI [AKP]
SIYALGIRI dial of BHILI [BHB]
SIYANG alt for CHIN, SIYIN [CSY]
SIYIN alt for CHIN, SIYIN [CSY]
SIYU alt for SIU dial of SWAHILI [SWA]
SIZAKI [SZK] lang, Tanzania
SIZANG alt for CHIN, SIYIN [CSY]
SIZI alt for DIZI [MDX]
SJIAGHA alt for SIAGHA-YENIMU [OSR]
SKAGIT [SKA] lang, USA
SKARANG alt for SEKARANG dial of IBAN [IBA]
SKCHIP alt for ALBANIAN, TOSK [ALN]
SKEPI CREOLE DUTCH [SKW] lang, Guyana
SKIDEGATE dial of HAIDA [HAI]
SKIDI dial of PAWNEE [PAW]
SKO [SKV] lang, Indonesia, Irian Jaya
SKOFRO alt for MANEM [JET]
SKOKOMISH alt for TWANA [TWA]
SKOKOMISH dial of TWANA [TWA]
SKOLT alt for SAAMI, SKOLT [LPK]
"SKOLT LAPPISH" alt for SAAMI, SKOLT [LPK]
SKOLT LAPPISH alt for SAAMI, SKOLT [LPK]
SKRUBU alt for SURUBU [SDE]
SLAI alt for HLAI [LIC]
SLAVE alt for SLAVEY [SLA]
SLAVEY [SLA] lang, Canada
SLAVEY dial of SLAVEY [SLA]
SLAVI alt for SLAVEY [SLA]
SLAVIC alt for MACEDONIAN [MKJ]
SLAVONIC, OLD CHURCH [SLN] lang, Russia,
   Europe
SLIAMMON dial of COMOX [COO]
SLN alt for DUTCH SIGN LANGUAGE [DSE]
SLOVAK [SLO] lang, Czechoslovakia, USA, Hungary,
   Russia, Europe, Yugoslavia
SLOVAKIAN alt for SLOVAK [SLO]
SLOVENE alt for SLOVENIAN [SLV]
SLOVENIAN [SLV] lang, Slovenia, Austria, Hungary,
   Italy
SLOVENIAN SIGN LANGUAGE dial of
   YUGOSLAVIAN SIGN LANGUAGE [YSL]
SLOVENIAN-CROATIAN dial of ROMANI, SINTE
   [RMO]
SLOVENIAN-CROATIAN ROMANI dial of ROMANI,
   SINTE [RMO]
SLOVINCIAN dial of KASHUBIAN [CSB]
SLUTSKO-MOZYR alt for SOUTHWEST
   BELORUSSIAN dial of BELORUSSIAN [RUW]
SLUUT alt for NORTH NAJDI dial of ARABIC, NAJDI
   [ARS]
SMALL FLOWERY alt for XIAO HUA dial of HMONG,
   WESTERN [HUJ]
SMALL NAMBAS alt for LETEMBOI [NMS]
SMITH RIVER alt for TOLOWA [TOL]
SMYRNA dial of ARMENIAN [ARM]
SNABI WATUBELA alt for WATUBELA [WAH]
SNOHOMISH [SNO] lang, USA
SNOQUALMIE dial of SALISH, SOUTHERN PUGET
   SOUND [SLH]
SO [SOC] lang, Zaïre
SO [SOX] lang, Cameroon

SÔ [SSS] lang, Laos, Thailand, Thailand, Viet Nam
SO alt for SOO [TEU]
SÔ alt for SÔ [SSS]
SO dial of KABA SO [KXJ]
SO MAKON alt for MANGKONG [XMK]
SO MAKON dial of SÔ [SSS]
SO PHONG dial of SÔ [SSS]
SO SLOUY dial of SÔ [SSS]
SO TRI [SZT] lang, Laos, Thailand, Thailand, Viet Nam
SO TRII alt for SO TRI [SZT]
SO TRONG dial of SÔ [SSS]
SO-BÊ alt for KIRMANJKI [QKV]
SOA alt for SO [SOC]
SOA dial of NGADA [NXG]
SOA alt for PERIPHERAL KONO dial of KONO [KNO]
SOAHUKU dial of AMAHAI [AMQ]
SOAI alt for KUY [KDT]
SOBA alt for HUPLA [HAP]
SOBANÉ alt for BAGA SOBANÉ [BSV]
SOBEI [SOB] lang, Indonesia, Irian Jaya
SOBEI dial of SOBEI [SOB]
SOBO alt for URHOBO [URH]
"SOBO" alt for ISOKO [ISO]
SOBOJO alt for MANGEI dial of TALIABU [TLV]
SOBOYO alt for MANGEI dial of TALIABU [TLV]
SOCHILE alt for NYAKYUSA-NGONDE [NYY]
SODDO alt for GURAGE, NORTH [GRU]
SODDO dial of GURAGE, NORTH [GRU]
SODIA alt for GUDWA dial of GADABA [GBJ]
SODOCHI dial of MAHASUI [BFZ]
SOFALA alt for NDAU [NDC]
SOGA [SOG] lang, Uganda
SOGA dial of SOGA [SOG]
SOGADAS alt for SOKODASA dial of KUNAMA [KUM]
SOGAL dial of BINE [ORM]
SOGAP alt for NGALA [NUD]
SOGH alt for MANTION [MNX]
SOGHAI alt for DUSUN SEGAMA dial of KINABATANGAN, UPPER [DMG]
SOGHAUA alt for ZAGHAWA [ZAG]
SÔGHOO dial of SENOUFO, MAMARA [MYK]
SOGILITAN alt for KADAZAN, LABUK-KINABATANGAN [DTB]
SOGO dial of JAPANESE [JPN]
SOGOBA alt for SUMARIUP [SIV]
SOGODAS alt for SOKODASA dial of KUNAMA [KUM]
SOGOKIRE dial of BOBO FING [BBO]
SOGOKIRI dial of BOBO FING [BBO]
SOGOO dial of OKIEK [OKI]
SOGORE alt for ME'EN [MYM]
SOHE dial of OROKAIVA [ORK]
SOHUR alt for YAQAY [JAQ]
SOI [SOJ] lang, Iran
SOIBADA alt for EASTERN TETUN dial of TETUN [TTM]
SOK [SKK] lang, Laos
SOKAKA alt for HIXKARYÁNA [HIX]
SOKHOK dial of PSOHOH [BCL]
SOKID dial of DUSUN, CENTRAL [DTP]
SOKILE alt for NYAKYUSA-NGONDE [NYY]
SOKILI alt for NYAKYUSA-NGONDE [NYY]
SOKIRIK dial of PATPATAR [GFK]
SOKNA alt for SAWKNAH [SWN]

SOKO alt for SO [SOC]
SOKO dial of NTOMBA [NTO]
SOKO alt for SUKA dial of KABA SO [KXJ]
SOKODASA dial of KUNAMA [KUM]
SOKORO [SOK] lang, Chad
SOKORO dial of SOKORO [SOK]
SOKOROK alt for SILIPUT [MKC]
SOKOTRI alt for SOQOTRI [SQT]
SOKTE dial of CHIN, TEDIM [CTD]
SOKYA alt for KOUYA [KYF]
SOLA [SOY] lang, Benin, Togo, Togo
SOLA DE VEGA MIXTECO alt for MIXTECO, AMOLTEPEC [MBZ]
SOLAMBA alt for SOLA [SOY]
SOLI [SBY] lang, Zambia
SOLLA alt for SOLA [SOY]
SOLO dial of JAVANESE [JAN]
SOLOMONS PIDGIN alt for PIJIN [PIS]
SOLON alt for EVENKI [EVN]
SOLONG alt for AROVE [AAW]
SOLOR alt for LAMAHOLOT [SLP]
SOLOR alt for SOUTH LAMAHOLOT dial of LAMAHOLOT [SLP]
SOLORESE alt for LAMAHOLOT [SLP]
SOLOS [SOL] lang, Papua New Guinea
SOLOTO dial of YURACARE [YUE]
SOLWA alt for KAGULU [KKI]
SOLWE alt for KONDOA dial of SAGALA [SBM]
SOM [SMC] lang, Papua New Guinea
SOM alt for WAB [WAB]
SOMA alt for TAMBERMA [SOF]
SOMAGE alt for MOMUNA [MQF]
SOMAHAI alt for MOMUNA [MQF]
SOMALI [SOM] lang, Somalia, Djibouti, Ethiopia, Kenya, United Arab Emirates, Yemen
SOMALINYA alt for SOMALI [SOM]
SOMATU alt for MADU dial of ENETS [ENE]
"SOMBA" alt for TAMBERMA [SOF]
SOMBA alt for DITAMMARI [TBZ]
SOMBA alt for BURUM-MINDIK [BMU]
SOME alt for TAMBERMA [SOF]
SOME dial of FASU [FAA]
SOMKHURI (ENA) alt for ARMENIAN [ARM]
SOMKHURI alt for ARMENIAN [ARM]
SOMO dial of GBAYA [GYA]
SOMONO dial of BAMBARA [BRA]
SOMORIKA alt for EMHALHE dial of OKPAMHERI [OPA]
SOMRA alt for NAGA, TANGKHUL [NMF]
SOMRAI [SOR] lang, Chad
SOMRAY [SMU] lang, Cambodia
SOMRE alt for SOMRAI [SOR]
SOMREI alt for SOMRAI [SOR]
SOMWADINA dial of DUAU [DUA]
SOMYEWE [KGT] lang, Nigeria
SON dial of VO [WBM]
SONA alt for KANASI [SOQ]
SONAHAA alt for SONHA [SOI]
SONAI dial of YAEYAMA [RYS]
SONAPAL dial of MURIA, WESTERN [MUT]
SONDE [SHC] lang, Zaïre
SONDER dial of TONTEMBOAN [TNT]
SONDOANG dial of ULUMANDA' [ULM]
SONDWARI [SCM] lang, India
SONDWARI dial of MALVI [MUP]

SONG [SOA] lang, Thailand
SONGA [SGO] lang, Zaïre
SONGA dial of SAAMIA [SBU]
SONGA dial of TSONGA [TSO]
SONGADI-KARISOA dial of BARUGA [BBB]
SONGAI [SON] lang, Mali, Burkina Faso, Niger
SONGAI alt for SONGAI [SON]
SONGAY alt for SONGAI [SON]
SONGBU dial of NAGA, RONGMEI [NBU]
SONGE [SOP] lang, Zaïre
SONGE alt for WESTERN KALEBWE dial of SONGE
  [SOP]
SONGHAI alt for SONGAI [SON]
SONGHAY alt for SONGAI [SON]
SONGISH dial of SALISH, STRAITS [STR]
SONGO [SOO] lang, Zaïre
SONGO alt for MBATI [MDN]
SONGO alt for NSONGO [NSX]
SONGOI alt for SONGAI [SON]
SONGOLA alt for OMBO [OML]
SONGOLA alt for SONGOORA [SOD]
SONGOLA alt for EKISONGOORA dial of NANDI
  [NNB]
SONGOMENO [SOE] lang, Zaïre
SONGOORA [SOD] lang, Zaïre
SONGU alt for SESA dial of FOLOPA [PPO]
SONGUM [SNX] lang, Papua New Guinea
SONGWA dial of NGEMBA [NGE]
SONGWE alt for SAFWA [SBK]
SONGYE alt for SONGE [SOP]
SONHA [SOI] lang, Nepal
SONIA [SIQ] lang, Papua New Guinea
SONINKE [SNN] lang, Mali, Burkina Faso, Côte
  d'Ivoire, Gambia, Guinea Bissau, Mauritania,
  Senegal
SONINKE alt for SONINKE [SNN]
SONJO [SOZ] lang, Tanzania
SONPARI dial of BAGHELI [BFY]
SONRAI alt for SONGAI [SON]
SONRHAI alt for SONGAI [SON]
SONSOGON [SGN] lang, Malaysia, Sabah
SONSOROL [SOV] lang, Micronesia
SONSOROLESE alt for SONSOROL [SOV]
SONTHAL alt for SANTALI [SNT]
SONYO alt for SONJO [SOZ]
SOO [TEU] lang, Uganda
SOOCHOW alt for SUZHOU dial of CHINESE, WU
  [WUU]
SOOK MURUT dial of PALUAN [PLZ]
SOOKE dial of SALISH, STRAITS [STR]
SOOLOO alt for TAUSUG [TSG]
SOONDE alt for SONDE [SHC]
SOOW HUHELIA alt for MANIPA [MQP]
SOP alt for USINO [URW]
SOP dial of KOHO [KPM]
SOPESE dial of FOLOPA [PPO]
SOPFOMO alt for NAGA, MAO [NBI]
SOPI dial of GALELA [GBI]
SOPI dial of BELI [BLM]
SOPOCNOVSKIJ dial of ITELMEN [ITL]
SOPPENG dial of BUGIS [BPR]
SOPPENG RIAJA alt for BARRU dial of BUGIS [BPR]
SOPVOMA alt for NAGA, MAO [NBI]
SOQOTRI [SQT] lang, Yemen
SOR alt for NGAING [NNF]
SOR alt for SAHARIA [SRX]

SOR dial of BIAK [BHW]
SOR dial of KUPSABINY [KPZ]
SÖR-LAPSKA alt for SAAMI, SOUTHERN [LPC]
SORA [SRB] lang, India
SORABE alt for WEND, LOWER [WEE]
SORABE alt for WEND, UPPER [WEN]
SORACHOLI dial of MAHASUI [BFZ]
SORADI dial of NEPALI [NEP]
SORANI dial of KURDI [KDB]
SORATHI alt for KATHIYAWADI dial of GUJARATI
  [GJR]
SORBIAN alt for WEND, LOWER [WEE]
SORBIAN alt for WEND, UPPER [WEN]
SORENDIDORI dial of BIAK [BHW]
SORI dial of SORI-HARENGAN [SBH]
SORI-HARENGAN [SBH] lang, Papua New Guinea
SORIDO dial of BIAK [BHW]
SORIMIN alt for ITERI [ITR]
SORIYALI dial of KUMAUNI [KFY]
SORK alt for SOK [SKK]
SORO alt for HADIYYA [HDY]
SOROAKO dial of MORI BAWAH [XMZ]
SOROGAMA alt for BOZO, SOROGAMA [BZE]
SOROUBA alt for SOLA [SOY]
SORSOGON BICOLANO alt for SORSOGON,
  MASBATE [BKS]
SORSOGON, MASBATE [BKS] lang, Philippines
SORSOGON, WARAY [SRV] lang, Philippines
SORSOGONON alt for GUBATNON dial of
  HANUNOO [HNN]
SORUBA alt for SOLA [SOY]
SORUNG alt for SIE dial of SIE [ERG]
SOS'VA alt for NORTHERN VOGUL dial of MANSI
  [MNS]
SOSE alt for SUSU [SUD]
SOSI alt for BASSOSSI [BSI]
SOSIA alt for SAHARIA [SRX]
SOSO alt for SUSU [SUD]
SOSU alt for SUSU [SUD]
SOSYVIN alt for NORTHERN VOGUL dial of MANSI
  [MNS]
SOTA alt for NORTH KANUM dial of KANUM [KCD]
SOTANG dial of KULUNG [KLE]
SOTATI-PO alt for SOTATIPO [SCS]
SOTATIPO [SCS] lang, China
SOTHO, NORTHERN [SRT] lang, South Africa
SOTHO, SOUTHERN [SSO] lang, Lesotho, South
  Africa, South Africa
SOTHO, SOUTHERN alt for SOTHO, SOUTHERN
  [SSO]
SOTIPURA alt for CENTRAL COLLOQUIAL MAITHILI
  dial of MAITHILI [MKP]
SOTO alt for MAQUIRITARI [MCH]
SOU [SQQ] lang, Laos
SOUBAKANEDOUGOU dial of CERMA [GOT]
SOUBRÉ dial of BÉTÉ, GUIBEROUA [BET]
SOUDHWARI alt for SONDWARI [SCM]
SOUEI alt for KUY [KDT]
SOUGB alt for MANTION [MNX]
SOUK alt for SOU [SQQ]
SOUKA alt for SUKA dial of KABA SO [KXJ]
SOULANI dial of WARA [WBF]
SOULETIN dial of BASQUE [BSQ]
SOUMO alt for SUMO [SUM]
SOUMRAI alt for SOMRAI [SOR]
SOUMRAY alt for SOMRAI [SOR]

SOUNGOR alt for SUNGOR [SUN]
SOUNRAI alt for SOMRAI [SOR]
SOURASHTRA alt for SAURASHTRA [SAZ]
SOUSOU alt for SUSU [SUD]
SOUSSOU alt for SUSU [SUD]
SOUTH AFRICA TAMIL dial of TAMIL [TCV]
SOUTH AFRICAN SIGN LANGUAGE [SFS] lang,
   South Africa
SOUTH ALASKA ESKIMO alt for YUPIK, PACIFIC
   GULF [EMS]
SOUTH ALBANIAN dial of ROMANI, VLACH [RMY]
SOUTH ALUNE dial of ALUNE [ALP]
SOUTH AMBRYM alt for DAKAKA [BPA]
SOUTH ARABIC alt for MAHRI [MHR]
SOUTH AWA dial of AWA [AWB]
SOUTH AWIN dial of AWIN [AWI]
SOUTH BANTAWA dial of BANTAWA [BAP]
SOUTH BAVARIAN dial of BAVARIAN [BAR]
SOUTH BELGIUM SIGN LANGUAGE dial of BELGIAN
   SIGN LANGUAGE [BVS]
SOUTH BINJA dial of SONGOORA [SOD]
SOUTH BOAZI dial of BOAZI [KVG]
SOUTH BUNA dial of BUNA [BVN]
SOUTH BUNUN dial of BUNUN [BNN]
SOUTH BURU alt for MASARETE dial of BURU [MHS]
SOUTH BUTON alt for CIA-CIA [CIA]
SOUTH CAROLINA dial of SEA ISLANDS CREOLE
   ENGLISH [GUL]
SOUTH CENTRAL IZON alt for BUMO dial of IJO,
   CENTRAL-WESTERN [IJC]
SOUTH CENTRAL TLAXIACO MIXTECO alt for
   MIXTECO, SAN ESTEBAN ATATLAHUCA [MIB]
SOUTH CH'UNGCH'ONG alt for CH'UNGCH'ONGDO
   dial of KOREAN [KKN]
SOUTH CHACHAPOYAS alt for LA JALCA dial of
   QUECHUA, CHACHAPOYAS [QUK]
SOUTH CHOLLADO alt for CHOLLADO dial of
   KOREAN [KKN]
SOUTH COAST MENGEN dial of MENGEN [MEE]
SOUTH COAST SIKKA alt for SIKKA NATAR dial of
   SIKKA [SKI]
SOUTH CONGO dial of KONGO [KON]
SOUTH DAMAR alt for DAMAR, EAST [DMR]
SOUTH DEDUA dial of DEDUA [DED]
SOUTH EAST KONGO dial of KONGO [KON]
SOUTH FORE alt for PAMUSA dial of FORE [FOR]
SOUTH HAMGYONGDO alt for HAMGYONGDO dial
   of KOREAN [KKN]
SOUTH HIBERNO ENGLISH dial of ENGLISH [ENG]
SOUTH HIJAZI dial of ARABIC, HIJAZI [ACW]
SOUTH IBANAG dial of IBANAG [IBG]
SOUTH IBIE dial of YEKHEE [ETS]
SOUTH ISLAND dial of MAORI [MBF]
SOUTH IZERE dial of IZERE [FIZ]
SOUTH KAMAYO dial of KAMAYO [KYK]
SOUTH KAMBERATARO dial of KAMBERATARO
   [KBV]
SOUTH KANUM dial of KANUM [KCD]
SOUTH KARAKELONG dial of TALAUD [TLD]
SOUTH KERALA dial of MALAYALAM [MJS]
SOUTH KHANA dial of KOANA [KEH]
SOUTH KHOWAR dial of KHOWAR [KHW]
SOUTH KITUI dial of KAMBA [KIK]
SOUTH KOMBIO dial of KOMBIO [KOK]
SOUTH KONGO dial of KONGO [KON]
SOUTH KWANDU dial of MASHI [MHO]

SOUTH KYONGSANGDO alt for KYONGSANGDO
   dial of KOREAN [KKN]
SOUTH LAAMANG dial of LAMANG [HIA]
SOUTH LAMAHOLOT dial of LAMAHOLOT [SLP]
SOUTH LOBALA dial of LOBALA [LOQ]
SOUTH LOLODA alt for LABA [LAU]
SOUTH LUWU dial of TAE' [ROB]
SOUTH MAKAA alt for MAKAA [MCP]
SOUTH MALAITA alt for SA'A [APB]
SOUTH MALO alt for ATARIPOE dial of MALO [MLA]
SOUTH MANUSELA dial of MANUSELA [WHA]
SOUTH MBUNDU alt for UMBUNDU [MNF]
SOUTH MEKAA alt for MAKAA [MCP]
SOUTH MENDI alt for ANGAL HENENG, SOUTH
   [AOE]
SOUTH MIGABAC dial of MIGABAC [MPP]
SOUTH MODOLE dial of MODOLE [MQO]
SOUTH MOEJOE alt for KATI, SOUTHERN [KTS]
SOUTH MORI alt for PADOE [PDO]
SOUTH MUYU alt for KATI, SOUTHERN [KTS]
SOUTH NAKAMA dial of NAKAMA [NIB]
SOUTH NGALIK alt for SILIMO [WUL]
SOUTH NKUNDO alt for PANGA dial of MONGO-
   NKUNDO [MOM]
SOUTH NORTHERN PAIUTE dial of PAIUTE,
   NORTHERN [PAO]
SOUTH NUK dial of NUK [NOC]
SOUTH NYALI alt for NYALI-TCHABI dial of NYALI
   [NLJ]
SOUTH OGBA dial of OGBAH [OGC]
SOUTH OLO alt for WAPI dial of OLO [ONG]
SOUTH ORAN dial of TAMAZIGHT [TZM]
SOUTH P'YONG'ANDO alt for P'YONG'ANDO dial of
   KOREAN [KKN]
SOUTH PAAMA dial of PAAMA [PMA]
SOUTH PALAWANO dial of PALAWANO, BROOKE'S
   POINT [PLW]
SOUTH PERMYAK dial of KOMI-PERMYAK [KOI]
SOUTH POHJANMAA dial of FINNISH [FIN]
SOUTH QATARI ARABIC dial of ARABIC, GULF
   [AFB]
SOUTH QUCHANI dial of KHORASANI TURKISH
   [KMZ]
SOUTH RAGA alt for PONORWAL dial of SA [SSA]
SOUTH RUSSIAN dial of RUSSIAN [RUS]
SOUTH SAISET alt for TUNGHO dial of SAISIYAT
   [SAI]
SOUTH SARDINIAN alt for SARDINIAN,
   CAMPIDANESE [SRO]
SOUTH SELEPET dial of SELEPET [SEL]
SOUTH SENA alt for SENA BANGWE dial of SENA
   [SEH]
SOUTH SIBERUT dial of MENTAWAI [MWV]
SOUTH TABASARAN dial of TABASSARAN [TAB]
SOUTH TABUKANG dial of SANGIR [SAN]
SOUTH THARAKA alt for THARAKA dial of
   THARAKA [THA]
SOUTH TIGAK dial of TIGAK [TGC]
SOUTH TIMBE dial of TIMBE [TIM]
SOUTH TORAJA alt for TORAJA-SA'DAN [SDA]
SOUTH TUGEN dial of KALENJIN [KLN]
SOUTH TUVALUAN dial of TUVALUAN [ELL]
SOUTH UDMURT dial of UDMURT [UDM]
SOUTH URAT dial of URAT [URT]
SOUTH WAIBUK dial of HARUAI [TMD]
SOUTH WALES dial of ENGLISH [ENG]

SOUTH WATUT alt for MARALANGO [MCY]
SOUTH WATUT alt for DANGAL [DAC]
SOUTH WEST BAY [SNS] lang, Vanuatu
SOUTH YAMDENA dial of YAMDENA [JMD]
SOUTH YAWA dial of YAWA [YVA]
SOUTH YEI dial of YEI [JEI]
SOUTHEAST ARABIAN COLLOQUIAL ARABIC alt for ARABIC, OMANI [ACX]
SOUTHEAST BANTAWA dial of BANTAWA [BAP]
SOUTHEAST BOBE dial of BUBE [BVB]
SOUTHEAST CAGAYAN alt for ROSO dial of AGTA, DUPANINAN [DUO]
SOUTHEAST DOBEL dial of DOBEL [KVO]
SOUTHEAST KAINGANG dial of KAINGÁNG [KGP]
SOUTHEAST KONGO dial of KONGO [KON]
SOUTHEAST LAMPUNG alt for KALIANDA dial of PESISIR, SOUTHERN [PEC]
SOUTHEAST MARIND alt for MARIND [MRZ]
SOUTHEAST METAFONETICA dial of SICILIAN [SCN]
SOUTHEAST NGADA dial of NGADA [NXG]
SOUTHEAST PASHTO dial of PASHTO, SOUTHERN [PBQ]
SOUTHEAST SELA dial of SELA [SLS]
SOUTHEAST SHONA alt for NDAU [NDC]
SOUTHEAST TOBA dial of TOBA [TOB]
SOUTHEAST VANUA LEVU dial of FIJIAN [FJI]
SOUTHEAST VITI LEVU dial of FIJIAN [FJI]
SOUTHEASTERN FINNISH dial of FINNISH [FIN]
SOUTHEASTERN KARAKALPAK dial of KARAKALPAK [KAC]
SOUTHEASTERN MACEDONIAN dial of MACEDONIAN [MKJ]
SOUTHEASTERN OCOTEPEC MIXTECO alt for MIXTECO, SOUTHWESTERN TLAXIACO [MEH]
SOUTHEASTERN POMO dial of POMO [POO]
SOUTHEASTERN TUVIN dial of TUVIN [TUN]
SOUTHEASTERN YI alt for YI, YUNNAN [NOS]
SOUTHEASTERN YI alt for YI, GUIZHOU [YIG]
SOUTHERN AKHVAKH dial of AKHVAKH [AKV]
SOUTHERN ALTAI alt for ALTAI PROPER dial of ALTAI, SOUTHERN [ALT]
SOUTHERN AMAMI-OSIMA alt for AMAMI-OSHIMA, SOUTHERN [AMS]
SOUTHERN AMIS dial of AMIS [ALV]
SOUTHERN ARAGONESE dial of ARAGONESE [AXX]
SOUTHERN ARAMIC dial of JUDEO-ARAMAIC [TRG]
SOUTHERN ARANDA dial of ARANDA, WESTERN [ARE]
SOUTHERN ASSYRIAN dial of ASSYRIAN [AII]
SOUTHERN ATTA alt for ATTA, FAIRE [ATH]
SOUTHERN BAAGANDJI alt for DARLING [DRL]
SOUTHERN BABOLE dial of BABOLE [BVX]
SOUTHERN BAJAU alt for SAMA, SOUTHERN [SIT]
SOUTHERN BAKOSSI dial of AKOOSE [BSS]
SOUTHERN BARASANO alt for BARASANA [BSN]
SOUTHERN BIRIFOR alt for BIRIFOR, GHANA [BIV]
SOUTHERN BISAYA alt for BISAYA, BRUNEI [BSB]
SOUTHERN BOLON alt for WHITE BOLON dial of BOLON [BOF]
SOUTHERN BONTOC alt for BONTOC, EASTERN [BKB]
SOUTHERN BULLOM alt for SHERBRO [BUN]
SOUTHERN BURUN alt for MABAAN [MFZ]
SOUTHERN BUTUNG alt for CIA-CIA [CIA]
SOUTHERN CAROLINIAN dial of CAROLINIAN [CAL]

SOUTHERN CHUMBURUNG dial of CHUMBURUNG [NCU]
SOUTHERN COAST KIWAI dial of KIWAI, SOUTHERN [KJD]
SOUTHERN CRIMEAN dial of CRIMEAN TURKISH [CRH]
SOUTHERN DAGARI alt for DAGAARI, SOUTHERN [DGA]
SOUTHERN DONG dial of DONG [KMC]
SOUTHERN DOS DE MAYO dial of QUECHUA, HUÁNUCO, SOUTHERN DOS DE MAYO-MARGOS CHAULÁN [QEI]
SOUTHERN EFATE alt for ERAKOR dial of EFATE, SOUTH [ERK]
SOUTHERN EJAGHAM dial of EJAGHAM [ETU]
SOUTHERN EJAGHAM dial of EJAGHAM [ETU]
SOUTHERN EMBERA alt for SOUTHERN EMPERA dial of EPENA SAIJA [SJA]
SOUTHERN EMPERA dial of EPENA SAIJA [SJA]
SOUTHERN ESTONIAN alt for TARTU dial of ESTONIAN [EST]
SOUTHERN FRENCH SIGN LANGUAGE alt for MARSEILLE SIGN LANGUAGE dial of FRENCH SIGN LANGUAGE [FSL]
SOUTHERN FUNGOM alt for OSO [OSO]
SOUTHERN GABRI alt for GABRI [GAB]
SOUTHERN GOURMANCHEMA dial of GOURMANCHÉMA [GUX]
SOUTHERN GUNU dial of NUGUNU [YAS]
SOUTHERN GURUNG alt for GURUNG [GVR]
SOUTHERN HEMA alt for HEMA-SUD [NIX]
SOUTHERN HUANCAYO QUECHUA alt for QUECHUA, HUANCA, HUAYLLA [QHU]
SOUTHERN ISAN. KORAT dial of TAI, NORTHEASTERN [TTS]
SOUTHERN JALE alt for NIPSAN [YAC]
SOUTHERN KALASHA dial of KALASHA [KLS]
SOUTHERN KARELIAN dial of KARELIAN [KRL]
SOUTHERN KAZAKH dial of KAZAKH [KAZ]
SOUTHERN KHAMS dial of KHAM [KHG]
SOUTHERN KHANTI dial of KHANTY [KCA]
SOUTHERN KIRGIZ dial of KIRGHIZ [KDO]
SOUTHERN KISAGALA alt for SAGALA [SBM]
SOUTHERN KORONDOUGOU dial of BOZO, SOROGAMA [BZE]
SOUTHERN KRAHN alt for SAPO [KRN]
SOUTHERN KURDISH alt for KURDI [KDB]
SOUTHERN LAHU alt for NYI dial of LAHU [LAH]
SOUTHERN LAPP alt for SAAMI, SOUTHERN [LPC]
SOUTHERN LENGUA dial of LENGUA [LEG]
SOUTHERN LIMBA dial of LIMBA, EAST [LMA]
SOUTHERN LISU alt for LISU [LIS]
SOUTHERN LUBA alt for SANGA [SNG]
SOUTHERN LUSHOOTSEED dial of LUSHOOTSEED [LUT]
SOUTHERN MAGAHI dial of MAGAHI [MQM]
SOUTHERN MAIDU alt for NISENAN dial of MAIDU [MAI]
SOUTHERN MAITHILI dial of MAITHILI [MKP]
SOUTHERN MALAY alt for PERAK dial of MALAY [MLI]
SOUTHERN MAMASA alt for PATTAE' dial of MAMASA [MQJ]
SOUTHERN MANINKA alt for MANINKA [MNI]
SOUTHERN MAO alt for ANFILLO [MYO]
SOUTHERN MARWARI dial of MARWARI [MKD]

SRADRI alt for SADANI [SCK]
SRANAN [SRN] lang, Surinam, Netherlands Antilles
SRANAN TONGO alt for SRANAN [SRN]
SRE dial of KOHO [KPM]
SREDNYAYA OB-KET dial of SELKUP [SAK]
SREM dial of ALBANIAN, TOSK [ALN]
SRI LANKA TAMIL dial of TAMIL [TCV]
SRI LANKAN CREOLE MALAY [SCI] lang, Sri Lanka
SRI LANKAN MALAY alt for SRI LANKAN CREOLE
    MALAY [SCI]
SRI LANKAN SIGN LANGUAGE [SQS] lang, Sri Lanka
SRIKAKULA dial of TELUGU [TCW]
SRINAGARIA dial of GARHWALI [GBM]
SRUBU alt for SURUBU [SDE]
SSIA alt for SERA [SRY]
SSO alt for SO [SOX]
SSU GHASSI alt for DZU/'OÃSI dial of KUNG-
    TSUMKWE [KTZ]
SSU GHASSI alt for DZU'OASI dial of KUNG-
    TSUMKWE [KTZ]
SSUGA alt for SUGA [SGI]
ST. BARTH CREOLE FRENCH dial of LESSER
    ANTILLEAN CREOLE FRENCH [DOM]
ST. FRANCIS alt for WESTERN ABNAKI dial of
    ABNAKI-PENOBSCOT [ABE]
ST. FRANCIS alt for WESTERN ABNAKI dial of
    ABNAKI-PENOBSCOT [ABE]
ST. LAWRENCE IROQUOIAN alt for LAURENTIAN
    [LRE]
ST. LAWRENCE ISLAND ESKIMO alt for YUPIK,
    CENTRAL SIBERIAN [ESS]
ST. LOUIS alt for LA CONCEPTION dial of CAAC
    [MSQ]
ST. LUCIA CREOLE dial of LESSER ANTILLEAN
    CREOLE FRENCH [DOM]
ST. LUCIAN ENGLISH dial of ENGLISH [ENG]
STAL dial of LEZGI [LEZ]
STANDARD ASSAMESE dial of ASSAMESE [ASM]
STANDARD FIJIAN alt for FIJIAN [FJI]
STANDARD FRENCH dial of FRENCH [FRN]
STANDARD GUJARATI dial of GUJARATI [GJR]
STANDARD HEBREW dial of HEBREW [HBR]
STANDARD KASHMIRI dial of KASHMIRI [KSH]
STANDARD KINNAURI alt for LOWER KANAURI dial
    of KANAURI [KFK]
STANDARD KONKANI dial of KONKANI, GOANESE
    [GOM]
STANDARD MAITHILI dial of MAITHILI [MKP]
STANDARD MALAY alt for MALAY [MLI]
STANDARD MARWARI dial of MARWARI [MKD]
STANDARD MUNA dial of MUNA [MYN]
STANDARD ORIYA alt for MUGHALBANDI dial of
    ORIYA [ORY]
STANDARD SOMALI alt for SOMALI [SOM]
STANDARD THAI alt for THAI [THJ]
STANG dial of DAYAK, LAND [DYK]
STAR alt for GEDAGED [GDD]
STAR HARBOUR alt for TAWARAFA dial of KAHUA
    [AGW]
STAR-RAGETTA alt for GEDAGED [GDD]
STEPPE BASHKIR alt for YURMATY dial of BASHKIR
    [BXK]
STEPPE CRIMEAN alt for NORTHERN CRIMEAN dial
    of CRIMEAN TURKISH [CRH]
STIENG [STI] lang, Viet Nam, Cambodia
STIMUL alt for PAIWAN [PWN]

STOCKBRIDGE dial of MOHEGAN-MONTAUK-
    NARRAGANSETT [MOF]
STOD dial of TIBETAN [TIC]
STOKAVIAN dial of SERBO-CROATIAN [SRC]
STONEY [STO] lang, Canada
STONY alt for STONEY [STO]
STOTPA alt for CHANGTHANG [CNA]
STRAITS alt for SALISH, STRAITS [STR]
STRIENG alt for TRIENG [STG]
STRIPED HMONG alt for HMONG GU MBA dial of
    HMONG DAW [MWW]
STRIPED HMONG alt for HMONG GU MBA dial of
    HMONG DAW [MWW]
STRIPED KAREN alt for YINCHIA [YIN]
SU alt for ISU [SZV]
SU alt for SOU [SQQ]
SU' alt for SOU [SQQ]
SUA [SSU] lang, Papua New Guinea
SUA alt for MANSOANKA [MSW]
SUA TO PADANG alt for SEKO PADANG [SKX]
SUABAU alt for INANWATAN [SZP]
SUABIAN alt for SWABIAN [SWG]
SUABO alt for INANWATAN [SZP]
SUAFA dial of LAU [LLU]
SUAHILI alt for SWAHILI [SWA]
SUAI alt for KUY [KDT]
SUAIN alt for ULAU-SUAIN [SVB]
SUANG LOTUD alt for LOTUD [DTR]
SUARMIN [SEO] lang, Papua New Guinea
SUARO alt for MAIA [SKS]
SUARU alt for MIANI [PLA]
SUAU [SWP] lang, Papua New Guinea
SUAU dial of SUAU [SWP]
SUB-BARBARICINO dial of SARDINIAN,
    CAMPIDANESE [SRO]
SUBA [SUH] lang, Kenya, Tanzania, Tanzania
SUBA alt for SUBA [SUH]
SUBANEN alt for SUBANUN, LAPUYAN [LAA]
SUBANEN, CENTRAL [SUS] lang, Philippines
SUBANON, TUBOY [STB] lang, Philippines
SUBANON, WESTERN [SUC] lang, Philippines
SUBANUN, LAPUYAN [LAA] lang, Philippines
SUBI alt for SHUBI [SUJ]
SUBIA [SBS] lang, Zambia, Botswana
SUBIYA alt for SUBIA [SBS]
SUBPAN dial of IDA'AN [DBJ]
SUBTIABA [SUT] lang, Nicaragua
SUBU alt for ISU [SZV]
SUCRE dial of QUECHUA, SOUTH BOLIVIAN [QUH]
SUD-EST alt for SUDEST [TGO]
SUDAIR alt for CENTRAL NAJDI dial of ARABIC,
    NAJDI [ARS]
SUDEST [TGO] lang, Papua New Guinea
SUEI alt for KUY [KDT]
SUENA [SUE] lang, Papua New Guinea
SUFRAI dial of TARPIA [SUF]
SUGA [SGI] lang, Cameroon
SUGALI alt for LAMANI [LMN]
SUGANGA [SUG] lang, Papua New Guinea
SUGBUANON alt for CEBUANO [CEB]
SUGBUHANON alt for CEBUANO [CEB]
SUGCESTUN alt for YUPIK, PACIFIC GULF [EMS]
SUGHU alt for GHARI [GRI]
SUGPIAK ESKIMO alt for YUPIK, PACIFIC GULF
    [EMS]
SUGPIAQ ESKIMO alt for YUPIK, PACIFIC GULF

[EMS]
SUGU alt for NUMANGGANG [NOP]
SUGUDI alt for SIGIDI dial of SAYA [SAY]
SUGUR alt for SUKUR [SUK]
SUGURTI dial of KANURI, YERWA [KPH]
SUGUT alt for DUSUN, SUGUT [KZS]
SUGUT KADAZAN alt for DUSUN, SUGUT [KZS]
SUHAID dial of MALAYIC DAYAK [XDY]
SUI [SWI] lang, China
SUI dial of KOL [KOL]
SUI AI dial of SUI [SWI]
SUI LI dial of SUI [SWI]
SUIEI dial of OKIEK [OKI]
SUIEI dial of OMOTIK [OMT]
SUIPO dial of SUI [SWI]
SUIT dial of BILIAU [BCU]
SUJAU alt for SAJAU BASAP [SAD]
SUK alt for PÖKOOT [PKO]
SUK alt for YUPIK, PACIFIC GULF [EMS]
SUKA alt for CHUKA [CUH]
SUKA dial of KABA SO [KXJ]
SUKADANA dial of MALAY [MLI]
SUKANG dial of KADAZAN, LABUK-
    KINABATANGAN [DTB]
SUKARAJA dial of LISABATA-NUNIALI [LCS]
SUKI [SUI] lang, Papua New Guinea
SUKI alt for WAIGALI [WBK]
SUKMA dial of DANDAMI MARIA [DAQ]
SUKU [SUB] lang, Zaïre
SUKU BATIN [SBV] lang, Indonesia, Sumatra
SUKUBATONG [SBT] lang, Indonesia, Irian Jaya
SUKULUMBWE alt for ILA [ILB]
SUKUMA [SUA] lang, Tanzania
SUKUR [SUK] lang, Nigeria
SUKURASE dial of DOGHOSIÉ [DOS]
SUKURUM [SBJ] lang, Papua New Guinea
SULA [SZN] lang, Indonesia, Maluku
SULA alt for DAJU, DAR SILA [DAU]
SULA MANGOLI alt for MANGOLE [MQC]
SULAKA alt for ARABIC, HASSANIYA [MEY]
SULAMU dial of BAJAU, INDONESIAN [BDL]
SULCITANO dial of SARDINIAN, CAMPIDANESE
    [SRO]
SULEIMANIYE alt for SORANI dial of KURDI [KDB]
SULIMA dial of YALUNKA [YAL]
SULKA [SLK] lang, Papua New Guinea
SULMELANG dial of WATUBELA [WAH]
SULOD [SRG] lang, Philippines
SULU alt for TAUSUG [TSG]
SULUD alt for KINARAY-A [KRJ]
SULUK alt for TAUSUG [TSG]
SULUNG [SUV] lang, India
SUMA dial of GBAYA [GYA]
SUMADEL dial of KALINGA, SOUTHERN [KSC]
SUMADEL-TINGLAYAN KALINGA alt for KALINGA,
    SOUTHERN [KSC]
SUMAMBU alt for TAGAL MURUT [MVV]
SUMAMBU dial of TAGAL MURUT [MVV]
SUMAMBU dial of TAGAL MURUT [MVV]
SUMAMBU-TAGAL alt for TAGAL MURUT [MVV]
SUMAMBUQ alt for TAGAL MURUT [MVV]
SUMAMBUQ alt for SUMAMBU dial of TAGAL
    MURUT [MVV]
SUMAMBUQ alt for SUMAMBU dial of TAGAL
    MURUT [MVV]
SUMARE-RANGAS dial of MAMUJU [MQX]

SUMARIUP [SIV] lang, Papua New Guinea
SUMAU [SIX] lang, Papua New Guinea
SUMBA [SMI] lang, Indonesia, Nusa Tenggara
SUMBANESE alt for SUMBA [SMI]
SUMBAWA [SMW] lang, Indonesia, Nusa Tenggara
SUMBAWARESE alt for SUMBAWA [SMW]
SUMBWA [SUW] lang, Tanzania
SUMBWA alt for MWERI dial of NYAMWEZI [NYZ]
SUMCHU alt for SHUMCHO [SCU]
SUMENEP dial of MADURA [MHJ]
SUMERI alt for TANAHMERAH [TCM]
SUMERINE alt for TANAHMERAH [TCM]
SUMO [SUM] lang, Nicaragua, Honduras
SUMOHAI alt for MOMUNA [MQF]
SUMOO alt for SUMO [SUM]
SUMOUN dial of PETATS [PEX]
SUMPO dial of DAYAK, LAND [DYK]
SUMRAI alt for SOMRAI [SOR]
SUMTSU alt for SHUMCHO [SCU]
SUMU alt for SUMO [SUM]
SUMWARI alt for NIKSEK [GBE]
SUNAM [SSK] lang, India
SUNBAR alt for SUNWAR [SUZ]
SUNDA [SUO] lang, Indonesia, Java, Bali
SUNDANESE alt for SUNDA [SUO]
SUNDEI dial of BIAK [BHW]
SUNDI dial of HALBI [HLB]
SUNDONI alt for BASINYARI dial of NUNI [NNW]
SUNGAI alt for SUNGAI, KINABATANGAN [DSB]
SUNGAI alt for TOMBONUWO [TXA]
SUNGAI alt for SUBPAN dial of IDA'AN [DBJ]
SUNGAI PIAH dial of TEMIAR [TMH]
SUNGAI, KINABATANGAN [DSB] lang, Malaysia,
    Sabah
SUNGAM alt for SUNAM [SSK]
SUNGEI alt for SUNGAI, KINABATANGAN [DSB]
SUNGEI alt for TOMBONUWO [TXA]
SUNGGARI dial of NANAI [GLD]
SUNGKAI [SUU] lang, Indonesia, Sumatra
SUNGKAI dial of SEMAI [SEA]
SUNGNAM alt for SUNAM [SSK]
SUNGOR [SUN] lang, Chad, Sudan, Sudan
SUNGOR alt for SUNGOR [SUN]
SUNGOR dial of SUNGOR [SUN]
SUNGU alt for TETELA [TEL]
SUNGU alt for NSONGO [NSX]
SUNKHLA alt for TASHON dial of CHIN, FALAM
    [HBH]
SUNÕÕ dial of SENOUFO, MAMARA [MYK]
SUNTAI alt for SAMBA LEKO [NDI]
SUNTAI alt for SAMBA LEKO dial of SAMBA LEKO
    [NDI]
SUNU TORBI dial of MAMBILA, CAMEROON [MYA]
SUNUWAR alt for SUNWAR [SUZ]
SUNWAR [SUZ] lang, Nepal
SUNWARI alt for SUNWAR [SUZ]
SUOI alt for KUY [KDT]
SUOMO dial of JIARONG [JYA]
SUÒNG PHÓNG alt for CHINESE, YUE [YUH]
SUOY [SYO] lang, Cambodia
SUP'IDE alt for SENOUFO, SUPYIRE [SPP]
SUPAI alt for SAMO-KUBO [SMQ]
SUPAN alt for SUBPAN dial of IDA'AN [DBJ]
SUPARI dial of ARAPESH, SOUTHERN [AOJ]
SUPAT dial of KUBU [KVB]
SUPEI-KUBOR alt for SAMO-KUBO [SMQ]

SUPHANABURI dial of UGONG [UGO]
SUPI alt for SOPI dial of BELI [BLM]
SUPIA alt for SUBIA [SBS]
SUPPIRE alt for SENOUFO, SUPYIRE [SPP]
SUPYIRE alt for SENOUFO, SUPYIRE [SPP]
SUQ alt for SOU [SQQ]
SUQUH dial of SALISH, SOUTHERN PUGET SOUND
 [SLH]
SURA alt for MWAGHAVUL [SUR]
SURABAYA dial of JAVANESE [JAN]
SURANI alt for SORANI dial of KURDI [KDB]
SURARA alt for YANOMÁMI [WCA]
SURATI alt for GAMADIA dial of GUJARATI [GJR]
SURBAKHAL dial of MASALIT [MSA]
SURBM alt for ME'EN [MYM]
SURCHI [SUP] lang, Iraq
SURGUCH dial of BALKAN GAGAUZ TURKISH [BGX]
SURGUJIA dial of CHATTISGARHI [HNE]
SURI alt for TAWBUID, EASTERN [BNJ]
SURI alt for SURMA [SUQ]
SURI alt for KACIPO [KOE]
SURI dial of FOLOPA [PPO]
SURIGAONON [SUL] lang, Philippines
SURIGAONON dial of SURIGAONON [SUL]
SURIN dial of KHMER, NORTHERN [KXM]
SURINAAMS alt for SRANAN [SRN]
SURINAM JAVANESE alt for JAVANESE,
 CARIBBEAN [JVN]
SURINAMESE alt for SRANAN [SRN]
SURINAMESE; SURINAM CREOLE ENGLISH alt for
 SRANAN [SRN]
SURIRÁ alt for SIRIANO [SRI]
SURMA [SUQ] lang, Ethiopia, Sudan
SUROA alt for MACUNA [MYY]
SUROI alt for SIROI [SSD]
SURSURUNGA [SGZ] lang, Papua New Guinea
SURU alt for TAPSHIN [TDL]
SURU-BO dial of APMA [APP]
SURU-MARANI dial of APMA [APP]
SURUBU [SDE] lang, Nigeria
SURUÍ [SRU] lang, Brazil
SURUÍ alt for SURUÍ DO PARÁ [MDZ]
SURUÍ DE RONDÔNIA alt for SURUÍ [SRU]
SURUÍ DO JIPARANÁ alt for SURUÍ [SRU]
SURUÍ DO PARÁ [MDZ] lang, Brazil
SURUVIRI dial of ASHKUN [ASK]
SURYA JAGANNATHI alt for JAGANNATHI [JAG]
SURYANA alt for SIRIANO [SRI]
SURYOYO [SYR] lang, Turkey, Iraq, Syria
SUSA dial of AZERBAIJANI, NORTH [AZE]
SUSHEN alt for NANAI [GLD]
SUSIUA alt for TACHELHIT [SHI]
SUSOO alt for SUSU [SUD]
SUSSEX dial of ENGLISH [ENG]
SUSU [SUD] lang, Guinea, Sierra Leone, Guinea
 Bissau, Sierra Leone
SUSU alt for SUSU [SUD]
SUTHU alt for SOTHO, SOUTHERN [SSO]
SUTI dial of JAGOI [SNE]
SUTO alt for SOTHO, SOUTHERN [SSO]
SUTU alt for NGONI [NGU]
SUUNDI dial of KUNYI [KNF]
SUUNDI dial of KONGO [KON]
SUWA alt for ARABIC, SHUWA [SHU]
SUWA dial of KWAMBA [RWM]
SUWAIRA dial of TAIRORA [TBG]

SUWANNAKHET alt for SAVANNAKHET dial of LAO
 [NOL]
SUWAWA [SWU] lang, Indonesia, Sulawesi
SUWAWA-BUNDA alt for SUWAWA [SWU]
SUYÁ [SUY] lang, Brazil
SUYUNG dial of HMONG, WESTERN [HUJ]
SUZHOU dial of CHINESE, WU [WUU]
SVAN [SVA] lang, Georgia
SVEA dial of SWEDISH [SWD]
SVENSK ROMMANI alt for TRAVELLER SWEDISH
 [RMU]
SWABIAN [SWG] lang, Germany
SWAGA dial of NANDI [NNB]
SWAGUP alt for NGALA [NUD]
SWAHILI [SWA] lang, Tanzania, Kenya, Mayotte,
 Mozambique, Somalia, South Africa, Uganda
SWAHILI alt for SWAHILI [SWA]
SWAHILI, ZAÏRE [SWC] lang, Zaïre
SWAKA dial of LALA-BISA [LEB]
SWARA alt for SORA [SRB]
SWAT KHOWAR dial of KHOWAR [KHW]
SWATI [SWZ] lang, Swaziland, Swaziland, South
 Africa
SWATOW alt for CHAO SHAN dial of CHINESE, MIN
 NAN [CFR]
SWAZI alt for SWATI [SWZ]
SWE'NGA alt for YAMBA [YAM]
SWEDISH [SWD] lang, Sweden, Estonia, Finland
"SWEDISH LAPP" alt for SAAMI, LULE [LPL]
SWEDISH LAPP alt for SAAMI, LULE [LPL]
SWEDISH SIGN LANGUAGE [SWL] lang, Sweden
SWETA dial of KURIA [KUJ]
"SWINA" alt for SHONA [SHD]
SWINOMISH alt for SKAGIT [SKA]
SWISS GERMAN alt for SCHWYZERDÜTSCH [GSW]
SWISS SIGN LANGUAGE [SSR] lang, Switzerland
SWOSE alt for BASSOSSI [BSI]
SYA dial of BOBO FING [BBO]
SYAN dial of MASABA [MYX]
SYANGJA GURUNG alt for SOUTHERN GURUNG dial
 of GURUNG [GVR]
SYÉMOU alt for SIAMOU [SIF]
SYENERE alt for SENOUFO, CEBAARA [SEF]
SYER dial of KARABORO, WESTERN [KZA]
SYER-TENYER alt for KARABORO, WESTERN [KZA]
SYIAGHA alt for SIAGHA-YENIMU [OSR]
SYLHETTI [SYL] lang, Bangladesh, United Kingdom
SYLHETTI BANGLA alt for SYLHETTI [SYL]
SYLT alt for SALRENG dial of FRISIAN, NORTHERN
 [FRR]
SYM dial of EVENKI [EVN]
SYMIARTA alt for SINYAR [SYS]
SYNTENG alt for PNAR [PBV]
SYRIA dial of ARMENIAN [ARM]
SYRIAC alt for SURYOYO [SYR]
SYRIAN ARAMAIC alt for SURYOYO [SYR]
SYRIEN alt for SYRIA dial of ARMENIAN [ARM]
SYRMIA alt for SREM dial of ALBANIAN, TOSK
 [ALN]
SYRYOYO alt for SURYOYO [SYR]
SYUBA alt for KAGATE [SYW]
SZEAK-BAGILI alt for GEDAGED [GDD]
SZEKELY dial of HUNGARIAN [HNG]
SZI alt for ATSI [ATB]
SZUCHI alt for TAISHUN dial of CHINESE, MIN NAN
 [CFR]

TAGAL alt for PENSIANGAN MURUT dial of TAGAL
MURUT [MVV]
TAGAL alt for PENSIANGAN MURUT dial of TAGAL
MURUT [MVV]
TAGAL MURUT [MVV] lang, Malaysia, Sabah,
Indonesia, Kalimantan
TAGALAGAD alt for BLAAN, KORONADAL [BIK]
TAGALE alt for TEGALI [RAS]
TAGALISA dial of LISELA [LCL]
TAGALOG [TGL] lang, Philippines, USA
TAGARA alt for DURUWA [PCI]
TAGARA dial of SENOUFO, CEBAARA [SEF]
TAGARO alt for KADAZAN-TAGARO dial of DUSUN,
CENTRAL [DTP]
TAGAU dial of PASHAYI, SOUTHWEST [PSH]
TAGAUR dial of OSETIN [OSE]
TAGBA alt for SÉNOUFO, SÌCÌTÉ [SEP]
TAGBA alt for TAGBU [TBM]
TAGBANA alt for SENOUFO, TAGWANA [TGW]
TAGBANWA [TBW] lang, Philippines
TAGBANWA, CALAMIAN [TBK] lang, Philippines
TAGBANWA, CENTRAL [TGT] lang, Philippines
TAGBARI dial of SENOUFO, CEBAARA [SEF]
TAGBO alt for TOGBO [TOR]
TAGBO alt for MAMBILA, CAMEROON [MYA]
TAGBO alt for TAGBU [TBM]
TAGBU [TBM] lang, Central African Republic, Zaïre,
Zaïre
TAGBU alt for TAGBU [TBM]
TAGBWALI alt for TOGBO [TOR]
TAGE alt for KREYE [XRE]
TAGGAL alt for PENSIANGAN MURUT dial of TAGAL
MURUT [MVV]
TAGGAL alt for PENSIANGAN MURUT dial of TAGAL
MURUT [MVV]
TAGHDANSH alt for AZER dial of SONINKE [SNN]
TAGINAMBUR alt for BUNDU dial of DUSUN,
CENTRAL [DTP]
TAGISH [TGX] lang, Canada
TAGKHUL alt for NAGA, TANGKHUL [NMF]
TÀGÓBÉ dial of AJA-GBE [AJG]
TAGOI [TAG] lang, Sudan
TAGOI dial of TAGOI [TAG]
TAGOL alt for TAGAL dial of TAGAL MURUT [MVV]
TAGOL alt for PENSIANGAN MURUT dial of TAGAL
MURUT [MVV]
TAGOL alt for PENSIANGAN MURUT dial of TAGAL
MURUT [MVV]
TAGOTA dial of MERIAM [ULK]
TAGOUNA alt for SENOUFO, TAGWANA [TGW]
TAGOY alt for TAGOI [TAG]
TAGUL alt for PENSIANGAN MURUT dial of TAGAL
MURUT [MVV]
TAGUL alt for PENSIANGAN MURUT dial of TAGAL
MURUT [MVV]
TAGULA alt for SUDEST [TGO]
TAGULANDANG alt for TAHULANDANG [THY]
TAGWANA alt for SENOUFO, TAGWANA [TGW]
TAHAGGART alt for HOGGAR dial of TAMAHAQ,
HOGGAR [THV]
TAHAMBA dial of BANDI [GBA]
TAHARI alt for GUHU-SAMANE [GHS]
TAHITIAN [THT] lang, French Polynesia, New
Caledonia, New Caledonia, New Zealand,
Vanuatu
TAHITIAN alt for TAHITIAN [THT]

TAHLTAN [TAH] lang, Canada
TAHOUA alt for TAMAJEQ, TAHOUA [TTQ]
TAHUERH alt for DAUR [DTA]
TAHULANDANG [THY] lang, Indonesia, Sulawesi
TAHUP alt for TAUP dial of JAGOI [SNE]
TAHUR alt for DAUR [DTA]
TAHUTA dial of MARQUESAN, SOUTH [QMS]
TAHYLANDANG alt for TAHULANDANG [THY]
TAI [TAW] lang, Papua New Guinea
TAI alt for DAI [TIZ]
TAI dial of KOANA [KEH]
TAI AHOM alt for AHOM [AHO]
TAI BLANC alt for TAI DÓN [TWH]
TAI CHE alt for DAI [TIZ]
TAI CHUANG alt for ZHUANG, NORTHERN [CCX]
TAI CHUNG alt for YA [YYA]
TAI DAENG [TYR] lang, Viet Nam, Laos
TAI DAM [BLT] lang, Viet Nam, China, Laos,
Thailand
TAI DENG alt for TAI DAENG [TYR]
TAI DO alt for TAI DAM [BLT]
TAI DÓN [TWH] lang, Viet Nam, China, Laos
TAI HANG TONG [THC] lang, Viet Nam
TAI ISLAM alt for THAI MALAY dial of TAI,
SOUTHERN [SOU]
TAI KA alt for TAI PONG dial of TAI NÜA [TDD]
TAI KAM TI alt for KHAMTI [KHT]
TAI KAO alt for TAI DÓN [TWH]
TAI KHUN alt for KHÜN [KKH]
TAI KONG alt for TAI NÜA [TDD]
TAI LAI alt for TAI DÓN [TWH]
TAI LAKA alt for LAKA [LBC]
TAI LAO alt for LAO [NOL]
TAI LATI alt for LATI [LBT]
TAI LE alt for TAI NÜA [TDD]
TAI LOI [TLQ] lang, Myanmar, Laos
TAI LOI dial of TAI LOI [TLQ]
TAI LONG [THI] lang, Laos
TAI LONG alt for TAI MAO dial of SHAN [SJN]
TAI LU alt for LÜ [KHB]
TAI LUANG alt for SHAN [SJN]
TAI LUE alt for LÜ [KHB]
TAI MAEN [TMP] lang, Laos
TAI MAN THANH [TMM] lang, Viet Nam
TAI MAO dial of SHAN [SJN]
TAI MUEAI alt for TÁY MU'Ò'I dial of TAI DAM
[BLT]
TAI MUEI alt for TAI MUOI dial of TAI DAM [BLT]
TAI MUOI dial of TAI DAM [BLT]
TAI NEUA alt for TAI NÜA [TDD]
TAI NOIR alt for TAI DAM [BLT]
TAI NÜA [TDD] lang, China, Myanmar, Laos,
Myanmar
TAI NÜA alt for TAI NÜA [TDD]
TAI NUEA alt for TAI NÜA [TDD]
TAI NUNG alt for NUNG [NUT]
TAI NUNG alt for CHINESE, YUE [YUH]
TAI NYA alt for TAI, NORTHERN [NOD]
TAI PAO [TPO] lang, Laos
TAI PHONG alt for PONG 1 [KPN]
TAI PONG alt for TAI NÜA [TDD]
TAI ROUGE alt for TAI DAENG [TYR]
TAI SEK alt for SAEK [SKB]
TAI SHAN alt for SHAN [SJN]
TAI TAK BAI alt for TAK BAI dial of TAI, SOUTHERN
[SOU]

TAKPA alt for NUPE CENTRAL dial of NUPE [NUP]
TAKPASYEERI dial of SENOUFO, CEBAARA [SEF]
TAKU alt for TAKUU [NHO]
TAKU alt for LIPO [TKL]
TAKU LISU alt for LIPO [TKL]
TAKUA [TKZ] lang, Viet Nam
TAKUDH alt for WESTERN CANADA GWICH'IN dial of GWICH'IN [KUC]
TAKUM dial of JUKUN TAKUM [JBU]
TAKUNA alt for TUCANO [TUO]
TAKUU [NHO] lang, Papua New Guinea
TAKWAMA alt for KOMA, NORTH [KMQ]
TAL [TAL] lang, Nigeria
TAL alt for TULU [TCY]
TALA [TAK] lang, Nigeria
TALA alt for WEMALE, SOUTH [TLW]
TALA dial of KOHO [KPM]
TALA INGOD dial of MANOBO, MATIGSALUG [MBT]
TALA'AI dial of SAHU [SUX]
TALAE alt for TERMANU-TALAE-KEKA dial of ROTI [ROT]
TALAHUNDRA dial of KALANGA [KCK]
TALAI [TLE] lang, Kenya
TALAINDJI alt for DHALANDJI [DHL]
TALAING alt for MON [MNW]
TALAING KAYIN alt for KAREN, PWO [PWO]
TALAING KAYIN alt for KAREN, PWO OMKOI [PWW]
TALAMANCA alt for BRIBRI [BZD]
TALANDI alt for DHALANDJI [DHL]
TALANDJI alt for DHALANDJI [DHL]
TALANG dial of KERINCI [KVR]
TALANG PADANG dial of PESISIR, SOUTHERN [PEC]
TALANGEE alt for DHALANDJI [DHL]
TALANGIT dial of ALTAI, SOUTHERN [ALT]
TALANGIT-TOLOS alt for TALANGIT dial of ALTAI, SOUTHERN [ALT]
TALANSI alt for TALNI dial of MAMPRULI [MAW]
TALANTANG dial of DUSUN, SUGUT [KZS]
TALASA alt for TALASSA dial of TUMTUM [TBR]
TALASSA dial of TUMTUM [TBR]
TALAU alt for TALLAU dial of LIGURI [LIU]
TALAUD [TLD] lang, Indonesia, Sulawesi
TALAUT alt for TALAUD [TLD]
TALAVIA alt for DUBLA [DUB]
TALE dial of KARI [KBN]
TALE dial of KARI [KBN]
TALENE alt for TALNI dial of MAMPRULI [MAW]
TALENG alt for MON [MNW]
TALENSI alt for TALNI dial of MAMPRULI [MAW]
TALESH alt for TALYSH [TLY]
TALI dial of BAI [PIQ]
TALI alt for TALE dial of KARI [KBN]
TALIABO alt for TALIABU [TLV]
TALIABU [TLV] lang, Indonesia, Maluku
TALIANG alt for TALIENG [TDF]
TALIÁSERI alt for TARIANO [TAE]
TALIENG [TDF] lang, Laos
TALIENG alt for TRIENG [STG]
TALIFUGU-RIPANG dial of ISNAG [ISD]
TALINGA-BWISI [TLJ] lang, Zaïre, Uganda
TALISE [TLR] lang, Solomon Islands
TALISE dial of TALISE [TLR]
TALISE dial of BAETORA [BTR]
TALISH alt for TALYSH [TLY]
TALISI alt for TALISE [TLR]
TALLA alt for KADUGLI dial of KATCHA-KADUGLI-

MIRI [KAT]
TALLAINGA alt for DHALANDJI [DHL]
TALLAU dial of LIGURI [LIU]
TALLENSI alt for TALNI dial of MAMPRULI [MAW]
TALLINN dial of ESTONIAN [EST]
TALLULEMBANGNA alt for MAKALE dial of TORAJA-SA'DAN [SDA]
TALLUMPANUAE alt for CAMPALAGIAN [CML]
TALNI dial of MAMPRULI [MAW]
TALNI dial of GURENNE [GUR]
TALO alt for TALLAU dial of LIGURI [LIU]
TALODDA alt for TALAUD [TLD]
TALODI [TLO] lang, Sudan
TALOINGA alt for DHALANDJI [DHL]
TALOKA alt for NGILE [MAS]
TALOKA alt for DALOKA dial of NGILE [MAS]
TALOKI [TLK] lang, Indonesia, Sulawesi
TALOMA alt for RUKAI [DRU]
TALONDO' [TLN] lang, Indonesia, Sulawesi
TALUKI alt for TALOKI [TLK]
TALUR [ILW] lang, Indonesia, Maluku
TALUTI alt for TELUTI [TLT]
TALYSH [TLY] lang, Azerbaijan, Iran, Iran
TALYSH alt for TALYSH [TLY]
TAMA [TEN] lang, Colombia
TAMA [TMA] lang, Chad, Sudan, Sudan
TAMA alt for MAJANG [MPE]
TAMA alt for NAMA [NAQ]
TAMA alt for TAMA [TMA]
TAMA dial of TAMA [TMA]
TAMACHEK alt for TAMAHAQ, HOGGAR [THV]
TAMACHEK alt for TAMAJEQ, AIR [THZ]
TAMACHEK alt for TAMAJEQ, TAHOUA [TTQ]
TAMACHHANG [RAX] lang, Nepal
TAMACHHANGE RAI alt for TAMACHHANG [RAX]
TAMAGARAST alt for TANASSFARWAT dial of TAMAJEQ, AIR [THZ]
TAMAGARIO [TCG] lang, Indonesia, Irian Jaya
TAMAHA alt for TSAMAI [TSB]
TAMAHAQ, HOGGAR [THV] lang, Algeria, Libya, Libya, Niger
TAMAHAQ, HOGGAR alt for TAMAHAQ, HOGGAR [THV]
TAMAJA alt for SAMAROKENA [TMJ]
TAMAJAQ alt for TAMAJEQ, TAHOUA [TTQ]
TAMAJEQ, AIR [THZ] lang, Niger
TAMAJEQ, TAHOUA [TTQ] lang, Niger, Mali, Nigeria
TAMAJEQ, TAHOUA alt for TAMAJEQ, TAHOUA [TTQ]
TAMAKO dial of SANGIR [SAN]
TAMAKWA alt for NAMA [NAQ]
TAMAL alt for TAMIL [TCV]
TAMAL EUY dial of OY [OYB]
TAMALSAN alt for TAMIL [TCV]
TAMALU dial of RAWANG [RAW]
TAMAN [TCL] lang, Myanmar
TAMAN [TMN] lang, Indonesia, Kalimantan
TAMAN alt for MALFAXAL [MLX]
TAMAN alt for HARUAI [TMD]
TAMAN DAYAK alt for TAMAN [TMN]
TAMANG, EASTERN [TAJ] lang, Nepal, India
TAMANG, NORTHWESTERN [TDG] lang, Nepal
TAMANG, SOUTHWESTERN [TSF] lang, Nepal
TAMANIK alt for TIMA [TMS]
TAMANRASSET dial of ARABIC, ALGERIAN [ARQ]
TAMARA alt for TAMARIA [TDB]

TAMARAW alt for TAMAGARIO [TCG]
TAMARI alt for TAMBERMA [SOF]
TAMARI alt for DITAMMARI [TBZ]
TAMARI alt for PAIWAN [PWN]
TAMARIA [TDB] lang, India
TAMASHEKIN alt for TAMAHAQ, HOGGAR [THV]
TAMASHEKIN alt for TAMASHEQ, TIMBUKTU [TAQ]
TAMASHEKIN alt for TAMAJEQ, TAHOUA [TTQ]
TAMASHEQ alt for TAMAHAQ, HOGGAR [THV]
TAMASHEQ alt for TAMAJEQ, TAHOUA [TTQ]
TAMASHEQ, TIMBUKTU [TAQ] lang, Mali, Burkina
    Faso
TAMAYA alt for SAMAROKENA [TMJ]
TAMAZIGHT [TZM] lang, Morocco, Algeria
TAMAZULAPAM MIXE alt for MIXE,
    NORTHEASTERN [MVE]
TAMAZUNCHALE AZTEC alt for NAHUATL,
    HUASTECA, WESTERN [NHW]
TAMBAGGO alt for TANGBAGO [TGM]
TAMBAHOAKA dial of MALAGASY [MEX]
TAMBANI dial of TAROF [TCF]
TAMBANUA alt for TOMBONUWO [TXA]
TAMBANUO alt for TOMBONUWO [TXA]
TAMBANUVA alt for TOMBONUWO [TXA]
TAMBANWAS alt for TOMBONUWO [TXA]
TAMBARO dial of KAMBAATA [KTB]
TAMBAS [TDK] lang, Nigeria
TAMBATU alt for PEMBA dial of SWAHILI [SWA]
TAMBE'E dial of MORI BAWAH [XMZ]
TAMBENUA alt for TOMBONUWO [TXA]
TAMBÉOPÉ dial of GUARANÍ, MBYÁ [GUN]
TAMBERMA [SOF] lang, Togo
TAMBES alt for TAMBAS [TDK]
TAMBO dial of MWANGA [MWN]
TAMBO dial of MWANGA [MWN]
TAMBO alt for BWAZZA dial of MBULA-BWAZZA
    [MBU]
TAMBOGO alt for TANGBAGO [TGM]
TAMBOKA alt for TUMBUKA [TUW]
TAMBOKI dial of MEKONGGA [MWK]
TAMBOPATA-GUARAYO alt for ESE EJJA [ESE]
TAMBOTALO [TLS] lang, Vanuatu
TAMBUKA alt for TUMBUKA [TUW]
TAMBUL alt for TAMIL [TCV]
TAMBUNAN alt for DUSUN, TAMBUNAN [KZT]
TAMBUNWAS alt for TOMBONUWO [TXA]
TAMBUOKI alt for TAMBOKI dial of MEKONGGA
    [MWK]
TAME alt for IDI [IDI]
TAME alt for AGÖB [KIT]
TAMEZRET [TMZ] lang, Tunisia
TAMHER TIMUR dial of WATUBELA [WAH]
TAMI [TMY] lang, Papua New Guinea
TAMIL [TCV] lang, India, Mauritius, South Africa,
    Malaysia, Peninsular, Singapore, Sri Lanka,
    Thailand
TAMIL alt for TAMIL [TCV]
TAMIL dial of TAMIL [TCV]
TAMILI alt for TAMIL [TCV]
TAMILOUW alt for SEPA [SPB]
TAMISO alt for CENTRAL dial of LIMBA, WEST-
    CENTRAL [LIA]
TAMKHUNGNYUO dial of NAGA, KONYAK [NBE]
TAMLU NAGA alt for NAGA, PHOM [NPH]
TAMMA alt for NAMA [NAQ]
TAMNIM alt for CITAK, TAMNIM [TML]

TAMOK alt for TAMA [TMA]
TAMONGOBO alt for TAMA [TMA]
TAMOT alt for TAMA [TMA]
TAMPASOK alt for DUSUN, TEMPASUK [TDU]
TAMPASSUK alt for DUSUN, TEMPASUK [TDU]
TAMPASUK alt for DUSUN, TEMPASUK [TDU]
TAMPELE alt for TAMPULMA [TAM]
TAMPIWI dial of CUIBA [CUI]
TAMPLIMA alt for TAMPULMA [TAM]
TAMPOLE alt for TAMPULMA [TAM]
TAMPOLEM alt for TAMPULMA [TAM]
TAMPOLENSE alt for TAMPULMA [TAM]
TAMPRUSI alt for TAMPULMA [TAM]
TAMPUAN [TPU] lang, Cambodia
TAMPUEN alt for TAMPUAN [TPU]
TAMPULMA [TAM] lang, Ghana
TAMPUON alt for TAMPUAN [TPU]
TAMPUR dial of GAYO [GYO]
TAMSANGMU dial of LEPCHA [LEP]
TAMUDES alt for TOMEDES [TOE]
TAMUN alt for CHRAU [CHR]
TAMUN dial of CHRAU [CHR]
TANA [TNQ] lang, Central African Republic
TANA AI dial of SIKKA [SKI]
TANA RIGHU dial of WEYEWA [WEW]
TANA TOA dial of KONJO, COASTAL [KJC]
TANA TOWA alt for TANA TOA dial of KONJO,
    COASTAL [KJC]
TANA-LINCHA dial of QUECHUA, YAUYOS [QUX]
TANACROSS dial of TANANA, UPPER [TAU]
TANAGHAI alt for TANDAI-NGGARIA dial of GHARI
    [GRI]
TANAH alt for AMIS [ALV]
TANAH dial of MINANGKABAU [MPU]
TANAH KUNU alt for LIO [LJL]
TANAH MERAH alt for TABLA [TNM]
TANAHMERAH [TCM] lang, Indonesia, Irian Jaya
TANAINA [TFN] lang, USA
TANALA dial of MALAGASY [MEX]
TANALANA dial of MALAGASY [MEX]
TANAN dial of RUKAI [DRU]
TANANA [TAA] lang, USA
TANANA, UPPER [TAU] lang, USA, Canada
TANAPAG alt for NORTHERN CAROLINIAN dial of
    CAROLINIAN [CAL]
TANASLAMT alt for TIMBUKTU dial of TAMASHEQ,
    TIMBUKTU [TAQ]
TANASSFARWAT dial of TAMAJEQ, AIR [THZ]
TANAY-PAETE dial of TAGALOG [TGL]
TANCHANGYA alt for TANGCHANGYA [TNV]
TANDA alt for LAMANI [LMN]
TANDA dial of LOBALA [LOQ]
TANDAI-NGGARIA dial of GHARI [GRI]
TANDANKE alt for BUDIK [TNR]
TANDEK dial of KIMARAGANG [KQR]
TANDIA [TNI] lang, Indonesia, Irian Jaya
TANDO alt for NDOLO [NDL]
TANDUBAS dial of SAMA, SOUTHERN [SIT]
TANE alt for TANA [TNQ]
TANEMA [TNX] lang, Solomon Islands
TANETE alt for BARRU dial of BUGIS [BPR]
TANG alt for SEDANG [SED]
TANG dial of NAGA, KONYAK [NBE]
TANG dial of LIMBUM [LIM]
TANGA alt for TANGGA [TGG]
TANGA dial of TANGGA [TGG]

TANGA alt for DOTANGA dial of BALUNDU-BIMA [NGO]
TANGAGO alt for TANGBAGO [TGM]
TANGALAN alt for KETANGALAN [KAE]
TANGALE [TAN] lang, Nigeria
TANGAMMA dial of WAAMA [WWA]
TANGAO alt for ATAYAL [TAY]
TANGARA' alt for TENGARA dial of BAUKAN [BNB]
TANGARARE alt for GHARI [GRI]
TANGBAGO [TGM] lang, Central African Republic, Sudan
TANGCHANGYA [TNV] lang, Bangladesh
TANGETTI alt for DYANGADI [DYN]
TANGGA [TGG] lang, Papua New Guinea
TANGGAL alt for DUSUN, SUGUT [KZS]
TANGGARAQ alt for TENGARA dial of BAUKAN [BNB]
TANGGU [TGU] lang, Papua New Guinea
TANGGUM alt for TANGGU [TGU]
TANGI dial of NANDI [NNB]
TANGKHUL alt for NAGA, TANGKHUL [NMF]
TANGKOU [TGK] lang, Indonesia, Sulawesi
TANGLAGAN dial of AGTA, DUPANINAN [DUO]
TANGLAPUI [TPG] lang, Indonesia, Nusa Tenggara
TANGLE alt for TANGALE [TAN]
TANGOA [TGP] lang, Vanuatu
TANGSA alt for NAGA, TASE [NST]
TANGSARR dial of RAWANG [RAW]
TANGSHEWI [TNF] lang, Afghanistan
TANGSHURI alt for TANGSHEWI [TNF]
TANGU alt for TANGGU [TGU]
TANGUAT [TBS] lang, Papua New Guinea
TANI alt for MIANI [PLA]
TANI alt for MAIANI [TNH]
TANIMA alt for TANEMA [TNX]
TANIMBAR KEI dial of KEI [KEI]
TANIMBILI [TBE] lang, Solomon Islands
TANIMUCA-RETUARÃ [TNC] lang, Colombia
TANJONG [TNJ] lang, Malaysia, Sarawak
TANJONG RAMBUTAN dial of TEMIAR [TMH]
TANJUNG BUNDA alt for SOUTH LAMAHOLOT dial of LAMAHOLOT [SLP]
TANKARANA dial of MALAGASY [MEX]
TANKAY alt for BEZANOZANO dial of MALAGASY [MEX]
TANKIRI alt for CENTRAL KONO dial of KONO [KNO]
TANNA, NORTH [TNN] lang, Vanuatu
TANNA, SOUTHWEST [NWI] lang, Vanuatu
TANNEKWE alt for GANI-KHWE [GNX]
TANNU-TUVA alt for TUVIN [TUN]
TANORIKI alt for MAEWO, CENTRAL [MWO]
TANORIKI dial of MAEWO, CENTRAL [MWO]
TANOSY dial of MALAGASY [MEX]
TAÑYGUÁ dial of GUARANÍ, PARAGUAYAN [GUG]
TAO dial of WOBE [WOB]
TAO-SUAMATO [TSX] lang, Papua New Guinea
TAO-SUAME alt for TAO-SUAMATO [TSX]
TA'OIH, LOWER [TTO] lang, Laos
TA'OIH, UPPER [TTH] lang, Laos, USA, Viet Nam
TAOKA alt for TAOKAS [TOA]
TAOKAS [TOA] lang, Taiwan
TAOKAT alt for TAOKAS [TOA]
TAOOLENDE dial of MOORE [MHM]
TAORI alt for TOLITAI [TDS]
TAORI-KAIY alt for KAIY [TCQ]
TAORI-KEI alt for KAIY [TCQ]

TAORI-SO alt for TOLITAI [TDS]
TAOS dial of TIWA, NORTHERN [TAO]
TAOSUG alt for TAUSUG [TSG]
TAOUJJOUT [TJJ] lang, Tunisia
TAOYUAN dial of CHINESE, HAKKA [HAK]
TAPA alt for NUPE CENTRAL dial of NUPE [NUP]
TAPACUA alt for XAVÁNTE [XAV]
TAPADAMTENG dial of DZONGKHA [DZO]
TAPAH dial of SIKULE [SKH]
TAPANGO alt for PANNEI [PNC]
TAPANGO dial of PANNEI [PNC]
TAPANGU dial of TSOU [TSY]
TAPANTA alt for ABAZA [ABQ]
TAPANTA dial of ABAZA [ABQ]
TAPAYÚNA alt for BEIÇO DE PAU dial of SUYÁ [SUY]
TAPEBA [TBB] lang, Brazil
TAPESSI alt for TIAPI dial of LANDOMA [LAO]
TAPIETÉ [TAI] lang, Paraguay, Argentina, Bolivia
TAPIRAPÉ [TAF] lang, Brazil
TAPIRO alt for EKARI [EKG]
TAPITN dial of MALAYIC DAYAK [XDY]
TAPOSA alt for TOPOSA [TOQ]
TAPPAH alt for NUPE CENTRAL dial of NUPE [NUP]
TAPPALANG dial of ULUMANDA' [ULM]
TAPSHIN [TDL] lang, Nigeria
TAPSHINAWA alt for TAPSHIN [TDL]
TAPU dial of CHINESE, HAKKA [HAK]
TAPUHOE dial of TUAMOTUAN [PMT]
TAR BAGRIMMA alt for BAGIRMI [BMI]
TAR BARMA alt for BAGIRMI [BMI]
TAR BINAMA alt for BINANA dial of KENGA [KYQ]
TAR CENE alt for CENGA dial of KENGA [KYQ]
TARA alt for PONGU [PON]
TARA dial of KAILI, LEDO [LEW]
TARA dial of TATAR [TTR]
TARA BAAKA alt for BAKA [BDH]
TARABA alt for NYA TARIYA dial of LONGUDA [LNU]
TARAHUMARA BAJA [TAC] lang, Mexico
TARAHUMARA, CENTRAL [TAR] lang, Mexico
TARAHUMARA, NORTHERN [THH] lang, Mexico
TARAHUMARA, SOUTHWEST [TWR] lang, Mexico
TARAIKA dial of AINU [AIN]
TARAKAN dial of TIDONG [TID]
TARAKIRI EAST dial of IJO, CENTRAL-WESTERN [IJC]
TARAKIRI WEST dial of IJO, CENTRAL-WESTERN [IJC]
TARALI KHAM alt for KAIKE [KZQ]
TARAM [TAX] lang, Cameroon
TARAMA-MINNA dial of MIYAKO [MVI]
TARANAKI dial of MAORI [MBF]
TARANCHI dial of UYGHUR [UIG]
TARANCHI dial of UYGHUR [UIG]
TARANCHI alt for ILI dial of UYGHUR [UIG]
TARANG alt for BLAGAR [BEU]
TARANGAN, EAST [TRE] lang, Indonesia, Maluku
TARANGAN, WEST [TXN] lang, Indonesia, Maluku
TARAO alt for NAGA, TARAO [TRO]
TARAON alt for DIGARO [MHU]
TARAPECOSI alt for CHIQUITANO [CAX]
TARASAG alt for NUME [TGS]
TARASCAN alt for TARASCO [TSZ]
TARASCO [TSZ] lang, Mexico
TARATARA dial of TOMBULU [TOM]

TARAVAIA alt for MIHIROA dial of TUAMOTUAN [PMT]
TARDROY alt for ANTARDROY 1 dial of MALAGASY [MEX]
TAREH alt for TRIENG [STG]
TAREMP alt for KATBOL [TMB]
TARENG [TGR] lang, Laos
TARFIA alt for TARPIA dial of TARPIA [SUF]
TARGARI alt for DHARGARI [DHR]
TARGUMIC alt for JUDEO-ARAMAIC [TRG]
TARIÂNA alt for TARIANO [TAE]
TARIANG alt for TARENG [TGR]
TARIANG alt for TALIENG [TDF]
TARIANO [TAE] lang, Brazil, Colombia, Colombia
TARIANO alt for TARIANO [TAE]
TARIFIT [RIF] lang, Morocco, Algeria
TARIMUKI dial of GUJARATI [GJR]
TARINO alt for WANECI [WNE]
TARIYA alt for CARA [CFD]
TARKARRI alt for DHARGARI [DHR]
TARMA-JUNÍN QUECHUA alt for QUECHUA, NORTH JUNÍN [QJU]
TAROBI alt for VERE dial of NAKANAI [NAK]
TAROF [TCF] lang, Indonesia, Irian Jaya
TAROF dial of TAROF [TCF]
TAROK [YER] lang, Nigeria
TAROKO [TRV] lang, Taiwan
TAROM dial of TAKESTANI [TKS]
TARON alt for RAWANG [RAW]
TARON dial of RAWANG [RAW]
TARPIA [SUF] lang, Indonesia, Irian Jaya
TARPIA dial of TARPIA [SUF]
TARTAR alt for TATAR [TTR]
TARTU dial of ESTONIAN [EST]
TARU alt for TAUNGYO [TCO]
TARUMBAL alt for BAYALI [BJY]
TARUNA dial of SANGIR [SAN]
TARUNGGARE alt for TUNGGARE [TRT]
TARUW alt for DANU dial of BURMESE [BMS]
TARYA dial of KAMORO [KGQ]
TASADAY dial of MANOBO, COTABATO [MTA]
TASAWAQ alt for NORTHERN SONGAI dial of SONGAI [SON]
TASE alt for NAGA, TASE [NST]
TASEMBOKO alt for LENGO [LGR]
TASEY alt for NAGA, TASE [NST]
TASHELHIT alt for TACHELHIT [SHI]
TASHILHEET alt for TACHELHIT [SHI]
TASHOM alt for TASHON dial of CHIN, FALAM [HBH]
TASHON dial of CHIN, FALAM [HBH]
TASI alt for HALIA [HLA]
TASI FETO alt for NORTHERN TETUN dial of TETUN [TTM]
TASI MANE alt for SOUTHERN TETUN dial of TETUN [TTM]
TASIKO dial of LEWO [LWW]
TASING alt for CAMPALAGIAN [CML]
TASIRIKI alt for AKEI [TSR]
TASMAN alt for NUKUMANU [NUQ]
TASMATE [TMT] lang, Vanuatu
TASOUSSIT alt for TACHELHIT [SHI]
TAT, HEBREW [TAT] lang, Iran, Russia, Europe, Russia, Europe
TAT, HEBREW alt for TAT, HEBREW [TAT]
TAT, MUSSULMAN [TTT] lang, Iran, Azerbaijan

TATA'ER alt for TATAR [TTR]
TATANA [TXX] lang, Malaysia, Sabah
TATANA' alt for TATANA [TXX]
TATANAQ alt for TATANA [TXX]
TATAR [TTR] lang, Russia, Europe, Afghanistan, China, Finland, Turkey
TATAR alt for TATAR [TTR]
TATAU dial of MANDARA [TBF]
TATE [TBD] lang, Papua New Guinea
TÂTE dial of BINE [ORM]
TATI alt for GABAKE-NTSHORI [GZZ]
TATI alt for TATE [TBD]
TATI alt for TAT, MUSSULMAN [TTT]
TATI dial of MAITHILI [MKP]
TATI BUSHMAN alt for GABAKE-NTSHORI [GZZ]
TATOG alt for DATOGA [TCC]
TATOGA alt for DATOGA [TCC]
"TATTARE" alt for TRAVELLER NORWEGIAN [RMG]
"TATTARE" alt for TRAVELLER SWEDISH [RMU]
TATU alt for TARTU dial of ESTONIAN [EST]
TATURU alt for DATOGA [TCC]
TATUTAPUYO alt for TATUYO [TAV]
TATUYO [TAV] lang, Colombia
TAU alt for TAKUU [NHO]
TAU dial of KWANGA [KWJ]
TAU alt for MASEMOLA dial of SOTHO, NORTHERN [SRT]
TAU OI alt for TA'OIH, UPPER [TTH]
TAU UBIAN alt for UBIAN dial of SAMA, SOUTHERN [SIT]
TAUADE [TTD] lang, Papua New Guinea
TAUATA alt for TAUADE [TTD]
TAUBUID alt for TAWBUID, EASTERN [BNJ]
TAUIRA alt for TAWIRA dial of MÍSKITO [MIQ]
TAUJJUT alt for TAOUJJOUT [TJJ]
TAULIL dial of TAULIL-BUTAM [TUH]
TAULIL-BUTAM [TUH] lang, Papua New Guinea
TAULIPANG dial of PEMON [AOC]
TAULIPANG alt for TAUREPAN dial of PEMON [AOC]
TAUMAKO dial of PILENI [PIV]
TAUNA dial of AWA [AWB]
TAUNG dial of SOTHO, SOUTHERN [SSO]
TAUNGTHU alt for KAREN, PA'O [BLK]
TAUNGYO [TCO] lang, Myanmar
TAUNITA dial of TEOP [TIO]
TAUP dial of JAGOI [SNE]
TAUPOTA [TPA] lang, Papua New Guinea
TAURA [TDM] lang, Nigeria
TAURAP alt for BURMESO [BZU]
TAUREPAN dial of PEMON [AOC]
TAUREPAN alt for TAULIPANG dial of PEMON [AOC]
TAUSE [TAD] lang, Indonesia, Irian Jaya
TAUSHIRO [TRR] lang, Peru
TAUSOG alt for TAUSUG [TSG]
TAUSUG [TSG] lang, Philippines, Indonesia, Kalimantan, Malaysia, Sabah
TAUU alt for TAKUU [NHO]
TAUYA [TYA] lang, Papua New Guinea
TAVA alt for RABAH dial of HRE [HRE]
TAVALA alt for TAWALA [TBO]
TAVARA alt for TAWALA [TBO]
TAVARA alt for TAWALA dial of TAWALA [TBO]
TAVAST alt for HÄME dial of FINNISH [FIN]
TAVDIN alt for SOUTHERN VOGUL dial of MANSI [MNS]

TAVEAK dial of AMBRYM, SOUTHEAST [TVK]
TAVETA [TVS] lang, Kenya, Tanzania, Tanzania
TAVETA alt for TAVETA [TVS]
TAVGI SAMOYED alt for NGANASAN [NIO]
TAVHA-TSINDI dial of VENDA [VEN]
TAVHATSINDI dial of VENDA [VEN]
TAVIAK alt for TAVEAK dial of AMBRYM,
    SOUTHEAST [TVK]
TAVOLA alt for VAGHUA [TVA]
TAVORA alt for TAWALA [TBO]
TAVOYA alt for TAUNGYO [TCO]
TAVOYAN [TVN] lang, Myanmar
TAVOYAN alt for TAUNGYO [TCO]
TAVUKI alt for KADAVU dial of FIJIAN [FJI]
TAVULA alt for VAGHUA [TVA]
TAVYTERA alt for PAI TAVYTERA [PTA]
TAW SUG alt for TAUSUG [TSG]
TAWAELIA alt for SEDOA [TVW]
TAWAILI-SINDUE alt for RAI dial of KAILI, LEDO
    [LEW]
TAWAKONI dial of WICHITA [WIC]
TAWALA [TBO] lang, Papua New Guinea
TAWALA dial of TAWALA [TBO]
TAWALLAMMAT TAN ATARAM dial of TAMAJEQ,
    TAHOUA [TTQ]
TAWALLAMMAT TAN DANNAG dial of TAMAJEQ,
    TAHOUA [TTQ]
TAWALLAMMET TAN DANNAG dial of TAMAJEQ,
    TAHOUA [TTQ]
TAWAN dial of TAGAL MURUT [MVV]
TAWANA dial of TSWANA [TSW]
TAWANXTE dial of NAMBIKUÁRA, NORTHERN
    [MBG]
TAWARA alt for TAWALA [TBO]
TAWARAFA dial of KAHUA [AGW]
TAWARI dial of GBAGYI [GBR]
TAWAU MURUT alt for KALABAKAN [KVE]
TAWAU MURUT alt for SERUDUNG MURUT [SRK]
TAWBUID, EASTERN [BNJ] lang, Philippines
TAWBUID, WESTERN [TWB] lang, Philippines
TAWE-TAVOY alt for TAUNGYO [TCO]
TAWINI alt for TALIFUGU-RIPANG dial of ISNAG
    [ISD]
TAWIRA dial of MÍSKITO [MIQ]
TAWIT alt for ITAWIT [ITV]
TAWKA alt for PECH [PAY]
TAWORTA [TBP] lang, Indonesia, Irian Jaya
TAWOYAN [TWY] lang, Indonesia, Kalimantan
TAWOYAN DAYAK alt for TAWOYAN [TWY]
TAWR alt for CHIN, TAWR [TCP]
TAXMAINITE dial of NAMBIKUÁRA, NORTHERN
    [MBG]
TAXWENSITE dial of NAMBIKUÁRA, NORTHERN
    [MBG]
TÀY alt for THO [THO]
TAY alt for TAI [TAW]
TAY alt for NUNG [NUT]
TAY BOI [TAS] lang, Viet Nam
TAY BOY alt for TAY BOI [TAS]
TÁY DÀ alt for TAI DÓN [TWH]
"TAY HAT" alt for O DU [TYH]
TAY HAY alt for KHANG [KJM]
TAY JO [TYJ] lang, Viet Nam
TAY KHANG [TNU] lang, Laos
TÁY KHAO alt for TAI DÓN [TWH]
TÀY MU'Ò'I dial of TAI DAM [BLT]

TAY MUEAI alt for TAI MUOI dial of TAI DAM [BLT]
TAY MUOI dial of TAI DAM [BLT]
TÀY MUÒNG alt for TAI HANG TONG [THC]
TAY NUNG alt for NUNG [NUT]
TAY PONG alt for PONG 1 [KPN]
TÁY THANH alt for TAI MAN THANH [TMM]
TÁY-DAM alt for TAI DAM [BLT]
TAY-JO alt for TAY JO [TYJ]
TÁY-MÔC-CHÂU alt for TAI DAENG [TYR]
TAYA alt for PECH [PAY]
TAYABA alt for TAYARI dial of NATENI [NTM]
TAYABAS dial of TAGALOG [TGL]
TAYAL alt for ATAYAL [TAY]
TAYANDO dial of KEI [KEI]
TAYARI dial of NATENI [NTM]
TAYART alt for AIR dial of TAMAJEQ, AIR [THZ]
TAYATO dial of ENGA [ENQ]
TAYEK alt for KAPIN [TBX]
TAYHAY alt for KHANG [KJM]
TAYING alt for DIGARO [MHU]
TAYOK dial of DAI [TIZ]
TAYPONG alt for PONG 1 [KPN]
TAZ dial of SELKUP [SAK]
TAZE alt for KREYE [XRE]
TAZOV-BAISHYAN alt for TAZ dial of SELKUP [SAK]
TBILISI dial of ARMENIAN [ARM]
TBOLI [TBL] lang, Philippines
TCAITI alt for TSHIDI-KHWE dial of SHUA [SHG]
TCENGUI alt for TSAANGI [TSA]
TCHAAKALAAGA alt for NGADJUNMAYA [NJU]
TCHADE alt for GUDE [GDE]
TCHAGA alt for ENGA [ENQ]
TCHAGIN dial of KWANG [KVI]
TCHAKIN alt for TCHAGIN dial of KWANG [KVI]
TCHAMBA alt for AKASELEM [AKS]
TCHAMBA alt for SAMBA DAKA [CCG]
TCHAMBULI alt for CHAMBRI [CAN]
TCHANG alt for YEMBA [BAN]
TCHANG alt for FOREKE DSCHANG dial of YEMBA
    [BAN]
TCHANGUI alt for TSAANGI [TSA]
TCHEDE alt for TSUVAN [TSH]
TCHEKE alt for GUDE [GDE]
TCHERE alt for GIZIGA, NORTH [GIS]
TCHERE-AIBA dial of KIMRÉ [KQP]
TCHEVI alt for SARUA [SWY]
TCHIDE dial of JINA [JIA]
TCHIEN dial of KRAHN, EASTERN [KQO]
TCHIKAI alt for BURARRA [BVR]
TCHINGALEE alt for DJINGILI [JIG]
TCHINI dial of NIELLIM [NIE]
TCHIRE alt for TCHERE-AIBA dial of KIMRÉ [KQP]
TCHOKOSSI alt for ANUFO [CKO]
TCHORNY alt for KARAKALPAK [KAC]
TCHOUVOK alt for CUVOK [CUV]
TE alt for GHOMALA SOUTH dial of GHOMALA'
    [BBJ]
TE MOTU dial of SANTA CRUZ [STC]
TEANU [TKW] lang, Solomon Islands
TEBAKANG alt for BUKAR SADONG [SDO]
TEBELE alt for NDEBELE [NDF]
TEBERA dial of FOLOPA [PPO]
TEBILIAN alt for TIBETAN [TIC]
TEBILUNG [TGB] lang, Malaysia, Sabah
TEBOU alt for TEDA [TUQ]
TEBOU alt for TUBU dial of TEDA [TUQ]

TEBU alt for TEDA [TUQ]
TEBU alt for TUBU dial of TEDA [TUQ]
TEBU alt for TUBU dial of TEDA [TUQ]
TECHING alt for DÉJÌNG dial of ZHUANG,
  SOUTHERN [CCY]
TECHU alt for CHAOCHOW dial of CHINESE, MIN
  NAN [CFR]
TECO alt for EMERILLON [EME]
TECO alt for TECTITECO [TTC]
TECTITÁN MAM alt for TECTITECO [TTC]
TECTITECO [TTC] lang, Guatemala, Mexico, Mexico
TECTITECO alt for TECTITECO [TTC]
TEDA [TUQ] lang, Chad, Libya, Libya, Niger
TEDA alt for TEDA [TUQ]
TEDA dial of TEDA [TUQ]
TEDA dial of TEDA [TUQ]
TEDI alt for NINGGERUM [NXR]
TEDIM alt for CHIN, TEDIM [CTD]
TEDONG alt for TIDONG [TID]
TEDURAY alt for TIRURAY [TIY]
TEE dial of GOLA [GOL]
TEEL alt for MONTOL [MTL]
TÉÉN [LOR] lang, Côte d'Ivoire, Burkina Faso
TEERE dial of DOYAYO [DOW]
TEFARO [TFO] lang, Indonesia, Irian Jaya
TEGAL dial of JAVANESE [JAN]
TEGALI [RAS] lang, Sudan
TEGALI dial of TEGALI [RAS]
TEGBO alt for TAFI [TCD]
TEGE alt for TEKE, NORTHERN [TEG]
TEGE alt for TEGEKALI dial of TEKE, NORTHERN
  [TEG]
TEGE alt for TEE dial of GOLA [GOL]
TEGEKALI dial of TEKE, NORTHERN [TEG]
TEGELE alt for TEGALI [RAS]
TEGEM alt for LAFOFA [LAF]
TEGEM alt for JEBEL TEKEIM dial of LAFOFA [LAF]
TEGESIE alt for TÉÉN [LOR]
TEGHE alt for TEKE, NORTHERN [TEG]
TEGINA alt for CINDA dial of KAMUKU [KAU]
TÉGUÉ alt for BOZO, TIÉYAXO [BOZ]
TÉGUÉ alt for TEGEKALI dial of TEKE, NORTHERN
  [TEG]
TEHID alt for TEHIT [KPS]
TEHIT [KPS] lang, Indonesia, Irian Jaya
TEHNU alt for KATCHAL dial of NICOBARESE,
  CENTRAL [NCB]
TEHORU alt for TELUTI [TLT]
TEHORU alt for WEST TELUTI dial of TELUTI [TLT]
TEHRI [THB] lang, India
TEHRI dial of GARHWALI [GBM]
TEHUA alt for WEST TELUTI dial of TELUTI [TLT]
TEHUANTEPEC dial of MIXE, COATLÁN [MCO]
TEHUELCHE [TEH] lang, Argentina
TEIMURI alt for TAIMURI dial of AIMAQ [AIQ]
TEIS-UMM-DANAB alt for KEIGA JIRRU [KEG]
TEITA alt for TAITA [DAV]
TEITA MIXTECO alt for MIXTECO, SAN
  BARTOLOMÉ YUCUAÑE [MVG]
TEIXEIRA PINTO dial of MANDYAK [MFV]
TEIXEIRA PINTO alt for BOK dial of MANDYAK
  [MFV]
TEIXEIRA PINTO alt for BOK dial of MANDYAK
  [MFV]
TEJUCA alt for TUYUCA [TUE]
TEKE alt for TEKE, NORTHERN [TEG]

TEKE dial of TURKMEN [TCK]
TEKE dial of TURKMEN [TCK]
TEKE, CENTRAL [TEC] lang, Congo, Zaïre, Zaïre
TEKE, CENTRAL alt for TEKE, CENTRAL [TEC]
TEKE, EASTERN [TEK] lang, Zaïre, Congo
TEKE, NORTHEASTERN [NGZ] lang, Congo
TEKE, NORTHERN [TEG] lang, Congo, Gabon, Gabon
TEKE, NORTHERN alt for TEKE, NORTHERN [TEG]
TEKE, SOUTH CENTRAL [IFM] lang, Congo
TEKE, SOUTHERN [KKW] lang, Congo
TEKE, WESTERN [TEZ] lang, Congo, Gabon, Gabon
TEKE, WESTERN alt for TEKE, WESTERN [TEZ]
TEKEIM alt for JEBEL TEKEIM dial of LAFOFA [LAF]
TEKEL alt for LEHALI [TQL]
TEKELA alt for SWATI [SWZ]
TEKELE alt for TEGALI [RAS]
TEKEZA alt for SWATI [SWZ]
TEKKE alt for TEKE dial of TURKMEN [TCK]
TEKKE alt for TEKE dial of TURKMEN [TCK]
TEKUTAMESO alt for KWERBA [KWE]
TELA'A alt for TELA-MASBUAR [TVM]
TELA-MASBUAR [TVM] lang, Indonesia, Maluku
TELANGANA dial of TELUGU [TCW]
TELANGIRE alt for TELUGU [TCW]
TELE alt for TANA [TNQ]
TELEEFOOL alt for TELEFOL [TLF]
TELEFOL [TLF] lang, Papua New Guinea
TELEFOL dial of TELEFOL [TLF]
TELEFOLMIN alt for TELEFOL [TLF]
TELEFOMIN alt for TELEFOL [TLF]
TELEGU alt for TELUGU [TCW]
TELEI alt for BUIN [BUO]
TELEKI alt for TSUVAN [TSH]
TELEKOSON alt for TOLOKOSON dial of TAGAL
  MURUT [MVV]
TELENGUT alt for ALTAI, NORTHERN [ATV]
TELEPOK alt for MENGGATAL dial of DUSUN,
  CENTRAL [DTP]
TELEUT alt for ALTAI, NORTHERN [ATV]
TELGI alt for TELUGU [TCW]
TELI dial of BHOJPURI [BHJ]
TELIRE dial of CABÉCAR [CJP]
TELLEM alt for KURUMFÉ [KFZ]
TELOM dial of SEMAI [SEA]
TELUGU [TCW] lang, India, Fiji, Singapore
TELUGU alt for TELUGU [TCW]
TELUGU dial of TELUGU [TCW]
TELUGU LAMANI alt for ANDHRA PRADESH
  LAMANI dial of LAMANI [LMN]
TELUK LILI dial of TUGUTIL [TUJ]
TELUKBETUNG dial of PESISIR, SOUTHERN [PEC]
TELUTI [TLT] lang, Indonesia, Maluku
TEM [KDH] lang, Togo, Benin, Ghana
TEMA alt for TEME [TDO]
TEMACIN dial of OUARGLA [OUA]
TEMAGERI dial of KANURI, YERWA [KPH]
TEMAINIAN alt for TEMEIN [TEQ]
TEMANE alt for JAPANESE SIGN LANGUAGE [JSL]
TEMBA alt for TEM [KDH]
TEMBAGLA dial of MEDLPA [MED]
TEMBÉ [TEM] lang, Brazil
TEMBE OF GURUPI dial of GUAJAJÁRA [GUB]
TEMBE' dial of TEMIAR [TMH]
TEMBEKUÁ dial of KAIWÁ [KGK]
TEMBENUA alt for TOMBONUWO [TXA]
TEMBI alt for TEMBE' dial of TEMIAR [TMH]

TEMBIMBE-KATBOL alt for KATBOL [TMB]
TEMBIS alt for TAMBAS [TDK]
TEMBO [TBT] lang, Zaïre
TEMBO [TMV] lang, Zaïre
TEMBO dial of TEMBO [TBT]
TEMBO alt for TAMBO dial of MWANGA [MWN]
TEMBOGIA alt for MBO-UNG 'MUX]
TEMBUNG dial of JAVANESE [JAN]
TEME [TDO] lang, Nigeria
TEMEIN [TEQ] lang, Sudan
TEMEN alt for THEMNE [TEJ]
TEMER alt for TEMIAR [TMH]
TEMIAR [TMH] lang, Malaysia, Peninsular
TEMILA dial of DAYAK, LAND [DYK]
TEMIRGOJ alt for BEZHEDUKH dial of ADYGHE
   [ADY]
TEMNE alt for THEMNE [TEJ]
TEMOGUN alt for TIMUGON MURUT [TIH]
TEMOQ [TMO] lang, Malaysia, Peninsular
TEMORAL alt for TAMARIA [TDB]
TEMPASOK alt for DUSUN, TEMPASUK [TDU]
TEMUAN [TMW] lang, Malaysia, Peninsular
TEMUAN dial of TEMUAN [TMW]
T'EN [TCT] lang, China
TEN alt for CHING [MKG]
TEN alt for ATEN [GAN]
TEN'A alt for KOYUKON [KOY]
TENA alt for MAKASSAR [MSR]
TENCH alt for TENIS [TNS]
TENDA alt for BUDIK [TNR]
TENDA alt for KONYAGI [COU]
TENDA BASARI alt for BASARI [BSC]
TENDANKE alt for BUDIK [TNR]
TENDE alt for KURIA [KUJ]
TENDE alt for TIENE [TII]
TENENGA dial of MAU [MXX]
TENERE dial of SENOUFO, CEBAARA [SEF]
TENET [TEX] lang, Sudan
TENETE alt for PITU ULUNNA SALU [PTU]
TENETEHAR alt for GUAJAJÁRA [GUB]
TENETEHÁRA alt for GUAJAJÁRA [GUB]
TENG alt for KHANG [KJM]
TENG dial of KISSI, NORTHERN [KQS]
TENGAH-TENGAH dial of TULEHU [TLU]
TENGARA dial of BAUKAN [BNB]
TENGGANU alt for KETIAR KRAU dial of JAH HUT
   [JAH]
TENGGARAQ alt for TENGARA dial of BAUKAN
   [BNB]
TENGGARONG alt for MALAY, TENGGARONG
   KUTAI [VKT]
TENGGARONG KUTAI dial of MALAY,
   TENGGARONG KUTAI [VKT]
TENGGER [TES] lang, Indonesia, Java, Bali
TENGGERESE alt for TENGGER [TES]
TENGIMA dial of NAGA, ANGAMI [NJM]
TENGO alt for MAMVU [MDI]
TENGOH dial of JAGOI [SNE]
TENGRELA alt for KANDERE dial of SENOUFO,
   CEBAARA [SEF]
TENGU alt for TELUGU [TCW]
TENH alt for KHMU [KJG]
TENHAREM alt for TENHARIM [PAH]
TENHARIM [PAH] lang, Brazil
TENHARIN alt for TENHARIM [PAH]
TÉNHÉ alt for TÉÉN [LOR]

TENINO [WAR] lang, USA
TENIS [TNS] lang, Papua New Guinea
TENOM MURUT alt for TIMUGON MURUT [TIH]
TENT GYPSY alt for ROMANO-SERBIAN [RSB]
TENTI alt for SENSI [SNI]
TENYER dial of KARABORO, WESTERN [KZA]
TEO alt for TYOO dial of TEKE, CENTRAL [TEC]
TEO alt for BALI dial of TEKE, EASTERN [TEK]
TEOCHEW dial of CHINESE, MIN NAN [CFR]
TEOCHEW alt for CHAO SHAN dial of CHINESE, MIN
   NAN [CFR]
TEOCHEW alt for CHAOCHOW dial of CHINESE, MIN
   NAN [CFR]
TEOCHOW alt for CHAOCHOW dial of CHINESE,
   MIN NAN [CFR]
TEOCHOW alt for CHAO SHAN dial of CHINESE,
   MIN NAN [CFR]
TEOCHOW alt for CHAOCHOW dial of CHINESE,
   MIN NAN [CFR]
TEOCHOW alt for CHAOCHOW dial of CHINESE,
   MIN NAN [CFR]
TEOCOCUILCO DE MARCOS PÉREZ ZAPOTECO alt
   for ZAPOTECO, WESTERN IXTLÁN [ZAE]
TEOP [TIO] lang, Papua New Guinea
TEOPISCA dial of TZOTZIL, CHAMULA [TZC]
TEOR [TEV] lang, Indonesia, Maluku
TEOTITLÁN MIXTECO alt for MIXTECO, SAN JUAN
   COATZOSPAN [MIZ]
TEP dial of MAMBILA, NIGERIA [MZK]
TEPANTEPEC alt for SAN MATEO TEPANTEPEC dial
   of MIXTECO, EASTERN [MIL]
TEPECANO [TEP] lang, Mexico
TEPEHUA, HUEHUETLA [TEE] lang, Mexico
TEPEHUA, PISA FLORES [TPP] lang, Mexico
TEPEHUA, VERACRUZ [TPT] lang, Mexico
TEPEHUAN, NORTHERN [NTP] lang, Mexico
TEPEHUAN, SOUTHEASTERN [STP] lang, Mexico
TEPEHUAN, SOUTHWESTERN [TLA] lang, Mexico
TEPERA alt for TABLA [TNM]
TEPERA dial of TABLA [TNM]
TEPES alt for SOO [TEU]
TEPETH alt for SOO [TEU]
TEPO dial of KRUMEN, SOUTHERN [TED]
TEPTYAR dial of TATAR [TTR]
TEQ alt for BATEK TEQ dial of BATEK [BTQ]
TEQEL alt for LEHALI [TQL]
TEQUENICA alt for YAMANA [YAG]
TEQUISTLATEC alt for CHONTAL OF OAXACA,
   HIGHLAND [CHD]
TEQURACA alt for ABISHIRA [ASH]
"TER LAPPISH" alt for SAAMI, TER [LPT]
TERA [TER] lang, Nigeria
TERA alt for CARA [CFD]
TERAKAN alt for TARAKAN dial of TIDONG [TID]
TERANGI alt for TELUGU [TCW]
TERAWIA alt for BIDEYAT [BIH]
TEREBU [TRB] lang, Papua New Guinea
TEREGO LUGBARA alt for LUGBARA, HIGH [LUG]
TEREI alt for BUIN [BUO]
TEREKEME dial of AZERBAIJANI, NORTH [AZE]
TEREMA alt for TIRMA dial of MURSI [MUZ]
TERÊNA [TEA] lang, Brazil
TERENO alt for TERÊNA [TEA]
TEREPU alt for TEREBU [TRB]
TERESSA [TEF] lang, India
TEREWENG dial of BLAGAR [BEU]

TERI alt for SAGALLA [TGA]
TERI dial of SAGALLA [TGA]
TERI-KALWASCH alt for KIMAGHAMA [KIG]
TERIA alt for CARA [CFD]
TERIBE [TFR] lang, Panama, Costa Rica
TERIK dial of TETUN [TTM]
TERIK dial of KALENJIN [KLN]
TERKI alt for TSUVAN [TSH]
TERMANU alt for TERMANU-TALAE-KEKA dial of
    ROTI [ROT]
TERMANU-TALAE-KEKA dial of ROTI [ROT]
TERNA alt for TIRMA dial of MURSI [MUZ]
TERNATE [TFT] lang, Indonesia, Maluku
TERNATE MALAY alt for MALAY, NORTH
    MOLUCCAN [MAX]
TERNATEÑO [TMG] lang, Indonesia, Maluku
TERNATEÑO dial of CHAVACANO [CBK]
TERNATEÑO CHAVACANO alt for TERNATEÑO dial
    of CHAVACANO [CBK]
TERNATENYO alt for TERNATEÑO [TMG]
TERRABA alt for TERIBE [TFR]
TERRI alt for CARA [CFD]
TERUTONG alt for MARGU [MHG]
TESHENNA alt for TISHENA dial of ME'EN [MYM]
TESHINA alt for TISHENA dial of ME'EN [MYM]
TESO [TEO] lang, Uganda, Kenya
TESUQUE dial of TEWA [TEW]
TETA alt for NYUNGWE [NYU]
TETALO alt for MBO-UNG [MUX]
TETE alt for DETI-KHWE [DET]
TETE alt for NYUNGWE [NYU]
TÊTE DE BOULE alt for ATIKAMEKW [TET]
TETELA [TEL] lang, Zaïre
TETELCINGO AZTEC alt for NAHUATL,
    TETELCINGO [NHG]
TETETE [TEB] lang, Ecuador
TETI alt for DETI-KHWE [DET]
TETO alt for TETUN [TTM]
TETON alt for LAKOTA [LKT]
TETTUM alt for TETUN [TTM]
TETUM alt for TETUN [TTM]
TETUN [TTM] lang, Indonesia, Nusa Tenggara
TETUN PRASA alt for DILI TETUN dial of TETUN
    [TTM]
TETUNG alt for TETUN [TTM]
TEU alt for KATU [KTV]
TEUEIA alt for MACUSHI [MBC]
TEÚI dial of KAIWÁ [KGK]
TEULA alt for LIANA-SETI [STE]
TE'UN [TVE] lang, Indonesia, Maluku
TEUSO alt for IK [IKX]
TEUTH alt for IK [IKX]
TEVE dial of MANYIKA [MXC]
TEVE dial of MANYIKA [MXC]
TEVORANG alt for TAIVOAN dial of SIRAIYA [FOS]
TEW alt for TUMBUKA [TUW]
TEWA [TEW] lang, USA
TEWA [TWE] lang, Indonesia, Nusa Tenggara
TEWATEWA dial of MISIMA-PANEATI [MPX]
TEWEYA alt for MACUSHI [MBC]
TEXAS dial of AFRO-SEMINOLE CREOLE [AFS]
TEXMELUCAN ZAPOTEC alt for ZAPOTECO, SAN
    LORENZO TEXMELUCAN [ZPZ]
TEZ dial of OROCH [OAC]
TFUEA dial of TSOU [TSY]
TGHUADE alt for DGHWEDE [DGH]

THAAYORE alt for THAYORE [THD]
THABINE-ROKA-NARENG alt for DZWABO dial of
    SOTHO, NORTHERN [SRT]
THADO-PAO alt for CHIN, THADO [TCZ]
THADO-UBIPHEI alt for CHIN, THADO [TCZ]
THADOU alt for CHIN, THADO [TCZ]
THAE alt for THE [THX]
THAGICHU dial of THARAKA [THA]
THAI [THJ] lang, Thailand, Singapore
THAI DANG alt for TAI DAENG [TYR]
THÁI DEN alt for TAI DAM [BLT]
THAI DEN alt for TAI DAM [BLT]
THAI DO alt for TAI DAENG [TYR]
THAI ISLAM alt for MALAY, PATTANI [MFA]
THAI KHE dial of DAI [TIZ]
THAI LU alt for LÜ [KHB]
THAI MALAY dial of TAI, SOUTHERN [SOU]
THAI SIGN LANGUAGE [TSQ] lang, Thailand
THAI SONG alt for SONG [SOA]
THÁI TRÁNG alt for TAI DÓN [TWH]
THAI YAI alt for SHAN [SJN]
THAI-CHE alt for TAI CHE dial of DAI [TIZ]
THAI-KHE alt for THAI KHE dial of DAI [TIZ]
THAKALI [THS] lang, Nepal
THAKARA alt for DURUWA [PCI]
THAKARI alt for THAKURI [THK]
THAKARI dial of KONKANI [KNK]
THAKRI alt for THAKURI [THK]
THAKUA alt for THAKURI [THK]
THAKURA alt for THAKURI [THK]
THAKURGAON SADRI dial of SADRI, ORAON [SDR]
THAKURI [THK] lang, India
THAL dial of KALAMI [GWC]
THALI dial of SIRAIKI [SKR]
THALU alt for TULU [TCY]
THALWEPWE alt for KAREN, PAKU [KPP]
THAMI [THF] lang, Nepal, China
THAMINYI alt for DAIR [DRB]
THANG dial of MUONG [MTQ]
THANGAL alt for NAGA, KHOIRAO [NKI]
THANGATTI alt for DYANGADI [DYN]
THANGATTY alt for DYANGADI [DYN]
THANGGAL alt for NAGA, KHOIRAO [NKI]
THANGKHULM alt for NAGA, TANGKHUL [NMF]
THANGNGEN dial of CHIN, THADO [TCZ]
THANY alt for ALIAP dial of DINKA, SOUTH
    CENTRAL [DIB]
THANY BUR alt for PALIET dial of DINKA,
    SOUTHWESTERN [DIK]
THAO [SSF] lang, Taiwan
THAP alt for KATU [KTV]
THAR alt for DHATKI BHIL dial of DHATKI [MKI]
THARADARI alt for KOLI, THARADARI [KXQ]
THARAKA [THA] lang, Kenya
THARAKA dial of THARAKA [THA]
THARELI dial of SINDHI [SND]
THARGARI alt for DHARGARI [DHR]
THARI dial of SINDHI [SND]
THARU dial of BHOJPURI [BHJ]
THARU dial of AWADHI [AWD]
THARU, CHITWAN [THE] lang, Nepal
THARU, DANG [THL] lang, Nepal
THARU, DEOKRI [THG] lang, Nepal
THARU, MAHOTARI [THN] lang, Nepal
THARU, RANA THAKUR [THR] lang, Nepal
THARU, SAPTARI [THQ] lang, Nepal

THARUMBAL alt for BAYALI [BJY]
THAT alt for KADO [KDV]
THAVUNG [THM] lang, Laos
THAYETMO alt for THAYETMYO dial of CHIN, ASHO [CSH]
THAYETMYO dial of CHIN, ASHO [CSH]
THAYETMYO dial of CHIN, ASHO [CSH]
THAYORE [THD] lang, Australia
THAYORRE alt for THAYORE [THD]
THAYPAN [TYP] lang, Australia
THE [THX] lang, Laos
THE CANT alt for SHELTA [STH]
THE LANGUAGE OF THE DEAF alt for AMERICAN SIGN LANGUAGE [ASE]
THEBARSHAD alt for SUNAM [SSK]
THEBARSKAD alt for SHUMCHO [SCU]
THEBARSKAD alt for JANGSHUNG [JNA]
THEBOR dial of SHUMCHO [SCU]
THEBOR alt for JANGSHUNG [JNA]
THEBOR alt for SUNAM [SSK]
THEBŎR SKADD alt for SHUMCHO [SCU]
THEBŎR SKADD alt for JANGSHUNG [JNA]
THEBŎR SKADD alt for SUNAM [SSK]
THEITHEI alt for SAKAJI [SKN]
THEMBU dial of XHOSA [XOS]
THEMNE [TEJ] lang, Sierra Leone
THENG alt for KHMU [KJG]
THENG alt for KHANG [KJM]
THEPHALABORWA alt for PHALABORWA dial of SOTHO, NORTHERN [SRT]
THET alt for KADO [KDV]
THIANG dial of NUER [NUS]
THIE dial of ROTI [ROT]
THIMBUKUSHU alt for MBUKUSHU [MHW]
THIN alt for MAL [MLF]
THIO alt for XARAGURE [ARG]
THIRO alt for TIRA [TIR]
THLANTLANG alt for KLANGKLANG dial of CHIN, HAKA [CNH]
THLAPING dial of TSWANA [TSW]
THLARO dial of TSWANA [TSW]
THLINGET alt for TLINGIT [TLI]
THLUKFU dial of BANA [FLI]
THO [THO] lang, Viet Nam, China
THÔ alt for THO [THO]
THOCHU dial of QIANG [CNG]
THOGNAATH alt for NUER [NUS]
THOI dial of DINKA, NORTHEASTERN [DIP]
THOK CIENG alt for ATUOT [ATU]
THOMPSON [THP] lang, Canada
THON alt for TUIC dial of DINKA, SOUTHWESTERN [DIK]
THONGA alt for TSONGA [TSO]
THOORGA alt for DHURGA [DHU]
THRO alt for SÔ [SSS]
THU alt for THO [THO]
THU alt for GELO [KKF]
THU LAO alt for THO [THO]
THUANGA alt for YUAGA [NUA]
THUANGA dial of YUAGA [NUA]
THUDAM BHOTE [THW] lang, Nepal
THUKUMI dial of NAGA, SANGTAM [NSA]
THULE ESKIMO alt for POLAR ESKIMO dial of INUIT, GREENLANDIC [ESG]
THULISHI alt for TULISHI [TEY]
THULU alt for TULU [TCY]

THULUNG [TDH] lang, Nepal, India
THULUNGE RAI alt for THULUNG [TDH]
THUNDAI-KANZA alt for PEREMKA [PEP]
THUNG CHAN PRAY alt for PHAI [PRT]
THURAWAL [TBH] lang, Australia
THURI [THU] lang, Sudan
TI dial of MUNGAKA [MHK]
TI alt for THIE dial of ROTI [ROT]
TI'ARA alt for BADA [BHZ]
TIAALA dial of GULA IRO [GLJ]
TIADJE alt for TOMINI [TXM]
TIAGBA alt for AIZI dial of AIZI [AHI]
TIAL dial of TULEHU [TLU]
TIALO alt for TOMINI [TXM]
TIAN-PAO alt for DIANBAO [TST]
TIANG [TBJ] lang, Papua New Guinea
TIAPI alt for LANDOMA [LAO]
TIAPI dial of LANDOMA [LAO]
TIARA alt for GEDAGED [GDD]
TIATINAGUA alt for ESE EJJA [ESE]
TIBA [TTB] lang, Nigeria
TIBAS SKAD alt for KANAURI [KFK]
TIBATE alt for TIBETAN [TIC]
TIBBU alt for TEDA [TUQ]
TIBBU alt for TUBU dial of TEDA [TUQ]
TIBBU alt for TUBU dial of TEDA [TUQ]
TIBEA [NGY] lang, Cameroon
TIBETAN [TIC] lang, China, Bhutan, India, Nepal, Taiwan
TIBETAN alt for TIBETAN [TIC]
TIBOLA alt for TSOU [TSY]
TIBOLAH alt for TSOU [TSY]
TIBOLAK alt for TSOU [TSY]
TIBOLAL alt for TSOU [TSY]
TIBOLI alt for TBOLI [TBL]
TIBU dial of BANGBA [BBE]
TICANESE [TIB] lang, Switzerland
TICHERONG alt for TICHURONG [TCN]
TICHURONG [TCN] lang, Nepal
TICINO alt for TICANESE [TIB]
TICUNA [TCA] lang, Peru, Brazil, Colombia
TID alt for MIDOB [MEI]
TID alt for TIRMA dial of MURSI [MUZ]
TID-N-AAL alt for MIDOB [MEI]
TIDAA MIXTECO alt for MIXTECO, NORTH CENTRAL NOCHIXTLÁN [MTX]
TIDDA alt for MIDOB [MEI]
TIDDIM alt for CHIN, TEDIM [CTD]
TIDI alt for NINGGERUM [NXR]
TIDIKELT [TIA] lang, Algeria
TIDOENG alt for SEMBAKUNG MURUT [SMA]
TIDOENG alt for TIDONG [TID]
TIDONG [TID] lang, Indonesia, Kalimantan, Malaysia, Sabah, Malaysia, Sabah
TIDONG alt for SEMBAKUNG MURUT [SMA]
TIDONG alt for TIDONG [TID]
TIDORE [TVO] lang, Indonesia, Maluku
TIDUNG alt for SEMBAKUNG MURUT [SMA]
TIDUNG alt for KALABAKAN [KVE]
TIDUNG alt for KUIJAU [DKR]
TIDUNG alt for TIDONG [TID]
TIDUNG alt for SERUDUNG MURUT [SRK]
TIDUNG dial of TIDONG [TID]
TIÉ alt for BOZO, TIÈMA CIÈWÈ [BOO]
TIE alt for BOZO, TIÉYAXO [BOZ]
TIE dial of KABA NA [KWV]

TINDAL dial of DUSUN, CENTRAL [DTP]
TINDI [TIN] lang, Russia, Europe
TINDIGA alt for HATSA [HTS]
TINDIN alt for TINDI [TIN]
TINGAL [TIG] lang, Sudan
TINGALUN alt for SEMBAKUNG MURUT [SMA]
TINGANESES alt for CHOLON [CHT]
TINGARA alt for TENGARA dial of BAUKAN [BNB]
TINGGALAN alt for SEMBAKUNG MURUT [SMA]
TINGGALUM alt for SEMBAKUNG MURUT [SMA]
TINGGUIAN alt for ITNEG, BINONGAN [ITB]
TINGKALA alt for TIKAR [TIK]
TINGUI alt for TINGUI-BOTÓ [TGV]
TINGUI-BOTÓ [TGV] lang, Brazil
TINGUIAN alt for ITNEG, BINONGAN [ITB]
TINIE alt for CENTRAL SONGAI dial of SONGAI
   [SON]
TINIÉ alt for CENTRAL SONGAI dial of SONGAI
   [SON]
TINITIANES alt for BATAK [BTK]
TINJAR SIBOP dial of KENYAH, SEBOB [SIB]
TINKIRE dial of BOBO FING [BBO]
TINNERS ROMANI dial of ROMANI, BALKAN [RMN]
TINO alt for SAMBAL, TINA [SNA]
TINOC dial of KALLAHAN, KAYAPA [KAK]
TINOC KALANGOYA alt for KALLAHAN, TINOC
   [TNE]
TINOMBO alt for LAUJE [LAW]
TINPUTZ [TPZ] lang, Papua New Guinea
TINTA dial of IPULO [ASS]
TINTEKIYA dial of KOCH [KDQ]
TIO alt for TYOO dial of TEKE, CENTRAL [TEC]
TIO alt for BALI dial of TEKE, EASTERN [TEK]
TIO'OR alt for TEOR [TEV]
TIOFFO dial of ABÉ [ABA]
TIOKOSSI alt for ANUFO [CKO]
TIONG alt for KENSIU [KNS]
TIOO alt for TYOO dial of TEKE, CENTRAL [TEC]
TIPAI [TIP] lang, Mexico
TIPININI dial of IPILI [IPI]
TIPPERA [TPE] lang, Bangladesh
TIPPERA-BENGALI alt for TIPPERA [TPE]
TIPPERAH alt for TIPPERA [TPE]
TIPPURAH alt for TIPPERA [TPE]
TIPRA alt for TIPPERA [TPE]
TIPRA alt for RIANG dial of KOK BOROK [TRP]
TIPUN alt for PYUMA [PYU]
TIPURA alt for TIPPERA [TPE]
TIPURA alt for CHIN, FALAM [HBH]
TIPURA alt for KOK BOROK [TRP]
TIRA [TIR] lang, Sudan
TIRA DAGIG alt for TIRA EL AKHDAR dial of TIRA
   [TIR]
TIRA EL AKHDAR dial of TIRA [TIR]
TIRA LUMUM dial of TIRA [TIR]
TIRA MANDI dial of TIRA [TIR]
TIRAHI [TRA] lang, Afghanistan
TIRAHUTIA alt for MAITHILI [MKP]
TIRAN alt for TIDONG [TID]
TIRHARI dial of KANAUJI [BJJ]
TIRHARI dial of BAGHELI [BFY]
TIRI [CIR] lang, New Caledonia
TIRIBI alt for TERIBE [TFR]
TIRIFIE alt for TARIFIT [RIF]
TIRIKI dial of IDAKHO-ISUKHA-TIRIKI [IDA]
TIRIMA alt for TIRMA dial of MURSI [MUZ]

TIRIO [TCR] lang, Papua New Guinea
TIRIÓ alt for TRIÓ [TRI]
TIRIO dial of TIRIO [TCR]
TIRIYA dial of DURUWA [PCI]
TIRIYÓ alt for TRIÓ [TRI]
TIRMA dial of MURSI [MUZ]
TIRMAGA alt for TIRMA dial of MURSI [MUZ]
TIRMAGI alt for TIRMA dial of MURSI [MUZ]
TIRO alt for KONJO, COASTAL [KJC]
TIRO alt for TIRA [TIR]
TIROLEAN alt for GERMAN, HUTTERITE [GEH]
TIRON alt for TAWBUID, EASTERN [BNJ]
TIRONES alt for TIDONG [TID]
TIROON alt for TIDONG [TID]
TIRRIBI alt for TERIBE [TFR]
TIRUMBAE alt for TAPIETÉ [TAI]
TIRURAI alt for TIRURAY [TIY]
TIRURAY [TIY] lang, Philippines
TISHENA dial of ME'EN [MYM]
TISMAN dial of REREP [PGK]
TISSA dial of KPAN [KPK]
TISVEL alt for KATBOL [TMB]
TIT [TIT] lang, Algeria
TITA [TDQ] lang, Nigeria
TITAN [TTV] lang, Papua New Guinea
TITIN BAJAYGUL alt for ASHURUVERI dial of
   ASHKUN [ASK]
TITO alt for TITAN [TTV]
TITU alt for PANGA dial of MONGO-NKUNDU [MOM]
TIUCHIU alt for CHAOCHOW dial of CHINESE, MIN
   NAN [CFR]
TIUCHIU alt for CHAOCHOW dial of CHINESE, MIN
   NAN [CFR]
TIV [TIV] lang, Nigeria, Cameroon
TIWA, NORTHERN [TAO] lang, USA
TIWA, SOUTHERN [TIX] lang, USA
TIWAL alt for MASAKIN TUWAL dial of NGILE
   [MAS]
TIWI [TIW] lang, Australia
TIWIRKUM alt for MOGHAMO dial of META' [MGO]
TIWORO alt for MUNA [MYN]
TIYA alt for BOI dial of KWANKA [BIJ]
TIYE alt for TIE dial of KABA NA [KWV]
TJABAKAI-THANDJI alt for DYAABUGAY [DYY]
TJABOGAIJANJI alt for DYAABUGAY [DYY]
TJAM alt for CHAM, WESTERN [CJA]
TJAM alt for CHAM, EASTERN [CJM]
TJAMORO alt for CHAMORRO [CJD]
TJAMPALAGIAN alt for CAMPALAGIAN [CML]
TJANKIR alt for DYAABUGAY [DYY]
TJANKUN alt for DYAABUGAY [DYY]
TJAPUKAI alt for DYAABUGAY [DYY]
TJAPUNKANDJI alt for DYAABUGAY [DYY]
TJARU alt for JARU [DDJ]
TJENDANA alt for SENDANA dial of MANDAR [MHN]
TJERAIT alt for TYARAITY [WOA]
TJIMBA alt for ZEMBA [DHM]
TJIMUNDO alt for ANGORAM [AOG]
TJINGILU alt for DJINGILI [JIG]
TJIREBON alt for CIREBON dial of JAVANESE [JAN]
TJITAK alt for CITAK [TXT]
TJITJAK alt for CITAK [TXT]
TJOKWAI alt for ROUKU [TCI]
TJUAVE alt for CHUAVE [CJV]
TJUDUN alt for TULU dial of BOHUAI [RAK]
TJUNBUNDJI alt for DYAABUGAY [DYY]

TJURA alt for NUGUNU [NNV]
TJURRURU [TJU] lang, Australia
TLACHICHILCO TEPEHUA alt for TEPEHUA, VERACRUZ [TPT]
TLACOAPA dial of TLAPANECO [TLL]
TLAHAPING dial of TSWANA [TSW]
TLAHUICA alt for MATLATZINCA, ATZINGO [OCU]
TLAHURA alt for MATLATZINCA, ATZINGO [OCU]
TLAPANECO [TLL] lang, Mexico
TLAPI alt for TLAHAPING dial of TSWANA [TSW]
TLAPI alt for THLAPING dial of TSWANA [TSW]
TLATSOP alt for KLATSOP dial of CHINOOK [CHH]
TLAZOYALTEPEC alt for SANTIAGO TLAZOYALTEPEC dial of MIXTECO, EASTERN [MIL]
TLETLE alt for DETI-KHWE [DET]
TLHAPING dial of TSWANA [TSW]
TLINGIT [TLI] lang, USA, Canada
TLINKIT alt for TLINGIT [TLI]
TLISI dial of BAGVALAL [KVA]
TLOKEANG alt for KATO [KTW]
TLOKOA alt for TLOKWA dial of SOTHO, NORTHERN [SRT]
TLOKWA dial of TSWANA [TSW]
TLOKWA dial of SOTHO, NORTHERN [SRT]
TLONGSAI dial of CHIN, MARA [MRH]
TLOUE alt for //XEGWI [XEG]
TLOUTLE alt for //XEGWI [XEG]
TLYADALY dial of BEZHTA [KAP]
TLYANUB alt for SOUTHERN AKHVAKH dial of AKHVAKH [AKV]
TMAGOURT [TMX] lang, Tunisia
TMAGURT alt for TMAGOURT [TMX]
TMOOY alt for KHMU [KJG]
TO 'LO dial of GELO [KKF]
TO [TOZ] lang, Cameroon, Central African Republic, Central African Republic
TO alt for TO [TOZ]
TO LA alt for TALA dial of KOHO [KPM]
TO PAMOSEAN alt for PANASUAN [PSN]
TO PANASEAN alt for PANASUAN [PSN]
TO RETE alt for TORETE dial of TULAMBATU [MFG]
TO RONGKONG alt for TAE' [ROB]
TO'ABAITA dial of TO'ABAITA [MLU]
TO'AMBAITA alt for TO'ABAITA [MLU]
TO'OLAKI alt for TOLAKI [LBW]
TO-BUAN dial of JARAI [JRA]
TOA alt for TOMA [TOD]
TOA dial of PARAUJANO [PBG]
TO'ABAITA [MLU] lang, Solomon Islands
TOAK dial of AMBRYM, SOUTHEAST [TVK]
TOALA' [TLZ] lang, Indonesia, Sulawesi
TOALA' dial of TOALA' [TLZ]
TOALA-PALILI alt for TOALA' [TLZ]
TOALE alt for TOMA [TOD]
TOALI alt for TOMA [TOD]
TOARIPI [TPI] lang, Papua New Guinea
TOARIPI dial of TOARIPI [TPI]
TOBA [TOB] lang, Argentina, Paraguay, Bolivia, Paraguay
TOBA alt for TOBA [TOB]
TOBA alt for EMOK [EMO]
TOBA BATAK alt for BATAK TOBA [BBC]
TOBA OF PARAGUAY alt for TOBA-MASKOY [TMF]
TOBA QOM alt for TOBA [TOB]
TOBA-EMOK alt for EMOK [EMO]

TOBA-MASKOY [TMF] lang, Paraguay
TOBA-PILAGÁ dial of PILAGÁ [PLG]
TOBADA' alt for BADA [BHZ]
TOBAKU dial of UMA [PPK]
TOBALO alt for TOBAU dial of PAMONA [BCX]
TOBANGA [TNG] lang, Chad
TOBAO alt for TOBAU dial of PAMONA [BCX]
TOBARU alt for TABARU [TBY]
TOBATI [TTI] lang, Indonesia, Irian Jaya
TOBAU dial of PAMONA [BCX]
TOBELO [TLB] lang, Indonesia, Maluku
TOBELO dial of TOBELO [TLB]
TOBILANG alt for TEBILUNG [TGB]
TOBILUNG alt for TEBILUNG [TGB]
TOBO [TBV] lang, Papua New Guinea
TOBOL dial of TATAR [TTR]
TOBOTE alt for NTCHAM [BUD]
TOBUNYUO dial of NAGA, KONYAK [NBE]
TOCENGA dial of TUKI [BAG]
TOCHIPO alt for CEP dial of ACIPA [AWA]
TOCHO alt for TACHO dial of MORO HILLS [TAZ]
TOCOD alt for TUKUDEDE [TKD]
TODA [TCX] lang, India
TODA alt for TAROKO [TRV]
TODA alt for TEDA [TUQ]
TODA alt for TEDA dial of TEDA [TUQ]
TODAGA alt for TEDA [TUQ]
TODAGA alt for TEDA dial of TEDA [TUQ]
TODELA alt for TUXÁ [TUD]
TODGA alt for TEDA [TUQ]
TODGA alt for TEDA dial of TEDA [TUQ]
TODI alt for KAIY [TCQ]
TODI alt for TODA [TCX]
TODRÁ alt for TODRAH [TDR]
TODRAH [TDR] lang, Viet Nam
TODZHIN alt for NORTHEASTERN TUVIN dial of TUVIN [TUN]
TOEMOETOE dial of KATI, NORTHERN [KTI]
TOENDE dial of KUSAAL, EASTERN [KUS]
TOF alt for KULERE [KUL]
TOFA alt for KARAGAS [KIM]
TOFA alt for TUVIN [TUN]
TOFALAR alt for KARAGAS [KIM]
TOFAMNA [TLG] lang, Indonesia, Irian Jaya
TOFIN alt for TOFIN-GBE [TFI]
TOFIN-GBE [TFI] lang, Benin
TOFOKE alt for POKE [POF]
TOGA [LHT] lang, Vanuatu
TOGA alt for TOGO dial of GIZRA [TOF]
TOGBO [TOR] lang, Zaïre, Central African Republic, Sudan
TOGHWEDE alt for DGHWEDE [DGH]
TOGO alt for GIZRA [TOF]
TOGOLE alt for TEGALI [RAS]
TOGOY alt for TOGOYO [TGY]
TOGOYO [TGY] lang, Sudan
TOHGBOH alt for TOGBO [TOR]
TOI alt for DIDINGA [DID]
TOI-OI alt for TA'OIH, UPPER [TTH]
TOICHO alt for TACHO dial of MORO HILLS [TAZ]
TOISHAN alt for TAISHAN dial of CHINESE, YUE [YUH]
TOISHANESE dial of CHINESE, YUE [YUH]
TOJOLABAL [TOJ] lang, Mexico
TOK PISIN [PDG] lang, Papua New Guinea
TOKA dial of TONGA [TOI]

TOKA dial of TONGA [TOI]
TOKAIMALO alt for NORTHEAST VITI LEVU dial of
    FIJIAN [FJI]
TOKAMA alt for TOKANO [ZUH]
TOKANO [ZUH] lang, Papua New Guinea
TOKAT alt for EWDOKIA dial of ARMENIAN [ARM]
TOKELAU alt for TOKELAUAN [TOK]
TOKELAUAN [TOK] lang, Tokelau, American Samoa,
    New Zealand
TOKHA alt for TUVIN [TUN]
TOKITA dial of KARATA [KPT]
TOKITIN alt for TOKITA dial of KARATA [KPT]
TOKKARU alt for DOGRI-KANGRI [DOJ]
TOKKO dial of EVENKI [EVN]
TOKMO-UPPER LENA dial of EVENKI [EVN]
TOKODÉ alt for TUKUDEDE [TKD]
TOKODEDE alt for TUKUDEDE [TKD]
TOKOLOR alt for TOUCOULEUR [TOU]
TOKONDINDI dial of PAMONA [BCX]
TOKOTU'A dial of MORONENE [MQN]
TOKU-NO-SHIMA [TKN] lang, Japan
TOKUNU alt for NASIKWABW dial of MISIMA-
    PANEATI [MPX]
TOKWA alt for TLOKWA dial of SOTHO, NORTHERN
    [SRT]
TOKWASA alt for ROUKU [TCI]
TOL [JIC] lang, Honduras
TOLAI [KSD] lang, Papua New Guinea
TOLAKI [LBW] lang, Indonesia, Sulawesi
TOLAMLEINYUA dial of NAGA, KONYAK [NBE]
TOLANGAN alt for TELUGU [TCW]
TOLDIL dial of GOLA [GOL]
TOLDIL dial of GOLA [GOL]
TOLE alt for EASTERN GUAYMÍ dial of GUAYMÍ
    [GYM]
TOLEE' dial of UMA [PPK]
TOLI alt for TOLI-GBE [TLH]
TOLI alt for NORTHERN KONO dial of KONO [KNO]
TOLI-GBE [TLH] lang, Benin
TOLILIKO alt for TOLIWIKU dial of PAGU [PGU]
TOLITAI [TDS] lang, Indonesia, Irian Jaya
TOLITOLI [TXE] lang, Indonesia, Sulawesi
TOLIWIKU dial of PAGU [PGU]
TOLO alt for TALISE [TLR]
TOLO dial of BAHNAR [BDQ]
TOLO dial of TALISE [TLR]
TOLOKIWA alt for AROP-LOKEP [APR]
TOLOKIWA alt for LUKEP [LOA]
TOLOKOSON alt for TAGAL MURUT [MVV]
TOLOKOSON alt for RUNDUM MURUT dial of
    TAGAL MURUT [MVV]
TOLOMAKO [TLM] lang, Vanuatu
TOLOMAKO-JEREVIU alt for TOLOMAKO [TLM]
TOLOU alt for TONDANO [TDN]
TOLOUR alt for TONDANO [TDN]
TOLOWA [TOL] lang, USA
TOLOWERI dial of BIMA [BHP]
TOLPAN alt for TOL [JIC]
TOLUBI alt for KATCHA dial of KATCHA-KADUGLI-
    MIRI [KAT]
TOM dial of TATAR [TTR]
TOM-KUZNETS TATAR alt for SHOR [CJS]
TOMA [TOD] lang, Guinea
TOMA dial of SAMO [SBD]
TOMA MA DALLA alt for KADUGLI dial of KATCHA-
    KADUGLI-MIRI [KAT]

TOMACHECK alt for TAMAJEQ, AIR [THZ]
TOMACHECK alt for TAMASHEQ, TIMBUKTU [TAQ]
TOMACHECK alt for TAMAJEQ, TAHOUA [TTQ]
TOMACHEK alt for TAMAHAQ, HOGGAR [THV]
TOMADINO [TDI] lang, Indonesia, Sulawesi
TOMAGE dial of IRARUTU [IRH]
TOMAHU alt for FOGI dial of BURU [MHS]
TOMANI dial of TAGAL MURUT [MVV]
TOMARAHO alt for CHAMACOCO BRAVO dial of
    CHAMACOCO [CEG]
TOMARAXA alt for CHAMACOCO BRAVO dial of
    CHAMACOCO [CEG]
TOMÁS-ALIS dial of QUECHUA, YAUYOS [QUX]
TOMBAGGO alt for TANGBAGO [TGM]
TOMBALU alt for TOMBULU [TOM]
TOMBATU alt for TONSAWANG [TNW]
TOMBELALA [TTP] lang, Indonesia, Sulawesi
TOMBMATA alt for WEST SONGAI dial of SONGAI
    [SON]
TOMBO dial of DOGON [DOG]
TOMBONUO alt for TOMBONUWO [TXA]
TOMBONUVA alt for TOMBONUWO [TXA]
TOMBONUWO [TXA] lang, Malaysia, Sabah
TOMBOUCTOU alt for TIMBUKTU dial of
    TAMASHEQ, TIMBUKTU [TAQ]
TOMBUCAS alt for TUMBUKA [TUW]
TOMBULA alt for TOMBULU [TOM]
TOMBULU [TOM] lang, Indonesia, Sulawesi
TOMBULU' alt for TOMBULU [TOM]
TOMEA dial of TUKANGBESI SOUTH [BHQ]
TOMEDES [TOE] lang, Colombia
TOMIA alt for TOMEA dial of TUKANGBESI SOUTH
    [BHQ]
TOMINI [TXM] lang, Indonesia, Sulawesi
TOMMAN alt for MALFAXAL [MLX]
TOMMOT dial of EVENKI [EVN]
TOMO alt for BATEK [BTQ]
TOMOHON dial of TOMBULU [TOM]
TOMOIP [TUM] lang, Papua New Guinea
TOMOIVE alt for TOMOIP [TUM]
TOMONI dial of PAMONA [BCX]
TOMOYP alt for TOMOIP [TUM]
TOMPAKEWA alt for TONTEMBOAN [TNT]
TOMPASO dial of TONTEMBOAN [TNT]
TOMPO alt for BARRU dial of BUGIS [BPR]
TOMPON dial of EVEN [EVE]
TOMPULUNG alt for KADAZAN, LABUK-
    KINABATANGAN [DTB]
TOMU [TOX] lang, Papua New Guinea
TOMU dial of ARANDAI [JBJ]
TOMU RIVER alt for TOMU [TOX]
TONA dial of RUKAI [DRU]
TONDA [IND] lang, Papua New Guinea
TONDAI dial of BUNUN [BNN]
TONDANO [TDN] lang, Indonesia, Sulawesi, USA
TONDANO dial of TONDANO [TDN]
TONDANOU alt for TONDANO [TDN]
TONG alt for TA'OIH, LOWER [TTO]
TÓNG alt for PA HNG [PHA]
TONG alt for PA HNG [PHA]
TONG alt for DONG [KMC]
TONG dial of PAK-TONG [PKG]
TONG dial of TA'OIH, LOWER [TTO]
TONG-PAK alt for PAK-TONG [PKG]
TONGA [TNZ] lang, Thailand, Malaysia, Peninsular
TONGA [TOG] lang, Malawi

TONGA [TOH] lang, Mozambique
TONGA [TOI] lang, Zambia, Zimbabwe, Zimbabwe
TONGA alt for TONGA [TOI]
TONGA alt for TONGAN [TOV]
TONGA alt for KENSIU [KNS]
TONGA alt for TSONGA [TSO]
TONGA dial of CHOPI [CCE]
TONGA dial of NDAU [NDC]
TONGA-INHAMBANE alt for TONGA [TOH]
TONGAN [TOV] lang, Tonga, American Samoa, Fiji, New Zealand
TONGAREVA alt for PENRHYN [PNH]
TONGARIKI ISLAND dial of NAMAKURA [NMK]
TONGBO alt for MAMBILA, CAMEROON [MYA]
TONGBO alt for MAMBILA, NIGERIA [MZK]
TONGIAN 1 dial of BAJAU, INDONESIAN [BDL]
TONGIAN 2 dial of BAJAU, INDONESIAN [BDL]
TONGKOU alt for TANGKOU [TGK]
TONGOA alt for NGUNA dial of EFATE, NORTH [LLP]
TONGOA ISLAND dial of NAMAKURA [NMK]
TONGOYNA alt for TUPURI [TUI]
TONGREN dial of BONAN [PEH]
TONGSHÍ dial of HLAI [LIC]
TONGTOU dial of CHINESE, MIN NAN [CFR]
TONGWE [TNY] lang, Tanzania
TONI alt for GWANDARA EASTERN dial of GWANDARA [GWN]
TONJ BONGO dial of BONGO [BOT]
TONJO dial of TUKI [BAG]
TONKAWA [TON] lang, USA
TONKINESE alt for NORTHERN VIETNAMESE dial of VIETNAMESE [VIE]
TONKO alt for MABAAN [MFZ]
TONKO alt for WESTERN LIMBA dial of LIMBA, WEST-CENTRAL [LIA]
TONORE alt for TXIKÃO [TXI]
TONSAWANG [TNW] lang, Indonesia, Sulawesi
TONSEA [TXS] lang, Indonesia, Sulawesi
TONSEA' alt for TONSEA [TXS]
TONTEMBOAN [TNT] lang, Indonesia, Sulawesi
TONTO dial of APACHE, WESTERN [APW]
TONTOLI alt for TOLITOLI [TXE]
TOO DII alt for TOLDIL dial of GOLA [GOL]
TOODII alt for TOLDIL dial of GOLA [GOL]
TOOGO dial of GBAYA [GYA]
TOOMA alt for TOMA [TOD]
TOORO alt for TORO dial of HEMA-SUD [NIX]
TOORO alt for TORO dial of NYORO [NYR]
TOOTOTOBI alt for YANOMAY dial of YANOMÁMI [WCA]
TOPADA dial of PAMONA [BCX]
TOPOIYO [TOY] lang, Indonesia, Sulawesi
TOPOKE alt for POKE [POF]
TOPOSA [TOQ] lang, Sudan, Ethiopia
TOPOTAA alt for TAA dial of PAMONA [BCX]
TOPOTHA alt for TOPOSA [TOQ]
TOPURA dial of WEDAU [WED]
TORÁ [TRZ] lang, Brazil
TORADJA alt for TORAJA-SA'DAN [SDA]
TORAJA alt for TORAJA-SA'DAN [SDA]
TORAJA BARAT dial of TORAJA-SA'DAN [SDA]
TORAJA TIMUR alt for TAE' [ROB]
TORAJA TIMUR alt for TOALA' [TLZ]
TORAJA-SA'DAN [SDA] lang, Indonesia, Sulawesi
TORAM [TRJ] lang, Chad
TORAU [TTU] lang, Papua New Guinea

TORAZ alt for TORÁ [TRZ]
TORBI alt for MAMBILA, CAMEROON [MYA]
TORBI alt for SUNU TORBI dial of MAMBILA, CAMEROON [MYA]
TORETE dial of TULAMBATU [MFG]
TORGHOUD alt for TORGUT dial of KALMYK-OIRAT [KGZ]
TORGHUD alt for TORGUT dial of KALMYK-OIRAT [KGZ]
TORGON dial of NANAI [GLD]
TORGUT dial of KALMYK-OIRAT [KGZ]
TORGUUD alt for TORGUT dial of KALMYK-OIRAT [KGZ]
TORI AIKWAKAI alt for SIKARITAI [TTY]
TORIKO alt for LIKA [LIK]
TORISHIMA dial of OKINAWAN, CENTRAL [RYU]
TORKOMANI alt for TURKMEN [TCK]
TORLAKIAN dial of SERBO-CROATIAN [SRC]
TORNASI alt for KELO [TSN]
TORNE dial of SAAMI, NORTHERN [LPR]
TORO dial of BAMBARA [BRA]
TORO dial of HEMA-SUD [NIX]
TORO dial of NYORO [NYR]
TORO alt for FALI-TINGUELIN dial of FALI, SOUTH [FLE]
TOROKO alt for TAROKO [TRV]
TOROM alt for TORAM [TRJ]
TOROMONA alt for TOROMONO [TNO]
TOROMONO [TNO] lang, Bolivia
TORONA dial of MORO HILLS [TAZ]
TORR alt for CHIN, TAWR [TCP]
TORRES alt for HIW [HIW]
TORRES alt for TOGA [LHT]
TORRES ISLAND alt for HIW [HIW]
TORRES STRAIT BROKEN alt for TORRES STRAIT CREOLE [TCS]
TORRES STRAIT CREOLE [TCS] lang, Australia
TORRES STRAIT PIDGIN alt for TORRES STRAIT CREOLE [TCS]
TORRICELLI [TEI] lang, Papua New Guinea
TORTI dial of MIDOB [MEI]
TORU alt for TAUNGYO [TCO]
TORUM alt for TORAM [TRJ]
TORWALI [TRW] lang, Pakistan
TOSK alt for ALBANIAN, TOSK [ALN]
TOTALI dial of NEWARI [NEW]
TOTELA [TTL] lang, Zambia
TOTO of DHIMAL [DHI]
TOTOK dial of NAGA, KONYAK [NBE]
TOTOLI alt for TOLITOLI [TXE]
TOTONACO, COYUTLA [TOC] lang, Mexico
TOTONACO, FILOMENO MATA-COAHUITLÁN [TLP] lang, Mexico
TOTONACO, NORTHERN [TOO] lang, Mexico
TOTONACO, OZUMATLÁN [TQT] lang, Mexico
TOTONACO, PAPANTLA [TOP] lang, Mexico
TOTONACO, PATLA [TOT] lang, Mexico
TOTONACO, SIERRA [TOS] lang, Mexico
TOTONACO, YECUATLA [TLC] lang, Mexico
TOTORE dial of BARUGA [BBB]
TOUAOURU alt for NUMEE [KDK]
TOUAOURU alt for NUMEE dial of NUMEE [KDK]
TOUAREG alt for TAMAHAQ, HOGGAR [THV]
TOUAREG alt for TAMAJEQ, AIR [THZ]
TOUAREG alt for TAMAJEQ, TAHOUA [TTQ]
TOUAT [TTA] lang, Algeria

TOUBAKAI alt for SONINKE [SNN]
TOUBOU alt for TEDA [TUQ]
TOUBOU alt for TUBU dial of TEDA [TUQ]
TOUBOU alt for TUBU dial of TEDA [TUQ]
TOUBOURI alt for TUPURI [TUI]
TOUCOULEUR [TOU] lang, Senegal, Gambia, Guinea, Mali, Mauritania
TOUGAN dial of SAMO [SBD]
TOUGGOURT alt for TOUGOURT [TJO]
TOUGOURT [TJO] lang, Algeria
TOULONNAIS alt for MARITIME PROVENÇAL dial of PROVENÇAL [PRV]
TOULOUR alt for TONDANO [TDN]
TOUMAK alt for TUMAK [TMC]
TOUMBULU alt for TOMBULU [TOM]
TOUNIA [TUG] lang, Chad
TOUNTEMBOAN alt for TONTEMBOAN [TNT]
TOUPOURI alt for TUPURI [TUI]
TOURA [NEB] lang, Côte d'Ivoire
TOURAGE alt for TAMAHAQ, HOGGAR [THV]
TOURAGE alt for TAMAJEQ, TAHOUA [TTQ]
TOURAI dial of MOUK-ARIA [MWH]
TOURKA alt for TURKA [TUZ]
TOUROU alt for TUR dial of HEDI [TUR]
TOUSSIAN, NORTHERN [TSP] lang, Burkina Faso
TOUSSIAN, SOUTHERN [WIB] lang, Burkina Faso
TOVOKE alt for POKE [POF]
TOWA alt for JEMEZ [TOW]
TOWAL alt for MASAKIN TUWAL dial of NGILE [MAS]
TOWANGARA dial of YANTA [YNT]
TOWARE alt for TAE' [ROB]
TOWARE alt for TOALA' [TLZ]
TOWARGARHI alt for BHADAURI dial of BUNDELI [BNS]
TOWE alt for TOWEI [TTN]
TOWEI [TTN] lang, Indonesia, Irian Jaya
TOWETAN alt for MALAVEDAN [MJR]
TOWI alt for NEYO [NEY]
TOWN BEMBA dial of BEMBA [BEM]
TOWOLHI alt for MACA [MCA]
TOYERI dial of HUACHIPAERI [HUG]
TOYOERI alt for TOYERI dial of HUACHIPAERI [HUG]
TOZHUMA alt for NAGA, YIMCHUNGRU [YIM]
TOZLUK TURKS dial of BALKAN GAGAUZ TURKISH [BGX]
TOZVI alt for LOZI [LOZ]
TRABZON dial of ARMENIAN [ARM]
TRADE JULA alt for DIOULA VÉHICULAIRE dial of BAMBARA [BRA]
TRADE MALAY alt for BAZAAR MALAY dial of MALAY [MLI]
TRAI alt for MIEN [YOC]
TRAKAY dial of KARAIM [KDR]
TRANSALPIN dial of PROVENÇAL [PRV]
TRANSITIONAL KANAUJI dial of KANAUJI [BJJ]
TRANSVAAL NDEBELE alt for NDEBELE [NEL]
TRANSVAAL SOTHO alt for SOTHO, NORTHERN [SRT]
TRANSYLVANIA dial of GERMAN, STANDARD [GER]
TRANSYLVANIAN dial of ROMANI, CARPATHIAN [RMC]
TRANSYLVANIAN dial of RUMANIAN [RUM]
TRAPEZUNT alt for TRABZON dial of ARMENIAN [ARM]
TRÀU alt for TRAW dial of CUA [CUA]

TRAUDE alt for DGHWEDE [DGH]
TRAVELLER DANISH [RMD] lang, Denmark
TRAVELLER NORWEGIAN [RMG] lang, Norway
TRAVELLER SCOTTISH [TRL] lang, United Kingdom, USA
TRAVELLER SWEDISH [RMU] lang, Sweden
TRAW dial of CUA [CUA]
TREGAMI [TRM] lang, Afghanistan
TREGORROIS dial of BRETON [BRT]
TREMBO dial of GREBO, GLOBO [GRV]
TREMEMBÉ [TME] lang, Brazil
TRENG alt for TRIENG [STG]
TRENG alt for BALAIT dial of LUNDAYEH [LND]
TRENGGANU dial of MALAY [MLI]
TRENTINO WESTERN dial of LOMBARD [LMO]
TREPO dial of KRUMEN, NORTHEASTERN [PYE]
TRETINE dial of VENETIAN [VEC]
TRI alt for SO TRI [SZT]
TRIBAL ORIYA alt for ORIYA, ADIWASI [ORT]
TRIENG [STG] lang, Viet Nam
TRIGAMI alt for TREGAMI [TRM]
TRING alt for TRINGUS [TRX]
TRING dial of KOHO [KPM]
TRINGUS [TRX] lang, Malaysia, Sarawak
TRINH alt for TRING dial of KOHO [KPM]
TRINIDAD CREOLE FRENCH [TRF] lang, Trinidad and Tobago
TRINIDAD VERNACULAR ENGLISH dial of ENGLISH [ENG]
TRINIDADIEN alt for TRINIDAD CREOLE FRENCH [TRF]
TRINITARIO [TRN] lang, Bolivia
TRINKAT alt for TRINKUT dial of NICOBARESE, CENTRAL [NCB]
TRINKUT dial of NICOBARESE, CENTRAL [NCB]
TRIÓ [TRI] lang, Surinam, Brazil
TRIOMETESEM alt for AKURIO [AKO]
TRIOMETESEN alt for AKURIO [AKO]
TRIPERAH alt for TIPPERA [TPE]
TRIPOLI dial of ARABIC, LIBYAN [AYL]
TRIPURA alt for TIPPERA [TPE]
TRIPURA alt for KOK BOROK [TRP]
TRIPURI alt for KOK BOROK [TRP]
TRIQUE, SAN ANDRÉS CHICAHUAXTLA [TRS] lang, Mexico
TRIQUE, SAN JUAN COPALA [TRC] lang, Mexico
TRIQUE, SAN MARTÍN ITUNYOSO [TRQ] lang, Mexico
TRIQUI alt for TRIQUE, SAN JUAN COPALA [TRC]
TROBIAWAN dial of BASAY [BYQ]
TROMOWA alt for GROMA [GRO]
TRONDHEIM dial of NORWEGIAN SIGN LANGUAGE [NSL]
TRONG GIA alt for BOUYEI [PCC]
TRUCIAL COAST ARABIC dial of ARABIC, GULF [AFB]
TRUE MOTU alt for MOTU [MEU]
TRUJ alt for DAR EL KABIRA dial of TULISHI [TEY]
TRUK [TRU] lang, Micronesia
TRUKÁ [TKA] lang, Brazil
TRUKESE alt for TRUK [TRU]
TRUKESE dial of TRUK [TRU]
TRUKHMEN alt for TURKMEN [TCK]
TRUKHMENY alt for TURKMEN [TCK]
TRUKMEN dial of TURKMEN [TCK]

TRUMAÍ [TPY] lang, Brazil
TRUNG alt for DRUNG [DUU]
TRUSAN dial of LUNDAYEH [LND]
TRUSAN dial of LUNDAYEH [LND]
TRUSAN alt for TRUSAN dial of LUNDAYEH [LND]
TS'AMAY alt for TSAMAI [TSB]
TS'EXA alt for HANDÁ [HNH]
TS'IXA alt for HANDÁ [HNH]
TS'OLE' dial of ATAYAL [TAY]
TSAAM alt for SAMBA [SMX]
TSAAM alt for BOK dial of MANDYAK [MFV]
TSAAM alt for BOK dial of MANDYAK [MFV]
TSAAMO dial of MANDYAK [MFV]
TSAANGI [TSA] lang, Gabon, Congo
TSAAYI dial of TEKE, WESTERN [TEZ]
TSAAYI dial of TEKE, WESTERN [TEZ]
TSAGA alt for ENGA [ENQ]
TSAGU [TGD] lang, Nigeria
TSAIWA alt for ATSI [ATB]
TSAIWA dial of ATSI [ATB]
TSAKHUR [TKR] lang, Russia, Europe, Azerbaijan
TSAKHURY alt for TSAKHUR [TKR]
TSAKONIA alt for TSAKONIAN [TSD]
TSAKONIAN [TSD] lang, Greece
TSALAGI alt for CHEROKEE [CER]
TSALISEN alt for RUKAI [DRU]
TSAMA alt for EBRIÉ [EBR]
TSAMAI [TSB] lang, Ethiopia
TSAMAKKO alt for TSAMAI [TSB]
TSAMAKO alt for TSAMAI [TSB]
TSAMANGKHA dial of KEBUMTAMP [KJZ]
TSAMBA alt for SAMBA [SMX]
TSAMBA alt for SAMBA DAKA [CCG]
TSANG alt for GTSANG dial of TIBETAN [TIC]
TSANGI alt for TSAANGI [TSA]
TSANGLA [TSJ] lang, Bhutan, China, China, India
TSANGLA alt for TSANGLA [TSJ]
TSANGLO alt for NAGA, ANGAMI [NJM]
TSANUMA alt for SANUMÁ [SAM]
TSARISEN alt for RUKAI [DRU]
TSAUDANGSI alt for CHAUDANGSI [CDN]
TSAUKWE alt for N/HAI-NTSE'E [NKT]
TSAUKWE dial of NHARON [NHR]
TSAURASYA [TSU] lang, Nepal
TSAXUR alt for TSAKHUR [TKR]
TSAYA alt for TSAAYI dial of TEKE, WESTERN [TEZ]
TSAYE alt for TSAAYI dial of TEKE, WESTERN [TEZ]
TSAYE alt for TSAAYI dial of TEKE, WESTERN [TEZ]
TSAYI alt for TSAAYI dial of TEKE, WESTERN [TEZ]
TSAYI alt for TSAAYI dial of TEKE, WESTERN [TEZ]
TSCHAKO alt for SHEKO [SHE]
TSCHETTI dial of IFÈ [IFE]
TSCHIOKLOE alt for CHOKWE [CJK]
TSCHIOKWE alt for CHOKWE [CJK]
TSCHOPI alt for CHOPI [CCE]
TSEGOB alt for SOUTHERN AKHVAKH dial of
    AKHVAKH [AKV]
TSEKU [TSK] lang, China, Bhutan, Nepal
TSEKU alt for TSEKU [TSK]
TSENAP alt for CHENAPIAN [CJN]
TSEPANG alt for CHEPANG [CDM]
TSEREKWE dial of NHARON [NHR]
TSESUNGÚN dial of HUILLICHE [HUH]
TSEZ alt for DIDO [DDO]
TSEZY alt for DIDO [DDO]
TSH'EREKHWE dial of DETI-KHWE [DET]

TSH'ITI alt for TSHIDI-KHWE dial of SHUA [SHG]
TSHAAHUI alt for CHAYAHUITA [CBT]
TSHALA alt for CHALA [CHA]
TSHALHIT alt for TACHELHIT [SHI]
TSHALINGPA dial of DZONGKHA [DZO]
TSHAMBERI alt for CHAMBRI [CAN]
TSHEENYA alt for ENYA [GEY]
TSHIDI-KHWE dial of SHUA [SHG]
TSHIGA alt for IGIKIGA dial of RWANDA [RUA]
TSHILUBA alt for LUBA-KASAI [LUB]
TSHINUK WAWA alt for CHINOOK WAWA [CRW]
TSHIRAMBO alt for BAMBALANG [BMO]
TSHIVENDA alt for VENDA [VEN]
TSHOGO alt for HUTU dial of RWANDA [RUA]
TSHOKWE alt for CHOKWE [CJK]
TSHOM-DJAPÁ [TSM] lang, Brazil
TSHUMAKWE alt for SHUA [SHG]
TSHUMKWE alt for KUNG-TSUMKWE [KTZ]
TSHUOSH alt for SAWOS [SIC]
TSHUWAU alt for HIECHWARE [HIE]
TSHUWAU alt for HIOTSHUWAU [HIO]
TSHWANA alt for TSWANA [TSW]
TSHWOSH alt for SAWOS [SIC]
TSIA alt for ZIA [ZIA]
TSIBATABAI alt for DIOS dial of TINPUTZ [TPZ]
TSIE alt for LIGBI [LIG]
TSIGADI alt for GADI dial of GADI-SHINGINI-VADI-
    BAANGI [KAM]
TSIGANE alt for ROMANI, SINTE [RMO]
TSIGANE alt for ROMANI, VLACH [RMY]
TSIGENE alt for DOMARI [RMT]
TSIGENE alt for ROMANI, VLACH [RMY]
TSÍHULI alt for CHITKULI [CIK]
TSIKIMBA alt for KIMBA dial of AGAUSHI-KIMBA-
    NGWANCI [KDL]
TSILMANO alt for ZILMAMU [ZIL]
TSIMANÉ [CAS] lang, Bolivia
TSIMIHETRY alt for TSIMIHETY dial of MALAGASY
    [MEX]
TSIMIHETY dial of MALAGASY [MEX]
TSIMPSHEAN alt for TSIMSHIAN [TSI]
TSIMSHIAN [TSI] lang, Canada, USA, USA
TSIMSHIAN alt for TSIMSHIAN [TSI]
TSINDIR alt for NAGA, LOTHA [NJH]
TSINGA dial of TUKI [BAG]
TSINGANI alt for ROMANI, VLACH [RMY]
TSIRACUA alt for AYOREO [AYO]
TSIRICUA dial of AYOREO [AYO]
TSIRIPÁ alt for CHIRIPA [NHD]
TSITKHULI alt for CHITKULI [CIK]
TSITSIKHAR alt for QIQIHAR dial of DAUR [DTA]
TSIVADI alt for VADI dial of GADI-SHINGINI-VADI-
    BAANGI [KAM]
TSIVILI alt for VILI [VIF]
TSLAGI alt for CHEROKEE [CER]
TSO alt for TSOU [TSY]
TSOBWA alt for PIANGA dial of BUSHOONG [BUF]
TSOCHIANG alt for ZUOJIANG dial of ZHUANG,
    SOUTHERN [CCY]
TSOGHAMI alt for NAGA, ANGAMI [NJM]
TSOGO [TSV] lang, Gabon
TSOKWAMBO alt for KOTOGÜT [KVZ]
TSOLA dial of TUYUCA [TUE]
TSONGA [TSO] lang, South Africa, Mozambique,
    Swaziland
TSONGA alt for TSONGA [TSO]

TSONGOL dial of MONGOLIAN, HALH [KHK]
TSONTSII alt for NAGA, LOTHA [NJH]
TSONTSU dial of NAGA, LOTHA [NJH]
TSOO alt for TSOU [TSY]
TSOROKWE dial of NHARON [NHR]
TSOTSI TAAL alt for FLY TAAL [FLY]
TSOTSO dial of LUYIA [LUY]
TSOU [TSY] lang, Taiwan
TSOVA-TUSH alt for BATS [BBL]
TSU-U alt for TSOU [TSY]
TSU-WO alt for TSOU [TSY]
TSUDAKHAR alt for CUDAXAR dial of DARGWA
  [DAR]
TSUGUMI alt for NAGA, ANGAMI [NJM]
TSUMANGGORUN dial of ADZERA [AZR]
TS'ÜN-LAO [TSL] lang, Viet Nam
TSUNARI alt for BANONI [BCM]
TSUNTIN alt for DIDO [DDO]
TSUOU alt for TSOU [TSY]
TSUREJA alt for RESHE [RES]
TSURESHE alt for RESHE [RES]
TSUVAN [TSH] lang, Cameroon
TSUWENKI dial of MARING [MBW]
TSWA [TSC] lang, Mozambique, Zimbabwe, South
  Africa, Zimbabwe
TSWA alt for TSWA [TSC]
TSWA dial of TSWA [TSC]
TSWA dial of TSWA [TSC]
TSWANA [TSW] lang, Botswana, South Africa,
  Namibia, South Africa, Zimbabwe
TSWANA alt for TSWANA [TSW]
TSWENE dial of SOTHO, NORTHERN [SRT]
TSWENI alt for TSWENE dial of SOTHO, NORTHERN
  [SRT]
TTA'O alt for MAKATAO dial of SIRAIYA [FOS]
TTHWARI alt for MACA [XMC]
TU [MJG] lang, China
TU DÍ alt for BOUYEI [PCC]
TU DÌN alt for BOUYEI [PCC]
TU NGORO alt for NGORO dial of TUKI [BAG]
TU'BORO alt for SAKPU dial of KARANG [KZR]
TU-LOP alt for NOP dial of KOHO [KPM]
TUAL dial of OSETIN [OSE]
TUAM alt for TUAM-MUTU [TUC]
TUAM dial of TUAM-MUTU [TUC]
TUAM-MUTU [TUC] lang, Papua New Guinea
TUAMOTUAN [PMT] lang, French Polynesia
TUARAN DUSUN alt for LOTUD [DTR]
TUAREG alt for TAMAHAQ, HOGGAR [THV]
TUAREG alt for TAMAJEQ, AIR [THZ]
TUAREG alt for TAMASHEQ, TIMBUKTU [TAQ]
TUAREG alt for TAMAJEQ, TAHOUA [TTQ]
TUAT alt for TOUAT [TTA]
TUAURU alt for NUMEE [KDK]
TUBA alt for LIGBI [LIG]
TUBA alt for TUVIN [TUN]
TUBA-KIZHI dial of TUVIN [TUN]
TUBAI dial of NAMOSI-NAITASIRI-SERUA [BWB]
TUBAL dial of LAMMA [LEV]
TUBANIWAI alt for NUCLEAR WESTERN FIJIAN dial
  of FIJIAN, WESTERN [WYY]
TUBAR [TBU] lang, Mexico
TUBARÃO [TBA] lang, Brazil
TUBARE alt for TUBAR [TBU]
TUBBI alt for ULUMANDA' [ULM]
TUBBIA dial of DAYAK, LAND [DYK]

TUBETA alt for TAVETA [TVS]
TUBETUBE [TTE] lang, Papua New Guinea
TUBIRUASA alt for URUANGNIRIN [URN]
TUBU alt for TEDA [TUQ]
TUBU dial of TEDA [TUQ]
TUBUAI dial of AUSTRAL [AUT]
TUBUAI-RURUTU alt for AUSTRAL [AUT]
TUBULAMO dial of SINAGORO [SNC]
TUBURI alt for TUPURI [TUI]
TUCANO [TUO] lang, Brazil, Colombia, Colombia
TUCHIA alt for TUJIA [TJI]
TUCHINAUA alt for TUXINÁWA [TUX]
TUCUNA alt for TICUNA [TCA]
TUDA alt for TEDA [TUQ]
TUDA alt for TODA [TCX]
TUDA alt for TEDA dial of TEDA [TUQ]
TUDAGA alt for TEDA [TUQ]
TUDAGA alt for TEDA dial of TEDA [TUQ]
TUDAHWE alt for PAWAIA [PWA]
TUDANCHI alt for ROR dial of PUKU-GEERI-KERI-
  WIPSI [GEL]
TUER-GALA dial of ZAGHAWA [ZAG]
TUERKE alt for ILI TURKI [ILI]
TUFTERA alt for HWANA [HWO]
TUGARA alt for DURUWA [PCI]
TUGARI dial of BARUGA [BBB]
TUGEN, NORTH [TUY] lang, Kenya
TUGERI alt for MARIND [MRZ]
TUGRAMA dial of IRARUTU [IRH]
TUGUN [TZN] lang, Indonesia, Maluku
TUGUN alt for MBEMBE, TIGON [NZA]
TUGURO-CHUMIKAN dial of EVENKI [EVN]
TUGURT alt for TOUGOURT [TJO]
TUGUTIL [TUJ] lang, Indonesia, Maluku
TUHUP dial of HUPDÈ [JUP]
TUIC dial of DINKA, SOUTHWESTERN [DIK]
TUIC dial of DINKA, SOUTHEASTERN [DIN]
TUJIA [TJI] lang, China
TUJIA alt for BOUYEI [PCC]
TUKA dial of GAGU [GGU]
TUKAIMI alt for NAGA, KHOIRAO [NKI]
TUKANA alt for TUCANO [TUO]
TUKÁNA alt for TUCANO [TUO]
TUKANG-BESI alt for TUKANGBESI SOUTH [BHQ]
TUKANGBESI NORTH [KHC] lang, Indonesia,
  Sulawesi, Singapore
TUKANGBESI SOUTH [BHQ] lang, Indonesia,
  Sulawesi
TUKEN alt for TUGEN, NORTH [TUY]
TUKEN alt for SOUTH TUGEN dial of KALENJIN
  [KLN]
TUKI [BAG] lang, Cameroon
TUKIUMU dial of RAWANG [RAW]
TUKKONGO alt for WONGO [WON]
TUKOLOR alt for TOUCOULEUR [TOU]
TUKOMBE alt for KOMBE dial of TUKI [BAG]
TUKONGO alt for WONGO [WON]
TUKPA [TPQ] lang, India
TUKUDE alt for TUKUDEDE [TKD]
TUKUDEDE [TKD] lang, Indonesia, Nusa Tenggara
TUKUDH alt for WESTERN CANADA GWICH'IN dial
  of GWICH'IN [KUC]
TUKULOR alt for TOUCOULEUR [TOU]
TUKULU alt for BAJUNI dial of SWAHILI [SWA]
TUKUMANFÉD [TKF] lang, Brazil
TUKUN alt for MBEMBE, TIGON [NZA]

TUKUNA alt for TICUNA [TCA]
TUKÚNA alt for TICUNA [TCA]
TUKURINA dial of JAMAMADÍ [JAA]
TULA [TUL] lang, Nigeria
TULAI alt for ZEEM dial of ZEEM [ZUA]
TULAMA alt for TULEMA dial of OROMO,
  WELLEGA-CENTRAL [GAZ]
TULAMBATU [MFG] lang, Indonesia, Sulawesi
TULAMBATU dial of TULAMBATU [MFG]
TULEHU [TLU] lang, Indonesia, Maluku
TULEHU dial of TULEHU [TLU]
TULEM alt for DANI, MID GRAND VALLEY [DNT]
TULEMA dial of OROMO, WELLEGA-CENTRAL [GAZ]
TULESH alt for TULISHI [TEY]
TULIM dial of NAGA, TASE [NST]
TULING alt for ELING dial of TUNEN [BAZ]
TULISHI [TEY] lang, Sudan
TULISHI dial of TULISHI [TEY]
TULLU alt for TULU [TCY]
TULON alt for HALIA [HLA]
TULU [TCY] lang, India
TULU dial of BOHUAI [RAK]
TULU dial of TULU [TCY]
TULU-BOHUAI alt for BOHUAI [RAK]
TULUN alt for HALIA [HLA]
TULUN alt for TULU dial of BOHUAI [RAK]
TULUNG alt for DRUNG [DUU]
TULUVA BHASA alt for TULU [TCY]
TUM [TMK] lang, Laos
TUMAC alt for TUMAK [TMC]
TUMAK [TMC] lang, Chad
TUMALE dial of TAGOI [TAG]
TUMANAO alt for BLAAN, SARANGANI [BIS]
TUMANIQ alt for TOMANI dial of TAGAL MURUT
  [MVV]
TUMARA alt for MUNIWARA [MWB]
TUMARIYA alt for TAMARIA [TDB]
TUMARU alt for MUNIWARA [MWB]
TUMAWO alt for SKO [SKV]
TUMBELE alt for MBERE dial of TUKI [BAG]
TUMBOKA alt for TUMBUKA [TUW]
TUMBUKA [TUW] lang, Malawi, Tanzania, Tanzania,
  Zambia
TUMBUKA alt for TUMBUKA [TUW]
TUMBUNWHA alt for TOMBONUWO [TXA]
TUMET alt for TUMUT dial of MONGOLIAN,
  PERIPHERAL [MVF]
TUMI alt for KITIMI [KKU]
TUMIE alt for TOMOIP [TUM]
TUMLEO [TMQ] lang, Papua New Guinea
TUMMA [TBQ] lang, Sudan
TUMMA dial of TUMMA [TBQ]
TUMMOK alt for TUMAK [TMC]
TUMTUM [TBR] lang, Sudan
TUMTUM dial of TUMTUM [TBR]
TUMU alt for KAIRI [KLQ]
TUMU alt for TWUMWU dial of TIKAR [TIK]
TUMUAONG dial of KALAGAN [KQE]
TUMUIP alt for TOMOIP [TUM]
TUMUT dial of MONGOLIAN, PERIPHERAL [MVF]
TUN alt for TOUNIA [TUG]
TUNA alt for TOLAI [KSD]
TUNA alt for KATCHA dial of KATCHA-KADUGLI-
  MIRI [KAT]
TUNBUMOHAS alt for TOMBONUWO [TXA]
TUNCELI dial of KIRMANJKI [QKV]

TUNDRA alt for YUKAGHIR, NORTHERN [YKG]
TUNDRA ENETS alt for MADU dial of ENETS [ENE]
TUNDRA YURAK dial of NENETS [YRK]
TUNDRE alt for YUKAGHIR, NORTHERN [YKG]
TUNEBO, ANGOSTURAS [TND] lang, Colombia
TUNEBO, BARRO NEGRO [TBN] lang, Colombia
TUNEBO, CENTRAL [TUF] lang, Colombia,
  Venezuela, Venezuela
TUNEBO, CENTRAL alt for TUNEBO, CENTRAL [TUF]
TUNEBO, WESTERN [TNB] lang, Colombia
TUNEN [BAZ] lang, Cameroon
TUNG alt for DONGXIANG [SCE]
TUNG alt for DONG [KMC]
TUNG dial of KISSI, SOUTHERN [KSS]
TUNG dial of KISSI, NORTHERN [KQS]
TUNG NU alt for PUNU [PNU]
TUNG-CHIA alt for DONG [KMC]
TUNGA alt for DOYAYO [DOW]
TUNGA dial of DADIYA [DBD]
TUNGAG [LCM] lang, Papua New Guinea
TUNGAK alt for TUNGAG [LCM]
TUNGAN alt for DUNGAN [DNG]
TUNGAN alt for MABAAN [MFZ]
TUNGARA alt for TENGARA dial of BAUKAN [BNB]
TUNGBO alt for DOYAYO [DOW]
TUNGGARE [TRT] lang, Indonesia, Irian Jaya
TUNGHO dial of SAISIYAT [SAI]
TUNGHSIANG alt for DONGXIANG [SCE]
TUNGI' dial of FE'FE' [FMP]
TUNGKAL dial of KUBU [KVB]
TUNGKAL ILIR dial of KUBU [KVB]
TUNGKUAN dial of CHINESE, YUE [YUH]
TUNGU dial of NGELIMA [AGH]
TUNGU dial of NGOMBE [NGC]
TUNGURAHUA QUICHUA alt for QUICHUA,
  HIGHLAND, TUNGURAHUA [QQS]
TUNGUS alt for EVENKI [EVN]
TUNGYEN dial of BONAN [PEH]
TUNIA alt for TOUNIA [TUG]
TUNIS dial of ARABIC, JUDEO-TUNISIAN [AJT]
TUNISIAN alt for ARABIC, TUNISIAN [AEB]
TUNISIAN SIGN LANGUAGE [TSE] lang, Tunisia
TUNJUNG [TJG] lang, Indonesia, Kalimantan
TUNJUNG dial of TUNJUNG [TJG]
TUNJUNG DAYAK alt for TUNJUNG [TJG]
TUNJUNG LINGGANG dial of TUNJUNG [TJG]
TUNJUNG LONDONG dial of TUNJUNG [TJG]
TUNJUNG TENGAH alt for TUNJUNG dial of
  TUNJUNG [TJG]
TUNJUR alt for SOKORO [SOK]
TUNKA dial of BURIAT, RUSSIA [MNB]
TUNNI [TQQ] lang, Somalia
TUNONG dial of ACEH [ATJ]
TUNULI alt for TXIKÃO [TXI]
TUNULOA alt for SOUTHEAST VANUA LEVU dial of
  FIJIAN [FJI]
TUNYA alt for TOUNIA [TUG]
TUNYA dial of TOUNIA [TUG]
TUOBO dial of GREBO, NORTHEASTERN [GRP]
TUOBO dial of GREBO, GBOLOO [GEC]
TUOM alt for TUAM-MUTU [TUC]
TUOMO dial of IJO, CENTRAL-WESTERN [IJC]
TUOTOMB [TTF] lang, Cameroon
TUPARÍ [TUP] lang, Brazil
TUPEN alt for BASAA [BAA]
TUPINAKI alt for TUPINIKIN [TPK]

TUPINAMBÁ [TPN] lang, Brazil
TUPINIKIN [TPK] lang, Brazil
TUPITIMOAKE alt for RANGATAU dial of
    TUAMOTUAN [PMT]
TUPURI [TUI] lang, Cameroon, Chad, Chad
TUPURI alt for TUPURI [TUI]
TUR dial of HEDI [TUR]
TURA alt for TOURA [NEB]
TURA dial of TATAR [TTR]
TURAKA [TRH] lang, Papua New Guinea
TURAMA alt for RUMA [RUZ]
TURAMA RIVER KIWAI alt for MORIGI [MDB]
TURATEA dial of MAKASSAR [MSR]
TURE alt for TULA [TUL]
TURFAN dial of UYGHUR [UIG]
TURI [TRD] lang, India
TURIJE'NE' alt for BAJAU, INDONESIAN [BDL]
TURIUARA alt for TURIWÁRA [TWT]
TURIWÁRA [TWT] lang, Brazil
TURKA [TUZ] lang, Burkina Faso
TURKANA [TUV] lang, Kenya
TURKI alt for TURKISH [TRK]
TURKISH [TRK] lang, Turkey, Bulgaria, Cyprus,
    Greece, Romania, Uzbekistan, Yugoslavia
TURKISH alt for TURKISH [TRK]
TURKLER alt for AZERBAIJANI, NORTH [AZE]
TURKMAN alt for TURKMEN [TCK]
TURKMANI alt for TURKMEN [TCK]
TURKMANIAN alt for TURKMEN [TCK]
TURKMEN [TCK] lang, Turkmenistan, Afghanistan,
    Iran, Pakistan, Turkey
TURKMENI alt for TURKMEN [TCK]
TURKMENLER alt for TURKMEN [TCK]
TURKOMAN alt for TURKMEN [TCK]
TURKOMANS alt for TURKMEN [TCK]
TURKPA alt for TURKWAM [TDV]
TURKWAM [TDV] lang, Nigeria
TUROHA alt for AURAMA dial of PAWAIA [PWA]
TUROYO alt for SURYOYO [SYR]
TURPAN alt for TURFAN dial of UYGHUR [UIG]
TURRA dial of NARUNGGA [NNR]
TURRUBUL alt for THURAWAL [TBH]
TURRUPAN alt for TOL [JIC]
TURU alt for NYATURU [RIM]
TURU alt for YAWA [YVA]
TURU alt for IAU [TMU]
TURU dial of IAU [TMU]
TURU alt for TUR dial of HEDI [TUR]
TURU-HIDE alt for HEDI [TUR]
TURUBA alt for NYA GUYUWA dial of LONGUDA
    [LNU]
TURUBU alt for TEREBU [TRB]
TURUJ alt for DAR EL KABIRA dial of TULISHI [TEY]
TURUKA alt for TURKA [TUZ]
TURUMASA alt for BAINAPI [PIK]
TURUMAWA alt for ETULO [UTR]
TURUMBU alt for LOMBO [LOO]
TURUNG [TRY] lang, India
TURUNGGARE alt for TUNGGARE [TRT]
TURUPU alt for TEREBU [TRB]
TURUTAP alt for MAIA [SKS]
TURVALI alt for TORWALI [TRW]
TURYOYO alt for SURYOYO [SYR]
TUSCAN dial of ITALIAN [ITN]
TUSCARORA [TUS] lang, Canada, USA
TUSH alt for BATS [BBL]

TUSH dial of GEORGIAN [GEO]
TUSHA alt for TUXÁ [TUD]
TUSIA alt for TOUSSIAN, SOUTHERN [WIB]
TUSIA alt for TOUSSIAN, NORTHERN [TSP]
TUSIAN alt for TOUSSIAN, SOUTHERN [WIB]
TUSIAN alt for TOUSSIAN, NORTHERN [TSP]
TUTAPI alt for OREJÓN [ORE]
TUTCHONE [TUT] lang, Canada
TUTET alt for CHAURA [CHO]
TUTLA MIXE alt for MIXE, MAZATLÁN [MZL]
TUTOH KENYA alt for KENYAH, TUTOH [TTW]
TUTONCANA dial of EVENKI [EVN]
TUTONG 1 [TTX] lang, Brunei, Malaysia, Sarawak,
    Malaysia, Sarawak
TUTONG 1 alt for TUTONG 1 [TTX]
TUTONG 2 [TTG] lang, Brunei
TUTRUGBU alt for NYANGBO [NYB]
TUTSINGO alt for TSINGA dial of TUKI [BAG]
TUTUBA [TMI] lang, Vanuatu
TUTUBELA dial of MOLIMA [MOX]
TUTUME alt for NOUMOU [NOW]
TUTUNG alt for TUTONG 2 [TTG]
TUTUNOHAN alt for APUTAI [APX]
TUTUNOHAN alt for TUGUN [TZN]
TUTUNOHAN alt for PERAI [WET]
TUUNO alt for DOYAYO [DOW]
TUVA alt for TUVIN [TUN]
TUVA-URIANKHAI alt for TUVIN [TUN]
TUVALU alt for TUVALUAN [ELL]
TUVALUAN [ELL] lang, Tuvalu, Fiji, Nauru, New
    Zealand
TUVAN alt for TUVIN [TUN]
TUVIA alt for TUVIN [TUN]
TUVIN [TUN] lang, Russia, Asia, China, Mongolian
    Peoples Republic
TUVINIAN alt for TUVIN [TUN]
TUWA-URIANKHAI alt for TUVIN [TUN]
TUWANG dial of LAWANGAN [LBX]
TUWARI [TWW] lang, Papua New Guinea
TUWAT alt for TOUAT [TTA]
TUWILI alt for BOWIRI [BOV]
TUXÁ [TUD] lang, Brazil
TUXINÁWA [TUX] lang, Brazil
TUYUCA [TUE] lang, Colombia, Brazil
TUYUKA alt for TUYUCA [TUE]
TUYUNERI alt for TOYERI dial of HUACHIPAERI
    [HUG]
TUZANTECO dial of MOCHO [MHC]
TUZU alt for TU [MJG]
TVER dial of KARELIAN [KRL]
TVRA-KA-MOLO alt for MOLO [ZMO]
TWA dial of LENJE [LEH]
TWA dial of RWANDA [RUA]
TWA alt for RUTWA dial of RWANDA [RUA]
TWA OF BANGWEULU dial of BEMBA [BEM]
TWA OF KAFWE dial of TONGA [TOI]
TWABO dial of GLARO-TWABO [GLR]
TWAMPA alt for UDUK [UDU]
TWANA [TWA] lang, USA
TWARE alt for KWALE [KSJ]
TWELVE DISTRICTS SHAN alt for DAI [TIZ]
TWENDI [TWN] lang, Cameroon
TWI alt for TUIC dial of DINKA, SOUTHEASTERN
    [DIN]
TWIC alt for TUIC dial of DINKA, SOUTHWESTERN
    [DIK]

TWICH alt for TUIC dial of DINKA, SOUTHWESTERN [DIK]
TWII alt for BAKONI dial of KENYANG [KEN]
TWIJ alt for TUIC dial of DINKA, SOUTHWESTERN [DIK]
TWOYU alt for DIZI [MDX]
TWUMWU dial of TIKAR [TIK]
TXAPACURA alt for URUPÁ [URP]
TXAPAKURA alt for URUPÁ [URP]
TXIKÁN alt for TXIKÃO [TXI]
TXIKÃO [TXI] lang, Brazil
TXIRIPÁ alt for CHIRIPA [NHD]
TXITXOPI alt for CHOPI [CCE]
TXOPI alt for CHOPI [CCE]
TXUNHUÃ DYAPÁ alt for TSHOM-DJAPÁ [TSM]
TXUNHUÃ-DJAPÁ alt for TSHOM-DJAPÁ [TSM]
TXUWABO alt for CHWABO [CHW]
TYAL alt for ATAYAL [TAY]
TYAMA alt for EBRIÉ [EBR]
TYAMUHI alt for CEMUHÎ [CAM]
TYANGA alt for TYENGA dial of SHANGA [SHO]
TYAP alt for KATAB dial of KATAB [KCG]
TYAPI alt for LANDOMA [LAO]
TYARAITY [WOA] lang, Australia
TYEBALA alt for SENOUFO, CEBAARA [SEF]
TYEBARA dial of SENOUFO, CEBAARA [SEF]
TYEE dial of TEKE, WESTERN [TEZ]
TYEFO alt for TIÉFO [TIQ]
TYEFORO alt for TIÉFO [TIQ]
TYELIBELE alt for SENOUFO, TYELIRI [TYE]
TYEMERI dial of NANGIKURRUNGGURR [NAM]
TYENGA dial of SHANGA [SHO]
TYEYAXO alt for BOZO, TIÉYAXO [BOZ]
TYHUA alt for HIOTSHUWAU [HIO]
TYM dial of SELKUP [SAK]
TYNESIDE NORTHUMBERLAND dial of ENGLISH [ENG]
TYO alt for TYOO dial of TEKE, CENTRAL [TEC]
TYO alt for BALI dial of TEKE, EASTERN [TEK]
TYOO dial of TEKE, CENTRAL [TEC]
TYOPI alt for LANDOMA [LAO]
TYREWUJU dial of KALIHNA [CRB]
TYROLESE alt for GERMAN, HUTTERITE [GEH]
TYUA alt for HIOTSHUWAU [HIO]
TYUMEN dial of TATAR [TTR]
TYURA alt for NUGUNU [NNV]
TYURAMA alt for TURKA [TUZ]
TYVA alt for TUVIN [TUN]
TZELTAL, BACHAJÓN [TZB] lang, Mexico
TZELTAL, HIGHLAND [TZH] lang, Mexico
TZO alt for TSOU [TSY]
TZOTZIL, CHAMULA [TZC] lang, Mexico
TZOTZIL, CHENALHÓ [TZE] lang, Mexico
TZOTZIL, HUIXTÁN [TZU] lang, Mexico
TZOTZIL, SAN ANDRÉS LARRAINZAR [TZS] lang, Mexico
TZOTZIL, ZINACANTECO [TZZ] lang, Mexico
TZUTUHIL alt for TZUTUJIL, EASTERN [TZJ]
TZUTUJIL ORIENTAL alt for TZUTUJIL, EASTERN [TZJ]
TZUTUJIL, EASTERN [TZJ] lang, Guatemala
TZUTUJIL, WESTERN [TZT] lang, Guatemala
U [UUU] lang, China
U alt for TIBETAN [TIC]
U dial of KHMU [KJG]
U NÍ alt for HANI [HNI]

UA HUKA dial of MARQUESAN, NORTH [MRQ]
UA POU dial of MARQUESAN, NORTH [MRQ]
UAB ATONI PAH METO alt for ATONI [TMR]
UADZOLI dial of CARÚTANA [CRU]
UAGEO [UAG] lang, Papua New Guinea
UAIAI dial of PAUMARÍ [PAD]
UAIANA alt for PIRATAPUYO [PIR]
UAIANA alt for WAYANA [WAY]
UAICANA alt for PIRATAPUYO [PIR]
UAIEUE alt for WAIWAI [WAW]
UAIKENA alt for PIRATAPUYO [PIR]
UAIMIRÍ alt for WAIMIRÍ dial of ATRUAHÍ [ATR]
UAINANA alt for PIRATAPUYO [PIR]
UAIORA alt for WAYORÓ [WYR]
UAIQUIARE alt for WOKIARE dial of YABARANA [YAR]
UAIUAI alt for WAIWAI [WAW]
UALAMO alt for WOLAYTTA [WBC]
UAMUÉ [UAM] lang, Brazil
UANANA alt for GUANANO [GVC]
UANANO alt for GUANANO [GVC]
UARDAI alt for ORMA [ORC]
UARE alt for KWALE [KSJ]
UARI alt for TUBARÃO [TBA]
UARIPI [UAR] lang, Papua New Guinea
UASE alt for PELE-ATA [ATA]
UASI alt for PELE-ATA [ATA]
UASILAU alt for PELE-ATA [ATA]
UASONA alt for WASONA dial of TUCANO [TUO]
UAURA alt for WAURÁ [WAU]
UBA alt for WOLAYTTA [WBC]
UBACH alt for JAWE [JAZ]
UBAE dial of NAKANAI [NAK]
UBAGHARA [BYC] lang, Nigeria
UBAMER alt for WUBAHAMER dial of AARI [AIZ]
UBANG [UBA] lang, Nigeria
UBANI alt for IBANI [IBY]
UBDÉ alt for HUPDË [JUP]
UBETENG alt for EHOM dial of UKPET-EHOM [AKD]
UBI alt for GLIO-OUBI [OUB]
UBIAN dial of SAMA, SOUTHERN [SIT]
UBILI alt for MELAMELA [MXM]
UBIR [UBR] lang, Papua New Guinea
UBIRI alt for UBIR [UBR]
UBOI alt for KOBIANA [KCJ]
UBONG dial of KAREN, PWO OMKOI [PWW]
UBU dial of TBOLI [TBL]
UBU UGU alt for UMBU-UNGU [UMB]
UBUIA dial of DOBU [DOB]
UBYE dial of EKPEYE [EKP]
UBYKH [UBY] lang, Turkey
UBYX alt for UBYKH [UBY]
UCAYALI alt for QUECHUA, SAN MARTÍN [QSA]
UCAYALI alt for COCAMA-COCAMILLA [COD]
UCAYALI dial of CAMPA, ASHÉNINCA [CPU]
UCHAMA dial of EVENKI [EVN]
UCHUR dial of EVENKI [EVN]
UCINDA alt for CINDA dial of KAMUKU [KAU]
UDAGAGA dial of KASUWERI [QKW]
UDAI alt for MAMUJU [MQX]
UDAI dial of TEMUAN [TMW]
UDEGEIS alt for UDIHE [UDE]
UDEKAMA alt for DEGEMA [DEG]
UDEKHE alt for UDIHE [UDE]
UDERI dial of MARIA [MDS]
UDI [UDI] lang, Azerbaijan, Georgia

UDIHE [UDE] lang, Russia, Asia
UDIN alt for UDI [UDI]
UDINY alt for UDI [UDI]
UDJIR alt for UJIR [UDJ]
UDLAM alt for WUZLAM [UDL]
UDMURT [UDM] lang, Russia, Europe
UDMURT alt for NORTH UDMURT dial of UDMURT
 [UDM]
UDO dial of AKOKO, NORTH [AKK]
UDOM alt for NDE dial of NDE-NSELE-NTA [NDD]
UDUK [UDU] lang, Sudan
UDUNG alt for WUTUNG [WUT]
UELLANSKIJ dial of CHUKOT [CKT]
UEN alt for NUMEE [KDK]
UEREQUEMA alt for GUAREQUENA [GAE]
UFAINA alt for TANIMUCA-RETUARÃ [TNC]
UFAUFA dial of IDUNA [VIV]
UFIA dial of ORING [ORI]
UFIA dial of BARAI [BCA]
UFIM [UFI] lang, Papua New Guinea
UFIOM dial of ORING [ORI]
UFUFU dial of IDUNA [VIV]
UGANA dial of LAVATBURA-LAMUSONG [LBV]
UGARE dial of MESAKA [IYO]
UGBALA dial of KUKELE [KEZ]
UGBE alt for ALEGE [ALF]
UGBEM dial of UBAGHARA [BYC]
UGE alt for ALEGE [ALF]
UGELE alt for UGHELE [UGE]
UGEP alt for LOKO [YAZ]
UGEP dial of LOKO [YAZ]
UGHBUG alt for KUBACHI dial of DARGWA [DAR]
UGHELE [UGE] lang, Solomon Islands
UGI alt for BUGIS [BPR]
UGI alt for UKI NI MASI dial of SA'A [APB]
UGI RIAWA alt for PASANGKAYU dial of BUGIS
 [BPR]
UGIE alt for NGIE [NGJ]
UGONG [UGO] lang, Thailand
UGUANO alt for AGUANO [AGA]
UHAMI-IYAYU [UHA] lang, Nigeria
UHEI KACHLAKAN alt for LIANA-SETI [STE]
UHEI KACHLAKAN alt for BENGGOI [BGY]
UHEI KACLAKIN alt for LIANA-SETI [STE]
UHEI KAHLAKIM alt for LIANA-SETI [STE]
UHEI-KACLAKIN alt for BENGGOI [BGY]
UHEI-KAHLAKIM alt for BENGGOI [BGY]
UHUNDUNI alt for DAMAL [UHN]
UIAKU alt for UYAKU dial of MAISIN [MBQ]
UIGHOR alt for UYGHUR [UIG]
UIGHUIR alt for UYGHUR [UIG]
UIGHUR alt for UYGHUR [UIG]
UIGUIR alt for UYGHUR [UIG]
UIGUR alt for UYGHUR [UIG]
UINA alt for DESANO [DES]
UIRAFED alt for WIRAFÉD [WIR]
UISAI [UIS] lang, Papua New Guinea
UIVE alt for YIIVE dial of TIV [TIV]
UJARRÁS dial of CABÉCAR [CJP]
UJIR [UDJ] lang, Indonesia, Maluku
UJJAINI alt for MALVI [MUP]
UJLTA alt for OROK [OAA]
UJUMCHIN dial of MONGOLIAN, PERIPHERAL [MVF]
UJUMCHIN alt for SHILINGOL dial of MONGOLIAN,
 PERIPHERAL [MVF]
UJUMUCHIN dial of MONGOLIAN, HALH [KHK]

UJUMUCHIN alt for UJUMCHIN dial of MONGOLIAN,
 PERIPHERAL [MVF]
UJUURAAN alt for AJURAN dial of GARREH-
 AJURAN [GGH]
UJUWA alt for MOKPWE [BRI]
UKAAN [KCF] lang, Nigeria
UKELE alt for KUKELE [KEZ]
UKERMARK alt for EAST LOW GERMAN dial of
 GERMAN, LOW [GEP]
UKFWO alt for KUO [OKU]
UKHRUL dial of NAGA, TANGKHUL [NMF]
UKHWEJO [UKH] lang, Central African Republic
UKHWEJO dial of UKHWEJO [UKH]
UKI alt for BOKYI [BKY]
UKI alt for NGORO dial of TUKI [BAG]
UKI NI MASI dial of SA'A [APB]
UKIT [UMI] lang, Malaysia, Sarawak
UKKIA alt for WAGAYA [WGA]
UKPE dial of UKPE-BAYOBIRI [UKP]
UKPE-BAYOBIRI [UKP] lang, Nigeria
UKPELLA alt for OKPELA dial of IVBIE NORTH-
 OKPELA-ARHE [ATG]
UKPET dial of UKPET-EHOM [AKD]
UKPET-EHOM [AKD] lang, Nigeria
UKRAINE-MOLDAVIA dial of ROMANI, VLACH [RMY]
UKRAINIAN [UKR] lang, Ukraine, Czechoslovakia,
 Poland, Romania, Yugoslavia
UKRAINIAN alt for UKRAINIAN [UKR]
UKRAINIAN VLACH ROMANI dial of ROMANI,
 VLACH [RMY]
UKU alt for KUO [OKU]
UKU alt for OKO dial of OKO-ENI-OSAYEN [OKS]
UKUE-EHUEN [UKU] lang, Nigeria
UKURIGUMA [UKG] lang, Papua New Guinea
UKWALI alt for UKWUANI dial of UKWUANI-ABOH
 [UKW]
UKWANI alt for UKWUANI dial of UKWUANI-ABOH
 [UKW]
UKWESE alt for KWESE [KWS]
UKWUANI dial of UKWUANI-ABOH [UKW]
UKWUANI-ABOH [UKW] lang, Nigeria
ULA alt for FUNGWA [ULA]
ULA-XANGKU alt for WULA dial of PSIKYE [KVJ]
ULANCHAB dial of MONGOLIAN, PERIPHERAL [MVF]
ULAU-SUAIN [SVB] lang, Papua New Guinea
ULAWA dial of SA'A [APB]
ULCH [ULC] lang, Russia, Asia
ULCHA alt for ULCH [ULC]
ULCHI alt for ULCH [ULC]
ULDEME alt for WUZLAM [UDL]
ULEME alt for UNEME [UNE]
ULI alt for OLI dial of DUALA [DOU]
ULINGAN alt for MAUWAKE [MHL]
ULIPE alt for KUNZA [KUZ]
ULITHI [ULI] lang, Micronesia
ULITHIAN alt for ULITHI [ULI]
ULKULU dial of KUNJEN [KJN]
ULLATAN [ULL] lang, India
ULSTER dial of GAELIC, IRISH [GLI]
ULTA alt for OROK [OAA]
ULU alt for MABAAN [MFZ]
ULU dial of MINANGKABAU [MPU]
ULU dial of RAMOAAINA [RAI]
ULU dial of KERINCI [KVR]
ULU AI' dial of DOHOI [OTD]
ULU AL dial of IBAN [IBA]

ULU CERES dial of JAH HUT [JAH]
ULU KAMPAR dial of SEMAI [SEA]
ULU KINTA dial of TEMIAR [TMH]
ULU LAKO dial of KUBU [KVB]
ULU LANGAT ORANG BUKIT dial of BESISI [MHE]
ULU MUAR MALAY alt for NEGERI SEMBILAN
  MALAY [ZMI]
ULU SELAMA dial of KENSIU [KNS]
ULU TEMBELING dial of JAH HUT [JAH]
ULUBUKUSU dial of MASABA [MYX]
ULUBUYA dial of MASABA [MYX]
ULUDADIRI dial of MASABA [MYX]
ULUKISU dial of MASABA [MYX]
ULUKWUMI [ULB] lang, Nigeria
ULULERA alt for HUTU dial of RWANDA [RUA]
ULUMANDA' [ULM] lang, Indonesia, Sulawesi
ULUMANDAK alt for ULUMANDA' [ULM]
ULUMBU alt for LOMBO [LOO]
ULUN-NO-BOKAN alt for BAUKAN dial of BAUKAN
  [BNB]
ULUN-NO-BOKON alt for BAUKAN dial of BAUKAN
  [BNB]
ULUNCHUN alt for OROQEN [ORH]
ULUNDA alt for ULUMANDA' [ULM]
ULUNYANKOLE alt for NYANKOLE [NYN]
ULUNYANKORE alt for NYANKOLE [NYN]
ULURAGOOLI alt for LOGOOLI [RAG]
ULYCH alt for ULCH [ULC]
UMA [PPK] lang, Indonesia, Sulawesi
UMA dial of AKPOSO [KPO]
UMA ARIA alt for UMA [PPK]
UMA BAKAH dial of KENYAH, WESTERN [XKY]
UMA BEM dial of KENYAH, KELINYAU [XKL]
UMA DARO dial of KAYAN, REJANG [REE]
UMA JALAM dial of KENYAH, KELINYAU [XKL]
UMA JUMAN dial of KAYAN, REJANG [REE]
UMA LAKAN dial of KAYAN, KAYAN RIVER [XKN]
UMA POH alt for LONG KEHOBO dial of KAYAN,
  REJANG [REE]
UMA RATU NGGAI dial of SUMBA [SMI]
UMA TAU dial of KENYAH, KELINYAU [XKL]
UMA TIMAI dial of KENYAH, WAHAU [WHK]
UMAIROF alt for YOLIAPI dial of HEWA [HAM]
UMALASA alt for PENDAU [UMS]
UMANAKAINA [GDN] lang, Papua New Guinea
UMANIKAINA alt for UMANAKAINA [GDN]
UMAR alt for YERETUAR [GOP]
UMARI alt for KAMORO [KGQ]
UMARI alt for YERETUAR [GOP]
UMATILLA [UMA] lang, USA
UMAUA alt for OMAGUA [OMG]
UMAWA alt for CARIJONA [CBD]
UMAYAMNON alt for OMAYAMNON dial of
  MANOBO, AGUSAN [MSM]
UMBAIA alt for WAMBAYA [WMB]
UMBERTANA alt for ADYNYAMATHANHA [ADT]
UMBINDHAMU [UMD] lang, Australia
UMBOI alt for KOVAI [KQB]
UMBRIAN dial of ITALIAN [ITN]
UMBU RATU NGGAI alt for UMA RATU NGGAI dial
  of SUMBA [SMI]
UMBU-UNGU [UMB] lang, Papua New Guinea
UMBUGARLA [UMR] lang, Australia
UMBULE dial of TSAURASYA [TSU]
UMBUNDU [MNF] lang, Angola
UMBUYGAMU [UMG] lang, Australia

UME alt for SAAMI, UME [LPU]
UME dial of GIDRA [GDR]
UMEDA [UPI] lang, Papua New Guinea
UMERA dial of GEBE [GEI]
UMIRAY AGTA alt for AGTA, UMIRAY DUMAGET
  [DUE]
UMIREY DUMAGAT alt for AGTA, UMIRAY
  DUMAGET [DUE]
UMM DOREIN dial of MORO [MOR]
UMM GABRALLA dial of MORO [MOR]
UMON [UMM] lang, Nigeria
UMOTÍNA [UMO] lang, Brazil
UMPILA [UMP] lang, Australia
UMUA alt for MACUNA [MYY]
UMUAHIA dial of IGBO [IGR]
UMURANO alt for OMURANO [OMU]
UMUTINA alt for UMOTÍNA [UMO]
UMWATE dial of BARAI [BCA]
UNA [MTG] lang, Indonesia, Irian Jaya
UNALASKAN alt for EASTERN ALEUT dial of ALEUT
  [ALW]
UNALE alt for OENALE-DELHA dial of ROTI [ROT]
UNAMBAL alt for WUNAMBAL [WUB]
UNAMI [DEL] lang, USA
UNANGAN alt for ALEUT [ALW]
UNANGAN alt for WESTERN ALEUT dial of ALEUT
  [ALW]
UNANGANY alt for ALEUT [ALW]
UNANGANY alt for WESTERN ALEUT dial of ALEUT
  [ALW]
UNANGHAN alt for ALEUT [ALW]
UNANK [UNA] lang, Papua New Guinea
UNDE dial of KAILI, DA'A [KZF]
UNDIMEHA dial of NDA'NDA' [NNZ]
UNDRI alt for URDU [URD]
UNDU dial of BERTA [WTI]
UNDUP dial of IBAN [IBA]
UNEME [UNE] lang, Nigeria
UNGA dial of BURIAT, RUSSIA [MNB]
UNGA dial of BEMBA [BEM]
UNGAMEHA dial of NDA'NDA' [NNZ]
UNGARINJIN alt for NGARINYIN [UNG]
UNGARINYIN alt for NGARINYIN [UNG]
UNGGUMI dial of WORORA [UNP]
UNGIE alt for NGIE [NGJ]
UNGOM alt for NGOM [NRA]
UNGORRI alt for KUNGGARI [KGL]
UNGU alt for IDUN [LDB]
UNGUJA dial of SWAHILI [SWA]
UNGWE alt for HUNGWORO [NAT]
"UNHAN" alt for INONHAN [LOC]
UNHUN dial of CURRIPACO [KPC]
UNI alt for HANI [HNI]
UNI alt for HONI [HOW]
UNIETTI alt for AFITTI [AFT]
UNINGANGK alt for URNINGANGG [URC]
UNKIA alt for FAIWOL [FAI]
UNSERDEUTSCH [ULN] lang, Papua New Guinea,
  Australia
UNSHOI alt for USUI [USI]
UNSUIY alt for USUI [USI]
UNTIB dial of AVAR [AVR]
UNUA [ONU] lang, Vanuatu
UNYAMA dial of MANYIKA [MXC]
UNYAMOOTHA alt for ADYNYAMATHANHA [ADT]
UNYEADA dial of OBOLO [ANN]

UNZA alt for NAGA, RENGMA [NRE]
UOLLAMO alt for WOLAYTTA [WBC]
UOMO alt for PAKAÁSNOVOS [PAV]
UPAIRÃ alt for TANIMUCA-RETUARÃ [TNC]
UPALE alt for NYANG'I [NYP]
UPATA dial of EKPEYE [EKP]
UPELLA alt for OKPELA dial of IVBIE NORTH-
   OKPELA-ARHE [ATG]
UPIALA-BITURI alt for AGÖB [KIT]
UPLAND YUMAN alt for HAVASUPAI-WALAPAI-
   YAVAPAI [YUF]
UPOTO alt for LIPOTO dial of LUSENGO [LUS]
UPPER ASARO alt for DANO [ASO]
UPPER ASARO dial of DANO [ASO]
UPPER AUGUST RIVER dial of MIANMIN [MPT]
UPPER BAL dial of SVAN [SVA]
UPPER BALONG alt for BAKONI dial of KENYANG
   [KEN]
UPPER BARAM KENJA alt for KENYAH, UPPER
   BARAM [UBM]
UPPER BELE dial of DANI, LOWER GRAND VALLEY
   [DNI]
UPPER BISAYA dial of BISAYA, SARAWAK [BSD]
UPPER CARNIOLA dial of SLOVENIAN [SLV]
UPPER CHINOOK alt for WASCO-WISHRAM [WAC]
UPPER CIRCASSIAN alt for KABARDIAN [KAB]
UPPER COLORADO RIVER YUMAN alt for
   HAVASUPAI-WALAPAI-YAVAPAI [YUF]
UPPER COQUILLE alt for COQUILLE [COQ]
UPPER EGYPT ARABIC alt for ARABIC, SÁIDI [AEC]
UPPER ENGADINE dial of RHETO-ROMANCE [RHE]
UPPER GIO dial of DAN [DAF]
UPPER GROMA dial of GROMA [GRO]
UPPER IRUMU alt for IRUMU [IOU]
UPPER KENYANG dial of KENYANG [KEN]
UPPER KOLYMA dial of EVEN [EVE]
UPPER LADAKHI alt for LEH dial of LADAKHI [LBJ]
UPPER LAMET dial of LAMET [LBN]
UPPER LOZYVIN alt for NORTHERN VOGUL dial of
   MANSI [MNS]
UPPER LUZH alt for OREDEZH dial of INGRIAN [IZH]
UPPER MANAGALASI alt for ÖMIE [AOM]
UPPER MBO alt for NKONGHO dial of MBO [MBO]
UPPER MOREHEAD alt for ARAMBA [STK]
UPPER MOREHEAD alt for ROUKU [TCI]
UPPER MORI alt for MORI ATAS [MZQ]
UPPER PIMAN alt for PAPAGO-PIMA [PAP]
UPPER PYRAMID dial of DANI, LOWER GRAND
   VALLEY [DNI]
UPPER TOR alt for BERIK [BER]
UPPER UGU RIVER dial of UMANAKAINA [GDN]
UPPER WASI-WERI dial of PRASUNI [PRN]
UPPER YAZGULYAM dial of YAZGULYAM [YAH]
UPSTREAM LESE alt for ARUMBI dial of LESE [LES]
UPURUI alt for WAYANA [WAY]
URA [UUR] lang, Vanuatu
URA alt for FUNGWA [ULA]
URADHI [URF] lang, Australia
URAK LAWOI' [URK] lang, Thailand
URAKHA-AKHUSH alt for AKUSHA dial of DARGWA
   [DAR]
URAKIN alt for URAT [URT]
URALI [URL] lang, India
URALI dial of KURUMBA [KFI]
URALIAN TATAR dial of TATAR [TTR]
URALY alt for URALI [URL]

URAMA dial of KIWAI, NORTHEAST [KIW]
URAMAT [URO] lang, Papua New Guinea
URAMBAL alt for BAYALI [BJY]
URAMET alt for URAMAT [URO]
URAMIT alt for URAMAT [URO]
URAMOT alt for URAMAT [URO]
URANG alt for KURUX [KVN]
URAON alt for KURUX [KVN]
URAON alt for KURUX, NEPALI [KXL]
URAPMIN [URM] lang, Papua New Guinea
URARICAA-PARAGUA alt for NORTHERN NINAM dial
   of NINAM [SHB]
URARINA [URA] lang, Peru
URAT [URT] lang, Papua New Guinea
URAT dial of MONGOLIAN, HALH [KHK]
URAT dial of MONGOLIAN, PERIPHERAL [MVF]
URAT alt for ULANCHAB dial of MONGOLIAN,
   PERIPHERAL [MVF]
URAXA-AXUSHA dial of DARGWA [DAR]
URBAREG dial of GURAGE, EAST [GRE]
URDU [URD] lang, Pakistan, Mauritius, South Africa,
   Afghanistan, India, Thailand
URDU alt for URDU [URD]
URENG dial of ASILULU [ASL]
UREPARAPARA alt for LEHALURUP [URR]
UREQUEMA alt for GUAREQUENA [GAE]
URFA of TURKISH [TRK]
URFA dial of ARABIC, SYRO-MESOPOTAMIAN [AYP]
URHOBO [URH] lang, Nigeria
URI [UVH] lang, Papua New Guinea
URI alt for NAGA, AO [NJO]
URI alt for AURAMA dial of PAWAIA [PWA]
URI VEHEES alt for URI [UVH]
URIA alt for ORYA [URY]
URIANKHAI alt for TUVIN [TUN]
URIANKHAI dial of KALMYK-OIRAT [KGZ]
URIANKHAI-MONCHAK alt for TUVIN [TUN]
URIGINA [URG] lang, Papua New Guinea
URIGINAU alt for URIGINA [URG]
URII alt for URI [UVH]
URIM [URI] lang, Papua New Guinea
URIMO [URX] lang, Papua New Guinea
URIPIV dial of URIPIV-WALA-RANO-ATCHIN [UPV]
URIPIV-WALA-RANO-ATCHIN [UPV] lang, Vanuatu
URITA dial of ARAPESH, BUMBITA [AON]
URIYA alt for ORIYA [ORY]
URKARAX alt for AKUSHA dial of DARGWA [DAR]
URLI alt for URALI [URL]
URMI dial of ASSYRIAN [AII]
URMI dial of ASSYRIAN [AII]
URMIA-MARAGHA alt for URMIA-MARAGHEH dial of
   ARMENIAN [ARM]
URMIA-MARAGHEH dial of ARMENIAN [ARM]
URMIA-MARAGHEH dial of ARMENIAN [ARM]
URMIY alt for URMI dial of ASSYRIAN [AII]
URMURI alt for ORMURI [ORU]
URNINGANGG [URC] lang, Australia
URO dial of AKOKO, NORTH [AKK]
UROHIMA alt for HIMA [HIM]
URRIGHEL dial of TARIFIT [RIF]
URRTI dial of MIDOB [MEI]
URSÁRI dial of ROMANI, BALKAN [RMN]
URTSUN alt for SOUTHERN KALASHA dial of
   KALASHA [KLS]
URU [URE] lang, Bolivia
URU dial of CHAGGA [KAF]

UZBEK, NORTHERN [UZB] lang, Uzbekistan, China
UZBEK, SOUTHERN [UZS] lang, Afghanistan,
Turkey, Pakistan, Turkey
UZBEK, SOUTHERN alt for UZBEK, SOUTHERN
[UZS]
UZBEKI alt for UZBEK, SOUTHERN [UZS]
UZBEKI ARABIC alt for KASHKADARYA ARABIC dial
of ARABIC, CENTRAL ASIAN COLLOQUIAL
[ABH]
UZBIN dial of PASHAYI, NORTHWEST [GLH]
UZEKWE [EZE] lang, Nigeria
UZEMCHIN alt for UJUMCHIN dial of MONGOLIAN,
PERIPHERAL [MVF]
UZHIL alt for AUSHI [AUH]
UZLAM alt for WUZLAM [UDL]
UZO alt for IJO, CENTRAL-WESTERN [IJC]
VA alt for VO [WBM]
VA alt for PARAUK [PRK]
VAADOO dial of TINPUTZ [TPZ]
VAAGRI BOOLI [VAA] lang, India
VAALPENS alt for XATIA dial of NG/AMANI [NMN]
VAALPENS alt for XATIA dial of NG/AMANI [NMN]
VAANEROKI alt for BOKYI [BKY]
VAAZIN dial of DII [DUR]
VACACOCHA alt for ABISHIRA [ASH]
VACAMWE alt for KAMWE [HIG]
VACH dial of KHANTY [KCA]
VADAGA dial of TELUGU [TCW]
VADAGU alt for BADAGA [BFQ]
VADANDA alt for DANDA dial of NDAU [NDC]
VADARA alt for VIDIRI [VIR]
VADARI alt for WADDAR [WBQ]
VADARI dial of TELUGU [TCW]
VADI dial of GADI-SHINGINI-VADI-BAANGI [KAM]
VADIYA alt for ORIYA [ORY]
VADODARI alt for GAMADIA dial of GUJARATI
[GJR]
VADONDE dial of MAKONDE [KDE]
VADVAL [VAD] lang, India
VAEDDA alt for VEDDAH [VED]
VAFSI [VAF] lang, Iran
VAGADI alt for WAGDI [WBR]
VAGALA alt for VAGLA [VAG]
VAGARI alt for WAGDI [WBR]
VAGARI alt for KOLI, KACHI [GJK]
VAGARI alt for KACHCHI dial of KOLI, KACHI [GJK]
VAGDI alt for WAGDI [WBR]
VAGED alt for WAGDI [WBR]
VAGERI alt for WAGDI [WBR]
VAGHRI [VGR] lang, Pakistan
VAGHRI alt for BAURIA [BGE]
VAGHRI alt for KOLI, KACHI [GJK]
VAGHRI alt for KACHCHI dial of KOLI, KACHI [GJK]
VAGHRI KOLI alt for VAGHRI [VGR]
VAGHUA [TVA] lang, Solomon Islands
VAGI alt for WAGDI [WBR]
VAGI alt for KAMBA [XAB]
VAGI alt for WAGI [FAD]
VAGILY alt for WESTERN VOGUL dial of MANSI
[MNS]
VAGLA [VAG] lang, Ghana, Côte d'Ivoire
VAGUA alt for VAGHUA [TVA]
VAHITU dial of TUAMOTUAN [PMT]
VAI [VAI] lang, Liberia, Sierra Leone, Sierra Leone
VAI alt for VAI [VAI]
VAIKENU alt for ATONI [TMR]

VAIKINO alt for ATONI [TMR]
VAIKINO alt for BIBOKI-INSANA dial of ATONI
[TMR]
VAILALA alt for OROKOLO [ORO]
VAIPEI alt for VAIPHEI [VAP]
VAIPHEI [VAP] lang, India
VAITUPU alt for SOUTH TUVALUAN dial of
TUVALUAN [ELL]
VAJIENG dial of CHRAU [CHR]
VAKAM dial of CITAK [TXT]
VAKHAN alt for WAKHI [WBL]
VAKUISE alt for KWISE dial of KWADI [KWZ]
VAKUTA dial of KIRIWINA [KIJ]
VAKWELI alt for MOKPWE [BRI]
VAKWENGO alt for XUN [XUU]
VAL-NOGLIKI dial of OROK [OAA]
VALAISIEN dial of FRANCO-PROVENÇAL [FRA]
VALE [VAE] lang, Central African Republic
VALE alt for GLAVDA [GLV]
VALE dial of VALE [VAE]
VALEIEN alt for GAVOT dial of PROVENÇAL [PRV]
VALENCIAN [VAC] lang, Spain
VALENCIANO alt for VALENCIAN [VAC]
VALIENTE alt for GUAYMÍ [GYM]
VALIENTE dial of GUAYMÍ [GYM]
VALLE D'AOSTA dial of FRANCO-PROVENÇAL [FRA]
VALLEY COVE dial of AGTA, DUPANINAN [DUO]
VALLEY TIHAAMAH dial of ARABIC, HIJAZI [ACW]
VALLEY TONGA alt for WE dial of TONGA [TOI]
VALMAN [VAN] lang, Papua New Guinea
VALMIKI alt for KUPIA [KEY]
VALMIKI ADIWASI ORIYA dial of ORIYA, ADIWASI
[ORT]
VALONGI alt for BALONG dial of BAFAW-BALONG
[BWT]
VALPAY alt for VALPEI [VLP]
VALPEI [VLP] lang, Vanuatu
VALPEI-HUKUA alt for VALPEI [VLP]
VALUGA alt for VOLOW dial of MOTLAV [MLV]
VALUVA alt for VOLOW dial of MOTLAV [MLV]
VALUWA alt for VOLOW dial of MOTLAV [MLV]
VALVI dial of BHILI [BHB]
VAMA'A alt for MBUGU [MHD]
VAMAKONDE dial of MAKONDE [KDE]
VAMALE [MKT] lang, New Caledonia
VAMALE dial of VAMALE [MKT]
VAMBENG alt for MOKPWE [BRI]
VAME-MBREME alt for PELASLA [MLR]
VAME-MORA alt for PELASLA [MLR]
VAMWALU dial of MAKONDE [KDE]
VAMWAMBE dial of MAKONDE [KDE]
VAN dial of ARMENIAN [ARM]
VAN KIEU alt for KATU [KTV]
VAN KIEU alt for BRU, EASTERN [BRU]
VANA alt for GBETE dial of MBUM [MDD]
VANAMBERE alt for WANAMBRE [WLN]
VANAPA RIVER dial of FUYUGE [FUY]
VANATINA alt for SUDEST [TGO]
VANAVARA dial of EVENKI [EVN]
VANECHI alt for WANECI [WNE]
VANGA alt for SUDEST [TGO]
VANGTEH dial of CHIN, TEDIM [CTD]
VANGUNU [MPR] lang, Solomon Islands
VANGUNU dial of VANGUNU [MPR]
VANIKOLO alt for VANO [VNK]
VANIKORO alt for VANO [VNK]

VANIMO [VAM] lang, Papua New Guinea, Indonesia, Irian Jaya
VANJARI alt for LAMANI [LMN]
VANKIEU alt for BRU, EASTERN [BRU]
VANNETAIS dial of BRETON [BRT]
VANO [VNK] lang, Solomon Islands
VANUA BALAVU dial of LAUAN [LLX]
VANUA LAVA alt for VATRATA [VLR]
VANUMA [VAU] lang, Zaïre
VANUMAMI dial of TOLAI [KSD]
VAO [VAO] lang, Vanuatu
VAPIDIANA alt for WAPISHANA [WAP]
VARA [VAX] lang, Central African Republic
VARESE alt for VARISI [VRS]
VARHADI-NAGPURI [VAH] lang, India
VARIEGATED alt for HUA dial of HMONG, WESTERN [HUJ]
VARIHÍO alt for HUARIJÍO [VAR]
VARISI [VRS] lang, Solomon Islands
VARISI dial of VARISI [VRS]
VARJAN dial of WAIGALI [WBK]
VARLI [VAV] lang, India
VARMALI alt for LAMENU [LMU]
VAROIS alt for MARITIME PROVENÇAL dial of PROVENÇAL [PRV]
VARSU alt for LEWO [LWW]
VARTASHEN dial of UDI [UDI]
VARTAVO alt for BURMBAR [VRT]
VARTO dial of KIRMANJKI [QKV]
VASAVA alt for VASAVI [VAS]
VASAVE alt for VASAVI [VAS]
VASAVI [VAS] lang, India
VASEKELA BUSHMAN [VAJ] lang, Namibia
VASKIA alt for WASKIA [WSK]
VASORONTU alt for ZOROTUA dial of KWADI [KWZ]
VASUII alt for TINPUTZ [TPZ]
VASYUGAN alt for VACH dial of KHANTY [KCA]
VATA dial of DIDA, LAKOTA [DIC]
VATEVE alt for TEVE dial of MANYIKA [MXC]
VATRATA [VLR] lang, Vanuatu
VATURANGA alt for NDI dial of GHARI [GRI]
VAUDOIS dial of FRANCO-PROVENÇAL [FRA]
VAUPÉS CACUA dial of CACUA [CBV]
VAYU [VAY] lang, Nepal
VAZAMA alt for XUN [XUU]
VAZEZURU alt for ZEZURU dial of SHONA [SHD]
VAZHIYAMMAR alt for MALARYAN [MJQ]
VEDA alt for VEDDAH [VED]
VEDANS alt for MALAVEDAN [MJR]
VEDDAH [VED] lang, Sri Lanka
VEDDHA alt for VEDDAH [VED]
VEHEES alt for VEHES [VAL]
VEHES [VAL] lang, Papua New Guinea
VEI alt for VAI [VAI]
VEIAO alt for YAO [YAO]
VEIPHEI alt for VAIPHEI [VAP]
VEJOS alt for WICHÍ LHAMTÉS VEJOZ [MAD]
VELE alt for VERE dial of NAKANAI [NAK]
VELICHE alt for HUILLICHE [HUH]
VELIPERI alt for WALIPERI dial of IPEKA-TAPUIA [PAJ]
VELLA LAVELLA alt for BILUA [BLB]
VEMGO alt for MABAS [VEM]
VEMGO dial of MABAS [VEM]
VENACO dial of CORSICAN [COI]
VENDA [VEN] lang, South Africa, Zimbabwe,

Zimbabwe
VENDA alt for VENDA [VEN]
VENETIAN [VEC] lang, Italy
VENETIAN PROPER dial of VENETIAN [VEC]
VENEZUELAN SIGN LANGUAGE [VSL] lang, Venezuela
VENGI alt for VENGO [BAV]
VENGO [BAV] lang, Cameroon
VENGOO alt for VENGO [BAV]
VENTIMIGLIESE alt for MONÉGASQUE dial of LIGURIAN [LIJ]
VEPS [VEP] lang, Russia, Europe
VEPSIAN alt for VEPS [VEP]
VERAGUAS SABANERO alt for BUGLERE [SAB]
VERE alt for MOM JANGO [VER]
VERE dial of NAKANAI [NAK]
VERKHOVSK dial of NEGIDAL [NEG]
VERON alt for PRASUNI [PRN]
VEROU alt for PRASUNI [PRN]
VERRE alt for MOM JANGO [VER]
VERUNI alt for PRASUNI [PRN]
VESERMYAN alt for NORTH UDMURT dial of UDMURT [UDM]
VESI alt for WUSHI [BSE]
VETAN dial of MALAVEDAN [MJR]
VETENG alt for KENSWEI NSEI [NDB]
VETTUVAN dial of MALAVEDAN [MJR]
VETUMBOSO dial of MOSINA [MSN]
VETWENG alt for KENSWEI NSEI [NDB]
VEZO dial of MALAGASY [MEX]
VHE alt for ÉWÉ [EWE]
VICCHOLI dial of SINDHI [SND]
VICE-ARXAVA dial of LAZ [LZZ]
VICHOLI alt for VICHOLO dial of SINDHI [SND]
VICHOLO dial of SINDHI [SND]
VICO-AJACCIO dial of CORSICAN [COI]
VICXIN dial of LAK [LBE]
VIDIRI [VIR] lang, Central African Republic, Sudan, Sudan
VIDIRI alt for VIDIRI [VIR]
VIDRI alt for VIDIRI [VIR]
VIDUNDA [VID] lang, Tanzania
VIDZEME alt for EASTERN LIVONIAN dial of LIV [LIV]
VIEMO alt for VIGE [VIG]
VIENTIANE dial of LAO [NOL]
VIET alt for VIETNAMESE [VIE]
VIET GOC MIEN alt for KHMER, CENTRAL [KMR]
VIETNAMESE [VIE] lang, Viet Nam, Cambodia, China, Laos, Thailand, New Caledonia
VIETNAMESE alt for VIETNAMESE [VIE]
VIETNAMESE PIDGIN FRENCH alt for TAY BOI [TAS]
VIGE [VIG] lang, Burkina Faso
VIGUÉ alt for VIGE [VIG]
VIGYE alt for VIGE [VIG]
VIGZAR alt for ZAAR dial of SAYA [SAY]
VIITTOMAKIELI alt for FINNISH SIGN LANGUAGE [FSE]
VIKHLIN alt for VIXLIN dial of LAK [LBE]
VIKZAR alt for ZAAR dial of SAYA [SAY]
VIL alt for BHILI [BHB]
VILA alt for BILA dial of TSONGA [TSO]
VILELA [VIL] lang, Argentina
VILI [VIF] lang, Congo, Gabon
VILI alt for VILI [VIF]
VILLA ALTA ZAPOTEC alt for ZAPOTECO,

YATZACHI [ZAV]
VILLA CORZO dial of TZOTZIL, HUIXTÁN [TZU]
VILLA JUÁREZ TOTONACO alt for TOTONACO,
  NORTHERN [TOO]
VIMTIM alt for VIN [VIM]
VIN [VIM] lang, Nigeria
VINCENTIAN dial of CARIB, ISLAND [CAI]
VINCENTIAN CREOLE ENGLISH dial of LESSER
  ANTILLEAN CREOLE ENGLISH [VIB]
VINMAVIS [VNM] lang, Vanuatu
VINZA [VIN] lang, Tanzania
VIRA alt for JOBA [JOB]
VIRA dial of ZYOBA [ZYO]
VIRAC alt for BICOLANO, SOUTHERN
  CATANDUANES [BLN]
VIRGINIA ALGONKIAN alt for POWHATAN [PIM]
VIRI alt for BELANDA VIRI [BVI]
VIRI alt for WINA dial of MASANA [MCN]
VIRYAL dial of CHUVASH [CJU]
VISAYAK alt for BISAYA, BRUNEI [BSB]
VISAYAK alt for BISAYA, SARAWAK [BSD]
VISAYAN alt for CEBUANO [CEB]
VISHAKAPATNAM dial of TELUGU [TCW]
VISHAVAN [VIS] lang, India
VISHOLI dial of SINDHI [SND]
VISIGOTH dial of GOTHIC [GOF]
VISIK dial of MABAS [VEM]
VISIK alt for VIZIK dial of MABAS [VEM]
VITA [VIT] lang, Central African Republic
VITAL-ARKHAVA alt for VICE-ARXAVA dial of LAZ
  [LZZ]
VITEB-MOGILEV alt for NORTHEAST BELORUSSIAN
  dial of BELORUSSIAN [RUW]
VITRÉ alt for EOTILE [EOT]
VITSKHIN alt for VICXIN dial of LAK [LBE]
VITU [WIV] lang, Papua New Guinea
VIVIGANA alt for IDUNA [VIV]
VIVIGANI alt for IDUNA [VIV]
VIWIVAKEU dial of AMAHUACA [AMC]
VIWULU-AUA alt for WUVULU-AUA [WUV]
VIXLIN dial of LAK [LBE]
VIZIK dial of MABAS [VEM]
VIZIK alt for VISIK dial of MABAS [VEM]
VLAAMS alt for DUTCH [DUT]
VLAAMSCH alt for DUTCH [DUT]
VLACH alt for ROMANI, VLACH [RMY]
VLAX alt for ROMANI, VLACH [RMY]
VLUM alt for VULUM dial of MUSGU [MUG]
VLUM alt for VULUM dial of MUSGU [MUG]
VO [WBM] lang, Myanmar, China
VO LIMKOU alt for LINGAO [ONB]
VOD [VOD] lang, Russia, Europe
VODERE alt for VIDIRI [VIR]
VODIAN alt for VOD [VOD]
VOGELKOP dial of BIAK [BHW]
VOGHERESE-PAVESE dial of EMILIANO [EML]
VOGUL alt for MANSI [MNS]
VOGULY alt for MANSI [MNS]
VOKO alt for LONGTO [WOK]
VOLGA alt for GRASSLAND MARI dial of MARI,
  LOW [MAL]
VOLGA OIRAT alt for KALMYK-OIRAT [KGZ]
VOLOF alt for WOLOF [WOL]
VOLOW dial of MOTLAV [MLV]
VONKUTU alt for VUKUTU dial of LESE [LES]
VONO alt for KIBALLO [KCH]

VONUN alt for BUNUN [BNN]
VOQTWAQ dial of CHRAU [CHR]
VORA alt for VARA [VAX]
VORA dial of SINAGORO [SNC]
VORE dial of BOBO FING [BBO]
VORU alt for VYRUS dial of ESTONIAN [EST]
VOTE alt for VOD [VOD]
VOTIAK alt for UDMURT [UDM]
VOTIAN alt for VOD [VOD]
VOTIAN alt for VOD [VOD]
VOTIC alt for VOD [VOD]
VOTISH alt for VOD [VOD]
VOTYAK alt for UDMURT [UDM]
VOUAOUSI alt for AUSHI [AUH]
VOUTE alt for VUTE [VUT]
VOUTERE alt for VUTE [VUT]
VOVO alt for BIERIA [BRJ]
VOVO dial of BIERIA [BRJ]
VOWAK alt for NORTHERN LENGUA dial of LENGUA
  [LEG]
VUITE alt for CHIN, PAITE [PCK]
VUKUTU dial of LESE [LES]
VULAA alt for HULA [HUL]
VULAVA dial of BUGHOTU [BGT]
VULUM dial of MUSGU [MUG]
VULUM dial of MUSGU [MUG]
VULUNG alt for THAO [SSF]
VUMBU [VUM] lang, Gabon
VUNADIDIR dial of TOLAI [KSD]
VUNAPU [VNP] lang, Vanuatu
VUNGUNYA dial of YOMBE [YOM]
VUNMARAMA alt for HANO [LML]
VUNUM alt for BUNUN [BNN]
VUNUN alt for BUNUN [BNN]
VUNUNG alt for BUNUN [BNN]
VUPURAN alt for PAPORA [PPU]
VURAS dial of MOSINA [MSN]
VUREAS alt for VURAS dial of MOSINA [MSN]
VUTE [VUT] lang, Cameroon, Nigeria, Nigeria
VUTE alt for VUTE [VUT]
VUTE DE BANYO alt for BUTE BAMNYO dial of
  VUTE [VUT]
VUTE DE DOUME alt for NUGANE dial of VUTE
  [VUT]
VUTE DE LINTE alt for NUJUM dial of VUTE [VUT]
VUTE DE MBANDJOK alt for VUTE MBANJO dial of
  VUTE [VUT]
VUTE DE NGORRO alt for NGORO dial of VUTE
  [VUT]
VUTE DE SANGBE alt for KUMBERE dial of VUTE
  [VUT]
VUTE DE TIBATI alt for NDUVUM dial of VUTE [VUT]
VUTE DE YANGBA alt for NUDOO dial of VUTE
  [VUT]
VUTE MBANJO dial of VUTE [VUT]
VUTEEN alt for YUPIK, SIRENIK [YSR]
VUTERE alt for VUTE [VUT]
VWELA alt for HWELA dial of LIGBI [LIG]
VWEZHI dial of GBAGYI [GBR]
VY alt for VAI [VAI]
VYRUS dial of ESTONIAN [EST]
WA alt for VO [WBM]
WA alt for PARAUK [PRK]
WA alt for BLANG [BLR]
WA BAMBANI alt for AGOI [IBM]
WA KHAWK dial of MARU [MHX]

WA LON dial of VO [WBM]
WA MAATHI alt for MBUGU [MHD]
WA PWI alt for VO [WBM]
WA'A alt for DGHWEDE [DGH]
WA'I alt for WADI dial of BATA [BTA]
WÁÁDÚ dial of TOURA [NEB]
WAAGAI alt for WAGAYA [WGA]
WAAGI alt for WAGAYA [WGA]
WAALI alt for WALI [WLX]
WAAMA [WWA] lang, Benin
WAAMA dial of WAAMA [WWA]
WAAMWANG [WMN] lang, New Caledonia
WAANA alt for BIDIO [BID]
WAANJAMA dial of MENDE [MFY]
WAANYI alt for WANJI dial of GARAWA [GBC]
WAAT alt for SANYE [SSN]
WAATA alt for BONI [BOB]
WAATA alt for SANYE [SSN]
WAATA dial of ORMA [ORC]
WAB [WAB] lang, Papua New Guinea
WABAG alt for MAE dial of ENGA [ENQ]
WABO alt for WORIASI [WBB]
WABONI alt for BONI [BOB]
WABUDA alt for KIWAI, WABUDA [KMX]
WABUI alt for HIXKARYÁNA [HIX]
WABULA dial of CIA-CIA [CIA]
WACHI alt for WACI-GBE [WCI]
WACI alt for WACI-GBE [WCI]
WACI-GBE [WCI] lang, Togo, Benin
WACIPAIRE alt for HUACHIPAERI [HUG]
WACIRI dial of PASHTO, CENTRAL [PST]
WACO dial of WICHITA [WIC]
WAÇU alt for WASU [WSU]
WADA [WDA] lang, Central African Republic, Sudan,
    Sudan
WADA alt for WADA [WDA]
WADA THURI alt for THURI [THU]
WADAGINAM [WDG] lang, Papua New Guinea
WADAGINAMB alt for WADAGINAM [WDG]
WADAI alt for MABA [MDE]
WADAI alt for ORMA [ORC]
WADAIËNS alt for MABA [MDE]
WADALEI dial of GALEYA [GAR]
WADAMAN alt for WARDAMAN [WRR]
WADAMKONG dial of RAWANG [RAW]
WADAPI-LAUT alt for AMBAI dial of AMBAI [AMK]
WADARIA alt for KOLI, WADIYARA [KXP]
WADAU dial of PASHAYI, NORTHWEST [GLH]
WADDAR [WBQ] lang, India
WADDAYEN alt for MABA [MDE]
WADEGA alt for JUMJUM [JUM]
WADEMA alt for YANOMAM dial of YANOMÁMI
    [WCA]
WADERMAN alt for WARDAMAN [WRR]
WADI dial of BATA [BTA]
WADI dial of JIMI [JIM]
WADI alt for OUEDGHIR dial of OUARGLA [OUA]
WADIBU dial of BIAK [BHW]
WADIMBISA dial of BUDU [BUU]
WADIRI alt for YANYUWA [JAO]
WADIWADI dial of THURAWAL [TBH]
WADIYARA dial of KOLI, WADIYARA [KXP]
WADJARI alt for WATJARI [WBV]
WADJERI alt for WATJARI [WBV]
WADJIGINY [WDJ] lang, Australia
WADJIGU [WDU] lang, Australia

WADONDO alt for DANDA dial of NDAU [NDC]
WADUMAN alt for WARDAMAN [WRR]
WADZOLI alt for UADZOLI dial of ĆARÚIANA [CRU]
WAE GEREN alt for CENTRAL BURU dial of BURU
    [MHS]
WAE KABO alt for CENTRAL BURU dial of BURU
    [MHS]
WAE RANA [WRX] lang, Indonesia, Nusa Tenggara
WAE SAMA dial of BURU [MHS]
WAENGATU alt for NHENGATU [YRL]
WAERANA alt for WAE RANA [WRX]
WAESAMA alt for WAE SAMA dial of BURU [MHS]
WAFFA [WAJ] lang, Papua New Guinea
WAGA alt for WAKAWAKA [WKW]
WAGADI alt for WAGDI [WBR]
WAGAI alt for WAGAYA [WGA]
WAGAJA alt for WAGAYA [WGA]
WAGANGA alt for MANGANJA dial of NYANJA
    [NYJ]
WAGANGA alt for MANGANJA dial of NYANJA
    [NYJ]
WAGAP alt for CEMUHÎ [CAM]
WAGARABAI alt for SUGANGA [SUG]
WAGARIA alt for KOLI, KACHI [GJK]
WAGARIA alt for KACHCHI dial of KOLI, KACHI
    [GJK]
WAGARINDEM alt for YAFI [WFG]
WAGAU dial of BUANG, MAPOS [BZH]
WAGAWAGA [WGW] lang, Papua New Guinea
WAGAWAGA alt for WAKAWAKA [WKW]
WAGAWAGA dial of WAKAWAKA [WKW]
WAGAWAGA alt for YALEBA dial of TAWALA [TBO]
WAGAYA [WGA] lang, Australia
WAGAYDY alt for WADJIGINY [WDJ]
WAGDI [WBR] lang, India
WAGELAK alt for RITARUNGO [RIT]
WAGEMAN [WAQ] lang, Australia
WAGGA alt for WAJA [WJA]
WAGGAIA alt for WAGAYA [WGA]
WAGHARI alt for WAGDI [WBR]
WAGHOLI alt for WAGDI [WBR]
WAGI [FAD] lang, Papua New Guinea
WAGI alt for KAMBA [XAB]
WAGIFA dial of BWAIDOKA [BWD]
WAGIMAN alt for WAGEMAN [WAQ]
WAGIMUDA alt for MAIANI [TNH]
WAGOW alt for TAMAGARIO [TCG]
WAGSOD dial of QIANG [CNG]
WAGUMI [WGM] lang, Papua New Guinea
WAHA alt for LAMANG [HIA]
WAHAI alt for SALEMAN [SAU]
WAHAI alt for MANUSELA [WHA]
WAHAKAIM dial of LIANA-SETI [STE]
WAHAU KAJAN alt for KAYAN, WAHAU [WHU]
WAHAU KENYA alt for KENYAH, WAHAU [WHK]
WAHE dial of GBARI [GBY]
WAHGI [WAK] lang, Papua New Guinea
WAHIBO alt for GUAHIBO [GUH]
WAHINAMA alt for MANUSELA [WHA]
WAHKE dial of RAWANG [RAW]
WAHMIRÍ alt for WAIMIRÍ dial of ATRUAHÍ [ATR]
WAHUA dial of CHINESE, HAKKA [HAK]
WAI alt for WAIGALI [WBK]
WAI alt for AJIË [AJI]
WAI dial of NAGA, YIMCHUNGRU [YIM]
WAI-ALA alt for WAIGALI [WBK]

WAIA [KNV] lang, Papua New Guinea
WAIA dial of TULAMBATU [MFG]
WAIAMPI alt for WAYAMPI, OIAPOQUE [OYA]
WAIBUK alt for HARUAI [TMD]
WAIBULA dial of IDUNA [VIV]
WAICÁ alt for AKAWAIO [ARB]
WAICÁ alt for YANOMÁMI [WCA]
WAIDINA alt for SOUTHEAST VITI LEVU dial of
 FIJIAN [FJI]
WAIDJELU alt for MANGILI-WAIJELO dial of SUMBA
 [SMI]
WAIDJEWA alt for WEYEWA [WEW]
WAIDORO dial of GIZRA [TOF]
WAIEMA dial of TAUPOTA [TPA]
WAIGALA alt for WAIGALI [WBK]
WAIGALI [WBK] lang, Afghanistan
WAIGAN dial of HANUNOO [HNN]
WAIGELI alt for WAIGALI [WBK]
WAIGEO [WGO] lang, Indonesia, Irian Jaya
WAIGIU alt for WAIGEO [WGO]
WAIJARA alt for OWENIA [WSR]
WAIKÁ alt for YANOMÁMI [WCA]
WAIKA alt for YANAMAM dial of YANOMÁMI
 [WCA]
WAIKHARA alt for PIRATAPUYO [PIR]
WAIKINO alt for PIRATAPUYO [PIR]
WAIKISU dial of NAMBIKUÁRA, SOUTHERN [NAB]
WAILAKI [WLK] lang, USA
WAILAPA [WLR] lang, Vanuatu
WAILBI alt for ADYNYAMATHANHA [ADT]
WAILBRI alt for WARLPIRI [WBP]
WAILEMI alt for IKOBI-MENA [MEB]
WAILPI alt for ADYNYAMATHANHA [ADT]
WAILU alt for AJIË [AJI]
WAIMA alt for RORO [RRO]
WAIMA dial of RORO [RRO]
WAIMA'A [WMH] lang, Indonesia, Nusa Tenggara
WAIMAHA [BAO] lang, Colombia, Brazil
WAIMAHA alt for WAIMA'A [WMH]
WAIMAJA alt for WAIMAHA [BAO]
WAIMIRÍ dial of ATRUAHÍ [ATR]
WAIMOA alt for WAIMA'A [WMH]
WAIN alt for NABAK [NAF]
WAINA alt for PIRATAPUYO [PIR]
WAINA alt for SOWANDA [SOW]
WAINANANA dial of TEOP [TIO]
WAING alt for GUWOT [GVE]
WAINUNGOMO alt for DE'CUANA dial of
 MAQUIRITARI [MCH]
WAINYI alt for WANJI dial of GARAWA [GBC]
WAIOLI [WLI] lang, Indonesia, Maluku
WAIPU alt for MEKWEI [MSF]
WAISARA alt for OWENIA [WSR]
WAIWAI [WAW] lang, Brazil, Guyana, Guyana
WAIWAI alt for WAIWAI [WAW]
WAJA [WJA] lang, Nigeria
WAJAKES dial of AMPEELI-WOJOKESO [APZ]
WAJAMLI alt for WAYAMLI dial of BULI [BZQ]
WAJANA alt for WAYANA [WAY]
WAJAO alt for YAO [YAO]
WAJAPI alt for WAYAMPI, OIAPOQUE [OYA]
WAJARU alt for WAYORÓ [WYR]
WAJEWA alt for WEYEWA [WEW]
WAJO dial of BUGIS [BPR]
WAJOLI alt for WAIOLI [WLI]
WAKA [WAV] lang, Nigeria

WAKAJA alt for WAGAYA [WGA]
WAKAL dial of HITU [HIT]
WAKALANGA alt for KALANGA [KCK]
WAKANDE alt for MBEMBE, CROSS RIVER [MFN]
WAKARI alt for WAPAN [JUK]
WAKASIHU dial of LARIKE-WAKASIHU [ALO]
WAKATOBI alt for TUKANGBESI SOUTH [BHQ]
WAKATOBI alt for TUKANGBESI NORTH [KHC]
WAKAWAKA [WKW] lang, Australia
WAKAYA alt for WAGAYA [WGA]
WAKDE alt for SOBEI [SOB]
WAKE alt for KWANGE dial of GBARI [GBY]
WAKHANI alt for WAKHI [WBL]
WAKHI [WBL] lang, Pakistan, Afghanistan, China,
 Tajikistan
WAKHI alt for WAKHI [WBL]
WAKHIGI alt for WAKHI [WBL]
WAKINDIGA alt for HATSA [HTS]
WAKKA alt for WAKAWAKA [WKW]
WAKKAJA alt for WAGAYA [WGA]
WAKOMBE alt for KOMBE dial of TUKI [BAG]
WAKONÁ [WAF] lang, Brazil
WAKORE alt for SONINKE [SNN]
WAKORIKORI alt for KOREKORE dial of SHONA
 [SHD]
WAKUE dial of MANAGALASI [MCQ]
WAKUT alt for VO [WBM]
WAKUT alt for TAI LOI [TLQ]
WALA alt for DAGAARI DIOULA [DGD]
WALA alt for WALI [WLX]
WALA alt for WAOLA dial of ANGAL HENENG,
 WEST [AKH]
WALA-RANO dial of URIPIV-WALA-RANO-ATCHIN
 [UPV]
WALACHIAN alt for MUNTENIAN dial of RUMANIAN
 [RUM]
WALAD DULLA dial of SUNGOR [SUN]
WALAF alt for WOLOF [WOL]
WALAHA dial of AMBAE, WEST [NND]
WALAK [WLW] lang, Indonesia, Irian Jaya
WALAMO alt for WOLAYTTA [WBC]
WALANE dial of GURAGE, EAST [GRE]
WALANG alt for KUNBARLANG [WLG]
WALANGU dial of GUPAPUYNGU [GUF]
WALAPAI dial of HAVASUPAI-WALAPAI-YAVAPAI
 [YUF]
WALARI alt for WALI [WLL]
WALARISHE alt for WALI [WLL]
WALBIRI alt for WARLPIRI [WBP]
WALESE alt for LESE [LES]
WALI [WLL] lang, Sudan
WALI [WLX] lang, Ghana
WALI dial of KHAM, TAKALE [KJL]
WALI BANUAH alt for SIKULE [SKH]
WALIA alt for MASANA [MCN]
WALIA dial of MASANA [MCN]
WALIMI alt for NYATURU [RIM]
WALING dial of BANTAWA [BAP]
WALIO [WLA] lang, Papua New Guinea
WALIPERI dial of IPEKA-TAPUIA [PAJ]
WALISI alt for LESE [LES]
WALJBI alt for ADYNYAMATHANHA [ADT]
WALJWAN alt for WAYILWAN dial of
 WANGAAYBUWAN-NGIYAMBAA [WYB]
WALLA WALLA [WAA] lang, USA
WALLACE dial of BAJAU, INDONESIAN [BDL]

WALLACH alt for ROMANI, VLACH [RMY]
WALLACHIAN alt for ROMANI, VLACH [RMY]
WALLAGA alt for MECHA dial of OROMO,
    WELLEGA-CENTRAL [GAZ]
WALLAMO alt for WOLAYTTA [WBC]
WALLAROO alt for NUGUNU [NNV]
WALLISIAN [WAL] lang, Wallis and Futuna, Fiji, New
    Caledonia, Vanuatu
WALLISIEN alt for WALLISIAN [WAL]
WALLON dial of FRENCH [FRN]
WALLON alt for WALLOON dial of FRENCH [FRN]
WALLOON dial of FRENCH [FRN]
WALMAJARRI [WMT] lang, Australia
WALMAJIRI alt for WALMAJARRI [WMT]
WALMALA alt for WARLMANPA [WRL]
WALMATJARI alt for WALMAJARRI [WMT]
WALMATJIRI alt for WALMAJARRI [WMT]
WALOMWE alt for LOMWE [NGL]
WALOOKERA alt for WARLUWARA [WRB]
WALPIRI alt for WARLPIRI [WBP]
WALSA alt for WARIS [WRS]
WALUGERA alt for WARLUWARA [WRB]
WALUNG alt for OLANGCHUNG GOLA [OLA]
WALUNGCHUNG GOLA alt for OLANGCHUNG GOLA
    [OLA]
WALURIDJI alt for MULURIDYI [VMU]
WALURIGI alt for AMBAE, EAST [OMB]
WALUWARA alt for WARLUWARA [WRB]
WALYA dial of MASANA [MCN]
WALYA alt for WALIA dial of MASANA [MCN]
WAM alt for WOM [WMO]
WAMA alt for AKURIO [AKO]
WAMAI alt for SURUVIRI dial of ASHKUN [ASK]
WAMAIS alt for ASHKUN [ASK]
WAMANYIKA alt for MANYIKA [MXC]
WAMAR alt for MANOBAI [WOO]
WAMAS [WMC] lang, Papua New Guinea
WAMAYI alt for ASHKUN [ASK]
WAMBA alt for NUNGU [RIN]
WAMBAIA alt for WAMBAYA [WMB]
WAMBAJA alt for WAMBAYA [WMB]
WAMBAYA [WMB] lang, Australia
WAMBAYA dial of WAMBAYA [WMB]
WAMBERA [WBX] lang, Ethiopia
WAMBISA alt for HUAMBISA [HUB]
WAMBON [WMS] lang, Indonesia, Irian Jaya
WAMBUTU alt for MANGBUTU [MDK]
WAMDIU dial of MARGHI SOUTH [MFM]
WAMESA alt for WANDAMEN [WAD]
WAMESA dial of WANDAMEN [WAD]
WAMIA alt for TESO [TEO]
WAMIN [WMI] lang, Australia
WAMOANG alt for WAAMWANG [WMN]
WAMOLA alt for WAMORA dial of KÂTE [KMG]
WAMORA dial of KÂTE [KMG]
WAMPANOAG [WAM] lang, USA
WAMPAR [LBQ] lang, Papua New Guinea
WAMPUR [WAZ] lang, Papua New Guinea
WAMSAK [WBD] lang, Papua New Guinea
WAMWAN dial of MUYUW [MYW]
WAN [WAN] lang, Côte d'Ivoire
WAN alt for VAN dial of ARMENIAN [ARM]
WAN WAN alt for ARINUA [AUK]
WANA alt for PAMONA [BCX]
WANA dial of KÂTE [KMG]
WANA alt for TAA dial of PAMONA [BCX]

WANAI alt for MAPOYO [MCG]
WANAM alt for YALE, KOSAREK [KKL]
WANAMBRE [WLN] lang, Papua New Guinea
WANAMI dial of MANAM [MVA]
WANANA alt for GUANANO [GVC]
WANÂNA alt for GUANANO [GVC]
WANANG dial of KOCH [KDQ]
WANAP [WNP] lang, Papua New Guinea
WANCHO alt for NAGA, WANCHO [NNP]
WANCI dial of TUKANGBESI NORTH [KHC]
WAND TAN alt for KAMASAU [KMS]
WANDA [WBH] lang, Tanzania
WANDABONG [WIA] lang, Papua New Guinea
WANDALA [MFI] lang, Cameroon, Nigeria, Nigeria
WANDALA alt for WANDALA [MFI]
WANDALA dial of WANDALA [MFI]
WANDAMEN [WAD] lang, Indonesia, Irian Jaya
WANDAMEN-WINDESI alt for WANDAMEN [WAD]
WANDARAN alt for WANDARANG [WND]
WANDARANG [WND] lang, Australia
WANDI dial of DASS [DOT]
WANDIA alt for WANDA [WBH]
WANDJI [WDD] lang, Gabon
WANDOMI dial of KAMASAU [KMS]
WANDYA dial of NYIHA [NIH]
WANE [HWA] lang, Côte d'Ivoire
WANECHI alt for WANECI [WNE]
WANECI [WNE] lang, Pakistan
WANETSI alt for WANECI [WNE]
WANG dial of MUONG [MTQ]
WANGA dial of LUYIA [LUY]
WANGAAYBUWAN dial of WANGAAYBUWAN-
    NGIYAMBAA [WYB]
WANGAAYBUWAN-NGIYAMBAA [WYB] lang,
    Australia
WANGADA alt for PINTIINI [PTI]
WANGANUI dial of MAORI [MBF]
WANGATA dial of MONGO-NKUNDU [MOM]
WANGDAY alt for WANDI dial of DASS [DOT]
WANGGAJI alt for PINTIINI [PTI]
WANGGAMADU alt for KOKATA [KTD]
WANGGAMALA [WNM] lang, Australia
WANGGANGURU [WGG] lang, Australia
WANGGO alt for WANGGOM [WNW]
WANGGOM [WNW] lang, Indonesia, Irian Jaya
WANGI-WANGI alt for WANCI dial of TUKANGBESI
    NORTH [KHC]
WANGKA dial of REMBONG [REB]
WANGKAJUNGA dial of MARTU WANGKA [MPJ]
WANGKAJUNGKA alt for WANGKAJUNGA dial of
    MARTU WANGKA [MPJ]
WANGKATJA alt for PINTIINI [PTI]
WANGKI alt for WANKI dial of MÍSKITO [MIQ]
WANGKUMARA alt for WONGKUMARA dial of
    NGURA [NBX]
WANGO alt for AROSI [AIA]
WANGOM alt for WANGGOM [WNW]
WANGUMARRA alt for WONGKUMARA dial of
    NGURA [NBX]
WANGURRI dial of DHANGU [GLA]
WANI dial of KOLAMI, NORTHWESTERN [KFB]
WANIABU alt for AMA [AMM]
WANIGELA dial of KEOPARA [KHZ]
WANINDILYAUGWA alt for ANINDILYAKWA [AOI]
WANINNAWA alt for KATUKÍNA, PANOAN [KNT]
WANJA alt for SOWANDA [SOW]

WANJE alt for WANCI dial of TUKANGBESI NORTH [KHC]
WANJI [WBI] lang, Tanzania
WANJI alt for LAMANI [LMN]
WANJI dial of GARAWA [GBC]
WANJI alt for WANCI dial of TUKANGBESI NORTH [KHC]
WANKI dial of MÍSKITO [MIQ]
WANMAN [WBT] lang, Australia
WANO [WNO] lang, Indonesia, Irian Jaya
WANONI alt for KAHUA [AGW]
WANSUM alt for PAHI [LGT]
WANTAKIA dial of BARUYA [BYR]
WANTJI alt for WANCI dial of TUKANGBESI NORTH [KHC]
WANTOAT [WNC] lang, Papua New Guinea
WANUKAKA [WNK] lang, Indonesia, Nusa Tenggara
WANUKAKA dial of WANUKAKA [WNK]
WANUMA alt for USAN [WNU]
WANYA alt for SOWANDA [SOW]
WANYAI alt for NYAI dial of KALANGA [KCK]
WANYATURU alt for NYATURU [RIM]
WANYIKA alt for MANYIKA [MXC]
WANYORO dial of ALUR [ALZ]
WAODANI alt for WAORANI [AUC]
WAOLA dial of ANGAL HENENG, WEST [AKH]
WAORANI [AUC] lang, Ecuador
WAPÃ alt for WAPAN [JUK]
WAPAN [JUK] lang, Nigeria
WAPATU alt for KALAPUYA [KAL]
WAPE alt for WAPI dial of OLO [ONG]
WAPI [WPI] lang, Papua New Guinea
WAPI dial of OLO [ONG]
WAPISHANA [WAP] lang, Guyana, Brazil
WAPISIANA alt for WAPISHANA [WAP]
WAPITXANA alt for WAPISHANA [WAP]
WAPITXÂNA alt for WAPISHANA [WAP]
WAPON dial of MAIWA [MTI]
WAPPO [WAO] lang, USA
WAR alt for MEOSWAR [MVX]
WAR dial of KHASI [KHI]
WARA [WBF] lang, Burkina Faso
WARA alt for LUWU dial of BUGIS [BPR]
WARABAL alt for BAYALI [BJY]
WARABAL dial of LOLA [LCD]
WARABORI dial of MARAU [MVR]
WARAGA dial of FOLOPA [PPO]
WARANDGERI alt for WIRADHURI [WRH]
WARAO [WBA] lang, Venezuela, Guyana, Surinam
WARAPICHE alt for CHAYMA dial of KALIHNA [CRB]
WARAPU [WRA] lang, Papua New Guinea
WARASAI alt for PASI [PSI]
WARASAI alt for YAW dial of YESSAN-MAYO [YSS]
WARAT alt for MADNGELE [ZML]
WARAWARA alt for NORTHERN LIMBA dial of LIMBA, EAST [LMA]
WARAY [WRZ] lang, Australia
WARAY alt for WARAY-WARAY [WRY]
WARAY dial of WARAY-WARAY [WRY]
WARAY-WARAY [WRY] lang, Philippines
WARDA'MAN alt for WARDAMAN [WRR]
WARDAMAN [WRR] lang, Australia
WARDAY alt for ORMA [ORC]
WARDEI alt for ORMA [ORC]
WARDMAN alt for WARDAMAN [WRR]
WARDO dial of BIAK [BHW]

WARDUJI [WRD] lang, Afghanistan
WARDUMAN alt for WARDAMAN [WRR]
WARE [WRE] lang, Tanzania
WARE alt for WARI dial of TUBETUBE [TTE]
WAREKENA alt for GUAREQUENA [GAE]
WAREKÉNA alt for GUAREQUENA [GAE]
WAREMA alt for YANOMAM dial of YANOMÁMI [WCA]
WAREMBORI [WSA] lang, Indonesia, Irian Jaya
WAREMBORI alt for WARABORI dial of MARAU [MVR]
WARENBORI alt for WAREMBORI [WSA]
WARES [WAI] lang, Indonesia, Irian Jaya
WARGARINDEM alt for YAFI [WFG]
WARGLA alt for OUARGLA [OUA]
WARI [WBE] lang, Indonesia, Irian Jaya
WARI alt for TUBARÃO [TBA]
WARI dial of BIAK [BHW]
WARI dial of TUBETUBE [TTE]
WARIADAI alt for MORIGI [MDB]
WARIAPANO alt for PANOBO [PNO]
WARIHÍO alt for HUARIJÍO [VAR]
WARIKIANA alt for KAXUIÂNA [KBB]
WARIKYANA alt for KAXUIÂNA [KBB]
WARILAU alt for KOLA [KVV]
WARIS [WRS] lang, Papua New Guinea, Indonesia, Irian Jaya
WARIYANGGA [WRI] lang, Australia
WARJA alt for WARJI [WJI]
WARJAWA alt for WARJI [WJI]
WARJI [WJI] lang, Nigeria
WARKAY-BIPIM [BGV] lang, Indonesia, Irian Jaya
WARKI alt for DILLING [DIL]
WARKIMBE alt for DILLING [DIL]
WARKYA alt for WAGAYA [WGA]
WARLANG alt for KUNBARLANG [WLG]
WARLMANPA [WRL] lang, Australia
WARLPIRI [WBP] lang, Australia
WARLUWARA [WRB] lang, Australia
WARM SPRINGS alt for TENINO [WAR]
WARMNU dial of IRARUTU [IRH]
WARNANG [WRN] lang, Sudan
WARNDARANG alt for WANDARANG [WND]
WARNMAN alt for WANMAN [WBT]
WARO alt for PALOR [FAP]
WARO-WARO alt for WOLOF [WOL]
WAROPEN [WRP] lang, Indonesia, Irian Jaya
WAROPEN KAI dial of WAROPEN [WRP]
WARPOK alt for ORYA [URY]
WARPU alt for ORYA [URY]
WARRA alt for NUGUNU [NNV]
WARRA-WARRA alt for YIDINY [YII]
WARRAI alt for WARAY [WRZ]
WARRAMUNGA alt for WARUMUNGU [WRM]
WARRANGOO alt for WIRANGU [WIW]
WARRAU alt for WARAO [WBA]
WARRGAMAY [WGY] lang, Australia
WARRI alt for ISEKIRI [ITS]
WARRIYANGKA alt for WARIYANGGA [WRI]
WARRYBOORA alt for YIDINY [YII]
WARSA dial of BIAK [BHW]
WARTAMAN alt for WARDAMAN [WRR]
WARU [WRU] lang, Indonesia, Sulawesi
WARU dial of WARU [WRU]
WARUMUNGU [WRM] lang, Australia
WARUNA [WRV] lang, Papua New Guinea

WARUNGU [WRG] lang, Australia
WARUWARU alt for YUWANA [YAU]
WASA [WSS] lang, Ghana
WASA [WSW] lang, Central African Republic, Sudan
WASANYE alt for BONI [BOB]
WASANYE alt for SANYE [SSN]
WASARE alt for KAPRIMAN [DJU]
WASAW alt for WASA [WSS]
WASCO-WISHRAM [WAC] lang, USA
WASE [JUW] lang, Nigeria
WASEDA alt for WASIDA dial of OROKAIVA [ORK]
WASEMBO [GSP] lang, Papua New Guinea
WASEPNAU alt for URAT [URT]
WASERA alt for WASIDA dial of OROKAIVA [ORK]
WASETA alt for WASIDA dial of OROKAIVA [ORK]
WASHKUK alt for KWOMA [KMO]
WASHKUK alt for KWOMA dial of KWOMA [KMO]
WASHO [WAS] lang, USA
WASHOE alt for WASHO [WAS]
WASI [WBJ] lang, Tanzania
WASI alt for PELE-ATA [ATA]
WASI-VERI alt for PRASUNI [PRN]
WASIDA dial of OROKAIVA [ORK]
WASIOR dial of WANDAMEN [WAD]
WASKIA [WSK] lang, Papua New Guinea
WASOI alt for TINPUTZ [TPZ]
WASONA dial of TUCANO [TUO]
WASSA alt for WASA [WSS]
WASSISI alt for WEASISI dial of WHITESANDS
    [TNP]
WASSU dial of JIARONG [JYA]
WASSULU alt for WASULU dial of MALINKE [MLQ]
WASSULUNKA alt for WASULU dial of MALINKE
    [MLQ]
WASSULUNKA alt for WASULU dial of MALINKE
    [MLQ]
WASSULUNKE alt for WASULU dial of MALINKE
    [MLQ]
WASSULUNKE alt for WASULU dial of MALINKE
    [MLQ]
WASU [WSU] lang, Brazil
WASULU dial of MALINKE [MLQ]
WASULU dial of MALINKE [MLQ]
WASUSU dial of NAMBIKUÁRA, SOUTHERN [NAB]
WAT dial of LIMBUM [LIM]
WATA alt for BONI [BOB]
WATA-BALA alt for BONI [BOB]
WATAKATAUI [WTK] lang, Papua New Guinea
WATALU alt for NAMIA [NNM]
WATALUMA [WAT] lang, Papua New Guinea
WATAM [WAX] lang, Papua New Guinea
WATANDE alt for DANDA dial of NDAU [NDC]
WATAPOR alt for ANGOR [AGG]
WATER BUSHMEN alt for XUN [XUU]
WATEVE alt for TEVE dial of MANYIKA [MXC]
WATIFA alt for DUMPU [WTF]
WATIWA alt for DUMPU [WTF]
WATJARI [WBV] lang, Australia
WATJARRI alt for WATJARI [WBV]
WATOM dial of TOLAI [KSD]
WATONGA alt for TONGA dial of NDAU [NDC]
WATUBELA [WAH] lang, Indonesia, Maluku
WATULAI alt for BATULEY [BAY]
WATUT alt for SILISILI [MPL]
WATUT alt for UNANK [UNA]
WATUT alt for HAMTAI [HMT]

WATYI alt for WACI-GBE [WCI]
WAUMEO [NOA] lang, Panama, Colombia
WAUNANA alt for WAUMEO [NOA]
WAUPE alt for KWATO [KOP]
WAURÁ [WAU] lang, Brazil
WAWA [WWW] lang, Cameroon
WAWA dial of BUSA-BOKO [BUS]
WAWAN dial of HANUNOO [HNN]
WAWILAG alt for RITARUNGO [RIT]
WAWOL alt for KAMULA [KHM]
WAWONII [WOW] lang, Indonesia, Sulawesi
WAWONII dial of WAWONII [WOW]
WAY LIMA dial of PESISIR, SOUTHERN [PEC]
WAYA dial of FIJIAN, WESTERN [WYY]
WAYA dial of SAPO [KRN]
WAYAMLI dial of BULI [BZQ]
WAYAMPI, AMAPARI [OYM] lang, Brazil
WAYAMPI, OIAPOQUE [OYA] lang, French Guiana,
    Brazil
WAYANA [WAY] lang, Surinam, Brazil, French
    Guiana
WAYÂNA alt for WAYANA [WAY]
WAYAPI alt for WAYAMPI, OIAPOQUE [OYA]
WAYÃPI alt for WAYAMPI, OIAPOQUE [OYA]
WAYAPÍ alt for WAYAMPI, OIAPOQUE [OYA]
WAYAPO alt for LISELA [LCL]
WAYARICURI alt for AKURIO [AKO]
WAYCHA dial of QUECHUA, HUANCA, HUAYLLA
    [QHU]
WAYHARA alt for YURUTI [YUI]
WAYILWAN dial of WANGAAYBUWAN-NGIYAMBAA
    [WYB]
WAYOLI alt for WAIOLI [WLI]
WAYOMBA alt for NGULU [NGP]
WAYOMBO alt for ZIGULA [ZIW]
WAYORÓ [WYR] lang, Brazil
WAYTO alt for WEYTO [WOY]
WAYU alt for VAYU [VAY]
WAYURÚ alt for WAYORÓ [WYR]
WAYUU alt for GUAJIRO [GUC]
WAZAIZARA alt for GUAJÁ [GUJ]
WAZAN dial of MOFU, NORTH [MFK]
WAZANG alt for WAZAN dial of MOFU, NORTH
    [MFK]
WAZEGUA alt for ZIGULA [ZIW]
WAZEZURU alt for ZEZURU dial of SHONA [SHD]
WAZIRI alt for WACIRI dial of PASHTO, CENTRAL
    [PST]
WE alt for FUNGOM [FUG]
WE dial of TONGA [TOI]
WE dial of TONGA [TOI]
WE alt for GHOMALA CENTRAL dial of GHOMALA'
    [BBJ]
WEASISI dial of WHITESANDS [TNP]
WEBO dial of GREBO, NORTHEASTERN [GRP]
WEDA alt for SAWAI [SZW]
WEDA alt for VEDDAH [VED]
WEDA dial of SAWAI [SZW]
WEDAU [WED] lang, Papua New Guinea
WEDAUN alt for WEDAU [WED]
WEDAWAN alt for WEDAU [WED]
WEDDO alt for VEDDAH [VED]
WEDEBO dial of GREBO, BARCLAYVILLE [GRY]
WEDEBO GREBO alt for GREBO, BARCLAYVILLE
    [GRY]
WEDJAH alt for WAYA dial of SAPO [KRN]

WEE alt for GUÉRÉ [GXX]
WEELA alt for LIGBI [LIG]
WEELA alt for HWELA dial of LIGBI [LIG]
WEEN alt for TOURA [NEB]
WEGAL dial of PASHAYI, SOUTHEAST [DRA]
WEGAM alt for KUGAMA [KOW]
WEGELE alt for GENGLE [GEG]
WEH [WEH] lang, Cameroon
WEI alt for DEBRI [DEB]
WEIDYENYE alt for MUNDURUKÚ [MYU]
WEILA alt for LIGBI [LIG]
WEILA alt for HWELA dial of LIGBI [LIG]
WEIM alt for GAL [GAP]
WEINING dial of HMONG, WESTERN [HUJ]
WEIWUER alt for UYGHUR [UIG]
WEKA alt for BAY ISLANDS ENGLISH dial of
    ENGLISH [ENG]
WELAM alt for NAGA, KHIAMNGAN [NKY]
WELAMO alt for WOLAYTTA [WBC]
WELAUNG [WEL] lang, Myanmar
WELE alt for WERI [WER]
WELEKI alt for WELIKI [KLH]
WELEMUR alt for APUTAI [APX]
WELI alt for WERI [WER]
WELIKI [KLH] lang, Papua New Guinea
WELLAMO alt for WOLAYTTA [WBC]
WELLEGA alt for MECHA dial of OROMO, WELLEGA-
    CENTRAL [GAZ]
WELLO dial of OROMO, WELLEGA-CENTRAL [GAZ]
WELSH [WLS] lang, United Kingdom, Canada
WEMALE, NORTH [WEO] lang, Indonesia, Maluku
WEMALE, SOUTH [TLW] lang, Indonesia, Maluku
WEMBA alt for BEMBA [BEM]
WEMBI alt for MANEM [JET]
WEME alt for WEME-GBE [WEM]
WEME-GBE [WEM] lang, Benin
WEMO dial of KÂTE [KMG]
WEN alt for NUMEE [KDK]
WENATCHEE-COLUMBIA alt for COLUMBIA-
    WENATCHI [COL]
WENCHANG alt for HAINANESE dial of CHINESE,
    MIN NAN [CFR]
WEND, LOWER [WEE] lang, Germany
WEND, UPPER [WEN] lang, Germany, Austria
WENDISH alt for WEND, LOWER [WEE]
WENDISH alt for WEND, UPPER [WEN]
WENMA dial of ZHUANG, SOUTHERN [CCY]
WENTA dial of HAMTAI [HMT]
WENYA dial of TUMBUKA [TUW]
WENZHOU dial of CHINESE, WU [WUU]
WEPPA WANO alt for UWEPA-UWANO dial of
    YEKHEE [ETS]
WERAFUTA dial of IRARUTU [IRH]
WERCHIKWAR dial of BURUSHASKI [BSK]
WERDERS alt for WADDAR [WBQ]
WERE [WEI] lang, Papua New Guinea
WERE alt for SAWAI [SZW]
WERE alt for MOM JANGO [VER]
WEREKENA alt for GUAREQUENA [GAE]
WERETAI alt for WARI [WBE]
WERI [WER] lang, Papua New Guinea
WERIAGAR dial of KEMBERANO [BZP]
WERIKENA alt for GUAREQUENA [GAE]
WERINAMA alt for BOBOT [BTY]
WERNI alt for WARNANG [WRN]
WEROGERY alt for WIRADHURI [WRH]

WERUGHA dial of TAITA [DAV]
WES COS alt for PIDGIN, CAMEROON [WES]
WESI alt for WATUBELA [WAH]
WEST AGAW alt for QIMANT [QIM]
WEST ALASKA ESKIMO alt for YUPIK, CENTRAL
    [ESU]
WEST ARABIAN COLLOQUIAL ARABIC alt for
    ARABIC, HIJAZI [ACW]
WEST ARCTIC ESKIMO dial of INUIT, NORTH
    ALASKAN [ESI]
WEST AWIN alt for AWIN [AWI]
WEST BAFWANGADA dial of BUDU [BUU]
WEST BANGGAI dial of BANGGAI [BGZ]
WEST BERAWAN dial of BERAWAN [LOD]
WEST BOIKIN dial of BOIKIN [BZF]
WEST BORNEO COAST MALAY dial of MALAY [MLI]
WEST CAPE AFRIKAANS alt for CAPE AFRIKAANS
    dial of AFRIKAANS [AFK]
WEST CENTRAL GOE alt for TOUGAN dial of SAMO
    [SBD]
WEST CENTRAL KLAOH dial of KLAO [KLU]
WEST CENTRAL KOMBA dial of KOMBA [KPF]
WEST CENTRAL KWOMTARI dial of KWOMTARI
    [KWO]
WEST CHACHAPOYAS alt for LAMUD dial of
    QUECHUA, CHACHAPOYAS [QUK]
WEST CIRCASSIAN alt for ADYGHE [ADY]
WEST COAST BAJAO alt for BAJAU, WEST COAST
    [BDR]
WEST COAST BAJAU dial of BAJAU, WEST COAST
    [BDR]
WEST COASTAL dial of JIMAJIMA [JMA]
WEST COUNTRY dial of ENGLISH [ENG]
WEST DANGALEAT dial of DANGALEAT [DAA]
WEST DANUBE dial of HUNGARIAN [HNG]
WEST ELEMA alt for OROKOLO [ORO]
WEST ENDE alt for NGA'O dial of ENDE [END]
WEST FUTUNA dial of FUTUNA-ANIWA [FUT]
WEST FUTUNA-ANIWA alt for FUTUNA-ANIWA
    [FUT]
WEST GIMI dial of GIMI [GIM]
WEST GORONTALO dial of GORONTALO [GRL]
WEST GREENLANDIC dial of INUIT, GREENLANDIC
    [ESG]
WEST GUADALCANAL alt for GHARI [GRI]
WEST GWARI alt for GBARI [GBY]
WEST HUNAN HMONG alt for HMONG, NORTHERN
    [MUQ]
WEST HUNGARIAN dial of HUNGARIAN [HNG]
WEST KALAMSE alt for LOGREMMA dial of
    KALAMSE [KNZ]
WEST KARA dial of KARA [LEU]
WEST KAREKARE alt for JALALUM dial of
    KAREKARE [KAI]
WEST KASEM dial of KASEM [KAS]
WEST KOITA dial of KOITA [KQI]
WEST KOMBA dial of KOMBA [KPF]
WEST KONGO dial of KONGO [KON]
WEST KONGO dial of KONGO [KON]
WEST LAMAHOLOT dial of LAMAHOLOT [SLP]
WEST LATVIAN dial of LATVIAN [LAT]
WEST MAFA dial of MAFA [MAF]
WEST MAIN CREE alt for CREE, CENTRAL [CRM]
WEST MAKUA alt for MAKHUWA-NIASSA [VMK]
WEST MAPE dial of MAPE [MLH]
WEST MARSELA alt for MASELA, WEST [MSS]

WESTERN KITUBA dial of KITUBA [KTU]
WESTERN KLAOH dial of KLAO [KLU]
WESTERN KOLIBUGAN dial of SUBANON, WESTERN [SUC]
WESTERN KUNDU alt for BALUE dial of BAKUNDU-BALUE [BDU]
WESTERN LAMPUNG alt for KRUI [KRQ]
WESTERN LAOTIAN alt for TAI, NORTHERN [NOD]
WESTERN LIMBA dial of LIMBA, WEST-CENTRAL [LIA]
WESTERN LIVONIAN dial of LIV [LIV]
WESTERN LOMBARD dial of LOMBARD [LMO]
WESTERN LOW NAVARRESE dial of BASQUE [BSQ]
WESTERN LUBA alt for LUBA-KASAI [LUB]
WESTERN MACEDONIAN dial of MACEDONIAN [MKJ]
WESTERN MACINA dial of FULFULDE, MAASINA [FUL]
WESTERN MAITHILI dial of MAITHILI [MKP]
WESTERN MAKUA alt for LOMWE [NGL]
WESTERN MAM alt for TACANECO [MTZ]
WESTERN MAM alt for MAM, CENTRAL [MVC]
WESTERN MANDARIN alt for HO dial of CHINESE, MANDARIN [CHN]
WESTERN MANGGARAI dial of MANGGARAI [MQY]
WESTERN MARWARI dial of MARWARI [MKD]
WESTERN MASALIT dial of MASALIT [MSA]
WESTERN MBUBE alt for MBE [MFO]
WESTERN MIXE alt for MIXE, TLAHUITOLTEPEC [MXP]
WESTERN MONGOL alt for KALMYK-OIRAT [KGZ]
WESTERN MONGOLIAN alt for KALMYK-OIRAT [KGZ]
WESTERN NYASA alt for TONGA [TOG]
WESTERN OKPAMHERI dial of OKPAMHERI [OPA]
WESTERN ORIYA dial of ORIYA [ORY]
WESTERN OROMO alt for OROMO, WELLEGA-CENTRAL [GAZ]
WESTERN POCOMCHÍ alt for POKOMCHÍ, WESTERN [POB]
WESTERN POINT dial of NIMOA [NMW]
WESTERN PUNJABI alt for PANJABI, WESTERN [PNB]
WESTERN QUICHÉ dial of QUICHÉ, WEST CENTRAL [QUT]
WESTERN RED BOBO alt for BOMU [BMQ]
WESTERN RENGAO dial of RENGAO [REN]
WESTERN SHONA alt for KALANGA [KCK]
WESTERN SHUSWAP dial of SHUSWAP [SHS]
WESTERN SICILIAN dial of SICILIAN [SCN]
WESTERN SOLA DE VEGA ZAPOTECO alt for ZAPOTECO, SANTA MARÍA ZANIZA [ZPW]
WESTERN STANDARD BHOJPURI dial of BHOJPURI [BHJ]
WESTERN SUDANESE dial of ARABIC, SUDANESE [APD]
WESTERN SURI alt for KACIPO [KOE]
WESTERN SWAMPY CREE dial of CREE, WESTERN [CRP]
WESTERN SYRIAC alt for SURYOYO [SYR]
WESTERN TARAHUMARA alt for TARAHUMARA BAJA [TAC]
WESTERN TAUBUID alt for TAWBUID, WESTERN [TWB]
WESTERN TEMNE dial of THEMNE [TEJ]
WESTERN TETUN dial of TETUN [TTM]

WESTERN TOPOSA dial of TOPOSA [TOQ]
WESTERN TUVIN dial of TUVIN [TUN]
WESTERN VOGUL dial of MANSI [MNS]
WESTERN WAKHI dial of WAKHI [WBL]
WESTERN YAGNOBI dial of YAGNOBI [YAI]
WESTERN YANOMAMI dial of YANOMAMÖ [GUU]
WESTERN YI dial of YI, SICHUAN [III]
WESTERN YIDDISH dial of YIDDISH [YDD]
WESTMORLAND dial of ENGLISH [ENG]
WESTPHALIAN alt for LOW SAXON dial of GERMAN, LOW [GEP]
WETAMUT [WWO] lang, Vanuatu
WETAN dial of LUANG [LEX]
WETANG alt for WETAN dial of LUANG [LEX]
WETAWIT alt for BERTA [WTI]
WETE dial of DEHU [DEU]
WETERE alt for VUTE [VUT]
WETU dial of JUR MODO [BEX]
WETUMBA alt for KAGULU [KKI]
WEWAW [WEA] lang, Myanmar
WEWEWA alt for WEYEWA [WEW]
WEWJEWA alt for WEYEWA [WEW]
WEYEWA [WEW] lang, Indonesia, Nusa Tenggara
WEYEWA dial of WEYEWA [WEW]
WEYOKO dial of DUAU [DUA]
WEYTO [WOY] lang, Ethiopia
WHANA alt for HWANA [HWO]
WHELNGO alt for LUSHAI [LSH]
WHITE BOLON dial of BOLON [BOF]
WHITE CLAY PEOPLE alt for GROS VENTRE [ATS]
WHITE KAREN alt for KAREN, S'GAW [KSW]
WHITE KAREN alt for KAREN, GEBA [KVQ]
WHITE KAREN alt for KAREN, PWO [PWO]
WHITE KHOANY dial of PHUNOI [PHO]
WHITE LACHI alt for LATI, WHITE [LWH]
WHITE LISU dial of LISU [LIS]
WHITE LISU dial of LISU [LIS]
WHITE LUM alt for HMONG DAW [MWW]
WHITE MEO alt for HMONG DAW [MWW]
WHITE MIAO alt for HMONG DAW [MWW]
WHITE MIAO alt for PEH dial of HMONG, WESTERN [HUJ]
WHITE MIAO alt for PETCHABUN dial of HMONG, WESTERN [HUJ]
WHITE MOUNTAIN dial of APACHE, WESTERN [APW]
WHITE NILE DINKA alt for DINKA, NORTHEASTERN [DIP]
WHITE NOGAI dial of NOGAI [NOG]
WHITE RUSSIA ROMANI dial of ROMANI, BALTIC [ROM]
WHITE RUSSIAN alt for BELORUSSIAN [RUW]
WHITE RUSSIAN ROMANI dial of ROMANI, BALTIC [ROM]
WHITE RUTHENIAN alt for BELORUSSIAN [RUW]
WHITE TAI alt for TAI DÓN [TWH]
WHITESANDS [TNP] lang, Vanuatu
WHITESANDS alt for WHITESANDS [TNP]
WI alt for KWANGE dial of GBARI [GBY]
WI-ISU dial of AGHEM [AGQ]
WIAKEI alt for WIAKI [WII]
WIAKI [WII] lang, Papua New Guinea
WIANG JAN alt for VIENTIANE dial of LAO [NOL]
WIANG PAPAO LUA alt for LAWA, EASTERN [LWL]
WIARI dial of NAMIA [NNM]
WICHÍ LHAMTÉS GÜISNAY [MZH] lang, Argentina

WICHÍ LHAMTÉS NOCTEN [MTP] lang, Bolivia, Argentina
WICHÍ LHAMTÉS VEJOZ [MAD] lang, Argentina, Bolivia
WICHITA [WIC] lang, USA
WIDEKUM alt for MOGHAMO dial of META' [MGO]
WIDIKUM-TADKON alt for META' [MGO]
WIELKOPOLSKA-KUJAWY dial of POLISH [PQL]
WIGA dial of SINAGORO [SNC]
WIGHOR alt for UYGHUR [UIG]
WIILA alt for LIGBI [LIG]
WIILA alt for HWELA dial of LIGBI [LIG]
WIINDZA-BAALI dial of NGOMBE [NGC]
WIIRATHERI alt for WIRADHURI [WRH]
WIK MUMINH alt for KUKU-MUMINH [XMH]
WIK NJINTURA alt for WIKNGENCHERA [WUA]
WIK-EPA [WIE] lang, Australia
WIK-IIYANH [WIJ] lang, Australia
WIK-KEYANGAN [WIF] lang, Australia
WIK-ME'ANHA [WIH] lang, Australia
WIK-MUMIN alt for KUKU-MUMINH [XMH]
WIK-MUNGKAN [WIM] lang, Australia
WIK-MUNKAN alt for WIK-MUNGKAN [WIM]
WIK-NANTJARA alt for WIKNGENCHERA [WUA]
WIK-NGANDJARA dial of WIKALKAN [WIK]
WIK-NGATHANA [WIG] lang, Australia
WIK-NGATHARA alt for WIKALKAN [WIK]
WIK-NGATHARRA alt for WIKALKAN [WIK]
WIKALKAN [WIK] lang, Australia
WIKNGATARA alt for WIKALKAN [WIK]
WIKNGENCHERA [WUA] lang, Australia
WILA-WILA alt for WILAWILA [WIL]
WILAWILA [WIL] lang, Australia
WILAWILA dial of NGARINYIN [UNG]
WILD `ALI alt for CENTRAL NAJDI dial of ARABIC, NAJDI [ARS]
WILD `ALI alt for CENTRAL NAJDI dial of ARABIC, NAJDI [ARS]
WILE dial of BIRIFOR, MALBA [BFO]
WILJAKALI dial of DARLING [DRL]
WILYAGALI alt for WILJAKALI dial of DARLING [DRL]
WIMBUM alt for LIMBUM [LIM]
WIN alt for TOUSSIAN, SOUTHERN [WIB]
WIN alt for TOUSSIAN, NORTHERN [TSP]
WINA alt for DESANO [DES]
WINA alt for SOWANDA [SOW]
WINA alt for TUPURI [TUI]
WINA dial of MASANA [MCN]
WINANTU-GIMPU dial of UMA [PPK]
WINDESI alt for WANDAMEN [WAD]
WINDESI dial of WANDAMEN [WAD]
WINDESSI alt for WANDAMEN [WAD]
WINDISCH alt for WEND, LOWER [WEE]
WINDISCH alt for WEND, UPPER [WEN]
WINGEI dial of AMBULAS [ABT]
WINIV dial of VINMAVIS [VNM]
WINIV dial of LAMETIN [LMB]
WINJI-WINJI alt for ANII [BLO]
WINNEBAGO [WIN] lang, USA
WINS dial of BUANG, MAPOS [BZH]
WINTU [WIT] lang, USA
WINTU dial of WINTU [WIT]
WINTUN alt for WINTU [WIT]
WINYE alt for KO [KST]
WIPI alt for GIDRA [GDR]

WIPIE alt for ADYNYAMATHANHA [ADT]
WIPIM dial of GIDRA [GDR]
WIPSI-NI alt for ZUKSUN dial of PUKU-GEERI-KERI-WIPSI [GEL]
WIPSI-NI alt for FER dial of PUKU-GEERI-KERI-WIPSI [GEL]
WIRÃ alt for DESANO [DES]
WIRA dial of JUR MODO [BEX]
WIRA-ATHOREE alt for WIRADHURI [WRH]
WIRADHURI [WRH] lang, Australia
WIRADJURI alt for WIRADHURI [WRH]
WIRADURI alt for WIRADHURI [WRH]
WIRAFÉD [WIR] lang, Brazil
WIRAIDYURI alt for WIRADHURI [WRH]
WIRAJEREE alt for WIRADHURI [WRH]
WIRAM alt for SUKI [SUI]
WIRANGU [WIW] lang, Australia
WIRASHURI alt for WIRADHURI [WRH]
WIRATHERI alt for WIRADHURI [WRH]
WIRI alt for DUVLE [DUV]
WIROFÉD alt for WIRAFÉD [WIR]
WIRONGU alt for WIRANGU [WIW]
WIRONGUWONGGA alt for WIRANGU [WIW]
WIRRACHAREE alt for WIRADHURI [WRH]
WIRRAI'YARRAI alt for WIRADHURI [WRH]
WIRRUNG alt for WIRANGU [WIW]
WIRRUNGA alt for WIRANGU [WIW]
WIRU [WIU] lang, Papua New Guinea
WISA alt for BISA dial of LALA-BISA [LEB]
WISCONSIN dial of WINNEBAGO [WIN]
WITA EA dial of MORONENE [MQN]
WITOTO alt for HUITOTO, MURUI [HUU]
WITU alt for WIRU [WIU]
WITU alt for VITU [WIV]
WIWA alt for MALAYO [MBP]
WIWIRANO dial of TOLAKI [LBW]
WIYAGWA dial of ANKAVE [AAK]
WIYAP alt for JIRU [JRR]
WIYAU alt for HARUAI [TMD]
WIYAW alt for HARUAI [TMD]
WIYEH dial of LIMBUM [LIM]
WIYOT [WIY] lang, USA
WIZA alt for BISA dial of LALA-BISA [LEB]
WIZA alt for BISA dial of LALA-BISA [LEB]
WLEPO dial of KRUMEN, NORTHEASTERN [PYE]
WLOPO dial of KRUMEN, SOUTHERN [TED]
WLUWE-HAWLO dial of KRUMEN, NORTHEASTERN [PYE]
WO alt for KULUNG [BBU]
WO alt for BASARI [BSC]
WO dial of YORUBA [YOR]
WO'OI alt for WOI [WBW]
WOBE [WOB] lang, Côte d'Ivoire
WODA alt for WOLANI [WOD]
WODA-MO alt for WOLANI [WOD]
WODANI alt for WOLANI [WOD]
WODIWODI alt for WADIWADI dial of THURAWAL [TBH]
WODO alt for WALAK [WLW]
WOGAITY alt for WADJIGINY [WDJ]
WOGAMUSIN [WOG] lang, Papua New Guinea
WOGEMAN alt for WAGEMAN [WAQ]
WOGEO [WOC] lang, Papua New Guinea
WOGGIL alt for YIDINY [YII]
WOGRI-BOLI dial of DOMARI [RMT]
WOGU alt for BAHINEMO [BJH]

WOI [WBW] lang, Indonesia, Irian Jaya
WOISIKA [WOI] lang, Indonesia, Nusa Tenggara
WOITAPE alt for FUYUGE [FUY]
WOJO [WJO] lang, Central African Republic
WOJOKESO alt for WAJAKES dial of AMPEELI-
WOJOKESO [APZ]
WOKAM alt for MANOBAI [WOO]
WOKIARE dial of YABARANA [YAR]
WOKO alt for LONGTO [WOK]
WOLAITA alt for WOLAYTTA [WBC]
WOLAITTA alt for WOLAYTTA [WBC]
WOLANE alt for WALANE dial of GURAGE, EAST
[GRE]
WOLANI [WOD] lang, Indonesia, Irian Jaya
WOLATAITA alt for WOLAYTTA [WBC]
WOLAYTA alt for WOLAYTTA [WBC]
WOLAYTTA [WBC] lang, Ethiopia
WOLEAIAN [WOE] lang, Micronesia
WOLIO [WLO] lang, Indonesia, Sulawesi, Malaysia,
Sabah, Malaysia, Sabah
WOLIO alt for WOLIO [WLO]
WOLLAMINYA alt for WOLAYTTA [WBC]
WOLLAMO alt for WOLAYTTA [WBC]
WOLLEGA alt for MECHA dial of OROMO,
WELLEGA-CENTRAL [GAZ]
WOLLEGARA alt for WARLUWARA [WRB]
WOLLO alt for WELLO dial of OROMO, WELLEGA-
CENTRAL [GAZ]
WOLMERI alt for WALMAJARRI [WMT]
WOLOF [WOL] lang, Senegal, Mauritania
WOLOF, GAMBIAN [WOF] lang, Gambia
WOLU alt for TELUTI [TLT]
WOLU alt for WEST TELUTI dial of TELUTI [TLT]
WOLYAMIDI dial of NGARINYIN [UNG]
WOM [WMO] lang, Papua New Guinea
WOM [WOM] lang, Cameroon, Nigeria, Nigeria
WOM alt for WOM [WOM]
WOM-BY-A alt for WAMBAYA [WMB]
WOMBOKO alt for WUMBOKO [BQM]
WOMBUNGEE alt for WANGAAYBUWAN dial of
WANGAAYBUWAN-NGIYAMBAA [WYB]
WOMBYA alt for WAMBAYA [WMB]
WOMSAK alt for KWANGA [KWJ]
WOMSAK alt for WAMSAK [WBD]
WONGA alt for PINTIINI [PTI]
WONGAGIBUN alt for WANGAAYBUWAN dial of
WANGAAYBUWAN-NGIYAMBAA [WYB]
WONGAI-I alt for PINTIINI [PTI]
WONGAIBON alt for WANGAAYBUWAN dial of
WANGAAYBUWAN-NGIYAMBAA [WYB]
WONGAIDYA alt for NUGUNU [NNV]
WONGAMARDU alt for KOKATA [KTD]
WONGAMUSIN alt for WOGAMUSIN [WOG]
WONGGAII alt for PINTIINI [PTI]
WONGHI alt for WANGAAYBUWAN dial of
WANGAAYBUWAN-NGIYAMBAA [WYB]
WONGHIBON alt for WANGAAYBUWAN dial of
WANGAAYBUWAN-NGIYAMBAA [WYB]
WONGKUMARA dial of NGURA [NBX]
WONGO [WON] lang, Zaïre
WONI alt for HONI [HOW]
WONI alt for KADO [KDV]
WONIE dial of GIDRA [GDR]
WONJHIBON alt for WANGAAYBUWAN dial of
WANGAAYBUWAN-NGIYAMBAA [WYB]
WONO alt for SEKO PADANG [SKX]

WONO alt for HONO' dial of SEKO PADANG [SKX]
WONTI alt for WAROPEN [WRP]
WOODS CREE dial of CREE, WESTERN [CRP]
WOOLWA alt for SUMO [SUM]
WOORAGURIE alt for WIRADHURI [WRH]
WOOTEELIT dial of YUPIK, CENTRAL SIBERIAN
[ESS]
WOPKEIMIN ? alt for BUSILMIN dial of TIFAL [TIF]
WORDAMAN alt for WARDAMAN [WRR]
WORDJERG alt for WIRADHURI [WRH]
WORGAI alt for WAGAYA [WGA]
WORGAIA alt for WAGAYA [WGA]
WORIA [WOR] lang, Indonesia, Irian Jaya
WORIASI [WBB] lang, Indonesia, Irian Jaya
WORIMI [KDA] lang, Australia
WORIN dial of YAU [YUW]
WORKAI alt for BARAKAI [BAJ]
WORKIA alt for WAGAYA [WGA]
WORKU dial of IGEDE [IGE]
WORO alt for ORLO dial of KRESH [KRS]
WORODOUGOU JULA dial of JULA [DYU]
WORORA [UNP] lang, Australia
WORORA dial of WORORA [UNP]
WORPEN alt for WAROPEN [WRP]
WORRORRA alt for WORORA [UNP]
WORUGL alt for RO dial of FOLOPA [PPO]
WOSERA dial of AMBULAS [ABT]
WOSKIA alt for WASKIA [WSK]
WOTAPURI-KATARQALAI [WSV] lang, Afghanistan
WOTU [WTW] lang, Indonesia, Sulawesi
WOULKI dial of MPADE [MPI]
WOUN MEU alt for WAUMEO [NOA]
WOUNAAN alt for WAUMEO [NOA]
WOURI alt for OLI dial of DUALA [DOU]
WOUTE alt for VUTE [VUT]
WOVAN alt for HARUAI [TMD]
WOVEA alt for BUBIA [BBX]
WOWO alt for BIERIA [BRJ]
WOWO alt for VOVO dial of BIERIA [BRJ]
WOWONII alt for WAWONII [WOW]
WRELPO dial of GREBO, JABO [GRJ]
WU alt for CHINESE, WU [WUU]
WU dial of VO [WBM]
WUASINKISHU alt for MOITANIK dial of MAASAI
[MET]
WUBAHAMER dial of AARI [AIZ]
WUBOMEI dial of LOMA [LOM]
WUBULKARRA dial of GUPAPUYNGU [GUF]
WUDING alt for HUBA [KIR]
WUDU [WUD] lang, Togo
WUHÁNA alt for MACUNA [MYY]
WUKAN dial of WAPAN [JUK]
WUKARI alt for WAPAN [JUK]
WUKINGFU dial of CHINESE, HAKKA [HAK]
WULA dial of PSIKYE [KVJ]
WULA dial of BOKYI [BKY]
WULAKI dial of DJINANG [DJI]
WULAMBA alt for DHUWAL [DUJ]
WULANGA dial of YELE [YLE]
WULIMA dial of LALA-BISA [LEB]
WULIWULI [WLU] lang, Australia
WULNA [WUX] lang, Australia
WULU dial of BELI [BLM]
WUM alt for AGHEM [AGQ]
WUMBOKO [BQM] lang, Cameroon
WUMBU alt for WUUMU dial of TEKE, SOUTH

CENTRAL [IFM]
WUMBVU [WUM] lang, Congo, Gabon, Gabon
WUMBVU alt for WUMBVU [WUM]
WUMING alt for ZHUANG, NORTHERN [CCX]
WUMNABAL alt for WUNAMBAL [WUB]
WUMVU alt for WUMBVU [WUM]
WUNA alt for MBUM [MDD]
WUNA alt for MUNA [MYN]
WUNAI alt for PUNU [PNU]
WUNAI dial of PUNU [PNU]
WUNAMBAL [WUB] lang, Australia
WUNAMBAL alt for KWINI [GWW]
WUNAMBAL dial of WUNAMBAL [WUB]
WUNAMBULLU alt for WUNAMBAL [WUB]
WUNAVAI dial of ANKAVE [AAK]
WUNCI alt for GHULFAN [GHL]
WUNCIMBE alt for GHULFAN [GHL]
WUNDU [WUW] lang, Sudan
WUNGU alt for BUNGU [WUN]
WUNINGAK alt for URNINGANGG [URC]
WUO dial of TEKE, CENTRAL [TEC]
WUPIWI alt for CHIRIPO dial of CUIBA [CUI]
WURANCI alt for WURI dial of GWAMHI-WURI [BGA]
WURAWA alt for WURI dial of GWAMHI-WURI [BGA]
WUREIDBUG alt for AMARAG [AMG]
WURI dial of GWAMHI-WURI [BGA]
WURI alt for OLI dial of DUALA [DOU]
WURKUM alt for JUKUN WURKUM [JUI]
WURKUM alt for PIYA [PIY]
WURKUM alt for KULUNG [BBU]
"WUSE" alt for E [EEE]
WUSHI [BSE] lang, Cameroon
WUSI [WSI] lang, Vanuatu
WUSI-KEREPUA alt for WUSI [WSI]
WUTE alt for VUTE [VUT]
WUTUNG [WUT] lang, Papua New Guinea
WUU alt for WUVULU dial of WUVULU-AUA [WUV]
WUUMU dial of TEKE, SOUTH CENTRAL [IFM]
WUVULU dial of WUVULU-AUA [WUV]
WUVULU-AUA [WUV] lang, Papua New Guinea
WUYA alt for WAJA [WJA]
WUYANGPU dial of TU [MJG]
WUZHOU dial of CHINESE, MANDARIN [CHN]
WUZLAM [UDL] lang, Cameroon
WYANDOT [WYA] lang, USA, Canada
XÁ alt for MIEN [YOC]
XA alt for KHANG [KJM]
XA AI alt for KHANG [KJM]
XA BUNG alt for KHANG [KJM]
XA CAU alt for KHMU [KJG]
XA CAU alt for KHANG AI dial of KHANG [KJM]
XA CHUNG CHÁ alt for NHANG [NHA]
XA DANG alt for KHANG [KJM]
XA DON alt for KHANG [KJM]
XA HOC alt for KHANG [KJM]
XA KHAO alt for LAHA [LHA]
XA KHAO alt for KHANG AI dial of KHANG [KJM]
XÁ LÁ VÀNG alt for MANG [MGA]
XÁ MANG alt for MANG [MGA]
XÁ Ố alt for MANG [MGA]
XÁ U NÍ alt for HANI [HNI]
XA XUA alt for KHANG [KJM]
XA-DIENG alt for STIENG [STI]
XAAYO alt for KHAYO dial of SAAMIA [SBU]
XADI alt for HEDI [TUR]
XAGUA alt for ACHAGUA [ACA]

XAJDAK alt for KAJTAK dial of DARGWA [DAR]
XAJRJUZOVSKIJ dial of ITELMEN [ITL]
XAKRIABÁ [XKR] lang, Brazil
XAKUCHI dial of ADYGHE [ADY]
/XAM [XAM] lang, South Africa
XAMANG alt for MANG [MGA]
XAMATARI alt for SANUMÁ [SAM]
XAMBIOÁ alt for KARAJÁ [KPJ]
XAMIN alt for XAMIR [XAI]
XAMIR [XAI] lang, Ethiopia
XAMTA [XAT] lang, Ethiopia
XAMTANGA [XAN] lang, Ethiopia
XAN alt for BOZO, HAINYAXO [BZX]
XANANWA alt for GANANWA dial of SOTHO,
    NORTHERN [SRT]
XANGA alt for CHANGA dial of NDAU [NDC]
XANTY alt for KHANTY [KCA]
XANYAXO alt for BOZO, HAINYAXO [BZX]
XAPUT dial of KRYTS [KRY]
XARACII alt for XARACUU [ANE]
XARACUU [ANE] lang, New Caledonia
XARAGURE [ARG] lang, New Caledonia
XARBUK dial of DARGWA [DAR]
XAROXA alt for DIDINGA [DID]
XARUA alt for HARUA dial of BOLA [BNP]
XASA alt for TIGRÉ [TIE]
XASONKE alt for KASSONKE [KAO]
XATIA dial of NG/AMANI [NMN]
XATIA dial of NG/AMANI [NMN]
XATYRSKIJ dial of CHUKOT [CKT]
XATYRSKIJ dial of KORYAK [KPY]
XATYRSKIJ alt for KHATYRKA dial of KEREK [KRK]
XAUNI alt for HANI [HNI]
XAVÁNTE [XAV] lang, Brazil
XAVIERANO alt for SAN JAVIER dial of
    CHIQUITANO [CAX]
XAYO alt for KHAYO dial of SAAMIA [SBU]
XEBERO alt for JEBERO [JEB]
XEDI alt for HEDI [TUR]
//XEGWI [XEG] lang, South Africa, Botswana,
    Namibia
XENQENNA dial of SONINKE [SNN]
XERÉNTE [XER] lang, Brazil
XEREU alt for HIXKARYÁNA [HIX]
XEREWYANA alt for HIXKARYÁNA [HIX]
XESIBE dial of XHOSA [XOS]
XETÁ [XET] lang, Brazil
XEVSUR dial of GEORGIAN [GEO]
XHOSA [XOS] lang, South Africa
XIAERBA alt for SHERPA [SCR]
XIAMEN alt for FUJIAN dial of CHINESE, MIN NAN
    [CFR]
XIAMEN alt for HOKKIEN dial of CHINESE, MIN NAN
    [CFR]
XIANG alt for CHINESE, XIANG [HSN]
XIANGTAN dial of CHINESE, XIANG [HSN]
XIANGXI MIAO alt for HMONG, NORTHERN [MUQ]
XIANYOU dial of CHINESE, MIN PEI [MNP]
XIAO HUA dial of HMONG, WESTERN [HUJ]
XIBBA alt for HUBA [KIR]
XIBE [SJO] lang, China
XIBITA alt for HIBITO [HIB]
XIBITAOAN alt for COCAMA-COCAMILLA [COD]
XIBITAONA dial of COCAMA-COCAMILLA [COD]
XIBO alt for XIBE [SJO]
XICAQUE alt for TOL [JIC]

XICHANGANA alt for CHANGANA dial of TSONGA [TSO]
XICHANGANA) alt for TSONGA [TSO]
XIDZIVI alt for TSWA dial of TSWA [TSC]
XIFANG dial of HLAI [LIC]
XIHUILA alt for JEBERO [JEB]
XIKRIN dial of KAYAPÓ [TXU]
XILULEKE alt for LULEKE dial of TSONGA [TSO]
XINALUG alt for KHINALUGH [KJJ]
XINCA [XIN] lang, Guatemala
XINGHUA alt for CHINESE, MIN PEI [MNP]
XINGHUA alt for HSINGHUA dial of CHINESE, MIN PEI [MNP]
XINGHUA alt for HENGHUA dial of CHINESE, MIN PEI [MNP]
XINGHUA MIN alt for CHINESE, MIN PEI [MNP]
XINGNING dial of CHINESE, HAKKA [HAK]
XINH MUL alt for PUOC [PUO]
XINH-MUN alt for PUOC [PUO]
XINJIANG MONGOLIAN alt for KALMYK-OIRAT [KGZ]
XIPAIA alt for KURUÁYA [KYR]
XIPINÁWA [XIP] lang, Brazil
XIRI [XII] lang, South Africa
XIRIÂNA [XIR] lang, Brazil
XIRIANA alt for NINAM [SHB]
XIRIANÁ alt for NINAM [SHB]
XIRIKWA alt for XIRI [XII]
XIRIWAI alt for NADËB [MBJ]
XIRONGA alt for RONGA [RON]
XISHUANG BANNA DAI alt for LÜ [KHB]
XITIBO alt for SHETEBO dial of SHIPIBO-CONIBO [SHP]
XITSONGA alt for TSONGA [TSO]
XITSWA alt for TSWA [TSC]
XIVARO alt for SHUAR [JIV]
XOCHISTLAHUACA dial of AMUZGO, GUERRERO [AMU]
XOCÓ alt for KARIRI-XUCO [KZW]
XODANG alt for SEDANG [SED]
XOKLENG [XOK] lang, Brazil
XOKÓ alt for KARIRI-XUCO [KZW]
XOKÓ-KARIRÍ alt for KARIRI-XUCO [KZW]
XONG alt for CHONG [COG]
XONGA dial of TSONGA [TSO]
XOPA dial of LAZ [LZZ]
XOSA alt for XHOSA [XOS]
XRE NOP alt for NOP dial of KOHO [KPM]
XRIKWA alt for XIRI [XII]
XTIENG alt for STIENG [STI]
XÛ alt for KUNG-TSUMKWE [KTZ]
XU alt for KUNG-TSUMKWE [KTZ]
XU alt for XUN [XUU]
XUI alt for CHINESE, MANDARIN [CHN]
XUKHWE alt for XUN [XUU]
XUKRU alt for XIKRIN dial of KAYAPÓ [TXU]
XUKURÚ alt for KIRIRÍ-XOKÓ [XOO]
XUKURÚ alt for KARIRI-XUCO [KZW]
XUKURU KARIRI alt for KARIRI-XUCO [KZW]
XUN [XUU] lang, Angola, Namibia, Botswana, Namibia
XUN alt for KUNG-TSUMKWE [KTZ]
XUN alt for XUN [XUU]
XUNZAL alt for HUNZIB [HUZ]
XUNZAX alt for KUNZAKH dial of AVAR [AVR]
XUÒNG dial of NUNG [NUT]

XURIMA alt for YANOMÁMI [WCA]
XURIWAI alt for NADËB [MBJ]
XVARSHI alt for KHVARSHI [KHV]
XVARSHI dial of KHVARSHI [KHV]
XWEDA alt for XWEDA-GBE [XWD]
XWEDA-GBE [XWD] lang, Benin
XWELA alt for XWELA-GBE [XWE]
XWELA-GBE [XWE] lang, Benin
XWLA alt for XWLA-GBE [XWL]
XWLA-GBE [XWL] lang, Benin
Y-LANG alt for JOLONG dial of BAHNAR [BDQ]
YA [YYA] lang, China
YA alt for TAI PONG dial of TAI NÜA [TDD]
YA LU alt for YUGUR, WEST [YBE]
YA'O alt for KUUKU-YA'U [QKL]
YA'UNK alt for YAHANG [RHP]
YAA dial of TEKE, WESTERN [TEZ]
YAA dial of MUMUYE [MUL]
YAA alt for YAKA dial of TEKE, WESTERN [TEZ]
YAADRE alt for MOORE [MHM]
YAAGA alt for SEEBA-YAGA dial of FULFULDE, JELGOOJI [FUM]
YAAKO alt for MARGU [MHG]
YAAKU [MUU] lang, Kenya
YAAKUA alt for YAAKU [MUU]
YAAMBA dial of MBOLE [MDQ]
YAAN dial of YAOURÉ [YRE]
YAAN alt for YANGA dial of MOORE [MHM]
YAANDE dial of MOORE [MHM]
YAANGELE alt for YANGELE dial of GBAYA [GYA]
YAÁYUWEE dial of GBAYA [GYA]
YAAYUWEE dial of GBAYA [GYA]
YABAÂNA [YBN] lang, Brazil
YABAN alt for ARANDAI [JBJ]
YABARANA [YAR] lang, Venezuela
YABARANA alt for YABAÂNA [YBN]
YABEKA dial of EWONDO [EWO]
YABEKANGA dial of EWONDO [EWO]
YABEKOLO dial of EWONDO [EWO]
YABEM [JAE] lang, Papua New Guinea
YABEN [YBM] lang, Papua New Guinea
YABI dial of EKARI [EKG]
YABIM alt for YABEM [JAE]
YABIO [YBX] lang, Papua New Guinea
YABIYUFA alt for YAWEYUHA [YBY]
YABONG [YBO] lang, Papua New Guinea
YABUTÍ alt for JABUTÍ [JBT]
YABYANG dial of BAKOKO [BKH]
YABYANG-YAPEKE alt for YABYANG dial of BAKOKO [BKH]
YACAN alt for YAKAN [YKA]
YACE alt for EKPARI [EKR]
YACHAM alt for DORDAR dial of NAGA, AO [NJO]
YACHE dial of AKPA-YACHE [AKF]
YACHUMI alt for NAGA, YIMCHUNGRU [YIM]
YACOUA alt for YAKPA [BYK]
YACOUBA alt for DAN [DAF]
YADË [NCE] lang, Papua New Guinea
YADENA alt for BUDUMA [BDM]
YADI alt for YANADI [YBF]
YAEYAMA [RYS] lang, Japan
YAFFI alt for YAFI [WFG]
YAFI [WFG] lang, Indonesia, Irian Jaya
YAG DII alt for DII [DUR]
YAGA dial of AGTA, DUPANINAN [DUO]
YAGALLO ZAPOTECO alt for ZAPOTECO,

NORTHERN VILLA ALTA [ZAR]
YAGAR YAGAR alt for KALA LAGAW YA [MWP]
YAGARIA [YGR] lang, Papua New Guinea
YAGAWAK [YGK] lang, Papua New Guinea
YAGBA dial of YORUBA [YOR]
YAGE dial of DUNGAN [DNG]
YAGHAN alt for YAMANA [YAG]
YAGHWATADAXA alt for GAVA dial of GUDUF
   [GDF]
YAGNOB alt for YAGNOBI [YAI]
YAGNOBI [YAI] lang, Tajikistan
YAGOMI [YGM] lang, Papua New Guinea
YAGOUA alt for YAGWA dial of MASANA [MCN]
YAGUA [YAD] lang, Peru
YAGWA dial of MASANA [MCN]
YAGWOIA [YGW] lang, Papua New Guinea
YAHADIAN [NER] lang, Indonesia, Irian Jaya
YAHANG [RHP] lang, Papua New Guinea
YAHOW alt for ZAHAO dial of CHIN, FALAM [HBH]
YAHUA alt for YAGUA [YAD]
YAHUANAHUA alt for YAWANAWA [YWN]
YAHUDIC [YHD] lang, Israel, Iraq
YAHUNA [YNU] lang, Colombia
YAHUP [YAB] lang, Brazil, Colombia
YAHUP MAKÚ alt for YAHUP [YAB]
YAI alt for NHANG [NHA]
YAI alt for IAAI [IAI]
YAIKOLE dial of MBOLE [MDQ]
YAIR [YIR] lang, Indonesia, Irian Jaya
YAISU dial of MBOLE [MDQ]
YAIWE alt for YAÁYUWEE dial of GBAYA [GYA]
YAIWE alt for YAAYUWEE dial of GBAYA [GYA]
YAJIMA alt for YALIMA dial of MONGO-NKUNDU
   [MOM]
YAKA [YAF] lang, Zaïre, Angola
YAKA alt for KAKO [KKJ]
YAKA dial of YAKA [YAF]
YAKA dial of TEKE, WESTERN [TEZ]
YAKA dial of GANZI [GNZ]
YAKA alt for YAA dial of TEKE, WESTERN [TEZ]
YAKAHANGA dial of NYAMBO [NYM]
YAKALAG alt for YAKALAK dial of BAKOKO [BKH]
YAKALAK dial of BAKOKO [BKH]
YAKAMUL [YKM] lang, Papua New Guinea
YAKAMUL dial of YAKAMUL [YKM]
YAKAN [YKA] lang, Philippines, Malaysia, Sabah
YAKAN alt for ARAKANESE [MHV]
YAKHA [YBH] lang, Nepal, India
YAKHAIN alt for ARAKANESE [MHV]
YAKHAING alt for ARAKANESE [MHV]
YAKIBA alt for MAIA [SKS]
YAKIMA [YAK] lang, USA
YAKIMA dial of YAKIMA [YAK]
YAKKHA alt for YAKHA [YBH]
YAKKHABA alt for YAKHA [YBH]
YAKO alt for LOKO [YAZ]
YAKO alt for MARGU [MHG]
YAKOKO dial of MUMUYE [MUL]
YAKOMA [YKY] lang, Central African Republic,
   Zaïre, Zaïre
YAKOMA alt for YAKOMA [YKY]
YAKORO alt for BEKWARRA [BKV]
YAKPA [BYK] lang, Central African Republic, Zaïre,
   Zaïre
YAKPA alt for YAKPA [BYK]
YAKPWA alt for YAKPA [BYK]

YAKUBA alt for DAN [DAF]
YAKURR alt for LOKO [YAZ]
YAKUSU alt for KELE [KHY]
YAKUT [UKT] lang, Russia, Asia
YAKWA alt for YAKPA [BYK]
YALA [YBA] lang, Nigeria
YALA IKOM alt for NKUM dial of YALA [YBA]
YALA OBUBRA alt for NKUM AKPAMBE dial of
   YALA [YBA]
YALA OGOJA dial of YALA [YBA]
YALACH alt for LACH dial of CZECH [CZC]
YALAHATAN [JAL] lang, Indonesia, Maluku
YALAPMUNXTE dial of NAMBIKUÁRA, NORTHERN
   [MBG]
YALARNNGA [YLR] lang, Australia
YALAYU dial of NYÂLAYU [YLY]
YALDIYE-HO alt for KANJU [KBE]
YALE, KOSAREK [KKL] lang, Indonesia, Irian Jaya
YALE-KOSAREK alt for YALE, KOSAREK [KKL]
YALEBA alt for BUHUTU [BXH]
YALEBA dial of TAWALA [TBO]
YALI OF PASS VALLEY alt for NIPSAN [YAC]
YALI, ANGGURUK [YLI] lang, Indonesia, Irian Jaya
YALI, NINIA [NLK] lang, Indonesia, Irian Jaya
YALI-NIPSAN alt for NIPSAN [YAC]
YALIAMBI dial of BUDZA [BJA]
YALIMA dial of MONGO-NKUNDU [MOM]
YALIMO alt for YALI, ANGGURUK [YLI]
YALINA dial of ZAPOTECO, SAN BARTOLOMÉ
   ZOOGOCHO [ZPQ]
YALLOF alt for WOLOF [WOL]
YALMBAU alt for MANGALA [MEM]
YALU [YLU] lang, Papua New Guinea
YALUNKA [YAL] lang, Guinea, Sierra Leone,
   Senegal, Sierra Leone
YALUNKA alt for YALUNKA [YAL]
YALUNKE alt for YALUNKA [YAL]
YALUTOROV dial of TATAR [TTR]
YALY alt for NIPSAN [YAC]
YALY alt for YALI, NINIA [NLK]
YAM alt for YANGA dial of MOORE [MHM]
YAMAI dial of BILIAU [BCU]
YAMALELE alt for IAMALELE [YML]
YAMALTU alt for NYIMATLI dial of TERA [TER]
YAMAMADÍ alt for JAMAMADÍ [JAA]
YAMANA [YAG] lang, Chile, Argentina
YAMANAWA alt for YAMINAHUA [YAA]
YAMAP [YMP] lang, Papua New Guinea
YAMBA [YAM] lang, Cameroon
YAMBASA alt for NUGUNU [YAS]
YAMBASSA alt for NUGUNU [YAS]
YAMBES [YMB] lang, Papua New Guinea
YAMBETA [YAT] lang, Cameroon
YAMBETTA alt for YAMBETA [YAT]
YAMBIYAMBI [YAP] lang, Papua New Guinea
YAMBO alt for ANUAK [ANU]
YAMBO alt for ANUAK [ANU]
YAMDENA [JMD] lang, Indonesia, Maluku
YAMEGI alt for KARA [KCM]
YAMEO [YME] lang, Peru
YAMI [YMI] lang, Taiwan
YAMIACA alt for ATSAHUACA [ATC]
YAMINAHUA [YAA] lang, Peru, Bolivia, Brazil
YAMINÁWA alt for YAMINAHUA [YAA]
YAMINAWA alt for YAMINAHUA [YAA]
YAMNA alt for SOBEI [SOB]

YAMONGERI [YMG] lang, Zaïre
YAMONGIRI alt for YAMONGERI [YMG]
YAMPHE alt for YANPHU [YBI]
YAMPHU RAI alt for YANPHU [YBI]
YAMUR dial of KAMORO [KGQ]
YAN alt for YANGA dial of MOORE [MHM]
YAN-NHANGU alt for JARNANGO [JAY]
YANA [YAN] lang, Burkina Faso, Togo
YANA [YNN] lang, USA
YANA alt for YANGA dial of MOORE [MHM]
YANABA dial of MUYUW [MYW]
YANADI [YBF] lang, India
YANAIGUA alt for TAPIETÉ [TAI]
YANAM alt for NINAM [SHB]
YANAMAM dial of YANOMÁMI [WCA]
YANANGU alt for JARNANGO [JAY]
YANBE alt for YANGBYE [YBD]
YANBYE alt for YANGBYE [YBD]
YANCHI alt for YANS [YNS]
YANDANG alt for YENDANG [YEN]
YANDAPO dial of ENGA [ENQ]
YANDERIKA alt for INDRI [IDR]
YANDIRIKA alt for INDRI [IDR]
YANDIS alt for YANADI [YBF]
YANDRUWANDHA [YND] lang, Australia
YANESHA' alt for AMUESHA [AME]
YANG alt for KAREN, BWE [BWE]
YANG KHAO alt for KAREN, S'GAW [KSW]
YANG SEK alt for RIANG [RIL]
YANG WAN KUN alt for RIANG [RIL]
YANGA alt for YANA [YAN]
YANGA dial of MOORE [MHM]
YANGARELLA alt for NYANGGA [NNY]
"YANGARO" alt for YEMSA [JNJ]
YANGBEN [YAV] lang, Cameroon
YANGBYE [YBD] lang, Myanmar
YANGELE dial of GBAYA [GYA]
YANGELE dial of GBAYA [GYA]
YANGERE [YAJ] lang, Central African Republic
YANGERE alt for YANGELE dial of GBAYA [GYA]
YANGGAL alt for NYANGGA [NNY]
YANGHAO dial of HMONG, EASTERN [HEA]
YANGHO [YNH] lang, Gabon
YANGHUANG alt for T'EN [TCT]
YANGLAM alt for RIANG [RIL]
YANGMAN [JNG] lang, Australia
YANGO [YNG] lang, Zaïre
YANGONDA dial of MBOLE [MDQ]
YANGORU alt for BOIKIN [BZF]
YANGTSEPAKHA alt for SALABEKHA dial of
    KEBUMTAMP [KJZ]
YÀNGUANG dial of ZHUANG, SOUTHERN [CCY]
YANGULAM [YNL] lang, Papua New Guinea
YANGYE alt for YANGBYE [YBD]
YANKOWAN alt for WASEMBO [GSP]
YANKTON alt for NAKOTA dial of DAKOTA [DHG]
YANKUNTATJARA [KDD] lang, Australia
YANKUNYTJATJARA alt for YANKUNTATJARA
    [KDD]
YANOAM alt for YANOMÁMI [WCA]
YANOAMA alt for YANOMAMÖ [GUU]
YANOMAM alt for YANOMÁMI [WCA]
YANOMAM dial of YANOMÁMI [WCA]
YANOMAMÉ alt for YANOMÁMI [WCA]
YANOMAME alt for YANOMAMÖ [GUU]
YANOMÁMI [WCA] lang, Brazil

YANOMAMI alt for YANOMAMÖ [GUU]
YANOMAMÖ [GUU] lang, Venezuela, Brazil
YANOMAY dial of YANOMÁMI [WCA]
YANPHU [YBI] lang, Nepal
YANRAKINOT dial of CHUKOT [CKT]
YANS [YNS] lang, Zaïre
YANSI alt for YANS [YNS]
YANTA [YNT] lang, Papua New Guinea
YANTILI dial of FIPA [FIP]
YANULA alt for YANYUWA [JAO]
YANYULA alt for YANYUWA [JAO]
YANYUWA [JAO] lang, Australia
YANZI alt for YANS [YNS]
YANZI alt for KIMBU [KIV]
YAO [YAO] lang, Malawi, Tanzania, Mozambique,
    Tanzania
YAO alt for YAO [YAO]
YAO alt for MIEN [YOC]
YAO MIN alt for BA PAI [BPN]
YAO YEN alt for LISU [LIS]
YAOSAKOR alt for ASMAT, YAOSAKOR [ASY]
YAOUNDE alt for EWONDO [EWO]
YAOURÉ [YRE] lang, Côte d'Ivoire
YAPANANI alt for YAWA [YVA]
YAPESE [YPS] lang, Micronesia
YAPO dial of KRUMEN, NORTHEASTERN [PYE]
YAPOA dial of WEDAU [WED]
YAPOMA dial of BAKOKO [BKH]
YAPRERÍA alt for JAPRERÍA [JRU]
YAPSI dial of ORYA [URY]
YAPUNDA [YEV] lang, Papua New Guinea
YAQAI alt for YAQAY [JAQ]
YAQAY [JAQ] lang, Indonesia, Irian Jaya
YAQUI [YAQ] lang, Mexico, USA, USA
YAQUI alt for YAQUI [YAQ]
YARAHUURAXI-CAPANAPARA dial of CUIBA [CUI]
YARAN dial of MARI, HIGH [MRJ]
YARAWATA [YRW] lang, Papua New Guinea
YARAWE alt for SUENA [SUE]
YARAWI alt for SUENA [SUE]
YARÊ alt for YADÊ [NCE]
YAREBA [YRB] lang, Papua New Guinea
YARÍ [YRI] lang, Colombia
YARIBA alt for YORUBA [YOR]
YARIBA dial of LEMBENA [LEQ]
YARKANDI alt for KASHGAR-YARKAND dial of
    UYGHUR [UIG]
YARKHUN dial of WAKHI [WBL]
YARSUN alt for SOBEI [SOB]
YARU dial of IRARUTU [IRH]
YARUKULA alt for YERUKALA [YEU]
YARUMÁ [YRM] lang, Brazil
YARUMARRA dial of NGURA [NBX]
YARURO [YAE] lang, Venezuela
YARURU alt for YARURO [YAE]
YARUS dial of ADZERA [AZR]
YAS alt for ASMAT, CENTRAL [AST]
YASA [YKO] lang, Cameroon, Equatorial Guinea,
    Equatorial Guinea
YASA alt for YASA [YKO]
YASA alt for PAWAIA [PWA]
YASGUA alt for YESKWA [YES]
YASHI [YBJ] lang, Nigeria
YASIN dial of WAKHI [WBL]
YASIN alt for WERCHIKWAR dial of BURUSHASKI
    [BSK]

YASING dial of MUNDANG [MUA]
YASING alt for YASING dial of MUNDANG [MUA]
YASOUKOU alt for YASSUKU dial of BAKOKO [BKH]
YASSA alt for YASA [YKO]
YASSING alt for YASING dial of MUNDANG [MUA]
YASSUKU dial of BAKOKO [BKH]
YASUG alt for YASSUKU dial of BAKOKO [BKH]
YASUKU alt for YASSUKU dial of BAKOKO [BKH]
YASYIN alt for YESSAN-MAYO [YSS]
YATÊ alt for FULNIÔ [FUN]
YATE alt for INOKE-YATE [INO]
YATEE-LACHIRUAJ alt for ZAPOTECO, SAN
  CRISTOBAL LACHIRUAJ [ZTC]
YATINI dial of NUNI [NNW]
YATYE alt for YACHE dial of AKPA-YACHE [AKF]
YATZACHI ZAPOTEC alt for ZAPOTECO, YATZACHI
  [ZAV]
YAU [YUW] lang, Papua New Guinea
YAU [YYU] lang, Papua New Guinea
YAU alt for PASI [PSI]
YAU alt for IAU [TMU]
YAU alt for YAW dial of YESSAN-MAYO [YSS]
YAUAGEPA alt for YAUGIBA [YEM]
YAUAN [YNA] lang, Papua New Guinea
YAUAPERI alt for JAWAPERI dial of ATRUAHÍ [ATR]
YAUARANA alt for YABARANA [YAR]
YAUGIBA [YEM] lang, Papua New Guinea
YAUL [YLA] lang, Papua New Guinea
YAULAPITI alt for YAWALAPITÍ [YAW]
YAUMA [YAX] lang, Angola, Zambia, Zambia
YAUMA alt for YAUMA [YAX]
YAÚNA alt for YAHUNA [YNU]
YAUNDE alt for EWONDO [EWO]
YAUR [JAU] lang, Indonesia, Irian Jaya
YAURAWA dial of RESHE [RES]
YAURE alt for YAOURÉ [YRE]
YAURI alt for GADI-SHINGINI-VADI-BAANGI [KAM]
YAURI alt for YAURAWA dial of RESHE [RES]
YAUTEFA alt for TOBATI [TTI]
YAVA alt for YAGUA [YAD]
YAVA alt for YAWA [YVA]
YAVAPAI dial of HAVASUPAI-WALAPAI-YAVAPAI
  [YUF]
YAVATMAL dial of GONDI, NORTHERN [GON]
YAVESIA ZAPOTECO alt for ZAPOTECO,
  SOUTHEASTERN IXTLÁN [ZPD]
YAVITA alt for MANDAHUACA [MHT]
YAVITA alt for BARÉ [BAE]
YAVITERO [YVT] lang, Venezuela
YAW alt for PASI [PSI]
YAW dial of YESSAN-MAYO [YSS]
YAW dial of BURMESE [BMS]
YAW YIN alt for LISU [LIS]
YAW-YEN alt for LISU [LIS]
YAWA [YVA] lang, Indonesia, Irian Jaya
YAWA [YWA] lang, Papua New Guinea
YAWALAPITÍ [YAW] lang, Brazil
YAWAN dial of YAU [YUW]
YAWANAWA [YWN] lang, Brazil
YAWARAWARGA [YWW] lang, Australia
YAWARETE TAPUYA alt for JAUARETE dial of
  CARÚTANA [CRU]
YAWENIAN alt for IWAM, SEPIK [IWS]
YAWEYUHA [YBY] lang, Papua New Guinea
YAWIYUHA alt for YAWEYUHA [YBY]
YAWOTATAXA alt for GAVA dial of GUDUF [GDF]

YAWURU [YWR] lang, Australia
YAY alt for NHANG [NHA]
YAYEYAMA alt for YAEYAMA [RYS]
YAYUNA alt for YAHUNA [YNU]
YAZDI alt for GABRI [GBZ]
YAZGULAM alt for YAZGULYAM [YAH]
YAZGULYAM [YAH] lang, Tajikistan
YAZIDI alt for GABRI [GBZ]
YAZORI dial of HANGA [HAG]
YAZVA dial of KOMI-ZYRIAN [KPV]
YBANAG alt for IBANAG [IBG]
YE dial of MON [MNW]
YE'CUANA alt for MAQUIRITARI [MCH]
YE'CUANA alt for MAYONGONG dial of
  MAQUIRITARI [MCH]
YEBA alt for MACUNA [MYY]
YEBAMASÃ alt for JEPA-MATSI [JEP]
YEBEKOLO alt for YABEKOLO dial of EWONDO
  [EWO]
YEBU alt for AWAK [AWO]
YECI dial of HOLU [HOL]
YEDIMA alt for BUDUMA [BDM]
YEDINA alt for BUDUMA [BDM]
YEDJI alt for YEJI dial of CHUMBURUNG [NCU]
YEEI alt for YEYE [YEY]
YEEI dial of YANS [YNS]
YEGA [YGG] lang, Papua New Guinea
YEGA alt for KEIGA [KEC]
YEGA dial of YEGA [YGG]
YEGA dial of KORAFE [KPR]
YEGHUYE alt for YAGWOIA [YGW]
YEGUA alt for YAGUA [YAD]
YEH alt for JEH [JEH]
YEH-JEN alt for LISU [LIS]
YEHEN alt for FWÃI [FWA]
YEHPÁ MAJSÁ alt for JEPA-MATSI [JEP]
YÊHUP alt for YAHUP [YAB]
YEI [JEI] lang, Indonesia, Irian Jaya, Papua New
  Guinea, Papua New Guinea
YEI alt for YEYE [YEY]
YEI alt for YEI [JEI]
YEIDJI alt for WUNAMBAL [WUB]
YEITHI alt for WUNAMBAL [WUB]
YEJI dial of CHUMBURUNG [NCU]
YEKHEE [ETS] lang, Nigeria
YEKORA [YKR] lang, Papua New Guinea
YEKUANA alt for MAQUIRITARI [MCH]
YEKUANA alt for MAYONGONG dial of
  MAQUIRITARI [MCH]
YELA [YEL] lang, Zaïre
YELA alt for YELE [YLE]
YELE [YLE] lang, Papua New Guinea
YELEJONG alt for YELE [YLE]
YELETNYE alt for YELE [YLE]
YELINDA dial of BULU [BUM]
YELLOW LAHU alt for LAHU SHI [KDS]
YELLOW LEAF alt for MLABRI [MRA]
YELLOW LEAF alt for KHA TONG LUANG [KHQ]
YELLOW RIVER alt for NAMIA [NNM]
YELLOW UIGHUR alt for YUGUR, WEST [YBE]
YELLOWKNIFE dial of CHIPEWYAN [CPW]
YELMEK [JEL] lang, Indonesia, Irian Jaya
YELMO alt for ADOMA dial of LELA [DRI]
YELOGU [YLG] lang, Papua New Guinea
YEMA alt for SUENA [SUE]
YEMBA [BAN] lang, Cameroon

YEMBA dial of YEMBA [BAN]
YEMBANA dial of BULU [BUM]
YEMBE alt for SONGE [SOP]
YEMBO alt for ANUAK [ANU]
YEMCHIDI alt for JAMSHIDI dial of AIMAQ [AIQ]
YEMENITE HEBREW alt for ORIENTAL HEBREW dial
   of HEBREW [HBR]
YEMMA alt for YEMSA [JNJ]
YEMSA [JNJ] lang, Ethiopia
YENADI alt for YANADI [YBF]
YENDAM alt for YENDANG [YEN]
YENDANG [YEN] lang, Nigeria
YENGEN alt for FWÃI [FWA]
YENGI HISSAR dial of UYGHUR [UIG]
YENGISAR alt for YENGI HISSAR dial of UYGHUR
   [UIG]
YENGONO dial of BULU [BUM]
YENGORU alt for BOIKIN [BZF]
YENICHE [YEC] lang, Germany, Switzerland
YENIMU alt for SIAGHA-YENIMU [OSR]
YENISEI OSTYAK alt for KET [KET]
YENISEI SAMOYEDIC alt for ENETS [ENE]
YENISEI TATAR alt for KHAKAS [KJH]
YENISEY OSTIAK alt for KET [KET]
YENKUANG alt for YÀNGUANG dial of ZHUANG,
   SOUTHERN [CCY]
YEPÁ MAXSÃ alt for JEPA-MATSI [JEP]
YEPÁ-MAHSÁ alt for JEPA-MATSI [JEP]
YERAKAI [YRA] lang, Papua New Guinea
YERAL alt for NHENGATU [YRL]
YERANI alt for GOROVU [GRQ]
YERAVA [YEA] lang, India
YERAWA alt for AKA-JERU [AKJ]
YERBOGOCEN dial of EVENKI [EVN]
YEREKAI alt for YERAKAI [YRA]
YERETUAR [GOP] lang, Indonesia, Irian Jaya
YERGAM alt for TAROK [YER]
YERGE alt for FUR [FUR]
YERGUM alt for TAROK [YER]
YERGYUCH dial of BUDUKH [BDK]
YERGYUDZH dial of KRYTS [KRY]
YERINGTON-SCHURZ alt for SOUTH NORTHERN
   PAIUTE dial of PAIUTE, NORTHERN [PAO]
YERKULA alt for YERUKALA [YEU]
YERONG [YRN] lang, China
YERU dial of KOMA [KMY]
YERUKALA [YEU] lang, India
YERUKALA-KORAVA alt for YERUKALA [YEU]
YERUKLA alt for YERUKALA [YEU]
YESKWA [YES] lang, Nigeria
YESOUM alt for BAMVELE dial of EWONDO [EWO]
YESSAN-MAYO [YSS] lang, Papua New Guinea
YETI alt for MANEM [JET]
YETIMARALA alt for BAYALI [BJY]
YETINJI alt for YIDINY [YII]
YEU alt for NYEU [NYL]
YEVANIC [YEJ] lang, Israel, USA
YEWA dial of NGOMBE [NGC]
YEWENA-YONGSU dial of TABLA [TNM]
YEWU dial of BWA [BWW]
YEY alt for YEI [JEI]
YEY alt for YEEI dial of YANS [YNS]
YEYE [YEY] lang, Botswana
YEYI alt for YEYE [YEY]
YEZO alt for HOKKAIDO dial of AINU [AIN]
YEZUM alt for BAMVELE dial of EWONDO [EWO]

YHUATA alt for OMAGUA [OMG]
YI alt for KWANGSHUN dial of HMONG, WESTERN
   [HUJ]
YI BE WU alt for BEBE [BZV]
YI, CENTRAL [YIC] lang, China
YI, GUIZHOU [YIG] lang, China
YI, SICHUAN [III] lang, China
YI, WESTERN [YIW] lang, China
YI, YUNNAN [NOS] lang, China
YIBAB dial of KAMASAU [KMS]
YIBARAMBU alt for BARAMA [BBG]
YIBWA alt for TIMA [TMS]
YICHIRA alt for SIRA [SWJ]
YIDANA alt for BUDUMA [BDM]
YIDDA alt for MADA [MDA]
YIDDINJI alt for YIDINY [YII]
YIDDISH [YDD] lang, Israel, Germany, Latvia
YIDDISH alt for YIDDISH [YDD]
YIDDISH SIGN LANGUAGE [YDS] lang, Israel
YIDENA alt for BUDUMA [BDM]
YIDGA alt for YIDGHA [YDG]
YIDGHA [YDG] lang, Pakistan
YIDI alt for YIDINICH dial of KWEGU [YID]
YIDIN alt for YIDINY [YII]
YIDINDJI alt for YIDINY [YII]
YIDINICH dial of KWEGU [YID]
YIDINIT alt for YIDINICH dial of KWEGU [YID]
YIDINY [YII] lang, Australia
YIDINY alt for YIDINY [YII]
YIGHA alt for LEYIGHA [AYI]
YIIVE dial of TIV [TIV]
YIJIA alt for ZHONGJIA dial of ZHUANG, NORTHERN
   [CCX]
YIL [YLL] lang, Papua New Guinea
YILIGELE dial of TOURA [NEB]
YILLARO alt for LARO [LRO]
YILPARITJA alt for YULPARITJA dial of MARTU
   WANGKA [MPJ]
YIMAS [YEE] lang, Papua New Guinea
YIMBA alt for LIMBA, WEST-CENTRAL [LIA]
YIMBA alt for LIMBA, EAST [LMA]
YIMBUN alt for ABUN [KGR]
YIMCHUNGER alt for NAGA, YIMCHUNGRU [YIM]
YIMCHUNGRE alt for NAGA, YIMCHUNGRU [YIM]
YIMCHUNGRU alt for NAGA, YIMCHUNGRU [YIM]
YIMCHUNGRU dial of NAGA, YIMCHUNGRU [YIM]
YIMTIM alt for VIN [VIM]
YIMWOM alt for KAM [KDX]
YIN alt for RIANG [RIL]
YINBAW alt for KAREN, YINBAW [KVU]
YINCHIA [YIN] lang, Myanmar
YINDI dial of CHIN, KHUMI [CKM]
YINDI alt for YINDU dial of CHIN, KHUMI [CKM]
YINDJIBARNDI [YIJ] lang, Australia
YINDJILANDJI [YIL] lang, Australia
YINDU dial of CHIN, KHUMI [CKM]
YINDU alt for YINDI dial of CHIN, KHUMI [CKM]
YINGA alt for SAA [SZR]
YINGGARDA [YIA] lang, Australia
YINIBU alt for ITERI [ITR]
YINIBU alt for ROCKY PEAK [ROK]
YINING dial for ILI dial of UYGHUR [UIG]
YINJEBI alt for NJEBI [NZB]
YINNET alt for YINCHIA [YIN]
YINTALE alt for KAREN, YINTALE [KVY]
YINTALET alt for KAREN, YINTALE [KVY]

YINZEBI alt for NJEBI [NZB]
YIPOUNOU alt for PUNU [PUU]
YIPUNU alt for PUNU [PUU]
YIR alt for IR [IRR]
YIR YORONT [YIY] lang, Australia
YIRA dial of NANDI [NNB]
YIREN alt for ZHONGJIA dial of ZHUANG,
 NORTHERN [CCX]
YIRMEL alt for JIR'JOROND dial of YIR YORONT
 [YIY]
YIRTANGETTLE alt for JIR'JOROND dial of YIR
 YORONT [YIY]
YIRTUTIYM alt for JIR'JOROND dial of YIR YORONT
 [YIY]
YIRU alt for NALI [NSS]
YIS [YIS] lang, Papua New Guinea
YISANGOU alt for SANGU [SNQ]
YISANGU alt for SANGU [SNQ]
YITINTYI alt for YIDINY [YII]
YIVOUMBOU alt for VUMBU [VUM]
YIWOM [GEK] lang, Nigeria
YIYANG dial of CHINESE, XIANG [HSN]
YLANOS alt for ILANUN [ILL]
YNÃ alt for KARAJÁ [KPJ]
YO alt for YOS [YOS]
YO alt for NYAW [NYW]
YOABOU alt for WAAMA [WWA]
YOABU alt for WAAMA [WWA]
YOADABE-WATOARE alt for MARING [MBW]
YOANA alt for YUWANA [YAU]
YOANGEN dial of MONGI [KGF]
YOANGGENG alt for YOANGEN dial of MONGI [KGF]
YOARI alt for JAUARI dial of YANOMÁMI [WCA]
YOBA [YOB] lang, Papua New Guinea
YOCOBOUE alt for LOZOUA dial of DIDA,
 YOCOBOUÉ [GUD]
YOFO alt for KUMBA [KSM]
YOFO dial of YENDANG [YEN]
YOFUAHA alt for CHOROTE, IYOJWA'JA [CRT]
YOGAD [YOG] lang, Philippines
YOGAM alt for GHOMALA CENTRAL dial of
 GHOMALA' [BBJ]
YOGLI dial of NAGA, TASE [NST]
YOGOR alt for YUGUR, EAST [YUY]
YŎGUR alt for YUGUR, EAST [YUY]
YOHORAA dial of TUCANO [TUO]
YOHOWRÉ alt for YAOURÉ [YRE]
YOI alt for YOY [YOY]
YOIDIK [YDK] lang, Papua New Guinea
YOIT alt for YUPIK, CENTRAL SIBERIAN [ESS]
YOKAN dial of SAAMI, SKOLT [LPK]
YOKARI dial of TABLA [TNM]
YOKOUBOUÉ alt for LOZOUA dial of DIDA,
 YOCOBOUÉ [GUD]
YOKU dial of SIE [ERG]
YOKULA alt for GANGGALIDA [GCD]
YOKUTS [YOK] lang, USA
YOLA alt for JOLA-FOGNY [DYO]
YOLIAPE alt for YOLIAPI dial of HEWA [HAM]
YOLIAPI dial of HEWA [HAM]
YOLMU alt for HELAMBU SHERPA [SCP]
YOLOTEPEC dial of CHATINO, LACHAO-
 YOLOTEPEC [CLY]
YOLOX dial of CHINANTECO, QUIOTEPEC [CHQ]
YOM alt for PILA [PIL]
YOMBE [YOM] lang, Zaïre, Angola, Congo

YOMBE dial of TUMBUKA [TUW]
YOMBE alt for YOOMBE dial of VILI [VIF]
YOMBE CLASSIQUE alt for VUNGUNYA dial of
 YOMBE [YOM]
YOMUD dial of TURKMEN [TCK]
YOMUD dial of TURKMEN [TCK]
YOMUT dial of TURKMEN [TCK]
YOMUT alt for YOMUD dial of TURKMEN [TCK]
YONAGUNI [YOI] lang, Japan
YONG [YNO] lang, Thailand
YONGBEI dial of ZHUANG, NORTHERN [CCX]
YONGCHUN [YUG] lang, China
YONGGOM [YON] lang, Papua New Guinea,
 Indonesia, Irian Jaya
YONGHO alt for YANGHO [YNH]
YONGJING dial of TU [MJG]
YONGKOM alt for YONGGOM [YON]
YONGNÁN dial of ZHUANG, SOUTHERN [CCY]
YONGO dial of MBANGALA [MXG]
YONGOLEI dial of BIANGAI [BIG]
YONGOM alt for YONGGOM [YON]
YONGREN dial of TAI NÜA [TDD]
YONGYASHA dial of NAGA, PHOM [NPH]
YONI dial of THEMNE [TEJ]
YOO dial of YAOURÉ [YRE]
YOOBA alt for YORUBA [YOR]
YOOI alt for YOY [YOY]
YOOMBE dial of VILI [VIF]
YOOMBE dial of VILI [VIF]
YOOY alt for YOY [YOY]
YORA [MTS] lang, Peru
YORDA alt for KPAN [KPK]
YORK CREE alt for CREE, CENTRAL [CRM]
YORO dial of MUMUYE [MUL]
YORON [YOX] lang, Japan
YORUBA [YOR] lang, Nigeria, Benin
YORUBA alt for YERAVA [YEA]
YOS [YOS] lang, Myanmar
YOSHKAR-OLIN alt for GRASSLAND MARI dial of
 MARI, LOW [MAL]
YOT alt for KOL dial of CUA [CUA]
YOTAFA alt for TOBATI [TTI]
YOTE alt for YOS [YOS]
YOTUBO alt for GIMNIME [KMB]
YOU alt for TAI PONG dial of TAI NÜA [TDD]
"YOUANNE" alt for TAI, NORTHERN [NOD]
YÒUJIANG dial of ZHUANG, NORTHERN [CCX]
YOULE alt for JINO [JIU]
YOULOU alt for YULU [YUL]
YOUMIAN dial of IU MIEN [IUM]
YOUNUO dial of PUNU [PNU]
"YOUON" alt for TAI, NORTHERN [NOD]
YOURÉ alt for YAOURÉ [YRE]
YOY [YOY] lang, Thailand, Laos
YOZA dial of HAYA [HAY]
YREPO dial of KRUMEN, SOUTHERN [TED]
YREWE dial of KRUMEN, NORTHEASTERN [PYE]
YU dial of MANDYAK [MFV]
YU dial of MANDYAK [MFV]
YU MIEN alt for MIEN [YOC]
YUAGA [NUA] lang, New Caledonia
"YUAN" alt for TAI, NORTHERN [NOD]
YUAN dial of KHMU [KJG]
YUANA alt for YUWANA [YAU]
YUANGA alt for YUAGA [NUA]
YUÁNMÉN dial of HLAI [LIC]

YUAPÍN alt for YARURO [YAE]
YUBANAKOR dial of KWANGA [KWJ]
YUCATEC MAYA alt for ITZÁ [ITZ]
YUCATECO [YUA] lang, Mexico, Belize
YUCATECO, CHAN SANTA CRUZ [YUS] lang,
    Mexico
YUCHI [YUC] lang, USA
YUCHIANG alt for YÒUJIANG dial of ZHUANG,
    NORTHERN [CCX]
YUCKAMURRI alt for NYANGGA [NNY]
YUCPA alt for YUKPA [YUP]
YUCUAÑE MIXTECO alt for MIXTECO, SAN
    BARTOLOMÉ YUCUAÑE [MVG]
YUCUAÑE-TEITA MIXTECO alt for MIXTECO, SAN
    BARTOLOMÉ YUCUAÑE [MVG]
YUCUHITI dial of MIXTECO, SOUTHWESTERN
    TLAXIACO [MEH]
YUCUNA [YCN] lang, Colombia
YUDGA alt for YIDGHA [YDG]
YUDGHA alt for YIDGHA [YDG]
YUDHIA alt for ORIYA [ORY]
YUDI [YUD] lang, Libya, Italy
YUE alt for CHINESE, YUE [YUH]
YUEH alt for CHINESE, YUE [YUH]
YUEYANG dial of CHINESE, XIANG [HSN]
YUFIYUFA alt for TOKANO [ZUH]
YUGAMBAL [YUB] lang, Australia
YUGAR alt for YUGUR, EAST [YUY]
YUGH [YUU] lang, Russia, Asia
YUGOSLAVIAN SIGN LANGUAGE [YSL] lang,
    Yugoslavia, Slovenia
YUGU alt for YUGUR, WEST [YBE]
YUGU alt for YUGUR, EAST [YUY]
YUGULDA alt for GANGGALIDA [GCD]
YUGUMBAL alt for YUGAMBAL [YUB]
YUGUMBE alt for BANDJALANG [BDY]
YUGUMBIR dial of BANDJALANG [BDY]
YUGUR, EAST [YUY] lang, China
YUGUR, WEST [YBE] lang, China
YUHUAN dial of CHINESE, MIN NAN [CFR]
YUHUP alt for YAHUP [YAB]
YUI alt for SALT-YUI [SLL]
YUIT alt for YUPIK, CENTRAL SIBERIAN [ESS]
YUK alt for YUPIK, CENTRAL SIBERIAN [ESS]
YUKAGHIR, NORTHERN [YKG] lang, Russia, Asia
YUKAGHIR, SOUTHERN [YUX] lang, Russia, Asia
YUKAGIR alt for YUKAGHIR, NORTHERN [YKG]
YUKAGIR alt for YUKAGHIR, SOUTHERN [YUX]
YUKALA alt for GANGGALIDA [GCD]
YUKAN alt for ATAYAL [TAY]
YUKI [YUK] lang, USA
YUKKABURRA alt for YIDINY [YII]
YUKO alt for YUKPA [YUP]
YUKPA [YUP] lang, Colombia, Venezuela
YUKU alt for YUGUR, WEST [YBE]
YUKUBEN [YBL] lang, Nigeria, Cameroon
YUKULTA alt for GANGGALIDA [GCD]
YUKUNA alt for YUCUNA [YCN]
YUKUTARE alt for BITARE [BRE]
YULBARIDJA alt for YULPARITJA dial of MARTU
    WANGKA [MPJ]
YULE-DELENA dial of RORO [RRO]
YULPARITJA dial of MARTU WANGKA [MPJ]
YULU [YUL] lang, Central African Republic, Sudan,
    Sudan, Zaïre
YULU alt for YULU [YUL]

YULU dial of YULU [YUL]
YUM alt for AGHEM [AGQ]
YUMÁ alt for JÚMA [JUA]
YUMA alt for QUECHAN [YUM]
YUMBA alt for LIMBA, WEST-CENTRAL [LIA]
YUMBA alt for LIMBA, EAST [LMA]
YUMBAR alt for ROUKU [TCI]
YUMBO alt for QUICHUA, LOWLAND, NAPO [QLN]
YUMBRI alt for MLABRI [MRA]
YUMINAHUA alt for YAMINAHUA [YAA]
YUMPIA alt for WAMBAYA [WMB]
YUNA alt for DUNA [DUC]
YUNDUM alt for YENDANG [YEN]
YUNG-CHU'UN alt for YONGCHUN [YUG]
YUNG-SHUN alt for YONGCHUN [YUG]
YUNGAY dial of QUECHUA, ANCASH, HUAYLAS
    [QAN]
YUNGCHENG dial of BONAN [PEH]
YUNGCHUN alt for YONGCHUN [YUG]
YUNGNAN alt for YONGNÁN dial of ZHUANG,
    SOUTHERN [CCY]
YUNGPEI alt for YONGBEI dial of ZHUANG,
    NORTHERN [CCX]
YUNGSHUN dial of CHINESE, XIANG [HSN]
YUNGUILLO-CONDAGUA dial of INGA, JUNGLE [INJ]
YUNGUR [YUN] lang, Nigeria
YUNGWE alt for NYUNGWE [NYU]
YUNNALINKA alt for WARLUWARA [WRB]
YUNNAN dial of BONAN [PEH]
YUNNAN SHANT'OU dial of DAI [TIZ]
YUNNANESE dial of CHINESE, MANDARIN [CHN]
YUNNANESE alt for HO dial of CHINESE, MANDARIN
    [CHN]
YUNNANESE SHAN alt for DAI [TIZ]
YUNO alt for YOUNUO dial of PUNU [PNU]
YUNUO alt for YOUNUO dial of PUNU [PNU]
YUPA alt for YUKPA [YUP]
YUPIK, CENTRAL [ESU] lang, USA
YUPIK, CENTRAL SIBERIAN [ESS] lang, USA, Russia,
    Asia, Russia, Asia
YUPIK, NAUKAN [YNK] lang, Russia, Asia
YUPIK, PACIFIC GULF [EMS] lang, USA
YUPIK, SIRENIK [YSR] lang, Russia, Asia
YUPNA [YUT] lang, Papua New Guinea
YUQUI [YUQ] lang, Bolivia
YURA alt for YORA [MTS]
YURA alt for YURACARE [YUE]
YURACARE [YUE] lang, Bolivia
YURAK alt for NENETS [YRK]
YURAK SAMOYED alt for NENETS [YRK]
YURI alt for KARKAR-YURI [YUJ]
YURI dial of GOLIN [GVF]
YURITI alt for YURUTI [YUI]
YURITI-TAPUIA alt for YURUTI [YUI]
YURMATY dial of BASHKIR [BXK]
YUROK [YUR] lang, USA
YURUK dial of BALKAN GAGAUZ TURKISH [BGX]
YÖRÜK dial of DOMARI [RMT]
YURÚNA alt for JURÚNA [JUR]
YURUPARI TAPUYA alt for JURUPARI dial of
    CARÚTANA [CRU]
YURUTI [YUI] lang, Colombia, Brazil
YURUTI-TAPUYA alt for YURUTI [YUI]
YUSUFZAI dial of PASHTO, EASTERN [PBU]
YUTA dial of GIDRA [GDR]
YUTNA alt for YUPNA [YUT]

lang, Mexico
ZAPOTECO, SAN LORENZO TEXMELUCAN [ZPZ]
   lang, Mexico
ZAPOTECO, SAN MIGUEL TILQUIAPAN [ZTS] lang,
   Mexico
ZAPOTECO, SAN RAYMUNDO XALPAN [ZTX] lang,
   Mexico
ZAPOTECO, SANTA CATARINA QUIERÍ [ZTQ] lang,
   Mexico
ZAPOTECO, SANTA CATARINA XANAGUÍA [ZTG]
   lang, Mexico
ZAPOTECO, SANTA MARÍA ZANIZA [ZPW] lang,
   Mexico
ZAPOTECO, SANTA MARÍA PETAPA [ZPE] lang,
   Mexico
ZAPOTECO, SANTIAGO LAPAGUÍA [ZTL] lang,
   Mexico
ZAPOTECO, SANTIAGO MATATLÁN [ZAQ] lang,
   Mexico
ZAPOTECO, SANTIAGO XANICA [ZPR] lang, Mexico
ZAPOTECO, SANTO TOMÁS MAZALTEPEC [ZPY]
   lang, Mexico
ZAPOTECO, SIERRA DE JUÁREZ [ZAA] lang, Mexico
ZAPOTECO, SOUTH CENTRAL ZIMATLÁN [ZPP]
   lang, Mexico
ZAPOTECO, SOUTHEASTERN IXTLÁN [ZPD] lang,
   Mexico
ZAPOTECO, SOUTHEASTERN YAUTEPEC [ZPK]
   lang, Mexico
ZAPOTECO, SOUTHEASTERN ZIMATLÁN [ZPN]
   lang, Mexico
ZAPOTECO, SOUTHERN EJUTLA [ZPT] lang, Mexico
ZAPOTECO, SOUTHERN RINCÓN [ZSR] lang, Mexico
ZAPOTECO, SOUTHERN VILLA ALTA [ZAD] lang,
   Mexico
ZAPOTECO, TEOTITLÁN DEL VALLE [ZTT] lang,
   Mexico
ZAPOTECO, WESTERN IXTLÁN [ZAE] lang, Mexico
ZAPOTECO, WESTERN MIAHUATLÁN [ZPS] lang,
   Mexico
ZAPOTECO, WESTERN OCOTLÁN [ZAC] lang,
   Mexico
ZAPOTECO, WESTERN TLACOLULA [ZAB] lang,
   Mexico
ZAPOTECO, WESTERN YAUTEPEC [ZPI] lang,
   Mexico
ZAPOTECO, WESTERN ZIMATLÁN [ZPH] lang,
   Mexico
ZAPOTECO, XADANI [ZAX] lang, Mexico
ZAPOTECO, YALALAG [ZPU] lang, Mexico
ZAPOTECO, YATZACHI [ZAV] lang, Mexico, USA
ZARA alt for BOBO DIOULA [BOD]
ZARABAON alt for BEU dial of GUÉRÉ [GXX]
ZARADAN alt for BOBO DIOULA [BOD]
ZARAMO alt for ZALAMO [ZAJ]
ZARAMU alt for ZALAMO [ZAJ]
ZARANDA dial of GEJI [GEZ]
ZARBARMA alt for DYERMA [DJE]
ZARGARI dial of ROMANI, BALKAN [RMN]
ZARI [ZAZ] lang, Nigeria
ZARI dial of ZARI [ZAZ]
ZARIWA alt for ZARI [ZAZ]
ZARMA alt for DYERMA [DJE]
ZARPHATIC [ZRP] lang, France
ZASKARI alt for ZANGSKARI [ZAU]
ZAUGE alt for ZAGHAWA [ZAG]

ZAUZOU [ZAL] lang, China
ZAWA [ZOA] lang, Tunisia
ZAYEIN alt for KAREN, ZAYEIN [KXK]
ZAYOLI dial of KASHMIRI [KSH]
ZAYSE [ZAY] lang, Ethiopia
ZAYSINYA alt for ZAYSE [ZAY]
ZAYSSE alt for ZAYSE [ZAY]
ZAZA alt for KIRMANJKI [QKV]
ZAZAKI alt for KIRMANJKI [QKV]
ZAZAKI alt for DIMLI [ZZZ]
ZAZAO [JAJ] lang, Solomon Islands
ZAZING alt for YASING dial of MUNDANG [MUA]
ZEBAK dial of SANGLECHI-ISHKASHIMI [SGL]
ZEBAKI alt for ZEBAK dial of SANGLECHI-
   ISHKASHIMI [SGL]
ZEBIE dial of BÉTÉ, GAGNOA [BTG]
ZEDDO dial of AARI [AIZ]
ZEDONG alt for TIDONG [TID]
ZEEM [ZUA] lang, Nigeria
ZEEM dial of ZEEM [ZUA]
ZEGACHE ZAPOTEC alt for ZAPOTECO,
   SOUTHEASTERN ZIMATLÁN [ZPN]
ZEGGAOUA alt for ZAGHAWA [ZAG]
ZEGHAWA alt for ZAGHAWA [ZAG]
ZEGUHA alt for ZIGULA [ZIW]
ZEGURA alt for ZIGULA [ZIW]
ZELGWA alt for ZULGWA [ZUL]
ZELGWA dial of ZULGWA [ZUL]
ZELMAMU alt for ZILMAMU [ZIL]
ZEMACHIAI alt for SHAMAITISH dial of
   LITHUANIAN [LIT]
ZEMAITIS alt for SHAMAITISH dial of LITHUANIAN
   [LIT]
ZEMAY alt for FULFULDE, ADAMAWA [FUB]
ZEMBA [DHM] lang, Namibia, Angola
ZEMI alt for NAGA, ZEME [NZM]
ZEMIAKI dial of GRANGALI [NLI]
ZENAG alt for ZENANG [ZEG]
ZENAGA [ZEN] lang, Mauritania
ZENANG [ZEG] lang, Papua New Guinea
ZENAP alt for CHENAPIAN [CJN]
ZERAOUA alt for ZAWA [ZOA]
ZERGULLA dial of ZAYSE [ZAY]
ZERGULLINYA alt for ZERGULLA dial of ZAYSE
   [ZAY]
ZERMA alt for DYERMA [DJE]
ZEYA-BUREYA dial of EVENKI [EVN]
ZEZURU dial of SHONA [SHD]
ZEZURU dial of SHONA [SHD]
ZHANG-ZHUNG alt for JANGSHUNG [JNA]
ZHEJIANG dial of CHINESE, MIN NAN [CFR]
ZHGABE alt for ALBANIAN, TOSK [ALN]
ZHILI dial of CHINESE, MANDARIN [CHN]
ZHIMOMI dial of NAGA, SEMA [NSM]
ZHIRE dial of HAM [JAB]
ZHIRU alt for JIRU [JRR]
ZHONGJIA dial of ZHUANG, NORTHERN [CCX]
ZHONGSHA dial of HLAI [LIC]
ZHONGSHAN dial of CHINESE, YUE [YUH]
ZHONJIGALI alt for WAIGALI [WBK]
ZHU'OASE alt for DZU/'OÃSI dial of KUNG-
   TSUMKWE [KTZ]
ZHU'OASE alt for DZU'OASI dial of KUNG-
   TSUMKWE [KTZ]
ZHU'OASI alt for KUNG-TSUMKWE [KTZ]
ZHUANG, NORTHERN [CCX] lang, China

ZUTIUA dial of GUAJAJÁRA [GUB]
ZUWADZA dial of ÖMIE [AOM]
ZUWARAH alt for ZUARA [ZOU]
ZWALL dial of SHALL-ZWALL [SHA]
ZWARA alt for ZUARA [ZOU]
ZWAY [ZWA] lang, Ethiopia
ZWN alt for BENDI dial of HLAI [LIC]
ZYOBA [ZYO] lang, Tanzania, Zaïre, Zaïre
ZYOBA alt for ZYOBA [ZYO]
ZYUDIN dial of KOMI-PERMYAK [KOI]
`AJMAAN alt for CENTRAL NAJDI dial of ARABIC,
    NAJDI [ARS]
`AWAAZIM alt for CENTRAL NAJDI dial of ARABIC,
    NAJDI [ARS]
`UMUUR alt for NORTH NAJDI dial of ARABIC,
    NAJDI [ARS]
`UTAIBA alt for CENTRAL NAJDI dial of ARABIC,
    NAJDI [ARS]